T0330067

THE LAWS OF INNKEEPERS

—For Hotels, Motels, Restaurants, and Clubs

THE LAWS
OF INNKEEPERS

—For Hotels, Motels, Restaurants, and Clubs

THIRD EDITION

JOHN E. H. SHERRY

Cornell University Press

ITHACA AND LONDON

Copyright © 1972, 1981, 1993 by Cornell University

All rights reserved. Except for brief quotations in a review, this book, or parts thereof, must not be reproduced in any form without permission in writing from the publisher. For information address Cornell University Press, Sage House, 512 East State Street, Ithaca, New York 14850.

First edition, by John H. Sherry, published 1972 by Cornell University Press.
Revised edition, by John E. H. Sherry, published 1981 by Cornell University Press.
Third edition, by John E. H. Sherry, published 1993 by Cornell University Press.

International Standard Book Number 0-8014-2508-5
Library of Congress Catalog Card Number 92-30561
Printed in the United States of America
Librarians: Library of Congress cataloging information
appears on the last page of the book.
♾ The paper in this book meets the minimum requirements
of the American National Standard for Information Sciences—
Permanence of Paper for Printed Library Materials, ANSI Z39.48-1984.

Preface

The original objectives of this book have not changed. These are to provide (1) a textbook for use in college-level schools of hospitality management; (2) a reference manual for use by hotel, motel, restaurant, and club owners and operators on site and by corporate executives managing multiple units; and (3) an aid for attorneys in the general practice of law who encounter legal problems in the field of public hospitality.

A new part, titled Selected Hospitality-related Legal Concerns, provides three new chapters: Employment Law (Chapter 24), Environmental Law and Land Use (Chapter 25), and Catastrophic Risk Liability (Chapter 26). These chapters selectively treat issues that are not normally contained in traditional hospitality-law books yet are of growing concern to an industry that is both labor-intensive and dependent upon the availability of scarce environmental resources for development. Moreover, catastrophes, natural and manmade, can have devastating effects on hotel employees, guests, and patrons. The risk of liability for such catastrophes as well as governmental regulation of employment and use of the environment impinges upon all aspects of the field of public accommodation and service.

The cases and commentary have been amended in this edition to reduce treatment of subjects that are no longer receiving judicial or regulatory attention. Procedural law aspects of decisions have been omitted, and the decisions have been edited to remove extraneous citations, although hospitality case citations have been retained for ready reference as sources of authority. Footnotes accompanying decisions have been deleted for the most part; where footnotes have been retained, the original numbering is used, and the notes immediately follow the decisions.

As preparation of the third edition began, a decision was made to provide a separate study guide for undergraduate students taking a law course as part of their hospitality management program. Such a guide has been prepared, one that meets the needs of students without deviating from the professional thrust of past editions of the textbook. The overall aim of the textbook / study guide combination is to maintain the utility and authority of the textbook to industry professionals, lawyers, and legal scholars while facilitating its use by instructors and students in academic programs.

The new edition has benefited substantially from the efforts of Maria Seda, a Stanford Law graduate, who researched both the text and cases, and those of Scott O'Connell, a law graduate, who made helpful editorial suggestions. Both my secretary, Bertha Hubbell, and Nancy Connors worked unstintingly to type the manuscript.

JOHN E. H. SHERRY

Ithaca, New York

Contents

Chapter 4. Discrimination in Places of Public Accommodation: Civil Rights 45

Chapter 5. Relationship of Innkeeper and Guest: Creation and Termination 105

Contents

Chapter 6. Legal Excuses for Failure to Receive a Guest and Right to Eject — 141

Chapter 7. Liability for Failure to Honor Reservations — 154

Chapter 8. Innkeeper's Duty to Guest: Courteous and Considerate Treatment — 197

PART II. TORT LAW: OWNER AND OPERATOR LIABILITY FOR GUEST'S SAFETY

Chapter 9. Duty to Provide Safe Premises   219

Chapter 10. Liability of Resort Facilities   274

Chapter 11. Responsibility for Conduct of Persons in the Inn   350

PART III. INNKEEPER'S RESPONSIBILITY FOR PROPERTY OF GUESTS AND PATRONS

Chapter 12. Innkeeper's Responsibility for Property of Guests   415

Chapter 13. Exceptions and Limitations to Liability for Guest's Property   471

Chapter 14. Innkeeper's Duty to Nonguests   **546**

Chapter 15. Responsibility of Restaurant Keeper
for Patron's Property   **564**

PART IV. GOVERNMENT REGULATION OF THE HOSPITALITY INDUSTRY

Chapter 16. Civil and Criminal Responsibility for Anticompetitive Marketing Activities   589

Chapter 17. Franchise Agreements: Legal Rights and Responsibilities of Franchisor and Franchisee   614

Chapter 18. Regulation Governing the Sale of Food, Beverages, and Intoxicants   622

Chapter 19. Responsibility Arising from the Sale of Food, Beverages, and Intoxicants

PART V. INNKEEPER CREDITOR-DEBTOR PROTECTION

Chapter 20. The Innkeeper's Lien

PART I

Introduction to the Laws
of Innkeepers: Responsibilities
to Guests and Patrons

1   Historical Development of the Business of Innkeeping

1:1   *Inns in the Ancient and Medieval World*

Houses of public entertainment have been maintained in all countries from early times. In the ancient world we hear of inns and taverns in all civilized countries: in Egypt, in Asia, in Palestine, in Greece, and in Italy. The beerhouses or taverns of ancient Egypt were furnished with mats, stools, and armchairs upon which customers sat side-by-side, fraternally drinking beer, wine, palm brandy, cooked and perfumed liquors. Slaves and maidservants served and entertained the customers and strived to maintain an atmosphere of ease and conviviality. The taverns of Babylon and Nineveh were owned by wealthy merchants who employed women managers, sold liquor on credit, and received payment in grain, usually after the harvest.

Inns and taverns were found throughout the Holy Land. A tavern in a town was in contrast with the caravanserai (unfurnished overnight resthouse) of the open road. The forerunners of the Greek inns were public places, lesches, where people gathered for gossip and amusement.

In ancient Rome publicans and their houses were held in general contempt just as they were in Greece. The Romans were a proud people who held that the business of conducting a tavern was a low form of occupation, and the running of such establishments was usually entrusted to slaves. The inns along the highways were of questionable reputation. Landlords were predatory and robberies of travelers were common. On the great highways leading to Rome, posthouses were located at various stages where horses could be baited and fresh ones obtained. These posthouses were great government inns used by the military as halting places where provender for men and beasts of the legions was provided. Officials were assigned to them for purposes of inspection and for the apprehension of dangerous or undesirable characters. Before any service could be obtained therein, it was necessary to present credentials.[1]

Throughout the Middle Ages the use of such houses continued all over the world. Travel abroad was much more common during the Middle Ages than we often realize; and the traveler returning to England might have brought home with him information about the trade of the innkeeper and suggested its establishment in his own land. But there is no reason to suppose that the English inns

---

[1]For a general discussion, *see* W. Firebaugh, The Inns of Greece and Rome (2d ed. 1928).

were not of indigenous growth; certain it is that they were noted as the cleanest, the best supplied, and the most attractive inns in the world. We must turn to the habits and needs of travel in medieval England to explain the origin, the nature, and the legal position of English inns.

1:2 *Study of History of English Inns to Understand the Law*

The laws regulating the rights and duties of an innkeeper are not in all respects what one might have looked for as applying to the innkeeper of today. The innkeeper occupies in our law a peculiar and apparently anomalous position: while not technically a bailee of the goods of his guests, he is held to the strictest responsibility which any bailee is under; and while apparently a mere individual householder with no corporate or other franchise specially granted, he is compelled, like the great railroad corporations, to receive and entertain strangers whether he will or not. These and other duties and responsibilities of the innkeeper will be considered at length later, but in order that we may understand the reason for the apparently peculiar doctrine of the law regulating the rights and liabilities of innkeepers, in order that we may learn the extent of their responsibilities and understand their limitations, we must examine briefly the early history of innkeeping in England, the character and nature of inns, and the functions which they performed in the social life of the English people at the time when the law of innkeepers was forming, that is, during the fourteenth and fifteenth centuries. The nature of the English inn in the Middle Ages determined the English law of innkeepers, and the principles thus established form the basis of the law of innkeepers in every place where the common law prevails.

1:3 *Conditions of Travel in Medieval England*

There was a surprising amount of traveling in England in the Middle Ages. The roads, to be sure, were very bad and in general were impassable for loaded wagons, and the transportation of goods from place to place was therefore almost impossible. While one portion of the country was well supplied with food, another portion not so far away might be in the throes of famine without a chance of relief so far as land transportation was concerned. Yet, in spite of this, the roads were sufficient for foot passengers or for lightly loaded horses, and they were used by multitudes of people on foot and on horseback. Carriers of goods existed, but they transported their goods in packs by means of horses.

The roads were not only bad, but they were infested with outlaws and robbers of all sorts. Between the villages there were long stretches of forest, and these forests were the refuge of the outlaws who formed a considerable proportion of the population of the country. They might at any time attack travelers by day, but that was unusual. Since it usually happened that travelers proceeded in companies, there was not much danger of attack during daylight hours; but at night the danger increased considerably.

1:4 *Houses of Accommodation for Travelers*

Such being the conditions of traveling, two results followed: a traveler had to carry the lightest weight baggage possible, and he had to secure protection at night from thieves and outlaws. He could not conveniently carry with him food for his journey, and he therefore had to find entertainment along the road. He could not safely sleep in the open and thus had to find some house which would offer him protection as well as entertainment for the night. These needs led naturally to the establishment of a course of business which should supply the demand. At the proper place on every main road of travel, houses were devoted to the business of furnishing food, drink, and safe lodging to hungry and weary travelers. Thus, out of the needs of the wayfarer and as an incident of travel from place to place, grew the English inn. It was established to supply the needs of the traveler along his journey, to wit, to furnish food and drink for man and beast and rest and safety for the night.

> Inns were intended for the middle class: merchants, small landowners, itinerant packmen, etc. A certain number of beds were placed in one room. . . . Each man bought separately what he wished to eat, chiefly bread, a little meat, and some beer. Complaints as to the excessive prices were not much less frequent then than now. . . . The people petitioned Parliament and the King interfered accordingly with his accustomed useless goodwill. Edward III [1312–1377] promulgated, in the twenty-third year of his reign [1350], a statute to constrain "hostelers et herbergers" to sell food at reasonable prices; and again, four years later, tried to put an end to the "great and outrageous cost of victuals kept up in all the realm by innkeepers and other retailers of victuals, to the great detriment of the people travelling through the realm."[2]

The inn was not the only accommodation which weary travelers might find in the course of their journey. The religious houses practiced hospitality and freely received certain classes of people. The nobles and magnates habitually resorted to them for refreshment and were received both in consideration of their own bounty and as representatives of the class to which the community owed its foundation and its wealth. The very poor also were received out of mere charity, for hospitality to the poor was one of the first requirements of religion as it was understood in the Middle Ages. To the houses of the friars, therefore, rich and poor resorted for entertainment; but the great middle class, the men who were able to pay their way, were not welcome there. If they had the means to pay for accommodation and were without special claim to favor, they had to go to those whose business it was to care for them. The great houses of nobles and gentry were also open to travelers who were in need of entertainment, but there, too, it was as a rule only the rich and the poor who were expected to avail themselves of the private hospitality. Anyone lost or benighted would of course be received; but the lord of the manor had no desire to compete with the innkeeper who had to make his livelihood from the wayfarer.

[2]J. Jusserand, English Wayfaring Life in the Middle Ages 61 (4th ed. L. Smith trans. 1961).

Besides these private houses and the inn for necessary entertainment, the ale-house or tavern supplied incidental refreshment of the traveler though generally intended to serve another purpose. This house primarily supplied the wants of the inhabitants of the place, for there the native found rest, heat, companionship, and beer. He could stay until the stroke of curfew, and then was turned out to find his way home as best he might, quarreling and fighting by the way, using his knife freely, or falling from his horse into a convenient stream, easy prey for enemies and robbers. The difference between the inn and the tavern is therefore obvious. The one was instituted for the weary traveler, the other for the native; the one furnished food that the traveler might continue his journey, the other furnished drink for the mere pleasure of neighbors; the one was open to the traveler for protection at night, the other turned its guest out at the very moment when he most needed protection, and left him to find it, if his remaining senses permitted him to do so, in his own home. A tavern, then, is not an inn, and the innkeeper's duties do not extend to the tavernkeeper.

1:5 *Development of Inns from Private Houses*

Such being the course of life among wayfarers in medieval England, the inn was a natural outgrowth of the conditions. The inn, the public house of entertainment, was evolved from the private house. Any householder might receive a stranger for the night, as indeed in rural communities many householders are still apt to do. If in the course of time one such householder came, either through the superiority of his own accommodation or by reason of the lack of competition, to receive all persons who in that village needed accommodation he would thereby have become an innkeeper. He would have done it perhaps gradually, without any distinct change marking the transition from private householder to public innkeeper; nor would the accommodation he offered be different in kind from the accommodation that would be offered by the private householder furnishing occasional accommodation to a transient guest. The inn was an outgrowth of the private house, and the kind of house employed and the general conduct of life in the house would be the same in the early inn and the private house of the same period. In order to discover the nature of the accommodation afforded by the inn, it is, therefore, worthwhile to examine the plan of life in the ordinary dwelling of the time.

The English houses of the thirteenth and fourteenth centuries differed greatly, of course, in size and in elegance, but the plan of life in all houses had certain common features. Indoor living centered about the great hall, the principal part of the house, to which other parts were added as they might be required. In the hall the days were spent, so far as they were spent indoors, meals were eaten, and at nighttime the tables were removed and the beds were spread. The mistress, to be sure, had a small room of her own, the bower, into which she could retire at any time, and the master of the house had a separate chamber in which he slept. But the retainers, the servants, and the ordinary guests slept together in the common hall. The house of a man who was well-to-do might have an additional chamber for guests, and a stable was usually attached to the hall at one end. The hall was warmed and lighted by a great fire. In each chamber there was a small fireplace for heat, and light was supplied by a candle.

The inn was undoubtedly built on this same plan, even when a building was built especially for an inn; in most cases, however, the inn had been built for an ordinary dwelling house. The weary traveler coming to the inn at nightfall would have his supper at the great table, and his bed would then be spread in the hall itself. Heat and such light as was necessary he would have from the hall fire. If he brought a horse and paid for his keep we are told he paid no extra charge for his bed, but the foot traveler paid a small sum for his lodging. A traveler of better estate would pay for and receive accommodation in a small chamber. There he would be served with food, and his bed would be spread; he would be charged not merely for the food and lodging, but also for his fire and candle. Even there he would not be likely to occupy the chamber alone, or even a bed alone; the king himself on his travels was expected to have a bedfellow, and a private person would be fortunate if he had only one. Still he was traveling in luxury if he shared with two or three others a private chamber, a private bed, and a private fire.

As time went on and the business of the innkeepers increased, especially in the great towns, buildings were built as inns, the number of chambers being greatly increased. In the sixteenth century we hear of inns in London which could accommodate one hundred guests. It must be clear that with so many guests the common hall would be needed for the reception and for the general table, and the guests must have all been put into special chambers for sleeping, but most of these were undoubtedly still common chambers, in which travelers were put as they happened to come, sharing not merely the chamber but the bed with strange bedfellows.

1:6 *Development of the Law*

Such being the business and such the customs of innkeepers, their responsibility, which through modern eyes seems anomalous, is easily explained. They undertake as a business to furnish food, protection, and shelter to the wayfaring guest. Having undertaken such a public business, and the public need being concerned, the innkeeper must supply his service to all; and in order to perform his undertaking he must furnish not merely sufficient food and a tight roof, but sufficient protection against the dangers of country traveling. To refuse shelter, to fail to provide food, or to permit robbers from outside to enter the inn would be a breach of his obligation and would render him liable to action. But this is not the limit of his obligation. If he puts a stranger into a common room with other strangers and bids him sleep, the innkeeper must undertake his care and protection during the night, not merely against persons outside but against strange bedfellows within the inn. It is interesting to notice how history repeats itself in this case. A much later invention, the sleeping car, brought back to modern life some of the obsolete features of the life of the Middle Ages. A number of persons, strangers to one another, were received to sleep in a common room open to persons from outside. The existence of the same conditions imposed a similar responsibility, and the proprietor of the sleeping car, like the innkeeper in the Middle Ages, was obliged to protect his guests as well as he could against danger from within and from without. The innkeeper's liability did not exist in the case of a private chamber, into which only the guest who engaged it or friends brought into it by the guest were allowed to enter. If a man engaged a room and was put in exclusive control of it, and was given the key, the protection which the innkeeper was obliged to furnish him was, therefore, merely against outsiders who might be permitted to break into the room without right. Against the inmates the guest had no right to call upon the innkeeper for protection. This is the reason for the stress laid in the old cases upon the fact that the innkeeper has given the guest the key of his room; this gift of key marked and symbolized the fact that the room was no longer in the innkeeper's disposal, that he could quarter no stranger in it, and that the guest and his friends alone could enter, and, therefore, against those who rightly entered the innkeeper undertook no responsibility.

The business of innkeeper having been carried on in this way, the distinctive features of the law are easily accounted for. The principles of the innkeeper's liability once being established have continued unchanged until the present day, and the hotelkeeper in the great cities of the United States derives his rights and traces his responsibilities to the host of the humble village inn of medieval England.

2 The Nature and Definition of an Inn and Other Places of Public Accommodation

2:1 *The Inn Is a Public House*

From the earliest times the fundamental characteristic of an inn has been its public nature. It is a public house, a house of public entertainment, or, as it is legally phrased, a common inn, a house kept "publicly, openly and notoriously, for the entertainment and accommodation of travellers and others, for a reward."[1]

The whole system of travel and communication in rural England, at the time the law of inns was in the making, required that the weary traveler should find, at convenient places beside the highway, houses of entertainment and shelter to which he might resort during his journey for food, rest, and protection. The ordinary laws of supply and demand would lead to the establishment of such houses by the roadside at places which would sufficiently serve the public convenience, but those laws could not be trusted to secure to each individual the benefit of the food and shelter therein provided. The desire for gain is not the only passion which moves men, innkeepers or others. Hatred, prejudice, envy, sloth, or undue fastidiousness might influence an innkeeper to refuse entertainment to a traveler, even though he could pay his score. The supply of food and shelter to a traveler was a matter of public concern, and the house which offered such food and shelter was engaged in a public service. The law must make injustice to the individual traveler impossible; the caprice of the host could not be permitted to leave a subject of the king hungry and shelterless. In a matter of such importance the public had an interest, and must see that, so far as was consistent with justice to the innkeeper, his inn was carried on for the benefit of the whole public, and so it became in an exact sense a public house.

2:2 *Innkeeper Professes a Public Business*

It follows from the nature of the inn that an innkeeper is one who professes to serve the public by keeping an inn. The most striking characteristic of his employment, that which distinguishes his employment from that of an ordinary person's, is the fact that his calling is a public one. He is a "common innkeeper," who, in quaint language of Lord Holt "has made profession of a trade which is

---

[1]State v. Stone, 6 Vt. 295, 298 (1834).

for the public good, and has thereby exposed and vested an interest of himself in all the King's subjects that will employ him in the way of his trade."[2] Whether a man is an innkeeper depends, therefore, in the first place upon whether he makes a profession of serving the public needs and in the second place upon whether his regular business is entertaining travelers.

2:3 *Distinction between Innkeeper and Private Host for Hire*

In many places where there are no inns, private householders occasionally, and even frequently, take in and accommodate travelers and receive compensation, but merely as a matter of accommodation, and without making a business of the practice. They receive the stranger and travel out of mere hospitality or from motives among which gain is merely incidental, and their livelihood is not derived from their hospitality. Such persons, though they receive compensation for the accommodation they furnish, are not innkeepers.[3]

Thus in *Howth v. Franklin*,[4] it was shown that a man had a house on the high road, much visited by travelers, who were uniformly entertained and charged; these facts were notorious and relied on by travelers. On the other hand, he often declared that he did not keep an inn, he refused to take boarders, and often entertained his friends and countrymen free of charge. The court held that the question whether he was or was not an innkeeper was for the jury and that the jury might on this evidence find him an innkeeper. In the course of his opinion Judge Roberts said:

> There are numerous farmers situated on the public roads of the country, who occasionally, and even frequently, take in and accommodate travellers, and receive compensation for it, who are not innkeepers, and are not liable as such. It is not their business or occupation, nor do they prepare and fit up their establishments for it. They yield to the laws of hospitality, in receiving and entertaining the stranger and the traveller, yet they cannot afford to do so without some compensation. This view of the subject the Court also presented to the minds of the jury, by telling them in substance, that if [the] defendant only occasionally entertained travellers for compensation, when it suited his own pleasure, he did not thereby become an innkeeper.[5]

Similarly, in *Lyon v. Smith*,[6] it was proved that the person alleged to be an innkeeper had entertained several individuals at his house overnight and been

---

[2]Lane v. Cotton, 88 Eng. Rep. 1458, 1464 (K.B. 1701).

[3]Lyon v. Smith, 1 Iowa 244 (1843); Goodyear Tire & Rubber Co. v. Altamont Springs Hotel Co., 206 Ky. 494, 267 S.W. 555 (1924); Kisten v. Hildebrand, 48 Ky. (9 B. Mon.) 72 (1848); State v. Steele, 106 N.C. 766, 11 S.E. 478 (1890); State v. Mathews, 19 N.C. 424 (1837); Howth v. Franklin, 20 Tex. 798 (1858); Southwestern Hotel Co. v. Rogers, 183 S.W.2d 751 (Tex. Civ. App. 1944), aff'd, 143 Tex. 343, 184 S.W.2d 835 (1945).

[4]20 Tex. 798 (1858).

[5]*Id.* at 802–803.

[6]1 Iowa 244 (1843).

paid a compensation for his care and attentions, but there was no proof that he held himself out in any manner as a common innkeeper, or that he was so regarded by the public. In the course of his opinion Chief Justice Mason said:

> To render a person liable as a common innkeeper, it is not sufficient to show that he occasionally entertains travelers. Most of the farmers in a new country do this, without supposing themselves answerable for the horses or other property of their guests, which may be stolen, or otherwise lost, without any fault of their own. Nor is such the rule in older countries, where it would operate with far less injustice, and be less opposed to good policy than with us. To be subjected to the same responsibilities attaching to innkeepers, a person must make tavern-keeping, to some extent, a regular business, a means of livelihood. He should hold himself out to the world as an *innkeeper*. It is not necessary that he should have a sign, or a license, provided that he has in any other manner authorized the general understanding that his was a public house, where strangers had a right to require accommodation. The person who occasionally entertains others for a reasonable compensation is no more subject to the extraordinary responsibility of an innkeeper than is he liable as a common carrier, who in certain special cases carries the property of others from one place to another for hire.[7]

If, however, the housekeeper does as a matter of fact receive every member of the public who applies for entertainment, as a regular course of business, he is an innkeeper, though he may claim that his house is still a private one.[8]

The question whether a house where a guest is entertained is a public inn or a private house is a question of fact, to be determined, like any fact, upon all the evidence. In determining the question, the facts may lead to a presumption against a party. Thus if a housekeeper does an act which he could not legally do unless he were an innkeeper, he will be presumed, in the absence of evidence to the contrary, to be an innkeeper. Thus in *Korn v. Schedler,*[9] it was held that when a man has applied for a license to sell liquor as a hotelkeeper, he cannot later deny liability for the loss of a guest's property on the ground that he does not keep a hotel.

2:4 Innkeeper Serves Transient Guests

The person whose needs the innkeeper undertakes to serve is the weary traveler, a person who stays with him merely a short time in the course of his journey. The inn is therefore primarily provided for transient guests, and one who does not profess to serve transient guests is not an innkeeper. (For this reason it was held necessary in the old cases to allege, in an action by a guest against an innkeeper, that the plaintiff was "transient.")

[7]*Id.* at 186.
[8]Jaquet v. Edwards, 1 Jamaica 70 (1867).
[9]11 Daly (N.Y.) 234 (Ct. C.P. N.Y. Co. 1882).

This characteristic of an innkeeper is the distinguishing feature between an inn and a boardinghouse. A boardinghouse is for the entertainment not of transient guests, who must find food and shelter at once, but of more or less permanent occupants, who may at their leisure make bargains with their host. The boarder being in this position, the housekeeper may exercise the same liberty. If the boarder may select and bargain for his boarding place, so the housekeeper may select and bargain with his guests. The distinction and the reason for it were brought out very neatly in *Bonner v. Welborn,* an early Georgia case.[10] The defendant, who was proceeded against on a statute affecting innkeepers, was the keeper of a hotel at a country watering place, who undertook, either in his hotel or in cottages near it which he rented, to entertain visitors for a season. In holding that he was not an innkeeper Judge Nesbet said:

> It is because inns and innkeepers have to do with the travelling public—strangers—and that for brief periods, and under circumstances which render it impossible for each customer to contract for the terms of his entertainment, that the law has taken them so strictly in charge. And it is because of the compulsion innkeepers are under, to afford entertainment to anybody, that the law has clothed them with extraordinary privileges. Now, under this (it is submitted), correct legal view of innkeepers, was the plaintiff in this case, an innkeeper? Was that his business? His business was, to rent his houses to families or persons who might contract with him for their occupancy. They are not his guests, they are beyond dispute, his tenants, and he their landlord. His business was, to furnish board, lodging and attention. But to whom? To the wayfaring world? No. But to persons who might resort to his healthful fountains and salubrious locality, for a season, that is, for the fall and summer months. They were not his guests for a day, or night, or week, but his lodgers or boarders for a season. They were not chargeable according to any tariff of rates, fixed by law, but according to contract, varied, beyond doubt, according to time, amount of accommodation, and other circumstances. These are not the characteristics of the business of innkeeping, but indicate a boarding house. As well might every private boarding house in the State, be adjudged an inn or a tavern, as this party's establishment. The object for which people are stated in the declaration, to have visited the springs, necessarily forbids the idea of their being travellers, and of plaintiff's house being a tavern. It was health, in the use of the medicinal waters. That object indicates abiding—permanency of location, for a season, at least. These waters cannot cure by seven draughts; or like the waters of Jordan, by seven washings.[11]

But the fact that a person receives those who are not transient guests does not prevent his being an innkeeper. Though in its origin the business of an innkeeper was to supply the needs of travelers, yet once in the business an innkeeper will naturally be quite willing to do a profitable business with other persons. An innkeeper will ordinarily receive and care for any proper person who applies, even

---

[10]7 Ga. 296 (1849).
[11]*Id.* at 307–308.

though, not being a traveler, he could not demand such reception as a legal right; and such reception of guests does not work a change of employment. One who keeps a house of entertainment for travelers is not the less an innkeeper because he also receives other persons.[12]

Even if the innkeeper caters to permanent guests, and makes his inn attractive for them, he is none the less an innkeeper if he professes also to supply the needs of travelers, as most hotelkeepers do. Thus the fact that a house stands upon enclosed grounds which are reserved for the exclusive use of guests, that the gates are closed at night, and that the house is thus rendered attractive as a pleasure resort and guests are thereby induced to remain a considerable time, does not prevent the house from being an inn if it is held out as a place of entertainment for travelers.[13]

And even in a case where the chief attraction of a hotel was a mineral spring connected with it, and it did not appear that persons resorted to the hotel except such as desired to use it as a watering place, it was assumed without argument that the hotel was an inn.[14]

> The function and purpose of hotels change with the period, methods of travel and conditions of society. [Citation omitted.] Now hotels are often devoted to the entertainment of guests seeking rest, recreation and pleasure. They are located in the mountains and at the seaside, where guests may go in the summer; or they may be located where there is a warm climate, to attract guests who wish to escape the rigors of winter. They differ in the main from purely commercial hotels only in respect to the greater attention they give to features of recreation and amusement, and in the usual duration of stay of the guests.[15]

2:5 Innkeeper Supplies the Needs of a Traveler

The innkeeper supplies all the entertainment which the weary traveler actually needs on the road, which in simplest terms are food, shelter, and protection. If the keeper of a house of entertainment does not undertake to furnish either food or shelter, he is not a common innkeeper, and this requirement distinguishes inns from many similar houses of public entertainment. Thus a house which does not supply lodging is not an inn, and this rule excludes from among inns a restaurant or eating house. On the same principle a coffeehouse or a bar and grill is not an inn. And for the same reason a house that furnishes only lodging without food, like a lodginghouse, or an apartment hotel, or a sleeping car, is not an inn.

---

[12]Wintermute v. Clark, 5 Sand. (N.Y.) 242 (Super. Ct. 1851).

[13]Fay v. Pacific Improvement Co., 93 Cal. 253, 26 P. 1099 (1892); Powers v. Raymond, 197 Cal. 126, 239 P. 1069 (1925).

[14]Willis v. McMahan, 89 Cal. 156, 26 P. 649 (1891); Perrine v. Paulos, 100 Cal. App. 2d 655, 224 P.2d 41 (Dist. Ct. App. 1950).

[15]Friedman v. Schindler's Prairie House, Inc., 224 A.D. 232, 236–37, 230 N.Y.S. 44, 50 (3d Dep't), aff'd mem., 250 N.Y. 574, 166 N.E. 329 (1928).

If all elements of entertainment required by a traveler are furnished him by the host the house may be an inn, notwithstanding they are independently furnished and separately charged. Thus a hotel is not less an inn though it is conducted on the so-called European plan; the fact that the food is separately obtained and paid for, and the guest may procure his food elsewhere if he chooses, does not alter the legal character of the house.

In the case of such a hotel it usually happens that food is supplied in a restaurant, connected with the hotel but open to everyone, not merely to guests of the hotel. It is this connection of the restaurant with the hotel as part of the same establishment that makes the hotel an inn.

The hotelkeeper cannot avoid the responsibility of an innkeeper by proving that the restaurant is in fact conducted by an independent person. If the hotel is held out to the public, as having a restaurant connected with it and forming part of it, it is an inn, and not a mere lodginghouse.

In *Johnson v. Chadbourn Finance Co.*[16] the court held that the establishment in question was a hotel even though it had no dining room or café since there was an independently operated café in the building to which there was access from the offices and sleeping quarters without going out of doors. Moreover the establishment itself was known as the Hotel Vendome and on its letterhead it was stated that there was a first-class café in connection with the hotel. Thus the Vendome, by its name and practices, masqueraded as a hotel and this was sufficient for the court to classify it as a hotel.

But, on the other hand, if there is no holding them out as parts of the same establishment, the fact that an independent restaurant is conducted under the same roof and is resorted to by lodgers, does not make a lodginghouse an inn,[17] nor does the fact that the keeper of the lodginghouse is in the habit of sending out to procure cooked food for his guests at their request.[18]

The common-law concept of an ''inn'' which requires that food and shelter both be furnished to travelers still prevails in New York and in the majority of jurisdictions. However, there is a strong minority trend toward relinquishing food service as a necessary requisite to innkeeping. Most state legislatures have enacted statutes governing the construction, maintenance, and operation of hotels, and the rights and duties of hotelkeepers to their guests and the public. Statutory definitions of hotels vary from state to state, depending upon the public policy of the state as well as upon the subject matter to which the statute applies. For example, hotels are defined in building codes, in fire regulations, in alcoholic beverage licensing laws, in labor laws, in public health codes, in penal statutes, in statutes limiting the liability of hotelkeepers for money or other property in their custody, and so forth. Statutory definitions are not necessarily uniform even within a single jurisdiction.

[16]89 Minn. 310, 94 N.W. 874 (1903). *See also* Asseltyne v. Fay Hotel, 222 Minn. 91, 23 N.W.2d 357 (1946).

[17]Cromwell v. Stephens, 2 Daly (N.Y.) 15, 3 Abb. Pr. (n.s.) 26 (Ct. C.P. N.Y. Co. 1867).

[18]Kelly v. Excise Comm'rs of New York, 54 How. Pr. (N.Y.) 327 (Ct. C.P. 1877).

2:6　*Innkeeper Defined*

The innkeeper is the person who on his own account carries on the business of an inn. In other words, he is the proprietor of the establishment. The person actually employed as manager, though he has the whole direction of the enterprise, is not an innkeeper if he is acting on behalf of someone else. Thus the salaried manager of a hotel owned or operated by a corporation is not to be held responsible as an innkeeper; the corporation is the innkeeper. Note, however, that, by statute, hotel managers and employees are often held personally liable for violations of, for example, liquor laws, labor laws, and sanitary codes. Note also the distinction between the *owner* of the physical hotel property, land, buildings, and equipment, and the *operator* of the hotel who is very often a lessee or managing or operating agent. While in such cases the one in actual charge of the conduct of the hotel business is the innkeeper, the owner of the property may also he held responsible by statute for the safe condition of the building.

It has been held, however, that a hotel owner, not in possession of the premises leased by him to a lessee operator, is not liable as insurer for the loss of a guest's personal property.[19]

The profession of readiness to serve the public need not be made in any particular way; it is enough that by word or act the innkeeper makes public his intention to become such. It has been usual, particularly in former times, to advertise his house by hanging out a sign; but it is not essential to a man's being an innkeeper that he should do so. If he in fact carries on the business publicly as innkeeper he will be held as such, although he never displayed a sign. The profession may be made by any method of soliciting the patronage of the public, as by advertising, by keeping a public register, by running a coach to a railroad station, and so forth.

What acts are sufficient to justify a finding that a man is an innkeeper is a question which has often been a subject of judicial decision. In a California case, the keeper of the What Cheer House insisted that his house was a lodginghouse and not an inn because, he said, the eating department was distinct from the lodging department. It appeared that in the basement of the What Cheer House, and connected with it by a stairway, there was a restaurant, which was conducted by the defendant and two other persons jointly, and that the three shared the profits. The court held that the What Cheer House was an inn.[20] In the course of his opinion Judge Rhodes said:

> Where a person, by the means usually employed in that business, holds himself out to the world as an innkeeper, and in that capacity, is accustomed to receive travellers as his guests, and solicits a continuance of their patronage, and a traveller relying on such representations goes to the house to receive such entertainment as he has occasion for, the relation of innkeeper and guest is created, and the innkeeper cannot be heard to say that his professions were false, and that he was not in fact an inn-

[19]Cohen v. Raleigh Hotel Corp., 153 N.Y.L.J. No. 71, 18 (Sup. Ct. 1965).
[20]Pinkerton v. Woodward, 33 Cal. 557 (1867).

keeper. The rules regulating the respective rights, duties and responsibilities of inn-keeper and guest have their origin in consideration of public policy, and were designed mainly for the protection and security of travellers and their property. They would afford the traveller but poor security if, before venturing to intrust his property to one who by his agents, cards, bills, advertisements, sign, and all the means by which publicity and notoriety can be given to his business, represents himself as an innkeeper, he is required to inquire of the employés as to their interest in the establishment, or take notice of the agencies or means by which the several departments are conducted. The same considerations of public policy that dictated those rules demand that the innkeeper should be held to the responsibilities which, by his representations, he induced his guests to believe he would assume. We think the jury were fully warranted by the evidence in finding that the "What Cheer House" was an inn.[21]

In a later case in the same state, the court dealt with a similar question as follows:

We think the evidence in this case is full and complete to the point that the Hotel Del Monte was a public inn. It not only had a name indicating its character as such, but it was also shown that it was open to all persons who have a right to demand entertainment at a public house; that it solicited public patronage by advertising and in the distribution of its business cards, and kept a public register in which its guest entered their names upon arrival, and before they were assigned rooms; that the hotel, at its own expense, ran a coach to the railroad station for the purpose of con-veying its patrons to and from the hotel; that it had its manager, clerks, waiters, and in its interior management all the ordinary arrangements and appearances of a hotel, and the prices charged were for board and lodging. These facts were cer-tainly sufficient to justify the court in finding, as it did, that the appellant was an innkeeper.[22]

2:7 Carrying on Other Business

An innkeeper may at the same time and on the same or neighboring premises carry on a different business, which though similar to that of the innkeeper is not identical with it. For instance, an innkeeper may maintain and operate an inde-pendent garage. In the same way, an innkeeper may establish under the same roof as his inn a restaurant for the accommodation of persons who are not his guests. If the restaurant is entirely distinct from the rooms proper to the inn, a person who resorts merely to the restaurant is not a guest. So where an innkeeper had the refreshment bar at the side of his building with a separate entrance it was held that one served there was not a guest.[23] On this principle one who, not being a lodger in the hotel on the European plan, resorts to the restaurant con-nected with the hotel for food is not a guest.[24] By the same token, a mere cus-

[21]*Id.* at 597.
[22]Fay v. Pacific Improvement Co., 93 Cal. 243, 259–60, 26 P. 1099, 1100 (1892).
[23]Regina v. Rymer, [1877] 2 Q.B.D. 136, 46 L.J.M.C. 108.
[24]Krohn v. Sweeney, 2 Daly (N.Y.) 200 (Ct. C.P. N.Y. Co. 1867).

tomer at a bar, a restaurant, a barbershop, or newsstand operated by a hotel is not a guest.[25]

2:8 *Inn and Hotel Defined*

CROMWELL V. STEPHENS
2 Daly (N.Y.) 15, 3 Abb. Pr. 26 (Ct. C.P. N.Y. Co. 1867)

[Application for an injunction prohibiting defendants, composing the Croton Aqueduct Board, from cutting off the Croton water from a building owned by plaintiff. The board, upon the assumption that plaintiff's building was a hotel, imposed a special tax applicable to hotels only. Plaintiff contends that he is operating a cheap lodginghouse. The question presented is whether the building is a "hotel."]

DALY, J.: " . . . Ordinarily, in a legal inquiry, it is sufficient to refer to some approved lexicographer to ascertain the precise meaning of a word. But this is a word of wide application, and as the meaning which is to be attached to it in this country, has been the subject of much discussion upon the argument, it may be well to refer to its origin and past history, as one of the means of determining its exact signification. The word is of French origin, being derived from *hostel,* and more remotely from the Latin word *hospes,* a word having a double signification, as it was used by the Romans both to denote a stranger who lodges at the house of another, as well as the master of a house who entertains travelers or guests. Among the Romans it was a universal custom for the wealthier classes to extend the hospitality of their house, not only to their friends and connections when they came to a city, but to respectable travelers generally. They had inns, but they were kept by slaves, and were places of resort for the lower orders, or for the accommodation of such travelers as were not in a condition to claim the hospitality of the better classes. On either side of the spacious mansions of the wealthy patricians were smaller apartments, known as the *hospitium,* or place for the entertainment of strangers, and the word *hospes* was a term to designate the owner of such a mansion, as well as the guest whom he received. [Citation omitted.] This custom of the Romans prevailed in the earlier part of the middle ages. From the fifth to the ninth century, traveling was difficult and dangerous. There was little security, except within castles or walled towns. The principal public roads had been destroyed by centuries of continuous war, and such thoroughfares as existed were infested by roving bands, who lived exclusively by plunder.

"In such a state of things there could be little traveling, and consequently the few inns to be found were rather dens to which robbers resorted to carouse and divide their spoils, than places for the entertainment of travelers. [Citation omitted.] The effect of a condition of society like this was to make hospitality not only a social virtue but a religious duty, and in the monasteries, and in all the

---

[25]Wallace v. Shoreham Hotel Corp., 49 A.2d 81 (D.C. Mun. Ct. App. 1946).

great religious establishments, provision was made for the gratuitous entertainment of wayfarers and travelers. Either a separate building, or an apartment within the monastery, was devoted exclusively to this purpose, which was in charge of an officer called the hostler, who received the traveler and conducted him to this apartment, which was fitted up with beds, where he was allowed to tarry for two days, and to have his meals in the refectory, while, if he journeyed upon horseback, provender was provided by the hostler for his beast in the stables. [Citation omitted.] In many countries this apartment, or guest hall, of a monastery retained the original Latin name of *hospitium*, but in France the word was blended with *hospes* and changed into *hospice*, and it afterward underwent another change. As civilization advanced, and the nobility of France deserted their strong castles for spacious and costly residences in the towns, they erected their mansions upon a scale sufficiently extensive to enable them to discharge this great duty of hospitality, as is still, or was very recently, the custom among the nobility and wealthier classes in Russia, and in some of the northern countries of Europe. Borrowing, by analogy, from an existing word, and to distinguish it from the guest house of the monastery, every such great house or mansion was called a *hostel*, and by the mutation and attrition to which these words are subject in use, the *s* was gradually dropped from the word, and it became *hôtel*. As traveling and intercourse increased, the duty upon the nobility of entertaining respectable strangers became too onerous a burden, and establishments in which this class of persons could be entertained by paying for accommodation sprung up in the cities, towns, and upon the leading public roads, which, to distinguish them from the great mansions or hotels of the wealthy, and at the same time to denote that they were superior to the *auberge* or *cabaret*, were called *hotelleries*, a name which has been in use in France for several centuries, and is still in use to some extent as a common term for inns of the better class, while the word hotel, in France, has long ceased to be confined to its original signification, and has become a word of a most extensive meaning. It is the term for the mansion of a prince, nobleman, minister of state, or of a person of distinction, or of celebrity. It is applied to a hospital, as Hôtel Dieu; or to a town hall, as Hôtel de Ville; to the residence of a judge, to certain public offices, and to any house in which furnished apartments are let by the day, week, or month. [Citation omitted.] . . .

" . . . [T]he word hotel came into use in England by the general introduction in London, after 1760, of the kind of establishment that was then common in Paris called an *hôtel garni*, a large house, in which furnished apartments were let by the day, week, or month. [In some early dictionaries,] . . . hotel is given as the proper pronunciation of *hostel*, an inn; [later,] . . . it is incorporated as an English word, and is defined in the latter to be 'an inn, having elegant lodgings and accommodations for gentlemen and genteel families. . . . '

"The word was introduced into this country about 1797. Before that time houses for the entertainment of travelers in this city were at first called inns, and afterward taverns and coffee-houses. In 1794, an association organized upon the principle of a tontine, erected in Wall Street what was then a very superior house for the accommodation of travelers, called the Tontine Coffee-house; the success of which led to the formation of another company for the erection of one upon a still more extensive scale in Broadway. This structure, which was called the Tontine Tavern, was built about 1796, upon the site of what had been a famous tavern or coffee-house in colonial times, and from the extensive accommodation it afforded, and the superior character of its appointments, it was then, and for many years afterward, the most celebrated establishment of the kind in the country. . . .

"It is to be deduced from the origin and history of the word, and the exposition that has been given to it by English and American lexicographers, that a hotel, in this country, is what in France was known as a *hotelerie*, and in England as a common inn of that superior class usually found in cities and large towns. A common inn is defined by Bacon to be a house for the entertainment of travelers and passengers, in which a lodging and necessities are provided for them and for their horses and attendants. . . . In *Thompson v. Lacy* (3 B. & A. 283), Justice BAYLEY declares it to be 'a house where a traveler is furnished with everything which he has occasion for while upon his way,' and in the same case, BEST, J., says it is 'a house, the owner of which holds out that he will receive all travelers and sojourners who are willing to pay a price adequate to the sort of accommodation provided, and who come in a situation in which they are fit to be received.' But a more practical idea of what was understood at the common law as common inns, may be gathered from Hollingshed's description of them, as they existed in the days of Elizabeth. 'Every man,' says that quaint chronicler, 'may in England use his inn as his own house, and have for his monie how great or how little varietie of vittals and whatsoever service himself shall think fit to call for. If the traveler have a horse, his bed doth cost him nothing, but if he go on foot, he is sure to pay a pennie for the same. Each comer is sure to be in clean sheets wherein no man hath been lodged since they came from the laundress, or out of the water wherein they were washed. Whether he be horseman or footman, if his chamber be once appointed, he may carry the key with him as of his own house as long as he lodgeth there. In all our inns we have plenty of ale, biere, and sundrie kinds of wine; and such is the capacity of some of them that they are able to lodge two hundred or three hundred persons and their horses at ease, and with very short warning (to) make such provision for their diet as to him that is unacquainted withall may seem to be incredible' (Hollingshed's Chronicle—Description of England). . . .

"In the above-mentioned case of *Thompson v. Lacy*, the defendant kept a house in London called the Globe Tavern and Coffee-house, where he furnished beds and provisions to those who applied. No stage, coaches, or wagons stopped there, nor were there any stables belonging to the house. The question was whether this was an inn, and it was held that it was. 'The defendant does not charge,' said BEST, J., 'as a mere lodging-housekeeper, by the week or month. . . . A lodging-house keeper, on the other hand, must make a contract with every man that comes, whereas an inn-keeper is bound, without making any special contract, to provide lodging and entertainment for all at a reasonable price.' . . .

"It follows from these authorities, that an inn is a house where all who conduct themselves properly, and who are able and ready to pay for their entertainment, are received, if there is accommodation for them, and who, without any stipulated engagement as to the duration of their stay, or as to the rate of compensation, are, while there, supplied at a reasonable charge with their meals, their lodging, and such services and attention as are necessarily incident to the use of the house as a temporary home."

In *Crapo v. Rockwell*,[26] excerpted below, the function of an inn was further explained:

> The primary and fundamental function of an inn seems clearly to have been to furnish entertainment and lodging for the traveler on his journey. This at all times seems to have been its distinguishing feature. This idea has been expressed in the literature of ages, in history, sacred and profane, in fiction and in poetry. So true is this that the term "inn" seems always to have been used in connection with the corresponding notion of travelers seeking the accommodation and protection of the inn. Thus the Christian era dawned on a Judean scene, where travelers away from home who had gone up to be taxed pursuant to the decree of the Roman emperor, sought refuge in a manger "because there was no room for them in the inn." Sir Walter Scott characterizes the inn of the old days of Merry England as "the free rendezvous of all travelers" of which the bonny Black Bear of Cumnor village, not conducted merely, but "ruled by Giles Gosling, a man of a goodly person," as landlord, was a typical instance. And so the most illustrious bard of England says, referring to the time of approaching twilight, with the west glimmering with streaks of day, "now spurs the lated traveler apace to gain the timely inn."
>
> In 1983, statutory hotel tenants sought rent abatement for defendant landlord's alleged breach of warranty of habitability. Finding in tenants' favor, the court then dealt with the further issue of whether tenants were entitled to rent reductions for landlord's alleged failure to provide customary hotel services.

WHITEHALL HOTEL v. GAYNOR
121 Misc. 2d 736, 470 N.Y.S.2d 286 (N.Y. City Civ. Ct. 1983)

McKAY, J.: " . . . Factually, the trial established that petitioner is currently providing to respondents the following services: desk service, including some mail service, some rough equivalent of bellboy services performed by one or two lobby attendants and minimal telephone service. New carpeting has also been provided to all respondents, but not upkeep of the carpeting. The parties stipulated that these services constitute 20% of all the hotel services set forth in the

---

[26]48 Misc. 1, 94 N.Y.S. 1122 (Sup. Ct. 1905).

METHISA [Metropolitan Hotel Industry Stabilization] Code, (although the list in the Code does not purport to be exhaustive). The remaining 80% which are services not provided by petitioner to respondents, are 'maid service, furnishings and laundering of linen, and use and upkeep of furniture and fixtures.' METHISA Code, § 13(h).

"The stipulation just referred to above also included an estimate of the relative value of the hotel services in relation to the respondents' rent. The stipulation reads in full as follows:

"1. That if all hotel services set forth in the Metropolitan Hotel Industry Stabilization Code were given to the respondent-tenants herein said services would constitute 25% of the rent charged for each of the respondents' apartments.

"2. It is conceded and stipulated that the petitioner-landlord is providing only 5% of the services and that the services that are not being provided to the respondents would comprise 20% of the rent being charged.

"3. This stipulation is in lieu of expert testimony and without prejudice to landlord's claim that it does not have to provide hotel services to the respondent-tenants herein.

"It should be emphasized here that consistent with all the petitions and as recognized and conceded by petitioner at trial, with no opposition from respondents' counsel, petitioner is a member of METHISA, and all of the units in question are currently governed by the METHISA Code. However, it is also apparent to this court that petitioner has been undergoing a serious 'identity crisis' as to whether in its newly renovated condition it should be, or even wants to continue to be, part of METHISA. For example, it advertised these newly renovated units as apartments, not as hotel rooms or suites, and it used the rent stabilized lease form and tenants' rights riders without reference to hotel stabilization or METHISA for each of respondents' leases. Furthermore, petitioner offered one and two years leases, instead of six months ones. Thus, with the exception of the name of the owner, 'Whitehall Hotel Corp.' and article 42 of the leases concerning the purported waiver of 'hotel services'—to be discussed below—there is not a single reference in these multi-page leases to the fact that this building is a hotel or that the lessees are supposed to be hotel tenants.

"Although these facts and circumstances demonstrate the ambivalent attitude of petitioner toward METHISA, these units are still currently under the METHISA Code and this court will not attempt to affect or alter this classification in the context of these non-payment summary proceedings. See Rent Stabilization Law ('RSL') § 43, N.Y.C. Admin. Code § YY51–3.1 as amended June 26, 1983.

"With respect to the waiver clause, article 42 of the leases referred to above, if the court were to find a valid, enforceable waiver here by each of the tenants, such a finding would seem to dispose of the 'hotel services' issue in favor of petitioner. This would require a careful analysis of the Code because Section 7 of the New Code declares certain waivers to be void. It reads as follows:

"WAIVER OF BENEFIT VOID—Any agreement by a tenant to waive the benefit of any provision of the RSL, the EPTA, or this Code shall be void unless permitted by this Code.

"Accordingly, the waiver clause in each of the leases is void if the hotel services purportedly waived comprise (1) benefits provided for in the METHISA Code or the enabling statute, RSL and (2) the waiver of such benefit is not otherwise permitted by the METHISA Code. Of course, the same careful analysis of the Code would be required to determine whether petitioner has violated the statute or the Code in the first place, apart from the validity of any waiver. We turn therefore to the analysis of the new Code.

"The first reference in the Code to 'hotel services' is found in 'DEFINITIONS', Section 3(h). That subsection reads in full as follows:

"Section 3. DEFINITIONS . . .

(h) 'Hotel'—Any Class A or Class B Multiple Dwelling containing six or more dwelling units which on June 1, 1968 was and still is commonly regarded as a hotel, transient hotel or residential hotel, which customarily provides hotel services such as maid service, furnishings and laundering of linen, telephone and bellboy service, secretarial or desk service and use and upkeep of furniture and fixtures.

"It should be noted here that one of the differences in this amended Code from its predecessor is found right in the definition of hotel. The prior Code included the words, 'provides or makes available hotel services such as . . . ', while the new Code eliminates the words 'or makes available.' This change made the Code definition identical with a definition of 'hotel' in the statute itself, the RSL, N.Y.C. Admin. Code § YY51–3.0(a)(l)(e), except that this particular statutory definition in RSL refers only to Class A multiple dwellings. The Commissioner of the Department of Housing Preservation and Development ('DHPD') in his Explanatory Statement to this new Code labels this difference as one of the 'more significant changes,' which 'requires the owner to actually provide customary hotel services instead of merely claiming that they are available in order to take advantage of the benefits under the Code. . . .'. . . .

"Without exception, every other reference in the Code to 'services' speaks exclusively in terms of services which were furnished or required to be furnished as of a certain date. In all cases, the controlling date is the date of the initial commencement of a given tenancy where such commencement is later than the base dates of May 31, 1968, May 29, 1974 or July 1, 1974. See subsection 3(p) of the Code. Any decrease in such required services is strictly regulated by the Code and the CAB. See § 42 of the Code. However, nowhere in this new Code is it specified which particular hotel services, if any, are required. Moreover, the official Rider for hotel tenants subsequently approved by DHPD [Department of Housing Preservation and Development] for attachment to hotel stabilized leases repeats the admonition of the Code that services provided or required on the date occupancy commences (or, if later, on the date the unit first became subject to Rent Stabilization) may not be decreased. This official Rider then goes on to state:

" . . . Required services include building-wide services such as heat, hot water, janitorial service, maintenance of locks and security devices, repair and maintenance and may include elevators, air conditioning, doorman and other amenities. . . . *Required services may also include* services within the dwelling unit, such as maintenance and repair of appliances, cleaning, linens and painting every three years. [Emphasis supplied.]

"It is understood that the Rider quoted above was published for informational purposes only and does not become part of any lease, nor does it replace or modify the RSL or the Code. Nevertheless, the Rider underscores the ambiguity which permeates the Code itself with respect to required hotel services, or put more positively, it demonstrates the studied decision of the drafters of the Code to refrain from specifying which particular hotel services would be required.

"It is therefore apparent to this court that the free market bargaining approach for the setting of agreed rents and services at the commencement of new tenancies, which has been traditionally employed in hotel stabilization, remains essentially intact under the new Code. The Code continues to provide for strict regulation of the increase or decrease in services from the base date, which for new tenants is the commencement of their tenancy.

"The threshold issue of what minimal hotel services, if any, or what minimum percentage of hotel services are mandated for this and other buildings to fit the definition of 'hotel' under the new Code, will have to be left to the CAB. . . .

"Based on the foregoing analysis, this court holds that the current METHISA Code does not require this petitioner to furnish any one or more specific hotel services to these respondents other than those few services already being provided.

"In view of this conclusion it follows that Section 7 of the Code ('Waiver of Benefit Void') does not apply to or render void the waiver of hotel services signed by these respondents. These tenants can and did agree to forego receiving the traditional hotel services, signified in part by the waiver clause (Article 42) in each of the leases, and by their overall agreement to pay the specified rents without these services. This may be contrary to the spirit of the new METHISA Code, but not to its letter, as read by this court. Hence, no reductions in rent are warranted at this time on account of the lack of those services. . . .

"This is not an unjust or inequitable result. Not one of these tenant-respondents ever even remotely suggested at trial that he or she wanted or expected these additional hotel services at the outset of their tenancy, nor is there any evidence that any of these tenants made inquiries or request of the landlord about these services. What they sought at trial, instead, were rent reductions. Clearly, they all had agreed to the rent fixed in their leases knowing full well that the rent did not include these services. Moreover, I credit the proof offered by petitioner that the rents would have been set significantly higher if these traditional hotel services were to have been provided and included, especially considering the fact that all utilities were already included in these rents."

In a holdover proceeding to remove an occupant from petitioner's residence, the court made the following observations.

YMCA OF GREATER NEW YORK MCBURNEY BRANCH V. PLOTKIN
136 Misc. 2d 950, 519 N.Y.S.2d 518 (N.Y. Civ. Ct. 1987)

FRIEDMAN, J.: " . . .

"The cause of action requires that the respondent prove that the YMCA is operating a 'hotel' or 'inn'. The facts in that regard are not in dispute. Petitioner operates a 'residence' that provides rooms for transient guests. The basic rental is a daily rate although there are 130 long term residents who rent by the week, either as 'students' or as 'permanent' residents. The petitioner provides education and recreational activities at the premises but does not serve meals. Petitioner claims that it rents only to 'members' but the testimony establishes that anyone who pays the membership fee as part of the room rental becomes a 'member.'

"The terms 'hotel' and 'inn' should first be examined in light of the customs and usage at the time GBL 206 was enacted. [Citations omitted.] The term ' "hotel" is in the common acceptance of the word synonymous with "inn", especially an inn of the better class.' (*Dixon v. Robbins*, 246 N.Y. 169, 172, 158 N.E. 63; *see Cromwell v. Stephens*, 3 Abb. Prac. [NS] 26 [1867]; *People v. Jones*, 54 Barb. 311, 316–317 [Gen. T. 1863].) The 'word "inn" at common law meant a place where a traveler is furnished with both lodging and entertainment, including food.' (*Dixon v. Robbins*, supra 246 N.Y. at 172, 158 N.E. 63; *People v. Jones*, supra at 316.) Under the common law definition petitioner does not operate an 'inn' since its residence does not provide ancillary services of the kind previously associated with 'inns'.

"Obviously, the conditions of travel and the nature of accommodations offered to transients have changed in the past century. (*See Freeman v. Kiamesha Concord*, 76 Misc. 2d 915, 921, 351 N.Y.S.2d 541, *supra; Friedman v. Schindler's Prairie House, Inc.*, 224 App. Div. 232, 236, 230 N.Y.S. 44 [3rd Dept 1928], *affd.* 250 N.Y. 574, 166 N.E. 329.) A more modern interpretation of the term 'hotel' includes any place where 'transient guests are received and lodged.' (*Dixon v. Robbins*, supra 246 N.Y. at 173, 158 N.E. 63; *Waitt Const. Co. v. Chase*, 197 App. Div. 327, 331, 188 N.Y.S. 589 [1st Dept 1921].)

"The courts have generally held that whether an establishment is a 'hotel' is, generally, a question of fact for the jury. (*Friedman v. Schindler's Prairie House, Inc.*, supra; *Goncalves v. Regent Intl. Hotels, Ltd.*, 58 N.Y.2d 206, 217, 460 N.Y.S.2d 750, 447 N.E.2d 693.) The court must, however, make a threshold determination as a matter of law whether there is a real controversy on the facts. [Citations omitted.] Without doubt, petitioner's establishment is a 'hotel' within the meaning of GBL 206. The only argument to the contrary is that petitioner caters only to 'members'. Under the undisputed testimony here, membership is open to anyone, without any requirement other than registration for a room. Thus, the court need not submit to a jury the question of whether this is a 'hotel'."

2:9 *Motel Defined*

The word "motel" is of comparatively recent origin. It is a modern coined word derived from, and an abbreviation of, the words "motorist's hotel." The word "motel" generally denotes a small hotel where lodgings are available for hire, with a minimum of personal service being furnished by the proprietor.

> [W]ith the great use of automobiles, there has been a tremendous develop-
> ment throughout the entire United States in the construction of buildings which
> furnish lodging accommodations for transients and which buildings are denomi-
> nated motels. . . . These motels have filled a required need for housing accommo-
> dations . . . quite generally more conveniently located for access by the general
> public than the normal hotel, and having greater facilities or accommodations for
> parking of automobiles immediately adjacent to the building itself. The mode of
> operation of the average motel results . . . in a great deal of "self-service" on the
> part of the guests and a reduction in the cost to the guest by way of gratuities.[27]

Hotels and motels are in point of fact of the same genus, differing only in style, design, appearance, location, and the type of service. They are both ser-vice establishments furnishing lodging, with or without meals, and a variety of other services to transients. A place which would otherwise be an inn or hotel does not lose its character as such because of its mode of construction, the name applied to it, or the fact that food or drink cannot be obtained therein. The same rules of law have been applied in cases of injuries to guests in motels as in ho-tels. Legal distinctions between hotels and motels, where they exist, are statu-tory, as in zoning ordinances, alcoholic beverage licensing laws, building codes, and other local ordinances. In *Gawzner Corp. v. Minier*,[28] the court held that statutory regulations which allowed hotels, but not motels, to display their rates outdoors were discriminatory and unconstitutional.

2:10 *Municipal Hotel-Room Use and Occupancy Taxes*

Many states have authorized city governments to impose hotel-room use and occupancy taxes under newly enacted constitutional home-rule powers available to cities that otherwise qualify. Since these taxes may be levied in addition to statewide sales taxes, affected local hotel and motel associations have resisted these burdens by challenging the legality of the cities' exercise of this new source of potential revenue-raising authority. See *Montana Innkeepers Associa-tion v. City of Billings*[29] and *Springfield Hotel-Motel Association v. City of Springfield*[30] for conflicting views as to the constitutionality of such tax levies.

In the following case, the Supreme Court of Pennsylvania upheld the consti-tutionality of the Philadelphia Convention Center Hotel Room Rental Tax. The court's opinion follows.

---

[27]Schermer v. Fremar Corp., 36 N.J. Super. Ct. 46, 50–51, 114 A.2d 757, 760 (1955).
[28]46 Cal. App. 3d 77, 120 Cal. Rptr. 344 (1975).
[29]206 Mont. 425, 671 P.2d 21 (Mont. 1983).
[30]119 Ill. App. 3d 753, 457 N.E.2d 1017 (1983).

LEVENTHAL v. CITY OF PHILADELPHIA
518 Pa. 233, 542 A.2d. 1328 (1988)

PAPADAKOS, J.: " . . .

"We assumed plenary jurisdiction in this matter to decide the narrow issue of whether the Convention Center Authority Act and the Hotel Room Rental Tax are constitutional as applied to Appellant under the Pennsylvania and the United States Constitutions. The challenge here is directed only to the portion of the tax which is dedicated to the Convention Center, and not to the past and continuing support for the Convention and Visitors Bureau. Resolution of the issue before us depends on whether our holding in *Allegheny County v. Monzo*, 509 Pa. 26, 500 A.2d 1096 (1985), is applicable to the facts presented in this case.

"On June 27, 1986, the General Assembly enacted the Convention Center Authority Act (Act), 53 Pa. S. § 16201, *et seq.*, which, among other things, created the Authority, 53 Pa. S. § 16204, and authorized cities of the first class to impose a hotel room rental tax, in part, for the use of the Authority for convention center purposes. 53 Pa. S. § 16223(b). In the event that construction of the main convention area is not commenced by December 31, 1988, all revenues collected under the tax can only be used for tourist promotion agency purposes, and not for convention center purposes. 53 Pa. S. § 16223(d)(5). Prior to the enactment of this Act, Philadelphia was imposing a three percent (3%) tax on hotel room rentals to support the Philadelphia Convention and Visitors Bureau.

"Pursuant to the Act, Philadelphia's City Council enacted a Hotel Room Rental Tax (Tax). Phila. Code § 19–2401, *et seq.* Philadelphia is the only city of the first class in Pennsylvania. The Tax imposes an excise tax on the consideration that each operator of a hotel in the city of Philadelphia receives from each transaction of renting a room or rooms to accommodate transients. Phila. Code § 19–2402. The Tax only applies to hotels in the City of Philadelphia. *Id.* . . . If an operator of a hotel fails to collect the tax, or pay the tax over to the City when due, that operator will be liable to the City for payment of the tax. Phila. Code § 19–2405(2).

"The Tax authorizes the Department to collect the tax from each hotel operator and deposit a portion of the revenues in a special fund for the use of the Authority for convention center purposes, which include: (1) projected annual debt service or lease payments of the Authority; (2) costs associated with financing, constructing, improving, maintaining, furnishing, fixturing and equipping the convention center; (3) costs associated with the development of the convention center, including, but not limited to, design, engineering and feasibility costs; (4) costs associated with the operation and management of the convention center; (5) costs associated with promoting, marketing and otherwise encouraging use of the convention center; and (6) general purposes of the convention center. Phila. Code § 19–2404(2).

"The Appellant is the owner/operator of the Guest Quarters Suite Hotel, previously known as Embassy Suites Hotel, located near the Philadelphia International Airport, approximately seven miles from the convention center, and approximately twenty minutes by motor vehicle from the downtown area of the

City of Philadelphia commonly referred to as Center City. Although the Appellant has complied and continues to comply with the mandates of the Tax, on June 8, 1987, Appellant filed a complaint against the Appellees seeking a declaratory judgment stating that the Tax and the Act are unenforceable as applied to the Partnership and that the portion of the Tax which supports a proposed convention center is void on its face. The trial court found that the Act and the Tax do not violate the Uniformity Clause of the Pennsylvania Constitution nor the Due Process and Equal Protection Clauses of the United States Constitution, and that neither constitutes special laws prohibited by Article III, Section 32 of the Pennsylvania Constitution. The trial court further found that this Court's decision in *Allegheny County v. Monzo, supra,* is distinguishable from the present challenge. We agree.

"The principles which govern analysis of the claims asserted here are well established. First, and foremost, is a presumption that tax enactments are constitutionally valid and the burden of proving invalidity is upon the person challenging the tax (citations omitted). *Monzo,* at 36, 500 A.2d at 1101. The Legislature, in the exercise of its taxing power, is subject to the requirements of the equal protection and uniformity clauses. *Alco Parking Corp. v. City of Pittsburgh,* 453 Pa. 245, 307 A.2d 851, *rev'd on other grounds,* 417 U.S. 369, 94 S. Ct. 2291, 41 L. Ed. 2d 132 (1974). However, the Legislature possesses wide discretion in matters of taxation. *Aldine Apartments v. Commonwealth,* 493 Pa. 480, 426 A.2d 1118 (1981).

" . . . Both the federal equal protection clause, as applied to taxing statutes, and the state constitutional requirement of uniformity of taxation 'upon the same class of subjects' (Pa. Const. Art. VIII, § 1) mandate that classification in a taxing scheme have a rational basis. In either case, a classification for tax purposes is valid when it 'is based upon some legitimate distinction between the classes that provides a non-arbitrary and "reasonable and just" basis for the different treatment.' *Leonard v. Thornburgh,* 507 Pa. 317, 321, 489 A.2d 1349, 1350 (1985), quoting *Aldine Apartments v. Commonwealth, supra.* Where there exists no legitimate distinction between the classes, and thus, the tax scheme imposes substantially unequal tax burdens upon persons otherwise similarly situated, the tax is unconstitutional. *Commonwealth v. Staley,* 476 Pa. 171, 180, 381 A.2d 1280, 1284 (1978). The controlling standard for determining whether a tax is violative of the Due Process Clause of the Fourteenth Amendment is ' . . . whether the taxing power exerted by the state bears a fiscal relation to protection, opportunities and benefits given by the state. The simple question is whether the state has given *anything* for which it can ask a return.' *Monzo,* 509 Pa. at 38, 500 A.2d at 1102, quoting *Wisconsin v. J.C. Penney Co.,* 311 U.S. 435, 444, 61 S. Ct. 246, 249, 85 L. Ed. 267 (1940) (emphasis added by *Monzo*). Where the benefit received and the burden imposed is palpably disproportionate, a tax is not only a taking without due process under the Fourteenth Amendment to the United States Constitution, but also an arbitrary form of classification in violation of equal protection and state uniformity standards. *Thomas v. Kansas City So. Ry.,* 261 U.S. 481, 43 S. Ct. 440, 67 L. Ed. 758 (1923).

"A taxing statute is subject to the same 'rational relationship test' under the special laws provisions of the Pennsylvania Constitution Act. 3, § 32, as under the equal protection clause. Legislation for a class is not an impermissible special law where the legislative classification 'is founded on real distinctions in the subjects classified, and not on artificial or irrelevant ones.' *Freezer Storage, Inc. v. Armstrong Cork Co.*, 476 Pa. 270, 275, 382 A.2d 715, 718 (1978) (quoting *Du Four v. Maize*, 358 Pa. 309, 313, 56 A.2d 675, 677 (1948)). . . .

"Applying these principles to the instant case, we find that the taxing scheme meets constitutional requirements and that our decision in *Monzo, supra,* is not applicable to the facts present in this case. In *Monzo,* we held that a tax violates the equal protection, due process and uniformity clauses if 'the benefit received and the burden imposed is palpably disproportionate.' 509 Pa. at 38, 500 A.2d at 1102. The hotel tax in *Monzo* failed this test because 'a substantial portion (perhaps a majority) of the class taxed are afforded no benefits whatsoever, while being significantly burdened.' *Id.* at 42, 500 A.2d at 1104. The *Monzo* decision was based on unique facts not present in the instant case.

"*Monzo* involved a challenge, based on the same constitutional principles invoked by the Appellant here to a hotel occupancy tax imposed upon all hotels located in Allegheny County, for the sole purpose of financing a convention center to be constructed in downtown Pittsburgh. The challenger, *Monzo,* was the operator of a hotel located in an outlying municipality near the Allegheny County line, and fifteen miles from downtown Pittsburgh. The tax at issue was an Allegheny County hotel occupancy tax ordinance enacted pursuant to the Hotel Room Rental Tax Statute of 1977,[5] which authorized second class counties to impose a one percent (1%) hotel room rental tax, the revenues of which were to be deposited in a special fund 'established solely for purposes of a convention center or exhibition hall.' 16 Pa. S. § 4970.2(c). Allegheny County is the only second class county in the Commonwealth and, due to the limited duration of the statute, there was no possibility that any other county would achieve second class status before the termination date of December 31, 1983. The record in *Monzo* established several uncontroverted facts which were critical to that decision and which are not present in the instant case.

"There was evidence that the Allegheny County tax and the convention center harmed Monzo's business by taking patrons away from his hotel and drawing them to downtown hotels near the convention center. There was also evidence that his hotel received no benefit as a result of the new Pittsburgh convention center. The effect of the tax was to require Monzo to subsidize his downtown competition in exchange for no observable benefit. Further, Monzo was able to show that because the tax increased the cost of an Allegheny County room, he lost business to competing hotels in Westmoreland County. In addition, officials of the Allegheny County Authority and the Pittsburgh Convention and Visitors Bureau testified that the convention center would only benefit hotels and other businesses in downtown Pittsburgh. They also testified that distance from the convention center was a critical factor and the further a hotel was from the center of Pittsburgh the less convention business it could expect. There was no proof of any kind—either legislative findings or factual evidence—that the Pittsburgh Convention Center would benefit the county. Moreover, the Allegheny County tax was levied upon all hotels in Allegheny County which encompasses several municipalities surrounding the City of Pittsburgh, in contrast to Philadelphia where the City and County are one and the same.

"The record before this Court in the instant case presents a quite different factual situation. In short, each of the critical factors upon which we relied in reaching the result in *Monzo* are absent here.

" . . . Appellant has failed to provide any evidence that the Tax or the new convention center will cause actual harm to the partnership business. The evidence of record shows that even Appellant's expert concedes that Appellant receives some benefit in the form of some convention business and displaced commercial demand. (Leventhal Report, App. 7a, 20a). Appellant has also failed to show that the taxing scheme imposes unequal tax burdens upon persons otherwise similarly situated. *Commonwealth v. Staley, supra,* 476 Pa. at 180, 381 A.2d at 1284. All hotels subject to the Tax are located in the City of Philadelphia and all stand to benefit from the proposed convention center. . . .

" . . . While Appellant claims that the Tax reduces its revenues and that the Tax has discouraged it from raising its rates, the trial court found that there was no evidence to substantiate these claims. The trial court further found that Appellant 'failed to prove that the three percent (3%) differential (resulting from the Tax) between its rates and the rates of its airport area competitors affects its business. Given Plaintiff's high occupancy rate, the Tax cannot be said to have resulted in an actual loss of business.' *Leventhal v. The City of Philadelphia,* June Term, 1987, No. 1849 (slip opinion at 11). The trial court also noted that this was in stark contrast to *Monzo,* where there was evidence that *Monzo's* hotel had lost considerable business because of that tax and the Pittsburgh Convention Center.

"Appellant has not only failed to prove any actual harm from the Tax, but has also failed to support its claim that it will not benefit from the new convention center. While conceding that the center will increase the demand for hotel rooms in Philadelphia, Appellant argues that individuals attending conventions will stay at center city hotels within walking distance of the Convention Center. Thus, claims Appellant, the Partnership will not benefit from this increased demand.

"Both the report submitted by Appellees' expert, Pannell Kerr Forster, and the accompanying affidavit of Thomas Muldoon, President of the Philadelphia Convention and Visitors Bureau, support the trial court's findings that because of overflow convention demand and displaced hotel room demand, hotels throughout Philadelphia will benefit from the increased demand generated by the new convention center. 'Hotels located in the airport area are particularly likely to benefit from increased room demand generated by the new Convention Center because of that market's location at the transportation gateway in the city, and because of the Airport High Speed Line.' (Pannell Report, App. 37a; Muldoon Affidavit, App. 99a). This evidence of benefit to Appellant and to other Philadelphia hotels not located in center city present yet another distinction between this case and the *Monzo* case. In *Monzo,* the evidence showed that Monzo would receive no convention business. Another critical difference between this case and *Monzo* is that here the Tax applies only to hotels in Philadelphia, whereas in *Monzo,* hotels in municipalities outside of Pittsburgh, but within Allegheny County, were subject to the tax. The record here clearly establishes that the Partnership will benefit from the proposed convention center, and that the burden imposed upon Appellant by the Tax is not palpably disproportionate to the benefit received. Nor do the Act and the Tax violate the Uniformity Clause of the Pennsylvania Constitution or the Equal Protection and Due Process Clauses of the United States Constitution. Under the previously enumerated applicable legal standards, the Act represents an appropriate exercise of the Legislature's power to enact taxes directed towards a legitimate public goal. . . .

"Accordingly, since we found no constitutional infirmity in either the Tax, or its enabling Act, the January 22nd order affirming the Order of the Court of Common Pleas of Philadelphia County was entered."

"5. Act of December 16, 1977, P.L. 323, No. 94, § 1, 16 Pa. S. § 4970.2."

2:11 *Other Public Houses Not in Public Calling*

Similar in many respects to inns are other houses maintained for use of the public; but none of them ministers to any absolute public necessity, and none of them, therefore, is regarded as engaged in a public calling. No part of the law of public callings, therefore, applies to these establishments. Furthermore, the law regulating the extent of liability of innkeepers is, as we shall see, in many respects peculiar and does not apply to keepers of other public houses. Nor does any keeper of such a house have a lien at common law, though, as will be seen, a lien has been given to some of them by statute. But in other respects the same principles of law apply to these houses of entertainment as to inns.

The following case illustrates the treatment of multiple dwellings within the New Jersey regulation of such entities.

ROTHMAN V. DEPARTMENT OF COMMUNITY AFFAIRS
226 N.J. Super. 229, 543 A.2d 1035 (N.J. Super. Ct. App. Div. 1988)

SKILLMAN, J. App. Div.: "The issue presented by this appeal is whether three buildings in Cliffside Park owned by appellants are 'multiple dwellings' as defined in N.J.S.A. 55:13A–3(k) and therefore subject to the regulatory authority of the Commissioner of Community Affairs (the Commissioner) under the Hotel and Multiple Dwelling Law, N.J.S.A. 55:13A–1 *et seq.* Appellants argue that the buildings, each of which contain four housing units, were converted into two separate buildings, each containing two units, when appellant Rothman Reality Corporation conveyed one half of each building to appellants Leonard and

Mildred Rothman, and that because a building must contain three or more housing units in order to be a 'multiple dwelling,' the buildings are not subject to the Hotel and Multiple Dwelling Law. The Commissioner rejected this argument and concluded that appellants' buildings are 'multiple dwellings.' Therefore, he asserted jurisdiction to determine whether there are violations in the buildings of regulations adopted under the Law. We affirm the Commissioner's decision. . . .

"The Hotel and Multiple Dwelling Law confers broad authority upon the Commissioner of Community Affairs to regulate the construction and maintenance of hotels and multiple dwellings. Thus, N.J.S.A. 55:13A–7 requires the Commissioner to adopt

" ' . . . such regulations as he may deem necessary to assure that any hotel or multiple dwelling will be constructed and maintained in such manner as is consistent with, and will protect, the health, safety and welfare of the occupants or intended occupants thereof, or of the public generally.

" ' . . . In order to be subject to these regulatory provisions, a building must be either a 'hotel' or a 'multiple dwelling.' See N.J.S.A. 55:13A–10, 11, 12 and 13. The term 'multiple dwelling' is defined in N.J.S.A. 55:13A–3(k) as

"'any building or structure of one or more stories and any land appurtenant thereto, and any portion thereof, in which three or more units of dwelling space are occupied, or are intended to be occupied by three or more persons who live independently of each other.

"In accordance with the legislative directive contained in N.J.S.A. 55:13A–2, we have liberally construed the Commissioner's jurisdiction under the Hotel and Multiple Dwelling Law. Thus, in *Rumson Country Club v. Comm'r of Community Affairs,* 134 N.J. Super. 54, 338 A.2d 219 (App. Div. 1975), *certif. den.* 68 N.J. 482, 348 A.2d 523 (1975), we upheld the Commissioner's determination that a country club with six bedrooms on its upper floors for the use of its employees and members was a multiple dwelling.' And in *Blair Academy v. Sheehan,* 149 N.J. Super. 113, 373 A.2d 418 (App. Div. 1977), we upheld the Commissioner's determination that a dormitory in a private school was a 'hotel' as defined in the Law. Most significantly, in *Bunting v. Sheehan,* 156 N.J. Super. 14, 383 A.2d 429 (App. Div. 1976), we affirmed the Commissioner's determination that a building which had two street addresses and an interior fire wall in the middle should nevertheless be treated as a single building in determining whether it had three or more dwelling units and hence was a multiple dwelling.' In our opinion we observed:

"It is of no moment that an interior fire wall, extending from the cellar to a point one foot below the roof line, separates the building into two halves with separate heating units and that for a number of years prior to the purchase of each half by appellant, they had been in separate ownership and had been separately taxed. [*Id.* at 16–17, 383 A.2d 429].

"The structure of appellants' buildings is similar to the building found to be a 'multiple dwelling' in *Bunting.* Each building consists of four apartments. Two apartments are on each side of the buildings, which are divided in the center by a fire wall. Each half of the buildings has a separate street address.

"Appellants do not dispute that their buildings, if held in common ownership, would be 'multiple dwellings' under our decision in *Bunting*. However, they argue that as a result of the conveyances of half the buildings from Rothman Realty to Leonard and Mildred Rothman, they are no longer 'multiple dwellings.' Appellants rely upon N.J.S.A. 55:13A–3(*l*), which provides that '[t]he term "owner" shall mean the person who owns, purports to own, or exercises control of any hotel or multiple dwelling.' Appellants argue that neither Rothman Realty nor Leonard and Mildred Rothman are 'owners' of 'multiple dwellings' because the half buildings owned by each party contain only two dwelling units.

"However, common ownership is not an element of the basic definition of a multiple dwelling. The only statutory condition for the classification of a building as a 'multiple dwelling' is that it contain 'three or more units of dwelling space [which] are occupied or intended to be occupied by three or more persons who live independently of each other.' N.J.S.A. 55:13A–3(k).

"Moreover, a reading of the entire definition of 'multiple dwelling' contained in N.J.S.A. 55:13A–3(k) indicates that the omission of any requirement of common ownership from the basic definition of a 'multiple dwelling' was not inadvertent. Thus, in addition to the basic definition of a 'multiple dwelling' previously quoted, a 1983 amendment to N.J.S.A. 55:13A–3(k), *L.* 1983, *c.* 447, § 1, added to the definition of a multiple dwelling

"any group of ten or more buildings on a single parcel of land or on contiguous parcels *under common ownership,* in each of which two units of dwelling space are occupied or intended to be occupied by two persons or households living independently of each other. [Emphasis added].

"If the Legislature had intended common ownership to be an element of the classification of a building containing three or more dwelling units as a 'multiple dwelling,' it could have expressly stated this requirement just as it did with respect to a cluster of duplexes. In addition, N.J.S.A. 55:13A–3(k) excludes from the definition of a multiple dwelling.

"any building section containing not more than two dwelling units held under a condominium or cooperative form of ownership, or by a mutual housing corporation, where all the dwelling units in the section are occupied by their owners, if a condominium, or by shareholders in the cooperative or mutual housing corporation, and where such building section has at least two exterior walls unattached to any adjoining building section and is attached to any adjoining building sections exclusively by walls of such fire-resistant rating as shall be established by the bureau in conformity with recognized standards.

"This carefully crafted exclusion of certain owner-occupied condominium and cooperative units from the definition of 'multiple dwelling' would have been unnecessary if each section of a building under separate ownership were required to be considered independently in determining whether it was a 'multiple dwelling.' Therefore, we conclude that common ownership of a building is not an element of the basic definition of a 'multiple dwelling' under N.J.S.A. 55:13A–3(k).

"Moreover, the Commissioner expressly found that common ownership had been established in this case. He cited N.J.S.A. 55:13A–3(*l*), which defines 'owner' as 'the person who owns, purports to own, *or exercises control of any hotel or multiple dwelling*.' [Emphasis added]. The Commissioner found that appellants Leonard and Mildred Rothman exercise control over all four units in each of the three buildings in question and therefore are 'owners' of all of the buildings. The Commissioner noted that Leonard and Mildred Rothman hold title to one half of each of the buildings in question while the other half is owned by Rothman Realty Corporation. He also noted that Leonard and Mildred Rothman own 50% of the stock in this corporation, the other 50% being owned by their son, their daughter and their son-in-law as trustee for their grandchildren. In addition, Leonard Rothman is president of the corporation and Mildred Rothman is Secretary and/or Vice President. Based on these factual circumstances, the Commissioner concluded that Rothman Realty Corporation is effectively controlled by Leonard and Mildred Rothman and therefore that both halves of each of the three buildings are under common ownership.

"The Commissioner's finding that both halves of the buildings in question are in common ownership is factual in nature. Therefore, it may not be disturbed on appeal unless there is a lack of substantial credible evidence in the record to support the finding. *Henry v. Rahway State Prison*, 81 N.J. 571, 579–580, 410 A.2d 686 (1980). We are satisfied from our review of the record that there is ample support for the Commissioner's finding.

"Accordingly, we affirm the Commissioner's determination that appellants' buildings are 'multiple dwellings' subject to regulation under the Hotel and Multiple Dwelling Law and remand the matter to him for hearings on appellants' alleged violations of the Department's building code regulations."

2:12 *Apartment Hotels*

The phrase "apartment hotel" originated about 1900, and has been used interchangeably with the words "family hotel" or "residential hotel" to describe hotels which made a practice of renting apartments, furnished or unfurnished, for fixed periods, the lessees or guests being treated in other respects like the transient guests of the house. The apartments are usually provided with kitchenettes or serving pantries for light housekeeping by the tenants. Section 181 of the New York Lien Law defines an apartment hotel as a "hotel wherein apartments are rented for fixed periods of time, either furnished or unfurnished, to the occupants of which the keeper of such hotel supplies food, if required." In addition to food service, apartment hotels generally provide other customary hotel services, such as maid service, linen service, secretarial and desk service, and bellman service.

2:13 *Rooming Houses, Boardinghouses, and Lodginghouses*

A "rooming house" is a building or a portion of a building in which non-housekeeping furnished rooms are rented on a short-term basis of daily, weekly, or monthly occupancy to more than two paying tenants, not members of the landlord's immediate family.[31] A rooming house is not necessarily a place of public accommodation to which any well-behaved person of means can go and demand lodging as a matter of right as he can do at a hotel. Subject to the provisions of applicable civil rights laws, the keeper of a rooming house may receive whom he will, reject whom he will, and usually makes special contracts with each of his guests concerning compensation and length of stay.

In the city of New York the operation of a rooming house requires a municipal permit.[32]

The only material difference between a rooming house and a "boardinghouse" is that a boardinghouse furnishes meals, in addition to lodging.

A "lodginghouse" differs from an inn or rooming house, in that it is a house in which persons are housed for hire for a single night, or for less than a week at one time.

In *Township of Ewing v. King,*[33] the New Jersey Supreme Court reversed a conviction of a violation of the township's zoning ordinance for allowing the occupancy of a dwelling owned by the defendant by more than four students.

> PER CURIAM: . . . A common definition of rooming houses, cited with approval by this court in *Pierro v. Baxendale,* 20 N.J. 17, 24 (1955), is that they are "places 'where there are one or more bedrooms which the proprietor can spare for the purpose of giving lodgings to such persons as he chooses to receive.' " *See also* 40 Am. Jur. 2d, *Hotels, Motels, etc.* § 6 at 904 (1968). It is perfectly obvious that here there was a letting of an entire building to a group of occupants for a fixed term. This did not constitute the conduct of a "rooming house" or a "student rooming house" in any normal acceptation of those terms. Plaintiffs in effect so conceded at the oral argument, as we believe they were, in all candor, compelled to do on this record.
>
> Reversed.

2:14 *Apartment Houses*

The term "apartment house" came into use about 1880. The term designates a multiple dwelling which is either rented, leased, or hired out for occupancy as the residence or home of three or more families living independently of each other. "An 'apartment' is that part of [an apartment house] consisting of one or more rooms containing at least one bathroom arranged to be occupied by [the] members of a family, which room or rooms are separated and set apart from all other rooms within [the building]."[34]

---

[31]Rent and Eviction Regulations of the New York State Housing Rent Commission, Pt. I, § 3–(6).
[32]Administrative Code, § D26-3.22.
[33]69 N.J. 67, 350 A.2d 482 (1976).
[34]New York Multiple Dwelling Law, § 4.

In *Eris v. City of Atlanta*,[35] the Supreme Court of Georgia interpreted the Atlanta City Code definition of "apartment house" to exclude condominium units for the licensing requirements imposed upon hotels.

WELTNER, J.: Grace Eris was convicted in the Municipal Court of Atlanta of the violation of Section 14–6172 of the Atlanta City Code, which prohibits the operation of a "hotel, lodging house, rooming house or similar place" without first applying to the bureau of police services for a permit to do so. This section of the ordinance does not define "a hotel, lodging house, rooming house or similar place." Section 14–6171, however, defines "rooming house." It defines also "apartment house" as a building in which "living facilities such as a living room, bedroom, kitchen and bath are provided for a person or family, and where the building is capable of accommodating two or more families who would have separate living facilities." Eris, who is a licensed real estate broker, was a principal in a real estate management firm that managed some two hundred condominium units in Peachtree Towers. The units which Eris rented consisted of a living room, one or two bedrooms, a kitchen and a bathroom.

Under the evidence of this case, there is no question but that each condominium unit in question was an "apartment," (as distinguished from being a "hotel, lodging house, rooming house or similar place") as this term is defined by Section 14–6171 of the Atlanta City Code. As such, Eris' conviction, therefore, must be vacated.

Judgment reversed.

2:15 Bed-and-Breakfast Establishment Defined

Since about 1980 a new form of accommodation has found favor with the public: bed-and-breakfast establishments. These establishments cater to the motorist who seeks a more homelike overnight sojourn, one which affords greater privacy and less congestion and services than more traditional inns, hotels, and motels. Such places can be defined as a collection of rooms, from one to generally no more than five, which are part of a private home owned and occupied by the homeowner, who provides accommodations for a stay generally limited to one night or a weekend. No valet, bell, waitstaff, or other typical hotel services are provided. Likewise, recreational amenities are kept to a minimum, namely, use of a swimming pool where available. The only meal provided is a breakfast prepared by the host-owner, who serves it in his private dining room.

Because of their small size, bed-and-breakfast establishments are akin to private hosts for hire and are exempt from federal and state civil rights laws governing places of public accommodation. However, their presence in a community may be prohibited by local law. If permitted, bed-and-breakfasts must conform to local building, fire, and safety codes, as well as comply with ordinances designed to protect the value of adjacent property, such as parking, signage, and noise ordinances. Such operations must also meet environmental regulations applicable to the residence, in addition to use and occupancy requirements.

[35]257 Ga. 178, 356 S.E.2d 885 (Ga. 1987).

In all other respects, the homeowner who operates a bed-and-breakfast establishment is subject to the same contract, tort, and agency laws governing reservations and care owed guests as for inns, hotels, and motels, except that the common law regarding innkeeper liability and statutes limiting that liability for loss of guest property *infra hospitium* do not apply.

2:16 *Restaurant Defined*

A "restaurant" is a public establishment where food is prepared, served, and sold for consumption on the premises. The term includes, but is not limited to, buffets, lunchrooms, lunch counters, cafeterias, grill rooms, and hotel dining rooms.

An "eating place" is an establishment, other than a restaurant, where food is prepared, served, and sold on the premises. It is of a more private character than a restaurant. The term includes, but is not limited to, dining rooms of clubs or associations, school lunchrooms, and eating places in factories or offices for personnel employed in such places.[36]

A "coffeehouse" is often used to refer to a popularly priced hotel dining room, while the term "café" is synonymous with restaurant. An "ordinary" is an eating house where regular meals are served at fixed prices.

The term "tavern" has come to be restricted to an eating and drinking place with limited kitchen facilities. In times past, the term was frequently used synonymously with inn or hotel, but the use of the word in this sense has become obsolete (*see also* section 1:4, *supra*). There is a similarity between a tavern and a "bar and grill," which is an establishment where the food volume is less than one-third of the entire volume of business.

A restaurant is not an inn, and a restaurant keeper is not engaged in a public employment in the sense that a carrier or innkeeper is. The distinctions between the duties and obligations of a restaurant keeper and an innkeeper will be pointed out in subsequent chapters.

2:17 *Air, Rail, Motor, and Maritime Carriers*

Common carriers are not innkeepers even though they furnish board, lodging, and ancillary services very often comparable to those provided by inns. The reason for this distinction is that the primary purpose of the carrier is to furnish transportation,[37] not lodging.

---

[36]New York City Health Code, § 87.01.

[37]An essential characteristic of common carriers is to furnish transportation for hire or reward, as a public employment, not as a casual occupation. 13 C.J.S. *Carriers* § 3b. This common-law definition is incorporated into the Revised Interstate Commerce Act, 49 U.S.C. § 10101 *et seq.* (1978). *See* U.S. v. Contract Steel Carriers, 350 U.S. 409 (1956), citing the predecessor statute, 49 U.S.C. § 363(a) (14) (15) [motor carriers].

Innkeepers and carriers, however, are often classified together in terms of their responsibilities to the person and property of guests and passengers.[38]

The common carrier is an insurer of the goods of a passenger at common law[39] and is subject to the same exceptions available to the innkeeper, that is, act of God, act of the public enemy, and negligence of the passenger contributing to the loss,[40] as well as the inherent nature of the goods[41] and acts of public authority.[42] Most jurisdictions permit the carrier to limit liability to the value declared by the passenger.[43] Interstate carriage of baggage is similarly protected by the Carmack Amendment to the Interstate Commerce Act.[44]

Unlike the innkeeper, the common carrier is held to the highest degree of care, skill, and diligence with respect to the safety, security, and well-being of its passengers.[45] This responsibility for safe transportation is due to the nature of the conveyance—that is, the passenger is confined, with no ability to come and go during carriage. The innkeeper is required to use only ordinary or reasonable care to protect the person of his guests in most instances.[46]

Another distinction between innkeepers and common carriers is that the common-carrier industry is regulated,[47] and, in some countries, common carriers are government owned. Although recent federal legislation to deregulate competition among air carriers has been adopted,[48] the safety and security of passengers and baggage is in no way diminished.

In all other respects the similarity between the services provided by maritime and air carriers and those provided by innkeepers is noteworthy. Air carriers furnish first-class passengers with berths on international flights as well as extensive meals and alcoholic and nonalcoholic beverages, not to mention food. Thus they are innkeepers in function if not innkeepers in the legal sense. The luxury liner is most readily comparable to an inn, since here all of the amenities normally found on land can be furnished at sea. Only the fact that the passengers are captives on board and cannot readily come and go from the carrier, although they have limited freedom of movement within the carrier, prevents the law from treating luxury liners as inns.

---

[38]For example *see* section 4:5, *infra*, regarding the duty of both carriers and innkeepers to refrain from discrimination in their treatment of passengers and guests.

[39]13 C.J.S. *Carriers* § 71. Rogers Walla Walla, Inc. v. Willis Shaw Frozen Express, Inc., 23 Wash. App. 540, 596 P.2d 669 (1979).

[40]13 C.J.S. *Carriers* §§ 76–78.

[41]*Id.* § 79.

[42]*Id.* § 86.

[43]*Cf.* U.C.C. § 7-309(2), a provision of the Uniform Commercial Code adopted in all states except Louisiana, governing requirements for making liability limitations effective.

[44]49 U.S.C. § 11707 (1978).

[45]13 C.J.S. *Carriers* § 678. Nieves v. Manhattan and Bronx Surface Transit Operating Authority, 31 A.D.2d 359, 297 N.Y.S.2d 743 (1st Dep't), *app. denied*, 24 N.Y.2d 1030, 250 N.E.2d 253 (1969).

[46]*See* Chapter 9, *infra*.

[47]49 U.S.C. 10101 *et seq.* (1978).

[48]49 U.S.C. 1302 *et seq.*, as amended by § 1551(a) (4), declaring that the Civil Aeronautics Board shall cease to exist on January 1, 1985. Pub. L. No. 96–192, §§ 2, 3, 94 Stat. 35, 36, Feb. 15, 1980.

3 The Innkeeper's Public Duty at Common Law

3:1 *The Law of Public Callings*

From the very beginning of our law it has been recognized that some kinds of business were of special importance to the public and that all persons engaged in such business owed the public certain duties. No one can be compelled to enter upon such employment, but if he chooses to do so, he thereby undertakes the performance of the public duties connected with it. The property which he devotes to the public employment becomes "affected with a publick interest, and [it] cease[s] to be *juris privati* only."[1]

In *Munn v. Illinois*,[2] the United States Supreme Court, in holding that grain elevators in Chicago were "affected with the public interest" and therefore subject to state regulation, quoted Lord Hale with approval, adding that:

> Property does become clothed with a public interest when used in a manner to make it of public consequence, and affect the community at large. When, therefore, one devotes his property to a use in which the public has an interest, he, in effect, grants to the public an interest in that use, and must submit to be controlled by the public for the common good, to the extent of the interest he has thus created. He may withdraw his grant by discontinuing the use; but, so long as he maintains the use, he must submit to the control.[3]

The duty placed upon one exercising a public calling is primarily a duty to serve every person as a member of the public. This primary duty requires that the service should be adequate, that only a reasonable price should be charged for it, and that all members of the public should be served equally and without discrimination.

3:2 *Innkeeper Is in the Public Employment*

The innkeeper has, from the earliest time, been recognized as being engaged in a public employment and, therefore, as subject to the duty of one engaged in

---

[1] Lord Hale, *De Portibus Maris*, 1 Hargrave's Law Tracts 78 (1787).
[2] 94 U.S. 113 (1876).
[3] *Id.* at 126

such employment.[4] Professor Bruce Wyman adds the following to what has already been said in Chapter 1 as the reasons for holding that an innkeeper's calling is a public one:

> The innkeeper is in a common calling under severe penalty if he does not serve all that apply, while the ordinary shopkeeper is in a private calling free to refuse to sell if he is so minded. The surrounding circumstances must again explain the origin of this unusual law. When the weary traveller reaches the wayside inn in the gathering dusk, if the host turn him away what shall he do? Go on to the next inn? It is miles away, and the roads are infested with robbers. The traveller would be at the mercy of the innkeeper, who might practise upon him any extortion, for the guest would submit to anything almost, rather than be put out into the night. Truly a special law is required to meet this situation, for the traveller is so in the hands of the innkeeper that only an affirmative law can protect him.[5]

3:3 *Duty to Admit the Public*

The fundamental duty of the innkeeper to the public, as a person engaged in a public employment, is to receive for entertainment at his inn all travelers who properly apply to be admitted as guests. This duty is symbolized by the traditional ceremony at the dedication of a new hotel or motel of throwing away a key to the inn, thus proclaiming to the world that the door to the hospitality of the inn will never be locked and that all weary travelers will always be welcome.

This duty to admit a traveler as a guest is not absolute, but is subject to the lawful excuses discussed in Chapter 5. However, subject only to such excuses, the duty binds the innkeeper from the time he opens his doors to the public.

The Supreme Court of New Jersey[6] recently reiterated the limitations that government may impose upon those in private business imbued with a public calling.

> Proprietors of privately owned quasi-public businesses may operate within a wide discretionary range, subject to limitations called for by the commonwealth. The nature, scope, and limitations of the innkeeper's discretion are illustrative. He was bound by common law to receive and lodge all comers in the absence of a reasonable ground of refusal. 21 Halsbury's Laws of England 445–446, 3d ed. (1957). A valid refusal had to be related to the inn's operations as an inn. *White's Case,* 2 Dyer 158b, 73 Eng. Rep. 343 (K.B. 1558). Full occupancy or the traveler's condition, such as drunkenness, which might offend other guests, constituted good cause for exclusion. On the other hand, arrival at a late hour or on a Sunday was held to be insufficient to deny lodging. *Rex v. Ivens,* 7 Car & P. 213, 173 Eng. Rep. 94 (K.B. 1835). There had to be a rational relationship, a causal nexus, between the reason for the refusal and the function of the inn.

---

[4]*See* sections 2:1 and 2:2, *supra.*

[5]Wyman, *The Law of the Public Callings as a Solution of the Trust Problem,* 17 Harv. L. Rev. 156, 159 (1903).

[6]Doe v. Bridgeton Hospital Ass'n, Inc., 71 N.J. 478, 483, 366 A.2d 641, 646 (1976), *cert. denied,* 433 U.S. 914 (1977).

3:4   *Definition of "Traveler"*

The public duty of the innkeeper is owed to travelers only, and one who is not a traveler cannot demand, as a matter of law, to be received at an inn. The rule laid down almost 400 years ago was that "common inns are instituted for passengers and wayfaring men . . . [a]nd therefore if a neighbour who is no traveller, as a friend, at the request of the innholder lodges there and his goods be stolen, etc. he shall not have an action. . . . "[7]

In early times, the courts construed the world "traveler" strictly to mean a person engaged in a journey. In the last hundred years, however, the cases are liberal in regarding anyone who calls at a hotel for admission as a traveler. "A townsman or a neighbor may be a traveler, and therefore a guest at an inn, as well as one who comes from a distance, or from a foreign country. . . . In short, any one away from home, receiving accommodations at an inn as a traveler, is a guest, and entitled to hold the inn-keeper responsible as such."[8]

In general, then, the guest is a transient who receives accommodations at an inn for compensation. It is the transient character of the visit, that is, its indefinite, temporary duration, which distinguishes a guest from a lodger, boarder, or tenant in the hotel, and the right to demand such transient accommodation is no longer contingent on traveling from afar.

3:5   *Duty to Receive Persons Incapable of Contracting*

The innkeeper's obligation to receive is not confined to the reception of persons with whom he can make a binding contract. Thus, the innkeeper has been held legally bound to receive a minor who applies for admission as a guest; the mere fact of infancy would not justify refusal to admit him.[9]

It should be noted that while the innkeeper is under a duty to admit minors and other travelers incapable of making binding contracts, provided they come in proper condition, he can collect charges only for "necessaries" furnished. "Necessaries" is a legal term of art, the technical definition of which, in the law of contracts, is beyond the scope of this work.[10] Generally, it encompasses food, clothing, and shelter purchased by the minor for the use of himself and his family.

In the context of hotel accommodations, what "necessaries" are depends on the circumstances of each case, such as the character of the hotel, the minor's station in life, the goods and services furnished, and the like. It has been held that money, although it will buy most necessities, is not itself a "necessary." A minor may, therefore, repudiate an obligation to reimburse the innkeeper for cash advances, unless it can be shown that the money was expended for nec-

---

[7]Calye's Case, 77 Eng. Rep. 520, 521 (1584).
[8]Walling v. Potter, 35 Conn. 183, 185 (1868).
[9]Watson v. Cross, 63 Ky. (2 Duv.) 147 (1865).
[10]2 S. Williston, Contracts §§ 241–242 (3d ed. 1959).

essaries, in which case an equitable right to recover may exist.[11] In general, however, making cash advances to minors is a practice that should not be encouraged.

3:6 *Reception May Be Demanded at Night*

While an inn may be closed at reasonable hours during the night,[12] it is clear that a traveler actually reaching the inn while it is closed may wake the innkeeper and demand admittance.

REX V. IVENS

7 Car. & P. 213, 173 Eng. Rep. 94 (1835)

[Indictment against an innkeeper for not receiving one Williams as a guest at his inn, and also for refusing to take his horse. Plea not guilty.

Williams, a law clerk from Newport, applied for admission at the Bell Inn at Chepstow, kept by the defendant. It was a Sunday evening, a few minutes before midnight. The inn was closed, the defendant and his wife having retired for the night. When Williams tapped at the door, Mrs. Ivens went to the window and asked for the caller's name. He answered, "What is that to you about my name?" Mrs. Ivens said, "At such a late hour I want to know your name and where you come from." Williams replied, "If you must know my name, it is Williams, and I come from Newport; and now you are as wise as you were before." There is some dispute as to whether he concluded this sentence with the words "and be damned to you." Mrs. Ivens testified that he did, while Williams specifically denied it.

Mrs. Ivens then shut the window and refused to admit Williams. He subsequently filed a complaint, initiating this prosecution.]

COLERIDGE, J.: "(in summing up). The facts in this case do not appear to be much in dispute; and though I do not recollect to have ever heard of such an indictment having been tried before, the law applicable to this case is this:—that an indictment lies against an innkeeper, who refuses to receive a guest, he having at the time room in his house; and either the price of the guest's entertainment being tendered to him, or such circumstances occurring as will dispense with that tender. This law is founded in good sense. The innkeeper is not to select his guests. He has no right to say to one, you shall come into my inn, and to another you shall not, as everyone coming and conducting himself in a proper manner has a right to be received; and for this purpose innkeepers are a sort of public servants, they having in return a kind of privilege of entertaining travelers, and supplying them with what they want. It is said in the present case, that Mr. Williams, the prosecutor, conducted himself improperly, and therefore ought not to have been admitted into the house of the defendant. If a person came to an inn

[11]Watson v. Cross, 63 Ky. (2 Duv.) 147 (1865).
[12]Commonwealth v. Wetherbee, 101 Mass. 214 (1869).

drunk, or behaved in an indecent or improper manner, I am of the opinion that the innkeeper is not bound to receive him. You will consider whether Mr. Williams did so behave here. It is next said that he came to the inn at a late hour of the night, when probably the family were gone to bed. Have we not all knocked at inn doors at late hours of the night, and after the family have retired to rest, not for the purpose of annoyance, but to get the people up? In this case it further appears, that the wife of the defendant has a conversation with the prosecutor, in which she insists on knowing his name and abode. I think that an innkeeper has no right to insist on knowing those particulars, and certainly you and I would think an innkeeper very impertinent, who asked either the one or the other of any of us. However, the prosecutor gives his name and residence; and supposing that he did add the words 'and be damned to you,' is that a sufficient reason for keeping a man out of an inn who has travelled till midnight? I think that the prosecutor was not guilty of such misconduct as would entitle the defendant to shut him out of his house. . . . It however remains for me next to consider the case with respect to the hour of the night at which Mr. Williams applied for admission; and the opinion which I have formed is, that the lateness of the hour is no excuse to the defendant for refusing to receive the prosecutor into his inn. Why are inns established? For the reception of travellers, who are often very far distant from their own homes. Now, at what time is it most essential that travellers should not be denied admission into the inns? I should say when they are benighted, and when, from any casualty, or from the badness of the roads, they arrive at an inn at a very late hour. Indeed, in former times, when the roads were much worse, and were much infested with robbers, a late hour of the night was the time, of all others, at which the traveller most required to be received into an inn. I think, therefore, that if the traveller conducts himself properly, the innkeeper is bound to admit him, at whatever hour of the night he may arrive. . . .

"Verdict—Guilty."

3:7 *Refusal to Receive Guests Made a Misdemeanor*

As we have seen, the refusal of an innkeeper, without just cause or legal excuse, to receive and entertain a guest was an indictable offense at common law. The refusal is also a civil wrong for which damages can be recovered in a civil action by the injured party.[13]

Several states have enacted legislation making a refusal to receive a guest a misdemeanor. The language of the New York statute is typical:

> A person who, either on his own account or as agent or officer of a corporation, carries on business as an innkeeper, or as a common carrier of passengers, and refuses, without just cause or excuse, to receive and entertain any guest, or to receive and carry any passenger, is guilty of a misdemeanor.[14]

[13]Cornell v. Huber, 102 A.D. 293, 92 N.Y.S. 434 (2d Dep't 1905).
[14]N.Y. Civ. Rights Law § 40-e (McKinney 1965).

The courts will not, however, allow such provisions to be used to justify violation of a statute prohibiting the operation of a house of ill repute. In *People v. McCarthy*,[15] the defendant innkeeper was prosecuted for keeping a bawdy house. The prosecution showed that on the night in question, the twenty-two rooms in the hotel were rented thirty-three times, making it obvious that at least some of the rooms were used by more than one patron during the night. Similar occurrences had happened on numerous occasions. The defendant's instructions to the desk clerks were to admit any couple who looked "over age." The defendant relied on § 513 of the New York Penal Law (now § 40-e of the Civil Rights Law), arguing that he was under a duty to admit all who applied, under penalty of law. The court rejected defendant's argument, stating that it was "aware of the provisions of section 513 of the Penal Law which make it a misdemeanor for an innkeeper to refuse to receive guests 'without just cause or excuse.' It certainly would not be without just cause or excuse to make a fair inquiry to ascertain whether the couple that desires accommodation are in fact married to each other; nor would it be a violation of section 40 of the Civil Rights Law to make such an inquiry."[16]

3:8 *Duty to Provide Adequate Facilities*

Not only must the innkeeper be willing to receive travelers as his guests; he must also be prepared to shelter and entertain them. From the duty to receive follows the duty to provide adequate facilities, for an innkeeper without a roof to cover the heads of his guests or sufficient food to appease their hunger would be as little regardful of his public obligation as one who would refuse admittance to his inn. The innkeeper's duty in this respect will be considered later in Chapter 9.

3:9 *Duty to Refrain from Discrimination*

Today, federal and state statutes are the basic framework prohibiting discrimination in inns and other places of public accommodation. This statutory scheme will be discussed in Chapter 4. However, long before the Fourteenth Amendment and the civil rights acts, the common law imposed a duty on innkeepers to refrain from discrimination. A brief examination of these principles will be helpful, even though the entire area of discrimination is now governed by the provisions discussed in the following chapter.

The law recognized that an innkeeper could perform his duty to the public only by refraining from discrimination in the treatment of his guests. If he were to give one man better service than another, or to serve him at a lower price, he would be fostering the interest of an individual against that of the public. Each traveler who applies for admittance to an inn does so as a member of the public and is entitled to all of the service which the innkeeper owes to the public.

[15]204 Misc. 460, 119 N.Y.S.2d 435 (Magis. Ct. 1953).
[16]*Id.* at 462, 119 N.Y.S.2d at 437–38.

" . . . [A]s they [innkeepers] cannot refuse to receive guests, so neither can they impose unreasonable terms on them."[17]

In referring to the duty of a common carrier, which duty is in most respects similar to that of innkeepers, the New Jersey Supreme Court stated that:

> A service for the public necessarily implies equal treatment in its performance, when the right to the service is common. Because the institution, so to speak, is public, every member of the community stands on an equality as to the right to its benefit, and therefore, the carrier cannot discriminate between individuals for whom he will render the service. In the very nature, then, of his duty and of the public right, his conduct should be equal and just to all.[18]

3:10 Duty to Make Reasonable Charges

Another rule following from the duty to receive all travelers as guests is that the innkeeper may charge only a reasonable amount for his services. If he could charge what he pleased, he could make any individual's right to be received valueless by requiring the payment of a prohibitive amount for accommodation. What constitutes reasonable compensation will be discussed in Chapter 21.

3:11 Duty to Receive and Serve Nonguests

Under some circumstances, the innkeeper may be obliged to admit to the inn persons who are not and do not intend to become guests. The nature and extent of this duty will be discussed in Chapter 14.

[17]Kirkman v. Shawcross, 6 East. 519, 101 Eng. Rep. 410, 412 (K.B. 1794).
[18]Messenger v. Pennsylvania R.R., 37 N.J. 531, 534 (1874).

4 Discrimination in Places of Public Accommodation: Civil Rights

4:1 *Innkeeper's Common-Law Duty to Admit All Who Apply*

We have already seen that at common law, a person engaged in a public calling, such as an innkeeper or public carrier, was held to be under a duty to the general public and was obliged to serve without discrimination all who sought service, whereas proprietors or purely private enterprises were under no such obligation, the latter enjoying an absolute power to serve whom they pleased.[1]

More recently, the New York Court of Appeals[2] recognized the continued vitality of this distinction but limited its application to purely private places of amusement, holding that the New York Racing Association was akin to a state instrumentality possessing monopoly power over thoroughbred racing and that to invoke the common-law immunity against a horse owner and trainer would be unwarranted.

JACOBSON v. NEW YORK RACING ASSOCIATION, INC.
33 N.Y.2d 144, 305 N.E.2d 765 (1973)

JASEN, J.: " . . . At common law a person engaged in a public calling, such as an innkeeper or common carrier, was under a duty to serve without discrimination all who sought service. On the other hand, proprietors of private enterprises, such as places of amusement and resort, had no such obligation and were privileged to serve whomever they pleased. In *Madden v. Queens County Jockey Club, Inc.* 296 N.Y. 249, 72 N.E.2d 697, . . . we recognized the common-law rule, as limited by the Civil Rights Law (section 40), that the operator of a racetrack licensed by the State may, without reason or sufficient excuse, exclude a patron from the premises provided the exclusion is not based on race, creed, color, or national origin. This rule was recently reaffirmed by this court in *People v. Licata*, 28 N.Y.2d 113, . . . 268 N.E.2d 787. . . .

A small portion of this chapter is reprinted from my article "Innkeeper's Liability for Failure to Honor Reservations" from May 1974 Cornell Hotel and Restaurant Administration Quarterly, with permission from the Cornell University School of Hotel Administration, © 1974.
[1]Madden v. Queens County Jockey Club, Inc., 296 N.Y. 249, 72 N.E.2d 697, *cert. denied*, 332 U.S. 761 (1947).
[2]33 N.Y.2d 144, 305 N.E.2d 765 (1973).

"On their facts, the *Madden* and *Licata* cases dealt with the right of a proprietor of a private racetrack to exclude a patron.

"In our view, it does not follow from the *Madden* and *Licata* cases that NYRA may, with impunity, exclude a licensed owner and trainer when that action allegedly causes injury. NYRA has virtual monopoly power over thoroughbred racing in the State of New York. Exclusion from its tracks is tantamount to barring the plaintiff from virtually the only places in the State where he may ply his trade and, in practical effect, may infringe on the State's power to license horsemen. In contrast to a racetrack proprietor's common-law right to exclude undesirable patrons, it would not seem necessary to the protection of his legitimate interests that the proprietor have an absolute immunity from having to justify the exclusion of an owner and trainer whom the State has deemed fit to license. (Horse Racing Act § 9-b, subd. 2, added by L.1951, ch. 324, § 4). Accordingly, plaintiff should have his opportunity to prove his allegations in an action for damages and, by the same token, defendant its opportunity to refute them. (*See Greenburg v. Hollywood Turf Club,* 7 Cal. App. 3d 968, 86 Cal. Rptr. 885; *see also, Martin v. Monmouth Park Jockey Club,* 145 F. Supp. 439, 441. . . .) In this regard, it will be plaintiff's heavy burden to prove that the denial of stall space was not a reasonable discretionary business judgment, but was actuated by motives other than those relating to the best interests of racing generally."

Subsequent to *Jacobson,* a New York appellate court upheld the common-law right to exclude without cause except where such exclusion is based on race, creed, color, or national origin, with regard to a private-for-profit harness-racing track.[3] The court maintained that since the trainers, drivers, and owners who brought the action could still race at six other tracks, there was not the requisite showing of "economic necessity" or "monopoly power" needed to invoke a *Jacobson*-type action. Moreover, regulation by the state, though heavy, was sufficient ground for a finding of state action. The dissent argued, however, that denying plaintiffs' use of the local track, with the subsequent damage to their reputations, had as great an impact from the plaintiffs' point of view as if there were no other facilities available.

The Supreme Court of Pennsylvania challenged the common-law concept that a patron may be arbitrarily excluded from a licensed racetrack without a hearing or any cause stated.

ROCKWELL v. PENNSYLVANIA STATE HORSE RACING COMMISSION
15 Pa. Commw. Ct. 348, 327 A.2d 211 (1974)

BLATT, J.: [Statement of facts omitted.]

"At common law, a person who was engaged in a public calling, such as an innkeeper or a common carrier, was held to be under a duty to the general public

---

[3]Arone v. Sullivan County Harness Racing Association, Inc., 90 A.D.2d 137, 457 N.Y.S.2d 958 (1982).

and was obligated to serve, without discrimination, all who sought service. *Horney v. Nixon,* 213 Pa. 20, 61 A. 1088 (1905). On the other hand, proprietors of private enterprises, such as places of amusement and resort, enjoyed the right to serve whomever they might please. *Horney, supra.* That right has been made subject now, of course, to civil rights statutes which prohibit the exclusion of persons from all places of public accommodation when such exclusion is based solely on the race, creed, color, or national origin of the persons seeking admission.

"Here the Association argues that, absent statutory or constitutional provisions specifically to the contrary, such as civil rights statutes, the common law right of private proprietors to eject or exclude would attach to operators of private racetracks just as it did to a theater operator in *Horney, supra.* The Association has not cited any precedents in this Commonwealth, nor have we found any. The Association asserts, however, that courts of other jurisdictions have held that the doctrine advanced in *Horney, supra,* does apply to racetrack operations. *Epstein v. California Horse Racing Board,* 222 Cal. App. 2d 831, 35 Cal. Rptr. 642 (1963); *Garifine v. Monmouth Park Jockey Club,* 29 N.J. 47, 148 A.2d 1 (1959); *Madden v. Queens County Jockey Club,* 296 N.Y. 249, 72 N.E.2d 697 (1947).

"Clearly if the common law doctrine does apply, an ejected racetrack patron merely has an action in contract, based on the purchase of the entrance ticket, for return of the admission price and no more. *Marrone v. Washington Jockey Club of the District of Columbia,* 227 U.S. 633 (1913). At least one commentator, however, has seen fit to argue that '[i]t might seem logical to conclude that the legal privilege of arbitrary expulsion of customers should be abolished.' Conrad, *The Privilege of Forcibly Ejecting an Amusement Patron,* 90 U. of Pa. L. Rev. 809, 819 (1942). This commentator points out that the doctrine is based only upon the notion that a patron has nothing more than a revocable license and has no property right in his seat. A property right, it is argued, can be given only by deed. *See Marrone v. Washington Jockey Club of the District of Columbia, supra.* Yet, the commentator adds, it strains the modern sense of justice to suggest that one has no right to a seat if he has no deed. As in fact, our own Supreme Court has postulated in a case regarding theater seats, 'as purchasers and holders of tickets for particular seats they [the patrons] had more than a mere license. Their right was more in the nature of a lease, entitling them to peaceable ingress and egress, and exclusive possession of the designated seats during the performance on that particular evening.' *Drew v. Peer,* 93 Pa. 234, 242 (1880). Such a position is especially compelling where, as in the instant case, a Commonwealth license virtually permits the existence of the amusement in question as a regulated monopoly. The public's access to this form of entertainment, therefore, is limited by the Commonwealth itself, and a patron would consequently seem entitled to the utmost protection. As was held in a recent New York case, 'the combined force of the factors establishing State involvement' in racetrack operations can be so great as to require the treatment of those operations as state actions subject to due process requirements, thus removing the common law defense of an absolute right to exclude otherwise available to a privately owned amusement operation. *Jacobson v. New York Racing Association, Inc.*, 41 A.D.2d 87, 341 N.Y.S.2d 333 (1973)."

Although the court ultimately grounded its decision in favor of the patron on a statutory right to appeal the Commission's decisions, the above observations point to an erosion of the traditional view that private entrepreneurs enjoy absolute discretion to turn away prospective patrons.

In *Shad v. Smith Haven Mall*, to follow, the New York Court of Appeals ruled that a private property owner, in this case a shopping mall, could constitutionally prohibit the distribution of political hand bills or pamphlets on its premises, because of lack of state action essential to trigger federal and New York constitutional free speech protections. In a concurring opinion, Judge Jasen cited prior New York public accommodations cases to require that any such policy of exclusion must be nondiscriminatory in practice.

SHAD v. SMITH HAVEN MALL
66 N.Y.2d 496, N.E.2d (1985)

JASEN, J.: "(concurring). While I concur in the opinion of Judge TITONE, I write to emphasize what I believe to be a critical limitation upon a shopping mall owner's right to exclude expressionist activity. In my view, where the owner of a shopping mall voluntarily and affirmatively creates a public forum or accommodation for expressionist activity, by inviting or permitting members of the general public to engage in noncommercial expressive conduct of a civic or community nature in the common areas of the mall, the owner cannot, at the same time, exclude particular expressionists upon purely discriminatory or arbitrary grounds.

"In the first instance, the exclusive choice and control rests with the property owner as to whether a mall shall be open or closed to noncommercial expressionist activity. As is true for any owner of private property, the mall owner may exercise his common-law right to exclude and, thereby, deny access to all individuals whose purpose is other than to engage in shopping, browsing, or other commercial or business activities. (*Madden v. Queens County Jockey Club*, 296 N.Y. 249, 253–254, *cert. denied* 332 U.S. 761.)

"However, once the owner of a shopping mall has opened the doors to the public to participate in the exchange of noncommercial ideas, such as to present or partake of cultural, educational, or political activities, the common-law right of the owner to exclude any expressionist from his private property must be limited to nondiscriminatory and nonarbitrary grounds. (*See, Matter of United States Power Squadron v. State Human Rights Appeal Bd.*, 59 N.Y.2d 401, 409–415; *Jacobson v. New York Racing Assn.*, 33 N.Y.2d 144, 149–150.) The owner may not exclude any person or group from the common areas of a mall, thus serving as a public forum or accommodation for expressionist purposes, on the bases of race, creed, color, gender, political belief, content of expression, or some other reason repugnant to the law or public policy of this State. (*See, Mat-*

ter of Walker, 64 N.Y.2d 354, 359; *Hollis v. Drew Theol. Seminary,* 95 N.Y. 166, 172.) Of course, a mall owner must still be permitted to regulate the expressive conduct so as to preclude disruption, vulgarity, incitement, or whatever else threatens the health or safety of the patrons or interferes with the primary commercial purpose of a mall. But persons otherwise welcome in a shopping mall for expressionist purposes cannot be excluded solely on the basis of the ideational content of their expression or for some other invidious reason.

"It is imperative that this court recognize, not only the absence of a constitutional right of free expression in a privately owned shopping mall, but also the presence of necessary limitations upon the owner's common-law right of exclusion. The principles which mandate these limitations constitute the most fundamental precepts of nondiscrimination and nonarbitrariness which underlie the decisional law, statutes and public policy of this State. (*See, e.g., Matter of United States Power Squadrons v. State Human Rights Appeal Bd., supra; Jacobson v. New York Racing Assn., supra; Madden v. Queens County Jockey Club, supra; Woollcott v. Shubert,* 217 N.Y. 212, 216–219; *Aaron v. Ward,* 203 N.Y. 351, 356–357; Civil Rights Law § 40; Executive Law §§ 292, 296.)

"Under the facts presented in this case, it cannot be said that the mall owner acted in a discriminatory or arbitrary fashion. The Smith Haven Mall does provide rent-free space to members of the general public for various expressionist activities, but plaintiffs have sought only to engage in the distribution of handbills which is uniformly prohibited by the mall owner. The absolute prohibition against this particular manner of expression, being an entirely content-neutral and reasonable means of avoiding litter, confrontation and interference with commercial activity, is a nonarbitrary rule which does not violate any antidiscrimination law or public policy. Consequently, in my view, the mall owner's ban against handbilling is a permissible exercise of the common-law right of exclusion."

4:2 *Restaurant Keeper's Common-Law Duty to Receive Members of the General Public*

Whether a restaurant keeper, as distinguished from an innkeeper, is legally required to admit members of the general public has not been conclusively decided. In *Madden v. Queens County Jockey Club, Inc.,* the Court of Appeals decided that places of amusement and resort, as distinguished from those engaged in a public calling, such as inns or common carriers, enjoy an absolute power to exclude those whom they please, subject only to the legislative restriction that they not exclude one on account of race, creed, color, or national origin. The court upheld the right of a race track to exclude Madden even though the exclusion was without cause.

In *Noble v. Higgins,*[4] the plaintiff was refused service in defendant's restaurant on purely personal grounds. He sought to recover damages, basing his action on sections 40 and 41 of the Civil Rights Law (*see* sections 4:12–4:15,

[4]95 Misc. 328, 158 N.Y.S. 867 (Sup. Ct. 1916).

infra). The court dismissed the complaint on the merits on the authority of *Grannan v. Westchester Racing Association,*[5] as extended and applied in *Woollcott v. Shubert,*[6] stating: "It may be conclusively determined after an examination of the last-quoted authorities that 'the legislature did not intend to confer upon every person all the rights, advantages and privileges in places of amusement or accommodations, which might be enjoyed by another. Any discrimination not based upon race, creed or color does not fall within the condemnation of the statute.' "[7] The court then added: "It would seem then that the common-law right still remains with those not engaged as common carriers, or in like occupations, to discriminate between persons according to rules established where the person applying for accommodation is objectionable for some reason. Otherwise, persons unclean, untidy, intoxicated or affected by disease might claim the same attention in a crowded restaurant or other public place as those against whom no objection could be urged. *Brandt v. Mink,* 38 Misc. Rep. 750. [38 Misc. 750, 78 N.Y.S. 1109 (Sup. Ct. 1902).]"

In the *Brandt* case, plaintiff was refused service in defendant's restaurant because he wore no collar. His action was predicated on sections 40 and 41 of the Civil Rights Law. The defense was that the defendant had established a rule in his restaurant not to serve any man who did not wear a collar. The court held that this rule was a reasonable one, applicable alike to all citizens of every race, creed, and color and, therefore, would come within the exception in the Civil Rights Law. The judgment was reversed but for some reason unexplained by the court a new trial was ordered.

Some doubt as to the private restaurant keeper's traditional unfettered authority to serve whom he pleases, subject to statutory restrictions already noted, has been created by the most recent New York appellate court case of *Harder v. Auberge Des Fougeres, Inc.*[8]

Here the court ruled that a restaurant proprietor should be under the same duty as an innkeeper to receive all patrons who present themselves in a fit condition, unless reasonable cause exists for a refusal to do so. This ruling was in response to defendant's motion to dismiss for legal insufficiency plaintiff's complaint that defendants "unlawfully, willfully, deliberately, and without just cause, refused to admit or seat plaintiff and his guests for dinner service even though plaintiff and his guests: (*a*) had made a bona fide reservation, (*b*) requested service, and (*c*) were ready, willing and able to pay any reasonable charges imposed by defendants for such meal."[9]

Conceding the existence of the universal rule that exonerates private enterprises from legal responsibility for refusal to admit patrons without cause, the majority of the court stated that: "For whatever benefit and purpose the rule once served in ancient times, it has no relevance in the 20th Century, and should

[5]153 N.Y. 449, 47 N.E. 896 (1897).
[6]217 N.Y. 212, 111 N.E. 829 (1916).
[7]95 Misc. 329, 158 N.Y.S. 868.
[8]40 A.D.2d 98, 338, N.Y.S.2d 356 (3d Dep't 1972).
[9]*Id.* at 98–99, 338 N.Y.S.2d at 357.

not be recognized for the purpose of distinguishing inns from other places of public accommodation. In our view, a restaurant proprietor should be under the same duty as innkeeper to receive all patrons who present themselves 'in a fit condition,' unless reasonable cause exists for a refusal to do so.''[10] The court concluded that an intentional tort had been properly pleaded and the case should be remanded for trial on the merits.

The same result was achieved in the prior New York case of *Moore v. Wood.*[11] Plaintiff sued to recover damages for injury to reputation predicated on defendant's deliberate refusal to serve plaintiff in its public restaurant. In denying defendant's motion for summary judgment, the court acknowledged defendant's contention that plaintiff's theory of liability—that is, the innkeeper's duty to serve all who properly present themselves must be distinguished from the duty of a place of public amusement—which is privileged to serve only those whom it pleases. Nonetheless, the court concluded that in the field of damage to reputation, the courts are delegated with the responsibility of protecting that right, and that it would be unlawful and unjust to dismiss the action at the stage of the proceedings.

The court ruled that the following issues would be dispositive at trial: (1) whether defendant's refusal to serve plaintiff was because of some established rules of the defendant restaurant; (2) whether the rule was unreasonable; and (3) whether plaintiff did, in fact, fail to comply therewith. Plaintiff would prevail only if these issues were decided in the negative, and plaintiff would then be required to prove the extent of his damages, if any.

What would constitute reasonable cause to justify a refusal to admit? Obvious past or present misbehavior, such as rowdyism, use of abusive and vile language, intoxication, belligerence, annoying other patrons, filthy appearance, having a communicable disease, or being known to be engaged in some unlawful or immoral occupation that would cause his continual presence to injure the reputation of the house, would clearly justify a refusal to admit. In a less obvious sense, a violation of any reasonable house rule would also withstand judicial scrutiny, predicated on the quality, class, and facilities of the establishment. Thus a more informal dress code that could be appropriate at a roadside fast-food outlet might be legally impermissible at a refined French formal dining room. In some situations local health ordinances require the wearing of shoes and other apparel on the premises, ruling out any discretion on that score.

In general, any person whose past or observable appearance, condition, or conduct would create a reasonable apprehension of harm to the entrepreneur, his personnel, and his property, as well as to the safety, comfort, and well-being of his patrons in their persons or property, could be properly excluded.

Once a house rule is found to exist and has been determined to be reasonable, such a rule must be adequately communicated to those persons who would wish to avail themselves of such services. This corollary to the reasonable rule re-

[10]*Id.* at 99, 338 N.Y.S.2d at 358.
[11]160 N.Y.L.J. 73 (Sup. Ct. N.Y. Co. 1968).

quirement is based on the settled concept that, in order to compel compliance, one must notify the person involved of its existence and give him a reasonable opportunity to comply. Posting house rules or tactful direct communication of those rules at the time and place at which the patron seeks admission is necessary.

In such cases, care must be taken to apply the rule uniformly and evenhandedly to all prospective patrons seeking admission. A house rule fair on its face may be discriminatory in its application and, if so, will not be sanctioned. Thus a restaurateur may not seat a number of patrons who are in violation of his house dress code requiring coats and ties and then attempt to enforce the dress rule on a customer who, although not in compliance with the dress code, is otherwise fit, but who has political views diametrically opposed to his own. Having admitted the previous patrons who were dressed in violation of the rule, he may not reinstate the rule for reasons unrelated to its purpose.

Finally, there must be an adequate showing that the alleged victim did in fact fail to comply with the house rule. If the victim can establish compliance, then the refusal to admit would be unjustified, absent some independent showing of unfitness that the proprietor would have to plead and prove by way of an affirmative defense.

4:3 Civil Rights Defined

A "civil right" may be defined as one which appertains to a person by virtue of his citizenship in a nation for the purpose of securing to him the enjoyment of his means of happiness. It includes the right to buy, sell, and to own property, freedom to make contracts, trial by jury, and the like. In another sense, the term also refers to certain rights secured to citizens of the United States by the Thirteenth, Fourteenth, and Fifteenth Amendments to the Constitution, and by various statutes, state and federal, commonly known as civil rights acts.

A principal object of such acts has been the securing of equal rights in places of public accommodation to all citizens without discrimination on account of race, creed, color, or national origin. It is in this latter sense that innkeepers and other public hosts throughout the nation are concerned with the subject.

4:4 Federal Civil Rights Act of 1964

The Civil Rights Act of 1964[12] became law on July 2, 1964. It is the first federal legislation on civil rights, other than voting, in ninety years. It is nationwide in its application and fills a void in the protection of civil rights in

---

[12]Title III of the Americans with Disabilities Act (ADA) of 1990, effective January 1992, prohibits discrimination on the basis of disability by anyone who owns, leases or leases to, or operates a place of public accommodation. Accommodations *not equal* to those afforded other individuals and accommodations that are *different* or *separate* are discriminatory. Stereotyping by others, patronizing attitudes, and fears or presumptions or both are expressly prohibited justifications for such discrimination. The prohibitions apply as well to discrimination on the basis of an individual's re-

states that failed to legislate on the subject. Title II of the act prohibits racial and religious discrimination in places of public accommodation. Title VII of the act prohibits similar discrimination in employment and also prohibits sex discrimination, a classification not contained in Title II.

4:5 *Injunctive Relief against Discrimination in Places of Public Accommodation: Title II*

The following definitions are given in section 201 of Title II:

Section 201. *Establishments Covered*
(a) All persons shall be entitled to the full and equal employment of the goods, services, facilities, privileges, advantages, and accommodations of any place of public accommodation, as defined in this section, without discrimination or segregation on the ground of race, color, religion, or national origin.

(b) Each of the following establishments which serves the public is a place of public accommodation within the meaning of this title if its operations affect commerce, or if discrimination or segregation by it is supported by State action:

(1) any inn, hotel, motel, or other establishment which provides lodging to transient guests, other than an establishment located within a building which contains not more than five rooms for rent or hire and which is actually occupied by the proprietor of such establishment as his residence;

(2) any restaurant, cafeteria, lunchroom, lunch counter, soda fountain, or other facility principally engaged in selling food for consumption on the premises, including, but not limited to, any such facility located on the premises of any retail establishment; or any gasoline station;

(3) any motion picture house, theater, concert hall, sports arena, stadium or other place of exhibition or entertainment; and

(4) any establishment (A) (i) which is physically located within the premises of any establishment otherwise covered by this subsection, or (ii) within the premises of which is physically located any such covered establishment, and (B) which holds itself out as serving patrons of such covered establishment.

(c) The operations of an establishment affect commerce within the meaning of this title if (1) it is one of the establishments described in paragraph (1) of subsection (b); (2) in the case of an establishment described in paragraph (2) of subsection (b), it serves or offers to serve interstate travellers, or a substantial portion of the food which it serves, or gasoline or other products which it sells, has moved in com-

---

lationship or association with another who is disabled. In addition, all places of public accommodation as well as other commercial facilities must be made accessible to and usable by the disabled.

Disability is defined to include: (1) a physical or mental impairment that substantially limits one or more of the major life activities of an individual, (2) a record of such impairment, or (3) the fact that an individual is regarded as having such an impairment. Proposed regulations issued in January 1991 require hotels and motels to make 5 percent of their guest rooms accessible; restaurants must make at least 5 percent of their tables and two-thirds of the eating area accessible. All meeting rooms at a conference center, hotel, or motel offering such services would have to be accessible to the disabled. Private clubs (*see* section 4:9, *infra*) are exempt. The accessibility requirements may not be imposed if they would constitute an undue hardship on the operation of the business. Specific factors excusing these requirements are set forth to qualify for such treatment.

merce; (3) in the case of an establishment described in paragraph (3) of subsection (b), it customarily presents films, performances, athletic teams, exhibitions, or other sources of entertainment which move in commerce; and (4) in the case of an establishment described in paragraph (4) of subsection (b), it is physically located within the premises of, or there is physically located within its premises, an establishment the operations of which affect commerce within the meaning of this subsection. For purposes of this section, "commerce" means travel, trade, traffic, commerce, transportation, or communication among the several States, or between the District of Columbia and any State, or between any foreign country or any territory or possession and any State or the District of Columbia, or between points in the same State but through any other State or the District of Columbia or a foreign country.

(d) Discrimination or segregation by an establishment is supported by State action within the meaning of this title if such discrimination or segregation (1) is carried on under color of any law, statute, ordinance, or regulation; or (2) is carried on under color of any customer or usage required or enforced by officials of the State or political subdivision thereof; or (3) is required by action of the State or political subdivision thereof.

(e) The provisions of this title shall not apply to a private club or other establishment not in fact open to the public, except to the extent that the facilities of such establishment are made available to the customers or patrons of an establishment within the scope of subsection (b).

Purpose and Construction of the Act

The general intent and overriding objective of the Act was to eliminate the humiliation and insult of racial discrimination in facilities that purport to serve the general public.[13] It is intended to end discrimination on the grounds of race, color, religion, or national origin.[14]

The Act must be given a liberal construction consistent with its avowed objectives.[15] The inns, hotels, motels, and other places serving transient guests are covered, except "Mrs. Murphy's boardinghouse," that is, a building with not more than five rooms for transient guests and which is also occupied by the proprietor himself. "Other places" have been held to include a YMCA,[16] apartments and cottages at a beach resort when they advertised for out-of-state patrons,[17] and a trailer park.[18] The fact that an institution serves transient guests by the week as well as by the night does not exclude it from coverage.[19]

On the other hand, a restaurant is covered only if it serves or offers to serve interstate travelers, *or* a substantial portion of the food or beverage which it

---

[13]Rousseve v. Shape Spa for Health & Beauty, Inc., 516 F.2d 64 (5th Cir. 1975), *cert. denied*, 425 U.S. 911 (1976).
[14]Daniel v. Paul, 395 U.S. 298 (1969).
[15]Olzman v. Lake Hills Swim Club, Inc., 495 F.2d 1333 (2d Cir. 1974).
[16]Nesmith v. Y.M.C.A., 397 F.2d 96 (4th Cir. 1968).
[17]United States v. Beach Associates, Inc., 286 F. Supp. 801 (D. Md. 1968).
[18]Dean v. Ashling, 409 F.2d 754 (5th Cir. 1969).
[19]United States by Mitchell v. Y.M.C.A., 310 F. Supp. 79 (D. S.C. 1970).

serves has moved in interstate commerce. In the *Ollie's Barbecue Case*,[20] a family-owned restaurant in Birmingham, Alabama, purchased some $150,000 worth of food in a year, of which some 46 percent was meat purchased from a local butcher who in turn procured it from outside the state. The restaurant was held to be subject to the Act.

A hotel or motel restaurant which serves transient guests who move in interstate commerce is subject to the Act.

The Supreme Court has held the service test satisfied when an establishment advertised in a magazine distributed to hotels and motels, over the radio, and in a newspaper distributed at an air base.[21] An offer to serve everybody is tantamount to an offer to serve interstate travelers.[22] Thus an offer to serve white strangers, not just local inhabitants, is sufficient to cause the Act to apply.[23] A carry-out shop offering to serve interstate travelers was held subject to the Act where the food was sold in a form fit for human consumption on the premises.[24]

The test to be applied on the issue of an offer to serve is an objective one; the subjective intent of the owner is disregarded.[25]

A hotel or motel barbershop, beauty salon, cigar stand, flower shop, laundry, Turkish bath, ticket agency, shoeshine parlor, or any other similar facility which serves transient, out-of-town guests, is subject to the Act, even though a barbershop across the street serving local people only may not be.

Bars and taverns serving only drinks are not covered by the Act.[26] However, when a bar is an essential or integral part of an establishment otherwise covered, it is also covered and may not discriminate.[27] Bars and taverns are also covered when they become places of entertainment through the use of jukeboxes, pinball machines, and the like which are manufactured out-of-state and are introduced through the channels of interstate commerce.[28]

But where a bar lounge did not serve food or offer any form of entertainment, the Act has been held not to apply.[29]

Additionally, it is a violation of the Act for a local government to require racial segregation at bars and cocktail lounges by a municipal ordinance.[30]

The term "place of entertainment" has been held to include a 232-acre amusement area which was held sufficiently to affect commerce because (1) it used fifteen paddleboats leased from an out-of-state supplier and (2) its jukebox

[20]Katzenbach v. McClung, 379 U.S. 294 (1964).
[21]Daniel v. Paul, 395 U.S. 298 (1969).
[22]Gregory v. Meyer, 376 F.2d 509 (5th Cir. 1967).
[23]Wooten v. Moore, 400 F.2d 239 (4th Cir. 1968), *cert. denied*, 393 U.S. 1083 (1969).
[24]United States v. Beach Associates, Inc., 286 F. Supp. 801 (D. Md. 1968).
[25]Wooten v. Moore, 400 F.2d 239 (4th Cir. 1968), *cert. denied*, 393 U.S. 1083 (1969).
[26]Selden v. Topza 1-2-3 Lounge, Inc., 447 F.2d 165 (5th Cir. 1971); Cuevas v. Sdrales, 344 F.2d 1019 (10th Cir. 1965), *cert. denied*, 382 U.S. 1014 (1966).
[27]United States *ex rel.* Clark v. Fraley, 282 F. Supp. 948 (D. N.C. 1968). Earlier the Supreme Court held unconstitutional a state law requiring the segregation of public facilities, Johnson v. Virginia, 373 U.S. 61 (1963).
[28]United States v. Purkey, 347 F. Supp. 1286 (D. Tenn. 1971).
[29]Selden v. Topza 1-2-3 Lounge, Inc., 447 F.2d 165 (5th Cir. 1971).
[30]United States v. Cantrell, 307 F. Supp. 259 (D. La. 1969).

was supplied from out-of-state, as were the phonograph records played.[31] That the amusement facility provides participatory recreational facilities rather than spectator or passive activities was not a valid defense.[32]

Incidentally covered establishments, such as a snack bar, have been held automatically to bring the entire facility within the ambit of the Act.[33] Conversely, a casino situated in a covered hotel would be subject to the Act.[34]

The Private Club Exemption

The Act exempts from coverage "private clubs or other establishments not in fact open to the public." No test or definition of a private club is set forth in the Act.

The United States Supreme Court has held an organization not to qualify as a private club when it lacks the attributes of self-government and member-ownership traditionally associated with private clubs.[35] Courts generally look to the totality of the facts to determine whether the organization is truly a private club within the meaning of the Act.[36]

> [A] common point of departure for all courts is an inquiry into the membership policies of the alleged private club. . . . Selectivity is the essence of a private club. . . . If there is no club machinery for screening membership applications, or if such machinery is ignored, then private club status is not indicated.
>
> If the facilities . . . are regularly used by nonmembers, who are not bona fide guests of members, then the facilities cannot be said to be private. . . . If membership has a voice in formulating the policies of the "club" then the balance is tipped in favor of club status. . . . If the club is operated for a profit; if it is a commercial enterprise operated for the benefit of one man or small group, then it is not a private club. . . . [C]ourts have considered the failure of organizations to claim the social club exemption under section 501(c) (7) of the Internal Revenue Code as indicating a lack of private club status. Finally, courts have considered publicity and advertising in the usual advertising media as being inconsistent with a claim of private club status. This is particularly true when the advertising is designed to increase patronage of the club's facilities.[37]

Mere limitation on the number of members does not prove that an establishment is a private club; nor does the fact that applicants who live in a defined area automatically become members upon paying a membership fee.[38]

The factors to be weighed have been enumerated most succinctly as follows:[39]

(a) Selectiveness of the group in the admission of members.

(b) The existence of formal membership procedures.

---

[31]Daniel v. Paul, 395 U.S. 298 (1969).
[32]Miller v. Amusement Enterprises, Inc., 394 F.2d 342 (5th Cir. 1968).
[33]Daniel v. Paul, 395 U.S. 298 (1969).
[34]Rosado Maysonet v. Solis, 400 F. Supp. 576 (D. P.R. 1975).
[35]Daniel v. Paul, 395 U.S. 298 (1969).
[36]Bell v. Denwood Golf & Country Club, Inc., 312 F. Supp. 753 (D. Md. 1970).
[37]Wright v. Cork Club, 315 F. Supp. 1143, 1151–52 (D. Tex. 1970).
[38]Olzman v. Lake Hills Swim Club, Inc., 495 F.2d 1333 (2d Cir. 1974).
[39]Cornelius v. Benevolent Protective Order of Elks, 382 F. Supp. 1182 (D. Conn. 1974).

(*c*) The degree of membership control over the internal governance of the organization, particularly with regard to new members.

(*d*) The history of the organization.

(*e*) The use of club facilities by nonmembers.

(*f*) The substantiality of dues.

(*g*) Whether the organization advertises.

(*h*) The predominance of the profit motive.

Neither the fact that a club received a tax exemption nor the fact that its individual members might use their membership to further their own business interests brought an otherwise bona fide private club under the provisions of Title II of the federal Civil Rights Act or constituted a denial of any rights guaranteed by the federal Constitution nor any denial of constitutional or statutory rights provided under New York law.[40]

Golden v. Biscayne Bay Yacht Club was ultimately resolved in favor of the club against those seeking admission to a private yacht club that had never admitted blacks or Jews except in one instance.[41] No state action was found in spite of the complainants argument that the lease of bay bottom land from the city of Miami, for a token fee, for maintenance of essential dock facilities, constituted state action under the authority of *Burton v. Wilmington Parking Authority*.[42] Rather, the later *Moose Lodge No. 107 v. Irvis* decision[43] was relied upon, in which the majority found *Burton* inapposite, because the Moose Lodge building was located on land owned by it, not by any public authority as in *Burton*, and because the Lodge discharged a purely private social function not otherwise performable by the public authority. These two criteria were met by the yacht club, thus compelling a finding of exempt status.

Persons or organizations claiming to operate private clubs have the affirmative burden of substantiating their status.[44] Thus the alleged victim of discrimination need only establish that he is a member of the protected class and that he was denied access or admission to the facility on the grounds proscribed by the Act. He need not prove that the facility was not a private club.

The Act does not force proprietors of covered establishments to accept undesirable customers. Persons who come in an improper condition to be received, those who are drunk, disorderly, filthy, inappropriately dressed, rude, or otherwise undesirable on legitimate grounds other than race or religion may be excluded.

In *Rosado Maysonet v. Solis*,[45] a claim of discrimination based on a gambling casino operator's refusal to admit the claimants was denied on a finding that

---

[40]Kiwanis Club of Great Neck, Inc. v. Board of Trustees of Kiwanis Int'l, 83 Misc. 2d 1075, 374 N.Y.S.2d 265 (Sup. Ct. 1975), *aff'd*, 41 N.Y.2d 1034, 363 N.E.2d 1378 (1977), *cert. denied*, 434 U.S. 859 (1977).

[41]530 F.2d 16 (5th Cir. 1975), *cert. denied*, 429 U.S. 872 (1976); *contra*, Citizens Council on Human Relations v. Buffalo Yacht Club, 438 F. Supp. 316 (W.D.N.Y. 1977).

[42]365 U.S. 715 (1961).

[43]407 U.S. 163 (1972).

[44]United States v. Richberg, 398 F.2d 523 (5th Cir. 1968).

[45]409 F. Supp. 576 (D. P.R. 1975).

the sole ground of exclusion from the premises was their unruly behavior and their unwillingness to comply with regulations established at the casino for the benefit of all patrons. Similarly, a Title II action was held inapplicable to convicted bookmakers who were barred from a racetrack because of their criminal records.[46]

Section 202 of the Act nullifies all state or local laws requiring or prescribing discrimination on grounds of race or religion, such as the Greenville, South Carolina, ordinance in *Peterson v. Greenville*.[47] The ordinance made it unlawful for all places of public accommodation to furnish meals to white persons and nonwhite persons in the same room, or at the same table, or at the same counter.

Section 203 of the Act forbids the intimidation, coercion, threatening, or punishing of any person for exercising or attempting to exercise his rights under the Act.

In holding that a Virginia golf club had not met its burden of establishing as a matter of law that it was a private club, legally entitled to bar nonwhite applicants from membership, the federal district court for the District of Virginia elaborated on the factors affecting private-club status in *Brown v. Loudon Golf & Country Club, Inc.*:[48]

> In determining whether an establishment is a truly private club, . . . [t]he key factor is whether the club's membership is truly selective. *See e.g., Wright v. Salisbury Club, Ltd.*, 632 F.2d 309 (4th Cir. 1980); *U.S. v. Eagles*, 472 F.Supp. 1174 (E.D. Wis. 1979); *Cornelius v. Elks*, 382 F. Supp. 1182, 1203 (D. Conn. 1974). Relevant here are the size of the club's membership fee, whether and how many white applicants have been denied membership relative to the total number of white applicants, *see Tillman v. Wheaton-Haven Recreation Association, Inc.*, 410 U.S. 431, 438 n.9, 93 S. Ct. 1090, 1094 n.9, 35 L. Ed. 2d 403 (1973); *Wright*, 632 F.2d at 312; *Eagles*, 472 F. Supp. at 1176, whether the club advertises its memberships, *Wright*, 632 F.2d at 312–13, and whether the club has well-defined membership policies, *Nesmith* [*v. Young Men's Christian Association*, 397 F.2d 96 (4th Cir. 1968)], 397 F.2d at 107. That the Club here has a substantial admission fee, a membership ceiling, a requirement that two members sign applications, and a requirement that the Board approve membership application does not, without more, establish that the Club's membership is sufficiently selective. The cases have held clubs to be actually open to the public despite the existence of one or more of these formal admission requirements. *See Tillman, supra* (membership ceiling); *Wright, supra* (2 member sponsorship & board approval requirements); *Nesmith, supra* (substantial annual dues & membership committee); *Eagles, supra* (2 member sponsorship & board approval requirements, membership committee). The crucial inquiry is whether formal admission procedures operate in practice to make the Club's membership selective. *Nesmith, supra* at 101.

[46]Bonomo v. Louisiana Downs, Inc., 337 So. 2d 553 (La. App. 1976).
[47]373 U.S. 244 (1963).
[48]573 F. Supp. 399 (E.D. Va. 1983) at 402–403.

4:6 *Discrimination on Account of Sex: Refusal to Serve Unescorted Women at Hotel or Restaurant Bars*

Significantly, Title II of the federal Civil Rights Act, governing racial and religious discrimination in places of public accommodation, does not prohibit sex discrimination. Such establishments may refuse to admit and serve unescorted females unless an applicable statute or local ordinance forbids such discrimination (*see* section 4:17, *infra*).

In *DeCrow v. Hotel Syracuse Corporation*,[49] the Federal District Court for the Northern District of New York (Port, D.J.) dismissed, on defendant hotel's motion, a compliant which stated that on December 20, 1967, the hotel refused service to plaintiffs at its bar in the Rainbow Lounge, a restaurant in the Hotel Syracuse, in keeping with its established policy of not serving an unescorted woman at its bar "[a]lthough she was sitting quietly and in no way disturbing any other patrons." (*But see* section 4:17, *infra*, for the New York statute which now outlaws such discrimination.)

Said the court:

> The conduct of hotels and restaurants is governed by section 201(a) of said Act (42 U.S.C.A. § 2000(a)). The full and equal enjoyment of public accommodations without discrimination on account of *"race, color, religion, or national origin"* (emphasis added), including the right to be served at a bar, has been guaranteed by Congress. No such guarantee has been made on account of *sex*. This court should not gratuitously do what Congress has not seen fit to do. Mrs. Kennedy's complaint should be addressed to Congress.

The court similarly dismissed plaintiff's contention that the complaint stated a claim under 42 U.S.C.A. §§ 1983 and 1985 in that plaintiffs were deprived of their rights, privileges, or immunities secured by the Constitution and laws and that defendant conspired to deprive plaintiffs of the equal protection of the laws or of equal privileges and immunities under the laws. Judge Port had this to say in disposing of plaintiffs' contention: "The short answer, so well established as not to require citation of authorities, is that these sections, like the Equal Protection Clause of the 14th Amendment, are only directed at State action, which is nowhere alleged in the complaint."

In *Seidenberg v. McSorley's Old Ale House, Inc.*,[50] plaintiffs, members of the National Organization for Women, sought to enjoin defendants, operators of a bar primarily engaged in serving alcoholic and nonalcoholic beverages, from continuing its 114-year practice of catering only to men. The defendant moved for an order dismissing the complaint for failure to allege sufficient facts to state a valid claim under 42 U.S.C.A. § 1983.

The Federal District Court for the Southern District of New York, (Tenney, D.J.) held that the court had jurisdiction of the action and that the complaint

---

[49]288 F. Supp. 530 (N.D. N.Y. 1968).
[50]308 F. Supp. 1253 (S.D. N.Y. 1969).

stated a claim for relief on the grounds that since a state license was required to operate a bar, there was sufficient state involvement to make the acts of the licensee those of the state itself and that the discrimination against women was unreasonable. "Bars or taverns, though a species of private property, are clearly in the public domain, 'affected with a public interest' and subject to more extensive State supervision than the lunch counters in *Garner* and *Lombard*,"[51] said Judge Tenney.

> Once we assume, for the purposes of defendant's motion, that its policy of excluding women may properly be considered the acts of the State, the Court must then determine whether such discrimination is founded in reason and thus a permissible classification within the meaning of the Fourteenth Amendment.
> . . . To adhere to practice supported by ancient chivalristic concepts, when there may no longer exist a need or basis therefor, may only serve to isolate women from the realities of everyday life, and to perpetuate, as a matter of law, economic and sexual exploitation. While members of each sex may at times relish the opportunity to withdraw to the exclusive company of their own gender, if it be ultimately found that the State has become significantly involved in a policy which mandates such seclusion, then considerable question is presented as to whether, for the purposes of the Fourteenth Amendment, this discrimination is founded upon a basis in reason.[52]

The question whether *McSorley's* prevents a hotelkeeper from reserving one of a number of its dining facilities for a group of male patrons, as a men's grill, has been dealt with in *Millenson v. The New Hotel Monteleone.*[53] The Fifth Circuit Court of Appeals affirmed the dismissal of a claim of the denial of equal protection based on the state issuance of a liquor licence to the hotel, on the ground that no action was involved, since the Louisiana liquor-licensing provisions were completely unrelated to the admission policies of the establishment. The *Moose Lodge No. 107 v. Irvis* case, involving a claim of racial discrimination against a private club, was used to support that holding.

The policy of noninterference with private clubs was clearly expressed by Justice Douglas in his dissenting opinion in *Moose Lodge:*[54] "My view of the First Amendment and the related guarantees of the Bill of Rights is that they create a zone of privacy which precludes government from interfering with private clubs or groups. . . . Government may not tell a man or woman who his or her associates must be. The individual can be as selective as he desires. . . . "

[51]Garner v. Louisiana, 368 U.S. 157 (1961); Lombard v. Louisiana, 373 U.S. 267 (1963).
[52]Seidenberg was not tried, and no appeal was taken from the district court's order, 317 F. Supp. 593 (1970). On motion for summary judgment the district court held that provision of the Civil Rights Act of 1964 guaranteeing to all persons the full and equal enjoyment of public accommodations without discrimination on account of race, color, religion, or national origin applies neither to discrimination on basis of sex nor to discrimination in a bar or tavern whose principal business is the sale of alcoholic beverages rather than food. But the court further held that the refusal of the ale house, which was primarily a bar serving alcoholic and nonalcoholic beverages and was subject to extensive and pervasive state regulation, to serve women denied women equal protection.
[53]475 F.2d 736 (5th Cir. 1973), *cert. denied*, 414 U.S. 1011 (1973).
[54]Moose Lodge No. 107 v. Irvis, 407 U.S. 163, 180 (1972).

In the *Moose Lodge* case, the majority of the Court determined that the mere issuance of a liquor license did not qualify as sufficient state involvement or action with respect to the club's admission policies so as to bring into play the equal protection clause of the federal Constitution. The Court, however, struck down a rule of the state liquor commission which mandated that the club comply with its own racial as well as other provisions contained in its constitution and bylaws. Justice Douglas dissented on the grounds that the issuance of the liquor license was sufficient state involvement to prevent the club from enforcing its discriminatory policies. No denial of membership to the club was at issue, since the black plaintiff was refused service as a guest of a member and was not seeking to join the club.

The Supreme Court refused to review the Fifth Circuit opinion in *Millenson* by denying *certiorari*. Whether *Millenson* is dispositive with respect to denial of access to areas admittedly public in nature remains for further resolution. If the argument adopted by *McSorley's* but implicitly rejected by the Fifth Circuit were to prevail, the only remedy would be by amendment of Title II to include sex-based discrimination as a violation. Currently the Fifth Circuit decision is binding only in those states within its jurisdiction lacking civil rights acts which outlaw such discrimination.

4:7 *Discrimination on Account of Age in Public Accommodations*

Title II of the federal Civil Rights Act does not prohibit age discrimination in places of public accommodation. No federal statutes address this issue, but several states do include age as a prohibited basis for treatment by owners or operators of public accommodations. Louisiana includes such a prohibition in its state constitution.[55]

The range of what is included as a public accommodation will vary from state to state, as will the age groups protected. The Illinois statute covers only persons aged forty to seventy.[56] In Connecticut, minors are not included.[57] Certain exceptions may exist to the statutes; in Connecticut, for example, federal- and state-aided housing and municipal housing are beyond reach of the statute.[58]

In *O'Connor v. Village Green Owners Ass'n*,[59] the Supreme Court of California held that a nonprofit condominium development association is a "business establishment" within the Unruh Civil Rights Act and thus barred an age restriction in the association's covenants that limited residency to persons over the age of eighteen. Because innkeepers market condominiums, this decision is important, since it reflects the stated public policy of a leading tourist real estate development jurisdiction.

---

[55]La. Const., article I, Section 12 (1977).
[56]III. Rev. Stat., chapter 68, 1–104 to 9–102 (Smith-Hurd Supp. 1982–83).
[57]Conn. Gen. Stat. Ann., Sections 46a–64(b)(4) (West Supp. 1983–84).
[58]*See generally* Howard C. Eglit, 1 Age Discrimination, chapter 11 (1983).
[59]33 Cal. 3d 790, 662 P.2d 427 (1983).

4:8 *Remedies and Penalties for Violations of Title II*

Injunctive relief is available against both public officials and private individuals "whenever any person has engaged or there are reasonable grounds to believe that any person is about to engage in any act or practice"[60] prohibited by the Act. Declaratory relief is also available.[61] No actions for damages are directly authorized under the Act,[62] but a violation may enable the victim to sue under other federal civil rights laws, so long as the right to be vindicated owes its existence to the Act.[63] There are no criminal penalties available under the Act. The statutory language makes the remedies indicated exclusive, "but nothing in this subchapter shall preclude any individual from asserting any right based on any other Federal or State law not inconsistent with this subchapter . . . or from pursuing any remedy, civil or criminal, which may be available for the vindication or enforcement of such right."[64]

Injunctive relief is available to a private party refused admission to play at a golf course covered by the Act. "Such injunctive relief must provide that, so long as defendant continues to make its golf course and related facilities available to local hotel patrons and other members of the general public, no distinctions are to be made on the basis of race in granting such access."[65]

Moreover, where a restaurant is found to persist in providing dual facilities, one for whites, the other for blacks, the court may order the black-only facility closed or limited to a carry-out business.[66]

Any violation of an injunctive order also empowers the court to hold the party in civil or criminal contempt and thereby levy appropriate fines and imprisonment or both.

Enforcement is by suit, by the person affected. The aggrieved person must bring a civil action for injunction in his own behalf. If he is unable to bring the suit himself because of lack of funds, or because of intimidation, the court in its discretion may permit the Attorney General to intervene, if he certifies that the case is of general public importance. But the Attorney General is denied the right to initiate suits in behalf of individuals.

The prevailing party in a suit may be allowed, at the discretion of the court, reasonable attorney's fees, as part of his costs.

In the words of the then Senator (later Vice-President) Humphrey:

> If the alleged discrimination occurs in a State or locality that has a public accommodations law covering the practice alleged, the individual cannot . . . bring his

[60]42 U.S.C. §§ 2000a-3200(a) (1976); Newman v. Piggie Park Enterprises, Inc. 390 U.S. 400 (1968).

[61]Heart of Atlanta Motel, Inc. v. United States, 379 U.S. 241 (1964).

[62]Newman v. Piggie Park Enterprises, Inc., 390 U.S. 400 (1968).

[63]Sherrod v. Pink Hat Cafe, 250 F. Supp. 516 (N.D. Miss. 1965).

[64]42 U.S.C. § 2000b (1976).

[65]Anderson v. Pass Christian Isles Golf Club, Inc., 488 F.2d 855 (5th Cir. 1974).

[66]United States v. Boyd, 327 F. Supp. 998 (S.D. Ga. 1970); United States v. Johnson, 390 U.S. 563 (1968) making criminal prosecution under 18 U.S.C. § 241 (1976) available against whites who assaulted blacks attempting to patronize a local restaurant, a right secured under Title II of the Civil Rights Act.

suit in Federal court until 30 days after he has registered a complaint with the proper State or local authorities. If these authorities then initiate enforcement proceedings under the State or local law and such proceedings have not been completed by the time suit is filed in Federal court, the Federal court may at its discretion stay the suit until such proceedings are terminated.

If the alleged discrimination has occurred in a State or locality without a public accommodations law, the individual who is aggrieved may bring suit in Federal court immediately. The court may refer such a case to the Federal Community Relations Service for efforts to settle the dispute by voluntary methods. The Service is authorized to investigate the case for that purpose. The time limit on such a referral to the Community Relations Service is 60 days, although, upon expiration of this period, the court may extend the referral for up to another 60 days, if it still believes there is a reasonable possibility of obtaining voluntary compliance.

Since the experience in States that have public accommodations laws is that most complaints can be settled by voluntary procedures, it is expected that discretionary referral under these provisions will further the purposes of the title without requiring Federal court orders in many cases.

At the same time . . . State and local officials [are given] a greater responsibility and a greater opportunity to achieve voluntary compliance without Federal action. The intent . . . is to preserve the power of the Federal courts as a last rather than a first step.

The Attorney General has two roles to play in public accommodations suits. One of these is to intervene, at the discretion of the court, in suits brought by aggrieved individuals. . . .

While the Attorney General would not have power to initiate suits in individual cases, he would have authority to initiate legal action on his own under Title II when "he has reasonable cause to believe that any person or group of persons is engaged in a pattern or practice of resistance to the full enjoyments of any of the rights secured by this title." In such cases the Attorney General need not refer the complaint to the Community Relations Service, although he could if he wanted to. Nor is there any requirement for exhaustion of State or local remedies beforehand. If the Attorney General files a certificate that the case is of general public importance, a three-judge court with a mandate to act expeditiously would be appointed. Provision is also made for expedited proceedings in cases filed by the Attorney General in which he does not ask for a three-judge court.

In short, where the Attorney General believes that a suit brought by an individual under title II is important—because, for example, the points of law involved in it are of major significance or because the particular decision will constitute a precedent for a large number of establishments—he may request intervention, in order to present the Government's point of view. And where he believes there is a pattern or practice designed to perpetuate discrimination, he may sue directly.

It is expected that this power of the Attorney General will be an important aid to maintaining public order in cases in which repeated discrimination in public accommodations has given rise to demonstrations and public violence. Since these are among the most explosive and disruptive instances of discrimination, [Congress] felt that the Attorney General had to have power to act quickly and decisively in the interest of public peace and harmony.

Legal assistance [is provided] to persons aggrieved: [Section 204 of the act] authorize[s] the court, in such circumstances as it deems just, to appoint an attorney for a person aggrieved and to permit his suit to be filed without the payment of fees, costs, or security. Relief would be possible for persons experiencing denial of their rights under Title II, who, for financial or other justifiable reasons, are unable to bring and maintain a lawsuit.[67]

Section 206 gives the Attorney General the right to bring an action for preventive relief only if he has reasonable cause to believe and pleads that a person or group of persons is engaged in a pattern or practice of discrimination intended to deny the full exercise of the rights under Title II.

4:9 *Discrimination in Employment under Title VII*

Title VII prohibits discrimination in employment on the basis of race, color, religion, sex, and national origin, but it excepts bona fide private membership clubs from its ambit. In *Equal Employment Opportunity Commission v. Wooster Brush Company Employees Relief Ass'n,*[68] the federal Circuit Court of Appeals ruled that the Association was not an employer but a bona fide private club. As such, it did not discriminate against female employees by refusing to pay pregnancy-related disability benefits although it did pay benefits for other disabilities that rendered pregnant employees unable to work. Only the Company had violated Title VII.

In the following North Carolina case, a former employee brought an action against defendant, a private club, alleging discrimination in employment on the basis of race. The court held that the uncontested status of the defendant as a private membership club within the meaning of the Civil Rights Act of 1964 was a sufficient ground for dismissal of the claim and that this exemption as an "employer" also protects such clubs from employment suits brought under the Civil Rights Act of 1866. The court reasoned as follows.

HUDSON v. CHARLOTTE COUNTRY CLUB, INC.
535 F. Supp. 313 (W.D. N.C. 1982)

POTTER, D.J.: "The Plaintiff, Alfred A. Hudson, was hired by the Defendant, Charlotte Country Club, Inc., in April of 1977 to perform various maintenance duties in and around the club's main clubhouse. However, in December of 1977, the Plaintiff was fired by the Defendant due to his behavior on several occasions toward female employees and guests of the club. The Plaintiff, a black, thereupon filed a complaint with the EEOC alleging that his termination was racially motivated, and that the payment and treatment accorded to him by his former employer had been less than that provided to white employees.

"Finding the Defendant to be a private club, exempt from the provisions of Title VII, the EEOC dismissed the Plaintiff's charge for lack of jurisdiction and granted him a 'right to sue' letter. The Plaintiff thereupon filed this suit pursuant

---

[67]110 Cong. Rec. 12712-13 (1964).
[68]727 F.2d 566 (6th Cir. 1984).

to 42 U.S.C. § 2000e, *et seq.* (Title VII) and 42 U.S.C. § 1981, alleging discrimination in employment on the basis of his race. . . .

III. The § 1981 Claim

"The only remaining issue for this Court to decide is whether the private club exemption of Title VII, by implication, exempts such clubs from discrimination in employment suits brought under § 1981.

"The Civil Rights Act of 1866, 42 U.S.C. § 1981 provides in pertinent part that

"All persons within the jurisdiction of the United States shall have the same right in every State and Territory to make and enforce contracts, . . . and to the full equal benefit of all laws and proceedings for the security of persons and property and is enjoyed by white citizens. . . .

"Case law has established that this statute 'affords a federal remedy against discrimination in private employment on the basis of race.' *Johnson v. Railway Express Agency,* 421 U.S. 454, 459–60, 95 S. Ct. 1716, 1719–20, 44 L. Ed. 2d 295 (1975). *See also, Jones v. Mayer Co.,* 392 U.S. 409, 88 S. Ct. 2186, 20 L. Ed. 2d 1189 (1968).

"In *Johnson,* the Supreme Court considered the question of whether the statute of limitations with regard to both a Title VII claim and a § 1981 claim was tolled by the EEOC filing in the Title VII claim. The Court held that Title VII and § 1981 offered distinct remedies and that by filing the Title VII claim, a plaintiff did not preserve his § 1981 claim. Consequently, the § 1981 claim filed over three years after the Title VII claim was barred by the statute of limitations.

"The private club exemption of Title VII was not before the Court in *Johnson,* yet the opinion includes *dicta* that touches on the subject. As a premise to finding that Title VII and § 1981 claims were governed by separate statutes of limitations, the Supreme Court necessarily found that

"the remedies available under Title VII and under § 1981, although related, and although directed to most of the same ends, are separate, distinct, and independent. 421 U.S. at 461, 95 S. Ct. at 1726.

"It is apparent from the *Johnson* opinion that, for the purpose of deciding the narrow statute of limitations question, the Supreme Court considered Title VII and § 1981, from a general standpoint, as creating separate and distinct causes of action. However, the Court did not address the possibility that the later Act, Title VII, might, in very specific situations, have preempted or limited certain causes of action under § 1981. Thus, the Supreme Court in *Johnson* cannot be fairly said to have directly decided the issue of whether the bar on suing private clubs in Title VII is also applicable, by statutory implication, to suits brought under § 1981.

"The term 'employer' under Title VII 'does not include . . . a bona fide private membership club (other than a labor organization) which is exempt from taxation under section 501 (c) of Title 26.' 42 U.S.C. § 2000e(b). To be exempt from Title VII coverage under the 'bona fide private membership club' exception, the club must be tax exempt and must be a private membership club. Tax exempt status alone under the Internal Revenue Code is insufficient to bring an organization within the Title VII exception. *See Quijano v. University Federal Credit Union,* 617 F.2d 129, 131 n.12 (5th Cir. 1980). *See also Tillman v. Wheaton-Haven Recreation Ass'n.,* 410 U.S. 431, 93 S. Ct. 1090, 35 L. Ed. 2d 403 (1973) (Title II); *Wright v. Cork Club,* 315 F. Supp. 1143 (S.D. Tex. 1970) (Title II).

"The Association's tax exempt status under 26 U.S.C. § 501(c)(9) is undisputed. The Court must therefore determine whether the Association is a private membership club under Title VII.

"The First Circuit Court of Appeals has articulated four criteria that must be met in order for an organization to achieve private membership club status. First, the organization must be club, i.e., an association of persons for social or recreational purposes or for promotion of a common literary, scientific, or political objective. Second, the organization's objective must be legitimate and not a sham. Third, the organization must be private, not public. Fourth, the organization must require meaningful conditions of limited membership. *Quijano v. University Federal Credit Union, supra* at 131.

"The Association was not created for social or recreational purposes or for promoting common literary, scientific, or political objectives. The sole reason for the Association's existence is to provide disability benefits for individuals who are members, i.e., for individuals who contribute to the Association and work for the Company. There is no evidence in the record that the members commingle in their capacity as Association members and with a common purpose.

"No one faults the origins of the Association as an organization originally established to aid fellow employees. Moreover, the Court finds that providing disability benefits is a legitimate reason for the Association's existence. The Court therefore declines to find that the Association is a sham for analysis of the Association's status as a bona fide private membership club under Title VII.

"The Court views the third and fourth criteria set out in *Quijano* as being closely related. While members of the general public are not admitted to the Association, neither does the Association impose meaningful conditions of limited membership. Access is premised, first of all, on being employed by the Company. Then, if a member meets the physical requirement and pays monthly dues, he or she can become and remain a member. As stated earlier, there is no common social, recreational, literary, scientific, or political prerequisite for Association membership. The binding objective of Association membership is personal benefit in case of disability while employed at the Company.

"The Court accordingly concludes that the Association is not a bona fide private membership club as intended under Title VII. *See Chattanooga Automobile Club v. Commissioner of Internal Revenue,* 182 F.2d 551, 554 (6th Cir. 1950) (denying tax exempt status to automobile clubs). The Association's contention, then, that it is excluded from Title VII coverage because of status as a private membership club, is rejected.

"The most recent significant statement by the Supreme Court in this area was made in *New York City Transit Authority v. Beazer*, 440 U.S. 568, 583–4 n.24, 99 S. Ct. 1355, 1364 n.24, 59 L. Ed. 2d 587 (1974). Although the private club exemption was not at issue, with regard to the relationship between claims brought under Title VII and § 1981 the Supreme Court held that

"Our treatment of the Title VII claim also disposes of the § 1981 claim without the need of a remand. Although the exact applicability of that provision has not been decided by this Court, it seems clear that it affords no greater substantive protection than Title VII.

"If § 1981 provides 'no greater substantive protection than Title VII,' then it would appear that a suit against a private club could not be brought under § 1981 when it is specifically barred by Title VII.

"This is the position that has been taken by the Fourth Circuit as stated in its opinion in *Tillman v. Wheaton-Haven Recreation Association, Inc.*, 451 F.2d 1211, 1214–15 (1971), *rev'd on other grounds*, 410 U.S. 431, 93 S. Ct. 1090, 35 L. Ed. 2d 403 (1973) with the Supreme Court specifically reserving a ruling on the present issue. In speaking of Title VII's exemption of private clubs with regard to membership practices, the Fourth Circuit in *Tillman* stated that

"[t]his exception to the ban on racial discrimination of necessity operates as an exception to the Act of 1866, in any case where that Act prohibits the same conduct which is saved as lawful by the terms of the 1964 Act. . . . If Wheaton-Haven is a private club as defined in the 1964 Act, the exemption contained in that Act is equally applicable to the earlier statutes.

"Several other courts in dealing with the specific issue have arrived at the same conclusion as that reached by the Fourth Circuit in *Tillman*, most notably, *Kemerer v. Davis*, 520 F. Supp. 256 (E.D. Mich. 1981); *Wright v. Salisbury Club, Ltd.*, 479 F. Supp. 378 (E.D. Va. 1979), *rev'd on other grounds*, 632 F.2d 309 (4th Cir. 1980); and *Cornelius v. Benevolent Protective Order of Elks*, 382 F. Supp. 1182 (D. Conn. 1974). The principal justification for finding that the private club exemption of Title VII supersedes and impliedly limits § 1981 actions insofar as they conflict, was best expressed by the District Court opinion in *Wright*, *supra*, in its analysis of Title VII's legislative history. Relying in part upon the *Tillman* decision, *supra*, the District Court found that

"When Congress enacted the 1964 legislation, it did not and could not have known about the conflict with the 1866 Act. Indeed, not until 1968, four years after the 1964 Act became law, did the Supreme Court first determine that the Civil Rights Act of 1866 prohibited 'private' as well as officially sanctioned discrimination. *Jones v. Mayer Co.*, 392 U.S. 409, 88 S. Ct. 2186, 20 L. Ed. 2d 1189 (1968). Thus the conflict between the two statutes was latent when Congress drafted the 1964 legislation, and the absence of express language in the 1964 Act limiting the 1866 Act is inconsequential.

"479 F. Supp. at 386.

"The Fourth Circuit reversed the district court's ruling in *Wright* on the grounds that the defendant was not truly a private club and thus did not rule upon the district court's holding that § 1981 was limited by the private club exemption in Title VII. 632 F.2d at 311, n.5.

"In light of the fact that the Fourth Circuit has not modified its holding in *Tillman,* in view of the analysis of Title VII's legislative history as expressed so well by the district courts in *Cornelius* and *Wright,* and with deference to the Supreme Court's recent statement in *New York City Transit Authority v. Beazer,* this Court finds that 42 U.S.C. § 1981 does not afford any greater degree of protection than Title VII, and that suits against private clubs that are barred by Title VII, are also barred under § 1981.

"Indeed, this ruling makes sense, from both the legislative and judicial viewpoints. As the Fourth Circuit noted in *Tillman,* 'it is unquestionable that in 1964 Congress acted in the belief that in outlawing discrimination . . . it was writing on a clean slate.' 451 F.2d at 1214 n.5. Thus, if private clubs, exempt from employment discrimination suits under Title VII, are nonetheless liable to suit under § 1981 for exactly the same alleged offense, then the exemption in Title VII has no meaning and no practical effect.

"Consequently, having previously found the Defendant in this case, Charlotte Country Club, Inc., to be a bona fide private club exempt from the provision of Title VII, this Court finds that such exemption in Title VII supersedes and limits § 1981 so as to bar the employment discrimination suit under § 1981 as well.

"THEREFORE IT IS HEREBY ORDERED . . .

"(2) that the Defendant's motion for summary judgment with regard to both the Title VII and § 1981 claims is granted, and the entire case is dismissed."[69]

4:10   *Supreme Court Holds Act Constitutional*

In the test case of *Heart of Atlanta Motel, Inc. v. United States,*[70] the Supreme Court, speaking through Justice Clark, unanimously sustained the constitutionality of the Act. Although Congress had purported to act under both the commerce clause and section 5 of the Fourteenth Amendment, the majority opinion relied solely upon the commerce clause to sustain the statute. (Justice Douglas wrote a concurring opinion urging that the statute should have been upheld simply on the basis of the Fourteenth Amendment. Justice Goldberg, also concurring, was content to rest upon the commerce clause but argued that the Fourteenth Amendment was a source more consonant with the act's basic purposes: what was involved, he stressed, was "the vindication of human dignities and not mere economics."[71] Clark found that Congress had a rational basis for finding that racial discrimination by motels and hotels adversely affected interstate commerce and that the means selected to eliminate that evil were reasonable and appropriate. He noted that the American people had become increasingly mobile; that blacks in particular had been the subject of discrimination in transient accommodations and often had been unable to obtain any; that

---

[69]*Contra;* Baptiste v. the Cavendish Club, Inc., 670 F. Supp. 108 (U.S.D.C., S.D. 1987).
[70]379 U.S. 241 (1964).
[71]*Id.* at 291.

these exclusionary practices were nationwide and hence significantly impaired the black traveler's pleasure; and that the net result of these factors was that interstate travel by a substantial portion of the black community was impeded and discouraged.

Although the Heart of Atlanta Motel served a substantial number of interstate travelers, in a companion case decided the same day, *Katzenbach v. McClung*,[72] the court held the Act constitutional as applied to a restaurant that neither solicited nor catered to interstate travelers but came within the Act only because a substantial portion of the food served therein had moved in interstate commerce.

4:11 State Civil Rights Laws

Following the Civil War, state legislatures in response to popular sentiment, particularly in the northern states, enacted civil rights laws, outlawing discrimination in places of public accommodation on account of race, creed, color, or national origin. Today, the majority of states have civil rights statutes of their own applicable to places of public accommodation, including hotels, motels, restaurants, theaters, barbershops, and a variety of other places.

4:12 Equal Rights in Places of Public Accommodation under the New York Civil Rights Law

New York was one of the first states to legislate on the subject of civil rights. Section 40 of the Civil Rights Law, originally enacted in 1895, provides that all persons are entitled to the full and equal accommodations, advantages, facilities, and privileges of any "place of public accommodation, resort or amusement," subject only to conditions and limitations established by law and applicable alike to all persons. The law further provides that no person shall refuse, withhold from, or deny to any person such accommodations or privileges by reason of *race, creed, color, or national origin*. A place of public accommodation is defined to include inns, hotels (including resort hotels), taverns, roadhouses, restaurants, barrooms, barbershops and beauty salons, and many other places.

4:13 Restriction on Advertising and Business Solicitation under the New York Civil Rights Law

Section 40 also prohibits the use of any circulars or advertisement, or the mailing of any written or printed matter which contains any statement, express or implied, that any of the accommodations, facilities, or privileges will be refused or denied on account of race, creed, color, or national origin, or that any person is unwelcome, not acceptable, not desired, or not solicited because of race, creed, color, or national origin.

[72]379 U.S. 294 (1964).

4:14   *Penalties under the New York Civil Rights Law*

Section 41 of the Civil Rights Law fixes a penalty for a violation of section 40 at not less than $100 nor more than $500 and gives the person who has been aggrieved the right to bring a *civil action* for such amount. In addition, the violation is made a misdemeanor and is punishable by a fine of not less than $100 nor more than $500, or imprisonment of not less than thirty days nor more than ninety days, or both.

4:15   *Protecting Civil and Public Rights under the New York Civil Rights Law*

The protection of section 40 applies to *any person,* irrespective of his citizenship or residence. Section 44-a (formerly section 514 of the Penal Law) makes it a misdemeanor for a person to exclude by reason of race, color, creed, national origin, or previous condition of servitude, a citizen of New York State from the equal enjoyment of any accommodations, facilities or privileges furnished by innkeepers or common carriers or to deny or aid another in denying to any other person, because of race, creed, color, or national origin, the full enjoyment of the accommodations, etc., of any hotel, inn, tavern, restaurant, or other place of public resort or amusement.

This section was originally enacted to secure blacks equal rights with white persons to the facilities furnished by carriers, innkeepers, taverns, restaurants, and places of public resort or amusement. It is similar in import to section 40.[73]

Since the enactment of the New York Civil Rights Law and Executive Law provisions prohibiting sex discrimination in places of public accommodation, twenty states have followed suit: Alaska, California, Colorado, Connecticut, Delaware, Florida, Idaho, Iowa, Kansas, Louisiana, Maine, Massachusetts, New Hampshire, New Jersey, New Mexico, Oregon, Pennsylvania, Utah, West Virginia, and Wisconsin.

Other states that have enacted statutes prohibiting sex discrimination in places of public accommodation include District of Columbia, Illinois, Kentucky (naming only restaurants, hotels, and motels), Maryland, Michigan, Minnesota, Missouri, Montana, Nebraska, North Dakota, Ohio, Rhode Island, South Dakota, Tennessee, and Wyoming.

4:16   *Cases Interpreting Sections 40 and 41 of the New York Civil Rights Law*

There is a difference between a "place of public accommodation" and a "place of public amusement." Theaters and concert halls are places of public amusement; restaurants and hotels are places of public accommodation.[74]

---

[73]People v. King, 110 N.Y. 418 (1888).
[74]People v. Keller, 96 Misc. 92, 161 N.Y.S. 132 (Ct. Gen. Sess. 1916).

Section 40 of the Civil Rights Law does *not* apply to a family or residential hotel, in which apartments are arranged in small suites, differing in no essential respect from those in an ordinary apartment house.[75]

Nor does the section apply to a private club, the facilities and privileges of which are available to members only. A club is not a place of public accommodation but rather an institution of a distinctly private nature. A complaint by club members based on ejection and use of language by other members describing plaintiffs in a derogatory manner but which failed to allege discrimination on account of "race, creed, color" was held defective.[76]

Application of the American Labor Party for a temporary injunction to prevent the Hotel Concourse Plaza in New York City from canceling a contract for the use of the hotel's grand ballroom was denied, since the cancellation was not based on race, creed, color, or national origin. The contract in question contained the following provision: "The hotel reserves the right to cancel engagements at any time where rules are not observed, or where functions are of a nature not acceptable to the hotel." The hotel canceled the contract when it learned that the ballroom was to be used for a rally to confer upon Paul Robeson the International Peace Award for which he was cited by the Warsaw World Peace Congress.[77]

In an action for recovery of a penalty under sections 40 and 41 of the Civil Rights Law, the defense that the defendant was out of food at the time was rejected as a sham and unworthy of belief.[78]

The employer was not guilty of violating sections 40 and 41 of the Civil Rights Law when a waiter refused to serve a black customer in violation of his employer's instructions to serve white and black customers alike, without discrimination.[79]

A rule in a restaurant, applicable alike to all citizens, that a person who did not wear a collar would not be served is a reasonable rule and is not within the proscription of the statute.[80]

Refusal to serve an unescorted female patron at the bar, despite willingness to serve her at a table near the bar, has been held not a violation of sections 40, 40-c, or 40-e of the New York Civil Rights Law in a state court action that paralleled the *DeCrow* federal case found in section 4:6, supra.[81] (*But see* section 4:17, *infra.*)

In 1982, however, section 40–c of the New York Civil Rights Law was amended to include sex, marital status, and disability as prohibited grounds for discrimination in a person's civil rights. Harassment, as defined in section

---

[75]Alsberg v. Lucerne Hotel Co., 46 Misc. 617, 92 N.Y.S. 851 (Sup. Ct. 1905).

[76]Garfield v. Sands Beach Club, Inc., 137 N.Y.S.2d 58 (Sup. Ct. 1954).

[77]American Labor Party v. Hotel Concourse Plaza, 200 Misc. 587, 102 N.Y.S.2d 413 (Sup. Ct. 1950).

[78]Wilson v. Razzetti, 88 Misc. 37, 150 N.Y.S. 145 (Sup. Ct. 1914).

[79]Hart v. Hartford Lunch Co., 81 Misc. 237, 142 N.Y.S. 515 (Sup. Ct. 1913).

[80]Brandt v. Mink, 38 Misc. 750, 78 N.Y.S. 1109 (Sup. Ct. 1902).

[81]DeCrow v. Hotel Syracuse Corp., 59 Misc. 2d 383, 298 N.Y.S.2d 859 (Sup. Ct. 1969).

240.25 of the penal law, in the exercise of civil rights was also prohibited. Section 40–c applies to all persons, firms, corporations, and institutions and to the state and any agency or subdivision of the state.

NOBLE V. HIGGINS
95 Misc. 328, 158 N.Y.S. 867 (Sup. Ct. 1916)

DAVIS (ROWLAND L.), J.: "On December 10, 1915, the plaintiff entered the restaurant of the defendants in the city of Oneonta, and asked to be served with certain food, offering at the same time to pay therefor. His request was refused and he was ordered to leave the premises. The plaintiff commenced an action to recover from the defendants a penalty pursuant to the provisions of chapter 6 of the Consolidated Laws, known as the Civil Rights Law, as amended by chapter 265 of the Laws of 1913.

"The evidence was brief, simple and practically undisputed. At the close of the evidence both sides moved for the direction of a verdict, and the jury was formally directed at the time to find a verdict for the plaintiff, which they did, assessing the penalty at $100. All proceedings after the entry of the verdict were stayed until the court could consider the legal questions involved in the controversy.

"The refusal to serve the plaintiff was apparently on purely personal grounds. The refreshment asked for by the plaintiff was not refused, withheld from or denied to him on account of race, creed, or color. Therefore, it seems that the interpretation of the Court of Appeals in *Grannan v. Westchester Racing Association*, 153 N.Y. 449 (1897), as extended and applied under the present statute in *Woollcott v. Shubert*, 217 N.Y. 212, forbids the application of the statute to the state of facts recited here.

"It may be conclusively determined, after an examination of the last-quoted authorities that 'the legislature did not intend to confer upon every person all the rights, advantages, and privileges in places of amusement or accommodation, which might be enjoyed by another. Any discrimination not based upon race, creed or color does not fall within the condemnation of the statute.'

"It would seem then, that the common-law right still remains with those not engaged as common carriers, or in like occupations, to discriminate between persons according to rules established where the person applying for accommodation is objectionable for some reason. Otherwise, persons unclean, untidy, intoxicated or affected by disease might claim the same attention in a crowded restaurant or other public place as those against whom no objection could be urged. *Brandt v. Mink*, 38 Misc. Rep. 750.

"Whether or not plaintiff had a remedy at common law for any indignity or humiliation caused by the act of the defendants need not be considered here, although some of the authorities cited on [*sic*] the plaintiff's brief discussed that question. The action is brought solely on the theory that the plaintiff is entitled to recover a penalty or forfeiture given under the Civil Rights Act where a violation occurs." [Complaint dismissed on the merits.]

HOBSON V. YORK STUDIOS, INC.
208 Misc. 888, 145 N.Y.S.2d 162 (Mun. Ct. 1955)

[The plaintiffs, Raymond S. Hobson, a black man, and his wife, a white woman, seek to recover statutory redress under section 41 of the Civil Rights Law, alleging that when they applied for a room in the defendant's hotel, they were rejected by reasons of their race.

It appeared that on May 6, 1953, Mrs. Hobson personally called at defendant's hotel, obtained a reservation for herself and her husband, paid a deposit of $5.00 and obtained a receipt.

The next day both husband and wife appeared to claim their reservation and to pay the balance due. Instead of admitting them, the desk clerk told Mr. Hobson that the hotel did not want "white and colored" living together in view of the tendency of another interracial couple, who had resided there previously, to fight all the time. The desk clerk then returned the plaintiff's deposit.]

WAHL, J.: "I have accepted the testimony of the plaintiffs, seemingly, respectable and worthy citizens, and I am convinced that both of them were discriminated against because of their race. The *post litem* contention that Mr. Hobson was offensive and abusive and that that was the basis of the refusal to give the plaintiffs accommodations is not convincing, nor was it pleaded as a matter of affirmative defense. It is natural that a defendant accused of racial discrimination will seek avoidance of statutory penalties therefor through 'explanations.' . . .

"I now come to an aspect of this case which is not free of difficulty: If the white plaintiff, Rose Hobson, was discriminated against because of her race, may she be given relief under the Civil Rights Law? . . .

"The words 'any person' [in the statute] . . . when given their usual meanings, must include protection for white persons as well as Negroes who are rejected because of race. To all but the naive, it is clear that a white woman may be the butt of a racial discrimination because she has elected to marry a Negro. I am convinced that both plaintiffs were rejected by the defendant because Mr. Hobson is a Negro and his wife is a white woman. Such a refusal, as applied to Mrs. Hobson, is a rejection of her because of her color. . . .

"In effect, what the defendant's desk clerk said to Mrs. Hobson was that if she had been married to a white man, her reservation for a room would have been honored. If the rejection was based upon some private theory of 'social acceptability,' where Negroes and whites are in intimate association, it is still offensive to the law. . . .

"The credible testimony confirms a racial discrimination against each of the plaintiffs. The Law Against Discrimination states its purpose to be 'the protection of the public welfare, health and peace of the people of this state' (Executive Law, § 290) [Laws of 1955, Ch. 340, Sec. 1]. This is inclusive of *all* people, white as well as Negro. The old cases which would limit the application of the Civil Rights Law to Negroes only are clearly negatived by recent legislative enactments. This legislation is remedial in concept and liberal in its scope; it represents the public policy of the State which applies to the entire public.

"For all of the foregoing reasons, I direct that the plaintiffs have judgment against the defendant in the amount of $100 each."

4:17   *Human Rights Law, New York State Executive Law*

This statute, passed in 1972, reads as follows:

Section 296. Unlawful Discriminatory Practices

2.(a) It shall be an unlawful discriminatory practice for any person, being the owner, lessee, proprietor, manager, superintendent, agent or employee of any place of public accommodation, resort or amusement, because of the race, creed, color, national origin, sex, or disability or marital status of any person, directly or indirectly, to refuse, withhold from or deny to such person any of the accommodations, advantages, facilities or privileges thereof, including the extension of credit, or, directly or indirectly, to publish, circulate, issue, display, post or mail any written or printed communication, notice or advertisement, to the effect that any of the accommodations, advantages, facilities and privileges of any such place shall be refused, withheld from or denied to any person on account of race, creed, color, national origin, sex, or disability or marital status, or that the patronage or custom thereat of any person of or purporting to be of any particular race, creed, color, national origin, sex or marital status, or having a disability is unwelcome, objectionable or not acceptable, desired, or solicited.

(b) Nothing in this subdivision shall be construed to prevent the barring of any person, because of the sex of such person, from places of public accommodations, resort or amusement if the division grants an exemption based on bona fide considerations of public policy; nor shall this subdivision apply to the rental of rooms in a housing accommodation which restricts such rental to individuals of one sex.

4:18   *Purpose and Construction of the New York State Executive Law*

BATAVIA LODGE V. DIVISION OF HUMAN RIGHTS
35 N.Y.2d 143, 316 N.E.2d 318 (1974)

WACHTLER, J.: "The unlawful discrimination committed in this case was blatant and intolerable. After being invited on the premises of the Moose Lodge for a fashion show, the black complainants were refused service at the private bar. White nonmembers who also attended the fashion show were freely served at the same bar. In addition several black complainants were verbally abused. It is evident that such conduct perpetrated in a place used as a public accommodation cannot be tolerated.

"The Commissioner of the Human Rights Division found there was enough corroborative evidence produced to warrant awarding each claimant $250 in compensatory damages.

"The majority of the Appellate Division modified the determination of the commissioner by striking out the damage award as being punitive in nature. The court implied that an award for compensatory damages required as a *sine qua non* proof of out of pocket expenses: 'there is no evidence that any respondent was put to expense or lost earnings or suffered any measurable damage by reason of the discrimination.'

"We do not agree that such a showing is necessary in order to validate an award for compensatory damages. For the most part we agree with the dissenters in the Appellate Division and the standards which they have spelled out for determining when damages for mental anguish may be awarded. However, recovery should not be based solely on common-law strictures as would be applied in determining liability for a tort. Recovery here, instead, is based on a statute which effectuates a State policy against discrimination.

"We have previously had occasion to speak of the strength and importance of the State's policy in combating discrimination [citations omitted], and there can be no doubt that the extensive powers granted to the Division of Human Rights in the Executive Law reflect the broad thrust of this fundamental policy (Executive Law, § 295). Indeed, it was 'undoubtedly, the need for a programmatic enforcement of the anti-discrimination laws which prompted the Legislature to create the State Commission for Human Rights and to vest it with broad powers to eliminate specified "unlawful discriminatory practices" ' [citation omitted] (see. . . Executive Law, § 296). Thus, the division is empowered to take appropriate action to eliminate and prevent discriminatory practices (Executive Law, § 297), and, if upon investigation, it finds that the statute has been violated, it is authorized to impose a variety of sanctions, including the 'awarding of compensatory damages to the person aggrieved by such practice, as, in the judgment of the division, will effectuate the purposes of this article' (Executive Law, § 297, subd. 4, par. c).

"In *Matter of State Comm. for Human Rights v. Speer* (29 N.Y.2d, 555) we held that the statute did authorize the awarding of compensatory damages for mental suffering and anguish to aggrieved individuals. There is nothing in the statute which would suggest that the commissioner does not have the power to make such an award and 'there is no exception carved out of the term "compensatory damages," removing his power to give an award for mental suffering as a traditional component of fair compensation' (dissent of HOPKINS, J., 35 A.D.2d 107, 113).

"The extremely strong statutory policy of eliminating discrimination gives the Commissioner of the Human Rights Division more discretion in effecting an appropriate remedy than he would have under strict common-law principles. The main goal of the common-law right spelled out by the dissenters below was to provide private remedies. In the case at bar, the right is statutory and involves a vindication of a public policy as well as a vindication of a particular individual's rights.

"We do not hold in this case that the commissioner may award what would amount to punitive damages solely on the finding that unlawful discrimination had occurred [citation omitted]. What we do hold is that due to the strong antidiscrimination policy spelled out by the Legislature of this State, an aggrieved individual need not produce the quantum and quality of evidence to prove compensatory damages he would have had to produce under an analogous provision, and this is particularly so where, as here, the discriminatory act is intentionally committed. The evidence produced in this case was adequate to meet the statutory standard and support the commissioner's determination. In addition, the size of the award was not unreasonably large under the circumstances. In all other respects we reverse on the dissent in the Appellate Division.''

It is significant that the court affirmed the finding of the intermediate appellate court that although the petitioner, Moose Lodge, was a private club, on the occasion in question it permitted its facilities to be used as a place of public accommodation.[82]

In a related factual setting, an appellate court has ruled that the totality of a plan or scheme to establish a private membership club otherwise exempt from the prohibitions of section 40 of the New York Civil Rights Law will be examined to see whether the club has met its required burden of proof and is not just a sham to conceal the truly public nature of the enterprise. That case, *Castle Hill Beach Club, Inc. v. Arbury*,[83] resulted in the court's approval of a commission order requiring an end of racial discrimination at a beach club found to be a "place of public accommodation, resort or amusement" within the scope of the law:

> The commission has found, and the record supports the conclusion, that the creation of the membership corporation was motivated by apprehension of the possible effect which the presence of Negroes might have on the profit-making potential of the recreational park. The membership corporation's president and general manager did not deny the statement attributed to him by the commission's field representative, "Our only reason for not wanting to admit negroes is" that "we are scared to death to admit them for fear of the untoward results which might follow their admission."
>
> It may be that the telephone listing, etc., as isolated facts, do not justify the conclusion that the membership corporation was a mere sham designed to conceal the truly public nature of the enterprise. But, in our judgment, the record, considered as a whole, leads to that conclusion. The various aspects of a plan or scheme, when considered singly, may very well appear innocent. The true nature of the plan or scheme is revealed only when the various aspects are viewed as a totality. Such is this case.
>
> Lastly, we find that the hearing conducted by the commission was fair and deprived the membership corporation of no constitutional right.[84]

Yet another indicator of the status of an ostensible private club as a "place of public accommodation" is the holding of conventions on the premises. In *Lake Placid Club, Inc. v. Abrams*,[85] the use of a booklet containing the language

[82]43 A.D.2d 807, 808, 350 N.Y.S.2d 273, 274 (4th Dep't 1973) *rev'd*, 35 N.Y.2d 143, 359 N.Y.S.2d 25, 316 N.E.2d 318 (1974).

[83]208 Misc. 622, 144 N.Y.S.2d 747 (Sup. Ct. 1955), *aff'd as mod.*, 1 A.D.2d 943, 150 N.Y.S.2d 367 (1st Dep't 1956).

[84]*Id.*

[85]6 A.D.2d 469, 179 N.Y.S.2d 487 (3d Dep't 1958), *aff'd*, 6 N.Y.2d 857, 160 N.E.2d 92 (1959).

"Serving Christian Clientele Since 1911" was held a violation of section 296(2), which makes it a discriminatory practice to publish or mail any communication to the effect "that the patronage or custom of any person belonging or purporting to be of any particular race, creed, color or national origin is unwelcome, objectionable or not acceptable, desired, or solicited."

4:19 *Other Forms of Discrimination*

HALES V. OJAI VALLEY INN AND COUNTRY CLUB
73 Cal. App. 3d 25, 140 Cal. Rptr. 555 (1977)

KINGSLEY, Acting Presiding Judge: "Plaintiffs appeal from an order dismissing their complaint, after an order sustaining, without leave to amend, a demurrer to that complaint. We reserve the order.

"The first cause of action is by plaintiff Hales, alleging a violation of the Unruh Civil Rights Act (Civ. Code, § 51); the second cause of action is by Hales, seeking damages for false advertising; the third cause of action is by plaintiff Losner, alleging a violation of the Unruh Act. All three causes of action seek both general and punitive damages. Since the briefs on appeal discuss only whether the complaint states any cause of action at all, we do not, on this appeal, reach the adequacy of the pleading as to the punitive damages claim.

"The first cause of action alleges that defendant conducts and conducted a public establishment for the service of food and drink. It then alleges: (1) that plaintiff Hales is a member of the male sex; (2) that he entered defendant's place of business, with his family, desiring to purchase food and drink; (3) that he was 'attired in a leisure suit'; (4) that he was told that he could not be served unless he wore a tie; and (5) that, at that time, food and drink were being served 'to female patrons who were similarly attired in leisure suits.'

"Based on those allegations, he alleges that he was the victim of discrimination because of sex.

"In *Stoumen v. Reilly* (1951) 37 Cal. 2d 713 [234 P.2d 969], the California Supreme Court recognized the right of homosexuals to obtain food and drink in a bar and restaurant under the Unruh Civil Rights Act, saying (at p. 716): 'Members of the public of lawful age have a right to patronize a public restaurant and bar so long as they are acting properly and are not committing illegal and immoral acts; the proprietor has no right to exclude or eject a patron "except for good cause," and if he does so without good cause he is liable in damages. (*See* Civ. Code, § § 51, 52).'

"The definitive interpretation of the Act was made in the case *In re Cox* (1970) 3 Cal. 3d 205 [90 Cal. Rptr. 24, 474 P.2d 992], when the California Supreme Court unanimously prohibited shopping centers from excluding individuals who wore long hair or unconventional dress. The court said (at p. 217): 'In holding that the Civil Rights Act forbids a business establishment generally open to the public from arbitrarily excluding a prospective customer, we do not imply that the establishment may never insist that a patron leave the premises. Clearly, an entrepreneur need not tolerate customers who damage property, injure others, or otherwise disrupt his business. A business establishment may, of course, promulgate reasonable deportment regulations that are rationally related to the services performed and the facilities provided.'

"*In re Cox* constructed the Unruh Act as prohibiting only arbitrary discrimination, not all discrimination. Whether the requirement that men wear ties but women need not is arbitrary or reasonable turns not on the bare facts pleaded by Hales but upon the facts. It requires a factual showing as to what is meant by the term 'leisure suit' and by a factual determination, based on the nature of defendant's establishment and on local community standards for dress for both sexes. Those are facts that can only be determined on trial and not on demurrer. Although, on a special demurrer, plaintiff may well, in the discretion of the trial court, be required to allege some of those facts in more detail, the first cause of action is sufficient to indicate the nature of plaintiff's contention. The general demurrer should not have been sustained.

"Hales' second cause of action alleges as follows:

"On or about March 15, 1976, Plaintiff received from Defendant, Ojai Valley Inn and Country Club, a brochure advertising its services 'in friendly surroundings in the Vista Room, Garden Room, and the Toppa Room,' as follows: 'Sports and casual clothes are in order during the day. A warm sweater or wrap is suggested for the evenings which are frequently cool. Gentlemen are requested to wear jackets and ties to dinner.'

"Plaintiff was induced by said advertising claim to reserve two rooms from Defendant, Ojai Valley Inn and Country Club for one week for use as a family vacation site.

"Defendant's advertising claim was false, in that Defendant did not merely 'request' men to wear jackets and ties to dinner, but actually required men, including Plaintiff, to wear a jacket and tie as a condition to serving them food and drink.

"At the time Defendant, Ojai Valley Inn and Country Club made said advertising claim, it did not intend to merely 'request' men to wear a jacket and tie, but intended to require men to wear a jacket and tie. If Plaintiff had known Defendant, Ojai Valley Inn and Country Club's true intention, he would not have made reservations with Defendant for his family vacation.

"A cause of action based on deceit-false advertising must allege: (1) a misrepresentation; (2) knowledge of falsity by the representor; (3) intent to deceive; and (4) reliance and resulting damage. (3 Witkin, Cal. Procedure (2d ed. 1971) § 573, pp. 2210–2211.) Tested by those rules, we conclude that the second cause of action sufficiently alleged enough facts to withstand a general demurrer. Hales alleges a misrepresentation, intent to deceive, and reliance on the false advertisement. That is enough. Whether the statement in the brochure was sufficient to put Hales on notice that the defendant's dress code might, in fact, be stricter than therein set forth is a matter of defense, to be raised by answer and not by demurrer.

"The so-called third cause of action is by plaintiff Losner, on his own behalf. It alleges:

"On August 21, 1976, Plaintiff entered the Ojai Valley Inn Cocktail Lounge to purchase a drink to be consumed on the premises. Plaintiff requested a drink, but Defendants refused him service since he was without a coat and tie. During this time, while Plaintiff was on the aforementioned premises, drink such as Plaintiff wished to order was sold and served to female patrons who were not wearing coats and tie, and who were attired in a fashion similar to Plaintiff.

"Defendants, and each of them, refused to serve food and drink to Plaintiff as aforesaid, and denied to Plaintiff the services, advantages, accommodations [sic], facilities, and privileges provided to other persons as aforesaid, solely on account of Plaintiff's sex. As a proximate result of the wrongful act of Defendants, Plaintiff has been generally damaged in the sum of Five Thousand Dollars ($5,000.00) and is entitled to recover further statutory damages in the sum of Two Hundred Fifty Dollars ($250.00) as provided in Section 52 of the Civil Code.

"For the same reasons that we held Hales' first cause of action to be sufficient as against a general demurrer, we hold that Losner has stated a sufficient cause of action.

"The judgment (order of dismissal) is reversed."

In rejecting the claim of exemption by reason of a Boy Scout council's private nonprofit associational status, thereby nullifying the council's expulsion of a male member on the ground of his homosexual preference, a California appellate court resolved the competing interests of free association and the commands of the Unruh Civil Rights Act as follows.

CURRAN V. MOUNT DIABLO COUNCIL OF BOY SCOUTS
147 Cal. 3d 712, 195 Cal. Rptr. 325 (1983), *appeal dismissed* 468 U.S. 1205, 104 S. Ct. 3574, 82 L. Ed. 2d 873 (1984)

THOMPSON, A.J.: " . . . [D]efendant argues that any construction of the Unruh Act to bring the Boy Scouts within the meaning of 'business establishment' would constitute an infringement of its rights of privacy and free association as a membership organization. The 'governing principle,' defendant asserts, is found in the following dissenting opinion of Mr. Justice DOUGLAS in *Moose Lodge No. 107 v. Irvis* (1972) 407 U.S. 163, 179–180, 92 S. Ct. 1965, 1974–1975, 32 L. Ed. 2d 627: 'The associational rights which our system honors permit all white, all brown, and all yellow clubs to be formed. They also permit all Catholic, all Jewish, or all agnostic clubs to be established. Government may not tell a man or woman who his or her associates must be. The individual can be as selective as he desires. So the fact that the Moose Lodge allows only Caucasians to join or come as guests is constitutionally irrelevant, as is the decision of the Black Muslims to admit to their services only members of their race.'

"Taking this principle literally as 'governing' would afford protection to the most flagrant form of discrimination under the canopy of the right of free association. The answer is, of course, that those with a common interest may associate exclusively with whom they please *only* if it is the kind of association which was intended to be embraced within the protection afforded by the rights of privacy and free association. (*See* Note, *Association, Privacy and Private Club: The Constitutional Conflict* (1970) 5 Harv. C.R.—C.L.L. Rev. 460, 466–467.) 'The character and extent of any interference with the freedom of association must be weighed against the countervailing interests.' (Note, *Sex Discrimination in Private Clubs* (1977) 29 Hastings L.J. 417, 422.)

"Accordingly, these constitutional provisions only restrain the Legislature from enacting anti-discrimination laws where *strictly* private clubs or institutions are affected. (*See, e.g., Burks v. Poppy Construction Co., supra,* 57 Cal. 2d 463, 471, 20 Cal. Rptr. 609, 370 P.2d 313; *Stout v. Y.M.C.A.,* (5th Cir. 1968) 404 F.2d 687. *Nesmith v. Y.M.C.A.* (4th Cir. 1968) 397 F.2d 96; *National Organization for Women, Essex Chapter v. Little League Baseball, Inc.,* (1974) 127 N.J. Super. 552 [318 A.2d 33].) . . .

"Since the essence of a private club or organization is exclusivity in the choice of one's associates, we find this approach ensures that private organizations remain protected. However, those entities which are not in fact private must comply with the mandate of the Unruh Act.

"Moreover, we find that to allow an organization to offer its facilities and membership to the general public, but exclude a class of persons on a basis prohibited by law would be contrary to the public policy expressed in the Unruh Act. Although our research discloses no California cases directly on point, cases decided under the federal and sister states' public accommodations statutes are persuasive here. For example, in *Tillman v. Wheaton-Haven Recreation Assn. Inc.* (1973) 410 U.S. 431, 438, 93 S. Ct. 1090, 1094, 35 L. Ed. 2d 403, a nonprofit recreational association open to all white residents in a certain area was found not to be a private club exempt from the Public Accommodation Law (Title II of the Civil Rights Act of 1964, as amended, 42 U.S.C. § 2000a, *et seq.*) because it had 'no plan or purpose of exclusiveness.' Similarly, in *Sullivan v. Little Hunting Park, Inc.* (1969) 396 U.S. 229, 236, 90 S. Ct. 400, 404, 24 L. Ed. 2d 386, a community park open to all area residents who were not black was held not to be a private club since '[i]t is not to be open to every white person within the geographic area, there being no selective element other than race.' In *National Organization for Women v. Little League Baseball, Inc., supra,* 127 N.J. Super. 522, 318 A.2d 33, a membership organization for boys was held to be a public accommodation under New Jersey's public accommodation law. There, the court said: 'Little League is a *public* accommodation because the invitation is open to children in the community at large, with no restriction (other than sex) whatever.' (318 A.2d at pp. 37–38.)

"We therefore conclude that the concept of organizational membership per se cannot place an entity outside the scope of the Unruh Act unless it is shown that the organization is truly private. . . . ''

The United States Supreme Court dismissed the Boy Scouts' appeal (no. 83–1513, July 5, 1984).

BRAUN V. SWISTON
72 Misc. 2d 661, 340 N.Y.S.2d 468 (Sup. Ct. 1972)

KRONENBERG, J.: "Defendant operates a restaurant and barroom, located in the City of Tonawanda, New York, and as such, it is open to the public. In the past few years, he has evolved a policy of refusing to serve long-haired male customers, presumably on the basis that such service would in some way jeopardize his liquor license. Plaintiffs are a class of persons, male, with long hair, who have been refused and who continue to be refused service in this restaurant and barroom. No refusal of service is known to have occurred concerning long-haired females at defendant's place of business.

"Plaintiff contends that the undenied action on the part of the defendant contravenes subdivision 2 of section 296 of the Executive Law which provides that it is an unlawful discriminatory practice for a place of public accommodation to deny the facilities to a person because of his or her sex. Defendant's premises are clearly a place of public accommodation as defined in said statute (Executive Law, § 292, subd. 9).

"Plaintiff has moved for summary judgment declaring the action on the part of the defendant is unlawful and enjoining the same.

"Plaintiff's contention that he is being discriminated against because he, as a man with long hair, will not be served, while a woman with even longer hair will be served is a unique contention. However, the fact of the matter is that the defendant will not serve a man with long hair and such refusal does constitute a discrimination and under the circumstances of this case it can be called a discrimination based on sex.

"Since there is no question of fact and since defendant's action is unlawful, plaintiff's motion for summary judgment should be granted permanently restraining defendant from refusing to serve male patrons due to the fact that their hair is long."

In a case of first impression in California, the Supreme Court of California ruled that the Unruh Civil Rights Act prohibits sex-based price discounts in nightclubs and car washes. (All references to the latter are omitted.) The high court reviewed the history and purpose of the California civil rights law in light of sexual stereotyping.

KOIRE V. METRO CAR WASH
40 Cal. 3d 24, 219 Cal. Rptr. 133 (1985)

BIRD, C.J.: "Does the Unruh Civil Rights Act (Civ. Code § 51) prohibit sex-based price discounts?

"In the spring of 1979, plaintiff. . . visited several bars which offered admission discounts to women, including a nightclub, Jezebel's. At trial, plaintiff testified that he heard a radio advertisement for Jezebel's. The ad publicized an event scheduled for the following weekend to celebrate the first opportunity for young adults 18 to 21 to patronize the establishment. The ad stated that all 'girls' aged 18 to 21 would be admitted free. Plaintiff, 18 years old at the time, went to Jezebel's and requested free admission which was refused.

"Jezebel's owner and manager testified that there had been no such advertisement and promotional discount as described by plaintiff. However, the nightclub does have a regular 'Ladies Night.' Women are admitted free but men must pay a $2 cover charge.

"Plaintiff filed suit against numerous . . . bars, claiming that their sex-based price discounts violated the Unruh Civil Rights Act (hereafter the Unruh Act or the Act.) He sought statutory damages and an injunction. He eventually went to trial against . . . Jezebel's.

"The trial court granted judgment for defendants on all causes of action. The court found that the sex-based price discounts did not violate the Unruh Act. Plaintiff appeals.

"The language of the Unruh Act is clear and unambiguous: 'All persons within the jurisdiction of this state are free and equal, and no matter what their sex . . . are entitled to the full and equal accommodations, advantages, facilities, privileges, or services in all business establishments of every kind whatsoever. . . . ' The Act is to be given a liberal construction with a view to effectuating its purposes. (*Orloff v. Los Angeles Turf Club* (1947); 30 Cal. 2d 110, 113, 180 P.2d 321; *Winchell v. English* (1976), 62 Cal. App. 3d 125, 128, 133 Cal. Rptr. 20.)

"The parties do not dispute that defendants are business establishments to which the Unruh Act applies. (*See generally, In re Cox* (1970) 3 Cal. 3d 205, 212–213, 90 Cal. Rptr. 24, 474 P.2d 922; 34 Ops. Cal. Atty. Gen. 230, 231–232 (1959). Nor can there be any dispute that the Act applies to classifications based on sex. Although the list of classes enumerated in the Act has been held to be illustrative rather than exhaustive (*Marina Point, Ltd. v. Wolfson* (1982) 30 Cal. 3d 721, 725, 180 Cal. Rptr. 496, 640 P.2d 115 [hereafter Marina Point]; *In re Cox, supra,* 3 Cal. 3d at p. 216, 90 Cal. Rptr. 24, 474 P.2d 992; [other citations omitted], the inclusion of 'sex' in the list clearly covers discrimination based on sex. (*See e.g., Easebe Enterprises, Inc. v. Alcoholic Bev. etc. Appeals Bd.* (1983) 141 Cal. App. 3d 981, 986 & fn.4, 190 Cal. Rptr. 678; *Hales v. Ojai Valley Inn & Country Club* (1977) 73 Cal. App. 3d 25, 28–29, 140 Cal. Rptr. 555.)

"Defendants argue that the Unruh Act prohibits only the exclusion of a member of a protected class from a business establishment. They claim the law allows discrimination based on admission prices and services. Defendants also argue that the Unruh Act prohibits only arbitrary discrimination, and that the sex-based price discounts at issue here fall within recognized exceptions to the Act. In addition, defendants argue that the sex-based discounts did not violate the Act because they did not injure the plaintiff. Finally, they contend that a prohibition on sex-based discounts will mean an end to all promotional discounts.

"Defendants' first contention, that the Act prohibits only the exclusion of prospective patrons from business establishments, is without merit. The Act guarantees 'full and equal accommodations, advantages, facilities, privileges, or services. . . . ' (§ 51). The scope of the statute clearly is not limited to exclusionary practices. The Legislature's choice of terms evidences concern not only with access to business establishments, but with equal treatment of patrons in all aspects of the business. . . .

"Contrary to defendants' assertions, the scope of the Unruh Act is not narrowly limited to practices which totally exclude classes or individuals from business establishments. The Act's proscription is broad enough to include within its scope discrimination in the form of sex-based price discounts.

"Defendants' primary argument is that sex-based price discounts do not constitute 'arbitrary' discrimination. Although the Unruh Act proscribes 'any form of arbitrary discrimination' (*O'Connor v. Village Green Owners Assn.* (1983) 33 Cal. 3d 790, 794, 191 Cal. Rptr. 320, 662 P.2d 427), certain types of discrimination have been denominated 'reasonable' and, therefore, not arbitrary. For example, the Act does not prevent a business enterprise from promulgating 'reasonable deportment regulations.' (*Ibid.; Marina Point, supra,* 30 Cal. 3d at pp. 725, 738–739, 180 Cal. Rptr. 496, 640 P.2d 115; *Orloff v. Los Angeles Turf Club* (1951) 36 Cal. 2d 734, 741, 227 P.2d 449.) ' " '[A]n entrepreneur need not tolerate customers who damage property, injure others or otherwise disrupt his business.' " ' (*O'Connor v. Village Green Owners Assn., supra,* 33 Cal. 3d at p. 794, 191 Cal. Rptr. 302, 662 P.2d 427; *Marina Point, supra,* 30 Cal. 3d at p. 737, 180 Cal. Rptr. 496, 640 P.2d 115; *In re Cox, supra,* 3 Cal. 3d at p. 217, 90 Cal. Rptr. 24, 474 P.2d 992.)

"In certain contexts, it has been said that the Act is inapplicable to discrimination between patrons based on the 'nature of the business enterprise and of the facilities provided.' (*O'Connor v. Village Green Owners Assn., supra,* 33 Cal. 3d at p. 794, 191 Cal. Rptr. 302, 662 P.2d 427; [other citations omitted]). However, few cases have held discriminatory treatment to be nonarbitrary based solely on the special nature of the business establishment. . . .

"Most often, the nature of the business enterprise or the facilities provided has been asserted as a basis for upholding a discriminatory practice only when there is a strong public policy in favor of such treatment. (*See Marina Point, supra,* 30 Cal. 3d at pp. 742–743, 180 Cal. Rptr. 496, 640 P.2d 115.) Public policy may be gleaned by reviewing other statutory enactments. For example, it is permissible to exclude children from bars or adult bookstores because it is illegal to serve alcoholic beverages or to distribute 'harmful matter' to minors. (*Id.,* at p. 741, 180 Cal. Rptr. 496, 640 P.2d 115, citing Bus. & Prof. Code s 25658 and Pen. Code, s 313.1.) This sort of discrimination is not arbitrary because it is based on a 'compelling societal interest' (*Marina Point, supra,* 30 Cal. 3d at p. 743, 180 Cal. Rptr. 496, 640 P.2d 115) and does not violate the Act.

"Defendants argue that sex-based price differences are not arbitrary because they are supported by 'substantial business and social purposes.' Essentially, they argue that the discounts are permissible because they are profitable.

"In *Marina Point*, this court held that the fact that a business enterprise was "proceed[ing] from a motive of rational self-interest" did not justify discrimination. (*Marina Point, supra*, 30 Cal. 3d at p. 740, fn.9, 180 Cal. Rptr, 496, 640 P.2d 115, disapproving *Newby v. Alto Riviera Apartments* (1976) 60 Cal. App. 3d 288, 302, 131 Cal. Rptr. 547.) This court noted that 'an entrepreneur may pursue many discriminatory practices "from a motive of rational self-interest," e.g., economic gain, which would unquestionably violate the Unruh Act. For example, an entrepreneur may find it economically advantageous to exclude all homosexuals, or alternatively all nonhomosexuals, from his restaurant or hotel, but such a "rational" economic motive would not, of course, validate the practice.' (*Marina Point, supra*, 30 Cal. 3d at p. 740, fn.9, 180 Cal. Rptr, 496, 640 P.2d 115.) It would be no less a violation of the Act for an entrepreneur to charge all homosexuals, or all nonhomosexuals, reduced rates in his or her restaurant or hotel in order to encourage one group's patronage and, thereby, increase profits. The same reasoning is applicable here, where reduced rates were offered to women and not men.

"Defendant Jezebel's argues that 'Ladies Night' encourages more women to attend the bar, thereby promoting more interaction between the sexes. This it deems to be a 'socially desirable goal' of the state. However, the 'social' policy on which Jezebel's relies—encouraging men and women to socialize in a bar— is a far cry from the social policies which have justified other exceptions to the Unruh Act. For example, the compelling societal interest in ensuring adequate housing for the elderly which justifies differential treatment based on age cannot be compared to the goal of attracting young women to a bar. (*Marina Point, supra*, 30 Cal. 3d at pp. 742–743, 180 Cal. Rptr, 496, 640 P.2d 115; [citations omitted]). The need to promote the 'social policy' asserted by Jezebel's is not sufficiently compelling to warrant an exception to the Unruh Act's prohibition on sex discrimination by business establishments.

"Next, defendants argue that their sex-based price discounts do not violate the Unruh Act because 'Ladies Day' discounts do no injury to either men or women. They contend that this plaintiff was not injured by the price differences. Defendants' argument fails for several reasons.

"First, it does not recognize that by passing the Unruh Act, the Legislature established that arbitrary sex discrimination by businesses is *per se* injurious. Section 51 provides that all patrons are entitled to equal treatment. Section 52 provides for minimum statutory damages of $250 for every violation of section 51, regardless of the plaintiff's actual damages.

"As this court noted in *Orloff v. Los Angeles Turf Club, supra*, 30 Cal. 2d at p. 115, 180 P.2d 321, construing an earlier version of the statute, the statute provides for damages aside from any actual damages incurred by the plaintiff. ' "This sum is unquestionably a penalty which the law imposes, and which it directs shall be paid to the complaining party. . . . [But], while the law has seen fit to declare that it shall be paid to the complaining party, it might as well have directed that it be paid into the common-school fund. The imposition is in its nature penal, having regard only to the fact that the law has been violated and its

majesty outraged." '. . . (*Accord MacLean v. First North. Industries of America*
(1981) 96 Wash. 2d 338, 635 P.2d 683, 690 (dis. opn. of UTTER, J.) [arguing
that the state of Washington's antidiscrimination laws recognize that discrimination 'injures not only the victim but the state and public in general,' and can
therefore be attacked 'despite an injury-free victim'].)

"Second, defendants ignore both the individual nature of a cause of action
under the Unruh Act [citation omitted] and the actual injury to this plaintiff. The
plaintiff was adversely affected by the price discounts. His female peers were
admitted to the bar free, while he had to pay. . . . In addition to the economic
impact, the price differentials made him feel that he was being treated unfairly.

"Moreover, differential pricing based on sex may be generally detrimental to
both men and women, because it reinforces harmful stereotypes. (*See* Babcock,
et al., Sex Discrimination and the Law (1975) p. 1069; Note, *Washington's
Equal Rights Amendment and Law against Discrimination—The Approval of the
Seattle Sonics' 'Ladies Night'* (1983) 58 Wash. L. Rev. 465, 473.)

"Men and women alike suffer from the stereotypes perpetrated by sex-based
differential treatment. (*See* Kanowitz, *'Benign' Sex Discrimination: Its Troubles
and Their Cure* (1980) 31 Hastings L.J. 1379, 1394; Comment, *Equal Rights
Provisions: The Experience under State Constitutions* (1977) 65 Cal. L. Rev.
1086, 1106–1107.) When the law 'emphasizes irrelevant differences between
men and women[,] [it] cannot help influencing the content and the tone of the
social, as well as the legal, relations between the sexes. . . . As long as organized legal systems, at once the most respected and most feared of social institutions, continue to differentiate sharply, in treatment or in words, between men
and women on the basis of irrelevant and artificially created distinctions, the
likelihood of men and women coming to regard one another primarily as fellow
human beings and only secondarily as representatives of another sex will continue to be remote. When men and women are prevented from recognizing one
another's essential humanity by sexual prejudices, nourished by legal as well as
social institutions, society as a whole remains less than it could otherwise become.' (Kanowitz, Women and the Law (1969) p. 4.)

"Whether or not these defendants consciously based their discounts on sex
stereotypes, the practice has traditionally been of that character. For example, in
Com., Pa. Liquor Control Bd. v. Dobrinoff (1984) 80 Pa. Cmwlth. 453, 471
A.2d 941, the trial court relied on just such a stereotype in upholding a tavern's
cover charge distinction based on sex. The court suggested that the purpose of
the discount was ' "chivalry and courtesy to the fair sex." ' (*Id.*, 471 A.2d at
p. 943.) The appellate court held, however, that a variance in admission charge
based 'solely upon a difference in gender, having no legitimate relevance in the
circumstances' violated the Pennsylvania Human Relation Act's prohibition
against sex discrimination. (*Ibid.*)

"Similarly, in striking down the New York Yankees 'Ladies' Day' promotion,
the New York State Human Rights Appeal Board observed that 'the stereotyped
characterizations of a woman's role in society that prevailed at the inception of
'Ladies' Day' in 1876' were outdated and no longer valid 'in a modern techno-

logical society where women and men are to be on equal footing as a matter of public policy.' (*Abosh v. New York Yankees, Inc.* (1972) No. CPS-25284, Appeal No. 1194, reprinted in Babcock, *et al.*, Sex Discrimination and the Law, *supra*, at pp. 1069, 1070.)

"With all due respect, the Washington Supreme Court also succumbed to sexual stereotyping in upholding the Seattle Supersonics' 'Ladies' Night.' (*MacLean v. First North. Industries of America, supra*, 635 P.2d at p. 684.) The court found that the discount was reasonable because, *inter alia*, 'women do not manifest the same interest in basketball that men do.' (*Ibid.*)

"This sort of class-based generalization as a justification for differential treatment is precisely the type of practice prohibited by the Unruh Act. [Citations omitted.] '[T]he Unruh Civil Rights Act prohibits all forms of stereotypical discrimination.' (*San Jose Country Club Apartments v. County of Santa Clara* (1982) 137 Cal. App. 3d 948, 952, 187 Cal. Rptr. 493.) These sex-based discounts impermissibly perpetuate sexual stereotypes. . . .

"In addition, classifications based on sex are considered 'suspect' for purposes of equal protection analysis under the California Constitution. (*Sail'er Inn, Inc. v. Kirby* (1971) 5 Cal. 3d 1, 20, 95 Cal. Rptr. 329, 485 P.2d 529.) California ratified the proposed Equal Rights Amendment to the United States Constitution on November 17, 1972, within one year of its passage by Congress. (Sen. Joint Res. No. 20, Stats. 1972 (Reg. Sess.) res. ch. 148, p. 3440.) In short, public policy in California mandates the equal treatment of men and women. . . .

"There may also be instances where public policy warrants differential treatment for men and women. For example, some sex-segregated facilities, such as public restrooms, may be justified by the constitutional right to personal privacy. (*See* Comment, *The Unruh Civil Rights Act: An Uncertain Guarantee* (1983) 31 UCLA L. Rev. 443, 462, fn.98.) However, defendants' discriminatory pricing policies are in no way based on privacy considerations, nor are they justified by any other public policy which might warrant differential treatment based on sex.

"The plain language of the Unruh Act mandates equal provision of advantages, privileges and services in business establishments in this state. Absent a compelling social policy supporting sex-based price differentials, such discounts violate the Act.

"Jezebel's argues that it will be forced to close its nightclub business if it cannot charge a lower cover price to women one evening each week. 'However, such a fact, if it be a fact, is not determinative.' (*Easebe Enterprises, Inc. v. Alcoholic Bev. etc. Appeals Bd., supra*, 141 Cal. App. 3d at p. 987, 190 Cal. Rptr. 678.)

"Moreover, Jezebel's has offered no reason why it could not charge a lower admission fee one night each week to men and women alike. This would encourage increased patronage by both sexes on equal terms. When faced with a similar question, the New York Human Rights Commission observed that '[p]erhaps, in their unending quest to serve best the social interests of the public, a Community Day at reduced prices irrespective of sex, rather than a Ladies Day with its attendant pricing based on sex, might well accomplish respondents' social concerns without violating the public policy of this State. . . . ' (*Abosh v. New York Yankees, Inc.*, reprinted in Babcock *et al.*, Sex Discrimination and the Law, *supra*, at p. 1070.) Such a solution might work equally well here.

"Courts are often hesitant to upset traditional practices such as the sex-based promotional discounts at issue here. Some may consider such practices to be of minimal importance or to be essentially harmless. Yet, many other individuals, men and women alike, are greatly offended by such discriminatory practices.

"The legality of sex-based price discounts depend on the subjective value judgments about which types of sex-based distinctions are important or harmful. The express language of the Unruh Act provides a clear and objective standard by which to determine the legality of the practices at issue. The Legislature has clearly stated that business establishments must provide 'equal . . . advantages . . . [and] privileges' to all customers 'no matter what their sex.' (§ 51.) Strong public policy supports application of the Act in this case. The defendants have advanced no convincing argument that this court should carve out a judicial exception for their sex-based price discounts. The straightforward proscription of the Act should be respected.

"The judgment is reversed and the cause remanded to the trial court for further proceedings consistent with the views expressed herein."

Citing *Koire*, the California Court of Appeal ruled that a group of San Diego topless bar owners violated the Unruh Civil Rights Act by refusing admission to persons wearing clothing with motorcycle club insignia. In the absence of evidence of violent or other objectional behavior, the court granted plaintiff's motion for a preliminary injunction in his favor.

RENTERIA V. DIRTY DAN'S INC.
198 Cal. App. 3d 1447 (1988)

REGAN, J.: " . . .

"Renteria's declaration is uncontradicted. Because he wore motorcycle club insignia, he was denied admission to and service at the bars. The defendants concede that persons wearing such insignia are excluded from entering or being served at their bars, claiming this exclusion is intended to regulate conduct as the presence of patrons wearing motorcycle club insignia is said to contribute to violent confrontations between members of competing motorcycle clubs. These allegations in the declarations of Levy and McClelland are, of course, pejorative conclusions and opinions without factual support. They fail to cite a single instance of confrontation between wearers of insignia denoting competitive clubs, violent or otherwise. There are no declarations, factual or otherwise, from patrons, police, employees or topless dancers, supporting the opinions and conclusions of Levy and McClelland. The only evidence before the court, then, is the exclusion of Renteria from the bars because he wore motorcycle club insignia. We conclude that evidence is insufficient to support denial of the preliminary injunction to restrain the operators of the bars from denying admittance to persons wearing motorcycle club insignia as violative of the Unruh Act. (*See IT Corp. v. County of Imperial* (1983) 35 Cal. 3d 63, 69 [196 Cal. Rptr. 715, 672 P.2d 121].)

"As we have seen, the Unruh Act accords every person an individual right against arbitrary discrimination of any kind whether or not expressed in the act. (*Isbister v. Boys' Club of Santa Cruz, Inc., supra,* 40 Cal. 3d 72, 86.) All arbitrary discrimination is prohibited. (*In re Cox, supra,* 3 Cal. 3d 205, 212.)

"*Koire v. Metro Car Wash, supra,* 40 Cal. 3d 24, 35–36, instructs that 'class-based generalization as a justification for differential treatment is precisely the type of practice prohibited by the Unruh Act' and the act ' "prohibits all forms of stereotypical discrimination." ' This sentiment was echoed in *Marina Point, Ltd. v. Wolfson, supra,* 30 Cal. 3d 721, 738–739, where the court discussed the nature of arbitrary discrimination. Though one may be excluded from a 'business enterprise' on an individual basis 'if he conducts himself improperly or disrupts the operations of the enterprise,' it is 'arbitrary' and therefore prohibited to exclude an entire class on the basis of stereotyped notions. (*See also Isbister, supra,* 40 Cal. 3d at p. 87; *In re Cox, supra,* 3 Cal. 3d at pp. 217–218.)

"Bars and restaurants like the defendants' establishments may not engage in arbitrary discrimination under the act. (*Koire, supra,* 40 Cal. 3d 24; *Easebe Enterprises, Inc. v. Alcoholic Bev. etc. Appeals Bd.* (1983) 141 Cal. App. 3d 981 [190 Cal. Rptr. 678, 38 A.L. R.4th 332]; *Rolon v. Kulwitzky* (1984) 153 Cal. App. 3d 289 [200 Cal. Rptr. 217]; *Hales v. Ojai Valley Inn & Country Club* (1977) 73 Cal. App. 3d 25 [140 Cal. Rptr. 555, 89 A.L.R.3d 1].)

"The bar owners concede Renteria cannot be excluded from the defendants' bars on the basis of membership in a motorcycle club. Discrimination on account of a person's association with others is prohibited by the Unruh Act. (*Winchell v. English, supra,* 62 Cal. App. 3d 125, 130 ['the discrimination of this case . . . was *arbitrary,* and based solely upon the subject's association with others']; *Hubert v. Williams* (1982) 133 Cal. App. 3d Supp. 1, 5 [184 Cal. Rptr. 161].) Discrimination on the basis of a person's appearance is prohibited by the act. (*In re Cox, supra,* 3 Cal. 3d 205, 217, 218.)

"The exclusion based on insignia cannot be justified as an attempt to maintain a certain ambiance by setting dress standards. A tuxedo-garbed Renteria would be excluded from the bars if his cummerbund contained a motorcycle club insignia. The dress regulations of defendant McFaddin San Diego 1139, Inc. required persons to be dressed neatly and cleanly. Motorcycle club insignia wearers meeting those standards are not excluded.

"The test for arbitrary discrimination is not whether an exclusionary policy is 'rational,' but whether it is based on a stereotype.

" '*Marina Point* made clear that "reason" and "good faith" are not enough to avoid a finding of "arbitrary" discrimination. Our opinion condemned the adults-only policy there at issue even to the extent it rested on *true* assumptions about the general difficulties of living with children. [Citation omitted.] There are any number of plausible reasons why the owner of a "business establishment" serving the public might wish, in good faith, to exclude or discriminate against a particular group. But the Legislature has decreed that, once a "business establishment" attains that public status, it has responsibilities to the entire community which cannot be lightly ignored. Were good faith and bare rationality sufficient to permit group discrimination, the Act would have little meaning.' (*Isbister v. Boys' Club of Santa Cruz, Inc., supra*, 40 Cal. 3d 72, 89, fn. 19.)

"Exclusion of Renteria cannot be excused or justified on the basis of a rational good faith belief that persons wearing insignia denoting membership in motorcycle clubs may be 'troublemakers.' The Unruh Act was specifically designed to prohibit exactly such stereotyping.

" 'As our prior decisions teach, the Unruh Act preserves the traditional broad authority of owners and proprietors of business establishments to adopt reasonable rules regulating the conduct of patrons or tenants; it imposes no inhibitions on an owner's right to exclude any individual who violates such rules. Under the act, however, an individual who has committed no such misconduct cannot be excluded solely because he falls within a class of persons whom the owner believes is more likely to engage in misconduct than some other group. Whether the exclusionary policy rests on the alleged undesirable propensities of those of a particular race, nationality, occupation, political affiliation, or age, in this context the Unruh Act protects individuals from such arbitrary discrimination.' " (*Marina Point, Ltd. v. Wolfson, supra*, 30 Cal. 3d 721, 725–726.)

"Unless a blanket exclusion serves a 'compelling societal interest,' a private exclusionary policy violates the mandate of the Unruh Act. (*Marina Point, Ltd. v. Wolfson, supra*, at p. 743.)

"Renteria was not excluded from bars for misconduct. The fact he is admitted to the bars when not wearing 'colors' denoting membership in a motorcycle club belies any claim his exclusion is based on reasonable rules for 'deportment.' There are no facts here which compel the conclusion he does not comport himself consistent with manners appropriate to a topless bar environment, whether wearing motorcycle club insignia or not.

"Wearing apparel can and frequently does include an element of communication implicating First Amendment concerns. Cases dealing with topless dancing in barrooms have established as much. (*Morris v. Municipal Court* (1982) 32 Cal. 3d 553, 564 [186 Cal. Rptr. 494, 652 P.2d 51], and cases cited therein.) Renteria was denied admission to the bars and excluded from enjoying the public accommodations not for the style of his clothing but for the insignia on his clothes. The exclusion rests squarely on his exercise of free speech rights. (*Cohen v. California* (1971) 403 U.S. 15, 18 [29 L. Ed. 2d 284, 289–290, 91 S. Ct. 1780].) Wearing the insignia of a motorcycle club cannot be deemed inherently inflammatory or provocative on the basis of the evidence adduced before the trial court. Based on the record here, membership in an association of motorcycle enthusiasts without more is not likely to cause a violent reaction in other people. (*Cohen v. California, supra*, 403 U.S. at p. 20 [29 L. Ed. 2d at p. 291].)

"The operators of the bars have offered no evidence that wearing of club insignia has ever caused any problems in their bars. McClelland's declaration fails to cite a single incident of inappropriate behavior caused by wearing motorcycle club insignia, although he claims 16 years of bar ownership experience. Levy claims a 'number of years of business experience,' but fails to cite a single incident of disorderly conduct traced to the wearing of motorcycle club insignia.

"That part of the order . . . denying injunctions against Dirty Dan's, Inc., Clubary, Inc., 10450 Friars Road, Inc., II.S., Inc. (erroneously sued as Club Royale In Spot II, Inc.), and The In Spot, Inc., is reversed and the court is ordered to issue a preliminary injunction enjoining and restraining those defendants, their agents and employees and all persons acting in concert with them, from enforcing a policy of denying admission to their business establishments or refusing to serve Michael Renteria and Clifford Dohrer while wearing clothing with insignia denoting membership in a motorcycle club."

4:20 *Marital Status*

The amendment of section 296(2) (a) to include exclusion based upon marital status as a discriminatory practice has not yet been interpreted by the New York courts. Under prior law, it was not a violation of the Civil Rights Law to make inquiry of a couple desiring hotel accommodations whether they were in fact married to each other.[86] Under the plain meaning rule of statutory construction, this customary hotel practice is no longer permitted. This change does not suggest that the legislature sought to condone immoral conduct, but rather reflects a realistic appreciation of a change in attitude with respect to consenting adults who seek to share the same room and register individually and not as Mr. and Mrs. The amendment does not envision prostitution, which is a crime, but voluntary acts for pleasure, which the courts have declared to be noncriminal and not grounds for exclusion solely because their conduct is not otherwise a violation of law.[87]

4:21 *Disability*

Another amendment to section (296)(2) (a) outlaws any form of discrimination based on a physical or mental handicap as such, absent proof that the person was incapable of functioning by reason thereof. This means that the innkeeper must make adequate provision for disabled or handicapped individuals and that the same legal obligations to provide for their comfort, convenience, and safety would apply as to nonhandicapped guests, taking into consideration the particular circumstances of each case.

---

[86]People v. McCarthy, 204 Misc. 460, 119 N.Y.S.2d 435 (City Ct. 1953).

[87]*See* Chapter 6, *infra*, with respect to the innkeeper's common-law right to deny admission under a house rule.

4:22　*Extension of Credit*

This new provision means simply that if a hotel chooses to extend credit, it must do so on a nondiscriminatory basis. It does not mean that a hotel or other place of public accommodation is required to extend credit. It does not mean that a hotel may not require adequate proof of financial responsibility or proper proof of identity since these are legitimate business considerations unrelated to the specified grounds of discrimination.[88]

4:23　*The Male-Only Civic Club*

The dichotomy of sex-based discrimination and the private club exception contained under federal and state law was forcefully presented in the following New York case. In a declaratory judgment action brought by a local chapter against its international organization seeking to nullify certain provisions of the international's constitution which restricted membership to men, the trial court found in favor of the defendant.

KIWANIS CLUB OF GREAT NECK, INC. V.
BOARD OF TRUSTEES OF KIWANIS INTERNATIONAL
83 Misc. 2d 1075, 374 N.Y.S.2d 265
(Sup. Ct. (1975), *aff'd*, 41 N.Y.2d 1034,
363 N.E.2d 1378 (1977), *cert. denied*, 434 U.S. 859 (1977)

BERMAN, J.: "The basic facts are not in dispute. Plaintiff, Kiwanis Club of Great Neck, Inc., hereinafter referred to as the local club, was duly chartered by Kiwanis International, hereinafter referred to as International. If was formed, organized and operated pursuant to the constitution and by-laws of International. Some time in 1973–74, several women, including the female plaintiffs, were admitted to membership in the local club despite the provisions of the International Constitution and By-Laws, which restrict membership to men. The International, upon being advised of such development, informed the local club that this was forbidden. When plaintiff, local club, refused to comply with the charter provision, the Board of Trustees of International voted to revoke the local club's charter. The club appealed this decision to the General Convention of the International body in June of 1975, but the decision of the International Board of Trustees was sustained.

"Plaintiffs contend that this discrimination by defendants against women is in violation of the Fifth and Fourteenth Amendments of the United States Constitution, the New York State Constitution, the Federal Civil Rights Law, Sec. 340 of the General Business Law in New York, and Article 15 of the Executive Law of New York.

"Neither in the pleadings, nor the moving papers, do plaintiffs claim any Federal or State governmental interest or involvement in Kiwanis nor in the oper-

---

[88]See Chapter 21, *infra*, regarding compensation of the innkeeper.

ation of International, except that defendants enjoy the benefits of tax exemption. However, plaintiffs claim that Kiwanis is largely a business organization and is made up of business and professional people; that commercial contacts are made by members through the channels of such organization; that the denial of membership to business and professional women is in violation of their rights under the Federal and State constitutions and statutes, and deprives them of opportunities to complete on an equal footing with men in the business community. Furthermore, and this is the crux of plaintiffs' case, they argue that Kiwanis is not truly a private club as defined in the 1964 Civil Rights Act.

"Article 22, Section 340 of the General Business Law of the State of New York, cited by plaintiffs, and which prohibits unlawful interference with the free exercise of any activity in the conduct of any business is not applicable to this situation; nor is the Executive Law of the State of New York, Section 290 (Human Rights Law) in any way pertinent. The latter deals primarily with discrimination in employment, public accommodation, resort and amusements and housing accommodations and to insure that every individual shall have an equal opportunity to participate fully in the economic, cultural, and intellectual life in the State. This law is not relevant, but in any event was not intended to deal with membership in a private club.

"All of the constitutional and statutory provisions cited and arguments advanced here by plaintiff were similarly urged in an almost identical case involving the Jaycees, a comparable national organization with local chapters, which also had a charter provision denying membership in any of its clubs to women. The Jaycees (Junior Chamber of Commerce) were sustained in their discriminatory charter provision restricting membership to men (*New York City Jaycees v. United States Jaycees*, 512 F.2d 856). The Second Circuit Court of Appeals in the latter case, which was decided as recently as March 7, 1975, held that the organization was immune from restrictions of the Fifth and Fourteenth Amendments to the Constitution, even though it was a recipient of federal funds and enjoyed tax exempt status. 'The mere receipt of public funds does not convert the activities of a private organization into state activities. . . . Similarly the grant of tax exemption to the Jaycees does not constitute significant government involvement in the organization's exclusionary membership policy.'

"The Court therein concludes: 'The Jaycees is a private organization acting in connection with its own enterprise, and the federal courts have no power to grant an injunction prohibiting its discriminatory membership policies.' *New York City Jaycees v. United States Jaycees (supra)*.

"In a similar case, also relating to the issue of sex discrimination in the same organization, the United States Court of Appeals, Tenth Circuit, in upholding the right of the Jaycees to discriminate against women in its Rochester club, in the case of *Junior Chamber of Commerce of Rochester, Inc., Rochester, New York v. United States Jaycees, Tulsa, Oklahoma*, 495 F.2d 883, held:

> "There is no dispute about the invalidity of discrimination by the state or federal Government based on sex and there is no dispute about the fact that the plaintiffs were excluded from membership in the organization purely on

the basis of sex. Therefore, the only issue is whether the discrimination can by reason of the circumstances present, be considered official (state or federal) action. *It must also be conceded that private discrimination does not give rise to a constitutional violation. See Moose Lodge No. 107 v Irvis,* 407 U.S. 163, 92 S. Ct. 1965, 32 L. Ed. 2d 627 (1972).

"It should be noted that the Jaycees is actually a Junior Chamber of Commerce whose prime object is to further the business interests of its members (*New York City Jaycees v. United States Jaycees, supra*). Thus, the decisions involving Jaycees are of considerable significance in the light of plaintiffs' claims of commercialism.

"It is abundantly clear from these and other similar decisions that Kiwanis is truly a private club, and as such has the unequivocal right to determine its own membership and to be discriminatory as to such membership, even though it may enjoy tax exemption. . . .

"It is the Court's conclusion that there is no valid basis to support plaintiffs' claims that Kiwanis is not a private club, or that the denial of membership to women is in any way violative of any constitutional or statutory provision, Federal or State. The Court further concludes that defendants' policy of restricting membership to men may not be disturbed by it."

On appeal to the New York Court of Appeals,[89] that court affirmed in the following memorandum opinion:

Plaintiffs failed to establish the existence of triable issues of fact which would support their claim that Kiwanis International is not within the "private club" exception to the Federal and State Constitutions and Civil Rights Laws. Although the Kiwanis Clubs' community-oriented activities may extend into the public sphere, the intrusion indicated on this record is not so extensive, or of the quality, as to permit governmental supervision of essentially private activity in the constitutional sense. Nor is it within the contemplation of our State's Human Rights Law. Therefore, summary judgment was properly granted.

In *Cross v. Midtown Club, Inc.*,[90] a Connecticut superior court held that a nonstock corporate club whose sole stated purpose was "to provide facilities for the serving of luncheon or other needs to members" acted *ultra vires*, or beyond its corporate purpose or authority, in excluding women as members or as guests of its members, and as such in derogation of its members' rights. The exclusion of women as members and guests was neither necessary nor convenient to the purpose for which the corporation had been organized, nor was such exclusion specifically authorized in the certificate of incorporation, the only means by which such purposes would be sanctioned under the Nonstock Corporation Act.

[89]41 N.Y.2d 1034, 363 N.E.2d 1378 (1977), *cert. denied,* 434 U.S. 859 (1977).
[90]33 Conn. Sup. 150, 365 A.2d 1227 (1976).

The court reasoned as follows: "It should be borne in mind that this club is one of the principal luncheon clubs for business and professional people in Stanford. It is a gathering place where a great many of the civic, business, and professional affairs of the Stanford community are discussed in an atmosphere of social intercourse. Given the scope of the entry of women today in the business and professional life of the community and the changing status of women before the law and in society, it would be anomalous indeed for this court to conclude that it is either necessary or convenient for the stated purpose for which it was organized for this club to exclude women as members or guests."[91]

In *Whitten v. Petroleum Club of Lafayette,*[92] women in the petroleum industry brought a class-action suit challenging the men-only policy of a petroleum-industry private membership club. The Petroleum Club of Lafayette, a tax-exempt and nonprofit membership club, had always prohibited women from membership, including professional women who had business at the club consistent with the purpose for which the club was formed and presently operating. The court found:

> Substantial dues, membership fees and entertainment expenses are "written off" by members or their companies each year. Approximately ninety per cent (90%) of the memberships are corporate memberships. The Petroleum Club, for all practicable purposes, is totally dependent financially on these corporate memberships, and without them, the club would probably have to close its doors.
>
> A great deal of business is carried on at the Petroleum Club. There is no doubt that women employed in the petroleum industries are at a distinct disadvantage in being denied the use of the facility and have suffered in the areas of career advancement, employment advantages, fringe benefits, and access to the market place, because that's where the action is and there is no substitute.

Despite these findings, the court granted the defendants' motion for summary judgment, asserting that the Petroleum Club did not act outside its rights as a private club.

In *United States Jaycees v. McClure,*[93] the Supreme Court of Minnesota construed the state's Human Rights Law as making the United States Jaycees "a place of public accommodation" and thus unable to bar females from the full membership privileges accorded males in its Minnesota chapters. The decision was made in response to a certified question raising this precise issue made by the United States District Court for the State of Minnesota.

The United States District Court upheld this application of the law to the United States Jaycees,[94] and the Jaycees appealed. The United States Court of Appeals for the Eighth Circuit reversed and remanded. In a two-to-one decision, the majority summarized its views as follows.

---

[91]*Id.* at 153–54, 365 A.2d at 1230–31.
[92]508 F. Supp. 765 (W.D. La. 1981).
[93]305 N.W.2d 764 (1981).
[94]534 F. Supp. 766.

UNITED STATES JAYCEES V. MCCLURE
709 F.2d 1560 (8th Cir. 1983), *rev'd sub nom.*, Roberts v. United States
Jaycees, 468 U.S. 609, 104 S. Ct. 3244, 82 L. Ed. 2d 462 (1984)

ARNOLD, C.J.: "The United States Jaycees, a young men's civic and service organization, does not admit women to full membership. A Minnesota statute, as amended in 1972, forbids discrimination on the basis of sex in 'places of public accommodation.' Minn. Stat. Ann. §§ 363.01 subd. 18, 363.03 subd. 3. The Supreme Court of Minnesota has interpreted this phrase to include the Jaycees, and the Minnesota Department of Human Rights has ordered the Jaycees to admit women to its local chapters in Minnesota. In this suit brought by the Jaycees, we are asked to declare the statute, as so applied and interpreted, unconstitutional, as in violation of the rights of speech, petition, assembly, and association guaranteed by the First and Fourteenth Amendments.

"We hold that the Jaycees, a substantial part of whose activities involve the expression of social and political beliefs and the advocacy of legislation and constitutional change, does have a right of association protected by the First Amendment. In our opinion, the interest of the state, in the circumstances of this case, is not strong enough to deserve the label 'compelling,' so as to override this right. In addition, the state law is unconstitutionally vague. The Jaycees is therefore entitled to an injunction restraining the state from efforts to prohibit its membership policy under state law as presently written. This is not to say that no state law could be written to redress this kind of nongovernmental discrimination. Still less do we intend to express our own view of what the Jaycees is doing. But if, in the phrase of Justice HOLMES, the First Amendment protects 'the thought that we hate,' it must also, on occasion, protect the association of which we disapprove. The First Amendment guarantees freedom of choice in a certain area. That freedom must, on occasion, include the freedom to choose what the majority believes is wrong. For reasons to be described, we think this is one of those occasions.[1]"

"1. The Jaycees' refusal to admit women has given rise to several other court or agency opinions. *See Junior Chamber of Commerce of Kansas City, Missouri v. Missouri State Junior Chamber of Commerce*, 508 F.2d 1031 (8th Cir. 1975) (receipt of federal funds (a practice since discontinued) does not make Jaycees a governmental actor for purposes of the Fifth Amendment); *New York City Jaycees, Inc. v. The United States Jaycees, Inc.*, 512 F.2d 856 (2d Cir. 1975) (same); *Junior Chamber of Commerce of Rochester, Inc. v. United States Jaycees*, 495 F.2d 883 (10th Cir.), *cert. denied*, 419 U.S. 1026, 95 S. Ct. 505, 42 L. Ed. 2d 301 (1974) (same); *United States Jaycees v. Bloomfield*, 434 A.2d 1379 (D.C. App. 1981) (Jaycees is not a 'place of public accommodation' within the meaning of the D.C. Human Rights Act of 1977, D.C. Code § 6–2241(a)(1)(Supp. 1978)); *Richardet v. Alaska Jaycees*, No. 3AN–79–424 CIV (Super. Ct. 3d Jud. Dist. of Alaska Sept. 15, 1980) (Jaycees is a place at which amusement or business services or commodities are offered to the public within the meaning of the Alaska public-accommodations law, Alaska Stat. §§ 18.80.230(1), .300(7)); *Fletcher v. U.S. Jaycees*, No. 78–BPA–0058–0071 (Mass. Comm'n Against Discrimination Jan. 27, 1981) (Jaycees is a place of public accommodation within the meaning of Mass. Gen. Laws Ann. ch. 272, §§ 92A, 98).

"The question has also been vigorously debated within the organization. On three occasions a resolution favoring the admission of women has been defeated, but each time a larger minority has voted for it."

Footnote 1 to the preceding case lists other relevant cases. Note that the Supreme Court of Alaska ruled that the United States Jaycees is not a place of public accommodation.[95] In an analogous situation, however, the New York Court of Appeals construed the New York State Human Rights Law broadly, following the precedent established by the Minnesota Supreme Court in *United States Jaycees v. McClure*.[96]

On appeal of the *McClure* decision the United States Supreme Court reversed the federal Circuit Court of Appeals, *sub nom. Roberts v. United States Jaycees*, which follows.

ROBERTS V. UNITED STATES JAYCEES
468 U.S. 609, 104 S. Ct. 3244, 82 L. Ed. 2d 462 (1984)

BRENNAN, J.: " . . . This case requires us to address a conflict between a State's efforts to eliminate gender-based discrimination against its citizens and the constitutional freedom of association asserted by members of a private organization. In the decision under review, the Court of Appeals for the Eighth Circuit concluded that, by requiring the United States Jaycees to admit women as full voting members, the Minnesota Human Rights Act violates the First and Fourteenth Amendment rights of the organization's members. We noted probable jurisdiction, ——U.S. ——, 104 S. Ct. 696, 79 L. Ed. 2d 162, and now reverse.

I

A

"The United States Jaycees (Jaycees), founded in 1920 as the Junior Chamber of Commerce, is a nonprofit membership corporation, incorporated in Missouri with national headquarters in Tulsa, Oklahoma. The objective of the Jaycees, as set out in its bylaws, is to pursue

> "such educational and charitable purposes as will promote and foster the growth and development of young men's civic organizations in the United States, designed to inculcate in the individual membership of such organization a spirit of genuine Americanism and civic interest, and as a supplementary education institution to provide them with opportunity for personal development and achievement and an avenue for intelligent participation by young men in the affairs of their community, state and nation, and to develop true friendship and understanding among young men of all nations. Quoted in Brief for Appellee 2.

"The organization's bylaws establish seven classes of membership, including individual or regular members, associate individual members, and local chap-

---

[95]United States Jaycees v. Richardet, 666 P.2d 1008 (Ala. 1983).
[96]*See* U.S. Power Squadron v. State Human Rights Appeal Bd., 59 N.Y.2d 401, 452 N.E.2d 1199 (1983), in which the Court of Appeals held that the Power Squadron was subject to the Human Rights Law, thus requiring it to admit female members.

ters. Regular membership is limited to young men between the ages of 18 and 35, while associate membership is available to individuals or groups ineligible for regular membership, principally women and older men. An associate member, whose dues are somewhat lower than those charged regular members, may not vote, hold local or national office, or participate in certain leadership training and awards programs. The bylaws define a local chapter as 'any young men's organization for good repute existing in any community within the United States, organized for purposes similar to and consistent with those' of the national organization. App. to Juris. Statement A98. The ultimate policymaking authority of the Jaycees rests with an annual national convention, consisting of delegates from each local chapter, with a national president and board of directors. At the time of trial in August 1981, the Jaycees had approximately 295,000 members in 7,400 local chapters affiliated with 51 state organizations. There were at that time about 11,915 associate members. The national organization's Executive Vice President estimated at trial that women associate members make up about two percent of the Jaycees' total membership. Tr. 56.

"New members are recruited to the Jaycees through the local chapters, although the state and national organizations are also actively involved in recruitment through a variety of promotional activities. A new regular member pays an initial fee followed by annual dues; in exchange, he is entitled to participate in all of the activities of the local, state, and national organizations. The national headquarters employs a staff to develop 'program kits' for use by local chapters that are designed to enhance individual development, community development, and members' management skills. These materials include courses in public speaking and personal finances as well as community programs related to charity, sports, and public health. The national office also makes available to members a range of personal products, including travel accessories, casual wear, pins, awards, and other gifts. The programs, products, and other activities of the organization are all regularly featured in publications made available to the membership, including a magazine entitled 'Future.'

B

"In 1974 and 1975, respectively, the Minneapolis and St. Paul chapters of the Jaycees began admitting women as regular members. Currently, the memberships and boards of directors of both chapters include a substantial proportion of women. As a result, the two chapters have been in violation of the national organization's bylaws for about 10 years. The national organization has imposed a number of sanctions on the Minneapolis and St. Paul chapters for violating the bylaws, including denying their members eligibility for state or national office or awards programs, and refusing to count their membership in computing votes at national conventions.

"In December 1978, the president of the national organization advised both chapters that a motion to revoke their charters would be considered at a forthcoming meeting of the national board of directors in Tulsa. Shortly after receiving this notification, members of both chapters filed charges of discrimination with the Minnesota Department of Human Rights. The complaints alleged that the exclusion of women from full membership required by the national organization's bylaws violated the Minnesota Human Rights Act (Act), which provides in part:

> "It is an unfair discriminatory practice:
> 'To deny any person the full and equal enjoyment of the goods, services, facilities, privileges, advantages, and accommodations of a place of public accommodation, because of race, color, creed, religion, disability, national origin or sex.' Minn. Stat. § 363.03, subd. 3 (1982).

"The term 'place of public accommodation' is defined in the Act as 'a business, accommodation, refreshment, entertainment, recreation, or transportation facility of any kind, whether licensed or not, whose goods, services, facilities, privileges, advantages or accommodations are extended, offered, sold, or otherwise made available to the public.' *Id.,* § 363.01, subd. 18. . . .

[The procedural aspects of the case are omitted. *See* p. 96, *supra.*]

II

"Our decisions have referred to constitutionally protected 'freedom of association' in two distinct senses. In one line of decisions, the Court has concluded that choices to enter into and maintain certain intimate human relationships must be secured against undue intrusion by the State because of the role of such relationships in safeguarding the individual freedom that is central to our constitutional scheme. In this respect, freedom of association receives protection as a fundamental element of personal liberty. In another set of decisions, the Court has recognized a right to associate for the purpose of engaging in those activities protected by the First Amendment—speech, assembly, petition for the redress of grievances, and the exercise of religion. The Constitution guarantees freedom of association of this kind as an indispensable means of preserving other individual liberties.

"The intrinsic and instrumental features of constitutionally protected association may, of course, coincide. In particular, when the State interferes with individuals' selection of those with whom they wish to join in a common endeavor, freedom of association in both of its forms may be implicated. The Jaycees contend that this is such a case. Still, the nature and degree of constitutional protection afforded freedom of association may vary depending on the extent to which one or the other aspect of the constitutionally protected liberty is at stake in a given case. We therefore find it useful to consider separately the effect of applying the Minnesota statute to the Jaycees on what could be called its members' freedom of intimate association and their freedom of expressive association.

A

"The Court has long recognized that, because the Bill of Rights is designed to secure individual liberty, it must afford the formation and preservation of certain kinds of highly personal relationships a substantial measure of sanctuary from unjustified interference by the State. *E.g., Pierce v. Society of Sisters*, 268 U.S. 510, 534–535, 45 S. Ct. 571, 573, 69 L. Ed. 1070 (1925); *Meyer v. Nebraska*, 262 U.S. 390, 399, 43 S. Ct. 625, 626, 67 L. Ed. 1042 (1923). Without precisely identifying every consideration that may underlie this type of constitutional protection, we have noted that certain kinds of personal bonds have played a critical role in the culture and traditions of the Nation by cultivating and transmitting shared ideals and beliefs; they thereby foster diversity and act as critical buffers between the individual and the power of the State. *See, e.g., Zablocki v. Redhail*, 434 U.S. 374, 383–386, 98 S. Ct. 673, 679–681, 54 L. Ed. 2d 618 (1978); *Moore v. City of East Cleveland*, 431 U.S. 494, 503–504, 97 S. Ct. 1932, 1937–38, 52 L. Ed. 2d 531 (1977) (plurality opinion); [citations omitted]. Moreover, the constitutional shelter afforded such relationships reflects the realization that individuals draw much of their emotional enrichment from close ties with others. Protecting these relationships from unwarranted state interference therefore safeguards the ability independently to define one's identity that is central to any concept of liberty. *See, e.g., Quillion v. Walcott*, 434 U.S. 246, 255, 98 S. Ct. 549, 554, 54 L. Ed. 2d 511 (1978); *Smith v. Organization of Foster Families*, 431 U.S. 816, 844, 97 S. Ct. 2094, 2109, 53 L. Ed. 2d 14 (1977); *Carey v. Population Services Int'l*, 431 U.S. 678, 684–686, 97 S. Ct. 2010, 2015–2016, 52 L. Ed. 2d 675 (1977); [citations omitted].

"The personal affiliations that exemplify these considerations, and that therefore suggest some relevant limitations on the relationships that might be entitled to this sort of constitutional protection, are those that attend the creation and sustenance of a family—marriage, *e.g., Zablocki v. Redhail, supra;* childbirth, *e.g., Carey v. Population Services Int'l, supra;* the raising and education of children, *e.g., Smith v. Organization of Foster Families, supra;* and cohabitation with one's relatives, *e.g., Moore v. City of East Cleveland, supra.* Family relationships, by their nature, involve deep attachments and commitments to the necessarily few other individuals with whom one shares not only a special community of thoughts, experiences, and beliefs but also distinctively personal aspects of one's life. Among other things, therefore, they are distinguished by such attributes as relative smallness, a high degree of selectivity in decisions to begin and maintain the affiliation, and seclusion from others in critical aspects of the relationship. As a general matter, only relationships with these sorts of qualities are likely to reflect the considerations that have led to an understanding of freedom of association as an intrinsic element of personal liberty. Conversely, an association lacking these qualities—such as a large business enterprise—seems remote from the concerns giving rise to this constitutional protection. Accordingly, the Constitution undoubtedly imposes constraints on the State's power to control the selection of one's spouse that would not apply to regulations affecting the choice of one's fellow employees. *Compare Loving v. Virginia*, 388 U.S. 1, 12, 87 S. Ct. 1817, 1823, 18 L. Ed. 2d 1010 (1967) with *Railway Mail Ass'n v. Corsi*, 326 U.S. 88, 93–94, 65 S. Ct. 1483, 1487, 89 L. Ed. 2072 (1945).

"Between these poles, of course, lies a broad range of human relationships that may make greater or lesser claims to constitutional protection from particular incursions by the State. Determining the limits of state authority over an individual's freedom to enter into a particular association therefore unavoidably entails a careful assessment of where that relationship's objective characteristics locate it on a spectrum from the most intimate to the most attenuated of personal attachments. *See generally Runyon v. McCrary,* 427 U.S. 160, 187–189, 96 S. Ct. 2586, 2602–2603, 49 L. Ed. 2d 415 (1976) POWELL, J., concurring). We need not mark the potentially significant points on this terrain with any precision. We note only that factors that may be relevant include size, purpose, policies, selectivity, congeniality, and other characteristics that in a particular case may be pertinent. In this case, however, several features of the Jaycees clearly place the organization outside of the category of relationships worthy of this kind of constitutional protection.

"The undisputed facts reveal that the local chapters of the Jaycees are large and basically unselective groups. At the time of the state administrative hearing, the Minneapolis chapter had approximately 430 members, while the St. Paul chapter had about 400. Report A–99, A–100. Apart from age and sex, neither the national organization nor the local chapters employs any criteria for judging applicants for membership, and new members are routinely recruited and admitted with no inquiry into their backgrounds. See I Tr. of State Administrative Hearing 124–132, 135–136, 174–176. In fact, a local officer testified that he could recall no instance in which an applicant had been denied membership on any basis other than age or sex. *Id.,* at 135. *Cf. Tillman v. Wheaton-Haven Recreation Ass'n,* 410 U.S. 431, 438, 93 S. Ct. 1090, 1094, 35 L. Ed. 2d 403 (1973) (organization whose only selection criteria is race has 'no plan or purpose of exclusiveness' that might make it a private club exempt from federal civil rights statute); *Sullivan v. Little Hunting Park, Inc.,* 396 U.S. 229, 236, 90 S. Ct. 400, 404, 24 L. Ed. 2d 386 (1969) (same); *Daniel v. Paul,* 395 U.S. 298, 302, 89 S. Ct. 1697, 1699, 23 L. Ed. 2d 318 (1969) (same). Furthermore, despite their inability to vote, hold office, or receive certain awards, women affiliated with the Jaycees attend various meetings, participate in selected projects, and engage in many of the organization's social functions. See Tr. 58. Indeed, numerous non-members of both genders regularly participate in a substantial portion of activities central to the decision of many members to associate with one another, including many of the organization's various community programs, awards ceremonies, and recruitment meetings. *See, e.g.,* 305 N.W. 2d, at 772; Report A102, A103.

"In short, the local chapters of the Jaycees are neither small nor selective. Moreover, much of the activity central to the formation and maintenance of the association involves the participation of strangers to that relationship. Accordingly, we conclude that the Jaycees chapters lack the distinctive characteristics that might afford constitutional protection to the decision of its members to exclude women. We turn therefore to consider the extent to which application of the Minnesota statute to compel the Jaycees to accept women infringes the group's freedom of expressive association.

B

"An individual's freedom to speak, to worship, and to petition the Government for the redress of grievances could not be vigorously protected from interference by the State unless a correlative freedom to engage in group effort toward those ends were not also guaranteed. *See, e.g., Rent Control Coalition for Fair Housing v. Berkeley,* 454 U.S. 290, 294, 102 S. Ct. 434, 456, 70 L. Ed. 2d 492 (1981). According protection to collective effort on behalf of shared goals is especially important in preserving political and cultural diversity and in shielding dissident expression from suppression by the majority. [Citations omitted.] Consequently, we have long understood as implicit in the right to engage in activities protected by the First Amendment a corresponding right to associate with others in pursuit of a wide variety of political, social, economic, educational, religious, and cultural ends. [Citations omitted.] In view of the various protected activities in which the Jaycees engage, . . . that right is plainly implicated in this case.

"Government actions that may unconstitutionally infringe upon this freedom can take a number of forms. Among other things, government may seek to impose penalties or withhold benefits from individuals because of their membership in a disfavored group, *e.g., Healy v. James,* 408 U.S. 169, 180–184, 92 S. Ct. 2338, 2345–2347, 33 L. Ed. 2d 266 (1972); it may attempt to require disclosure of the fact of membership in a group seeking anonymity, *e.g., Brown v. Socialist Workers '74 Campaign Committee,* 459 U.S. 87, 91–92, 103 S. Ct. 416, 419–421, 74 L. Ed. 2d 250 (1982); and it may try to interfere with the internal organization or affairs of the group, *e.g., Cousins v. Wigoda,* 419 U.S. 477, 487–488, 95 S. Ct. 541, 547, 42 L. Ed. 2d 595 (1975). By requiring the Jaycees to admit women as full voting members, the Minnesota Act works as infringement of the last type. There can be no clearer example of an intrusion into the internal structure or affairs of an association than a regulation that forces the group to accept members it does not desire. Such a regulation may impair the ability of the original members to express only those views that brought them together. Freedom of association therefore plainly presupposes a freedom not to associate. *See Abood v. Detroit Board of Education, supra,* 431 U.S., at 234–235, 97 S. Ct., at 1799.

"The right to associate for expressive purposes is not, however, absolute. Infringements on that right may be justified by regulations adopted to serve compelling state interests, unrelated to the suppression of ideas, that cannot be achieved through means significantly less restrictive of associational freedoms. [Citations omitted.] We are persuaded that Minnesota's compelling interest in eradicating discrimination against its female citizens justifies the impact that application of the statute to the Jaycees may have on the male members' associational freedoms. . . .

"By prohibiting gender discrimination in places of public accommodation, the Minnesota Act protects the State's citizenry from a number of serious social and personal harms. In the context of reviewing state actions under the Equal

Protection Clause, this Court has frequently noted that discrimination based on archaic and overbroad assumptions about the relative needs and capacities of the sexes forces individuals to labor under stereotypical notions that often bear no relationship to their actual abilities. It thereby both deprives persons of their individual dignity and denies society the benefits of wide participation in political, economic, and cultural life. [Citations omitted.] These concerns are strongly implicated with respect to gender discrimination in the allocation of publicly available goods and services. Thus, in upholding Title II of the Civil Rights Act of 1964, 78 Stat. 243, 42 U.S.C. § 2000a, which forbids race discrimination in public accommodations, we emphasized that its 'fundamental object . . . was to vindicate "the deprivation of personal dignity that surely accompanies denials of equal access to public establishments." ' *Heart of Atlanta Motel v. United States,* 379 U.S. 241, 250, 85 S. Ct. 348, 354, 13 L. Ed. 2d 258 (1964). That stigmatizing injury, and the denial of equal opportunities that accompanies it, is surely felt as strongly by persons suffering discrimination on the basis of their sex as by those treated differently because of their race.

"Nor is the state interest in assuring equal access limited to the provision of purely tangible goods and services. *See Alfred L. Snapp & Son, Inc. v. Puerto Rico,* 458 U.S. 592, 609, 102 S. Ct. 3260, 3270, 73 L. Ed. 2d 995 (1982). A State enjoys broad authority to create rights of public access on behalf of its citizens. *Pruneyard Shopping Center v. Robins,* 447 U.S. 74, 81–88, 100 S. Ct. 2035, 2040–2044, 64 L. Ed. 2d 741 (1980). Like many States and municipalities, Minnesota has adopted a functional definition of public accommodations that reaches various forms of public, quasi-commercial conduct. *See* 305 N.W.2d at 768; Brief for National League of Cities *et al.* as *Amicus Curiae* 15–16. This expansive definition reflects a recognition of the changing nature of the American economy and of the importance, both to the individual and to society, of removing the barriers to economic advancement and political and social integration that have historically plagued certain disadvantaged groups, including women. [Citations omitted.] Thus, in explaining its conclusion that the Jaycees local chapters are 'place[s] of public accommodations' within the meaning of the Act, the Minnesota court noted the various commercial programs and benefits offered to members and stated that, '[l]eadership skills are "goods," [and] business contacts and employment promotions are "privileges" and "advantages". . . . ' 305 N.W.2d at 772. Assuring women equal access to such goods, privileges, and advantages clearly furthers compelling state interests.

"In applying the Act to the Jaycees, the State has advanced those interests through the least restrictive means of achieving its ends. Indeed, the Jaycees have failed to demonstrate that the Act imposes any serious burdens on the male members' freedom of expressive association. *See Hishon v. King & Spalding,* ——U.S. ——, ——, 104 S. Ct. 2229, 2235, 80 L. Ed. 2d ——(1984) (law firm 'has not shown how its ability to fulfill [protected] function[s] would be inhibited by a requirement that it consider [a woman lawyer] for partnership on her merits'); *id.,* at ——, 104 S. Ct., at 2236 (POWELL, J., concurring); [Citations omitted]. To be sure, as the Court of Appeals noted, a 'not insubstantial part' of the Jaycees activities constitutes protected expression on political, economic, cultural, and social affairs. 709 F.2d at 1570. . . . There is, however, no basis in the record for concluding that admission of women as full voting members will impede the organization's ability to engage in these protected activities or to disseminate its preferred views. The Act requires no change in the Jaycees' creed of promoting the interests of young men, and it imposes no restrictions on the organization's ability to exclude individuals with ideologies or philosophies different from those of its existing members. *Cf. Democratic Party v. Wisconsin,* 450 U.S., at 122, 101 S. Ct., at 1019 (recognizing the right of political parties to 'protect themselves "from intrusion by those with adverse political principles" '). Moreover, the Jaycees already invite women to share the group's view and philosophy and to participate in much of its training and community activities. Accordingly, any claim that admission of women as full voting members will impair a symbolic message conveyed by the very fact that women are not permitted to vote is attenuated at best. *Cf. Spence v. Washington,* 418 U.S. 405, 94 S. Ct. 2727, 41 L. Ed. 2d 842 (1974); *Griswold v. Connecticut,* 381 U.S., at 483, 85 S. Ct., at 1681. . . .

" . . . In the absence of a showing far more substantial than that attempted by the Jaycees, we decline to indulge in the sexual stereotyping that underlies appellee's contention that, by allowing women to vote, application of the Minnesota Act will change the content or impact of the organization's speech. [Citations omitted.]

"In any event, even if enforcement of the Act causes some incidental abridgement of the Jaycees' protected speech, that effect is no greater than is necessary to accomplish the State's legitimate purposes. As we have explained, acts of invidious discrimination in the distribution of publicly available goods, services, and other advantages cause unique evils that government has a compelling interest to prevent—wholly apart from the point of view such conduct may transmit. Accordingly, like violence or other types of potentially expressive activities that produce special harms distinct from their communicative impact, such practices are entitled to no constitutional protection. *Runyon v. McCrary,* 427 U.S. 160, 175–176, 96 S. Ct. 2586, 2596–2597, 49 L. Ed. 2d 415 (1976). [Citations omitted.] In prohibiting such practices, the Minnesota Act therefore 'responds precisely to the substantive problem which legitimately concerns' the State and abridges no more speech or associational freedom than is necessary to accomplish that purpose. See *City Council v. Taxpayers for Vincent,* ——U.S. ——, ——, 104 Ct. 2118, 2132, 80 L. Ed. 2d 772 (1984).

[Court's rejection of argument that State Act unconstitutionally vague omitted.]

IV

"The judgment of the Court of Appeals is *Reversed.*

"Justice REHNQUIST concurs in the judgment.

"The CHIEF JUSTICE and Justice BLACKMUN took no part in the decision of this case."

[Concurring opinion of Justice O'CONNOR omitted.]

After the *Roberts* decision, the City of New York adopted a law prohibiting discrimination by private clubs which have over 400 members or which provide benefits to business entities and persons other than their own members. Such clubs forfeit the "distinctly private" exemption provided by law. A consortium of such clubs brought suit seeking a ruling declaring the city law unconstitutional by reason of the right of privacy of association guaranteed under the federal and New York constitutions. The New York Court of Appeals affirmed lower court decisions holding the law constitutional.[97] The United States Supreme Court affirmed,[98] holding that the law was not unconstitutional on its face, and that the consortium had failed to establish that the exemption providing that benevolent orders and religious corporations were distinctly private entities violated the equal protection clause of the federal Constitution.

4:24 *Remedies and Penalties under the New York Executive Law*

Section 297(9) authorizes any person claiming to be aggrieved to have a cause of action in any court of appropriate jurisdiction for damages and such other remedies as shall be appropriate, unless such person has filed a complaint with the appropriate human rights commission.

Section 299 makes any willful violation of an order issued under this law a misdemeanor, punishable by imprisonment for not more than one year, or by a fine of not more than $500, or both.

4:25 *Overlap of New York Civil Rights Law and Executive Law*

The Civil Rights Law sections 40 *et seq.*, previously discussed, were intended to vindicate equal rights, violated by discriminatory conduct, by means of private lawsuits based on common-law concepts. The Executive Law was intended to permit the state itself to intercede and to investigate, hear, and punish instances of wrongdoing, with appeal to the courts being provided from cease-and-desist orders. Obviously a private lawsuit could not be pursued by someone who is unable to afford private counsel but who is above the minimum income threshold to qualify for legal aid. Moreover, the State Commission for Human Rights would be in a better position to develop rules and to oversee compliance than would an individual resorting to private litigation and remedies.

[97] 69 N.Y.2d 211, 505 N.E.2d 915.
[98] New York State Club Ass'n, Inc. v. City of New York, 108 S. Ct. 2225, 101 L. Ed. 2d—— (1988).

5 Relationship of Innkeeper and Guest: Creation and Termination

5:1 *Notice to Innkeeper of Traveler's Intention to Become Guest*

To become the guest of an inn, the traveler must first give the innkeeper an opportunity to receive or to reject him. No person can make himself a guest without the innkeeper's assent. The required assent may be and is usually given by an employee entrusted with the duty of receiving or rejecting travelers, such as the desk clerk or assistant manager if the traveler seeks room accommodations, or the headwaiter or other person in charge of the dining room if he visits the inn for food or refreshments. There need be no formal bargain, for the acceptance of a traveler as a guest will be implied when a room is assigned to him, or when food or refreshments are furnished to him, at his request, although the service of victuals does not automatically confer such status.

In the case of *Gastenhofer v. Clair*,[1] the plaintiff was invited by his uncle to dinner in defendant's hotel. Not finding his uncle on arrival, plaintiff had dinner alone; having finished his meal, he met his uncle in the lobby and went with him to the dining room. Plaintiff left his overcoat on a chair near the entrance to the dining room where there was no attendant. The coat having disappeared through no fault or negligence on defendant's part, it was incumbent on plaintiff to prove that he was a guest. In this he failed. The court held that he was not a guest. Said Judge Daly:

> It is not the fact that a person does or does not take lodgings or partake of refreshments in the inn that makes him a guest. It is the motive with which he visits the place: whether to use it even for the briefest period or the most trifling purpose as a public house or not; and I think it will be long before the courts will be disposed to hold landlords liable for the property of persons who call to visit their guests, and incidentally enjoy the hospitality of the house. The taking of the dinner without notice to the proprietor or the clerk no more constituted plaintiff a guest than his sitting in the parlor, using the reading-room or writing-room, etc. for any period, while waiting for his host to appear.[2]

[1]10 Daly (N.Y.) 265 (Ct. C.P. 1881).
[2]*Id.* at 267.

In the case of *Hill v. Memphis Hotel Co.*,[3] plaintiff, a resident of Oklahoma, motoring en route to New Orleans, stopped at the Gayoso Hotel in Memphis, Tennessee. Without registering or speaking with the clerk on duty, he went directly to the hotel restaurant, had a meal there, then relaxed for awhile in the hotel lobby where he bought a cigar. Plaintiff was held to be a guest. He was a traveler; he was assisted upon arrival by the hotel doorman who placed plaintiff's baggage in the lobby; he was seated and served in the dining room and paid his check in the customary manner; it was not incumbent upon him to give notice to the desk clerk or some particular officer or agent of the hotel company in order to become a guest.

A traveler may, however, enter a public room at an inn without at once presenting himself as a guest; in such case, the relation of host and guest is not established between the innkeeper and himself. So a traveler who enters a public room of an inn for a temporary purpose, without intending to lodge or be otherwise entertained at the inn, is not a guest.[4]

As soon as the relation is established, the guest must compensate the innkeeper for his services; however, it must be clear that one who enters an inn does not by that mere fact become liable to pay the innkeeper's charges. Bearing this in mind, we can agree in the correctness of the decision in an English case where it appeared that a traveler went to an inn and gave his luggage to a porter, intending to stay at the inn, but upon being handed a telegram which had been sent there for him, he decided not to stop, but to continue his journey at once. It was held that he had not become a guest.[5]

The burden appears to be on the applicant to give notice to the innkeeper that he desires to be received as a guest. In *Hawthorne v. Hammond,* where a person was traveling at night, and came to an inn after it was shut up for the night, and knocked, it was held that the innkeeper must, in order to be liable for not admitting the guest, have heard the knocking, and in addition must reasonably have concluded that the person was a bona fide guest. Park, B., said, in charging the jury:

> There is no doubt that the law is, that a person who keeps a public inn is bound to admit all persons who apply peaceably to be admitted as guests. You will therefore have to say whether you are satisfied that the noise made by yon plaintiff's brother was really heard by the defendant; and if so, whether you think that she ought to have concluded from it that the persons so knocking at the door were persons requiring to be admitted as guests, or whether she might have concluded that they were drunken persons, who had come there to make a disturbance. You will take the case into your consideration, and find, by your verdict, whether you think that the noise made at the door implied that the persons who made it wanted to be admitted as guests or not.[6]

---

[3]124 Tenn. 376, 136 S.W. 997 (1911).
[4]Bernard v. Lalonde, 8 Leg. News 215 (Can. 1885).
[5]Strauss v. County Hotel and Wine Co., Ltd., [1883] 12 Q.B.D. 27.
[6]Hawthorne v. Hammond, 174 Eng. Rep. 866, 869 (1844).

The requirement of giving notice of intention to become a guest has been held satisfied by a request for accommodation or entertainment and by furnishing same in the customary manner. "The traveler receiving lodging without food, or food without lodging, or any other form of refreshment which the innkeeper publicly professes to serve in the usual and customary way in which travelers are entertained, thereby becomes a guest."[7]

In *Langford v. Vandaveer*,[8] one of the men in a party of four, consisting of two men and two women, asked for overnight accommodation for "four oil men" in defendant's motor court. Defendant was unaware that two members in the party were women, the register having been signed by one of the men as "C. P. Howe and party." Plaintiff, one of the women, was seriously injured by a gas heater explosion in the cabin assigned to and occupied by the party. She predicated her right of recovery on defendant's negligence in the maintenance of the heater, and claimed that she was a "lawful guest for pay." Defendant took the position that plaintiff was a trespasser. The trial court instructed the jury that plaintiff was a guest as a matter of law. On appeal, judgment for plaintiff was reversed. Said the court:

> In the case at bar, the intention of the young lady to become a guest in the legal sense is apparent. The question is whether or not she was intentionally or knowingly received as such by the proprietor of the motor court. Generally, an innkeeper, though the conductor of a semipublic institution, is not under obligation to receive as a guest everyone who applies. He has the right to reject or expel persons whom he reasonably deems objectionable. [Citations omitted.] Under this rule of law a person may not impose himself upon the proprietor and become a guest without his knowledge or intention to receive him. One becomes a guest only if he is received to be treated as a guest and the intention to become such must be communicated to the innkeeper or his agent. This is a fact to be proved by evidence, definite or circumstantial. [Citations omitted.][9]

5:2 *Duty to Receive Baggage or Luggage with Guest*

The cases clearly establish that an innkeeper is under duty to admit not only the person, but the baggage of his guest as well. It is also clear, however, that not all goods which the guest may bring with him can be considered "baggage." In this connection, it has been held that

> [l]uggage and baggage are essentially the bags, trunks, etc., that a passenger takes with him for his personal use and convenience with reference to his necessities or to the ultimate purpose of his journey, and in this connection it has been held that,

---

[7]Hill v. Memphis Hotel Co., 124 Tenn. 376, 380–81, 136 S.W. 997, 998–99 (1911).
[8]254 S.W.2d 498 (Ky. 1953).
[9]*Id.* at 501.

within limits, the same include such jewelry as may be adapted to the tastes, habits and social standing and be necessary for the convenience, use and enjoyment of the traveler either while in transit or temporarily staying at a particular place.[10]

5:3   *Innkeeper May Not Investigate Ownership of Guest's Luggage*

In order to demand admittance for the luggage he brings, the guest is not bound to prove that it is his own. A guest may come to an inn with the goods of another, and the ownership of the goods is no business of the innkeeper.

> He has not to inquire whether the goods are the property of the person who brings them or of some other person. If he does so inquire, the traveller may refuse to tell him, and may say, "What business is that of yours? I bring the goods here as my luggage, and I insist upon your taking them in"; or he may say "They are not my property, but I bring them here as my luggage, and I insist upon your taking them in"; and then the innkeeper is bound by law to take them in.[11]

The innkeeper may undoubtedly refuse to receive goods known to him to be stolen when they are brought to the inn by the thief; but in the ordinary case he need not and cannot investigate the question of title.

If the traveler brought something exceptional which is not luggage—such as a tiger or a package of dynamite—the innkeeper might refuse to take it in; but the custom of the realm is that, unless there is some reason to the contrary in the exceptional character of the things brought, he must take in the traveler and his goods.

Whether an animal which is not dangerous, like a dog, could be refused on the ground that there are no facilities at the inn to prevent the dog from becoming a nuisance to the guests is more doubtful. It could not be restrained from annoyance by a regulation, like a piano; and on the whole it would seem that unless the inn has, or considering the nature of its business, ought to have, special facilities for caring for animal pets they may be excluded from the inn.

In a related case, a Florida appellate court ruled that a guest injured by slipping on dog fecal matter could recover on the following theories of liability: (1) lack of adequate facilities for and supervision of guest pets admitted on the premises and (2) advertising that pets were welcome as establishing a duty of reasonable supervision. A jury verdict for the injured guest was sustained.[12]

5:4   *Reception of Traveler Establishes Relation of Host and Guest*

When a traveler comes to an inn and is received by the innkeeper for the purpose of entertaining him during his journey, the relation of host and guest is

---

[10]Waters v. Beau Site Co., 114 Misc. 65, 68, 186 N.Y.S. 731, 732 (N.Y. City Ct. 1920).
[11]Lord Escher, M.R., in Robins v. Gray, [1895] 2 Q.B. 501, 504.
[12]Fountainhead Motel, Inc. v. Massey, 336 So.2d 397 (Fla. App. 1976).

thereby established.[13] No lapse of time is required for the establishment of this relation; if the guest presents himself for entertainment and is accepted, the relation "is instantly established between them."[14]

5:5 *Refusal of Innkeeper to Accept Guest*

Not only must the guest communicate his intention to the innkeeper; the latter must consent to receive him as a guest. If the innkeeper refuses to receive a person as a guest, whether the refusal is legal or illegal, the relation is not established. Therefore when an innkeeper refuses to receive a guest (whether justifiably because his house is full, or unjustifiably), such person cannot, by placing his property in the inn, make the innkeeper liable for it.[15]

If the refusal is wrongful, the remedy is by action for the refusal; if it is lawful, the applicant has no right to force the obligation on the innkeeper. Thus, where the innkeeper having said his inn was full, the applicant nevertheless placed his goods in the inn, and induced a guest to share his bed with him, without the consent of the innkeeper, it was held that the latter was not responsible for the goods as innkeeper.[16]

So where an innkeeper refused to accept a guest because he was going to serve on a jury next morning, and the traveler at his request received the keys to look out for himself, the relation of host and guest was not established.[17]

5:6 *Reception in a Capacity Other Than as Guest*

A person may be received in an inn by the innkeeper, but in another capacity than as guest. He may, for instance, come to the inn on the invitation of the innkeeper as his friend, and not on the footing of a paying guest.[18] Or, he may be a prospective employee hired to commence employment at some future date but, having arrived earlier, admitted to occupy a room in the inn prior to the commencement of his employment.[19] The relation of host and guest is not established in such cases, and the responsibility of the innkeeper does not come into existence.

5:7 *Guest Need Not Resort to Inn for Both Food and Lodging*

It is not necessary, in order that one received at an inn should become a guest there, that he should resort to the inn for both food and lodging. The traveler

---

[13]Pinkerton v. Woodward, 33 Cal. 557 (1867); Healey v. Gray, 68 Me. 489 (1878); Norcross v. Norcross, 53 Me. 163 (1865); Ross v. Mellin, 36 Minn. 421, 32 N.W. 172 (1887).
[14]Norcross v. Norcross, 53 Me. 163 (1865); *accord*, Ross v. Mellin, 36 Minn. 421, 32 N.W. 172 (1887).
[15]Bennett v. Mellor, 101 Eng. Rep. 154 (K.B. 1793); Bird v. Bird, 123 Eng. Rep. 47, 337 (C.P. 1558).
[16]Bird v. Bird, 123 Eng. Rep. 47, 337 (C.P. 1558); White's Case, 73 Eng. Rep. 343 (K.B. 1558).
[17]Y-B Anon. 11 Hen. 4, f. 45, pl. 18 (1409).
[18]Anonymous, 1 Rolle's Abr. 3, pl. 4; Taylor v. Hamphreys, 142 Eng. Rep. 519 (C.P. 1861).
[19]Powers v. Raymond, 197 Cal. 126, 239 P. 1069 (1925).

may stop on his way at an inn merely for food and drink, or for either one of
them, and proceed on his journey the same day, or he may arrive at the inn late
at night, needing lodging only, and leave the inn early in the morning without
stopping for breakfast. In either case he is a guest. Currently the innkeeper need
not furnish both food and lodging (*see* section 2:5).

So it has been held that a traveler resorting to an inn for food and drink only
is a guest.[20] Upon this principle, where a person came to an inn in the afternoon,
intending to leave by a late train that night, and therefore took no room, but
remained in the public room of the inn, waiting for his train, and intending to get
supper there, it was held that he was a guest.[21] And so where one called at
an inn for the purpose of dining only, and was supplied with dinner in the
dining room, he was held to be a guest.[22] Even if he resorts to the inn for drink
only, he may thereby become a guest.[23] Of course, a man could not be said to
be a traveller who goes to a place merely for the purpose of taking refreshment.
But, if he goes to an inn for refreshment in the course of a journey, whether of
business or of pleasure, he is entitled to demand refreshment.''[24] So in an English case where the servant of the plaintiff, having the plaintiff's goods, asked
if he could leave the goods until next week, and upon the innkeeper's saying he
could not yet tell whether he would have the room to keep them, the servant
set down the goods and had some liquor, and while he was drinking the goods
were stolen, it was held that the relationship of host and guest had been established and the innkeeper had become liable for the goods.[25]

5:8 *Whether Guest Must Be Personally Entertained*

In the case of *Ticehurst v. Beinbrink,*[26] the plaintiff recovered a judgment
against the defendant, an innkeeper, for the value of a horse, which was stolen
while in the defendant's stable. The plaintiff, a veterinary surgeon, intending to
drive his horse from Oyster Bay, Long Island, to New York City, decided, when
he reached Hollis, Long Island, not to go any further with his horse at that time.
He stopped at the hotel or inn of the defendant. He tied his horse under a shed,
and he went into the inn, and asked the person whom he found in charge if he
could leave his horse at the inn-stable during the night, as he intended to return
to the borough of Brooklyn. The person in charge of the inn said, "We don't
board no horse here, and don't keep no livery stable," but finally consented that
the horse might be left there during the night. While in the inn, the plaintiff
received and paid for a drink of whisky and a cigar. The horse was unharnessed

[20]Hill v. Memphis Hotel Co., 124 Tenn. 376, 136 S.W. 997 (1911).
[21]Overstreet v. Moser, 88 Mo. Ct. App. 72 (1901).
[22]Read v. Amidon, 41 Vt. 15 (1868); Orchard v. Bush & Co., [1898] 2 Q.B. 284.
[23]McDonald v. Edgerton, 5 Barb. (N.Y.) 560 (Sup. Ct. 1849).
[24]Cockburn, C. D., in Atkinson v. Sellers, 141 Eng. Rep. 181, 183 (C.P. 1858).
[25]Bennett v. Mellor, 101 Eng. Rep. 154 (K.B. 1793).
[26]72 Misc. 365, 129 N.Y.S. 838 (Sup. Ct. 1911).

and put in the stable attached to the inn. The plaintiff returned to the inn, and after waiting at the inn about twenty minutes boarded a trolley car and rode to Jamaica, where he took a train for the borough of Brooklyn, New York City. During that night the horse was stolen from the stable of the defendant.

The evidence failed to establish any negligence on the part of the defendant, and the sole question before the court was whether he was liable as an innkeeper whose liability, as such, arises only when the relation of host and guest exists.

The court, in reversing the judgment in favor of the plaintiff, held that plaintiff was not a guest and not entitled to recover. Said the court, after review of the leading authorities:

> "A guest is a transient person who resorts to, or is received at, an inn for the purpose of obtaining the accommodations which it purports to offer." [Citation omitted.]
>
> A guest may be such actually or constructively.
>
> The real or presumed intention to become a guest is controlling factor in determining whether one is in fact to be considered as a guest.
>
> If a guest leaves the inn intending to return, the relation of host and guest is, in the absence of evidence to the contrary, deemed to continue in the interim as to animate but not as to inanimate property, because the innkeeper gains a profit from the former but none from the latter.
>
> Where one makes a contract with an innkeeper to stable and care for his horse, but does not become or intend to become a guest, the innkeeper is not liable as such for the loss of the horse.
>
> The fact that one making such a contract received refreshments at the inn, under a contract separate and distinct from that under which the horse is cared for, does not of itself constitute such person a guest.

In *Adler v. Savoy Plaza Inc.*,[27] it appeared that plaintiff was accustomed to staying at defendant's hotel whenever she visited New York and had been a guest of the hotel many times. She and her husband had requested reservations for May 15, 1946. Upon their arrival at ten o'clock that morning, they were advised that their reservation was for the following day, but that the hotel would try to accommodate them, so they registered hoping that a room might be assigned during the day. At the same time, they delivered their luggage to the bell captain, and it was deposited in a section of the lobby set aside for luggage of arriving and departing guests. Plaintiff's husband attended to business during the day while plaintiff was in and out of the hotel. When both returned to the hotel in the afternoon, they found that a room was still not available, so they whiled away some time in the lounge bar and had dinner in the room of a friend who was a guest of the hotel.

All during the day defendant's manager was seeking accommodations for the couple but was unable to locate them in the hotel. He finally secured accom-

[27]279 A.D. 110, 108 N.Y.S.2d 80 (1951).

modations for them for the night at the Sherry Netherland Hotel where they registered at about 8:00 P.M., taking with them two suitcases and a cosmetic case, and leaving the suitcase with the valuables and two matching cases at defendant's hotel.

When plaintiff returned to defendant's hotel the next morning, to take up a residence for two or three weeks, and requested delivery of her luggage, the large suitcase was missing. During the night the suitcase had been delivered by the night manager of the hotel to an impostor.

> The circumstances of this delivery are not altogether clear as the night manager was deceased at the time of the trial. Whether there was some complicity on the part of one or more of the hotel employees, as plaintiff suggests, we are not called upon to surmise. It is quite apparent that defendant was negligent, probably grossly negligent, and if the case would be determined simply on a question of negligence, plaintiff would be entitled to recover the amount of her loss.

The court ruled, *as a matter of law,* on the admitted facts, the plaintiff was a guest in defendant's hotel, notwithstanding that at the time of the loss she was registered and resided at the Sherry Netherland.

5:9   *Entertainment of Employee or Child as Making Employer or Parent a Guest*

Where a person's employee (or minor child) with his property is received at an inn, it has been said that the employer (or parent) is a guest, and has the rights of such.[28] It is clear, however, that the employee or child who is personally present at the inn is himself a guest, even if the employer or parent accompanies him and pays the bill and even if the employer or parent is not present. If a head of household goes with his family to an inn, each member of the family is a guest, even though the head of household is responsible for payment of the innkeeper's charges. Generally, every person who is received as a guest is a guest, irrespective of whether he is responsible for his bill.[29] It would seem that since there is but one person present obtaining entertainment and as but one guest is paid for, there is but one guest; and the absent employer or parent is therefore not properly a guest. The point actually decided in the cases is therefore that the innkeeper is directly liable to the employer or parent, as owner, for a loss of the goods. In other words, because the parent or employer is in legal possession of the goods while they are in the hands of the employee or family member, the parent or employer may sue the innkeeper directly, as the person whose possession has been infringed.

[28]Epps v. Hinds, 27 Miss. 657 (1854); Coykendall v. Eaton, 55 Barb. 188 (N.Y. Sup. Ct. 1869); Robinson v. Waller, 81 Eng. Rep. 599 (K.B. 1617).
[29]Holland v. Pack, 7 Tenn. 151 (1823).

5:10 *Resorting to Inn to Attend Banquet or Other Function*

Where a banquet or a ball is held at an inn, a guest at such banquet or ball is not a guest of the innkeeper, and the latter is not liable, in the absence of negligence, for any goods lost by the guest.[30] In such a case Judge Blodgett said:

> . . . [A]s to the banquet where the loss occurred, and which they attended on the invitation and at the expense of the club, the plaintiffs are justly to be regarded as its guests, and not of the defendant, as innkeeper or otherwise, who simply provided the banquet as caterer under a contract with the club, without any lien or claim for compensation against its guests, and with no right or power to exclude anybody from participating in its festivities whom the club might properly invite.
>
> Neither by contract nor by operation of law was the defendant acting in the character of innkeeper as to the club, and still less as to its guests, who would have had no right whatever to attend except upon its invitation. Both the club and its guests came not as ordinary travelers to an inn, but as to a banquet, for the purpose of participating in and enjoying its festivities.[31]

The fact that the innkeeper himself supplies the banquet, so that the persons present are being furnished entertainment by him for hire, does not alter the case. The case is the same even if the guest at the ball or banquet deals in other ways directly with the innkeeper, as by buying liquor, or putting up his horse in the stable of the inn.[32]

Nor is the case altered even if the innkeeper is himself the person who gives the entertainment and invites the public to be present. So, where an innkeeper gave a ball and furnished food and drink to a person attending the ball, he was held not to be an innkeeper in so doing, though one who resorted to him as an innkeeper and was provided with the same refreshment would become a guest. In this case the innkeeper, the court said, was in the position of any owner of a ballroom who should do the same. It is not the amount of refreshment but the character under which the person buys it that makes him a guest.[33]

In the more recent case of *Ross v. Kirkeby Hotels, Inc.*,[34] the plaintiffs, husband and wife, were to be married in the Hotel Warwick in New York City. The husband arrived at the hotel in his car on the morning of his wedding day. He issued specific instructions to place the car in the hotel garage. Instead the doorman left it on the street, where it was broken into and the contents carried off.

In an action against the hotel for the recovery of the loss, the issue was whether plaintiffs were guests of the hotel at the time of the loss. If they were guests, the hotel was entitled to the statutory limitation of liability for the loss of the property of guests; absent innkeeper-guest relationship, the plaintiffs were entitled to the full value of their loss.

---

[30]Carter v. Hobbs, 12 Mich. 52 (1863); Amey v. Winchester, 68 N.H. 447, 39 A. 487 (1895).

[31]Amey v. Winchester, 68 N.H. 447, 39 A. 487 (1896).

[32]Carter v. Hobbs, 12 Mich. 52 (1863); Fitch v. Casler, 17 Hun. (N.Y.) 126 (Sup. Ct. 1879).

[33]Fitch v. Casler, 17 Hun. (N.Y.) 126 (Sup. Ct. 1879).

[34]8 Misc. 2d 750, 160 N.Y.S.2d 978 (1st Dep't 1957).

The court held that plaintiffs were not guests, ruling that a person renting hotel facilities solely for a wedding is not a guest within the meaning of section 201 of the General Business Law, the New York statute limiting a hotelkeeper's liability for the property of guests.

5:11   One Not Entitled to Admittance Received as Guest

Even a person not entitled to demand admittance, not being a bona fide traveler, will become a guest and entitled to all the rights of a guest if he is received voluntarily in the inn upon the same footing as a guest. The innkeeper has a right to refuse to receive him, but that right may be waived by consenting to receive the guest. Thus it is usually stated that one who lives in the same town with the innkeeper cannot be a guest, since he is not a traveler seeking entertainment during a journey. While it is true that such a person is often received to be entertained out of friendship alone, and therefore is not a guest, yet if he is really received on the footing of a guest the relation of host and guest is thereby established.[35]

5:12   Guest at Inn for Illegal Purpose

Where a person went to an inn with a prostitute and took a room which he occupied with her, it was held that on account of his misconduct he did not become a guest, any more than would a thief who took a room in order to steal from the guests.[36] It is clear in this case, as the court says, that if the innkeeper had been aware of the party's purpose in applying for the room, he might have refused to receive him; and even after the applicant had been received, he could have been ejected, once his purpose became known. It does not follow, however, as the court appeared to hold, that therefore he was not a guest. The court says that if he had been a guest, "he could not have been turned into the street, though his profligate conduct was outraging all decency and ruining the reputation of the hotel."[37] This dictum can hardly be supported; for, as has been seen, the innkeeper would certainly have a right to turn out a guest under such circumstances (*see* section 6:3). And although the innkeeper would have been justified in refusing to receive the applicant as a guest, it by no means follows that if he was received, the applicant did not occupy the exact position of a guest. The innkeeper can doubtless waive his right to refuse admittance and accept an applicant as his guest; though it is equally clear that he may, if he chooses, accept him on such terms that he will not be a guest (*see* section 5:11). In this case the applicant was received as a guest. He, however, was guilty of fraud in asking for accommodation for himself and wife; and the decision may probably best be supported on the ground that the guest was precluded from recovery in the case because of his fraud.

[35]Walling v. Potter, 35 Conn. 183 (1868); Orchard v. Bush & Co., [1898] 2 Q.B. 284.
[36]Curtis v. Murphy, 63 Wis. 4, 22 N.W. 825 (1885).
[37]*Id.* at 8.

5:13   *Guest at Inn as Result of Illegal Act*

Regardless of the status of the guest who is acting illegally while in the inn, it is clear that he is none the less a guest because he may have been guilty of an illegal act in coming to the inn, if his illegal conduct has ceased. Thus, in a similar case to the one just discussed, where the man remained after the woman had left the inn, and lost his goods, it was held that he might recover from the innkeeper. Even assuming that such misconduct would have barred him while the misconduct continued, the loss here happened after his misconduct ceased, and his previous immorality could not affect his subsequent status as a guest.[38]

In *Cramer v. Tarr,*[39] plaintiffs falsely registered in defendant's lodginghouse as husband and wife. A fire broke out and plaintiffs were injured while escaping from their room. They sued to recover damages for personal injuries which they alleged resulted from defendant's negligence. Defendant moved for summary judgment for dismissal of the complaint on the theory that plaintiffs, not being married, were trespassers by reason of their unlawful purpose, and that no duty of reasonable care was owed them.

The court denied defendant's motion. Said the court:

> In the absence of any showing of a causal connection between plaintiffs' alleged statutory violation and their injuries, it is the considered opinion of this Court that neither false registration nor an illegal or immoral purpose in occupying a room in the defendant's boarding house would affect the status of the plaintiffs as guests to whom the defendant owed the duty of reasonable care. It follows, therefore, that plaintiffs would not be barred from maintaining these actions even if false registration for an illicit purpose could be inferred. . . .
>
> In accord with the general principle thus stated and applied by the Maine court, the better view of the law and the greater weight of authority is specifically to the effect that false registration in an inn or lodging house for an immoral or illegal purpose will not preclude recovery for injuries resulting from the innkeeper's negligence where there is no showing of a causal connection between the illegality and the plaintiff's injuries. . . . To the extent that *Curtis v. Murphy,* 1885, 63 Wis. 4, 22 N.W. 825, and related cases express views in conflict with the foregoing, they are considered by this Court to be unsound.
>
> The Court is of the opinion, therefore, that even if false registration for the purpose of fornication were established, these plaintiffs would yet be guests to whom the defendant owned a duty of reasonable care for their safety and the defendant would not be entitled to judgment as a matter of law.[40]

---

[38]Lucia v. Omel, 46 A.D. 200, 61 N.Y.S. 659 (2d Dep't 1900). The facts differed from Curtis v. Murphy, 63 Wis. 4, 22 N.W. 825 (1885), which was distinguished in the opinion, in two important particulars. In the Wisconsin case, the plaintiff was a resident of the same town, which does not seem to have been true in this case; and the innkeeper had wrongfully refused to take charge of the property before its loss.

[39]165 F. Supp. 130 (D. Me. 1958).

[40]*Id.* at 132.

The minority view is illustrated by the Supreme Court of North Carolina in *Jones v. Bland.*[41] The court in that case held that an innkeeper owes no duty to a person going to the room of a guest, upon the latter's invitation, for the purpose of gambling, except not willfully or intentionally to injure him. The court's theory appears to have been that the innkeeper's duty does not extend to wrongdoers who come upon the premises for an unlawful purpose, and that even though invited by a guest of the inn, such person has the status of a trespasser in his relation with the innkeeper.

In any event, the guest's misconduct should be set up by the innkeeper as an affirmative defense, as was pointed out in *Rapee v. Beacon Hotel Corp.*[42] In that case, plaintiff and his fiancée registered at defendant's hotel as husband and wife under an assumed name. While in the hotel, plaintiff was injured as a result of falling into the pit at the bottom of an elevator shaft, the door having been left open through the negligence of the defendant. Defendant claimed that plaintiff's fraudulent misrepresentation of his personality made him a trespasser on the hotel premises. The Court of Appeals refused to assent to defendant's argument: "Foremost on the defendant's part was an intention to contract with the man and the woman who had put signatures on the register and, that being so, the plaintiff became a guest of the hotel, though the defendant may perhaps have been deceived as to his identify."[43] Plaintiff's trickery was not set up as an affirmative defense and thus was of no avail to defendant on appeal.

The New York Court of Appeals has abolished the distinctions between the legal duty of a landowner owed to an invitee or licensee, namely, to warn him of any dangerous conditions, and that owed to a trespasser, a party not legally upon the premises, not to inflict willful or intentional harm upon him.

In *Basso v. Miller,*[44] the facts established at trial were as follows. On September 3, 1976, there was an accident in the scenic park operated by Ice Cave Mountain, Inc. in Ellenville. On hearing of the accident, Miller, the defendant, rode up to the mountain on his motorcycle with Basso, the plaintiff, as his passenger in order to participate in the rescue operations. There was conflicting testimony as to whether they entered the park with the permission of the entrance guard, whether they remained on the scene of the accident with the permission of the owner of the park, and whether they actually participated in the rescue operation.

While leaving the park, the defendant hit a series of holes in the road causing his motorcycle to go out of control. He and the plaintiff were thrown onto rocks at the side of the road.

The trial court charged the jury that the plaintiff's status on the mountain was determinative of the duty of care owed to him by Ice Cave Mountain. The trial court stated, *inter alia,* that the duty of care owed a licensee was to warn him of

---

[41]182 N.C. 70, 108 S.E. 344 (1921).
[42]293 N.Y. 196, 56 N.E.2d 548 (1944).
[43]*Id.* at 199.
[44]40 N.Y.2d 233, 352 N.E.2d 868 (1976).

any dangerous conditions. Ice Cave Mountain took exception to this charge and appeals after the jury found that Ice Cave Mountain was liable to the plaintiff.

The Court of Appeals, in remanding the case for a new trial, overruled the trial court:

> The excepted charge was erroneous. . . . [T]he distinctions between trespasser, license and invitee are no longer determinative of the degree of care owed by the landowner to one injured on his property. There is a single standard of care to be applied: ''reasonable care under the circumstances whereby foreseeability shall be a measure of liability. . . . [T]he duty of care of keeping the roads of Ice Cave Mountain in repair should not vary with the status of the person who uses them, but rather, with the foreseeability of their use and the possibility of injury resulting therefrom. . . . [W]hile status is no longer determinative, considerations of who plaintiff is and what his purpose is upon the land are factors which, if known, may be included in aiming at what would be reasonable care under the circumstances.''

The abolition of the invitee-trespasser distinction is the minority rule, but the minority is growing.[45]

5:14 *Registration as Establishing the Relation of Host and Guest*

While registration is the customarily recognized method of establishing the innkeeper-guest relationship, it has been held that one may become a guest at an inn without registering.

MOODY v. KENNY

153 La. 1007, 97 So. 21 (1923)

[Action against the defendants, owners of the Monteleone Hotel in New Orleans, to recover the sum of $10,000 for damages. Verdict and judgment for $5,000, from which defendant appeals.

One Mr. Bradley was a guest of the Hotel Monteleone in New Orleans. His friends, Mr. and Mrs. Moody, arrived at the hotel but could obtain no rooms. Bradley then offered them his room, and he went to lodge elsewhere. Bradley spoke about this arrangement to the day clerk of the hotel, but this clerk forgot to say anything about it to the night clerk.

The Moodys retired in their room for the night when the house officer passing by heard Mrs. Moody's voice inside. This particular section of the hotel was reserved for men, so the house officer reported the presence of a woman to the clerk on duty, who checked the register and found the room assigned to Mr. Bradley; he then called the room on the phone. Not having received a reply, he sent up the house officer to investigate. The latter verified the facts and reported back to the clerk who sent him back to the room with the night watchman. The testimony differs as to what happened. Moody and his wife claimed that they

---

[45]See Recent Developments, 45 Fordham L. Rev. 682 (December 1976).

were grossly insulted and ejected and dragged down to the front office for explanation, while the house officer testified that he merely asked for an explanation of the lady's presence in the room.

It was admitted that neither Moody nor his wife was registered as a guest at the hotel. The defense of the hotel was that the plaintiff's not being guests, the hotel was justified in making inquiry of their presence in a room assigned to another man.]

LAND, J.: "While a mere guest of the registered occupant of a room at a hotel, who shares such room with its occupant without the knowledge or consent of the hotel management, would not be a guest of the hotel, as there would be no contractual relations in such case between such third person and the hotel proprietor; at the same time, when the registered occupant of a room, with the knowledge and consent of the hotel management, turns his room over to another person, and the hotel clerk delivers the key of the room to that person, he becomes an accepted guest of the hotel and is not a mere licensee. The fact that such person fails to register, or is not required to register, is immaterial; as the registration of guests at a hotel is no part of the contract between the hotel proprietor and the guest, but the purpose of a register is to keep track of the number of people in the house and to keep the books straight. A register is kept solely for the benefit and convenience of the hotel proprietor.

"A guest may be accepted at a hotel, without registration, by the mere delivery to him of the key to the room by the clerk. There is no law in this state requiring a guest to sign a hotel register as the evidence of a contract between the parties. Such contracts are mere matters of oral consent, and are legal without further formality." [Judgment reduced to $500 and affirmed as so amended.]

O'NIELL, C.J. (dissenting): "I respectfully dissent from the statement in the majority opinion in this case that a hotel register is kept solely for the benefit and convenience of the proprietor. A hotel register is as necessary to protect a guest in his exclusive right to occupy a particular room, as it is necessary to protect the proprietor in his right to collect what the guest owes for occupying the room.

" . . . I do not know how the clerks who hand out the room keys to the guests in large hotels identify the guests and avoid the mistake of giving a key to one who is not entitled to it. I imagine it would cause much embarrassment if the key clerks should require the guests to be identified every time one of them asks for the key to his room. For that reason, I suppose that the key clerks in the large hotels must rely upon their judgment of the honesty of the men who ask for keys to their rooms. . . .

" . . . [W]hatever mistake was made by the hotel clerk, or by the house detective, in this instance, was a pardonable mistake . . . [and] I am not in favor of allowing damages for a pardonable mistake, when the injury . . . cannot be measured in dollars and cents and the condemnation therefore would be very much like an infliction of punishment. I do not know how the management of the large hotels can maintain their respectability if they cannot with impunity inquire into the right of a strange man and woman to occupy a room where another man is registered as a guest of the hotel."

5:15 *Statutes Requiring the Keeping of Hotel Registers*

At common law an innkeeper is not required to keep a register of guests in the house. However, statutes in New York and several other states now mandate the keeping of registers. The New York statute is section 204 of the General Business Law, which reads as follows:

> The owner, lessee, proprietor or manager of any hotel, motel, tourist cabins, camp, resort, tavern, inn, boarding or lodging house shall keep for a period of three years a register which shall show the name, residence, date of arrival and departure of his guests. Such record may be kept within the meaning of this section when reproduced on any photographic, photostatic, microfilm, microcard, miniature photographic or other process which actually reproduced the original record.

In addition to the requirements of section 204 of the General Business Law, the Election Law, in order to prevent frauds at elections, imposes certain duties on innkeepers. Section 61(1) provides:

> Every keeper of a hotel, lodging house, boarding house or rooming house in a town or city, shall cause to be kept for a period of one year a record showing the name and residence and the date of arrival and departure of his guests or lodgers and the room, rooms or bed occupied by them, which record shall have a space in which each guest or lodger shall sign his name. The keeping of but one person as a guest or lodger in any building shall not constitute such building either a boarding house or a rooming house within the meaning of this section.

Section 60 of the Election Law which applies only to hotels, lodging, boarding, and rooming houses of less than fifty rooms, located anywhere in the state, empowers the local board of elections to require a special report by the keepers of such hotels, etc., at any time, giving the names, length of residence, and other information of every resident over twenty-one years of age in the house. A misstatement in such report is punishable by a civil penalty of one thousand dollars.

5:16 *Preregistration: Must Guest Register Personally?*

In the interests of greater efficiency and better service, some innkeepers have adopted the practice of preregistering incoming guests. The registration card is completed by the hotel personnel in advance of the guest's arrival, so as to save him the time and inconvenience of registering in person. In New York, there is no legal prohibition against this practice. The risks involved therein are, of course, obvious, in terms of identifying those in the house, in the collection of charges, and in matters of security.

5:17 *True-Name Registration*

A number of states have enacted so-called true-name registration statutes, the purpose of which is to aid law enforcement agencies to trace and identify individuals charged with criminal offenses. As an example, in Massachusetts (General Laws, Ch. 140, § § 27–29), every innholder and every lodginghouse keeper, etc., is required to keep, in permanent form, a register in which shall be recorded the true name or name in ordinary use and the residence of every person engaging or occupying a private dining room not containing a bed or couch, or opening into a room containing a bed or couch, for any period of the day or night in any part of the premises controlled by the licensee, together with the true and accurate record of the room assigned to such person and of the day and hour when such room is assigned. The guest is required to sign his own name and shall not be allowed to occupy any room in the house without so registering. The register shall be kept for a period of one year from the date of the last entry therein. The violation of the law is punishable by a fine of from $100 to $500 or by imprisonment for not more than three months, or both.

The Massachusetts law further provides that no person shall write or cause to be written, or if in charge of a register knowingly permit to be written, in any register in any lodginghouse or hotel any other or different name or designation than the true name or name in ordinary use of the person registering or causing himself to be registered therein. No person occupying such room shall fail to register or fail to cause himself to be registered. Violation of the law is punishable by a fine of from $10 to $25.

Indiana and New Jersey have also enacted compulsory registration laws.

The Supreme Judicial Court of Massachusetts dealt with the issue of criminal responsibility of an innkeeper stemming from failure to produce a hotel register to a law enforcement agent. The court ruled that the statute requiring production was not unconstitutional on search and seizure grounds.

COMMONWEALTH v. BLINN
399 Mass. 126, 503 N.E.2d 25 (1987)

NOLAN, J.: "The defendant, Brian P. Blinn, appeals from a judgment of conviction by a jury of six in the Salem Division of the District Court. The defendant was found guilty of violating G.L. c. 140, § 27 (1984 ed.), for refusing to produce a motel register when requested to do so by a State trooper. The defendant now argues that G.L. c. 140, § 27 (1984 ed.), violates the Fourth Amendment of the United States Constitution and art. 14 of the Declaration of Rights of the Massachusetts Constitution. We allowed the defendant's petition for direct appellate review. We disagree and affirm the conviction.

"The facts are not in dispute. On September 21, 1984, Massachusetts State Trooper Robert Smith went to the Howard Johnson Motor Lodge in Danvers. Trooper Smith asked the defendant, the manager of the motel, to produce the motel's guest register for inspection. The defendant refused to allow Trooper Smith to see the register unless Trooper Smith obtained a search warrant. Trooper Smith left the motel and returned with a copy of G.L. c. 140, § 27, and again demanded to see the register. Even though the statute required the defendant to show the register to the police, the defendant refused to do so because the State trooper did not have a search warrant. The trooper again left the motel and returned with two other troopers about an hour and a half later. At this time, the defendant produced the register, but he was subsequently charged with violating G.L. c. 140, § 27, for failing to produce the register for inspection when first requested to do so. At no time did Trooper Smith obtain a search warrant requiring the defendant to produce the guest register for inspection.

"Our inquiry begins by examining whether the conduct of the trooper constituted a search in the Fourth Amendment sense. The Fourth Amendment does not prohibit all searches *per se*, but it does bar police intrusions into areas where a defendant has a 'legitimate expectation of privacy in the particular circumstances.' *Commonwealth v. Podgurski,* 386 Mass. 385, 387, 436 N.E.2d 150 (1982), *cert. denied,* 459 U.S. 1222, 103 S. Ct. 1167, 75 L. Ed. 2d 464 (1983), quoting *Sullivan v. District Court of Hampshire,* 384 Mass. 736, 741–742, 429 N.E.2d 335 (1981). Thus, if the defendant had no legitimate expectation of privacy in the motel register, the trooper's request pursuant to G.L. c. 140, § 27, does not require a search warrant under the Fourth Amendment.

"The United States Supreme Court has held that the government 'has ''greater latitude to conduct warrantless inspections of commercial property'' because ''the expectation of privacy that the owner of commercial property enjoys in such property differs significantly from the sanctity accorded an individual's home.'' ' *Dow Chemical Co. v. United States,*——U.S.——, 106 S. Ct. 1819, 1826, 90 L. Ed. 2d 226 (1986), quoting *Donovan v. Dewey,* 452 U.S. 594, 599, 101 S. St. 2534, 2538, 69 L. Ed. 2d 262 (1981). The Court has emphasized that, unlike a homeowner's interest in his dwelling, '[t]he interest of the owner of commercial property is not one in being free from any inspections.' *Id.* The test in determining whether a particular defendant has a reasonable expectation of privacy is essentially an objective one: whether the expectation is one that society is prepared to recognize as reasonable. *Michigan v. Clifford,* 464 U.S. 287, 292, 104 S. Ct. 641, 646, 78 L. Ed. 2d 477 (1984).

"Based on the facts presented at the defendant's trial, we conclude that the defendant had no reasonable expectation of privacy in the motel's guest register. In reaching this conclusion, we rely on several factors. First, as noted above, in business premises a person enjoys less of an expectation of privacy than in a home. Second, the guest register at issue was required to be kept by statute, thereby placing the defendant on notice that the register was subject to police inspection. The fact that a statute gives advance notice of warrantless inspections, though not determinative, is a factor to be considered in determining whether a defendant's expectation of privacy is legitimate. *United States v. Biswell,* 406 U.S. 311, 316, 92 S. Ct. 1593, 1596, 32 L. Ed. 2d 87 (1972). 3 W. LaFave, Search and Seizure § 10.2(c), 221 (1978). Third, all motel guests are presumed to be aware that the defendant was required by law to keep an accurate register because the laws regarding the register are required to be posted. G.L. c. 140, § 31 (1984 ed.). Thus, the defendant's argument that he could withhold the register in order to protect the privacy of his guests must fail because the guests had no legitimate expectation that their names in the register could be withheld from the police.

"Finally, it is important to note that the defendant was not the target of a criminal investigation by the State police. Had the police sought the register for the purpose of obtaining evidence against the defendant in a criminal proceeding, the defendant arguably may have had an expectation of privacy in the register. However, where, as here, the police are seeking the register to ascertain whether a criminal suspect is registered at the hotel, the hotel manager's expectation of privacy in the register is significantly diminished, if it exists at all. The record indicates that the defendant did not know that he was not a criminal suspect, but this fact alone is not sufficient to warrant reversal. The fact that the defendant was not the target of a criminal investigation, when combined with the other three factors discussed above, indicates that the defendant had no legitimate expectation of privacy in the motel register in the circumstances of this case. Accord, *King v. Tulsa,* 415 P.2d 606, 610–612 (Okla. Crim. App. 1966) (upholding a hotel guest register inspection ordinance which was challenged as an unconstitutional search and seizure; an inspection pursuant to the ordinance is not unreasonable when the police request is limited to a specific period of time); *Allinder v. Homewood,* 254 Ala. 525, 531–533, 49 S.2d 108 (1950) (statute requiring guest register to be open for police inspection for two years after the date of the last register entry does not violate innkeeper's constitutional right to be free from 'obnoxious force and seizure'). . . .

"*Judgment affirmed.*"

5:18 *Patron of Hotel Restaurant as Guest of Hotel*

ALPAUGH v. WOLVERTON
184 Va. 943, 36 S.E.2d 906 (1946)

[Proceeding by notice of motion for judgment based on the refusal of defendant, a hotel and restaurant keeper, to serve food and drink to plaintiff. Dismissed and plaintiff brings error. Affirmed.

Plaintiff alleged that he was a member in good standing of the Manassas, Va., Chamber of Commerce; that the defendant was the owner and operator of a certain hotel and restaurant in said town; that defendant entered into an arrangement to furnish lunch, food and drink to members of said Chamber of Commerce on Tuesdays of each week and that although plaintiff was a member in good standing of said organization and tendered the price of the meal, yet the defendant, in utter disregard of his "duties and obligations" to the plaintiff, "wilfully, wickedly, wantonly and maliciously" refused to serve plaintiff with food and drink on Tuesday, October 31, 1944, while plaintiff was seated at the dining table of the "hotel" along with other members of said organization, thereby maliciously humiliating him and bringing him into ridicule, disrespect and disgrace.

The second count is identical with the first, except that it charges defendant with refusal to serve plaintiff at a Kiwanis dinner on Friday, November 10,1944.]

EGGLESTON, J.: "The defendant filed a demurrer which, in substance, challenged the sufficiency of the notice of motion . . . [in that] it failed to allege that the defendant had violated any legal duty which he owed to the plaintiff. . . .

"The plaintiff insists that the allegations of the notice of motion for judgment are sufficient to show that in furnishing and agreeing to furnish the meals, under the circumstances stated, the defendant was a hotel operator or an innkeeper; that, as such, he 'was not entitled to say whom he would serve and whom he would not so serve,' but that 'he was legally bound to entertain and serve each and every one requesting such service and entertainment,' whether he be a local resident or a traveler from a distance.

"The defendant, on the other hand, insists that the allegations show that the relation established, or sought to be established, between the parties was not that of innkeeper and guest, but merely that of a restaurateur and customer, and that under the latter relation there was no common-law duty on the part of the defendant to serve the plaintiff, or any other customer, with meals.

[After stating the duties of an innkeeper in relation to guests the court continued:] " . . . The proprietor of a restaurant is not subject to the same duties and responsibilities as those of an innkeeper, nor is he entitled to the privileges of the latter. [Citations omitted.] His rights and responsibilities are more like those of a shopkeeper. [Citations omitted.] He is under no common-law duty to serve everyone who applies to him. In the absence of statute, he may accept some customers and reject others on purely personal grounds. [Citations omitted.]

"Everyone patronizing or seeking to patronize the facilities of a hotel or inn does not necessarily become a 'guest' of the establishment within the technical meaning of that term. It is well settled that the proprietor of a hotel may be a technical 'innkeeper' as to some of his patrons and a 'boarding housekeeper' as to others. . . .

"No one would seriously contend that a casual patron of a barbershop located in a hotel, or one who purchases a newspaper or cigar from a hotel newsstand, or one who uses the pay-telephone in the hotel lobby, by virtue of such patronage alone, thereby became a 'guest' of the hotel in a technical sense.

"And so, too, where a hotel operator operates a restaurant for the accommodation both of its guests and of the public in general, he may be an innkeeper as to some of his patrons and a restaurateur as to others. Clearly, one who goes into a restaurant, to which the general public is invited, for a meal, should be entitled to no greater privileges and subject to no greater liabilities because the establishment is operated by one who also operates a hotel, rather than by one who furnishes only food to his customers. In either case the customer seeks only restaurant service.

"We do not mean to imply that the relationship of innkeeper and guest may not arise where the patron partakes of a single meal at the hotel. . . . But in these cases there were other circumstances which indicated an intent to create the relationship.

"Indeed, the controlling factor in determining whether the relationship of innkeeper and guest has been established is the intent of the parties. [Citations omitted.]

"Applying these principles to the case before us, it is clear that the allegations of the notice of motion do not show the establishment of the relation of innkeeper and guest between the parties. On the contrary, they show merely the relationship of restaurateur and patron.

"There is no allegation that the plaintiff sought or intended to seek to become a guest of the hotel, or that he, or the proprietor, or the latter's servants or employees, did anything to indicate the intention to create such relation. There is no allegation that the plaintiff sought any of the other accommodations furnished by the establishment. On the contrary, it is clear that he sought merely to patronize the restaurant, as such. The allegation is that the defendant had entered into an 'arrangement and agreement' with two social clubs, under the provisions of which the defendant was to serve certain meals on certain days to the members of these clubs, including the plaintiff. It was while the plaintiff was seated at a table in the restaurant, pursuant to these arrangements, that he sought and was refused service of meals on two occasions.

"Since the notice of motion for judgment charges the defendant with the breach of no legal duty, the demurrer thereto was properly sustained. The judgment is *affirmed.*"

One who is merely a customer at a bar, restaurant, barbershop, or newsstand operated by a hotel does not thereby establish the relationship of innkeeper and guest.[46] The intention to do so, communicated to and accepted by the innkeeper, is the critical requirement (*see* section 5:1, *supra*).

But once guest status is established, all of the rights of the innkeeper are in effect, including the right to rely on the appropriate statute limiting his liability for losses of guest property. The use by the guest of a public restaurant maintained by the hotel does not change guest status to that of a restaurant patron.

SUMMER v. HYATT CORP.
153 Ga. App. 684, 266 S.E.2d 333 (1980)

SHULMAN, J.: "Plaintiff brought this action to recover damages for loss or theft of valuables from her purse, contending that the loss or theft was due to the negligence of defendant or to the maintenance of a nuisance by defendant. The loss or theft occurred in the rotating Polaris restaurant, operated by defendant

---

[46]Wallace v. Shoreham Hotel Corp., 49 A.2d 81 (D.C. Mun. Ct. App. 1946).

and located atop the Hyatt Regency hotel owned by defendant. While plaintiff was registered as a guest at the hotel, she went into the restaurant and took a seat on the rotating portion of the structure, placing her purse on the stationary portion of the structure. Plaintiff's seat rotated away from her purse. When the purse was recovered, valuables were missing from it.

"Defendant moved for and received summary judgment on the basis of plaintiff's admitted noncompliance with the hotel's regulations concerning the safekeeping of guests' valuables. *See* Code Ann. § 52–108 *et seq.; Jones v. Savannah Hotel Co.,* 141 Ga. 530(2), 81 S.E. 874. Plaintiff contends in this appeal . . . that her status as an invitee of the restaurant, rather than her status as a hotel guest, controls the rights and liabilities of the parties to this action.

"Although this precise question has not been decided in Georgia (that is, whether an 'inn' guest retains guest status when such guest avails herself of a restaurant facility located on the premises of the hotel structure), several cases imply that the relationship of guest-innkeeper would remain in effect during the guest's occupation of a hotel's restaurant and bar. (*See Alpaugh v. Wolverton,* 184 Va. 943(2), 36 S.E.2d 906). For example, in *Walpert v. Bohan,* 126 Ga. 532, 534, 55 S.E. 181, 182, it was stated that: ' "[O]ne who keeps a public house may, not inconsistently, *carry on a restaurant,* cater to a select company, *serve liquors at a bar,* keep a shaving saloon, or permit outside parties to get up a ball on his premises; [but] *as to strangers who avail themselves* of such extraneous service, he is no innkeeper at all." ' (Emphasis supplied.)

"What *Walpert* implies is that an innkeeper who provides the above service to a guest of the inn remains in the status of an innkeeper in regard to such guest. As to a stranger, however; that is, one who is not a guest of the inn, the fact that an innkeeper provides the above services does not establish a guest-innkeeper relationship. The duties normally flowing from the position of innkeeper, therefore, are not owed to a stranger, but they are owed to a guest.

"*Diplomat Restaurant v. Townsend,* 118 Ga. App. 694, 165 S.E.2d 317, likewise implies that a guest retains his guest status while patronizing a hotel restaurant. In *Diplomat Restaurant,* this court refused to apply the innkeeper statutes to one who 'merely operated a restaurant and a bar for serving liquors,' impliedly holding that its decision would have been contrary had the defendant likewise operated an inn.

"Moreover, this court has previously found the relationship of innkeeper-guest to exist despite the fact that the guest was availaing himself of facilities other than those used solely for lodging (rooms) and integral connecting portions of the hotel (lobby, elevators, etc.). *See* in this regard *Traylor v. Hyatt Corp.,* 122 Ga. App. 633(1), 178 S.E.2d 289, wherein the court held the innkeeper statutes applicable to a guest's loss of property from his car parked (for a separate fee) in the hotel's parking lot. *See also Ellerman v. Atlanta American Motor Hotel Corp.,* 126 Ga. App. 194(2), 191 S.E.2d 295.

"We do not hold that an innkeeper retains his status as an innkeeper towards guests of the inn in regard to all extraneous services provided by the innkeeper, of which hotel guests as well as the general public partake (such as 'boats for rowing and sailing . . . a public race course or golf links or a baseball park. . . .' *Walpert, supra,* 126 Ga. p. 535, 55 S.E., p. 182).

"But, under the circumstances of the case at bar, in view of the fact that plaintiff was in defendant's restaurant within the hotel structure, we conclude that plaintiff retained her guest status, as a matter of law, and that defendant continued to owe plaintiff the duties of an innkeeper, and that plaintiff accordingly was bound by the regulations established under Code Ann. ch. 52–1.

"That being so, plaintiff, as a guest, was required to comply with the posted rules in regard to the safety deposit of her valuables in order to recover against the defendant. The failure to do so precludes her recovery from defendant on the claims asserted. *See Jones, supra,* 141 Ga. p. 534, 81 S.E. 874.

"Judgment affirmed."

5:19 *Deposit of Chattels with Innkeeper*

When the baggage of a transient is received by the innkeeper and the transient thereafter accepts some service for which he pays, or obligates himself to pay, such transient will be considered a guest of the innkeeper from the time the baggage was received.[47]

FREUDENHEIM V. EPPLEY

88 F.2d 280 (3d Cir.), *appeal dismissed,* 302 U.S. 769 (1937)

[Action by J. Freudenheim & Sons, a partnership, against the receivers of the Pittsburgh Hotels Corporation to recover damages suffered by the alleged negligence of the defendant in failing to safely keep some $40,000 worth of its diamonds deposited with defendant by Sol J. Freudenheim, one of the partners, who was an alleged guest of the hotel. On trial, a verdict was had for the plaintiff for $41,893.13. The court below entered judgment in favor of the defendant n.o.v. (judgment notwithstanding the verdict) on the ground that plaintiff was not a guest of the defendant's hotel at the time of the deposit, that the deposit was a gratuitous bailment, and that there was no proof of gross negligence on the part of defendant. This is an appeal by plaintiff from said judgment.]

BUFFINGTON, C.J.: ". . . [T]he uncontradicted facts in the case showed that Freudenheim was the traveling salesman of his diamond firm, and . . . was accustomed to visit. . . Pittsburgh. . . . [He was accustomed, when trade justified, to stay] at hotels which had vaults for the deposit of valuables and he left his bag containing diamonds in their vaults. Prior to 1922–23, he had stopped at other hotels in Pittsburgh, but since then had stopped at the William Penn. Prior to 1930 he came to Pittsburgh eight or nine times a year and stayed at the William Penn two, three, or four days at a time, depending on trade conditions. In 1933 he was twice in Pittsburgh, received his mail at the hotel, but did not stay overnight. On every one of his trips to Pittsburgh he used the vault at the

---

[47]Burton v. Drake Hotel Co., 237 Ill. App. 76 (1925).

William Penn. On the morning of December 5, 1933, after visiting other cities, he arrived in Pittsburgh from Cincinnati before 7:00 A.M. After checking his personal bag at the railroad station, he went to the hotel. His proof was: 'I intended to stay . . . as long as I could do business here.' He arrived at the hotel around 7:00 o'clock, but the cashier's office, where the hotel had vaults, was not open, and the cashier, Schaller, had not arrived. . . . [Around 7:30, he again went back to the cashier's cage and Schaller there greeted him, saying, "I suppose you want a box."] He knew Freudenheim quite well. He took a set of two keys from a board and handed Freudenheim an interlocking printed check used at the hotel for vault service. One [part of this check] was the stub check given to Freudenheim, in form following:

WILLIAM PENN HOTEL
VAULT CHECK
C 6306

Checked by _____
Room _____

"The other [part] was a corresponding numeral, 6306, signed by Freudenheim and retained by the hotel. . . . [The cashier then inserted one of the two keys in the metal box in the safe, turned it and withdrew it. Freudenheim then inserted the other key, opened the box, and put his brief case with the merchandise in it right inside that box, closed the door, and went downstairs.] . . . From these facts, could an inference be reasonably drawn that Freudenheim was a guest of the hotel?

"In the first place, we have the fact that Freudenheim was known to the hotel as a past guest and that there was the possibility of his lodging at the hotel if trade warranted such stay. There was, therefore, in the minds of both parties that the hotel would have Freudenheim as a guest. He was recognized by the cashier; inquiry was made whether he wanted a box; he was given the box; his merchandise was deposited; and the operation recognized by both parties by the corresponding vault checks with similar numbers. This was a service or accommodation which the hotel had extended before and Freudenheim had enjoyed before.

" . . . Now it is clear that vault service for valuables is a customary hotel accommodation and that it was the intention of both parties that Freudenheim should have that accommodation, and the relation of guest and hotel being once established, the doctrine in *Wright v. Anderton*, 1 K.B. 209, applies, viz.: 'The responsibility of an innkeeper for the safety of a traveller's property begins at the moment when the relation of guest and host arises, and that relation arises as soon as the traveller enters the inn with the intention of using it as an inn, and is so received by the host. It does not matter that no food or lodging has been supplied or found up to the time of the loss. It is sufficient if the circumstances show an intention of the one hand to provide and on the other hand to accept such accommodation.'

"Moreover, later on, and before he left, Freudenheim . . . did take his dinner in the general dining room of the hotel. It is true he did not take a room and register, but his omission to do so does not put him out of guest protection. *See Moody v. Kenny*, 153 La. 1007, 97 So. 21, 22, 29 A.L.R. 474, wherein it is said: 'The fact that such person fails to register, or is not required to register, is immaterial; as the registration of guests at a hotel is no part of the contract between the hotel proprietor and the guest, but the purpose of a register is to keep track of the number of people in the house and to keep the books straight. A register is kept solely for the benefit and convenience of the hotel proprietor.'

"This is in accord with cases cited in 14 Ruling Case Law, 518, which says: 'It is not necessary that a traveller shall register at an inn as a guest in order to become such, but it is sufficient if he visits the inn for the purpose of receiving entertainment and is entertained accordingly.'

"The jury having found a verdict in favor of the plaintiff, and the court having erred in holding as a matter of law that Freudenheim was not a guest, the judgment below is vacated, and the record is remanded, with instruction to the court to enter judgment on the verdict in favor of the plaintiffs."

[Rehearing denied March 23, 1937. Petition for *certiorari* dismissed. 302 U.S. 769.]

It would seem, therefore, that to entitle a person visiting an inn to be treated as a guest, and to hold an innkeeper responsible for money deposited with him for safekeeping, it must appear that such visit was for the purposes which the common law recognizes as the purposes for which inns are kept. When such visit is made by one who does not require the present entertainment or accommodations of the inn, but whose purpose is simply to deposit his money for safekeeping, he is not a guest of the inn or hotel.

5:20 *Length of Stay as Affecting Status of Guest*

One who seeks accommodations in an inn with a view to permanency, so as to make the inn his home, is not a guest. The length of stay, however, is not ordinarily decisive for he will continue to be a guest as long as he retains his transient status. The question whether a person receiving accommodations at an inn is a guest or a lodger, boarder, or tenant, is one of fact.[48]

In *Holstein v. Phillips and Sims*,[49] the plaintiff, a resident of South Carolina, stopped at defendant's hotel and was charged ten dollars per week for board. She was to stay two or three weeks, but no agreement was made for any particular

---

[48]Hancock v. Rand, 94 N.Y. 1 (1883).
[49]146 N.C. 366, 59 S.E. 1037 (1907).

time. In an action to recover for the loss of valuables, the defense was that plaintiff was not a guest. (It appeared that defendant failed to comply with the statute limiting his liability as innkeeper.) Judgment for plaintiff was affirmed, the court stating:

> She came to the hotel from her home in South Carolina for a short stay; she was a stranger to the parties defendant, and entered as a guest, so far as appears, without any prearrangement as to terms or time, but on the implied invitation held out to the public generally. She was there for no definite time, and, in our opinion, she was transient in every sense of the term and within every reason that gave her the right to the protection on which she insists. And, where this is true, all the authorities— certainly those having the better reason—are to the effect that the mere fact that she was to pay board by the week, or even at a reduced rate, does not alter her position as guest or deprive her of the right to hold defendants as insurers.[50]

In *Petti v. Thomas*,[51] plaintiff sued for the loss of her property destroyed by fire in defendant's hotel. The defense was that plaintiff was not a guest and that defendant was therefore not liable as innkeeper for the loss. It appeared that plaintiff paid her bills weekly and received a special rate, but that there was no agreement as to how long she would stay.

Judgment for plaintiff was affirmed on appeal, the court stating:

> [T]he fact that a person had been at a hotel for more than a week, and paid the reduced weekly rate, does not make him a boarder, rather than a guest, in the absence of an agreement as to the time he would remain at the hotel. Neither does the fact that one makes an arrangement to pay a reduced rate per meal, or per day, or per week, take away his character as a guest, where there is no agreement as to the time he will remain at the hotel. And the question whether one is a boarder or guest is one of fact, to be determined by the jury under proper instructions from the court.[52]

In *Kaplan v. Stogop Realty Co.*,[53] it was held that a person who occupied a suite in defendant's hotel for a period of eleven months, paying rent on a monthly basis, the defendant furnishing maid service, linens, towels, soap, light, and telephone service, was not a transient person and, therefore, not a guest. And in the later case of *Mason v. Hotel Grand Union*,[54] a person who resided in the hotel from August 1, 1940 to May 30, 1942, when he was robbed, and who paid on a monthly basis and had no other home or residence, was a tenant and not a guest.

[50]*Id.* at 372.
[51]103 Ark. 593, 148 S.W. 501 (1912).
[52]*Id.* at 600.
[53]133 Misc. 611, 233 N.Y.S. 113 (Sup. Ct. 1929).
[54]41 N.Y.S.2d 309 (N.Y. City Ct. 1943).

5:21 *Employee as Guest*

An employee residing in a hotel pursuant to his contract of employment is not a guest.[55] An employee, discharged at a late hour of the day, and permitted to occupy a room for the night, because of the lateness of the hour of her discharge, is not a guest.[56]

5:22 *Lodgers, Boarders, and Tenants Distinguished from Guests*

The nature and extent of the legal obligations of an innkeeper to persons in the inn depend on their relationship to the innkeeper. At common law, he is an insurer of the property of his guests in the house subject to exceptions and limitations; for the property of lodgers, boarders, and tenants his responsibility depends upon the exercise of reasonable care. He owes a high degree of care for the personal comfort and safety of guests, to whom he owes a duty of courtesy as well. He may lock out a guest, lodger, or boarder for nonpayment of his reasonable charges, but must resort to legal process to dispossess a tenant. It is, therefore, important, in ascertaining legal rights and obligations, to understand the distinction between guests and nonguests. The determination is not an easy one, and where there is any doubt as to the status of a person, particularly in cases of lockout, the innkeeper should seek legal advice before taking action.

The following case distinguishes between guest and nonguest status.

STATE V. ANONYMOUS
34 Conn. Supp. 603, 379 A.2d 1 (1977)

SHEA, J.: "General Statutes § 53a–119(7) provides, in pertinent part: 'A person is guilty of theft of services when: (1) With intent to avoid payment . . . for services rendered to him as a transient guest at a hotel, motel, inn, tourist cabin, rooming house or comparable establishment, he avoids such payment by unjustifiable failure or refusal to pay, by stealth, or by any misrepresentation of fact which he knows to be false. . . . ' The question which is decisive of this appeal is whether there was sufficient evidence that the defendant was a 'transient guest' within the meaning of this statute.

"There was testimony that the defendant rented an efficiency apartment at a motel on a weekly basis for four weeks. The efficiency apartments of the motel were not rented on a daily basis, as were the regular motel rooms. They were provided with cooking facilities and did not receive maid service, unlike the other units. There was no provision for renting the efficiency apartments for a period of less than one week. The rent of $58.35 per week was payable in advance on the first day of each weekly period. The defendant paid the rent as it fell due each week. On the day when the next weekly payment was due and was not made, the room of the defendant was checked and some of his belongings

---

[55]Powers v. Raymond, 197 Cal. 126, 239 P. 1069 (1925).
[56]Morrison v. Hotel Rutledge Co., 200 A.D. 636, 193 N.Y.S. 428 (1st Dep't 1922).

were still in the room. Two days later a woman came to the motel, removed the remaining property of the defendant and left the key at the motel office. The next day the complainant telephoned the defendant at an address which was obtained from his room registration card and informed him that he owed the rent for one week. The defendant claimed that he had vacated his motel room and was not responsible for rent for an additional week.

"It is fundamental that the state had the burden of proving every element of the offense charged beyond a reasonable doubt. *State v. Brown*, 163 Conn. 52, 64, 301 A.2d 547. Proof that the defendant was a 'transient guest' at the motel was essential for a conviction under the statute. The word 'transient' means '[a] person passing through a place or staying there only temporarily.' Ballentine's Law Dictionary, p. 1293 (3d ed.). 'To be a guest of an inn or hotel it is essential, at least at common law, that the person should be a transient, that is, that he should come to the inn for a more or less temporary stay, for if he comes on a permanent basis he will be deemed a boarder or lodger rather than a guest.' 43 C.J.S. *Innkeepers* § 3, p. 1140. Although it has been said that a guest must be a traveler, that is meant in a broad sense to include anyone away from home who enjoys the same accommodations which are offered to travelers. *Walling v. Potter*, 35 Conn. 183, 185. The length of stay, the existence of a special contract for the room, the fact that a person has another abode and the extent to which he has made the room his home for the time being are material circumstances in determining whether the relationship is that of a guest or a lodger. 43 C.J.S., *supra*, p. 1138.

"The defendant, who acted as his own counsel, never raised any claim that he was not a 'transient guest.' It was essential, nevertheless, that the evidence establish beyond a reasonable doubt that he had that status. That standard has not been met in this case. The testimony bearing upon this issue indicates that the defendant may have been a roomer rather than a 'transient guest.' Apparently he was not a traveler in the literal sense. The rental arrangement and the nature of the accommodations differed from those pertaining to the regular motel rooms. The duration of the occupancy was not so brief as to justify a conclusion that it was merely temporary in character. Whether the defendant intended the room to be a more or less permanent residence or whether he had a home elsewhere are questions unanswered by the testimony. In sum, there is insufficient evidence to support a conclusion that the defendant was a 'transient guest.'

"There is error, the judgment is set aside and the case is remanded with direction to render a judgment of not guilty."

5:23 Dispossession of Tenants by Summary Proceedings

Since the distinction between a lodger and a tenant is often a shadowy one, in case of any doubt, it would seem best to assume that a person who has resided in the hotel on a weekly or monthly rate basis for more than thirty days is a tenant, and to proceed against him accordingly. This view is reinforced by the provisions of Section 711 of the New York Real Property Actions and Proceedings Law, which became effective September 1, 1963, and which reads, in part, as follows: "An occupant of one or more rooms in a rooming house in a city having a population of one million or more, who has been in possession for thirty consecutive days or longer is a tenant under this article; he shall not be removed from possession except in a special proceeding."

Poroznoff v. Alberti
161 N.J. Super. 414, 391 A.2d 984 (Dist. Ct. 1978), *aff'd*, 168 N.J. Super. 140, 401 A.2d 1124 (App. Div. 1979)

Reiss, P.J.D.C.: "This case raises an issue of first impression in this state whether a guest or roomer in a hotel, motel or guest house may be dispossessed from his room without resort to legal process.

"The facts appear to be uncontroverted. Plaintiff was living in a room at the Young Men's Christian Association in the City of Passaic (hereinafter Y.M.C.A.) on a week-to-week basis. During the week of June 5, 1978 plaintiff became drunk and disorderly, was arrested by the local police and subsequently released. Returning to the Y.M.C.A., plaintiff found his room locked and was told not to re-enter the building.

"Plaintiff, represented by Legal Aid, moved at an order to show cause hearing to be allowed to re-enter his room. Also, he filed a complaint for recovery of possession or treble damages pursuant to N.J.S.A. 2A:39-8 '(Forcible Entry and Detainer).'

"Plaintiff did not appear to dispute the grounds for removal, but rather the method used by the agents for the Y.M.C.A. Plaintiff argues that the 'lock-out' or self-help remedy employed by the Y.M.C.A. is violative of the legal procedures for eviction as mandated by N.J.S.A. 2A:18-61.1 and N.J.S.A. 2A:18-53 *et seq.*

"Defendant, however, submits that the Y.M.C.A. is in the category of a hotel, motel or guest house and is excluded from the provisions of N.J.S.A. 2A:18-61.1 and N.J.S.A. 2A:18-53.

"A dispossess action is initially governed by N.J.S.A. 2A:18-61.1 *et seq.*, which establishes guidelines for the removal of resident tenants 'from any house, building, mobile home . . . or tenement leased for residential purposes, other than . . . *a hotel, motel or other guest house or part thereof rented to a transient guest or seasonal tenant. . . .* ' (Emphasis supplied.)

"If the Y.M.C.A. were deemed to be a multiple-dwelling apartment operation falling within N.J.S.A. 2A:18-61.1, then any lawful lock-out must conform to the appropriate judicial procedures provided by statute. Inasmuch as counsel for both parties conceded that the Y.M.C.A. was not an apartment house, further inquiry into this status is unnecessary. Now in order for the Y.M.C.A. to be contemplated as a hotel the next appropriate statute should be reviewed.

"N.J.S.A. 2A:18-53 provides:

"Except for residential lessees and tenants included in [N.J.S.A. 2A:18-

61.1] any lessee or tenant at will or sufferance, or for a part of a year . . . of any houses, buildings, lands or tenements, . . . may be removed from such premises by the county district court . . . in the following cases: . . .

"c. Where such person (1) shall be so disorderly as to destroy the peace and quiet of the landlord or other tenants or occupants living in said house or neighborhood . . . and shall hold over and continue in possession of the demised premises . . . after the landlord or his agent . . . has caused a written notice of the termination of said tenancy to be served upon said tenant and a demand that said tenant remove from said premises within 3 days from the service of such notice.

"The distinguishable words of this statue are 'lessee' and 'tenant.' Can a week-to-week resident of a Y.M.C.A. be designated a 'lessee' or 'tenant' for the purpose of the summary dispossess statute N.J.S.A. 2A:18–53? Plaintiff's attorney stated that while plaintiff could be so qualified, this distinction was not the issue before the court.

"Plaintiff's attorney submitted that it makes no difference whether plaintiff was staying at a hotel or in an apartment. Indeed, as indicated earlier, plaintiff's attorney admitted that the Y.M.C.A. was, in this case, operating as a hotel and not as an apartment building.

"Plaintiff's argument essentially rested upon his action at law under the forcible entry and detainer statute, N.J.S.A. 2A:39–1, which states:

"No person shall enter upon or into any real property or estate therein and detain and hold the same, except where entry is given by law, and then only in a peaceable manner. With regard to any real property occupied solely as a residence by the party in possession, such entry shall not be made in any manner without the consent of the party in possession unless the entry and detention is made pursuant to legal process as set out in N.J.S.A. 2A:18–53 *et seq.* or 2A:35–1 *et seq.*

"Plaintiff's position, then, was that he was a party in possession of his residence at the Y.M.C.A. and, despite any distinction between hotel rooms or apartments, his residence was entered in violation of the forcible entry and detainer statute.

"The distinguishable words in this statute are 'residence' and 'possession.' Was plaintiff a resident at the Y.M.C.A. or a 'party in possession,' within the meaning of the forcible entry and detainer statute? And was he a lessee or tenant for the purposes of N.J.S.A. 2A:18–53?

"Resolution of these questions initially hinges upon a determination of whether the Y.M.C.A. was a hotel or an apartment building.

"The Hotel and Multiple Dwelling Law defines the term 'hotel' as " . . . any building . . . which contains 10 or more units of dwelling space or has sleeping facilities for 25 or more persons and is kept, used, maintained, advertised as, or held out to be, a place where sleeping or dwelling accommodations are available to transient or permanent guests. [N.J.S.A. 55:13A–3(j)]

"A multiple dwelling on the other hand, means

" . . . any building . . . in which three or more units of dwelling space are occupied . . . by three or more persons who live independently of each other, provided, that this definition shall not be construed to include any building or structure defined as a hotel in this act, or, registered as a hotel with the Commissioner of Community Affairs . . . , or occupied or intended to be occupied exclusively as such . . . [N.J.S.A. 55:13A–3(k)].

"Therefore, if a Y.M.C.A.,

"1. maintains, advertises or holds itself out as a hotel *i.e.* a place where sleeping accommodations are available to transient or permanent guests; and

"2. the contractual arrangement or understanding between the parties is that of an innkeeper and guest; and

"3. the Y.M.C.A. is occupied or is intended to be occupied as a hotel, and

"4. the Y.M.C.A. is registered with the Commissioner of the Department of Community Affairs as a hotel,

"then it is indeed a hotel.

"With this point established, the question then arises whether a guest occupying a hotel has the same legal relationship with his innkeeper, as a tenant does with his landlord. The leading New Jersey case on this is *Johnson v. Kolibas,* 75 N.J. Super. 56, 182 A.2d 157 (App. Div. 1962), *certif. den.* 38 N.J. 310, 184 A.2d 422 (1962). There the court stated:

"The chief distinction between a tenant and a lodger or roomer lies in the character of their possession. The criterion is the right of exclusive possession. While the tenant has exclusive legal possession of the premises, the lodger only has the right to use the premises, subject to the landlord's retention of control and right of access to them. [75 N.J. Super. at 62–63, 182 A.2d at 160.]

"This distinction is upheld in the majority of other jurisdictions. The lodger, or roomer, or guest is a mere licensee and only has a right of use of the room he occupies. However, the tenant has the more substantial estate and the law gives him the right of exclusive possession and control for the term of his leasehold. [Citations omitted.] In Connecticut this distinction between a tenant and a lodger was held to be a substantial one: 'The tenant may maintain ejectment, *quare clausum fregit,* and trespass. The lodger may not.' [Citations omitted.]

"Even though New Jersey case law clearly distinguishes the relationship between a guest and a tenant, there is very little authority on whether an innkeeper may summarily remove a guest for nonpayment or disorderly behavior. Therefore, appropriate reference must be made to the law in other jurisdictions.

"Generally, because an innkeeper has a different legal relationship with his guest than a landlord, the innkeeper is not required to submit to the statutory procedures in evicting the guest. In a similar case to the one at bar, *Tamamian v. Gabbard,* 55 A.2d 513 (D.C. Mun. App. 1947), held that the forcible entry and detainer statute does not apply to actions by an innkeeper. Thus, the court also stated:

"Plainly, in the ordinary case of a roomer there is no forcible entry and detainer; nor is there unlawful entry, without force, and a forcible detainer. This leaves only the case of unlawful detention by a tenant after expiration of his tenancy. As we have already seen however, a roomer is not a tenant and has no tenancy. We, therefore, fail to see how an action under this section (Wash. D.C. Rent Act of 1940) could be sustained against a roomer, and as this is our only statute relating to summary possession, we conclude that the trial court was in error in instructing the jury that it was necessary to institute court proceedings against plaintiff for possession of the room [at 516] [citations omitted].

"In *Sawyer v. Congress Square Hotel Co.*, 157 Me. 111, 170 A.2d 645 (Sup. Jud. Ct. 1961), plaintiff had been a guest for a long period of time. She brought an action for damages against the hotel from which she had been summarily evicted due to her delinquent account. There the court held that plaintiff was not entitled to notice or process under the Maine tenancy law when ' . . . where as here a person occupies a room in a hotel, registers as others do, receives mail service, and has the benefit of the other incidental services, that the hotel gives, she is a guest, and this is true in spite of the fact that her stay there may be a long one and that she pays on a weekly or monthly basis. . . . ' [at 647]

"Finally, in the case of *Roberts v. Casey*, 36 Cal. App. Supp. 2d 767, 93 P.2d 654 (D. Ct. App. 1939), the court treated at length the question of whether notice under California procedural law must be given before an occupant of an apartment hotel can be evicted. The court made the distinction between a tenant and lodger, and finding that plaintiff's situation was that of a guest, it concluded that 'so soon as a guest or lodger has, either by default in making payments due or otherwise, breached his contract he may by appropriate proceedings be ousted without the requirement of any advance notice.' 93 P.2d at 659. Any other method "would be absurd . . . to require either a demand, or notice to quit.' *Id.* The *Roberts* court felt that a prior demand or notice to quit or any other remedies at law would similarly be absurd and '[s]uch a ruling would make the operations of hotels and lodging houses virtually impossible and . . . manifestly cannot be the law.' *Id.* at 659.

"Because New Jersey case law has not directly dealt with the issue here, this court is guided by the wealth of other decisions which find that an innkeeper may rightfully eject a guest who is either seriously delinquent on his bill or who is so unruly and disorderly as to offend the sensibilities of a reasonably conscientious hotelkeeper.

" . . . Consequently, plaintiff's petition for permanent relief or damages is denied and the case is dismissed."

5:24 *Termination of the Relation of Innkeeper and Guest*

The general rule is that when the guest pays his bill and departs, the strict liability does not cease at once, but continues for a reasonable time within which to remove the baggage; and if the host undertakes to deliver the baggage to a common carrier thereof, strict liability continues until the delivery is made.[57]

The relation, with its strict liability, may and does continue during the mere temporary absence of the guest from the inn. The length of time during which the absence may continue without terminating the relation is not fixed by law; the question of this duration in a given case is important only as evidence to determine whether the relation of host and guest continues in the interim. In order for this relation to continue during the guest's absence from the inn, however, the law does prescribe certain conditions which must be fulfilled:

(a) There must be on the part of the guest an *animus revertendi,* which must be known to the innkeeper, or he must be properly chargeable therewith.

(b) The intent must be to return within a reasonable time.

(c) The liability to compensate the innkeeper, on the part of the guest, must continue during the absence. The right of the host to charge the guest is the criterion of the former's strict liability as host to the latter.[58]

In the Ohio case of *Hotel Statler Co., Inc. v. Safier,*[59] plaintiff was a guest in defendant's hotel each week for about four days. Each time he left the hotel, he had his trunk delivered to the hotel storage room; upon his return it was redelivered to him. About August 1, 1917, when plaintiff returned again, he was told that his trunk and contents had been lost. The plaintiff, while technically a guest when the arrangement for storage was made, was not a guest during the period of storage. The statutory limitation of liability of the guest's property was not available to the hotel.

Courts in New York and Kentucky have taken a different view of liability for property remaining in the hotel after a guest's departure. In *Dilkes v. Hotel Sheraton, Inc.,*[60] upon facts substantially similar to those found in the *Safier* case, the limitation of liability for the property of guests was held to remain in full force and effect after departure of the guest.

SALISBURY V. ST. REGIS-SHERATON HOTEL CORP.
490 F. Supp. 449 (S.D. N.Y. 1980)

LASKER, D.J.: "On the morning of November 22, 1978, Mr. and Mrs. Roger Salisbury concluded a three day stay at the St. Regis-Sheraton Hotel in New York. While Mr. Salisbury paid the bill and surrendered their room key, Mrs. Salisbury checked their luggage with a bellhop in the lobby. The couple was to spend the day in town and return for the luggage that afternoon. Mrs. Salisbury did not inform the hotel, when she checked the luggage, that one of their pieces, a cosmetics case, contained jewelry and cosmetics worth over $60,000, and did

---

[57]Kaplan v. Titus, 64 Misc. 81, 117 N.Y.S. 944 (Sup. Ct. 1909), aff'd, 140 A.D. 416, 125 N.Y.S. 397 (1st Dep't 1910).
[58]Watkins v. Hotel Tutwiler Co., 200 Ala. 386, 388, 76 So. 302, 304 (1917).
[59]103 Ohio St. 638, 134 N.E. 460 (1921).
[60]282 A.D. 488, 125 N.Y.S.2d 38 (1st Dep't 1953).

not ask that the case be kept in the hotel's safe. Nor did she inform the hotel that the value of the case and its contents exceeded $100.

"When the Salisburys returned to the hotel to retrieve their luggage at about 4:30 that afternoon, the cosmetics case containing the jewelry was missing. Mrs. Salisbury sues to recover the value of the case and its contents.

"It is undisputed that posted conspicuously in the public areas of the hotel was a notice informing guests that the hotel provided a safe for the safekeeping of their valuables, and notifying them of the provisions of sections 200 and 201 of the New York General Business Law. . . . Relying on these provisions, the hotel moves for summary judgment on the grounds that the undisputed facts establish that its liability cannot exceed $100., and therefore federal subject matter jurisdiction is lacking. Mrs. Salisbury cross-moves for summary judgment, asserting that sections 200 and 201 are inapplicable here because she was no longer a 'guest' of the hotel at the time the loss occurred.

"The question, then, is whether Mrs. Salisbury ceased to be a 'guest' within the meaning of sections 200 and 201 when she checked out of the hotel, even though she arranged to have the hotel hold her luggage for the day. The two cases on which Mrs. Salisbury relies are clearly distinguishable. In one, *Crosby v. Fifth Ave. Hotel Co.*, 173 Misc. 595, 20 N.Y.S.2d 227 (N.Y.C. Mun. Ct. 1939), *modified*, 173 Misc. 604, 17 N.Y.S.2d 498 (App. T. 1st Dept. 1940), a departing guest stored two trunks with the defendant hotel, and returned to reclaim them several years later only to discover that the hotel had sold them. The court concluded that the relationship involved was not that of innkeeper and guest, but rather that of bailee and bailor. Here, however, the lost luggage was not stored with the hotel for a lengthy period, but simply held for the day as an accommodation to departing guests. In the other case relied on by Mrs. Salisbury, *Ticehurst v. Beinbrink*, 72 Misc. 365, 129 N.Y.S. 838 (App. T. 1911), the plaintiff arranged to leave his horse at an inn while he continued his journey by train. The court held that the plaintiff, who simply sought to board his horse, was not a 'guest,'—'a transient person who resorts to or is received at an inn for the purpose of obtaining the accommodations which it purports to offer.' This definition, however, applies quite well to the Salisburys.

"It is not uncommon for a hotel to hold luggage for a few hours after guests check out as an accommodation to them. This would appear to be one of the services which a hotel performs for its guests in the normal course of its business, and there is no reason why it should be deemed to alter the otherwise existing legal relationship between them. Accordingly, we conclude that sections 200 and 201 are fully applicable in the circumstances of this case, and precludes any recovery against the hotel for the loss of Mrs. Salisbury's jewelry, and limits any recovery for the loss of the case and its other contents to $100. [Citation omitted.]

"While we thus conclude that the hotel has an absolute defense to Mrs. Salisbury's suit for the value of her jewelry, we note that even if the relationship involved here were deemed a gratuitous bailment, as Mrs. Salisbury contends it should be, the hotel's liability would be limited to the value of articles ordinarily found in a cosmetics case, even if Mrs. Salisbury could establish that the hotel was grossly negligent in caring for her case. [Citation omitted.] *Waters v. Beau Site Co.*, 114 Misc. 65, 186 N.Y. Supp. 731 (N.Y.C. Civ. Ct. 1920). Even under her own view of the law, Mrs. Salisbury could not recover the value of her lost jewelry.

"Since the most that could be recovered in this action is $100., it is evident that the amount in controversy does not exceed $10,000., and therefore federal subject matter jurisdiction is lacking. . . . ''

In *Kentucky Hotel v. Cinotti*,[61] the statutory limitation of liability was held to apply to property lost subsequent to the guest's departure from the hotel. "As the absence was to be temporary and the guest intended to return shortly and secure personal accommodations, the relationship of innkeeper and guest continued during the interval insofar as liability for the safekeeping of the property is concerned."[62]

5:25 *Penalty for Charging Guest after Departure*

The New York statute, section 206 of the General Business Law, which mandates innkeepers to post "a statement of the charges or rate of charges by the day and for meals furnished and for lodging" also provides a treble damage penalty for charges made after the guest's departure, that is to say, after the termination of the innkeeper-guest relationship.

5:26 *Penalty for Charging Guest for Services Not Actually Rendered*

Section 206 of the General Business Law is designed to penalize the innkeeper for charging the guests for services they do not actually receive. Included in this category would be blanket charges for services which some guests receive but which other guests do not.

STATE BY LEFKOWITZ V. WALDORF-ASTORIA CORP.
67 Misc. 2d 90, 323 N.Y.S.2d 917 (Sup. Ct. 1971)

BAER, J.: "Petitioner brings this special proceeding under subdivision 12 of section 63 of the Executive Law to permanently enjoin and restrain the respondents from conducting and transacting their business in a 'persistently fraudulent and illegal manner,' and to direct restitution to all consumers of the amount charged for services not rendered, plus triple damages, pursuant to section 206 of the General Business Law.

"The General Business Law does require every hotel to post 'a statement of the . . . charges by the day and for meals furnished and for lodging.' It further

---

[61]298 Ky. 88, 182 S.W.2d 27 (1944).
[62]*Id.* at 91.

provides that 'No charge or sum shall be collected or received by any such hotel keeper or inn keeper for any service not actually rendered.'

"Between December 2, 1969 and May 21, 1970 the respondents did add to each bill of each customer a 2% charge for sundries. The respondents contend that this was a proper charge because of the peculiar needs of their clientele, and the capital cost and maintenance cost of their internal communications system. They also contend that counsel for the New York State Hotel and Motel Association, of which they are members, advised of the propriety of such charges. This latter contention is not borne out by an advisory letter dated April 17, 1970, wherein respondents were advised that it was 'Improper to charge guests for interior calls or interior service other than through his room rent.' They were advised in the same communication that such charges should be 'included in the room rent' or 'if separately stated, should be clearly identified.'

"The respondents' plea in defense or amelioration is grossly mistaken. Of course, they could charge more for the room but it was fraudulent and deceitful to add to each billing after the room charge 'Sund's' without any explanation, itemization or identification.

"Respondents argue that there was no violation of section 206 of the General Business Law because that section only prohibits charges 'for any service not actually rendered' and that message services in fact were rendered. However, even respondents admit that all of their customers did not receive special, costly messenger service. They contend that 77% did receive such service but admit that 23% did not. None of their customers received any explanation or itemization of the charge for sundries. All of them were charged this 2% during the period in question.

"In any event, the practice was fraudulent within the meaning of subdivision 12 of section 63 of the Executive Law, wherein fraud is defined as 'any device, scheme or artifice to defraud and any deception, misrepresentation, concealment . . . or unconscionable contractual provisions.' [Citation omitted.] Although the 2% charge was discontinued after an inquiry by the petitioner, this in no way restricts the court from restraining the practice. [Citations omitted.]

" 'The business of an innkeeper is of a *quasi* public character, invested with many privileges and burdened with correspondingly great responsibilities.' [Citation omitted.] The charge for message services delineated as sundries was fraudulent and unconscionable. Accordingly, petitioner's application is granted to the extent that respondents are permanently enjoined from engaging in the fraudulent and illegal acts and practices complained of herein.

"The amount of money to be refunded is admitted. The petitioner, by its Bureau of Consumer Frauds and Protection, investigated the records of the respondents and claims that the 2% charge for sundries during the period in question involved 64,338 customers and amounts to $113,202.83. Frank A. Banks, vice-president and manager of respondent, in an affidavit of June 10, 1971, states that during the period in question transient room sales amounted to $6,329,484. The 2% charge would therefore be over $126,000. However, the exact amount is not important, as the respondents are ordered to refund to each and every customer during the period in question all charges for unexplained sundries. These refunds are to be made within 60 days of the date of service of the judgment herein with notice of entry. Within 30 days thereafter canceled vouchers of copies thereof will be exhibited to the petitioner. If payment cannot be made to any customer for any reason, the amounts thereof will be deposited with the petitioner, who will deposit same with the court if restitution cannot be made (Abandoned Property Law, § 600). Petitioner may suggest another method of creating a fund to assure restitution upon settlement of judgment, if so advised.

"If there be disagreement as to the amount involved in the restitution herein ordered, either party may submit an order at the time of settling judgment, for an assessment of damages.

"The demand for treble damages is denied. The Executive Law provides for restitution only. The General Business Law provides for treble damages to the injured parties. The injured parties may seek such punitive damages but the petitioner may only obtain restitution for them. The petitioner, in addition to one bill of costs against respondents, is granted an allowance of $2,000 against the respondent Hotel Waldorf-Astoria Corporation (CPLR 8303, subd. [a], par. 6)."

6 Legal Excuses for Failure to Receive a Guest and Right to Eject

6:1 *Refusal to Receive and Ejection in General*

Notwithstanding the innkeeper's common-law duty to admit all who apply or the provisions of the civil rights laws, there are circumstances under which an innkeeper may refuse to admit one who applies to be received as a guest or may eject one who has already been admitted as a guest.

Generally, if, after the admission of a guest, circumstances occur which would have justified the innkeeper in refusing to admit him had they existed when he applied for admission, they will equally justify the innkeeper in ejecting him. Once admitted, a guest is perhaps in a better position to demand the services of the innkeeper than when he first applied for admission, but probably this advantage is merely tactical. While the burden is on one who applies for admission to prove himself entitled to demand it, once he has been received as a guest, the burden is placed on the innkeeper to justify the act of ejecting him. But as far as substantive rights go, it is doubtful that the guest gains any by securing admission to the inn.

CAMPBELL V. WOMACK
345 So. 2d 96 (La. Ct. App. 1977)

EDWARDS, J.: "This suit was brought by Elvin Campbell and his wife for damages resulting from breach of contract and embarrassment, humiliation and mental anguish, sustained by Mrs. Campbell as a result of the defendants' refusal to admit Mrs. Campbell to her husband's motel room. The defendants' motion for summary judgment was granted and the action was dismissed. From this dismissal, plaintiffs have appealed.

"Plaintiff, Elvin Campbell, is engaged in the sand and gravel business. Since the nature of his business often requires his absence from his home in St. Francisville, Mr. Campbell generally obtains temporary accommodations in the area in which he is working. For this purpose, Mr. Campbell rented a double room on a month to month basis at the Rodeway Inn, in Morgan City, Louisiana. The room was registered in Mr. Campbell's name only.

"From time to time, Mr. Campbell would share his room with certain of his employees; in fact he obtained additional keys for the convenience of these employees. It also appears that Mr. Campbell was joined by his wife on some weekends and holidays, and that they jointly occupied his room on those occasions. However, Mrs. Campbell was not given a key to the motel room. On one such weekend, Mrs. Campbell, arriving while her husband was not at the motel, attempted to obtain the key to her husband's room from the desk clerk, Barbara Womack. This request was denied, since the desk clerk found that Mrs. Campbell was neither a registered guest for that room nor had the registered guest, her husband, communicated to the motel management, his authorization to release his room key to Mrs. Campbell. Plaintiffs allege that this refusal was in a loud, rude, and abusive manner. After a second request and refusal, Mrs. Campbell became distressed, left the Rodeway Inn, and obtained a room at another motel. Mr. Campbell later joined his wife at the other motel, and allegedly spent the weekend consoling her. Shortly thereafter, suit was filed against the motel and the desk clerk, Barbara Womack.

"Plaintiffs' main contention is that Mrs. Campbell was entitled to a key to her husband's room since she had acquired the status of a guest from her previous stays with her husband in the motel room. The leading pronouncement in Louisiana on the creation of a guest status is found in *Moody v. Kenny,* 153 La. 1007, 97 So. 21 (1923). There it is stated at page 22: ' . . . a mere guest of the registered occupant of a room at a hotel, who shares such room with its occupant without the knowledge or consent of the hotel management, would not be a guest of the hotel, as there would be no contractual relations in such case between such third person and the hotel. . . . ' Plaintiffs would have us conclude from this statement that once the motel management gained knowledge on the previous occasions that Mrs. Campbell was sharing the motel room with the registered occupant, the motel was thereafter estopped to deny Mrs. Campbell the key to that room. The fallacy of this argument is apparent, since under it even a casual visitor to a hotel guest's room would be entitled to return at a latter time and demand a key to the guest's room, so long as the hotel management had knowledge of the initial visit.

"The motel clerk was under no duty to give Mrs. Campbell, a third party, the key to one of its guest's rooms. In fact, the motel had an affirmative duty, stemming from a guest's rights of privacy and peaceful possession, not to allow unregistered and unauthorized third parties to gain access to the rooms of its guest (*cf.* LSA–C.C. art. 2965-67). This duty is the same regardless of whether we consider the contractual relationship one of lessor-lessee or motel-guest.

"The additional fact that Mrs. Campbell offered proof of her identity and her marital relation with the room's registered occupant does not alter her third-party status; nor does it lessen the duty owed by the motel to its guest. The mere fact of marriage does not imply that the wife has full authorization from her husband at all times and as to all matters, (LSA–C.C. art. 2404). Besides, how could Mrs. Campbell prove to the motel's satisfaction that the then present marital situation was amicable? This information is not susceptible of ready proof.

"Having found that Mrs. Campbell was not entitled to demand a key to the motel room, and further that no authorization to admit her was communicated to the motel by her husband, there was no breach of contract. . . .

"Affirmed."

6:2 *Refusal to Receive Guest Due to Lack of Accommodations*

When the innkeeper's accommodations are exhausted, he may refuse to receive an applicant as a guest. If all of his sleeping rooms are occupied, he need not admit a guest to sleep in a sitting room or to share the room of another, at least not in modern times. A turn-of-the-century English case describes how the concept of considering an inn "full" has changed over time.

The plaintiff has been refused admission to an inn because the inn was full. At the trial, he proved that the coffee room had been unoccupied and that there had been room without overcrowding, for him to have slept in a room with another guest. In upholding on appeal the trial court's decision in favor of defendant-innkeeper, the court said:

> No doubt an innkeeper is bound to provide accommodation for travellers, but he is not bound to do so at all risks and all costs. He is only bound to provide accommodation so long as his house is not full; when it is full he has no duty in that respect. The question then arises, when an innkeeper's house may properly be said to be full. I do not think that the old cases can help one very much, because in olden times people were in the habit of sleeping many in one room, and several in one bed. People who were absolutely unknown to each other would sleep in the same room. . . . Therefore, if we got a definition of "full" in one of the old cases, I should not be surprised to find that what was called "full" then we should now call "indecent overcrowding." It is the habit now of people to occupy separate bedrooms, and, having regard to the ordinary way of living at the present time, I think an inn may be said to be full for the purpose of affording accommodation for the night if all the bedrooms are occupied.[1]

That exhaustion of his accommodations will excuse an innkeeper in turning away prospective guests has long been recognized by American courts.[2] It might be added that any rooms held under reservations for incoming guests can be said to be occupied[3] and that rooms that are "out of order" or under repair may properly be said to be unavailable for occupancy.

6:3 *Refusal and Ejection of Persons of Objectionable Character or Condition or for Improper Conduct*

The improper conduct or objectionable character or condition of a guest or prospective guest will generally be held to be grounds for ejection or refusal to admit. This is so partially because an innkeeper has a duty to all of his guests to protect their persons and property[4] and therefore must be able to exclude persons who are likely to injure or disturb other guests. Also, the public interest which

---

[1]Browne v. Brandt, [1902] 1 K.B. 696, 698.

[2]Kisten v. Hildebrand, 48 Ky. (18 B. Mon.) 72 (1948); Jackson v. Virginia Hot Springs Co., 209 F. 479 (W.D. Va. 1913); Dold v. Outrigger Hotel, 54 Hawaii 18, 501 P.2d 368, 373 (1972) (citing with approval Browne v. Brandt).

[3]*See* Chapter 7, *infra,* on breach of reservations concerning the innkeeper's obligation to holder of such reservation if he should let the room to another applicant.

[4]*See* section 7:1, *infra.*

the law seeks to protect in imposing the duty to receive all guests would hardly be served by requiring the innkeeper to receive and accommodate undesirables.

What constitutes objectionable character or condition or improper conduct is not easily defined. As mores change over time, so do the standards of conduct which the law will consider improper. In an English case, *Regina v. Sprague*,[5] a jury acquitted an innkeeper on an indictment for refusal to entertain a woman clad in a bicycling outfit. Such a case even arising today is inconceivable—imagine the Hilton Hawaiian Village objecting to a female guest's wearing a bikini. This is not to say, however, that the management would not be justified in requiring that such attire not be worn in the main dining room.

It has been held that an innkeeper "would be entitled by way of justification [for refusal to receive] to show, if he could, that plaintiff was a card sharper, or a hotel thief, or was intoxicated, or engaged in some unlawful or immoral occupation that rendered him unfit to stay among respectable people at a respectable hotel."[6]

In *Raider v. Dixie Inn*[7] the court, in upholding an innkeeper's right to eject a common prostitute, enumerated the types of undesirable conduct which have been held to justify exclusion from an inn:

> It appears, therefore, fully settled that an innkeeper may lawfully refuse to entertain objectionable characters, if to do so is calculated to injure his business or to place himself, business, or guests in a hazardous, uncomfortable, or dangerous situation. The innkeeper need not accept anyone as a guest who is calculated to and will injure his business [citation omitted]. A prizefighter who has been guilty of law breaking may be excluded. *Nelson v. Boldt*, 180 F. 779 [E.D. Pa. 1910]. Neither is an innkeeper required to entertain a card sharp, *Watkins v. Cope*, 84 N.J.L. 143, 86 A. 545 [1913]; a thief, *Markham v. Brown*, 8 N.H. 523 [1837]; persons of bad reputation or those who are under suspicion, *Goodenow v. Travis*, 3 Johns. (N.Y.) 427 [Sup. Ct. 1808]; drunken and disorderly persons, *Atwater v. Sawyer*, 76 Me. 539 [1884]; one who commits a trespass by breaking in the door, *Goodenow v. Travis, supra;* one who is filthy or who subjects the guests to annoyance, *Pidgeon v. Legge*, 5 Week. Rep. 649, [21 J.P. 743 (Ex. 1857)].[8]

It will be noted that the cases on ejection and refusal to receive for undesirable character are quite old. This is because this question is simply not litigated today. The tendency of hotel and motel management in recent years has been one of restraint in the exclusion of "undesirables," in contrast to the policy of decades ago of employing house detectives to wander the halls, listening at doors and peeping through keyholes for signs of "immoral conduct."[9]

---

[5]63 J.P. 233 (Surrey Quarter Sessions 1899).
[6]Watkins v. Cope, 84 N.J.L. 143, 148, 86 A. 545, 548 (1913).
[7]198 Ky. 152, 248 S.W. 229 (1923).
[8]*Id.* at 154, 248 S.W. at 229–30.
[9]A number of cases cited in the first edition of this book (published in 1972) arose out of the prowlings of house detectives. They have been omitted from the present work as being of minimal relevance in modern practice, but still make interesting historical reading. *See, e.g.,* Warren v.

If the need should arise to exclude a person as undesirable, reasonableness should be used as a guide, since this is the standard which a court would employ if called upon to determine whether the exclusion was justified.

The rights of an innkeeper to effect a citizen's arrest of a patron who refused to leave the premises when informed that he was in violation of the dress code enforced in defendant's exclusive Virgin Islands night club was reviewed by the Federal Court of Appeals for the Third Circuit in *Moolenar v. Atlas Motor Inns, Inc.*[10] In an action brought for false arrest, the jury had awarded the patron both compensatory and punitive damages. The trial court had refused defendant's request to charge the jury, among other things, on the law contained in two Virgin Island statutes authorizing hotelkeepers to evict persons under certain circumstances, e.g., for intoxication, disorderly conduct, or violation of the hotel's stated rules and regulations. The trial court had ruled that the statutory authority to evict for a stated violation of house rules was limited to registered guests and not to public patrons and that defendant could arrest the patron without liability if the patron had been guilty of disorderly conduct, but not otherwise.

The circuit court held that the statutes applied to all persons, but were relevant only on the issue of the jury's finding of punitive damages, not on the issue of the hotel's liability. The court held that the statutes authorized an eviction, but not a citizen's arrest, since the latter is appropriate only for the commission of a felony or "public offense" in the hotel's presence. However, since a criminal trespass was a public offense, and the trial court failed to instruct the jury on the question whether the defendant had committed such a trespass, the case was remanded for a new trial.

6:4 *Refusal or Ejection for Inability or Refusal to Pay Innkeeper's Lawful Charges*

An innkeeper is obliged to provide accommodations "only [for] such as are capable of paying a compensation suitable to the accommodation provided."[11]

From the earliest times, the rule was that an innkeeper had the right to demand payment before furnishing accommodations. By the nineteenth century, it had become customary not to demand payment in advance,[12] though the right to do so remained.[13] In response to this practice, the law developed various mechanisms for securing payment for the innkeeper, notably the innkeeper's lien,[14] and more recently, statutes making it a crime for patrons to defraud an innkeeper of his lawful charges.[15] Also, modern credit card practices provide security for

---

Penn-Harris Hotel Co., 91 Pa. Super. 195 (1927); Boyce v. Greeley Square Hotel Co., 181 A.D. 61, 168 N.Y.S. 191 (2d Dep't 1917), *aff'd*, 228 N.Y. 106, 126 N.E. 647 (1920).

[10]616 F.2d 87 (3d Cir. 1980).

[11]Thompson v. Lacy, 3 B. & Ald. 283, 285, 106 Eng. Rep. 667 (K.B. 1820).

[12]Rex v. Ivens, 7 Car. & P. 213, 173 Eng. Rep. 94 (1835).

[13]Mulliner v. Florence, 3 Q.B.D. 484 (1878).

[14]*See* Chapter 20, *infra.*

[15]*See* Chapter 22, *infra.*

the innkeeper. However, if the management feels compelled in a particular case to demand payment before receiving a guest, it may do so without violating its duty to receive.

The hotel bill accrues and is due day by day on demand. Though again custom dictates that payment will be made upon the guest's departure, the innkeeper has a right to demand payment of charges as they accrue. The refusal of a guest to pay charges on demand constitutes a basis for ejection from the inn. The classic case on ejection for refusal to pay is *Morningstar v. Lafayette Hotel Co.*

MORNINGSTAR V. LAFAYETTE HOTEL CO.
211 N.Y. 465, 105 N.E. 656 (1914)

CARDOZO, J.: "The plaintiff was a guest at the Lafayette Hotel in the city of Buffalo. He seems to have wearied of the hotel fare, and his yearning for variety has provoked this lawsuit. He went forth and purchased some spareribs, which he presented to the hotel chef with a request that they be cooked for him and brought to his room. This was done, but with the welcome viands there came the unwelcome addition of a bill or check for $1, which he was asked to sign. He refused to do so, claiming that the charge was excessive. That evening he dined at the café, and was again asked to sign for the extra service, and again declined. The following morning, Sunday, when he presented himself at the breakfast table, he was told that he would not be served. This announcement was made publicly, in the hearing of other guests. He remained at the hotel till Tuesday, taking his meals elsewhere, and he then left. The trial judge left it to the jury to say whether the charge was a reasonable one, instructing them that it if was, the defendant had a right to refuse to serve the plaintiff further, and that if it was not, the refusal was wrongful. In this, there was no error. An innkeeper is not required to entertain a guest who has refused to pay a lawful charge. Whether the charge in controversy was excessive, was a question for the jury.

"The plaintiff says, however, that there was error in the admission of evidence which vitiates the verdict. In this we think that he is right. He alleged in his complaint that the defendant's conduct had injured his reputation. He offered no proof on that head, but the defendant took advantage of the averment to prove what the plaintiff's reputation was. A number of hotel proprietors were called as witnesses by the defendant, and under objection were allowed to prove that, in their respective hotels, the plaintiff's reputation was that of a chronic faultfinder. Some of them were permitted to say that the plaintiff was known as a 'kicker.' Others were permitted to say that his reputation was bad, not in respect of any moral qualities, but as the guest of a hotel. The trial judge charged the jury that they must find for the defendant if they concluded that the plaintiff had suffered no damage, and this evidence was received to show that he has suffered none.

"It is impossible to justify the ruling. The plaintiff, if wrongfully ejected from the café, was entitled to recover damages for injury to his feelings as a result of the humiliation [citations omitted]; but his reputation as a faultfinder was certainly not at issue. The damages recoverable for such a wrong were no less because the occupants of other hotels were of the opinion that he complained too freely. In substance, it has been held that the plaintiff might be refused damages for the insult of being put out of a public dining room because other innkeepers considered him an undesirable guest.'' [Judgment reversed and a new trial granted.]

6:5 *Eviction of Guest Who Has Overstayed Agreed Term*

An innkeeper may, particularly in times of high demand for accommodations, require that the guest agree to limit his stay to a specified period. The agreement limiting the stay should be in writing and signed by the guest, though this is not a prerequisite to an enforceable agreement. Innkeepers have adopted the practice of printing or stamping the limitation on the registration card. If this practice is followed, the limitation notice should not be in an unusually inconspicuous location or in unusually small type, since this may deprive it of legal effect if the guest is unaware of it.

The guest who overstays the agreed time limit may be required to leave. If he refuses, he may be evicted in a reasonable manner, not inflicting unnecessary injury or undue humiliation upon the guest. The usual method is to remove the guest's luggage from his room during his absence and to double-lock the door so as to deny reentry.

Even in the absence of a specific agreement limiting the term of a guest's stay, at least one court has held that, since the purpose of an inn is to serve travelers, ''a person is not entitled to stay indefinitely, and on reasonable notice may be ejected without any other reason.''[16] While this is probably the correct rule, it is advisable to set a definite period as described above, due to the inherent ambiguity of what constitutes a reasonable stay.

In some jurisdictions it is illegal for an innkeeper to evict a holdover,[17] that is, a traveler who extends his stay beyond its scheduled duration, while in others it involves a civil process similar to that used by a landlord to evict a tenant.[18] Hawaii recently enacted a statute[19] that treats a holdover much like a trespasser, and Puerto Rico requires its police to remove a holdover physically upon request by an innkeeper.[20]

---

[16]McBride v. Hosey, 197 S.W.2d 372, 374 (Tex. Civ. App. 1946).

[17]*See, e.g.,* N.Y. Real Prop. Law § 853 (McKinney 1979). *But cf.* Neely v. Lott Hotels Co., 334 Ill. App. 91, 78 N.E.2d 659 (1948) (innkeeper may evict for failure to pay, and may use whatever reasonable force is necessary); Sawyer v. Congress Square Hotel Co., 157 Me. 111, 170 A.2d 645 (1961) (guest not entitled to notice or legal process before eviction); Poroznoff v. Alberti, 161 N.J. Super. 414, 391 A.2d 984 (Dist. Ct. 1978), *aff'd,* 168 N.J. Super. 140, 401 A.2d 1124 (A. D. 1979) (innkeeper not required to resort to legal procedures when evicting guest).

[18]*See, e.g.,* Conn. Gen. Stat. Ann. § 47a-23 (West 1978).

[19]Hawaii Rev. Stat. § 486K-8 (Supp. 1978).

[20]P. R. Laws Ann. Tit. 10 § § 719, 720 (1976).

6:6 *Ejection for Illness*

If a guest at the inn becomes ill, it is the duty of the innkeeper to treat him
with the consideration due to a sick person. In the discharge of his duty, the
innkeeper may call a physician to examine the guest, and if so requested by the
guest, to treat him. Many hotels keep a doctor on call for such contingencies. If
the guest refuses treatment or medical services and if, in the opinion of the physician who examined him, the guest's condition is serious, the guest may be removed to a hospital. In the event the diagnosis is one of a contagious disease, the
guest must be moved to a hospital promptly and under medical supervision to
protect the other guests in the house and to preserve public health.

Of primary importance in dealing with an ill guest is caution and consideration for the guest's condition. The following case illustrates the kind of impru-
dent course of action which an innkeeper should carefully avoid.

McHUGH v. SCHLOSSER

159 Pa. 480, 28 A. 291 (1894)

WILLIAMS, J.: "The defendants are hotelkeepers in the city of Pittsburgh.
McHugh was their guest and died in an alley appurtenant to the hotel on the
second day of February, 1891. Mary McHugh the plaintiff is his widow, and she
seeks to recover damages for the loss of her husband, alleging that it was caused
by the improper conduct of the defendants and their employees. . . . McHugh
came to the Hotel Schlosser late on Friday night, January 30th, registered, was
assigned to and paid for a room for the night, and retired. On Saturday and Sunday he complained of being ill and remained most of both days in bed. A physician was sent for at his request, who prescribed for him. He also asked for and
obtained several drinks during the same time, and an empty bottle or bottles
remained in his room after he left it. During the forenoon of Monday he seemed
bewildered and wandered about the hall on the floor on which his room was.
About the middle of the day the housekeeper reported to Schlosser that he
[McHugh] was out of his room and sitting half dressed on the side of the bed in
another room. Schlosser and his porter both started in search of McHugh, and
Schlosser seems to have exhibited some excitement or anger. He was found and
the porter led him to his room. While this was being done Schlosser said to him
'You can't stay here any longer'; to which McHugh replied 'I'll git.' The porter,
on reaching his room, put his coat, hat and shoes on him and at once led him to
the freight elevator, put him on it, and had him let down to the ground floor. He
then took him through a door, used for freight, out into an alley some four or five
feet wide, that led to Penn avenue. Rain was falling, and the day was cold. A
stream of rain water and dissolving snow was running down the alley. McHugh
was without overshoes, overcoat or wraps of any description. When the porter
had gotten him part way down the alley he fell to the pavement. While he was
lying in the water and the porter standing near him, a lady passed along the

sidewalk on Penn avenue and saw him. She walked a square, found Officer White, and reported to him what she had seen. He went to the alley to investigate; and when he arrived McHugh had gotten to his feet, but was leaning heavily against the wall of the hotel, apparently unable to step. The porter was behind him with his hands upon him, apparently urging him forward. What followed will be best told in the officer's own words. He says: 'I asked what's the matter with this man, Mr. Powers? He says, he's sick. I says he ought to have something done for him, and at that time he fell right in the alley on his back. He had his coat open, no vest, and his shoes were untied. He had strings in his shoe, but not tied.' The officer was asked if the man spoke, after he reached the place where he was; and he replied thus: 'He spoke to me. Somebody said he was drunk. He rolled his eyes up and he says, "Officer, I am not drunk; I am sick; I wish you would get an ambulance and have me taken to the hospital." Then I ran to the patrol box.' It required about twenty minutes to get an ambulance on the ground. During all this time the man continued to lie on the pavement in the alley. At length, after an exposure of about half an hour in the storm and on the pavement, the ambulance came. He was placed on the stretcher, lifted into the ambulance and taken to police headquarters and thence to the hospital but all signs of life had disappeared when he was laid on the hospital floor. The postmortem examination disclosed the fact that the immediate cause of death was valvular disease of the heart. The theory of the plaintiff was that the shock from exposure to wet and cold in the alley had, in his feeble and unprotected condition, brought on the heart failure from which he died; and as the exposure resulted from the conduct or directions of the defendants, they were responsible for his death.

"Three principal questions were thus raised: First, what duty does an inn keeper owe to his guest? Second, what connection was there between the defendant's disregard of their duty, if they did disregard it in any particular, and the death of Mr. McHugh? Third, if the plaintiff be entitled to recover, what is the measure of her damages?

" . . . [As to the first of these questions the trail judge, in charging the jury, had stated the rule thus:] 'If [the annoying acts] . . . were the result of sickness, although they might under certain circumstances remove him, such removal must be in a manner suited to his condition.' This was saying that if McHugh was intoxicated, and the disturbances made by him were due to his intoxication, he might be treated as a drunken man; but if he was sick, and the disturbances caused by him were due to his sickness, he must be treated with the consideration due to a sick man. This is a correct statement of the rule. In the delirium of a fever a sick man may become very troublesome to a hotelkeeper, and his groans and cries may be annoying to the occupants of rooms near him, but this would not justify turning him forcibly from his bed into the street during a winter storm. What the condition of the decedent really was, went properly to the jury for determination. If they found the fact to be that he was suffering from sickness, then the learned judge properly said that, if his removal was to be undertaken, it should be conducted in a manner suited to one in his condition.

"[Second] . . . The question which the defendants were bound to consider before putting the decedent out in the storm, was not whether such exposure 'would' surely cause death, but what was it reasonable to suppose might follow such a sudden exposure of the decedent in the condition in which he then was? What were the probable consequences of pushing a sick man, in the condition the decedent was in, out into the storm without adequate covering, and when he fell from inability to stand on his feet, leaving him to lie in the stream of melting ice and snow that ran over the pavement of the alley, for about half an hour in all, in the condition in which officer White found him?

"[Third] . . . The true measure of damages is the pecuniary loss suffered, without any solatium for mental suffering or grief; and the pecuniary loss is what the deceased would probably have earned by his labor, physical or intellectual, in his business or profession, if the injury that caused death had not befallen him, and which would have gone to the support of his family. In fixing this amount, consideration should be given to the age of the deceased, his health, his ability and disposition to labor, his habits of living and his expenditures." [Judgment for plaintiff reversed and a new trial ordered, limited solely to the issue of recoverable damages.]

The innkeeper's right to evict a guest for cause extends to restaurant and bar patrons as well. It has been held that it is the duty of a restaurant keeper to accord protection to his patrons from insult or annoyance while they are in his restaurant. In putting a stop to the annoyance, he may eject the person guilty of the offense and in so doing may use all necessary force.[21]

6:7 Ejection of Unauthorized Intruders: Criminal Trespass

The modern inn is not only a home for the traveler away from home; it is a center for community affairs, social and business functions, exhibits, conferences, entertainment, a magnet that attracts people from all walks of life, desirable and undesirable as well. Among the undesirables are the daily intruders, who, in the mistaken belief that the inn is a public house open to all, arrogate to themselves the right to remain in the public areas of the house without invitation or permission and challenge the innkeeper to put them out.

A person who, regardless of his intent, enters or remains in or upon premises which are at the time open to the public does so with license and privilege unless he defies a lawful order not to enter or remain, personally communicated to him by the owner of such premises or other authorized person. A license or privilege to enter or remain in a building which is only partly open to the public is not a license or privilege to enter or remain in that part of the building which is not open to the public.

The innkeeper in possession or control of the premises of the inn, is justified in using physical force upon an intruder when and to the extent that he reason-

---

[21]Chase v. Knabel, 46 Wash. 484, 90 P. 642 (1907).

ably believes it necessary to prevent or terminate the commission or attempted commission of a criminal trespass in or upon the premises.

It would seem important to limit the application of the foregoing to those undesirables whose presence in the inn is or may become harmful to the guests or to the security of the house. In this class are any known prostitutes who find hotel lobbies favorite places of resort and the class of obnoxious persons known as "lobby lizards" who spend nothing but time at the inn (*see* section 14:1, *infra*). If, after a polite but firm request to leave, any such undesirable individual persists in remaining in the inn, police assistance may be called, and an arrest on a complaint may be made. Of course, the innkeeper or his security officer should, whenever possible, consult legal counsel before making an arrest. In the same vein, hiring off-duty law enforcement officers to police restaurant premises and enforce house rules prohibiting overstays by patrons may be risky. The court's dismissal of the criminal complaint in *People on Information of Fanelli v. Doe*[22] invites a civil action for false arrest, and if the officer acts in a private capacity for his employer, the employer could be held liable.

The following case illustrates the principle that even the constitutional right of free speech does not immunize the news media from a claimed trespass upon restaurant premises.

Le Mistral, Inc. v. Columbia Broadcasting
61 A.D.2d 491, 402 N.Y.S.2d 815 (1st Dep't 1978)

Lupiano, J.: "Defendant Columbia Broadcasting System in its capacity as owner and operator of Television Channel 2 in New York, on July 6, 1972, directed defendant Lucille Rich, its employee, and a camera crew to visit a number of restaurants which had been cited for health code violations by the Health Services Administration of New York City. Plaintiff restaurant was on the list. The camera crew and Ms. Rich entered the restaurant at approximately 2:00 P.M. with the camera working ('rolling'), which necessitated the utilization of bright lights for filming purposes. After entering the premises in this fashion, Ms.Rich and the camera crew were commanded to leave by plaintiff's president. It appears that these CBS employees were on the premises for a period of time during which the camera continued to roll. Plaintiff, insofar as its action for trespass is concerned, was awarded compensatory and punitive damages by a jury. The trial court on defendant CBS's motion upheld the jury verdict in finding that the conduct of this defendant constituted a trespass, but set aside the damage awards.

"Initially, we are confronted with defendant CBS's claim that despite the tort committed, defendant is insulated from any damage award by virtue of the First Amendment to the United States Constitution. Clearly, the First Amendment is not a shibboleth before which all other rights must succumb. This Court 'recognizes that the exercise of the right of free speech and free press demands and

---

[22]85 Misc. 2d 592, 380 N.Y.S.2d 549 (1976).

even mandates the observance of the co-equal duty not to abuse such right, but to utilize it with right reason and dignity. Vain lip service to ''duties'' in a vacuous reality wherein ''rights'' exist, sovereign and independent of any balancing moral or social factor creates a semantical mockery of the very foundation of our laws and legal system' (*Bavarian Motor v. Manchester*, 61 Misc. 2d 309, 311, 305 N.Y.S.2d 593, 596). In *Dietemann v. Time, Inc.*, 449 F.2d 245, 249 (9th Cir. 1971), it was observed that '[t]he First Amendment has never been construed to accord newsmen immunity from torts or crimes committed during the course of news-gathering. The First Amendment is not a license to trespass. . . .' Similarly, the Second Circuit Court of Appeals in *Galella v. Onassis*, 487 F.2d 986, 995–996, stated: 'Crimes and torts committed in news gathering are not protected. [Citations omitted.] *See* Restatement of Torts 2d § 652(f), comment K (Tent. Draft No. 13, 1967). There is no threat to a free press in requiring its agents to act within the law.'

''Scrutiny of the record demonstrates an adequate basis to justify the compensatory damage award rendered by the jury and, accordingly, such award must stand. Regarding punitive damages, it is well recognized that such damages 'are penal in their nature and are different, both in nature and purpose, from compensatory damages. Such damages are allowed in addition to compensatory damages, and are awarded upon public consideration as a punishment of the defendant for the wrong in the particular case, and for the protection of the public against similar acts, to deter the defendant from a repetition of the wrongful act, and to serve as a warning to others' (14 N.Y. Jur., *Damages* § 176). 'As a general rule, exemplary damages are recoverable in all actions *ex delicto* based upon tortious acts which involve ingredients of malice, fraud, oppression, insult, wanton or reckless disregard of the plaintiff's rights, or other circumstances of aggravation, as a punishment of the defendant and admonition to others. . . . Punitive damages have been allowed in actions for trespass. . . . ' (14 N.Y. Jur., *supra*, § 180). The award of punitive damages under circumstances warranting the allowance of same rests in the discretion of the jury, or in the court where the case is tried without a jury. The basis for an award of exemplary damages depends upon a showing that the wrong is aggravated by evil or a wrongful motive or that there was wilful and intentional misdoing, or a reckless indifference equivalent thereto.

''The trial court in setting aside the jury award of punitive damages, did so because of its exclusion of certain testimony by defense witness Dessartz relevant to defendant CBS's motive and purpose in entering the plaintiff's premises unannounced 'with cameras rolling.' The court noted: 'As punitive damage involves malice, evidence of motivation and purpose are admissible, at least in mitigation of damages.' As recovery of punitive damages depends upon the defendant acting with evil or wrongful motive or with a wilful and intentional misdoing, or with a reckless indifference equivalent thereto, '(a)ll . . . circumstances immediately connected with the transaction tending to exhibit or explain the motive of the defendant are admissible' (14 N.Y. Jur., *supra*, § 189).

Defendant CBS was entitled to demonstrate and explain its motive and the curtailment of this right by the trial court mandates re-trial of the punitive damage issue.

"Accordingly, the order of the Supreme Court, New York County, entered January 19, 1977 which vacated the jury's award of $1,200 in compensatory damages and $250,000 in punitive damages and directed a new trial on the issue of damages, should be modified, on the law, to the extent of reinstating the jury's award of compensatory damages, severing the claim to punitive damages and remanding the matter for a trial on the issue of punitive damages, and as so modified, should be affirmed, without costs and without disbursements."

MURPHY, P.J. (dissenting in part): "While I agree with the majority that defendant CBS committed a trespass and is accountable in compensatory damages therefor, I would not award punitive damages on the particular facts in this case. It is clear from the record that, in dispatching reporters to plaintiff restaurant, defendant was not motivated by actual malice or such an intentional disregard of plaintiff's rights as would justify the imposition of punitive damages (87 C.J.S. *Trespass* § 112, p. 1068). The defendant was merely pursuing a newsworthy item in the overly aggressive but good faith manner that characterizes the operation of the news media today. To the date of this opinion, it may be safely said that the news media has rarely been taken to task for the type of unwarranted intrusion presented in this proceeding. (*See generally,* 28 A.L.R. Fed. 904, *First Amendment as Immunizing Newsman from Liability for Tortious Conduct While Gathering News*). In this sensitive and evolving First Amendment area, I would permit this precedent-setting opinion to stand as a warning to all news gatherers that future trespasses may well be met with an award of punitive damages. [Citation omitted.]"

7 Liability for Failure to Honor Reservations

7:1 *Responsibility at Common Law*

One of the historical foundations felt to support the common-law doctrine of nondiscriminatory accommodations was the accepted fact of life that the medieval traveler had to have access to a place of safety, in particular after dark, in order to avoid being robbed or molested or worse by criminal highwaymen who made travel perilous after nightfall. This reality was said to justify the innkeeper's duty at common law to accommodate, without discrimination, all travelers who presented themselves at the inn in a fit condition, that is, able to pay for their lodging and other amenities.[1]

Surely today the vast growth of a great variety of highway hostelries and the concomitant decline in highway crimes no longer justifies the doctrine's historical antecedents. Yet the doctrine persists.

Contrast this doctrine with the duty owed the traveler who, in advance of arrival, has confirmed his reservation by payment in advance of his first night's room charge. It is in this narrower area that the innkeeper should indeed be admonished to honor his end of the bargain by providing the guest with the service which both innkeeper and guest agreed upon—a clear manifestation of the meeting of the minds of the parties. And it is here where the law has made inroads by insisting that both parties maintain their bargain. This is most notably the case in regard to the innkeeper; as yet the guest's countervailing responsibility has not received definitive treatment.

As noted previously, the public duty of the innkeeper at common law was to accommodate all persons who apply for admission as guests unless reasonable grounds exist for refusing to do so.[2] The considerations of public policy which the courts have fashioned to support this uniform rule are well stated by Professor Wyman in his article *The Law of the Public Callings as a Solution to the Trust Problem:* "[I]n public business (in contrast to private callings), one must serve all who apply without exclusive conditions, provide adequate facilities to

---

This chapter reproduces in part my article "Innkeeper's Liability for Failure to Honor Reservations" from the May 1974 *Cornell Hotel and Restaurant Administration Quarterly,* with permission from the Cornell University School of Hotel Administration, © 1974.

[1]*See* section 1:3, *supra.*
[2]*See* Chapter 6, *supra.*

[154]

meet all the demands of the consumer, exact only reasonable charges for the services that are rendered and between customers under similar circumstances make no discriminations."[3]

7:2 A Reservation as a Contractual Obligation

No less an authority than Williston admits that the innkeeper-guest relationship is essentially consensual, but not necessarily contractual. Williston states:[4] "The obligations of an innkeeper arising from the common-law relation of innkeeper and guest are imposed by law irrespective of contract, and may arise when no contract is or can be made. There is, nevertheless, frequently a contract between the parties fixing the terms of their relation within the limits which the law permits."

Since most authorities agree that the duties stemming from this relation can be implied from law, little reference is made as to whether a reservation is treated as a contractual obligation, with attendant duties imposed upon both innkeeper and guest. Williston continues, "it is not often material to determine whether the obligation is imposed not only by virtue of general public policy, but also by virtue of mutual assent."

Courts have recognized the validity of a contract to provide hotel accommodations and have granted recovery for breach of reservation on the theory of contract.[5] In *Kellogg v. Commodore Hotel*[6] the parties entered into a written contract for hotel accommodations. The defendant hotel, for value received, promised to provide the plaintiff with a room for four days. Upon defendant's refusal to honor this contract, made two weeks in advance, the plaintiff recovered $5,000 for the extra expenses caused by the defendant's cancellation of the contract.

In *Thomas v. Pick Hotels Corporation*,[7] the plaintiffs, who were black, were refused hotel accommodations because of their race. The defendant hotel had previously agreed in writing and later by telephone to provide the plaintiffs lodging on a specified date.

The court held that plaintiffs' complaint, based on such facts, stated a claim on an express written contract. The plaintiffs' reservations were held to constitute a contractual obligation. By refusing to honor this reservation, the hotel breached that contract. The *Thomas* court stated that there was no statutory, common-law, or public policy barrier preventing the parties from entering into a valid and enforceable contract for hotel accommodations. In fact, the common law and the Kansas Civil Rights statute sanctioned such a contract.

[3]17 Harv. L. Rev. 156 (1903).
[4]Williston on Contracts, § 1070.
[5]*See, e.g.*, Kellogg v. Commodore Hotel, 187 Misc. 319, 64 N.Y.S.2d 131 (Sup. Ct. 1946); Thomas v. Pick Hotels Corp., 224 F.2d 604 (7th Cir. 1955); Dold v. Outrigger Hotel, 54 Hawaii 18, 501 P.2d 368 (1972).
[6]187 Misc. 319, 64 N.Y.S.2d 131 (Sup. Ct. 1946).
[7]224 F.2d 604 (7th Cir. 1955).

The Supreme Court of Hawaii has recognized the validity of a reservation contract in *Dold v. Outrigger Hotel*.[8] Here, the plaintiffs made their reservations through a third party, the American Express Company. It was the hotel's policy that a reservation was deemed to be confirmed when a deposit was paid or when the reservation was made by a booking agent that had established credit with the Outrigger Hotel. In lieu of a deposit, the hotel accepted the American Express Company's guarantee that it should pay the first night's deposit if the plaintiffs failed to show up. The hotel claimed that the reservations were not "confirmed." The court awarded damages to the plaintiffs for breach of contract. The plaintiffs were refused lodging because there was no available space at the hotel.

Under such circumstances, the court agreed that an innkeeper was not liable on his common-law duty to accommodate. But such circumstances did not relieve the hotel from its contractual duties. The concurring opinion in the Hawaii case supports the finding of contractual liability: " . . . I encounter no difficulty in finding that a contract for accommodations existed between the parties. Furthermore, I construe the contract as including both an aesthetic expectation on the part of the plaintiffs and a particular type of accommodation, namely, one in a hotel located on the beach as is the Outrigger."

In *Dold*, the hotel referred the plaintiffs to a less expensive hotel not located on the beach. The record revealed that during the week in question, February 15–22, the Outrigger made 134 referrals to the less expensive Pagoda Hotel. Ordinarily, the Outrigger made a profit on these referrals. (*Dold* is discussed further in section 7:8, *infra*.)

Although these three courts recognized the existence of a contract based on prior hotel reservations, the cases shed little light on what are the necessary elements of such a reservation contract. There is a suggestion in all of the cases that "confirmation" is a key element.

As a result, a reservation will be treated as a contract when there can be found an offer and an acceptance. The necessary consideration is supplied by the guest's confirmation of the reservation in compliance with the hotel's policy, for example, payment of a deposit.

In support of the argument that confirmation is a necessary element of a reservation's being treated as a contract, it is well to note the unreported case of Judge Kadela. The judge and his family had confirmed reservations at the New York Statler Hilton. When the reservations were not honored, the judge and his family staged a sit-in in the hotel's dining room. Later, the judge sued the hotel for $3 million. The case was settled out of court for a fraction of the amount requested.

The fact that the judge even attempted to bring suit supports the argument that a reservation will be treated as a contract when confirmed. Had the judge's reservations not been "confirmed," perhaps his counsel would not have advised

[8]501 P.2d 368 (Hawaii 1972).

him to bring suit, despite the adverse publicity which the judge undoubtedly wanted to bring upon the hotel.

The question arises whether a guest or patron may sue to compel specific performance of a function contract in lieu of an action to recover damages arising out of its breach by the innkeeper. A negative answer was rendered by a New York trial court in *Vincent, Berg, Russo, Marcigliano & Zawacki v. Americana of New York*,[9] for the reason that substitute performance was readily available, making damages the appropriate remedy:

> This is a motion by plaintiffs for a mandatory temporary injunction requiring defendants specifically to perform an agreement renting to them the Americana suite as [*sic*] the Americana Hotel for the evening of May 5–6, 1978.
>
> The Maritime Law Association is holding its annual dinner at the Americana Hotel on the evening of May 5, 1978. Plaintiffs, who are members of the Association, invited clients to attend the dinner, and contemplated a reception for them. Accordingly, they sought to and, by telephone and letter dated March 20, 1978, did make the reservation. On that day a check in payment for the rental of the suite was forwarded to the hotel. The hotel deposited the check on March 24 and by letter dated April 3 confirmed the reservation.
>
> At or about the same time, the hotel, through some inadvertence, took the reservation of another law firm for the same suite. That reservation was confirmed by the hotel's letter of March 23. Based upon priority in confirmation dates, the hotel has decided to honor the reservation of the other law firm.
>
> There are a number of reasons why the injunction sought cannot be granted. To begin with, we [were] asked to adjudicate the rights of a party—the law firm whose reservation the hotel has decided to honor—in the absence of that law firm. More importantly, however, the injuries resulting from the breach of the contract sought to be specifically enforced is compensable in damages. Thus, the intervention of equity is unwarranted. Finally, plaintiffs have not established the clear legal right necessarily incident to the relief sought by them.
>
> Under all the circumstances, and without prejudice to plaintiffs' right to pursue their action for damages, the motion is denied.

In *Barton v. Wonderful World Travel, Inc.*,[10] a hotelkeeper's failure to inform both a travel agent and a hotel guest holding a confirmed reservation of changed accommodations after a reserved room had become unavailable constituted negligence. In this case the guest found the promised Florida accommodations to be nonexistent, because the hotel was closed, chained, and guarded.

7.3 Requirements of Contract Formation

Generally the elements outlined below are required to form a *legally binding agreement*, which is the basic definition of a contract. The *Restatement of Con-*

[9]179 N.Y.L.J. 82 (Sup. Ct. N.Y. Co., Mar. 28, 1978).
[10]28 Ohio Misc. 2d 6,502 N.E.2d 715 (Ohio Mun. Ct. 1986).

tracts (2d ed. 1964), section 1 expands that basic definition as follows: "A contract is a promise or set of promises for the breach of which the law gives a remedy, or the performance of which the law in some way recognizes as a duty."

The first requirement is that of agreement, meaning the existence of two or more parties who are legally competent to enter into a contractual agreement who have consented to do so voluntarily. It is not necessary that the minds of the parties meet; it is sufficient that from all objective manifestations, determined objectively, not from the secret or unexpressed intentions of the parties, that a contract was intended. Consent is usually expressed orally or, in commercial dealings, by signing a written document setting out all the terms and conditions agreed upon. However, a party who signs a contract without reading it is not excused from performing his or her promises. The fact that the party signing did not read the contract or read it carelessly in no way relieves the signing party of liability. A contract is presumed valid until the contrary is established. Therefore a party who does not understand the contract should seek legal advice before executing it.

Reaching agreement is preceded by negotiation or dickering until all terms are agreed upon. Normally, the offeror makes an offer to the party with whom the offeror wishes to do business. Since an offer, once accepted, creates a contractual obligation, the common law requires that the offer be (1) definite and (2) communicated to the intended party. If the offer is vague or indefinite, it will not create a contract upon acceptance, and thereby permits the other party to avoid performing it. In this regard, see *Hotel Del Coronado Corp. v. Food Service Equipment Distributors Ass'n*,[11] dealing with the definiteness of reservation convention prices, a topic also noted at section 7:9.

Like the offeror, the offeree, the party to whom the offer is made, must accept the offer according to its terms. Any acceptance that does not meet this requirement will be treated as a counteroffer, which will not result in a contract unless the offeror treats it as a new offer, which the offeror may accept or reject.

At this point, it is important to note that the common law of contracts with which we have been dealing has been modified by the Uniform Commercial Code (UCC), which liberalizes some of the strict requirements of offer and acceptance, as well as other matters. However, the UCC generally applies to sales of goods, not services. Thus the common law governs real estate, employment, and other service transactions, whereas the UCC governs sales of personal property such as hotel inventory and other purchase items of tangible movable property.

The next requirement is that the contract must be supported by consideration; that is, it must be a bargained-for agreement. There must be an exchange of promises to do or not to do something in exchange for promises to do or not to do something in return. In commercial dealings we normally associate consideration with money (i.e., a person seeking accommodation at a hotel pays in advance by a one-night deposit if that is what the innkeeper requires to guarantee

---

[11]783 F.2d 1323 (9th Cir. 1986).

the reservation for future arrival), but consideration may also be valid by the exchange of mutual promises, even in the absence of money changing hands. Such was the case in *Hotel Del Coronado Corp. v. Food Service Equipment Distributors Ass'n,* noted above. In that case the reservation was not accompanied by a money deposit or credit card, but merely by agreement to show at the time and place agreed upon. In such a case the reservation is confirmed, with the understanding that the reservation is good only if the party takes it up at the time and date agreed upon. If the party fails to do so, the innkeeper is free to terminate the confirmation and rent the room to another.

The next requirement is that the contract must be legal in purpose and in method of performance. This means, among other things, that the contract does not restrain one's right to earn a living, or does not by its terms exonerate or excuse a party's liability for personal injuries that normally would be legal rights available to the other party. Such contract provisions may or may not be enforceable, depending upon whether or not the law finds them against public policy. For example, courts generally will not permit an innkeeper to exonerate himself from liability for his gross negligence or malicious or reckless conduct injuring a guest. But some states will allow the innkeeper and guest to agree to exonerate the innkeeper for liability arising out of his ordinary negligence.

An otherwise enforceable contract may be set aside if the parties' consent has been obtained by fraud, mistake, duress, or undue influence. Fraud is the most likely avenue a party will use to avoid performance of a contract or to sue to set aside a contract or to recover damages. Fraud essentially is a material misrepresentation of fact intended to induce and which does induce the other party to justifiably rely upon that fact to his or her detriment. Where fraud is established, the innocent party may recover punitive or exemplary damages in addition to purely compensatory damages.[12]

Another, less-frequent, requirement is that the contract must be in writing to be enforceable. Normally the lack of a writing does not affect contract enforcement. Many deals are sealed by a handshake or over the phone. However, a number of contracts must be in writing or may be overturned if the party against whom the contract is sought to be enforced did not sign a written document. The most important of these is real estate contracts and contracts not to be performed within one year of their execution. The case to follow illustrates this issue as well as questions of good faith and fair dealing to which all parties to a contract must comply.

An unsuccessful seller of a hotel sued the purchaser, others, and purchasers' alleged partners to recover for breach of contract, negligent and intentional misrepresentation, breach of covenant of good faith and fair dealings, and unfair business practices. In the following case, the court dealt with these and the issue of the validity of the liquidated damages clause raised by plaintiff. (All other issues are omitted from the extract.)

[12]See Reinah Development Corp. v. Kaaterskill Hotel Corp., 59 N.Y.2d 482, 452 N.E.2d 1238 (1983), also noted at section 7.7, *infra.*

KONA HAWAIIAN ASSOCIATES V. THE PACIFIC GROUP
680 F. Supp. 1438 (U.S.D.C. Hawaii 1988)

2. Liquidated Damages Clause

LETTS, D.J.: " . . . In opposition to the merits of this motion, KHA [Kona Hawaiian Associates] states that the parties did not intend the liquidated damages clause to be included in the Purchase Agreement as extended by the extension agreements and that, even if it were included, it is unenforceable under Hawaii law.

"a. Contract Interpretation: The construction and legal effect of a document is a question of law for the Court. *Hanagami v. China Airlines, Ltd.,* 67 Hawaii 357, 688 P.2d 1139, 1144 (1984). Determining whether or not the document is ambiguous is also a question of law. *Id.; Bishop Trust Co., Ltd. v. Central Union Church of Honolulu,* 3 Hawaii App. 624, 656 P.2d 1353, 1356 (1983). The interpretation of any ambiguity and intent, however, lies within the province of the jury. *Bishop Trust Co.,* 656 P.2d at 1356.

"KHA attempts to preclude summary judgment by raising the issue of the parties' intent to be bound by the liquidated damages clause, thus claiming that the contract is ambiguous. The extrinsic evidence presented by KHA, however, does not render ambiguous the clear language of the various agreements. There are three separate agreements which purport to set forth the buyer's contract obligations to KHA as the seller of the Hotel. The DROA [Deposit, Receipt, Offer, and Acceptance] and Purchase Agreement both contained the same liquidated damages clause. Both provided that if Pacific failed to close the transaction, the $400,000 deposited with KHA would be retained as liquidated damages and the parties waived all other remedies. Both clauses unambiguously and expressly set forth the $400,000 was the exclusive remedy available to KHA for breach.

"Moreover, the liquidated damages clauses are entirely consistent with the remainder of the agreements. Neither the DROA nor the Purchase Agreement contained any representations about the financial condition of the Pacific defendants, of the ability of Pacific to close the transaction, or of the ability of Pacific to respond in damages for any failure on their part to meet their obligations. These agreements required only that Pacific was to deliver a non-refundable sum of $400,000 by April 15, 1985 in order to secure the *right* to close the transaction, and that in order to close, Pacific was required to deliver the balance of the purchase price, or lose the $400,000. The clear intent and legal impact of these documents was that Pacific acquired for $400,000 an option to purchase the Hotel which, if not exercised, would cause it to be the option purchase price.

"The transaction did not close on the date stated. KHA retained the deposit money, subsequently transferred it to the Bishop Estate for its continued forebearance on the First Mortgage. In the June 9 Extension, the parties extended the closing date to July 31, 1985, provided that Pacific would be responsible for KHA's costs in contemplation of closing. The June 9 Extension also provided that *if* closing was extended further, the purchase price would be increased by net operating losses.

"KHA argues that this extension demonstrates that it was contemplated that damage remedies would be reinstated if the transaction did not close on July 31, 1985. In fact, however, the extension demonstrates just the opposite. The DROA and Purchase Agreement *never* contemplated a damage remedy. Accordingly, there was no such remedy to reinstate. . . .

"The documents are unambiguous and consistent. They make no reference whatsoever to any notion that the remedies which were expressly waived in the liquidated damages provision were ever reinstated. Accordingly, KHA is only entitled by contract to the initial $400,000 deposit which it has already received and any costs in contemplation of closing as provided in the June 9 Extension.

"b. Enforceability of the Provision: KHA argues that under Hawaii law, the liquidated damages clause is unenforceable as a penalty. Hawaii law is clear that a liquidated damages clause that constitutes a penalty will not be enforced. If the breach was not in bad faith, the nonbreaching party may be required to return any amount in excess of what is reasonably related to the its damages. *Ventura v. Grace*, 3 Hawaii App. 327, 650 P.2d 620, 622–23 (1982); *Gomez v. Pagaduan*, 1 Hawaii App. 70, 613 P.2d 658, 661–62 (1980). . . .

"KHA in essence sold Pacific an option to purchase the Hotel for a price of $400,000. This price is approximately 10% of the roughly $4,000,000 value which is ascribed to the KHA equity by the Purchase Agreement. The option created by the Purchase Agreement reflected the product of arm's length bargaining. KHA retained full freedom to negotiate with other parties for the sale of the property if the option were not exercised. Were the property worth the purchase price, so that other buyers could be readily found, upon failure by Pacific to exercise the option, KHA could have sold the property to another party and kept the $400,000. That KHA was unable to find another buyer at any acceptable price strongly suggests that $15,000,000 was a seller's price. It all the more suggests the basic option nature of the Purchase Agreement. For that option, the $400,000 option price was not a bargain.

"The Purchase Agreement made clear on its face that there was doubt about Pacific's ability to raise financing. Both parties bargained for the liquidated damages clause. KHA, which still retained both the property and the deposit at the time of breach cannot now be heard to complain that its estimate was too low and that Pacific, which never claimed the financial wherewithall to close the Purchase Agreement should now be required to do so. The parties had the chance to modify the clause and did not do so.

"In sum, KHA will be held to its own initial estimate of damages. The liquidated damages clause is enforceable and remained in effect without modification. The damages on KHA's breach of contract claim are thereby limited to $400,000.

3. Scope of Clause

"Finally, KHA asserts that, if in effect and enforceable, the liquidated damages clause precludes a suit for damages only on the contract causes of action. Here, KHA is correct. The clause is unambiguous and waives damages for breach of contract. A waiver of the parties' right to recover for the torts of negligent or intentional misrepresentation cannot be inferred absent some evidence supporting that interpretation. Further, such a disclaimer of tort liability would be construed strictly and would be required to state explicitly on its face a limitation of tort liability for negligence and will not be interpreted to cover intentional torts. *See* Prosser, Dobbs, Keeton, and Owen, Prosser and Keeton on Torts 484 (5th Ed. 1984).

"Accordingly, the liquidated damages clause prohibits KHA from recovering damages in excess of $400,000 for its breach of contract claim only. The tort causes of action remain unaffected as to the damages actually incurred after the date of any misrepresentation or omissions which can be proven at trial.

B. Statute of Frauds

"The USHP [United States Hotel Properties] defendants also contend in this motion that the statute of frauds bars proof of the alleged oral partnership agreement between the USHP defendants and Pacific to acquire an equity interest in the Hotel. The Court agrees.

"As previously indicated, all parties to the negotiations concerning the transaction in question were represented by competent counsel who understood sophisticated transaction documentation. Counsel demonstrated in the DROA that they knew how to draft a document which temporarily bound the parties pending the drafting of a more detailed agreement. Counsel demonstrated in the Purchase Agreement that they knew how to draft a detailed binding agreement for the purchase of property. They demonstrated in the June 9 Extension that they knew how to draft binding agreements in letter form which include express statements as to what is *agreed* between the parties. Finally, they showed in the Letter Understanding that they could draft a document which avoided the use of the words "agree" and "agreement" and used words such as "understanding" and "approved" to signify that the letter represented no more than an expression of nonbinding understandings rather than a legally binding contract.

"The suggestion that parties to a negotiation of a multi-million dollar contract, all represented by competent counsel, intended to become bound to an oral contract without any signed documentation to reflect it, demeans beyond recognition the important role which transaction lawyers play in our society and the protections which they afford for which their clients, quite willingly, pay very handsome fees. Courts must not confuse agreements in principle or understandings reached before transaction lawyers are called upon to draft legal agreements with those agreements that are legally binding. To do so would seriously destroy the process by which transaction lawyers and their clients arrive at legally binding agreements.

"Hawaii's statute of frauds requires that any contract for an interest in land and any authority for the signing party to buy land be in writing. Hawaii Rev. Stat. Section 656–1. In the case here, KHA cannot enforce the USHP defendants' alleged oral promise to purchase the Hotel for two reasons. First, the USHP defendants are not signatories to the Purchase Agreement or any of the extensions. Under the statute of frauds, KHA cannot do so without some *writing* evidencing the agreement signed by the party to be charged, USHP. Hawaii Rev. Stat. Section 656–1.

"Second, while partnership agreements in general do not have to be in writing to be enforced, the alleged partnership agreement between Pacific and the USHP defendants contemplated only the transfer of a specific piece of land. It is not alleged that there was ever an intent to form a general partnership in which Pacific and any USHP defendant would go into the general business of buying and selling real estate. Under Hawaii law, therefore, because the writing contemplating transfer of the land, the partnership agreement here, must be in writing. *Honolulu Memorial Park, Inc. v. City and County of Honolulu,* 50 Hawaii 189, 436 P.2d 207 (1967); *Harrison v. Bruns,* 10 Hawaii 395 (1896).

"This is almost a paradigm case, for application of the statute of frauds. This is not a case in which there are no documents. The oral contract which is urged to exist between Pacific and the USHP defendants is wholly inconsistent with the copious paper trail produced by the lawyers who represented the parties in this transaction. In the view of the Court, the documents presented for purposes of these motions go far toward proving the USHP defendants' assertions that they did not enter into any contract with anyone for the purchase of the Hotel. Even Smith's November Notes and December Notes evidence different deals, if they evidence any deal at all. This suggests that the parties present knew that no deal had solidified and that no one expected to become bound to any specific contract which was not drafted and reviewed by counsel, and executed by the parties.

"Accordingly, KHA and Pacific may not attempt to enforce an oral agreement to buy land against the USHP defendants. The USHP defendants' motions for summary judgment as to these breach of contract claims are therefore granted.

C. KHA's Fifth Claim for Relief: Breach of the Covenant of Good Faith and Fair Dealing

"The USHP defendants request summary judgment as to KHA's fifth claim for relief, breach of duty of good faith and fair dealing. Here, the Court holds that KHA does not have a claim for breach of duty of good faith and fair dealing against the USHP defendants.

"Courts interpreting the law of Hawaii have been reluctant to recognize claims for breach of an implied covenant of good faith and fair dealing. Even if this Court were to apply the reasoning of the jurisdictions which do imply a covenant of good faith, KHA's claim here still would fail. In California, for example, the covenant of good faith and fair dealing is implied into every contract. *Crisci v. Security Ins. Co.,* 66 Cal. 2d 425, 58 Cal. Rptr. 13, 426 P.2d 173 (1967). As discussed above, however, there is no binding contract between KHA and the USHP defendants from which to imply a covenant of good faith.

"Furthermore, even in California, where courts have held that a *tort* claim for breach of the covenant of good faith also may exist, in order to establish such a claim, a "special relationship" must be present between the parties to the contract. *See Seaman's Direct Buying Service, Inc. v. Standard Oil Company of*

California, 36 Cal. 3d 752, 768–69, 686 P.2d 1158, 206 Cal. Rptr. 354 (1984). Because the courts of Hawaii are reluctant to imply a covenant of good faith in situations where a contract exists, *see Parnar,* 65 Hawaii at 377, 652 P.2d 625, this Court, applying Hawaii law, will not imply a *tort* claim in a situation where no contract exists.

"Accordingly, KHA's fifth claim for relief against the USHP defendants fails and the USHP defendants' motion for summary judgment as to this claim is granted.

D. KHA's Sixth Claim for Relief: Unfair and Deceptive Business Practice

"The USHP defendants also request summary judgment as to KHA's unfair and deceptive business practice claim. The Court grants this motion.

"In order to state a claim under Hawaii Revised Statutes Section 480–13, a plaintiff must establish either that: (1) the defendants are "merchants"; or (2) the plaintiff's suit against the defendants is in the public interest. *See Island Tobacco Co. v. R.J. Reynolds,* 63 Hawaii 289, 301, 627 P.2d 260 (1981); *Ai v. Frank Huff Agency, Ltd.,* 61 Hawaii 607, 607 P.2d 1304 (1980).

"The USHP defendants here are not "merchants" within the meaning of Chapter 480. In order to be a merchant, a person must be a dealer in goods or services which are the subject of the transaction challenged as an unfair and deceptive practice. *Ailetcher v. Beneficial Finance Co. of Hawaii,* 2 Hawaii App. 301, 632 P.2d 1071, 1075–76 (finance company not a merchant). The transaction here, a real estate transaction involving the sale of a hotel, is not a transaction involving goods or services. *See, e.g., Lacey v. Edgewood Home Builders, Inc.,* 446 A.2d 1017 (R.I. 1982); *Wendling v. Cundall,* 568 P.2d 888 (Wyo. 1977). Accordingly, in this transaction, as a matter of law, the USHP defendants are not merchants within the meaning of the Unfair Business Practices Act.

"Moreover, there is no showing that the dispute here is in the public interest. The transaction was a purely private transaction, involving the sale of the Hotel from one private party to another, and is not sufficiently in the public interest to support an unfair business practice claim under Section 480–13. *See Ai v. Frank Huff Agency, Inc.,* 61 Hawaii at 614, 607 P.2d 1304; *Ailetcher,* 632 P.2d at 1076.

"Summary judgment therefore is granted in favor of the USHP defendants as to KHA's sixth claim for relief."

A word about discharge of contracts is in order. Normally, contracts are performed satisfactorily by all parties, at which point the contract is at an end, either by performance (in the case of a construction contract) or by agreement of the parties (a hotel management contract for a fixed period which has now arrived). However, situations arise that are beyond the control of the parties which may make it impossible or commercially impracticable to perform the agreement (i.e., destruction of subject matter of contract). It is here that the courts are called upon to excuse performance of one or the other party. At common law the contract had to be literally impossible to perform for the court to exercise its discretion to excuse or mitigate performance. Under the UCC the doctrine of commercial impracticability is somewhat more flexible. In the latter case, performance will be excused if the risk-causing factor could not have been reasonably anticipated and dealt with by the seller, and the cost of performance under the risk would be very unreasonable (ten times normal cost). In most cases, the courts are willing to use the doctrine if the elements noted are present.

Lastly, contract interpretation and construction are needed in cases where the parties differ over the meaning (interpretation) and legal effect (construction) of the contract language. Normally, the courts seek to determine the objective of the contract, to judge the intentions of the parties from an objective standard, to carry out the intentions of both parties, and to presume that the parties intended their agreement to be legal, reasonable, and effective.

In *John W. Cowper Co., Inc. v. Buffalo Hotel Development Venture*,[13] the New York Appellate Division, Fourth Department dealt with a claim to recover sums borrowed by a construction contractor as reimbursement for borrowing at greater-than-prime interest rates. The sums were borrowed from the developer to meet cash flow demands allegedly caused by the developer's intentional withholding of payments due under the contract. The court ruled that the claim did not state a cause of action, explaining that only the legislature can cure such a problem. In view of the plain language of the contract, plaintiff is bound by his undertaking to accept interest "at the legal rate prevailing at the place of the project."

In the following case, delay in performance of a hotel construction contract was in issue. Delay, if established, may support a reduction in payment if the contract so provides. The Federal Circuit Court for the Fourth Circuit, applying Virginia law, overturned a trial court decision on the delay aspects of the case.

McDevitt and Street Co. v. Marriott Corp.
922 F.2d 723 (4th Cir. 1990)

PER CURIAM: "In this contract action, McDevitt and Street Company (McDevitt), the general contractor on a hotel building project, sued Marriott Corporation (Marriott) for the unpaid portion of the contract between the parties. Marriott counterclaimed for damages arising out of construction delays. . . . McDevitt appeals the denial of some of its claims and the grant of certain of Marriott's counterclaims. Marriott cross-appeals the denial of one of its counterclaims. We reverse the order as to the denial of two of McDevitt's claims, and we affirm the denial of the remainder of its claims as well as the denial of the counterclaim. Because the reversal necessitates the recalculation of all the delay-related damages, we remand for further proceedings.

"McDevitt contracted with Marriott to construct a hotel in Herndon, Virginia. The contract called for completion by December 21, 1986. The hotel was not completed until May 1, 1987. The adjusted contract price was $4,946,668;

---

[13]91 A.D.2d 1183, 459 N.Y.S.2d 175 (A.D. 4th 1983).

Marriott, citing the extra costs and losses incurred due to this 132-day delay, which it asserted was entirely McDevitt's fault, withheld $424,998 from the contract price.

"McDevitt then filed this diversity action for the withheld amount. The gist of McDevitt's claim was that the entire delay in completion was the fault of Marriott. Marriott counterclaimed for, inter alia, management fees lost as a result of the delay in the opening of the hotel. After a bench trial, the district court entered an order that essentially laid the entire 132-day delay at McDevitt's feet and offset the agreed-upon contract figure by various delay- related costs incurred and losses suffered by Marriott.

"McDevitt's claim was for contract damages, i.e., the unpaid portion of the construction contract. Inasmuch as Marriott received a hotel which met contract specifications, albeit later than planned, the contract price is not in dispute. What is disputed are issues of responsibility for the various delays. After the length of delay for which McDevitt was to be held responsible was determined, the court had to quantify each component of Marriott's loss, e.g., lost rental fees. Marriott's losses were then deducted from the contract price, and this figure was compared to the amount actually paid to McDevitt. The district court found that the total amount due McDevitt under the contract was $514,986.68, and that McDevitt's breaches of the contract left it liable to Marriott in the amount of $416,823.00. Therefore, the final judgment below was an award to McDevitt for $98,163.68. We find error in only two aspects of the district court's order. First, the court erroneously held McDevitt liable for the 19-day delay involving the question of what type of foundation to use in Building D. Second, the lower court should have offset the lost-interest award to Marriott by the interest earned on amounts retained by Marriott due to the delay. We discuss each in turn.

"The construction contract provided for extensions of the completion date if delays in construction were caused by "any act or neglect" of Marriott. McDevitt's complaint claimed that it was entitled to a 19-day extension because of Marriott's inaction in deciding whether to use a structural form or a slab-on-grade foundation in one of the hotel buildings. A finding in McDevitt's favor would reduce the delay for which it could be held responsible (from 132 to 113 days), and this in turn would act to proportionately reduce each of the delay-related components of the judgment. Allocation of responsibility is primarily a finding of fact, and we review the trial court's factual determinations under a "clearly erroneous" standard. Fed. R. Civ. P. 52(a).

"On this issue, the court found that on August 8, 1986, McDevitt submitted a written request for a final decision from Marriott on whether to use a slab-on-grade or a structural slab in Building D of the project. Inadequate compaction in the structural fills at two other sections of the complex had previously resulted in the use of structural slabs instead of the slab-on-grade called for in the contract, and, according to the court, uncertainty still remained regarding Building D. Marriott responded to the request on August 20 to say only that additional information would be forthcoming from a structural engineering firm. Marriott then tentatively approved the slab-on-grade pending confirmation of suitability by Soils Consultants, Inc., a company which had tested the soil on May 7 and whose May 28 report approved the use of slab-on-grade. Upon receiving this confirmation, McDevitt immediately began installing slab-on-grade on September 2.

"In the conclusions of law, the district court stressed that McDevitt waited until August 8 to "formally" bring to Marriott's attention the potential need for a structural slab in Building D. The court concluded that Marriott responded with "reasonable promptness" and, therefore, that McDevitt failed to demonstrate that the delay was excusable.

"There is no dispute that the delay from August 14 to September 2 constituted a 19-day delay in the project's "critical path." It is also undisputed that McDevitt was prepared to begin installing the slab-on-grade on August 14. After consideration of all the circumstances surrounding the delay, we hold that it was clear error to hold McDevitt responsible for any portion of this delay.

"The construction contract specified that the Marriott representative was to be the sole judge of whether adequate soil compaction existed. The compaction issue had arisen with regard to two other sites at which structural slabs were used instead of slab-on-grade, and the Building D site had been tested some three months earlier. In fact, representatives from Marriott's engineering firm, Meyer Associates, were present at the May 7 soil test, and, in a letter to Marriott of the same date, Meyer informed Marriott of possible compaction problems. Meyer even submitted a design for a structural slab to Marriott a full month prior to the beginning of the delay. The potential for a problem, then, was evident to Marriott or its representatives for months prior to August 14. Any problems were in the eyes of Meyer, the firm retained by Marriott. McDevitt's consultant on the issue, however, tested and found adequate compaction, and this view remained unchanged from May 7 through the date on which Marriott decided to authorize slab-on-grade. The district court's focus on the August 8 request fails to give proper weight to events leading up to this "formal" request for a decision. We hold that the lower court's ruling that the delay was McDevitt's fault was clear error, and we therefore reverse with regard to this 19-day delay component of the final damage award.

"Another delay-related component of the final award was based on the loss of interest on the sales price. Since the sale by Marriott was delayed by 132 days, the district court ruled that Marriott was entitled to interest on the sales price for the period of time it was deprived of this amount. We find no error in this ruling as far as it goes. However, McDevitt contends that the interest amounts should be offset by interest earned by Marriott on the portion of the contract price retained by Marriott because of the delay. We agree.

"It is black letter law that damages for a breach of contract are intended to put the non-breaching party in the position he would have been in had the breach not occurred. *Appalachian Power Company v. John Stewart Walker, Inc.*, 201 S.E.2d 758, 767 (Va. 1974). The district court's award put Marriott in a substantially better position. On remand, the lost interest figure should be recomputed to allow for the retainage during the delay. Of course, the delay in the sale date should also be adjusted to take into consideration the reduction in the delay period for which McDevitt is responsible.

"The delay for which McDevitt may be held responsible is reduced by 19 days, and McDevitt should be given credit against the lost use-of-sales-proceeds interest damages for the interest earned by Marriott on the contract amounts retained due to the delay. Subject to adjustments based on the 19-day reduction in the delay period, all other portions of the district court's order are affirmed on the reasoning of the district court.

"AFFIRMED IN PART, REVERSED IN PART, AND REMANDED."

7:4 *Excuses for Breach*

Where parties are under a contractual duty to each other, few excuses for breach are permissible under the ordinary law of contracts. Impossibility might be a sufficient excuse for nonperformance by the hotel, for example, when a fire destroys a hotel. Courts are reluctant to interfere with contracts because of the principle of freedom of contract. In *Dold*[14] and *Kellogg*,[15] lack of available space did not serve as an excuse for breach of contract, though a "full house" can excuse an innkeeper from his common-law duty to accommodate. In *Thomas*,[16] the court disregarded racial discrimination as means to relieve a hotel from honoring reservations.

Even where a hotelkeeper finds other accommodations for a guest whose reservation was not honored, as was done in *Dold*, the court may not relieve a hotel from liability in the form of contract damages. The Hawaii case leaves unanswered the question: had there been no such pattern of substantial overselling, would the hotel have been held liable in spite of its referrals to another hotel? In short, the Hawaii court does not reveal the role which the substantial overbooking policy played in the assessment of its finding of a breach of contract of reservation.

One other caveat is in order. In *Archibald v. Pan American World Airways, Inc.*,[17] the plaintiff's confirmed economy seat reservations were not honored by the airline. The plaintiffs were bumped off because of overselling and were placed on the next available flight. The *Archibald* court stated: "Some overselling is an economic necessity for an airline in view of inevitable cancellations and no-shows. However, when a flight is thus oversold, the airline must fill the plane in a reasonable and just manner."[18]

The dicta in the *Archibald* opinion indicates that at least with respect to airlines, some overselling is permissible for economic reasons. If so, where does

[14]Dold v. Outrigger Hotel, 54 Hawaii 18, 501 P.2d 368 (1972).
[15]Kellogg v. Commodore Hotel, 187 Misc. 319, 64 N.Y.S.2d 131 (Sup. Ct. 1946).
[16]Thomas v. Pick Hotels Corp., 224 F.2d 604 (7th Cir. 1955).
[17]460 F.2d 14 (19th Cir. 1972).
[18]*Id.* at 16.

one draw the line as to permissibility? What happens then to the underlying security factor of reservation contracts? Should it be applied to hotel-guest reservation contracts? That "some overselling is an economic necessity" implies that the policy is reasonable. Yet, it leaves unsettled the problem of hotel overbooking.

The most recent airline overbooking case decided by the United States Supreme Court[19] raised the question whether the provisions of the Federal Aviation Act, which created a statutory claim for damages arising out of an overbooked reservation when the passenger is bumped, confer immunity upon the air carrier from any common-law liability arising out of the overbooking itself. The court held that the common-law remedy survived the Act. Although the case dealt with a claim of misrepresentation in that the carrier failed to inform the passenger in advance of its deliberate overbooking practices, the court stated that the common-law remedy applied to the breach-of-contract claim itself under the applicable Civil Aeronautics Board Order.[20]

7:5 Contractual Duties Imposed upon the Guest

When the contractual obligations of innkeeper and guest are based upon a written reservation, the terms of the contract dictate the performance that is required of both parties. In short, the normal rules of contract law govern.

If a traveler cannot honor his reservation, he is under a duty to inform the hotel promptly. Under the contract rule of mitigation of damages, the hotel is bound to try to rerent the room. If this is done, the hotel should return any deposit that had been made prior to the cancellation.

Even under a written reservation contract, a guest should present himself in a proper manner as a condition to the innkeeper's duty to accommodate. The existence of a contract should not relieve a traveler of his duty to appear in an acceptable manner, able and willing to pay for services rendered.

A New York Civil Court decision, *Freeman v. Kiamesha Concord, Inc.*,[21] held that a reservation solicited by a guest who tendered a deposit for a minimum duration, which was accepted by a resort hotel, constituted a valid, enforceable contract imposing liability for payment for the full reservation period upon the guest who elected without justification to check out prior to the agreed minimum period.

The court reasoned that had the innkeeper failed to provide accommodation for the guest upon his arrival, the innkeeper would have breached its reciprocal duty owing to the guest under the contract. Plaintiff sought treble damages against the hotel under section 206 of the General Business Law (McKinney Supp. 1972), which provides such relief whenever a hotelkeeper charges for any service not actually rendered or for a longer period than the guest actually re-

[19]Nader v. Allegheny Airlines, Inc., 426 U.S. 290 (1976).
[20]C.A.B. Order ER-503, 32 Fed. Reg. 11943; 426 U.S. at 305–307.
[21]76 Misc. 2d 915, 351 N.Y.S.2d 541 (Small Claims Ct. N.Y. Co. 1974).

mained at the hotel. The claimed lack of service, based upon misrepresentation of entertainment, was found to be without merit. The court construed the statute as not intended to apply to situations such as this one, where it found that the hotel stood ready and willing to provide the services contracted for and the guest arbitrarily refused to accept such services.

The court reasoned further that such statutory construction would permit a guest to break his contract with impunity and thus obligate only one of the contracting parties to its performance, a result clearly at variance with settled principles of contract law and which would have far-reaching detrimental economic consequences not sanctioned by the public policy of the state.

The decision is significant in establishing the proposition that both innkeeper and guest have contractual rights and responsibilities by reason of a reservation and that an innkeeper may hold a guest liable in damages for its breach, absent any finding of misfeasance or nonfeasance on the innkeeper's part that would justify a contrary result.

In the case to follow, the court held that a hotel guest who canceled his reservation was entitled to recover his deposit because the hotel did not suffer any damage owing to the cancellation.

2625 BUILDING CORP. v. DEUTSCH
179 Ind. App. 425, 385 N.E.2d 1189 (1979)

MILLER, J.: "This is an appeal by Defendant, 2625 Building Corporation, d/b/a The Marriott* Hotel (Marriott), from a judgment for the Plaintiff (Deutsch) granting recovery of his advance payment for hotel rooms which were reserved for the 1973 Indianapolis '500' Mile Race weekend but were not used.

"A summary of the facts shows that on December 7, 1972, Deutsch, a resident of Connecticut, made reservations by telephone for six rooms at the Marriott for the 1973 '500' Mile Race weekend (May 27, 28, 29). Marriott requested advance payment for the rooms. Deutsch complied with Marriott's demand and paid by check in the amount of $1,008.00 in full for the reserved rooms. At the end of March, or the beginning of April, 1973, Deutsch, by telephone, cancelled the reservations and requested the return of his advance payment. Marriott refused his demand. Deutsch did not use the rooms and later brought action against Marriott to recover the $1,008.00 advance payment alleging the above facts and, in addition, that Marriott had relet the rooms and was not harmed by the cancellation.

"At trial before the court, after Deutsch presented his evidence and rested, Marriott moved for dismissal on the ground that Deutsch had failed to present evidence in support of his allegation that Marriott had relet the rooms and was not harmed, and, therefore, had failed to establish a *prima facie* case. The judge

---

*In the original report, the hotel name was spelled *Marott*. The spelling has been corrected to *Marriott* throughout.—J.E.H.S.

took the motion under advisement, reserving his ruling until the conclusion of all the evidence. Marriott presented no evidence and rested. The judge . . . entered . . . judgment in favor of Deutsch and against Marriott. . . .

"On appeal Marriott argues that the decision of the trial court was not sustained by sufficient evidence, that the decision of the trial court was contrary to law in that the court found the contract between the parties to be an executory contract and to contain a provision for a penalty upon cancellation, and that the trial court abused its discretion in deeming Deutsch's complaint amended to conform to the evidence without a request from Deutsch and without any indication of the court's intention to do so before he entered judgment.

"We affirm.

"Initially we examine Marriott's contention that the court erred in finding the room reservation to be an oral special contract which was executory in nature and which contained a provision for a penalty upon cancellation. In absence, Marriott argues that the contract was fully executed at the time Deutsch tendered his advance payment for the reservations and thereafter it was obligated to hold the rooms open and available for Deutsch on the dates reserved. Hence, Marriott argues it was not required to refund Deutsch's advance payment when the reservations were cancelled.

"An executory contract is defined in 17 Am. Jur. 2d, *Contracts* § 6, p. 341, as follows:

> "*An executory contract is one in which a party binds himself to do or not to do a particular thing, whereas an executed contract is one in which the object of the agreement is performed and everything that was to be done is done.* The distinction would seem to relate to the legal effect of a contract at two different stages. An executory contract, it is said, conveys a chose in action, while an executed contract conveys a chose in possession. (Emphasis added.)

"Contrary to Marriott's contention, the contract was not fully executed at the time the reservations were cancelled. Under the facts of this case the contract was executory in nature, part of which had been executed when Deutsch cancelled his reservations. That is to say, the portion of the contract pertaining to Deutsch's tender of payment in full and Marriott's acceptance of said payment was an executed portion of the contract and the obligation of Marriott to provide its facilities for Deutsch's use remained executory until Deutsch's cancellation. Marriott's further contention that it was obligated to keep the rooms available for Deutsch after he cancelled his reservations is also without merit. Deutsch's repudiation of the contract was an anticipatory breach thereof which relieved Marriott from its future obligations and enabled it, if it desired, to sue at that time for damages caused by such breach. [Citations omitted.]

"We next examine Marriott's claim that the evidence did not support the trial court's conclusion that full payment for the rooms constituted a penalty. The general nature of an agreement for hotel reservations was recently defined in *Freeman v. Kiamesha Concord, Inc.* (1974), 76 Misc. 2d 915, 351 N.Y.S.2d 541, as follows:

"The solicitation of a reservation, the making of a reservation by the transmittal of a deposit and the acceptance of the deposit constituted a binding contract in accordance with traditional contract principles of offer and acceptance.

"In *Freeman, supra,* the guest paid the hotel a $20.00 deposit in advance for a three day reservation, used the hotel's facilities for two days but refused to use them on the third day because of his dissatisfaction with the entertainment. The hotel insisted upon full payment for the three days in accordance with the reservation. The guest paid under protest and sued to recover for the amount paid for the unused portion of the reserved period. . . .

"The Marriott cites this decision in support of its proposition that it had a right to refuse to refund $1,008.00 to Deutsch when he cancelled his reservations. However, we find the facts in the case at hand to be clearly distinguishable. In *Freeman* the guest had checked into the hotel pursuant to the contract whereas in this case Deutsch had not. Moreover, *Freeman* involved a 'last minute' checkout prior to the end of the contract period, whereas Deutsch gave the Marriott approximately two months advance notice of his cancellation.

"We do not disagree with the reasoning in *Freeman* as applied to the facts therein and such reasoning is certainly applicable in 'last minute' cancellation cases, especially at resort type hotels. Thus, we recognize there may be instances when a guest's cancellation of reservations would not justify a refund of an advance payment. As noted previously, the making and acceptance of the reservation in this case constituted a binding contract. Upon Deutsch's breach Marriott was entitled to *actual damages* in accordance with traditional contract principles. [Citations omitted.] However, we agree with the trial court that to allow Marriott to retain damages representing payment for use of all the rooms, regardless of the fact that damages could be ascertained, would be to enforce a penalty or forfeiture. [Citation omitted.] To hold otherwise under the facts and circumstances of this case would be inconsistent 'with the principles of fairness and justice under the law' as set down in *Skendzel v. Marshall* (1973), 261 Ind. 226, 301 N.E.2d 641: . . .

" . . . If the damages are unreasonable, i.e., if they are disproportionate to the loss actually suffered, they must be characterized as penal rather than compensatory. (Citations omitted.]

"The evidence in the record reveals that Deutsch made reservations, tendered full payment for the use of the rooms in advance and, approximately two months prior to Marriott's time for performance, cancelled the reservations and demanded refund, which demand was refused. In addition, we take judicial notice that the Indianapolis '500' Mile Race has the largest attendance of any single, one-day, arena-type sporting event in the world. The influx of dedicated racing fans to the Indianapolis metropolitan area in order to witness this spectacle of racing is legend. Attendant with this influx is the overwhelming demand for and shortage of hotel accommodations.

"Therefore, we find that the facts of this case justified the trial court's conclusion that assessing Deutsch for the full amount of his room payments would cause him to suffer a loss which was wholly disproportionate to any injury sustained by Marriott. Since there was no evidence that Marriott sustained any damage, we cannot say, as a matter of law, that the trial court erred in allowing Deutsch full refund of his money.''

7:6 *Measure of Damages for Guest's Failure to Honor Reservations*

It is now well settled that a guest can recover compensatory damages resulting from an innkeeper's breach of a reservation contract.[22] Under proper circumstances, he may recover additional consequential damages.[23] A more serious issue for the innkeeper is whether the guest may be awarded punitive or exemplary damages, that is, damages not to compensate for direct loss, but to punish the wrongdoer for intentional injury to feelings and reputation.[24] But what recourse does the innkeeper have against the no-show guest? The scope and extent of the innkeeper's damage claims are examined in this section.

If a guest does not honor his reservation and makes no reasonable effort to notify the hotel that he cannot do so, the hotel ought to be able to treat the previously tendered deposit, usually the first night's room charge, as liquidated damages. If a guaranteed reservation is made without any advance deposit and the guest's absence is without justification, then the normal rule of compensatory damages, recovery of out-of-pocket expenses, should prevail.

The problem facing the innkeeper in the latter case is the stark fact that the amount in question, normally the cost of an overnight stay, is so small as not to justify the time and expense of electing to sue the absent guest. The amount generally recoverable is simply too minimal to support legal action. There are situations, however, in which the innkeeper may find his measure of damages substantial and thus worthy of legal redress.[25]

Let us assume that a major enterprise books a large complement of guest rooms and function rooms for an annual convention a year in advance, making it a virtual certainty that the hotel will be filled to capacity on the convention dates. Let us further assume that a required deposit of an appropriate sum has been paid in advance, and that at the last possible moment the convention host reneges on the agreement, for no reason or for reasons that are not economically justified, that is, the convention host willfully and deliberately refuses to honor its commitment. Under these circumstances, is the hotel able not only to keep the deposit but to sue for consequential damages?

The answer from a management standpoint would be to insert a provision in its reservation and function contracts fixing both cancellation and damages. Such protective clauses would go far toward establishing adequate legal grounds for recovery of lost profits in excess of out-of-pocket expenses.

---

[22]*See, e.g.,* note 5, *supra.*

[23]*See* section 7:9, *infra.*

[24]*See* section 7:7 and 7:8, *infra.*

[25]King of Prussia Enterprises, Inc. v. Greyhound Lines, Inc., 457 F. Supp. 56 (E.D. Pa. 1978), *aff'd,* 595 F.2d 1212 (3rd Cir. 1979) quoted in this section.

Moreover, is the hotelkeeper able to sue not only for compensatory damages but for punitive damages if the guest or patron's cancellation is willful, wanton, or oppressive? As will be seen hereafter,[26] damages may be recovered in proper circumstances by the wronged guest for "mental suffering" and "emotional distress" when the innkeeper's refusal to honor the reservation is deliberate and his treatment of the guest causes humiliation and indignity.

May the same measure of damages be recovered by the injured innkeeper? Clearly the likelihood of willful or wanton conduct inflicted upon management by a guest in cancelling his prior reservation is unlikely. However, in the case previously posed, the recovery of consequential damages should be afforded the innkeeper; similarly, exemplary or punitive damages should be awarded in the case of deliberate provocation. (*See* section 7:7, *infra.*)

KING OF PRUSSIA ENTERPRISES, INC.
v. GREYHOUND LINES, INC.
457 F. Supp. 56 (E.D. Pa. 1978), *aff'd*, 595 F.2d 1212 (3d Cir. 1979)

DITTER, D.J.: "This suit was brought to recover damages for hotel rooms engaged but not occupied. The matter is presently before the court on Loyal Travel's motion for a new trial and for judgment notwithstanding the verdict.

"Plaintiff's Valley Forge Hilton Hotel is located near Philadelphia. In 1976, it was expected that 48 million visitors might come to the Philadelphia area in celebration of the nation's bicentennial. In addition, the Forty-first International Eucharistic Congress was planned for July 31 to August 8, 1976, and it alone was expected to attract more than a million visitors. As a result of a bid submitted to the Chicago Archdiocese, Loyal was designated as the exclusive agent to provide travel services for those from the Chicago area who would be attending the Congress. The Congress also created a housing bureau to refer hotel and motel rooms to the various travel agencies which would be dealing directly with the general public. Both plaintiff and defendant knew of the housing bureau, had agreed to work through it, and were aware that the housing bureau had suggested a payment schedule for any rooms committed. At no time was it intended that the housing bureau contract with any hotel, motel, or travel agent, impose any terms on anyone, or interfere with the right of a hotel and travel agent to reach whatever agreement might be mutually satisfactory.

"Hoping to obtain better rooms through direct contact than it had been allocated by the Eucharistic Congress' housing bureau, Loyal sent its area manager, Jose C. Ros, to the Philadelphia area in February, 1976. He visited several hotels or motels seeking the commitment of rooms for Loyal's clients. On February 11, 1976, he came to plaintiff's hotel and talked with Louis Serafine, director of sales, and Milos Hamza, plaintiff's general manager. At trial Hamza testified that Ros wanted to engage all of plaintiff's available rooms, 200 in number, for the period from July 27 to August 9, agreeing to pay $12.50 per person with the

---

[26]*See* section 7:8, *infra.*

understanding that four persons would occupy each room. Hamza also said that he agreed to commit all 200 rooms to Loyal, which he knew to be a subsidiary of Greyhound, only if there would be a ten percent, non-refundable deposit with the balance to be paid 60 days prior to the arrival of the guests. However, up to the 60-day deadline, the rooms could be cancelled and only the ten percent deposit forfeited. In addition, Hamza said that he told Ros that there were two-bedroom apartments at a nearby Hilton building and that additional apartments were available at the Presidential Apartment complex in Philadelphia. Ros was interested in all of these accommodations. As a result of their conversation, Hamza testified he dictated a letter to Ros setting forth the offer of the rooms as outlined in their conversation. Ros took the letter with him and returned to Chicago. By check dated February 27, 1976, Loyal sent $10,000. to plaintiff marking the attached voucher, "Deposit for 200 Rms. at $50. each, four persons max., arrival 7/31/76–8/09/76, Eucharistic Congress." Similar deposits were sent to plaintiff for the two-bedroom Hilton Apartments and the Presidential Apartments. Hamza accepted and deposited all three checks. In view of the change of expected arrival time from that originally discussed, July 27, to that shown on the voucher accompanying the checks, July 31, Hamza expected the balances of payments on May 31. In mid-May he talked with Ros on the telephone and was assured that arrangements were proceeding in a satisfactory way. Not having received a further payment on May 31, Hamza called Ros on June 4 and was assured by Ros that checks for the balances due, a total of $116,800., were in the mail. Hamza called again on June 10 or June 11 and was told by Ros that the checks were not being forwarded from Chicago but from Phoenix and were therefore taking longer than he had expected to reach Hamza. A week later Hamza called again and Ros said that with a big corporation like Loyal and Greyhound, the forwarding of checks took time but that Hamza should not worry about the matter. On June 21, 1976, Hamza received a letter signed by Ros dated June 10 and postmarked June 18 stating that Loyal was cancelling all of its reservations and asking for a refund of all deposits made.

"Ros testified that he only had a momentary conversation with Hamza and that all of his arrangements had been made with Serafine. Ros denied he had agreed that the rooms would not be subject to cancellation, denied that he had agreed to pay for any rooms not used, and denied he had agreed the ten percent deposit was to be non-refundable. He described his extensive experience in the travel industry and said that he had never made an arrangement with any hotel on the basis of which the right to cancel a reservation had been surrendered or that he had ever agreed to pay for a room not utilized. He also said that the custom in the travel industry is to reserve rooms on the basis of a ten percent deposit with an additional 40 percent within a certain time and the remaining 50 percent 30 days before rooms are to be used. He had never heard of any travel agency which had lost more than its initial deposit of ten percent, and then only if the reservations were not cancelled within the time for the payment of the remaining balance. Ros also said that he was aware of guidelines stated by the Eucharistic Congress, working through its housing bureau, which required a ten percent deposit to secure the commitment of rooms by the hotel, an additional 40 percent 60 days before arrival, and the balance 30 days before arrival. He said the arrangements with plaintiff were cancelled because Loyal's attempts to interest Chicagoans in the Eucharistic Congress were a complete failure.

"Two other witnesses appeared for the defendant. Raymond J. O'Brien, a representative of the Eucharistic Congress housing authority, and Richard Lupinacci, the head of a large Philadelphia travel agency. O'Brien testified as to the organization of the housing bureau and its publication of guidelines for the travel and hotel industry. Lupinacci testified as to his experiences in booking tours, reserving hotel rooms, and the practices of the travel industry and its customs. Both O'Brien and Lupinacci said that there were estimates in early 1976 that as many as 48 million people might visit Philadelphia that year and that highly unusual conditions and circumstances then prevailed.

"By separate interrogatories submitted to it, the jury concluded there had been a contract between plaintiff and defendant which defendant had breached and that plaintiff was entitled to $58,900. for direct damages. No award was made for consequential damages and no award was made for any loss which the plaintiff may have suffered from defendant's failure to pay for the Hilton two-bedroom apartments. Defendant's motions seeking a new trial and judgment notwithstanding verdict must be refused for the following reasons:

"1. There was sufficient testimony to prove the existence of a contract: from Hamza's testimony the jury could have found he offered 200 hotel rooms to Ros on the basis of a non-refundable deposit of ten percent to secure commitment of the rooms (but without additional liability if the rooms were cancelled 60 days prior to the start of the Eucharistic Congress); that this offer was set forth in writing (Exhibit 1); and that the mailing of Loyal's check dated February 27, 1976, constituted a counter-offer, which was accepted by plaintiff's deposit of said check.

"Plaintiff's evidence through its witness John Dailey and its daily logs (Exhibits 17A through I) provided sufficient basis for the jury's finding that the damages it awarded were:

"*(a)* such as would naturally and ordinarily follow from the breach of contract;

"*(b)* reasonably foreseeable and within the contemplation of the parties at the time the contract was entered into;

"*(c)* proven with reasonable certainty, Restatement of Contracts § § 330 and 331. . . .

"Defendant had provided testimony that the custom in the travel industry and the guidelines published by the Eucharistic Congress were the same, rooms could *always* be cancelled and a refund obtained. . . .

"Defendant's witness, O'Brien, specifically stated that hotels and motels were free to strike their own deals and that the housing bureau made no attempt to impose any terms on anyone. . . .

"5. It was not error to refuse to charge on liquidated damages. There was no evidence from any witness that if the rooms were not utilized plaintiff's recovery was to be limited to defendant's deposit. . . . It is axiomatic in the law that provisions for the limitation of damages must be clear and unequivocal—the language here is nonexistent. . . .

" . . . One of the major pillars of Loyal's defense was that 'no travel agent would ever enter into such a contract such as that asserted by plaintiff, wherein he would become responsible for the entire dollar amount of the rooms reserved.' (Brief of Loyal Travel, Document 39, page 6.) To substantiate this defense, Loyal presented the testimony of Lupinacci as to his experiences in the travel industry and its customs. The relevance and indeed the admissibility of much of what he said was questionable. Lupinacci did testify, however, that the travel industry and hotel industry in early 1976 were expecting as many as 48 million visitors to Philadelphia, that the situation was unique in Philadelphia travel history, and that it would be possible that under the circumstances, a travel agent would have been willing to pay money down to tie up rooms even though he had not previously sold them to the public. . . .

"8. The court did not err by charging that plaintiff's liability evidence was not ambiguous—what the court charged was that the purpose of the evidence concerning custom and usage was to help understand what the parties intended and understood *if* there was uncertainty or ambiguity. The court said that the plain terms of the contract prevail over a trade usage or custom, that evidence of custom or usage cannot be considered to destroy a contract, or to make the rights and liabilities of the parties to a contract other than those created by the contract terms. The court also said that custom and usage evidence cannot create an ambiguity where none exists and that where the terms of an express contract are clear and unambiguous, they cannot be varied or contradicted because they differ from those usually found in a particular trade of business. Whether or not there was ambiguity was left to the jury.''

7:7 *Punitive Damages for Breach of Contract: In General*

The common-law rule, to which there were qualifications and exceptions, stated simply that punitive damages may not be assessed in an action for breach of contract, no matter what the circumstances of malice, abuse, wantonness, or oppression that attended the breach. The reason for this refusal to assess punitive damages in contract actions was a fear of introducing confusion and uncertainty into business transactions, combined with the notion that substituted performance in terms of compensatory damages was an adequate remedy for the aggrieved party to a contract. To turn a jury loose with power to give to the plaintiff not only a dollar sum equal to the value to the plaintiff of defendant's promised performance but in addition an amount many times that sum as punitive damages seemed an unequal weighting of the scales between the contending parties not justified by any factor of punishment or deterrence.

There were certain narrow categories of exception to this rule. Where a breach of contract precipitated mental distress as well as disappointment, recovery for such distress was sometimes possible. (*See also* section 7:8, *infra.*) Professor Williston has observed that

> [m]ental suffering caused by breach of contract, though it may be a real injury, is not generally allowed as a basis for compensation in contractual actions. Pecuniary loss is the usual measure. There are, however, exceptions conceded in many jurisdictions. Where other than pecuniary benefits are contracted for, damages have been allowed for injury to the feelings. Wherever exemplary damages are allowed, mental suffering is always considered; and in other cases where an element of tort exists, the same is true. Unjustifiable expulsion or mistreatment of passengers by carriers, or of guests by innkeepers, are illustrations. . . . Damages will be given for mental suffering for "wanton or reckless breach of a contract to render a performance of such a character that the defendant had reason to know when the contract was made that the breach would cause mental suffering for reasons other than pecuniary loss" (citing Restatement of Contracts).[27]

The only other relevant exceptions are where an innkeeper or common carrier has intentionally and willfully insulted and abused a guest or passenger, or where a proprietor of a public resort has publicly and wrongfully ejected a patron.

In *Dalzell v. Dean Hotel Co.*,[28] plaintiff and her husband, while attending a convention, were guests in defendant's hotel. The day after their arrival, plaintiff's husband left the room, and while he was away, defendant's clerk, honestly but mistakenly believing, because of an error in the checkout records, that plaintiff and her husband had checked out, sold the room to another guest and ejected plaintiff (then pregnant) from possession. In an action for breach of contract, plaintiff demanded compensatory and exemplary damages. The trial judge instructed the jury that if they found for the plaintiff, they could allow her only nominal damages. The jury thereupon returned a verdict for plaintiff for $5.

The judgment was reversed on appeal on the following grounds: Even though there was no actual malice in the case, in that defendant did not know that it was doing wrong, *legal malice* may be presumed "from gross and culpable negligence in omitting to make suitable and reasonable inquiries."[29] No ill will or hatred or personal spite is necessary to create legal malice. The jury might infer legal malice from the fact that plaintiff was refused a chance to prove that defendant was wrong, though plaintiff repeated three times that there was a mistake.

In *Emmke v. DeSilva*,[30] plaintiff registered on April 1 at defendant's hotel and was assigned to a room. She told the desk clerk at the time that her husband would arrive in a few days and would be with her at the hotel from time to time,

---

[27]5 Williston on Contracts, § 1340A.

[28]193 Mo. App. 379, 186 S.W. 41 (1916).

[29]*Id.* at 401, 186 S.W. at 48 (1916), Story, J., quoting Stubbs v. Mulholland, 168 Mo. 47, 77, 67 S.W. 650, 659 (1902), in turn quoting Wiggin v. Coffin, 29 F. Cas. 1157, 1159 (No. 17624) (C.C.D. Me. 1836).

[30]293 F. 17 (8th Cir. 1923).

but that his business would require him to be elsewhere on occasion and that he would not be with her constantly.

Plaintiff's husband came to the hotel on April 11, spent the night and day with her and returned to the hotel on the 16th and occupied the room with her that night. About one o'clock the next morning, Emmke, president of defendant hotel company and himself a codefendant, entered plaintiff's room, which was then dark, awakened plaintiff and her husband, and according to plaintiff "maliciously and insultingly accused plaintiff of unchastity and in her presence spoke of her husband in loathsome terms of vulgarity, whereby plaintiff suffered nervous strain and mental anguish, was greatly insulted and humiliated."

Defendant objected to the sufficiency of the complaint and to the evidence in support of it on the ground that neither showed personal violence or injury to the plaintiff. The jury found for plaintiff for $3,500 as damages, of which $2,000 were stated as actual and $1,500 as exemplary damages.

On appeal, the judgment entered on the jury's verdict was affirmed as to the $2,000 actual damages and reversed as to the $1,500 punitive damages. Said the court: "notwithstanding no physical injury was inflicted, plaintiff was entitled to recovery on account of the mental anguish and humiliation to which she was subjected."[31]

In *Gefter v. Rosenthal,*[32] plaintiff sued to recover damages for humiliation and mental suffering he alleged he received because at a dinner celebrating his twenty-fifth wedding anniversary his guests were charged a fifteen-cent tip for each coat checked. Plaintiff had entered into a written agreement with the caterers that he would pay defendants fifteen cents per coat checked, and there would be no tipping for cloakroom services. Plaintiff claimed that defendants' wanton and intentional violation of their written agreement and their charge of fifteen cents per coat checked caused him humiliation and mental suffering to the extent of $15,000, plus $5,000 punitive damages. There was no claim for physical injuries.

The court dismissed plaintiff's amended complaint. "There can be no recovery for humiliation, disappointment, anxiety, or mental suffering, or emotional distress when unconnected with physical injury or physical impact [citations omitted]."[33]

In *Frank v. Justine Caterers, Inc.,*[34] where the dismissal of plaintiff's complaint for mental anguish suffered by reason of poisoned food served by defendant caterer to plaintiff's guests was affirmed on appeal, the court stated: "The alleged cause of action does not come within any exception to the general rule that mental suffering resulting from a breach of contract is not a subject of compensation."

[31]*Id.* at 21.
[32]384 Pa. 123, 119 A.2d 250 (1956).
[33]*Id.* at 125, 119 A.2d at 251.
[34]271 A.D. 980, 68 N.Y.S.2d 198 (2d Dep't 1947) (mem. opinion).

In *New York Hotel Statler Co., Inc. v. Levine,*[35] a dinner dance in honor of the bar mitzvah of the defendant's son was held at the Hotel Statler. Upon defendant's failure to pay the bill, plaintiff sued for its recovery. Defendant counterclaimed for $3,000 for alleged humiliation, ridicule, and criticism suffered by or directed at her by reason of plaintiff's alleged breach of contract in serving certain non-Kosher foods at the "Kosher-style" dinner she ordered. In addition, she alleged that she "has been upset and nervous as a result of plaintiff's breach of contract." The court granted plaintiff's motion to strike out the counterclaim so as to remove same from consideration of the jury at the trial.

Air Carrier's Liability

Noting with gratitude that it was not bound by state rules against awarding punitive damages in contract actions, a federal district court happily awarded $5000 exemplary damages to a passenger who had been bumped from an overbooked flight on which he had reserved a seat.[36] The action was brought under 8404(b) of the Civil Aeronautics Act of 1938, which provides that: "[n]o air carrier . . . shall make, give or cause any undue or unreasonable preference or advantage to any particular person . . . any unjust discrimination or any undue or unreasonable prejudice or disadvantage in any respect whatsoever."[37]

The federal statute itself does not provide for an award of punitive damages; nonetheless the court created and justified this remedy as "a needed force to assure full compliance with the requirements of the Act.[38] Plaintiff's out-of-pocket losses as a result of being bumped from defendant's flight were $1.54, the cost of a telephone call made from St. Louis to his wife in Los Angeles to explain his delayed arrival. In granting punitive damages, the court noted:[39] "[t]he fact that a plaintiff's pecuniary loss, proximately resulting from unjust discrimination, is inconsequential should not rule out exemplary relief since it is the vindication of his rights as a passenger from future encroachment, which warrants the assessment of damages over and above the passenger's actual injury."

The more recent federal decision[40] involving Ralph Nader and Allegheny Airlines illustrates vividly how costly such an award may be. A finding of intentional overbooking on the airline's part resulted in a $25,000 punitive damage award to Nader and an identical sum to a citizen action group, as against compensatory damage awards $10 and $51, respectively, to each aggrieved party.

The issue of under what circumstances punitive or exemplary damages are available in a hotel real estate contract fraud action was the subject of a New York Court of Appeals decision in the following case.

---

[35]Mun. Ct. of New York City, Man. 9th Dist., 1957, not officially reported.
[36]Wills v. Trans World Airlines, Inc., 200 F. Supp. 360 (S.D. Cal. 1961).
[37]49 U.S.C. 1374(b) (1958).
[38]200 F. Supp. at 365.
[39]*Id.* at 367.
[40]Nader v. Allegheny Airlines, Inc., 365 F. Supp. 128 (D.D.C. 1973), *rev'd,* 512 F.2d 527 (D.C. Cir. 1975), *rev'd and remanded,* 426 U.S. 290 (1976).

REINAH DEVELOPMENT CORP. V. KAATERSKILL HOTEL CORP.
59 N.Y.2d 482, 452 N.E.2d 1238 (1983)

JASEN, J.: "This appeal requires us to determine whether the evidence presented in this fraud action was sufficient to justify an award of punitive or exemplary damages.

"The underlying transaction involved in this action related to the sale of real property, including a hotel, located in Liberty, New York. The purchaser of the property, plaintiff Reinah Development Corp. (Reinah), intended to develop it into condominium units. When plaintiff experienced difficulty arranging financing, defendant Kaaterskill Hotel Corp. (Kaaterskill), the holder of a purchase-money second mortgage, loaned plaintiff additional funds to enable it to pay back real estate taxes. As security for that loan and to insure that payments would be made on the first mortgage, not held by Kaaterskill, plaintiff delivered to Kaaterskill a deed to the property which was to be held in escrow until August 15, 1970. It was agreed in writing that in the event the plaintiff failed to repay the loan by the specified date or to pay the interest and amortization due on the first mortgage on or before August 20, 1970, defendant Kaaterskill was authorized to record the deed. Plaintiff defaulted in repayment to Kaaterskill of the loan and in payment of the amortization and interest due on the first mortgage. However, Kaaterskill extended the time to meet these obligations. The new deadline fixed is a point of contention between the parties. Defendants, believing September 15 to be the last date for plaintiff to make the necessary payments, demanded payment, and when none was received recorded the deed on September 22, which deed bore the caption, 'This Deed is Given in Lieu of Foreclosure'. Plaintiff asserted that the extended date to repay the loan was September 30 and that defendant Kaaterskill had no right to record the deed when it did.

"The recorded deed, however, was insufficient to pass marketable title, as it did not have the required consents of the stockholders and the board of directors of plaintiff corporation. (Business Corporation Law, § 909). Therefore, plaintiff asserts, defendants Kaaterskill and Alan Portnick, as president and principal of Kaaterskill, induced plaintiff to forbear from suing Kaaterskill for the breach of their agreement, and defendants in turn agreed that, upon a sale of the property to a third party, plaintiff would be reimbursed, out of the proceeds of the sale, for the actual cash investment made by it in its original purchase of the property. Plaintiff delivered the necessary certificate certifying that the shareholders and directors of the corporation had approved the delivery of the deed to defendant Kaaterskill.

"Subsequently, defendant Kaaterskill completed the sale of the hotel to a third party. When plaintiff demanded payment in the amount of his investment, defendants refused and an action for compensatory and punitive damages was commenced. Two of the eight causes of actions alleged, all sounding in fraud, were charged to the jury; the remaining six were dismissed.

"The jury was instructed that 'under the law and under the June 10th and 15th agreements [related to the loan from defendant] the plaintiff was obligated and required to provide the stockholder consent once the defendant recorded the deed on September 22nd'. There was no objection to this portion of the charge, nor to the court's later instruction that punitive damages could only be allowed if they determined that the conduct of the defendant's president constituted fraud and was malicious and reckless in its nature. Accordingly, the court's charge on these issues is the law governing this case. (*Bichler v. Lilly & Co.*, 55 N.Y.2d 571, 581, 584, 450 N.Y.S.2d 776, 436 N.E.2d 182.)

"The jury returned a verdict awarding plaintiff nominal compensatory damages and $225,000 in punitive damages, apparently having determined that defendant's president, Alan Portnick, had acted fraudulently in this transaction. Defendants moved to set aside the verdict as to both compensatory and punitive damages. The motion was denied as to compensatory damages, but was granted as to punitive damages. In deciding the motion, the Trial Judge stated that the evidence was insufficient for the jury to conclude, as the charge required them to, that Portnick's behavior was 'malicious, vindictive or morally reprehensible [demonstrating the] intent of wanton and reckless behavior.' The Appellate Division, 86 A.D.2d 50, 448 N.Y.S.2d 686, unanimously reversed, on the law, the facts and in the exercise of discretion, and reinstated the jury verdict. For the reasons which follow, we conclude that the result reached by the trial court should be upheld.

"We hold that the jury, as charged, could not have found that Portnick's conduct, even if fraudulent was malicious and vindictive to justify awarding punitive damages or that his conduct was wanton and reckless.

"No fraudulent or morally culpable conduct could have been found to exist on the basis of the court's instruction to the jury, without exception, that the giving of the stockholders' consent certificate to the defendant 'is not a factor to be considered by you as to whether or not the plaintiff justifiably relied on [defendants'] promise of money because under the law and under the June 10th and 15th agreements, the plaintiff was obligated and required to provide the stockholder consent once the defendant recorded the deed on September 22nd' and that plaintiff may 'not now justifiably claim that he was induced to give the stockholder consent to the defendant in reliance on defendant's promise for money.' The court went on to charge that 'the testimony with respect to the stockholders' consent, although not a factor to be considered on the issue of fraud as such, it may be taken into consideration by you as effecting the credibility of the parties.'

"The further conduct complained of that defendants fraudulently induced the plaintiff to forbear from suing the defendants for the breach of their agreement to extend the time for the plaintiff to repay its loan to the defendant Kaaterskill and to refrain from pursuing an action against the defendants to set aside the deed improperly recorded in violation of their agreement, while perhaps constituting a breach of contract, does not demonstrate a malicious, vindictive or reckless act to support an award of punitive damages.

"While promises made to settle a dispute prior to litigation should be honestly made and honored, there was no proof presented, as required by the charge, that defendant acted 'maliciously' or 'recklessly' at the time he promised to reimburse plaintiff for his losses. All that has been shown is that defendant breached his agreement. Thus, the jury's determination that defendant should be punished by assessing punitive damages is not supported by the record and that portion of the verdict should be set aside.

"Accordingly, the order of the Appellate Division should be reversed, with costs, and the judgment of Supreme Court, New York County, setting aside the jury verdict should be reinstated.

"COOKE, C.J., and JONES, WACHTLER, MEYER and SIMONS, JJ., concur.

"Order reversed, with costs, and the judgment of Supreme Court, New York County, reinstated."

7:8 *Recovery for Mental Suffering and Emotional Distress*

Under the quaint rubrics of "mental suffering," "nervous upset," or "emotional distress," damages have been allowed in excess of a normal contract recovery where an innkeeper has refused to honor a reservation made in advance of the disappointed guest's arrival.

In *Aaron v. Ward,*[41] insulting words were added to the injury of expulsion from a bathhouse, and the plaintiff was allowed to recover $250—a windfall one thousand times the 25-cent purchase price of the bathhouse ticket. Plaintiff in this case, a woman, had purchased a ticket from a bathing establishment on Coney Island and stood in line to receive a key admitting her to a bathhouse. She purchased her 25-cent ticket. When she approached, a dispute arose between her and bathhouse employees as to the right of another person not in the line to receive his key in advance of plaintiff. As a result of the dispute, plaintiff was ejected from the bathhouse premises. The annoyed employees refused to furnish her with the accommodations for which she had contracted.

Plaintiff sued for breach of her contractual right to enter the bathhouse, not for tortious expulsion. Bypassing a pure contract recovery, the court reflected on the nature of the indignity plaintiff suffered in being ejected from the line of waiting patrons:

> It may be admitted that, as a general rule, mental suffering resulting from a breach of contract is not universal. It is the settled law of this state that a passenger may recover damages for insulting and slanderous words uttered by the conductor of a railway car as a breach of the company's contract of carriage. (Cite omitted.) The same rule obtains where the servant of an innkeeper offers insult to his guest. *DeWolf v. Ford,* 193 N.Y. 397 (1908). And it must be borne in mind that a recovery for indignity and wounded feelings is compensatory and does not constitute exemplary damages. . . . The defendant having voluntarily entered into a contract with her admitting her to the premises and agreeing to afford facilities for bathing, her status became similar to that of a . . . guest of an innkeeper, and in case of her improper expulsion she should be entitled to the same measure of damages as obtains in actions against carriers or innkeepers when brought for breach of their contracts. The

[41]203 N.Y. 351, 96 N.E. 736 (1911).

reason why such damages are recoverable . . . is not merely because the defendants are bound to give the plaintiffs accommodation, but also because of the indignity suffered by a public expulsion.[42]

The damages awarded in *Aaron v. Ward, supra,* are designated compensatory and allowed for humiliation, indignity, and emotional distress suffered. The $250 award being one thousand times in excess of a simple contract recovery seems more punitive than compensatory, especially since plaintiff's claim of indignities suffered is not rooted in any evidence of concomitant physical or nervous upset which required medical attention. Plaintiff's action is for breach of contract; she does not claim an independent tort was committed. A jury determined substantial damages were in order, perhaps not incorrectly, but the court was clearly eager to call these damages compensatory, not punitive.

A like situation was presented in *Kellogg v. Commodore Hotel,*[43] wherein plaintiff, having contracted with defendant to furnish lodging, arrived at the hotel and was informed by desk clerk that no room was available. Plaintiff sued for breach of contract demanding $5,000. He also asked relief for nervous upset, shock, and depression, demanding another $5,000. The court struck the second prayer for relief for emotional upset and offered two reasons for doing so. The first of these reasons was that plaintiff failed to allege "intentional or willful injury on the part of the (hotel) management," nor were there any "allegation(s) of indecent, improper or insulting remarks on the part of the room clerk or other employees of the hotel that would submit the plaintiff to humiliation."[44]

While the court stipulated that "disappointment cannot amount to injury to feelings,"[45] the real reason motivating the court to strike the prayer for damages for emotional upset is contained in the last part of the opinion wherein the court takes judicial notice of wartime housing shortages, the practice of the government to commandeer blocks of hotel rooms to house its various officers, and the inability of a hotel manager in those chaotic world-war circumstances to honor all commitments. The weightier reason for striking the prayer for relief for emotional distress was the exonerating circumstance of war and not the improperly alleged emotional distress. This case suggests the prayer for relief for nervous shock would not have been struck under less extreme national circumstances.

More recently the Supreme Court of Hawaii allowed damages for emotional distress to stand with no allegations of willfulness or wantonness on the part of hotel management.[46] Again, interestingly, the court was careful to point out that these damages were not punitive, merely compensatory.[47]

---

[42]*Id.* at 354–57.
[43]187 Misc. 319, 64 N.Y.S.2d 131 (1946).
[44]*Id.* at 324, 64 N.Y.S.2d at 136.
[45]*Id.* at 326, 64 N.Y.S.2d at 138.
[46]Dold v. Outrigger Hotel, 54 Hawaii 18, 501 P.2d 368 (1972).
[47]Although the state courts do seem willing to award such damages when a plaintiff can point to abusive behavior on the part of the innkeeper or his employees, the courts are more willing to label an award punitive damages. But where the disappointment of the plaintiff is more visible than the misconduct which caused it, the same award will usually be labeled compensatory.

DOLD V. OUTRIGGER HOTEL
54 Hawaii 18, 501 P.2d 368 (1972)

KOBAYASHI, J.: "This is an appeal by the plaintiffs, Mr. and Mrs. D. F. Dold and Mr. and Mrs. Leo Manthei, from a judgment in their favor. Plaintiffs' amended complaint prayed for actual and punitive damages and alleged three counts for recovery, breach of contract, fraud, and breach of an innkeeper's duty to accommodate guests. . . . Though the judgment was favorable to them, the plaintiffs contended that the trial judge erred in not allowing an instruction on the issue of punitive damages. This is the issue before the court.

Facts

"The plaintiffs, mainland residents, arranged for hotel accommodations from February 18 to February 23, 1968, through the American Express Company, the agent of the defendant, Outrigger Hotel, hereinafter referred to as 'Outrigger.' Hawaii Hotels Operating Company, Ltd., managed and operated the Outrigger. Both are Hawaii corporations.

"Upon arrival at the Outrigger on February 18, 1968, the plaintiffs were refused accommodations and were transferred by the Outrigger to another hotel of lesser quality because the Outrigger lacked available space. On February 19 and 20 the plaintiffs again demanded that the defendants honor their reservations but they were again refused.

"Though the exact nature of the plaintiffs' reservations is in dispute, the defendants claim that since the plaintiffs made no cash deposit, their reservations were not 'confirmed' and for that reason the defendants justifiably dishonored the reservations. Plaintiffs contend that the reservations were 'confirmed' as the American Express Company had guaranteed to Outrigger a first night's payment in the event that the plaintiffs did not show up. Further, the plaintiffs claim that this guarantee was in fact the same thing as a cash deposit. Thus, plaintiffs argue that the defendants were under a duty to honor the confirmed reservations. Although the jury awarded $600 to the Dolds and $400 to the Mantheis, it is not known upon which count the recovery was based.

"An examination of the record in the instant case shows the following:

"(1) It was the policy of the Outrigger that a reservation was deemed confirmed when either a one night's cash deposit was made or the reservation was made by a booking agent which had established credit with the Outrigger.

"(2) The plaintiffs made their reservations through the American Express Company, which had established credit with the Outrigger.

"(3) In lieu of a cash deposit, the Outrigger accepted American Express Company's guarantee that it would pay the first night's deposit for the plaintiffs.

"(4) On February 18, 1968, the Outrigger referred 29 parties holding reservations at the Outrigger to the Pagoda Hotel which deemed these referrals 'overflows.'

"(5) On February 18, 1968, the Outrigger had 16 guests who stayed beyond their scheduled date of departure.

"(6) From February 15 to 17 and 19 to 22, 1968, the Outrigger also had more reservations that it could accommodate. Plaintiffs' exhibits Nos. 23 to 29 indicate the number of overflows and referrals of the above-mentioned reservations made by the Outrigger to the Pagoda Hotel on the following dates:

February	15	20	referrals
"	16	20	"
"	17	32	"
"	19	44	"
"	20	9	"
"	21	9	"
"	22	20	"

"(7) Evidence was adduced that the Outrigger made a profit from its referrals to the Pagoda Hotel. Upon advance payment for the rooms to American Express who in turn paid Outrigger, the plaintiffs were issued coupons representing the prepayment for the accommodations at the Outrigger. On referral by the Outrigger, the Pagoda Hotel's practice was to accept the coupons and bill the Outrigger for the actual cost of the rooms provided. The difference between the coupon's value and the actual value of the accommodations was retained by the Outrigger.

"Plaintiffs prevented a profit from being made by the Outrigger by refusing to use the coupons and paying in cash for the less expensive accommodations.

May Plaintiffs Recover Punitive Damages for Breach of Contract?

"The question of whether punitive damages are properly recoverable in an action for breach of contract has not been resolved in this jurisdiction.

"In the instant case, on the evidence adduced, the trial court refused to allow an instruction on the issue of punitive damages but permitted an instruction on the issue of emotional distress and disappointment.

"In a case involving a similar pattern of overbooking of reservations the court in *Wills v. Trans World Airlines, Inc.*, 200 F. Supp. 360 (S.D. Cal. 1961), stated that the substantial overselling of confirmed reservations for the period in question was a strong indication that the defendant airline had wantonly precipitated the very circumstances which compelled the removal of excess confirmed passengers from its flights.

"In *Goo v. Continental Casualty Company*, 52 Haw. 235, 483 P.2d 563 (1970), we affirmed the public policy considerations behind the doctrine of punitive damages and acknowledged the fact that some jurisdictions allow a recovery of punitive damages where the breach of contract is accompanied by some type of contemporaneous tortious activity. However, the *Goo* case did not afford the proper factual setting for this court to consider the propriety of an assessment of punitive damages in contract actions.

"Various jurisdictions have adopted their own rules regarding the nature of the tortious activity necessary to recover punitive damages in a contract action. Some require that the breach be accompanied by an independent willful tort [citations omitted], or by a fraudulent act [citation omitted], or by a concurrent breach of a common law duty [citation omitted].

"We are of the opinion that the facts of this case do not warrant punitive damages. However, the plaintiffs are not limited to the narrow traditional contractual remedy of out-of-pocket losses alone. We have recognized the fact that certain situations are so disposed as to present a fusion of the doctrines of tort and contract. [Citation omitted.] Though some courts have strained the traditional concept of compensatory damages in contract to include damages for emotional distress and disappointment (*Kellogg v. Commodore Hotel,* 187 Misc. 319, 64 N.Y.S.2d 131 (1946)), we are of the opinion that where a contract is breached in a wanton or reckless manner as to result in a tortious injury, the aggrieved person is entitled to recover in tort. Thus, in addition to damages for out-of-pocket losses, the jury was properly instructed on the issue of damages for emotional distress and disappointment.

May Plaintiffs Recover Punitive Damages for Breach of an Innkeeper's Duty to Accommodate?

"We now consider count III of plaintiffs' complaint. It has long been recognized that an innkeeper, holding himself out to the public to provide hotel accommodations, is obligated, in the absence of reasonable grounds for refusal, to provide accommodations to all persons upon proper request. *Perrine v. Paulos,* 100 Cal. App. 2d 665, 224 P.2d 41 (1950). This duty traditionally extended to the traveller who presented himself at the inn. However, where the innkeeper's accommodations had been exhausted, the innkeeper could justly refuse to receive an applicant. [Citations omitted.] It is well recognized that punitive damages are recoverable for breach of an innkeeper's duty to his guest where the innkeeper's conduct is deliberate or wanton. [Citations omitted.] We are not aware of any jurisdiction that renders an innkeeper liable on his common law duty to accommodate under the circumstances of this case. Consequently, plaintiffs are not entitled to an instruction on punitive damages on count III of their complaint.

"Judgment is affirmed."

The traditional view that exemplary damages as such or as relabeled by the Supreme Court of Hawaii in *Dold v. Outrigger*[48] are not available in a contract action for breach of reservation is reaffirmed in *Brown v. Hilton Hotels Corp.*[49] Here a married couple had prepaid and were guaranteed a reservation for two rooms for a party of four, but upon arrival were offered only one room with a cot. They refused these accommodations and were forced to fly home because of a lack of any other space in the locality. This resulted in an aggravation of the wife's preexisting heart condition. The court held that compensatory damages, that is, the prepaid room rate, were recoverable, but that no tort action for re-

---

[48] 501 P.2d at 372.
[49] 133 Ga. App. 286, 211 S.E.2d 125 (1974).

covery of medical costs or exemplary damages could be maintained since the hotel's failure to honor the reservation was nonfeasance rather than misfeasance or active negligent performance of the contract.

There are generally no degrees of negligence that limit or restrict recovery in breach-of-contract cases. Rather the issue is whether the breach was willful or intentional, rather than merely negligent or careless. Thus a breach of reservation based on misfeasance, that is, a failure to provide the guaranteed reservation not intentionally caused, does not sanction recovery for emotional distress or other forms of consequential damages. By its very nature, however, overbooking, that is, the acceptance of more reservations than there are accommodations available and gambling that some guaranteed reservation holders will not show, or if they do, will accept rooms in a less desirable facility previously arranged by the hotel where the guaranteed reservation was made, is an intentional, premeditated act. The fact that it was economically necessary has not yet caused the courts to hold that hotel overbooking is reasonable. It is this active negligence, a willful breach of contract, that has caused the courts to permit recovery of either punitive damages or damages for emotional or mental distress arising out of the breach.

The caterer or restaurant keeper who breaches his contract is not immune from liability. In a recent unpublished decision,[50] a Canadian court held that a caterer who failed to perform a wedding reception under a written function contract was responsible not only for out-of-pocket losses but for the grave emotional harm caused the plaintiffs, especially the bride, compounded by the fact that the cause was not defended. The full amount claimed, $10,000, was awarded. Judge Phelan reasoned:

> In addition to the recovery of the amounts claimed the plaintiffs seek general damages for breach of contract. Counsel for the plaintiffs has referred me to the English decisions which I mentioned earlier; *Jarvis v. Swan Tours Limited,* 1 Q.B., 233 (1973), a decision of the English Court of Appeal in which the principal judgment is written by Lord Justice Denning; *Jackson v. Horizon Holidays Limited* W.L.R., 1468 (1975), another decision of the Court of Appeal in England, again Lord Denning giving the principal judgment; *Cox v. Phillips Industries Limited* W.L.R., 638 (1976), a decision of Mr. Justice Lawson of the Queen's Bench Division; *Heywood v. Wellers,* 1 Q.B. Div. 446 (1976), this being still another decision of the English Court of Appeal, again with Lord Denning having written the judgment.
>
> It appears from these decisions that in certain breach of contract cases, the English Courts have allowed damages for mental distress in the same manner as damages for shock have been recovered in tort actions. The cases referred to involve situations where contracts were broken resulting in disappointment, distress, upset and frustration to the offended party as a result of the breach. The English cases involve situations where the plaintiffs made arrangements for holidays, which arrangements were frustrated because of the actions of the defendants.

[50]Cacares v. Anthony's Villa, File No. 65063 (County Court, York District of Toronto, Ontario, Feb. 23, 1978).

In the case at bar, I find it difficult to contemplate a situation which could cause more discomfort, vexation, inconvenience or distress than this one. These words, indeed, seem completely inadequate to express what surely would be heartbreak experienced, especially by the bride—female plaintiff in this case. The [ruin of the] greatest event in her life . . . [was] occasioned by the failure of the defendants to live up to the written agreement which has been entered into. Irreparable damage was done by these defendants, and it is certainly an experience which, I am certain, will remain with these plaintiffs as long as they live. It is difficult to visualize a more traumatic experience in the lives of these young people than the one they did experience in September 1977—the day of their wedding. Money can never really make up for the mental distress and vexation which has been caused to them, and I point out the defendants have been completely callous about the whole affair. They haven't seen fit to defend this action, or to appear at trial, or give any explanation whatsoever for their actions.

7:9 *Group Reservations: Conventions and Tours*

In *Cardinal Consulting Co. v. Circo Resorts, Inc.,*[51] plaintiff, a group tour promoter, entered into a reservation contract for a block of 58 rooms in defendant's Las Vegas Circus Circus Hotel. When the defendant allegedly breached the contract by its unjustified cancellation, plaintiff sued to recover compensatory and punitive damages, to include lost profits. A jury found defendant liable for breach of contract and awarded damages to include loss of profits. On a posttrial motion to vacate and set aside the jury verdict, enter judgment of dismissal, or order a new trial in the alternative, the court denied the motion,[52] holding that lost profits were adequately established.

CARDINAL CONSULTING CO. v. CIRCO RESORTS, INC.
297 N.W.2d 260 (Minn. 1980)

SHERAN, C.J.: " . . . On appeal from a jury verdict for Cardinal, Circo raises the following issues:

"1. Was there a binding contract between Cardinal and Circo that was breached by Circo?

"2. Did Cardinal prove lost profits with sufficient certainty to permit recovery?

"3. Was the amount of the jury verdict supported by the evidence?

"1. Circo takes the position that it did not breach the contract by cancelling the rooms reserved for Cardinal because the contract expressly and by custom recognized the parties' mutual right of cancellation upon 30-days written notice. Alternatively it argues that, if the hotel had no right to cancel, the contract would be void as a matter of law because it lacked mutuality of obligation or consideration. . . .

---

[51]File No. 81724, Minn. Dist. Ct., First Jud. Dist. County of Dakota (1978) (case remanded from federal district court and tried in state court).

[52]Order on motion dated Oct. 3, 1978.

"Our perusal of the record convinces us that there was sufficient evidence from which the jury could have found a contract for the reservation of 50 rooms at the Circus Circus Hotel from January 22 to April 29, 1976, which permitted Cardinal to cancel by 30-days notice, oral or written, without according an equal right to Circo. Haas, O'Neill and Valentine, Circo's national sales manager at the time the agreement was made, all testified that they had never discussed the hotel's reservation of a right to cancel the entire contract on 30-days written notice. Although Larson, who replaced Valentine in the Circo hierarchy, claimed that the contract as written merely recited the terms discussed by the parties, the strong, negative response of Haas and O'Neill to the suggestion that they sign it supported a jury finding to the contrary.

"Similarly, there was sufficient evidence to permit the jury to find that it was not the usual custom and practice in Las Vegas to allow for mutual rights of cancellation by either party upon 30-days written notice. Although Circo introduced expert testimony that all Las Vegas contracts had such clauses, Cardinal's experts disagreed. Moreover, both Valentine and the director of travel at Minnesota AAA explained why tour operators need more cancellation flexibility than hotel operators.

"Circo's argument that the contract lacked mutuality and, thus, was not binding on the parties has no merit. The concept of mutuality has been widely discredited in contract law, and it is now generally recognized that the obligations of the parties need not be substantially equal for there to be a binding contract. 1 S. Williston, Contracts §§ 105, 105A (3d ed. 1957); 1A A. Corbin Contracts §§ 152, 160, 161, 164 (1963). Moreover, 'Minnesota has long recognized the principle that where a contract is supported by valuable consideration (such as a detriment incurred in exchange for a promise . . .), then a right of one party to terminate it at will does not render it invalid for lack of mutuality.' *Clausen & Sons, Inc. v. Theo. Hamm Brewing Co.*, 395 F.2d 388, 391 (8th Cir. 1968).

"Although Circo takes the position that Cardinal's interpretation of the contract permitted it to cancel at will without limitation, Cardinal introduced evidence that it recognized and complied with the 30-day cancellation period. Haas and O'Neill testified that they advised Valentine in October that the tours in early January might have to be cancelled, and that they in fact orally cancelled on December 10 and December 13, both of which were within the 30-day cancellation period. Cardinal also maintained that by advertising its relation with Circus Circus it not only acted to its detriment but conferred a benefit upon Circo, both of which are sufficient to satisfy the consideration requirement. Thus, it was not improper for the court to reject the mutuality argument.

"2. Circo next contends that Cardinal's claim for lost profits should have been dismissed because Cardinal was not an established business and could not prove its lost profits with the requisite degree of certainty to support recovery. It attacks the damage award on three grounds: (1) that Cardinal did not prove the fact of lost profits because it could show no past or future profitability; (2) that Cardinal did not prove causation because other factors, such as its undercapitalization and lack of advertising, more plausibly explained its failure; and (3) that Cardinal incorrectly calculated and inadequately documented the amount of lost profits.

"The general rule in Minnesota is that damages in the form of lost profits 'may be recovered where they are shown to be the natural and probable consequences of the act or omission complained of and their amount is shown with a reasonable degree of certainty and exactness. This means that the nature of the business or venture upon which the anticipated profits are claimed must be such as to support an inference of definite profits grounded upon a reasonably sure basis of facts. . . . This rule does not call for absolute certainty.' *Appliances, Inc. v. Queen Stove Works, Inc.*, 228 Minn. 55, 63, 36 N.W.2d 121, 125 (1949) (quoting from *Johnson v. Wright,* 175 Minn. 236, 239, 220 N.W. 946, 948 (1928)). The controlling principle is that speculative, remote, or conjectural damages are not recoverable. [Citations omitted]; Restatement of Contracts § 331 (1) (1932); C. McCormick, Handbook on the Law of Damages § 26 (1935). Our earlier cases held that lost profits of unestablished businesses were not recoverable because they were speculative, remote, or conjectural, and thus incapable of proof [citation omitted], but this is no longer the law in Minnesota. *See, Leoni v. Bemis Co.*, 255 N.W.2d 824 (Minn. 1977). 'Although the law recognizes that it is more difficult to prove loss of prospective profits to a new business than to an established one, the law does not hold that it may not be done.' *Id.* at 826. As the Nebraska Supreme Court noted in *El Fredo Pizza, Inc. v. Roto-Flex Oven Co.*, 199 Neb. 697, 705, 706, 261 N.W.2d 358, 363–64 (1978),

"The rule that lost profits from a business are too speculative and conjectural to permit the recovery of damages therefor . . . "is not a hard and fast one, and loss of prospective profits may nevertheless be recovered if the evidence shows with reasonable certainty *both* their *occurrence* and the *extent* thereof. . . . Uncertainty as to the *fact* of whether any damages were sustained at all is fatal to recovery, but uncertainty as to the *amount* is not.' . . .

" . . . The fact that a business is new is relevant only insofar as that fact affects the certainty of proof of lost profits; it does not establish as a matter of law that damages for lost profits may not be recovered. (Emphasis in original.)

"While we have not yet addressed the issue of how a new business can prove its lost profits, other courts have suggested substitutes for past profitability that will remove a plaintiff's anticipated profits from the realm of speculation and support such a damage award. *See, e.g., Edwards v. Container Kraft Carton & Paper Supply Co.*, 161 Cal. App. 2d 752, 327 P.2d 622 (1958) (past performance as employee plus subsequent success); *El Fredo Pizza, Inc. V. Roto-Flex Oven Co.*, 199 Neb. 697, 261 N.W.2d 358 (1978) (subsequent success); *Butler v. Westgate State Bank*, 3 Kan. App. 2d 403, 596 P.2d 156 (1979) (other examples of that type of business); *Alliance Tractor & Implement Co. v. Lukens Tool & Die Co.*, 204 Neb. 248, 281 N.W.2d 778 (1979) (plaintiff's skill and expertise together with proven existence of a market for the product). What is important is that the loss be established with reasonable certainty, *and this depends upon the circumstances of the particular case. Smith Dev. Corp. v. Bilow Enterprises, Inc.*, 112 R.I. 203, 308 A.2d 477, 482 (1973). *Accord, Vickers v. Wichita State Univ., Wichita*, 213 Kan. 614, 518 P.2d 512, 515 (1974).

"We agree with Circo that the evidence relating to lost profits that was presented by Cardinal lacks precision. Nevertheless, we can not say that it was unreasonable for the jury to award lost profits to Cardinal, given the unusual circumstances of this particular enterprise and the devastating effect of Circo's breach.

"Although Cardinal was able to demonstrate no past or future profitability, one of several substitutes was available in the evidence presented at trial. Haas and O'Neill were portrayed as persons with extensive experience in arranging tours who were also familiar with Las Vegas. They entered the OTC market early with packages and others, such as retail agencies or social clubs would be selling for them. Moreover, the market they chose was a fertile one. Las Vegas was very popular with the people from the Upper Midwest, and the small cities on which they were concentrating offered an untapped source of tour participants. Temporally, they were planning to operate their tours during the peak tourist period when 75 percent of the Midwest's tourists visit Las Vegas. This same market and time period have been extremely profitable for those travel agencies who began OTC packages the following year. Thus the jury could have reasonably based its decision that Cardinal lost profits either on evidence of the skill and expertise of plaintiff's principals plus the proven existence of a market, *Alliance Tractor & Implement Co. v. Lukens Tool & Die Co.*, 204 Neb. 248, 281 N.W.2d 778 (1979), or on evidence of profitability of OTC programs operated by other travel agencies in the same general geographic area at the same time of year, *Butler v. Westgate State Bank*, 3 Kan. App. 2d 403, 596 P.2d 156 (1979).

"Similarly, the evidence, although weak, supports the inference that were it not for the cancellation by Circo, Cardinal would have been able to fill all its flights, except the first three. The jury could reasonably have based such a finding on the fact that Cardinal sold out the eight trips it actually ran, which could not have been accomplished but for the energy and skill of Haas and O'Neill and the significant unmet demand for a travel service of this kind. That they were able to do so well on such short notice is persuasive to us, particularly because the substituted hotel, being new, lacked the appeal that the better known and advertised Circus Circus Hotel would have had for prospective customers. What is significant is that Cardinal had moved into a travel field that opened up as a result of a change in CAB regulations and had, by virtue of its contracts with North Central Airlines and Circo, placed itself in control of the essential elements of a successful enterprise. Thus, it was reasonable for the jury to determine that what doomed Cardinal's tour program was the change of management at Circus Circus and the cancellation of the 50 rooms. As the wrongdoer, Circo should not be permitted to evade its liability, just because its wrongful cancellation involved a new business rather than an established one. *Bigelow v. RKO Radio Pictures Inc.*, 327 U.S. 251, 264–65 . . . (1946). . . .

"3. Finally, Circo contends that the damage award was excessive and seeks either a reduction of the amount or a new trial on the issue of damages. The general rule in Minnesota, however, is that the trial court has broad discretion in determining whether defendant should get a new trial for excessive damages. *Lambertson v. Cincinnati Corp.*, 257 N.W.2d 679, 684 (Minn. 1977); *Bisbee v. Ruppert*, 306 Minn. 39, 235 N.W.2d 364 (1975). '[T]he primary responsibility for the reduction of excessive damages lies in the trial court, and . . . a trial court's ruling on this point will only be disturbed where a clear abuse of discretion is demonstrated.' *Bigham v. J.C. Penney Co.*, 268 N.W.2d 892, 898 (Minn. 1978).

"Of the total verdict of $71,500, $69,595 consisted of lost profits. The court was satisfied that this figure represented what Cardinal lost by not being able to run its tour package from January 22, 1976, until April 25, 1976, with its costs fixed as they were on January 5, 1976, when Circo wrongfully breached the contract. We do not believe it abused its discretion in so determining.

"Affirmed."

Group reservations are also discussed in *King of Prussia Enterprises, Inc. v. Greyhound Lines, Inc.* in section 7:6, *supra*.

Under what circumstances is a group hotel reservation contract enforceable in the absence of a specific price and method of payment? The federal Circuit Court of Appeals for the Ninth Circuit, applying California law, held that a reservation contract which specified that the current stated prices which were quoted to the convention at the time of contract execution were base prices subject to adjustment at the time of performance was sufficiently definite to render the contract enforceable against the convention's claim that the contract lacked definiteness as to price and method of payment.[53]

In a more recent case, the federal Circuit Court for the Tenth Circuit reviewed the sufficiency of the evidence to support a jury award to the Rainbow Travel Service for breach of contract and fraud. The contract claim was reversed. The fraud claim was affirmed. The fraud and contract portions of the court's decision are set forth below.

RAINBOW TRAVEL SERVICE V. HILTON HOTELS CORP.
896 F.2d 1233 (10th Cir. 1990)

BROWN, J.: [Statement of facts omitted.]

Fraud

"Appellants next argue that the evidence was insufficient to support the jury's verdict on fraud. Under Oklahoma law, fraud consists of a false material representation made as a positive assertion which is known either to be false, or is

---

[53]*See* Hotel Del Coronado Corp. v. Food Service Equipment Distributors Ass'n, 783 F.2d 1323 (9th Cir. 1986).

made recklessly without knowledge of the truth, with the intention that it be acted upon by a party to his or her detriment. *Tice v. Tice,* 672 P.2d 1168, 1171 (Okla. 1983). As the jury was instructed, fraud must be shown by clear and convincing evidence. *Id.* Rainbow argued in the district court that a Hilton agent's assurances that rooms would be available amounted to fraud because the representations were made recklessly without knowledge of the truth. Most of the evidence at trial centered on whether Hilton knew or should have known there would be a shortage of rooms at the Fontainebleau on September 26, 1986. Interpreting the evidence in the light most favorable to the plaintiff, we find there was sufficient evidence to raise a question of fact for the jury on the issue of fraud.

"Rainbow presented evidence that Hilton accepted reservations for more rooms than were available on September 26, 1986. Hilton admitted that its policy was to book the Fontainebleau up to one hundred and fifteen per cent of its capacity, but argued that it did so based on a historic fifteen per cent 'no-show' rate for guests with reservations. Hilton insisted that this policy allowed the hotel to honor almost all of its reservations. Although Hilton showed that an exceedingly high percentage of reservations were in fact honored over the course of the year, Rainbow presented evidence showing that on fifty per cent of those occasions when the hotel was operating at capacity the hotel had to dishonor reservations. Additionally, Rainbow presented evidence tending to show that Hilton was aware of a substantial likelihood that Rainbow's reservation might be dishonored. Rainbow showed that Hilton knew at least one month in advance that a large number of rooms would be closed for maintenance during September of 1986. Rainbow also argued that departure figures from the Fontainebleau showed that the hotel knew that a substantial number of people would stay over past their announced departure date. Additionally, Rainbow showed that on the date in question Hilton gave a block of rooms to a group from the University of Oklahoma even though the group had not reserved the rooms. Despite these factors, and pursuant to Hilton policy, Rainbow was not informed of the practice of overbooking and was not told there was a possibility that 'guaranteed' reservations might be dishonored. Instead, Hilton assured Rainbow that the rooms would be available.

"Hilton argued strenuously in the district court that the overbooking situation was due to factors beyond its control, such as guests extending their stay at the Fontainebleau and rooms being out of order for repairs. These explanations may have sounded rather hollow to the jury, however, in light of a portion of the Fontainebleau's policy manual which read:

Overboard

"We never tell a guest we 'overbooked.'

"If an overboard situation arises, it is due to the fact that something occurred that the hotel could not prevent.

"Examples:

"1. Scheduled departures do not vacate their rooms.

"2. Engineering problems with a room (pipe bursted, thus water leaks, air conditioning, heating out of commission, broken glass, etc.)

"Always remain calm and as pleasant as possible.

"(Plaintiff's Exhibit 25–2). . . .

" . . . [W]e find substantial evidence in the record that Hilton was aware of having overbooked the hotel to such an extent as to create a substantial likelihood that Rainbow's reservation would be dishonored. *Cf. Marriott Corporation v. American Academy of Psychotherapists, Inc.*, 157 Ga. App. 497, 277 S.E.2d 785 (1981). Despite this, Hilton repeatedly told Rainbow that its rooms would be available and did not tell Rainbow that the group might be 'bumped.' Based on this and all of the evidence in the record before us, we find that a reasonable juror could find by clear and convincing evidence that Hilton recklessly made statements without knowledge of their truth, that Hilton did so with the intention that plaintiff rely on them, and that plaintiff relied on the statements to its detriment. *See Tice v. Tice*, 672 P.2d 1168, 1171 (Okla. 1983) ('When fraud is properly alleged by one party and denied by the other party, the existence or nonexistence of fraud becomes a question of fact.') *See also Federal Deposit Insurance Corp. v. Palermo*, 815 F.2d 1329, 1335 (10th Cir. 1987). . . .

V. Damages for Breach of Contract

"Appellants contend that the jury's award of $5,493.10 for breach of contract was not supported by the evidence. We have examined the record in detail and we agree with appellant that this figure is not supported by the record. There was little evidence presented as to damages from the breach of the contract. Rainbow did not seek damages for lost profits from the Miami trip. Indeed, the evidence was that the travel agency realized its expected profit from the trip. Rainbow only suffered out of pocket expenses of $796.00 from the breach. Aside from these expenses, however, Rainbow sought to recover $8,740.00, which was the amount paid by Rainbow's clients to Rainbow for the Miami trip (excluding airfare). A. J. Musgrove testified that he would like to repay his customers since they did not get the rooms that Rainbow promised they would get. Hilton argued that this was an improper attempt to recover on behalf of Rainbow's clients. Rainbow's response was to argue that this was a necessary expense to help repair Rainbow's good will.

"We agree that under the evidence in this case it was improper to allow Rainbow to recover an amount to pay back to its customers. Clearly, Rainbow had no right to recover on behalf of its clients. Thus, the amounts paid by Rainbow's customers were only relevant insofar as Rainbow's good will was concerned. Awarding Rainbow both the full extent of injury to its good will, however, *and* the means to repair that damage amounts to a double recovery. Mr. Musgrove's opinion that Rainbow had suffered damage to its good will did not take into account the effect of giving refunds to its customers for the Miami trip. In fact, Rainbow's argument that its good will had been injured relied heavily on the fact that its customers had not been paid back. Yet, under the instructions on the fraud count, the jury was told that if it found fraud it should fully compensate Rainbow for any loss of good will arising from Hilton's conduct. The jury did so, awarding $37,500.00 in damages attributable to loss of good will. Rainbow cannot have it both ways. It cannot recover the full extent of damage to its good will while seeking additional money that it claims is necessary to repair the injury to good will. In view of this fact, there is simply no evidence to support the jury's award of $5,493.10 for breach of contract.

"Under the instructions given to the jury in this case, the defendants were entitled to a setoff of $5,892.90 on any damages arising from a breach of the parties' agreement. This setoff was due to the fact that Hilton refunded a portion of Rainbow's initial payment for the hotel rooms. Accordingly, we must offset the amount of $5,892.90 against the $796.00 loss claimed by Rainbow. When this is done, it is apparent that Rainbow is not entitled to recover any damages from Hilton for the breach of contract. . . .

Conclusion

"The judgment is AFFIRMED in all respects except as to the damages for breach of contract; on that issue we REVERSE the judgment as unsupported by the evidence.

"IT IS SO ORDERED."

8 Innkeeper's Duty to Guest:
Courteous and Considerate Treatment

8:1 *Common-Law Duties of Innkeeper to Guest*

The common-law duties of the innkeeper require that he furnish his guests: (1) shelter, (2) protection, and (3) food. He is thus called upon to provide safe premises, to protect the guest against personal harm, and to furnish a sufficient quantity of wholesome food.

8:2 *Innkeeper's Right of Access to Guest's Room*

It is a basic legal principle governing the relationship of innkeeper and guest that the innkeeper holds himself out as able and willing to entertain guests for hire, and, in the absence of a specific contract, the law implies that he will furnish such entertainment as the character of his inn and reasonable attention to the convenience and comfort of his guests will afford.

If the guest is assigned to a room upon the express or implied understanding that he is to be the sole occupant thereof during the time that it is set apart for his use, the innkeeper retains a right of access thereto only at such proper times and for such reasonable purposes as may be necessary in the general conduct of the inn or in attending to the needs of a particular guest. If, for instance, there should be an outbreak of fire, a leakage of water or gas, or any other emergency calling for immediate action in a room assigned to a guest, the innkeeper and his servants must necessarily have the right to enter without regard to the time of day or night and without consulting the guest. It is equally clear that the innkeeper and his servants must have access to the room at all such reasonable times as will enable him to fulfill his express or implied contract to furnish his guest with such convenience and comfort as the inn affords. No hard and fast rule on right of entry can be laid down, for what would be reasonable in a case where a room is occupied by two or more guests, or where access to one room can be had only through another, might be highly unreasonable where a separate room is assigned to the exclusive use of a single guest. It is also proper and necessary that an innkeeper have the right to make and enforce reasonable rules designed to prevent immorality, drunkenness, or any form of misconduct that may be offensive to other guests, or that may bring his inn into disrepute, or that may be radically inconsistent with the generally recognized proprieties of life. The guest must submit to these reserved rights of the innkeeper.

Should an emergency arise, calling for immediate and unpremeditated action on the part of the innkeeper or his employees to secure the safety or protection of the guests or of the building in which they are housed, the usual rules of decency, propriety, convenience, or comfort might be disregarded without subjecting the innkeeper to liability for mistake of judgment or delinquency in conduct. But for all other purposes any occasional or regular entries into a guest's room are subject to the fundamental consideration that it is for the time being *his* room and that he is entitled to respectful and considerate treatment at the hands of his host. Such treatment necessarily implies an observance by the innkeeper and his employees of the proprieties as to the time and manner of entering the guest's room and of civil deportment toward him when such an entry was either necessary or proper.[1]

8:3 *Exclusive Right of Guest to Use and Possession of Assigned Room*

The guest also has affirmative rights which the innkeeper is not at liberty willfully to ignore or violate. When a guest is assigned to a room for his exclusive use, it is his for all proper purposes and at all times until he gives it up. This exclusive right of use and possession is subject to occasional entries by the innkeeper and his servants as necessary in the reasonable discharge of their duties, but these entries must be made with due regard to the occasion and at such times and in such manner as are consistent with the rights of the guest. A guest at a public inn has the right to insist upon respectful and decent treatment at the hands of the innkeeper and his servants. That right is an essential part of the contract, whether express or implied, and necessarily implies an obligation on the part of innkeeper that neither he nor his servants will abuse or insult the guest or indulge in any conduct or speech that may unnecessarily bring upon him physical discomfort or distress of mind. The innkeeper, it is true, is not an insurer of the safety, conveniences, or comfort of the guest. But he is bound to exercise reasonable care that neither he nor his servants shall by uncivil, harsh, or cruel treatment destroy or minimize the comfort, convenience, and peace that the guest would ordinarily enjoy if the inn were properly conducted, due allowance being always made for the grade of the inn and the kind of accommodation which it is designed to afford.[2]

8:4 *Authority of Management and Law Enforcement Agents to Enter Guest's Room and Seize Guest's Property*

In case of quarrelsome or other objectionable conduct in a guest's room, such as shouting, screaming, or fighting, an innkeeper may deem it necessary to call for police assistance. Under what circumstances may a police officer enter an occupied guest room solely at the behest of the innkeeper?

[1]DeWolf v. Ford, 193 N.Y. 397, 86 N.E. 527 (1908).
[2]*Id.*

In *People v. Gallmon*,[3] the night manager of a rooming house summoned the police to investigate noisy conduct in a guest room. The officers, in company of the night manager, knocked on defendant's door and after waiting for a minute for defendant to open the door, directed the night manager to open it with his pass key. Defendant was found stripped to the waist with a narcotic instrument in his right hand and was arrested, prosecuted, and convicted for unlawful possession of the contraband. Defendant's motion to suppress the evidence obtained against him was denied.

The license to the landlord does not afford the police an unqualified privilege to engage in an otherwise unlawful practice merely on the consent of the hotel proprietor. But where the police are called in to aid the manager in the performance of his duty to the occupants of the building, their entry is investigatory in its nature, not based on consent or license, and may be made without consent.

SUMDUM V. STATE
612 P.2d 1018 (Alaska 1980)

MATTHEWS, J.: "The defendant, Rick Sumdum, contends that the police entry into his motel room was the product of an illegal search, and that the evidence of stolen goods found on his person pursuant to that entry should be suppressed. The superior court denied the motion to suppress and we affirm.

"At 5:30 A.M., May 7, 1978, Pete Heger was awakened by an intruder in his motel room at the Driftwood Lodge in Juneau. Later that morning, Heger's roommate, Roy Claxton, discovered that his watch, cash, and marijuana were missing. The Driftwood's manager, Leona Gran, was notified of the theft, and the police were summoned. In the presence of the police, Heger described the burglar to other lodgers, one of whom pointed to room 38 and said Rick Sumdum was the one they wanted.

"This identification was made at approximately 12:30 P.M., some one and one-half hours after the Driftwood's posted checkout time of 11:00 A.M. Gran informed the police that room 38 was registered in the name of one K. Brown, and that neither the registered guest nor anyone else had yet reregistered.

"At the suppression hearing Gran testified that it was her responsibility to ascertain whether guests who had failed to appear by 11:00 A.M. were 'skips,' and if they were not, whether they intended to vacate their room or reregister. Her customary procedure was to telephone the occupants of the room, knock on their door, and enter their room, in that order, if such steps were necessary for the determination she was required to make. Though she had not yet done so when room 38 was suggested as the suspected burglar's quarters, the manager testified that she intended to and certainly would have followed her customary procedures even if the police had not been present.

"On her own initiative, Gran telephoned room 38 and received no answer. Thereupon, Gran, Peter Heger, Dave Heger, Roy Claxton, and two police offi-

[3]19 N.Y.2d 389, 227 N.E.2d 284 (1967).

cers, walked over to room 38. Gran knocked on the door, received no response, and retrieved the key from her office. She then opened the door. From the doorway, the two men could be seen, both apparently asleep. Also clearly visible, on the outstretched wrist of the man on the cot closest to the door, was a distinctive watch which Claxton immediately identified as his own. In addition, the clothing worn by the man fit the description given earlier by Heger. The police officers then entered the motel room and arrested and handcuffed the suspect, Rick Sumdum. They searched his person, finding sixty dollars in cash, and searched under his cot, finding a buckknife. At the station house, a bag of marijuana was found strapped to Sumdum's leg. . . .

"A guest in a motel has a constitutionally protected right to privacy in his motel room and motel personnel cannot consent to a search of the guest's room. *Stoner v. California,* 376 U.S. 483, 490, . . . *rehearing denied* 377 U.S. 940, . . . (1964); *Finch v. State,* 592 P.2d 1196, 1197 n. 3 (Alaska 1979); [citation omitted]. But after the rental period has terminated, a guest's reasonable expectations of privacy are greatly diminished with respect to the right of motel management to enter. [Citation omitted.] . . . Gran testified that motel guests frequently left without paying their bill. After checkout time, she tried to contact Sumdum by phoning his room and by knocking at his door, but there was no response. Gran then opened the door to his room in order to determine whether he had vacated. Her authority to do so, at the time she would normally have done so, in accordance with her customary procedure, was not altered by the presence of the police. Assuming the police were in a location which did not violate Sumdum's rights before the door was opened, Gran's opening of the door for a legitimate private purpose did not constitute an illegal search merely because the police were present. . . .

"The judgment of the Superior Court is affirmed."

In *People v. Minervini,*[4] defendants' motions to suppress the evidence and to set aside an information charging them with burglary of hotel property, granted below, were reversed. In rejecting defendants' argument that the entry into the guest room by the hotel manager constituted an unconstitutional search and seizure, the court stated:

> More important however, is the rule that if the manager had a right to enter the rooms because of circumstances affecting the relationship between him and the defendants and between him and his property, that right would not be diminished if he sought police assistance in exercising that right or even if he was encouraged by the police to so exercise it. [Citations omitted.]
>
> In the case at bench, it is significant that any "search" by the manager was not conducted to discover or examine the effects of guests, or to observe their activities, but to secure the premises themselves and to prevent theft of property belonging to the motel.

[4] 20 Cal. App. 3d 832, 98 Cal. Rptr. 107 (1971).

It is abundantly clear that hotel management retains control over all premises including rooms occupied by guests.

The customer in a motel is a "lodger" or a guest, not a tenant. . . . He has a personal contract and no interest in the realty. The contract contains certain implied reciprocal rights and duties. As a minimum the guest impliedly covenants not to damage or steal motel property. A breach of such a covenant gives the proprietor a right to treat the contract of occupancy as terminated.

Thus a guest may be excluded from the premises and his privilege of occupancy forfeited because of his unlawful conduct.

As a method of preserving his rights in the contract the proprietor retains rights of reasonable access to prevent damage to or destruction of the property.

"A 'lodger' has only the right to use the premises, subject to the landlord's retention of control and *right of of access to them.*" (Italics added.) (*Stowe v. Fritzie Hotels, Inc.*, 44 Cal. 2d 416, at p. 421 [282 P.2d 890].) Inspection of the property in the face of information reasonably indicating an ongoing burglary or theft was within the concept and bounds of reasonable access by management.

In the case at bar it is questionable whether these respondents acquired the status of a genuine "guest." Their purpose in registering and gaining entry into the rooms was neither shelter nor sanctuary, but the opportunity to commit theft.

A person does not become a guest by obtaining a room at an inn solely for the accomplishment of an unlawful purpose.

Thus, the manager had a right under the circumstances to enter the rooms and to treat the occupancy of respondents as terminated. It is clear that a claimed agency relationship between police and management could not extinguish this right. . . .

The philosophy expressed in several decisions [citations omitted], is pertinent: "A trespasser—or burglar—cannot make another man's home his castle."

The conduct of the clerk, manager and police was above reproach, and no evidence obtained by them was subject to exclusion or suppression. . . .

Additional support for the general rule concerning the guest's right to privacy is found in *People v. Cohen.*[5] In *United States v. Cowan*[6] the United States Court of Appeals for the Second Circuit rejected the argument that a seizure of luggage of a nonpaying guest under an existing innkeeper's statutory lien was an invasion of the guest's privacy requiring suppression of the evidence that the luggage in question constituted stolen property:

Cowan contends that the search and seizure of the luggage were unlawful. We hold that appellant does not have standing to raise this issue. . . .

The Supreme Court's decisions in *Stoner v. State of California*, 376 U.S. 483 . . . (1964) and *Chapman v. United States*, 367 U.S. 610 . . . (1961), upon which appellant relies, recognized that protection of privacy requires suppression in some circumstances where property interests have not been violated. Here there was no invasion of Cowan's right to privacy. He had lost his right to use the room and with this the law gave the hotel the right to seize the property. Although Cowan concedes that the hotel was entitled to remove the luggage from the room, and pre-

[5]59 Cal. App. 3d 241, 130 Cal. Rptr. 656 (1976).
[6]396 F.2d 83 (2d Cir. 1968).

pare it for sale, he argues that he retained all other rights in the property and therefore the hotel manager's consent was not sufficient to authorize the search. This argument is unsound because, whatever Cowan's rights to reclaim the luggage might be under New York Law, it is clear that by leaving the luggage in the room and failing to pay his bill, Cowan forfeited the right to occupy the room undisturbed and, as to the luggage, the right to retain possession and any claim to privacy concerning it and its contents.

In view of the information given to the F.B.I. the hotel had the right, if not the duty, to render every assistance to determine who were the lawful owners of the luggage and its contents. . . . *Miranda v. State of Arizona*, 384 U.S. 436, 477–78 (1966).

Under these circumstances, Cowan's privacy was not invaded when the hotel manager permitted the federal agents to examine the contents of the baggage at the hotel or when the agents seized the baggage after Cowan's arrest. And since the hotel, not Cowan, was entitled to retain possession at the time when the baggage was seized there was no interference with Cowan's property rights, such as they were, in the luggage. . . .

Moreover, we agree with Judge Weinfeld that the luggage had been abandoned at the time of the search. *United States v. Cowan*, 37 F.R.D. 215, 217 (S.D.N.Y. 1965). . . . Cowan's conduct supports the district court's inference that he intended to relinquish possession of the property. Appellant failed to pay his hotel bill on March 28 and did not return to or communicate with the hotel prior to his arrest on April 8 although he had told the clerk when he took the room that he only intended to stay one night. Judge Weinfeld's finding is amply supported by the record and is not clearly erroneous. . . .

The judgment is affirmed.

In *Holt v. State*[7] the Alabama Court of Criminal Appeals rejected the right of an intruder to claim the room of an absent guest as a sanctuary from arrest. The court reasoned:

> The defendant was arrested in a hotel room not his own. The registered guest was not present. The night manager of the hotel opened the door with a pass key.
>
> The defendant approached a police officer, drew a revolver and pulled the trigger twice. The gun misfired both times. The officer disarmed Holt.
>
> The defendant, on the record before us, has no standing to assert that the officer was a trespasser. True, the night manager was not cloaked with any apparent blanket authority by the registered guest. *Stoner v. California*, 376 U.S. 483. . . . However, an innkeeper who knows of an intruder in an absent guest's room has a right to enquire by whose permission, if any, he has entered. *Compare United States v. Jeffers*, 342 U.S. 48. . . .
>
> Such limitation on the authority of the landlord vis-a-vis the guest is not by any analogy a restraint on the landlord when confronted with a burglar. A hotel room is entitled to the protection of the burglary statute. *Avinger v. State*, 29 Ala. App. 161, 195 So. 279.

---

[7]46 Ala. App. 555, 246 So. 2d 85 (Cr. App. 1971).

. . . Though we have not extended this opinion to discuss each and every point raised in briefs, nevertheless from a consideration of the entire record we conclude that the judgment of the lower court is one to be
Affirmed.

In the case that follows, the U.S. Court of Appeals, for the Eighth Circuit, applying Minnesota law, held that a warrantless entry into defendant's hotel room was lawful, justifying a search of the room, where the defendant was ejected by the police upon request of the hotel manager for committing disorderly conduct.

UNITED STATES V. RAMBO
789 F.2d 1289 (8th Cir. 1986)

GIBSON, C.J.: [Statement of facts and other issues omitted.]

"Rambo argues, in the alternative, that even if we conclude that the officers' entry and arrest was authorized by state law, their actions, under these circumstances, violated the fourth amendment. Specifically, Rambo contends, a warrantless arrest in a dwelling place, such as a hotel room, is permitted only under exigent circumstances, which Rambo contends were not present here. Moreover, he argues, the Supreme Court's recent decision in *Welsh v. Wisconsin*, 466 U.S. 740, 104 S. Ct. 2091, 80 L. Ed. 2d 732 (1984), suggests that where the suspected offense is only a minor misdemeanor, as he asserts disorderly conduct is, warrantless entry to arrest is prohibited as a matter of law, regardless of the presence of any exigent circumstances.

"We do not doubt that the protections against warrantless intrusions into the home announced in *Payton v. New York*, 445 U.S. 573, 100 S. Ct. 1371, 63 L. Ed. 2d 639 (1980), apply with equal force to a properly rented hotel room during the rental period. *See United States v. Morales*, 737 F.2d 761, 764 (8th Cir. 1984); *see also United States v. Baldacchino*, 762 F.2d 170, 175–76 (1st Cir. 1985); *United States v. Bulman*, 667 F.2d 1374 (11th Cir.), *cert. denied*, 456 U.S. 1010, 102 S. Ct. 2305, 73 L. Ed. 2d 1307 (1982); 2 W. LaFave, Search and Seizure § 6.1, at 157 (Supp. 1986). In the present case, however, Rambo was asked to leave the hotel by the officers, acting at the request of and on behalf of the hotel manager, because of his disorderly behavior. Magistrate's Report at 1–2. Thus, Rambo was justifiably ejected from the hotel under Minnesota law, *see* § 327.73 subd. 1, and the rental period therefore had terminated. *See United States v. Haddad*, 558 F.2d 968, 975 (9th Cir. 1977). At that time, control over the hotel room reverted to the management. Rambo no longer had a reasonable expectation of privacy in the hotel room, and therefore is now without standing to contest the officers' entry (search) into the hotel room. *United States v. Clifford*, 664 F.2d 1090, 1092 (8th Cir. 1981); *accord United States v. Underwood*, 717 F.2d 482, 484 (9th Cir. 1983), *cert. denied*, 465 U.S. 1036, 104 S. Ct. 1309, 79 L. Ed. 2d 707 (1984); *United States v. Robinson*, 698 F.2d 448, 454 (D.C.

Cir. 1983). Rambo cannot assert an expectation of being free from police intrusion upon his solitude and privacy in a place from which he has been justifiably expelled. . . .

"Rambo also argues that regardless of the officers' authority to enter his hotel room and arrest him, their subsequent search of his belongings and the hotel room violated the fourth amendment, and the evidence of the cocaine and currency must be suppressed. The magistrate held that Rambo had validly consented to the search, and, in the alternative, that the search was justified as incident to arrest or an inventory search, and the items seized were thus admissible.

"For the same reason which led us to conclude that Rambo has no standing to challenge the officer's entry to arrest, he has no standing to challenge the seizure of the small bag of cocaine which was discovered by the officers under the mattress during their search. *See Rawlings v. Kentucky,* 448 U.S. 98, 104–05, 100 S. Ct. 2556, 2561–62, 65 L. Ed. 2d 633 (1980). *Cf. United States v. Lee,* 700 F.2d 424, 426 (10th Cir.), *cert. denied,* 462 U.S. 1122, 103 S. Ct. 3094, 77 L. Ed. 2d 1353 (1983) (evidence discovered in motel under bed during search consented to by manager after rental period elapsed admissible as defendant had no reasonable expectation of privacy in area). Whether Rambo has standing to challenge the officers' search of his locked luggage raises a more difficult question. *Cf. Donovan v. A.A. Beiro Construction Co., Inc.,* 746 F.2d 894, 901–902 (D.C. Cir. 1984) (search conducted pursuant to consent of third party does not include areas or objects in which absent owner has manifested high expectation of privacy); *Lee,* 700 F.2d at 426 (same); *United States v. Block,* 590 F.2d 535, 541 (4th Cir. 1978) (same). However, we need not address this question for we find that Rambo validly consented to the search of this luggage.

"An individual may validly consent to an otherwise impermissible search if, in the totality of circumstances, consent is freely and voluntarily given, and not the product of implicit or explicit coercion. *Schneckloth v. Bustamonte,* 412 U.S. 218, 226–27, 93 S. Ct. 2041, 2047–48, 36 L. Ed. 2d 854 (1973); *United States v. Dennis,* 625 F.2d 782, 793 (8th Cir. 1980). Although the fact of custody, alone, does not render consent involuntary, the government bears a heavy burden of proving that consent granted by an individual under arrest was not the product of coercion. *United States v. Slupe,* 692 F.2d 1183, 1188 (8th Cir. 1982). Whether consent was voluntarily given is a question of fact. *United States v. Kampbell,* 574 F.2d 962, 963 (8th Cir. 1978).

"We recognize that Rambo was possibly under the influence of a narcotic at the time of his arrest, Magistrate's Report at 5, and was highly disturbed. However, the mere fact that one has taken drugs, or is intoxicated, or mentally agitated, does not render consent involuntary. *See United States v. Gay,* 774 F.2d 368, 377 (10th Cir. 1985); *United States v. Elrod,* 441 F.2d 353, 355 (5th Cir. 1971). In each case, '[t]he question is one of mental awareness so that the act of consent was the consensual act of one who knew what he was doing and had a reasonable appreciation of the nature and significance of his actions.' *Elrod,* 441 F.2d at 355.

"The magistrate found that Rambo was not cowed by authority, and answered questions intelligently. After the officers advised Rambo of his *Miranda* rights, he responded that he would answer only certain questions. He responded coherently and rationally to the officers' requests for identification, and voluntarily directed them to his luggage. When Officer Tucker was unable to find any identification in Rambo's garment bag, Rambo directed him to his other luggage, and informed the officers where he kept the key to the padlocks on the various compartments. Rambo told the officers, when they first discovered the cocaine in his luggage, that it was for his personal use only, indicating an appreciation and comprehension of his circumstances. The officer's search was brief and its scope was consistent with the desire to secure identification; there is no evidence that the officers tried to coerce Rambo's consent to the search of his belongings. While it is clear that Rambo was in need of assistance and, indeed, needed to be subdued physically, we believe there is substantial evidence that Rambo was competent to understand the nature of his acts, and his consent was fully and voluntarily given.

"We affirm the judgment of the district court."

8:5 *Authority to Record Telephone Calls and Transmit to Police*

The Supreme Court of California in *People v. Blair* [8] has rejected the right of an innkeeper to transmit a list of a guest's telephone calls to the police without a search warrant or other legal process.

We next consider whether the police acted improperly in obtaining from an employee of the Hyatt House, without legal process, a list of telephone calls made from defendant's room while a guest at the hotel. Among those calls was one to Wellman on the day of the murders.

In *People v. McKunes* (1975) 51 Cap. App. 3d 487 [124 Cal. Rptr. 126], it was held . . . that the police may not, without legal process, obtain from the telephone company records revealing the calls dialed by a defendant from his home or office. The court reasoned that, as with bank records, a telephone subscriber has a reasonable expectation that the calls he makes will be utilized only for the accounting functions of the telephone company and that he cannot anticipate that his personal life, as disclosed by the calls he makes and receives, will be disclosed to outsiders without legal process. As with bank records, concluded the court, it is virtually impossible for an individual or business entity to function in the modern economy without a telephone, and a record of telephone calls also provides "a virtual current biography."

The fact that the telephone calls in the present case were made by defendant from a hotel room rather than his home does not render the *McKunes* rationale inapplicable. As in the case of a telephone call from a private residence, a hotel guest may reasonably expect that the calls which he makes from his room are recorded by the hotel for billing purposes only, and that the record of his calls will not be transmitted to others without legal process. The People argue that because there is no "on-

[8]25 Cal. 3d 640, 602 P.2d 738 (1979).

going relationship'' between a hotel and a guest who rents a room for a limited period, the situation is distinguishable from *McKunes.* . . . But the hotel room is in reality a residence, however temporary. Thus the critical issue is whether there is an expectation of privacy in the information sought; such an expectation may exist even in the briefest encounter between the persons who impart and receive the information. We conclude, therefore, that the motion to suppress should have been granted as to the telephone call which defendant made from the Hyatt House to Wellman on December 14.

We have concluded above that the trial court erred in failing to suppress the evidence regarding . . . the telephone call made by defendant to Wellman from the Hyatt House. Under all the circumstances, these errors were not prejudicial. . . . The evidence that defendant called Wellman from Oakland on the day of the murders did not significantly advance the prosecution's case. . . . It is not reasonably probable that a result more favorable to defendant would have been reached in the absence of the trial court's errors in admitting this evidence. [Citation omitted.]

The judgment is affirmed.

The following case deals with a related subject, the authority to eavesdrop by telephone upon a guest.

PEOPLE V. SOLES
68 Cal. App. 3d 418, 136 Cal. Rptr. 328 (1977)

CHRISTIAN, A.J.: ''Gayle E. Soles appeals from a judgment of imprisonment which was rendered after a jury found her guilty of possession of heroin. [Citation omitted.]

'' . . . Appellant contends that the evidence seized in the motel room occupied by appellant and her associates should have been excluded because the entry was based on information obtained by telephone eavesdropping on the part of the motel manager. . . .

''Although the possible effect of section 632 of the Penal Code (electronic eavesdropping on confidential communications) is not mentioned in appellant's brief, the issue was argued in the trial court and will therefore be discussed briefly. The statute does not prohibit eavesdropping in general; it applies only to the use of 'any electronic amplifying or recording device' to eavesdrop upon or record a confidential communication. A telephone extension, not equipped with features for amplification or recording, is not an 'electronic amplifying or recording device.' The action of the motel manager in staying on the line was not electronic eavesdropping within the meaning of the statute.

''Moreover, the telephone conversations of the tenants, in aid of criminal activity, were not confidential, within the meaning of the statute, as against the manager of the motel. She had reason to suspect that the tenants were engaged in prostitution or in selling narcotics. Her awareness of such activities might ripen into guilty knowledge, subjecting her to penalties for maintaining a place where narcotics are sold [citation omitted] or maintaining a house of prostitution [citation omitted]. Her lawful right and duty to guard against misuse of her property for purposes of prostitution or narcotics trafficking excluded the tenants from entertaining a reasonable expectation of privacy, as against the manager. [Citation omitted.] Therefore, the conversations were not confidential within the meaning of the statute, as against the manager. This result is congruent with the rule that when there is reason to suspect that a hotel room is being used for an illicit purpose, the management may reassert control to the extent necessary to carry out a protective search. (*See People v. Minervini* (1971) 20 Cal. App. 3d 832, 98 Cal. Rptr. 107.)''

8:6 *Authority to Identify Guest to Police*

SMITH V. JEFFERSON HOTEL CO., INC.
48 Ga. App. 596, 173 S.E. 456 (1934)

[Action for damages against the Jefferson Hotel on account of the alleged conduct of the servant and agent of the defendant toward plaintiff while she was a guest in the hotel.

Plaintiff alleged that she was in the habit of staying at the defendant's hotel as guest on Saturday nights. On the night of March 11, 1933, which was a Saturday night, she applied for a room at defendant's hotel. While standing at the desk, the clerk informed her that there had been a telephone call for her and after receiving the desired room, she seated herself in the lobby waiting for a repetition of the telephone call. While reading her paper there, she was arrested by two detectives, and, although she asked for assistance from the hotel clerk, who was a witness of the whole occurrence, he failed to respond. Plaintiff further alleged that while she was seated in the hotel lobby, the clerk on duty received information over the telephone that a woman was wanted by the police, and the desk informed the officers that the woman wanted was at the hotel. Plaintiff alleged that the officers arrested her on the identification of the clerk. It was shown that the arrest was illegal and plaintiff was dismissed from the custody without any explanation.

Plaintiff's complaint was dismissed.]

PER CURIAM: '' . . . One conducting a hotel is not under a duty to prevent the arrest of a guest of the hotel by officers of the law who are seemingly acting within their authority. There is no duty on the part of a hotel company the violation of which will make it liable in damages because it has not investigated and determined for itself whether or not such an arrest, within the apparent scope of the officers' authority, is legal.

'' . . . There can be no question that if the hotel company or its agents in charge of its guest wilfully and wantonly made false statements to the police as to the identity of a guest and thus caused his or her arrest illegally, the hotel company would be liable. . . .

''Judgment affirmed.''

[Dissenting opinion omitted.]

8:7   *Damages for Unlawful Intrusion into Guest's Room*

When a guest of a hotel is occupying his room and is neither engaged in nor permitting improper conduct therein nor affording any just ground to suspect such, it is an unjustified intrusion upon the guest and a trespass upon his rights incident to his occupancy of the room for the hotelkeeper, uninvited and unpermitted, to enter the room to ascertain whether improper conduct by the guest or anyone else is transpiring therein.

In *McKee v. Sheraton-Russell, Inc.,*[9] the plaintiff, June McKee, sought to recover for injuries she alleged she had sustained when her room in defendant's hotel was invaded.

Shortly after midnight of Saturday, September 4, 1954, plaintiff, who had reached New York that evening from Detroit, arrived at the Sheraton-Russell, registered, and was assigned a room with bath on the seventh floor.

She testified that when she retired on Sunday night, September 5, she locked her door and attached a "Do Not Disturb" sign to the outside doorknob. About 6:45 A.M. on September 6, she arose and went to her bathroom. Reentering her bedroom she discovered, crouched near the end of her bed, the bellboy who upon her arrival at the hotel had shown her to her room. Plaintiff was undressed and, attempting to cover herself, tried to get the bellboy to leave. He remained, however, for some twelve to twenty minutes, making remarks which the court regarded as suggestive, and, near the end of his stay, he advanced upon her with hands outstretched. She finally managed to get him out of the room without being physically touched by him but shortly thereafter he returned and attempted to persuade her not to tell anyone what had happened. She suffered fright and shock and also proffered evidence tending to show that this occurrence had aggravated a preexisting urinary ailment.

The bellboy, who was called to the witness stand by the court, corroborated the plaintiff's story that he was in fact in her room that morning. He testified, however, that he was not on duty, that he believed Miss McKee had checked out and that her room was unoccupied, that he wanted to take a radio from there to the locker room for his own use, and that he was not in Miss McKee's room in the course of, or in furtherance of, the business of the hotel. He stated that he had obtained the passkey he used from the hotel desk where room keys were readily accessible to the bellmen. He denied that he was in the room for as long a time as plaintiff claimed and denied that he was other than respectful to her.

The jury awarded plaintiff $5,000 compensatory and $5,000 punitive damages. The judgment entered on the jury's verdict was reserved on appeal and a new trial ordered. In the new trial the jury again found for the plaintiff for $10,000 compensatory damages, which on defendant's motion, the court reduced to $5,146.25.

In *Dixon v. Hotel Tutwiler Operating Co.,*[10] the plaintiff and his wife registered as guests in defendant's hotel. Through an error at the front desk, the reg-

---

[9]268 F.2d 669 (2d Cir. 1959).
[10]214 Ala. 396, 108 So. 26 (1926).

istration card, prepared by the clerk, showed the name of the husband alone as a guest. Subsequently, a house officer entered plaintiff's room during the night, interrupting their sleep.

Mere suspicion of improprieties or indecencies will not authorize a violation of well-recognized rights of a guest, said the court. The grounds should be more than a mere suspicion; they should be reasonable; there should be a proper inquiry for the truth and facts in the premises.

The decision below permits recovery for physical discomfort arising out of a wrongful intrusion.

POLLOCK v. HOLSA CORP.

98 A.D.2d 265, 470 N.Y.S.2d 151 (A.D. 1st Dep't. 1984)

MURPHY, P.J.: "The first cause of action was dismissed by the trial court at the close of plaintiff's case. . . . At trial, plaintiff testified that, at about 3:30 A.M. on May 5, 1978, he discovered that the defendants had placed another individual in his hotel room. He further testified that his reservation for that room was not to terminate until later that morning. Although defendants' night clerk was most courteous, plaintiff found himself without a room in the middle of the night. He was forced to drive home in the early morning hours.

"Clearly, this testimony indicated that defendants had breached their duty in their role as innkeeper. The evidence strongly suggested that plaintiff had been wrongfully evicted from his room by defendants' employees (*DeWolf v. Ford*, 193 N.Y.397, 404, 405, 89 N.E.527.) In a colloquy with plaintiff's counsel, the trial court conceded that plaintiff had established a *prima facie* case against defendants. However, the trial court found that the injuries claimed by plaintiff were not compensible. Therefore, it dismissed the first cause. The Appellate Term agreed and it affirmed the judgment dismissing the first cause (114 Misc. 2d 1076, 454 N.Y.S.2d 582).

"The damages sought under the first cause are enumerated in paragraph Eleventh of the complaint: 'ELEVENTH: As a result of Plaintiff's eviction from his assigned hotel room and refusal to provide alternate sleeping accommodations, Defendants did breach their contract with Plaintiff, causing Plaintiff to suffer great humiliation and indignity by public expulsion for [sic] his room as aforesaid, as well as physical discomfort and distress of mind, all to Plaintiff's damage in the sum of $25,000.00.'

"There was no evidence in the record that plaintiff was abused or insulted by defendants' night clerk. Therefore, we agree with the trial court and the Appellate Term that plaintiff was not entitled to recover compensatory damages for allegedly suffering (i) humiliation, (ii) indignity and (iii) distress of mind. (*Boyce v. Greeley Square Hotel*, 228 N.Y. 106, 111, 126 N.E. 647.) Likewise, we agree with their determination that plaintiff was not entitled to punitive damages (*DeWolf v. Ford, supra*, 193 N.Y. at 406, 89 N.E. 527). We disagree with their conclusion that the portion of the first cause as sought damages for 'physical discomfort' should also be dismissed.

"A plaintiff may be entitled to recover damages for 'physical discomfort' resulting from a breach of contract where those damages may reasonably be held to have been within the contemplation of the parties (22 Am. Jur. 2d, *Damages*, 47, p. 75; *cf. McConnell v. United States Exp. Co.*, 179 Mich. 522, 146 N.W. 428). In this proceeding, the plaintiff was required to drive to his home in Roslyn, Long Island at 4:00 A.M. after he had spent many hours entertaining clients. The 'physical discomfort' experienced by plaintiff as a result of this inconvenience is an item of damage that was within the contemplation of the parties at the time plaintiff became a guest in this inn. Therefore, that item of damage should have been submitted to the jury for its consideration. Even if the defendants acted unintentionally in breaching their duty to plaintiff, they must still answer in damages.

"The case of *Odom v. East Avenue Corp.*, 178 Misc. 363, 34 N.Y.S.2d 312, *aff'd* 264 A.D.2d 985, 37 N.Y.S.2d 491, does not dictate a different determination. In *Odom*, the plaintiff alleged in the second cause of action that defendant hotel had refused to serve him in a restaurant because of racial discrimination. The Fourth Department affirmed the Supreme Court's order which denied defendant's motion to dismiss that second cause. In the course of its decision, the Supreme Court stated (178 Misc. at 366, 34 N.Y.S.2d 312): 'It seems apparent that once the relationship of innkeeper and guest is obtained, the innkeeper must not only provide such facilities as the character of his inn will afford but must also refrain from insulting, abusing or indulging in any conduct that may necessarily bring upon his guest physical discomfort or distress of mind. A violation of these duties gives rise to a cause of action and a cause of action known to common law.'

"It is true that an innkeeper should not insult or abuse a guest because such activity might cause 'physical discomfort' to the guest. This statement in *Odom* does not preclude the possibility that other acts of wrongdoing on the part of the innkeeper may cause 'physical discomfort.' As was developed above, the wrongful eviction of a guest by the innkeeper may cause damages flowing from the 'physical discomfort' experienced by the guest. . . .

"Order, Appellate Term, First Department, entered on June 24, 1982, unanimously modified, on the law, by vacating so much thereof as affirmed the dismissal of that portion of the first cause as sought damages for physical discomfort, and by directing a new trial on that portion of the first cause. As modified, the Appellate Term's order is affirmed, without costs and without disbursements."

8:8 *Duty to Furnish and Right to Assign and Change Guest Accommodations*

It is the duty of the innkeeper to supply the guest with such accommodations as he needs, due allowance being made for the grade of the inn and its facilities. The inn, though a public house, does not, however, become in any sense the house of the guest; the innkeeper continues to be the housekeeper, and the management of the house remains absolutely and at all times in his hands, subject only to the right of the guest to receive reasonable entertainment.

The assignment of a guest to a room is in no sense a lease; it is a mere revocable license. It follows that the innkeeper, in the course of his management, has the absolute right to assign the guest to any proper room, and he may at will change the room and assign the guest, with or without his consent, to another room.

As the innkeeper may assign the guest to any chamber he pleases, so he may serve him with food in any room he pleases, provided it is a decent and proper room; the guest cannot complain if the innkeeper refuses to serve him in the common dining room. This question was involved in the interesting case of *Regina v. Sprague.*[11] The suit was an indictment for refusing to supply Lady Harberton with food. Lady Harberton was cycling, clad in the "rational costume," so called, and she stopped for luncheon at the defendant's inn. The defendant refused to serve her in the coffee room unless she put a skirt over the "rational costume," but offered to serve her in a private room behind the bar. On looking into the room Lady Harberton found it was occupied by men, some of whom were smoking, and refused to enter; thereupon the prosecution was instituted, at the Surrey Quarter Sessions. The defendant urged that no person had a right to choose a particular room, to which the court replied, "Suppose a landlord said he would only supply victuals in the coal cellar?" The defendant said that was an extreme case, but would an indictment lie against a landlord because a fastidious lady disliked the smell of smoke? The court left the question to the jury. The question was whether there was a refusal to supply food in a decent and proper place. The innkeeper could select the room provided it was a decent and proper place. In his opinion, a guest was not entitled to have a room exactly to his or her taste. The jury must judge by the requirement of ordinary and reasonable persons. The court then asked the jury to consider whether the bar parlor was a decent and proper room for a guest to have lunch in. The jury brought in a verdict of not guilty. It may be doubted whether an American jury would have been so ungallant, but the action of the court was unquestionably correct.

At the same time the innkeeper cannot go further than determine the kind of accommodation to be furnished to the guest; he cannot demand that the guest make any particular use of the accommodation. He may place such reasonable food as he chooses before the guest, but he cannot complain if the guest refuses to eat it; nor can he object if the guest refuses to occupy his bed, but chooses to sit up all night. So in the course of the argument in *Fell v. Knight,*[12] Baron Alderson, said: "A traveller is not bound to go to bed: he may have business to attend to, which would render it necessary for him to sit up all night. An innkeeper cannot be justified in turning his guest out because he refuses to sleep."

---

[11]63 J.P. 233 (Surrey Quarter Sessions 1899).
[12]151 Eng. Rep. 1039 (Exch. 1841).

The innkeeper must, of course, provide a reasonable number of common rooms, but he may refuse to furnish light and heat for the guest to occupy his chamber as a reading or writing room, or a common room as a sleeping apartment. So where a guest refused to sleep in the chamber assigned to him, and requested that candles should be furnished him that he might sit up all night in a chamber, the innkeeper was justified in refusing, at least where he offered to allow the guest to sit up and have light in the regular reading room. In *Fell v. Knight*, Lord Abinger, C.B., said: "I do not think a landlord is bound to provide for his guest the precise room the latter may select. . . . All that the law requires of him is, to find for his guests reasonable and proper accommodation: if he does that, he does all that is requisite."[13]

A landlord is not bound to provide a traveler with a particular room, nor to permit him to occupy a bedchamber as a sitting room if he offers him another room fit and proper for the purpose. He is to provide him with a room affording reasonable accommodation, but not any room which the caprice of guest may lead him to select.

8:9   *Right of Guest to Display Business Signs in Lobby*

One who rents a room in a hotel does not acquire the right to use the hotel for advertising purposes. In *Samuel v. Boldt*,[14] plaintiff checked into the Bellevue Stratford in Philadelphia and was given a room on a day-to-day basis to be used as a millinery shop. There was nothing in the agreement about the use of display signs. Shortly after she had taken possession of the room, plaintiff put up signs in the lobby which were immediately removed by the management. She was then given notice to vacate her room. She complained that the management refused to permit her the public display of placards announcing her business and prevented her from operating her shop and finally dispossessed her. The court had no hesitation in directing judgment for the defendant innkeeper.

8:10   *Duty to Furnish Telephone Service*

The innkeeper is under no duty to furnish telephone service to his guests. In point of fact, however, hotel rooms are almost universally provided with telephones for the convenience of guests. A question may well arise, therefore, as to the liability of an innkeeper for damages arising as a result of failure to provide service.

In *Lewis v. Roescher*,[15] the action was brought by an executrix against the owner and operator of a hotel and was based on two counts. The first count alleged that the defendant had furnished her deceased husband with tainted food from which he contracted ptomaine poisoning. The second count stated that the

---

[13]*Id.* at 1042.
[14]77 Pa. Super. 144 (1921).
[15]193 Ark. 161, 98 S.W.2d 956 (1963).

decedent contracted for a room which was equipped with a telephone, that the telephone was defective, or the defendant's clerk was inattentive, that the decedent became desperately ill and was unable to leave his room, and that when his repeated efforts to telephone failed, he was forced to suffer and vomit excessively until the following morning when he finally obtained a physician. The complaint alleged that the defendant breached her contract in failing to provide facilities for communicating the decedent's illness, but there was no allegation of defendant's knowledge of either the defective phone or the guest's illness. The lower court dismissed the complaint. On appeal, the Supreme Court of Arkansas reversed on the first count but upheld the lower court's determination on the second.

The court held as follows: The hotel was under no duty to furnish Lewis with a telephone in his room, and would not be liable because the telephone furnished was defective or because he was unable to get communication with the clerk. Special damages claimed because of the failure to furnish telephone connection could be recovered only where the hotel had knowledge of the circumstances and conditions. There was no implied warranty that Lewis would be furnished with telephone service, and there was no allegation in the complaint that the hotel had knowledge of the fact that the telephone was defective. Nor was there any allegation that the hotel had knowledge that Lewis was either sick or that he was likely to become sick and suffer.

It would seem that if the innkeeper had knowledge of the circumstances and had negligently failed to provide telephone services and the results to the guest were foreseeable, damages would have been recoverable.

8:11 *Liability for Failure to Furnish Guest with Key and to Awaken Guest*

GUMBART v. WATERBURY CLUB HOLDING CORP.
27 F. Supp. 228 (D. Conn. 1938)

[Plaintiff seeks to recover damages for personal injuries received in a fall while attempting to enter through a window.]

HINCKS, D.J.: "For purposes of this memorandum, I assume throughout that the relationship plaintiff and defendants was that obtaining between guest and innkeepers.

"The first count, insofar as it is based upon the defendants' failure to supply the plaintiff with a key to the premises, fails to state a cause of action. *Neither common law nor statute require an innkeeper, unrequested to supply every guest with a key to the inn or to keep the entrance either unlocked or under attendance during the night* [emphasis supplied]. . . .

"The first count also fails to state a cause of action insofar as it is based upon the maintenance of an outside window in the defendant's building. To be sure, it is stated that this window was unprotected and "open and easily accessible to anyone from the outside"; that inside the window there was a drop of some

25 feet to the floor of the gymnasium; and that the gymnasium was unlighted at the time in question. The complaint, however, fails to show that the defendants invited the plaintiff to enter by the window, either by express invitation or by an invitation which might be implied from a walk leading to the window or from any other features of the lay-out of the premises. A guest's implied invitation of entry may not be expanded to include such a means of entrance. [Citations omitted.] And the same rule is applicable to gratuitous licenses. [Citations omitted.] Since from the facts stated it appears affirmatively that the plaintiff in attempting to enter by a window was neither invitee nor licensee, the remaining facts alleged are insufficient to show the violation of any duty on the part of the defendants. . . .

"The third count also sounds in tort, and must also be held to be insufficient in law. *For I can find nothing in the common law nor any statute which imposes a mandatory duty upon innkeepers to awaken guests from their slumbers at a requested hour.* [Emphasis supplied.] Indeed, the proposition is tacitly abandoned in plaintiff's brief.

"Furthermore, this count fails to state facts from which it could be found that the defendant's alleged negligence was the proximate cause of the only injury complained of. For if the defendants had called the plaintiff at 7:30 and had thus learned that he was not in his room, they would have been under no duty to search for him in the gymnasium. In other words, the defendants' negligence (assuming it to have been negligence) in failing to call the plaintiff was not a substantial factor in bringing about the aggravation of the plaintiff's injuries, and hence not a legal cause thereof." [Citation omitted.] [Complaint dismissed.]

8:12   *Liability for Failure or Delay in Delivering Messages, Mail, and Telegrams*

There is no common-law or statutory duty imposed on innkeepers to deliver messages and telegrams addressed to guests. Such duty, if there be any, is voluntarily assumed by the innkeeper and is contractual in its nature. Liability is the result of breach of promise to perform a service implied from the nature of the business.

The innkeeper is sometimes confronted with claims for special damages for mental suffering and also for the loss of profits in business transactions which were not consummated because of failure or delay in delivery of a letter, telegram, or message.

In the majority of jurisdictions damages are not recoverable for mental suffering consequent on delay in the delivery of a telegraphic message, nor for sickness and physical suffering resulting from such mental distress. It is also well settled that a hotelkeeper is not liable for special damages in the nature of loss of profits in an unconsummated business transaction unless he has knowledge of the fact that delay or failure of delivery will result in such special damages.

The innkeeper should be intelligently informed about postal regulations applicable to the handling of mail addressed to guests in the hotel. He should obtain from the local post office a copy of the Official Postal Guide which contains regulations specially applicable to hotels. In general, a hotel may be liable for negligence in failing to use reasonable care in the delivery or handling of mail. The duty, the breach of which may be the foundation of such liability, may be assumed by voluntary agreement, or it may be implied from the custom and service practice of the hotel upon which the aggrieved guest relied or had a right to rely. It is invariably unwise for an innkeeper to commit himself to a guest by agreement to hold mail for any period longer than ten days. In the large transient hotels it might be wise to post a notice in a conspicuous place at the mail desk with respect to the handling of mail after departure. Special care should be used with respect to registered mail, C.O.D. packages, and parcel post.

In *Joslyn v. King*,[16] plaintiff was a letter carrier. He had a registered letter addressed to a guest at defendant's hotel. The plaintiff delivered the letter to the clerk of the hotel who signed for it. The clerk placed the letter in the letter box and then left the desk for six hours to get some sleep. When the clerk returned he discovered that the letter had been purloined. The plaintiff being under a duty to deliver the letter only to the addressee was held liable for the loss. The letter had contained $100 and this amount the plaintiff paid the guest. The plaintiff then sued the hotel owner and the clerk. The defense was twofold: (1) the plaintiff was himself negligent in not delivering the letter to the addressee; and (2) the plaintiff did not communicate the value of the letter to the clerk when he delivered it. The trial court entered judgment for the plaintiff. On appeal, the judgment was affirmed.

The court reasoned: The negligence of the plaintiff in delivering the letter in no way relieved the defendants of their own negligence. The fact that the letter had to be signed for was notice that the letter was of more than ordinary importance and that special care was required. The bailment was voluntarily assumed and care should have been proportionately increased.

There are no reported cases involving innkeepers on the subject of damages recoverable for failure to deliver messages, telegrams, or a trunk or other property, for that matter. Such situations usually involve a negative wrong of failing to perform a usual or ordinary service to which a guest was entitled either because of a promise made to him or because a promise of service was implied from the usual practice of hotelkeepers.

In the vast majority of cases, a hotelkeeper would not be liable for damages to a guest in the nature of "loss of business," loss of commission on some anticipated deal, or loss of compensation for services the guest has been unable to perform by reason of the hotelkeeper's failure to perform some service, such as awakening the guest at a requested hour, or delivering a message, telegram, letter, or the like. The courts usually hold such claims vague, general, and meaningless. The rule with respect to such claims has been succinctly stated in the Pennsylvania case of *Macchia v. Megow*.[17]

[16]27 Neb. 38, 42 N.W. 756 (1889).
[17]355 Pa. 565, 569–70, 50 A.2d 314, 316 (1947).

Anticipated profits on a resale are not recoverable unless in contemplation of the parties when the original contract was made [citations omitted]: "Parties, when they enter into contracts, may well be presumed to contemplate the ordinary and natural incidents and consequences of performance or nonperformance; but they are not supposed to know the conditions of each other's affairs, nor to take into consideration any existing or contemplated transactions, not communicated nor known, with other persons. Few persons would enter into contracts of any considerable extent as to subject-matter or time if they should thereby incidentally assume the responsibility of carrying out, or be held legally affected by, other arrangements over which they have no control and the existence of which are *[sic]* unknown to them": Sutherland on Damages, 4th ed. vol. 1, p. 182, § 47.

The exception to the rule is where the hotelkeeper, or his duly authorized representative, being made fully aware of the consequences to the guest of failure to perform the service, nevertheless makes a binding commitment to perform. In this connection, it would seem doubtful that a telephone operator, a mail clerk, or bellman, or even an assistant manager, would have implied authority to commit the hotelkeeper.

PART II

Tort Law:

Owner and Operator

Liability for Guest's Safety

9   Duty to Provide Safe Premises

9:1   *Innkeeper's Duty of Reasonable Care for Personal Safety of Guests*

It is the duty of an innkeeper to take reasonable care of the persons of his guests, so that they may not be injured while in the inn by want of such care on his part. He is not, however, an insurer of the guest's safety; his responsibility is limited to the exercise of reasonable care, and he may be held liable only for injuries caused by his negligence.

9:2   *Innkeeper's Duty to Social Invitees of Guests*

Two state reviewing courts extended the reasonable-care rule to include social visitors, invited by guests, on innkeepers' premises: Maryland, in *Murrey v. Lane*[1]; and North Carolina, in *Hockaday v. Morse*.[2]

9:3   *Innkeeper's Duty to Business Invitees of Tenants or Guests*

The innkeeper's duty of reasonable care has been found to extend to business invitees of guests as well. In *Davis v. Garden Services, Inc.*,[3] the plaintiff, employed by a corporation to furnish a band to play for a party to be held in the hotel ballroom rented to the corporation, brought a personal injury action against the hotel to recover for injury sustained when he fell from a temporary bandstand situated in the hotel ballroom. The court of appeals reversed a directed verdict for the hotel entered by the superior court. The Georgia Court of Appeals held: (1) plaintiff was an invitee rather than a mere licensee, even though the engagement to play for the party was entered into with the corporate tenant rather than directly with the hotel; (2) the evidence did not mandate a finding in favor of the owner on the issue of negligence. Said Chief Judge Deen: "The general rule that an innkeeper has the duty of exercising ordinary care to keep its premises safe for its tenants applies equally to guests of such tenants.

---

[1]51 Md. App. 597, 444 A.2d 1069 (1982).
[2]57 N.C. App. 109, 290 S.E.2d 763 (1982), *petition for review denied* 306 N.C. 384, 294 S.E.2d 209 (N.C. 1982).
[3]155 Ga. App. 34, 270 S.E.2d 228 (1980).

Those coming on the based premises for business purposes beneficial to the tenant, and those doing business with him are there by the tenant's invitation and stand in his shoes insofar as they suffer injury due to the negligence of the owner or occupier of the premises."[4]

9:4 *Negligence as Basis of Liability for Injuries*

The standard of care is the care which a reasonably prudent person would exercise under the circumstances to avoid a reasonably foreseeable harm. This is neither the highest care nor the lowest. To choose the highest care would avoid many accidents, but the additional safety would be attained at too great a cost of public convenience. By reducing the maximum rate of speed for automobiles to 20 mph, many accidents would be avoided, but the inconvenience to travelers and the harm to business would be intolerable.

The standard of conduct of a reasonable man may be determined either by legislation as in building codes that prescribe fire exits in hotels, by judicial decisions, or as applied to the facts of a case by judge or jury, if there is no statute, regulation, or decision.

While the standard of care remains the same, all circumstances must be taken into account in its application. The care in crossing the street on a summer day differs from the care required in crossing an icy street in winter. The care with respect to a small child differs from that with respect to an adult.

The law exacts from each person in his conduct only the care of a reasonably prudent person *under the same circumstances.* The standard of care for a skilled person and an unskilled person is the same, but in determining whether in either case ordinary skill has been exercised, the fact of the profession or nonprofession of skill is a circumstance that must be considered. Thus, the standard of care of a physician is measured by his professional standards. If a person who holds himself out as skilled in surgery injures his patient in an operation which he knows he is not competent to perform, he is negligent even though he does as well as any unskilled person would have done under the same circumstances. He is responsible because he professed to have skill when a person of ordinary prudence would not have made that profession.

One sage commentator had this to say:

> The Common Law of England has been laboriously built about a mythical figure—the figure of "The Reasonable Man." . . .
> It is impossible to travel anywhere or to travel for long in that confusing forest of learned judgments which constitutes the Common Law of England without encountering the Reasonable Man. He is at every turn, an ever-present help in time of trouble, and his apparitions make the road to equity and right. There never has been a problem, however difficult, which His Majesty's judges have not in the end been able to resolve by asking themselves the simple question, "Was this or was it not the conduct of a reasonable man?" and leaving that question to be answered by the jury.

[4]*Id.* at 35, 270 S.E.2d at 229.

This noble creature . . . is one who invariably looks where he is going, and is careful to examine the immediate foreground before he executes a leap or bound; who neither star-gazes nor is lost in meditation when approaching trap-doors or the margin of a dock; who records in every case upon the counterfoils of cheques such ample details as are desirable, scrupulously substitutes the word "Order" for the word "Bearer," crosses the instrument "a/c Payee only," and registers the package in which it is dispatched; who never mounts a moving omnibus and does not alight from any car while the train is in motion; who investigates exhaustively the *bona fides* of every mendicant before distributing alms, and will inform himself of the history and habits of a dog before administering a caress; who believes no gossip, nor repeats it, without firm basis for believing it to be true; who never drives his ball till those in front of him have definitely vacated the putting-green which is his own objective; who never from the year's end to another makes an excessive demand upon his wife, his neighbors, his servants, his ox, or his ass; who in the way of business looks only for that narrow margin of profit which twelve men such as himself would reckon to be "fair," and contemplates his fellow-merchants, their agents, and their goods, with that degree of suspicion and distrust which the law deems admirable; who never swears, gambles, or loses his temper; who uses nothing except in moderation, and even while he flogs his child is meditating only on the golden mean. Devoid, in short, of any human weakness, with not one single saving vice, sans prejudice, procrastination, ill-nature, avarice, and absence of mind, as careful for his own safety as he is for that of others, this excellent but odious character stands like a monument in our Courts of Justice, vainly appealing to his fellow-citizens to order their lives after his own example. . . .

To return, however, as every judge must ultimately return, to the case which is before us—it has been urged for the appellant, and my own researches incline me to agree, that in all that mass of authorities which bears upon this branch of the law *there is no single mention of a reasonable woman.*[5]

9:5 *The Elements of a Cause of Action for Negligence*

Negligent conduct may be active or passive. Active negligent conduct is the commission of an act resulting in injury to another, in breach of a legal duty owed to such other, and falling below the standard of the reasonably prudent person under the circumstances. Passive negligent conduct is the failure to act, in violation of the actor's legal duty under the circumstances, resulting in injury to another.[6]

As noted in section 9:1, *supra*, the innkeeper owes his guest or others similarly situated the legal duty to provide reasonably safe premises. The interest the law seeks to compensate is that of protecting a guest or other person against the infliction of unintentional harm.[7]

---

[5]A. P. Herbert, Misleading Cases in the Common Law, 9–13 (6th ed. 1931) (emphasis in original).

[6]Restatement (Second) of Torts § 282 (1965). [hereinafter cited as Restatement Second].

[7]Restatement Second, *supra*, § 281(a).

Four conditions must be met by a party seeking compensation from an innkeeper or other owner or occupier of land. First, the party must prove that he is a member of a protected class and that the defendant owed him some legal duty of protection.[8]

Second, actions or failures to act on the part of the innkeeper must create an unreasonable risk of harm to the protected person or class.[9] "Reasonableness" in this context must be understood to mean a flexible standard relative to the situation and circumstances of each case. A hotel window lacking a screen or guard might well constitute no risk to an adult occupant, but the risk that such a window might create to a small child could be deemed sufficiently serious to warrant characterizing it as unreasonable. The same analysis might be true of an unattended playground or wading pool. Thus the legal significance of the risk rests upon the ability of the injured party to apprehend it and to apply corrective self-help within the existing time and physical conditions.

A famous New York jurist stated the irreducible common denominator which exemplifies the requirement as "the risk reasonably to be perceived defines the duty to be obeyed."[10] Thus the requirement is synonymous with the test of foreseeability of risk discussed later in this section.

Essentially the law of negligence seeks to achieve an equitable accommodation between the value of protecting the victim from physical or mental harm, and the threat to the economic interest of the owner or occupier measured by the severity and likelihood of recurrence of his act or omission. The less the degree of severity and repetition, the less the scope of protection afforded the victim. It also gauges the seriousness or unreasonableness of the risk created in terms of the ambit or outer limits of that risk. Assume that a hotel employee drives a hospitality van during the course of his employment at excessive speed and in so doing runs a stop sign in front of the hotel building causing injury to Tommy Tucker, a 12-year-old hotel guest who was properly crossing the street. There would be no doubt that Tommy could recover for his injuries if all of the above facts were established to the satisfaction of a court and jury. Assume further that Tommy's mother, Teresa, pregnant at the time, observes the accident from her hotel room window. In her haste to reach the scene, she falls and suffers a miscarriage. Is Teresa also entitled to recover, on the theory that she would not have suffered the miscarriage were it not for the negligent conduct of the hotel driver? No. The courts[11] have uniformly held that the injury inflicted was not foreseeable in the normal course of events, even though the conduct giving rise to it was negligent, and Teresa, herself a hotel guest, was entitled to the same standard of reasonable care as was her son Tommy. In other words, extending the ambit of responsibility to Teresa would be disproportionate to the economic harm inflicted upon the innkeeper. The risk of harm was unreasonable in Tommy's situation, but was reasonable in Teresa's and thus nonactionable.

[8]Restatement Second, *supra,* § 281(b).
[9]Restatement Second, *supra,* § 281, Comment f.
[10]Cardozo, J., Palsgrafi v. LIRR Co., 284 N.Y. 399, 162 N.E. 99 (1928).
[11]*Cf.* Niederman v. Brodsky, 436 Pa. 401, 261 A.2d 84 (1970).

Another essential corollary of the standard of reasonable care is the requirement that the owner or occupier, our hypothetical innkeeper, had actual or constructive notice of the defective condition of the premises. Actual notice means notice imparted to him by his own observation or by the observation of others, such as employees or guests. Constructive notice means that the defective condition should have been noted by him or his employees in the exercise of reasonable care because of the nature and duration of its existence. In both cases the owner or occupier must have had reasonable time either to warn the protected class of its existence or to remedy the condition. Only if these conditions are met can the owner or occupier be said to have breached or violated his legal duty to protect his guests and patrons from defective premises.

Third, it is necessary that the negligence of the actor be a legal cause of the harm inflicted upon the injured guest or patron. This means that the negligence giving rise to the lawsuit must proximately cause or contribute to the injuries suffered by the party seeking to recover damages.

In *Pearce v. Motel 6, Inc.*,[12] plaintiff slipped in defendant motel's shower stall. The court found reversible error in the trial court's failure to instruct the jury that the inn's reasonable-care duty was triggered only if the inn had actual or constructive knowledge that the condition of the shower created an unreasonable risk of harm.

The courts[13] have developed some guidelines that are helpful in dealing with this necessarily broad subject and in retaining the flexibility essential to do justice to the parties:

(a) The test of status—is there an existing legal relationship between the parties?

(b) The test of temporal duration—is the occurrence of the injury tied to the claimed negligent act or omission within a reasonable period of time?

(c) The test of spatial relation—is the occurrence of the injury close or far in distance from the point of the claimed negligent act or omission?

(d) The test of forseeability—is the claimed negligent act or omission reasonably predictable as a cause of the occurrence of the injury?

(e) The test of public policy—is there an identifiable policy which either protects the victim of the injury or forbids liability for the injury?

Fourth, it is necessary that the party seeking to hold the owner or occupier liable suffered legal damages as a result of the foregoing circumstances. Damages are critical to any legally sanctioned cause of action. Without damages, the cause of action will fail, irrespective of findings favorable to the party suing on the issues of breach of legal duty and proximate cause.

9:6 Burden of Proof

The burden of alleging and proving negligence, including all of the elements of negligence, is always on the party seeking to recover. In some jurisdictions

[12]28 Wash. App. 474, 624 P.2d 215 (1981).
[13]*See* Pagan v. Goldberger, 51 A.D.2d 508, 382 N.Y.S.2d 549 (2d Dep't 1976).

this burden includes proof that the victim was himself not guilty of contributory negligence. However, the majority rule is to treat this issue as well as the corollary issue of assumption of risk as affirmative defenses that must be alleged and proved by the defendant.

9:7 *Duty to Furnish Safe Premises Is Nondelegable*

The innkeeper is bound to provide reasonably safe premises. The innkeeper cannot escape this duty by delegating it to another, even though the latter is a skilled and generally careful person. The innkeeper is responsible if his delegate is negligent. Thus, where an innkeeper had his elevator inspected in the usual manner by competent employees of the elevator manufacturing company which originally installed the elevator, and the latter negligently failed to find a defect, the innkeeper was held liable to a guest who was injured by reason of the defect.[14]

PAGE V. SLOAN
281 N.C. 697, 190 S.E.2d 189 (1972)

HUSKINS, J.: "What standard of care is required of innkeepers with respect to their guests?

"An innkeeper is not an insurer of the personal safety of his guests. He is required to exercise due care to keep his premises in a reasonably safe condition and to warn his guests of any hidden peril. [Citation omitted.] The duties thus imposed upon an innkeeper for the protection of his guests 'are nondelegable, and liability cannot be avoided on the ground that their performance was entrusted to an independent contractor.' 40 Am. Jur. 2d, *Hotels, Motels, and Restaurants* § 81. [Citation omitted.] *See* Prosser on Torts (4th ed. 1971), § 71 at p. 470.

"The rule of nondelegability is grounded on the premise that an innkeeper's duty to use due care for the safety of his guests is a responsibility so important to the public that he should not be permitted to transfer it to another. The Restatement of the Law of Torts expresses and illustrates the rule as follows: 'One who employs an independent contractor to maintain in safe condition land which he holds open to the entry of the public as his place of business, or a chattel which he supplies for others to use for his business purposes or which he leases for immediate use, is subject to the same liability for physical harm caused by the contractor's negligent failure to maintain the land or chattel in reasonably safe condition, as though he had retained its maintenance in his own hands.' Restatement of Torts 2d, § 425. The second illustration following this section is especially pertinent: '2. A operates a hotel. He employs B as a plumber to install a shower bath. B negligently transposes the handles so that the hot water pipe is

---

[14]Stott v. Churchill, 15 Misc. 80, 36 N.Y.S. 476 (Ct. C.P. 1895), *aff'd mem.*, 157 N.Y. 692, 51 N.E. 1094 (1898).

labeled cold. *C*, a guest, deceived by the label, turns on the hot water and is scalded. *A* is subject to liability to *C*.'

"The rule of nondelegability has been applied where plaintiff was injured by the negligent operation or maintenance of an elevator located in defendant's premises. [Citations omitted.] Even where the company which manufactured and installed the elevator had by contract assumed responsibility for the inspection, repair and maintenance of the elevator, the rule was applied and defendant owner of the premises was held liable. [Citations omitted.]

"Thus, depending on the evidence offered at the trial, defendants in this case could be liable on any of the following bases:

"1. Failure to use due care for the safety of their guests by employing a plumber instead of an electrician to repair the electrical heating element on the water heater, thereby failing 'to exercise reasonable care to employ a competent and careful contractor (*a*) to do work which will involve a risk of physical harm unless it is skillfully and carefully done, or (*b*) to perform any duty which the employer owes to third persons.' Restatement of Torts 2d, § 411. While making repairs to the heating element of an electric water heater is not 'inherently' or 'intrinsically' dangerous work, it involves work which will likely cause injury if proper safety precautions are not observed. *Compare Evans v. Rockingham Homes, Inc.*, 220 N.C. 253, 17 S.E.2d 125 (1941). If defendants knew, or in the exercise of due care should have known, that a plumber was not competent to do such work and if the plumber's negligence was a proximate cause of the explosion and ensuing death of plaintiff's testate, defendants would be liable.

"2. Since the duties imposed upon an innkeeper for the protection of his guests are nondelegable and liability cannot be avoided on the ground that their performance was entrusted to an independent contractor, defendants would be subject to the same liability for an injury or death caused by the plumber's negligent failure properly to repair the electrical heating element on the water heater as if they had made the repair themselves. . . .

"Due consideration of the supporting documents and materials presented by defendants leads us to the conclusion that the granting of summary judgment by the trial court was erroneous. We hold that defendants have failed to carry the movant's burden of proof. . . .

"In our opinion reasonable men could reach different conclusions on the evidentiary material offered by defendants to support their motion for summary judgment. Were defendants negligent in selecting a plumber instead of an electrician to repair an electrical element on the water heater? [Citations omitted.] Was the plumber negligent in making the repairs? Was his negligence a proximate cause of the explosion and ensuing injury? The evidentiary material offered by defendants would permit a jury to answer all these questions in the affirmative as well as the negative. These are material issues of fact and demonstrate that the movants have failed to satisfy the burden of 'clearly establishing the lack of any triable issue of fact by the record properly before the court.'

[Discussion of applicability of *res ipsa loquitur* doctrine omitted.]

"For the reasons stated the decision of the Court of Appeals reversing the entry of summary judgment in favor of defendants is
"Affirmed."

In *Bardwell Motor Inn, Inc. v. Accavallo,*[15] the Supreme Court of Vermont reiterated the rule that an innkeeper or motor inn operator has a nondelegable duty to keep his premises reasonably safe for business invitees. In that case, a guest had suffered injury as the result of a negligently constructed front door, and the innkeeper was permitted to recover indemnity from the contractors hired to repair the door who had failed to do so in a reasonably careful manner.

9:8 Liability by Reason of Defective Premises: Doctrine of Res Ipsa Loquitur

Whereas the burden of proving all elements of negligence, including proximate cause, rests upon the party seeking to recover, there are situations in which the burden of explanation shifts to the defendant. A typical case justifying the doctrine is that involving injury to a guest caused by the collapse of the ceiling in his guest room.

In such a case it would be unfair and unreasonable to require the injured plaintiff to prove the elements of defendant's negligence. The plaintiff has no access to the necessary factual information as to the date and method of construction, the materials used, the care and skill of the construction crew and the plasterers, and the inspection and maintenance procedures of defendant with respect to the condition of guest rooms—all such information is much more readily available to the defendant than to the plaintiff.

So, in the interests of fairness and justice, the law has developed a rule of evidence called the doctrine of *res ipsa loquitur* (the thing speaks for itself). In order for the rule to apply:

(a) The instrumentality of injury must be within the exclusive control and supervision of the defendant.

(b) The injury must be of a nature that would normally not happen but for the negligence of the defendant under the circumstances.

When these two conditions are met to the court's satisfaction, the burden of going forward with the evidence shifts from the plaintiff to the defendant to explain, if he can, that the injury was the result of some act or omission other than by his negligence. For example, in our ceiling case, it might appear that an explosion of gas in the neighborhood or blasting for an excavation was the activating cause of the ceiling defect which was the proximate cause of plaintiff's injury. If such were the case, the defendant might escape liability.

In addition to the requirements of exclusive control by the defendant and the event not occurring in the absence of negligence, "the event must not have been

---

[15]135 Vt. 571, 381 A.2d 1061 (Vt. 1977).

due to any voluntary act or contribution on the part of the plaintiff (*Corcoran v. Banner Super Market,* 19 N.Y.2d 425, 430, 280 N.Y.S.2d 385, 387 . . .)."[16]

The doctrine was applied in *Deming Hotel Co. v. Prox,*[17] a case involving the fall of a mirror from the wall of a restaurant operated by the defendant. Under Indiana law, when the plaintiff alleges facts that invoke the doctrine, these facts give rise to a permissive inference of negligence, requiring the defendant to come forward with an explanation. In this case it was found that the restaurant patron was entitled to a safe place to eat, and there was sufficient evidence to support the jury verdict for the patron.

In *Terrell v. Lincoln Motel, Inc.,*[18] plaintiff guest was injured when he slipped through the door of a shower stall while attempting to escape an unexpected burst of hot water. The New Jersey Superior Court reversed the trial court's decision for defendant and remanded the case because the trial court failed to instruct the jury that the doctrine of *res ipsa loquitur* should apply if the jury believed the plaintiff's testimony.

9:9 *Common-Law Liability for Defective Equipment, Fixtures, and Furnishings*

The traditional common-law theory of liability for defects in products furnished to guests and patrons is predicated upon negligent construction, maintenance, and supervision, resulting in the creation of unreasonable risk of harm to the user. This theory requires injured guests to prove that the owner/occupier of the premises neglected to maintain the object causing harm in a reasonably safe manner. Absent proof of fault causing harm, the guest or patron cannot recover.

In *Freeman v. Rock-Hil-Uris, Inc.,* guests at the New York Hilton hotel sued to recover damages for personal injuries sustained as a result of a fall over an electric light cord situated on the floor of their hotel room. The New York Court of Appeals[19] affirmed the dismissal of their complaint:

> Undoubtedly, the plaintiffs could rely on circumstantial evidence in their efforts to explain how the condition which is alleged to have precipitated the fall came about. Yet, even inferring that the condition was reasonably attributable to the acts of defendant or his agents there is a complete failure of proof on the issue of proximate cause. The record itself is vague, and relevant facts such as the length of the cord, its point of emanation or the immediate facts attending Mrs. Freeman's movements just prior to the accident are conspicuously omitted.
>
> The trial court's action in dismissing the complaint for failure to make out a *prima facie* case should be sustained. . . .

---

[16]Moeller v. Pearl, 78 A.D.2d 540, 432 N.Y.S.2d 96 (2d Dep't 1980).
[17]142 Ind. App. 603, 236 N.E.2d 613 (1968).
[18]183 N.J. Super. 55, 443 A.2d 236 (1982).
[19]30 N.Y.2d 742, 284 N.E.2d 155 (1972).

BURKE, BREITEL and GIBSON, JJ., dissent and vote to reverse and grant a new trial on the ground that there was an issue of fact with respect to the conduct of hotel employees in placement of the electric cord which allegedly caused the accident.

Order affirmed, without costs, in a memorandum.

In *Wysong v. Little Creek Hotel Courts, Inc.*,[20] plaintiff suffered carbon monoxide poisoning when a gas heater burned up the oxygen in his room. The appellate court upheld the trial jury's verdict for the defendant, finding that the heater was not defective and that the jury could reasonably find that the sole cause of the accident was the plaintiff's use of the heater at a higher setting over an extended period of time.

A broken chair that caused injury to a patron was the subject of the following case.

DILLMAN v. NOBLES
351 So. 2d 210 (La. App. 1977)

BEER, J.: "On the evening of February 27, 1975, plaintiff-appellee, Shirley Dillman, in company with Darlene C. Musso and Beverly Alexander, attended the Scorpio Lounge in Marrero where they danced and had some drinks over a period of about two and one-half hours. When Dillman returned from the dance floor to her table and sat down in the chair she had previously occupied, the right rear leg allegedly broke, causing her to fall to the floor. She sustained a fracture of her coccyx. Her description of the incident is confirmed by Musso and Alexander, who also confirm Dillman's testimony that a waitress named 'Mary' came to her assistance, picked up the broken chair leg and waved it in the air while beckoning to 'Johnny' (John S. Nobles), who did not respond.

"John S. Nobles is president of Country Shindig, Inc., owner of the Scorpio Lounge. The lounge was sold by him to Country Shindig, Inc., in 1970. He manages the Scorpio, acknowledges that it is his sole source of livelihood, but denies liability for Dillman's alleged damages on the ground that if anyone is liable, it is the corporation. He also denies that the chair broke, contending that Dillman had been drinking and slipped from the chair as she attempted to sit down. He denies that any waitress waved a broken chair leg or that he was informed of the leg breaking incident.

"The trial judge found that the chair did, in fact, collapse, causing Dillman's injuries. He further concludes:

"The Court is of the opinion that the lounge operator owed a duty of reasonable care to the plaintiff to provide a safe place to sit. Further the Court finds that . . . the chairs and tables . . . were within the exclusive possession and control of the defendant. There was testimony that the defendant inspected the chairs every week but the Court does not find this testimony credible and finds that the chairs were in fact never inspected at all. Since

[20]614 S.W.2d 852 (Tex. Civ. App. 1981).

there is no direct evidence indicating negligence on the part of the defendant this Court feels that the doctrine of *res ipsa loquitur* is applicable. A plausible conclusion fairly drawn from the facts is that this accident would not ordinarily happen in the absence of negligence. This inference drawn from the failure to explain the accident's cause, together with the facts and circumstances of this case, is that the defendant did not exercise proper care. *See Pear v. Labiche's, Inc.*, La., 301 So. 2d 336.

" . . .

"In *Gonzales v. Winn-Dixie Louisiana*, 326 So.2d 486 (La. 1976) and *Kavlich v. Kramer*, 315 So. 2d 282 (La. 1974), the Louisiana Supreme Court described the order of proof required in cases such as this: when plaintiff has established that the cause of the accident was some allegedly negligent act of defendant, '(t)he burden then shifts to the defendant to go forward with the evidence to exculpate itself from the presumption that it was negligent.'

"The *Kavlich-Gonzales* rule seems as applicable to a procedure for the maintenance of chairs as to the maintenance of floors when applied to one in whose sole control those chairs are maintained.

"Appellant further contends that since Dillman (as an 'unescorted lady') received free drinks on the night in question, she was not an invitee but merely a gratuitous guest to whom no more than ordinary care was due.

"It is a ready inference that the lounge owner's giving free drinks to unescorted ladies was motivated as much by business reasons as by a munificent spirit toward unescorted females. We view the arrangement as one for mutual benefit. Such was held to be the basis of invitee status in *Brown v. State Farm Fire & Casualty Company*, 252 So. 2d 909 (La. App. 2nd Cir. 1971). . . .

"The trial judge found that Nobles did not inspect the chairs weekly, as his uncontradicted testimony indicated. Thus, the court made a factual conclusion that he had breached the applicable standard of care."

[The court sustained the judgment for plaintiff.]

In *Jones v. Keetch*,[21] the Supreme Court of Michigan, adopting the Virginia rule enunciated in *Schnitzer v. Nixon*,[22] held that the innkeeper breached his implied warranty of fitness when a room chair collapsed causing a guest serious injuries, independently of any claim predicated on negligence. It remanded the case for trial on the warranty theory, overruling the appellate court that had denied the warranty claim on the ground that it was not cognizable under existing Michigan common law.

The reasoning of *Jones, supra*, and *Schnitzer, supra*, was reexamined in *Ely v. Blevins*,[23] in which the plaintiff brought an action alleging negligence and breach of warranty against hotel owners after being burned while showering when the hot-water valve failed to shut off the hot water. The court upheld the

---

[21]388 Mich. 164, 200 N.W.2d 227 (1972).
[22]439 F.2d 940 (4th Cir. 1971).
[23]706 F.2d 479 (4th Cir. 1983).

negligence count but stated that under Virginia law an innkeeper is not, in fact, to be held liable for an implied warranty of suitability.

Defective hotel-room chairs have subjected innkeepers to liability in Georgia[24] and in Oregon.[25]

9:10 Strict Liability under the Uniform Commercial Code for Defective Equipment, Fixtures, and Furnishings

Plaintiffs who sue inns for injuries resulting from safety defects have begun to prevail upon an alternate theory of liability. This theory rests on a breach of warranty of fitness of the product for intended use by guests and patrons under the Uniform Commercial Code, which governs sales of goods to consumers. This theory eliminates proof of negligence and imposes strict liability upon the provider of the product. The cases of *Bidar v. AMFAC, Inc.*[26] and *Livingston v. Bigay*, presented below, illustrate two methods used by courts to resolve product liability claims in the innkeeper-guest setting.

In *Bidar*, plaintiff guest tried to use the towel rack in her bathroom to support herself as she rose from the toilet. The rack tore loose from the wall, and plaintiff fell. In response to plaintiff's claim that product liability law applied, the court said: "[A] portion of a leased or rented premises . . . [that] prove[s] defective [citation omitted]" does not equal a "product" for purposes of product liability law.[27] The court was careful, however, to distinguish "identified component[s] of a prefabricated building," which can be a "product."[28]

In *Livingston*, the court engaged in a more policy-oriented analysis of plaintiff's product liability claim. Both courts rejected the imposition in Virginia of strict liability in *Schnitzer v. Nixon*[29] and followed in *Jones v. Keetch*[30] by the Supreme Court of Michigan.

Livingston v. Begay
98 N.M. 712, 652 P.2d 734 (1982)

Payne, J.: "This case presents various questions concerning the liability of a hotel operator for the death of a guest caused by allegedly defective fixtures in the hotel room.

"Peter Begay, plaintiff's decedent, was found dead in his hotel room the morning after he had checked in. The cause of death was asphyxiation by carbon monoxide gas which apparently escaped from a disconnected exhaust vent attached to a gas space heater located in the room. Plaintiff sued the Livingstons,

---

[24]Gary Hotel Courts, Inc. v. Perry, 148 Ga. App. 22, 251 S.E.2d 37 (Ga. App. 1978).
[25]Weaver v. Flock, 43 Or. App. 505, 603 P.2d 1194 (1979).
[26]66 Haw. 547, 669 P.2d 154 (1983).
[27]*Id.* at 161.
[28]*Id.*
[29]439 F.2d 940 (4th Cir. 1971).
[30]388 Mich. 164, 200 N.W.2d 227 (1972).

owners and operators of the hotel at the time of death, the prior owner, Nellie Livingston (Nellie); Montgomery Ward and Company, Inc., the alleged supplier of the heater; and Gas Company of New Mexico, supplier of the gas. Plaintiff's complaint included allegations of negligence, *res ipsa loquitur,* and strict liability. The trial court granted summary judgments for the defendants on all counts of the complaint involved here. . . .

"However, the Court of Appeals reversed the grant of summary judgment in favor of the Livingstons on Count IV, thereby applying the doctrine of strict liability to a hotel operator. We hold that this was error and reverse on this point.

"The general rule is that a hotel operator owes its guests a duty to use reasonable care in promoting their safety. Annot., 18 A.L.R.2d 973, 974 (1951). Although a hotel operator must use reasonable care, he is not an insurer of the safety of his guests. The rule has been that the duty of reasonable care applies to cases involving injuries to guests caused by defective furnishings or conditions in their rooms. *Id.* This rule has been followed in cases involving unsafe heating fixtures. *See* cases cited *id.* at § 7. This reasonable care standard of liability has been applied to motel owners in New Mexico. *Withrow v. Woozencraft,* 90 N.M. 48, 559 P.2d 425 (Ct. App. 1976), *cert. denied,* 90 N.M. 255, 561 P.2d 1348 (1977).

"Plaintiff cites no authority for holding a hotel operator strictly liable for injuries to a guest by inherent defects in fixtures or furnishings in a hotel room. Plaintiff proposed to the Court of Appeals that it hold the Livingstons strictly liable on the authority of two California cases, *Golden v. Conway,* 55 Cal. App. 3d 948, 128 Cal. Rptr. 69 (1976), and *Fakhoury v. Magner,* 25 Cal. App. 3d 58, 101 Cal. Rptr. 473 (1972). The Court of Appeals, with one dissent, obliged.

"*Golden* and *Fakhoury* held landlords strictly liable for injuries to tenants caused by inherent defects in fixtures and furnishings provided as part of the lease. Other courts have refused to apply strict liability to lessors of real estate. *Old Town Development Company v. Langford,* 349 N.E.2d 744 (Ind. App. 1976); *Dwyer v. Skyline Apartments, Inc.,* 123 N.J. Super. 48, 301 A.2d 463 (Ct. App.), *aff'd. mem.* 63 N.J. 577, 311 A.2d 1 (1973). The question is one of first impression in New Mexico. Therefore, a brief review of the law of strict liability in New Mexico is necessary.

"In *Stang v. Hertz Corporation,* 83 N.M. 730, 497 P.2d 732 (1972), we approved the rule of strict products liability expressed in Restatement (Second) of Torts § 402A (1964). There we applied strict liability to a lessor of an automobile, reasoning that there is no logical basis for differentiating between a seller of defective automobile and a lessor of such an automobile. In a lengthy analysis of the development of strict liability, we noted that the theory was adopted '[b]ecause of the shortcomings of the early theories. . . . ' *Stang, supra* at 731, 497 P.2d at 733. These theories—negligence and breach of warranty—imposed limitations and difficulties particularly onerous to purchasers of products. The difficulty in proving that a manufacturer was negligent, the common lack of privity between manufacturer and the ultimate purchaser, as well as other contract and sales rules, required development of strict liability as applied to manufacturers.

Liability extends to retailers and distributors as well as manufacturers because each is an integral part of the marketing process, *Vandermark v. Ford Motor Company,* 61 Cal. 2d 256, 37 Cal. Rptr. 896, 391 P.2d 168 (1964), and because the shortcomings of the earlier theories are equally applicable to such dealers. In *Rudisaile v. Hawk Aviation, Inc.,* 92 N.M. 575, 592 P.2d 175 (1979), we also noted that an important reason for imposing strict liability was to encourage manufacturers to take care in production activities and to provide adequate warning of dangers. In *Stang* we held that these same rationales apply to lessors of particular products. We reaffirmed this application of *Rudisaile.* However, we decline to extend the § 402A definition of 'seller' to persons in the class represented by the Livingstons.

"The lessors involved in *Stang* and *Rudisaile* were involved in leasing particular products. Leasing automobiles and airplanes is a common means of making these products available to consumers. Henszey, *Application of Strict Liability to the Leasing Industry,* 33 Bus. Law 631 (1978). The relationship between such lessors and the manufacturers is substantially the same as that between retail dealers and manufacturers. Thus, it would be illogical to distinguish between such lessors and retailers or other retail dealers.

"The Court of Appeals apparently considered the Livingstons to be lessors of the hotel room, as well as lessors of the fixtures placed therein. Thus, as in *Golden* and *Fakhoury,* the Livingstons could be strictly liable for injuries caused by defects in the fixtures, much as the lessors in *Stang* and *Rudisaile* were held liable.

"Plaintiff argues that there were three defective products involved: the room itself as a whole, the gas heater, and the vent. Because each of these 'products' has distinctive characteristics, we shall examine the application of strict liability principles to each 'product' separately.

"Plaintiff asserts that Room 7 was a defective product because it had an inherently unsafe design. (The heater was placed near the sink where a guest would be likely to bump it.) Accordingly, plaintiff claims that by offering the room to prospective guests, the Livingstons placed a defective product on the market. We decline to accept this line of reasoning. Although other courts have held that a house is a product for purposes of holding a contractor liable to the initial and subsequent purchasers, we think such an application is neither required nor advisable in the circumstances of this case. The rationales behind application of strict liability do not apply when the injured party necessarily has a direct relationship with the defendant, when proof of negligence is not difficult, and when traditional remedies have proven adequate. The unsafe design of a hotel room is simply not the type of defect for which strict liability was fashioned as a remedy.

"Any inherent defect in the gas heater would, of course, create strict liability in the manufacturer and distributors, including the seller to Nellie Livingston. The question here is whether the Livingstons should be treated as part of the 'chain of distribution,' or, in other words, whether the Livingstons placed the heater in the 'stream of commerce.' A major consideration in holding lessors of commercial products strictly liable was that such lessors possessed expert knowledge of the characteristics of the equipment or machines they leased. *Booth Steamship Co. v. Meier & Oelhaf Co.*, 262 F.2d 310 (2d Cir. 1958). Another consideration is that such lessors, like retailers, deal continually with their suppliers, giving them an enduring relationship which permits them to seek contribution and indemnification. These considerations do not apply when a motel operator makes a one-time purchase of furnishings and fixtures about which he has no special expertise. Therefore, we hold that a motel operator is not strictly liable for defects in the fixtures and furnishings of the rooms he holds out to the public.

"Finally, plaintiff claims the exhaust vent was defective. It appears that this vent was fabricated by the installer. Therefore, there is no chain of distribution to pursue, and liability, if any, can fall only on the Livingstons. The traditional duty imposed upon hotel operators as discussed *supra* is adequate to cover any claim by plaintiff, and strict liability will not be imposed as to this item.

"Accordingly, we hold that a hotel operator may not be held strictly liable for injuries suffered by hotel guests when the injuries are caused by defects inherent in the fixtures or furnishings of the hotel rooms. This holding in no way diminishes the hotel operator's liability under alternative theories. *See Wagner v. Coronet Hotel*, 10 Ariz. App. 296, 458 P.2d 390 (1969).

"We reverse the Court of Appeals as to this issue."

9:11 *Floors*

In a wet-floor slip-and-fall case, excerpted below, the Court of Appeals of California ruled in plaintiff's favor that the jury should have been instructed on defendant's duty to warn. The court's decision reversed a jury award for a restaurant owner.

WILLIAMS V. CARL KARCHER ENTERPRISES, INC.
182 Cal. App. 3d 479, 227 Cal. Rptr. 465 (Cal. App. 1986)
review denied 212 Cal. App. 3d 903

SONENSHINE, J.: "Stephanie Williams was injured when she slipped and fell on the wet tile floor at a fast food establishment. A jury verdict was rendered in favor of the restaurant's owner. On appeal, Williams contends the court committed prejudicial error in refusing to instruct the jury a business proprietor has a duty to either remove a dangerous condition on its premises or warn of its presence. We agree and reverse.

I

"The accident occurred on a Friday evening, around the dinner hour. Williams, on a break from her job at the Sears Automotive Center in South Coast Plaza, had gone to Carl's Jr. inside the mall for something to eat. She was accompanied by two coworkers.

"The surface of the floor in the front section of the restaurant was made of ceramic tile; the rear dining room was carpeted. After picking up their order,

Williams and her companion left the tiled area and proceeded to a table in the rear. Ten or twenty minutes later they got up to empty their trash and, ultimately, to return to work.

"As Williams crossed from the carpeted area onto the tile floor, she fell, landing on her right knee. When she got up, she noticed the side of her skirt was wet. Apparently the floor was also wet although not visibly. Williams was wearing rubber soled wedge-type shoes, about one and one-half inches in height. She was walking no differently than usual.

"Williams returned to work to complete her shift. The next day, after noticing her leg was swollen, she obtained treatment at a local hospital emergency room. An infection thereafter developed, necessitating further treatment and a lengthy hospitalization.

"Williams recalled that upon entering the restaurant she saw a man mopping the ceramic tile floor. Nearby were a bucket and an orange cone bearing the word 'caution.' When she got up to leave, she noticed the man and the bucket were gone but the cone was still there.

"The employee who had done the mopping testified he was instructed by the manager to wash the floor before the dinner hour. He used three 'wet signs,' including a bucket which he characterized as such. On each side of the bucket were the words 'caution wet floors.' He used a cleaning solution consisting of about five or six gallons of water and a handful of soap powder. After he finished the job he left behind the wet signs and the bucket. When he returned to the site after the accident, he noticed the bucket had been removed; however, the other signs were still there. He recalled having performed the same task three or four times previously. He did not remember if he ever removed the excess soap between cleanings.

"The restaurant manager testified it was customary to mop the floor, at management's discretion, at least once day during operating hours. It was also customary to allow the floor to dry naturally. Contrary to the testimony of Williams and her two friends, she said business was light at the time of the accident. And although she did not observe the fall, she recalled seeing Williams as she approached the tiled area in the direction of the exit. She said Williams was chatting with one of her friends as she walked. The manager recalled the wet signs were still in place; however, she identified the area where Williams had fallen as being outside their perimeter. She assumed the floor was wet, not because it looked wet but because it had just been mopped. She had last seen the individual who had done the mopping about 15 minutes earlier. To her knowledge, no one, with the exception of a customer who spilled a drink, had ever fallen on the tile floor.

"Williams's accident reconstruction expert testified he had conducted tests on the tile floor surface. In his opinion, the surface when wet was unsafe to walk on with rubber soled shoes. He recommended routine maintenance be done before or after business hours, when customers are not present. Alternatively, he suggested the floor be roped off until it is thoroughly dry and the detergent be removed with clear water to avoid soap buildup.

"In closing argument, defense counsel acknowledged '[t]here is no question that the floor was wet and slippery. You put water on a ceramic tile floor, it's going to be slippery.' However, it was his position Carl's 'took every reasonable effort to inform the public' of this fact; that it was Williams's fault for walking into an area that was a 'known, open obvious danger, and you can't stop people from doing that.'

"The jury was charged with the standard . . . instructions on negligence . . . and contributory negligence. . . . It was also instructed, at Carl's request, with respect to a landowner's duty to exercise ordinary care in the management of its premises.

" . . . Williams requested a number of special instructions pertaining to a business proprietor's duty to remedy a dangerous condition on its premises or to warn of its existence. The trial court refused to give any of these special instructions, except for a portion of one of them.

"Williams contends the court failed to instruct on the heart of her case: a business proprietor's duty to remove a dangerous condition or *adequately* warn of its presence. Although the jury was instructed generally on the law of negligence, no reference was made to a 'dangerous condition.' Had the jury been properly instructed, she asserts, it could have concluded Carl's efforts were *inadequate* to fulfill its affirmative duty. She argues this is particularly true in light of the evidence she fell outside the perimeter of the signs. . . .

"According to Williams' theory of the case, the wet tile floor, due to its slippery condition, was unsafe to walk on, irrespective of any warning to that effect. Under California law, 'the proprietor of a store who knows of, or by the exercise of reasonable care could discover, an artificial condition upon his premises which he should foresee exposes his business visitors to an unreasonable risk, and who has no basis for believing that they will discover the condition or realize the risk involved, is under a duty to exercise ordinary care either to make the condition reasonably safe for their use or to give a warning adequate to enable them to avoid the harm. [Citations.]' (*Bridgman v. Safeway Stores, Inc.* (1960) 53 Cal. 2d 443, 446 [2 Cal. Rptr. 146, 348 P.2d 696]; [citations omitted]). Williams was entitled to have the jury so instructed. . . .

"Without being instructed in terms of Carl's duty to remedy or warn, the jury could not have determined if a dangerous condition existed, and if so, whether the warning was adequate to enable Williams to foresee the full extent of the hazard. Indeed, if a floor is slippery and constitutes a dangerous condition, precautionary measures may not necessarily shield the landowner from liability. (*See, e.g., Scott v. Alpha Beta Co.* (1980) 104 Cal. App.3d 305, 308–309 [163 Cal. Rptr. 544, 20 A.L.R. 4th 511].) 'When required whether a warning is effective to give protection is a jury question. [Citation.]' (*Beauchamp v. Los Gatos Golf Course, supra*, 273 Cal. App. 2d 20, 27.)

"It is of no moment none of the proposed instructions embrace the concept of 'adequacy.' Had the jury been properly instructed, Williams' counsel would then have had a basis upon which to argue the warning was inadequate. True, he endeavored in closing argument to inform the jury Carl's use of warning signs had nothing to do with the case; the true issue was whether the signs were adequate to caution Williams the wet floor created a hazardous condition. And in so doing, he pointed out no evidence had been produced tending to show the floor was wet to the naked eye; thus, Williams had a right to assume the floor was safe to walk on. However, without the instruction, the jury was free to conclude Carl's had satisfied its duty of ordinary care merely by attending to the placement of the signs. It might even have determined their use was gratuitous.

"The duty owed by Carl's was, after all, the crux of the case. '[I]t is the duty of the court to see that jurors are guided on controlling legal principles. . . .' (7 Witkin, Cal. Procedure (3d ed. 1985) Trial, § 243, p. 250.) Its failure to do so here constitutes error.

IV

"The crucial question is whether the error was prejudicial, requiring reversal. (Cal. Const., art. VI, § 13.) Generally, 'if it appears that error in [refusing to give a proper instruction] was likely to mislead the jury and thus to become a factor in its verdict, it is prejudicial and ground for reversal. [Citation.]' (*Henderson v. Harnischfeger Corp.* (1974) 12 Cal. 3d 663, 670 [117 Cal. Rptr. 1, 527 P.2d 353].) . . . ". . . Our problem in the case at bench . . . [involves] not the sufficiency of the evidence, but rather the effect on the jury of an improper instruction.' (*Id.*, at p. 674 . . .) Viewing the matter in this light, we conclude the judgment must be reversed.

"There was evidence the floor was not visibly wet. There was also evidence to support Williams' contention the accident was a result of Carl's failure to take sufficient precautionary measures. Thus, while Williams acknowledged she saw the cone just prior to the fall, the thrust of her case entailed the inadequacy of the warning. Something more was required—the floor should have been dried by hand, roped off, or cleaned before or after business hours.

"The jury should have been permitted to weigh this evidence in accordance with appropriate instructions. Indeed, it could not have determined if Carl's duty had been satisfied without knowing what that duty was. 'Judgment obtained based upon a wrong application of law cannot stand.' (*McGee v. Cessna Aircraft Co.* (1978) 82 Cal. App. 3d 1005, 1019 [147 Cal. Rptr. 694].) . . .

"The judgment is reversed and the matter is remanded to the trial court for a new trial in accordance with the views expressed herein."

In *Harmon v. Cova*,[31] the Court of Appeals of Georgia ruled that it was an error to grant defendant nightclub's motion for summary judgment dismissing a patron's complaint as a matter of law. It was for the jury to determine whether a history of the toilet overflow problem in defendant's restroom was sufficient to confer superior knowledge of risk upon defendant in a slip-and-fall case.

---

[31] 180 Ga. App. 805, 350 S.E.2d 774 (Ga. App. 1986).

In another bathroom slip-and-fall case, a hotel guest was denied recovery on the ground that he failed to prove that the shower where the fall occurred contained any defect which created an unreasonable risk of harm. Such a defect is a necessary element in establishing strict premises liability under Louisiana law.[32]

9:12 *Doors*

WINKLER V. SEVEN SPRINGS FARM, INC.
240 Pa. Super. 641, 359 A.2d 440 (1976)

JACOBS, J.: "Mrs. Winkler, plaintiff below, sustained personal injuries as a result of a fall out a screen door on appellant's premises. Appellant Seven Springs Farm, Inc., argues to this Court that its motion *non obstante veredicto* should have been granted because the plaintiff failed to show that any negligence on the part of appellant caused her fall. We agree that appellant should not be held liable for Mrs. Winkler's injuries.

"Seven Springs Farm is a mountain resort which operates, among other facilities, ten chalets for its guests. On August 25, 1971, Mrs. Winkler, a woman 62 years of age, together with four other ladies, arrived at Seven Springs intending to rent one of the chalets for a short holiday. Because the prior guests had not yet moved out, the ladies sat outside while the departing guests and appellant's employees who were cleaning the unit went in and out attending to their tasks. During this time no one experienced any difficulty with the front screen door which was in constant use. When Mrs. Winkler moved in with her party, she herself used the door without difficulty. A problem was first encountered when one member of the group, Mrs. Rosenberg, sought to leave. Although another lady had exited without incident only moments before, Mrs. Rosenberg was heard to swear at the screen door, complaining that it was stuck. She exited safely, however, and shortly thereafter Mrs. Winkler tried the screen door, finding it stuck. She pushed the screen door a number of times with her hand but it could not be moved, so putting her elbow against it she put her strength into another push and the screen door opened. Mrs. Winkler lost her balance as the screen door opened and fell out onto the step outside, breaking her ankle. Testimony further revealed that the chalet had been built about ten years earlier of a rustic wood construction and it had two exits. The exit where the accident occurred had a step between the screen door, which opened out, and the ground. It was also stated that it had rained earlier in the day on the date of the accident. . . .

"In order to find the defendant liable for her injuries, plaintiff must show that the defendant either knew or, by the exercise of reasonable care, should have

---

[32]*See* Connor v. Motel 6, Inc., 521 So. 2d 1248 (La. App. 1988). To the same effect *see* Malvicini v. Stratfield Motor Hotel, Inc., 206 Conn. 439, 538 A.2d 690 (1988).

known that the screen door in her chalet was sticking and was likely to cause her harm. A number of principles of law are applicable to the plaintiff's proof of this hypothesis. A possessor of land is not an insurer of his business invitees, and plaintiff's evidence must establish some degree of negligence on defendant's part in order to recover. [Citations omitted.] Furthermore, a jury cannot be permitted to return a verdict based on speculation and not supported by adequate evidence or reasonable inferences. 'We have said many times that the jury may not be permitted to reach its verdict merely on the basis of speculation or conjecture, but that there must be evidence upon which logically its conclusion may be based.' *Smith v. Bell Telephone Co.*, 397 Pa. 134, 138, 153 A.2d 477, 479 (1959). Circumstantial evidence is adequate to prove the plaintiff's case and '[i]t is not necessary, under Pennsylvania law, that every fact or circumstance point unerringly to liability. . . . '[*I*]*d*. at 138, 153 A.2d at 480, however, the mere happening of an accident is no evidence of negligence and does not raise a presumption of negligence. [Citation omitted.]

"It is apparent from the facts of record that the appellee-plaintiff failed to produce any evidence upon which a trier of fact could conclude that appellant somehow breached its duty to Mrs. Winkler. Rather than showing the appellant had knowledge that the screen door represented an unreasonable risk of harm, appellee showed that appellant could not possibly have such knowledge: appellant's employees had been using that door while cleaning the chalet without any difficulty only moments before Mrs. Winkler's fall. Moreover, there was no showing that the allegedly dangerous condition of the door could or should have been discovered by a proper or reasonable inspection. From all the evidence it appeared the door had been working perfectly when it suddenly became stuck. No evidence whatsoever was introduced to show that the stickiness was caused by some discoverable condition or structural defect of which the appellant could have been aware had it performed an inspection. [Citations omitted.] Because no evidence was submitted to show that the door was in any way defective or that it had ever stuck prior to Mrs. Rosenberg's and Mrs. Winkler's use of it, I cannot say that the condition of the door would support an inference of negligence on the part of appellant.

"Nor is this a case where the concept of *res ipsa loquitur*, as defined in the Restatement (Second) or Torts § 328D (1965), can be applied to raise the inference that the accident was the result of appellant's negligence. We are not persuaded that a sticking screen door is the type of event contemplated by the Restatement as being of a kind which ordinarily does not occur in the absence of negligence. Common human experience suggests numerous explanations for a sticking door, many of which do not involve negligence. Furthermore, no attempt was made by the appellee to eliminate the possibility of responsible causes other than the negligence of the appellant. [Citation omitted.] The totality of these circumstances cannot be viewed to raise an inference of negligence, and as it is still the plaintiff's burden to advance some evidence to support her claim, we find no support for the jury's result in this case. [Citation omitted.]

"The appellee-plaintiff in the present case failed to prove more than the mere happening of an accident while she was a business visitor on appellant's premises. The conclusion that appellant was negligent toward her could only be based on speculation unsupported by evidence. [Citations omitted.]

"Judgment reversed."

In *Karna v. Byron Reed Syndicate #4*,[33] the federal district court sitting in Nebraska held, after trial, without a jury, that even where the placement of a hotel check-in counter in close proximity to the inner glass entry doors of the premises constituted gross negligence, the prior knowledge of the dangerous condition by the guest constituted more than slight negligence, barring any recovery.

The same result will apply to bar recovery by a minor plaintiff injured when she went through a closed sliding glass panel door at defendant's private swimming club, where club rules in effect prohibit "horseplay," including running, in the swimming pool enclosure, and the plaintiff was aware of these rules. The Louisiana Court of Appeal[34] concluded that the twelve-year-old victim was heedless of her own welfare by blindly running without looking and was thus guilty of contributory negligence, requiring reversal of a judgment rendered below in her favor and the dismissal of her action.

In a ruling to the contrary, the Supreme Court of Nevada affirmed a judgment for an elderly patron injured by the premature closing of the hotel's automatic sliding lobby glass doors. In doing so, it reviewed the doctrine of *res ipsa loquitur* and concluded that the trial court had properly instructed the jury on that issue.[35]

Likewise, the federal Court of Appeals for the Eighth Circuit, applying Missouri law, affirmed a substantial nonjury award in favor of a minor patron and his mother for injuries sustained by the minor when he fell through a sliding glass door in a hotel. The court found that the door specifications provided by the hotel were unreasonably dangerous.[36]

In another sliding door case, a nonguest of a hotel was injured when the door struck her as she entered the hotel lobby. The Louisiana Court of Appeal held that the hotel failed in its obligation to use reasonable care by not warning invitees of the risk of the sliding door. The trial court properly apportioned the liability and damages among the hotel, the employee engaged in the work, and the employer who was responsible for installing the automatic lobby door.[37]

9:13 *Stairways*

In general, the same legal concepts that apply to hotel doors govern proof of negligence and the defenses of contributory negligence and of assumption of risk in cases of innkeeper liability for safe stairways. The essential elements of neg-

---

[33]374 F. Supp. 687 (D. Neb. 1974).

[34]Williamson v. The Travelers Ins. Co., 235 So. 2d 600 (1970), *reh'g denied*, 256 La. 818, 239 So. 2d 345 (1970).

[35]*See* Landmark Hotel and Casino, Inc. v. Moore, 757 P.2d 361 (1988).

[36]*See* Jenkins v. McLean Hotels, Inc., 859 F. 2d 598 (8th Cir. 1988).

[37]*See* Johnson v. Beavers, 496 So. 2d 1251 (La. App. 1986).

ligence are contained in *Campbell v. Bozeman Community Hotel*,[38] in which the Supreme Court of Montana denied a guest recovery because of lack of evidence that the hotel stairway was defective. In *Buck v. Del City Apartments*,[39] the Supreme Court of Oklahoma ruled that the failure of a motel guest to observe snowfall and act accordingly on the outdoor stairs precluded recovery. However, a restaurant patron was permitted to recover when a steep drop-off on an entry stairway was found to constitute a concealed or hidden trap, requiring reversal of a trial court entry summary judgment on the pleadings. The Illinois Appellate Court ruled that the issues of negligence and contributory negligence were proper ones for the jury to resolve at trial.[40]

In accord with *Buck* is the case of *Kittle v. Liss*,[41] in which the court held that a property owner is not liable for injuries occurring on the property that result from natural accumulations of ice and snow, in this case on a stairway, unless the owner caused or aggravated the accumulation. The court, however, hastened to add that the presence of ice and snow on property does not abrogate an owner's duty to provide a safe means of ingress and egress for invitees. See, in accord, *Chadwick v. Barba Lou, Inc.*[42]

In *Rocoff v. Lancella*,[43] which dealt with a fall on a staircase, an Indiana reviewing court applied the rule of reasonable care for the safety of business invitees and found that the defendants were negligent. The court rejected the argument on appeal that plaintiff was contributorily negligent as a matter of law.

A patron at an Air Force club who sought damages for a fall on a dark stairway leading to an area of the club closed to the public at that time was denied recovery. Her actions were deemed negligent, thus requiring dismissal by the Federal District Court for the District of Columbia.[44]

Adequacy of lighting and visibility as factors for the jury to consider on the issue of safe premises was raised in *McNally v. Liebowitz*.[45] In that case, the Supreme Court of Pennsylvania affirmed a jury verdict for a patron in a public restaurant injured because of an inadequately lighted ladies' restroom.

In the case that follows, the issue was whether proof of defendant's compliance with the local building code was sufficient to preclude a finding of negligence.

LUXEN v. HOLIDAY INNS, INC.
566 F. Supp. 1484 (N.D. Ill. 1983)

BUA, D.J.: " . . . [Plaintiff brought suit for injuries that occurred in a fall while she was climbing a set of stairs on the hotel premises.]

---

[38]160 Mont. 327, 502 P.2d 1144 (1972).
[39]431 P.2d 360 (Okla. 1967).
[40]*See* Allgauer v. Le Bastille, Inc., 101 Ill. App. 3d 978, 428 N.E.2d 1146 (1981).
[41]108 Ill. App. 3d 922, 439 N.E.2d 972 (1982).
[42]69 Ohio St. 2d 222, 431 N.E.2d 660 (1982).
[43]145 Ind. App. 440, 251 N.E.2d 582 (1969).
[44]*See* Roberts v. United States, 514 F. Supp. 712 (D.D.C. 1981).
[45]498 Pa. 163, 445 A.2d 716 (1982).

"Plaintiff's final claim is that defendant's failure to provide a handrail on the wall side of the stairway proximately caused plaintiff's injuries. Defendant counters by asserting that summary judgment is warranted because there is no dispute that the premises were in compliance with the applicable building codes.

"On March 5, 1979, the City of Hazelwood, Missouri passed Bill No. 1350, Ordinance No. 1320–79, thus codifying the 1978 BOCA Basic Building Code. Under the BOCA code, unless an inspector finds the exitways to be 'inadequate for safety,' the exitways in an existing building shall be deemed to be in compliance with the Code. BOCA Basic Building Code (1978), § 604.2-1. Because the inspector did not find the stairway to be inadequate for safety, there can be no issue as to whether the stairway was in compliance with the BOCA code. That the stairway was in compliance with the BOCA code is supported by the deposition testimony of experts for both plaintiff and defendant. Furthermore, because the BOCA code specifically sets out requirements in existence prior to its enactment and because it expressly states that all prior codes are 'hereby repealed and held for naught,' there can be no question that the code as enacted in 1979 was the applicable code at the time of the incident. Therefore, no issue of material fact exists that a violation of the code provision was a proximate cause of plaintiff's injury. This does not, however, end the Court's inquiry.

"Plaintiff alleges that the failure to provide a handrail was the proximate cause of plaintiff's injury. While defendant may well have been in compliance with the applicable building and safety code provisions, such compliance does not preclude a determination that, under the circumstances, defendant was nevertheless negligent. As Prosser notes, compliance with a statute does not necessarily mean that due care was used. W. Prosser, Law of Torts, 4th ed., § 36, at 203 (1971). Thus, where specific circumstances present situations beyond those which the statute was designed to meet, a plaintiff may prove that the defendant was negligent in not taking extra measures. [Citations omitted.] Defendant is only entitled to summary judgment on the issue of statutory compliance. Whether defendant was nevertheless negligent remains in issue."

In *Sussman v. Tutelman*,[46] a hotel resident, after descending from a stairway, tripped over the cane of a hotel guest seated in the lobby. The Florida Court of Appeals reversed a jury verdict for the resident. The evidence failed to demonstrate that the injury was caused by any violation of a legal duty.

In *Morton v. F.B.D. Enterprises*,[47] absent proof of a factual causal connection between the occurrence of an accident and a violation of a dinner theater operator's duty to exercise reasonable care in the maintenance of a two-step stairway leading to a dinner buffet line, a patron's cause of action in negligence was reversed for failure to make out a *prima facie* case.

[46]445 So. 2d 1081 (Fla. App. 1984).
[47]141 Ill. App. 3d 553, 490 N.E.2d 995 (1986), *appeal denied*.

9:14   *Bathrooms and Showers*

APPER v. EASTGATE ASSOCIATION
28 Md. App. 581, 347 A.2d 389 (1975)

ORTH, C.J.: "On 11 February 1969 Leonard Apper, a wholesale camera salesman, checked into the Towne Motel in Hagerstown, Maryland, owned by Eastgate Associates and others, as an overnight guest. He dined at a nearby restaurant and returned to his motel room. He watched television for a time, telephoned his wife and, around 10:00 P.M., took a bath. Upon completion of his bath, he drained the water and started to get out of the tub. 'I went to raise myself to get out of the tub. I put my right elbow on the right side of the tub and I grabbed this handhold with my left hand and attempted to assist myself in getting up and the handhold broke away from the wall and it was a massive handhold . . . and it broke away from the wall and hit me across . . . the bridge of my nose.' He fell back and hit his head, back and neck. He blacked out. 'The next thing that I remembered was I opened my eyes and there was blood streaming down my face and my chest and that is the next thing that I recollect.' He called for help and was taken to the hospital. The cut on the bridge of his nose was sutured. He suffered injuries to his back and neck. The 'handhold' was a ceramic fixture set in the wall above the tub. It was known in the ceramic tile trade as a 'soap and grab' and was intended to be used by bathers to help themselves in and out of the bathtub. It was installed with the expectation that bathers would so use it. Apper was alone in the room at all times, made no prior examination of the fixture, and noticed nothing unusual about it. It appeared to be securely fastened and was not loose to the touch. There were no warning signs or notices in regard to the fixture or its use. He used it as he had previously used similar fixtures on many other occasions in many other hotels.

"On 13 January 1972 Apper and his wife instituted an action in tort in the Circuit Court for Washington County against Eastgate. He sought damages for the injuries he suffered which he alleged were caused by Eastgate's negligence. He and his wife sought damages for loss of consortium. . . .

"The action was tried before a jury on 26 November 1974. From a grant of defendant's motion for a directed verdict, plaintiffs appeal. . . .

"[I]n this jurisdiction, there are three elements which a plaintiff must show to invoke the doctrine of *res ipsa loquitur.* [Citation omitted.] . . .

"1. A casualty of a sort which usually does not occur in the absence of negligence.

"2. Caused by an instrumentality within the defendant's exclusive control.

"3. Under circumstances indicating that the casualty did not result from the act or omission of the plaintiff.

"We consider the elements necessary to invoke the doctrine of *res ipsa loquitur* in the light of the evidence adduced to prove them, but we do so in the order inverse to the listing of them.

The Act of the Person Injured

"A person injured must eliminate his own conduct as a cause of injury. He may do so by showing that he has done nothing abnormal with the instrumentality causing the injury and has used it in the manner and for the purpose for which it was intended. *Sweet v. Swangel,* 166 N.W. 2d 776, 778 (1969), quoting W. Prosser, Res Ipsa Loquitur *in California,* 37 Calif. L. Rev. 183, 202 (1949): ' "The plaintiff need only tell enough of what he did and how the accident happened to permit the conclusion that the fault was not his. Again he has the burden of proof by a mere preponderance of the evidence; and even though the question of his own contribution is left in doubt, *res ipsa loquitur* may still be applied under proper instructions to the jury." ' The evidence is clear that Apper did nothing abnormal with the fixture. He used it in the manner and for the purpose for which it was intended. It was designed and installed to assist a bather to get in and out of the tub and that is precisely the use he made of it. . . . On the evidence Apper could be found to be exonerated from any responsibility for the accident. It permitted a conclusion that he was injured through no fault of his own while engaged in a customarily innocuous course of conduct—getting out of a bathtub. We find that there was evidence to show the third element.

Exclusive Control

"There was also evidence sufficient in law to prove the second element, that the casualty was caused by an instrumentality within the exclusive control of the defendant. The fixture was exclusively under the control and maintenance of Eastgate, and Eastgate had exclusive knowledge of the care exercised in the control and maintenance of that instrumentality. Apper was a guest in the motel. The motel owed him the duty of providing accommodations that were reasonably safe for the use contemplated, and, where it furnished appliances, of furnishing them in such a condition that with ordinary use they would be reasonably safe. The motel rented the room and appliances and it had them under its exclusive control with respect to installation and maintenance. It retained such control of the equipment it furnished, notwithstanding that it furnished Apper with possession of the equipment while he was a guest. . . . The hotel's duty to plaintiff was singular and it certainly was not divided with plaintiff . . . at the point where plaintiff assumed occupancy of the room.' Eastgate had the exclusive responsibility as well as the sole capability for keeping the 'soap and grab' in good order and condition. *See Brown Hotel Company v. Marx,* 411 S.W.2d 911, 915 (Ky. 1967).

The Nature of the Casualty

"The evidence fully warranted the inference of negligence permitted by the *res ipsa* doctrine. Not only was it legally sufficient to show that the fixture was within the exclusive control of Eastgate and that Apper was exonerated from any responsibility for the accident, but, also, the casualty was of the sort which usually does not occur in the absence of someone's negligence. In the ordinary instance, no injurious operation is to be expected from the use of the fixture unless from a careless construction, maintenance or user. We think that the jury could have properly inferred the injury was probably caused by some negligent act on the part of Eastgate.

"We look first at *Byrne v. Boadle*, 2 Hurl. & Colt. 722 (1863) which launched the *res ipsa* doctrine into the orbit of tort law. Chief Baron POLLOCK said, at 726:

> "The learned counsel was quite right in saying that there are many accidents from which no presumption of negligence can arise, but I think it would be wrong to lay down as a rule that in no case can presumption of negligence arise from the fact of an accident. The present case upon the evidence comes to this, a man is passing in front of the premises of a dealer in flour, and there falls down upon him a barrel of flour. I think it apparent that the barrel was in the custody of the defendant who occupied the premises, and who is responsible for the acts of his servants who had the control of it; and in my opinion the fact of its falling is *prima facie* evidence of negligence, and the plaintiff who was injured by it is not bound to show that it could not fall without negligence, but if there are any facts inconsistent with negligence it is for the defendant to prove them.

"We see a parallel between the casualty there and the casualty here. Just as the barrel could not roll out of a warehouse without some negligence, the 'soap and grab' could not pull out from the wall without some negligence. The fixture was in the control of Eastgate, and the fact of its pulling loose from the wall was *prima facie* evidence of negligence. Apper was not bound to show directly that it could not have pulled loose without negligence. . . .

"Having shown the three elements which a plaintiff must prove to invoke the doctrine of *res ipsa loquitur*, Apper was entitled to have the doctrine applied. Upon its application, there would have been such evidence of negligence as to make unwarranted the grant of Eastgate's motion for a directed verdict at the close of evidence offered by Apper. We hold that the court erred in granting the motion. Apper should be afforded a new trial.

"We emphasize that the doctrine of *res ipsa loquitur* merely provides a permissible inference of negligence. . . . Negligence may be rebutted by testimony and evidence produced on behalf of Eastgate. In the words of Chief Baron POLLOCK: '[I]f there are any facts inconsistent with negligence it is for the defendant to prove them.' *Byrne v. Boadle, supra*, at 726.

"Appeal dismissed; case remanded for further proceedings in accordance with this opinion. . . . ''

In a similar case, *Bidar v. AMFAC, Inc.*[48] (see section 9:9, *infra*), the majority of the court held that a genuine issue of material fact existed with respect to whether a hotel should foresee that guests will grab nearby towel racks to assist themselves in rising from the toilet. In a persuasive dissent, however, Judge Spencer concluded that a reasonable guest knows better than to use a towel rack

---

[48]66 Haw. 547, 669 P.2d 154 (1983).

to support his or her weight. Therefore, the court should find that no material issue of fact exists as to the hotel's use of reasonable care.

9:15   *Fire Liability in General*

The federal Hotel and Motel Fire Safety Act of 1989, is the first comprehensive law indirectly establishing uniform minimum fire standards for hotel and motel owners and operators in order to qualify for occupancy by federal employees. The Act prohibits federal travelers from obtaining reimbursement for expenses incurred at a hotel or motel that does not install federally approved automatic room sprinkler systems and smoke detectors. The Act exempts those hotels and motels that are three stories or lower or any other lodging establishment located within a building that contains no more than five rooms for rent or hire and that is actually occupied as a residence by the proprietor. A list of approved accommodations must be provided to all federal agencies according to a cumulative percentage of available establishments over a six-year period, at which time the Act will be fully effective (1995).

The Alaska Supreme Court's discussion, to follow, of *per se* negligence would include violation of this federal law. Moreover, as the court notes, compliance with such statutes does not obviate a jury finding of negligence based upon proof that the owner or operator should have done more under the circumstances.

NORTHERN LIGHTS MOTEL, INC. v. SWEANEY
561 P.2d 1176, *rehearing*, 563 P.2d 256 (Alaska 1977)

CONNOR, J.: "In the early morning hours of September 19, 1972, Kenneth Stumbaugh died in a fire while staying at the Northern Lights Motel in Anchorage, Alaska. His personal representative sued the motel and was awarded a total judgment of $313,650.82 after a trial by jury. Northern Lights Motel, Inc., appeals from the judgment on a variety of grounds. The central issues on appeal concern the application of the doctrine of negligence *per se*.

"The fire started in a chair in room 15 and spread to room 10 where Stumbaugh was staying. It was not determined at trial whether it was caused by a lighted cigarette left in the chair by the room occupants or whether it was deliberately set by an arsonist.

"The fire was discovered by two men. Magnuson and Nyquist, while they were driving along Fireweed Lane. After learning from the deceased's roommate that Stumbaugh was still in his room, Magnuson attempted a rescue. He entered the smoke-filled room, located Stumbaugh, and tried to drag him out, feet first. Stumbaugh struggled and kicked, grabbing a table and chair to prevent being pulled. As Magnuson reached the door and breathed some fresh air, Stumbaugh kicked loose and moved back into the room. At about that time, 'whatever it was that was smoldering in there burst into flames,' and Magnuson was prevented from going back into the room. After several unsuccessful attempts to put out the flames, he and Nyquist went on to get the rest of the occupants out of the building. Stumbaugh died from carbon monoxide asphyxia, according to the autopsy report. . . .

"The Northern Lights Motel was inspected by the borough fire department twice before the fire. Various deficiencies were noted, including a need to enclose the furnace room in one-hour construction, and these were promptly remedied by the management. The inspector failed to note the construction of the east-west wing, although his report indicated the north-south ceiling construction. The borough department did not consider the building to be a threat to human life. Borough Fire Chief Hildreth did testify, however, that had he known of the ceiling construction in the east-west wing he would have required additional safety devices. In 1970 the department considered the building to be an 'existing building' under the state fire code, including the Uniform Building Code. The department permitted such buildings to continue operating without one-hour construction or alternative safeguards such as sprinkler systems or smoke detectors, as long as the department determined that they presented no unreasonable threat to human life. . . .

Uniform Building Code Standard as Negligence *Per Se*

"In *Ferrell v. Baxter*, 484 P.2d 250, 263 (Alaska 1971), we adopted the principles expressed in the Restatement (Second) of Torts concerning negligence *per se:*

"The court may adopt as the standard of conduct of a reasonable man the requirements of a legislative enactment or an administrative regulation whose purpose is found to be exclusively or in part

"(*a*) to protect a class of persons which includes the one whose interest is invaded, and

"(*b*) to protect the particular interest which is invaded, and

"(*c*) to protect that interest against the kind of harm which has resulted, and

"(*d*) to protect that interest against the particular hazard from which the harm results. [Restatement (Second) of Torts § 286 (1965.]

"Where these criteria are met, the trial court may, in its discretion, adopt the statute or regulation in question rather than the usual common law reasonable person standard as the applicable standard of care. [Citations omitted.] Substitution of an administrative or legislative enactment as the applicable standard of safety is appropriate where the rule of conduct contained therein is expressed in specific concrete terms. Substitution is not appropriate where the statute merely sets out a general or abstract standard of care. [Citations omitted.]

"The construction requirement contained in the U.B.C. meets the criteria developed in *Ferrell* and its progeny. Defendant claims, however, that *Ferrell* is inapposite because it was limited to traffic violations and its principles should not be applied to a building code. However, in *Bachner* [*Bachner v. Rich*, 554 P.2d 430, 440–41 (Alaska 1976)] . . . we extended application of the doctrine of negligence *per se* beyond traffic regulations. . . .

"Defendant further argues that the provisions of the U.B.C. are 'obscure,' and not generally known and obeyed. . . .

"The trial court here exercised its discretion in favor of giving the negligence *per se* instruction. We hold that the trial court did not abuse its discretion in ruling that a reasonably prudent person might be aware of the U.B.C. provisions and of their applicability to the instant case. The Code has been in effect in Alaska since at least 1959. There was evidence that the U.B.C. was recognized in Anchorage in 1964. . . .

"Thus the court could reasonably have concluded, in its discretion, that the U.B.C. was not so 'obscure' or 'unknown' to warrant a refusal to give the negligence *per se* instruction. ' "Obviously cases will be relatively infrequent in which legislation directed to the safety of persons or property will be so obsolete, or so unreasonable, or for some other reason inapplicable to the case, that the court will take this position; but where the situation calls for it, the court is freed to do so." ' *Ferrell, supra* at 264 n. 23, quoting Restatement (Second) or Torts § 286, comment d (1965).

"The U.B.C. Provisions in question are not so arcane or unreasonable that compliance with them would be virtually impossible. Nor does the application of the U.B.C. in the case at bar impose liability without fault. Objections to its use as a standard should be analyzed as excuses. This would shift the burden to the defendant to show why compliance was unreasonable. [Citations omitted.]

"Defendant's argument that regulations based on the U.B.C. should not be adopted as negligence *per se*, is not persuasive. That these are regulations rather than statutes has no effect on their applicability as a standard of care in civil cases. [Citations omitted.] A fire regulation need not specifically impose civil liability in order for a violation to be the basis of negligence *per se*. [Citations omitted.] *See generally Sanchez v. J. Barron Rice, Inc.,* 77 N.M. 717, 427 P.2d 240, 244–45 (1967); *Rietze v. Williams,* 458 S.W.2d 613, 617 (Ky. 1970) (violations of plumbing or plumbing gas codes held to be negligence *per se*); *Derboven v. Stockton,* 490 S.W.2d 301, 313 (Mo. App. 1973) (negligence *per se* applicable to fire ordinance and statute violations).

"We hold, therefore, that the trial court's instruction set forth in full on page 1180 *supra* on the effect of a violation of the U.B.C. was not error. . . .

Evidence of Additional Safeguards

"Courts generally hold that there is no common law duty to maintain a ' "fire proof hotel." ' *Mozer v. Semenza,* 177 So. 2d 880, 882 (Fla. App. 1965). But the *Mozer* court, after reviewing the authorities, concluded that 'it is the duty of an innkeeper to provide reasonably safe premises for the housing of its guests,' and held that the maintenance of an unenclosed stairwell constituted a violation of that duty. *Id.* We found a similar duty in *Silverton v. Marler,* 389 P.2d 3, 4 (Alaska 1964) (lodge operator owes paying guest duty to keep premises in reasonably safe condition). [Citation omitted.] Thus the evidence of lack of a resident manager (and sprinkler system and smoke detectors) is relevant under the ordinary negligence standard.

"The lack of any evidence of a community standard should not prevent the introduction of this evidence. Even assuming there was no other hotel or motel in the Anchorage area taking any such precautions, and that a community custom against use of such devices was established, that custom would still not be conclusive. 'Even an entire industry, by adopting such careless methods to save time, effort or money, cannot be permitted to set its own uncontrolled standard.' W. Prosser, The Law of Torts § 33, at 167 (4th ed. 1971). Conformity with such a standard might, in some cases, permit a directed verdict that there was no negligence, if there were nothing in the evidence or in common experience to suggest otherwise. But 'where common knowledge and ordinary judgment will recognize unreasonable danger, what everyone does may be found to be negligent. . . . ' *Id.* at 168. . . . [Citations omitted.]

"Affirmed."

In *Darby v. Checker Co.*,[49] an Illinois appellate court held that in the absence of statute or municipal ordinance it was reversible error to instruct the jury that the hotel was negligent in failing to extinguish a hotel fire and in failing to provide assistance to the plaintiff in leaving the premises. A new trial was ordered where a guest fell from a makeshift bed clothes "rope" after climbing out the window of her fourth floor room in an attempt to escape a fire of unknown origin. The appellate court also ruled that the injury was warranted in deciding for her on the issues of lack of adequate warning of fire, delay in notifying the fire department, and failure to prevent the fire from spreading. The jury finding of no contributory negligence was sustained on the ground that in an emergency one need not exercise the same degree of self-possession and judgment necessary under ordinary circumstances.

In *Barrous v. Knotts*,[50] the Texas Court of Civil Appeals concluded that a failure to warn a guest who died in the fire of the existence of a fire was actionable negligence despite the absence of any statute governing the hotel requiring fire escapes or a fire alarm or warning system.

Also see *Hassan v. Stafford*,[51] where the U.S. Court of Appeals for the Third Circuit, applying Delaware law, held that a jury verdict of no negligence in a wrongful death action arising out of a motel fire was sustainable even though the testimony of the local fire marshal that the hotel did not conform to current standards for fire safety devices was uncontradicted. Such testimony did not establish the liability of the hotel operator as a matter of law in view of the fact that the hotel was not required to conform to the current Delaware safety regulations governing alarm systems and fire doors.

The following case illustrates two issues: (1) the rescue doctrine and (2) what constitutes proof of the rescuer's contributory negligence sufficient to deny recovery.

---

[49] 6 Ill. App. 3d 188, 285 N.E.2d 217 (1972).
[50] 482 S.W.2d 358 (Tex. 1972).
[51] 472 F.2d 88 (3d Cir. 1973).

ALTAMURO V. MILNER HOTEL, INC.
540 F. Supp. 870 (E.D. Pa. 1982)

McGlynn, D.J.:

Findings of Fact

"1. The Milner Hotel is located at 111 South 10th Street in Philadelphia, Pennsylvania and is owned by the defendant The Milner Hotel, Inc., a corporation maintaining its registered office at 1526 Center Street, Detroit, Michigan.

"2. During the morning of October 11, 1978, Patricia DeLoss, a guest in Room 706 at the Hotel, went to the Hotel's Lobby and there told the Desk Clerk, William T. Wilson, that the television in her room was not receiving a picture and requested that it be repaired. After speaking to Wilson, Ms. DeLoss left the Hotel.

"3. Wilson then summoned Edwin Jennings, the maintenance man employed by the Hotel, and instructed him to proceed to Ms. DeLoss' room on the seventh floor to inspect the television.

"4. Mr. Jennings went to Room 706 and turned the power-switch of the television to the 'on' position, but the switch did not activate the set.

"5. Jennings then moved the television and placed the plug into another receptacle in the same room. When he did this, the television began to emit a 'burning' odor and made a 'popping' or 'crackling' sound. Jennings removed the plug from the receptacle and then placed the television in its former position reinserting the plug into the original receptacle with the power switch still in the 'on' position.

"6. Jennings then returned to the Lobby and reported to Wilson that he thought the television had a 'short' in it. In response, Wilson asked Jennings if he turned the television off. Jennings replied, 'No, I don't think I did.' Wilson then told Jennings to return to Room 706 and turn off the TV set. As Jennings began to ascend the stairs, an unidentified man came in and stated that there was smoke coming out of one of the Hotel's windows on the third floor.

"7. Wilson called the Fire Department and then, using the switchboard, called all the rooms in the Hotel, alerting the residents to the fire.

"8. About fifteen minutes later, Harry E. Vonada, the Manager of the Hotel, entered the Lobby, and after being apprised of the fire by Wilson, he and Jennings went to the third floor but were unable to locate the source of the smoke. Vonada then telephoned Wilson from one of the rooms on the third floor and told him that there was no fire at that level. Wilson then went outside, observed that the fire was on the seventh floor, and so advised Vonada.

"9. About fifteen minutes before Wilson told Vonada that the fire was on the seventh floor, Altamuro, who operated the newsstand in front of the Hotel, and who was known to Wilson, rushed into the Lobby and shouted to Wilson that smoke was pouring out of one of the rooms.

"10. Altamuro then boarded an elevator alone and went to one of the upper floors to alert the residents.

"11. Wilson testified that he warned Altamuro not to go because the Fire Department was called and would be soon arriving.

"12. Wilson also stated that Altamuro came back down to the Lobby, stayed there for approximately ten minutes and then boarded the elevator a second time. Wilson again warned him 'not to go up.'

"13. Wilson testified that Altamuro went up alone the second time and that this is the last time he saw him alive.

"14. At about this time, Officer Edward Markowski of the Philadelphia Police Department noticed the fire while driving in his patrol car. He pulled up in front of the Hotel, went into the Lobby and informed the Clerk at the desk that there was a fire in the Hotel. He then went out to his patrol car and radioed the Fire Department and then returned to the Hotel Lobby.

"15. While there, Officer Markowski met Jennings and Altamuro, with whom the Officer was acquainted. The officer said to Jennings: 'Let's get upstairs and see what's happening.' Altamuro asked if he could also go along to see if 'he could give them a hand.' Officer Markowski said it was all right with him, 'but if anything went wrong, he'd have to get out.'

"16. All three men then boarded the elevator and went up to the seventh floor. They were joined by Vonada, the Manager.¹

"17. All four men went to Room 706 where the fire had started. Officer Markowski tried to open the door but the door was locked. The Officer asked Jennings if he had a key to the room. Jennings said he did. Officer Markowski said: 'Open the door.' Mr. Vonada ordered Jennings to keep it closed in order to keep the fire contained in the room. Officer Markowski countered by telling Jennings: 'I am the law. Open up the door.'² Jennings complied with his command. When the door was opened, black smoke poured out of the room and into the hallway and filled the entire corridor. The lights in the hallway then went out.

"18. The men then became nauseous and the police officer began vomiting. Officer Markowski ordered the men downstairs, which order the men obeyed.

"19. While on the seventh floor, Officer Markowski found a woman unconscious on the floor. He picked the woman up and placed her on his shoulder and carried her down to the fifth floor.

"20. When on the fifth floor, Officer Markowski saw Altamuro knocking on doors informing guests of the fire. The police officer asked Altamuro to take the woman down to the Lobby for him. Altamuro carried the woman downstairs and Officer Markowski returned to the seventh floor.

"21. When he returned to the seventh floor, Officer Markowski found a tall slender Black male, assisted him to the Lobby, and then across the street away from the Hotel.

"22. The officer returned to the Lobby, but at this time, the fire was spreading rapidly. Flaming debris had fallen on the Hotel's marquee and consequently the firemen in the Lobby ordered all policemen and civilians out of the building.

"23. Officer Markowski testified that at the time the firemen made this announcement, he observed the presence of Mr. Wilson and Mr. Altamuro in the

Lobby and that immediately after this announcement, he escorted these men to the outside of the Hotel.

"24. Officer Markowski testified that this was the last time he saw Altamuro alive and never saw him return to the Hotel.

"25. The decedent's body was found in Room 710 sometime after he had left the Hotel to go across the street with Officer Markowski. The cause of death was 'inhalation of fumes and carbon monoxide poisoning' and there were burns on his body and 'skin slip of the face.'

"26. The fire at the Milner Hotel had been in progress for an undetermined length of time before the Philadelphia Fire Department arrived.

"27. There were four means of access to the seventh floor from the Lobby: two elevators, a stairway and a fire tower.

"28. Fire Department personnel had no knowledge of the activities of Officer Markowski and/or the decedent and were unaware of the uses to which the elevators and stairwells were put prior to their arrival at the scene.

"29. Fire Department personnel only used the stairway for access to the seventh floor of the Hotel.

"30. The decedent's death occurred after the Philadelphia Police Department and Philadelphia Fire Department arrived at the Milner Hotel and ordered all civilians to vacate the premises.

"31. The fire that occurred at the Hotel on October 11, 1978 originated in the defective television set owned by the Hotel in Room 706. . . .

Discussion

1. Defendant Milner Hotel

"Plaintiff's case against the defendant, Milner Hotel, is based principally on the 'rescue doctrine', which provides that when one person is exposed to peril of life or limb by the negligence of another, the latter will be liable for damages for injuries received by a third person in a reasonable effort to rescue the one so imperiled. *Guca v. Pittsburgh Railways Co.*, 367 Pa. 579, 80 A.2d 779 (1951); *Toner v. Pennsylvania Railroad Co.*, 263 Pa. 438, 106 A. 797 (1919); *Corbin v. City of Philadelphia*, 195 Pa. 461, 45 A. 1070 (1900); *Truitt v. Hays*, 33 Pa.D. & C.2d 453 (C.P. Ven. 1963); W. Prosser, The Law of Torts § 44, at 277 (4th ed. 1971); Annot., 91 A.L.R.3d 1202 (1979).[4]

"Perhaps the most quoted articulation of this doctrine was that by then New York Court of Appeals Justice CARDOZO:

"Danger invites rescue. The cry of distress is the summons to relief. The law does not ignore these reactions of the mind in tracing conduct to its consequences. It recognizes them as normal. It places their effects within the range of the natural and probable. The wrong that imperils life is a wrong to the imperiled victim; it is a wrong also to his rescuer. The state that leaves an opening in a bridge is liable to the child that falls into the stream, but liable also to the parent who plunges to its aid. . . . The risk of rescue, if only it be not wanton, is born of the occasion. The emergency begets the man. The wrongdoer may not have foreseen the coming of the deliverer. He is accountable as if he had. . . .

"*Wagner v. International Railway Co.*, 232 N.Y. 176, 180, 133 N.E. 437, 438 (1921). . . . In applying the rescue doctrine, I must first determine the negligence *vel non* of The Milner Hotel.

A. The Negligence of the Hotel Caused a Peril to Its Guests

"Under Pennsylvania law, a hotel keeper, while not an insurer or guarantor of the safety of his guests, must nonetheless exercise ordinary or reasonable care to keep them from injury. *Lyttle v. Denny,* 222 Pa. 395, 71 A. 841 (1909); *Winkler v. Seven Springs Farm, Inc.,* 240 Pa. Super. Ct. 641, 359 A.2d 440 (1976), *aff'd,* 477 Pa. 445, 384 A.2d 241 (1978); *Hunter v. Hotel Sylvania Co.,* 153 Pa. Super. Ct. 591, 34 A.2d 816 (1943). . . .

"Here, the fire at The Milner Hotel on October 11, 1978 originated in the defective television set in Room 706. The defective condition of the television was known to the Hotel through its employee, Jennings, who nevertheless left the set plugged in, unattended and with the power switch in the 'on' position. I have no difficulty in concluding that, under these circumstances and given the substantial risk of fire resulting from a short-circuited or otherwise faulty television set, Jennings' conduct clearly amounted to negligence and that his negligence was a substantial factor in placing the lives of the Hotel guests in peril. The very least a reasonably prudent person would have done would have been to disconnect the power source by turning the set off or removing the plug. Of course, Jennings' negligence is imputed to his employer under the doctrine of respondeat superior. *Wagaman v. General Finance Co.,* 116 F.2d 254, 257 (3d Cir. 1940).

"That a fire in a ten-story hotel presents an imminent danger to the residents cannot be gainsaid. The Hotel employees, the police and firemen as well as Altamuro recognized the need for immediate action. The prompt action taken by them at considerable risk to themselves was undoubtedly responsible for preventing a catastrophic loss of life.

B. Contributory or Comparative Negligence

"Having decided that the Hotel's negligence placed the lives of the guests in imminent peril, the next question is whether any conduct on the part of Altamuro would bar recovery.

"Defendant Hotel argues that since Altamuro's death occurred after the firemen ordered all civilians out of the Hotel and because it can be inferred from the evidence that the deceased heard the command by his conduct in immediately leaving the Hotel, then his final rescue effort was so unreasonable as to preclude recovery by his administratrix. The test, as enunciated in *Corbin v. Philadelphia,* 195 Pa. 461, 45 A. 1070 (1900), is whether the rescuer 'acted with due regard for his own safety, or so rashly and imprudently' as to bar recovery. *Id.*

at 473, 45 A. at 1074. The court stated that 'where another is in great and imminent danger, he who attempts a rescue may be warranted, by surrounding circumstances, in exposing his limbs or life to a very high degree of danger. In such a case, he should not be charged with the consequences of errors of judgments resulting from the excitement and confusion of the moment. . . . '' 195 Pa. at 472, 45 A. at 1074. . . . [5] Thus the standard of care for a rescuer is not to act rashly or imprudently.

"In any event, Pennsylvania has abolished the defense of contributory negligence and has replaced it with comparative negligence. See 42 Pa. Cons. Stat. Ann. § 7102 (Purdon Supp. 1981). Although no reported case has applied Pennsylvania's Comparative Negligence Statute to the rescue doctrine, the instant case clearly falls within the literal language of Act, which states that the Act is to be applied to '*all actions* brought to recover damages for negligence resulting in death or injury to person or property. . . . ' 42 Pa. Cons. Stat. Ann. § 7102(a) (Purdon Supp. 1981) (emphasis added). Courts in other jurisdictions have applied their comparative negligence schemes in similar circumstances, holding that if 'the trier of fact finds that the rescue is unreasonable or unreasonably carried out the factfinder should then make a comparison of negligence between the rescuer and the one whose negligence created the situation to which the rescue was a response.' *Cords v. Anderson*, 80 Wis. 2d 525, 548, 259 N.W.2d 672, 683 (1977). *Accord, Ryder Truck Rental, Inc. v. Korte*, 357 So. 2d 228, 230 (Fla. Dist. Ct. App. 1978). While I believe Pennsylvania courts would reach a similar result, it is not necessary for me to decide the issue because I find that Altamuro did not act rashly, imprudently or so unreasonably as to constitute negligence on his part under the rescue doctrine.

"There is no dispute that during the initial phase of the fire, Altamuro busied himself warning guests at the Hotel of the fire, and later he assisted Officer Markowski in helping people out of the building. The last time Altamuro was seen alive was when he left the Hotel after the firemen ordered all civilians out of the building. There was no evidence as to how Altamuro got back into the building. What prompted his return can only be surmised but, having been successful in two prior missions to the upper floors of the Hotel, I am not convinced that it was unreasonable for him to conclude that he could successfully complete another mission without unduly imperiling his own safety even though he disobeyed the order of the firemen by returning to the building.[7]

II. Third-Party Defendant City of Philadelphia

"The Milner Hotel joined the City of Philadelphia as a third-party defendant alleging that the City took possession and control of the building during the fire-fighting efforts; that the City was negligent in failing to prevent Altamuro from slipping back into the Hotel after the Fire Department personnel ordered all civilians to leave the building; and that this negligence was the proximate cause of Altamuro's death and therefore the Hotel should be entitled to contribution and/or indemnity from the City. The plaintiff has not asserted any claim directly against the City.

"Assuming, without deciding, that the City had a duty to use reasonable care to prevent the plaintiff's decedent from entering the Hotel while it was in flames and thus exposing himself to harm, and assuming further that the Political Subdivision Tort Claims Act, 42 Pa. Cons. Stat. Ann. §§ 8541–8564 (Purdon Supp. 1981), would permit an action against the City in these circumstances, nevertheless, I find that the City did not breach this duty, but rather exercised reasonable care under the circumstances. The evidence is clear that once it became apparent to the fire personnel at the scene that the conflagration posed a grave danger, all persons were ordered out and a barricade was erected. There is no evidence that either the firemen or the police became aware that Altamuro had reentered the Hotel. The City is not an insurer or guarantor of a person's safety, *see Chapman v. City of Philadelphia,* 290 Pa. Super. Ct. 281, 434 A.2d 753 (1981), but is liable only for negligent acts which cause him harm. The Hotel's claim against the City must fall simply because it lacks proof. Accordingly, the Hotel is not entitled to recover from the City for contribution and/or indemnity.

"Accordingly, I arrive at the following

Conclusions of Law

"1. The Court has jurisdiction over the subject matter and the parties.

"2. The defendant, The Milner Hotel, Inc., by the acts of its employees, was negligent, and this negligence placed the lives of the residents in imminent peril. Such negligence was the cause of the death of Joseph S. Altamuro.

"3. The plaintiff's deceased, Joseph S. Altamuro, did not act rashly, imprudently or unreasonably in his efforts to alert the residents of The Milner Hotel to the imminent danger of the fire and in aiding in their removal from the building.

"4. The City of Philadelphia was not negligent and therefore is not liable to the defendant-third party plaintiff.

"5. Plaintiff is entitled to judgment in her favor and against defendant The Milner Hotel, Inc. in the amount of $396,373.

"6. The third-party defendant City of Philadelphia is entitled to judgment in its favor and against third-party plaintiff The Milner Hotel, Inc.

"1. Officer Markowski's testimony that he met Edward Jennings in the Lobby and went upstairs with him, see N.T., 11/24/81, at 95–96, appears to be in direct conflict with Jennings' testimony. Jennings testified that the first time he met Officer Markowski was on the elevator on the third floor of the Hotel where he along with Harry Vonada joined the Officer and then together went to the seventh floor. *See* Vonada Deposition at 6–7; Jennings deposition at 8. However, because this fact is not of crucial importance to the disposition of this case, I will assume that the Officer's account of his first meeting with Jennings is correct.

"2. Officer Markowski later testified that he ordered the door opened because he was told by Mr. Jennings that there was a possibility that the room was occupied. N.T., 11/24/81, at 96. Mr. Vonada expressed his reason for wanting the door to remain closed thus:

'Q. Why didn't you want Jennings to open the door?

'A. Any stupid bastard knows you don't open up a door when there is a fire in the room.

Vonada Deposition at 24–25. It was subsequently learned that no one was present in Room 706 during the fire.'

"4. The parties agree that Pennsylvania law is to be applied to the substantive issues in the case.

"5. *Cf.* Stebner v. YMCA, 428 Pa. 370, 374, 238 A.2d 19, 21 (1968) ('A building owner responsible for placing an invitee in a dangerous situation cannot escape responsibility for an injury resulting to the invitee, merely because the victim, in fright, frenzy or panic adds to his danger by an act which, in a later serene moment of contemplation, might seem to have been unwise.').

"7. *Cf.* Clayton v. Blair, 254 Iowa 372, 117 N.W.2d 879 (1962) (While plaintiff's decedent was warning others of danger during apartment house fire she was within the doctrine of rescue and, although it did not appear why decedent had returned from second floor of building to third floor, where her apartment was located and her daughter and personal belongings were, jury should have been instructed as to doctrine of rescue.)"

The following case involves an incident in which a hotel guest was injured when descending stairs after the outbreak of a fire. A New York reviewing court, the Appellate Division, reinstated a jury verdict in the guest's favor on liability and remanded only on the issue of damages.

TAIEB V. HILTON HOTELS CORP.
131 A.D.2d 257, 520 N.Y.S.2d 776 (N.Y.A.D. 1987), *appeal dismissed* 72 N.Y.2d 1040, 531 N.E.2d 656 (1988)

ROSENBERGER, J.: "On the evening of August 13, 1979, appellants Bella and Maurice Taieb were in their corner room on the 38th floor of the New York Hilton Hotel when a minor fire broke out several stories below them. Hearing sirens, Mr. Taieb looked out of the window and saw several fire engines stop and park around the hotel. Aware of the fact that several weeks before 48 persons had died in a hotel fire in Spain, Mr. Taieb urged his wife to hurry and finish dressing while he went down the hall to alert their children. The Taiebs at first went to the elevator but there was smoke inside it and they saw a sign directing guests to use the stairway in case of fire. Although no fire alarm was sounded, the Taiebs proceeded down the cement stairway where they were joined by more and more people as they descended. The group on the stairs was moving very fast and, on the 15th floor, Mr. Taieb told his wife to remove her shoes so that she could keep up with them. The Taiebs did not encounter any hotel personnel in the stairwell on their descent to the lobby. By the time they were out on the street Mrs. Taieb, who was taking medication for high blood pressure, was in pain and her left foot and leg began to swell. She was subsequently treated by a doctor in New York whom the hotel recommended and, upon her return to France, she allegedly underwent treatment for phlebitis.

"Appellants instituted this action against respondent Hilton Hotels Corporation and the New York Hilton, Inc., seeking damages for the permanent injury allegedly suffered by Mrs. Taieb and for her husband's loss of services and support. The jurors unanimously found that the respondents were negligent and that this negligence was the proximate cause of Mrs. Taieb's injuries. They awarded $150,000 to Mrs. Taieb and $20,000 to her husband. On appeal to Appellate Term, 132 Misc. 2d 892, 506 N.Y.2d 810, the jury verdict was reversed and the complaint dismissed.

"Appellate Term, in reversing the jury's verdict, concluded that the evidence was insufficient to support a finding of negligence. However, this conclusion rests on a misreading of the record and is clearly contradicted by the documents offered in evidence at trial. Appellate Term also determined, as a matter of law, that 'the hotel's overall response to the fire was reasonable' despite testimony from appellants' expert witness to the contrary which raised a triable question of the fact for the jury. . . .

" . . . To conclude as a matter of law that the evidence is not sufficient to support the jury's verdict, essentially the court must find that the evidence does not present a valid question of fact for the jury [citation omitted]. In this case, we find that appellants presented sufficient evidence to raise triable questions of fact regarding respondents' negligence for the outbreak and spread of the fire and the actions of hotel employees to ensure the safety of the guests after they learned of the fire.

"While it is true that a hotel keeper is not an insurer of the guests' personal safety, at common law the hotel keeper has a duty to exercise reasonable care for the guests' safety (*Friedman v. Schindler's Prairie House, Inc.*, 224 App. Div. 232, 234, 230 N.Y.S. 44 [3d Dept., 1928], *affd.* 250 N.Y. 574, 166 N.E. 329 [1929]). 'One who collects a large number of people for gain or profit must be vigilant to protect them' (*Tantillo v. Goldstein Bros. Amusement Co.*, 248 N.Y. 286, 290, 162 N.E. 82 [1928]; *Tapley v. Ross Theatre Corp.*, 275 N.Y. 144, 9 N.E.2d 812 [1937]). The duty to safeguard hotel guests from known danger persists even if the danger arose through no fault attributable to the hotel keeper. In *Owen v. Straight*, 242 App. Div. 892, 893, 275 N.Y.S. 1000, *revd. on other grounds*, 267 N.Y. 453, 196 N.E. 395 [1935], the Court of Appeals held that 'irrespective of the origin of the fire, it was a question of fact whether the defendant had used reasonable care to safeguard his guests.' We find that, in this case, the evidence was sufficient not only for the jury to find that the origin of the fire was attributable to respondents' negligence but also that appellant failed to take reasonable precautions to safeguard the guests from injury in their attempt to escape what they believed to be a life-threatening situation in a high rise building. . . .

"It was established that the area in which the fire started and the route by which it spread were under the exclusive control of respondents' personnel. The hotel's security director testified that both the linen and trash chutes in the service areas from the lobby through the 44th floor were kept locked. As the trial court correctly instructed the jury, the mere fact that there was a fire at the hotel does not, of itself, establish negligence. However, the start or spread of a fire due to a failure to exercise reasonable care in operating or maintaining the hotel would be sufficient basis for such a finding. Thus the evidence was legally sufficient to raise a valid question of fact and it was error for Appellate Term to dismiss the complaint. [citation omitted].

"From the evidence presented at trial it was permissible for the jurors to infer, and rational for them to conclude, that careless acts by respondents' personnel and deficiencies in the respondents' maintenance 'permitted a fire to break out,' as appellants alleged in the complaint. That conclusion finds further support in the fire-fighters' report that the parts of the chutes which had been recently cleaned did not catch fire while the chute from the fourth through the eighth floors, which had not been cleaned for ten months, did. As a factual matter, therefore, it cannot be said that the jury's verdict was against the weight of the evidence. Respondents did not challenge the Fire Department's theory as to the cause of the fire and respondents' claim that the chutes had been recently cleaned was contradicted by their own records.

"A party's liability for negligent acts or omissions extends to all injuries which are a foreseeable consequence thereof provided that the negligent conduct was the proximate, or legal cause of the injuries sustained. 'Given the unique nature of the inquiry in each case, it is for the finder of fact to determine legal cause, once the court has been satisfied that a prima facie case has been established' (*Derdiarian v. Felix Contracting Corp.*, 51 N.Y.2d 308, 315, 434 N.Y.S.2d 166, 414 N.E.2d 666 [1980]). It is entirely foreseeable that persons in a burning building may be injured either by fire, smoke, or in the attempt to escape the building. Respondents, however, presented evidence to show that appellants were not endangered by the fire and there was no need for them to take flight. The fire-fighters who responded to the scene quickly contained the blaze and determined that there was no danger to the guests. The Fire Department did not issue an evacuation order and no alarm was sounded. The hotel's assistant manager testified that he and other hotel personnel then went from floor to floor knocking at doors to tell the guests that things were under control and not to be alarmed by the smoke. However, he did not recall if he or any other hotel employee went to appellants' floor and appellants testified that they saw no one from the hotel staff either on their floor or in the stairwell. Indeed, the assistant manager acknowledged that no hotel employees were stationed in the stairwells which hotel guests were instructed to use in case of fire. According to appellants, this was also a breach of respondents' duty of care.

"Appellants' expert witness, George Friedel, a former Chief of the New York City Fire Department, stated that, in his opinion, it was 'totally incorrect' for the hotel not to station employees in the stairwell to assist guests in the event of a fire. The hotel's Fire Emergency Plan which was introduced by respondents reveals that no employees are assigned to the stairwells to insure orderly evacuation during a fire, although the maids on each floor are assigned to stations at the fire stairway doors and security personnel are posted at the fire exit doors. Appellants' expert maintained that because the Hilton 'is about a block square, there would be areas in this particular case that would be free from smoke and fire,' and it was therefore unnecessary for guests to go down 38 floors to escape from the building. In his opinion someone from the hotel should have been in the stairwell 'to give them guidance and direction, whether or not to stop, don't go any further, it's not necessary'.

"This expert testimony raised a question of fact as to the reasonableness of respondents' conduct after hotel employees learned of the fire and smoke conditions in the hotel. 'That there was evidence to the contrary does not justify dismissing the complaint on the ground that the jury's verdict was not based on legally sufficient evidence . . . '[citation omitted]. . . .

"An international hotel opens its doors to guests of all ages and in all states of health, some of whom might have trouble walking down 38 flights of steps under the best of circumstances. Given that the hotel instructed guests to use the stairs in case of fire, and the ever present danger of panic in such a situation, the jury was warranted in finding that a reasonably prudent person would have foreseen the risk of injury under the circumstances and taken the precaution of having hotel employees in the stairwell to direct and give guidance to the guests.

"Appellate Term, having rejected the jury's verdict on liability, did not reach the issue of damages other than to note that the damage award was clearly excessive given the quality of medical proof in this case. On this issue, we find that the jury's award was against the weight of the evidence. . . .

"Appellants' expert medical testimony, which was tenuous and speculative, was not sufficient, in our view, to support the substantial award in appellants' favor. We therefore remand for a new trial on the issue of damages. . . .

"All concur."

9:16 *Standard of Care Required of Innkeeper to Child Guest*

The special circumstances surrounding the protection of an infant hotel guest is the subject of the following case.

BAKER v. DALLAS HOTEL CO.
73 F.2d 825 (5th Cir. 1934)

SIBLEY, C.J.: "Mr. and Mrs. Robert F. Baker sued the Dallas Hotel Company, owners and operators of a hotel in Dallas, Tex., under the Texas death statute, . . . for the death of their infant son, Bobby, who fell from a window of the twelfth story of the hotel. On the evidence, the judge held that no actionable negligence appeared on the part of the defendant and that there was contributory negligence on the part of the plaintiffs and directed a verdict for the hotel company. Mr. and Mrs. Baker appeal, and assign as the sole error the refusal to permit the jury to pass upon the issues of negligence.

" . . . [T]he Bakers, having with them the child 2 years and 5 months old, registered as guests of the hotel and were assigned to a room with adjoining bath on Wednesday. At about 9 o'clock the next Saturday morning Mrs. Baker had just bathed the child and left him playing with his blocks on the floor near the center of the room while she was washing something in the adjoining bathroom. Mr. Baker was in bed, awake, but with his back toward the window a few feet away. The sash was raised, but the opening was covered by a wire window screen which they knew was there, but had never examined. The windowsill was about the height of Bobby's face. In front of it was a radiator which did not extend the whole length of the sill, but left a space on each side. The cut-off valve of the radiator was under one of these spaces, and Bobby could have stepped upon this valve and climbed onto the window. Neither Mr. nor Mrs. Baker knew he was near the window until after a short absence she returned from the bathroom and saw him sitting sideways on the windowsill with his head pressed against the screen, and before she could reach him the screen opened outwards and he fell below and was killed. An examination of the screen showed that it was hinged at the top and was intended to be secured from opening outwards by two spring plungers of metal, one on each side near the bottom of the screen frame, which passed through the frame into holes in the wooden window facing. The screen was old, and the springs had become weak, and the window facing had grooves worn by the ends of the plungers from each hole outwards so that the plungers got but little hold in the facing. A slight pushing of the screen was found by experiment sufficient to open it. The hotel company had employees whose duty it was to inspect windows and screens. This screen had not been reported as out of order to the superintendent, but he did not know whether it had been reported to the housekeeper or carpenter. There were heavy iron grills outside of some of the windows of the hotel, but none on this window.

" . . . An innkeeper is not the insurer of the safety of his guests, but owes to them ordinary care to see that the premises assigned to them are reasonably safe for their use and occupancy. [Citations omitted.] When a child of tender years is accepted as a guest, the inexperience and the natural tendencies of such a child become a part of the situation and must be considered by the innkeeper. We do not mean that the innkeeper becomes the nurse of the child, or assumes its control when accompanied by its parents, but only that he is bound to consider whether his premises, though safe enough for an adult, present any reasonably avoidable dangers to the child guest. The control and general responsibility for the child accompanied by a parent or nurse is with the latter, who are also bound to exercise ordinary care to keep the child from harm. As has been stated, when parents are complaining of the negligence of the innkeeper, their own negligence which contributes to the injury is a good defense to their suit. Negligence is not attributable as such to a child of 2½ years. [Citation omitted.] The conduct of such a child being natural, spontaneous, and instinctive, is like that of an animal, and is similarly to be anticipated and guarded against by those charged with any duty in respect to the child. What then should this innkeeper and these parents have anticipated that this child might do, and what have they respectively done or failed to do that was negligent? There is no statutory requirement respecting hotel windows or window screens, obedience to which would be diligence and failure to comply with which would be negligence *per se*. There is no course of decisions establishing any rule applicable specially to children and hotel windows. The only available standard of care is the conduct of the ideal person of ordinary prudence, to be judged of by the jury as a question of fact. . . . The innkeeper and the parents perhaps ought equally to have anticipated the danger of a child trying to get into the window, but the duty of inspecting the screen is not the same. The responsibility for the premises is primarily on the innkeeper, and the guest may generally assume that they are safe. But it is argued that the screens are there to keep insects out and not to keep children in, and there is no duty on the innkeeper to have them safe for the latter purpose, and parents have no right to rely on them for such purposes. [Citation omitted.] But yet if the screen to all appearances, and as screens are usually found, would serve to protect the child, the false appearance of an insecurely fastened screen might easily mislead the parent or even inspire confidence in a child to lean against it. [Citation omitted.] Though there was no original duty to have any screen in the window for the purpose of keeping the child in, the jury might conclude that prudence would as respects this child, have required that it be as securely fastened as screens customarily are, lest it prove a deception and a trap. We agree with the trial judge that the failure to have protecting grills at the windows is not negligence. . . . '' [Reversed and remanded.]

The reasoning of the court in *Baker v. Dallas Hotel Co.* was adopted by the Supreme Court of Appeals of Virginia in *Crosswhite v. Shelby Operating Corp.*[52] In that case the testimony indicated that in the early morning of June 24, 1943, Mrs. Fitzgerald and her two small daughters, the elder of whom was Sheridan Fitzgerald, about three years old, had registered as guests at defendant's hotel, and were assigned to a room on the fourth floor. They went to the room assigned. The mother left Sheridan playing in the bedroom and went into an adjoining bathroom to wet a cloth for use about the toilet of the smaller child. When she came back she saw Sheridan standing on the windowsill with her back to a wire screen. Seeing the danger in which this child stood, she rushed to her rescue, but before she could reach her, the child leaned against this wire screen, which gave way, she fell through the window and was killed.

The child's administrator sought to recover damages from the Shelby Operation Corporation. The trial court dismissed the complaint for failure to state a cause of action. On appeal, the judgment of dismissal was reversed and the case was remanded for trial to a jury on the issue of negligence.

In *Roberts v. Del Monte Properties Co., Inc.,*[53] plaintiff, seven-year-old son of a tenant in defendant's hotel building, was playing by jumping and sliding on some mattresses piled in the hall near a window on the fifth floor of defendant's hotel. While plaintiff was on the top mattress, he accidentally tumbled backward toward the open window behind the pile. The screen in the window gave way and the boy and screen fell down into a patio. Plaintiff was seriously injured. There was evidence that the screen was in a weakened and defective condition. Judgment for the plaintiff infant was affirmed.

The court held that the action of playing on such a pile of mattresses would not render plaintiff a trespasser or licensee to whom the hotel operator owed no duty of care except to refrain from overt or intentional acts, and that violation of statute by a seven-year-old child does not constitute contributory negligence on the part of the child as a matter of law and whether its violation constituted contributory negligence is for the jury.

In *Waugh v. Duke Corp.,*[54] the infant plaintiff, a guest in defendant's motor lodge, walked into a glass panel adjacent to the door of the guest room. The

[52]182 Va. 713, 30 S.E.2d 673 (1944).
[53]111 Cal. App. 2d 69, 243 P.2d 914 (1952).
[54]248 F. Supp. 626 (M.D.N.C. 1966).

child believed that the panel, running from floor to ceiling, was an open space giving direct access to the courtyard. The glass broke, the broken fragments fell into the room and cut the child about the face, leg, arms, and knee, requiring surgical operation to camouflage a facial scar resulting from the accident.

The court entered judgment for plaintiff, having found as a fact that the defendent was negligent in that it failed to warn the child plaintiff of the existence of the floor-to-ceiling glass panel, and failed to construct guards around such panel.

9:17 *Vermin, Insects, Animals*

An innkeeper who negligently fails to keep his premises in a clean and safe condition is responsible for injuries to his guests caused by rats, mice, or insects.

In *DeLuce v. Fort Wayne Hotel*,[55] plaintiff, an actress, was a guest in defendant's hotel. On the day after her arrival, she was to present a review of a show at the home of a local business executive, and intending to use the pool at her host's home, took along her swim equipment, including hand and foot fins. Upon her return to the hotel that evening, she left her swimming equipment on a chair in the lobby while she was at a desk inquiring for messages that may have been left for her. Someone in the lobby picked up one of her swim fins, hit the top of a radiator in the lobby with it and dropped it behind the radiator. When plaintiff reached down to retrieve it, she felt a sharp bite on her hand. A rat, approximately a foot long, was hanging from her finger. She was given a tetanus antitoxin injection and later developed postencephalitic Parkinsonism.

The trial court instructed the jury that a relevant statute of Michigan made it mandatory for a hotelkeeper to keep his premises free from rats, and that if plaintiff had been bitten by a rat while on the hotel premises, the hotel would be guilty of negligence as a matter of law and plaintiff entitled to recover.

A judgment for plaintiff for $25,000 was set aside and a new trial ordered on the ground that the jury instruction was erroneous. The Seventh Circuit held that the defendant hotelkeeper was liable only if he knew or should have known of the presence of rats on his premises. If, however, the rat in question was on the premises at the time of the accident because of failure to use due care to keep his premises free of rats, the court stated the defendant would be guilty of a violation of the statute, and, therefore, negligent *per se*.

In *Del Rosso v. F.W. Woolworth Co.*,[56] it appeared that while plaintiff was eating her luncheon in defendant's restaurant, she was aroused by outcries of other persons and saw a big rat coming toward her; that it ran directly beneath the table at which she was sitting; that she jumped and fell and received severe injuries; that the rat came from the kitchen of the defendant, went back of a lunch counter, then came upon the restaurant floor and ran back of another lunch counter. A directed verdict in favor of defendant was affirmed on appeal.

[55]311 F.2d 853 (6th Cir. 1962).
[56]293 Mass. 424, 200 N.E.2d 277 (1936).

There was no evidence, said the court, that the presence of this or other rats on its premises had ever come to the knowledge of the defendant. There was nothing in the record to show circumstances calculated to arouse apprehension that rats were on its premises. The court said:

> The rat is commonly recognized as an enemy of mankind. It is offensive from almost every point of view. . . . It is not a domestic animal but is *ferae naturae*. [Citation omitted.] There is nothing in this record to indicate effective and practicable means to keep occupied premises entirely clear of this vermin. The record does not show that the defendant failed to try to preserve its premises free from the pest. . . . The facts here disclosed do not warrant the finding of any act or omission on the part of the defendant in violation of a legal duty owed by it to the plaintiff.[57]

The difference between "causing" and "contributing to" guest injuries relating to the presence of a beehive as a predicate for a finding of innkeeper liability is illustrated by the following case.

BRASSEAUX V. STAND-BY CORP.
402 So. 2d 140 (La. Ct. App.), *writ denied*, 409 So. 2d 617 (La. 1981)

CHIASSON, J.: " . . . We will first consider the question of liability since we pretermitted that issue in the first appeal. The trial court found that the accident occurred as contended by the plaintiff. We find there is a causal relationship between the bees attacking and stinging the plaintiff and his slipping and falling in the shower injuring his left wrist.

"We next consider the duty owed by the motel's personnel toward this plaintiff-guest. The duty owed by an innkeeper to his guests or patrons is that of exercising reasonable and ordinary care including maintaining the premises in a reasonably safe and suitable condition and the warning of guests or patrons of any hidden or concealed perils which are known or reasonably discoverable by the innkeeper. *Brown v. Southern Ventures Corporation*, 331 So. 2d 207 (La. App. 3d Cir. 1976), writ refused 344 So. 2d 211 (La. 1976), and *Jarvis v. Prout*, 247 So. 2d 244 (La. App. 4th Cir. 1971).

"The trial court found that the defendants breached this duty in failing to remove the bees and in failing to warn the plaintiff that there were bees about the premises. We agree with this finding. The bees were known to be on the outside of the building for a sufficient amount of time that the defendants could have had them removed. In addition, the defendants should have warned occupants of the rooms in the immediate vicinity of the existence of bees in the area and the possibility of the bees entering the rooms. We find the risk involved in this case, plaintiff slipping in a shower from warding off bees, would be encompassed within the duty to keep the premises reasonably safe and warning him of this hidden peril.

[57]*Id.* at 425, 200 N.E. at 277–78.

"Defendants argue that they had no control over the bees and that they were not the insurer of safety of their guests under the theory of strict liability. Because we hold defendants are liable under the negligence theory we need not address the theory of strict liability. With reference to not having control over 'Mother Nature's' insects, we agree with defendants but that does not relieve them from the duty to inspect their premises and rid it of any perils that might confront their patrons or guests. In this case the defendant's, knowing of the presence of the beehive, should have had the hive removed or at least warned their patrons of its presence. Additionally, we find no merit in defendants' contention that the plaintiff was contributorily negligent or that he assumed the risk."

9:18 Condition of Areas outside the Inn

The duty of an innkeeper to maintain his premises in a safe condition extends to areas under his control as well as inside the inn.

MARHEFKA v. MONTE CARLO MANAGEMENT CORP.
358 So. 2d 1171 (Fla. App. 1978)

CARROLL (Ret.), A.J.: "This appeal is by the plaintiffs below from an order and a judgment by which their second amended complaint was dismissed with prejudice. We find error and reverse.

"The appellants filed a complaint against Monte Carlo Management Corporation, doing business as Monte Carlo Hotel, and its liability insurer, for damages for personal injuries suffered by Margaret Marhefka, herein referred to as the plaintiff, and for derivative damages resulting to her husband.

"By the second amended complaint it was alleged that at the time of the incident involved the plaintiffs, who were residents of New Jersey, were guests of the Monte Carlo Hotel, as defined in Section 509.013(3), Florida Statues (1975); that as a means by which guests of the hotel were furnished access to the Atlantic Ocean the defendant had constructed and maintained 'a set of wooden steps leading from the pool-cabana area of said hotel down to the beach'; that the defendant invited its guests to use and enjoy the beach and ocean and had advertised that said beach and ocean were available to its guests; that the steps were owned by and under the exclusive care and control of the defendant; that when the ocean tide was high the steps extended into the water, in which debris, logs and other partially submerged articles collected; that the wooden steps leading into the water were not protected from the debris at such times and were a dangerous condition; that the defendant did not close such steps to use by its guests during periods of high tide, and did not warn its guests of the above described dangerous condition of the steps, which was known or should have been known to defendant; further that defendant was negligent by failing to barricade or otherwise block use of the steps by its guests during such periods, in which the use thereof was thus dangerous, as it was known or should have been known to the defendant; that while the plaintiff was using said steps to descend to the ocean beach area she was struck violently and forcibly by a floating wooden plank causing her injuries.

"The defendants moved to dismiss, stating as grounds that the amended complaint failed to state a cause of action, failed to disclose any duty owed by the defendant to the plaintiff, and failed to state any relationship between the action of the debris in the ocean and the steps. . . .

"The defendant was under a duty to the hotel guests to maintain the premises in a reasonably safe condition. That duty extended to the means which the defendant had provided expressly for use by the hotel guests for ingress to the ocean beach area, and the complaint alleged a dangerous condition of the latter as a breach of the defendant's duty to the plaintiff hotel guest. Whether such occurred involved factual questions to be determined by the trier of the facts.

"In *McNulty v. Hurley*, 97 So. 2d 185, 187 (Fla. 1957) the Supreme Court said: ' . . . The owner or occupant owes an invitee the duty of keeping the premises in a reasonably safe condition, and, as plaintiff contends, also to guard against subjecting such person to dangers of which the owner or occupant is cognizant or might reasonably have foreseen. *First Federal Sav. & Loan Ass'n v. Wylie*, Fla. 1950, 46 So. 2d 396 and *Messner v. Webb's City, Inc.*, Fla. 1952, 62 So. 2d 66.'

"The position taken by the defendant-appellee was that the duty of the defendant to its hotel guests to keep the premises in a reasonably safe condition did not extend beyond its premises, and could not be intended to [govern] the steps facility which were not shown to be on its premises. That proposition is not applicable to the steps involved in this case, where as alleged, the steps were furnished by the hotel operator as the exclusive means of access to the ocean from its property, and when such facility represented an invitation to its guests to use that means for ingress and egress between its property and the immediately adjacent beach (at low tide) and to the ocean waters (at high tide). [Citations omitted.]

"For the reasons stated, the judgment [in defendant's favor] is reversed and the cause is remanded for further proceedings."

In *Naponic v. Carlton Motel, Inc.*[58] a Pennsylvania superior court held that the motel owner owed an injured employee an affirmative duty of keeping its premises reasonably safe for business invitees and of giving warning for any failure to maintain them in that condition.

In the following case, a lawsuit predicated on an innkeeper's failure to remove unnatural shrubbery from its driveway, resulting in an automobile accident that injured a hotel guest, was held to state a cause of action.

---

[58]221 Pa. Super., 287, 289 A.2d 473 (1972).

DESCHAMPS V. HERTZ CORP. [AND THE RAMADA INN]
429 So. 2d. 75 (Fla. App. 1983)

PER CURIAM: "This appeal arises from a judgment on the pleadings in favor of appellees/third party defendants, Charles and Nancy Thornburgh, owners of the Key West Ramada Inn. Alexanda Stefaniw, a guest at the Ramada, was involved in an automobile accident with Richard Deschamps while attempting to exit the motel's driveway. Plaintiff, Deschamps, sued Stefaniw and Hertz Corporation, owner of the car Stefaniw was driving, in an action grounded in negligence. The defendants then impleaded the Thornburghs as third party defendants alleging that they failed to maintain their property in a safe condition in that unnatural shrubbery was positioned so as to obstruct the view of Stefaniw as he attempted to exit. Furthermore, the defendants alleged that the Thornburghs violated certain county and municipal ordinances. Plaintiff, Deschamps, also filed a direct action against the Thornburghs as defendants. The defendants/third party defendants moved for judgment on the pleadings contending there was no legal liability on their part to any of the parties. The trial court granted this motion and this appeal follows.

"Although we affirm the trial court's determination that the county and municipal ordinances were inapplicable to this case, we are compelled to reverse its decision on the remainder of the complaint. We hold that the plaintiff and the defendants stated a cause of action in their respective complaints against the Thornburghs. *See Cook v. Martin*, 330 So. 2d 498 (Fla. 4th D.C.A. 1976). Accordingly, this matter is remanded to the trial court for further proceedings consistent with this opinion.

"AFFIRMED IN PART; REVERSED IN PART; AND REMANDED.

"LETTS, C.J., and BERANEK and DELL, JJ., concur."

In the case below, the New York Appellate Division, Second Department, ruled that a hotel guest who was thrown from a horse could not recover from the hotel because the accident occurred on nonhotel property and the riding was not supervised or controlled by the hotel. The court also denied recovery for alleged misrepresentations contained in defendant's travel brochure.

BARBER V. PRINCESS HOTEL INTERNATIONAL INC.
134 A.D.2d 312, 520 N.Y.S.2d 789 (1987)

MEMORANDUM BY THE COURT: " . . . The plaintiff, an experienced horseback rider, sustained serious physical injuries when she was thrown from the horse on which she was seated after her guide, a nonparty to this action, had negligently removed the horse's bridle. At the time of the accident, the plaintiff was a guest at the Acapulco Princess Hotel.

"Although an innkeeper must exercise reasonable care to protect his guests, while on his premises, against injury at the hands of third persons who are not employees of the hotel, he is not an insurer of their safety (*Barry v. Merriman*,

215 App. Div. 294, 214 N.Y.S. 66). Because the horseback riding incident in which the plaintiff was injured was arranged by local Mexican residents having no affiliation with the hotel and since the accident occurred on property owned by the Mexican government, the defendants owed no duty to the plaintiff and cannot be held liable for her injuries (*see, Palsgrafi v. Long Island R.R. Co.,* 248 N.Y. 339, 162 N.E. 99).

"Similarly, the plaintiff has failed to make out a cause of action to recover damages for misrepresentation. The travel brochure which merely stated that horseback riding was available did not express a direct promise upon which the plaintiff could be expected to reasonably rely (*see, White v. Guarente,* 43 N.Y.2d 356, 401 N.Y.S.2d 474, 372 N.E.2d 315). The subject brochure merely stated that horseback riding was available but did not precisely indicate how or where appropriate arrangements could be made. The horseback riding activity was neither arranged, operated nor maintained by the defendants (*see, Weiner v. British Overseas Airways Corp.,* 60 A.D.2d 427, 401 N.Y.S.2d 91, *lv. denied* 45 N.Y.2d 706, 408 N.Y.S.2d 1024, 380 N.E.2d 337, *rearg. denied* 45 N.Y.2d 839, 409 N.Y.S.2d 1031, 381 N.E.2d 630). . . . "

The Court of Appeals of Oregon rejected a claim based on a guest's fall from a cliff while lowering herself from a ledge on her way to a beach adjacent to the hotel. The adjacent property was held to be beyond the ambit of the hotel's responsibility to its guests.

BEAUREGARD V. BARRETT
92 Or. App. 707, 759 P.2d 337 (1988)

PER CURIAM: "Plaintiff appeals from a directed verdict entered in favor of defendant after a jury trial. She sued for personal injuries sustained when she fell from a cliff. We affirm.

"Plaintiff, her family, and their dog stayed at defendant's motel on the Oregon coast. Plaintiff took the dog for a walk. She followed what she thought was a path from defendant's property to the beach. The path zigzagged steeply down to a five-foot cliff. Because plaintiff was unable to go back up the path, she sat on the ledge and tried to lower herself to the beach. She still could not reach the ground, so she dropped to the beach, breaking her hip.

"Plaintiff claimed that defendant was negligent in failing to warn of 'dangerous conditions on the property,' failing to inspect to determine whether dangerous conditions existed 'on the premises,' and failing to correct or to protect plaintiff from 'dangerous conditions on the premises.' Even viewing the evidence in the light most favorable to plaintiff, no rational jury could find that she fell on defendant's property. Defendant's liability as an innkeeper does not extend to hazards on adjacent property. *Fuhrer v. Gearhart by the Sea, Inc.,* 79 Or. App. 550, 553, 719 P.2d 1305 (1986), *rem'd* 303 Or. 171, 734 P.2d 1348, *aff'd* 87 Or. App. 219, 742 P.2d 58 (1987), *rev. allowed* 304 Or. 405, 745 P.2d 1225 (1987).

"Affirmed."

The Louisiana Court of Appeals was confronted with an unusual case of an injury suffered by a hotel guest who was carried away by the sexual antics of Mardi Gras participants and fell from his hotel balcony while attempting to mimic their ribald behavior. In affirming a jury verdict for the hotel, the court used a duty-risk analysis to find that the guest had assumed the risk of his own injuries, thus negating any duty of care on the hotel's part.

ELDRIDGE V. DOWNTOWNER HOTEL
492 So. 64 (La. App. 1986)

ARMSTRONG, J.: "Plaintiff, Edward Eldridge, filed suit against the defendants, The Downtowner Hotel ('Downtowner') and its insurer, Liberty Mutual Insurance Company ('Liberty'), for damages sustained when plaintiff fell off the balcony of the Downtowner. Following a trial on the merits, the jury returned a verdict in favor of defendants. It is from this verdict that plaintiff appeals.

"The record reflects that on February 7, 1978, Mardi Gras day, plaintiff was the guest of a patron of the Downtowner in the French Quarter. While on the second floor balcony of the hotel, he observed various individuals on other balconies toying with the crowds below by exposing their breasts or 'mooning' the crowds by exposing their bare buttocks. Spurred on by the wild atmosphere in the Quarter, plaintiff climbed on the balcony railing and mooned the crowd. While on the railing plaintiff fell to the street below and was seriously injured.

"Plaintiff filed suit for 1.75 million dollars arguing that Downtowner was negligent in failing to have a protective screen or a uniformed guard on the balcony to prevent just such accidents as occurred herein.

"The primary issue before this Court is whether, under the circumstances of this case, the trial court committed reversible error in failing to charge the jury on a duty-risk analysis of negligence liability. We think not and we affirm. . . .

" . . . [I]t is . . . abundantly clear that even under a duty-risk analysis plaintiff was not entitled to recover.

"Under a duty/risk analysis, the pertinent inquiries are:

"I. Whether the conduct of which plaintiff complains was a cause-in-fact of the harm;

"II. Whether there was a duty on the part of the defendant which was imposed to protect against the risk involved;

"III. Whether there was a breach of that duty; and

"IV. Damages.

"*Vicknair v. Hibernia Bldg. Corp.*, 479 So.2d 904 (La. 1985); *Harris v. Pizza Hut of Louisiana, Inc.*, 455 So. 2d 1364, 1370 (La. 1984).

"The record reflects that plaintiff's fall resulted solely from his own conduct. Plaintiff was not pushed off the railing, and he was neither enticed nor encouraged by defendant to sit on the railing. Moreover, the railing was not defective. It is clear, therefore, that plaintiff's fall was in fact caused by his own want of skill, that is, in exercising bad judgment by sitting on the railing *and* in losing his balance. Thus, the question becomes whether Downtowner had a duty to protect plaintiff from his own conduct.

" 'The principal juridical element of an action in negligence is a duty, apparent to reason and common sense, to avoid acts and omissions which engender an unreasonable risk of harm to others.' *Stephens v. State, Through Department of Transportation,* 440 So.2d 920, 925 (La. App. 2nd Cir. 1983), *writ denied,* 443 So. 2d 1119 (La. 1984). Implicit in this notion of duty is that there are some risks which are reasonable. An individual encountering such risks bears the responsibility of dealing with and/or avoiding them.

"Thus, a 'visitor assumes the obvious, normal or ordinary risks attendant on the use of the premises and owners are not liable for injuries to a visitor when those injuries result from a danger which he should have observed in the exercise of reasonable care.' *Calhoun v. Royal Globe Ins. Co.,* 398 So. 2d 1166, 1168 (La. App. 2nd Cir. 1981); see *Bell v. Marriott Hotels, Inc.,* 411 So. 2d 687 (La. App. 4th Cir. 1982), *writ denied,* 413 So. 2d 908 (La. 1982); [citation omitted].

"Here the risk of harm was that of falling while sitting on a railing on a second floor balcony. Such a risk is an obvious and reasonable risk of harm which the defendant had no duty to protect against.

"But plaintiff argues that because of the wild atmosphere of Mardi Gras and the fact that traditionally women would expose themselves from the balconies, defendant should have foreseen that an accident was likely and was under an obligation to protect plaintiff from himself. We find no merit in this argument for two reasons: first, absolutely no evidence was offered at trial demonstrating that anyone had ever fallen from the balcony during Mardi Gras or even that people sat on the balcony railings. Second, cases cited by plaintiff in support of his argument involved plaintiffs that were in some way incapacitated, i.e., minority, intoxication, insanity, etc. [citation omitted]. . . . In the instant case, no evidence was introduced demonstrating that plaintiff was in any way incapacitated. In fact, he knowingly and voluntarily placed himself at risk.

"We also note that plaintiff's reliance on *Boyer v. Johnson,* 360 So. 2d 1164 (La. 1978) is misplaced. *Boyer* held that the defendant was liable because he violated a statute designed to prevent the type of risk and harm encountered by the minor plaintiff. In the case before us, Downtowner was not in violation of any statute at the time of plaintiff's injury.

"For these reasons we hold that the trial court was not required to charge the jury that the defendant had a duty to protect patrons from the type of conduct engaged in by the plaintiff herein. Accordingly, the trial court did not err in refusing to charge the jury on a duty/risk analysis.

"For the foregoing reasons, the judgment of the trial court is affirmed." [Concurring opinion omitted.]

9:19 Parking Lots

A note with respect to parking lots is in order. The construction of a parking lot should afford adequate space for ingress, egress, and maneuverability of cars. The ground surface should be free of potholes and obstructions. Strips and barriers should be painted in bright colors, and adequate lighting should be maintained for patrons to move about safely at night.

LARREA V. OZARK WATER SKI THRILL SHOW, INC.
562 S.W.2d 790 (Mo. App. 1978)

TITUS, J.: "Plaintiff, a 68-year-old female, fell on defendant's parking lot and was injured. The jury gave her a verdict but the trial court entered judgment for defendant n.o.v. and plaintiff appealed. As the matter concerns us, the chief question for determination is whether plaintiff made a submissible case for the jury.

"On July 26, 1972, defendant operated a water ski show at Paradise Cove on the Lake of the Ozarks. Its premises, 'about 300 feet long [north and south] and probably about 150 feet wide [east and west],' were situated on the west side of the cove and sloped downward from west to east to the water's edge. Patrons viewed the show from facilities located at the northeast corner of the property adjacent to the lake; a parking lot occupied the southwest part of the premises. According to the main instruction proffered by plaintiff and given by the court, 'defendant's parking lot was irregular and uneven and was covered with rocks and gravel.' Growing trees were interspersed about the parking area. The casualty occurred near 8 P.M. By taking judicial notice of the time of sunset [citation omitted], we know that on the date and at the place of the accident sunset occurred at 8:27 P.M. [Citation omitted.] Also, we are aware that "When lighted lamps are required" [for motor vehicles upon the highways] means at any time from a half-hour after sunset. . . . ' § 307.020(9), V.A.M.S. Consequently, we may confidently assume it was daylight at the time concerned.

"Plaintiff, a business invitee, arrived at defendant's parking lot as a back-seat passenger in a four-door car driven by her son who shared the front seat with his wife and three-year-old daughter. In accordance with directions given by attendants, the automobile was parked near the south side of a tree, headed west, parallel in a row with previously parked vehicles. Carrying her daughter, the wife left the car, walked around the tree and headed for the seating and viewing area. Plaintiff . . . was '[l]ooking to the lake, toward the lake' and following her daughter-in-law. Plaintiff walked past the tree a few feet where she stepped on top of a rock. Her foot slipped off the rock causing her to fall and be injured. The rock, said to have been 'imbedded tightly in the ground,' apparently had a fairly flat surface and measured approximately three inches wide by five inches long. Its surface was described as sloping down towards the lake with its highest elevation being about one and three-quarters inches above ground level. Neither plaintiff nor her daughter-in-law observed the rock until after the fall. . . .

"An invitee who goes upon a paved sidewalk, paved passageway or paved parking lot, or who enters upon the premises of a store, theater, hotel, motel, or office building, is entitled to expect that the possessor thereof will have made far greater preparation to secure the safety of his invitees than will have been made by the possessor of a primordial lakeside parking area which obviously conforms to its inclined terrain, is irregular, uneven, covered with dirt, rocks and creek gravel and which, intermittently, accommodates trees native to the property. [Citations omitted.]

"Defendant-possessor owed to plaintiff-invitee only the duty to provide a reasonably safe parking lot, but defendant did not owe plaintiff absolute safety for it was not an insurer of her safety. [Citation omitted.] Furthermore, defendant is not liable to plaintiff for injuries which result from an open and obvious condition which is or must have been known to plaintiff in the exercise of due care for her own safety, and if plaintiff was or should have been aware of the condition and of the consequences of disregarding it, she may not recover. Possessors of premises are not obliged to anticipate that their invitees, in the exercise of ordinary care, will fail and neglect to appreciate dangers generally which are known to be inherent in obvious conditions. [Citation omitted.] The attention which an invitee must give his surroundings and come by an appreciation of them in governing his actions is not a legal absolute but is to be judged by the concomitant circumstances and conditions and the environment in which he finds himself. [Citations omitted.]

"The bucolic nature of the parking area was patent. In the exercise of ordinary care for her own safety, plaintiff should have recognized that the semi-sylvan plot as it inclined to meet the lake was rugose, overlaid with coarse gravel and rocks and that its rustic terrain demanded near-constant scrutiny by all desiring safe passage. No duty reposed in the possessor of such a lot to maintain its surface absolutely smooth. The wary, using due care, would realize that in such a surface there would be depressions, rises and rocks and that danger was a probable consequence of disregarding these conditions. Consequently, it cannot be responsibly said that it is negligent to allow such impedimenta of nature to remain so long as they are only those as may be expected in such a place. We conclude that there was no actionable negligence insofar as the surface of the particular parking lot in question was concerned and that had plaintiff, instead of looking at the lake, used the care as should have been used by an ordinarily prudent person walking on such a surface, should not have been injured. [Citations omitted.]

"Judgment affirmed."

RAPPAPORT V. DAYS INN OF AMERICA, INC.
296 N.C. 382, 250 S.E.2d 245 (1979)

HUSKINS, J.: "The sole question presented by this appeal is whether plaintiff's evidence, considered in the light most favorable to her, is sufficient to repel the motion for a directed verdict and carry the case to the jury. We hold that it is.

"We commence with the observation that an innkeeper is not an insurer of the personal safety of his guests but is required 'to exercise due care to keep his premises in a reasonably safe condition and to warn his guests of any hidden peril.' *Page v. Sloan*, 281 N.C. 697, 190 S.E.2d 189 (1972). The owner of the premises is liable for injuries resulting from his failure to exercise ordinary care to keep in a reasonably safe condition that part of the premises where, during business hours guests and other invitees may be expected. 'The owner's duty extends to a parking lot provided by the owner for the use of the invitees.' A guest who enters upon the premises by invitation, express or implied, is an invitee. Plaintiff has the burden of showing negligence and proximate cause, and allegations of negligence not supported by the evidence must be disregarded. [Citations omitted.]

"With respect to contributory negligence as a matter of law, '[t]he general rule is that a directed verdict for a defendant on the ground of contributory negligence may only be granted when the evidence taken in the light most favorable to plaintiff establishes her negligence so clearly that no other reasonable inference or conclusion may be drawn therefrom. Contradictions or discrepancies in the evidence even when arising from plaintiff's evidence must be resolved by the jury rather than the trial judge.' *Clark v. Bodycombe*, 289 N.C. 246, 221 S.E.2d 506 (1976). [Citation omitted.]

"When tested by these rules what does the evidence show? Plaintiff's daughter testified that no parking spaces were available on the same side of the building where their rooms were located and her husband pulled into a parking space that was available 'right behind the building'; that 'the lighting conditions in the area where plaintiff fell was dark. I did not see any spotlight. The only lights that I saw was a dim glow from far away . . . but there was no light where we were. . . . When we arrived back from the hospital in the early morning we parked in the same spot and I noticed from the distance the bulbs or spots [spotlights] and it was not lighted. We continued registered in that motel for about a week after March 25th. I did not ever notice that light on at any other time and I don't remember lights on a post in that general vicinity. . . . You cannot see the motel porch from where we parked that night so I don't know whether the lights on the motel porch were on or not. I did not see a spotlight. . . . When I got out of the car it was dark. . . . '

"It was stipulated and agreed that the deposition of plaintiff, taken in Rockville, Maryland, would be offered into evidence. In her deposition plaintiff testified in pertinent part: 'When I got out I realized that I was on hard surface, but there were no lights in that area. It was approximately nine o'clock and it was nighttime and dark. . . . I was walking and I made a step, I think, or it was so dark that I couldn't see what it was. And I must have put my foot on the little place there. All I know is that I fell back. . . . When I fell back I hit nothing but pavement. . . . '

"The foregoing evidence, considered in the light most favorable to plaintiff, would permit but not require a jury to find that plaintiff was an invitee on defendant's premises; that defendant failed to exercise ordinary care to provide adequate lighting for the parking lot designed for the use of defendant's invited guests; and that such failure was the proximate cause of plaintiff's fall resulting in injury to her. Plaintiff's evidence, taken as true, tends to show that the parking lot was not only inadequately lighted but that it was in total darkness, *i.e.*, 'pitch dark.' Since the owner of premises is under a duty to exercise ordinary care to keep that portion of his premises designed for use by his invitees in a reasonably safe condition so as not to expose them unnecessarily to danger [citation omitted], and since the duty to keep the premises in a reasonably safe condition implies the duty to make reasonable inspection and to correct unsafe conditions which a reasonable inspection would reveal [citation omitted], such breach of duty would constitute actionable negligence on defendant's part and would support a verdict in plaintiff's favor. [Citations omitted.]

"Under the evidence in this case the mere fact that plaintiff attempted to go to her room in the darkness does not constitute contributory negligence *as a matter of law.* Reasonable men may differ as to whether plaintiff was negligent at all in attempting, despite the darkness, to reach the room to which she had been assigned. What would any reasonably prudent person have done under the same or similar circumstances? Only a jury may answer that question because the evidence, taken in the light most favorable to plaintiff, fails to establish plaintiff's negligence so clearly that no other reasonable inference may be drawn therefrom. This is true because an invited guest, when confronted with inadequate lighting on a motel parking lot while on the way to her room in the nighttime, is not ordinarily required to elect whether to remain indefinitely in her car or, at her own peril, to grope in the darkness for walkways that perchance might lead to her assigned room. [Citations omitted.] . . .

"[Pertinent to the decision were findings that plaintiff was 82 years of age, had never been at defendant's motel previously, and that the vehicle was parked in the area designated by defendant's front desk clerk, and that the fall occurred as plaintiff was following her daughter and son-in-law from the vehicle up a seven-inch step up to the concrete sidewalk at night.]

"At the close of plaintiff's evidence defendant moved for a directed verdict on the grounds that plaintiff's evidence failed to disclose any actionable negligence on defendant's part and showed contributory negligence as a matter of law. The motion was allowed, and plaintiff appealed to the Court of Appeals. That court affirmed, with Judge WEBB dissenting. Plaintiff thereupon appealed to this court as of right.

"Reversed and remanded."

In *Pope v. Holiday Inns, Inc.,*[59] the U.S. Court of Appeals for the Fifth Circuit, applying Texas law, held that where the precise hazard causing the guest to fall, the layer of ice hidden beneath the snow in the motel parking lot, is "open and obvious," the guest is charged with knowledge of the risk as a matter of law. However, Texas permits the jury to find that the guest was reasonably ignorant of the risk. This meant that the trial court erred in granting the motel's motion for judgment notwithstanding the verdict, requiring its reinstatement on appeal.

The issue of superior knowledge of the owner-operator of hotel as to the existence of a condition that could subject a hotel guest to unreasonable risk injury was decided in favor of the guest in *Robinson v. Western International Hotels*

[59]464 F.2d 1303 (5th Cir. 1972).

Co.[60] In that case the guest fell while leaving the key booth at defendant's parking garage. The guest's alleged contributory negligence was held to be a jury question, because the heavy traffic in and about the booth could be viewed as an unavoidable distraction and a judgment notwithstanding the verdict in the guest's favor was held reversible error.

[60]170 Ga. App. 812, 318 S.E.2d 235 (Ga. App. 1984).

10 Liability of Resort Facilities

10:1 *General Rule*

An innkeeper who provides resort facilities for the comfort and convenience of his guests is not an insurer of the safety of guests who avail themselves of such facilities. His only duty is to use ordinary and reasonable care in the construction, maintenance, and operation of the facility and to provide an adequate degree of general supervision so as to render the facility reasonably safe for the use of his guests.[1]

Hooks v. Washington Sheraton Corp.
578 F.2d 313 (D.C. Cir. 1977)

Robb, C.J.: "This diversity case arose out of the injuries suffered by 18-year old Thomas Hooks when he dove from the three-meter diving board at the Sheraton Park Hotel in Washington, D.C., in June 1971. The pool was equipped with a high performance aluminum 'Duraflex' board that propelled Hooks, who was not an experienced diver, into shallow water where he struck his head on the bottom. As a result Hooks is a quadriplegic. Hooks and his parents sued the operator of the pool, the Washington Sheraton Corporation (hereafter Sheraton) and its parent, ITT, alleging negligence in the construction and operation of the pool. Specifically, plaintiffs alleged that the depth of the water in the diving area of the pool did not comply with applicable District of Columbia regulations and that it was too shallow for a three-meter Duraflex diving board.

"The District Court held a bifurcated trial on the issues of liability and damages. The jury found Sheraton liable to the plaintiffs and awarded $6,000,000 to Thomas Hooks and $1,000,000 to his parents. On motion by Sheraton the District Court ordered a new trial on the issue of damages unless plaintiffs filed remittiturs of the amounts exceeding $4,500,000 and $180,000 respectively. Plaintiffs filed the remittiturs.

---

[1]40 Am. Jur. 2d, *Hotels, Motels and Restaurants*, § 84 at 958; A.L.R.2d 1203, § 2 and authorities cited therein.

"In its appeal from the finding of liability Sheraton contends that the District Court improperly instructed the jury on the standard of care owed by hotelkeepers to their guests, and on the issue of negligence *per se.*

"Sheraton contends that the District Court improperly instructed the jury on a hotelkeeper's duty of care, that contrary to the law of the District of Columbia the instruction required Sheraton to give what Sheraton calls an 'absolute warranty of safety' to its guests. Sheraton cites *Bellevue v. Haslup,* 80 U.S. App. D. C. 181, 182, 150 F.2d 160, 161 (1945) (PER CURIAM); [citation omitted]. Appellees argue that the doctrine of implied warranty is now the law of the District of Columbia. Whether the *Bellevue* decision remains the law of the District of Columbia is an issue we need not reach because read in context the instruction here is not a warranty charge.

"The District Court began its instructions on the issue of negligence by properly instructing the jury that

"the owner of a hotel is liable for failure to use reasonable care to keep safe such parts of the premises as he may retain under his control either for his own use or for the common use of the guests or tenants of the hotel.

"*It is the duty of the tenants or guests to exercise ordinary care for their own safety. In other words, the owner of a hotel is not an insurer of the safety of his guests, but he does owe to them the duty to exercise reasonable care for their safety.* [Emphasis added.]

"The court then proceeded to instruct the jury on the general law of negligence, negligence *per se,* contributory negligence, and assumption of risk. The court's reference to warranty came in the context of the instruction on assumption of risk.

"Before this rule [assumption of risk] is applied to defeat the plaintiff's claim, however, you must be satisfied by a preponderance of the evidence that the danger or hazard which caused the injuries of the plaintiff was open and apparent that he was aware of it, or that in the exercise of reasonable care should have been aware of it, and that he voluntarily exposed or subjected himself to whatever hazard or danger might reasonably have been involved.

"*You are instructed that the owner or the operator of a hotel warrants to its patrons that the facilities of said hotel are safe for the use by its patrons, free from defects and dangerous designs, and that such facilities can be used in the use and manner for which they were intended without danger or risk of injury and that such facilities are reasonably fit and suitable for their intended use.*

"When a patron of such a hotel uses such facilities in the manner and method they were intended to be used, he does not assume the risk of injury and is not chargeable with contributory negligence if he sustains an injury in so doing. [Emphasis added.]

"It is apparent from the language before and after the sentence relating to warranty that in this sentence the court was explaining to the jury that when using the defendant's pool in the manner for which it was intended, Thomas Hooks did not assume the risk of injury from defects or dangerous design, of which he was not aware, and that he was entitled to rely on the hotel's representation that there were no such hidden perils. We think the jury could not have understood the one sentence, delivered in the course of seven pages dealing with negligence, to mean that the hotel owed an 'absolute warranty of safety' to its guests. This we think is plain in light of the clear statement at the outset, that the hotel is not an insurer and that it owes its guests a duty of reasonable care. Accordingly we reject the argument that the instruction improperly imposed upon Sheraton a duty to give its guests an absolute warranty of safety.

"Sheraton also contends that the District Court erred in instructing the jury on the issue of negligence *per se* because Sheraton had explained that any possible violations of the applicable District of Columbia regulations were consistent with due care. At trial Hooks offered evidence from which the jury could conclude that the pool failed to meet District of Columbia regulations concerning the depth of water required to be directly under as well as extending out from the end of the three-meter diving board. . . .

" . . . In an effort to explain any violations, Sheraton called Mr. Brink, the chief of the District of Columbia Bureau of Air and Water Quality, to testify that the plans for the pool had been approved by his Bureau.

"In *H.R.H. Construction Corp. v. Conroy,* 134 U.S. App. D.C. 7, 411 F.2d 722 (1969), this court drew a distinction between cases in which the defendant offers no explanation of a violation of a statute or regulation and those in which the defendant introduces evidence tending to show that its failure to comply with the statute or regulation is consistent with the exercise of due care. The instruction on negligence *per se* is proper only when no explanation is made. [Citation omitted.] Sheraton urges us to hold that its evidence of the approval of the plans, the custom of inspection during construction, and the issuance of the operating license for the pool was enough to negative the inference of negligence *per se*. We disagree.

"Mr. Brink testified that he personally approved the plans for the pool in 1960. He also testified that it is the custom for inspectors to check compliance during construction, and that a license to operate the pool would not have issued unless the pool had been built according to the plans. Mr. Brink did not testify from personal knowledge that the pool was so constructed, nor did anyone else. As it turned out, the pool was not so constructed. The approved plans called for a wooden diving board. In 1968 Sheraton replaced the original board with a high performance aluminum 'Duraflex' board. Several experts, including the 1976 U.S. Olympic diving coach, testified that this type of board at the three-meter height is unsafe for the inexperienced divers likely to use a hotel pool. Moreover, the aluminum board extended five inches farther into the pool than the original wooden board. This seems at first a small modification, but it is of particular importance to the question whether the pool depths violated District of Columbia regulations. The regulations require ten feet of water directly under the board and extending out from it for twelve feet. Thereafter the bottom may incline toward the surface at a rate of one foot of depth for every three feet of distance from the board. Obviously as the board extends farther over the water, the distance from the end of the board to the point where the bottom inclines toward the surface is reduced. The area where the bottom slopes up is where the injury occurred. Finally, plaintiffs introduced evidence that on the day of the accident, the pool's water level was several inches low. This too would reduce the depth of the water under and out from the diving board. There was no showing that the District of Columbia approved these deviations from the plans approved by Mr. Brink in 1960. We conclude, therefore, that the negligence *per se* instruction given here was proper under the circumstances.

"Affirmed."

In *Blanc v. Windham Mountain Club, Inc.*,[2] a member of a private club and his wife sued the club to recover for injuries she had sustained while using the club's skiing facilities. The club counterclaimed for indemnification from the husband on the basis of an exculpatory clause in the club's bylaws wherein members agreed to hold the club harmless from claims of any kind, including employee negligence, which the plaintiffs alleged in this action. The club's motion for summary judgment dismissing the complaint was denied; the plaintiffs' cross-motion striking the affirmative defense and counterclaim was granted.

The court found first that the plaintiff wife, not being a member of the club, could not be held to any covenant barring her recovery arising out of the alleged incident relating to such membership. Second, the club's defense was insufficient as against the plaintiff husband, a member of the club, because there was no proof that the members had ever been notified of the exculpatory clause. Finally, the court held that the club was a "place of . . . recreation, or similar establishment" within the scope of the General Obligations Law, section 5–326, which prohibits such organizations, where the owner or operator receives a fee for the use of its facilities, from making covenants, agreements, or understandings that exempt the owner or operator from liability caused by or resulting from the negligence of the owner, the operator, or their agents, servants, or employees, as void against public policy. As such, the club's exculpatory clause was invalid as against public policy. The court stated that General Obligations Law, section 5–326, applied to both public and private organizations.

In *Stein v. Lebowitz-Pine View Hotel*,[3] the New York Appellate Division, Third Department, concluded that a hotel guest's executrix was entitled to recover for the wrongful death by drowning of her husband in defendant's resort swimming pool on the basis of a coroner's report as to causation and the absence of a lifeguard.

[2]115 Misc. 2d 404, 454 N.Y.S.2d 383 (Sup. Ct. 1982), *aff'd*, 92 A.D.2d 529, 459 N.Y.S.2d 447 (1st Dep't 1983).
[3]111 A.D.2d 572, 489 N.Y.S.2d 635 (A.D. 3rd Dep't 1985).

10:2   *Duty to Warn of Known Concealed Perils*

TARSHIS V. LAHAINA INVESTMENT CORP.
480 F.2d 1019 (9th Cir. 1973)

PER CURIAM: "This appeal is from a summary judgment of dismissal awarded to Lahaina Investment Corporation, d/b/a Royal Lahaina Hotel, on the ground that no genuine issue of material fact was involved.

"Appellant, a citizen of New York, registered with her husband at the Royal Lahaina Hotel at Kaanapali, Maui, on January 27, 1969. The Royal Lahaina with a beach frontage of 400 feet, advertised in brochures that: '[T]he Royal Lahaina Beach resort stretches along a 3-mile secluded white sand beach on the West side of the Island of Maui. . . . The sea is safe and exhilarating for swimming. . . . '

"However, on the day of appellant's accident, appellee alleges that four signs were posted along the frontage of the beach, two of which read: 'CAUTION Red flag on beach indicates dangerous surf conditions. Guests please use swimming pools. Mahalo.' The other two signs read: 'NOTICE to our guests, Red Flag on Beach indicates dangerous surf. Please use swimming pools. Mahalo.'

"The red flags (allegedly six in number) were positioned along the edge of Royal Lahaina's beach frontage, and were admittedly seen by appellant on January 28 when she, her husband and friends, went to the beach to swim in the ocean. Appellant, however, in her affidavit, stated that she did not see the signs warning of dangerous surf conditions, not did she receive verbal warnings from appellee concerning those conditions. Noting the existence of 'slight waves,' appellant and her companions entered the water where, five to ten minutes later, appellant was injured as the result of being thrown on the beach by a 'huge wave.'

"In granting appellee's motion for summary judgment the district court assumed, without deciding, that appellee owed appellant the duty to warn her of dangerous conditions in the Pacific Ocean along its beach frontage 'which were not known to her or obvious to an ordinarily intelligent person and either were known or in the exercise of reasonable care ought to have been known to the [appellee].' We find this to be a correct statement of the law. [Citations omitted.]

"The court held, however, that the dangers inherent in swimming in the ocean on the day of the accident 'should have been known to the [appellant] as an ordinarily intelligent person' and hence appellee was under no duty to warn appellant of the dangerous surf conditions.

"Whether or not the ocean fronting appellee's property would have appeared dangerous to an ordinarily intelligent person is a question of fact inappropriate for summary adjudication. We have recently noted that ' "[i]ssues of negligence are ordinarily not susceptible of summary adjudication." ' *Arney v. United States*, 479 F.2d 653 (9th Cir. 1973).

"Appellant contends that she observed only 'slight waves,' and saw nothing to indicate the powerful force exerted by some of them. Appellee presented evidence that the surf on the day of the accident was 'like that usually experienced during a typical trade wind day,' but came forward with nothing to show that appellee should have known that the surf was dangerous as the hotel itself cautioned in its signs.

"On the basis of this evidence, appellant is entitled to present to a trier of fact her theory that the existence of the powerful, surging surf represented an unapparent, dangerous condition which appellee knew about and of which it failed to adequately warn her.

"The judgment is reversed and the cause remanded to the district court."

BLANKENSHIP v. DAVIS
251 So. 2d 141 (Fla. App. 1971)

"WIGGINTON, J.: "Plaintiffs have appealed an adverse judgment based upon a jury verdict rendered in favor of defendants. The points on appeal challenge the correctness of the trial court's ruling which denied appellants' motion for a directed verdict on the issue of negligence by defendants, and on the issues of assumption of risk and contributory negligence pleaded as affirmative defenses to the cause of action sued upon. Appellants also challenge the propriety of the instructions given the jury on the issues of assumption of risk and contributory negligence over plaintiffs' objection.

"Plaintiffs sued defendants for damages resulting from personal injuries sustained by Jimmie Lou Blankenship while using a sliding board furnished by defendants as a recreational facility to their paying guests stopping at their motel in Escambia County. Plaintiffs and their children traveled to Escambia County where they intended to spend part of their vacation. They registered at defendants' motel at Pensacola Beach and proceeded to the bathing area set apart for the enjoyment of the guests. Defendants had erected and maintained a T-shaped pier extending out into the water from the shore, to which was attached a sliding board for the entertainment of the bathers. Plaintiff Jimmie Lou Blankenship walked out onto the pier and proceeded to slide down the board into the water below. She had used sliding boards at other bathing facilities on prior occasions and testified that her slide was made in a normal manner. The water beneath the lower end of the slide was less than three feet deep, and after entering the water plaintiff's feet struck the bottom with such force that it broke her foot. Although before mounting the slide she observed the surface of the water around and beneath the end of the slide, she did not take soundings of the area around the pier for the purpose of determining the depth of the water at the point near the lower end of the board where a person would enter the surf at the terminus of his slide. There were no signs posted on the pier or around the slide warning that the water was shallow in the vicinity of the board or giving notice that it would be dangerous for an adult to use the board in view of the shallowness of the water beneath it.

"The owner of the motel testified that at low tide the water would recede to a depth of from three to four feet in the vicinity of the slide although at high tide the depth reached approximately five feet. She further testified that she had discussed with her co-owner husband on several occasions the advisability of placing the slide in deeper water, but they were fearful if they did so, young children would be unable to use it. It was because of this consideration that they continued to maintain the slide in relatively shallow water. There is no evidence in the record that plaintiffs knew the shallow depth of the water at the lower end of the slide or that it would be dangerous for a normal adult to use this facility. The record is likewise silent of any warnings by defendants to their invited guests as to the true condition which existed or that it would be dangerous for an adult to use the slide during periods of low tide.

"It is undisputed that plaintiffs were paying guests at defendants' motel at the time of the injury complained about and, as such, were invitees to whom defendants owed a duty to warn against any latent or concealed perils existing on the premises of which they had knowledge. In the early case of *Turlington v. Tampa Electric Co.* our Supreme Court held:

> "Where a party maintains a bathhouse or a diving or swimming place for the use of the public for hire, and negligently permits any portion of the same or its appurtenances, whether in the house or the depth of the water, or in the condition of the bottom or in things thereon, to be in an unsafe condition for its use in the manner in which it is apparently designed to be used, a duty imposed by law is thereby violated; and, if an injury to another proximately results from a proper use of the same without contributory negligence, a recovery of compensatory damages may be had. . . .

"The undisputed facts disclosed by the record before us conclusively establish the defendants were guilty of negligence as a matter of law by maintaining a sliding board over such shallow water that those guests invited to use it might strike the bottom with such force as to injure themselves in the manner suffered by plaintiff without giving adequate warning of the dangerous condition or cautioning against use of the slide during periods of low tide. Defendants may not absolve themselves from negligence by the mere showing that during periods of high tide the water beneath the end of the slide has a depth of about five feet when twice during each twenty-four hours the low tide reduces the depth of the water to only three feet at that point, resulting in the perilous condition which proximately caused plaintiffs' injuries. . . .

[Discussion of assumption of risk doctrine omitted.]

"For the reasons and upon the authorities hereinabove cited, the judgment appealed is reversed and the cause remanded with directions that an order be entered granting plaintiff's post-trial motion for a new trial on all issues."

In *First Arlington Investment Corporation v. McGuire*,[4] a Florida appellate court affirmed a substantial jury verdict for an invitee who was paralyzed from his shoulders down when he dived off of defendant's resort hotel pier. No signs warning persons not to dive into the gulf waters or warning of the shallow depth from the pier were in existence. The court concluded that the duty to warn ex-

---

[4]311 So. 2d 146 (Fla. App. 1975).

tended not only to ordinary uses of the facilities but also to customary uses of it known to the proprietor.

In *Meyer by Meyer v. Smiley Brothers Inc.*,[5] the New York Appellate Division held that the resort (Mohonk Mountain House) has no duty to warn a mountain hiker of alleged defects in a gazebo from which he fell, since there was insufficient proof of any unreasonable risks to require reversal of a jury verdict in favor of the resort.

The Supreme Court of Montana in the following case—a suit brought by a resort guest who slipped and fell on an ice-covered sundeck around a swimming pool open for guests in winter—ruled that the trial court erred in overturning a jury verdict for defendant. The court found that the safety measures to avoid falls employed by the resort, which the high court found substantial, warranted the jury verdict.

NELSON V. FAIRMONT HOT SPRINGS RESORT INC.
234 Mont. 452, 763 P.2d 1135 (1988)

TURNAGE, C. J.: " . . .

"We reverse.

"[Kathryn] Nelson was on the Fairmont premises on December 30 and 31, 1984, while visiting relatives, who leased a Fairmont time-share condominium. After dinner and drinks, Nelson and her companions decided to go swimming in the Fairmont pools. Fairmont closes its pools to the general public at 10:00 P.M. However, hotel guests and condominium owners can still access the pools with a special key. It was just after midnight when they accessed the pools with one of these keys.

"After swimming indoors for a short time, they decided to go outside to the outdoor pool to experience the cold. Although it was a cold December evening, near zero degrees, the Nelson party wanted to swim in the outdoor heated pools while experiencing the cold weather around them, and they went outside for this express purpose.

"While hurrying back indoors along the pathway leading to the indoor pool, Nelson slipped and fell and injured herself. She made no report to the resort management of her fall and injuries; however, she filed complaint against them on May 5, 1986, and a jury trial was had in September 1987. The jury returned a defense verdict. Plaintiff made post-trial motions for judgment N.O.V. or, in the alternative, for a new trial. . . .

New Trials

The Trial Record

"Nelson's complaint alleged that Fairmont was negligent in failing to warn the plaintiff of the hazardous condition on the deck area around the outside pool and by failing to maintain and police the same.

[5]145 A.D. Ed. 674, 535 N.Y.S. 2d 217 (N.Y.A.D. 1988).

"The defendant maintained that it took all reasonable steps to eliminate hazards and adequately warned of any possible hazards. Additionally, it asserted that Nelson assumed the risk of swimming past 10:00 P.M. at night and her accident was caused by her own negligence by swimming after consuming alcohol and by failing to use ordinary care in negotiating the obviously icy pathway. Lastly, the defense contended that the head, neck, back and shoulder injuries suffered by Nelson were not proximately caused by her fall at Fairmont since she was subsequently involved in an altercation in which her nose was broken and then involved in a car wreck which rendered her unconscious. . . .

"It was clear that guests who swam after 10:00 P.M. did so at their own risk. Ten o'clock P.M. was the time when the lifeguards went off duty and the doors were locked to the general public. There were large signs on the entrance to the pool area and on the door to the outside pool stating this policy. . . .

"There was ice present on the walkway in the early morning hours of December 31, 1984. This condition was open and obvious. Certainly there was a jury question as to whether a hazard existed; whether Fairmont negligently allowed the hazard, if any, to exist; and whether it adequately warned patrons of the possible hazard. The jury was properly instructed on these issues and determined them accordingly based on the foregoing substantial credible evidence. The jury's verdict of 'not negligent' is supported by the evidence of precautionary steps taken and warnings given by Fairmont. This Court will not substitute its judgment for that of the jury when no misconduct or abuse of discretion has been shown. We do not hesitate to reinstate a verdict supported by substantial credible evidence. *Nelson v. Hartman* (1982), 199 Mont. 295, 648 P.2d 1176.

"Based on the lengthy trial record and the foregoing evidence recited, appellant convinces this Court that the District Court abused its discretion by setting aside the verdict and awarding a new trial.

"The order granting new trial is vacated. The jury's verdict of September 22, 1987 is reinstated."

In the following case, the Supreme Court of Oregon ruled that innkeepers and possessors of land have an affirmative duty to warn paying guests of foreseeable unreasonable risks of physical harm. However, the duty does not extend to all possible risks of the premises as a matter of law or to the provision of safety equipment to protect against hazards off the premises. In a suit brought by a relative of a hotel guest who drowned while rescuing children, also guests, who were struggling in ocean surf, plaintiff's failure to allege that the innkeeper knew or should have known of dangerous surf at an adjacent beach rendered his wrongful death claim insufficient as a matter of law.

FUHRER V. GEARHART BY THE SEA, INC.
306 Or. 434, 760 P.2d 874 (1988)

LENT, J.: "The issue is whether plaintiff has stated ultimate facts sufficient to constitute a claim for relief against defendants for defendants' failure to warn plaintiff's decedent and others of the hazards of the ocean surf and for defendants' failure to provide safety measures to protect against those hazards. Defendant Gearhart By the Sea, Inc. (Gearhart) moved to dismiss on the theory that it 'owed no duty' to warn or protect from hazards not located on its premises. Defendant Department of Transportation, State of Oregon (the state), moved to dismiss on the theory that the state has no duty to warn of natural conditions on public property and no duty to protect against natural conditions. The circuit court granted both motions to dismiss. The Court of Appeals affirmed the dismissals. *Fuhrer v. Gearhart by the Sea, Inc.*, 79 Or. App. 550, 719 P.2d 1305 (1986). We remanded to the Court of Appeals for reconsideration in light of *Fazzolari v. Portland School Dist. No. 1J*, 303 Or. 1, 734 P.2d 1326 (1987); *Kimbler v. Stillwell*, 303 Or. 23, 734 P.2d 1344 (1987); and *Donaca v. Curry Co.*, 303 Or. 30, 734 P.2d 1339 (1987). 303 Or. 171, 734 P.2d 1348 (1987). On remand, the Court of Appeals again affirmed the dismissal. 87 Or. App. 219, 742 P.2d 58 (1987). We also affirm the judgments of dismissal, although for different reasons from those stated by the Court of Appeals. . . .

"The following facts are alleged in the complaint.

"Plaintiff's decedent was a paying guest at defendant Gearhart's resort. The hotel is adjacent to an ocean beach owned by the state. The state had jurisdiction over the beach pursuant to ORS 390.635.

"While on the beach, decedent saw some children struggling in the ocean surf, apparently caught in an undertow, riptide or other hazardous condition of the waters adjacent to the beach. The children and their parents were also paying guests at the resort. Decedent and others attempted to save the children. The children were saved by the efforts of decedent and the other rescuers, but decedent died from drowning or cardiac arrest caused by his rescue efforts.

"Gearhart did not warn its guests of the dangerous undertow, riptide or other hazardous conditions of the surf. It did not provide lifeguards, lifesaving equipment or warning flags. It also did not rescue or aid the rescue of decedent or the children. The state likewise did not warn, have lifeguards on duty or provide lifesaving equipment or warning flags. Plaintiff alleged that decedent's death was the result of defendants' failure to warn or provide safety measures.

"To determine whether plaintiff has stated ultimate facts sufficient to constitute a claim, we first determine what is the law concerning a failure to warn or a failure to provide safety measures. We shall refer to the failure to supply the various safety measures as a failure to protect.

"The law traditionally has been that a defendant is liable for a failure to warn or protect only if the defendant had a 'duty' to warn or protect. This court discussed the concept of duty in negligence cases in *Fazzolari*, *Kimbler* and *Donaca*. In those cases, we held that the concept of duty was not always a useful tool with which to analyze common-law negligence. There may be specific duties established by statute, status or relationship, but the absence of such duties does not insulate a defendant from liability. In the absence of a duty arising from a source of that kind, a defendant may be liable for conduct which is unreasonable in the circumstances if that conduct results in harm to a plaintiff and the risk of harm to the plaintiff or the class of persons to whom the plaintiff belongs was foreseeable.

"In this case, we must determine whether the analytical approach of *Fazzolari*, *Kimbler* and *Donaca* should be used when the negligence alleged is a failure to warn or protect. The answer to that is clear. *Fazzolari* and *Donaca* involved a failure to warn or provide protection, and *Kimbler* involved failure to take appropriate safety measures. In each we held that the facts should be analyzed to determine whether the risk of harm was foreseeable. Whether negligence involves the commission of a negligent act or the taking of no action when the lack of action creates a foreseeable unreasonable risk of harm, the analysis should be the same.

"Failure to warn or protect should be analyzed in terms of foreseeability and unreasonable conduct. If a specific affirmative duty is imposed by statute, status or relationship, an analysis based on that specific duty is also appropriate. As noted in *Fazzolari*, the difference between a traditional duty analysis and a foreseeability analysis may be only semantic. In 'duty' terms, a defendant may be found to have a duty to warn another of an undue risk of harm to a protected interest of the other if the defendant knows of the risk. *See* the discussion of Prosser and Keeton, The Law of Torts (5th ed. 1984), and Harper, James & Gray, The Law of Torts (2d ed. 1986), in *Fazzolari*, 303 Or. at 9, 734 P.2d 1326. If the defendant has a specific duty to the plaintiff, the defendant may also be liable without knowledge of the risk; that depends on the terms of the particular duty. Absent an affirmative duty, the existence of a 'duty' in the given circumstances is a conclusion to be reached, not a means of analysis.

"In *Fazzolari*, we stated that the issue was 'whether that conduct unreasonably created a foreseeable risk to a protected interest of the kind of harm that befell the plaintiff.' 303 Or. at 17, 734 P.2d 1326. The Court of Appeals' decision on remand in this case held that defendants did not create the risk of harm in that they did not 'create' the dangerous condition of the surf. This does not bear on whether defendants unreasonably failed to warn or protect others who were at risk. In a warning case, the risk of harm created is exposure to a danger known to the defendant. In *Fazzolari*, the defendant school district did not create the rapist or the rape that injured the plaintiff in that case, but a jury could have found that the school district was or should have been aware of the risk of sexual assault and neither warned plaintiff nor took other action to protect plaintiff and others in her position. The risk in a failure-to-warn case is not the hazard itself, but the chance that someone predictably will be exposed to danger, be it rape or dangerous surf, if no warning is made.

"A defendant may be liable if the defendant can reasonably foresee that there is an unreasonable risk of harm, a reasonable person in the defendant's position would warn of the risk, the defendant has a reasonable chance to warn of the risk, the defendant does not warn of the risk, and the plaintiff is injured as a result of the failure to warn.

"Courts frequently have prevented juries from considering the second question, whether a reasonable person in the defendant's position would warn of the risk, by deciding either that the defendant had a duty or had no duty to warn.

There are four factors to be considered in determining whether action or a failure to act is reasonable: the likelihood of harm, the severity of the possible harm, the 'cost' of action that would prevent harm,[2] and the defendant's position, including the defendant's relationship with the plaintiff. . . .

"Plaintiff alleges that Gearhart, as an innkeeper or possessor of land, should have warned its paying guests of the dangers of the ocean surf. Although Gearhart did not warn decedent of the danger, the danger may have been apparent to decedent when he saw the children struggling in the surf. If that is so, a warning would not have made decedent more aware of the danger, and the failure to warn decedent did not expose him to any greater risk of harm than if he had been warned. However, we do not know this, and decedent might have chosen other means of rescue if he had been warned and if other means had been available. A trier of face could find that a warning could have made a difference.

"The children who were rescued were also paying guests of Gearhart. A trier of fact could find that a failure to warn the children or their parents did expose the children to the danger of the surf. If a danger is foreseeable, under most circumstances including this one, an attempted rescue is foreseeable. *See* Prosser and Keeton. The Law of Torts 307–309 (5th ed. 1984), and cases cited therein. The failure to warn the children could have created a foreseeable unreasonable risk of harm to decedent as a rescuer. Inherent in the concept of rescue is that the rescuer knows of the risk but may disregard the risk to effect the rescue; therefore, Gearhart might be liable if the failure to warn the children or their parents were negligence.

"Gearhart argues that innkeepers, as a matter of law, are not liable for failure to warn of risks not located on property owned or controlled by the innkeeper. The traditional view of the duty of an innkeeper in this situation is stated by Comment c to section 314A of the Restatement (Second) of Torts:

> " 'A carrier is under no duty to one who has left the vehicle and ceased to be a passenger, not is an innkeeper under a duty to a guest who is injured or endangered while he is away from the premises. Nor is a possessor of land under any such duty to one who has ceased to be an invitee.'

"Under the traditional rule, Gearhart had no affirmative duty to its guests concerning any hazard away from Gearhart's premises. Support for the traditional rule is no longer universal. Some jurisdictions have imposed an affirmative duty on possessors of property to warn business invitees of known dangers immediately adjacent to the premises. *Banks v. Hyatt Corp.*, 722 F.2d 214, *reh. den.* 731 F.2d 888 (5th Cir. 1984); *Ollar v. Spakes (George's Place)*, 269 Ark. 488, 601 S.W.2d 868 (1980); *Piedalue v. Clinton Elem. School Dist. No. 32*, 692 P.2d 20 (Mont. 1984); *Southland Corp. v. Superior Court*, 203 Cal. App. 3d 656, 250 Cal. Rptr. 57 (1988).

"One case, *Tarshis v. Lahaina Investment Corporation*, 480 F.2d 1019 (9th Cir. 1973), involved facts very similar to the facts in this case. The defendant in *Tarshis* operated an ocean-front hotel in Hawaii. The court held that the operator had a duty to warn its guests of dangerous conditions in the ocean which were known or should have been known to the operator but of which the guests were unaware, if the dangerous conditions were not obvious. The court then held that the trier of fact was to determine whether the dangerous condition was obvious.

"In a recent case, *Mostert v. CBL & Associates*, 741 P.2d 1090 (Wyo. 1987), the Wyoming Supreme Court held, as a matter of law, that the operators of a movie theater owed to its paying guests 'an affirmative duty to exercise reasonable or ordinary care for their safety which includes an obligation to advise them of off-premises danger that might reasonably be foreseeable.' 741 P.2d at 1096.

"We believe that the courts in *Tarshis* and *Mostert* may have been too specific in holding as a matter of law that there was an affirmative duty to warn in the situations presented in those cases. The duties of innkeepers and other operators of commercial establishments to their guests are to 'protect them against unreasonable risk of physical harm' and to aid them if they are ill or injured. Restatement (Second) of Torts § 314A. Traditionally they include an affirmative duty to warn of dangerous conditions on the premises that are not obvious, but we do not extend the duty to warn of all possible dangers off the premises as a matter of law or to provide safety equipment to protect against off-premises hazards. It is the role of the trier of fact to determine whether it is unreasonable not to warn of a danger or otherwise provide protection in the specific circumstances of each case. Innkeepers and possessors of land have an affirmative duty to warn their paying guests and invitees of foreseeable unreasonable risks of physical harm; when the risk involves a dangerous condition off the premises, the trier of fact must decide the reasonableness of the failure to warn in all the circumstances.

"In the present case, there is no allegation in the complaint that Gearhart knew or should have known of the dangerous condition of the ocean surf. Without knowledge of a dangerous condition or reason to know of the condition, Gearhart could not have foreseen an unreasonable risk of harm. If plaintiff were able to prove all the facts alleged in the complaint, plaintiff would still not have proved one element necessary to recovery, the foreseeability to defendant of an unreasonable risk of harm to persons in plaintiff's position. Even if Gearhart had an affirmative duty to take reasonable steps to warn and protect, the duty would extend only to warn of and protect from knowable risks. Because plaintiff might prove all the facts alleged and still not be entitled to recover, the complaint was properly dismissed. . . .

"The judgment of dismissal of the circuit court and the decision of the Court of Appeals are affirmed.

"2. 'Cost' includes more than economic cost. Time, effort and risk to defendant are the primary considerations, although monetary cost may also affect the reasonableness of taking action."

10:3 *Constructive Notice of Concealed Perils*

MONTES V. BELCHER
480 F.2d 1128 (8th Cir. 1973)

NICHOL, D. J.: "On the warm Sunday afternoon of July 13, 1968, 35 year old Fernando Montes, a citizen of Nebraska, took a running dive off a short dock which served the Appellants' resort, one of the many enhancing Minnesota's beautiful lakes. He surfaced with a severely lacerated scalp and a vertebral fracture. Shortly after the incident, a jagged piece of concrete was recovered from the lake floor in the general area where plaintiff had entered the water. The concrete piece resembled the home-made boat anchors constructed by Appellants to use in the boats which frequented the boat dock.

"Plaintiff, Montes, a proficient swimmer and diver, claims that he executed a flat, 'racing' dive because he knew he was plunging into shallow water. The water depth was variously described to be from 27 in. to waist level. Montes testified, however, that his ultimate purpose was to grab the ankles of a friend who was standing in the water 15 feet from the end of the dock, a purpose which would require either a deep dive or a subsequent submergence.

"Montes was very familiar with the swimming area, and had executed dives from the boat dock on numerous previous occasions. Never before had he encountered rocks or blocks in the water. He admitted to having imbibed two or three drinks on the afternoon of the accident.

"The Appellants, Mr. and Mrs. Belcher, citizens of Minnesota, had owned the resort since 1963. They charged $10 per day for cabin accommodations. Although the area surrounding the boat dock was perennially in use by Appellants' swimmer-patrons and although Mr. Belcher had seen swimmers jump off the boat dock, he testified that he had never made any special attempt to inspect the lake bottom for debris nor had he ever 'raked' the shoreline lake bottom. Never had he erected signs warning of the dangers of diving in the shallow water or the possible presence of debris in the swimming area. Never had he placed floats in the water to discourage the intrusion of boats into the swimming and diving area; in fact there was no segregation whatsoever of swimming waters from boating waters.

"The case went to the jury on a comparative negligence instruction. The jury adjudged defendants 90% negligent and the plaintiff 10% negligent. The Appellants-defendants challenge the sufficiency of the evidence to support submission to the jury and the Trial Court's refusal to instruct on assumption of risk.

"A jury must not be denied the right to make reasonable inferences from the evidence. [Citation omitted.] Given that premise, we conclude that the jury could have reasonably inferred that the Appellee came into contact with the concrete block rather than with the bottom of the lake.

"Appellants' challenge to the submission of the case to the jury is based upon a contention that the Trial Court was mistaken in the formulation of Appellants' duty to their guests. They first contend that a riparian owner is not responsible for the safe maintenance of property beyond the meander line of a lake, which line marks the boundary between Appellants' shoreline land and submerged land which belongs to the state. But even if Appellants are held responsible for the maintenance of submerged lands, Appellants contend, that responsibility extends only to the remedy of dangerous conditions known to Appellants or of which they could have acquired knowledge had they been in the exercise of reasonable care. Since there was no evidence that Appellants knew of the presence of the cement block nor that it had been there long enough to mandate an invocation of constructive knowledge, Appellants contend the case should not have gone to the jury.

"The Trial Court correctly rejected these formulations of duty (or lack thereof). Relying upon the case of *Hanson v. Christensen*, 275 Minn. 204, 145 N.W.2d 868 (1966), the Court held a resort owner who avails himself of the advantages of riparian ownership for resort purposes owes to his patrons a duty of reasonable care which includes 'active vigilance' in their protection from foreseeable risks. [Citations omitted.] The Court thus rejected the necessity of showing actual knowledge of the existence of the dangerous condition or of showing that the condition was of sufficient duration to afford constructive notice, which are the ordinary standards of care in the business invitee situation.

"The jury was perfectly justified in determining that Appellants had violated this duty in any one or more of three respects: (1) their failure to warn of the dangers of diving off the boat dock; (2) their failure to periodically 'rake' the swimming-diving area in search of dangerous obstructions; (3) their failure to segregate swimming areas from boating areas. In the absence of any evidence of an intervening-superseding cause, the jury was also justified in concluding that the Appellants' omissions were the cause of Appellee's injuries. The jury's allocation of negligence between the Appellants and the Appellee pursuant to Minnesota's comparative negligence statute, Minn. Stats. Ann. Sec. 604.01 (1969), is determinative absent a showing that there was no evidence to support it. [Citations omitted.] . . .

[Discussion of assumption of risk defense omitted.]

"We therefore find that there was sufficient evidence to support a plaintiff's verdict and that the defense of assumption of risk is inapplicable to this fact situation.

"Affirmed."

10:4   *Tortious Breach of Contract*

In general, courts do not authorize recovery of punitive damages arising out of contract claims (see Chapter 7, section 7:7, *supra*). In the following case, a federal circuit court of appeals distinguished between Alabama's statutory wrongful death action, which cannot arise out of a breach of contract claim because of its punitive damage basis, and an independent wrong based upon a violation of a contractual duty, which authorizes a wrongful death claim.

BAROCO V. ARASERV, INC.
621 F.2d 189 (5th Cir. 1980)

KRAVITCH, C.J.: "In this wrongful death action the jury returned a verdict for the appellee in the amount of $500,000. Appellants claim errors below including instructions to the jury, denial of a motion for directed verdict and failure to reverse as excessive the jury's award. We find these claims to be without merit; therefore, we affirm.

"On April 10, 1973 the appellant Araserv and its subsidiary entered into a contract with the state of Alabama for the operation of a recreation facility at Gulf Shores, Alabama. The contract expressly provided that it was entered into for the benefit of the public. Specifically, the contract required that Araserv operate a pavilion at the Gulf Shores beach area. Pursuant to § 16 of the contract, the appellants were obligated to provide two lifeguards for the pavilion area and to furnish all necessary life-saving equipment. Moreover, the appellants were required to take all proper safeguards for the prevention of injuries or damage to the public. The contract was scheduled to terminate five years from the opening of the Gulf Shores Park in 1974, although the precise date for the opening was not provided. Only one lifeguard was hired, however, and he was not advised of the availability of any life-saving equipment, nor had such equipment been purchased at the time of the death involved here. The lifeguard reported for work on May 12, 1974.

"May 12, 1974 was also the day on which Anthony Baroco, appellee's decedent, took his wife and family to the Gulf Shores Beach. Upon their arrival at the beach, Baroco noticed two teenagers at play in the water. Later, one of the teenagers approached Mr. Baroco and informed him that her playmate was in danger and asked for his assistance. Although the water was choppy and the waves were high, Baroco, after instructing the teenager to summon the lifeguard, went to the young girl's aid. As soon as the lifeguard was informed of the plight of the teenaged swimmer and the rescue attempt of Mr. Baroco, he also attempted a rescue. Although the lifeguard was able to swim the nearly 150 yards to the pair, he was unable to save either: the teenager already appeared dead and Baroco had panicked preventing rescue. Because the rescue attempts failed, Baroco drowned.

"Appellee filed a wrongful death action in a two-count complaint charging tortious breach of contract and negligence. At trial, this claim was submitted to the jury, which returned a verdict against the appellants, awarding appellee $500,000.

"The appellants urge several grounds for reversal: *inter alia* (1) that a breach of contract claim cannot support a wrongful death action. . . .

"Appellants first argue that the court erred in submitting the tortious breach of contract claim to the jury. Appellants base their argument on the punitive nature of Alabama's wrongful death statute: damages recoverable are punitive rather than compensatory, and because punitive damages are not recoverable in contract actions in Alabama, then a wrongful death action may not be maintained in a breach of contract claim. As the appellants contend, the Supreme Court of Alabama has specifically held that a contract claim cannot support a wrongful death action. *Clinton Geohagan v. General Motors Corp.*, 291 Ala. 167, 279 So. 2d 436 (1973). The appellants are correct as far as the argument goes. The appellants have failed to focus, however, on the *tortious* nature of the instant breach of contract action. Here, the appellee did not claim that the death occurred as a result of a breach of contract, but rather the death resulted from the nonperformance of a duty *established* by the contract. In *Thaggard v. Vafes,* 218 Ala. 609, 119 So. 647 (1929), the Supreme Court of Alabama expressly held that a wrongful death action may be maintained for such tortious breach of contract. In the instant case, as provided in the contract, appellant Araserv owed a duty to patrons of the beach as third party beneficiaries of the contract to provide two lifeguards and life-saving equipment. The appellants failed to observe this duty and testimony established that the failure proximately caused the death of Baroco. Thus, the court was correct in submitting this claim to the jury. . . .

"[Affirmed.]"

10:5 *Duty of Adequate Supervision*

Swimming Pools

What is adequate supervision? That depends on the circumstances of each case. In *McKeever v. Phoenix Jewish Community Center,*[6] a parent sued the defendant club for the death by drowning of a ten-year-old child in the club's pool. The trial resulted in judgment for the club, which was affirmed by the Supreme Court of Arizona.

From the testimony at the trial it appeared that plaintiff and his family were members of the defendant club. On the day of the accident the whole family, including plaintiff, his two sons, and his nine-year-old and ten-year-old daughters, were using the pool. The young children were using the shallow end of the pool, which was separated from the deep end by a rope supported by buoys.

Plaintiff's ten-year-old daughter, Mary Agnes, with two young girl friends, moved over to the deep side of the safety rope. In their play the girls jumped into the deep water and successfully climbed back to jump several times. It seems that none but the nine-year-old sister of Mary Agnes saw these children in this game, although there were roughly forty other children and a *lifeguard* at the pool. An older brother of Mary Agnes testified that approximately five minutes passed from the time he saw the three little girls in the shallow part of the water until he knew of the accident. During that period Mary Agnes was left alone at that part of the pool, her two girl friends having returned to other areas. Immediately thereafter, the body of Mary Agnes was discovered at the bottom of the pool by two other swimmers.

The evidence also indicated that the lifeguard was on duty at the time, that he observed the three little children at the deep end of the pool, and that they appeared reasonably able swimmers to him. The lifeguard got to the scene of the accident as fast as was humanly possible, and made every effort to revive the child, without success.

Plaintiff's doctor testified that a drowning could result from very little water on the back of a person's throat causing a spasm of the glottis which closes off the airway. This could occur within a matter of seconds. Consequently, several

[6] 92 Ariz. 121, 374 P.2d 875 (1962).

factors other than the defendant's alleged negligence could conceivably be said to have contributed to the child's death. One such factor could have been the parents' leaving her without immediate and direct supervision in an inherently dangerous body of water, where drowning is not only possible but may be expected in the event of misjudgment on the part of the child. Even an unnoticed chance fall by a child from a pool's edge into the water could be the cause.

In *Cohen v. Suburban Sidney-Hill, Inc.,*[7] the minor plaintiff was an eight-year-old boy whose father was a member of the club operated by defendant. The boy had the privilege of using the pool located on the club premises. There were at least three lifeguards on duty at the pool on the date of the accident. The minor plaintiff was going up on a ladder which led to a high diving board approximately twenty feet above the concrete flooring which extended around the pool. The ladder and the diving board were wet. There were a number of other children trying to climb this ladder to get on the diving board. There were no lifeguards attempting to regulate the number of children going up on this diving board. The minor plaintiff was near the top as other children were climbing up the ladder. He slipped and went over on his back on the concrete flooring around the pool. Upon the conclusion of an opening statement by plaintiff's counsel, the trial judge granted defendant's motion for a directed verdict.

On appeal, the judgment entered on the verdict was affirmed. Said the court:

> There is nothing in the opening statement to show or to justify an inference as to what it was that caused the minor to slip and fall from the ladder. It is as likely that he fell simply because he lost his foothold, or because he did not grip the ladder while ascending, or because the ladder was wet, as that he fell because of the lack of supervision by the defendant. . . . The [plaintiff was] required to show that it was more likely that the injury was occasioned by the negligence of the defendant than by a cause for which the defendant was not liable. . . . [The verdict] for the defendant [was] rightly directed.[8]

In *Wagenschnur v. Green Acres Recreation Ass'n,*[9] the minor plaintiff was a nine-year-old girl who attended a swimming party at defendant's swimming pool. She asked for and received permission to remove from the storeroom, and to play with, certain hard plastic floats. In the course of such play, one of the floats bobbed up far enough out of the water to strike and break a portion of one of her front teeth. There was a lifeguard on duty at or near the pool at the time the floats were in use, but he did not feel it was necessary to give more specific supervision to the plaintiff's use of the floats.

In her action to recover for the damage to her front teeth, plaintiff contended that defendant's lifeguard was negligent in permitting children to use the float and in failing to supervise its use. Judgment for the defendant was affirmed on appeal. Said the court, "[O]ne who participates in an active sport accepts the

[7]343 Mass. 217, 178 N.E.2d 19 (1961).
[8]*Id.* at 219, 178 N.E.2d at 21.
[9]196 A.2d 401 (Del. Super. Ct. 1963).

obvious dangers connected therewith and the operator of the facility in the exercise of reasonable care cannot be held liable for those dangers which are inherent in such activity and are obvious to the participant."[10]

Athletic Facilities

GINSBERG V. LEVBOURNE REALTY COMPANY, INC.
28 A.D.2d 874, 282 N.Y.S.2d 601 (2d Dep't 1967)

MEMORANDUM: "In an action to recover damages for personal injuries allegedly sustained by the plaintiff while he was a guest at the defendant's hotel, . . . defendant's motion to set aside the jury's verdict in plaintiff's favor for $55,000 and for a new trial was denied upon all grounds other than excessiveness, and a new trial limited to the issue of damages was granted unless plaintiff consented to a reduction of the verdict. . . . Judgment, insofar as appealed from, reversed on the law and the facts, and a new trial granted, with costs to abide the event, unless, within 30 days after entry of the order hereon, plaintiff shall serve and file a written stipulation consenting to . . . reduce to $30,000 the amount of the verdict in his favor, and to the entry of an amended judgment accordingly. While the jury was warranted in determining that defendant was negligent in failing to maintain the basketball court in a reasonably safe manner for the anticipated use of the guests (*Ginsberg v. Levbourne Realty Co.*, 25 A.D.2d 440; [citation omitted]), we are of the opinion that an award of $30,000 is fair and adequate for all the damages and injuries sustained by the plaintiff. . . . BENJAMIN and MUNDER, JJ., dissent and vote to reverse the judgment and to dismiss the complaint, with the following memorandum: Plaintiff, while a guest at defendant's Summer resort hotel, slipped and fell while playing basketball on an outdoor basketball court, which was paved with macadam and was bounded on three sides by grass and dirt. He has recovered a verdict on the theory that the presence of a minuscule quantity of sand on the court evidenced a breach of defendant's obligation of reasonable care and thus established actionable negligence. We cannot agree with this result nor with the theory on which it is based. So small was the quantity of sand that allegedly caused plaintiff's fall that it could not be seen until the viewer was right 'on top of it.' We do not believe that the presence of such quantity of sand on a resort hotel's outdoor basketball court, surrounded by grass and by dirt which can be tracked onto the court by every passing guest, by every ball player, and by the elements themselves, evidences lack of reasonable care by the owner of the hotel. To require the owner to keep such outdoor play area as immaculate as a ballroom dance floor would be to impose an impossible and clearly unreasonable burden upon him. And it is undisputed on this record that defendant did provide supervision and 'housecleaning' service for this play area that clearly met the requirements of reasonable care in light of all the circumstances. In our opinion, plaintiff has not established

[10]*Id.* at 403.

actionable negligence on defendant's part, the verdict in his favor is contrary to the evidence as a matter of law, his judgment should be reversed, and his complaint should be dismissed."

Diving Areas

Diving activities involve greater risk of injury than ordinary use of a swimming pool, and supervision should therefore be commensurate with the risks involved.

In *Allon v. Park Central Hotel Co.*,[11] plaintiff sued the defendant hotel and its pool concessionaire for injuries sustained in the hotel pool. It appeared that plaintiff was swimming down the hotel pool from the shallow end, and as he approached the diving board at the deep end, somebody did a back dive and they met head-on. As a result, plaintiff sustained rupture of the right ear drum, followed by acute traumatic mastoiditis.

Plaintiff claimed that defendant was negligent in failing to have a sufficient number of employees in the swimming pool to prevent patrons from diving off the diving board at the time when patrons using the pool were immediately below the diving board. Although the court, at defendant's request, charged the jury that "the plaintiff in the exercise of reasonable care was required to adjust his conduct to other persons who were using the pool at the time or who reasonably could be expected to use the pool by right," the jury nevertheless brought in a verdict for plaintiff, which was affirmed on appeal.

In the subsequent case of *Byron v. St. George Swimming Club*,[12] plaintiff sustained her injury while diving from the high board in defendant's swimming pool. No one was using the diving section at the time plaintiff jumped, making a swan dive. As she reached the water her head struck a boy who was swimming underneath the water in the diving section, looking for a lost cap. The boy, made codefendant in the action, had no right to be swimming in the diving section, and his presence there was obviously a danger to any person diving from the boards. There were signs in the pool to warn swimmers and divers, reading "Diving at your own risk" and "Look before you dive."

Plaintiff grounded her action on the defendant club's negligence in failing to restrict the diving area to divers and in failing to give warning to plaintiff and others that the rules would be relaxed to allow a nondiver to enter the diving area to search for his cap. The trial court dismissed the action at the end of the plaintiff's case, and the appellate division affirmed. But the Court of Appeals reversed and remanded the case for a new trial. Said the court, "The risk of injury from diving under the conditions obtaining at the place and time of the accident was not, as a matter of law, assumed by the plaintiff.[13]

The court also pointed out, as another ground for reversal, the exclusion by the trial court of evidence that it was the uniform custom and practice of the

[11]272 N.Y. 631, 5 N.E.2d 366 (1936) (mem. opinion).
[12]283 N.Y. 505, 28 N.E.2d 934 (1940) (per curiam).
[13]*Id.* at 508, 28 N.E.2d at 937.

defendant in the maintenance of the pool and in the protection of its diving patrons, to maintain two guards to keep the diving section of the pool free from swimmers when patrons were diving.

Fairgrounds

In the following case, the Supreme Court of Michigan found a fairgrounds owner liable for a discharge of a firearm that injured a patron.

BAUER v. SAGINAW COUNTY AGRICULTURAL SOCIETY
349 Mich. 616, 622–23, 628, 84 N.W.2d 827, 833–34, 839 (1957)

EDWARDS, J.: "The parties in their briefs and the trial judge in a careful opinion agree upon at least 2 basic propositions. As stated by the appellant, they are:

" 'The appellant concedes that the law of Michigan requires it to maintain a reasonably safe place for visitors to the fair, and appellant further concedes that in the case of firearms, whether used by appellant's agents or anyone on their fairgrounds that a high degree of care is owed to patrons of the fair to the area where firearms are used reasonably safe.'

"The first of these propositions is quoted thus in *Sullivan v. Detroit & Windsor Ferry Co.*, 255 Mich. 575, 576, 577:

" ' "The duty assumed by the owners of places to which the public thus resort in large numbers is manifestly analogous to that which the law imposes upon carriers of passengers. Nevertheless it has been measured by the standard of *ordinary care*. Doubtless the true theory is that such persons assume the obligation of exercising reasonable care, and that what will be reasonable care will be a degree of care proportioned to the danger incurred, and to the number of persons who will be subjected to that danger. . . . Such being the nature of the obligation, it is obvious that the proprietor of such a building is under a *continuing duty of inspection*, to the end of seeing that it is reasonably safe for the protection of those whom he invites to come into it; and that, if he neglects his duty in this respect, so that it becomes unsafe, the question of his *knowledge* or *ignorance* of the defect which renders it unsafe is immaterial." ' 1 Thompson on Negligence (2d ed.), § 996, pp. 913, 914.

"The second is best stated in *Bahel v. Manning*, 112 Mich. 24, 29, 30 (36 LRA 523, 67 Am. St. Rep. 381):

" 'The general rule . . . is that a very high degree of care is required from all persons using firearms in the immediate vicinity of others, no matter how lawful or even necessary such use may be. 7 Am. & Eng. Enc. Law (1st ed.), p. 523. This same principle is stated in 2 Shearman & Redfield, Negligence (4th ed.), § 686. In *Morgan v. Cox*, 22 Mo. 373 (66 Am. Dec. 623), it was held that, where injury to another is caused by an act that would have amounted to trespass *vi et armis* under the old system of actions, it is no defense that the act occurred through inadvertence, or without the wrongdoer's intending it; it must appear that the injury done was inevitable, and utterly without fault on the part of the alleged wrongdoer.'

"With the above disposed of, the dispute on appeal hinges on whether or not there were facts from which the trial judge as trier of the facts could have found negligence on the part of defendant which was a proximate cause of the boy's injury. The contested finding was as follows:

> " 'Here it was known that guns in a shooting gallery were to be used in close proximity to large crowds of people invited there by the defendant, Saginaw County Agricultural Society, whose negligence in not exercising a reasonable degree of continuous supervision, control and inspection of the shooting gallery was the proximate cause of the accident to plaintiffs, who certainly were not guilty of any contributory negligence.'

"It is apparent from this record that defendant had the power and opportunity to control and regulate its concessionaires. Defendant exercised those rights only to the extent of seeing that steel backs and sides were provided for the booth and that the guns were chained to the counter. Beyond these 2 gestures, it apparently felt it had no duty to go. It provided no rules, made no inspections, exercised no supervision over the employees of the concessionaire. . . .

"The small son of plaintiff in our instant case was plainly a guest invited to the fair by defendant. The duty of reasonable care owed to the boy at defendant's fair must be viewed in relation to the twin circumstances of the regular use of dangerous weapons authorized by defendant and carried on in close proximity to large crowds of people who felt assured against any danger. Thus viewed, the duty owed is plainly that of the high degree of care previously cited from *Bahel*, *supra*.

"We believe that there is ample evidence in this record from which the trial judge could have found the defendant's failure to prescribe any rules for or to exercise any sort of supervision over the operation of the shooting gallery was negligence which was a proximate cause of the boy's injury.

"We believe that the holding above accords with perhaps the least debatable definition of legal duty called to our attention during consideration of this case:

> " 'No better general statement can be made, than that the courts will find a duty where, in general, reasonable men would recognize it and agree that it exists.' Prosser, Law of Torts (2d ed.), ch. 6 § 36, p. 168.

"The judgment of the court below in both cases is affirmed."

10:6 *Death or Injury as Presumption of Negligence*

In general, the fact of the death or injury of a swimming-pool patron is not conclusive proof of negligence and does not even raise a presumption of negligence on the part of the pool operator.

In *Rovegno v. San Jose Knights of Columbus Hall Association*,[14] a mother sued to recover damages for the death of her nineteen-year-old son, who died in a swimming pool in a building owned by the defendant and used for social and athletic purposes by its members. The action was grounded on alleged negli-

---

[14]108 Cal. App. 591, 291 P. 848 (1930).

gence by reason of defendant's failure to provide an experienced lifeguard at the pool. The evidence disclosed that young Rovegno and a boy guest went swimming in the pool at a time when no one was present at the pool and no member or officer of defendant had notice or knowledge that the boys intended to swim or that they were swimming in the pool at the time. Notices were posted in the locker rooms and in the pool, reading: "Bathers using pool do so at their own risk."

Rovegno's companion swam across the pool first. When he turned around, Rovegno, who was concededly not a good swimmer, started across. At a point about halfway across the pool, he was seen to jump up and down in deep water. His face was white and bore a frightened look or horrible expression. His companion, unable to assist him from the pool, went outside for help. Rovegno was found lying at the bottom of the pool at the nine-foot depth, dead. An autopsy revealed that death resulted from a cardiac condition "more than anything else" rather than from "real drowning."

The trial court, by granting defendant's motion for nonsuit, took the case from the jury. On appeal, the judgment of nonsuit was reversed and the case remanded for trial to a jury. The court reasoned that whether death occurred by drowning or not was a question for the jury to determine. Just what would have happened had a lifeguard been present was a matter of speculation or of inference and one for the jury and not for the court. It was similarly for the jury to determine whether defendant's negligence was the proximate cause of young Rovegno's death and whether the arrangements made by defendant were such as ordinarily prudent persons, situated as defendant was, would have done.

The court also rejected defendant's contention that the deceased was bound by the notice, "Bathers using pool do so at their own risk," and therefore assumed the risk of drowning. Said the court, "This action is based upon alleged negligence, while the last suggested defense, if it be a defense, arises from contract. Even though it might have been available against the decedent had he lived and brought suit for damages on account of personal injuries, it cannot operate to defeat his mother's independent statutory right of action."[15]

A contrary result was reached by a New York court in a substantially similar action in the case of *Laut v. Brooklyn & Queens Y.M.C.A.*[16] In that case, a mother sued to recover for the death by drowning in defendant's pool of her twenty-three-year-old son. It appeared that the boy went into the pool alone. There were no attendants or supervisors or anyone else there at the time. There were posted rules in the locker rooms and in the pool, reading:

DO NOT SWIM ALONE
NOTIFY THE ATTENDANT BEFORE ENTERING THE POOL
YOU USE THE POOL AT YOUR OWN RISK
PRACTICE SAFETY FIRST

[15]*Id.* at 598, 291 P. at 850.
[16]262 A.D. 1038, 30 N.Y.S.2d 425 (2d Dep't 1941), *aff'd mem.*, 289 N.Y. 593, 43 N.E.2d 722 (1942).

The action was predicated on defendant's alleged negligence in not having an employee present in the pool for lifesaving purposes and for supervision of neophyte swimmers; failing to give the deceased any instructions as to the use of the pool under the circumstances existing at the time of the drowning; failing to supervise the pool's use so as to prevent the deceased from entering, and allowing the deceased to enter the pool knowing that no supervisors were present.

The jury returned a verdict in favor of plaintiff. The judgment entered on the verdict was reversed on appeal. The court found no affirmative evidence of negligence causing the accident, nor any evidence to warrant an inference of negligence.

Some jurisdictions, however, apply a *res ipsa loquitur* standard in drowning cases when the exact cause of death cannot be established.

BROWN V. SOUTHERN VENTURES CORP.
331 So. 2d 207 (La. App.), *cert. denied*, 334 So. 2d
211 (1976)

DOMENGEAUX, J.: "This is a wrongful death action tried by jury. Plaintiffs are the surviving spouse and children of the decedent, James Brown. Defendants are Southern Motor Lodges of Alexandria, Inc., lessee and builder of the Howard Johnson's Motor Lodge in Alexandria, Louisiana, and Insurance Company of North America, its liability insurer.

"The pertinent facts of this case are as follows:

"On the afternoon of January 14, 1973, a party was given by some Alexandria businessmen and their wives at the Bayou Room of the Howard Johnson's Motor Lodge in that city. The party was to coincide with the 'Superbowl' football game and was given for the purpose of watching the contest amid friends. At approximately 2:30 P.M. the decedent, James Brown, arrived at the gathering and began to mill about and enjoy himself. Liquor flowed freely at the party and there is evidence that Mr. Brown indulged, but no one testified that he was noticeably intoxicated. During the party a number of the guests, including Mr. Brown, noticed and commented upon a phenomenon created by a combination of the poor lights and by steam rising from the motel swimming pool some ninety-three feet away and visible from the Bayou Room. At one point during the evening the decedent and another guest planned to walk over to the pool and observe it more closely but for some reason abandoned the idea. At about 7:00 P.M. Mr. Brown and another man who remained unidentified entered the motel restaurant and each had two cups of coffee. The manager of the restaurant knew Mr. Brown and testified that he was talking rather loudly about the game with his companion but that neither man gave the impression that he was intoxicated. No one saw Mr. Brown after he left the restaurant some time after 7:00 P.M. At approximately 1:30 A.M. a city policeman found the decedent's body floating in the shallow end (four feet) of the motel swimming pool which is located near the restaurant. The coroner ruled that the cause of death was drowning. There were no witnesses.

"The defendants raise the following specifications of error:

"1. The jury erred in finding the proximate cause of Mr. Brown's death to be the allegedly dangerous condition existing around the motel swimming pool.

"2. The jury erred in failing to find that Mr. Brown's alleged intoxication contributed substantially to his death.

The Motel's Negligence

"In order to determine the duty owed to the decedent by the defendants while on the latters' premises, we must first ascertain the status which the decedent enjoyed while at the motel.

"In the case of *Savoy v. G.F. Poole Mortuary*, 60 So. 2d 108 (La. App. 1st Cir. 1952), the 'invitee' was described in the following manner: ' . . . an invitation to enter upon or use premises may be express or implied, and an invitation may be implied when the owner or occupant engages in some business which fairly indicates to the person entering the premises that his entry and use of the property is consistent with the intentions and purposes of the owner or occupant.' [Citations omitted.]

"Mr. Brown entered onto the motel property at the express invitation of his hosts, occupants of the Bayou Room. The Bayou Room is a large room used almost exclusively for parties of this type. Under the test set forth in *Savoy, supra,* we find that the motel acted in such a fashion so as to clearly indicate its intentions that the room and motel premises be used as they were by the persons attending the 'Superbowl' party. Furthermore, we find that after the termination of the party Mr. Brown became a paying customer in his own right when he purchased coffee in the restaurant. For these reasons, we are firmly of the opinion that Mr. Brown was a member of that class of persons deemed 'invitees' as far as his relationship with the motel was concerned.

"Under our jurisprudence the duty owed to an invitee is that of exercising reasonable and ordinary care including maintaining the the premises in a reasonably safe and suitable condition and warning invitees of any hidden or concealed perils which are known or reasonably discoverable. [Citations omitted.]

"On the afternoon of the decedent's funeral, approximately two days after his death, some members of his family visited the scene of the drowning. They discovered that much of the coping or slanted tile border (which extends approximately one inch over the edge of the pool wall) around the edge of the pool was loose and in a somewhat shaky or wobbly condition. In fact, one member of this party testified that all of the coping on the shallow end of the pool was loose. Mr. C. E. Ewing, Jr., a former swimming pool contractor, and now a swimming pool maintenance man, testified that he had inspected the Howard Johnson's pool in 1972 or 1973, and found that approximately 25% of the cement coping around the pool had to be replaced and that some pieces were completely loose. There was also some conflicting testimony as to the effect of standing on a piece of loose coping. One individual testified that he did not think the coping would be shaky or wobbly if a person stood on it, while others testified to the contrary. An employee of the motel, Raymond Gaines, testified that he noted some loose coping and reported that condition to the motel manager some time prior to Mr. Brown's death, however, the motel manager denies that such information was communicated to her. We find that the opinion of the majority of those witnesses who testified was that uncemented or loose coping would be more hazardous to an individual standing on it than coping which would be firmly cemented. As to the exact cause of death, Doctor Edward C. Uhrich, the physician who performed the autopsy testified as follows:

"Now, there is a condition and this could fit this case very well, where the man fell into the water and on a real cold night, and if you will check the records, it was about 36 degrees that night. He fell into the pool and I maintain that—or I think that he had a laryngeal spasm. I think that—uh—that the epiglottis here cut off his air instantly and he had no chance at all, of swimming or yelling or doing anything. I think he died from a laryngeal spasm and this his—uh—as he died, almost instantly, I think the lungs filled up with water, and all the other things happened. That's an honest opinion. That's what I told the coroner and that's what I believe and there's nobody here can shake me out of that.

"Confronted with the above outlined circumstantial evidence, the jury was forced to make a determination of the causation of Mr. Brown's death.

"We find that the principle of *res ipsa loquitur* as set forth in the case of *Boudreaux v. American Insurance Company*, 262 La. 721, 264 So. 2d 621 (La. 1972) particularly applicable to this case. In *Boudreaux* the Supreme Court stated:

"In this respect, the principle of '*res ipsa loquitur*' (the thing speaks for itself) sometimes comes into play as a rule of circumstantial evidence, whereby negligence is inferred on the part of a defendant because the facts indicate this to be the more probable cause of injury *in the absence of other as-plausible explanation* by witnesses found credible. [Citations omitted.] Thus, by this principle where properly applied, the circumstantial evidence indicates that the injury was caused by some negligence on the part of the defendant, without necessarily proving just what negligent act caused the injury. . . .

" . . . [W]e have in our most recent decision on the issue noted that the real test of applying *res ipsa loquitur* to be as follows: 'Do the facts of the controversy suggest negligence of the defendant, rather than some other factors, as the *most plausible* explanation of the accident?' *Pilie v. National Food Store*, 245 La. 276, 158 So. 2d 162, 165 (1963).

"In light of the duty which the motel owed Mr. Brown as an invitee we find a reasonable basis in the evidence to support the jury's determination that the motel breached said duty when it failed to maintain the pool in a safe condition or at least warn Mr. Brown of the potential danger attendant thereto. Furthermore, in applying the above cited doctrine of *Boudreaux*, we cannot say that the jury committed manifest error in determining that the dangerous condition in existence around the motel pool was the 'most plausible explanation' of the causation of Mr. Brown's entry into the pool."

[Discussion of decedent's contributory negligence omitted.]

10:7 *Boisterous Conduct*

In *Gordon v. Hotel Seville, Inc.,*[17] plaintiff, Ethel Gordon, sued to recover for personal injuries she suffered in defendant's swimming pool. It appeared that a number of boys were engaged in boisterous conduct and horseplay, including pushing or throwing boys into the pool, and that such activities were permitted to go unrestrained for some time.

On the day of the accident, Mrs. Gordon went into the pool at the shallow end. A short time later, while she was swimming there face down, a body landed on her, following which she blacked out or fainted, was assisted from the pool, and became hysterical. A pool attendant rendered first aid, and Mr. Gordon, husband of the plaintiff, stated in his deposition that the pool attendant made an admission to him that "these fellows picked one another up bodily and threw him into the pool, and one of them landed on her head."

The trial court granted a motion for summary judgment in defendant's favor. On appeal, the judgment was reversed and the case remanded. The causal connection between the horseplay and the injury was held to be supplied by the admission of the pool attendant, a hotel employee who was in the performance of duties as a pool attendant, that the accident resulted from the horseplay at the pool.

See also Williamson v. The Travelers Insurance Co., previously noted at section 9:12 at note 34, where horseplay was held to constitute contributory negligence barring recovery by an infant plaintiff.

In the case that follows, the Supreme Court of Appeals of West Virginia reviewed the doctrine of assumption of risk and ruled that it was reversible error for the trial court not to instruct the jury on that defense.

VENTURA v. WINEGARDNER
357 S.E. 2d 764 (1987)

BROTHERTON, J.: " . . .

"On April 27, 1984, Diane Ventura was a college senior and a member of the Rutgers tennis team. That year she had played at the number three position and compiled a 15–4 record. She was staying with the team at the Holiday Inn in Star City, West Virginia, while the team competed in the Atlantic 10 Tennis Tournament being held at West Virginia University. That night fellow members of the team surprised Diane with a water battle. She attempted to run away from her friends, and ran thirty feet beyond a walkway, into an unlit area, and fell over a steep bank. The fall injured her right knee. The injury has shown not to be a crippling one, but it has given her continuing trouble in several areas, such as climbing stairs and running or jumping, and, most notably, has interfered with her ability to play competitive tennis. She sued for negligence in the Circuit Court of Monongalia County. The jury awarded Ventura $147,000 for the injury. Holiday Inn raises several assignments of error which we now discuss. . . .

[17]105 So. 2d 175 (Fla. Dist. Ct. App. 1958), *cert. denied,* 109 So. 2d 767 (Fla. 1959).

"Holiday Inn . . . argues that Ventura had the burden of proving that the hazard, *i.e.*, the steep bank, was on Holiday Inn property or that Holiday Inn had knowledge of the dangerous condition. We agree. The owner of a hotel can only be held liable for failing to warn a guest about a defect on property not his if the property is immediately adjacent to the hotel, the hotel knew or should have known of the defect, and the defect is of such a nature that a reasonable hotel operator would have warned his guests. *See generally* Annotation, *Liability of Operator of Business Premises to Patron Injured by Condition of Adjacent Property*, 39 A.L.R.3d 579 (1971). Nevertheless, in this case it is clear that Holiday Inn knew of the defect. The area was inspected by Holiday Inn's director of safety and was quite open and obvious to all concerned. It was also an obvious hazard. Holiday Inn could hardly argue that it had never noticed the steep embankment a few feet from its property line. . . .

" . . . evidence showed that the Rutgers' women's tennis team often conducted water fights at the hotels where they stayed. During previous matches at other hotels there had been several such fights. On one occasion certain hotel rooms had to be dried out because the walls were soaked with water. Ventura had participated in some of these fights in the past. A question arises as to the extent of the innkeeper's liability for an injury to a guest caused, at least in part, by horseplay of the victim and other guests. The general rule is that the hotel must exercise reasonable care to restrain its guests where there is a foreseeable risk of danger. *See, e.g.*, syl. pt. 1, *Connolly v. Nicollet Hotel*, 254 Minn. 373, 95 N.W.2d 657 (1959), *aff'd*, 258 Minn. 405, 104 N.W.2d 721 (1960). . . .

" . . . Holiday Inn objects to the trial court's refusal of an instruction to the jury on assumption of risk. Generally, a jury instruction should be given if there is evidence in the trial which would support such an instruction and it was requested. *See* syl. pt. 2, *Brammer v. Taylor*,——W. Va.——,388 S.E.2d 207 (1985). In this case there was evidence to support an assumption of risk defense. The elements of an assumption of risk defense are: (1) knowledge of the danger; (2) an appreciation of the danger; and (3) voluntary exposure to the danger. *See Spurlin v. Nardo*, 145 W. Va. 408, 418–19, 114 S.E.2d 913, 920 (1960). Ventura knew her surroundings, having been a guest at the Holiday Inn during daylight hours and passed the area where the embankment was located going to and from her room. By her own testimony, she went running at a full sprint into a dark, unlit area, with her eyes unadjusted to the night. She testified that her field of vision was only about five feet. While Ventura may not have realized the specific danger of the embankment, she had to know that running at a fast rate of speed in the dark is a danger—a danger which any reasonable person would appreciate, and to which she voluntarily exposed herself as she ran from her team mates, who sought to throw water on her as they had in the past.

"Analogous cases support our holding that assumption of risk is a proper defense in this situation. In *Newell v. Zurich Ins. Co.*, 325 So. 2d 745 (La. App. 1976), the court upheld a judgment against the plaintiff on the grounds of assumption of risk where the plaintiff had been running across a wet sidewalk with bare feet in rainy weather. The court held that no discussion of the assumption of risk by the plaintiff was necessary. Anyone who runs on a wet sidewalk with bare feet assumes a known and well-understood danger. *See* 325 So. 2d at 747. In *Moss v. Atlanta Housing Authority,* 160 Ga. App. 555, 556, 287 S.E.2d 619, 620 (1981), the Georgia Appeals Court held that the plaintiff, a guest at the defendant's building, assumed the risk by walking into an unlit area. This case, with Ventura running into an unlit area on uncertain ground, potentially presents a stronger assumption of risk defense than either of the above cases.

"Thêre being sufficient evidence before the jury from which it could have found an assumption of risk by the plaintiff, the defendant, Holiday Inn, was entitled to an instruction on that defense. It was error for the court to withhold it.

"For the above reasons, the decision of the Circuit Court of Monongalia County is reversed, and the case is remanded for further proceedings consistent with this opinion.

"Reversed and remanded."

10:8 *Violation of Statutory Duty*

HAFT v. LONE PALM HOTEL
3 Cal. 3d 756, 478 P.2d 465 (1970)

TOBRINER, J.: "Plaintiffs Mrs. Ethel Haft and her daughter Roberta Haft appeal from a defense judgment, entered upon a jury verdict, in this wrongful death action, brought in connection with the drowning deaths of Mr. Morris M. Haft and Mark Haft, father and son, in defendants' motel pool. Plaintiffs raise numerous contentions challenging the trial court's (1) refusal to take several matters from the jury, (2) refusal to give a requested instruction, and (3) exclusion of various evidentiary matters. As we explain below, we have concluded that under the facts presented at trial, plaintiffs, in demonstrating defendants' failure to provide a lifeguard at the pool as required by statute, sustained their initial burden of proof and that defendants then bore the burden of showing that this statutory violation was not a cause of the deaths. Although defendants failed to meet this burden at the initial trial, we have determined that inasmuch as the parties' respective burdens were not clearly defined at that time, the judgment should be reversed and the cause be remanded for a new trial.

1. The Facts

"On June 26, 1961 Mr. and Mrs. Haft, and their five-year-old son Mark, traveled to Palm Springs and stayed at the Lone Palm Hotel, operated by defendants. The Lone Palm Hotel is a 90-unit motel, with rooms on both sides of a six-lane through street, Indian Avenue. The motel office, a restaurant and a swimming pool are located on the east side of Indian Avenue: on the west side there are rooms, a swimming pool and a wading pool. The Hafts were given a room on the west side and it was in the west pool that father and son drowned.

"In the morning of the day following the Hafts' arrival, the weather was typically hot for June in Palm Springs, with the temperature around 115 degrees. Mrs. Haft left to go shopping early that morning as Mr. Haft and Mark prepared to take advantage of the motel's inviting pool facilities. At trial, Mrs. Haft testified that although she could not say that her husband and son were 'real swimmers' they both could dog-paddle and tread water well enough to get around the pool; this evaluation of the decedents' swimming abilities was confirmed by Mrs. Haft's sister and brother-in-law, who had spent numerous vacations with the Hafts on prior occasions and thus were familiar with the decedents' swimming skills. Mr. Ollson, a guest at the Lone Palm on the day of the drownings, testified for the defense, however, that after hearing of the tragedy Mrs. Haft had exclaimed: "My husband, my son, I told them not to swim—' and that Mrs. Haft had also admitted that 'they couldn't swim,' 'they couldn't put their faces under water.'

"No one witnessed the actual drownings of the two Hafts. Ollson testified that on the morning of the tragedy, he first noticed the two in the wading pool and later observed them in the regular pool; he testified that he saw no other persons in the vicinity of the pools that entire morning. (The summer is off-season in Palm Springs and the motel was apparently not at all crowded.) When the Hafts were in the main pool, Ollson testified that Mr. Haft was lying on two rubber floating rafts, with Mark astride his stomach; the two were laughing and playing. At the time Ollson first observed the Hafts in the main pool, as he walked by the pool on his way to his motel room, father and son were in the shallow end; when Ollson later viewed the two from his motel room they appeared to be near the deeper end of the pool. This was apparently the last time Mr. Haft and Mark were observed alive.

"More than a half hour thereafter Ollson left his room and returned to the pool area, where he observed two bodies submerged in the deep end of the pool. At first Ollson entered the pool but, being unable to swim, found he could not reach the bodies; he then ran to his room to telephone for help. Ultimately an ambulance attendant went into the pool and retrieved the bodies.

"Although no direct evidence revealed the manner in which the drownings occurred, the evidence did establish, without conflict, that while defendants had furnished the lounging space, wading pool and swimming pool essential for their guests' recreation, the motel had failed to provide *any of the major safety measures required by law* for pools available for the use of the public.

"Thus the record shows that, with defendants' knowledge, no lifeguard was present at the pool and no sign advising guests of this fact was posted. (*See* Health & Saf. Code, § 24101.4.) No markings on the edge of the pool stated the various depths of the water or indicated the break in the slope between the deep and shallow portions of the pool (*see* Cal. Admin. Code tit. 17, § 7788). No sign warned that children were not to use the pool without an adult in attendance (*see* Cal. Admin. code, tit. 17, § 7829). No telephone numbers of the nearest ambulance, hospital, fire or police rescue services, physician and pool operator were posted in the pool area (*see id.*). No diagrammatic illustrations of artificial respiration procedures were posted, nor were there any instructions provided to indicate that, in emergencies manual or mouth-to-mouth resuscitation should be begun and continued until the arrival of a physician or mechanical resuscitator (*see id.*). No 12-foot-long life poles were available (*see id.*). In short, when measured against state safety standards, it would be difficult to find a pool that was more dangerous than the attractive facility which the Lone Palm offered its guests and in which Mr. Haft and Mark drowned.

"In failing to satisfy all of these mandatory safety requirements, which were clearly designed to protect the class of persons of which the victims were members, defendants of course were unquestionably negligent as a matter of law. [Citations omitted.] Plaintiffs requested the trial judge to direct the verdict for plaintiffs on the issue of liability or, alternatively, to instruct the jury that defendants were negligent as a matter of law and that the negligence was a proximate cause of the deaths. Plaintiffs also asked for an instruction that, under the evidence presented at trial, Mark was not contributorily negligent as a matter of law.

"Defendants contended, in response, that the facts did not establish the requisite causation as a matter of law, and also maintained that, under the evidence, the jury should be permitted to find that the wrongful death action as to either or both decedents was barred by contributory negligence. The trial judge, apparently agreeing with the defendants, declined to take either the issue of negligence and proximate causation or the issue of the minor's contributory negligence from the jury. The jury returned a verdict for all defendants on both causes of action.

"Plaintiffs raise several contentions on this appeal. Initially, they assert that the trial judge erred in declining to find that defendant's most serious statutory violation—the failure to provide lifeguard services or to erect a sign so notifying their guests—constituted a proximate cause of the deaths as a matter of law. Second, plaintiffs strongly urge that absolutely no evidence supports a finding that Mark Haft, a five-year-seven-month-old child in the care of his father, was contributorily negligent, and that the court thus committed error in permitting the jury so to find. Third, plaintiffs challenge the trial court's exclusion of certain inspection reports which they argue were clearly relevant to the issue of defendants' alleged 'willful and wanton misconduct.'

"We proceed to discuss each of these contentions in turn.

2. *Under the facts in the instant case plaintiffs, in proving defendants' violation of the statutory lifeguard requirement, sustained their initial burden of proof on the issue of causation; the burden then shifted to defendants to show that their violation was not a proximate cause of the deaths.*

"Although the proof of the numerous statutory and regulatory safety violations established defendants' negligence as a matter of law, this proof of negligence alone, of course, did not automatically establish liability; plaintiffs still bore the initial burden of showing that defendants' negligence was a proximate cause of the deaths. [Citation omitted.] Of course the breach of a statutory duty itself will often suffice to give rise to an inference from which a jury may find that a given injury was the actual and proximate result of the violation. [Citations omitted.] The jury returned a verdict for defendants, however, and defendants now argue that in the light of this verdict, we must infer that the jury concluded that plaintiffs failed to establish the requisite causal relationship between any of the negligent violations and the fatal accidents.

"Plaintiffs, however, contend here, as they did before the trial court, that the evidence established as a matter of law that defendants' breach of the most significant safety regulation—the statuory lifeguard requirement—was a proximate cause of the deaths and that the issue properly should not have been submitted to the jury at all. For the reasons discussed below, we have concluded that after plaintiffs proved that defendants failed to provide a lifeguard or to post a warning sign, the burden shifted to defendants to show the absence of a lifeguard did not cause the deaths. Because these respective burdens were not clear at the time of the initial trial, we have determined that justice will best be served by a remand of the cause for a new trial.

"Clearly, the failure to provide a lifeguard greatly enhanced the chances of the occurrence of the instant drownings. In proving (1) the defendants were negligent in this respect, and (2) that the available facts, at the very least, strongly suggest that a competent lifeguard, exercising reasonable care, would have prevented the deaths, plaintiffs have gone as far as they possibly can under the circumstances in proving the requisite causal link between defendants' negligence and the accidents. To require plaintiffs to establish 'proximate causation' to a greater certainty than they have in the instant case, would permit defendants to gain the advantage of the lack of proof inherent in the lifeguardless situation which they have created. [Citations omitted.] Under these circumstances the burden of proof on the issue of causation should be shifted to defendants to absolve themselves if they can.

a. Under section 24101.4 pool owners who fail either to provide lifeguard services or to post a sign warning of the absence of a lifeguard are, as a matter of statutory policy, responsible for the consequences attributable to a failure to provide lifeguard services.

"Section 24101.4 of the Health and Safety Code provides that for swimming pools such as the one involved in the instant case 'lifeguard service shall be provided or signs shall be erected clearly indicating that such service is not provided.' The evidence clearly establishes that defendants neither provided 'lifeguard service' nor erected a sign warning of the absence of a lifeguard. At trial plaintiffs requested an instruction that defendants' violation of this section was a proximate cause of the deaths of the two Hafts as a matter of law. Plaintiffs argued that since defendants had failed to comply with the alternative of erecting a sign, they were under a mandatory obligation to provide lifeguard service; given this duty, plaintiffs urged that any reasonable jury would be compelled to conclude from the facts disclosed at trial that the presence of a reasonably attentive lifeguard would have averted the tragedies. The merit of plaintiffs' argument turns initially on the accuracy of their reading of the duty imposed by section 24101.4. . . . That section recognizes that a primary obligation of 'public' pool ownership is the maintenance of adequate 'life guard service'; the section, however, does permit owners of certain public pools to satisfy their primary duty of providing 'lifeguard services' by erecting a sign 'clearly indicating' that no lifeguard is on duty.

"Defendants suggest that since their pool falls into the category of pools in which the statutory obligation would be satisfied by the posting of an adequate sign, the consequences of their failure to meet the statutory demands ought to be limited to harm caused by the non-erection of the warning notice. The language of the section makes clear, however, that the underlying requirement of this statute, for pools of *either* category, is the provision of 'lifeguard service,' and we believe that the legislative intent would be nullified if a pool owner were permitted to avoid this important requirement by pointing to the fact that he *failed* to comply with the statutory substitute as well.

"Defendants' factual argument in this case duly illustrates the manner in which the protection afforded by section 24101.4 would be undermined by an adoption of their interpretation of this requirement. Although they failed to fulfill either statutory alternative, defendants attempt to avoid liability by contending that since the decedents were the only people in the pool area, the absence of a lifeguard must have been obvious; if the absence of a life guard was obvious, the argument continues, defendants' failure to post a sign notifying decedents of this absence could be of no significance. Defendants thus conclude that this negligence was not a 'proximate cause' of the resulting injury. We have no doubt that this is an argument which would commonly be made by noncomplying pool owners in such cases.

"Although there is some superficial persuasiveness in such a position, the main strength of the argument derives not from its own merit but, instead, from the difficulty of proof facing an injured party attempting to counter this position. The sign required by section 24101.4 and California Administrative Code, title 17, section 7829 does considerably more than indicate to potential swimmers that no lifeguard is present. It gives notice of the general hazards present in the given swimming pool and most importantly serves as a *continuing warning* of the potential danger to the novice swimmer; the mere absence of a lifeguard hardly provides such cautionary advice.

"A pool owner, however, can facilely assert that a given individual would have gone in swimming even if there had been a 'no lifeguard' sign posted; it is quite difficult in contrast, for a plaintiff, especially in a wrongful death action, to prove that a warning sign would have had the intended cautionary effect. We do not believe that the Legislature, in giving some pool owners the option of fulfilling the lifeguard requirement by posting an adequate sign, intended, in effect, to withdraw the protection of section 24101.4 in a significant percentage of all cases. Yet, because of the uncertainty surrounding the probable effectiveness of a sign, such substantial eradication of the provision would be the practical result of an adoption of defendant's construction of section 24101.4. In view of the ease with which a pool owner can comply with this section, we cannot choose defendants' construction and remain faithful to the salutary policies underlying this provision.

"Moreover, as stated above, to hold that a pool owner, who has failed to satisfy either of the section's alternative requirements, may limit his liability to that resulting from his 'lesser' failure to erect a sign, would of course effectively read out of the section the primary requirement of providing life guard service. To avoid this undermining of the vital purposes underlying the lifeguard provision, we interpret the section as requiring that the liability of a pool owner, who has neither provided a lifeguard nor erected a warning sign, be measured with respect to his wrongful omission to provide lifeguard services. The Court of Appeal so held in *Lucas v. Hesperia Golf & Country Club* (1967) 255 Cal. App. 2d 241, 251 [63 Cal. Rptr. 189], and we concur in that conclusion.

b. Upon defendants' failure to provide lifeguard services, the burden shifted to them to prove that their violation was not a proximate cause of the deaths; in the absence of such proof, defendants' causation of such death is established as a matter of law.

"Defendant's failure to provide lifeguard service is of course only of consequence if such negligence was a 'proximate cause' of either or both of the drownings at issue in the instant case. In view of the absence of any direct evidence on the actual events which resulted in the deaths of the father and son, the problem of 'causation' has loomed large in this case from the very outset.

"In analyzing this 'causation' issue, we must preliminarily reject defendants' contention that the alleged negligence of Mr. Haft could properly be considered as an 'intervening,' and 'superseding' cause which 'broke the chain of proximate causation' with respect to the deaths of father or son. Without doubt, one of the principal dangers in swimming pools that the statutory lifeguard requirement sought to control, was the danger to careless swimming novices who might negligently overrate their aquatic skills. That some swimmers would be imperiled through their own negligence was clearly one of the foreseeable risks which motivated the issuance of section 24101.4's requirements; under recognized principles [citations omitted] such negligence could not properly be designated as a 'superseding cause' which would automatically relieve defendant of all liability.

"The fallacy of defendants' contention as to 'superseding cause' is perhaps most clearly illuminated by its application to the cause of action relating to the death of five-year-old Mark. In that context the claim that defendants' responsibility to Mark was 'cut off' by Mr. Haft's alleged negligence is in reality no more than an attempt to resurrect the doctrine of 'imputed contributory negligence' between a minor and his parent, a theory which the California courts have long repudiated. [Citations omitted.] The 'imputed contributory negligence' formula transferred the negligence of a parent (in not carefully supervising his child [citation omitted] to a plaintiff child so as to bar the child's recovery against an admittedly negligent defendant; defendants seek to obtain a like dispensation through the jury's application (in reality, misapplication) of the nebulous 'superseding cause' doctrine. This argument has no more merit phrased in 'superseding cause' terms than it had in the context of 'imputed contributory negligence.' [Citations omitted.]

"Our rejection of defendants' 'superseding cause' theory, however, does not in itself resolve the question of whether, on the basis of the facts adduced at trial, the absence of a lifeguard was a proximate cause of the deaths as a matter of law. The troublesome problems concerning the causation issue in the instant case of course arise out of the total lack of direct evidence to the precise manner in which the drownings occurred. Although the paucity of evidence on causation is normally one of the burdens that must be shouldered by a plaintiff in proving his case, the evidentiary void in the instant action results primarily from defendents' failure to provide a lifeguard to observe occurrences within the pool area. The main purpose of the lifeguard requirement is undoubtedly to aid those in danger, but an attentive guard does serve the subsidiary function of witnessing those accidents that do occur. The absence of such a lifeguard in the instant case thus not only stripped decedents of a significant degree of protection to which they are entitled, but also deprived the present plaintiffs of a means of definitively establishing the facts leading to the drownings.

"Without such a shift in the burden of proof in the instant case, the promise of substantial protection held out by our statutory lifeguard requirement will be effectively nullified in a substantial number of cases. One purpose of the statute is to prevent a drowning in a pool where no one else is present to witness it and possibly prevent it. If the pool owner can disregard the statute and retreat to the sanctuary of the argument that the plaintiff must prove the 'cause' of the death which obviously is unknown he can, without liability, expose his paying patron to the very danger that the statute would avoid. Since the pool-owner violates the statute, since he creates the dangerous condition and exercises control over it, since the death occurs upon his premises with which he is familiar, since he profits from the presence of the pool, he cannot take refuge in the position that the burden of proof rests with the probable victim of his statutory violation.

"Under the facts presented at the initial trial defendants did not sustain their burden on this issue and thus theoretically the court erred in declining to take the matter from the jury. Because the obligation of defendants to bear the burden on this issue was not clearly defined at the time of the trial, however, principles of fairness counsel that defendants be afforded the opportunity of meeting that burden of proof. [Citations omitted.] Under these circumstances, we reverse the judgment and remand the case for a new trial, at which both parties will be fully advised as to their respective burdens. . . .

3. The trial court erred in refusing to instruct the jury that Mark Haft was not contributorily negligent as a matter of law.

"At trial plaintiffs requested an instruction that 'the evidence in this case fails to show any negligence on the part of the decedent Mark Brian Haft. . . . ' The trial judge refused to give this instruction, but instead instructed the jury, on defendants' request, that 'if you find from a preponderance of the evidence *ei-*

ther decedent was guilty of negligence which contributed as a proximate cause of his death, no recovery of damages may be had by *the plaintiffs for the death of that decedent who was contributorily negligent . . .* ' (original italics). We agree with plaintiff's contention that on the evidence presented the trial court erred in failing to give the instruction which they requested.

"We note initially that plaintiffs do not suggest that they were entitled to the requested instruction simply by virtue of Mark's tender age [citations omitted]; rather plaintiffs ground their contention on the failure of defendants to introduce sufficient evidence with respect to an issue on which defendants bore the burden of proof. Under traditional standards plaintiffs were entitled to have the question of Mark's contributory negligence withdrawn from the jury if 'disregarding conflicting evidence and giving to [defendants'] evidence all the value to which it is legally entitled . . . the result is a determination that there is no evidence of sufficient substantiality to support' a finding that the drowned child was contributorily negligent. [Citation omitted.] ' "In order to justify the submission of any question of fact to a jury, the proof must be sufficient to raise more than a mere conjecture or surmise that the fact is as alleged. It must be such that a rational . . . mind can reasonably draw from it the conclusion that the fact exists, and when the evidence is not sufficient to draw such inference, the court should refuse to submit the question to the jury." ' [Citations omitted.]

"Although some evidence indicated that Mark was not a good swimmer and possibly demonstrated that Mark was sufficiently familiar with swimming pools to appreciate their potential dangers to him *if he were by himself,* all the testimony presented at trial disclosed that Mark was *not* by himself but, instead, under the direct care and supervision of his father. Even if a child of Mark's age, size, intelligence and capacity should reasonably have been aware of the dangers of the pool, no one could reasonably find such a child 'negligent' in entering the pool under his parent's instruction and guidance. Although we might take judicial notice of the increasing tendency of children to question and challenge their parents, surely even the most 'liberated' five-year old cannot reasonably be expected to reject a father's invitation to play with him in the 'adult' swimming pool.

"From all the available information, Mark only entered the large pool, where he met his death, with the consent and under the direction of his father and remained in the pool only under the most direct supervision of his parent. Viewing these facts in the light most favorable to defendants, we cannot find evidence of sufficient substantiality to support a finding of Mark's contributory negligence. In the event that equivalent evidence is presented at a new trial, plaintiffs would be entitled to have this issue withdrawn from the jury's consideration.

"A careful review of the California precedents and of the case law of our sister states has not disclosed a single instance in which a young child was found negligent while following the instructions of his parent; rather, minor children have been held contributorily negligent only in situations in which the child was acting either without or contrary to parental or similar guidance. [Citations omitted.] In cases in which an accident occurred while a parent was in direct control of the child's actions, courts have traditionally analyzed the propriety of permitting a defense of contributory negligence only in terms of the viability of the doctrine of 'imputed contributory negligence,' which imputes the negligence of the *parent* to the child to bar recovery. [Citations omitted.] In looking only to the negligence of the controlling parent in these instances, the numerous decisions reflect a generally unspoken premise that a child, obeying the directions of his parent, cannot reasonably be found to be negligent in his own right.

"The judgment of the Superior Court of Los Angeles County is reversed and the cause is remanded for further proceedings consistent with this opinion."

In the case below, the Florida District Court of Appeal reviewed the scope and effect of the negligence *per se* role in a drowning which occurred in a hotel swimming pool.

FIRST OVERSEAS INVESTMENT CORP. v. COTTON
491 So. 2d. 293, 79 A.L.R. 4th 455 (Fla. App. 1986)

HENDRY, J.: "Defendants First Overseas Investment Corp. d/b/a Monte Carlo Hotel and its insurers appeal a final judgment in favor of plaintiffs . . . in plaintiffs' action for wrongful death. . . .

"At trial the following testimony was adduced. Cleophus Cotton and his wife were guests at the Monte Carlo Hotel (hotel). Mr. Cotton went swimming in the shallow end of the hotel pool. The pool water was extremely cloudy as the pool attendant had that morning dumped a bucketful of soda ash into it to 'sweeten' the pH. The pool attendant testified that the pool's soda ash feeder was inoperable, hence his practice of dumping the soda ash directly into the pool. Expert testimony was offered that soda ash should never be dumped directly into a pool and that a bucketful was ten to twelve times more than is needed. Soda ash increases turbidity and makes the water cloudy until completely filtered. The pool attendant testified that he had no training in first aid or in the use of lifesaving apparatus. He further testified that the pool's filtration system was inoperable. The pool did not have lifesaving apparatus such as a shepherd's hook, an elevated lifeguard's chair, or first aid equipment.

"Michael Wolfe testified that he observed Mr. Cotton swimming in the shallow end of the pool. Mr. Wolfe turned away from the pool for about 60 seconds and when he looked back, Mr. Cotton was gone. Mr. Wolfe went to the side of the pool and looked for Mr. Cotton, but did not see him. He asked another hotel guest, Daniel Jones, if he had seen Mr. Cotton. Mr. Jones indicated that he had not seen him. Mr. Wolfe told the pool attendant that he thought Mr. Cotton was in the pool. The pool attendant and Mr. Wolfe stood at the edge of the pool and looked for Mr. Cotton, but still did not see him. Subsequently, Mr. Wolfe and Mr. Jones began swimming the length of the pool at the bottom, looking for Mr. Cotton. They testified that they did not find Mr. Cotton on the bottom until they were practically on top of him. They then brought him up to the side of the pool. Mr. Jones ran down the beach to get a lifeguard. A lifeguard was located by Mr. Jones. The lifeguard attempted to resuscitate Mr. Cotton, but his efforts were unsuccessful, as were the efforts of a fire rescue squad which arrived at the scene shortly after the lifeguard.

"Mr. Wolfe testified that twelve to twenty minutes elapsed between the time he first started looking for Mr. Cotton and the time resuscitation efforts were first made. According to expert testimony, there was a high probability of Mr. Cotton's survival if he had been rescued within four to five minutes after disappearing. It was plaintiffs' contention that Mr. Cotton would have been rescued within four to five minutes and would not have drowned if the hotel had complied with the following Florida Department of Health and Rehabilitative Services (HRS) rules:

Rule 10D–5.66(3)

"All items of equipment designed for recirculation, filtration, disinfection, and pool water treatment, shall be kept in service at all times and shall be properly maintained to perform the functions of the units and protect the swimming pool water from contamination.

Rule 10D–5.68(6)

"Clearness—At all times the pool water shall be sufficiently clear so that the main drain or drains are clearly defined when viewed from the pool deck.

Rule 10D–5.81(1)

"All owners, managers, and/or other attendants in charge of a public swimming pool shall be responsible for supervision and safety of the pool. The attendant, if provided, shall be in full charge of bathing, shall have authority to enforce all rules, and shall be trained in first aid and the use of lifesaving apparatus.

Rule 10D–5.81(2)

"Lifesaving apparatus—All swimming pools shall be provided with a shepherd's hook securely attached to a one piece pole not less than sixteen (16) feet in length, and at least one (1) eighteen (18) inch diameter lifesaving ring with sufficient rope attached to reach all parts of the pool from the pool deck. Lifesaving apparatus shall be mounted in a conspicuous place and be readily available for use. Pools greater than fifty (50) feet in length shall have multiple units with at least one (1) shepherd's hook and one (1) lifesaving ring located along each of the longer sides of the pool.

Rule 10D–5.81(3)

"Lifeguard chairs—One elevated lifeguard chair of [sic] platform shall be provided for pools having over two thousand (2,000) square feet up to four thousand (4,000) square feet of pool water surface area. One additional lifeguard chair or platform shall be provided for each two thousand (2,000) square feet, or major fraction thereof, of pool water surface area above four thousand (4,000) square feet. The lifeguard chair(s) or platform(s) shall be located to allow a clear and unobstructed view of the pool bottom in the area of surveillance.

Rule 10D–5.81(6)

"First aid equipment and materials—Each pool shall have available first aid equipment and materials sufficient for use in connection with injuries which may occur in the pool or on the pool deck.

"Plaintiffs contended that Mr. Cotton would not have drowned if the pool's filtration system had been operating properly; the water in the pool had been clear; an elevated lifeguard chair had been in place affording a clear and unobstructed view of the pool; there had been lifesaving apparatus and first aid equipment available; and the pool attendant had been trained in the use of lifesaving apparatus and first aid. . . .

"The jury found the hotel negligent and awarded damages to plaintiffs. A final judgment was entered pursuant to the verdict. . . .

"The primary contention raised by defendants on appeal is that the trial court erred in giving a negligence per se instruction with regard to the violation of the six HRS rules. We disagree.

"The well established rule is that it is 'negligence *per se*' for a defendant to violate a statute which establishes a duty to protect a particular class of persons from a particular type of injury. [Citations omitted]. This applies to violations of HRS rules as well. *H.K. Corp. v. Estate of Miller*, 405 So. 2d 218 (Fla. 3d D.C.A. 1981). We find that all of the HRS rules at issue obligated the hotel to protect a particular class of persons (guests using the pool), from a particular type of harm (drowning). All of the rules were designed to ensure a clear view of swimmers in distress and/or the capability of saving them from drowning. This is consistent with our holding in *H.K. Corp. v. Estate of Miller*, that the violation of an HRS rule prescribing minimum water depths for diving boards at public swimming pools was negligence *per se*. We found in *H.K. Corp.*, 405 So. 2d at 219, that the rule 'obligated the hotel to protect a particular class of persons (swimming pool divers), from a particular type of harm (hitting the bottom of the pool).' *Cf. Kelly v. Koppers Co.*, 293 So. 2d 763 (Fla. 3d D.C.A.) (HRS rule requiring floors and walls of swimming pools to be light in color was promulgated for purposes of sanitation, health and cleanliness, and not for safety purposes), *cert. denied*, 302 So. 2d 415 (Fla. 1974). Therefore, we find the trial court did not err in instructing the jury that violations of the HRS rules were negligence *per se*.

"We have considered the remaining issues raised by defendants and find them to be without merit. . . .

"Affirmed."

In *Quality Inn South, Inc. v. Weiss*,[18] the Florida District Court of Appeal ruled as a matter of law that a guest who dove into a swimming pool, hit bottom,

---

[18]505 So. 2d 509 (Fla. App. 1987).

and was injured could not recover. The basis for the ruling was that no proof was offered to show that either the construction, design, or maintenance of the pool was defective or otherwise created an unreasonable risk of harm.

10:9   Comparative Knowledge of Operator and Injured Party as Test of Liability

A swimming-pool operator may be held liable for injuries caused in connection with use of a swimming pool, the dangerous character of which is known to him but is not known to the injured patron.

GAULT v. TABLADA

400 F. Supp. 136 (S.D. Miss. 1975), *aff'd*, 526 F.2d 1405 (5th Cir. 1976)

NIXON, D.J.: "The decedent's mother, Jo Ann Gault, was employed as a waitress in the restaurant at the defendants' motel (Moody's) by Mrs. Elizabeth Bond, its manager, who oversaw the entire operation of the defendant's motel, including the restaurant, lounge and motel itself, after having been recommended by Mrs. Gertrude Kimm, the assistant manager and supervisor of the morning shift, which included the restaurant operation, to whom Mrs. Gault had applied for a job.

"Moody's consisted of seventy-three rental units, including nine apartments, and employed approximately sixty-five persons in its several departments at its rather extensive location on the north side of U.S. Highway 90 in Gulfport, Mississippi.

"Pursuant to the suggestion of the defendants' management, Mr. and Mrs. Gault and their six children, including the deceased minor, moved into Apartment 'A' at Moody's as paying guests where they resided until approximately one week subsequent to the drowning death of Maynard, Jr., paying a rental of $130.00 per month. Although Mrs. Gault was discharged as a waitress by Moody's on February 14, 1974, she, Mr. Gault and the children continued to reside as tenants in their apartment on the premises and were business invitees at the time that their six and one-half year old son drowned in the defendants' swimming pool which was provided for the use and enjoyment of all paying guests or business invitees. When they did vacate the premises of their own volition after Maynard, Jr., drowned, their rent was fully paid.

"Maynard Gault, Jr., a twin brother of Marcy Ann, was six and one-half years of age at the time of his death on February 18, 1974, when he drowned in Moody's swimming pool at the motel late in the afternoon. Earlier that day he had accompanied his mother and his brother, John, to a nearby store to purchase groceries and to sell some bottles which the children had collected. While there, the two boys bought some bright colored balloons and after arriving back at their apartment went out to play while Mrs. Gault began preparing supper for the children and her husband, who usually arrived home at approximately 5:30 or 6:00 P.M. from his job as an 'oiler' of heavy equipment used in mechanical construction at Litton Industries in Pascagoula, approximately thirty-five miles away. He regularly worked during the week and on holidays and overtime whenever such work was available.

"When Mr. Gault arrived home on February 18, 1974 at approximately 5:30 P.M. he inquired of the whereabouts of John and Maynard, Jr. and was informed by Mrs. Gault that they were out playing. He sent one of his daughters to the pool area to look for them because that child had stated that they had been playing around the pool which was located on the defendants' premises a short distance south of their apartment. This child came back and informed the Gaults that Maynard, Jr. was 'down in the pool,' at which time Mr. and Mrs. Gault ran to the pool area and observed Maynard, Jr.'s body at the bottom of the pool in its deepest part. Mr. Gault dived into the pool and retrieved Maynard's body, handing it to Mrs. Gault who, together with another guest at the motel, began administrating artificial respiration and also attempted to utilize oxygen from a small tank which was owned by another guest. The child was rushed to Memorial Hospital in Gulfport where he was pronounced dead on arrival as a result of drowning.

"Maynard, Jr. did not enjoy swimming and could not swim, although he could 'dog paddle' a little. He, unlike some of the other Gault children, did not like the water but had played frequently in the swimming pool area, although he had been cautioned by both Mr. and Mrs. Gault about playing in that area. Samuel Wright, a former maintenance man for the defendants, testified that he had previously run the deceased child away from the pool area on one occasion as he had likewise done to many other small children practically every day that he worked at Moody's for a period of approximately one year prior to the time that Maynard, Jr. drowned. It was established that Moody's experienced considerable trouble with minor children playing in the pool area, particularly in the summertime when the pool was being utilized. The defendants' manager also had cautioned the deceased child to stay away from the pool area on other occasions, and she and Mrs. Kimm, the assistant manager, acknowledged that the Gault children frequently played in the area of the pool and the restaurant, which was located near the pool, and that they and other children frequently ran around the motel premises in the pool area which was easily accessible to children.

"Mrs. Bond, the defendants' manager, acknowledged that she felt 'someone was going to get hurt around the pool area, and that the minor Gault child did, i.e., he drowned.'

"Mr. Wright, the defendants' former maintenance man, frequently talked to and played with Maynard, Jr. and earlier on the afternoon that he drowned had been requested by the child to fill his last balloon with water but the laundry room was already closed for the day and this could not be done. When the child's body was found, his balloon was observed floating in the swimming pool.

"On the date of the drowning the swimming pool was full of leaves and was very dirty. It had not been drained after the summer season, and in fact was not capable of being drained, according to Mrs. Bond. It was not covered, although

Mrs. Bond admitted that she knew that it could have been, and there was no rope or any safety or lifesaving equipment at or near the pool and no life guard had at any time been assigned to duty at the swimming pool. There were no signs posted at or near the pool at the time that Maynard, Jr. drowned, and although Mrs. Bond testified that there was a sign posted during the summer which had been taken down for painting at the time of the Gault child's drowning, she did not relate what the sign stated nor was there any offer of the sign or any picture thereof. The former maintenance man testified that during the entire year that he had worked at Moody's prior to the time of this drowning that he had never seen any sign of any kind containing rules or regulations posted in the area of the swimming pool, and the Court finds that there was none. Although there was a four foot metal fence enclosing the entire pool there were approximately four openings for entrance to the pool through this fence with no gates thereon.

"The evidence further disclosed that although Mrs. Gault was a very competent waitress, nevertheless she had a tendency to drink alcoholic beverages and that she and Mr. Gault had had a violent argument which involved some physical contact in the lounge at Moody's while she was off duty. On another occasion, when she was called to perform special work after her regular duty hours approximately two weeks prior to Maynard, Jr.'s drowning she was intoxicated, and spilled some food and was discharged. There was no evidence either that she had imbibed on or shortly before the date on which Maynard, Jr. drowned.

"Despite the fact that Moody's management testified concerning the alleged trouble that they had with the Gault children, including the two year old baby, running unsupervised around the court and their consequent admonitions to Mrs. Gault, they at no time had ever requested the Gaults to vacate the premises or took any steps to discharge Mrs. Gault for that reason. Neither had they placed any gates around the pool area, covered the pool nor provided any other safety measures or equipment at or near the pool area despite their knowledge that many children, both guests and neighborhood children, frequented the pool area and had to be frequently run away, and were fully aware of the danger to these children because of the water-filled unprotected pool.

"Mr. and Mrs. Gault were required to work in order to support themselves and their children, and employed a baby sitter to watch the six minor children during that period of time.

"Maynard Gault, Jr. was a shy, introverted child who did not easily make friends. He and the other Gault children, with the exception of the two year old baby, were attending school, Maynard, Jr. being a first grade student who had been put into a 'special education' class because his principal was of the opinion that he was 'immature' and had a learning disability.

"When his body was recovered from the swimming pool, he was fully clothed wearing long pants, a shirt, shoes and socks, which makes it rather doubtful that he was engaged in swimming at the time that he drowned, but in all probability was attempting to fill his balloon with water from the pool in view of the conversation which he had had with the maintenance man and the fact that his balloon was found partially filled with air and floating on the pool when his body was recovered from the bottom thereof.

"Although Mr. and Mrs. Gault at times did not enjoy a harmonious marital relationship, they nevertheless loved and were concerned about their children, including Maynard, Jr., who was a rather affectionate child. This was evidenced by the testimony of the former maintenance man and Mrs. Kimm, whom Maynard, Jr. finally befriended in response to her friendly overtures toward him.

"This Court has jurisdiction of the parties and of the subject matter.

"In this diversity case this Court is . . . bound to apply the substantive law of the State of Mississippi to the foregoing facts.

"In *Mock v. Natchez Garden Club*, 230 Miss. 377, 92 So. 2d 562 (1957), 8 A.L.R.2d 1315, the Mississippi Supreme Court held that the owner or operator of a bathing resort and swimming pool owed a duty to use ordinary or reasonable care for the safety of patrons or to guard against injury to them, and must exercise reasonable care and diligence to provide a reasonably safe place or accommodations and maintain the premises in a reasonably safe condition for their use. This duty varies according to the risk involved and the age of the invitees on the premises, and the defendents were bound to consider whether the pool area, although perhaps safe enough for adult guests, presented any reasonably avoidable dangers to children of tender age. [Citations omitted.] Thus, the known presence of Maynard, Jr. as well as various other children who were guests at the defendants' motel, imposed a duty of care upon the defendants commensurate with the facts and circumstances then existing. [Citations omitted.] It was established without dispute that minor children were accustomed to playing around the pool premises and that the management and the employees of the motel were aware of this and of the danger presented thereby, yet failed to take any reasonable steps or do anything to discharge their foregoing duties to protect them, including the plaintiff's decedent. [Citation omitted.]

"In *City of Jacksonville v. Stokes* . . . [74 So. 2d 278 (Fla. 1954)] the Court in discussing the actions of minor children stated: 'It takes more indication of danger to alert a child than to alert an adult. "Children are necessarily lacking in the knowledge of physical causes and effects. . . . They must be expected to act upon childish instincts and impulses, and must be presumed to have less ability to take care of themselves than adults have." '

"In spite of the fact that many minor children stayed at the defendants' motel with their parents, including the Gault children, with the full knowledge and realization of the defendants through their management, that it was necessary to chase the children, including the minor plaintiff, away from the pool area on several occasions prior to the date that Maynard Gault, Jr. drowned, and that the defendants' manager was fully aware of the existence of danger presented to children playing in the pool area, nevertheless (1) no life guard was ever assigned to duty at the defendants' pool, even during the summertime or the swimming season when the pool was being fully utilized; (2) although a four foot high fence had been erected around the pool, there were four openings therein on which no gates had ever been hung or placed; (3) no cover had ever been placed over this pool at any time during the off-swimming season, including the period in question, to protect minor children who were playing near the pool from falling therein and drowning; and (4) there was no lifesaving equipment owned or utilized by the defendants or warning signs or instructions posted near the pool.

"In view of the foregoing undisputed facts, this Court finds and is of the opinion that the defendants wholly failed to discharge their duty to use reasonable and ordinary care to provide protection for minor children playing at or near its swimming pool. They were therefore negligent and their negligence was the sole proximate cause of Maynard Gault, Jr.'s death by drowning.

"As the defendants concede in their post-trial Proposed Findings of Fact and Conclusions of Law submitted to this Court, a minor child under the age of seven is not possessed with that discretion which would permit him to be charged with any contributory negligence. [Citations omitted.]

"Neither can this Court say that under all the facts and circumstances of this case that the deceased's father or mother was guilty of any contributory negligence which proximately caused or contributed to cause the drowning death of their six and one-half year old minor child. [Citation omitted.] [E]ven if Mrs. Gault had been negligent and her negligence had proximately contributed to cause the death of Maynard, Jr. which this Court does not find, the other plaintiffs had a separate and independent right to unmitigated recovery of all damages incurred by them through the loss of a minor child. [Citations omitted.] . . . "

The following case involving a federal district court ruling applies Georgia law to deny a motion for summary judgment for defendant hotel. The case reviews the death of a three-year-old child whose father was a hotel guest. Questions of the child's status, whether contributory negligence or assumption of risk defenses are available as to the child and, separately, as to the parents, are examined.

ENGLISH V. 1ST AUGUSTA LTD.
614 F. Supp. 1406 (S.D. Ga. 1985)

BOWEN, D.J.: " . . . Defendants own and operate the Oasis Motor Hotel located in Augusta, Georgia. Plaintiffs have brought this action seeking to hold the defendants legally responsible for the death of plaintiffs' three-year-old son. The child drowned in the swimming pool at the Oasis while visiting his father who was staying at the hotel. Plaintiffs seek to recover damages for their son's funeral expenses and for his pain and suffering. They also seek to recover damages for the loss of services of their minor child and for the full value of his life. Additionally, plaintiffs seek punitive damages.

"Jurisdiction is based upon diversity of citizenship and is not disputed.

"The complaint states twelve specific allegations of negligence. In summary, plaintiffs allege that defendants negligently maintained the pool. As defendants concede, the allegations of negligence are taken as true for purposes of considering the motion for summary judgment. Defendants argue that they are entitled to summary judgment, however, because the plaintiffs were aware of the pool's defects. According to defendants, 'the plaintiffs were aware of the alleged conditions of the premises which they now contend were dangerous, yet the plaintiffs failed to prevent the child from being in a position where he could enter the pool area alone, which failure led to the tragic drowning.' (Defendants' Brief in Support of Motion for Summary Judgment at 2.) In other words, the defendants' 'summary judgment motion is premised on the failure of the parents to properly supervise and care for their child as required by Georgia law.' (*Id.* at 7)

"Whether or not plaintiffs and defendants were negligent as a matter of fact or law is a matter of dispute. What is clear is that the child was not negligent as a matter of law. A child of three years of age is conclusively presumed to be incapable of contributory negligence. Further, any negligence on the part of the parents is not imputable to the child. *See, e.g., Hyde v. Bryant,* 114 Ga. App. 535, 537, 151 S.E.2d 925, 926 (1966). *See also* Ga. Code Ann. § 51-2-1(b) (1982) ('In an action by an infant, the fault of the parent or of custodians selected by the parents is not imputable to the child.') Therefore, if plaintiffs are barred from recovery, they are barred by their own negligence or assumption of the risk.

"Defendants have argued that the plaintiffs were aware of the alleged defective condition in which the pool was maintained. A review of the transcripts of the deposition testimony of the plaintiffs reveals that they were aware, prior to the death of their child, of the conditions at the Oasis Motel which they now contend were unreasonably dangerous. Defendants insist that they are not relying upon a theory of contributory negligence. Rather, defendants argue that the 'equal knowledge' of the pool's defects requires judgment for the defendants as a matter of law.

"Knowledge alone, however, will not bar plaintiffs' recovery. The plaintiffs must have been aware of the danger inherent in the conditions surrounding the pool and not merely aware of the existence of the conditions. *Robinson v. Western International Hotels,* 170 Ga. App. 812, 814, 318 S.E.2d 235, 237 (1984). Further, although the knowledge a party possesses is an element to consider when determining whether the party was negligent or assumed the risk of injury, that consideration is in most instances for a jury. This Court is unwilling to declare as a matter of law that the plaintiffs' negligence, if any, was *the* 'proximate cause' of the child's death or that the plaintiffs assumed the risk of their child's death. *Keating v. Jones Development of Missouri, Inc.,* 398 F.2d 1011 (5th Cir. 1968); [Georgia State citations omitted]; *Butler v. Sports Haven International,* 563 P.2d 1245 (Utah S. Ct. 1977); *Kandrach v. Chrisman,* 63 Tenn. App. 393, 473 S.W.2d 193, 198 (1971); *Lynch v. Motel Enterprises, Inc.,* 248 S.C. 490, 151 S.E.2d 435, 437 (1966). 'Even when evidence in a case is not in conflict, the determination of negligence is ordinarily within the province of the trier of fact because of the peculiarly elusive nature of negligence and the necessity that the trier of fact assess the reasonableness of the conduct under all the circumstances.' *Decker v. Gibson Products Co. of Albany, Inc.,* 679 F.2d 212, 216 (11th Cir. 1982). . . .

" . . . Whether defendants choose to base their defense upon a theory that plaintiffs' negligence caused the death of plaintiffs' child or upon the theory that plaintiffs assumed the risk of the death of their child or both theories, this Court reiterates its inability to grant summary judgment for the defendants.

"The question of parental negligence is for the jury to determine. 'It is normally the duty of parents, by their presence or training, to keep young children from going into places of obvious danger.' *Augusta Amusements, Inc. v. Powell*, 93 Ga. App. 752, 755, 92 S.E.2d 720, 724 (1956). . . .

" '[T]he true test of parental negligence *vel non* is whether in the exercise of ordinary care he should have anticipated that harm would result from the unsupervised activities of the child and whether, if so, he exercised the proper degree of care to guard against this result.' *Hill v. Morrison*, 160 Ga. App. 151, 286 S.E.2d 467 (1981). 'However, parents are not required to do the impossible in caring for their children. They are not required to watch them every minute.' 57 Am. Jur. 2d *Negligence* § 377 (1971). Courts are reluctant to hold as a matter of law that parents are negligent in not keeping constant and unremitting watch and restraint over their children. *Atlanta & Charlotte Air-Line Railway v. Gravitt*, 93 Ga. 369, 375, 20 S.E. 550, 552 (1893). . . .

"The Court will not, at least at this stage of the case, determine as a matter of law the status of the deceased child. If, however, the hotel did in fact encourage adults to stay at the hotel by allowing their children to stay for free, then it would seem that the child was an invitee. *See Anderson v. Cooper*, 214 Ga. 164, 169, 104 S.E.2d 90, 94 (1958). . . . 'The courts have usually recognized that persons upon the premises of the inn in response to an invitation, either express or implied, for the purpose of visiting or calling upon registered guests at proper times, for lawful purposes, and who remain within the boundaries of their invitation are, or are to be treated as invitees. . . . ' Annot. 58 A.L.R.2d 1201, 1203 (1958). . . .

"The Court reserves ruling on the question of whether the father's negligence, if any, is imputable to the mother, but questions the validity of such an assertion in this case. The parents were divorced. The father had visitation rights. The mother was obligated to cooperate and allow the father his visitation rights. Nothing in the present record indicates that the mother had any reason to doubt the father's fitness as a parent.

"The Court has discussed some of the issues of this case perhaps at greater length than necessary to reach its ruling on the summary judgment motion. The discussion is meant to provide some guidance to counsel in the preparation of this case for trial. In conclusion, the Court DENIES defendants' motion for summary judgment."

10:10 *Selection of Competent Employees*

Apart from the question whether an employee who negligently or intentionally injures a guest was acting within the scope of his employment, so as to make his misconduct imputable to his employer, recovery may be based on the hiring or retention of an incompetent or otherwise unsuitable employee whose incompetence or incapacity proximately causes the injury inflicted. In this context the employer is primarily responsible, whereas in the case of imputed liability the employer is secondarily liable. Primary responsibility may entail a greater measure of damages, including punitive damage and criminal responsibility in the case of a violation of a statutory duty, and thus ought to be avoided.

The following case illustrates the importance of the issue of responsibility in the context of the operation of resort amusement facilities by an employee who might be subject to physically incapacitating seizures.

Ellingsgard v. Silver
352 Mass. 34, 223 N.E.2d 813 (1967)

Spalding, J.: "We summarize the evidence in this action of tort as follows: On August 16, 1961, Mary Ellingsgard was injured when a motorboat struck the dock on which she was standing. The dock, owned by a third person, extended into Pontoosuc Lake near Pittsfield. Shortly before the boat struck the dock, Perley Brace, the owner and operator, suffered a heart attack and lost control of the boat. His death occurred 'some time prior to the striking of the dock.' The cause of death was 'probable coronary thrombosis.' Brace was an employee of the defendant and was acting in the course of his employment when the heart attack occurred.

"The defendant conducts Pontoosuc Lodge, a summer resort. The defendant's daughter, Mrs. Barbara Kolodkin, was authorized to hire employees for the lodge, and employed Brace to 'take people out for water skiing or for boat rides.' His employment commented on July 2, 1961, and continued until the time of the accident. . . .

"The plaintiffs are husband and wife and their declaration is in four counts. The first and third counts are for personal injuries sustained by the plaintiff Mary, and the second and fourth are for consequential damages sustained by the plaintiff Charles. The first and second counts allege negligent operation of the motorboat. The third and fourth counts allege negligence in hiring and employing Brace.

" . . . The case comes here on two bills of exceptions brought respectively by the defendant and the plaintiffs. The questions raised by the defendant's exceptions relate to the denial of her motion for a directed verdict on each count, the denial of her motion for a new trial, and several rulings on evidence. The plaintiffs' exceptions relate to the denial of their motion for a new trial on counts 3 and 4, several evidentiary rulings, and certain portions of the charge. . . .

"We consider first the defendant's exception to the denial of her motion for directed verdicts on counts 1 and 2. These counts are based upon the negligent operation of the boat. The judge rightly charged the jury that there was no evidence of negligence in the manner in which the boat was operated prior to the heart attack. And it has been held that 'a sudden and unforeseeable physical seizure rendering an operator unable to control his motor vehicle cannot be termed negligence.' *Carroll v. Bouley*, 338 Mass. 625, 627. [Citation omitted.] The plaintiffs' theory, however, is that Brace's seizure was reasonably foreseeable; that Brace was therefore incompetent to operate the boat; and that the operation of the boat in these circumstances was negligent.

"We know of no decision of this court, and our attention has been directed to none, which has considered the validity of the plaintiffs' theory. The few jurisdictions which have considered the question, however, have held that the operation of a motor vehicle, without more, may be the basis for negligence when the operator knew or should have known that he was likely to be subject to an incapacitating physical seizure. [Citations omitted.] But even if we were to adopt that rule, we are of opinion that the evidence was insufficient to warrant a finding that the operation of the boat constituted a failure to exercise reasonable care and foresight.

"The evidence relating to Brace's physical condition was: At the time of his death he was forty years old. He was a prisoner of the Japanese for several months during World War II and had a heart attack in 1949. He had other heart attacks in 1957, 1958, and early in 1961. . . . He was admitted to a hospital after each of his three most recent attacks, and since 1957 had been taking anticoagulent drugs. Brace's physician testified that it was likely that the attacks would continue. . . . In 1959, after examining Brace, the physician reported that he was able to 'lead a moderately normal life.' Mrs. Kolodkin testified that Brace was a 'robust looking man' who 'didn't look ill in any way' and 'seemed always very jolly.' She said that when she interviewed him for the job she knew he had driven a school bus and drove his own car, but did not know he had a 'heart condition.' She did not inquire about the state of his health.

"In those jurisdictions which have held that negligence may be based upon the operation of a motor vehicle when the operator should foresee a physical seizure, foreseeability has been found in two types of circumstances. One is when the operator suffers from a condition which indicates, from a medical viewpoint, a fairly immediate likelihood that it will result in an attack rendering him unconscious. [Citation omitted.] The other is when the operator suffers warning symptoms of a physical failure during actual operation, but neglects to heed such warnings and continues to operate the vehicle. [Citation omitted.] We know of no case which holds that, absent medical testimony, previous symptoms of the sort suffered by Brace would warrant a finding that an incapacitating seizure was foreseeable. [Citations omitted.] To hold the contrary would impose a severe limitation upon the substantial number of persons who, with medical advice and treatment, attempt to live moderately normal lives despite heart conditions and other infirmities. [Citation omitted.]

"The evidence would not warrant findings that the incapacitating seizure suffered by Brace was foreseeable and that he was therefore incompetent to operate the boat. . . . "

10:11 *Contributory Negligence of Patron*

The patron of a swimming pool is under a duty to exercise ordinary care for his own safety. Thus, if a patron knew of a particular danger or would have known of it by the exercise of ordinary care, or was duly warned, but nevertheless placed himself in peril, thereby causing or contributing to his injury or death, he is guilty of contributory negligence which in a majority of jurisdictions serves as an absolute bar to the recovery of damages. On the other hand, the patron has the right to assume that the owner or operator has discharged his duty of providing a reasonably safe place for his patrons.

In *Ryan v. Unity, Inc.,*[19] plaintiff, employed as doorman in the Delmonico Hotel in Miami Beach, got off from work at 2:30 A.M. Thereafter, in company with three females, he visited a bar and restaurant. From there he and his girl friends went to the Surrey Hotel, arriving there at about 4:30 A.M. The party then decided to take a swim, and while it was still dark and visibility was still low, they all proceeded to the swimming pool. Plaintiff immediately went to the diving board and dived headlong into the swimming pool, which contained approximately two feet of water at the deepest end where the diving board was located, and thereby sustained severe head injuries. The pool had been drained for cleaning at the time.

Summary judgment for defendant was affirmed on appeal. Said the court:

> From a careful study of the record it appears that appellant failed to exercise ordinary care for his own safety when, during the early morning hour of approximately 5:00 A.M. while it was still dark and visibility was low, he dove headlong into the swimming pool without giving the slightest heed to existing conditions at that particular time. By doing so, he directly contributed to his own injury and made his own negligent act a concurring proximate cause of his injury.[20]

In *Biltmore Terrace Associates v. Kegan,*[21] a minor guest of defendant's hotel and his father sued for injuries to the minor guest who dived from beyond a four-foot wall at the edge of the ocean and was permanently injured when he struck bottom.

The minor was fifteen years old at the time of the accident and had been a guest of the hotel for twelve days. The defendant operated a patio-pool resort hotel and provided a patio-pool area between the hotel proper and the ocean. This structure was located landward of the mean high-water line, but the tides on occasion brought the water up to the wall and to a depth of several feet. The ocean side of the patio-pool area was enclosed by a wall approximately four feet high. On the day of the accident, the pool was closed because of bad weather. No lifeguard was on duty, nor was any person of authority present to oversee the recreation area.

[19] 55 So. 2d 117 (Fla. 1951).
[20] *Id.* at 117–18.
[21] 130 So. 2d 631 (Fla. Dist. Ct. App. 1961), *writ of certiorari discharged and case dismissed,* 154 So. 2d 825 (Fla. 1963).

Plaintiff and a young friend climbed over the wall and stood on the slanted ledge on the opposite side of the wall. After waiting for a large wave, plaintiff's friend dived into the ocean. Shortly thereafter, plaintiff took a dive, struck the bottom of the shallow water and suffered a complete and permanent paralysis from the neck down. The jury returned a substantial verdict for the plaintiff. On appeal, the judgment entered on the verdict was reversed by the Supreme Court of Florida, and the complaint was dismissed. The court held that it was the duty of the trial court to direct a verdict for the defendant at the close of the plaintiff's case. Said the court:

> It is suggested that the hotel violated this duty [of reasonable care for the safety of its patrons] in one or more of the following ways: 1. It failed to maintain a lifeguard on duty. 2. It failed to maintain a guard rail. 3. It failed to post signs or other warnings against use of the subject wall or the beams protruding therefrom as a means of diving or jumping into the ocean. . . . We think that the plaintiffs, in all of the above contentions, overlook the fact . . . that there was a four-foot wall at the end of the patio area. The plaintiff found it necessary to climb over this wall and assume a precarious position outside of the wall area in order to get a footing from which to dive. There was no other way by which one could enter the ocean except to climb over the wall. . . . To require a warning under such circumstances would be as ludicrous as requiring a sign on the top of an office building reading "don't jump off here." . . .
>
> In view of our holding that the plaintiffs failed to prove negligence on the part of the defendant, it is not necessary for us to discuss in an extended fashion our holding that the plaintiff was guilty of contributory negligence as a matter of law.[22]

MULLERY V. RO-MILL CONSTRUCTION CORP.
76 A.D.2d 802, 429 N.Y.S.2d 200 (1st Dep't 1980), *rev'd* 54 N.Y.2d 888,
444, N.Y.S.2d 912, 429 N.E.2d 419 (1981)

MEMORANDUM: "Defendants appeal from a judgment in favor of the plaintiff-executrix after a jury trial. The deceased, a member of a private health club owned and operated by the defendants, sustained fatal injuries on February 17, 1975, in the swimming pool maintained by the club. After swimming in the pool for a period of time, the deceased left the pool, suddenly mounted a tower alongside it on which the lifeguard's chair was located and dived into the shallow portion of the pool, fracturing his cervical spine.

"The theory of liability advanced at the trial was that the deceased was intoxicated, that employees of the defendants knew or should have known of his condition, and that the defendants were negligent in not excluding the deceased from the area of the swimming pool.

"We agree that there was sufficient evidence of intoxication to raise a factual issue as to the negligence of the defendants. On the other hand, it seems quite

[22]*Id.* at 634.

clear that the deceased's own actions were negligent as a matter of law. In the absence of circumstances that would permit the application here of the last clear chance doctrine (*see* Anno: *Last Clear Chance-Intoxicated Person*, 26 A.L.R.2d 308, § 12 at pp. 345–346) the liability of the defendants may be sustained only on the theory, in effect presented to the jury in the court's charge, that the defendants had violated a special duty of care to the deceased as an intoxicated person.

"The concept of a special duty was developed with regard to the obligations of common carriers to intoxicated passengers. [Citations omitted.] Its essential principles were succinctly set forth in *Fardette v. New York & Stamford R. Co.* at 546, 180 N.Y.S. at 181–182, as follows:

"In cases where there is no special duty resting upon the defendant to protect the plaintiff from the results of his own intoxication, the fact that the plaintiff was intoxicated, if it was a contributing cause of the injury, is a bar to the action [citations omitted]. But this rule is modified in cases where a defendant, like a common carrier, owes to a passenger plaintiff a special duty to protect him because of the fact that he is intoxicated [citation omitted]. In such cases intoxication is considered a condition only under which the problem must be solved, and a remote, not proximate, cause of the injury, although it may have been present and may have affected the conduct of the plaintiff at the time of the accident. Obviously, if the defendant was under an obligation to protect the plaintiff against the results of his intoxication, and the accident happened partly through the failure of the defendant to furnish such protection, the very condition against which the defendant was to protect the plaintiff cannot bar the right of action arising from the failure of the duty to protect him.

"We are aware of no case in which the special duty principle has been applied to a defendant other than a common carrier. [Citation omitted.] In *Olsen v. Realty Hotel Corp.*, 2 Cir., 240 N.Y.S.2d 277, 210 F.2d 785, the only case cited by plaintiff as embodying such an application, it is immediately apparent from an examination of the opinion that the court did not undertake to consider the issue presented here.

"We do not exclude the possibility that there may be circumstances under which an extension of the special duty concept would merit consideration, although the force of the argument for such an extension has been significantly weakened by the enactment into the law of this state of the doctrine of comparative negligence (C.P.L.R. art. 14–A), a doctrine regrettably not applicable to this pre-September 1975 death. In any event, the evidence here does not disclose such circumstances. For while there is evidence that the deceased was to some extent intoxicated, the totality of the evidence discloses no basis for the conclusion that the defendants knew or should have known that the deceased was so intoxicated that he was unable to take care of himself and that his judgment was so impaired that he was likely to undertake such a dangerous action.

"Accordingly, the judgment in favor of the plaintiff is reversed and the complaint dismissed.

"All concur except MARKEWICH, J., who dissents in a memorandum as follows:

" . . . The difficulty I find with the majority writing is that it . . . goes on to talk of subjects not really apropos as presented: of a special duty owed by common carriers to intoxicated passengers—obviously an area beclouded by considerations of contract of safe carriage—and, without specification, the application of the doctrine of last clear chance, and then concludes by second guessing the jury in respect of its finding 'that the defendants knew or should have known that the deceased was so intoxicated that he was unable to take care of himself and that his judgment was so impaired that he was likely to undertake such a dangerous action.'

"Let us take last things first. At argument, we were told that the deceased could not have been far under the influence because, before he climbed to the vacant lifeguard's seat, he had vigorously engaged in swimming back and forth. Such an exercise requires no operation of judgment; indeed, drunks are notoriously able to display great physical prowess, usually expressed in fighting. The deceased's judgment was impaired, else he would not have climbed the stand and essayed a directly downward dive in water too shallow to perform such a maneuver safely. In this respect, he possessed no more than the judgment of a small child, and there can be no doubt that, had a tiny infant wandered into the potentially dangerous, slick, wet area of a swimming pool, he would have been taken by the hand and gently led away. Perhaps there are no cases to cite on removing intoxicated persons from a swimming pool area because, by ordinary standards, no lifeguard worthy of the descriptive title, or pool attendant worthy of his pay, would even consider permitting a drunk to remain in such a dangerous place. The duty of avoiding disaster by last clear chance reaction did not arise when 'the deceased left the pool, suddenly mounted a tower . . . and dived. . . . ' That was too late. The duty to react by removing the deceased, intoxicated, as the witnesses who testified knew and as the attendant should have known, arose when he arrived at this potentially dangerous swimming pool, where no one with impaired judgment should have been permitted to come. Of course, this bizarre particular danger was not to be specifically foreseen, but one who operates a potentially dangerous place for profit should have a duty to foresee that one whose judgment is impaired should not be permitted to enter.

"To return to basics: 'It is familiar doctrine that a man placed in a responsible situation must guard against a risk of danger to others where reasonable foresight would suggest a good chance of occurrence and reasonable care suggests steps in avoidance. As the doctrine of tort developed, predictability of casualty became the main element; and this in turn, as always in the case of social predictability, rested on the experience of society. The judgment required to be applied, as well as the risk of liability to be assumed, was based on what a man would regard as likely to happen, and this could be predicated only on what he knew, or should have learned, had happened in the past. The rule of tort liability was never regarded as an insurance against all casualty; it was a selective process of protection against the injury to the innocent which common sense dictated should be guarded against.' *McPartland v. State*, 277 App. Div. 103, 106, 98 N.Y.S.2d 665, 667–68.

" 'Ordinary care must be in proportion to the danger to be avoided and the consequences that might reasonably be anticipated from the neglect. It must be commensurate with known dangers. The risk reasonably to be perceived defines the duty to be obeyed. A man placed in a responsible situation must guard against a risk of danger to others where a reasonable foresight would suggest a good chance of occurrence and reasonable care suggests steps in avoidance.' 41 N.Y. Jur. 30, *Negligence* § 18.

"There has been some mention of contributory negligence. Displayed how? By getting drunk? Such a dictum has no place in this discussion of last clear chance to avoid the consequences of negligence, except as discussed above. By climbing and diving? To risk repetition, that was the result only of not having seized upon the early clear chance of eliminating all danger by immediate expulsion. The verdict as to liability should stand, and denial of the motion to set it aside should be affirmed."

The Court of Appeals reversed the Appellate Division in *Mullery v. Ro-Mill Construction Corp.*, 54 N.Y.2d 888, 429 N.E.2d 419 (1981), holding:

> MEMORANDUM.
> The order of the Appellate Division, 76 A.D.2d 802, 429 N.Y.S.2d 200, should be reversed, with costs, and the matter remitted to that court for review of the facts (C.P.L.R. 5613). Under the charge given by the trial court the jury was instructed to determine whether the decedent was so intoxicated as to be rendered incapable of understanding or appreciating the danger which confronted him. In view of this charge, to which no exception was taken, and on the evidence adduced at trial, it cannot be said, as a matter of law, that the decedent was contributorily negligent.

Contributory negligence of a child patron is discussed in *Haft v. Lone Palm Hotel* in section 10:8, *supra*.

10:12 *Assumption of Risk Inherent in Skiing and Other Recreational Activities*

Traditionally, at common law, owners of recreational facilities have been able to escape responsibility for injuries suffered by participants in such activities on the theory that the injured participant had assumed such risks by voluntarily undertaking that activity. The Latin term *volenti non fit injuria* is often contained in the treatises and decisions on this subject.

"In its simplest sense, assumption of risk means that plaintiff, in advance, has expressly given his consent to relieve the defendant of any legal obligation or legal duty which the defendant would otherwise have owed him. A second situation where the doctrine is applicable is when the plaintiff with knowledge of the risk enters into a relationship with the defendant which will necessarily involve that risk, and so is regarded as implicitly agreeing to take his chances. In the third type of situation the plaintiff, aware of the risk already created by defendant's negligent conduct, proceeds voluntarily to encounter it.''[23]

Nowhere are the assumption of risk doctrine and the perils of too facile reliance upon it more evident than in the ski resort industry. Most of the cases that follow are drawn from that field, but generally represent principles that would apply equally to other recreational activities.

The legal relationship of ski resort owner or operator and skier is generally that of landowner-inviter and guest or patron-invitee.[24] Thus the ordinary rules noted in other areas apply, requiring the operator to use ordinary care to protect the skier from such hazards as may be reasonably discovered and prevented.[25] Reasonable care must be used to keep the premises in a safe and suitable condition so that skiers will not be unnecessarily or unreasonably exposed to danger.

At this juncture a distinction should be made between man-made or artificial risks and natural risks. With respect to ski lifts constructed by the owner or his predecessor, the resort operator is held to a more demanding standard of care, akin to that of "common carriers," which requires that the utmost care be exercised for the safety of the passenger.[26] With regard to injuries caused by natural obstacles that may confront the skier on any downhill slope, a general statement of what is required of the operator can be distilled from prior case law as follows:

> A duty to maintain its premises reasonably safe for those whose business it solicited whether a skier or non-skier [and] a duty to use reasonable care to keep its premises in a safe and suitable condition so that the plaintiff would not be unnecessarily or unreasonably exposed to danger, and if a hidden danger existed known to the defendant, but unknown and not reasonably apparent to the plaintiff, to give warning of it to the plaintiff, who had a right to assume that the premises, aside from obvious dangers, were reasonably safe for the reasons that he was upon them and make them so.[27]

There are a number of accident-causing conditions that often constitute common-law evidence of negligence on the part of the ski operator, such as exposed lift towers, trees, and telephone poles. In the past, unpadded obstacles have caused severe injuries. Other common causes of injury include: (1) inadequate lighting for nighttime skiing; (2) negligent operation of trail-grooming vehicles; (3) clouds of snow thrown over trails by snow-making machines;

[23]M. Farrow, *Ski Operators and Skiers—Responsibility and Liability*, 14 New Eng. L. Rev. 262 (1978).

[24]*Id.* at 266.

[25]C. Manby, *Assumption of Risk after Sunday v. Stratton Corporation: The Vermont Sports Injury Liability Statute and Injured Skiers*, 3 Vt. L. Rev. 129, 135 (1978).

[26]*Id.* at 133.

[27]M. Farrow, *Ski Operators and Skiers, supra* note 20, at 266.

(4) failure to patrol ski trails adequately; (5) failure to warn of known hazards; (6) faulty rental equipment; and (7) failure to seal off closed areas adequately.

In the now notorious case of *Sunday v. Stratton Corporation*,[28] the Vermont Superior Court found the resort operator at fault for allowing an unforeseeable hazard to exist below the surface of the snow on a downhill ski slope. In so doing the court departed from the assumption of risk doctrine most recently enunciated in Vermont in *Wright v. Mt. Mansfield Lift, Inc.*[29] in a closely related factual pattern. In *Sunday* the court ruled that this defense was no longer available under a recently enacted comparative negligence statute.

It is noteworthy that the court found Sunday was a rank novice, 21 years old at the time, who while skiing on a novice trail caught his ski or binding on a piece of snow-covered brush while executing a "very slow" snowplow turn. Upon falling, he hit his head on a rock located a distance off the trail itself. As a result he was paralyzed from the shoulders down, has no excretory control, and will be confined to a wheelchair for the balance of his life.

Under the Vermont comparative negligence statute[30] no mention is made of assumption of risk. The doctrine is not automatically included or excluded; the judge may apply it or ignore it based on his own evaluation of its relevance. Some jurisdictions have expressly abolished assumption of risk, while others have specifically retained it.[31] Colorado[32] has qualifiedly abolished the doctrine, unless there is a written consent to assume all risks. Thus the court in *Sunday* had no out-of-state precedents to which to refer for persuasive authority. Ironically, however, the court in *Sunday* chose to ignore a more recent Vermont precedent:[33] In *Leopold v. Okemo Mountain* the comparative negligence statute was in effect, but the court nonetheless held for the operator on the basis of assumption of risk. In *Sunday* the jury found Stratton 100 percent liable for the injuries suffered by Sunday and awarded him $1,500,000 in damages.

The Vermont Supreme Court[34] noted a critical flaw in Stratton's arguments on appeal to overturn the adverse judgment rendered by the lower court as not stating a legally cognizable claim. First Stratton argued that the disputed piece of brush, the culprit, could not have been on the ski slope because of their superior standards of slope maintenance. Standing alone, this might have carried the day, on the theory that no negligence causing the injuries had been established as a matter of law. But Stratton then argued the doctrine of assumption of risk. Taken together, these arguments are mutually exclusive. If trail grooming is

---

[28]No. C83–75 Cn. C. (Vt. Super. Ct., May 31, 1977), *aff'd*, 136 Vt. 293, 390 A.2d 398 (1978).

[29]96 F. Supp. 786, 791 (D. Vt. 1951).

[30]Vt. Stat. Ann. Tit. 12, § 1036 (1973).

[31]Among the statutes that have expressly abolished assumption of risk are Massachusetts (Mass. Ann. Laws, ch. 231, § 85 (Michie 1974)), Oregon (Or. Rev. Stat. § 18,475 (2) (1977)), and Utah (Utah Code Ann. § 78-27-37 (1977)). The doctrine has been specifically retained, whether by statute or decisional law, in Arkansas, Mississippi, and Texas.

[32]Col. Rev. Stat. § 33–44–110(2) (1979).

[33]Leopold v. Okemo Mountain, Inc., 420 F. Supp. 781, 786–87 (D. Vt. 1976).

[34]136 Vt. 293, 390 A.2d 398 (1978).

so complete that a hidden piece of brush cannot exist, then the risk of tripping on such a piece of brush is not one that a skier should have to "assume." The Supreme Court thereupon affirmed the decision below.[35]

Another aspect of the operator's conduct requires comment. Prior to 1976 Stratton boasted in its advertising literature of the "fairway-like trails" and meticulous grooming of its resort. Such advertising offered what amounted to an express warranty of the hazard-free condition of its ski trails and slopes. Such a guarantee of safe downhill slopes could not have been lost upon the trial court and jury.

Ordinary care may be delineated by industry standards of maintenance, or, where available, by state legislation regulating ski resort operations. Industry standards normally dictate that each ski area remove as many potentially dangerous hazards as possible from ski trails during the off season.[36] In addition, once the ski area is open, the use of special grooming equipment and snow-making machines to ensure a safe, even snow cover is practically universal as is the practice of padding all lift towers with foam. The unjustified absence of any of these commonplace upkeep programs or pieces of equipment from a particular resort area might suffice to establish lack of the requisite standard of care.

Some states, such as Washington,[37] have delineated the duties owed the skier through legislation. Presumably if the resort meets all of the legislative criteria, it is protected from legal recourse by an injured skier. Many "snow belt" states have passed special legislation designed to protect the ski industry from unwarranted law suits while furthering the interests of the skiing public.[38] One such enactment, the Massachusetts Ski Act,[39] a part of which is printed as an appendix to this chapter, illustrates a typical legislative response to the *Sunday v. Stratton* case.

The Act sought to achieve two principal objectives: (1) to decrease the financial menace to the ski operator by limiting his liability and (2) to make the sport safer through mandatory safety precautions.

Unlike New Hampshire,[40] where the statute precludes the jury from judging whether or not reasonable care had been exercised, Massachusetts saw fit to allow the jury to make that determination, on a case-by-case basis. It would appear, however, that the jury will consider compliance by the owner with all of the statutory safety provisions as evidence of reasonable care.

Other beneficial contributions provided under the Massachusetts Ski Act include: (1) an improved system of evaluating the difficulty of various slopes; (2) new regulation of the manner in which skiers are warned of known hazards; (3) power to revoke or amend the rules governing the safety sign system vested

[35]*Id.*
[36]C. Manby, *Assumption of Risk after Sunday, supra* note 22, at 134.
[37]Wash. Rev. Code Ann. § 70:117 (1977).
[38]Colorado, Massachusetts, New Hampshire, New Mexico, Vermont, and Washington have enacted such legislation.
[39]1978 Mass. Acts, ch. 455.
[40]N.H. Rev. Stat. Ann., ch. 225 A-26 (Equity 1977).

in the state recreational tramway board, thus allowing for necessary additional safety measures without the otherwise arduous process of statutory amendment; (4) fines for noncompliance; and (5) a fine imposed on any person who leaves the scene of a skiing accident without offering identification and assistance.

Certain deficiencies in the legislation deserve mention. The Act does not offer a reasonable standard of safety for the novice or handicapped skier.[41] The Act does not regulate the operation of ski schools,[42] leaving the implication that ski students may be found by the courts to have assumed risks encountered during ski class of which they had no knowledge or prior experience.

The Act does not require any padding on ski towers, even when they protrude from the center of a skiable trail. Although the Vermont federal district court in *Leopold v. Okemo Mountain, Inc.*[43] had ruled that the assumption of risk rule would bar recovery in a downhill ski slope accident similar to that found in *Sunday v. Stratton*, this same court charged the jury in an earlier case[44] that the doctrine required knowledge by the skier of the existence of that particular risk and that participation in the sport itself is not tantamount to an automatic assumption of all risks. In that case the skier collided with an unguarded lift tower after falling in an unmarked icy spot in an otherwise well-groomed trail. Granted, tramway towers are among the most obvious risks of skiing. To reduce the frequency and severity of injuries to skiers, simple and relatively inexpensive padding of such towers would be prudent policy.

The Act makes no provision for the presence of ski patrols. Most sizable ski resorts voluntarily employ such patrols, and it would seem advisable for others to do so as well.[45]

The Act fails to mandate liability insurance coverage by the resort for ski accidents.[46] Since such a provision benefits all parties, it should come as no surprise that virtually all ski resorts voluntarily assume adequate coverage as a sound business practice.

BAZYDLO V. PLACID MARCY CO.
422 F.2d 482 (2d Cir. 1970)

PER CURIAM: "Carolyn A. Bazydlo and a girl friend were using a toboggan run on January 17, 1965 as guests of the Hotel Marcy, owned by the appellants, Placid Marcy Co., Inc. The toboggan run had been designed and built by the hotel for the use of its guests. The hotel also furnished toboggans for its guests. During the fourth or fifth time down the elevated chute and along the snow cov-

---

[41]M. Farrow, *Ski Operators and Skiers, supra* note 20, at 273.

[42]*Id.* at 273–74.

[43]420 F. Supp. 781 (D. Vt. 1976).

[44]Gemza v. Mt. Snow Development Corp., No. 71–36 (D. Vt. Feb. 24, 1971).

[45]It is well documented that the use of ski patrols has added significantly to the safety of skiing. C. Manby, *Assumption of Risk after Sunday, supra* note 22.

[46]Washington, on the other hand, does have such a requirement. *See* Wash. Rev. Code Ann. § 70.117.040.

ered track, the toboggan failed to negotiate a turn. It went over the foot-high snow sidewall maintained by the hotel to keep the toboggan on the track. Just six feet from the turn was the steel A-frame of a swing in a children's playground. The toboggan hit a steel pole; Miss Bazydlo's knee hit the pole; she turned a somersault and hit the ground.

"Appealing from a judgment entered on a jury verdict in favor of Miss Bazydlo, the hotel maintains that it has not been shown negligent and that Miss Bazydlo assumed the risk as a matter of law. We find sufficient evidence in the record to support the jury's finding on the issue of liability. The hotel recognized the risk that a toboggan might leave the run and failed to maintain the sidewalls sufficiently to turn the toboggan away from obstructions. [Citation omitted.]

"During its deliberation, the jury requested a: '[r]ereading of his Honor's charge on preponderance of evidence and contributory negligence, specifically if there is any degree of contributory negligence on the part of the plaintiff, must we find for the defendant.'

"The trial court responded: '[If] you find that the plaintiff's own negligence was a substantial factor—I repeat that—was a substantial factor in causing her accident, then she was guilty of contributory negligence and cannot recover. It doesn't matter how great or small her negligence was, but you must find that it was a substantial factor in causing the accident.'

"The hotel, relying on *Bacon v. Celeste,* 30 A.D.2d 324, 292 N.Y.S.2d 54 (1st Dep't 1968), contends that the charge might have led the jury to believe that there must be substantial negligence on the part of the plaintiff to bar her recovery. In the *Bacon* case, the New York court, recognizing 'substantial factor in causing the [accident]' as correct in explaining proximate cause, nevertheless found that language to be confusing in the circumstances there presented. The facts of *Bacon* reveal that language was used there to correct a confusing supplementary charge which contained the words 'substantially contributed' in a description of the degree of contributory negligence. The potential for confusion of the jury was much greater in *Bacon* than in the circumstances presented on this appeal.

"A distinction must be made between the quantum of contributory negligence which bars recovery (which need be only 'slight') and the causal relation between that negligence and the accident (which must be negligence that is 'a substantial factor in bringing about the harm.' Restatement (Second) of Torts § 431 (1965). Prosser, Torts 431 (3d ed. 1964) quoted with approval in *Juaire v. Narden,* 395 F.2d 373, 380 n. 1 (2d Cir. 1968). Here, the language in the charge, 'It doesn't matter how great or small her negligence was' refers to the quantum of negligence, while the language 'substantial factor in causing her accident' refers to proximate cause. Neither element was so overemphasized as to cause the confusion present in *Bacon, supra.* We do not believe the charge to be too subtle to be grasped by the ordinary jury.

"Although high, we do not find the verdict of $55,000 to be 'so high that it would be a denial of justice to permit it to stand.' [Citations omitted.]

"Judgment affirmed."

In *Lawrence v. Danos,*[47] the court affirmed the rejection by the trial court of a suit instituted by a patron injured by reason of a fall from a ski lift. It was established that the patron had failed to use the safety chain provided with the lift. The claim, based on *res ipsa loquitur,* was rejected since there could be a reasonable inference that failure to use the chain was the cause of his injuries.

In *Murray v. Ramada Inns, Inc.*, which follows, the Supreme Court of Louisiana decided that the assumption of risk doctrine does not serve as a complete bar to recovery by plaintiffs in negligence or strict liability cases, but results only in reducing recovery in accordance with Louisiana's comparative fault statute. The case dealt with the death of a hotel guest who dove into the shallow end of the hotel's pool with actual knowledge of the risk of doing so.

Murray v. Ramada Inns, Inc.
521 So. 2d 1123 (La. 1988)

Calogero, J.: "Today we are called upon to resolve the role, if any, which the assumption of risk defense continues to play in Louisiana tort law, given the Legislature's adoption of a comparative fault system. The issue has presented itself in a case certified to us by the United States Court of Appeals for the Fifth Circuit, *Murray v. Ramada Inns, Inc.*, 821 F. 2d 272 (1987). The certified question is as follows:

"Does assumption of risk serve as a total bar to recovery by a plaintiff in a negligence case, or does it only result in a reduction of recovery under the Louisiana comparative negligence statute?

"We accepted certification, 514 So. 2d 21 (La. 1987), and now answer that assumption of risk does not serve as a total bar to a plaintiff's recovery in a negligence case.

"We also note at the outset that the certified question comes to us in a case where the defendants were found strictly liable under La. Civ. Code Ann. art. 2317 (West 1979), the jury having been instructed by the trial judge to apply the provisions of that article when determining whether or not the defendants were liable. Because of that fact, and in order to provide an unambiguous response to the certified question, we further answer that assumption of risk should not operate as a total bar to recovery regardless of whether the defendant is found negligent or strictly liable.

"Assumption of risk terminology has been utilized to describe three basic types of plaintiff conduct. In the vast majority of cases that have involved the assertion of the defense, the plaintiff conduct at issue was in reality a form of contributory negligence. Such conduct henceforth should be exclusively adjudged by the comparative fault principles set forth in La. Civ. Code Ann. art. 2323. (West Supp. 1988). In a relative handful of other cases, the assumption of risk defense has been used to deny recovery on the ground that the plaintiff expressly agreed to release the defendant from liability. Our decision here does not

[47]46 A.D.2d 41, 360 N.Y.S.2d 730 (3d Dep't 1974).

require a different result in such cases, which may be resolved in favor of a defendant without resort to assumption of risk. Finally, the defense has been used in a few cases to bar recovery by plaintiffs who have opted to place themselves in situations which involve virtually unpreventable risks, the textbook example being the sports spectator who has the misfortune of being hit by an errant ball. Our decision also does not necessarily call for a different outcome in cases of this type, which may be resolved in appropriate cases on the simple ground that the defendant is not negligent.

"Regardless of the context in which it has been utilized, the assumption of risk defense has produced confusion and conceptual difficulties. The doctrine is easily replaceable by other established principles of tort law which more readily comport with civilian tradition, such as comparative fault and duty/risk analysis. Accordingly, and given the Legislature's adoption of a comparative fault system, we conclude that the assumption of risk defense no longer has a place in Louisiana tort law.

(I) Facts and Proceedings in Federal Court

"On July 30, 1983, Gregory Murray and two of his brothers began doing shallow water dives in the pool at a Ramada Inn Motel in Shreveport. After making two dives without incident, Murray made a third dive and struck his head on the bottom of the pool. Murray suffered instant paralysis, from which he never recovered. He died of his injuries five months later, and his wife and son subsequently brought this wrongful death action in federal district court against the companies which franchised, owned and operated the motel, as well as their respective liability insurers.

"At trial, it was established that no lifeguard was on duty at the time of the accident, and that the absence of a lifeguard was a violation of the Louisiana Sanitary Code. It was further established that there were no signs in the area which warned against diving into the shallow end of the pool, even though other Ramada Inn pools had signs which prohibited diving. Other testimony indicated that the motel had previously removed the diving board from the pool, in order to curtail diving.

"Gregory knew how to dive, his brother Carl testified, for Gregory had told him that shallow water diving was dangerous. He further stated that shortly before the accident, Gregory had warned his brothers to 'be careful' while diving into the pool. There was also a sign near the pool which stated 'NO LIFE GUARD—SWIM AT OWN RISK.'

"At the close of the evidence, the defendants asked the trial judge to instruct the jury on the elements of assumption of risk. They also urged that assumption of risk, if found applicable by the jury, should act as a complete bar to the plaintiffs' recovery. The trial judge denied the request and refused to instruct the jury on assumption of risk, concluding that the defense has been replaced by comparative negligence. The jury's verdict was returned in the form of responses to special interrogatories, the pertinent interrogatories and responses being as follows:

"(1) Under the circumstances and facts of this case, did the swimming pool as it was being operated present an unreasonable risk of harm which was a proximate cause of Gregory Murray's injury and death?

"Answer: Yes.

"(2) Do you find that Gregory Murray was himself negligent and that such negligence was a proximate cause of his own injury or death?

"Answer: Yes.

"The jury further assessed Murray's negligence at 50%, and awarded $250,000 in damages (before reduction for comparative negligence) to each plaintiff.

"On appeal to the United States Fifth Circuit, the defendants argued that the trial judge erred by refusing to instruct the jury on assumption of risk, and by failing to hold that that defense, distinct from comparative negligence, was available as a total bar to recovery. Reviewing the evidence, the Fifth Circuit concluded that 'testimony supports the jury's conclusion that Murray knew, appreciated, and voluntarily exposed himself to the risk of diving into the shallow end of the swimming pool.' 821 F.2d at 276. . . . With due respect to our Fifth Circuit brethren, the jury did not make such a specific finding, at least not as is evident from the record. Instead, the jury responded in the affirmative to an interrogatory which asked whether Murray was negligent. However, we take this language in the opinion to mean simply that the Fifth Circuit panel, after reviewing the evidence, concluded that Murray assumed the risk of his injury and subsequent death.

"However, the Fifth Circuit also noted that the impact of an assumption of risk finding is 'unsettled' in Louisiana in light of the Legislature's adoption of a comparative fault system. 821 F.2d at 274. Thus, they have asked us to decide on certification whether the defense serves 'as a total bar to recovery in a negligence case,' or results only 'in a reduction of recovery under the Louisiana comparative negligence statute.' *Id.* at 276.

(II) The Origins and Evolution of the Assumption of Risk Defense

(A) Development at Common Law

"Assumption of risk is a common law doctrine 'not well developed in Louisiana,' *Rozell v. Louisiana Animal Breeders Cooperative, Inc.,* 496 So. 2d 275, 278 (La. 1986), and has been described as a concept 'more difficult to understand and apply than almost any other in the law of torts.' Mansfield, *Informed Choice in the Law of Torts,* 22 La. L. Rev. 17, 17 (1961). In its various attempts to interpret and explain the supposedly distinct nature of the defense, this Court has usually turned to non-civilian sources, such as the Restatement (Second) of Torts. *See, e.g., Dorry v. Lafleur,* 399 So. 2d 559, 560–61 (La. 1981); *Langlois v. Allied Chemical Corp.,* 258 La. 1067, 1087, 249 So. 2d 133, 141 (La. 1971). Accordingly, we will preface our analysis of the certified question with a discussion of the development of the defense at common law, and the subsequent attempts of Louisiana courts to incorporate the doctrine into civilian jurisprudence.

(1) Contractual Roots

"The original premise of the assumption of risk defense appears to have been contractual rather than delictual. Early assumption of risk cases were based on the theory that the plaintiff could not recover because he had actually consented to undertake the risk of injury posed by a given situation, and therefore could not be heard to complain when such an injury occurred. *See generally,* Wade, *The Place of Assumption of Risk in the Law of Negligence,* 22 La. L. Rev. 5 (1961). The doctrine was described by the maxim '*volenti non fit injuria,*' meaning 'no wrong is done to one who is willing.' W. Prosser and J. Wade, Cases and Materials on Torts 534 (5th ed. 1971).

"Thus, the defense appeared frequently in early common law cases which involved servants or employees who were injured while performing their employment duties. The right of such employees to recover damages from their employers was barred under the rationale that, as an implied provision of the employment contract, the servant assumed all risks incidental to his normal employment duties. [Citations omitted.]

"The philosophy of the defense, premises on the idea that a plaintiff who confronts a known danger necessarily must have chosen to do so, was 'a terse expression of the individualistic tendency of the common law,' which regarded 'freedom of individual action as the keystone of the whole [legal] structure.' Bohlen, *Voluntary Assumption of Risk,* 20 Harv. L. Rev. 14, 14 (1906). Consequently, assumption of risk was thereafter extended in application far beyond the master-servant relationship. On the theory that '[a] true contract may be indicated by conduct as well as by express language,' courts presumed that plaintiffs in certain situations had agreed to accept the risk of injury, even though actual consent was a fiction. Wade, *supra,* 22 La. L. Rev. at 8.

"For example, a plaintiff who accepted an invitation to a party at the defendant's home could not recover for an injury he suffered on the premises because he was 'presumed to accept such generous entertainment with an understanding that he accommodates himself to the conditions of his host.' *Comeau v. Comeau,* 285 Mass. 578, 579, 189 N.E. 588, 589–90 (1934). Similarly, the baseball fan who purchased a ticket to a ballgame was usually presumed to have accepted responsibility for the risks inherent in watching a game, including the possibility of being struck by an errant ball. *See Kavafian v. Seattle Baseball Club,* 105 Wash. 219, 181 P. 679 (1919). As this contractual doctrine began to acquire a separate identity as a tort defense, the need arose to distinguish the assumed risk concept from another tort defense, contributory negligence.

(2) Similarity to Contributory Negligence

"As early as 1906, a distinguished commentator expressed the view that it was 'essential' that contributory negligence and assumption of risk 'should be kept quite distinct.' Bohlen, *supra,* 20. Harv. L. Rev. at 18. But at an even earlier date, there were indications that Professor Bohlen's hopes in this regard were in vain. In *Eckert v. Long Island R.R.,* 43 N.Y. 502, 3 Am. Rep. 721

(1871), plaintiffs sued the railroad company after their decedent was killed in the process of removing a small child from the path of an oncoming train. The New York Court of Appeal affirmed the trial court's judgment in favor of the plaintiffs, but there were two dissenting opinions. One dissent urged that the plaintiff should not recover on the ground that he was contributorily negligent; the other dissenting opinion posited that the plaintiff should not recover because he had assumed the risk. Neither of the dissenting opinions discussed the other, nor attempted to distinguish between the two defenses.

"Nonetheless, other courts insisted that there was a distinction between the two doctrines. Contributory negligence was described as the inadvertent or unintentional failure of the plaintiff to exercise due care for his own safety. *See* James, *Contributory Negligence,* 62 Yale L.J. 691, 723 (1953). The defense called for an objective inquiry into whether the plaintiff's conduct fell below the standard required of a 'reasonable man of ordinary prudence' under the circumstances. W. Prosser and J. Wade, Cases and Materials on Torts, *supra* at 505 n. 6. Assumption of the risk, on the other hand, was purportedly distinguishable from contributory negligence because it was governed by a subjective test, which required an inquiry into whether the plaintiff actually knew of the risk and voluntarily confronted the danger. *See, e.g., Bartlett v. Gregg,* 77 S.D. 406, 92 N.W.2d 654 (1958); *Landrum v. Roddy,* 143 Neb. 934, 12 N.W.2d 82 (1943). *See also Cincinnati, N.O. & T.P.R. Co. v. Thompson,* 236 F. 1, 9 (6th Cir. 1916) ('Knowledge is the watchword of assumption of risk.'). This distinction has been preserved in the Restatement (Second) of Torts, which explains the theory of assumption of risk as follows:

"The basis of assumption of risk is the plaintiff's consent to accept the risk and look out for himself. Therefore, he will not be found, in the absence of an express agreement which is clearly so to be construed, to assume any risk unless he has knowledge of its existence. This means that he must not only be aware of the facts which create the danger, but must also appreciate the danger itself and the nature, character and extent which make it unreasonable. Thus the condition of premises upon which he may enter may be quite apparent to him, but the danger arising from the condition may be neither known nor apparent, or if known or apparent at all, it may appear to him to be so slight as to be negligible. In such a case the plaintiff does not assume the risk. His failure to exercise due care either to discover or understand the danger is not properly a matter of assumption of risk, but of the defense of contributory negligence.

"Restatement (Second) of Torts, § 496, comment (b). . . .

"However, the theoretical distinctions between the two defenses are often most difficult to maintain in practice. A conceptual difficulty arises from the fact that a plaintiff who knowingly and voluntarily encounters an unreasonable risk of injury may usually be described as one whose conduct has fallen below the standard of due care which would be exercised by a reasonable man under similar circumstances. *See Meistrich v. Casino Arena Attractions, Inc.,* 31 N.J. 44, 55, 196 A.2d 90, 96 (1959) (describing a plaintiff's decision to incur a known risk as failure 'to use the care of a reasonably prudent man under all of the circumstances.'); *see also* Lowndes, *Contributory Negligence*, 22 Geo. L.J. 674, 680 (1934) ('A voluntary and unreasonable assumption of risk affords a defense . . . not because the plaintiff has consented to the injury, but because he has acted imprudently.') . . . ; V. Schwartz, *Comparative Negligence, supra* at 155 ('Often when a plaintiff assumes a risk, he does not act as a reasonable man and therefore he is also contributorily negligent.') Accordingly, the two defenses often overlap, and '[t]he vast majority of assumption of risk cases involve nothing more than a particular form of plaintiff negligence.' Robertson, *Ruminations on Comparative Fault, Duty-Risk Analysis, Affirmative Defenses, and Defensive Doctrines in Negligence and Strict Liability Litigation in Louisiana,* 44 La. L. Rev. 1341, 1372 (1984).

(3) Common Law Categories

"Yet another difficulty which arises when attempting to analyze this doctrine is that the term 'assumption of risk' has been used to describe widely differing types of plaintiff conduct. . . .

"Even so, in answering the certified question, we must be cognizant of the fact that 'assumption of risk' has been used to refer to different concepts in different cases. In order to provide an unambiguous answer to the certified question, we will briefly review the three most commonly utilized categories of assumption of risk, and will specify in Section III of this opinion how our answer to the certified question should affect the disposition of cases in each category.

"The first category has been called 'express assumption of risk,' and it includes those cases, infrequent in occurrence, where the plaintiff 'expressly contracts with another not to sue for any future injuries which may be caused by that person's negligence.' *Anderson v. Ceccardi,* 6 Ohio St. 3d 110, 451 N.E.2d 780, 783 (1983). *See also* V. Schwartz, Comparative Negligence [§ 9.1, 154 (1974)], *supra* at 154; *Keegan v. Anchors Inns, Inc.,* 606 F.2d 35, 37–38 (3rd Cir. 1979). Express consent, which might also be called 'waiver' or 'release,' will usually bar recovery by the plaintiff 'unless there is a statute or established public policy against it.' Wade, *supra,* 22 La. L. Rev. at 8.

"A second category of cases involves what has been called 'implied primary' assumption of risk. In such cases, the plaintiff has made no express agreement to release the defendant from future liability, but he is presumed to have consented to such a release because he has voluntarily participated in a 'particular activity or situation' which involves inherent and well known risks. *Duffy v. Midlothian Country Club,* 135 Ill. App. 429, 90 Ill. Dec. 237, 241, 481 N.E.2d 1037, 1041 (1985). Implied primary assumption of risk has been described as 'an alternative expression of the proposition that the defendant was not negligent, *i.e.,* either owed no duty or did not breach the duty owed. *Meistrich v. Casino Arena Attraction, Inc.,* 31 N.J. 44, 155 A.2d 90, 93 (1959).

"The third and largest category of assumption of risk cases are those in which the plaintiff is said to assume the risk of the defendant's negligence. Even though the defendant in such cases is found to be at fault, the plaintiff is barred from recovery on the ground that he knew of the unreasonable risk created by the defendant's conduct and voluntarily chose to encounter that risk. The plaintiff conduct at issue has been labeled 'implied secondary' assumption of risk. However, most common law courts now agree that the plaintiff conduct involved in these cases is nothing more and nothing less than contributory negligence. *See Duffy*, 90 Ill. Dec. at 241–42, 481 N.E.2d at 1041–42 and authorities cited therein; *Meistrich*, 155 A.2d at 93–96.

(4) Abandonment of Assumption of Risk

"The high courts in a number of states lost patience with the assumption of risk doctrine and abolished it even prior to the widespread adoption of comparative negligence. *See, e.g., Rosenau v. City of Estherville*, 199 N.W.2d 125, 133 (Iowa 1972); *Leavitt v. Gillaspie*, 443 P.2d 61, 68–69 (Alas. 1968); *Parker v. Redden*, 421 S.W.2d 586, 592–93 (Ky. 1967); *Bulatao v. Kauai Motors, Ltd.*, 49 Haw. 1, 406 P.2d 887, 894–96 (1965); *Boulder Valley Coal Co. v. Jernberg*, 118 Colo. 486, 197 P.2d 155, 156 (1948). In those statements, conduct which previously had been described as assumption of risk was re-classified as contributory negligence.

"Many other states were spurred to eliminate the assumption of risk doctrine by the adoption of a comparative fault system. In some of these states, the comparative fault statute enacted by the legislature specifically indicates that conduct which had been described by assumed risk terminology should be reclassified as comparative fault (and should thereby operate only as a comparative reduction of the plaintiff's recovery, rather than a complete bar). *See, e.g.*, Ariz. Rev. Stat. Ann. § 12–2505 (Supp. 1987); Mass. Gen. Laws Ann. ch. 231 § 85 (West 1985). In other jurisdictions which have adopted comparative fault statutes that do not expressly refer to assumption of risk, the courts have subsequently determined that assumption of risk should not survive as a distinct defense that totally bars recovery. *See, e.g., Mizushima v. Sunset Ranch, Inc.*, 737 P.2d 1158, 1161 (Nev. 1987); *Salinas v. Vierstra*, 107 Idaho 984, 695 P.2d 369, 372–75 (1985); *Wilson v. Gordon*, 354 A.2d 398, 401–03 (Me. 1976).

"Some states have retained assumption of risk terminology only for the purpose of referring to 'express' or 'contractual' consent cases. *See, e.g., Mizushima*, 737 P.2d at 1161; *Wilson*, 354 A.2d at 401–03; *Segoviano v. Housing Auth. of Stanislaus City*, 143 Cal. App. 3d 162, 191 Cal. Rptr. 578, 583 (1983). Other jurisdictions have insisted on the total elimination of the defense, most notably New Jersey in *McGrath v. American Cyanamid Co.*, 41 N.J. 272, 196 A.2d 238, 240–41 (1963). There, the court stated that the term assumption of risk is 'so apt to create mist that it is better banished from the scene. We hope we have heard the last of it.' *Id.*

"All told, it appears that sixteen states have totally abolished the defense, and seventeen more have eliminated the use of assumption of risk terminology in all cases except those involving express or contractual consent by the plaintiff. *See* H. Woods, Comparative Fault §§ 6.1–6.8 (2d ed. 1987). After long ago arriving in the torts arena as a refugee from contract law, assumption of the risk now appears to be passing from the scene in most common law jurisdictions. . . .

"Thus, by 1980, when the comparative fault system adopted by the Legislature became effective, the status of the law of assumption of risk could charitably be described as confusing. As discussed above, the defense seemed indistinguishable from contributory negligence in most cases, yet could be asserted in strict liability cases even when the defense of contributory negligence was legally unavailable. This case squarely presents the issue of whether the assumption of risk doctrine should have continuing viability now that Louisiana is a comparative fault jurisdiction.

(III) Answer to the Certified Question

"In 1979, Louisiana Civil Code article 2323 was rewritten to eliminate the judicially created rule that contributory negligence was a complete bar to the plaintiff's recovery, and to substitute a procedure by which any negligence on the part of the plaintiff would operate as a percentage reduction of his recovery:

"When contributory negligence is applicable to a claim for damages, its effect shall be as follows: If a person suffers injury, death or loss as the result partly of his own negligence and partly as the result of the fault of another person or persons, the claim for damages shall not thereby be defeated, but the amount of damage recoverable shall be reduced in proportion to the degree or percentage of negligence attributable to the person suffering the injury, death or loss. (Amended by Acts 1979, No. 431 § 1, eff. Aug. 1, 1980).

"One question which this change in the law presented was whether assumption of risk should continue to operate as a complete bar to the plaintiff's recovery, even though contributory negligence no longer constitutes such a bar. Noting that Louisiana courts of appeal have taken 'divergent views' on this issue, the Fifth Circuit certified to us the question of whether assumption of risk bars recovery totally, or only results in a reduction of recovery under article 2323.

"Our response is that the common law doctrine of assumption of risk no longer has a place in Louisiana tort law. The types of plaintiff conduct which the defense has been used to describe are governed by civilian concepts of comparative fault and duty/risk. Assumption of risk should not survive as a distinct legal concept for any purpose, and certainly can no longer be utilized as a complete bar to the plaintiff's recovery.

"Because the term 'assumption of risk' is almost always used to describe plaintiff conduct that is indistinguishable from contributory negligence, it would make no sense for us to hold otherwise. Under article 2323, plaintiff negligence results only in a comparative reduction of recovery, and it would be anamolous for us to hold that the same conduct which results only in a reduction of recovery when it is described as 'comparative negligence' somehow should operate as a total bar to recovery when described as 'assumption of risk.' As another state supreme court considering this issue has concluded, 'it would be the ultimate legal inconsistency to reject contributory negligence as an absolute defense yet at the same time allow its effect to continue under the guise of assumption of risk.' *Salinas v. Vierstra,* 107 Idaho 984, 695 P.2d 369, 374 (1985).

"Defendants argue that because article 2323 does not expressly mention assumption of risk, the Legislature intended that the defense would survive the adoption of comparative fault as a complete bar to recovery. Their reasoning is that the Legislature had to be aware of the existence of the defense at the time article 2323 was enacted, and if the Legislature had intended to alter the application of the doctrine, it would have expressly referred to assumption of risk in the code article. Instead, the article simply states it is applicable '[w]hen contributory negligence is applicable to a claim for damages,' and does not refer to assumption of risk.

"However, the fact that article 2323 does not contain the words 'assumption of risk' is not dispositive of the issue. As we have noted elsewhere, it is equally plausible to argue that if the Legislature had intended to preserve the defense as a total bar to recovery, it could have easily and expressly stated that intention in article 2323. *Turner v. New Orleans Public Service, Inc.,* 476 So. 2d 800, 804 (La. 1985). The dispositive factor here should be that there is no doubt that the Legislature intended by article 2323 to eliminate contributory negligence as a complete bar to recovery and to make comparative fault applicable to those cases in which the plaintiff's conduct may result in a reduction of recovery. *Bell v. Jet Wheel Blast,* 462 So. 2d 166, 171 (La. 1985). Beyond that clearly expressed intention, we have observed that the Legislature left the 'tough details' regarding the scope and application of article 2323 'for the courts to decide.' *Turner,* 476 So. 2d at 804. The issue we are called upon to decide here is whether the survival of assumption of risk as a defense which totally bars recovery would be consistent with the Legislature's expressed intention of eliminating the total bar of contributory negligence.

"The answer is that the survival of assumption of risk as a total bar to recovery would be inconsistent with article 2323's mandate that contributory negligence should no longer operate as such a bar to recovery. The arguments raised by the defendants in support of a rigid construction of the wording of article 2323 do not take into consideration the fact that, in all but a relative handful of cases (the express and implied primary assumption of risk cases, which are affected by this opinion in the manner discussed below), 'assumption of risk' is simply a term that has been used to describe a form of contributory negligence. The statute clearly dictates that contributory negligence shall no longer operate as a complete bar to recovery, and the intent of the statute should not be frustrated by the unfortunate practice of describing certain plaintiff conduct as 'assumption of the risk.' To the contrary, the true intent of the statute will be fulfilled by the application of comparative fault principles to such alleged plaintiff negligence, thereby eliminating the inequities inherent in the 'all or nothing' recovery rules that prevailed prior to the adoption of comparative fault. *Turner,* 476 So. 2d at 800. As we stated in *Bell v. Jet Wheel Blast,* 'the adoption of a system of comparative fault should, where it applies, entail the merger of the defenses of misuse and assumption of risk into the general scheme of assessment of liability in proportion to fault.' 462 So. 2d at 172.

"Thus, in any case where the defendant would otherwise be liable to the plaintiff under a negligence or strict liability theory, the fact that the plaintiff may have been aware of the risk created by the defendant's conduct should not operate as a total bar to recovery. Instead, comparative fault principles should apply, and the victim's 'awareness of the danger' is among the factors to be considered in assessing percentages of fault. *Watson v. State Farm Fire & Cas. Ins. Co.*, 469 So. 2d 967, 974 (La. 1985).

"In order to avoid further confusion in this area of the law, we believe that the courts, lawyers and litigants would best be served by no longer utilizing the term assumption of risk to refer to plaintiff conduct. We belatedly join the New Jersey Supreme Court in expressing our view that assumption of risk terminology 'is better banished from the scene.' *McGrath v. American Cyanamid Co.*, 196 A.2d at 240–41.

"However, our answer to the certified question does not change the law in those cases where the plaintiff, by oral or written agreement, expressly waives or releases a future right to recover damages from the defendant. Assuming that the existence of a voluntary and express pre-accident agreement is proven, and that no public policy concerns would invalidate such a waiver (*see also* La. Civil Code art. 2004), the plaintiff's right to recover damages may be barred on a release theory. Applying duty/risk analysis to this situation, it can be concluded that the defendant has been relieved by contract of the duty that he otherwise may have owed to the plaintiff.

"Nor does our decision today mean that the result reached in the sports spectator or amusement park cases (common law's 'implied primary' assumption of risk cases) was incorrect. However, rather than relying on the fiction that the plaintiffs in such cases implicitly consented to their injuries, the sounder reasoning is that the defendants were not liable because they did not breach any duty owed to the plaintiffs.

"For example, in the classical baseball spectator setting, the case for negligence may often fall short on the question of whether the defendant breached a duty owed to the plaintiff. While a stadium operator may owe a duty to spectators to provide them with a reasonably safe area from which they can watch the game, it is generally not considered reasonable to require the stadium operator to screen all spectator areas from flying baseballs. Even while applying assumption of risk terminology to these types of cases, courts have simultaneously recognized that the defendant was not negligent because his conduct vis-a-vis the plaintiff was not unreasonable. *See Lorino v. New Orleans Baseball & Amusement Co.*, 16 La. App. at 96, 133 So. at 408 ('It is well known . . . that it is not possible . . . for the ball to be kept at all times within the confines of the playing field.') On the other hand, the failure to protect spectator areas into which balls are frequently hit, such as the area behind home plate, might well constitute a breach of duty. These types of cases will turn on their particular facts and may be analyzed in terms of duty/risk. The same analysis applies in other cases where it may not be reasonable to require the defendant to protect the plaintiff from all of the risks associated with a particular activity. *See, e.g., Bonanno v. Continental Casualty Co.*, 285 So. 2d at 592 (operator of haunted house provided adequate supervision and space for patrons, and therefore was not negligent).

(IV) Application of the Answer to the Certified Question to the Facts of This Case

"Having reviewed the impact that our answer to the certified question will have on the different types of cases in which courts have relied on assumption of risk terminology, we return to the facts of this case. The defendants urge that the plaintiffs' decedent assumed the risk of his injuries by diving into the shallow end of a swimming pool, even though, according to the evidence, he had actual knowledge of the dangers associated with that activity. The same conduct which is described by the defendants as assumption of risk, however, also constitutes contributory negligence, since it may be said that a reasonable, prudent person exercising due care for his own safety would not have engaged in shallow water diving. While defendants concede that the successful assertion of the contributory negligence argument can only result in a percentage reduction of recovery under article 2323, they argue that the same evidence used by the jury to assess comparative negligence at 50% should be used to bar recovery under the assumption of risk doctrine. For reasons previously discussed, the law cannot allow such an anamoly. The plaintiffs should be entitled to recover the full amount of their damages, minus a percentage assessed as comparative fault.

"An attempt to analyze this plaintiff's conduct in terms of assumption of risk highlights the weakness of the underlying premise of the defense: the fiction that the plaintiff who disregards a known risk necessarily has consented to his own injury and agreed to relieve the potential defendant of liability for that injury. It cannot be seriously contended that Murray, by attempting to dive into the shallow end of the pool, consented to the risk that he would suffer a fatal blow to his head on the bottom of the pool, and thus agreed in advance to relieve the defendants from liability for his injury. To the contrary, it is obvious from the record that Murray thought that he could safely dive into the shallow end of the pool, an assumption on his part which turned out to be a grave mistake. As Prosser has noted, a miscalculation of the risk constitutes contributory negligence:

"Suppose . . . that the plaintiff dashes into the street in the middle of the block, in the path of a stream of automobiles driven in excess of the speed limit. Given these facts, the ordinary entering law student would immediately say that he had of course assumed the risk. Yet by no stretch of the imagination can such conduct be regarded as manifesting consent that the drivers shall be relieved of the obligation of care for the plaintiff's safety. Rather it clearly indicates a demand, and an insistence, that they shall look out for him and use all reasonable care to protect him. No consent that they shall not is implied on any rational basis. This is an ordinary case of contributory negligence, and not assumption of risk at all.

"W. Prosser & J. Wade, Cases and Materials on Torts, *supra*, at 535.

"Another argument raised by the defendants deserves attention here, because in light of our holding today, similar arguments might arise in future cases. Defendants suggest that, leaving aside the doctrine of assumption of risk, they should not be liable because they had no duty to protect the decedent from a danger of which he had knowledge. In essence, defendants contend here that they were not negligent because the plaintiff voluntarily encountered the risk.

"The Fifth Circuit wisely rejected this contention. 821 F.2d at 276. If accepted, defendants' argument would inject the assumption of risk doctrine into duty/risk analysis 'through the back door.' By that, we mean that the argument attempts to define the defendant's initial duty in terms of the plaintiff's actual knowledge, and thereby seeks to achieve the same result which would be reached if assumption of risk were retained as a defense, i.e., a total bar to the plaintiff's recovery.

"A defendant's duty should not turn on a particular plaintiff's state of mind, but instead should be determined by the standard of care which the defendant owes to all potential plaintiffs. See Robertson, *supra*, 44 La. L. Rev. at 1378. Here, for example, the defendants owed a duty to all potential users of the pool to operate that facility in a reasonably safe fashion. Further, the defendants faced strict liability under civil code article 2317 if the pool constituted an unreasonably dangerous thing over which they had custody and control.

"The jury found that the pool was operated in an unreasonably dangerous manner after hearing evidence on the absence of warning signs regarding diving, the removal of the diving board and the absence of a lifeguard. The jury further determined that the unreasonably dangerous manner in which the pool was operated was a cause of the decedent's injuries and subsequent death. Once these determinations were made, it was then proper for the jury to consider the decedent's alleged fault. It would not have been proper for the jury to turn this analytical process on its head by finding, as urged by the defendants, that this particular plaintiff's knowledge of the risk rendered the pool operator free from fault. If such a finding were allowed to stand, the decedent's negligent disregard for the risk, i.e., his contributory negligence, would bar recovery despite defendants' fault, and the comparative fault rules of article 2323 would be circumvented.

"Again, this is not to say that a duty is owed or breached in all situations that involve injury. We have held, for example, that the duty which a landowner owes to persons entering his property is governed by a standard of reasonableness, and that a potentially dangerous condition that should be obvious to all comers is not, in all instances, unreasonably dangerous. *See, e.g., Shelton v. Aetna Casualty & Surety Co.*, 334 So. 2d 406, 410–11 (La. 1976). However, the key to a finding of no liability in such cases is not the plaintiff's subjective awareness of the risk, but the determination that the defendant did not act unreasonably vis-a-vis the plaintiff, or injure the plaintiff through the instrumentality of an unreasonably dangerous thing in his custody. The determination of what the plaintiff knew regarding the risk of injury is made after fault on the part of the defendant has been established, and is governed by the comparative fault principles enunciated in La. Civ. Code art. 2323 (West Supp. 1988). . . . ''

10:13 *Emerging Higher Standard of Care*

In *DiSalvo v. Armae, Inc.*[48] the New York Court of Appeals held that a resort owner, as an occupier of land, owed a very high degree of care to his paying guests. In that case an infant guest was run over by a pickup truck traversing a private road dividing the property during a festive gathering organized by the resort management. The court concluded that it was error to dismiss the infant's cause of action on the ground that she was within the immediate supervision of her parents. The road under these circumstances constituted a hazard to minors, and the resort was under a duty to close off or prevent motor traffic during that time of day and under those circumstances. A new trial was ordered.

This is a significant departure from the prior rule of responsibility, that is, that of providing reasonable care to protect guests and patrons from unsafe premises. The only other cases in which a more stringent standard of care is imposed are those dealing with employee or intruder assaults upon invitees (*see* section 11:1, *infra*). This holding is still the minority viewpoint, but it portends a reexamination and possible modification of the traditional rule with the result that any commercial owner or occupier of land will be compelled to exercise more than ordinary care toward paying customers, irrespective of the cause of the injury or harm inflicted.

10:14 *Summary*

The law does not impose an absolute duty on the operator of the facility to maintain that facility in a safe condition. Thus the operator is not an insurer of the safety and security of invitees. The operator, however, has an affirmative duty to warn the invitee of concealed or hidden dangers or risks that are or should have been known to the operator, as well as to exercise at least ordinary or reasonable care in the construction, maintenance, and supervision of the facility. (*See* section 10:13, *supra*.)

The operator is not liable for dangers inherent in the use of the facility and obvious to the user, except when there are state statutory enactments that adopt a comparative negligence rule as to contributory negligence and assumption of risk doctrines that would otherwise bar recovery.

The operator is required, as part of his duty of reasonable supervision, to comply with all statutory or municipal requirements governing the activity he provides. Any failure to do so causally related to the injuries suffered by the invitee constitutes either negligence *per se* or evidence of negligence.

[48]41 N.Y.2d 80, 359 N.E.2d 391 (1976).

The operator is required to hire and retain competent employees whom he engages to operate the recreational activities. It is negligence to hire or retain persons unfit to manage, supervise, or operate the activity who might cause or contribute to the injuries suffered by the invitee. Some activities involve greater risk and call for supervision and operational skill commensurate with the risk.

The comparative knowledge of the operator and the injured party will be weighed by the courts in applying the normal standard of reasonable care. A minor or handicapped person will not be held to the same degree of understanding and ability to escape risks that might be dispositive in the case of an adult. This fact is especially critical in those states that have adopted comparative negligence statutes. But it also is important in determining whether the injured party was capable of contributory negligence or assumption of risk where those rules otherwise remain in full force. A minor is always treated with some deference, depending on his age and level of development. Always bear in mind that issues of negligence, contributory negligence, and assumption of risk are normally questions of fact for the jury to resolve upon proper instructions on the law by the court. So long as no egregious errors were committed in the course of the charge to the jury on the law, and there is sufficient evidence in the record of the case to support a jury finding on these questions, the reviewing court will not overturn any verdict rendered.

Whereas it is literally true that the mere fact of death by drowning does not create any inference of negligence, some jurisdictions apply the *res ipsa loquitur* doctrine to establish such a presumption or other evidence of negligence.

A total absence of supervision over a recreational facility such as a swimming pool should be avoided, especially if the resort is family oriented and there are children using the facility. The very absence of supervision might be viewed as a special risk that would attract children and would thus constitute a breach of the duty otherwise owing for reasonable care for their safety. For example, the risk of drowning in an unattended pool would more than likely be greater in the case of a person of tender years, and leaving such a pool unattended could be viewed as making the risk of such harm foreseeable and thus actionable, whereas this theory of foreseeability would not apply in the case of an adult.

Appendix.   *Excerpts from the Massachusetts Ski Act*

SKI OPERATORS AND SKIERS—
RESPONSIBILITY AND LIABILITY

CHAPTER 455.

An Act clarifying the responsibility and liability of ski operators and skiers.

Whereas, The deferred operation of this act would tend to defeat its purpose, which is to clarify the responsibility and liability of ski operators and skiers, therefore it is hereby declared to be an emergency law, necessary for the immediate preservation of the public convenience.

Be it enacted, etc., as follows:

SECTION 1. said section 71I of said chapter 143 is hereby further amended by adding the following four definitions—

"Skier," any person utilizing the ski area under control of ski area operator for the purpose of skiing, whether or not that person is a passenger on a recreational tramway, including riders during a non-skiing season.

"Ski area," all of the slopes and trails under the control of the ski area operator, including cross-country ski areas, slopes, and trails, and any recreational tramway in operation on any such slopes or trails administered or operated as a single enterprise but shall not include base lodges, motor vehicle parking lots and other portions of ski areas used by skiers when not actually engaged in the sport of skiing.

"Ski area operator," the owner or operator of a ski area, including an agency of the commonwealth or a political subdivision thereof, or the employees, agents, officers or delegated representatives of such owner or operator, including the owner or operator of a cross-country ski area, slope or trail, and of any recreational tramway in operation on any such slope or trail administered or operated as a single enterprise.

"Ski slope or trail," an area designed by the person or organization having operational responsibility for the ski area as herein defined, including a cross-country ski area, for use by the public in furtherance of the sport of skiing, meaning such designation as is set forth on a trail map or as otherwise designated by a sign indicating to the skiing public the intent that the area be used by skiers for purpose of participating in the sport.

SECTION 2. Section 71J of said chapter 143, as so appearing, is hereby amended by inserting after the first sentence the following sentence:

The board shall in like manner adopt, and from time to time amend or revoke, rules and regulations for a system of signs to be used by a ski area operator in order to promote the safety of skiers. Such system shall incorporate standards in general use in the skiing industry to evaluate the difficulty of slopes and trails and to adequately alert skiers to the known danger of any slope or trail of the ski area.

SECTION 3. Said chapter 143 is hereby further amended by striking out sections 71N and 71O, as so appearing, and inserting in place thereof the following six sections.

Section 71N.

A ski area operator shall:

(1) whenever maintenance or snowmaking equipment is being employed on any ski slope or trail open to the public, conspicuously place or cause to be placed, notice at or near the top of any ski slope or trail being maintained that such equipment is being so employed, and shall conspicuously indicate the location of any such equipment in a manner to afford skiers reasonable notice of the proximity of such equipment;

(2) mark and identify all trail maintenance and emergency vehicles, including snowmobiles, and furnish such vehicles with flashing or rotating lights, which shall be operated during the time that said vehicles are in operation within the ski area;

(3) with respect to the emergency use of vehicles within the ski area, including but not limited to uses for purposes of removing injured or stranded skiers, or performing emergency maintenance or repair work to slopes, trails or tramway equipment, not be required to post such signs as is required by clause (1), but shall be required to maintain such lighting equipment required by clause (2);

(4) mark the location of any hydrants used in snowmaking operations and located within or upon a slope or trail;

(5) conspicuously place within the ski area, in such form, size and location as the board may require, and on the back of any lift ticket issued notice, in plain language, of the statute of limitations and notice period established in section seventy-one P; and

(6) maintain a sign system on all buildings, recreational tramways, ski trails and slopes in accordance with rules and regulations promulgated by the board and shall be responsible for the maintenance and operation of ski areas under its control in a reasonably safe condition or manner, provided, however, that ski area operators shall not be liable for damages to persons or property, while skiing, which arise out of the risks inherent in the sport of skiing.

Section 71O

No skier shall embark or disembark upon a recreational tramway except at a designated location and during designated hours of operation, throw or expel any object from any recreational tramway while riding thereon, act in any manner while riding on a recreational tramway that may interfere with its proper or safe operation, engage in any type of conduct which may injure any person, or place any object in the uphill ski track which may cause another to fall while traveling uphill on a ski lift, or cross the uphill track of a recreational tramway except at designated locations. A skier shall maintain control of his speed and course at all times, and shall stay clear of any snow-grooming equipment, and vehicle, towers, poles, or other equipment.

A skier who boards a recreational tramway shall be presumed to have sufficient abilities to use the same, and shall follow any written or oral instruction given regarding its use and no skier shall embark on a recreational tramway without authority of the operator. A skier skiing down hill shall have the duty to avoid any collision with any other skier, person or object on the hill below him, and, except as otherwise provided in this chapter, the responsibility for collisions by any skier with any other skier or person shall be solely that of the skier or person involved and not that of the operator, and the responsibility for the collision with any obstruction, man-made or otherwise, shall be solely that of the skier and not that of the operator, provided that such obstruction is properly marked pursuant to the regulations promulgated by the board. No skier shall ski on any ski slope or trail or portion thereof which has been designated closed, nor ski on other than an identified trail, slope or ski area. Any person skiing on other than an open slope or trail within the ski area shall be responsible for any injuries resulting from his action. A skier shall, prior to his entrance onto the slope or trail, other than one designated for cross-country skiing, or embarking on any recreational tramway, have attached on his skies, a strap or other device for the purpose of restraining or preventing a runaway ski. A ski area operator who finds a person in violation of this section, may issue an oral warning to that individual. A person who fails to heed the warning issued by such ski area operator shall forfeit his recreational tramway ticket and recreationl tramway use privileges and may be refused issuance of another such ticket to the recreational tramway.

Section 71P.

For the purpose of sections seventy-one I to seventy-one R, inclusive, in any action brought against a ski area operator on negligence, it shall be evidence of due care where the conduct of an operator has conformed with the provisions of this chapter or rules or regulations of the board made pursuant to section seventy-one J.

No action shall be maintained against a ski area operator for injury to a skier unless as a condition precedent thereof the person so injured shall, within ninety days of the incident, give to such ski area operator notice, by registered mail, of the name and address of the person injured, the time, place and cause of the injury. Failure to give the foregoing notice shall bar recovery, unless the court finds under the circumstances of the particular case that such ski area operator had actual knowledge of said injury or had reasonable opportunity to learn of said injury within said ninety-day period, or was otherwise not substantially prejudiced by reason of not having been given actual written notice of said injury within said period. In a case where lack of written notice, actual knowledge, or a reasonable opportunity to obtain knowledge of any injury within said ninety-day period is alleged by such ski area operator, the burden of proving substantial prejudice shall be on the operator.

An action to recover for such injury shall be brought within one year of the date of such injury.

Section 71Q.

Any person who is knowingly involved in a skiing accident and who departs from the scene of such accident without leaving personal identification or otherwise clearly identifying himself and obtaining assistance knowing that any other person involved in the accident is in need of medical or other assistance shall be punished by a fine of not less than one hundred dollars.

Section 71R.

Whoever violates any provision of sections 71K, 71N, or any rule or regulation made under the provisions of section 71J, shall be punished by a fine of not more than two hundred dollars; provided, however, that any person who operates a recreational tramway, after the license therefore has been suspended or revoked, shall be punished by a fine of one hudred dollars for each day of such operation.

. . .

Approved July 17, 1978.

11 Responsibility for Conduct of Persons in the Inn

11:1 *Protection against Injury by Third Parties: The Trend toward Stricter Standards*

An innkeeper must take at least reasonable care to protect the guest against injuries at the hands of "third parties" while the guests are on—and sometimes outside—the premises. The term "third parties" denotes guests and patrons of the establishment as well as strangers and intruders. In some cases, the innkeeper's obligation has been interpreted to extend beyond warning the guest of danger, to include the responsibility of taking positive action to forestall injuries.[1]

Examining an array of cases, one sees the justices' growing concern with the circumstances and the nature of an apprehended danger. For example, in *Dean v. Hotel Greenwich Corp.*,[2] a hotel patron was assaulted in the hotel's lobby only minutes after a guard gave him assurances of protection upon the patron's telling the guard he had been threatened by the assailants. The New York Supreme Court found that the "duty or degree of care to be expected depends upon [the] danger to be apprehended. . . . " The court observed further: " . . . there is no fixed degree of care . . . it depends on circumstances . . . the degree of care that [the] hotel keeper is required to exercise varies with the grade and quality of accommodations offered." This case was one of the first in which the social milieu (i.e., the environment in or around the hotel) was used as a criterion for establishing a standard of care: "The defendant hotel is a place where assault, theft and kindred events are a daily occurrence. . . . [T]he plaintiff made out a *prima facie* case under the law against the defendant if under the circumstances there were insufficient guards or incompetent guards."[3] Courts have since interpreted the reasonable-care rule as including "the duty to police the premises

---

This chapter reproduces in part an article by John E. H. Sherry and David Bruce Wallace titled "Hotel Security: The Innkeeper's Dilemma" from the May 1978 issue of the Cornell Hotel and Restaurant Administration Quarterly, with permission from the Cornell University School of Hotel Administration. © 1978.

[1] 43A C.J.S. 1176 and authorities cited therein.
[2] 193 N.Y.S.2d 712 (Sup. Ct. 1959).
[3] *Id.* at 715.

where necessary to control the conduct of those present and prevent them from injuring others'' and have also concluded that the obligation may extend off the premises.[4]

In addition to evidence with respect to a hotel's "social milieu," a court can hear evidence concerning security measures taken at substantially similar area hotels and motels for the purpose of determining whether the hotel at issue adequately protects its guests from third-party misconduct. In the Missouri case of *Anderson v. Malloy,*[5] plaintiff was raped while she was staying at a defendant hotel. The court held that differences in the physical layout between the defendant hotel and area hotels notwithstanding, evidence concerning security measures at similar area hotels was relevant to the adequacy of the defendant's security measures.

The case to follow illustrates the judicial trend toward relating standards of reasonable care for the physical safety of hotel guests from third-party criminal misconduct to the size, class, and quality of services represented to the public. Moreover, and of equal importance, the case disallows the defense that the industry, lacking any standards, thus immunizes itself from liability. The jury is permitted reasonable latitude to set its own standards in such cases.

ORLANDO EXECUTIVE PARK, INC., v. P.D.R.
402 So. 2d 442 (Fla. App. 1981)
pet. for rev. denied,
411 So. 2d 384 (1981), *decision approved, Orlando Executive Park, Inc. v. Robbins,* 433 So. 2d 491 (Fla. 1983)

ORFINGER, J.: " . . . On October 22, 1975, [plaintiff] was in Orlando performing the duties of her employment. She telephoned the Howard Johnson's Motor Lodge involved in this action at approximately 9:30 P.M. and made a room reservation. Approximately ten minutes later she left the restaurant and drove directly to the motor lodge. When she arrived, she signed the registration form which had already been filled out by the desk clerk and was directed to her room which was located on the ground level in building 'A', the first building behind the registration office. Plaintiff parked her car, went to her room and left her suitcase there. She then went back to her car to get some papers and when starting back to her room, she noticed a man standing in a walkway behind the registration office. Having reentered the building and while proceeding back along the interior hallway to her room, she was accosted by the man she had seen behind the registration office, who struck her very hard in the throat and on the back of her neck and then choked her until she became unconscious. When consciousness returned, plaintiff found herself lying on the floor of the hallway with her assailant sitting on top of her, grabbing her throat. Plaintiff was phys-

---

[4]*See, e.g.,* Vale v. Yawarski, 357 N.Y.S.2d 791 (Sup. Ct. 1974).
[5]700 F.2d 1208 (8th Cir. 1983).

ically unable to speak and lapsed into an unconscious or semi-conscious state. Her assailant stripped her jewelry from her and then dragged her down the hallway to a place beneath a secluded stairwell, where he kicked her and brutally forced her to perform an unnatural sex act. He then disappeared in the night and has never been identified.

"Plaintiff's action for damages was based on her claim that defendants owed her the legal duty to exercise reasonable care for her safety while she was a guest on the premises. And she alleged that this duty had been breached by, *inter alia,* allowing the building to remain open and available to anyone who cared to enter, by failing to have adequate security on the premises either on the night in question or prior thereto so as to deter criminal activity against guests which had occurred before and which could foreseeably occur again, failing to install TV monitoring equipment in the public areas of the motel to deter criminal activity, failing to establish and enforce standards of operation at the lodge which would protect guests from physical attack and theft of property, and failure to warn plaintiff that there had been prior criminal activity on the premises and that such activity would or might constitute a threat to her safety on the premises. . . .

"There was evidence submitted tending to show serious physical and psychological injury as a result of this assault which was susceptible of the conclusion that within a year following the assault, plaintiff lost her job because of memory lapses, mental confusion and inability to tolerate and communicate with people. There was evidence from which the jury could conclude that this injury was permanent and that she would require expensive, long-term medical and psychiatric treatment, and that she had suffered a great loss in her earning capacity. . . .

"There was no regular security force at the motor lodge, nor were there other security devices such as TV monitors in hallways or other common areas. One security guard was employed from time to time, on a sporadic basis. For the six-month period prior to the incident in question, management of the motor lodge was aware of approximately thirty criminal incidents occurring on the premises. While most of these involved burglary, some of them involved direct attacks upon the guests. Following one of the attacks, approximately ten weeks prior to the incident in question, the motor lodge owners had hired a full-time security guard, but he was terminated a short time later. Anticipating high occupancy, one security guard had been employed for the evening in question commencing at 10:00 P.M. While it is not clear whether the attack occurred during the period this guard was on duty, the jury could have concluded that he was not on duty at the time, although he was on the premises becoming familiar with the layout because he had never been on the property before. Additionally, the evidence indicated that the guard had been employed to patrol the parking areas, and not the motor lodge buildings. The security service which provided the guards from time to time, had recommended the employment of two to three guards on a full-time basis. Plaintiff's security expert testified that three guards on staggered shifts would be necessary to deter criminal activity, although he agreed that there were no industry standards for security guards and that it was impossible to say that the assault would not have occurred if three guards had been on the premises. He did, however, testify that in his opinion, a proper security force would serve as a deterrent to this type of activity and the chance of this happening would be slight.

I. Liability of Orlando Executive Park, Inc.

"It seems clear in Florida registered guests in a hotel or motel are business invitees to whom the hotel or motel owes a duty of reasonable care for their safety. *Phillips Petroleum Company of Bartlesville, Oklahoma v. Dorn*, 292 So. 2d 429 (Fla. 4th D.C.A. 1974). While recognizing this principle and conceding this duty, appellants say, nevertheless, that there is no evidence of a breach of their duty, since the injury to appellee was caused by the criminal act of a stranger, thus acting as an intervening efficient cause for which they are not responsible.

"The evidence clearly shows numerous criminal activities on the premises in the six-month period immediately prior to this occurrence. The testimony of a security expert produced by plaintiff indicated adequate security at this motor lodge required the presence of at least three full-time security guards. Thus the question becomes one of foreseeability. Could a jury, under the facts of this case reasonably conclude that the absence of adequate security would lead to the robbery and attack here? Such is ordinarily a question for the jury. *Rosier v. Gainesville Inns Associates, Ltd.*, 347 So. 2d 1100 (Fla. 1st D.C.A. 1977). . . . We first reject, as entirely fallacious, the defendant's claim that the brutal and deliberate act of the rapist-murderer constituted an 'independent intervening cause' which served to insulate it from liability. It is well-established that if the reasonable possibility of the intervention, criminal or otherwise, of a third party is the avoidable risk of harm which itself causes one to be deemed negligent, the occurrence of that very conduct cannot be a superseding cause of a subsequent misadventure. . . .

"Appellant continues, however, with its argument that there was no evidence that security was inadequate or more to the point, that any specific quantity of security guards or other measures would have prevented this robbery and attack. They say that since there are no standards for security in the motel industry, there is no way for a jury to determine the reasonableness (or unreasonableness) of any particular security measure. The absence of industry standards does not insulate the defendants from liability when there is credible evidence presented to the jury pointing to measures reasonably available to deter incidents of this kind, against which the jury can judge the reasonableness of the measures taken *in this case*.

"Obviously, a six-unit, one building 'Mom and Pop' motel will not have the same security problems as a large highrise thousand room hotel, or of a three hundred room motor lodge spread out over six buildings. Each presents a peculiar security problem of its own. How the means necessary to fulfill the duty of care varies with the peculiar circumstances of each case is explained by the Wisconsin Supreme Court in *Peters v. Holiday Inns, Inc.*, 89 Wis. 2d 115, 278 N.W.2d 208 (1979). . . .

"Here, the jury had the right to consider that the size and layout of the complex, its various accessory uses and the apparent ease of entrance into the motel buildings, and could have concluded that these factors required *some* security measures. They could also conclude from the evidence that the type of activity within the complex increased the security risk and that no security was provided at the time of this attack.

"And while appellant suggests plaintiff was required to show the attack would have been prevented had reasonable measures been taken, this is not the test. Causation, like any other element of plaintiff's case, need not be demonstrated by conclusive proof:

"and it is enough that [plaintiff] introduces evidence from which reasonable men may conclude that it is more probable that the event was caused by the defendant, than that it was not. The fact of causation is incapable of mathematical proof, since no man can say with absolute certainty what would have occurred if the defendant had acted otherwise.

"W. Prosser, Law of Torts, § 41 at 242 (4th ed. 1977). Plaintiff adduced evidence that reasonable measures were not taken. Expert testimony, as well as reasonable inferences from the suggested measures, allowed a conclusion that the chance of this attack was 'slight' had reasonable measures been taken. Thus the question of whether defendant's negligence was the proximate cause of plaintiff's injury was properly a jury question. *See Helman v. Seaboard Coast Line Railroad Co.*, 349 So. 2d 1187, 1189 (Fla. 1977); *Yamada v. Hilton Hotel Corp.*, 17 Ill. Dec. at 233, 376 N.E.2d at 232.

"Plaintiff also proved that the area under the stairwell where she was dragged was dark and secluded and was in itself a security hazard which should have been boarded up as had other similar stairwells in the motel. OEP management actively discouraged criminal investigations by sheriff's deputies, minimizing any deterrent effect they may have had. Thus, the totality of the circumstances presented a jury question regarding causation. . . . It cannot be said that there was a complete absence of probative facts to support the jury's conclusion. *See Yamada v. Hilton Hotel Corp.*, 17 Ill. Dec. at 233, 376 N.E.2d at 232. . . .

"The judgment appealed from is affirmed."

In *Davenport v. Nixon*,[6] the defendant innkeeper's check-in window was located in the hotel parking lot. The plaintiff was assaulted and robbed in the parking lot, immediately in front of the check-in window, by an assailant who had watched plaintiff expose a large quantity of money while paying the desk clerk. The court held that the defendant's check-in method unreasonably increased the risk of attacks on patrons.

Courts have increased innkeepers' duty of care by expanding the scope of "constructive notice." In particular, a court will charge an innkeeper with constructive notice of a criminal incident even if previous criminal incidents that

---

[6]434 So. 2d 1203 (La. Ct. App. 1983).

have occurred on the inn's premises have differed both in kind and in location from the incident at bar.[7]

In *Urbanov v. Days Inns of America, Inc.*,[8] the court held that the existence of twelve criminal episodes on the motel premises, including one armed robbery and several illegal entries during the three months preceding the assault at issue, was sufficient to give the innkeeper constructive notice that security measures in the parking lot where plaintiff was assaulted were inadequate.

In *Virginia D. v. Madesco Investment Corp.*,[9] the Missouri Supreme Court charged the defendants with possessing sufficient constructive notice of a criminal attack on the basis of a few, dissimilar prior acts of misconduct.

One of the most significant New York cases is the now notorious "Connie Francis Case," *Garzilli v. Howard Johnson's Motor Lodges, Inc.*[10] The well-known entertainer Connie Francis was sexually assaulted in November 1974 by an assailant who entered her motel room through the sliding patio door. The traumatized singer and her husband collected almost $1.5 million in damages—for pain, suffering, mental anguish, humiliation, and loss of earnings. In reviewing the case, the New York District Court noted that, although the doors to the singer's room gave the appearance of being locked, they were quite easily opened from the outside. It was also observed that the motel had been burglarized four times by intruders who gained access using the patio doors[11] and that although safer locks had been ordered by the motel, they had not been received and installed at the time of the attack. At least in New York State, an innkeeper who operates a property in a high-crime area or with a history of recent on-premises crimes is well advised to take special precautions against such crimes if he wishes to avoid staggering lawsuits. When master keys for major New York City hotels are available "on the street" for $500,[12] one might justifiably expect some future court to find that a traditional keying system no longer satisfies the innkeeper's duty of "reasonable care." If this should happen, and if the damages in the case were large, the industry might be forced to adopt new systems almost overnight.

In an Illinois case, *Kiefely v. Las Vegas Hacienda, Inc.*[13] a U.S. District Court reviewed a motel assault case on several procedural grounds. One of the questions the district judge raised was, "Did the assault proximately result from

---

[7]But *cf.* Highlands Insurance Co. v. Gilday, 398 So. 2d 834 (Fla. Dist. Ct. App. 1981), *petition for rev. denied*, 411 So. 2d 382 (Fla. 1981) (previous misconduct, including disgruntled employee's threat and a breaking and entering, held not to give hotel sufficient constructive notice that guests were inadequately protected against criminal attacks); McCoy v. Gay, 165 Ga. App. 590, 302 S.E.2d 130 (1983) (previous purse-snatching and robbery on hotel premises not sufficient to give hotel constructive notice that parking lot was inadequately secured).

[8]58 N.C. App. 795, 295 S.E.2d 40 (1982).

[9]648 S.W.2d 881 (Mo. 1983).

[10]419 F. Supp. 1210 (E.D.N.Y. 1976).

[11]19 A.T.L.A. Newsletter 306–307 (1976).

[12]C. Wintrey, *Hotels Trying to Stem Rise in Thefts,* N.Y. Times, Sept. 7, 1977 at B1.

[13]39 F.R.D. 592 (N.D. Ill. 1966), *aff'd,* 404 F.2d 1163 (7th Cir. 1968), *cert. denied,* 395 U.S. 908 (1969).

defendant's negligence in failing to provide an adequate lock on the door or in not maintaining sufficient security guard in the corridor?'' While the question was not specifically answered in that case, an expanding, court-inspired innkeeper's duty to protect his guests from unexpected assaults is again evident.

In *Nordmann v. National Hotel Co.*,[14] a case tried in Louisiana, the complainant charged the defendant with:

(*a*) Permitting criminals, sex deviates, and vagrants to wander indiscriminately about the hotel.

(*b*) Failure to maintain a competent staff of employees.

(*c*) Failure to maintain adequate security personnel.

(*d*) Failure to summon the police immediately.

(*e*) Failure to have the hotel security officer investigate the incident as soon as it was reported to a hotel employee.

This case involved a sexual attack perpetrated upon a female guest, whose struggle was overheard by the guest next door; the second guest immediately called the hotel switchboard for help, but no action was taken for almost an hour. The court interpreted the law as imposing at least ordinary- or reasonable-care standards on innkeepers and found that the evidence supported the jury's verdict of negligence. In fact, the Fifth Circuit Court of Appeals concluded that the damages awarded were too modest. The charges enumerated above are an indication of what steps the jury considered it reasonable for the hotel to take.

In *Phillips Petroleum Co. of Bartlesville, Oklahoma v. Dorn*[15] the court found that the degree of care required to protect the guest was the same whether the guest was in his room or in other common areas of the hotel. This distinction is important because many of the guests attacked in the infamous New Orleans sniper case, *Steagall v. Civic Center Site Development Co., Inc.*,[16] were in the hotel's public areas at the time. The plaintiffs in that case alleged that the innkeeper breached his duty of reasonable care to protect his guests from injuries at the hands of third persons by: (1) failing to design and maintain safe premises; (2) failing to warn the victims against the sniper; and (3) failing to provide adequate security guards and other safety devices. The jury found that the innkeeper's omissions contributed to the plaintiffs' injuries, and damages were high, both in court and in out-of-court settlements.

Two other hotel cases merit examination: *Adams v. Holiday Inns of America*[17] and *Moore v. Florida Innkeepers, Inc., and Holiday Inns, Inc.*[18] In *Adams*, the plaintiff had been attacked in his room by a gunman, and the criminal history of the property's location and allegedly inadequate security measures were evidentiary factors considered in the trial. In *Moore*, a guest who was shot at an ice machine in a St. Augustine, Florida, Holiday Inn settled out-of-court for substantial damages. The innkeeper-defendants were charged with failing to provide

---

[14]425 F.2d 1103 (5th Cir. 1970).
[15]292 So. 2d 429 (Fla. 1974).
[16]No. 74-3 (E.D. La. July 2, 1975).
[17]15 A.T.L.A. Newsletter 411–12 (1972).
[18]20 A.T.L.A. Newsletter 152–54 (1977).

guards and other protective measures, including adequate illumination, and for falsely advertising Holiday Inns as reliable and safe places to stay.

The continued erosion of the reasonable care standard and the substitution of a stricter degree of care upon those who own or operate places of public accommodation are illustrated by the Wisconsin Supreme Court's ruling in *Peters v. Holiday Inns, Inc.*[19] Here, the fortuitous presence of the police at the scene was held not sufficient to preclude a jury trial on the issues of liability.

In sum, although the innkeeper has not been considered an insurer of the safety and well-being of the guest, he has been found liable in cases of assault and injury when, through fault or negligence, he has caused or contributed to the injury suffered. Moreover, his duty to exercise care has been increased to reflect dissatisfaction with the traditional standard of ordinary care adopted in the early cases.

It is appropriate here to ask how the law could support the notion that the innkeeper must anticipate and guard against the intentional misconduct of third persons that could result in injury to the guest. Surely it stands to reason that an innkeeper cannot assume a third party on the premises will violate the criminal law; hence, the innkeeper cannot foresee such events and should not be held to suffer the consequences when they occur. However, an innkeeper *is* required by law to protect his guests against such criminal misconduct, especially when he has created or exposed the guest to a recognizably high degree of risk of harm.

A mitigating condition should be noted. The duty of care, however defined, is applicable only where the innkeeper has actual knowledge of the presence upon his premises of an intruder or trespasser, whether through personal observation or that of his staff, other guests, or law-enforcement agencies; or where the innkeeper may be said to have constructive notice, by reason of prior incidents of a similar nature, that the situation requires corrective action. In this regard, the location of the premises in a high-crime area does not in and of itself give rise to a duty to act, but may be considered by the jury as one factor with bearing on the issue of liability. Simply stated, the innkeeper is not bound to anticipate and guard against the unusual and abnormal. He is currently required to take action only when he has reason to believe, from what he has observed or from experience, that the conduct of a third party will be dangerous to the guest.

In the following case, the Supreme Court of Hawaii made extensive reference to the issues of legal duty and proximate cause in a negligence action arising out of a fatal shooting of a hotel guest by a third person on the premises. (Only the issue of proximate cause is excerpted.)

KNODLE V. WAIKIKI GATEWAY HOTEL, INC.
69 Haw. 376, 742 P.2d 377 (1987)

NAKAMURA, J.: "Linda Kay Knodle, a flight attendant then employed by Continental Air Lines, Inc., was murdered by George Patrick Murphy on November 26, 1974 in the Waikiki Gateway Hotel.

---

[19] 89 Wis. 2d 115, 278 N.W.2d 208 (1979).

"Linda Knodle arrived in Honolulu on the fateful day at about 2:00 A.M. on a Continental Air Lines flight from Guam. She was not one of the attendants assigned to duty on the flight; she was 'riding on a pass given by her employer and going back to Chicago' for the Thanksgiving holiday. Shortly after the plane landed, the two flight attendants who 'worked' the flight left the airport in a taxicab to go to the Waikiki Gateway Hotel, where Continental's flight crews were housed during 'layovers' in Honolulu. Linda Knodle could not leave with them because she was detained in Customs. She caught a ride later with several Continental pilots and reached the hotel shortly before 5:00 A.M.

"When they arrived, the pilots carried Linda Knodle's bags into the lobby. She went to the front desk where she was greeted by the Assistant Manager and the Night Auditor, both of whom she knew from previous stays at the hotel. She then asked the Night Auditor to place a telephone call to the pilot who had been the Captain of the flight from Guam. After a half-hour conversation with the Captain, in which they talked about the possibility of having a party on his boat but decided not to, Ms. Knodle resumed her conversation with the two hotel employees. The pilots with whom she rode to the hotel were gone, having left earlier upon learning the Captain was reluctant to host a party.

"Ms. Knodle then started to fill out a guest registration card. But before she finished, she asked the Assistant Manager about the two attendants on the flight from Guam and the rooms they were occupying. Upon learning one was in a room with two beds, she asked for a key to the room, Room 1006. The Assistant Manager handed her a key to the tenth-floor room and tore up the registration card. Ms. Knodle then carried two pieces of her luggage to one of the hotel's three elevators and went back to fetch the remaining bags.

"Meanwhile, George Murphy came into the lobby, walked to the elevators, and entered the one in which Ms. Knodle had placed her bags. The Assistant Manager saw this and yelled, '[h]old the elevator.' Murphy held the door open while Ms. Knodle picked up the rest of her luggage and entered the elevator. The door then closed, and the elevator ascended to the upper floors. The two employees at the front desk resumed what they had been doing earlier.

"At about 6:30 A.M., the Night Auditor was informed by a guest who was checking out that there was 'some extra luggage [in] the elevator.' The Auditor removed the bags from the elevator and took them to the front desk. When he examined the luggage tags, he realized the bags belonged to Ms. Knodle. He discussed the matter with the Assistant Manager, but they decided not to disturb her because they assumed she was asleep in her room.

"A maintenance man who came to work at 7:00 A.M. found the key to a tenth-floor guest room later on in a fourth-floor hallway. He 'noticed . . . the key didn't belong on that floor,' asked the first guest he saw whether the guest had misplaced the key to his room, and 'took the key downstairs to the clerk's counter' thereafter, telling the desk clerk 'I found the key on the fourth floor.'

"Shortly after 9:00 A.M., Linda Knodle's body was discovered in a restroom adjoining the laundry room on the fourth floor. A guest came upon Ms. Knodle's inert form, assumed she was ill, and called the Manager, informing him that 'someone is ill in the bathroom.' The Manager responded to the call, but discovered she was dead. She had been strangled to death by George Patrick Murphy sometime between 5:15 A.M. and 9:00 A.M.

"John Knodle filed suit on November 24, 1976, nearly two years after the lamentable occurrence. His first complaint named Murphy, Waikiki Gateway Hotel, Inc. and John Does 1 through 20 as defendants and alleged, *inter alia,* that Murphy 'brutally assaulted and murdered [Linda Kay Knodle] on the premises of the Waikiki Gateway Hotel' and Waikiki Gateway Hotel, Inc. and Does 1 through 5 did not 'provide safe accommodations for . . . Linda Kay Knodle' and 'adequate security to protect [her] from the unreasonable risk of physical harm.' Continental Air Lines and the owners and operators of the hotel were identified subsequently as the originally unidentifiable defendants.

"The plaintiff proceeded to trial against the hotel's owners and operators after conducting extensive discovery and twice amending his complaint. The claims tried were: '(1) That the defendants were negligent; and (2) That the defendants acted wantonly and with reckless disregard for the safety of Linda Knodle.' The jury found the defendants had breached no duty owing to Linda Knodle, and John Knodle appeals from the judgment entered on the verdict returned by the jury. . . .

" 'Proximate cause,' the term employed by many courts to characterize this legally sufficient causal relation, is 'in itself an unfortunate term.' W. P. Keeton, *supra,* § 41, at 264. It might have been apt in an earlier time; but in the complex society of the late twentieth century, a negligent tort is as likely as not to have plural or concurring causes. And it is not only the 'next' or 'nearest' cause that the law considers close enough to make a defendant responsible for the injury suffered by the plaintiff. . . .

"Some courts stepping away from literal 'proximate causation' adopted a 'but for' rule. Thereunder, '[t]he defendant's conduct is a cause of the event if the event would not have occurred but for that conduct; conversely, the defendant's conduct is not a cause of the event, if the event would have occurred without it.' *Id.* at 266. . . . The test serves to explain culpable causation in most cases. *Id.* 'The problem with the "but for" test is that it may not cover the situation where two or more causes [can be perceived yet] none of them alone would have produced the result[ing harm].' 1 J. Dooley, Modern Tort Law § 8.02, at 227 (1982). . . .

" . . . Under the guidelines developed by the American Law Institute (A.L.I.) in its Restatement of Torts, '[t]he actor's negligent conduct is a legal cause of harm to another if (a) his conduct is a substantial factor in bringing about the harm. . . . ' Restatement (Second) of Torts, *supra,* § 431. Finding this measure of blameworthiness was '[t]he best definition and the most workable test of proximate or legal cause so far suggested,' we adopted it in *Mitchell v. Branch,* 45 Haw. 128, 132, 363 P.2d 969, 973 (1961). In affirming a judgment in favor of the plaintiff, we said the defendant's negligence 'need not have been the whole cause or the only factor [in bringing about the harm]. It was enough that his negligence was a substantial factor in causing plaintiff's injuries.' *Id.* (citation omitted). . . .

"The plaintiff in this case argues '[t]he trial court's instruction to the jury on proximate causation and foreseeability was improper.' Considering the judge's charge to the jury as a whole, as we must, [citations omitted], we conclude he erred, as plaintiff avers. . . .

"After apprising the jury that the assailant George Patrick Murphy failed to respond to the complaint and should be considered liable for the harm sustained, the judge proceeded to explain the negligence claim brought by the plaintiff against the hotel's owners and operators. The relevant instruction read:

"The plaintiff's first claim against the defendants is that they were negligent. In order to find that the defendants were negligent, you must find the following elements:

"(1) That the defendants owed Linda Knodle a duty;

"(2) That the defendants breached that duty;

"(3) That Linda Knodle's death was proximately caused by that breach of duty.

"The instruction thus served to delineate the elements of negligence as viewed by the judge and directed the jury to find the defendants were negligent only if they owed Linda Knodle a duty, the duty was breached, and her death was 'proximately caused' by the breach. . . .

" 'The "proximate cause" of an injury' was then defined as 'that cause which in direct, unbroken sequence, produces the injury, and without which the injury would not have occurred.' This was clearly a misstatement of the law. We have moved beyond the strictures of 'direct, unbroken sequence' in the consideration of legal causation. It was error also to speak of legal cause as that 'without which the injury would not have occurred' in the face of our holding in *Mitchell v. Branch* [*supra*]. . . .

"The judge's definition of 'proximate cause' was followed by explanations of plural and concurring causes. We cannot fault the judge as far as these instructions are concerned. But he went on to advise the jury that:

"The independent acts of Mr. Murphy may be found by a preponderance of the evidence to supersede or excuse the negligence of a defendant in failing to provide adequate security at the Waikiki Gateway Hotel.

"However, if you find by a preponderance of the evidence that a defendant's negligence in failing to provide adequate security at the Waikiki Gateway Hotel created a reasonably foreseeable risk of criminal harm to Linda K. Knodle, you are instructed that the independent acts of Mr. Murphy do not operate, excuse any defendant found by you to be negligent.

"An act is reasonably foreseeable if it appears to have been ordinary or usual under all the circumstances then existing.

"The plaintiff argued the instruction fashioned by the court was improper; and as we observed, his claim of error regarding instructions is centered on this instruction. The defendants also objected, but they now maintain the error was harmless because the jury did not reach the issue of causation. We cannot agree. . . .

"In the paragraph following the discussion of independent acts and superseding causes, the judge instructed the jury that the independent acts of George Murphy did not excuse a defendant if its failure to exercise due care created a reasonably foreseeable risk of criminal harm to Linda Knodle. We cannot fault the judge here, but in the succeeding paragraph he informed the jury that '[a]n act is reasonably foreseeable if it appears to have been ordinary or usual under all the circumstances then existing.' We fail to see how murder can be 'ordinary or usual' under any circumstance. We could say the same about lightning striking at any given place or time; yet since 'the possibility is there, . . . it may require precautions for the protection of inflammables.' [Citation omitted.] The test is whether 'there is some probability of harm sufficiently serious that [a reasonable and prudent person] would take precautions to avoid it.' *Tullgren v. Amoskeag Manufacturing Co.*, 82 N.H. at 276, 133 A. at 8. It is not whether the act or risk 'appears to have been ordinary or usual under all the circumstances.' . . .

"The judgment of the circuit court is vacated, and the case is remanded for a new trial."

In *Knott v. Liberty Jewelry and Loan, Inc.*, excerpted below, the Supreme Court of Washington also made reference to foreseeability. In this case, the lack of foreseeability required affirmance of the dismissal of a suit brought by a guest who was shot by another guest.

KNOTT V. LIBERTY JEWELRY AND LOAN INC.
50 Wash. App. 267, 748 P.2d 661 (Wash. App. 1988)

RINGOLD, Acting C.J.: "The plaintiff, Norma Knott, guardian ad litem for Douglas Knott, appeals from the trial court's dismissal of all claims on defendants' motions to dismiss and motions for summary judgment. We affirm. . . .

"On July 31, 1984, [Joseph] Bates shot Douglas Knott in a stairwell at the Publix Hotel, where both men resided. Bates then returned to his room and committed suicide. Knott suffered severe injuries and is now a ventilator-dependent quadriplegic. Knott's mother, as guardian *ad litem* for Douglas Knott, commenced this action. . . .

Claims against Hotel Operator

"The plaintiff first assigns error to the trial court's dismissal of the negligence claim against Hashi Taniguchi, the proprietor and manager of the Publix Hotel. Knott alleged in her complaint that Taniguchi knew or should have known of Bates' violent nature, and failed to fulfill his duty to warn Knott of Bates' dangerous propensities or to protect him from injury. The trial court found no facts on the record suggesting that Taniguchi knew or had reason to know Bates posed a danger to other hotel guests. Without this knowledge, the trial court concluded, Taniguchi had no legal duty to warn other guests of the danger presented by Bates or to prevent Bates from carrying his weapon.

"Knott's evidence concerning Taniguchi's alleged knowledge of Bates' dangerous propensities consisted of the affidavit of an investigator and deposition testimony from another resident of the Publix Hotel. Each alleged Taniguchi knew on the day of the shooting that Bates was carrying a concealed gun. Knott also offered evidence showing other hotel residents found Bates to be 'strange.' According to Knott, Bates recently had glared at and intentionally bumped into other hotel guests, had reached into a bag as if to grab a gun, and had verbally threatened other guests. The plaintiff offered no evidence any guest reported these acts to Taniguchi or his employees or that Taniguchi or any of his employees ever witnessed Bates behaving in a belligerent or threatening manner. Taniguchi testified at his deposition that he thought Bates to be a very quiet man.

"After considering the evidence, the trial court held that even if Taniguchi knew Bates owned and carried a gun, that knowledge alone could not be found to have imparted knowledge of Bates' dangerous character and propensity for violence:

"I don't see any way that Mr. Taniguchi could possibly have foreseen that this would happen, and I just do not see a duty on his part to warn Mr. Knott or the other tenants.

" . . .

"The essential elements of actionable negligence are: (1) the existence of a duty owed to the complaining party; (2) a breach thereof; (3) a resulting injury; and (4) a proximate cause between the claimed breach and resulting injury. . . .

"The general rule followed in Washington is that an innkeeper owes to his guests the duty to exercise reasonable care to protect them from injury at the hands of a fellow guest. *Miller v. Staton,* 58 Wash. 2d 879, 883, 365 P.2d 333 (1961). The scope of this duty is limited to the range of danger foreseeable to the innkeeper. *See Bernethy v. Walt Failor's, Inc.,* 97 Wash. 2d 929, 653 P.2d 280 (1982).

"Reviewing the evidence before the trial court, we find Taniguchi had no knowledge of facts which should have alerted him to Bates' dangerous propensities and that the shooting of Knott was not reasonably foreseeable. Taniguchi was therefore under no legal duty to warn or protect guests of the Publix Hotel. We hold the trial court acted properly in granting Taniguchi's motion for summary judgment.

"We affirm the orders granting summary judgment and dismissing the plaintiff's claims."

In *Gray v. Kurcher,*[20] the California Court of Appeals affirmed a nonsuit (dismissal) in favor of a hotel catering to homosexuals where a guest was shot by another guest who was antigay. There was no proof of a history of violent behavior on the part of the assailant or proof that the assailant possessed a gun.

[20]193 Cal. App. 3d 1069, 236 Cal. Rptr. 891 (1987).

Thus, there was no proof of foreseeability on the hotel's part that could be rationally connected to the failure to provide reasonable care to the injured guest.

In *Nalle v. Quality Inn, Inc.*,[21] the Court of Appeals of Georgia reviewed an assault case involving a hotel guest who was attacked and robbed in the hotel parking lot. In affirming the granting of the hotel's motion for summary judgment dismissing the case, the court held that the evidence of prior criminal activity was not sufficiently similar to the assault in question to sustain a finding of superior knowledge of the risk on the hotel's part so as to create a duty to provide security.

The following case applies the Illinois comparative negligence statute to a claim of willful and wanton negligence on the part of motel owners who failed to warn a female guest of a neighborhood's dangers or of previous crimes committed against guests. The Federal Circuit Court of Appeals for the Seventh Circuit rejected the claim and affirmed a jury verdict, finding the guest 97 percent to blame for an assault in her room.

WASSELL V. ADAMS
865 F.2d 849 (7th Cir. 1989)

POSNER, Cir. J.: " . . .

"The common law refused to compare the plaintiff's and the defendant's negligence. See 4 Harper, James and Gray, The Law of Torts § 22.1 (1986). The negligent plaintiff could recover nothing, unless the defendant's culpability was of a higher degree than simple negligence. *See id.,* §§ 22.5, 22.6, and the discussion of 'degrees' of negligence in *Alvis v. Ribar, supra,* 85 Ill. 2d at 9–10, 52 Ill. Dec. at 26–27, 421 N.E.2d at 889–90. Susan [the plaintiff] argues that the defendants were willful and wanton, which, she says, would make her negligence as irrelevant under a regime of comparative negligence as it would be in a jurisdiction in which contributory negligence was still a complete defense. *See id.,* 85 Ill. 2d at 10, 52 Ill. Dec. at 27, 421 N.E.2d at 890; 4 Harper, James and Gray, *supra,* § 22.6.

"Both the premise (that the Adamses were willful and wanton) and the conclusion (that if so, her own negligence was irrelevant) are wrong. As we guessed in *Davis v. United States,* 716 F.2d 418, 429 (7th Cir. 1983), that it would, Illinois appears to be lining up with the states that allow the plaintiff's simple negligence to be compared with the defendant's 'willful and wanton conduct,' *see State Farm Mutual Automobile Ins. Co. v. Mendenhall,* 164 Ill. App. 3d 58, 115 Ill. Dec. 139, 517 N.E.2d 341 (1987); [citation omitted]; *Soucie v. Drago Amusements Co.,* 145 Ill. App. 3d 348, 99 Ill. Dec. 262, 495 N.E.2d 997 (1986). . . .

"As we noted in *Davis,* there are two lines of 'willful and wanton' decisions in Illinois. One, which seemed to be in the ascendancy when we wrote *Davis,*

[21]358 S.E.2d 281 (Ga. App. 1987).

and is the position taken in section 342 of the Second Restatement of Torts (1965), indeed regards 'willful and wanton' is merely a heightened form of 'negligent.' Section 342 requires only that the defendant 'knows *or has to reason to know* of the [dangerous condition of his premises] and *should* realize that it involves an unreasonable risk of harm' (emphasis added). But the cases since *Davis* appear to have swung round to the narrower concept, under which willful and wanton conduct denotes 'conscious disregard for . . . the safety of others,' *Rabel v. Illinois Wesleyan University,* 161 Ill. App. 3d 348, 356, 112 Ill. Dec. 889, 895, 514 N.E.2d 552, 558 (1987), or 'knowledge that [the defendant's] conduct posed a high probability of serious physical harm to others.' *Albers v. Community Consolidated #204 School,* 155 Ill. App. 3d 1083, 1085, 108 Ill. Dec. 675, 677, 508 N.E.2d 1252, 1254 (1987). *See also Soucie v. Drago Amusements Co., supra,* 145 Ill. App. 3d at 352, 99 Ill. Dec. at 264, 495 N.E.2d at 999. These formulations come close to—perhaps duplicate—the standard of recklessness that we limned in *Duckworth v. Franzen,* 780 F.2d 645, 652 (7th Cir. 1985), a prisoners' suit involving a claim that reckless disregard for prisoners' safety violates the Eighth Amendment's prohibition against cruel and unusual punishments. *Bresland v. Ideal Roller & Graphics Co.,* 150 Ill. App. 3d 445, 457, 103 Ill. Dec. 513, 522, 501 N.E.2d 830, 839 (1986), describes willful and wanton misconduct as 'so close to . . . intentional misconduct that a party found liable on that basis should not be able to obtain contribution [from his joint tortfeasors].'

"If the more recent formulations are authoritative, this would undermine the argument in *Davis* and *Mendenhall* for allowing a plaintiff's simple negligence to be compared with a defendant's willful and wanton misconduct. But it would not help Susan Wassell win her case. No rational jury could find that the Adamses *consciously* disregarded a *high* probability of serious physical harm. *Cf. Doe v. United States,* 718 F.2d 1039 (11th Cir. 1983). . . .

"It is careless to open a motel or hotel door in the middle of the night without trying to find out who is knocking. Still, people aren't at their most alert when they are awakened in the middle of the night, and it wasn't crazy for Susan to assume that Michael [her fiancé] had returned without telling her, even though he had said he would be spending the night at the base. So it cannot be assumed that the cost—not to her (although her testimony suggests that she is not so naive or provincial as her lawyer tried to convince the jury she was), but to the reasonable person who found himself or herself in her position, for that is the benchmark in determining plaintiff's as well as defendant's negligence, *see, e.g., Blacconeri v. Aguayo,* 132 Ill. App. 3d 984, 988, 88 Ill. Dec. 231, 234–35, 478 N.E.2d 546, 549–50 (1985); 4 Harper, James and Gray, *supra,* § 22.10, at pp. 334–38—was zero, or even that it was slight. As innkeepers (in the increasingly quaint legal term), the Adamses had a duty to exercise a high degree of care to protect their guests from assaults on the motel premises. *See, e.g., McCarty v. Pheasant Run, Inc.,* 826 F.2d 1554, 1558 (7th Cir. 1987) (Illinois law); *Yamada v. Hilton Hotel Corp.,* 60 Ill. App. 3d 101, 112, 17 Ill. Dec. 228, 237, 376 N.E.2d 227, 236 (1977); *Mrzlak v. Ettinger,* 25 Ill. App. 3d 706, 712,

323 N.E.2d 796, 800 (1975); *Fortney v. Hotel Rancroft, Inc.*, 5 Ill. App. 2d 327, 125 N.E.2d 544, 546, 548 (1955); *Peters v. Holiday Inns, Inc.*, 89 Wis. 2d 115, 278 N.W.2d 208 (1979). And the cost to the Adamses of warning all their female guests of the dangers of the neighborhood would have been negligible. Surely a warning to Susan would not have cost the Adamses 32 times the cost to her of schooling herself to greater vigilance.

"But this analysis is incomplete. It is unlikely that a warning would have averted the attack. Susan testified that she thought the man who had knocked on the door was her fiancé. Thinking this, she would have opened the door no matter how dangerous she believed the neighborhood to be. The warning that was not given might have deterred her from walking alone in the neighborhood. But that was not the pertinent danger. Of course, if the Adamses had told her not to open her door in the middle of the night under any circumstances without carefully ascertaining who was trying to enter the room, this would have been a pertinent warning and might have had an effect. But it is absurd to think that hoteliers are required to give so *obvious* a warning, any more than they must warn guests not to stick their fingers into the electrical outlets. Everyone, or at least the average person, knows better than to open his or her door to a stranger in the middle of the night. The problem was not that Susan thought that she *should* open her bedroom door in the middle of the night to anyone who knocked, but that she wasn't thinking clearly. A warning would not have availed against a temporary, sleep-induced lapse. . . .

" . . . During its deliberations, the jury sent the judge a question about the duty to warn (the judge did not answer it). This is some indication that the jury thought that the Adamses' negligence consisted in failing to warn Susan. But it is equally plausible that the jury didn't think the Adamses were negligent at all toward Susan, but, persuaded that she had suffered terribly, wanted to give her a token recovery. Concern with sympathy verdicts appears to lie behind Illinois' new statute barring the plaintiff from recovering any damages if he is more than 50 percent negligent. . . .

"It may be more than coincidence that the jury awarded Susan just enough money to allow her to undertake the recommended course of psychological therapy. We are not supposed to speculate about the jury's reasoning process, *see, e.g.*, Fed. R. Evid. 606(b), and we have just seen that it would not necessarily strengthen Susan's case if we did. The issue for us is not whether this jury was rational and law abiding but whether a rational jury could, consistently with the evidence, have returned the verdict that this jury did.

"If we were the trier of fact, persuaded that both parties were negligent and forced to guess about the relative costs to the plaintiff and to the defendants of averting the assault, we would assess the defendants' share at more than 3 percent. But we are not the trier of fact, and are authorized to upset the jury's apportionment only if persuaded that the trial judge abused his discretion in determining that the jury's verdict was not against the clear weight of the evidence. We are not so persuaded. It seems probably wrong to us, but we have suggested an interpretation of the evidence under which the verdict was consistent with the evidence and the law. And that is enough to require us to uphold the district judge's refusal to set aside the verdict.

"AFFIRMED."

In *Alster v. Palace Co.*,[22] the New York Appellate Division, First Department, ruled as a matter of law that plaintiff, a trespasser, assumed the risk of his own misconduct in entering a private function and attempting to disrupt the gathering.

In *Millman v. Howard Johnson's Co.*,[23] the Florida Third District Court of Appeal ruled that the Florida innkeeper's statute that limits liability for loss of guest property was not applicable to damages sought for mental pain and suffering, anguish, and humiliation. Plaintiff was a guest who was assaulted and robbed by an armed intruder who broke into plaintiff's locked guest room.

The Supreme Court of Virginia held in *Wright v. Webb*[24] that a motel owner owed no duty to protect the victim, a theater patron, from criminal assault in a joint theater and motel parking lot. The ruling was made in spite of recognition that the patron was a business invitee of the motel and notwithstanding a prior physical assault upon a female guest in her motel room and a prior double murder in the parking lot of an adjacent property. Justice Poff's concurring opinion follows:

> I concur in the result the majority has reached but cannot subscribe to the negligence standard which I understand the Court has adopted. I would endorse the logic underlying the Restatement (Second) of Torts § 344 (1965). This rule has been adopted in nearly every jurisdiction that has considered it. *See id.* app. at 523–43 (1986).
>
> A business invitor is not an insurer of the safety of his invitees, and, ordinarily, he has no duty to protect them from criminal assaults by third persons. If, however, the character of his business or his past experience in the conduct of his business is such that a reasonable person should anticipate criminal assaults committed on the premises by third persons, an invitor may have a duty to warn his invitees or to take other precautionary measures to protect them from bodily harm. *Id.* comment f (1965). A number of courts have found that such a duty may exist if an invitor knows or should know of a history of prior criminal assaults committed on his business premises that poses a reasonable likelihood that other invitees may be the victim of criminal assaults. *See, e.g., Stevens v. Jefferson*, 436 So. 2d 33, 34–35 (Fla. 1983); *Early v. N.L.V. Casino Corp.*, 100 Nev. 200, 203–04, 678 P.2d 683, 684–85 (1984); *Butler v. Acme Markets, Inc.*, 89 N.J. 270, 277–81, 445 A.2d 1141, 1145–46 (1982); *Nallan v. Helmsley-Spear, Inc.*, 50 N.Y.2d 507, 519–20, 407 N.E.2d 451, 458, 429 N.Y.S.2d 606, 613 (1980); *Murphy v. Penn Fruit Co.*, 274 Pa. Super. 427, 432–35, 418 A.2d 480, 483–84 (1980). Although I agree that the prior criminal assaults reflected in the evidence in this case would not raise such a duty, I would not categorically foreclose the possibility of a duty stemming from a history of prior assaults.

[22] 126 A.D.2d 465, 510 N.Y.S.2d 611 (1987).
[23] 533 So. 2d 901 (Fla. App. 1988).
[24] 234 Va. 527, 362 S.E.2d 919 (1987).

In *Crinkley v. Holiday Inns, Inc.*,[25] the Federal Circuit Court of Appeals for the Fourth Circuit, applying North Carolina law, affirmed a jury verdict for plaintiffs against both a hotel franchisor and a franchisee arising out of an assault by third persons who forced plaintiffs into their motel room, beating one and threatening the other. This decision should be compared with that of *Wright v. Webb*, excerpted above, in which the Supreme Court of Virginia refused to impose liability upon an innkeeper for the assault of an invitee in a motel parking area.

11:2 *Liability of Occupiers of Premises Other Than Hotels*

There has been almost exponential growth in cases outside the hotel area that involve negligence in the form of inadequate or nonexistent security standards. Because the charges raised are similar to those that might be raised in future hotel and motel cases, consideration of these cases is pertinent to the present discussion. Moreover, in some instances—particularly in landlord-tenant cases, which are discussed in section 11:3, *infra*—the courts base findings of negligence and breach of duty on arguments derived from hotel law.

Slapin v. Los Angeles International Airport[26] arose from a mugging in the airport's parking lot. Although the plaintiffs did not recover from the city for its failure to police the lot, they were able to charge the governmental entity "for injuries caused by a combination of a dangerous condition of public property and the wrongful acts of third parties." The Court of Appeals found that the plaintiffs could recover on the ground that there was insufficient lighting, if it could be shown that this condition is conducive to muggings.

A quite opposite approach was taken in *Davis v. Allied Supermarkets*,[27] where a plaintiff brought action against the grocery-store owners for failing to provide adequate lighting and personnel in their parking lot, located in a high-crime area. Here the court reasoned:

> If there had been enough guards, the offence would not have occurred. This being true, to sustain the appellants' position would for all practical purposes put the business owner in the position of an insurer. An insurer against what? Crime.
>
> One may argue the social advantages of shifting or equalizing the burden of victims of crime, but aside from the question of propriety in this litigation, it does not seem that shifting the financial loss caused by crime from one innocent victim to another innocent victim is proper.

A similar decision was issued in *Cornpropst v. Sloan*,[28] involving a female shopper assaulted at a Tennessee shopping center. The state supreme court found

[25]844 F.2d 156 (4th Cir. 1988).
[26]65 Cal. App. ed. 484, 135 Cal. Rptr. 296 (1977).
[27]547 P.2d 963 (Okla. 1976).
[28]528 So. 2d 188 (Tenn. 1975).

that the individual shopkeepers had no duty to guard their patrons against third-party criminal acts of a sudden and unexpected nature. In a lengthy dissent, however, Justice Henry remarks that, while he would impose only the duty of reasonable care, the standard announced in the majority opinion "affords virtually no protection" and is "not in the best interests of the consuming public."[29] Justice Henry's dissent demonstrates some courts' tendency to view the overall context as a cause for social concern. Justice Henry senses evolving tort liabilities arising out of the modern shopping center, which he likens to a city within a city. He feels that new protections and liabilities are formed by new institutions and situations; consequently, he does not hold the more literal majority view. It is this situational perspective—this view toward the larger social picture—that seems to be a trend in some courts. Its potential impact on the owners of premises, including hoteliers, is serious.

Illustrative of a trend toward subjecting shopping centers and malls to higher standards of care is the decision of the North Carolina Supreme Court in *Foster v. Winston-Salem Joint Venture.*[30] In *Foster,* plaintiff was assaulted in the parking lot of defendant's mall during the Christmas season. The evidence showed that defendant had only one guard assigned to the large mall parking lot during the busy season and that thirty-one incidents of crime, including four or five assaults, had occurred in the lot during the previous year. Consequently, the court reversed a summary judgment granted in the lower court in favor of the defendant and concluded that a reasonable jury could find that the defendant could have foreseen the assault upon the plaintiff at bar.

11:3   *Liability in Landlord-Tenant Relations*

Landlord-tenant cases are applicable to hotel law not only because they highlight the evolving nature of tort liability but also because many of them make repeated references to innkeepers' standards of care in defending more strictly construed standards for landlords. Since the courts may eventually apply more stringent interpretations in landlord-tenant cases, it is prudent to track any discernible tendencies in related landlord-tenant decisions.

One case that imposes an affirmative duty of protection on landlords, at least in the District of Columbia, is *Kline v. 1500 Massachusetts Avenue Apartment Corp.*[31] A female tenant assaulted in the common hallway of her apartment house brought action against her landlord. The U.S. Court of Appeals found that the landlord had both actual and constructive notice that: tenants were the objects of criminal attacks in the common areas of the building; the building was subject to a rising wave of crime; further criminal attacks were likely; and the landlord was under a duty of protection. In addition, the landlord was liable for his failure to maintain the original standards of security that existed when the

[29]*Id.* at 199–200.
[30]303 N.C. 636, 281 S.E.2d 36 (1981).
[31]439 F.2d 477 (D.C. Cir. 1970).

tenant moved in. According to Circuit Judge Wilkey, "There is . . . a duty . . . placed on a landlord to take steps to protect tenants from foreseeable criminal acts committed by third parties."[32] After discussing the criminal history of the building and of the surrounding neighborhood, the court goes on to say: "The duty is the landlord's because by his control of the areas of common use and common danger he is the only party who has the *power* to make the necessary protection . . . he certainly is no bystander."[33]

It is important to note that the court compares the landlord's responsibility to the innkeeper's liability, which is similarly based on his supervision, care, or control of his premises: "The most analogous relationship to that of the modern day urban apartment house dweller is not that of a landlord and tenant, but that of innkeeper and guest."[34] The court adds, as a seeming afterthought, that the discharge of this affirmative duty will be costly to landlords, but that this does not deter the justices in their decision. The seriousness of this judgment can only be appreciated fully when one learns that many of the security precautions the majority finds suitable are not available in Washington's hotels.

It seems fair to conclude that a number of courts are leaning toward making private corporations and institutions in general liable for the criminal acts of others—and that innkeepers are among those likely to be held responsible for larger social problems.

Since *Kline v. 1500 Massachusetts Avenue Apartment Corp.*,[35] courts have approached the issue of landlords' liability for criminal attacks upon tenants in two different ways. Some courts, like the *Kline* court, find an implied warranty of habitability running in favor of tenants.[36] Other courts, also like the *Kline* court, deem the landlord-tenant relationship a "special relationship" in which the landlord owes the duty to protect the tenant from third-party misconduct.[37]

In *Feld v. Merriam*,[38] the Supreme Court of Pennsylvania held that a landlord is under no duty to protect tenants from foreseeable criminal acts by third parties. In that case, the plaintiff was robbed and raped in the defendant's apartment-building garage. The court stated that a duty to protect tenants from criminal intrusion could be incurred voluntarily by a landlord only by a specific agreement or by providing a program of security.

In *Lay v. Dworman*, the Supreme Court of Oklahoma held that a residential apartment tenant stated a cause of action in negligence but not in breach of warranty arising out of the tenant's rape by a third party within her apartment. The decision is set forth below.

[32]*Id.* at 478.
[33]*Id.* at 481.
[34]*Id.* at 485.
[35]*Id.*
[36]*See* Trentacost v. Brussel, 82 N.J. 214, 412 A.2d 436 (1980).
[37]*See* Kwaitkowski v. Superior Trading Co., 123 Cal. App. 3d 324, 176 Cal. Rptr. 494 (1981). But *cf.* Riley v. Marcus, 125 Cal. App. 3d 103, 177 Cal. Rptr. 827 (1981), and King v. Ilikai Properties, Inc., 2 Haw. App. 359, 632 P.2d 657 (1981), in which the ordinary negligence standard was used.
[38]506 Pa. 383, 485 A.2d 742 (1984).

Lay v. Dworman
732 P.2d 455 (Okla. 1990)

Lavender, J.: "Appellant, Rhonda Lynn Lay, was assaulted and raped in her apartment in an apartment/condominium complex in Tulsa, Oklahoma. This suit was initiated against the parties owning interests in the complex at the time appellant rented her apartment and at the time of the assault. The petition and later amended petition sought recovery on two theories—negligence and breach of warranty. Appellant also sought the recovery of punitive damages, alleging that appellees were guilty of gross negligence in subjecting appellant to an unsafe residence. Demurrers were sustained to appellant's initial petition and to her amended petition on the ground that they had failed to state a cause of action. Upon the sustainment of the demurrer to the amended petition appellant elected to stand upon her pleading and the case was dismissed. Appellant then initiated the present appeal.

"This case was initially assigned to the Oklahoma City Divisions of the Court of Appeals. The Court of Appeals affirmed the trial court's ruling without opinion in an accelerated docket disposition. Appellant subsequently petitioned this Court for writ of *certiorari* to review that disposition. We have previously granted *certiorari*. . . .

"The present case, at threshold level, requires that this Court examine the question of a landlord's duty to protect a tenant from the criminal activities of third parties. In support of her position, appellant urges this Court to adopt an expanded view of this duty typified by the United States Court of Appeals for the District of Columbia in the case of *Kline v. 1500 Massachusetts Avenue Apartment Corp.* (439 F.2d 477 (D.C. Cir. 1970). . . .

"In order to state a cause of action for recovery under a negligence theory certain elements must be present. These elements are: the existence of a duty; a subsequent breach of that duty; and an injury to the plaintiff proximately flowing from the breach of that duty. . . .

"In the oft-cited *Kline* case the District of Columbia Court reexamined the basic nature of the landlord-tenant relationship in reaching the conclusion that there was a duty to protect tenants from foreseeable criminal activities. In doing so the court concluded that the relationship of innkeeper-guest as recognized in the common-law courts was more attuned to the actual relationship of landlord-tenant as it exists in modern apartment dwellings. The court determined that the modern lease should be treated as a contract and that one of the terms implied in the contract was the innkeeper's duty to exercise reasonable care in protecting the guest/tenant.

"*Kline*, however, dealt with an assault on a tenant in a common area of the apartment building. Upon consideration we do not feel that an expansion of the possible liability of a landlord of the magnitude imposed in *Kline* is either necessary or desirable. Under present Oklahoma law a landlord has the duty to use ordinary care to maintain the common portions of leased premises, over which he has retained control, in a safe condition. [Citation omitted.] . . .

"Applying this principle to the landlord-tenant situation we can define the duty owed by the landlord as being a duty to use reasonable care to maintain the common areas of the premises in such a manner as to insure that the likelihood of criminal activity is not unreasonably enhanced by the condition of those common premises.

"Aside from the duty of the landlord arising from traditional principles relating to the duty to maintain common areas of the premises, this case also requires consideration of the landlord's duty to maintain the actual security of the leased premises themselves. Where the premises provided are inadequately secured due to ineffective or defective materials, a duty on the part of the landlord to provide repairs or modifications would arise upon notification of the defect by the tenant. This duty arises from the landlord-tenant contract and from the implication that the landlord is to provide services under the contract in a diligent manner. . . . That the landlord must furnish these services is in turn necessarily implied under Oklahoma law in order to insure the reasonability of the contractual agreement. (*See Keel v. Titan Construction Corp.,* 639 P.2d 1228 (Okla.1981).)

"Every person is under a duty to exercise due care in using that which he controls so as not to injure others, but in order for such duty to arise, the person to be charged therewith must have knowledge or notice that his act or omission involves danger to another. . . . Thus, by retaining control over aspects of the premises such as door and window locks or alarm devices which directly relate to security, the landlord faces potential liability when the circumstances are such that a reasonable man would realize that a failure to act would render one relying on those actions susceptible to criminal acts.

"These principles appear to form the foundation for the landlord's liability in other jurisdictions in cases involving criminal acts within the rented premises. The element of foreseeability in these cases has been found from a history of criminal activity in the apartment complex or building, (*See Warner v. Arnold,* 133 Ga. App. 174, 210 S.E.2d 350 (1974); *Ten Associates v. McCutchen,* 398 So. 2d 860 (Fla. Ct. App.1981); and *Riley v. Marcus,* 125 Cal. App. 3d 103, 177 Cal. Rptr. 827 (1981).) or strictly from the nature of the defect in the premises. (*See Braitman v. Overlook Terrace Corp.,* 68 N.J. 368, 346 A.2d 76 (1975) (dead bolt lock in apartment had been reported as defective, burglars slipped a second, inadequate door lock.)) . . .

"Based upon the foregoing analysis, appellant's amended petition does state an extant duty on the part of appellees flowing from their averred knowledge of criminal activities in the complex and the knowledge of the defective lock in appellant's apartment. The petition further avers a breach of that duty by alleging that appellees had been informed by appellant of the defective lock and had failed to make necessary repairs. Finally the petition avers that an unknown intruder gained entrance to her apartment and that she was assaulted and suffered injury as a result of this intrusion. . . .

"Axiomatically, in order to state a cause of action in negligence an alleged breach of duty must proximately result in the injury to the party seeking to recover for that injury. . . . The question here is whether, from the facts stated, a reasonable inference may be drawn that the unknown assailant did enter as a result of the defective lock and thus complete the link between appellees' alleged breach of duty and the injury to appellant. This fact is not specifically averred. However, we find that a reasonable inference may be drawn from the facts stated that the proximate causation link has been asserted. Such a result is in keeping with the court's duty to construe the facts stated and inferences to be drawn therefrom liberally in favor of appellant. For this reason we find the demurrers to appellant's amended petition were not properly sustained as to appellant's first stated theory of recovery. . . .

"Appellant's amended petition also sought recovery under breach of warranty theory. To support this theory appellant alleged: (1) that appellees had warranted to the general public and to appellant that the apartment complex was secure and had security; (2) that appellant had relied on these warranties and the implied warranty of habitability in occupying her apartment; (3) that appellees breached these warranties by failing to provide a safe apartment, by failing to provide a sufficient number of security personnel, and by failing to provide a properly lighted apartment area; and (4) that as a result of these breaches of warranty appellant suffered injury.

"In order to find that appellant's second theory of recovery would support a claim for relief, we would be required to consider the allegations concerning the general warranty of security by appellees to give rise to an assumption of absolute insurance of appellant's safety. Otherwise appellant's amended petition may not be found to have shown any causative link between the alleged 'breach' of these warranties and the injury to appellant. To find a cause of action arising from the mere fact that appellees allegedly stated the complex to be secure and the fact that an intruder gained access to appellant's apartment runs directly afoul of the factors which we considered in limiting a landlord's possible tort liability by the application of traditional tort concepts.

"We have rejected the concept that the landlord-tenant relationship itself gives rise to the landlord's being placed in a position of quasi-guarantor of the tenant's safety. We also reject the concept that a statement regarding the security of a complex, in and of itself, establishes a landlord's liability for criminal activities within the complex in the absence of facts establishing a causal connection between the alleged breach of warranty and the injury. In this case appellant alleged the breach and alleged the injury but failed to show how the existence of the breach resulted in the injury. We are presented instead with a mere conclusion that the alleged breach was responsible for the injury. The absence of facts to support the element of causation in appellant's amended petition rendered that pleading incapable of stating a claim upon which relief could be granted. . . .

"The opinion of the Court of Appeals in this matter is VACATED. The order of the trial court as it relates to the sustainment of demurrers to appellant's first pled theory of recovery is REVERSED. The order of the trial court as it relates to the sustainment of demurrers to appellant's second pled theory of recovery is

AFFIRMED. The cause is REMANDED to the trial court for further proceedings consistent with this opinion.''

11:4 *Protection against Injury by Employees: In General*

As the innkeeper must protect the guest against third persons, *a fortiori* he must protect him against injuries from his own employees. And since the employees are provided, among other things, for the purpose of protecting guests, every injury inflicted upon the guest by an employee, either intentionally or negligently, is a breach of his duty of protection and renders the innkeeper liable to the guest. The innkeeper's duty, the breach of which by his employee causes the injury, is not the negative duty not to assault the guest, but the affirmative duty to protect him from assault. The employee, in assaulting the guest, is committing the tort for himself, but he is breaching the obligation of protection which rests on the innkeeper, and which the employee has himself been employed to carry out.

New York innkeepers are required to exercise only reasonable care to prevent injuries to guests resulting from defects in the hotel premises or from the acts of nonemployees. If, on the other hand, the injury is caused by an employee acting within the scope of his employment, the innkeeper—like other employers—is responsible. The major problem derives from guests injured by employees who are acting outside the scope of their employment. Recent New York decisions and commentaries have been sufficiently strict to render the innkeeper generally liable for his employees' acts, even when committed outside the scope of their employment.

In *Tobin v. Slutsky*,[39] for example, the U.S. Court of Appeals for the Second Circuit found the defendant hotelkeepers liable for a guest's injury even though the hotel employee was not acting within the scope of his employment when he molested a fifteen-year-old guest. The court also held the "hotel's advertisement was admissible as to representations of quality and care made by the hotel; that under New York law an innkeeper is obliged to use reasonable care, commensurate with the quality of the accommodations offered, to see that his guests are not injured, abused or insulted by his employees; that the hotel is not an insurer of the guest's safety; [and] that evidence generated [a] jury question whether it was reasonable to have no policing of the lobby or the elevators to prevent incidents such as that at issue.''[40] The *Tobin* finding is based on *McKee v. Sheraton-Russell, Inc.*,[41] a case involving injuries inflicted on a woman guest by a bellboy. The Circuit Court found on appeal that a hotel does not have an absolute duty to its guests, but only a duty of reasonable care, depending on the

[39]506 F.2d 1097 (2d Cir. 1974). *But see* Moritz v. Pine Hotels, Inc., 52 A.D.2d 1020, 383 N.Y.S.2d 704 (3d Dep't 1976).

[40]506 F.2d at 1097.

[41]268 F.2d 669 (2d Cir. 1959).

grade and quality of the accommodations offered. The court also ruled that the employee need not be acting within the scope of his employment for the hotel to be liable.

According to a 1974 commentary by the New York supreme court justices, *Pattern Jury Instructions,* an employer is generally responsible for his own negligence in selecting or retaining an incompetent employee, for the wrongful act of an employee within the scope of his employment, or for the breach of an implied condition of the contract establishing the relationship between the employer and the plaintiff.[42] The commentary also compares the innkeeper-guest relationship to the stricter carrier-passenger relationship. Significantly, this commentary suggests the innkeeper in New York should have absolute liability for assaults or insults committed by employees, unless caused by the guest's own improper act.

Although "failure to make more than a routine check of an employee's background is not negligence as a matter of law,"[43] in the state of New York, an employer has a responsibility to select competent employees. Although the innkeeper is well advised to screen his prospective employees carefully—if for no other reason than to reduce assaults by those in his hire—he should recognize that he may still not escape liability for his employees' subsequent actions.

Generally, the reasonable-care rule is applicable to cases involving assaults by employees in New York and other states. Thus the innkeeper is not an insurer of the safety of his guests, but he must observe reasonable care of their persons, and he is liable for injury to a guest resulting from his own negligence.[44]

Moreover, just as the trend in dealing with third-person criminal assaults is toward establishing stricter standards of care, one can expect a hand-in-hand movement toward stricter duties regarding property stolen from the guest's room or person, if such acts were foreseeable in a climate of crime and violence. Stronger standards of care for a guest's person cannot be disassociated from those for his property, which indeed impose a stricter liability under the common law.

In applying the appropriate legal theory with which to impose liability for employee-caused injuries upon guests and patrons the majority of jurisdictions apply the "federal" rule enunciated in *Clancy v. Barker.*[45] Under that rule, the test of whether an innkeeper is liable for the negligent or willful acts of his employees resulting in injury to his guests rests upon a finding that the employee was acting within the scope of his employer's duties at the time the harm was inflicted. The fact that the injury took place on the premises of the hotelkeeper was not conclusive on this issue. Rather, the fact that the employee was off duty was found to establish nonliability on the part of his employer for a negligent discharge of a firearm which injured an infant hotel guest. In the case of an intentional tort, such as a bodily assault, self-defense or some provocation for the

---

[42]New York Pattern Jury Instruction 516.
[43]*Id.* at 565, citing Stevens v. Lankard, 25 N.Y.2d 640, 254 N.E.2d 339 (1969).
[44]43A C.J.S. 1174.
[45]131 F. 161 (8th Cir. 1904).

assault would also aid the innkeeper, but only by way of an affirmative defense. The fact that the employee disobeyed instructions or deviated from the authority granted does not itself immunize the innkeeper as a matter of law. California and Pennsylvania exemplify the majority rule.

A minority of jurisdictions, including New York and Massachusetts, apply a contract theory of responsibility enunciated by the Supreme Court of Nebraska in *Clancy v. Barker.*[46] Under this rule there is an implied contractual undertaking that the guest be treated with due consideration for his safety and comfort. The fact that the employee committed the wrongful act is immaterial. Equally immaterial is the question whether the employee was actively engaged in the discharge of his responsibilities at the time the harm was inflicted. The duty is a continuing one, irrespective of the on-duty or off-duty status of the employee at any given time. Nor is it material whether the injury was inflicted negligently or intentionally. The contractual duty affirmatively to protect the guest encompasses both types of misconduct.

The anomalous result of two rules, one federal and one state, emanating from the same jurisdiction adopting diametrically opposed theories on the same facts is explained by the fact that the federal courts were able to enunciate their own federal common law at the time the case was decided, independently of the law of the state in which the federal court was sitting. Today federal courts are bound by the substantive law of the state, whether statutory or the decisional law of the court of last resort of the state, except as to matters governed by the federal Constitution or federal statutes. This uniform rule, adopted by the Supreme Court in *Erie R.R. v.. Tompkins,*[47] was to eliminate forum-shopping whereby the case might be decided merely upon the law of the federal or state forum, irrespective of the merits and irrespective of the fact that not all parties to the lawsuit might have a choice of forums open to them.

11:5 *Protection against Injury to Employees*

Whether an employer has a "special relationship" with the employees that creates a duty on the employer to provide adequate protection from third-party misconduct has not been clearly decided by any court. In an Illinois decision dealing with innkeepers, however, the court "assumed" such a special relationship when it analyzed the facts, although it did not specifically hold that such a relationship existed.[48] The plaintiff, a seventeen-year-old boy, was assaulted by two guests while he was delivering beer to their room. The court held that even if a duty existed on the part of the innkeeper to protect its employees from third-party misconduct, the hotel was not liable here because there had been no previous criminal attacks of any kind in the hotel; this attack, therefore, was completely unforeseeable.

---

[46]71 Neb. 83, 98 N.W. 440 (1904); *adhered to on reh'g,* 71 Neb. 91, 103 N.W. 446 (1905).
[47]304 U.S. 64 (1938).
[48]Ozmeni v. Lance, 107 Ill. App. 3d 348, 437 N.E.2d 930, *cert. denied,* 119 Ill. App. 3d at 276 (1982).

11:6   *Firearm Assaults by Employees*

Another crucial matter for hotelkeepers is liability for injuries inflicted upon a hotel guest by an employee, or contract employee, using a firearm. In a Justice Department study conducted by the Rand Corporation, titled *Private Police in the United States: Findings and Recommendations*, it was reported that 45 percent of the analyzed insurance claims against a large contract security agency that dealt with operational security abuses involved assault or the use of unnecessary force.[49] From complaints to state and local regulatory agencies, it was discovered that "incidents involving deaths or shootings caused by security personnel are reported relatively frequently, compared to incidents involving assault without the use of a gun . . . [and] the types of complaints registered are probably indicative of the major types of abuses occurring."[50] Among many private guards, according to the study, "firearms training is woefully inadequate."[51] Although only 50 percent of the guards surveyed were armed, only 19 percent of those had received any training. Buzby and Paine, writing in *Hotel and Motel Security Management*, point out that where the law is restrictive, legal complexities are reduced, but where it is permissible for contract employees or for the hotel's own force to be armed, the legal problems are more complicated. While it is certainly possible that in the New Orleans Howard Johnson's sniper case,[52] for example, an armed security employee might have saved lives, it would still be extremely detrimental—not only legally but from the standpoint of public relations—for a hotel's guest to suffer serious injury or death at the hands of an armed security employee.[53]

If a hotel develops its own force, it must be adequately trained. According to the *New York Pattern Jury Instructions*, the liability imposed by an employer's negligence in selecting or keeping an incompetent employee in a situation where he may harm others is based upon the same legal principle involved when an instrument is furnished to an employee not competent to handle it. Furthermore, a thorough background check is in order when selecting employees who will be armed, because "retention of an employee who has a known psychiatric disorder in a position which gives him access to guns" may result in liability.[54] Given the special nature of the innkeeper-guest relationship and the added duty of care arising from arming an employee, it seems likely that a very strict standard of care would be the finding of the court, whatever the jurisdiction. Thus, as Buzby and Paine suggest,[55] hiring armed guards from a contract service—especially a

---

[49]H. S. Ursic and L. E. Pagano, Security Management Systems 177 (1974). Although the study is old, the premises on which it is based are still valid. *See* R. C. Ellis, Security and Loss Prevention Management 17–27 (1986).

[50]*Id.* at 124.

[51]*Id.* at 129.

[52]Steagall v. Civic Center Site Development Co., Inc., No. 74-3 (E.D. La. July 2, 1975). (*See* section 11:1, *supra*, at 356).

[53]W. J. Buzby and D. Paine, Hotel and Motel Security Managment at 29–30 (1976).

[54]1 New York Pattern Jury Instructions, 565.

[55]Buzby and Paine, *supra* note 36, at 30.

reputable, licensed firm—has much to recommend it. The hotel should also see that a ''save harmless'' clause is included in the contract to ensure that the contractor will be responsible for his employees' acts. By a carefully drawn contract, the right of control passes to the agency supplying the personnel, and the innkeeper cannot be held liable for the negligent acts of the agency's personnel when they are performing work under the contract. It should be noted, however, that if the contract guard commits an intentional tort, the innkeeper may still be liable. Similarly, if the innkeeper's agents by some means participate in or ratify the negligent act, the innkeeper may be held liable vicariously, or as a joint tort-feasor.[56]

11:7 *Employee's Abusive Conduct*

In *Arky v. Leitch,*[57] plaintiff and her friend failed to receive a room with private bath in defendant's hotel, but were assigned to a room with a connecting bath. They suffered great inconvenience and embarrassment by having their bathroom entered by someone from the other room connected therewith. When they complained to the clerk in charge, he treated them in an offensive and insulting manner. In an action for the recovery of damages for the offensive treatment, the testimony tended to establish willfulness or gross inattention to duty by the defendant, sufficient to go to the jury. There was no evidence of pecuniary damage. A verdict for $1,000 in plaintiff's favor was reduced to one-half on appeal.

But compare *Pollock v. Holsa Corp.*[58] (see section 8:7, *supra*), in which an employee was held not to be ''discourteous'' or ''abusive'' when he mistakenly terminated plaintiff's stay one day early, preventing plaintiff from returning to room during early-morning hours. On appeal, the trial court's dismissal of the plaintiff's claim for damages resulting from emotional harm was affirmed. The appellate court, however, reversed the trial court's dismissal of the plaintiff's claim of physical harm. Compare *Eckhart v. Robert E. Lee Motel,*[59] in which a sleeping guest was not entitled to a refund after a man had entered her motel doorway, apparently by mistake.

11:8 *Employee's Inattention to Duty*

Sheridan v. Hotels Statler Co., Inc.[60] involved an action for personal injuries based on negligence. Plaintiff, in leaving defendant's hotel, desired to take a taxicab. The doorman opened the cab door for her and stood holding the door while she entered.

---

[56]*See, e.g.,* 38 A.L.R.3d 1336.
[57]131 Miss. 14, 94 So. 855 (1922).
[58]114 Misc. 2d 1076, 454 N.Y.S.2d 582 (App. Term. 1st Dep't 1982), *aff'd as modified,* 98 A.D.2d 265, 470 N.Y.S. 2d 151 (1st Dep't 1984).
[59]20 Ohio App. 3d 80, 440 N.E.2d 824 (1981).
[60]282 Mass. 456, 185 N.E. 33 (1933).

The plaintiff had got in, faced about, and, with her hand brushing the door or the side of the cab near the hinges of the door, which were toward the rear of the vehicle, she was seating herself, when the doorman shut the cab door. Her finger was caught in the hinge and was injured. The jury found for the plaintiff. The only questions were whether there was sufficient evidence of negligence by the doorman or of lack of due care by the plaintiff to justify submitting those issues to the jury. Said Justice Wait:

> A majority of the court think that there was. It could be found that the duty of the doorman was to use reasonable care to make sure that those upon whom he was attending were so arranged within the cab that the door could be closed without injury to them, and that, in closing it while looking elsewhere, he was not perform-ing that duty. It could also be found that while it was the duty of the plaintiff to use due care to see that her fingers were not in a place of danger when the door was closed, and although she had seen the doorman looking elsewhere and attending to some extent to another than herself as he was closing the door, she still might rely upon him to give his whole attention to her and to allow her to be fully seated in safety before completing the closing. Exceptions overruled. . . .

In *Giles v. Pick Hotels Corp.*,[61] plaintiff was injured while he and a bellboy employed by defendant were engaged in removing luggage from plaintiff's car in front of defendant's hotel in Detroit. While the bellboy was taking luggage out of the rear seat of the car, plaintiff reached into the front seat to remove a brief case. In doing so, he supported himself by placing his left hand on the center pillar to which the rear door was hinged, with his fingers in a position to be injured if the rear door was closed. The bellboy closed the rear door, and as a result a part of plaintiff's left index finger had to be amputated.

The trial judge found plaintiff guilty of contributory negligence as a matter of law and directed a verdict for defendant. On appeal, affirmed. "Ordinarily a door jamb or crack is not the place for fingers," said the court.[62]

11:9 *Agency Law: Employer's Liability under the Doctrine of* Respondeat Superior

In *Fruit v. Schreiner*, below, the Supreme Court of Alaska dealt with the doc-trine of *respondeat superior* in a case in which the plaintiff sued both Fruit, an employee of the Equitable Life Insurance Company, and Equitable for injuries sustained in an automobile accident for which it was alleged that Fruit was re-sponsible because of intoxication arising out of and within the scope of his employment.

---

[61]232 F.2d 887 (6th Cir. 1956) (per curiam).
[62]*Id.* at 888, quoting, a bit inaccurately, Abent v. Michigan Cab Co., 279 Mich. 617, 618, 273 N.W. 289, 290 (1937).

FRUIT V. SCHREINER
502 P.2d 133 (Alaska 1972)

BOOCHERER, J.: "The jury found that Fruit was an employee acting within the course and scope of his employment for Equitable at the time and place of the accident. Under the doctrine of *respondeat superior* (which simply means 'let the employer answer') Equitable would thus be liable for Fruit's acts of negligence despite lack of fault on Equitable's part.

"Equitable argues, however, that the evidence was insufficient to establish that Fruit was acting within the course and scope of his employment. Equitable contends that any business purpose was completed when Fruit left the Waterfront Bar and Restaurant. It cites cases holding that an employee traveling to his home or other personal destination cannot ordinarily be regarded as acting in the scope of his employment. But Fruit was not returning to his home. He was traveling to the convention headquarters where he was attending meetings as a part of his employment.

"In addition, Equitable seeks to narrow the scope of *respondeat superior* to those situations where the master has exercised control over the activities of employees. Disposition of this issue requires an analysis of the doctrine of *respondeat superior*, one of the few anomalies to the general tort doctrine of no liability without fault.

"The two theories which carry the greatest weight in contemporary legal thought are respectively, the control theory which finds liability whenever the act of the employee was committed with the implied authority, acquiescence or subsequent ratification of the employer, and the enterprise theory which finds liability whenever the enterprise of the employer would have benefited by the context of the act of the employee but for the unfortunate injury.

"Since we are dealing with vicarious liability, justification may not be found on theories involving the employer's personal fault such as his failure to exercise proper control over the activities of his employees or his failure to take proper precautions in firing or hiring them. Lack of care on the employer's part would subject him to direct liability without the necessity of involving *respondeat superior*.

"The concept of vicarious liability is broad enough to include circumstances 'where the master has been in no way at fault; where the work which the servant was employed to do was in no sense unlawful or violative of the plaintiff's rights; where there has been no delegation of a special duty; where the tortious conduct of the servant was neither commanded nor ratified; but nevertheless the master is made responsible.' This liability arises from the relationship of the enterprise to society rather than from a misfeasance on the part of the employer.

"The aspect of the relationship most commonly advanced to delimit the theory is the 'scope of employment' of the employee-tortfeasor.

" 'Scope of employment' as a test for application of *respondeat superior* would be insufficient if it failed to encompass the duty of every enterprise to the social community which gives it life and contributes to its prosperity. "The meaning of the legal sword of Damocles forged for [the enterprises'] penalization is rightly to be found, not in the particular relation they bear to their charge, but in the general relation to society into which their occupation brings them.'' [Laski, *The Basis of Vicarious Liability,* 26 Yale L.J. 105, 113 (1916).] The basis of *respondeat superior* has been correctly stated as 'the desire to include in the costs of operation inevitable losses to third persons incident to carrying on an enterprise, and thus distribute the burden among those benefited by the enterprise.' The rule of *respondeat superior . . .* is limited to requiring an enterprise to bear the loss incurred as a result of the employee's negligence. The acts of the employee need be so connected to his employment as to justify requiring that the employer bear that loss.

'' . . . Employees' acts sufficiently connected with the enterprise are in effect considered as deeds of the enterprise itself. Where through negligence such acts cause injury to others it is appropriate that the enterprise bear the loss incurred.

''Consistent with these considerations, it is apparent that no categorical statement can delimit the meaning of 'scope of employment' once and for all times. Applicability of *respondeat superior* will depend primarily on the findings of fact in each case. In this particular case, Clay Fruit's employment contract required that he attend the sales conference. Each employee was left to his own resources for transportation, and many of the agents, including Fruit, chose to drive their own automobiles. By the admission of Equitable's agency manager, the scope of the conference included informal socializing as well as formal meetings. Social contact with the out-of-state guests was encouraged, and there is undisputed evidence that such associations were not limited to the conference headquarters at Land's End.

''When Fruit left for the Waterfront Bar and Restaurant his principal purpose was to join the out-of-state guests. This testimony of his was further confirmed by the fact that once he discovered that they were not present at the Waterfront he departed immediately. Had he been engaged in a 'frolic of his own' it would appear likely that he would have remained there. There was evidence from which the jury could find that he was at least motivated in part by his desire to meet with the out-of-state guests and thus to benefit from their experience so as to improve his abilities as a salesman.

''Because we find that fair-minded men in the exercise of reasonable judgment could differ as to whether Fruit's activities in returning from Homer to the convention headquarters were within the scope of his employment, we are not disposed to upset the jury's conclusion that liability for damages may be vicariously imputed to Equitable.

''In addition to finding that Equitable was liable for the negligence of its employee the jury by its answers to interrogatories held that Equitable itself was negligent in 'its planning and conducting the summer conference, and that such negligence was a proximate cause of the accident.'

''To reach this conclusion the jury must have believed that the convention involved improper use of intoxicating beverages which proximately caused the collision. We have grave doubts as to whether the record would sustain a finding that the collision was due to intoxication. . . .

"Moreover, the great weight of authority holds that the gratuitous provider of alcohol cannot be held liable to one injured by an intoxicated driver in the absence of other facts. The rule has been applied to persons injured by intoxicated drivers who obtained liquor at company office parties and at a company picnic.

"Cases cited by Schreiner involve additional affirmative acts on the part of the defendant justifying imposition of liability, such as plying a minor with intoxicants at a company Christmas Party and then placing him in a car so that he could drive home.

"There is no indication that Fruit's presence on the highway was the direct result of affirmative action by Equitable placing him there or ordering him to undertake the fateful trip. Equitable may have created the environment in which one so inclined might behave as Fruit did, but we cannot go so far as to hold, as a matter of law, that the necessary degree of causation exists for direct negligence.

"Even with the evidence viewed most favorably to the plaintiff, we find that it was insufficient to present a jury question on Equitable's direct liability."

What Employee Conduct Is Foreseeable

RIVIELLO V. WALDRON
47 N.Y.2d 297, 391 N.E.2d 1278 (1979)

FUCHSBERG, J.: "Plaintiff Donald Riviello, a patron of the Pot Belly Pub, a Bronx bar and grill operated by the defendant Raybele Tavern, Inc., lost the use of an eye because of what was found to be negligence on the part of Joseph Waldron, a Raybele employee. The jury having decided for the plaintiff, in due course the trial court entered a judgment in his favor for $200,000 plus costs and interest from the date of the verdict. It later amended the judgment to reflect a payment of $25,000 which the plaintiff had received in advance of trial from Waldron's personal liability insurer in return for a general release conditioned upon a reservation of plaintiff's rights against Raybele.

"On plaintiff's appeal to us, the principal issues we confront are: (1) whether, as a matter of law, Waldron's negligence, which Riviello sought to impute to Raybele on the theory of *respondeat superior,* was outside the scope of the employment and, if not, (2) whether, under section 15-108 of the General Obligations Law, the prejudgment settlement between plaintiff and Waldron operated to bar any recovery by plaintiff against Raybele, an assertion on which, in the light of the ground for the Appellate Division's decision, it did not have to pass. For the reasons which follow, we believe both questions should be answered in the negative.

"The relevant facts are easily set forth. And, because, in the posture in which the case comes to us, our examination focuses on whether plaintiff established a *prima facie* case against Raybele, we, of course, do so in the light most favorable to the plaintiff [citation omitted].

"As was customary, on the Friday evening on which Riviello sustained his injuries, only two employees manned the Pot Belly. One was the bartender. The other was Waldron, who, in this modest-sized tavern, wore several hats, primarily that of short-order cook but also the ones that went with waiting on tables and spelling the bartender. Though his services had been engaged by Raybele's corporate president in the main to improve business by introducing the sale of food, his testimony showed that the fact that, as a local resident, he was known to most of the customers in this neighborhood bar figured in his hiring as well. There was also proof that, in the time he had been there, when not preparing or serving food or relieving the bartender, he would follow the practice of mingling with the patrons.

"Nor was Riviello a stranger when he entered the premises that night. Living nearby, he had frequented the establishment regularly for some years. The two men knew one another and, after a while, Riviello gravitated to the end of the bar near the kitchen, where, during an interval when he had no food orders to fill, Waldron and another patron and mutual friend, one Bannon, were chatting. Riviello joined in the discussion, which turned to street crime in the neighborhood. In the course of the conversation, Waldron exhibited a knife, variously described as a pocketknife or, according to Bannon, a boy scout knife, containing a small blade and screwdriver attachment, which he said he carried for protection. At this point Waldron broke away to go to the kitchen to fill a food order for another patron. Several minutes later, while Waldron was returning from his chore to rejoin Bannon and Riviello, the latter suddenly turned and, as he did so, his eye unexpectedly came in contact with the blade of the knife which Waldron still had in his hand. On defendant's case, Waldron largely confirmed these facts, but added that he was 'flipping' the knife, presumably as one might flip a coin, as he was coming from the direction of the kitchen and inadvertently struck the plaintiff. No one else so testified.

"Applying the pertinent legal precepts to this factual framework, we first note what is hornbook law: the doctrine of *respondeat superior* renders a master vicariously liable for a tort committed by his servant while acting within the scope of his employment [citations omitted]. The definition of 'scope of employment,' however, has not been an unchanging one.

"Originally defined narrowly on the theory that the employer could exercise close control over his employees during the period of their service, as in other tort law contexts (*see, e.g., Codling v. Paglia*, 32 N.Y.2d 330, 339–341), social policy has wrought a measure of relaxation of the traditional confines of the doctrine (*see* Restatement, Agency 2d, § 219, Comment [*a*]. Among motivating considerations are the escalation of employee-produced injury, concern that the average innocent victim, when relegated to the pursuit of his claim against the employee, most often will face a defendant too impecunious to meet the claim, and that modern economic devices, such as cost accounting and insurance coverage, permit most employers to spread the impact of such costs (*see* Prosser, Torts [4th ed.], § 69; Seavey, Agency, § 83).

"So, no longer is an employer necessarily excused merely because his employees, acting in furtherance of his interests, exhibit human failings and perform negligently or otherwise than in an authorized manner. Instead, the test has come to be ' ''whether the act was done while the servant was doing his master's work, no matter how irregularly, or with what disregard of instructions'' ' (*Jones v. Weigand*, 134 App. Div. 644, 645, quoted in *Baker v. Allen & Arnink Auto Renting Co.*, 231 N.Y. 8, 12–13 [POUND, J.]).

"Thus formulated, the rule may appear deceptively simple but, because it depends largely on the facts and circumstances peculiar to each case, it is more simply said than applied [citation omitted]. For, while clearly intended to cover an act undertaken at the explicit direction of the employer, hardly a debatable proposition, it also encompasses the far more elastic idea of liability for 'any act which can fairly and reasonably be deemed to be an ordinary and natural incident or attribute of that act' (2 Mechem, Agency [2d ed.], § 1879, p. 1461). And, because the determination of whether a particular act was within the scope of the servant's employment is so heavily dependent on factual considerations, the question is ordinarily one for the jury [citations omitted].

"That is not to say there are no useful guidelines for assessing whether the conduct of a particular employee, overall, falls within the permissible ambit of the employment. Among the factors to be weighed are: the connection between the time, place and occasion for the act; the history of the relationship between employer and employee as spelled out in actual practice; whether the act is one commonly done by such an employee; the extent of departure from normal methods of performance; and whether the specific act was one that the employer could reasonably have anticipated [citations omitted].

"The first of these criteria need not detain us. The Pot Belly was the arena in which Waldron worked, and the evening was the time when he did so. The route from the kitchen where he would hold forth as chef to the patrons in the public room in which he performed his other functions could hardly be claimed to be a physical deviation. As to past employment practices, there was evidence that the friendly relations which Waldron enjoyed with the majority of the pub's patrons and the expectation that these would be exploited to enhance the popularity of the pub entered into the hiring itself. The implementation of this plan, pursued continuously until the day Riviello was injured, almost of necessity had to depend largely on Waldron's own personality and his judgment of how different patrons were to be handled. Pertinently, we suggest that, even if the jury had found no express understanding that Waldron would socialize, it could have drawn the inference from the nature of his job that his interaction with those visiting the premises would be a concomitant of the employment.

"Surely, the fact that Waldron, at the precise instant of the occurrence, was not plying his skills as a cook, waiter and bartender did not take him beyond the range of things commonly done by such an employee. The intermittent demands of his work meant that there would be intervals in which his function was only to stand by awaiting a customer's order. Indeed, except perhaps in a world of complete automation as portrayed for instance in Charlie Chaplin's classic film 'Modern Times,' the busiest of employees may be expected to take pauses and, when they do, engage in casual conversation, even punctuated, as here, by the exhibition to others of objects they wear or carry on their persons.

"We turn then to the extent of Waldron's departure, if it may be so characterized, from the normal methods of his performance, and to whether the specific act of carrying the pocketknife in his hand was one that the employer could reasonably have anticipated. Initially, it bears noting that for an employee to be regarded as acting within the scope of his employment, the employer need not have foreseen the precise act or the exact manner of the injury as long as the general type of conduct may have been reasonably expected [citation omitted]. As indicated earlier, it suffices that the tortious conduct be a natural incident of the employment. Hence, general rather than specific foreseeability has carried the day even in some cases where employees deviated from their assigned tasks [citations omitted].

"Indeed, where the element of general foreseeability exists, even intentional tort situations have been found to fall within the scope of employment (*see, e.g., Sims v. Bergamo,* 3 N.Y.2d 531, 534–535 [assault of unruly patron by bartender to protect employer's property and to maintain order on premises]; [citation omitted].

"Given all this, it was permissible to find as a fact that Raybele could have anticipated that in the course of Waldron's varied activities in the pursuit of his job, he might, through carelessness, do some injury. The specifics of the act, though it was not essential that they be envisaged, could be, as here, the product of an inattentive handling of the pocketknife he had described to Riviello and Bannon, or a similar mishandling of a paring knife he could have had in his hand as he left the kitchen, or perhaps a steak knife with which he was on his way to set a table. Or, perchance, instead of a knife, with equal nonmalevolence it could in similar fashion have been a pen, a comb, a nail file, a pencil, a scissors, a letter opener, a screwdriver or some other everyday object that he was displaying. In any of these cases, an instant of inattention could render such an instrument of injury.

"Further, since, as a result of our decision, this case will return to the Appellate Division for consideration of the facts, it is not amiss to add the following observations: Waldron's own testimony that he had 'flipped' the knife (though not intending any injury) was no part of plaintiff's case. If it had been, it is not to be assumed that this kind of motion, any more than would the twirling of a chain containing sharp-pointed keys or the tossing of a coin, or some other gesture, whether used as an aid to communication or an outlet for nervous energy, would be beyond the broad ambit of the employer's general expectation. For one employing men and women takes them subject to the kind of conduct normal to such beings. . . .

[Discussion of effect of prejudgment settlement and general release omitted.]

"Accordingly, the order of the Appellate Division should be reversed, with costs, and the case remitted for review of the facts."

When the nature of an employee's duties are such that the employer necessarily contemplates that the employee will occasionally be required to use force, the employer is not necessarily relieved of liability merely because the employee uses more force than is necessary in the performance of a particular job.

In *Sage Club v. Hunt*,[63] the bartender at the defendant's club assaulted a patron who disagreed with him over the amount that the patron owed for drinks. The court affirmed the holding of the lower court that the bartender was acting within the scope of his duties when he assaulted the plaintiff. The court said:

> Here Mr. Thyfault's [the bartender's] duties included collecting money for drinks, and he lost his temper over that matter. His duties also included keeping order in the bar and removing disruptive customers which Thyfault apparently tried to do by pushing appellee down the stairs. . . . Appellant evidently allowed Thyfault to use force at his discretion, and he was performing work of the kind he was employed to perform. . . . This Court will therefore not indulge in nice distinctions to determine whether excessive force was motivated by personal reasons.[64]

In *Cappo v. Vinson Guard Services Inc.*,[65] the court held that the defendant restaurant was liable for the acts of its parking-lot guard when the guard struck the plaintiff during a dispute over parking privileges. The court found that the dispute occurred in the course of the guard's duties in enforcing parking regulations.[66]

11:10 Employer Estopped to Deny Responsibility for Acts of Independent Contractor

The following Illinois appellate decision illustrates the danger of representing oneself as engaged in a business in which some act of negligence on the part of a supposed independent contractor may be imputed to the business for the purpose of imposing liability.

WALSH v. PHEASANT RUN, INC.
25 Ill. App. 3d 769, 323 N.E.2d 855 (1975)

DRUCKER, J.: "On June 14, 1969, plaintiff, a guest at the lodge owned and operated by defendant, was injured when she fell from a horse at a nearby riding stable. She filed a complaint alleging that both defendant and Homestretch, Inc., owned and maintained the stable, and that their negligence in maintaining their equipment and training their employees was the proximate cause of her injuries. . . . In its answer Homestretch admitted ownership and control of the stable but denied plaintiff's other allegations. Defendant denied ownership and control of the stables. The case proceeded to trial.

[63]638 P.2d 161 (Wyo. 1981).
[64]*Id.* at 163.
[65]60 A.D.2d 615, 400 N.Y.S. 2d 148 (1981).
[66]*Id.* at 151.

''We need summarize only that evidence which is relevant to the issues raised on appeal.

'' . . . Edward McCardle, president of defendant, was called by plaintiff. He testified that in June 1969 defendant owned a resort complex known as Pheasant Run Lodge consisting of 10 or 11 buildings and approximately 170 acres of land. Defendant's employees ran various facilities for the benefit of guests at the lodge. Prior to June 1, 1969, these included the bars, swimming pool, restaurant, tennis courts and equestrian stable. After June 1, 1969, the stable was rented to Jerry Farmer under an oral lease. McCardle personally owned the land on which the stable and riding ring were located but some years earlier had leased the land to defendant. For 5 or 6 months prior to June 1, 1969, Farmer had been an employee of defendant. Following the rental of the stable to Farmer, a sign saying 'Homestretch' was erected in front of those facilities. After June 1, 1969, defendant had nothing to do with the day-to-day operation of the stable. Its employees there were placed on Farmer's payroll. The public was not specifically alerted that defendant no longer ran the stable. After June 1, 1969, defendant referred all inquiries made by lodge guests concerning the stables to that facility. The lodge had a telephone extension to the stable for the convenience of guests who wished to make riding reservations.

''Defendant employed a public-relations manager. Advertisements were placed in Chicago newspapers and radio ads may have been used as well. Defendant distributed printed material to lodge guests explaining the various services which were available to them. These brochures were placed at the front desk and possibly in the rooms. An informational or 'locater' sheet (plaintiff's Exhibit 1) was admitted into evidence. It consisted of a map of the resort complex and depicted the availability of the stables directly across North Avenue from the lobby and offices. A brochure (plaintiff's Exhibit 2) was admitted into evidence which portrayed the activities available to lodge guests. Prominently pictured were two people riding horses. The brochure included the following copy: 'Of course, there are also, all of the usual activities found at a fine resort . . . shuffleboard, horseback riding, tennis, billiards, pingpong, skeet shooting, water skiing and fishing.' A receipt (plaintiff's Exhibit 3) bearing the letterhead:

'PHEASANT RUN FARMS
P.O. Box 64
St. Charles, Illinois, 60174
RACE HORSES-HUNTERS-JUMPERS'

was admitted into evidence. The post office box and telephone number listed on the receipt were defendant's. The receipt was dated June 14, 1969.

''Plaintiff's counsel read into the record McCardle's answers to interrogatories wherein he acknowledged defendant's ownership of the tacking equipment and riding stock used at the stable on June 14, 1969.

''Suzanne McCutcheon testified for defendant that she had been employed by defendant in May 1969. On June 14, 1969, she worked for Homestretch, Inc.

Many townspeople as well as guests of the lodge used the stables. On June 14, 1969, there was a large sign in front of the stables that said 'Homestretch.' Although she did not know for sure, there may have been a procedure for charging use of the stables to a lodge guest's bill.

"Jerry Farmer testified for defendant that beginning in May 1969 and culminating on June 1, 1969, the stable and restaurant operations were gradually transferred from defendant to Homestretch, Inc. By June 14, 1969, a large 'Homestretch' sign had been painted and erected in front of the stable. He decided to operate the stable after a discussion with McCardle. He had a month-to-month lease which included rental of tack equipment, horses and use of the facilities. . . . A dual billing system was employed so that lodge guests' bills were collected by defendant and repaid to Homestretch. . . .

"At the close of evidence plaintiff was permitted to file a second amended complaint inserting the following paragraphs:

"5. That at the time and place aforesaid the plaintiff relied on the reputation of the defendant insofar as providing safe and proper supervision over those recreational activities which were represented as being conducted by defendant, Pheasant Run, Inc.

"6. That relying upon these representations the Plaintiff became a patron of the Pheasant Run riding stables which stable operation was being conducted on the premises of Pheasant Run.

"Defendant raised no objection to this portion of the proposed amendment. . . .

"Defendant has also contended that even if the second amended complaint was properly before the court, 'the evidence did not support the necessary elements of estoppel.' Defendant argues that in order to establish an equitable estoppel, plaintiff was required to prove that its misleading conduct was the proximate cause of her injuries. Consequently it is claimed that since negligent acts or omissions at the stable caused her injuries, and not representations as to who owned it, defendant cannot be held liable. We disagree.

"Where a defendant holds 'itself out as one engaged in maintaining and operating [a] business in the course of which the negligence arose,' it may be held liable. [Citation omitted.] . . . [F]or example, where defendant proprietor of a store building granted a license to a merchant to operate a beauty parlor in the building, the court held that since defendant held itself out as the owner and operator of the beauty shop, and these representations were reasonably relied upon by a patron of that facility, defendant could properly be held liable for injuries she suffered when she received a permanent wave of her hair [citation omitted].

"In the instant case we believe that the evidence clearly demonstrates that defendant held itself out as the owner and operator of the stables. Defendant distributed to its guests brochures and promotional literature indicating the availability of horseback riding facilities at the resort. This material was placed in the lobby and guest rooms of the lodge even after June 1, 1969, the ostensible date of the transfer of the stables to Homestretch. The manner in which the stables were operated was apparently unaffected by the transfer. Guests continued to charge their horseback riding expenses to their bills at the lodge. The stables continued to issue receipts headed 'Pheasant Run Farms.' . . . Although evidence was introduced to the effect that a 'Homestretch' sign had been placed in front of the stables, . . . the mere presence of a sign labeled 'Homestretch' was more than counterbalanced by the manifestations of continued ownership and operation of the stables by defendant.

"The record also demonstrates that plaintiff relied on defendant's representations of ownership and operation of the stables. . . .

"In light of this record, we believe that a finding that defendant was estopped from denying ownership and thus was liable was not against the manifest weight of the evidence. Accordingly, the judgment entered below is affirmed.

"Affirmed."

A hotelkeeper's nondelegable duty to maintain the premises in good structural repair is the subject of the following case.

FITZGERALD V. 667 HOTEL CORP.
103 Misc. 2d 80, 426 N.Y.S.2d 368 (Sup. Ct. 1980)

GREENFIELD, J.: "In the late afternoon on August 3, 1973, a portion of a building known as the Broadway Central Hotel at 673 Broadway in Manhattan collapsed. Four persons were killed in the wreckage, many others were hurt and a number of businesses sustained substantial property damage giving rise to the 43 consolidated actions at bar. Named as defendants were, among others, the owners of the building, the net lessee, the mortgagee, a tenant who was having structural renovation done on its portion of the premises and the contractor it employed for that purpose. . . . Thus, the case raises both factual and legal questions as to the responsibility for the disaster and the court must apportion the liability among those responsible. . . .

"The Multiple Dwelling Law imposes upon an owner (which is defined to include a lessee directly or indirectly in control of the premises) a duty to keep every part of the premises in good repair. (MDL § 78). The testimony clearly established that the hotel was a multiple dwelling and this fact is conceded by the owners, Matilda Edwards and Gertrude Latham.

"The duties imposed by § 78 are non-delegable, *Rogers v. Dorchester Associates,* 32 N.Y.2d 553, 347 N.Y.S.2d 22, 300 N.E.2d 403; however, the owner or a lessee is not the insurer of the safety of persons and property upon the premises. Fault and actual or constructive notice of the defective condition must be shown in order to impose liability under § 78. [Citation omitted.] Thus, an owner will not be held liable where he has so completely parted with possession and control that he cannot perform the duty to keep the premises in good repair. However, the burden is on the owner to make such a showing.

"The owners in this case did not sustain this burden. To the contrary, the evidence established that the owners retained sufficient control to subject them to liability. Although the premises were under a net lease, the owners had a right to enter and inspect the premises and make repairs, thus retaining sufficient control to subject them to liability.

"Moreover, the evidence supports a finding that the owners had constructive, if not actual notice of the dangerous condition. As noted above, cracks in the bearing wall were evident as early as 1970, and by early 1973, the crack had widened and extended to the second floor. Owners of a building cannot absolve themselves of liability by failing to avail themselves of their contractual right of access and then claim that they did not have notice of condition. Where, as here, the owners have the right to enter the premises and make repairs, the continued existence of a dangerous condition, which the evidence established was actually known to the net lessee, justifies a finding that the owners had constructive notice of the condition. [Citation omitted.]

"In addition, there was evidence that Mr. Edwards, defendant Matilda Edwards' husband, had actual notice of the condition. Mr. Edwards, who acted on behalf of the owners on more than one occasion, may be considered their agent, at least for purposes of notice. Based on the foregoing, the court finds the owners liable.

"667 Hotel Corporation, as the net lessee of the premises, in addition to having an obligation of reasonable care, *Putnam v. Stout,* 38 N.Y.2d 607, 381 N.Y.S.2d 848, 345 N.E.2d 319 (1976), had the right under its lease and, in fact, had covenanted to make repairs to the building.

"Although the net lessee engaged architect Alvin Fisher two days after Mr. Clark's inspection, this did not fulfill the lessee's duties. No repairs were undertaken and plans were not even filed until May of 1973. Although Mr. Fisher testified that he was called again in April, probably in connection with a violation that was issued in February concerning the bulge on the Broadway facade, no plans for any repairs were submitted until May 2, 1973. Moreover, Mr. Fisher testified that the plans were filed simply to gain time, since it was not expected that they would be approved. In addition, based on the testimony adduced at trial, had any of Mr. Fisher's plans been implemented, the collapse would not have been prevented. Accordingly, the court finds that the net lessee is also liable. Neither the owners nor the net lessee can avoid liability because the Department of Buildings admittedly issued a defective violation in February which only referred to the facade of the building and made no mention of the second bearing wall. . . . "

11:11 *Duty to Rescue and Aid Guests*

As a general rule, there is no duty to aid or rescue another person and hence no tort liability for harm to him for failing to do so. Thus one may stand idly by and watch another person bleed to death or drown, although with no risk to himself he could have easily saved the victim.

The harshness of this rule has been modified in certain areas where the parties in question are not strangers but stand in some relationship which the law deems sufficiently close to require the taking of active steps by the one to rescue the other. Thus an employer owes a duty to rescue an employee who is injured in the course of his employment and to care for or furnish medical aid to an ill employee.[67]

When the hotel keeper has been responsible for bringing about the situation that imperils the guest or patron, there is to some extent a duty upon him to extend aid, particularly when he was at fault in so exposing the victim to harm.[68]

Stahlin v. Hilton Hotels Corporation[69] raises two issues with respect to the duty, if any, of an innkeeper to render medical assistance to a guest who is ill and calls for help: (1) the duty to render such aid and (2) the duty to render proper aid when such aid is provided. In affirming a jury verdict in favor of the plaintiff, the court reviewed the Illinois law on this subject as follows:

> We believe the evidence was sufficient to support a finding that Hilton was negligent in sending Fredarica Anderson to Stahlin's room in response to Bishop's request for help. Whether Bishop specifically requested a doctor and whether the assistant manager represented that a doctor would be sent are not determinative of this question. Bishop related the circumstances of Stahlin's problem and Hilton undertook to render assistance. As the trial court correctly charged the jury, "the operator of a hotel owes no duty to provide any service for a guest who may be ill or injured. If, however, it undertakes to provide such service for any person, it must exercise ordinary care to provide such services that it has undertaken to give." . . .
> We agree with plaintiffs that the duty undertaken by Hilton was more than merely "sending someone up" to Stahlin's room. Reasonable care under the circumstances required that the hotel send a doctor, or at the very least a licensed nurse, to provide the medical assistance requested on behalf of Stahlin. Moreover, while Hilton denied that it had knowledge of Mrs. Andersen's lack of a license, there is ample evidence in the record from which the jury could find that the failure to inquire as to her qualifications constituted negligence on the part of Hilton. Hilton knew she was making room calls on sick and injured guests and charging the same amount as a doctor. It was the established practice of the hotel to send her to a guest's room in response to a request for a doctor. Under these circumstances, since Hilton knew she was not a doctor, the jury could reasonably find the hotel chargeable with such further knowledge which a reasonable investigation would have revealed—that is, that Mrs. Andersen was not a licensed nurse. Hilton relies on *Tansey v. Robinson*, 24 Ill. App. 2d 227, 164 N.E.2d 272 (1960), in support of its position that plaintiffs were required to show that the hotel had actual knowledge of Mrs. Andersen's lack of qualifications. However, the court in *Tansey, supra,* held that liability for the negligent acts of an independent contractor may be predicated upon a failure to exercise reasonable care in selecting a careful and competent contractor. . . . Hilton states in its brief that both Dr. Addenbrooke and Mrs. Andersen were independent contractors. Thus, under the rule stated in *Tansey, supra,* Mrs. Andersen's lack of a nursing license in Illinois was a matter which could have been determined by Hilton upon inquiry, and it was a matter which the jury could properly take into consideration

[67]64 A.L.R.2d 1108.
[68]*See* McLean v. University Club, 97 N.E.2d 174 (Mass. 1951).
[69]484 F.2d 580 (7th Cir. 1973).

in determining whether Hilton was negligent in carrying out its voluntary undertaking to provide medical assistance for Stahlin.

In *Boles v. La Quinta Motor Inns*,[70] a Texas decision, plaintiff, Mrs. Boles, was bound, gagged, and raped in her room while a guest at the defendant motel. She managed to telephone the motel's front desk but was forced to speak to several different motel employees before one of them, a desk clerk, would contact the police. Plaintiff claimed that the desk clerk spoke sarcastically to her and refused to send motel employees to help her, though plaintiff told the clerk that she feared the rapist's return. Unknown to the plaintiff, two relief managers stood outside her door, listening to her terrified screams but failing to comfort her, while they waited for the police to arrive.

The court of appeals found the defendant negligent in failing to respond more quickly to the plaintiff's peril. Plaintiff was awarded $43,000 in damages for the mental anxiety she suffered while waiting for the hotel employees to respond to her situation.

Whether a duty initially exists to come to the aid of another, it is clear that once the hotelkeeper does come to the aid of the guest or patron, he will be liable to the guest if through his negligence he puts him in a worse condition than that in which he found him or causes the guest to refrain from taking any steps for his protection by causing him to rely on the hotelkeeper's assistance.

Because of the possibility of fraud occasioned by the above rule, a number of states have adopted "good samaritan" statutes which bar recovery against the rescuer in the absence of proof of willful or wantonly inflicted harm. The New York Education Law, section 6527, exempts from civil liability licensed physicians who gratuitously render first aid or treatment at the scene of an accident or other emergency to a person who is ill, unconscious, or injured except in the case of gross negligence. Section 6611 applies this exemption to dentists, and section 6908 applies it to registered nurses and licensed practical nurses.

The responsibility to exercise care in ejecting an ill guest was discussed in section 6:6, *supra*.

The following case reiterates a basic rule of the law of negligence in the delivery of medical aid to a hotel guest. The delay in rendering such aid, no matter how unreasonable, must be the proximate cause of the guest's injuries, including pain and suffering, to be actionable.

Room v. Caribe Hilton Hotel
659 F.2d 5 (1st Cir. 1981)

Campbell, C.J.: "Plaintiff Herbert Room commenced this diversity action to recover damages allegedly arising out of a heart attack he suffered on November 24, 1976, while a guest at defendant Caribe Hilton Hotel. At the close of plaintiff's case-in-chief, the district court granted a directed verdict for defendant and plaintiff appeals. We affirm.

[70]680 F.2d 1077 (5th Cir. 1982).

"The facts as viewed in the light most favorable to plaintiff, *see, e.g., Carlson v. Amercian Safety Equipment Corp.*, 528 F.2d 384, 385 (1st Cir. 1976), are as follows. Herbert Room arrived in Puerto Rico on November 24, 1976 and registered as a guest at the Caribe Hilton Hotel in San Juan. That evening, Room gambled at the hotel casino. As he was leaving the casino, he began to feel weak and returned to his room. Upon arriving there, he felt nauseous, and therefore called the hotel operator, after reading the following section in the hotel service directory:

"A registered nurse is on duty, and a qualified physician is available at all times. Call doctor's office for appointment 8:30 A.M. to 5:00 P.M., Monday through Friday. After hours and Saturdays and Sundays, call: Telephone operator. Nurse will be glad to make dental appointments. Call: Ext. 1740.

"This first call to the operator took place, according to Room, at 7:30 P.M. He requested a doctor, although he did not describe his symptoms, and testified that the operator told him she would get him one. At 11:30 P.M., he called the operator and again requested a doctor, again making no mention of his symptoms. The operator tried to call one of three doctors listed on a hotel roster as available to treat guests, but his line was busy. She then called Room, who told her to keep trying. Five or ten minutes later she tried again to call the doctor, but his line was still busy. She informed Room, who again asked her to keep trying. She tried to call the other doctors on the list, but was unable to make contact with any of them. Once again, she called Room, who again asked her to keep trying. At no time did she call the 24-hour emergency number of the San Jorge Hospital, although that number was also listed on her roster. Eventually, Room called some friends in Puerto Rico, who advised him to take a cab to the Presbyterian Hospital, which he did. They also called the hotel operator and informed her that she could stop trying to call the doctor.

"Room arrived at the hospital at approximately 1:15 A.M. His condition was diagnosed as a myocardial infarction, or heart attack. He remained hospitalized for almost a month. In the course of that time, he suffered two more serious incidents involving his heart, acute cardiac failure on November 30, and paroxysmal tachycardia on December 8.

"After being released from the hospital, Room returned to his home in New York and took a job as a converter in the textile industry. He quit approximately nine months later because he was unable to keep enough information in his head to do his job satisfactorily. He now suffers from a poor memory and head pains, complaints he never had before his heart attack.

"Room sued the hotel, alleging that it had breached a duty under Puerto Rico law to provide him with adequate medical care by failing to put him in touch with a doctor from the time he first called the operator until he left for the hospital. Room alleged that this delay caused him permanent brain damage, and claimed $1 million in damages for hospital and medical expenses, loss of earnings, and pain and suffering. In directing a verdict for the defendant, the district court found, *inter alia,* that the delay in providing plaintiff with medical attention was not a proximate cause of his injuries.

"Assuming *arguendo* that the defendant breached a duty to exercise reasonable care in providing medical care to its guests,[2] the plaintiff must still establish a causal relation between the defendant's negligence and the plaintiff's injury. *See, e.g., Portilla v. Carreras Schira*, 95 P.R.R. 785, 793 (1968). In discussing this issue, it is necessary to distinguish the plaintiff's permanent brain damage from any pain and mental anguish he may have suffered during the time when the defendant failed to provide him with a doctor. We shall address the permanent injuries first.

"The plaintiff's sole expert testimony concerning his medical condition was given by Dr. Jose Luis Freyre, a clinical neurologist. Dr. Freyre examined the plaintiff on November 1, 1978. He had no contact with plaintiff at any time prior to this; specifically, he did not treat plaintiff during his hospitalization in 1976.

"Dr. Freyre testified as to plaintiff's loss of some cerebral function, and testified further that the heart attack of November 24 could have caused this condition. On cross-examination, however, he admitted that the hospital's records of plaintiff's condition at the time of his admission were not complete enough to determine with any degree of certainty whether the November 24 attack did indeed cause any brain damage. In particular, the lack of any information as to plaintiff's blood pressure at the time of admission made it impossible for Dr. Freyre to ascertain whether the attack had resulted in any significant decrease in blood flow to the brain.

"Most significantly, Dr. Freyre was unable to determine which of the three heart-related incidents suffered by plaintiff caused the brain damage. The following colloquy took place between the court and Dr. Freyre:
"THE COURT: [C]ould the second [heart failure] have been the cause of [plaintiff's] condition?
"THE WITNESS: It could have.
"THE COURT: Is there any way of telling whether it was the second or the first?
"THE WITNESS: No way of telling whether it was the first, second or third.

"It is not disputed that the delay in rendering medical assistance on November 24 was not a cause of the two subsequent cardiac incidents. There was no evidence that the delay on November 24 was a more likely cause of plaintiff's condition than were the other two incidents. In such a situation, any determination by the jury that the delay did cause the injury would be pure speculation and conjecture. Such speculation is not permitted. *Widow of Delgado v. Boston Insurance Co.*, 99 P.R.R. 693, 702–04 (1971); W. Prosser, Handbook of the Law of Torts § 41, at 241 (4th ed. 1971). The directed verdict for defendant as to plaintiff's permanent brain damage was therefore proper.

"The evidence of any mental anguish[3] that plaintiff may have suffered during the delay in obtaining medical treatment was also insufficient to overcome defendant's motion for a directed verdict. Plaintiff's sole evidence on this issue is as follows. He testified that during the time he was in the hotel room waiting for the operator to contact a doctor, he was weak and had few lucid moments. He said he had some pains in his back and arms, and that at one point they became very severe, at which time he felt that he was going to die.

"There was, however, no evidence that the delay alone caused any pain or mental suffering. Defendant quite rightly points out that the heart attack itself—an event for which defendant was not responsible—would be accompanied by some pain, regardless of the speed with which help arrived. There was no attempt by plaintiff to show the extent to which prompt medical attention would have alleviated his pain, if at all. Given this failure even to attempt to apportion the damages between the delay and the heart attack,[4] no reasonable jury could conclude that the delay alone caused any pain or mental suffering.

"Similarly, the proof of mental anguish based on plaintiff's fear that he was going to die was insufficient. Again, there is no evidence that he would not have feared for his life even after receiving medical attention. The fact that he suffered two more cardiac-related crises while in the hospital certainly suggests that he was not out of danger even after his hospitalization. Moreover, plaintiff did not describe how long he feared for his life or how great that fear was. Any attempt by the jury to assign a dollar value to this injury based on the testimony described above could only be the result of speculation and conjecture. While plaintiff's tetimony may amount to a scintilla of evidence that the delay caused him substantial mental anguish, that is not sufficient to overcome a motion for a directed verdict. *See, e.g., Trinidad v. Pan American World Airways, Inc.*, 575 F.2d 983, 985 (1st Cir. 1978).

"*Affirmed.*

"2. We do not decide whether such a duty actually existed or whether it was breached in this case.
"3. Under Puerto Rico law, a plaintiff may recover damages for mental suffering, even without any physical injury being alleged or proven. *See Compagnia Nationale Air France v. Castano*, 358 F.2d 203 (1st Cir. 1966); *Murial v. Suazo*, 72 P.R.R. 348 (1951); *Rivera v. Rossi*, 64 P.R.R. 683 (1945).
"4. Defendant is not, of course, responsible for that portion of the injury resulting solely from the heart attack. *See generally* W. Prosser, Handbook of the Law of Torts § 52, at 317–20."

In a unique California case, the court even went so far as to hold a tavern liable for the wrongful death of a patron in a tavern *across the street*. In *Soldano v. O'Daniels*,[71] plaintiff's husband was shot and killed in a bar across the street from the defendant's bar (the Circle Inn). A patron of the other bar came into the Circle Inn and asked the bartender if he could use the phone to call the police to break up a fight that was going on at the other bar. The bartender refused, and plaintiff's husband was subsequently shot and killed during the fight in the other bar. The court held that the bartender at the Circle Inn was negligent in refusing the use of the phone to the patron. While the court acknowledged that no "special relationship" existed between the bartender at the Circle Inn and plaintiff's husband, the court viewed its holding as a natural extension of the principle that people are liable for negligent interference with a person attempting to render necessary aid.

[71] 141 Cal. App. 3d 443, 190 Cal. Rptr. 310 (1983).

11:12 *Emergency Medical Care of Guests*

As a part of the hotel's duty to protect guests from harm, the hotel has a duty to assist a guest in obtaining medical care in case of emergency. No legal problem arises when the guest seeks the aid of the hotel and the hotel either gives the guest the information as to where to find medical aid or takes him there. As long as the hotel has acted in a reasonable manner and has used reasonable care in dealing with the guest, it is not liable for any subsequent negligence or fault of the doctor or the hospital to whom it has directed or taken the guest.

What should the hotel do if it finds that a guest is unconscious? If the guest is outside of his room and is unconscious, the hotel is under a duty to see that medical care and attention are provided for the guest. The hotel is not liable for any harm as long as it exercises reasonable care in selecting the physician or hospital for the guest. Moreover, as the hotel is acting in an emergency, it is not negligent when it makes the best of circumstances as it finds them, although when viewed in the light of the event after it has occurred, the hotel may not have made the most judicious decision.

If the unconscious guest is in his room, a technical question arises as to how the hotel can reach the guest without violating the guest's right of privacy. The matter becomes very difficult for the hotelkeeper when he is not certain whether the guest is unconscious and in need of medical help. Thus the hotelkeeper is faced with the following alternatives: (1) the guest is not in need of help, and, accordingly, entry into his room may constitute an invasion of privacy for which the hotel would be liable, or (2) the guest is in fact in need of medical help, and if the hotelkeeper does not enter the guest's room to take care of him, the hotel may be liable for the harm, and possible death, that may result from the neglect of the guest. The solution to this dilemma lies in favor of entering to rescue the guest. Society places a high value on giving the guest necessary medical care and perhaps saving his life than it gives to protecting his injured feelings from an invasion of his privacy. In terms of monetary liability it is reasonably certain that the same jury would return a greater verdict against a hotel for failure to provide necessary aid than it would for making an unnecessary invasion of privacy. Moreover, since the potential of harm to the guest is so great, it is more than likely that the jury would be eager to find that the hotelkeeper had reasonable cause to enter to rescue the guest although in fact there was no need for rescue.

The manner of entry is important. The entry should be made if possible by a high-ranking employee and a physician if they are available and time permits their being summoned. If not, and if reasonable ground exists for believing that there is an emergency, the hotelkeeper should take the chance of making a mistake and enter to save the guest.

The condition of the guest when last seen or heard from is important in determining whether the hotel has acted with reasonable care. For example, if the guest comes into the hotel very intoxicated, the hotel is entitled to assume that the reason it does not hear from him the next morning is that he is sleeping off his indulgence. The hotel is not required to play the role of nursemaid and assume that the worst has happened to one of its wards. In such circumstances, the hotel is justified in believing that everything is normal and that there is no emergency.

A difficult situation may arise if the guest appears to be in need of medical treatment but insists that he is all right and refuses to go for or receive such treatment. If in fact he appears fully possessed of his faculties and knows what he is doing, the hotel will not be liable because it leaves him alone, even though in fact he required medical attention. If it appears to a reasonable man that the guest needs medical care and that the guest is too stricken to make an intelligent choice, he should be treated the same as an unconscious guest. The best solution, of course, is to get a doctor as soon as possible and let him decide what action should be taken. Once the hotel, in the exercise of reasonable care, has procured a doctor for the guest, it need go no further unless requested or advised to do so by the doctor, in which case it is protected from liability for its conduct to the same extent as though the act directed or requested of it had been performed personally by the doctor.

What should be done if the person considered in the previous situations is not a guest but a patron at the restaurant or a lodger, boarder, or tenant? As a starting point, the distinction can be made that it is only to the guest that the duty of care is owed. As a practical matter, the hotelkeeper should ignore this distinction and should treat anyone on its premises as a guest. First, there may not be any time to check on the identity and classification of the afflicted person; thus anyone on the premises should be cared for by the hotel, which holds its place out as safe for members of the public. Second, the question whether a person is a guest or a public patron may present a difficult legal problem, and it would be absurd to require the hotel to analyze its legal status before it could determine whether it should act as a good samaritan.

In any case, the sensible solution is to get a physician to take charge of the patron, for from that moment the problem rests with the doctor; the hotel is no longer responsible for the patron if it has exercised reasonable care in finding a physician to minister to the patron.

If the patron is a guest, tenant, lodger, or boarder in the hotel and is removed for emergency medical care, the hotel must take reasonable steps to protect his property while he is away. In the case of a guest, protecting property may give rise to an insurer's liability, although statutory limitations of liability exist in almost all states.

If the hotelkeeper does not lock up the guest's property in the guest's room, he should remove the property for safekeeping. Before he does so, an inventory should be prepared carefully, listing all items of property which have been removed, under supervision of a high-ranking employee of the hotel.

11:13 *Suicide*

In a Georgia case, *Sneider v. Hyatt Corp.*,[72] the survivors of a woman who committed suicide in a hotel alleged that the hotel employees' negligence con-

---

[72]390 F. Supp. 976 (D. Ga. 1975).

tributed to the woman's death. The defense was that a hotel cannot, as an absolute rule, be held liable for a guest's suicide—a kind of first-person injury. The U.S. District Court in Atlanta held, however, that a hotel should have a duty to protect and care for its troubled guests, and that imposing no liability for a suicide translates into no standard of care. The implications of this court's decision are overwhelming. What is a hotelkeeper to do with a troubled guest? Resorting to physical restraint or putting a guest under strict surveillance is a legally risky alternative and could in itself result in lawsuits. Moreover, people who look troubled check into hotels every day without posing problems for innkeepers. Obviously, this is a very complex and difficult question.

11:14 *Restaurant Keeper's Duty to Protect Patrons*

EASTEP V. JACK-IN-THE-BOX
546 S.W.2d 116 (Tex. Ct. Civ. App. 1977)

BROWN, C.J.: "Paula Eastep and her husband, Danny Eastep (the Easteps or appellants), filed suit against Jack-in-the-Box, Inc. (appellee) and others to recover damages for injuries received by Paula while at a restaurant owned and operated by Jack-in-the-Box. All defendants other than Jack-in-the-Box were discharged prior to the submission of the case to the jury. The jury answered all liability issues favorably to appellants and found damages. The trial court granted the defendant's motion . . . for judgment *non obstante veredicto.* Judgment was entered that the plaintiffs take nothing.

"On the night of August 24, 1973, Paula and Danny Eastep, along with Danny's brothers Lloyd and Kenneth, and Kenneth's wife, Charlene, went dancing at a local night club. When the club closed they went to a Jack-in-the-Box restaurant near their apartment in Pasadena, Texas, arriving there around 2:00 A.M. They placed their orders and sat down. Shortly thereafter, four men (the McDonalds) entered the restaurant, placed their orders, and also sat down. When the Eastep party's food was ready, Danny went to the counter to obtain it. As he passed by the McDonald party's table, they cursed him loudly. Further cursing and obscenities were exchanged between the two tables, whereupon the McDonalds jumped up and at least two of them drew out knives. After several minutes of taunting by the McDonalds, a fight ensued. The two women in the Eastep party made their way to one of the restaurant's exit doors. However, Paula Eastep, apparently seeing her husband in danger of being stabbed or cut by the largest of the McDonalds, went back into the melee and grabbed the aggressor by the hair, pulling him over a table. Having retained the grasp on his knife, this individual got up and began slashing wildly at Paula. She threw up her hands to protect her face and sustained a severe laceration on her right arm. The fight ended a few minutes after Paula was cut, and the police arrived almost immediately thereafter.

"In answer to Special Issue No. 1, the jury found that Jack-in-the-Box, acting through its employees, were [*sic*] negligent in: (1) failing to demand that the McDonalds leave the premises before the fight began; (2) failing to timely notify the police; and (3) failing to warn the Easteps of the McDonalds' acts and condition before the fight began. In answer to Special Issue No. 2, the jury found each of the above omissions were [*sic*] a proximate cause of Paula Eastep's injuries. The jury further found that Paula's actions were reasonable under the circumstances and did not constitute negligence. The trial court disregarded the jury's answers to Special Issue No. 2 and entered judgment *non obstante veredicto* for Jack-in-the-Box.

''Appellants' two points of error assert that the trial court erred in granting appellee's motion for judgment n.o.v., and in failing to grant appellants' motion for judgment.

''The owner of land is under a duty to exercise reasonable care for the safety of his invitees. [Citation omitted.] The weight of authority now recognizes that the duty of a proprietor of a restaurant, inn or similar establishment includes the exercise of reasonable care to protect his patrons from intentional injuries inflicted by third persons. [Citations omitted.] Such a duty has been recognized in Texas for owners of public theatres. [Citations omitted.] As patrons, appellants were invitees of appellee; therefore, appellee owed appellants a duty of reasonable care to protect them from the assaults of third persons while on the premises.

''Section 344 of the Restatement (Second) of Torts (1965) states that a possessor of land held open to the public for business purposes is liable for patrons' injuries that are caused by the intentional acts of third persons *and* by 'the failure of the possessor to exercise reasonable care to (*a*) discover that such acts are being done or are likely to be done, or (*b*) give a warning adequate to enable the visitors to avoid the harm, or otherwise to protect them against it.' The portion of the rule requiring notice to the possessor that acts of violence are likely to be done 'does not require a long and continued course of conduct to find that the proprietor had knowledge of the violent disposition of the other patron—all that is necessary is that there be a sequence of conduct sufficiently long to enable the proprietor to act for the patron's safety. It is not necessary that the proprietor know of a history of a series of offenses against the peace. [Citations omitted.]

''In the instant case the evidence showed that at the time of the incident there were four or five Jack-in-the-Box employees on duty and eight to twelve patrons present in addition to the McDonalds. Paula Eastep testified that she first noticed the McDonalds because they were talking loudly and banging on the counter where orders are taken. She said that they were acting 'weird.' The Easteps' order was called 'two or three minutes' later, after the McDonalds had sat down. It took Danny about a minute to get the food. Paula stated that after Danny came back with their order the Mcdonalds began shouting obscenities and making obscene gestures at them. After one of the Easteps returned an obscenity, the Mcdonalds jumped up and drew out their knives. She testified that after the McDonalds got up there was about a two-minute period before any blows were struck, during which time the Easteps were trying to stall off a fight while the McDonalds were hurling epithets, obscenities, and taunts at them. The fight then began, and it was, in her estimation, another two-and-a-half to five minutes before she was cut. She stated that the police arrived four-and-a-half or five minutes after she was cut. Kenneth and Lloyd Eastep also testified that they first noticed the McDonalds when they were 'loudmouthing' at the front counter.

"Steve Gregg, a patron in the Jack-in-the-Box when the fight started, testified that the McDonalds 'were kind of tough acting, you know, like there was a couple of big guys, a couple of medium size guys. They were, looked like they were hopped up on something, a little high or something like that. They come in, sat down and acted kind of tough and slouchy. They were kind of cussing among themselves. I could hear the cussing.'

"He stated that from the time that the McDonalds entered the restaurant until they sat down was about four minutes. From the time they sat down until they got up and took out their knives was another two or three minutes.

"Randall Kimmel, Gregg's roommate, was also in the Jack-in-the-Box when the fight started. He testified that the McDonalds were talking loud and 'looking for trouble, it looked like.' He stated that 'I was eating at the time they were up at the counter and I heard them talking to the manager. There was profanity.'

"The person in charge of the restaurant at the time of the incident was Ismael Cavazos, the assistant manager. He testified that when the McDonalds entered the restaurant, he was away from the counter preparing another order. He asked them to 'hold on a second,' to which the largest of the McDonalds replied, 'Hold on, sh—.' Cavazos stated that this comment was loud enough to have been heard by some of the other patrons. Although he was busy with something else, Cavazos stated that when this abusive language was directed at him, 'I got the impression he was in a nasty mood, so I went ahead and hurried and got their order.' He also testified that he thought one of them had a knife or a gun: 'He had his hand in his pocket and, you know, when he approached me with that expression of "Hold on, hell," you know, I thought to myself, well, you know, this guy must be armed or something.' He recalled stating in a deposition that he was 'scared, [McDonald] was going to start a fight.' Cavazos stated that the McDonalds had red eyes and slurred their worlds, and that he was 'pretty sure' they had been drinking. After he had taken their order, Cavazos said he heard them using other vulgar language.

"Cavazos testified that Jack-in-the-Box employees are instructed to ask anyone using profanity to leave, and to call the police if they do not leave. However, he did not ask the McDonalds to leave even after hearing them use vulgar and abusive language, some of which was directed at him.

"Cavazos stated that as he was preparing food in the 'fry area,' he heard loud noises from the dining room and when he looked, he saw the two groups faced off and the McDonalds' knives drawn. He testified that his 'mind went blank for awhile,' and he did nothing until the fight actually began. He admitted that there might have been time for him to get out in the dining room while the two groups were still just talking. When the fighting did start he said he then told one of the other employees to call the police. However, he also stated that the other employees were more shocked than he was: 'They weren't moving; they were just sitting there. . . . '

"Cavazos testified that he had called the police to come to that Jack-in-the-Box on many occasions. He said that it took an average of five or ten minutes for them to arrive. He stated that on this particular occasion the police arrived 'almost' as the McDonalds were going out the back door.

"L. G. Lilleux, a member of the Pasadena Police Department, testified that the police records indicated that on this occasion a call was received by the police department at 2:36, and the police arrived on the scene at 2:39. Cavazos stated that he thought the fighting lasted a total of five or ten minutes. Robert Harrah, another Jack-in-the-Box employee present that night, testified on deposition that he thought the fight lasted ten or fifteen minutes.

"We hold that the record contains some evidence of probative value to support the jury findings that appellee, through its employees, was negligent in failing to demand that the McDonalds leave the premises before the fight began, in failing to timely notify the police, and in failing to warn appellants of the acts and condition of the McDonalds before the fight began.

"While strongly urging that it owed appellants 'no duty' and was not negligent, appellee primarily contends that there was 'no evidence' to support the jury's findings on proximate cause. The elements of proximate cause are: (1) cause in fact, and (2) foreseeability. We believe the evidence outlined above is sufficient to show the presence of the element of foreseeability. The question narrows, then, to whether the negligent acts of appellee's employees were a cause in fact of Paula Eastep's injury. '[W]hether a particular act of negligence is a cause in fact of an injury has been said to be a particularly apt question for jury determination.' *Farley v. M M Cattle Co.,* 529 S.W.2d 751, 756 (Tex. Sup. 1975). [Citation omitted.]

"In the instant case the time sequence of the particular events is crucial. Steve Gregg estimated that the length of time that the McDonalds were in the restaurant before they jumped and drew out their knives was a total of six or seven minutes. Randy Kimmel estimated this period to be five minutes. Paula and Lloyd Eastep estimated that there were two minutes between the time the McDonalds jumped up and the actual beginning of the fight. Danny estimated this time as two or three minutes. From the time the fight started until Paula was cut was estimated by Kimmel to be three or four minutes. Danny estimated this period to be two or three minutes, and Paula's estimate varied between two-and-a-half and five minutes. Danny estimated that the fight ended from one to three minutes after Paula was cut. Cavazos stated that the police arrived 'right after' the fight ended, almost as the McDonalds were going out the back door.

"The total length of time of the fight was estimated by Danny to be two to four minutes, by Kenneth Eastep to be four or five minutes, by Cavazos to be five or ten minutes, and by Robert Harrah to be ten or fifteen minutes. As noted previously, police records showed that the police arrived three minutes after they were called. Cavazos, who took the McDonalds' orders, had notice of their condition and conduct soon after they arrived; however, he did not ask them to leave. Robert Harrah testified that when a patron is asked to leave the dining room because of the way he is conducting himself, that usually is sufficient. In those instances in which an offensive or abusive patron does not leave when asked, a call to the police usually will produce a quick exit before the police arrive. When asked how such an individual knows they are calling the police, Harrah answered: 'They can see us. The phone is right there, all we've got to do is dial the number and they know I am calling the police.' He said they had the police telephone number 'right there.'

"Had the Jack-in-the-Box employees demanded that the McDonalds leave as soon as they had notice of the likelihood that the McDonalds might commit acts of violence, the fight probably would never have gotten started. Certainly the jury could have believed that the police would have arrived before Paula Eastep was injured.

"Moreover, it is a reasonable inference that if the Jack-in-the-Box employees had acted as soon as they saw weapons displayed, the police would have arrived before Paula was cut. There was evidence that the McDonalds taunted the Easteps with knives drawn for two or three minutes before the first blow was struck. It was during this time that the employees saw the confrontation but were 'paralyzed' and did nothing. There was evidence that Paula was not cut until as long as five minutes after the first blow. The police arrived three minutes after being called. This is sufficient to support a finding of cause in fact.

"We hold that the record contains some evidence of probative value that the negligent acts of the employees of appellee were a proximate cause of the injuries sustained by Paula Eastep. Appellants' points of error are sustained. The judgment of the trial court is reversed, and judgment is here rendered that appellants, Paula Eastep and Danny Eastep, recover from appellee, Jack-in-the-Box, Inc., the damages found in accordance with the verdict of the jury.

"Reversed and rendered."

In *Kimple v. Foster*,[73] the question of foreseeability of the risk, which triggers the duty either to intervene and prevent the injurious conduct or to restore order, was discussed. The Supreme Court of Kansas concluded that a four-hour period of time during which a gang of toughs were abusing customers in full view of the tavernkeeper was sufficient to hold him derelict in not acting affirmatively to maintain order. Also see *Alonge v. Rodriquez*,[74] in which the Wisconsin Supreme Court reviewed a tavernkeeper's duty to maintain order and allowed a host to sue for indemnification for damages recovered by a minor patron.

ALLEN v. BABRAB, INC.
438 So. 2d 356 (Fla. 1983)

McDONALD, J.: "The petitioner, Pearl Allen, and a companion were patrons of the Gemini Club on the evening of October 1, 1977. As the two women left the club in the early morning hours and proceeded to their car in the Gemini

---

[73]205 Kan. 415, 469 P.2d 281 (1970).
[74]89 Wis. 2d 544, 279 N.W.2d 207 (1979).

Club's parking lot, a male patron of the club, Leroy Allen (not related to the plaintiff), approached them. Pearl Allen and her companion rebuffed Leroy Allen's advances, and the trio exchanged harsh words. After pouring his drink on the companion, Leroy Allen hurled the empty glass, which struck Ms. Allen in the face and permanently blinded her in the left eye. . . .

" . . . Implicit in the district court opinion is the view that a tavern owner may be liable for injuries to its patrons caused by the tortious conduct of third parties only if the tavern owner knew or should have known of the dangerous propensities of that specific assailant. This is the very proposition we recently rejected in *Stevens* [*Stevens v. Lankard,* 254 N.E.2d 339] The proprietor of a place of public entertainment will not be held liable for the unforeseeable acts of third persons, but, as we emphasized in *Stevens,* specific knowledge of an individual's dangerous propensities is not the exclusive method of proving foreseeability. It can be shown by proving that, based on past experience, a proprietor knew of or should have recognized the likelihood of disorderly conduct by third persons in general which might endanger the safety of the proprietor's patrons. Foreseeability of an intervening cause is a question for the trier of fact. *Gibson v. Avis Rent-a-Car System, Inc.,* 386 So. 2d 520 (Fla. 1980).

"The Gemini Club had a history of fighting and other disturbances. Prior to October 1, 1977 Babrab had employed a 'bouncer' to maintain security on the premises. The bouncer's duties included patrolling the parking lot and preventing patrons from removing glasses from the bar. Despite urgings to the corporate officers by the bartenders that such security was needed, no such employee was on duty the night of Pearl Allen's assault.

"The evidence was sufficient for the jury reasonably to find that Babrab should have known of the likelihood of injury to patrons caused by disorderly conduct on the part of third parties in general and failed to do anything about it. It is a close question as to whether this failure caused or contributed to the plaintiff's injuries, but the jury could have reasonably concluded that, if Babrab had continued its previous policy of hiring security personnel to take glasses from patrons as they left the club and to patrol the parking lot, the injury suffered by Pearl Allen would have been prevented. This being so, the jury verdict should stand.

"The decision below is quashed, and the district court is ordered to reinstate the judgment rendered by the trial court in favor of Ms. Allen.

"It is so ordered.

"ALDERMAN, C.J., and ADKINS, OVERTON AND EHRLICH, JJ., concur.

"BOYD, J., dissents.''

In the following case, the Supreme Court of Kansas reaffirmed its prior decision in *Kimple v. Foster,*[75] imposing an affirmative duty upon restaurant keepers to exercise reasonable care for their patrons. Here a shift manager looked on while other patrons assaulted the victim. Moreover, the high court ruled that the

---

[75]205 Kan. 415, 469 P.2d 281 (1970).

trial court properly submitted the issue of punitive damages to the jury. (Only the issue of punitive damages is excerpted below).

GOULD v. TACO BELL
239 Kan. 564, 722 Pd.2d 511 (1986)

HERD, J.: " . . .

"As its final point on appeal, appellant argues the trial court erred in submitting this case to the jury on the issue of punitive damages.

"We discussed the nature of punitive damages in *Wooderson v. Ortho Pharmaceutical Corp.*, 235 Kan. 387, 681 P.2d 1038, *cert. denied*——U.S.——, 105 S. Ct. 365, 83 L. Ed. 2d 301 (1984), and held as follows:

" 'Punitive damages are permitted whenever the elements of fraud, malice, gross negligence, or oppression mingle in the controversy.'

" 'Punitive damages are allowed not because of any special merit in the injured party's case, but are imposed to punish the wrongdoer for malicious, vindictive or willful and wanton invasion of the injured party's rights, the purpose being to restrain and deter others from the commission of like wrongs.'

"Before discussing this issue any further, we will first set out the general rule regarding the liability of a corporation for punitive damages awarded for a tort committed by its employee:

" 'A corporation is not liable for punitive damages awarded for an employee's tortious acts within the scope of employment unless (*a*) a corporation or its managerial agent authorized the doing and manner of the act; (*b*) the employee was unfit and the corporation or its managerial agent was reckless in employing or retaining him; (*c*) the employee was employed in a managerial capacity and was acting within the scope of employment; or (*d*) the corporation or its managerial agent ratified or approved the act of the employee. Following Restatement (Second) of Torts § 909 (1977); Restatement (Second) of Agency § 217C (1957). *Kline v. Multi-Media Cablevision, Inc.*, 233 Kan. 988, . . . 666 P.2d 711 (1983).'

"*See also Plains Resources, Inc. v. Gable*, 235 Kan. 580, . . . 682 P.2d 653 (1984).

"In the present case, plaintiff alleges the failure of Taco Bell's manager, Mark Wills, to call the police or intervene to prevent the fight provided a sufficient basis upon which to award punitive damages. Since Wells was employed in a managerial capacity and was acting within the scope of his employment, the corporation can be held liable if Wells' failure to act was willful, wanton, or grossly negligent.

"Appellant argues it cannot be held liable for punitive damages for negligent omissions amounting to wantonness. Rather, appellant contends punitive damages are recoverable only for affirmative acts, as opposed to a failure to act. This argument is without merit.

"57 Am. Jur. 2d, *Negligence* § 105, p. 457, defines 'wanton' as follows:

" 'Generally speaking, inherent in wanton negligence is the ideal of moral fault arising from the doing *or failing to do* an act with consciousness that the act *or omission* would probably cause serious injury, and with reckless indifference to consequences.'

"We have defined a 'wanton act' as something more than ordinary negligence but less than a willful act. It must indicate a realization of the imminence of danger and a reckless disregard and indifference to the consequences. *See Bowman v. Doherty*, 235 Kan. 870, 686 P.2d 112 (1984); *Willard v. City of Kansas City*, 235 Kan. 655, 681 P.2d 1067 (1984); *Britt v. Allen County Community Jr. College*, 230 Kan. 502, 638 P.2d 914 (1982); *Friesen v. Chicago, Rock Island & Pacific Rld.*, 215 Kan. 316, 524 P.2d 1141 (1974). 'Wantonness' refers to the mental attitude of the wrongdoer rather than a particular act of negligence. It follows that acts of omission as well as acts of commission can be wanton since reckless disregard and indifference are characterized by failure to act when action is called for to prevent injury.

"Appellant also contends its conduct could not be 'wanton' because, to constitute wantonness, the act must indicate a realization of the imminence of danger and a reckless disregard or complete indifference or an unconcern for the probable consequences of the wrongful act. *Britt v. Allen County Community Jr. College*, 230 Kan. at 510, 638 P.2d 914. Specifically, Taco Bell argues its conduct could not be wanton because it had no reason to know that harm was imminent. This argument is not supported by the facts. The evidence at trial indicated that the shift manager, Mark Wills, saw Karen Brown strike the plaintiff while the plaintiff was still sitting in the booth, but he did nothing. As the parties moved toward the door, Wills came out from behind the food counter to an area within a few feet of the assailant and the plaintiff. He again failed to call the police or attempt to intervene, but instead observed a second attack upon Gould. It was not until Gould's friend, Theresa Holmberg, broke away from Karen Brown and ran inside and threatened to jump over the counter in order to phone the police that Wills finally called the police.

"Evidence was also presented that Mark Wills believed Karen Brown had been the cause of a disturbance in the restaurant a couple of weeks before the present incident occurred, yet he failed to intervene or call the police when she began attacking Gould.

"In addition, Mark Walters, the store manager, testified that since he became manager of the restaurant in August 1981 the late night patrons had been 'destructive' and 'uncontrollable.' He stated that the late night business in Taco Bell originated in the neighboring bars and that the customers were rowdy and used loud, vulgar and obscene language, and engaged in verbal fights and occasional physical fights. He also testified there was not sufficient help to handle such crowds and that Taco Bell's written policy was to call the police in case of disruptive customer behavior.

"These facts indicate that Taco Bell was aware of the 'imminence of danger' yet failed to intervene or warn plaintiff of such danger. There was substantial evidence to support the jury's award of punitive damages.

"The judgment of the trial court is affirmed.''

11:15   *Injuries to Strangers by Objects Thrown from Hotel Windows*

In *Holly v. Meyers Hotel & Tavern, Inc.*[76] plaintiff sued to recover for personal injuries inflicted upon her by a bottle thrown from a room in defendant's hotel. Said room was occupied by five Canadian sailors who became noisy. When guests in adjoining rooms complained about them, the clerk on duty warned them on the telephone and twenty minutes later went to their room and told them to pipe down or be ejected. Nothing significant happened until two hours later when plaintiff, while walking on the sidewalk alongside the hotel, was struck by a Coca-Cola bottle thrown out of a window in the sailors' suite.

The trial court granted defendant's motion for the dismissal of the complaint, on the theory that although defendant owed the plaintiff a duty of care, yet defendant was not put on any notice which would require it to take any further or more drastic action than it did. The clerk warned the people in the room, they promised to become quiet, and the defendant heard nothing further about it until after the accident. The Appellate Division reversed and held that the factual issue as to whether the clerk acted with reasonable prudence should have been submitted to the jury.

The New Jersey Supreme Court reversed the Appellate Division and reinstated the judgment of dismissal. In the court's view, there was no occasion for affirmative action on the clerk's part during the two-hour period between his warning to the sailors and plaintiff's injury, and under the admitted circumstances no inference of fault or neglect might reasonably be drawn from his inaction. The contrary view, the court suggested, would tend to ignore the real relation between the hotel and its transient guests and the limited extent of control or supervision which may properly be exercised by the former over the latter.

CONNOLLY v. NICOLLET HOTEL

254 Minn. 373, 95 N.W.2d 657 (1959), *order denying motion for new trial aff'd*, 258 Minn. 405, 104 N.W.2d 721 (1960)

[Action for injuries sustained when plaintiff was struck by some substance falling from above her as she walked on a public sidewalk adjacent to defendant's hotel where a convention was being conducted. The jury found for plaintiff. Defendant then moved for judgment notwithstanding the verdict. The trial court granted defendant's motion and entered judgment for the defendant, from which plaintiff appealed.

The accident occurred about midnight June 12, 1953, during the course of the National Junior Chamber of Commerce Convention at defendant's hotel. It was occasioned when plaintiff was struck in her left eye by a substance falling from above her as she walked on a public sidewalk adjacent to the hotel. The blow which struck plaintiff caused her to lose her balance but not to fall. Following the blow, she could not open her left eye. A dark substance which looked like mud was found imbedded in her left eye, as a result of which plaintiff lost the sight of her injured eye.

---

[76] 9 N.J. 493, 89 A.2d 6 (1952).

It appeared that during the course of the convention a mule was stabled in the lobby, and a small alligator was kept on the fourth floor. Guns were fired in the lobby. Broken bottles and broken glass were strewn on the sidewalk, and it was necessary to clean the sidewalk at least twice a day during the convention. Property of the hotel was damaged on several floors; the window of the credit manager's office was broken, and so were chairs, screens, and doors. Carpets and walls were spotted with liquor and water; mirrors were pulled off the walls; lights and toilet bowls were smashed. In general the disorderly behavior of the hotel guests created a hazard to defendant's property.]

MURPHY, J.: " . . . 1. [The general rule is] that a hotel owner or innkeeper owes a duty to the public to protect it against foreseeable risk of danger attendant upon the maintenance and operation of his property [citations omitted]; and to keep it in such condition that it will not be of danger to pedestrians using streets adjacent thereto. [Citation omitted.]

" . . . The plaintiff contends that the act which caused the injury was foreseeable and that the defendants failed in their duty to exercise reasonable care to restrain their guests or to prevent injury.

" . . . It is recognized that one who assembles a large crowd of people upon his premises for the purpose of financial gain to himself assumes the responsibility for using all reasonable care to protect others from injury from causes reasonably to be anticipated. In the exercise of this duty it is necessary for him to furnish a sufficient number of guards or attendants and to take other precautions to control the actions of the crowd. Whether the guards furnished or the precautions taken are sufficient is ordinarily a question for the jury to determine under all of the circumstances.

"3. The common-law test of duty is the probability or foreseeability of injury to the plaintiff. . . .

"4. For the risk of injury to be within the defendants' 'range of apprehension,' it is not necessary that the defendants should have had notice of the particular method in which an accident would occur, if the possibility of an accident was clear to the person of ordinary prudence. . . .

"7. . . . That the dropping of objects from the hotel windows by certain of those occupying the premises was within the range of foreseeability is evidenced by the fact that the hotel company, prior to the convention, took the precaution of cutting the corners out of hotel laundry bags so as to prevent their use as water containers. Moreover, it seems to us that in light of what had happened prior to the accident the management of the hotel must have been aware of the fact that in the indiscriminate throwing of glasses, bottles, and other objects in and about the hotel they might expect as part of that course of conduct that objects might be thrown from the windows to the sidewalk below. It is our view that these facts and circumstances presented a question for the jury to determine as to whether the negligent act which caused the plaintiff's injuries was within the defendants' range of foreseeability.

"8. We turn next to inquire as to what precautions were taken by the defendants to protect the plaintiff as a member of the public from such foreseeable risk. It appears from the record that, after the hotel manager received the report the water bags had been dropped to the street, he said they patrolled the house and in rooms where they found 'they were doing entertaining we told them to be careful about throwing out anything.' He said that it wouldn't have done any good to try to find out the room from which the water bags were thrown, apparently for the reason that the convention was 'out of control. . . . '

"The record establishes that the defendants made no complaint as to the conduct of the guests and invitees to any responsible official of the Junior Chamber of Commerce. Had one been made, it may be assumed that the officers of the convention could have controlled their own members. Neither did the management of the hotel complain to the authorities or ask for additional police protection. . . . [W]e think that evidence of the defendants' failure to hire additional guards, to secure additional police protection, or to appeal to responsible officers of the convention presented a fact question as to whether the defendants exercised due care commensurate with the circumstances. The argument may well be advanced that by 'turning the other cheek,' to use an expression of the hotel's managing director, the defendants acquiesced in the misuse of their property and became for all practical purposes participants in such misuse.

"9. The defendants further contend that there can be no liability to the plaintiff for the reason that she was neither an invitee nor patron of their establishment. They argue that they cannot be held liable for the unauthorized acts of a third person who, while on their premises, causes injury to an occupant of a public sidewalk. It may be briefly said that, even though the plaintiff was not a patron or a guest of the defendants, a relationship existed between them at the time and place of the injury which gave rise to a legal duty on the part of the defendants. That relationship imposed an affirmative duty upon the defendants to guard the public from danger flowing from the use of their property by their guests and invitees, even though that use was not authorized by the defendants. There was a duty on the part of the defendants to members of the public at large to protect them from injury by forces set in motion as a result of the use which the defendants permitted to be made of their property. Here the plaintiff was a pedestrian within her rights as an occupant of the sidewalk on a street adjacent to the defendants' hotel. There was evidence form which a jury could find that she was injured as a result of disorderly conduct upon the premises, the risk of which was foreseeable and in regard to which the defendants after notice failed to take measures to protect her as a member of the public. . . .

"We think the authorities relied upon by the defendants may be distinguished. *Wolk v. Pittsburgh Hotels Co.*, 284 Pa. 545, 131 A. 537, 42 A.L.R. 1081, where it was held that an innkeeper is not liable for injuries caused by a transient guest's placing of objects on a window sill, which objects fell to the street injuring a person in an automobile, and *Larson v. St. Francis Hotel*, 83 Cal. App. (2d) 210, 211, 188 P. (2d) 513, 514, where a pedestrian was injured when a guest of the defendant hotel as ' the result of the effervescence and ebullition of San Franciscans in their exuberance of joy on V-J Day' tossed an armchair out of a hotel window, may be distinguished in that they deal with instances of sporadic or isolated acts of which the owner did not have notice and in regard to which he had no opportunity to take steps to remove the danger. We think that *Holly v. Meyers Hotel & Tavern, Inc.* 9 N.J. 493, 89 A. (2d) 6, may also be distinguished. Under the facts in that case the court concluded (9 N.J. 496, 89 A. [2d] 7): ' . . . there was no occasion for any affirmative action' during the 2-hour period between the time the guests of the hotel who were responsible for the accident were warned by the hotel management and the time the accident occurred. These cases do not deal with facts establishing a course of disorderly conduct continuing over a period of days and under circumstances where the defendants admitted that they had lost control of the orderly management of their property and failed to do anything about it. . . .

"Reversed."

[Dissenting opinions omitted.]

11:16 *Anticipated Future Standards of Care*

Standards of care related to injuries suffered by guests at the hands of employees or third persons will probably be even more rigorous in the future. Massachusetts law,[77] for example, finds the innkeeper to be the virtual insurer of his guest through a contract relationship; other states, such as Illinois,[78] apply a very high standard of care to assault situations, with reasonable care applying only to defective-premises situations. There are several areas where many existing properties may fail to satisfy reasonable-care requirements in the foreseeable future:

(*a*) Vulnerable traditional lock-and-key systems.

(*b*) Inadequate identification of persons requesting keys.

(*c*) Inadequate surveillance of hallways, elevators, lobbies, and other common areas in urban properties.

(*d*) Inadequate fencing, lighting, and surveillance of parking lots, walkways, and outside common areas in motel properties.

(*e*) Inadequate room-door visual identifiers (i.e., no peepholes).

(*f*) Inadequate security personnel or guards.

(*g*) Inadequate preemployment screening programs.

Rectification of the above inadequacies would still not ensure absolute security; other possibilities include elaborate employee-identification devices coupled with a system of restricted access to individually coded areas, camera or fingerprint identification systems for room guests, metal or x-ray detectors at employee entrances and exits, and so on.

---

[77]Crawford v. Hotel Essex Boston Corp., 143 F. Supp. 172 (D. Mass. 1956), citing Frewen v. Page, 238 Mass. 499, 131 N.E. 475 (1921).
[78]Yamada v. Hilton Hotels Corp., 60 Ill. App. 3d 101, 376 N.E.2d 227 (1977).

Possibly, Louisiana is joining Illinois in holding hotels to a "high standard of care" with respect to providing adequate protections to patrons. In *Kraaz v. La Quinta Motor Inns, Inc.,*[79] the court said: "The innkeeper's position vis-a-vis his guests is similar to that of a common carrier toward its passengers. [Citation omitted.] Thus a guest is entitled to a high degree of care and protection."[80] Whether the court in *Kraaz* actually applied a stricter standard of care, however, is not clear for two reasons. First, the court later said: "The innkeeper has a duty to take reasonable precautions against criminals."[81] Second, the result in the case—holding the defendant liable because the desk clerk negligently gave a hotel passkey to a stranger—would certainly have been reached under either standard of care.

In *Margreiter v. New Hotel Monteleone, Inc.,*[82] the court held that under applicable Louisiana law, the defendant hotel had inadequately protected plaintiff from a criminal attack. The court noted that the hotel had no security cameras, no heat-sensing devices, and no adequate alarm system.

Effective January 1, 1982, the New York legislature added the following to section 204 of the New York General Business Law (governing hotel registration records): "204-a. Safety chain latches required. Every person, firm or corporation engaged in the business of furnishing public lodging accommodations in hostels, motels or motor courts shall install and maintain, on the inside of each entrance door to every rental unit for which there is a duplicate or master key which would afford entry to said unit by one other than the occupant, a safety chain latch."

Although no New York court decision imposing liability for a failure to provide such a device, thereby causing personal injury or loss of guest property, has been found, the new requirement manifests a significant legislative concern for guests' safety in their rooms. At the very least, failure to install such devices could be interpreted as violating the growing stricter standard of care for the person of a guest who, as a result, is assaulted by an intruder whose access to the room is facilitated by the absence of such devices. See also section 11:1.

In *Montgomery v. Royal Motel,*[83] the Nevada Supreme Court ruled that a Las Vegas municipal ordinance requiring deadbolt locks, but not self-locking doors, at residential housing units applied also to motel guest rooms, but also that the motelkeeper had not violated that statute. An unknown assailant had entered the guests' room and assaulted the plaintiffs. It was established that the door was not locked, but deadbolt locks were provided. Absent proof that the motelkeeper could reasonably foresee or anticipate a criminal act under these circumstances and injury resulting therefrom, summary judgment granted by the trial court as a matter of law was affirmed.

[79]410 So. 2d 1048 (La. 1982).
[80]*Id.* at 1053.
[81]*Id.*
[82] 640 F.2d 508 (5th Cir. 1981).
[83]98 Nev. 240, 645 P.2d 968 (Nev. 1982).

A more recent decision reflecting the increased standard of care required of innkeepers for guests' safety from the criminal misconduct of third parties is *Banks v. Hyatt Corp.* That Louisiana case, excerpted below, involved the death of a guest who was shot by an armed robber four feet from the doors to the hotel entranceway and underneath an overhang that formed the second floor of the New Orleans Hyatt-Superdome complex. At trial, in affirming the judgment that imposed liability upon the innkeeper, the Court of Appeals for the Fifth Circuit set forth the public-policy arguments supporting innkeeper liability.

BANKS v. HYATT CORP.

722 F.2d 214 (5th Cir.), *reh'g denied,* 731 F.2d 888 (1984)

WINTER, C.J.: ''Tort law has become increasingly concerned with placing liability upon the party that is best able to determine the cost-justified level of accident prevention. *See* G. Calabresi, The Costs of Accidents: A Legal and Economic Analysis (1970); Calabresi and Hirschoff, *Toward a Test for Strict Liability in Torts,* 81 Yale L.J. 1055, 1060 (1972); Posner, *A Theory of Negligence,* 1 J. Legal Stud. 29, 33 (1972). Holding a negligent innkeeper liable when there is a third-party assault on the premises is sensible, not because of some abstract conceptual notion about the risk arising within 'the course of the relation', but because the innkeeper is able to identify and carry out cost-justified ('reasonable') preventive measures on the premises. If the innkeeper has sufficient control of property adjacent to his premises so that he is capable of taking reasonable actions to reduce the risk of injury to guests present on the adjacent property, the innkeeper should not be immune from liability when his failure to take such actions results in an injury to a guest. As between innkeeper and guest, the innkeeper is the only one in the position to take the reasonably necessary acts to guard against the predictable risk of assaults. He is not an insurer, but he is obligated to take reasonable steps to minimize the risk to his guests within his sphere of control.

''The security measures adopted by Hyatt, especially the 'perimeter patrol', demonstrate that Hyatt had the power to take preventive action within the immediate surrounding area. As noted above, the jury found that Hyatt did not go far enough. Allowing the jury's finding of negligence to stand should induce Hyatt to determine and to put in effect cost-justified preventive measures covering both the premises of the hotel and such adjacent areas as are sufficiently within its control to permit reasonable preventive action. . . .

''Our decision in this case is strongly influenced by the peculiar facts with which we are presented. Dr. Banks's death occurred only four feet from the entrance doors to the mall and hotel, underneath an overhang that is actually the second floor of the complex. The defendants were aware of the crime problem in the plaza complex and its immediate environs, and were capable of taking reasonable action to reduce the risk to guests and invitees in these areas.

''We affirm the judgment n.o.v. [notwithstanding the verdict] in favor of Refco [the owner of the Superdome complex], because that defendant's duty of care to invitees does not include a duty to adopt precautionary measures to reduce the general risk of criminal assault. Hyatt's duty to its guests, however, does embrace a responsibility to take reasonable precautionary measures. We reject Hyatt's argument that its duty cannot, as a matter of law, extend to the location of Dr. Banks's death. Dr. Banks did not make it through the entrance doors to the complex. We refuse to transform those doors into an impregnable legal wall of immunity.

"The judgment of the district court is AFFIRMED."

Chain hotel properties in particular are caught in a difficult position. As discussed in section 11:1, *supra*, the law regarding the innkeeper's duty to his guest varies from one jurisdiction to the next. At first glance the most prudent action would seem to be adoption of the standards required by the strictest jurisdiction. Thus, a chain might take steps in all properties to satisfy the standards set in New York, for example. Once such standards are established, however, they must be maintained. If an innkeeper provides extensive security measures initially, but later reduces them, he runs the risk of liability if subsequent criminal acts might have been forestalled by his earlier safeguards. On the other hand, if he provides only minimum security, he might also be held liable for failing to meet standards of reasonable care. Perhaps the best approach is one of cost-benefit—that is, striking a balance between the expenditures for reasonable security measures and the cost of reasonably anticipated litigation damages.

Given the continually rising crime rate in U.S. hotels and motels and the stricter judicial interpretations of reasonable-care rules in hotel and similar cases, one must look for more than a crisis solution.

PART III

Innkeeper's Responsibility
for Property of
Guests and Patrons

12 Innkeeper's Responsibility for Property of Guests

12:1 *Origin of Rule of Responsibility*

The liability of the innkeeper for the goods of the guest has been enforced from the earliest times. Inns were established originally for the entertainment of travelers on their journey and particularly to protect them against the bands of marauders and outlaws that infested the roads at night. The most important function of the innkeeper, therefore, after the furnishing of food and drink, was protecting the weary traveler against nocturnal robbers. If a traveler was robbed at an inn, it was necessarily from defect of care of the innkeeper, since he undertook to protect against such misfortune.

It was decided, therefore, as early as the year 1367 that the innkeeper is responsible for the goods of his guest stolen from the inn. In the earliest case, the loss was alleged to be "for defect of guard of the innkeeper and his servants."[1]

With the progress of commercial development, of course, the conditions in which the common-law liability of the innkeeper to his guest originated have passed away. But other conditions exist which render it wise and expedient that the modern hotelkeeper should respond for the loss of his guests' property; consequently, there has been no relaxation in the rule of his common-law liability, except as such liability has been modified by statute, as we will see in Chapter 13.

12:2 *Innkeeper as Insurer: The Common-Law Rule*

In the majority of American jurisdictions, the liability of an innkeeper for loss or damage to the property of a guest is governed by the rule of insurer's liability. This is the rule that applies to common carriers for loss or damage to goods entrusted to the carrier. Under this rule, the innkeeper is responsible for any loss or damage, regardless of the presence or absence of negligence on his part, unless the loss was caused by negligence or fraud of the guest or by an act of God or the "public enemy."

> An innkeeper is responsible for the safekeeping of property committed to his custody by a guest. He is an insurer against loss, unless caused by the negligence or

[1] Y.B. 42 Edw. 3, 11, pl. 13 (1367).

fraud of the guest, or by the act of God or the public enemy. This liability is recognized in the common law as existing by the ancient custom of the realm. . . .

This custom, like the kindred case of the common carrier, had its origin in considerations of public policy. It was essential to the interests of the realm, that every facility should be furnished for secure and convenient intercourse between different portions of the kingdom. The safeguards, of which the law gave assurance to the wayfarer, were akin to those which invested each English home with the legal security of a castle. The traveler was peculiarly exposed to depredation and fraud. He was compelled to repose confidence in a host, who was subject to constant temptation, and favored with peculiar opportunities, if he chose to betray his trust. . . . The care of the property was usually committed to servants, over whom the guest had no control, and who had no interest in its preservation, unless their employer was held responsible for its safety. In case of depredation by collusion, or of injury or destruction by neglect, the stranger would of necessity be at every possible disadvantage. He would be without the means either of proving guilt or detecting it. . . . The sufferer would be deprived, by the very wrong of which he complained, of the means of remaining to ascertain and enforce his rights, and redress would be well-nigh hopeless, but for the rule of law casting the loss on the party entrusted with the custody of the property, and paid for keeping it safely.[2]

More recently, the Supreme Court of Hawaii has restated the rule of the innkeeper's liability as insurer of guests' property and the reasons behind it:

At common law an innkeeper was practically an insurer of the goods of a guest lost in the inn. With the exception of a loss occurring by act of God or a public enemy or by the fault or negligence of the guest himself, the innkeeper was liable for the loss of a guest's property, however occurring. To recover, all the guest had to prove was that his property was lost while in the inn. It made no difference that the innkeeper may have used the greatest care to protect the guest's property. The innkeeper's liability was absolute to him other than the mentioned exceptions. No business, with the possible exception of common carriers, was more rigorously governed by common law than that of innkeepers.

The imposition of strict liability on the innkeeper found its origin in the conditions existing in England in the fourteenth and fifteenth centuries. Inadequate means of travel, the sparsely settled country and the constant exposure to robbers left the traveler with the inn practically his only hope for protection. Innkeepers themselves, and their servants, were often as dishonest as the highwaymen roaming the countryside and were not beyond joining forces with the outlaws to relieve travelers and guests, by connivance or force, of their valuables and goods. Under such conditions it was purely a matter of necessity and policy for the law to require the innkeeper to exert his utmost efforts to protect his guests' property and to assure results by imposing legal liability for loss without regard to fault.[3]

---

[2]Hulett v. Swift, 33 N.Y. 571, 572–75 (1865).
[3]Minneapolis Fire & Marine Ins. Co. v. Matson Navigation Co., 352 P.2d 335, 337 (Hawaii 1960).

12:3   *The* **Prima Facie** *Liability Rule*

While the common-law insurer's rule still prevails in most American jurisdictions, subject to statutory limitations on liability discussed in the following
chapter, several states have laid down a much less stringent rule. In these jurisdictions, the innkeeper is responsible only for losses that occur through his negligence. Under this *prima facie* liability rule, which prevails in Indiana, Illinois,
Kentucky, Maryland, Texas, and Vermont, an innkeeper is only *presumed* to be
liable for loss or damage to goods of the guest and may exculpate himself by
proving that the loss did not happen through any fault or negligence on his part
or that of his servants. The rationale for this rule was explained long ago by the
Supreme Court of Indiana in *Laird v. Eichold:*

> Innkeepers, on grounds of public policy, are held to a strict accountability for the
> goods of their guests. The interests of the public, we think, are sufficiently sub-
> served, by holding the innkeeper *prima facie* liable for the loss or injury of the
> goods of his guest; thus throwing the burden of proof upon him, to show that the
> injury or loss happened without any default whatever on his part, and that he ex-
> ercised the strictest care and diligence. And it is more in accordance with the prin-
> ciples of natural justice, to permit him to exonerate himself by making such proof,
> than to shut the door against him, and hold him responsible for an accident hap-
> pening entirely without his default, and against which strict care and prudence
> would not guard.[4]

The Illinois Supreme Court explained how this rule operates in practice in
Rockhill v. Congress Hotel Co.:

> An innkeeper owes the duty and assumes the obligation of safely keeping the
> property of his guests, and, if the property is lost, all that is necessary to make a
> *prima facie* case is to show the relation of innkeeper and guest and the loss. The
> burden is then cast on the innkeeper to exonerate himself, and this he may do by
> showing that there has been no negligence on the part of himself or his servants, or
> that the loss was caused by the personal negligence of the guest or some one for
> whom the guest was responsible, or some superior force. The loss of the goods of
> the guest while at an inn raises a presumption of negligence on the part of the inn-
> keeper or his servants.[5]

12:4   *Liability before the Beginning of the Innkeeper-Guest Relationship*

When the goods are actually given to the innkeeper, his liability as innkeeper
begins at the moment of delivery to him. The innkeeper may therefore become
responsible for the goods of the guest even before the relationship of host and

---

[4]10 Ind. 212, 215 (1858).
[5]237 Ill. 98, 99, 86 N.E. 740, 741 (1908).

guest is established. If the innkeeper sends a conveyance to an airport, railroad station, or steamship to bring guests to his inn and a traveler gives his baggage to the porter or other person authorized by the innkeeper to take it, the innkeeper becomes liable for it all at once, provided the traveler later becomes a guest.

In all these cases, though, the responsibility of the innkeeper is predicated on the owner of the goods becoming a guest within a reasonable time. If he changes his mind and does not become a guest, the innkeeper will be regarded as not responsible as such for the goods. So where the traveler gave his luggage to the porter of the inn at the railroad station, and the porter carried it to the inn, but the owner never became a guest, it was held that the innkeeper never became responsible for it as innkeeper.[6] And in a similar case, where the traveler went to the office of the inn, but there found a telegram addressed to him, in consequence of which he did not register but went to another place, the innkeeper did not become responsible.[7]

In either of these cases, if the traveler had become a guest, the innkeeper's responsibility for the goods would have dated from the moment the porter took charge of them at the railroad station; but since the owner never became a guest, the innkeeper was not liable as such even during the time while the traveler was on his way to the hotel. In other words, during that period the responsibility is doubtful and is settled only by the event.

Where the check for the baggage is delivered to the porter of the hotel by one who does not intend to become a guest, it is obvious that the porter has no authority to accept the goods on behalf of the hotel, and the innkeeper would not be responsible for the goods even as bailee. Even if he deposited the goods in the hotel office, without calling the attention of the proper clerk to it, the innkeeper is not responsible as innkeeper or even as ordinary bailee. "It is the same as if the porter had gratuitously brought up the valise of a friend or a stranger, and put it down in the hotel office, without calling any attention to it, or giving the hotel employees any notice of it, and no occasion existed for them to take charge of it."[8] The porter individually is the bailee.

The case would seem to be different if the owner, at the time he gives his goods to the porter, bona fide intends to become a guest within a reasonable time. The porter's authority, as distinguished from the innkeeper's responsibility, must be determined by the facts existing at the time he takes the goods. At that time the facts are the same as in any case of the sort where the owner carries out his intention and becomes a guest. If the owner acts bona fide, the porter has authority to receive the goods for the innkeeper and the latter is a gratuitous bailee. In *Tulane*, however, the owner intended, at the time he gave his valise to the porter, to become a guest; but the distinction indicated was not made by the court, and the innkeeper was held not to be even a bailee.

---

[6]Tulane Hotel Co. v. Holohan, 112 Tenn. 214, 79 S.W. 113 (1903).
[7]Strauss v. County Hotel and Wine Co. Ltd., 12 Q.B.D. 27 (1883).
[8]Tulane Hotel Co. v. Holohan, 112 Tenn. 214, 218, 79 S.W. 113, 114 (1903).

12:5 *Property in Transit to or from the Inn*

DAVIDSON v. MADISON CORP.
257 N.Y. 120, 177 N.E. 393 (1931)

KELLOGG, J.: "The plaintiff had been a guest of the Madison Hotel in New York city, which was owned and operated by the defendant Madison Corporation. At the conclusion of a temporary visit to Norfolk, Va., she purchased a railroad ticket from the Pennsylvania Railroad and boarded one of its trains for New York city. Prior to leaving she had caused her trunk to be delivered to the railroad and had checked it to the same destination. On arrival, the plaintiff returned to her quarters in the Madison Hotel. The check for the trunk was delivered to the head porter with instructions 'to get the trunk in' promptly. The head porter handed the check to a licensed expressman, Peter J. Coen, with similar instructions. Coen delivered the check to a truckman employed by him, who obtained the trunk from the railroad and placed it on his truck. On the return journey to the hotel the truckman was required to pick up another trunk at the Hotel Buckingham. He parked his car at the curb in the vicinity of that hostelry; stopped his motor, leaving the ignition key in the lock; and went into the hotel, leaving the truck unattended. When he returned to the curb the truck had disappeared, and with it had gone the plaintiff's trunk. The car and the trunk had been stolen. The contents of the trunk, consisting of expensive furs and dresses, were worth $10,000, and for that sum the plaintiff has recovered a verdict against the Madison Corporation.

" 'An innkeeper is an insurer of the safety of the property of his guest, brought *infra hospitium*. He is liable for its loss, whether by burglary, theft, fire or negligence, unless it arises from the neglect or misconduct of the guest, the act of God or the public enemies.' (*Wilkins v. Earle*, 44 N.Y. 172, 178; *Hulett v. Swift*, 33 N.Y. 571.) The innkeeper's liability, at common law, did not originally extend to cover property not within the walls of the inn, or the buildings used in connection therewith. . . . In several States of the Union, other than this, the innkeeper's liability has been greatly extended. The innkeeper has been held liable in respect to baggage never within the hotel precincts, lost in the course of transportation thereto from a railroad station, while in the custody of an independent transfer agent to whom the innkeeper had delivered railroad checks, received from his guest, for the purpose of securing the baggage and bringing it to the inn. [Citations omitted.] The basis of the recovery in each of these cases was said to be the common-law liability of an innkeeper to his guest.

"We are not greatly impressed with the reasoning of these cases. . . . When the baggage is received by a transfer agent, to whom the check has been delivered, the custody is that of an independent contractor, not the custody of the innkeeper or his agent. The whole theory of the innkeeper's liability, that the things of his guest, which are within the walls of his inn, must be defended . . . against nearly all conceivable perils, fails of application where the circumstances are those of the cases cited. Never having had custody or possession of the things of his guest, never having assumed a relationship in the least degree resembling that of a bailee, it is difficult to see how the duty of an innkeeper to safeguard and defend the possessions of his guest may have arisen. . . .

"The proprietor of the Madison testified that the hotel made 'charges for the transportation of baggage'; that 'if the porter receives instructions to go and get trunks, he makes his charge.' He was asked: 'Mr. Titze, you make a charge to your guests for the transportation of baggage, do you not?' and he replied, 'We do, yes.' We have, then, an innkeeper maintaining a system for the transportation of the baggage of his guests for which a charge is made, an order by the guest to the hotel porter to get her baggage and bring it to the hotel; an acceptance of the order and an undertaking to perform the service. How can it be gainsaid that the defendant, for a consideration, promised to obtain the baggage and transport it to the hotel, using at least ordinary care in the fulfillment of the promise? If the defendant chose to perform its contract through an independent contractor, it may have been within its rights. Nevertheless, it could not thereby escape liability for its nonperformance through the negligence of one to whom the contract duty was assigned. 'The performance in such a case is indeed in legal contemplation rendered by the original obligor, who is still the party liable if the performance is in any respect incorrect.' (1 Williston on Contracts, § 411.) In this instance there was evidence to support the conclusion that the contract duty to transport was negligently performed and that there was no negligence on the part of the plaintiff. We prefer, therefore, to affirm the recovery upon this ground. We do not determine that the defendant was or was not liable for the breach of a duty owed by an innkeeper to his guest.''

[Judgment affirmed, with costs. All concur.]

As a result of the *Davidson* case, the New York State Legislature enacted sections 203-a and 203-b of the General Business Law, which limit a hotelkeeper's liability for property in transit to or from the hotel to the sum of $250, "unless at the time of delivering the same such value in excess of two hundred and fifty dollars shall be stated by such guest and a written receipt stating such value shall be issued by such keeper; provided, however, that where such written receipt is issued the keeper shall not be liable beyond five hundred dollars unless it shall appear that such loss or damage occurred through his fault or negligence."

A contrary view, namely, that delivery of a railroad baggage check is symbolical delivery of the baggage which the check represents so as to make the innkeeper liable as insurer for its loss, is held in Colorado.

In *Keith v. Atkinson*,[9] plaintiff and his wife arrived at defendant's hotel at about 11 P.M. on August 20, 1902, and were shown to a room which they occupied that night. The following morning plaintiff rang for a bellboy, gave him his railroad check for his baggage with instructions to give it to the clerk on duty so as to have it brought up from the depot, which the bellboy agreed to do. The

---

[9] 48 Colo. 480, 111 P. 55 (1910).

trunk did not come. It was never found, and the check was never returned to the plaintiff. Judgment in favor of defendant hotel was reversed on appeal.

The Colorado court held that "one who becomes the guest of a hotel, by giving his baggage checks into its possession, places the goods they represent into its custody, so far as to make the innkeeper responsible for goods which, by means of the possession of such checks, his representative or agent receives, although the baggage be never brought within the walls of the hotel."[10]

12:6 *Loss of Property Delivered to Innkeeper by Third Person for Guest*

In order for the innkeeper to be responsible for a guest's goods, it is not necessary that the innkeeper receive the goods from the guest himself. The goods may be delivered to the innkeeper by a third person to hold for or to deliver to the guest. In that case the responsibility for the goods is that of an innkeeper. The leading common-law authority is *Needles v. Howard.*[11]

In *Berlow,* to follow, the Texas Court of Civil Appeals ruled that acceptance of a package for a departing guest in violation of that guest's instructions does not fall within the innkeeper's statute limiting liability for its loss.

BERLOW V. SHERATON DALLAS CORP.
629 S.W.2d 818 (Tex. App. 1982)

WHITHAN, J.: "This is an appeal from a judgment, on an alternative motion by defendant Sheraton Dallas Corporation (the hotel) for judgment on the verdict or judgment notwithstanding the verdict, that plaintiff (Berlow) take nothing in her suit against the hotel for the loss of a package containing jewelry. We reverse and render judgment in favor of Berlow.

"Berlow, a designer and manufacturer of jewelry, frequently authorized her parents (the Soifers) to represent her in showing and selling jewelry to fashionable department stores. In January, 1978, Berlow authorized the Soifers to show ten pieces of jewelry in Dallas. Berlow arranged to have a package containing the jewelry delivered by United Parcel Service (UPS) to her parents at the hotel. The package was marked 'insured' on the outside and showed Berlow's return address. The package did not arrive at the hotel during the four-day stay of the Soifers. During their stay, each of the Soifers asked frequently about it at the front desk and, before checking out, the Soifers informed front desk personnel that this was a very important package, although they deliberately refrained from telling them the contents or value of the package. They asked that the hotel refuse delivery of it, and personnel at the front desk agreed to refuse its delivery. Agreeing to and subsequently refusing delivery of packages upon the oral instructions of guests to front desk attendants was standard procedure for the hotel. Contrary to its agreement, however, when the package arrived the hotel took

---

[10]*Id.* at 481, 111 P. at 56.
[11]1 E.D. Smith (N.Y.) 54 (Ct. C.P. 1850).

delivery of it, stored it at the front desk for a month, and then turned it over to the United States Post Office (USPO) without postage, marked 'Return to Sender.' This, too, was standard procedure for the hotel in dealing with packages stored at the front desk. No attempt was made to determine if the Soifers had been recent guests at the hotel, nor to contact Berlow. The package was lost. At trial, Berlow testified that the fair market value of the jewelry was $10,231.00. . . .

"Berlow moved for judgment on the verdict and the hotel moved alternatively for judgment on the verdict or judgment notwithstanding the verdict. The trial court granted the hotel's motion and rendered judgment for it, without specifying on which ground judgment was being rendered. On appeal, if the judgment is proper in either respect, the trial court must be affirmed; thus a discussion of each ground on which judgment could have been entered is necessary.

I. The Hotel's Motion for Judgment on the Verdict

"The hotel contends that a judgment was proper on its motion for judgment on the verdict because, under Tex. Rev. Civ. Stat. Ann. art. 4593 (Vernon 1976), the risk of loss of the package was placed on Berlow as a matter of law. We do not agree. Article 4593 provides:

"Whenever any person shall allow his baggage or other property to remain in any hotel, apartment hotel or boarding house after the relation of innkeeper and guest has ceased without checking same, or shall leave his baggage or other property in the lobby of any hotel, apartment hotel or boarding house prior to checking it or becoming a guest, or shall forward any baggage to such hotel, apartment hotel or boarding house before becoming a guest, said hotel, apartment hotel or boarding house keeper may, at his option, hold such baggage or other property at the risk of the said owner.

"Under this statute, a hotel's liability is limited only under specifically enumerated circumstances, and, under the facts of this case, no such circumstances exist which would limit the hotel's liability. Berlow did not 'allow' the package to remain at the hotel, instead she, through the Soifers, elicited a promise from the hotel *not* to permit the package to enter the premises and was unaware that this promise was not carried out. Nor did Berlow forward the package to the hotel at her risk before the Soifers became guests. This section of the statute contemplates that the property reaches the hotel before the guest and awaits the guest's arrival at the owner's risk. In the present case, Berlow's package arrived only after the Soifers left. The hotel was not entitled to a judgment on the verdict under Article 4593.

"The hotel was likewise not entitled to a judgment on the verdict under the jury's finding that it was not grossly negligent. The hotel argues that the bailment of the package was merely gratuitous and, as a gratuitous bailee, it can be held liable only for gross negligence. See, *Citizen's National Bank v. Ratcliff & Lanier*, 253 S.W. 253 (Tex. Com. App. 1923, judgment adopted). Because we find for reasons explained below that the bailment of the package was a bailment for mutual benefit and not a gratuitous bailment, the hotel was liable for its ordinary negligence. *Citizens National Bank v. Ratcliff & Lanier,* 253 S.W. at 255; *Shamrock Hilton Hotel v. Caranas,* 488 S.W.2d 151 (Tex. Civ. App.—Houston [14th Dist.] 1972, writ ref'd n.r.e.). The hotel was not entitled to a judgment on the verdict on this ground.

II. The Hotel's Motion for Judgment Notwithstanding the Verdict

"Because judgment for the hotel was not proper on the verdict, the trial court may be affirmed only if it properly rendered judgment notwithstanding the verdict. Before a judgment notwithstanding the verdict is proper, there must be no evidence of probative force upon which the jury could have made the findings relied upon. *Harbin v. Seale,* 461 S.W.2d 591, 592 (Tex. 1970); Tex. R. Civ. P. 301. On appeal, all evidence must be considered in the light most favorable to the jury's findings, disregarding all contrary evidence. *Elliott v. Elliott,* 597 S.W.2d 795, 800 (Tex. Civ. App.—Corpus Christi 1980, no writ). *See also Rogers v. Searle,* 544 S.W.2d 114, 115 (Tex. 1976). We find that a bailment was established as a matter of law, that the bailment was one of mutual benefit as a matter of law, and that there was some evidence to support the jury's findings on negligence, proximate cause, and damages. Because the form or omission of special issues on some of the elements of bailment for mutual benefit are complained of in crosspoints by the hotel, each element will be discussed.

"In order to constitute a bailment there must be a contract, express or implied, delivery of the property to the bailee, and acceptance of the property by the bailee. *Sanroc Co. International v. Roadrunner Transportation, Inc.,* 596 S.W.2d 320, 322 (Tex. Civ. App.—Houston [1st Dist.] 1980, no writ). Uncontroverted evidence showed that the hotel, rather than refusing delivery, took possession of Berlow's package and stored it on the premises, under lock and key, for one month. Assuming custody of the package in this manner established an implied contract to bail the package. Delivery of the package and acceptance of it by the hotel were stipulated; thus bailment of the package was established as a matter of law. *See Sanroc Co. International v. Roadrunner Transportation, Inc.,* 596 S.W.2d at 322.

"That the bailment was one for mutual benefit and not merely gratuitous was also established as a matter of law. A bailment is for the mutual benefit of the parties, although nothing is paid directly by the bailor, where property of the bailor is delivered to and accepted by the bailee as an incident to a business in which the bailee makes a profit. *Wilson v. Hooser,* 573 S.W.2d 601, 602–603 (Tex. Civ. App.—Waco 1978, writ ref'd n.r.e.). The Soifers were paying guests at the hotel. It is not unusual for patrons to have packages delivered to them at a hotel, and, in this case, the evidence showed that the practice occurred frequently enough that the hotel developed standard procedures for dealing with packages. Although no direct charge was made, the price paid for the room also included the incidental services provided by the hotel. This provided consideration for the implied agreement to bail Berlow's package and established a bailment for mutual benefit as a matter of law.

"Having entered into a bailment for mutual benefit, the hotel became liable for its ordinary negligence. *Citizen's National Bank v. Ratcliff & Lanier,* 253 S.W. 253 (Tex. Com. App. 1923, judgmt. adopted); *Shamrock Hilton Hotel v. Caranas,* 488 S.W.2d at 155. The jury found that the hotel was negligent in its acceptance, care, and handling of the package, and there was some evidence to support this finding. The evidence showed that the hotel violated its own standard procedure, as well as its express agreement with the Soifers, to refuse delivery of packages when requested to do so. The evidence also showed that the package was stored for one month, during which the hotel made no attempt to contact the Soifers or Berlow, then delivered to USPO without postage. This raises some evidence upon which the jury could find the hotel negligent.

"By crosspoint, the hotel argues that, as a matter of law, it was not negligent. According to the hotel, because the package was delivered to USPO for return to Berlow, the liability for any loss rested with USPO as a subsequent bailee and not with the hotel. We do not agree. While the evidence showed that Berlow's package was lost while in the custody of USPO, it also showed that the hotel gave the package, which was insured when delivered to the hotel by UPS, to USPO without insurance or postage. This was evidence of negligence by the hotel sufficiently strong to require submission of the issue to the jury. The hotel, therefore, did not establish its non-negligence as a matter of law.

"There was also some evidence to support the jury's finding that the hotel's negligence was a proximate cause of Berlow's loss. In Texas, proximate cause is cause in fact plus foreseeability. *McClure v. Allied Stores of Texas, Inc.,* 608 S.W.2d 901, 903 (Tex. 1980). The evidence showed that instead of refusing delivery of the package, and thereby causing its immediate return to Berlow by UPS, the hotel took the package and attempted to return it, without insurance or postage, by a different method. This is some evidence that Berlow's loss was caused, in fact, by the hotel's negligent handling of the package. Moreover, because the package was given to USPO without postage, the jury could find that the hotel should have reasonably foreseen that the package would never reach Berlow.

"Likewise, there was some evidence to support the jury's finding that it was foreseeable that the package contained property of substantial dollar value. In *Shamrock Hilton Hotel v. Caranas,* 488 S.W.2d 151 (Tex. Civ. App.—Houston [14th Dist.] 1972, writ ref'd n.r.e), the court upheld a hotel's liability for the loss of a woman's purse containing jewelry worth $13,000. The evidence showed that the woman left the purse in the hotel dining room where a bus boy found it and turned it over to the cashier. The cashier gave the purse to a man who claimed it, and the purse and jewelry were lost. Rejecting the hotel's argument that it was not foreseeable that the purse contained jewelry worth $13,000, the court, holding that foreseeability is a question for the jury to decide, stated 'it is known that people who are guests in hotels such as the Shamrock Hilton . . . not infrequently bring such expensive jewelry with them.' *Id.* at 155. In the present case, this 'known' practice of guests having valuables in hotels, together with evidence showing that the hotel provided a safe, used often, in which guests could store valuables and evidence showing that the package marked 'insured', was some evidence from which the jury could find it reasonable for the hotel to foresee that guests would bring or deliver items of value to the hotel. *See also Ampco Auto Parts, Inc. v. Williams*, 517 S.W.2d 401 (Tex. Civ. App.—Dallas 1974, writ ref'd n.r.e.). . . .

"Because there was some evidence on each element of recovery on Berlow's theory that she and the hotel entered into a bailment for mutual benefit, the trial court erred in granting the hotel's motion for judgment notwithstanding the verdict; thus judgment should be rendered for Berlow. The hotel, however, alternatively complains by crosspoint that the evidence was insufficient to support the jury's findings and requests reversal and remand rather than rendition. *See Muro v. Houston Fire and Casualty Insurance Co.*, 329 S.W.2d 326, 332, 333 (Tex. Civ. App.—San Antonio 1959, writ ref'd n.r.e.); Tex. R. Civ. P. 324; Calvert, *'No Evidence' and 'Insufficient Evidence' Points of Error*, 38 Tex. L. Rev. 1 (1960). We have reviewed the evidence and find it sufficient to support the jury's findings. The hotel's crosspoints on this ground are overruled. . . .

"Reversed and judgment rendered in favor of Berlow for $10,231.00 damages and $10,500.00 attorney's fees."

The case of *Peet v. Roth Hotel Co.*,[12] raises the question whether a bailment is created if the person in possession of the bailed property, a ring, does not declare its value when delivering it to a hotel employee for a hotel guest. The court rejected the argument that there was no bailment as a matter of law because mutuality of assent was lacking. The identity of the ring was not concealed, and its value was obvious. "A bailee of jewelry is not relieved of liability because of his own erroneous underestimate of its value."

In *Van Cleef & Arpels, Inc. v. St. Regis Hotel Corp.*,[13] plaintiff, a well-known jewelry firm, sued defendant hotel in bailment and in negligence, for $19,000 for the loss of a pair of platinum and diamond earrings given to some unauthorized person by the hotel. Plaintiff moved to strike out the hotel's affirmative defense that its liability, if any, was limited to $500 by sections 200 and 201 of the General Business Law. The court denied the motion on the ground that the question involved was a mixed one of law and fact properly determinable on the trial. The court stated:

> Plaintiff left the earrings at the hotel to be delivered to a guest of the hotel, informing the hotel that the package contained jewelry. The hotel delivered the earrings to the guest. Plaintiff had agreed with the guest that, if he decided against the purchase, he would leave the earrings with the hotel to be picked up by plaintiff. The next day the guest returned the earrings to the hotel to be picked up by plaintiff, signed out of the hotel and left for Europe. The hotel put the earrings in its safe and recorded the package in its "Valuables Deposit" record, noting that it was for plaintiff firm. One week later plaintiff called and asked for the package. The hotel

[12]191 Minn. 151, 253 N.W. 546 (1934).
[13]160 N.Y.L.J. No. 103, 2 (Sup. Ct. N.Y. Co. 1968).

stated that it had turned it over to some unknown person, whose signed name was illegible in the valuable deposit record.

The statute provides that whenever a hotel has a safe in its office for the safe-keeping of any jewels, &c., belonging to its guests and gives due notice thereof, the hotel shall not be liable for loss sustained by theft or otherwise if such property is not delivered to its office for deposit in such safe; and shall not be liable in excess of $500 for loss of any property, which is deposited, in the absence of special written agreement.

Plaintiff urges that the statute has no application to plaintiff's claim, that the statute regulates only the liability of a hotel to its guests, that the earrings did not belong to a guest, that the hotel was simply a bailee in this transaction and should be treated vis-a-vis plaintiff in the same manner as any bailee.

Defendant concedes that it was an ordinary bailee from the time it received the package from plaintiff and placed it in its safe up to the time it delivered it pursuant to plaintiff's instructions to its guest. It maintains, however, that on the next day, when it received the package from its guest and deposited it in its safe to be picked up by plaintiff, the statute applied, limiting its liability to $500 in the absence of a written agreement with the guest.

In the court's view the question rests on the hotel's knowledge of the nature of the transaction at the time that the guest delivered the package to it. If the hotel was informed that the package contained jewelry which belonged to plaintiff, not the guest, and that it was to be picked up by plaintiff because the guest had decided not to purchase the jewelry delivered to him the previous day through the hotel as bailee, then the transactions of the two days should be deemed to be continuous so far as the hotel's status is concerned. In such case the statute regulating the hotel's liability to its guest for the safekeeping of property belonging to him would not be applicable. Conversely, if the hotel merely was informed that a package being left by its guest and deposited in its safe would be picked up by plaintiff, the statute would appear to apply. Since the facts on this aspect of the case have not been fully established, the motion is denied.

12:7 *Property for Which Innkeeper Is Responsible*

The general rule at common law is that the innkeeper's responsibility is not confined to property of any particular kind, but, subject always to statutory limitations, extends to money and all other personal property brought by the guest to the inn and used by or suitable to the use of the guest.[14] The rule does not, however, apply to merchandise brought into the inn for sale or display by the guest.

In *Myers v. Cottrill*[15] plaintiff sought to recover the value of watches, chains, and various kinds of jewelry that he brought into defendant's hotel for the purpose of commercial exhibit and sale in one of the guest rooms therein, rented for that purpose. The articles were stolen from the room, which was used by plain-

[14]Watkins v. Hotel Tutwiler Co., 200 Ala. 386, 76 So. 302 (1917); Stoll v. Almon C. Judd Co., 106 Conn. 551, 138 A. 479 (1927).
[15]17 F. Cas. 1099 (No. 9985) (C.C.E.D. Wis. 1873).

tiff and his wife as a bedroom as well, while they were out for breakfast. It appeared that defendant failed to comply with the statute limiting his responsibility as an innkeeper.

In charging the jury, Drummond, circuit judge, said:

> I think this is the true rule on the subject. If a person, going into a hotel as a guest, takes to his room not ordinary baggage, not those articles which generally accompany the traveller, but valuable merchandise, such as watches and jewelry, and keeps them there for show and sale, and from time to time invites parties into his room to inspect and to purchase, unless there is some special circumstance in the case showing that the innkeeper assumes the responsibility as of ordinary baggage, as to such merchandise, the special obligations imposed by the common law do not exist, and the guest, as to those goods, becomes their vendor and uses his room for the sale of merchandise, and really changes the ordinary relations between innkeeper and guest.

Whether a room is used for the exhibit or sale of merchandise and whether the articles lost constitute baggage or merchandise is a question of fact for the determination of the jury: "If a guest applies for a room in an inn, for a purpose of business distinct from his accommodation as a guest, the particular responsibility does not extend to goods lost or stolen from that room."[16]

Statutes in the various states should be consulted with respect to the obligations of innkeepers for merchandise and merchandise samples brought into their hotels. In New York, an innkeeper's liability for merchandise samples or merchandise for sale is conditioned upon the delivery to him by the guest of a "prior written notice of having the same in his possession, together with the value thereof, the receipt of which notice the hotel-keeper shall acknowledge in writing over the signature of himself or his agent, but in no event shall such keeper be liable beyond five hundred dollars, unless it shall appear that such loss or damage occurred through his fault or negligence."[17]

12:8 *Property Brought by Guest into Inn after His Arrival*

In *Mateer v. Brown,*[18] the court stated:

> One point further remains to be considered. It appears from the testimony that the bundle, which is claimed to have contained the gold dust, was not taken to the defendant's inn until several days after the plaintiff became his guest. As, in order to entitle the plaintiff to recover, it is necessary for him to establish the character of guest in the inn of the defendant, so also it is equally necessary that it should appear that his goods were taken there in the capacity of guest. [Citation omitted.] The liability of the innkeeper results from the relation of guest in which the traveller stands to him, and extends only to those things which properly pertain to him in that

---

[16]2 Kent Comm. 596, cited with approval in Fisher v. Kelsey, 121 U.S. 383, 385–86 (1887).
[17]N.Y. General Business Law, § 201 (McKinney 1968).
[18]1 Cal. 221, 230–31, *adhered to on rehearing,* 1 Cal. 231 (1850).

relation. [Citation omitted.] It does not necessarily follow that the strict responsibility can be imposed on an innkeeper for all property, which his guest may choose to bring into the inn after he has been received *infra hospitium;* or that the latter may make the former a compulsory depository of any amount of goods or treasure, which, during his sojourn in the inn, he may desire to keep secure. The innkeeper is bound by law to receive the traveller and his goods, and, for his refusal, in case he has sufficient accommodations for him, he is liable not only to an action on the case for the private damage, but to indictment for the public wrong. [Citations omitted.] Inns are instituted for passengers and wayfaring men; and the keepers thereof can be held to the strict legal liability only for such goods as are brought into their inns by travellers in the character of guests. It would be too great a responsibility if that liability could be extended so as to cover any conceivable amount of money or gold dust, which the traveller, after he has become a guest, might be disposed to thrust into the custody of his host, and thus compel him to become the insurer of its safety.

It is a question of fact for the jury to determine in what character goods have been taken into a hotel.

12:9   *Loss of Property Deposited in Hotel Lobby*

SWANNER V. CONNER HOTEL CO.
205 Mo. App. 329, 224 S.W. 123 (Springfield Ct. App. 1920)

[Plaintiff, a traveling salesman, went to the Conner Hotel in Joplin about 11:30 A.M. on a certain day in May, 1919, to obtain a room as a guest. Being familiar with the hotel, plaintiff went directly to the bellboys' bench where it was the custom to leave grips, and set his grip by the bench. On previous occasions when plaintiff was a guest at this hotel he had seen the bellboy set his grip by this bench, and had seen the grips of other guests set by this bench. No room being vacant at the time, plaintiff had lunch at the hotel, went out and returned at about 5:30 P.M. Still there was no vacancy, but he was told there would be vacancies later. After 10:00 P.M. plaintiff succeeded in getting a room, registered, but by that time his grip was gone. None of the bellboys handled it or knew of it, and plaintiff did not call anyone's attention to it. Defendant maintained a checkroom in the hotel, and plaintiff knew of this fact and could have checked his bag without any inconvenience. An attendant was present at all times in the checkroom. Plaintiff never looked for his grip, nor gave it any attention from the time he set it down until after 10 o'clock that night.

The cause was tried before the court, and at the close of the case defendant demurred to the evidence, and was overruled. The correctness of this ruling is the only question here. It was conceded or rather not questioned that the relation of innkeeper and guest was created and existed.

In Missouri, an innkeeper is liable for the loss of the goods of his guest not arising from the negligence of the guest, the act of God, or public enemies. *Batterson v. Vogel,* 10 Mo. App. 235.]

BRADLEY, J.: "Defendant urges that plaintiff's baggage was never *infra hospitium*, that is, in the care and under the custody of the innkeeper, and that, therefore, no liability attached. As stated, the fact that plaintiff was a guest is not questioned. He had put his baggage where it was customary to put baggage while a guest was registering and seeing about a room. . . . He was told there would be a room, and he waited for the room. His baggage was where it should have been at least up to the time he asked for and failed to get a room.

"In *Read v. Amidon,* 41 Vt. 15, 98 Am. Dec. 560, [the court said:] . . . The guest is not relieved from all responsibility in respect to his goods on entering an inn; he is bound to use reasonable care and prudence in respect to their safety so as not to expose them to unnecessary danger of loss. Whether the plaintiff was so careless, in laying down his gloves in the manner he did, as to exonerate the innkeeper is a fact to be determined by the jury, in view of all the circumstances.' [Citations omitted.]

" . . . We do not think that plaintiff's negligence was any more than a question for the trier of the facts, and therefore we decline to sustain appellant on this feature.

" . . . The judgment below is affirmed."

FARRINGTON, J. concurs.

STURGIS, J. (dissenting): " . . . The innkeeper is an insurer only where the guest is not negligent in respect to his loss. The guest cannot recover if his negligence enters into the loss and the negligence on the part of the guest which will defeat his recovery is the want of that ordinary care which a reasonably prudent man would take under the circumstances of the case. . . .

" . . . Certainly, if the plaintiff in making his case admits by his own evidence the facts showing his contributory negligence and such facts so clearly and unmistakably establish contributory negligence that reasonable minds cannot differ then the question is one of law and the court should direct a verdict for the defendant. This rule is so universal that citation of authorities is unnecessary.

" . . . Certainly the defendant hotel had provided every reasonable means for caring for the baggage of the guest, all of which were familiar to plaintiff and of which he could avail himself without cost or inconvenience. . . .

"If plaintiff's own evidence does not show him guilty of negligence in exposing his hand grip to peril without the slightest excuse for so doing, I do not know what he could have done that would be negligence. Plaintiff has no one to blame for his loss except himself and should not be allowed damages. The judgment should be reversed."

In *Widen v. Warren Hotel Co.,*[19] plaintiff applied for a room in defendant's hotel. The room plaintiff requested was occupied, but plaintiff was told that it would become vacant later in the day. The clerk told plaintiff that he could check his baggage while waiting for a room or leave it in the lobby and the bell-

[19]262 Mass. 41, 159 N.E. 456 (1928).

boy would take it to his room when he returned. The plaintiff left it in the lobby where it disappeared.

In conspicuous places throughout the hotel defendant posted regulations, one of which was: "Baggage may be left in charge of the porter, for which checks will also be given; when sent for, a written order must accompany the checks for the same. For articles not thus checked the management will not be responsible."

It was held that the regulation was duly brought to plaintiff's notice, that it was reasonable, and that the loss was caused by plaintiff's failure to comply with the regulation. The clerk had no authority to waive the regulation.

In *Clarke v. Hotel Taft Corp.*,[20] the plaintiff arrived at the hotel by cab, was escorted to the lobby by a bellboy who also took the baggage (three suitcases) from the cab, carried them to the lobby and deposited them in a portion of the lobby reserved for the baggage of incoming and outgoing guests. The plaintiff registered, was assigned a room and was ready to proceed when she found that the suitcases were gone. They were never found.

The defendant was held liable for $2,350, the full value of plaintiff's loss, without benefit of the statutory limitation provided in section 201 of the General Business Law as it then existed. The limitation then applied only to property delivered "for storage or safekeeping in the storeroom, baggage room or other place elsewhere than in the room or rooms assigned" to guests. The court held that there was no such delivery for safekeeping or storage and that until plaintiff deposited them for storage or safekeeping, the statute did not apply.

The statute has since been amended to apply to property in the lobby, hallways, or in the room or rooms assigned to guests.

12:10 *Property Must Be within the General Control of Innkeeper*

While it is not necessary, in order to make the innkeeper responsible for the property of a guest, that it should be delivered into his possession, still the property must be within his general care and control. If the guest himself undertakes the care of it, or if he makes a special arrangement by which the control of it is removed from the innkeeper, the innkeeper is not liable. Thus in an old case the innkeeper gave notice to a guest that he could not receive him because he was obliged to leave at once to serve on a jury. The guest then requested that he might himself take the keys and take care of the goods. The innkeeper gave him the keys and went away and the goods were lost. It was held that the innkeeper was not liable.[21]

12:11 *Liability for Loss by Fire*

Loss by fire, where the innkeeper was not negligent, charges the innkeeper or not according to the rule prevailing in the jurisdiction concerned. In a state

---

[20]128 N.Y.L.J. No. 53, 478 (N.Y. City Ct. 1952).
[21]Y.B., 11 Henry 4, 45, pl. 18 (1410).

where stringent liability was imposed at common law, as in the state of New York, the innkeeper was liable for a loss by accidental fire. But in states that hold the innkeeper liable only for negligence or breach of undertaking, he was not responsible where the goods were lost by accidental fire.

Whatever view is adopted, it is agreed that upon loss or injury to the property being shown the innkeeper is *prima facie* liable, and the burden is upon him to prove such facts as will exonerate him.

The liability of innkeepers for loss of or damage to property caused by fire is now limited in many states by statute. The New York statute[22] provides that "no hotel or motel keeper shall be liable for damage to or loss of such property by fire, when it shall appear that such fire was occasioned without his fault or negligence."

The property referred to in the above quoted portion of the New York statute is wearing apparel or other personal property in the lobby, hallways, or in the room or rooms assigned to guests or deposited with the innkeeper for storage or safekeeping. As to whether the exemption applies to other property such as money, jewelry, and valuables required to be deposited in the hotel safe, or situated in other parts of the hotel building has not yet been the subject of judicial decision.

In *Hyman v. South Coast Hotel Co.*,[23] the court ruled that where the innkeeper had voluntarily removed valuables deposited in the hotel safe in order to prevent them from burning, the statute limiting liability enacted to protect the innkeeper would not apply to their subsequent loss caused by the innkeeper's negligence.

In the following case, the motel sued a guest for property damage sustained in the guest's room by reason of a fire alleged to have been caused by his negligence. One of the issues raised was the legal sufficiency of a jury verdict which found the motel contributorily negligent. The Supreme Court of Minnesota, in affirming the verdict, set forth the Minnesota law on negligence and proximate cause as follows:

EDGEWATER MOTELS, INC. v. GATZKE
277 N.W.2d. 11 (Minn. 1979)

SCOTT, J.: [Facts and procedural issues omitted.]

"Edgewater contends that the jury's findings relating to Edgewater's contributory negligence are not reasonably supported by the record. It first claims that it owed no duty to protect against its guests' negligence. This court, in *Jacobs v. Draper*, 274 Minn. 110, 142 N.W.2d 628 (1966), stated that: ' . . . there are many situations in which a reasonable man is expected to anticipate and guard against the conduct of others.' 274 Minn. 116, 142 N.W.2d 633. In that case we quoted from Prosser, Torts (3 ed.), § 33 at 173, as follows, in part: ' . . . In

---

[22]N.Y. General Business Law, § 201 (McKinney 1968).
[23]146 A.D. 341, 130 N.Y.S. 766 (2d Dep't 1911).

general, where the risk is relatively slight, he is free to proceed upon the assumption that other people will exercise proper care. . . . But when the risk becomes a serious one, either because the threatened harm is great, or because there is an especial likelihood that it will occur, reasonable care may demand precautions against ''that occasional negligence which is one of the ordinary incidents of human life and therefore to be anticipated.'' ''It is not due care to depend upon the exercise of care by another when such reliance is accompanied by obvious danger.'' . . .' 274 Minn. 116, 142 N.W.2d 633.

"The record indicates that Edgewater had notice of its guests' practice of placing cigarette materials in their motel rooms' plastic wastebaskets. The Edgewater maid who regularly cleaned the room in which Gatzke was staying testified that she had seen cigarette butts in the wastebasket in Gatzke's room. She also stated that, in her experience, she had observed that many other motel residents would often 'dump' ash trays and cigarettes in their motel rooms' plastic wastebaskets. She further testified that the head housekeeper had knowledge of the motel guests' habit of leaving cigarette butts in these plastic baskets. In light of these facts, and consistent with the principle articulated in *Jacobs v. Draper, supra,* it was reasonable for the jury to find that Edgewater had a duty to protect against the dangers which might flow from its guests' disposal of smoking materials in the motel rooms' wastebaskets.

"Edgewater further contends that defendants failed to prove that the use of a plastic wastebasket in and of itself can amount to a breach of a duty of due care. Again, however, the record does not support this contention. Edgewater's own expert witness, Dr. Anderson, testified that the plastic material out of which the wastebasket was made 'burns readily.' In fact, he had no difficulty igniting the remains of the wastebasket with a common household match. Based on this alone, the jury could quite reasonably conclude that a motel owner, aware that smoking materials were often dumped into wastebaskets, breached a duty of due care by providing a highly combustible plastic wastebasket.

"Edgewater finally claims that, even if its use of a plastic wastebasket was negligent, such negligence was not a proximate cause of the fire damage. This contention is premised on the theory that the evidence does not show that the fire originated in the wastebasket. Plaintiff's expert. Dr. Anderson, in reference to the origin of the fire, testified on direct examination as follows:

" . . .

"Q Where, in your opinion, with reference to the wastebasket, did the fire originate, Doctor?

"A Basically in the wastebasket. . . .

"Q All right, Sir. Now, is that—Can you tell us whether that opinion that the fire originated in the wastebasket, is that consistent with all of the pointers and all of the char and all of the burn that you saw in that area, or is it not?

"A Yes, it is consistent. . . .

[Following the noon recess the questioning continued as follows:]

"Q Doctor Anderson, at the noon break I was talking to you about the place of origin of the fire and I think—tell us, again, where did you say you felt that it originated?

"A I felt—it's my opinion that it originated right in the wastebasket or right next to it where I put the 'X' on the figure. . . .

"The above testimony, coupled with the reasonable inferences which may be drawn from the facts of this case (i.e., a person would presumably dispose of a cigarette in a wastebasket, rather than next to it), provides a reasonable basis from which the jury finding of proximate cause is supported.

"The trial court's granting of judgment to Walgreen is hereby set aside, and the jury's verdict is hereby reinstated in its entirety.

"Reversed in part; affirmed in part."

HERBERG v. SWARTZ
89 Wash. 2d 916, 578 P.2d 17 (1978)

STAFFORD, J.: "Appellant Real Estate Consultants, Inc., appeals a judgment entered on a jury verdict in two actions which were consolidated for trial. We affirm.

"Appellant purchased the Chieftain Hotel in August of 1973. On October 19, 1973, the hotel was inspected for compliance with the state's minimum fire and life safety standards for transient accommodations. Although approximately 23 state fire code violations were discovered, appellant was given 5½ months to correct them.

"Two months later, on December 19, 1973, an arson fire was started on the hotel's first floor. At this time most of the fire code deficiencies were still uncorrected. Appellant notified the City of Yakima (City) fire department sometime in the midafternoon and evacuated all tenants. Before the fire department could arrive the fire had spread throughout the hotel. The fire's rapid spread was caused by at least five, and potentially by twenty, of the uncorrected fire code deficiencies. One serious deficiency in particular, open pipe chases which ran vertically and horizontally throughout the building, accelerated and spread the fire, acting as a series of open chimney flues.

"That evening the fire mushroomed from the pipe chases into the attic, causing the roof to collapse. Thereafter efforts to suppress the fire were limited to the exterior of the building.

"The fire continued to burn throughout the evening and into that night. At 3 A.M. on December 20, the east wall collapsed. By the afternoon of December 20, the fire was creating such a hazard that the City determined demolition of the remaining walls was necessary. Consequently, appellant engaged Carrell Trucking (Carrell) to reduce the walls to a safe level.

"After Carrell had demolished the west wall, only the north wall and the centrally-located elevator shaft remained standing. As Carrell began demolition of the elevator shaft, the crane's cable became entangled. During efforts to extricate the cable from the shaft, the north wall collapsed and fell on the adjoining store owned by respondent Herberg.

"In one action respondent tenants sued appellant for loss of their personal property. Appellant asserted a common-law claim for indemnity against the City based upon the City's alleged active negligence in its fire fighting procedures and its failure to contain the fire.

"In a second action respondent Herberg sued appellant *and* Carrell alleging negligence. Appellant, in turn, asserted common-law indemnity claims against *both* the City and Carrell. Carrell thereafter asserted its written contract of indemnity against appellant and also sought common-law indemnity from the City.

"The two actions were consolidated for trial. Prior to trial, the court entered a summary judgment that the written indemnity contract between Carrell and appellant was supported by consideration. The court also granted a summary judgment that appellant was negligent *per se* for operating the hotel in violation of RCW 70.62. . . .

"During trial, and in response to respondents' motions to exclude evidence of the superseding or intervening negligence of the City and Carrell, appellant's common-law indemnity claim against the City was dismissed and the evidence was excluded. With all claims against the City and Carrell having been dismissed, settled, or nonsuited, the consolidated actions were submitted to the jury with appellant as the sole defendant.

"The jury returned verdicts for both respondent hotel tenants and respondent Herberg. The court entered judgment on the verdicts and later denied appellant's motions for judgment n.o.v. or for a new trial. The Court of Appeals certified the appeal to this court.

"We turn first to the determination that appellant was negligent *per se* for operating the hotel in violation of the minimum fire and life safety standards promulgated under the Transient Accommodations Act, RCW 70.62.290. Appellant asserts that its duties to the tenants and to Herberg should have been tested by the common-law standards of sections 343, 353, 364, and 366 of the Restatement (Second) of Torts (1965). It is argued that under those sections the reasonableness of appellant's actions during the 2 months preceding the fire would have presented a question of material fact. Thus, appellant urges, summary judgment was inappropriate. We disagree.

"The concept of negligence *per se* permits a court to substitute legislatively required standards of conduct for lesser common-law standards of reasonableness. *Bayne v. Todd Shipyards Corp.*, 88 Wn. 2d 917, 568 P.2d 771 (1977); *Kness v. Truck Trailer Equip. Corp.*, 81 Wn. 2d 251, 501 P.2d 285 (1972); Restatement (Second) of Torts § 286 (1965). As W. Prosser in Laws of Torts § 36 (4th ed. 1971) states at page 190: 'When a statute provides that under certain circumstances particular acts shall or shall not be done, it may be interpreted as fixing a standard for all members of the community, from which it is negligence to deviate.' Thus, if a defendant violates an applicable statutory duty, the court may properly instruct the jury that the defendant was in fact negligent. [Citations omitted.] Prosser, *supra*, § 36, at 200. If the statutory duty applies, lesser common-law duties necessarily become irrelevant. [Citation omitted.]

"It is clear that at the time the arson fire was discovered appellant was still in violation of several state fire and life safety standards. Further, the undisputed evidence considered on summary judgment demonstrates that at least five of these violations *caused the fire to spread.* These are the only facts material to a determination of whether appellant was negligent *per se.* Consequently, whether summary judgment was proper depends on whether the trial court properly adopted the statutory standards as the duty required of appellant.

"We said in *Bayne v. Todd Shipyards Corp., supra* at 920 and in *Kness v. Truck Trailer Equip. Co., supra* at 257:

"The court may adopt as the standard of conduct of a reasonable man the requirements of a legislative enactment, or an administrative regulation whose purpose is found to be exclusively or in part

"(a) to protect a class of persons which includes the one whose interest is invaded, and

"(b) to protect the particular interest which is invaded, and

"(c) to protect that interest against the kind of harm which has resulted, and

"(d) to protect that interest against the particular hazard from which the harm results.

"Thus, we must determine whether the fire and life safety standards were intended to protect either or both the tenants and Herberg.

"RCW 70.62.200 provides that the purpose of the Act is 'to promote the protection of the health and welfare of individuals using such accommodations. . . . ' Further, the fire marshal is specifically directed to promulgate rules and regulations and to enforce the fire and life safety standards. *See* RCW 70.62.290; WAC 248-144-035; WAC 212-12-010(1)(g). These standards were adopted to provide 'the highest degree of public safety from fire' consistent with normal use and occupancy of the building. WAC 212-12-010(2). Each of the applicable standards is mandatory. Respondent tenants were residents of the transient accommodation and were harmed by the very danger sought to be prevented. Given the legislature's clear statement of purpose to protect such persons, we hold the trial court properly adopted the statutory and regulatory standards as the appropriate duty owed these tenants by appellant.

"The trial court also correctly adopted the standards of RCW 70.62 as the duty owed by appellant to respondent Herberg. That the legislature intended the same protective policy to extend to landowners in the immediate vicinity of the danger is based on the Act, the regulatory standards, and on common sense.

"RCW 70.62.290 provides: 'Rules and regulations establishing fire and life safety requirements, not inconsistent with the provisions of this chapter, *shall* continue to be promulgated and *enforced* by the state fire marshal's office.' (Italics ours.) Unlike RCW 70.62.200, this mandatory directive is not expressly limited to mere protection of persons actually 'occupying such accommodations.' Rather, in considering other statutory duties of the state fire marshal we find that he is authorized to enter 'upon all premises and into all buildings except private dwellings for the purpose of inspection to ascertain *if any fire hazard exists, and to require conformance with minimum standards for the prevention of fire and for the protection of life and property against fire and panic* as to use of premises. . . . ' (Italics ours.) RCW 48.48.040(1). When the fire marshal finds any fire hazard 'dangerous to the safety of the building, premises, or to the public,' he must order such condition remedied. RCW 48.48.050(1). These statutes are interrelated and must be so considered. Viewed from this perspective, we must conclude that the Transient Accommodations Act was not intended merely to protect transient occupants but was also intended to protect the *public reasonably expected to be endangered* by the fire hazard.

"Further, a review of the state fire marshal's regulations reveals that they too are designed to promote 'the *highest* degree of *public* safety from fire.' WAC 212-12-010(2). In fact, several of the statutory and regulatory standards violated herein were concerned exclusively with preventing the *spread* of fire, thus clearly evidencing an intent to protect those reasonably expected to be within the zone of danger from such spread. For example, Standard No. 3 required interior stairways to be enclosed or cut off at floor level. The explanatory comment states: "Past fire experience in multi-story buildings, substantiated by the school fire tests, have [*sic*] conclusively established that the single-most factor in life loss and fire spread is open stairways, which serve as chimneys, accelerating and spreading fire throughout the building in a matter of minutes.' However, Standard No. 4 is even more stringent in its treatment of vertical openings, such as pipe chases. The explanatory comment notes the 'chimney effect' caused by such vertical openings and, unlike stairways, the standard pertaining to *pipe chase* enclosures is *mandatory*. No alternative corrective device is permitted. It is evident that these safety standards were designed to prevent the precise harm which occurred here. Safety legislation is to be liberally construed, and for good reason. [Citations omitted.]

"These standards, admittedly violated, were intended to preclude the rapid spread of fire. Respondent Herberg was a member of that public reasonably expected to be endangered by the contemplated hazards involved. Thus, the trial court correctly adopted the legislative standard as the one by which to measure appellant's duty vis-a-vis Herberg. . . .

"Appellant's trial theory was that the negligence of the City and/or Carrell was a superseding or intervening cause of the harm. Appellant here argues it should have been allowed to introduce evidence of such claimed superseding or intervening negligence. We find no error.

"The terms 'intervening' and 'superseding' cause are often used interchangeably. [Citations omitted.] However, the theoretical underpinning of an *intervening* cause which is sufficient to break the original chain of causation is the *absence of its foreseeability*. [Citations omitted.] Further, insofar as here applicable the question of whether the intervening act is a *superseding* cause depends upon whether it brings about a different kind of harm or whether it operates independently of the situation created by the actor's negligence. [Citations omitted.]

"In the instant case neither theory applies. The trial court correctly determined, as a matter of law, that appellant could reasonably have foreseen that *both* the assistance of the fire department and demolition efforts would be necessary in the event of a fire. Negligence, if any, of either the City or Carrell was activated by appellant's own negligence in failing to correct the many code deficiencies which caused the fire to spread. Appellant argues no other theory at trial which might have made such evidence relevant. Since the trail court correctly determined that appellant could reasonably have foreseen the need for assistance by both the City and a demolition team, the proffered evidence was irrelevant and properly excluded. Finding no error in excluding such evidence there was no error in the trial court's refusal to instruct the jury on the issue."

12:12 *Liability for Loss by Theft*

Loss of goods because of theft by the innkeeper's employees clearly charges the innkeeper under any rule. Even if the goods are stolen by a stranger without actual negligence on the part of the innkeeper (unless they are stolen by someone for whom the guest is responsible), there is a breach of the innkeeper's obligation, and he should be held liable under any theory of liability.

In *Wies v. Hoffman House,*[24] the plaintiff and his wife registered at defendant's hotel and were duly assigned to a room. During their absence from the hotel, on the following evening, plaintiff's traveling bag and its contents, together with some wearing apparel, were stolen. Prior to their departure, the plaintiff had locked the room and handed the key to the night clerk. There was no proof of fraud or negligence on plaintiff's part. Plaintiff was allowed to recover for the loss, measured by the market value of the goods at the time of the loss.

The common-law rule has been modified by statutes limiting liability for such losses enacted in all states. This subject is treated in section 13:24, *infra*.

12:13 *Responsibility for Automobiles and Their Contents*

At common law, the innkeeper was held to a strict liability for the loss of or damage to a guest's horse or carriage when placed within the confines of the inn, that is, *infra hospitium*. The innkeeper was excused from liability only if the loss, or damage, occurred by an act of God, an act of the public enemy, or the fault of negligence of the guest himself.[25]

The common-law rule of strict liability was later extended to cover the automobile.[26] The rule required (1) that the claimant be a guest of the innkeeper and (2) that the automobile be within the confines of the inn, *infra hospitium*.

---

[24]28 Misc. 225, 59 N.Y.S. 38 (Sup. Ct. 1899).

[25]Hulett v. Swift, 33 N.Y. 571 (1865).

[26]Park-O-Tell Co. v. Roskamp, 203 Okla. 493, 223 P.2d 375 (1950).

In *Plant v. Howard Johnson's Motor Lodge*,[27] the Indiana Court of Appeal held that the Indiana statute limiting innkeeper's liability for loss of guest property applied only to property brought into the hotel and did not govern a guest van stolen from a motel parking lot.

12:14 Scope of the infra Hospitium Requirement

The concept of what constitutes property *infra hospitium* has been expanded by the courts. At first the *hospitium* was held to be merely the inn itself with its attendant buildings (such as stables and garages). However, the innkeeper might, by his actions, extend the confines of his *hospitium*. In *Calye's Case*,[28] it was held that if an innkeeper, without direction from the guest, put a horse to pasture, he would be held strictly liable for its loss. The same principle applied to a guest's gig left by the innkeeper on a public street outside of the inn.[29]

In the much later case of *Aria v. Bridge House Hotel (Staines) Ltd.*,[30] the plaintiff, while a guest at defendant's hotel, parked his car in the parking lot adjoining the hotel, as he was directed by one of the defendant's employees. While plaintiff was at dinner in the hotel, his car was stolen. The court held that the insurance liability of an innkeeper for the goods of his guest extended also to the guest's automobile parked in a space adjoining the hotel, as directed by the porter, and that the defendant hotel was liable for the loss of the car stolen while the guest was at dinner.

The high point of English case law holding an innkeeper strictly liable as insurer for the loss of a guest's car was reached in the case of *Williams v. Linnitt*.[31] In that case the plaintiff, a local resident, called at defendant's inn for liquid refreshments only. He parked his car in an open lot provided free of charge for that purpose. The car was stolen. The court held that the plaintiff was a guest,[32] that the parking lot was *infra hospitium*,[33] and that hence the innkeeper was strictly liable for the theft of the car. By providing the free parking space, the innkeeper extended an invitation[34] to the guest to park there, which invitation

---

[27]500 N.E.2d 1271 (Ind. App. 1986).

[28]77 Eng. Rep. 520 (K.B. 1584).

[29]Jones v. Tyler, 110 Eng. Rep. 1307 (K.B. 1834).

[30]137 L.T.R. (n.s.) 299 (K.B. 1927).

[31][1951] 1 K.B. 565 (C.A. 1950).

[32]Asquith, L. J., felt that the broad construction given the term "traveler" to constitute plaintiff a guest did after all exclude, "for instance, (a) the innkeeper's family living in the inn; (b) the innkeeper's servants; (c) the innkeeper's private guests; (d) lodgers at the inn; (e) persons resorting to the inn for purposes unconnected with the enjoyment of the facilities it provides as an inn." *Id.* at 579.

[33]The test applied by Lord Tucker in deciding whether the parking lot was *infra hospitium* was: "[I]s the place in question a part of the inn premises intended and suitable for use in connection with some part of the innkeeper's business?" *Id.* at 577.

[34]For a case drawing a distinction between an invitation which serves to extend the *hospitium* and mere permission, *see* Watson v. People's Refreshment House Ass'n Ltd., [1952] 1 K.B. 318. (Mere permission to park a motor coach on runway of hotel-owned gas station does not extend the *hospitium* and does not create liability for loss of motor coach.)

was sufficient to constitute the lot as within the *hospitium* of the inn. The court also held, with one dissent, that the defendant innkeeper could not limit his liability by merely posting a notice to that effect.

In the New York case of *Lader v. Warsher,*[35] plaintiff, a traveling salesman, parked his automobile in a parking lot provided free of charge for that purpose for guests of defendant's hotel, the St. Charles, in Hudson, New York. Plaintiff locked his car and retired for the night. During the night the car was jimmied and plaintiff's sample case was stolen.

The court, in affirming judgment for the defendant, held that none of plaintiff's property was ever "within the walls of the inn," *infra hospitium.* Said the court:

> [T]he rule of absolute liability of an innkeeper for loss of property of a guest under the common law has always . . . been limited and applied to cases where the property was within the walls of the inn itself and not outside them; or if outside the walls the goods must have been in the care and under the charge of the innkeeper. [Citations omitted.]
>
> Where property is damaged or lost outside the inn itself the landlord's liability is measured by a different rule; it may be one of the many and various rules relating to contract or negligence or agency or bailment or what have you. . . .
>
> [Defendant], at the most, was a bailee, and his responsibility and liability must be measured by rules applicable to that relationship.
>
> If [defendant] was a bailee for hire on the theory that he derived some indirect benefit or profit in his business by providing a free parking place for automobiles belonging to his guests, he is held to the rule of ordinary care [citation omitted]; or if he was a gratuitous bailee he was liable only for gross negligence.
>
> In either case the burden of proof was on the [plaintiff]. [Citation omitted.][36]

The majority of jurisdictions in the United States have adopted the strict rule of insurance liability of an innkeeper for the goods of his guest *infra hospitium.* In a few jurisdictions (*see* section 12:3), the liability is not that of an insurer, but is predicated on negligence or wrongful acts. In these latter jurisdictions the loss or damage to the property creates a *prima facie* case against the innkeeper, which he can rebut by proving that the loss or injury was not due to any fault or neglect on his part. All states have enacted statutes limiting the innkeeper's liability for the goods of his guest.

Of the numerous jurisdictions that have passed on the problem of an innkeeper's liability for a guest's car and its contents, only two, Oklahoma and Utah, have imposed insurer's liability on the innkeeper. In most states the liability is predicated on a bailment relationship between the guest and the innkeeper.

Clearly, where no innkeeper-guest relationship exists, there is no case for imposing strict insurance liability. A person attending a banquet has been held not

[35]165 Misc. 559, 1 N.Y.S.2d 160 (Columbia County Ct. 1937).
[36]*Id.* at 561, 1 N.Y.S.2d at 162.

to be a guest of the hotel.[37] A bridegroom who entered the hotel solely for the purpose of getting married, without any intent of occupying a room, was not considered a guest.[38]

The two states that have held the innkeeper to an insurer's liability had no trouble deciding that the car in question was *infra hospitium*. In one case, decided by the Supreme Court of Oklahoma,[39] the car had been parked in the hotel garage, which was advertised as a special feature of the hotel. The court held that at common law as well as under the relevant statute it is not necessary, in order to render the innkeeper liable for their loss, that the goods be placed under his special care, or that notice be given of their arrival. It is sufficient if they are brought into the inn in the usual and ordinary way and are not retained under the exclusive control of the guest, but are under the general and implied control of the innkeeper.

In the other case,[40] the car had been parked at a loading platform situated in front of the hotel. The Supreme Court of Utah found that the clerk had instructed the guest to leave it there and the hotel would take care of it.

For the most part, the courts have refrained from facing the issue of whether or not a guest has placed his car *infra hospitium*. Where, on the facts, the innkeeper is liable under either a strict liability theory or as a bailee for hire, the courts have generally decided the case without passing on the issue of *infra hospitium*.[41]

GOVERNOR HOUSE v. SCHMIDT
284 A.2d 660 (D.C. App. 1971)

NEBEKER, A.J.: "This appeal results from (1) a directed verdict in favor of a hotel patron who left his car containing personal property with the doorman for parking in the basement garage under the hotel; and (2) from a judgment in favor of a garage on a cross-claim styled as 'indemnification of contribution' by the hotel. The pleadings and trial centered around a claim of breach or ordinary care duty owed by the hotel as bailee and the subbailee garage. The trial judge, in directing the verdict at the close of all the evidence, ruled that the hotel was an insurer of the patron's property under the theory of 'infra hospitium' since the garage was an integral part of the hotel. The factual issue of ordinary care was thus taken from the jury—leaving only the question of damages to be argued. . . .

[37]Edwards Hotel Co. v. Terry, 185 Miss. 824, 187 So. 518 (1939). Plaintiff's car was stolen from the hotel's free parking lot while he was attending a banquet held in the hotel. The court held that the plaintiff was not a guest of the hotel.

[38]Ross v. Kirkeby Hotels, Inc., 8 Misc. 2d 750, 160 N.Y.S.2d 978 (1st Dep't 1957).

[39]Park-O-Tell Co. v. Roskamp, 203 Okla. 493, 223 P.2d 375 (1950).

[40]Merchants Fire Assur. Corp. v. Zion's Securities Corp., 109 Utah 13, 163 P.2d 319 (1945).

[41]*See, e.g.,* Zurich Fire Ins. Co. v. Weil, 259 S.W.2d 54 (Ky. 1953). The guest parked his car in front of the hotel, preparatory to its being sent to the garage. The bellboy took the key from the desk and damaged the car. The court, in holding the innkeeper liable, stated: "We are not required to decide in this case whether the hotel could be held liable as an innkeeper. . . . The [hotel] owed . . . at least the duty of a bailee for hire." *Id.* at 56.

"The gravamen of the appeal by the hotel centers around the conclusion by the trial judge that the doctrine of *infra hospitium* applied to the case, thus to give rise to innkeeper liability of the hotel as an insurer. . . .

"It is the holding of this court that the directed verdict in favor of the patron was proper. To the extent that the judgment precluded the jury from deciding the issue of lack of due care arising out of the bailment of the car, the judgment must be reversed. . . .

"The hotel's major point on appeal . . . is that it was error for the trial judge to have concluded, as a matter of law, that the garage was an integral part of the hotel. It appears all parties agree that this court correctly stated the law in this type of case in *Hallman v. Federal Parking Services*, D.C. Mun. App., 134 A.2d 382, 384 (1957). There we observed:

"[O]nce the property of a guest is taken into the custody and control of the innkeeper the goods are considered *infra hospitium* and the liability for loss or destruction of the goods imposed is that of an insurer, unless the property is lost or destroyed by an act of God, the public enemy, or by fault of the guest. This is undoubtedly the rule of common law having its source in the ancient case of *Calye* which dealt with the innkeeper's liability for the loss of a guest's horse put to pasture. The common-law rule is of force in this jurisdiction. The doctrine of *infra hospitium* has been applied in cases where a car or its contents are lost while in the exclusive care and custody of a hotel. However, where the hotel takes custody of the vehicle, as here, and delivers it to a lot or garage not an integral part of the hotel and thereafter a loss of the property occurs, the better rule imposes the liability of a bailee for hire on the hotel. *Id.*

"In the instant case, unlike *Hallman*, the garage was physically a part of the hotel structure, and access to it was only through the hotel lobby or by way of the ramp. The fact that the cost of parking by hotel patrons using the garage facilities was absorbed by the hotel adds weight to the determination that the garage was for this purpose an integral part of the hotel. [Citation omitted]. Moreover, it should make no difference that another business entity operated the garage or that the ticket handed the patron contained both the hotel and garage names. There was certainly no privity between the patron and the garage. Viewed through the patron's eyes the garage reasonably was an integral part of the hotel. The disposition of the patron's claim on the basis of *infra hospitium* was therefore proper.

"In this connection we observe that where the doctrine of *infra hospitium* is properly applied it is irrelevant that the hotel was not on notice as to the contents of the automobile left in its custody. [Citation omitted.] Therefore, the hotel's contention that notice of 'bailed' goods was required is without merit in this situation where the hotel is an insurer. To the extent that the record may be susceptible of a reading that notice as to the nature of contents was not given the hotel, no error exists. . . .

"The cross-claim, treated by the trial judge as an equitable claim for indemnification, can be read as asserting a breach of duty in a bailment relationship.

We do not believe that application of the doctrine of *infra hospitium* to the hotel should preclude it from having the jury decide the question of negligence as raised in its cross-claim. Whether characterized as contribution or indemnification the facts asserted posed an issue of negligence which pertained to the relationship between the hotel and the garage. The garage attendant admitted having custody of the car and also testified regarding the failure to redeliver, thereby establishing a *prima facie* case of liability in bailment. The liability of the garage for damages relating to nonuse of the automobile asserted in the hotel's cross-claim presented an issue of negligence that should have been submitted to the jury. We therefore reverse and remand the case for a new trial on the factual issues pertaining to liability arising from the relationship between the garage and the hotel.''

In *Vilella v. Sabine, Inc.,*[42] reported at 12:17 *infra,* the Supreme Court of Oklahoma interpreted its innkeeper's liability statute as imposing liability for the loss of a guest's car and contents, absent proof of actual notice or delivery to an authorized employee. The statutory requirement "placed under his [the innkeeper's] care" was met by proof that the property was brought in to the inn in the usual and ordinary way and was not retained under the guest's exclusive control. A vehicle parked in an outside, unenclosed parking lot that was provided for the use of guests and was patrolled during the night was held within the ambit of innkeeper liability.

In the case below, the Tennessee Court of Appeals (an intermediate review court) reversed a dismissal of a claim arising from an accident in which an off-duty hotel employee lost control of his personal car and crashed into a guest's vehicle. The guest's car was parked in the hotel's valet parking lot and was found to be in the complete care and control of the hotel. Excerpts from the majority and concurring opinion follow.

SHEPHERD FLEET, INC. V. OPRYLAND USA, INC.
759 S.W.2d 914 (Tenn. App. 1988)

TODD, P.J.: '' . . . Defendant asserts that the strict common law rule does not apply because plaintiff's automobile was not '*infra hospitium*' because it was not 'stored and kept within the four walls of the inn'. Such is not the meaning or intent of the expression '*infra hospitium*'. The meaning is 'in the care and custody of the innkeeper'. Black's Law Dictionary Fourth Edition, p. 919. *Davidson v. Madison Corporation,* 247 N.Y.S. 789, 231 App. Div. 421 (1931). . . .

"This Court is satisfied that the rule as adopted in Tennessee includes any property delivered and accepted into the exclusive custody of the innkeeper and that the term '*infra hospitium*', includes all property deposited and accepted in exclusive control of the innkeeper, wherever the innkeeper elects to physically store the property, whatever its character, so long as it is not the type of property for which special statutory provision exists.

---

[42]293 Okla. 636, 652 P.2d 759 (1982).

"This Court notes with concern the present incongruous state of the law in this State regarding the liability of innkeepers.

"The innkeeper is 'practically an insurer' (liable without fault) of personal property of the guest '*infra hospitium*'. However, the innkeeper is not in a like position in regard to the person of a guest; and the liability of the innkeeper is eliminated or sharply limited as to valuables and baggage by T.C.A. §§ 62-7-103, 104, 105, 106. This is a subject which merits legislative investigation and action. . . .

"REVERSED AND REMANDED."

KOCH, J. (concurring).

"The majority's opinion reaches a proper result, albeit by a circuitous route. I have prepared this separate opinion to address the points raised in the briefs and during argument concerning the significance of the Tennessee Supreme Court's decision in *Dispeker v. New Southern Hotel Co.,* 213 Tenn. 378, 373 S.W.2d 904 (1963).

I.

"After tracing Tennessee's common law back to its roots, the majority concludes that the common law standard of liability of innkeepers to their guests is part of the law of this state. This is undoubtedly true, except to the extent that the common law standard has been modified by the Tennessee Supreme Court or by the General Assembly.

"Unfortunately, the majority's opinion leaves the impression that the common law is immutable and that once a principle of common law is recognized or followed, it becomes an indelible part of our jurisprudence. This is simply not the case. Tennessee's common law is not static. It continues to grow and change to accommodate the needs of modern society. *Powell v. Hartford Accident & Indem. Co.,* 217 Tenn. 503, 509–10, 398 S.W.2d 727, 730–31 (1966); *Box v. Lanier,* 112 Tenn. 393, 407, 79 S.W. 1042, 1045 (1904); *Jacob v. State,* 22 Tenn. (3 Hum.) 493, 515 (1842).

"Were it not for the Tennessee Supreme Court's specific approval of and reliance on the common law standard of an innkeeper's liability in *Maxwell Operating Co. v. Harper,* 138 Tenn. 640, 641–42, 200 S.W. 515, 516 (1918), I would conclude that the common law standard is no longer necessary or appropriate. The law of bailments, as it presently exists, adequately recognizes and balances the respective interests of inn keepers and their guests.

"The *stare decisis* value of *Maxwell Operating Co.* is open to question. Ever since this case was decided, the courts have gone to some length to avoid relying on the common law standard of inn keeper's liability. *Dispeker v. New Southern Hotel Co.,* 213 Tenn. 378, 373 S.W.2d 904 (1963); *Kallish v. Meyer Hotel Co.,* 182 Tenn. 29, 184 S.W.2d 45 (1944); *Sewell v. Mountain View Hotel,* 45 Tenn. App. 604, 325 S.W.2d 626 (1959); *Andrew Jackson Hotel v. Platt,* 19 Tenn. App. 360, 89 S.W.2d 179 (1935).

"However, this Court should not presume to modernize or modify the decisions of the Tennessee Supreme Court. [Citations omitted.] Any further modification of an inn keeper's common law liability must be left to the Tennessee Supreme Court or the General Assembly.

II.

"Opryland seeks to avoid the common law standard of liability in two ways. First, it insists that Mrs. Crocker's automobile was not '*infra hospitium*,' or in its exclusive custody. . . .

"The facts in this case . . . clearly support the applicability of the common law standard of liability. The determining factor is whether the guest's property was placed in the custody and control of the hotel. *Governor House v. Schmidt*, 284 A.2d 660, 661 (D.C. Ct. App. 1971); *Vilella v. Sabine, Inc.*, 652 P.2d 759, 763 (Okla. 1982) (OPALA, J., concurring). That a garage or parking lot is open to the public or is not enclosed or contiguous to the hotel is not controlling as long as an automobile has been placed in the hotel's care and custody. *Plant v. Howard Johnson's Motor Lodge*, 500 N.E.2d 1271, 1272–73 (Ind. Ct. App. 1986).

"Mrs. Crocker turned her automobile and keys over to a hotel employee when she checked in. An Opryland employee parked the automobile in the hotel's 'valet parking' area and kept the keys. This parking lot was on Opryland property adjacent to the hotel, and access to the lot was limited to hotel employees. Neither Mrs. Crocker nor any member of the public was permitted in the lot. In light of these facts, it is difficult to argue that Mrs. Crocker had not placed her automobile in Opryland's custody and that the automobile was not '*infra hospitium*' at the time it was damaged.''

12:15 *Liability as Bailee*

In the following case, the federal court of appeals for the District of Columbia reiterated the rule that the strict liability of an innkeeper for loss of guest property does not apply to public patrons of a hotel restaurant.

BLAKEMORE V. COLEMAN
701 F.2d 967 (D.C. Cir. 1983)

MIKVA, C.J.: " . . .

I. Background

"The decision in this case turns uniquely on the facts. The Blakemores were in Washington, D.C. to celebrate President Reagan's inauguration, staying as overnight guests at a hotel in Georgetown. Before returning home, they decided to have lunch at The Jockey Club. . . . Upon arriving at the restaurant, which was then part of The Fairfax hotel, the Blakemores . . . carried two pieces of hand luggage—a briefcase and a small, carry-on bag—into the hotel themselves. It was the carry-on bag that contained the jewelry that eventually disappeared; specifically, the missing jewelry was in one of the two small jewelry pouches that the Blakemores had stored in the bag. . . .

"When the Blakemores entered the hotel, they checked their two bags with the hotel bellman, who proceeded to place the bags in a small holding room or checkroom adjacent to the lobby. That room had neither a door separating it from the lobby nor any posted sign that would limit the defendant's liability under D.C. Code Ann. § 34-101 (1981) (allowing hotels to limit liability if, *inter alia*, they conspicuously post such notice). The Blakemores did not inform the bellman of the valuable jewelry contained in their bags or ask about locked storage areas; neither did the bellman inquire whether such valuables existed or inform the Blakemores that safety deposit boxes or other locked storage compartments were available for their use.

"Following their lunch in the restaurant, the Blakemores returned to the hotel lobby to retrieve their belongings. Having done so, Mrs. Blakemore immediately opened the carry-on bag only to discover that one of the jewelry pouches was missing. It was at this point that the defendants actually were notified of the jewelry's existence and apparent disappearance. A search of the hotel by employees of The Fairfax and the police was unsuccessful in locating the missing pouch or any of the jewelry that it contained. . . .

II. Innkeeper's Liability

"Before discussing the issue of constructive knowledge that is central to this appeal, we must consider an alternative basis urged by the Blakemores for upholding the judgment of the district court. Specifically, the Blakemores argue that the trial judge should have found the defendants subject to innkeeper's liability, making them responsible for the contents of luggage belonging to their guests regardless of their knowledge about those contents. *See, e.g., Governor House v. Schmidt*, 284 A.2d 660 (D.C. 1971). It is true that application of the strict liability imposed on innkeepers would require affirmance of the district's court's judgment; but the Blakemores misconstrue the basis on which D.C. law premises an innkeeper-guest relationship. Indeed, in the latest case to define the scope of that relationship, *Wallace v. Shoreham Hotel Corp.*, 49 A.2d 81 (D.C. Mun. App. 1946), the D.C. Municipal Court of Appeals explicitly held that '[o]ne who is merely a customer at a bar, a restaurant, a barber shop or [a] newsstand operated by a hotel does not thereby establish the relationship of innkeeper and guest.' *Id.* at 82; *cf. Governor House*, 284 A.2d at 661–62 (applying innkeeper's liability in action brought by overnight guest of hotel); *Hotel Corp. of America v. Travelers Indemnity Co.*, 229 A.2d 158 (D.C. App. 1967) (same). Absent any indication that the D.C. courts have subsequently modified that definition, the federal courts are bound to follow that holding when applying D.C. law.

"Nor is there any sound justification for distinguishing between the Blakemores and other restaurant patrons simply because the restaurant they happened to visit is located within a hotel. *Cake v. District of Columbia*, 33 App. D.C. 272 (D.C. Cir. 1909), heavily relied on by the Blakemores, is not to the contrary. In that case, the court defined 'bona fide registered guests' to include customers partaking of a hotel's food or lodging. *Id.* at 277. That court, however, was interpreting language included in a criminal statute, and was not delineating the scope of the innkeeper-guest relationship created by the common law. Thus, the district court was correct to conclude that the Blakemores could not premise their action on the strict liability imposed on innkeepers.

III. Constructive Knowledge

"The Blakemores can sustain their damages award, therefore, only under a bailee-for-hire theory. The law of bailment for the District of Columbia, which the defendants admit is applicable to this case, requires that the subject matter of the bailment be delivered to, and accepted by, the bailee. It is not required, however, that the bailee have actual knowledge of the property in its custody in order to be liable for the property's eventual loss. Rather, when the property that is subject to the bailment is enclosed within a container, responsibility for its disappearance may rest with the bailee even though the bailee has only constructive or imputed knowledge of its existence. *See Dumlao v. Atlantic Garage, Inc.*, 259 A.2d 360 (D.C. App. 1969) (contents of an automobile); *Hallman v. Federal Parking Services*, 134 A.2d 382 (D.C. Mun. App. 1957) (same). Such constructive knowledge about the contents of a container has been defined to include those items that are in plain view, *see Dumlao*, 259 A.2d at 362, or that could be expected, given 'common knowledge and experience,' to be in a container under the specific facts and circumstances of a particular case, *see Hallman*, 134 A.2d at 385.

"The mere articulation of this legal standard inescapably leads to the conclusion that a finding of constructive knowledge is a mixed question of law and fact. As with a finding of negligence, the specific facts underlying a given situation must be determined by the trier of fact before the legal standard can be properly applied. In the usual trial setting, the trial judge will explain the legal standard in his or her instructions, but the jury, uniquely qualified to make factual determinations, will apply that standard to the particular facts at issue. *See generally* W. Prosser, Handbook of the Law of Torts § 37 (4th ed. 1971) (discussing respective functions of court and jury in finding of negligence). In the present case, therefore, whether the defendants had constructive knowledge that the Blakemores' carry-on bag might contain valuable jewelry should have been left to the jury.

"The district court ruled first that '[t]he evidence mandated a finding of constructive notice, leaving no question of fact for the jury in this regard,' RE 8, and then that '[a]rticles of jewelry are, as a matter of law, commonly and appropriately carried in hand luggage,' *id*. Both rulings, which had the effect of conclusively removing this issue from the jury's deliberations, were erroneous.

"The first ruling quoted above—that the evidence 'mandated a finding' of constructive knowledge—effectively concluded that every reasonable juror necessarily would have found that the defendants had implied notice of the valuable jewelry contained in the Blakemores' carry-on bag. Although such a finding would not be clearly erroneous if the trial judge were serving as the trier of fact, the trial court committed reversible error when it removed the issue from the jury. The only fact that was conclusively established at trial was that the bag had some tangible contents. Whether those contents were valuable jewelry or just dirty laundry, however, could not be considered a foreclosed issue. Indeed, facts clearly existed from which conflicting inferences could be drawn. For example, it is conceded that the Blakemores arrived at the hotel only to have lunch, that they neither mentioned the valuables stored inside the bag or complained when the bag was placed in an unlocked holding room, and that the bag itself was unlocked. By themselves, these facts would seem to require submission of the case to the jury. . . . This is especially true when, as in this case, tha trial judge takes an issue from the jury by ruling in favor of the party that bears the burden of persuasion. Cf. *Lucas v. Auto City Parking,* 62 A.2d 557, 559 (D.C. Mun. App. 1941) (burden on plaintiff to prove bailment).

"Nor can we approve of the district court's ruling that valuable jewelry is, 'as a matter of law, commonly and appropriately carried in hand luggage.' To support that ruling, the trial judge relied on *Hasbrouck v. New York Cent. & H.R.R.,* 202 N.Y. 363, 95 N.E. 808 (N.Y. 1911), and the Blakemores cite *Sherman v. Pullman Co.,* 79 Misc. 52, 139 N.Y.S. 51 (App. Div. 1913). Even if these New York cases are somehow controlling in a diversity case applying D.C. law, they do not stand for the proposition stated. In *Hasbrouck,* for example, the specific paragraph relied on, 95 N.E. at 813, was an appellate court conclusion that there was sufficient evidence to support the trial judge's findings of fact, no conclusion of law about jewelry was made at the trial level. Similarly, in *Sherman,* the appellate court simply held that the lower court's conclusion that the term 'baggage' included jewelry found inside was not 'against the weight of the evidence.' 139 N.Y.S. at 52. Thus, in both cases the courts were affirming findings of fact made by trial judges serving as triers of fact; neither opinion is appropriate precedent for the lower court's action in the present case.

"In sum, a straightforward application of the law of bailment for the Distirct of Columbia requires that the jury determine whether the defendants in this case had constructive knowledge of the existence of valuable jewelry in the Blakemores' carry-on bag. To this extent, the district court's judgment must be reversed, and the case remanded for a new trial.

IV. Proceedings on Remand

"Our holding requires that a retrial on all issues be held. Any decision concerning the defendant's constructive knowledge of valuable jewelry is too enmeshed with the other issues presented to allow for separate consideration.

"Even assuming the jury concludes that the defendants had constructive knowledge that valuable jewelry was contained in the Blakemores' carry-on bag, it does not follow that the defendants would be liable for an unlimited amount or value of jewelry. The defendants had a right to assume that patrons of the restaurant would not check articles having an unreasonably high value without informing the bellman. Thus, the trial judge should further instruct the jury to limit its potential damage award to the maximum value of goods which the defendants reasonably could expect to be left in baggage checked under the particular circumstances of the present case. Only in this way can the necessary and appropriate limits be set on the liability that might be imposed on the defendants.

"*It is so ordered.*"

12:16 *Liability as Bailee: Parking Lot Transactions*

ELLERMAN V. ATLANTA AMERICAN MOTOR HOTEL CORP.
126 Ga. App. 194, 191 S.E.2d 295 (1972)

[Plaintiff, a guest at a motor hotel operated by the defendant, placed his automobile in the defendant's parking facility. He was required by the defendant to leave the ignition key with the defendant's employee, and the latter parked the vehicle in an area unknown to plaintiff. At the time, plaintiff was given a claim check which was admitted in evidence at trial and which plaintiff in his testimony admitted reading. It provided in part as follows: "Liability. Cars parked at owner's risk. Articles left in car at owner's risk. We reserve privilege of moving car to other section of lot. No attendant after regular closing hours." Prior to delivering the ignition key and the car to the attendant, the plaintiff removed a raincoat from the interior, placed it in the trunk of the car, and kept the trunk key. When plaintiff checked out of the motel his car was found missing. The car and its contents have never been recovered. The plaintiff's suit sought to recover the value of the items of personalty contained in the trunk which he alleged [were] allowed to be stolen through the defendant's negligence. Plaintiff had been paid by his insurance company for the loss of the automobile. The trial judge directed a verdict for the defendant.]

BELL, C.J.: " . . . The defendant contends that the depositing of the automobile with the defendant's attendant under these circumstances does not give rise to a bailment relationship because of the disclaimer of liability printed on the claim check given to plaintiff. He relies upon our decision in *Brown v. Five Points Parking Center,* 121 Ga. App. 819 (175 S.E.2d 901) as controlling. As we view this issue, *Brown* is not in point. *Brown* dealt with an ordinary parking lot. There is no special statute governing that operation. This case involves a parking facility operated by a motel as a part of its service and this creates the relationship of innkeeper and guest. This latter relationship is influenced by special statutory provisions. Code Ch. 52-1; *Traylor v. Hyatt Corp.,* 122 Ga. App. 633 (178 S.E.2d 289).

"It is recognized that an ordinary bailee by contract may limit or completely exculpate himself from any liability for loss or damage to the bailed property as a result of his own simple negligence. *Evans & Pennington v. Nail,* 1 Ga. App. 42 (1, 2) (57 S.E. 1020). However, an innkeeper is not an 'ordinary' bailee. Many courts and texts have described an innkeeper as a 'professional' bailee. See 8 Am. Jur. 2d 1026, § 131, and Ann. 175 A.L.R. 111 *et seq.* and particularly *ibid.*, § 69, p. 149. Unlike an 'ordinary' bailee the 'professional' bailee is often precluded from limiting by contract liability for his own negligence as violative of public policy. The reasoning utilized is that the public, in dealing with innkeepers, lacks a practical equality of bargaining power and may be coerced to accede to the contractual conditions sought by the innkeeper or else be denied the needed services. We think that both the principle precluding the limitation of liability and the reasoning underlying it are sound. The General Assembly by Code § 52-111 authorizing a limitation of liability has pre-empted the field on that subject. We are therefore constrained to hold that the legislative pre-emption cannot be avoided by a special contract and that any such contract purporting to further exculpate the innkeeper is contrary to the public interest and policy and cannot be enforced.

"Judgment reversed."

In *Peralta v. Port of New York Authority*,[43] a New York City Civil Court (a trial court of limited monetary jurisdiction) adopted a very liberal attitude in finding a bailment relationship created with respect to self-service-type public parking facilities. Applying prior New York case law which found a bailment to exist with respect to airport parking lot patrons whose cars were stolen, the court extended their reasoning to enable an airport parking lot employee whose automobile was stolen from such a lot to recover.

On appeal, the judgment for plaintiff employee was reversed.[44] The Appellate Term of the Supreme Court, the appropriate reviewing court, held that there was no bailment. The last sentence of its per curiam decision states, "Nor was there any proof of a negligent act or omission in the facts as stipulated,"[45] indicating that absent any bailment relationship the plaintiff must introduce independent evidence of negligence on the part of the parking lot operator to establish liability.

A later decision, *Garlock v. Multiple Parking Services, Inc.*, which follows, rejects the no bailment–no liability theory as violative of the public policy of the city of Buffalo, which requires each commercial parking lot operator to obtain insurance coverage not exceeding $20,000 for personal injury theft and vandalism covering vehicles of parking patrons as a condition of securing a license to operate such a facility.

GARLOCK V. MULTIPLE PARKING SERVICES, INC.
103 Misc. 2d 943, 427 N.Y.S.2d 670 (Buffalo City Ct. 1980)

MCCARTHY, J.: "The plaintiff, on June 13, 1971, at about 7:30 P.M., entered a parking lot operated by (but not owned by) the defendant corporation. Plaintiff

---

[43]68 Misc. 2d 302, 326 N.Y.S.2d 776 (Civ. Ct. Queens Co. 1971).

[44]76 Misc. 2d 1086, 351 N.Y.S.2d 787 (Sup. Ct. 1973).

[45]*Id.* at 1086, 351 N.Y.S.2d at 788. *But see* Motors Ins. Corp. v. American Garages, Inc., 98 Misc. 2d 881, 414 N.Y.S.2d 841 (Sup. Ct. 1979).

paid the attendant the parking fee, (defendant said this was a nominal flat rate of $.50 at that time) and was directed to park his 1968 Chevrolet Corvette Roadster, and take his keys with him.

"At approximately 11:30 P.M., the plaintiff returned to the parking lot and found his auto had been burglarized and vandalized. He further stated that the attendant appeared to be in an intoxicated condition when the plaintiff returned, but had seemed sober when he had first left his car.

"The convertible top had been slashed; driver door window smashed; driver door upholstery slashed; seats slashed; dash panel slashed, and a stereo tape deck and eight cartridge tapes were stolen. Total damage, which is not disputed by the defendant, was five hundred and six dollars ($506.00).

"The defendant, in its answer, generally denied the plaintiff's allegations. In its affidavit in support of its later motion for summary judgment, the defendant indicated that this incident took place at 505 Washington Street in downtown Buffalo.

"The defendant said it was the operator of the parking lot, but not the owner. It further alleged that the lot had a sign posted showing rates, and the fact that the lot closed at 9:00 P.M. The lot was not fenced, and the lot attendant did not take possession of the autos or their keys. Defendant's president said it was not customary for the lot attendant to remain after the 9:00 P.M. closing time, but he did not know personally whether or why the attendant remained until the 11:30 P.M. discovery time.

"The unfenced lot had available ingress and egress on Washington Street, Ellicott Street, and through an adjacent lot to Huron Street. The Court takes notice of the fact that that location was on the East side of downtown Buffalo. Further, that in June, 1971, that location was on the westerly edge of what could euphemistically be called a 'high crime area.' There was no indication by either party as to the time the alleged vandalism occurred.

"The defendant denies liability on the basis that it never took possession of the plaintiff's auto; that the claim ticket contained a liability disclaimer, and that the damage occurred after closing, so that they were no longer responsible. . . .

"It is clear, from [Citations omitted], that the rationale which was originally used to protect the rights and property of persons leaving their goods with others, now effectively frustrates those rights. This is because the less the indicia of bailment, the less the protection for the goods, and the greater the likelihood of unreimbursed losses. . . .

"In our society today, the use of the automobile as the main mode of transportation is irrefutably established (with the possible exception of the City of New York). A person does not really choose where to park; he parks as close to his destination as possible. The fee he pays depends more on the distance he must then walk to the main business district or other specific area of attraction, rather than the perceived amount of security offered by supposedly competing operators.

" . . . [T]he less an operator spends, the less likely he will be found liable for damage or loss of a vehicle. . . . Therefore, he saves money by putting on a 'ticket spitter' instead of an attendant; or posts disclaimer notices which some courts have found significant as evidence of a supposed implied contractual understanding; or by not fencing his lot; or by not providing adequate lighting; or by not providing a guard for security; or by any combination of these factors. The net result is that he saves further sums because he is not found liable for damage or loss to vehicles. This last conclusion may not be entirely true, today in the City of Buffalo, as we shall soon see.

"In the City of Buffalo, the money-saving bailment rationale is in violation of public policy. Public policy can be established by this Court taking notice of the ordinances of the City of Buffalo. Chapter V, section 393, of the Ordinances of the City of Buffalo states: 'Every application for a license here under (annually applied for license of a parking lot) shall be accompanied by a policy of . . . legal liability insurance up to twenty thousand dollars ($20,000.00) for fire, theft, and vandalism, covering vehicles parked or stored on the licensed premises.' (Parking lot is defined under section 340 of Chapter V, Ordinances of the City of Buffalo, as 'any open, outdoor space . . . where more than five (5) motor vehicles may be parked. . . . ')

"It should be amply clear that the City fathers intended that those who profit from the storage of vehicles should include the risks of loss or damage to those vehicles as a cost of doing business. This means they determined that increases in rates or loss of insurability should be considered by the operator as a factor in determining whether to fence, light, and how to guard a lot.

"The present state of the law in the First and Second Departments of this State seems to force the owner to rely on his own insurance if his auto is stolen or vandalized in a parking lot. That assumes that the owner has theft and comprehensive coverage, or perhaps collision coverage (none of which are mandatory). It fails to take into account that, even with such coverage, there is usually a deductible and higher rates, and non 'risk pool' insurability may be affected by the filing of a claim. . . .

"All of this exploration and analysis leads this Court to one conclusion: the 'bailment theory' as a basis for recovery in parking lot cases is no longer appropriate. . . .

"The new standard to be followed . . . was to be ' . . . reasonable care under the circumstances whereby foreseeability shall be a measure of liability' (*Basso v. Miller,* 40 N.Y.2d 233, cf. 241, . . . 352 N.E.2d 868, 872) [1976]. . . .

" . . . Therefore, this Court need not decide whether a bailment was created in the instant case. The measure we will apply is that of the *Basso* case (*supra*): 'reasonable care under the circumstances whereby foreseeability shall be a measure of liability' (40 N.Y.2d 233, at 241, 386 N.Y.S.2d 564, at 568, 352 N.E.2d 868, at 872.) In doing thus, this court is not making new law. We are only stripping away the excusatory verbiage from those cases where liability was found for a damaged or stolen auto, under a finding of bailment, but where it was clear that the gravamen was lack of reasonable care. . . .

"The presence of insurance shows both the City's determination that public property demands that owners or operators of parking lots should be responsible and financially able to pay for damage or theft, and that the owners are in fact able to pay.

"When one considers the initial cost today of a passenger vehicle, plus its financing costs; the ravages of depreciation; the cost of repair; the costs of insurance and license fees; the wear and tear of potholes and salt corrosion, and costs of parking itself, it is a small thing to ask that a parking lot owner at least keep it from being stolen or damaged.

"This Court finds that the defendant failed to properly protect the plaintiff's vehicle from damage through the acts of a vandal. The possibility of such acts were clearly foreseeable considering the parking lot's location, size, and general accessibility. The failure to fence or provide a guard, or to at least direct the patron to a location close to the attendant's booth are acts of omission which, as a matter of law, constitute negligence.

"The Court further finds that the attendant's failure to observe the acts of vandalism—which, by nature of the damage caused, had to be overt and observable—was also negligence, attributable to the defendant. This is true, whether the attendant was officially on duty or not, since the defendant cannot establish when the damage took place. Even though the plaintiff has the burden of proof, since he wasn't present and the defendant's employee was, the burden of coming forward with those facts shifts to the defendant.

"The plaintiff's burden is met by his showing that the defendant failed to exercise ' . . . reasonable care under the circumstances, whereby foreseeability shall be a measure of liability.' (*Basso v. Miller,* 40 N.Y.2d 233, at 241, . . . 352 N.E.2d 868, at 872.)"

In Illinois, self-service parking lots have fared better in obtaining immunity from liability for loss of automobiles. In *Wall v. Airport Parking Co.,*[46] plaintiff car owner parked his car on an airport parking lot and retained the ignition key. His only contact with the parking-lot employee was on making payment upon leaving the lot. The court held that there was no bailment, but merely a lease of land so that although the plaintiff's car concededly disappeared, the burden of proof was on the plaintiff owner to prove defendant's negligence. The court found that such negligence was not shown by the mere disappearance of the car.

Other courts have adopted "foreseeability" as a measure of liability in parking lot cases. In *Danielenko v. Kinney Rent A Car, Inc.,*[47] the car that the plaintiff rented from the defendant (defendant both rented cars and owned the garage in New York City where he stored the cars) exploded when a bomb detonated under the front passenger seat while the plaintiff was driving. The plaintiff survived with serious injuries, and the blast destroyed some of the payroll that he was transporting.

The court held the defendant not liable, stating that sabotage of the type that occurred was not foreseeable. The court held that the "most foreseeable event that [could be] gleaned from the record is that defendant's automobiles could be

[46]40 Ill. 2d 506, 244 N.E.2d 190 (1969).
[47]57 N.Y.2d 198, 455 N.Y.S.2d 555 (1982).

stolen or parts taken from them." (*Id.* at 558.) The defendant met the duty to protect against such vandalism by renting the plaintiff a car that was in sound operating condition.

In *McGlynn v. Newark Parking Authority,*[48] while the court abandoned the "bailment" theory of responsibility and adopted the foreseeability standard, it did *not* abandon the presumption of negligence that attaches to the garage owner under the bailment theory. The court cited the garage owner's superior ability to control access to his garage as the reason for retaining the presumption.

In accord with *Garlock* are *Gauther v. Allbright New Orleans, Inc.,*[49] and *McGlynn v. Newark Parking Authority.*[50]

12:17 Liability for Loss of Articles Left in Automobiles

Generally, the liability of a bailee for hire for the loss or damage to personal articles left in an automobile is made to depend on the presence of notice or knowledge of such articles.[51] The notice necessary need not be actual or express.

The courts have shown little hesitation in making an innkeeper liable for the loss of a car's contents. Where the car has been held to be *infra hospitium,* its contents have also been held *infra hospitium,* without need for specific notice.[52] Where the liability has been based on a bailment theory, the bailment has been held to include such items as a traveler may "reasonably be expected to leave in the car such accessories, equipment and baggage as they had no occasion to use while at the hotel."[53] The damages may even include cost of alternative transportation for the plaintiff.[54]

In the New York case of *Lader v. Warsher,*[55] the court held that, where a guest himself parked his automobile in the parking lot provided free of charge for that purpose, the car had not been placed *infra hospitium* and the hotelkeeper was not liable as insurer for personal articles rifled during the night from the automobile. The court suggested that the hotel's liability in such cases would have to be on a theory other than insurance liability, probably on a bailment theory.

[48]86 N.J. 551, 432 A.2d 99 (1981).

[49]417 So. 2d 376 (La. App. 1982).

[50]86 N.J. 551, 432 A.2d 99 (1981).

[51]For a Canadian case dealing with this problem, *see* George v. Williams, [1965] 5 D.L.R. 2d 21, where the court held that a car parked by plaintiff in the hotel's parking lot was *infra hospitium,* but its contents, which were stolen, were not. The only articles within a car for which an innkeeper was to be held liable were those associated with a car such as "cushions and knee-robes." For a criticism of this decision, *see Comment,* 34 Can. Bar. Rev. 1203 (1956).

[52]Annot., 27 A.L.R.2d 796 (1953). *See also,* Hallman v. Federal Parking Services, Inc. 134 A.2d 382 (D.C. Mun. App. 1957).

[53]Park-O-Tell Co. v. Roskamp, 203 Okla. 493, 223 P.2d 375 (1950).

[54]Campbell v. Portsmouth Hotel Co., 91 N.H. 390, 20 A.2d 644 (1941) (per curiam). This was an action for negligence in care of automobile left by plaintiff with defendant hotel company. The car was stolen. The court held that the contract of bailment included both the car and its contents.

[55]165 Misc. 559, 1 N.Y.S.2d 160 (Columbia County Ct. 1937).

In the more recent case of *Schibilia v. Kiamesha Concord, Inc.*,[56] the plaintiff's car was damaged while in the defendant hotelkeeper's garage. The court decided the case in favor of plaintiff on a theory of bailment and stated that the return of the car to plaintiff in damaged condition created a *prima facie* case of negligence, shifting to defendant the burden of coming forward with proof.

These cases are authorities for the proposition that in New York an automobile parked outside the hotel proper is not regarded *infra hospitium* and in the event of loss or damage do not subject the innkeeper to insurance liability.

In *Swarth v. Barney's Clothes, Inc.*,[57] a parking-lot operator was held not liable for the loss of a sum of money in a wallet which was left on the seat of a car and concerning which he had no notice. Said the court:

> [A parking-lot operator who accepts an automobile for parking becomes its bailee and assumes the liabilities flowing from that relation.] It by no means follows, however, that [he] thereby also undertook the bailment of the wallet [containing $350 in cash], whose presence in the car was neither disclosed nor reasonably to be expected. Delivery, actual or constructive, to the person sought to be held as bailee is not enough to create a bailment; acceptance, actually or constructively, by the [bailee] is equally essential. [Citations omitted.] Acceptance is absent when the property is not such as is usually and customarily left with a custodian in like circumstances and no disclosure of this fact is made. In that situation, the person sought to be charged as bailee having no reason to suppose the property has been delivered to him, is liable only if on express notice, "for the bailee cannot by artifice be compelled to assume a liability greater than he intended." [Citation omitted.] Self-evidently valuable and easily stolen articles are not left in parked automobiles, and the operator of a parking lot, without notice that they have been so left, is not liable as bailee in respect to them. [Citations omitted.][58]

On the other hand, it has been held that, for the purpose of imposing liability on a parking lot owner under a "foreseeability" theory, cassettes and a tape deck are items reasonably found in cars today.[59]

In most states, an innkeeper must be shown to have accepted complete and exclusive control over a guest vehicle and contents in order for a bailment to exist. In the case to follow, the Supreme Court of Oklahoma interpreted its innkeeper's statute to apply to a vehicle and contents under the care of the innkeeper.

VILELLA v. SABINE, INC.
293 Okla. 636, 652 P.2d 759 (1982)

SIMMS, J.: " . . . The cause of action arose under the following facts: On February 8, 1979, plaintiff's sons registered as paying guests at a motel in Okla-

---

[56]16 A.D.2d 504, 229 N.Y.S.2d 729 (3rd Dep't 1962).
[57]40 Misc. 2d 423, 242 N.Y.S.2d 922 (Sup. Ct. 1963).
[58]*Id.* at 424, 242 N.Y.S.2d at 923.
[59]McGlynn v. Newark Parking Authority, 86 N.J. 551, 432 A.2d 99 (1981).

homa City operated by the predecessor corporation to defendant Sabine. Acting as his agents, plaintiff's sons were transporting his personal property to Pennsylvania in a truck and trailer. They inquired about a patrolled area where they could park the truck and trailer and were advised that the motel had an open parking lot, patrolled by a security guard during the night areas. During the evening hours of February 3 or the early morning hours of February 4, 1979, the vehicle and its contents were stolen from said parking lot. The defendant as owner and operator of the motel fully complied with the provisions of 15 O.S. 1981, § 503 and 503(a) in maintaining safety features for the motel doors, a safety deposit box for valuables, etc.

"The United States District Court certifies the following questions of law which may be determinative of the issues involved:

"1. Is a motel guest's vehicle and its contents parked in an outside, unenclosed, patrolled (at night) parking lot, provided for the use of the motel's guest, placed under the care of the motel within the meaning of 15 O.S. § 501?

"2. If yes, do the limitations of liability in § 503b apply to such vehicle and its contents stolen from such a parking lot described above when the motel complies with § 503?

I

"We answer question one in the affirmative on the basis of prior case law. In *Park-O-Tell Co. v. Roskamp*, 203 Okl. 493, 223 P.2d 375 (1950) the court found that property under 15 O.S. 1941, § 501, included an auto and its contents. § 501 is a codification of the common law which made the innkeeper a virtual insurer of the safety of property entrusted to his care by a guest. *Busby Hotel & Theatre Co. v. Thom*, 125 Okl. 239, 257 P. 314 (1927). Innkeepers were made strictly liable not only because of the traveler's vulnerability and the necessity of reliance on the innkeeper's good faith, but the innkeeper was considered in a better position to protect himself from loss by regulating charges to indemnify himself. Exceptions to this high standard of duty were the intervention of an Act of God, the public enemy, or negligence of the guest.

"For the property to be 'under the care of the motel' it need not be exclusively within the control of the innkeeper. *Park-O-Tell, supra* quoting an earlier case, [footnote omitted] clarified the meaning of the phrase under 15 O.S. 1981, § 501:

"The provision of this statute that the innkeeper is liable for goods of his guests, 'placed under his care', is declaratory of the common law, not restrictive thereof. Under such provisions it is not necessary, in order to render the innkeeper liable for their loss, that the goods be placed under his special care, or that notice be given of their arrival. It is sufficient if they are brought into the inn in the usual and ordinary way and are not retained under the exclusive control of the guest, but are under the general and implied control of the innkeeper.

''Some jurisdictions require the automobile to be in the custody and control of the innkeeper in a literal sense (e.g., the owner retains the keys, the innkeeper does not control the locking of the car or does not charge an extra fee for parking.) Neither *Park-O-Tell, supra,* nor our statute requires a showing of custody and control, only that the property be under the care of the innkeeper. Moreover, our legislature has not limited the liability of an innkeeper for the loss of an automobile by changing the common law rule and making the innkeeper liable as a bailee for hire.

II

''We answer the second question in the negative. The limitations of liability in 15 O.S. 1981, § 503b do not apply to a vehicle and contents, unless the items would fall under the provisions of § 503b.

''While we agree with defendant that the purpose of § 503a and b was to limit the liability of innkeepers in derogation of the common law, the limitation applies to only certain types of property as enunciated in § 503a, 'valuable property of small compass', and § 503b, providing for types of property that cannot be placed in a safety deposit box: 'trunks', 'valise', 'box or bundle', 'miscellaneous effects and property'. An early decision of our Court, *Busby Hotel & Theatre Co. v. Thom, supra,* agreed with the contention that the intent of § 501 was to make innkeepers insurers of all losses to personal property placed under their care, except where *specifically exempted.*

''The 10th Circuit in *Solomon v. Downtowner of Tulsa,* 357 F.2d 449 (1966) recognized that § 503b was an exception to the strict liability rule of § 501 for certain kinds of property brought within the inn's care. *Solomon* involved an action against a motel owner for loss of jewelry (merchandise samples) from an automobile left in a motel parking lot while the plaintiff was checking out. Both car and jewelry were stolen, though the car was retrieved. The court upheld the award of damages to the car but denied recovery for the merchandise samples because the plaintiff had not followed the provisions of § 503b. The 10th Circuit, then, limited liability because of the nature of the property involved which fell specifically under § 503b; the court in no way intimated that liability would be so limited if a car and its contents [excluding items listed in § 503a and b] were stolen from the motel's parking lot.

''With no Oklahoma or 10th Circuit opinion directly on point, we look to another jurisdiction which has construed its statute limiting innkeeper's liability. In *Kushner v. President of Atlantic City, Inc.,* 105 N.Y. Super. 203, 251 A.2d 480 (1969) plaintiff filed suit against an innkeeper for recovery of the value of his automobile which was allegedly lost or stolen while parked in the motel's lot. The defendant contended that the 'chattel' in the following statute included all kinds of property, including an automobile, and therefore defendant motel was liable only for a sum not to exceed $100.00:

'' . . . nor shall any such proprietor be liable for in any sum for the loss of any article or articles of wearing apparel, cane, umbrella, satchel, valise, bag, box, bundle or other chattel belonging to such guest, the same not being in a room or rooms assigned to such guest, unless the same shall be specially intrusted to the care and custody of such proprietor or his duly authorized agent, and if such property shall be so specially intrusted, the proprietor shall not be liable for the loss of the same in any sum exceeding one hundred dollars.

"The court held that such a construction would not be within the intention of the legislature which only sought abrogation of absolute liability for loss of a guest's personal property, *infra hospitium causa hospitandi*. Furthermore, the court said:

" . . . the rule of *ejusdem generis* would mitigate against the asserted interpretation made by defendant. The list of articles in the second clause of R.S. 29; 2–3, N.J.S.A. other than the term 'chattel', is specific in scope, i.e., 'articles of wearing apparel, cane, umbrella, satchel, valise, bag, box, bundle, or other chattel belonging to such guest, the same not being in a room or rooms assigned to such guests . . . ' *Ejusdem generis* may be applied to general words in conjunction with words of specific meaning, to limit them to the class expressly mentioned.

"We agree with the reasoning of the New Jersey Court and believe it expresses the intent of our legislature to limit liability under § 503b only to those items listed—such items of personal use, convenience, instruction or amusement which the ordinary innkeeper and traveler would regard as baggage or luggage and which it is customary or reasonable to expect a guest to consign or keep with the room assigned to him by the innkeeper—rather than to *all* personal property. . . . "

12:18　*Apparent Authority of Hotel or Motel Employees for Automobiles*

A frequently litigated issue in these cases, whether the ultimate decision is based on a strict liability or on a bailee theory, is that the extent of the "authority" of the employee who takes control of the car. Does a footman or bellboy who hands a guest a check for his car,[60] or suggests to him that the hotel has made arrangements for parking,[61] have the authority to do so, thus binding the hotel to a relationship in which the hotel is eventually held liable for the loss of or damage to the car? With but few exceptions,[62] the courts have stated that the

[60]Campbell v. Portsmouth Hotel Co., 91 N.H. 390, 20 A.2d 644 (1941) (per curiam).

[61]Bidlake v. Shirley Hotel Co., 133 Colo. 166, 292 P.2d 749 (1956). The guest delivered his car keys to the night porter wearing the hotel's uniform. The porter took the car for a "joy ride," damaged it, and also took some personal property from the glove compartment. The court held the hotel liable to the guest; the porter had at least apparent authority to accept the car. In Todd v. Natchez-Eola Hotels Co., 171 Miss. 577, 157 So. 703 (1934), plaintiff left his car in care of the attendant in a parking lot operated by the defendant hotel. The attendant took the car for a ride and wrecked it. The court held that the defendant was the agent of the hotel even though he received his pay in tips. His taking the car from its place of safekeeping violated the hotel's duty as a bailee. *See also* Zurich Fire Ins. Co. v. Weil, 259 S.W.2d 54 (Ky. 1953).

[62]In Smith v. Robinson, 300 S.W. 651 (Tex. Civ. App. 1927), the guest's car was taken from the garage by a bellboy and was damaged. In an action against the hotel for the recovery of the damage,

"apparent authority" of such employees is sufficient to bind the hotel. The guest is under no duty to search behind the uniform to find whether or not the employee has actual authority.[63] Even the fact that the employee was expressly forbidden to take control of the car has been held not sufficient to save the innkeeper from liability.

BROWN v. CHRISTOPHER INN CO.

45 Ohio App. 2d 279, 344 N.E.2d 140 (1975)

McCORMAC, J.: "In her second assignment of error, plaintiff contends that the statement made by the porter that her property would be safe raises an issue of fact to be determined by the jury as to whether the statement constituted a warranty or guarantee. In support of this contention, plaintiff has cited only one case as authority, *Compton v. The M. O'Neil Co.*, 101 Ohio App. 378, 1 O.O.2d 315 (1955). In that case, the plaintiff purchased a pressure cooker which exploded, injuring her. At the time the pressure cooker was purchased, plaintiff asked the saleslady if it was safe, and the reply was 'absolutely, it is safe, because M. O'Neil's stands back of everything they sell.' The Court of Appeals reversed a trial court ruling that the saleslady's statement was an express warranty as a matter of law, holding that the statement presented a question of fact to the jury, whether or not it amounted to an express warranty. The basis for the ruling was a provision of the sales act stating that any affirmation of fact or promise relating to the goods is an express warranty if the natural tendency of the statement is to induce the buyer to purchase the goods and the buyer does so, relying thereon.

"The statute, now R.C. § 1302.26, relied upon in the *Compton* case has no application to this case because there was no sale of goods as defined under the

---

the court held that the hotel doorman who was authorized to inquire as to the garaging of the car had not only apparent, but also actual authority to store the car, and that the hotel was estopped from denying his authority. *See also* Merchants Fire Assurance Corp. v. Zion's Securities Corp., 109 Utah 13, 163 P.2d 319 (1945).

[63]In Andrews v. Southwestern Hotel Co., 184 Ark. 982, 44 S.W.2d 675 (1931), the plaintiff registered at defendant's hotel and inquired as to garage facilities. The clerk told plaintiff that a bellboy would take charge of the car and drive it to the garage. The bellboy damaged the car. The court held that in order to recover, the plaintiff must prove that the clerk on duty authorized or directed the bellboy to take charge of plaintiff's car. In Andrew Jackson Hotel, Inc. v. Platt, 19 Tenn. App. 360, 89 S.W.2d 179 (1935), the guest arranged with defendant's doorman to have the guest's car sent to a garage to have the car repaired. While being driven back from the garage by one of the garage hands, the car was damaged. In an action against the hotel for recovery of the damage, the court held that the doorman acted as the agent of the guest in transmitting the latter's request that the car be repaired, not as the hotel's agent. In Smith v. Hotel Antler's Co., 126 Ind. App. 385, 133 N.E.2d 89 (1956), the guest's car was damaged while being driven by a bellboy. The car keys were given to the bellboy at a party to which he had been invited by the guest and while he was out of uniform. In an action against the hotel, the court held that the bellboy was acting as the guest's agent, not the hotel's agent. Of the three cases, only the Arkansas decision is an exception to the general rule of imputing at least apparent authority to a bellboy, doorman, or porter. The other two cases can be limited to their respective fact situations.

Uniform Commercial Code. In addition, the bargain had already been struck, as plaintiff had registered at the hotel prior to the conversation taking place.

"More importantly, however, the statement of a porter—who was directed by the room clerk to show plaintiff, a registered guest, to a parking location—that the contents of her car will be 'safe' cannot reasonably be interpreted to be a binding commitment, guaranteeing or warranting the safety of the contents. The directed verdict test is whether *reasonable* minds could come to but one conclusion, construing all inferences favorably to the nonmoving party. In this particular instance, reasonable minds could come to the conclusion that the statement, at most, gave assurance that the hotel would take reasonable steps to provide for the safety of the contents of articles left in guests' automobiles, but not that the hotel assumed the status of an insurer or guarantor of those contents. Since no evidence was produced to indicate that the hotel did not take reasonable steps to provide for the safety of the contents, a directed verdict was justified.

"Furthermore, plaintiff seeks to hold the employer responsible rather than the person who made the statement. A party who claims that a principal is responsible for the acts of an employee is obligated to prove the agency and scope of his authority. [Citation omitted.] The only proof produced concerning the extent of the porter's authority was the statement by the room clerk that the porter would assist with parking, and the help provided and statements made by the porter in the parking garage. Arguably, that would be sufficient proof of actual or apparent authority to bind the principal for liability arising from erroneous statements of fact about the parking conditions and the existence of a security guard. That is, however, a far cry from the argument that the porter has apparent authority to bind the hotel to be absolutely responsible for the safety of the contents of a car being parked with the key taken by the patron. Construing all inferences most favorably to plaintiff, no proof of that authority, actual or apparent, was presented. Consequently, a directed verdict is also justified on that basis.

"For the reasons expressed herein, plaintiff's assignments of error are overruled and the judgment of the trial court is affirmed."

12:19 *Agreement between Hotel and Independent Garage*

Where a hotel does not have its own facilities for parking a car, it usually arranged with a private garage or parking-lot operator for space in which to park its guests' cars. The private arrangement made by the hotel and the garage in no way intrudes upon the relationship between the guest and the hotel. It is immaterial that only the garage's employees are permitted to collect the cars or to take payment,[64] or whether the garage pays for this service or not.[65] The garage is

---

[64]Bidlake v. Shirley Hotel Co., 133 Colo. 166, 292 P.2d 749 (1956); Smith v. Robinson, 300 S.W. 651 (Tex. Civ. App. 1927).
[65]*Id.*

usually considered the innkeeper's agent in his relations with the guest.[66] Indeed, in one case where the plaintiff-guest sued both the innkeeper and the parking-lot operator, the court held that only the innkeeper was liable.[67]

12:20 *Contractual Disclaimers of Liability for Automobiles*

The general rule in the United States is that a bailee of an automobile, whether he is a garage keeper, a parking-lot operator, or an innkeeper, cannot limit his liability for negligence by contract.[68] In some states this prohibition is regulated by statute.[69] In any event, the courts have looked with disfavor upon contracts printed on the back of claim checks or notices on walls.[70] These prohibitions do not affect the applicability of statutes limiting such liability.[71]

In *Horowitz v. Ambassador Associates, Inc.*,[72] an exculpatory clause in an agreement governing storage of a tenant's vehicle in landlord's residential garage was held void as violative of N.Y. Gen. Obligations Law, section 5-325 (discussed in footnote 71).

12:21 *Statutory Limitations of Liability for Automobiles*

In the United States, all states have statutory provisions limiting the liability of an innkeeper for loss of his guest's property. A question arises as to the applicability of such statutes to a guest's car and its contents.

---

[66]In most cases the hotel receives a payment for sending cars to a garage. *See* Kallish v. Meyer Hotel Co., 182 Tenn. 29, 184 S.W.2d 45 (1944). Even where no payment is made to the hotel, the courts assume that a hotel derives some benefit from being able to extend a parking service to its guests. *See* Hallman v. Federal Parking Services, Inc., 134 A.2d 382 (D.C. Mun. App. 1957); Zurich Fire Ins. Co. v. Weil, 259 S.W.2d 54 (Ky. 1953). Often the hotel's employees are instructed that they are not to drive the cars to the garage, that the garage keeper will supply the drivers. These arrangements do not prevent the imposition of liability on the hotel, as the guest is not charged with knowledge of these "internal arrangements." *See* Bidlake v. Shirley Hotel Co., 133 Colo. 166, 292 P.2d 749 (1956).

[67]Kallish v. Meyer Hotel Co., 182 Tenn. 29, 184 S.W. 2d 45 (1944). A private garage with which the hotel had an arrangement to park its guests' cars turned plaintiff's car over to another person. The garage was held to be the hotel's agent; therefore the hotel was held liable for damages caused by its agent's negligence.

[68]Hallman v. Federal Parking Services, Inc., 134 A.2d 382 (D.C. Mun. App. 1957).

[69]See 9 Williston on Contracts 1069 (rev. ed. 1967) (semble); Hallman v. Federal Parking Services, Inc., 134 A.2d 382 (D.C. Mun. App. 1957).

[70]Klar v. H. & M. Parcel Room, Inc., 270 A.D. 538, 61 N.Y.S.2d 285 (1st Dep't 1946), *aff'd mem.*, 296 N.Y. 1044, 73 N.E.2d 912 (1947).

[71]N.Y. Gen. Oblig. Law § 5–325 (McKinney 1964) disables garage keepers and parking-lot operators from making agreements exempting them from liability for negligence. A New York appellate court has held that although an innkeeper charged its guests no specific fee for parking but took exclusive control of the automobile and automobile keys from the time the automobile arrived at the hotel entrance, the totality of services paid for by the guest constituted "other consideration" within the statute. The trial court properly denied any effect to the supposed exculpatory clause appearing on the claim check issued by the hotel. Mindlin v. Kiamesha Concord Inc., 31 A.D.2d 988, 297 N.Y.S.2d 1008 (3rd Dep't 1969).

[72]437 N.Y.S.2d 608 (N.Y. City Civ. Ct. 1981).

At present, few states have dealt with this issue. The Oklahoma Supreme Court held that the language of the Oklahoma statute, declaratory of the common law, was broad enough to encompass both a car and its contents as "property."[73] Kentucky has held that a hotel statute limiting recovery for loss of or damage to a guest's property did not apply to any action based on negligence. This decision may be limited to the state, however, as it was based on a provision of the Kentucky constitution which prohibits limitations in negligence actions.[74]

The application of these statutory limitations to a car and its contents are important in light of the great increase in the number of motels.

Only two jurisdictions have enacted statutes applicable directly to a guest's car and its contents. Chapter 35, section 715 of the laws of Puerto Rico provides:

> *Liability for motor vehicles and property therein.*
> No innkeeper shall be liable to any guest, or other person, for any loss sustained by reason of theft of, or damage done to, any motor vehicle or other conveyance while parked in any free parking lot maintained by such innkeeper, or for any loss sustained by reason of the theft of, or damage done to any personal property left in such vehicle or other conveyance while so parked; provided, however, that nothing contained in this section shall be construed as to relieve any person of liability for his own willful act.

Under section 711(e), which defines the term *free parking,* the performance of regular services by employees for the business of the hotel is not deemed to constitute the payment of consideration for the use of parking accommodations.

Section 105.7 of the Iowa hotelkeepers statute entitled "Nonliability for conveyance" provides:

> No keeper or owner of any hotel, inn or eating house shall be liable by reason of his innkeeper's liability or his responsibility as innkeeper to any guest for the loss of or damage to the automobile or other conveyance of such guest left in any garage not personally owned and operated by such hotel, inn or eating house or the owner or keeper thereof.

---

[73]Park-O-Tell Co. v. Roskamp, 203 Okla. 493, 223 P.2d 375 (1950). The relevant statutory language reads: "An innkeeper or keeper of a boarding house is liable for all losses of or injuries to, personal property placed by his guests or boarders under his care, unless occasioned by an irresistible superhuman cause, by a public enemy, by the negligence of the owner, or by the act of someone whom he brought into the inn or boardinghouse, and upon such property the innkeeper of a boarding house has a lien and a right of detention for the payment of such amount as may be due him for lodging, fare, boarding or other necessaries by such guest or boarder; and the said lien may be enforced by a sale of the property in the manner prescribed for the sale of pledged property." 15 Okla. Stat. Ann. § 501 (1941). In Vilella v. Sabine, Inc., 652 P.2d 759 (Okla. 1982) (reported at 12:17, *supra*), however, the court held that a vehicle and its contents are *not* "property" within the meaning of statutes limiting an innkeeper's liability for the lost property of guests.

[74] Zurich Fire Ins. Co. v. Weil, 259 S.W.2d 54 (Ky. 1953). The relevant statutory language reads: "*Injuries to person or property; recovery not limited*—The general assembly shall have no power to limit the amount to be recovered for injuries resulting in death, or for injuries to personal property." Ky. Const. § 54.

This provision exempts the hotel or restaurant keeper from vicarious responsibility for the acts or omissions of an independent garage keeper with whom he may contract for the storage of guest vehicles.

Section 105.8 makes the hotel or restaurant keeper who owns or operates such a garage a bailee for hire as to both vehicle and contents, but limits liability for contents to $50 unless the guest lists the contents with the hotel or restaurant keeper at the time the vehicle is left in the garage.

12:22   *Lost and Found Property*

It is human to be careless at times, and hotel guests are human. The number and variety of articles lost or misplaced by guests vary with the size and type of the hotel or motel. Whenever an article is ''lost'' and ''found'' within a hotel or motel premises, a question arises as to its ownership. (*See* 12:23) The purpose of the following sections is to acquaint the innkeeper with the legal principles applicable to lost property and to give him legal guidance for handling lost property.

12:23   *Title to Lost or Misplaced Personal Property*

At common law the finder acquired a right to a found article good against the whole world except the true owner. Among the questions that developed in this area of the law was whether an article had been *lost, mislaid,* or *abandoned.* Property is never ''lost'' unless the owner parts with it unintentionally and does not at any time thereafter know where to find it. Mislaid property is that which the owner voluntarily and intentionally lays down in a place where he can find it again, but which he then forgets. Abandoned property is that which the owner voluntarily discards with no intention of reclaiming. The law requires that title to the article must be in someone and as a practical matter, the finder, whether he is an employee or a stranger to the hotel, and the innkeeper on whose premises the property was found will each insist that he or she has title.

Except where a statute otherwise provides, title to lost or mislaid property remains with the true owner. But the true owner may never become known. Thus it is important to determine who is entitled to possession. The answer to this question may depend on the place where the property is found, that is, whether in a private room or public place within the hotel. As a rule, a guest room in a hotel is considered to be a private rather than a public space, and the innkeeper rather than the finder is entitled to the possession of articles found therein. On the other hand, lobbies, dining rooms, ballrooms, function rooms, halls and the like, to which the public has access, have been held public places. The cases generally hold that the finder, that is, the person who first discovers and takes possession, is entitled to articles found in public places. The right to mislaid property is generally held to be in the owner of the premises where the property is found.

12:24   *Statutes and Local Ordinances Governing Lost and Found Property*

Most states have enacted statutes or authorized municipalities to adopt local ordinances that require finders to report found property and deposit the property in a designated public place, usually the local police department.

The New York statute abolishes the distinction between lost and mislaid property, treats all such property as lost, and excepts only "instruments" (documents of title, such as checks, notes, drafts, warehouse receipts, stock certificates, bonds, and insurance policies, which need not be deposited with the police and which, if negotiable, may be transferred to others who acquire full ownership rights) from the definition of property. If the property exceeds ten dollars in value, it must be returned to the owner, if known; if unknown, to the police department. Failure to return it or turn it over to the police is a misdemeanor. The police will issue a receipt for the property and are required to hold it for a prescribed period of time, depending on the value of the property. If the property remains unclaimed after that period of time, the finder obtains both title and possession, even against the true owner.

A finder who is an employee will relieve himself of further responsibility by turning the property over to the innkeeper. The finder is normally provided a reasonable grace period, ten days under the New York City ordinance, to locate the owner so that the owner may reclaim the item before it is delivered to the police. To avoid possible adverse claims between employees and innkeepers, all employees should be required by the terms of their employment contract to turn over to the innkeeper all property found within the hotel, no matter where found, and to waive any rights they might otherwise claim as finders.

A finder is guilty of larceny if, without taking reasonable steps to return such property to the owner, he intentionally exercises control over the property of another which he knows to be lost or mislaid or to have been delivered because of a mistake about the identity of the recipient or the nature or amount of the property. The New York Penal Law defining larceny is representative of penal statutes in most states on this subject.

The prudent innkeeper should acquaint himself with the legal mandates governing the disposition of lost or mislaid property, not only as a matter of good will, but to avoid the civil and criminal penalties that may otherwise be invoked.

The companion problem of how to dispose of unclaimed guest property has also been the subject of statutory regulation. For example, section 207 of the New York General Business Law authorizes the sale at public auction of unclaimed articles held for a period of six months. Care must be exercised to determine whether such property is in fact abandoned property, since a mistake may render such a sale violative of the property rights of the guest. The New York case described below illustrates the severe consequences that may follow a sale of property which was not abandoned.

In *Dajkovich v. Hotel Waldorf Astoria Corporation*,[75] plaintiff deposited fifteen pieces of baggage with defendant's hotel. Some five years later, a friend of

---

[75]285 A.D. 421, 137 N.Y.S.2d 764 (1st Dep't 1955), *aff'd mem.*, 309 N.Y. 1005, 133 N.E.2d 456 (1956).

plaintiff called at the hotel to inquire about the baggage and was told that it was still within the hotel intact and in good order and that it would be held until plaintiff's return. Within two months after such assurance and promise, defendant sold the baggage at public auction, pursuant to section 207, in the mistaken belief that it was abandoned by plaintiff. In an action by plaintiff for the conversion of the baggage, the court held for plaintiff, stating:

> Section 201 affords an innkeeper a limited liability, under certain circumstances, for the "loss of or damage to" a guest's property. There was no "loss" or "damage" in this case, and no misadventure of the kind which is contemplated by the statute. There was a sale and disposition of plaintiff's property as the voluntary, intentional and deliberate act of defendant as a matter of claimed right under section 207 of the General Business Law. This section of the law prescribes an innkeeper's rights under certain circumstances, in which defendant purported to act, and affords its own defined protection. The issue litigated at the trial was whether defendant was entitled, on the facts disclosed, to the protection of this statute. It has been held, and we affirm, that defendant did not bring itself within the statute and is, therefore, liable in conversion for its unlawful act.
>
> We think there is no room for section 201 of the General Business Law then to come into play. It was not the contemplation of that section of the law to limit an innkeeper's liability for its own misappropriation of a guest's property, albeit without *animus furandi,* and to give the innkeeper a secondary protection of limited liability in those cases in which it has failed in its assertion of right under section 207.

In selling unclaimed property, extreme caution must be used to comply strictly with the requirements of the appropriate statute. In every case, the property in question must be held for the minimum period of time specified. Local counsel should be consulted to ascertain whether any additional holding period is required.

12:25 *Internal Procedure for Handling Lost and Found Property*

Every hotel or motel should have a proper system for handling lost and found property. All employees should be instructed to deliver articles found by them or turned in to them by a patron to a designated responsible person or office, *promptly.* A record should be made in a lost and found record book of the date, the place where found, the description of the article, the name of the finder, and, if found in a guest room, the name and address of the last occupant, together with any appropriate "remarks." The article should be deposited in a safe place, presumably in the hotel safe, until claimed by the owner or until delivered to the police according to law. Prompt efforts should be made to ascertain the owner.

FLAX v. MONTICELLO REALTY CO.
185 Va. 474, 39 S.E.2d 308 (1946)

[Plaintiff was a guest in defendant's hotel, the Monticello Hotel in Norfolk, Va. Immediately prior to checking out, he noticed on the dresser in his room something wrapped in tissue paper. Upon examination, it contained a pear-shaped brooch, which plaintiff supposed at first sight to be a piece of worthless costume jewelry. Plaintiff took the article to the suite of some friends in the hotel, and later in the evening, at the suggestion of one of them, to a jeweler who appraised it as a genuine diamond brooch worth between $3,750.00 and $4,000.00.

The jewel was thereafter delivered to the hotel manager for custody until it should be called for by the true owner. Plaintiff called several times to ascertain if the owner had made claim for it and when he found that no such claim was asserted, he made demand for the jewelry. Upon refusal, he commenced this action. The jury returned a verdict for plaintiff which was set aside by the court as contrary to law and the evidence.

Investigation revealed the fact that the maid who was employed at the hotel, upon dismantling the bed in plaintiff's room, thinking that plaintiff was about to check out found the brooch wrapped in tissue paper, in the crevice of the margin of the mattress. In accordance with the hotel instructions and custom, as plaintiff occupant of the room had not actually departed, she placed the article on the bureau, on the supposition that it belonged to him.

It was plaintiff's contention (1) that the brooch was abandoned property and that he, as finder, was entitled to keep it as against everyone, except the true owner; (2) that his delivery of the brooch to the hotel manager constituted a bailment and that his bailee was estopped to deny his bailor's right to the possession of the brooch.]

BROWNING, J., delivered the opinion of the court: " . . . As to the contention that the brooch was abandoned property, the observation of the learned trial judge is sufficient to refute it. [The court quoted from the opinion of the trial judge, as follows:]

" 'It is contrary to human experience that the owner of a $3,750.00 brooch would place it in a mattress in a hotel room and intentionally leave it there because of a desire no longer to possess it. On the other hand, the probability is so strong as to amount to proof that it was left at the hotel room as a result of inadvertence. Failure of the owner to make claim for it may be explained by a number of hypotheses more reasonable than that of voluntary abandonment.'

" . . . The plaintiff in this case was not the finder of the jewel. He appropriated it and claimed it as his own. We may say at this time that the maid made no claim for it and does not do so. The claimant by mere coincidence found himself in an advantageous position to assert some sort of right thereto.

"In the adjudications which we have found a very controlling circumstance as to the rightful authority and custody of the article is the control over the *locus in quo* in which the thing is found. The *locus in quo* here is, of course, a private room in the hotel of the defendant.

"This court said in the case of *Crosswhite v. Shelby Operating Corp.*, 182 Va. 713, 30 S.E. (2d) 673, 153 A.L.R. 573: 'An innkeeper (as distinguished from a landlord) is in direct and continued control of his guest rooms.'

"Some of the cases have held that where money and bonds and packages of bills have been found in such public places as lobbies, dining rooms, halls and the like, to which the public has access, the finder is entitled to the property found, as against everyone except the rightful owner, but a private room in a hotel or an inn is a very different *locus in quo*. As to mislaid or forgotten property, which, we think this unquestionably was, the innkeeper, as the custodian, owed the duty to the owner of the chattel. He is treated in some of the cases as representing the owner and has the paramount custody, notwithstanding any agreement as that alleged. . . .

"The plaintiff in the case before us urged the contention that the defendant was his bailee and was thus estopped to deny his bailor's right to the possession of the brooch. . . .

"If the rule of law on the subject of bailment is present at all, it is found in the fact that the defendant occupied the position as bailee, *in invitum,* for the true owner of the chattel, and if it made the agreement alleged, it would constitute a breach of trust and would have been unenforceable.

" . . . A very pertinent excerpt is found in a passage in Pollack and Wright's Essay on Possession in the Common Law. . . . '[T]he general principle seems to me to be that where a person has possession of house or land, with a manifest intention to exercise control over it and the things which may be upon or in it, then, if something is found on that land, whether by an employee of the owner or by a stranger, the presumption is that the possession of the thing is in the owner of the *locus in quo*.'

"The plaintiff, Flax, has no legal standing as a claimant to the brooch. Were he successful in his claim, in Biblical language, he would reap where he has not sown and would gather where he has not strawed, an abhorrent thought."

[Judgment affirmed.]

JACKSON v. STEINBERG

186 Or. 129, 200 P.2d 376 (1948), *reh'g denied,* 186 Or. 140, 205 P.2d 562 (1949)

[Action by Laura I. Jackson against Karl Steinberg, doing business as the Arthur Hotel, for money had and received. From an adverse judgment, defendant appeals. Reversed. The plaintiff, Mrs. Jackson, was employed by defendant innkeeper, as chambermaid in his hotel. On December 30, 1946, while cleaning one of the guest rooms, she found eight one-hundred dollar bills, U.S. currency, concealed under the paper lining of a dresser drawer. The bills were stacked neatly and her attention was drawn to them only by reason of their bulk having made a slight bulge in the lining. She removed the bills and delivered them immediately to the manager of the hotel, in order that they might be restored to the true owner, if he could be found, and subject to her claims as finder.

Defendant made an unsuccessful attempt to discover the true owner of the bills, by communicating, by mail, with each of the persons who had occupied this particular room from mid-October through December 31, 1946. Plaintiff then demanded of defendant that he return the money to her as finder, but he refused. This action for money had and received followed. Defendant's affirmative defense was that as innkeeper, he is required, both at common law and by the Oregon statute, to hold the bills as bailee for the rightful owner. Defendant's theory is that the bills constitute mislaid property, presumed to have been left in the room by a former guest of the hotel, and that, as innkeeper, he is entitled to custody of the bills and bound to hold them as bailee for the true owner. Plaintiff, on the other hand, claims the right to possession of the bills as treasure trove, as against all persons but the true owner.]

HAY, J. [after recital of facts]: "Lost property is defined as that with the possession of which the owner has involuntarily parted, through neglect, carelessness, or inadvertence. [Citation omitted.] It is property which the owner has unwittingly suffered to pass out of his possession, and of the whereabouts of which he has no knowledge. [Citation omitted.]

"Mislaid property is that which the owner has voluntarily and intentionally laid down in a place where he can again resort to it, and then has forgotten where he laid it. [Citations omitted.]

"Abandoned property is that of which the owner has relinquished all right, title, claim, and possession with the intention of not reclaiming it or resuming its ownership, possession or enjoyment. [Citations omitted.]

" 'Treasure trove consists essentially of articles of gold and silver, intentionally hidden for safety in the earth or in some secret place, the owner being unknown.' Brown, Personal Property, § 13. . . .

"From the manner in which the bills in the instant case were carefully concealed beneath the paper lining of the drawer, it must be presumed that the concealment was effected intentionally and deliberately. The bills, therefore, cannot be regarded as abandoned property. [Citation omitted.]

"With regard to the plaintiff's contention that the bills constituted treasure trove, it has been held that the law of treasure trove has been merged with that of lost goods generally, at least so far as respects the rights of the finder. [Citations omitted.]

"The natural assumption is that the person who concealed the bills in the case at bar was a guest of the hotel. Their considerable value, and the manner of their concealment, indicate that the person who concealed them did so for purposes of security, and with the intention of reclaiming them. They were, therefore, to be classified not as lost, but as misplaced or forgotten property [citation omitted], and the defendant, as occupier of the premises where they were found, had the right and duty to take them into his possession and to hold them as gratuitous bailee for the true owner. [Citations omitted.]

"The decisive feature of the present case is the fact that plaintiff was an employee or servant of the owner or occupant of the premises, and that, in discovering the bills and turning them over to her employer, she was simply performing the duties of her employment. She was allowed to enter the guest room solely in order to do her work as chambermaid, and she was expressly instructed to take to the desk clerk any mislaid or forgotten property which she might discover. . . .

"On this branch of the case, the terse comment of a distinguished text writer will suffice our own view: 'In those cases where the servants are hired to clean up premises it seems that there might well be held that in finding things in the course of such cleaning the found property should belong to the master on this ground alone.' Aigler, *Rights of Finders*, 21 Mich. L. Rev. 664, 681 [1923] (footnote).

"The position of the defendant in the case at bar is fortified by the fact that, as an innkeeper, he is under common law and statutory obligation in respect to the found bills. 'When a guest gives up his room, pays his bill, and leaves an inn without an intention of returning, the innkeeper's liability as such for the effects of the former guest left in his charge ceases, and he is liable thereafter merely as an ordinary bailee, either gratuitous or for hire, depending upon the circumstances.' 28 Am. Jur. *Innkeepers*, section 94. Our statute (section 55-203, O.C.L.A.), in effect when the facts of this case transpired, provides that, when baggage or property of a guest is suffered to remain in an inn or hotel after the relation of guest and innkeeper has ended, the innkeeper may, at his option, hold such property at the risk of such former guest.

"Where money is found in an inn on the floor of a room common to the public, there being no circumstances pointing to its loss by a guest, the finder, even if an employee of the innkeeper, is entitled to hold the money as bailee for the true owner. *Hamaker v. Blanchard* (90 Pa. 377, 35 Am. Rep. 664, 665). It would seem that, as to articles voluntarily concealed by a guest, the very act of concealment would indicate that such articles have not been placed 'in the protection of the house' (Brown, Personal Property, section 14), and so, while the articles remain concealed, the innkeeper ordinarily would not have the responsibility of a bailee therefor. Upon their discovery by the innkeeper or his servant, however, the innkeeper's responsibility and duty as bailee for the owner becomes fixed. . . .

"The plaintiff in the present case is to be commended for her honesty and fair dealing throughout the transaction. Under our view of law, however, we have no alternative other than to reverse the judgment of the lower court. It will be reversed accordingly."

[All concur.]

ERICKSON v. SINYKIN
223 Minn. 232, 26 N.W.2d 172 (1947)

[Action to determine the ownership of $760 in currency. Defendants were the owners and operators of the Kenesaw Hotel in Minneapolis. They employed plaintiff to decorate several rooms therein. In the course of his work, plaintiff found it necessary "to raise up a rug which was on the floor, and under this rug he found $760.00 in the form of thirty-three old twenty-dollar bills around which was wrapped a new one-hundred-dollar bill.''']

"Plaintiff reported his finding of this money to defendants, who informed him 'that they knew the true owner thereof, and that they would deliver said money' to the owner. Upon that representation, 'plaintiff delivered the money' so found to them. No evidence was offered at the trial that defendants knew who the true owner was or that they had made any effort to find him.''

[As conclusions of law, the court determined that plaintiff was entitled to the money. Defendants' motion to vacate and set aside the finding or for a new trial was denied, and judgment entered for plaintiff.]

OLSON, J.: "[After recital of facts] . . . We are limited in this action solely to a determination of the rights and remedies of the parties to the cause. The original owner is unknown. He has made no appearance and is not a party to the action. This is a proceeding in personam, not one in rem. Therefore, until the actual owner appears and establishes his ownership, there can be no final determination of his rights.

"When plaintiff found this money under the circumstances we have related, he thereby came into physical possession of it. While that possession was a qualified one, he nevertheless had immediate dominion over the money. This possession and dominion as to any third person, including defendants, was adequate to sustain his cause until his adversary showed a better right. . . .

"In the instant case, the trial judge, in passing upon defendants' motion for a new trial, carefully reconsidered the matter of whether the money had been 'abandoned or lost,' characterizing the situation as a 'serious question.' After such reconsideration, he—'reached the conclusion that it was a question of fact for the court to determine. . . . In reaching the conclusion that it was abandoned, the court has taken into consideration circumstances existing since the finding of the money, that is, that the real owner has not stepped forth and claimed it. There is no way of knowing beyond the eighteen-month period how long this money remained under the carpet. It appears to the court that it is a reasonably clear case of an abandonment of the money.'

"Defendants challenge this finding as not sustained by the evidence. They take the view that since they were operating a hotel they owed a duty to their guests to see to it that property overlooked or forgotten by such guests is taken care of by them until such guest shall appear and demand a return of it. The case most heavily relied upon is *Flax v. Monticello Realty Co.*, 185 Va. 474, 39 S.E. (2d) 308, and the cases there cited. . . .

"The facts here are clearly distinguishable from those in the *Flax* case. . . .

"Defendants have done nothing to find the actual owner. Instead, they cling to it upon the theory that their possession of it as hotel proprietors now and ever since obtaining it from plaintiff is sufficient to defeat his cause. If their representation to plaintiff was truthful, then in the language we have italicized, it was their duty to comply with [Minn. Stat. (1945) and M.S.A. § 622.11,] which provides: '*Every person who shall find lost property under circumstances which give him knowledge or means of inquiry as to the true owner,* who shall appropriate such property to his own use, or to the use of another person not entitled thereto, without having first made reasonable effort to find the owner and restore the property to him, shall be guilty of larceny.' (Italics supplied [by court].)

"The question whether the money found by plaintiff was abandoned by the person placing it in this peculiar and unusual hiding place is an important one. In a general sense, abandonment 'means the act of intentionally relinquishing a known right absolutely and without reference to any particular person or purpose.' 1 Am Jur., *Abandonment*, § 2. . . . Its characteristic element is the voluntary relinquishment of ownership so that thereby the property subject to such ownership becomes the subject of appropriation by the one who thereafter first takes it. *Id.* § 3. . . . While mere lapse of time does not in and of itself establish abandonment, it nevertheless is of persuasive importance on the question of the former owner's intention. *Id.* § 8. . . . And, since his intention is the important element to be considered, all relevant facts and circumstances may be shown, and considerable latitude is allowed in the taking of testimony. Generally, it is not necessary to support such a claim that there be any expressed declaration on the part of the former owner; rather, it may be inferred from the situation of the property and the conduct of the person who has placed it so as to lead to the conclusion that it has been abandoned. . . . While . . . lapse of time and nonuser may not be conclusive, such facts are competent evidence of an intent to abandon and in many instances 'are entitled to great weight when considered with other circumstances' shown in the particular case. *Id.* § 15. . . .

"Initially, this money was neither lost nor abandoned. It was purposely hidden, for reasons which seemed adequate to the possessor—no doubt to keep it out of sight of subsequent users of the room so that he might later come back and repossess it. As to the respective rights and remedies of the parties to this case (and they are the only parties presently involved), we are of the view that in either case plaintiff's rights are superior to defendants' claim. . . .

"In the light of adjudicated cases . . . we think that the question whether the money so found was abandoned or lost was a fact issue and that the evidence reasonably supports the conclusions reached by the trial court. A period of more than 15 years had elapsed since the time when our paper currency was changed until this money was found, and at least another two years have elapsed since then, yet no one claiming to be the actual owner has appeared. Defendants' silence and inactivity cannot be said to have been due to any excess of modesty on their part nor attributable to any good faith in their claimed interest in the original owner's rights. The judgment should be and is affirmed."

13 Exceptions and Limitations to Liability for Guest's Property

13:1 *Losses Chargeable to Guest*

The innkeeper is not liable for losses chargeable in any way to the guest himself. Thus the innkeeper is not liable for property of his guest stolen by the guest's own servant or roommate[1] or by one authorized by the guest to handle the goods.

Similarly, where the guest gives explicit directions as to the care of the goods, and the loss happens through following such directions, the innkeeper is not liable.

13:2 *Contributory Negligence of Guest*

The loss of goods is most commonly chargeable to the guest himself by reason of contributory negligence on the part of the guest. A guest cannot recover for the loss of his goods from an inn if his own negligence contributed to the loss. And the care required of the guest must not be such care as will cause him serious personal inconvenience; the innkeeper cannot call upon the guest seriously to inconvenience himself in such a matter.[2] A fortiori the guest cannot be called upon to run into danger.[3]

Whether the negligence of the guest did contribute to the loss is a question of fact,[4] and the burden of proof of this fact is on the innkeeper.[5] If the innkeeper might subsequently have avoided the effect of the guest's negligence but failed to do so, he cannot escape liability.[6]

In *Medawar v. Grand Hotel Company,*[7] the plaintiff sued the defendant innkeeper for the loss of certain jewelry. The plaintiff came to the inn and found it full, with the exception of one room which had been engaged in advance by another person. The plaintiff, however, was allowed to dress in the room and keep

---

[1]Calye's Case, 77 Eng. Rep. 520 (K.B. 1584).
[2]Maltby v. Chapman, 25 Md. 310 (1866).
[3]Jefferson Hotel Co. v. Warren, 128 F. 565 (2d Cir. 1904).
[4]Of course, the facts may be so clear that the court will decide the question without leaving it to the jury. Lanier v. Youngblood, 73 Ala. 587 (1883).
[5]Jefferson Hotel Co. v. Warren, 128 F. 563 (2d Cir. 1904).
[6]Watson v. Loughran, 112 Ga. 837, 38 S.E. 82 (1901) (discovered that the guest left door unlocked and yet did not lock it); Medawar v. Grand Hotel Company, [1891] 2 Q.B. 11 (C.A.).
[7][1891] 2 Q.B. 11(C.A.).

it until the arrival of the person who had engaged it. He went to the room, opened his bag, and took out a stand which contained various implements for the toilet and the jewelry which was lost and for which he sued. After he finished dressing, he went out, leaving the stand on the dressing table and the door of the room unlocked and left the inn to attend the races. While he was absent, the person who had engaged the room arrived, and, in order to clear the room for his occupancy, the stand with the plaintiff's other luggage was placed in the corridor, where it remained until the plaintiff's return that night. While the luggage was in the corridor, the jewelry was stolen. The High Court held that the innkeeper was not liable, but the court of appeals reversed the decision. On the point here under discussion Lord Esher, master of the rolls, remarked:

> [T]here was contributory negligence on the part of the plaintiff while the goods were in the room; but, when the defendants' servants went into the room and became aware of the plaintiff's negligence, they were bound to take reasonable care of the property. When they saw the negligence of the plaintiff they ought to have taken care not to be negligent themselves. If the jewellery was stolen while it was in the corridor, it was stolen not in consequence of the plaintiff's negligence, but by reason of the defendants' negligence.[8]

The negligence must, of course, have to do with the loss of the goods themselves, and evidence of careless conduct by the guest either before or after the time he was at the inn will not be received.[9]

It is obvious that the question is the same whether the owner of the goods is guest, boarder, or lodger, since contributory negligence will bar them all. The cases of all will therefore be considered together.

13.3 *Failure to Lock Door or Window*

In accordance with the general doctrine, it is a question of fact in each case whether a guest's failure to lock his door at night constitutes such negligence as to prevent him from recovering from the innkeeper the value of the goods stolen from his room; and it is a question for the jury unless the facts are so plain that the court will not leave it to the jury.

All the circumstances are to be considered by the jury in determining this fact: for instance, that the inn was a London inn, where bad characters might be expected to seek entry,[10] or that the valuable goods or money had been publicly displayed.[11]

Failure of the guest, after locking the door, to bolt it, when he did not see the bolt or have it called to his attention, is so clearly not contributory negligence

---

[8]*Id.* at 22.

[9]Burrows v. Trieber, 21 Md. 320 (1864).

[10]Filipowski v. Merryweather, 175 Eng. Rep. 1063 (Nisi Prius 1860).

[11]Oppenheim v. White Lion Hotel Co., L.R. 6 C.P. 515 (1871); Dunbier v. Day, 12 Neb. 596, 12 N.W. 109 (1882).

that the court will not allow the jury to pass on the question, but will direct the jury that such failure will not defeat the action.[12]

Where the guest saw the bolts, failure to use them was relied on as one element of negligence to bar his recovery.[13] Failure to notify the innkeeper that the lock is out of repair is not negligence on the part of the guest.[14]

COHEN v. JANLEE HOTEL CORP.

276 App. Div. 67, 92 N.Y.S.2d 852 (1st Dep't 1949)

rev'd mem., 301 N.Y. 736, 95 N.E.2d 410 (1950)

[Anna Cohen sued the Janlee Hotel Corporation for damages for loss of plaintiff's coat from a room that plaintiff occupied as a guest in defendant's hotel].

DORE, J.: "By the determination of Appellate Term appealed from, affirming judgment in plaintiff's favor after nonjury trial in the Municipal Court, defendant has been held liable in damages for loss of plaintiff's Persian Lamb fur coat from the room she occupied as a guest in defendant's hotel. The trial court granted plaintiff judgment on the merits for $250 and judgment with interest and costs was entered in plaintiff's favor for $315.75.

"At common law an innkeeper was liable as an insurer of the property of guests lost by the theft unless the loss was occasioned by the negligence or fault of the guest. [Citations omitted.]

"Plaintiff admitted that on January 27, 1946, at 10:00 P.M. she undressed in her hotel room, suite 1206, and went to bed leaving the door of her room unlocked. She deliberately left the door unlocked so as to avoid the inconvenience of getting up to open the door for her girlfriend who shared the room with her and who was coming in later. Plaintiff had all the room lights lit and sat up in bed intending to read the papers while waiting for her friend, but later she fell asleep; and when she awoke about midnight, her Persian Lamb fur coat which she had in the closet of the room had disappeared.

"The hotel is a large metropolitan hotel, to the corridors of which thousands of persons necessarily have access. Defendant's evidence showed that there were 1,500 rooms in the hotel, accommodating about 2,300 guests at night; that in the month in question there was a check-out of 300 or 400 guests a day; that several thousand persons passed through the hotel during an average business day and ten or fifteen hundred persons used the ballrooms in the hotel; and that all of such persons had access to all the floors in the hotel. The hotel employed sixteen officers, seven in plain clothes and nine in uniform, and the latter patrolled the floors and observed hotel room doors after midnight; and if doors were found unlocked the guests were requested to lock them, and in the absence of the guest the doors are locked by the house officer.

"The action was for breach of contract of bailment, but there was no proof of bailment. The fur coat at the time of the loss was in plaintiff's room and in plain-

[12]Spring v. Hager, 145 Mass. 186, 13 N.E. 479 (1887).

[13]Hulbert v. Hartman, 79 Ill. App. 289 (1898).

[14]Lanier v. Youngblood, 73 Ala. 587 (1883).

tiff's exclusive custody and control. [Citation omitted.] Under the circumstances disclosed, plaintiff in failing to take the simple ordinary precaution of locking the door of her room before she went to bed when she knew she had in the room a valuable fur coat, acted in a manner that facilitated the theft and was guilty of contributory negligence; on this record such negligence was at least a contributing cause of the loss. [Citation omitted.]

"In supplemental briefs requested by the court, both parties concede that Section 201 of the General Business Law is not herein applicable.

"Accordingly, we vote to reverse the determination of the Appellate Term and the judgment of the Municipal Court and to dismiss the complaint."

SHIENTAG, J. (concurring in result): "I concur in the result and vote for reversal and dismissal of the complaint on the ground that the implied finding of the trial court that the plaintiff was free from contributory negligence is against the weight of the evidence."

COHN and CALLAHAN, JJ. (dissenting): "Whether there was contributory negligence was a question of fact for the trial court. As there was sufficient evidence to sustain the findings of the trial court to the effect that plaintiff was not guilty of contributory negligence, we vote to affirm the determination of the Appellate Term."

[The court of appeals reversed the appellate division on the ground that the question as to plaintiff's contributory negligence was one of fact and not of law and remitted the case to the appellate division for determination upon the questions of fact raised in that court. Thereupon the appellate division made the order and judgment of the court of appeals its own order and judgment, and reversed the determination of the appellate term and the judgment of the municipal court, and dismissed the complaint.]

13:4   *Failure to Deliver Valuables to Innkeeper*

In the absence of special circumstances, it is not negligence to leave goods in a public room in the inn, if it is with the assent of the innkeeper or his servants, even though the innkeeper informed the guest that the goods would be safer elsewhere. Thus where the goods were left in the lobby of the inn and were lost, the innkeeper was liable.[15]

Where, however, the guest's act is not expressly permitted by the innkeeper, though known to him, the question of liability is for the jury. Thus where the guest laid down a valuable pair of gloves on a bench in a public room in the presence of the innkeeper, and they were lost, the question of contributory negligence might be determined by the jury.[16]

The fact that a custom exists to deposit valuables with the innkeeper does not render the guest negligent for not doing so, if the custom was unknown to him. If he knew of it, though, it might be negligent for him to fail to comply with it.[17]

[15]Clarke v. Hotel Taft Corp., 128 N.Y.L.J. No. 53, 478 (N.Y. City Ct. 1952).
[16]Read v. Amidon, 41 Vt. 15 (1868).
[17]Berkshire Woollen Co. v. Proctor, 61 Mass. (7 Cush.) 417 (1851).

Where, however, the guest has express notice that he takes the risk of loss if he does not deposit his valuables with the innkeeper, he is negligent if he fails to comply with the notice.[18] So where the guest asked if the goods would be safe in his room and was told he must leave them at the bar, but notwithstanding this warning he kept them in his room and they were lost, he was barred from recovery by his negligence.[19]

The notice, in order to impose the risk of loss upon the guest, must be clear. In a New York case, a notice saying that packages of value may be deposited in the office safe and cautioning guests against leaving money or valuables in a guest's room was held insufficient to put the risk of loss of goods left in the room upon a guest:

This may very well have been understood, as Forbes appears to have understood it, as merely cautioning him against leaving money or valuables loose or exposed about his room. If the landlord, to enable him the more effectually to secure the property, requires something to be done by the guest, it must appear that what was required was in itself reasonable, and that the guest was distinctly informed of what was necessary to be done on his part. Whether the request was made orally or in the form of a printed notice, it should be in terms so clear and unmistakable as to leave room for no reasonable doubt as to what was intended. The traveller should know precisely what he is to do before he can be chargeable with negligence for not doing it; and as the notice did not apprize him that he was not to leave money locked up in his trunk, he cannot be regarded as guilty of negligence in so leaving it.[20]

13:5 *Failure to Inform Innkeeper of Value of Goods Deposited*

In the absence of statutory requirement, it is not negligence to fail to inform the innkeeper that a package put into his possession or that of his servants contains valuables.[21] This common-law rule has been modified by innkeepers' liability statutes, which place the burden of declaring valuables either on the guest, as does New York, or on the innkeeper, as does Virginia. The New York statute is explicit on this point, whereas the Virginia statute has been interpreted to impose this responsibility on the innkeeper.

13:6 *Publicly Exhibiting Money or Valuables*

Opening or counting one's money or exhibiting valuable goods in a public place is not of itself such negligence as will bar recovery by the guest,[22] but it is one of the circumstances to be considered by the jury, which may find the act

---

[18]Jalie v. Cardinal, 35 Wis. 118 (1874).

[19]Wilson v. Halpin, 30 How. Pr. 124 (N.Y. Ct. C.P. 1865).

[20]Van Wyck v. Howard, 12 How. Pr. 147, 150–51 (N.Y. Ct. C.P. 1856).

[21]Sagman v. Richmond Hotels, Inc., 138 F. Supp. 407 (E.D. Va. 1956); Stoll v. Almon C. Judd Co., 106 Conn. 551, 138 A. 479 (1927); Fowler v. Dorlon, 24 Barb. 384 (N.Y. Sup. Ct. 1856).

[22]Dunbier v. Day, 12 Neb. 596, 12 N.W. 109 (1882); Cunningham v. Bucky, 42 W. Va. 671, 26 S.E. 442 (1896).

negligent.[23] In *Armistead v. Wilde*,[24] the plaintiff was a guest at an inn and had lost from a box which he brought to the inn a parcel containing several hundred pounds in bank notes. Upon the facts being examined, the evidence showed that the plaintiff had boasted of the sum he possessed and had ostentatiously rolled up the notes and put them in the box in the travelers' room in the presence of several persons. He had then left the box in the travelers' room, imperfectly secured. One of the persons to whom the plaintiff had shown the notes was probably the thief. The judge directed the jury to find a verdict for the defendant if they thought the plaintiff "had been guilty of gross negligence in leaving the money in the travellers' room"; and the jury accordingly found a verdict of not guilty. The plaintiff had the temerity to move for a new trial on the ground of misdirection, but the rule was discharged. Lord Chief Justice Campbell said:

> Suppose a guest were to count out his money and leave it lying loose on the table of the public room; surely that might be such gross negligence as to be the cause of the loss. The facts here do not go so far as that; but there was evidence that the plaintiff's servant, in a public room, took out a large sum of money, counted it and shewed it, and then left it there in a box capable of being opened without using a key. These facts might or might not amount to negligence; but they were evidence of it; and it was a fair question for the jury.[25]

13:7 *Intoxication of Guest*

Intoxication of the guest is not in itself contributory negligence, but if it contributes in any way to the loss, it bars the recovery.

CUNNINGHAM v. BUCKY
42 W. Va 671, 26 S.E. 442 (1896)

[Appeal from a judgment for $254.00 obtained by plaintiff against defendant in the Circuit Court of Randolph County.]

DENT, J.: "Plaintiff went to the defendant's hotel, called the 'Valley Hotel,' to stop for a few days at the most. His home was in Virginia. . . . On this occasion, he had received payment of a draft; was drinking, and slightly intoxicated; exhibited his money freely; was arrested, fined, and paid the same. Mrs. Bucky, during the day, asked him to let her take charge of his money. This he declined to do, saying he was able to take care of his own money. . . . He examined his pocketbook, to see that his money was in it, then placed it down in his coat pocket, and hung his coat on the bedpost, and retired for the night. On awakening in the morning, he noticed the pocketbook had been disturbed, and, on examining it, found his money gone. He got up, went out, found the . . . porter, and acquainted Mr. Bucky with his loss. . . .

---

[23]Cashill v. Wright, 119 Eng.Rep. 1096 (Q.B. 1856); Armistead v. Wilde, 117 Eng. Rep. 1280 (Q.B. 1851).
[24]117 Eng. Rep. 1280 (Q.B. 1851).
[25]*Id.* at 1281.

"It is plainly evident who committed this theft [the court recited testimony indicating that defendant's . . . porter was the thief]; and the sole question is, on whom does the law fix the loss? We have no statute on the subject, and must be governed by the common law. . . .

"There is no question that the plaintiff was a guest at the defendant's hotel, and that while there he was robbed in his room while asleep, from within the defendant's family, including his servants. That he had been drinking, was careless with his money and trusted in the honesty of defendant's household, and refused the services of Mrs. Bucky as to the care of his money, will not excuse the defendant from the dishonesty of those admitted to his employment. . . . As Judge Dixon says in *Jalie v. Cardinal,* above cited [35 Wis. 118 (1874)]: 'If drunk, the plaintiff might still have claimed the protection of his host, as did Falstaff when he fell asleep "behind the arras," and might say with him: "Shall I not take mine ease in mine inn, but I shall have my pocket picked?"' ' . . . "

[Judgment affirmed.]

In *Shultz v. Wall,*[26] plaintiff sued for the loss of money which had been stolen while he was a guest in defendant's hotel. It appeared that plaintiff was assigned to a room on the door of which was a lock with the key upon the inside, and also an inside sliding bolt. A notice was printed at the head of each sheet of the hotel register, which read as follows: "Money, jewelry and other valuables must be placed in the safe. . . . Otherwise the proprietor will not be responsible for loss." Defendant claimed to have called plaintiff's attention to this notice.

Plaintiff testified that he both locked and bolted his bedroom door before retiring, but that the next morning he found it standing partially open. Plaintiff's vest was found downstairs carefully folded and laid between two lap blankets on the hat rack in the dining room with the pocket book and everything intact, but the money gone. There was some testimony that plaintiff, though a sober man, was not a total abstainer, and had been drinking that evening. The trial court refused to submit the question of plaintiff's contributory negligence to the jury. On appeal, the ruling of the trial court was reversed, and a new trial granted: "[I]t is now held in our own case of *Walsh v. Porterfield* [87 Pa. 376 (1878)] that intoxication is no excuse for the negligence of a guest which contributes to his loss."[27]

13:8 *Loss Caused by Act of God*

In *Wolf Hotel Co. v. Parker,*[28] plaintiff was a long-term guest in defendant's hotel. Defendant had stored several of plaintiff's trunks containing a quantity of clothing in a basement room of the hotel. One July evening there was a heavy rainfall, which caused the water from the streets and alleys in the vicinity of the

[26]134 Pa. 262, 19 A. 742 (1890).
[27]*Id.* at 275, 19 A. at 744.
[28]87 Ind. App. 333, 158 N.E. 294 (1927).

hotel to back up into the basement of the hotel and into the room where the trunks were stored, thus damaging the clothing.

In an action to recover for the damages sustained, the complaint alleged that defendant was negligent in not having traps, valves, or shutoffs installed in the sewer and drain system of the hotel to prevent the street sewer from flooding the basement. The complaint also alleged that defendant was negligent in that it knew that its basement had been flooded several times previously and yet with such knowledge had placed plaintiff's trunks on the floor of the basement, where they were damaged.

Defendant contended that the flood was an act of God against which it could not guard with reasonable precaution; that defendant was merely a gratuitous bailee; and that the damage was due to plaintiff's failure to open her trunk after the flood and unpack her apparel.

The trial court instructed the jury, *inter alia*, that an act of God which would excuse defendant from liability must not only be a proximate cause of the loss, but must also be the sole cause thereof; that if the damage was caused by an act of God commingled with the negligence of defendant and would not have occurred except for such negligence, defendant would be liable, unless plaintiff was contributorily negligent; "that if [defendant] knew, or by reasonable diligence could have known, the hotel basement flooded after heavy rainfall, and took no steps to prevent it by placing the usual and common devices to prevent such flooding, or if it placed the trunk of [plaintiff] on the basement floor with such knowledge, and that such devices would have prevented the overflow of the basement, the fact that there was an unusual rainfall would be no defense"; and that it made no difference whether plaintiff was a guest or a roomer, if the damage was caused by defendant's negligence.

After a judgment entered upon a jury verdict for plaintiff, defendant appealed. The appeals court affirmed the lower court's decision. There was no error in any of the instructions.

The term *act of God*, used to express the cause of loss or damage which will exonerate the innkeeper from all liability for the guest's property, means some casualty resulting from natural or physical causes without the intervention of any human agency. Thus losses caused by lightning, earthquake, frost, rain, snowstorms, tornadoes, freezing of canals and rivers, floods, and the like are due to acts of God.

The terms *inevitable accident* and *irresistible force* are sometimes used as synonymous with *act of God*, but they lack the suggestion that the loss may be due to causes other than those of human agency, and are, therefore, unsatisfactory. *Inevitable accident* includes *act of God*, but the term *inevitable accident* is not equivalent to *act of God*, because inevitable accident, such as incendiary or accidental fire, robbery, theft, etc., may be due solely to human agency.

It has been said that the act of God must have been the proximate cause of the loss. If there has been any intervention of a human agency, the innkeeper is not excused. The true test for an act of God seems to be the entire absence of any human agency in producing the loss.

13:9   *Loss Caused by Acts of the "Public Enemy"*

JOHNSTON V. MOBILE HOTEL CO.
27 Ala. App. 145, 167 So. 595 (1936), *cert. denied,*
232 Ala. 175, 167 So. 596 (1936)

[Action for loss of property by R. P. Johnston against the Mobile Hotel Company, Inc. From a judgment for defendant, plaintiff appeals.]

RICE, J.: "Appellant was, admittedly, a guest of the hotel; he testified that, while such guest, he was 'held up and robbed,' at the point of a gun, by two men, of the money and valuables on account of the loss of which he sues.

"Both parties submit that the decisive question in the case is 'whether or not an innkeeper . . . is liable at common law for a loss of money and valuables . . . of his guest, occasioned by *robbery* within the inn, without negligence on the part of the innkeeper or his responsible agents.' . . .

"The phrase 'public enemy' is universally understood to mean some power with whom the government is at open war. It does not include robbers. [Citations omitted.] . . .

"If appellant's testimony is to be believed, it is plain that his loss was neither caused by an 'act of God' nor by 'his own act.' And since we have declared a 'robber' not to be included in the phrase 'public enemy,' it appears that appellant is entitled to recover—should the jury believe his testimony. [Citation omitted.]

"Reversed and remanded."

13:10   *Statutory Limitations of Liability: In General*

All American jurisdictions have enacted statutes limiting the liability of innkeepers for the property of guests. These statutes vary considerably from state to state in both their coverage and their requirements. A discussion of the general principles underlying these statutes follows, with examples from several jurisdictions. However, given the disparate provisions of various statutes, this discussion cannot substitute for reference to the statutes of one's own state. The Hawaii innkeeper's statute (Hawaii Revised Statutes, Chapter 486K, Rights and Liabilities of Hotel Keepers and Guests), reenacted in 1978, serves as a model act. It appears as Appendix A to this chapter. Appendix B is a list of limitation of liability statutes for the fifty states and the District of Columbia as well as for Guam, Puerto Rico, and the Virgin Islands.

13:11   *Limited Liability for Money and Valuables*

In New York the statute limiting the innkeeper's liability was first enacted in 1855. As modified and amended, it is now part of the General Business Law. Separate sections relate to money and valuables, to personal property other than money and valuables, to property in transit to and from the hotel, and to property destroyed by fire. No section of the law limits the liability of a discotheque owner for the loss of patrons' property.[29]

Most statutes follow New York's pattern of treating money and valuables separately from other types of property because valuables create a greater likelihood of excess liability for the innkeeper and thus require special treatment.

The federal Court of Appeals for the Ninth Circuit, applying Nevada law, held that a jewelry salesman who checked his sample case with a hotel was a guest for purposes of being bound by the Nevada innkeeper's statute limiting liability for loss of valuables to $750.

PACHINGER V. MGM GRAND HOTEL—LAS VEGAS
802 F.2d 363 (9th Cir. 1986)

FARRIS, C.J.: " . . .

" . . . [W]e must first determine whether § 651.010 applies to Pachinger. Section 651.010(2) states that where a hotel provides a safe deposit box and notice of this service either is personally given to a guest or is posted in the office and the guest's room, the hotel is not liable for property not offered for deposit unless the hotel was grossly negligent. Appellant was personally given notice of the existence of the safe deposit box service when he checked his bags and received in return a claim check stating that the hotel assumed only limited liability for checked baggage and that a safe deposit box service for valuables was available in the hotel. Thus, in Pachinger's case, proper notice under § 651.010 was effected.

"Appellant contends, however, that he was not a guest at the time he received his claim check, and that § 651.010 is therefore inapplicable to him. We disagree. Pachinger behaved as a guest of the hotel and made use of the baggage check service provided specifically for guests of the hotel. As the district court properly remarked, 'the legal relationship of innkeeper and guest was established at the time plaintiff checked his luggage with the hotel and received his claim check containing the declaration of liability limitations. Order Granting Defendant's Motion to Dismiss, at 3, *Pachinger v. MGM Grand Hotel, Inc.*, (D. Nev. 1985). 618 F. Supp. 218. The district court did not err in holding that Pachinger was a guest and that, as a result, his recovery was limited by § 651.010 to $750. . . .

"Pachinger also raises the argument, not reached by the district court, that the claim check's limitation of liability is ineffective. We need not address this argument since we agree with the district court that § 651.010 is applicable. Because § 651.010 limits Pachinger's potential recovery to $750, the claim check's limitation on liability is immaterial.

"AFFIRMED."

[29]Conboy v. Studio 54, Inc., 113 Misc. 2d 403, 449 N.Y.S.2d 391 (Civ. Ct. 1982).

13:12　*Constitutionality of Statutory Limitations of Innkeeper Liability*

In two cases, set forth below, a state and a federal appellate court were confronted with a challenge of first impression as to the constitutionality of statutory enactments limiting the liability of innkeepers with respect to guest property. In the state action, the Colorado statute was sustained against the claims that it was a denial of due process to limit liability in derogation of the common-law rule of strict responsibility and that it was a denial of equal protection to sanction unlimited liability for personal injuries at common law and to enact legislation limiting liability for property losses, where both losses arose simultaneously out of the same criminal misconduct. The state court reasoned that the common law did not vest personal rights as a matter of constitutional law in perpetuity and that the legislature could alter common-law rights not explicitly protected by that state's constitution. Therefore no due process rights of the petitioners were violated. Nor was any constitutional denial of equal protection established, since there was no invidious discrimination and the statutory limitations enacted were rationally related to protecting the legitimate interests of innkeepers against excessive liability claims of guests.

In the federal case, the court held that there was no "state action" established because the legislation was permissive, not mandatory, and the innkeeper was free to increase his liability by special agreement with the guest. The court reasoned further that there was no delegation of state power to resolve private disputes, since the innkeeper "would have been free, without the statute, to limit its liability through its contract" with the guest.

State action in the constitutional sense is derived from the explicit language of the federal Constitution, which limits a constitutional remedy to actions of the states, not of private individuals or entities. Thus a finding of no state action means that there is no constitutional remedy for the court to apply. Absent any explicit state action, such as a legislative enactment, state action may be implied. Petitioners sought to establish such implied action by arguing that the legislature had delegated to innkeepers legislative authority to settle private disputes. The federal court rejected this argument by concluding that the innkeeper always had authority to limit his liability under his contract with his guests. (*But see* section 13:13, *infra*.)

PACIFIC DIAMOND CO., INC. V. SUPERIOR COURT
85 Cal. App. 3d 871, 149 Cal. Rptr. 813, *reh'g denied*, Dec. 20, 1978

FEINBERG, J.: " . . . Do sections 68-1-5 and 68-1-6, as herein construed, violate the due process and equal protection clauses of the Colorado Constitution or the Fourteenth Amendment to the Constitution of the United States?

"We hold that they do not.

"Preliminarily, we had occasion to question whether a California court has jurisdiction to rule upon the constitutionality of Colorado statutes. Petitioner has called two cases to our attention where state courts have ruled on the constitutionality of state legislation other than their own. . . . [Citations omitted.]

"No cases that we are aware of have held that a state court which has jurisdiction of a cause lacks jurisdiction to rule upon the constitutionality of a sister state statute when that is an issue raised in the cause.

"Since concededly we have jurisdiction and the constitutional issues have been raised reluctantly, and since we have no alternative, we address the issue of the constitutionality of the Colorado statutes in question.

"A. As to the due process argument, petitioner seems to argue that since at common law there was a cause of action based on unlimited strict liability of the innkeeper for the goods of his guests, it is violative of due process for a state to modify or abrogate this cause of action. It is not our understanding that the due process clause was intended to embalm as a constitutional principle common law causes of action any more than as Justice Holmes said, dissenting, in *Lochner v. New York* (1905) 198 U.S. 45, 74, 75, . . . the Fourteenth Amendment was intended to enact into constitutional law Mr. Herbert Spencer's Social Statistics. . . .

"The Colorado Supreme Court has had occasion to consider such a question in *O'Quinn v. Walt Disney Productions, Inc.* (1972) 177 Colo. 190 [493 P.2d 344]. At issue in *O'Quinn* was the Colorado workmen's compensation statutes which denied an employee of a subcontractor any relief, in tort, for the negligence of the general contractor or the owner of the land upon which the work was performed, relegating the employee to his workers' compensation benefits. The employee contended that insofar as the statutes deprived him of his common law action in tort against the general contractor and landholder, it deprived him of property without due process of law and of equal protection of the laws in violation of the Colorado and federal Constitutions. The court held:

"As to plaintiff's . . . [due process] argument, this court and others have many times considered whether or not the abrogation of a common law remedy constitutes a taking under Fifth and Fourteenth Amendments to the United States Constitution and article II, section 25 of the Colorado constitution. As a general proposition, courts have concluded that, so long as a statute in abrogation of the common law does not attempt to remove a right which has already accrued, there is no taking. [Citations omitted]; *Lowman v. Stafford*, 226 Cal. App. 2d 31, 37 Cal. Rptr. 681.

"In *Lowman, supra*, the court stated: 'Although rights of property which have been created by the common law cannot be taken away without due process, the law itself, as a rule of conduct, may be changed at will by the Legislature. . . . " . . . It may create new rights or provide that rights which have previously existed shall no longer arise, and it has full power to regulate and circumscribe the methods and means of enjoying those rights, so long as there is no interference with constitutional guarantees." ' (493 P.2d at p. 345.)

"At the time of the robbery, sections 68-1-5 and 68-1-6 had been in effect for many years; no common law right could have accrued in petitioner, it follows that petitioner's due process argument must fail.

"B. We address now the question of equal protection.

"We begin with an inquiry into the purposes of sections 68-1-5 and 68-1-6 and we shall conclude with an examination as to whether the sections rationally relate to that purpose. [Citation omitted.]

"It is clear that the purpose of sections 68-1-5 and 68-1-6 is to protect the hotel against unrestricted liability for articles of value belonging to a guest that can be conveniently stored in a safe or some similar secure receptable where the hotel doesn't even know that the guest has such valuables provided that the hotel makes available such a secure facility and posts notice to that effect. If the guest chooses not to avail himself of that secure facility, having notice thereof, it is surely not an unreasonable legislative decision to exculpate the hotel from any liability if the guest thereafter sustains the loss of or damage to those valuable articles. On the other hand, if the guest does place his valuables in the safe, if then there is loss or damage, the hotel is liable up to the value declared by the guest but not more than $5,000. Even in these days of inflation, $5,000 is not a minimal sum, as petitioner suggests, for such valuables as the ordinary hotel guest carries with him. In any event, we cannot say that such a limitation is irrational. In addition, section 68-1-6 permits the guest to seek a greater liability from the hotel if the hotel is willing to assume it.

"Further, if the hotel does not provide a safe or put the guest on notice that there is a safe available, then, as we read the statutes, under sections 68-1-11, there is unlimited liability either in negligence or on a theory of strict liability as to valuables that could be stored in a safe. In addition, there is unlimited liability for all other personal property of the guest.

"We need not examine all the permutations or combinations possible under the Colorado innkeeper statutes for it appears to us that the means employed by the Colorado Legislature to effectuate its legislative purpose are rationally related thereto.

"We conclude by noting that '[t]he prohibition of the Equal Protection Clause goes no further than the invidious discrimination. We cannot say that the point has been reached here.' (*Williamson v. Lee Optical Co.* (1955) 348 U.S. 483, 489). . . .

"Accordingly, insofar as the trial court held California law applicable in its order of November 3, 1977, the trial court is directed to set aside its order and the cause is remanded to the trial court for such further proceedings as may be appropriate and not inconsistent with views expressed herein. . . . ''

RUDISILL V. WESTERN INTERNATIONAL HOTELS CO.
601 F.2d 599 (7th Cir. 1979) (*without opinion*),
pet. for writ of cert. filed Aug. 28, 1979

Order

"Plaintiff appeals from the dismissal of his *pro se* civil rights suit under 42 U.S.C. § 1983 on the ground that the complaint failed to allege a deprivation of a constitutional right. We affirm.

I. Facts

"On checking out of defendant's hotel in Detroit, Michigan, plaintiff left a suitcase with the hotel for the day and received a claim check which states the hotel's undertaking to safeguard plaintiff's property. Plaintiff returned later that day and presented the claim check. Hotel employees informed plaintiff that his suitcase could not be found and it has never been recovered. Plaintiff presented a claim for the suitcase and its contents to defendant and its insurer in the amount of $669.30. Defendant and its insurer refused to pay plaintiff more than $250, relying on a Michigan statute which limits an innkeeper's liability for a guest's personal property to that amount. Mich. Comp. Laws § 424.101 (Mich. Stat. Ann. § 18.311 [Callaghan 1971]).

"Plaintiff then brought this action under 42 U.S.C. § 1983, alleging that his property was lost or stolen through defendant's negligence and in breach of its contract with him. The complaint alleges that defendant's refusal to pay the full value of that property deprived plaintiff of his property without due process and of equal protection of law. The district court granted the defendant's motion to dismiss, holding that the complaint failed to allege a deprivation of a right protected by the constitution.

II. Discussion

"A cause of action under § 1983 has two elements: (1) deprivation of a right 'secured by the Constitution and laws' of the United States, (2) by a person acting 'under color of any statute . . . of any state. . . . ' *Flagg Bros., Inc. v. Brooks,* 436 U.S. 149, 155 (1978); *Adickes v. Kress & Co.,* 398 U.S. 144, 150 (1970); *Sparkman v. McFarlin,* No. 76-1706, slip op. at 6–7 (7th Cir. May 2, 1979) (SPRECHER, J., concurring). The district court correctly held that plaintiff failed to allege the first element of such a cause of action.

"Plaintiff's due process claim is that defendant's refusal to pay more than $250 in reliance on the Michigan statute 'deprives plaintiff of his right to full compensation for injuries suffered due to defendant's tort and breach of contract.' Appellant's Br. at 7. While full compensation for injuries may be, at least colorably, a property right subject to Fourteenth Amendment protection [citations omitted], that protection extends only to deprivations by the states. *Flagg Bros., Inc. v. Brooks, supra,* 436 U.S. at 156–157. Thus the substantive constitutional rights asserted by plaintiff require 'state action.'

"Plaintiff contends that the complaint alleges state action in two ways. First, he contends that the Michigan statute compelled defendant to deny full compensation. The terms of the statute, however, contradict that contention. The statute expressly permits innkeepers to assume a greater liability for guests' property. The statute no more than authorizes or encourages the limitation of liability; it does not compel it. Thus, defendants [*sic*] conduct may not be described as state action on this theory. *Flagg Bros., supra,* 436 U.S. at 164–166. Second, plaintiff argues that the statute delegates to defendant the state's sov-

ereign power to resolve private disputes by allowing defendant to limit its liability. This argument has no merit because private dispute resolution is not an
exclusive governmental function. Here for example, defendant presumably
would have been free, without the statute, to limit its liability through its contract with plaintiff. *See Flagg Bros., supra,* at 160–163. Plaintiff argues that
Flagg Bros. is distinguishable on this point because there the Court, according
to plaintiff, stressed that alternative remedies existed under the New York statute
considered there. A careful reading of the Court's opinion shows that the decision is not based on alternative judicial remedies, but on the fact that private
dispute resolution 'is not traditionally an exclusive public function.' *Id.* at 161.
One of the alternatives 'stressed' by the Court was the possibility of changing
the result authorized by the statute through the parties' contract. As noted on the
compulsion issue above, the Michigan statute expressly provided that alternative
to plaintiff here. Thus *Flagg Bros.* is controlling on this point also.

"Since plaintiff has not alleged sufficient state action to show a deprivation
of a right protected under the Fourteenth Amendment, the district court correctly held his § 1983 due process claim insufficient. His equal protection claim
fails for the same reason.

"The judgment of the district court is affirmed."

A Nevada innkeeper statute limiting the recovery on guests' property loss to
$750 was upheld against an equal protection challenge in *Morris v. Hotel Riv-
iera, Inc.*[30] because the statute was reasonably designed to foster a legitimate
state interest in enhancing the tourist trade. The court noted that the statute reduced the possibility of fraudulent claims and properly considered the difficulties of preventing crimes related to personal property.

13:13 *Contractual Limitations of Liability for Guest's Property*

Like other persons engaged in a public employment—for instance, the common carrier—the innkeeper may not limit his liability for loss of the guest's
property by a contract with the guest. It is the necessity of the guest which leads
to the innkeeper's obligation to receive him. This same necessity puts the guest
at the mercy of the innkeeper; he must not be required to consent to the limitation of liability as a condition of his being received. The parties are not on an
equal footing, and public policy requires that the guest be protected from over-
reaching by the innkeeper. A contract for limitation of the innkeeper's liability,
therefore, will not be enforced by the courts as a matter of public policy.

In this connection, however, the defendant contends that the maximum amount of
the coverage is fixed in the amount of Twenty-five ($25) Dollars by the statement on
the reverse side of the check delivered to the plaintiff. Said statement is as follows:

---

[30] 704 F.2d 1113 (9th Cir. 1983).

"Hotel Biltmore
"Oklahoma City, Okla.
"Check Room
"Contract Releasing Liability

"In consideration of the receipt and free storage of the property (no value stated) for which this check is issued, it is agreed by the holder, in accepting this check, that the hotel shall not be liable for loss or damage to said property unless caused by negligence of the hotel, in which event only hotel shall be liable for a sum not to exceed $25.00. The hotel shall not in any event be liable for loss or damage to said property by fire, theft or moth, whether caused by its own negligence or otherwise. The hotel is authorized to deliver property to any person presenting this check without identification. Not responsible for articles left over 30 days." . . .

Such alleged contractual limitations upon liability in such bailment cases in this jurisdiction are contrary to public policy and void.[31]

In addition to such public policy considerations, the existence of statutes limiting liability has been held to preclude any contractual limitations by an innkeeper.[32]

In *Frockt v. Goodloc*,[33] the North Carolina Federal District Court held that the North Carolina innkeeper's statute was unavailable to limit liability for a hotel guest's loss of jewelry cases because the hotel had failed to post notices in compliance with the statute and, additionally, that its contractual disclaimer of liability was void as against public policy. The court also concluded that the guest's damage claim was limited to the actual market value of the jewelry and that lost profits were not recoverable because the proof was insufficient to warrant such an award.

13:14 *Common-Law Right of Innkeeper to Require Deposit of Property ("Rules of the Inn")*

Statutory schemes exist in every state to allow an innkeeper to limit his liability for the property of guests. However, it should be noted that, from the earliest times, the common law allowed an innkeeper to condition his liability for loss on the guest complying with reasonable rules which the innkeeper might require.

One Spencer, an innkeeper of Brodeway, was sued in an action upon the law and custom of the realm, by one Sanders, for a piece of cloth stolen out of the inn by some delinquents. And he for his excuse shewed that he gave warning to the plaintiff that he should lay his goods in packs in a certain chamber within the inn, under a lock and key provided for that purpose, and that if he would do so he would undertake to warrant them safe, otherwise not, but he, notwithstanding the said admonition, laid them in an outer court at large, where they were stolen by the default of the plaintiff himself, &c. upon which the plaintiff demurred in law. And the opinion of the Court was against the plaintiff.[34]

---

[31]Oklahoma City Hotel v. Levine, 189 Okla. 331, 333, 116 P.2d 997, 998–99 (1941).
[32]Hackney v. Southwest Hotels, 210 Ark. 234, 195 S.W.2d 55 (1946).
[33]670 F. Supp. 163 (W.D.N.C. 1987).
[34]Sanders v. Spencer, 73 Eng. Rep. 591 (Q.B. 1566).

Thus when the innkeeper placed the guest on notice that all valuables were required to be deposited in the hotel safe, a guest failing to do so could not hold the innkeeper liable for any loss.[35] Of course, such a requirement could be made only as to property which could conveniently be left in a safe, not to property that the guest needed to keep with him, such as clothing and articles of daily use.[36] Obviously, a guest must have these things with him in his room. He cannot go to the innkeeper's office every time he needs an article of clothing or a toothbrush. It is therefore not reasonable for an innkeeper to require the surrender of such items.

13:15 *Provision of Safes for Valuables*

Typically, limitation-of-liability statutes provide that an innkeeper must maintain a safe or vault for the deposit of guests' money and valuables. If he does so and posts notice as required by the statute, he will be relieved of liability should a guest fail to deposit.

Some jurisdictions (Iowa, for example) require the innkeeper to provide "a metal safe or vault, in good order and fit for the safekeeping of such property." Others, such as Arizona, require "a fireproof safe."

The safe or the deposit boxes should be located near the cashier's section in the front office so as to be accessible to and in full view of guests so that they may be eyewitnesses to every phase of the transactions involving their money or valuables. A separate vault room or enclosure, adjacent to the front office providing safety and privacy, is most desirable.

The New York statute specifies that a safe must be provided, but does not specify the type of safe. In the absence of a specific statutory mandate, most hotels prefer the individual lock box type, also in use in the safety deposit vaults of banks. A significant protective feature of this type of safety box is that it can be opened only by the simultaneous insertion of a guard or master key in the possession of the hotel *and* the individual lock box key in the possession of the guest.

In the following case, the New York Court of Appeals reviewed to what extent the innkeeper must make a safe available in order to secure the protection of section 200 of the General Business Law limiting its liability for guest valuables.

ZALDIN v. CONCORD HOTEL

48 N.Y.2d 107, 397 N.E.2d 370 (1979)

FUCHSBERG, J.: "We treat here with section 200 of the General Business Law, a statute delineating the responsibilities of the hotel industry with regard to the valuables of its millions of patrons.

"Plaintiffs, registered guests, bring suit on a theory of absolute liability for the loss of two valuable diamond rings which disappeared from their hotel room.

---

[35]Stanton v. Leland, 4 E.D. Smith 88 (N.Y. Ct. C.P. 1855).

[36]Johnson v. Richardson, 17 Ill. 302 (1855).

In its answer, the defendant hotel pleaded section 200 by way of affirmative defense. Asserting that the hotel's vault was not available to guests at the time they attempted to place the jewelry there for safekeeping, plaintiffs moved for summary judgment . . . or, in the alternative, for an order striking the defense. . . . Special Term held, *inter alia,* that the hotel's failure to provide access to its safe at all times did not necessarily preclude it from claiming the protection of section 200, and, concluding that the 'reasonableness of the vault hours should be left to the judgment of the triers of fact,' denied the motion. On review, the Appellate Division in effect ruled that, since the statute does not speak of 'reasonable hours,' a hotel's maintenance of vault facilities, even when available to guests only at limited times, generally entitles the hotel to the statutory benefits; on that basis, the court granted summary judgment to the defendant, dismissing the complaint on the law.

"On our review, we hold that a hotel may not claim the limitations on liability afforded it by section 200 of the General Business Law at times when it fails to make a safe available to its guests. We therefore determine that summary judgment should not have been granted and the complaint, accordingly, should be reinstated. Our reasons follow.

"Section 200 of the General Business Law reads: 'Whenever the proprietor or manager of any hotel, motel, inn or steamboat shall provide a safe . . . for the safe keeping of any money, jewels, ornaments, bank notes, bonds, negotiable securities or precious stones, belonging to the guests . . . and shall notify the guests or travelers thereof by posting a notice stating the fact that such safe is provided . . . in a public and conspicuous place and manner in the office and public rooms . . . and if such guest or traveler shall neglect to deliver such property . . . for deposit in such safe, the proprietor or manager . . . shall not be liable for any loss of such property, sustained by such guest or traveler by theft or otherwise.' Beyond this, in the absence of a special agreement in writing, the statute goes on to limit a hotel's liability for property so deposited with it, whether the loss is sustained 'by theft or otherwise,' to a sum not exceeding $500. [Citation omitted.] . . .

" . . . It is agreed that on Friday afternoon the plaintiffs William and Shelby Modell, accompanied by their daughter and son-in-law, checked into the defendant's large resort hotel. No one disputes but that the hotel provided a safe-deposit vault for the use of its guests and that, shortly after the plaintiffs' arrival, the daughter requested and was assigned one of its boxes. Plaintiffs allege that she then placed two diamond rings belonging to her mother in the box and that, late the following afternoon, she withdrew them from the box for her mother to wear while attending the Saturday evening festivities sponsored by the hotel.

"Sometime after midnight, however, upon the conclusion of the hotel's night club performance and before retiring, when the Modells and their daughter attempted to redeposit the jewelry, a hotel desk clerk informed them that the vault was closed and that they would have to retain possession of their valuables until it was opened in the morning. The defendant concedes that it would not allow guests access to the vault between the hours of eleven in the evening and eight in the morning. The Modells claim they thereupon secreted the jewelry in their room only to find, upon arising at about 9:00 A.M. that the chain lock with which they had secured the room had been cut from the outside and the rings were missing. They promptly notified the hotel and police of what they took to be a theft.

"In now applying the statute to this factual framework, we first remark on the obvious: the statute's wording is plain. This is not a new observation. Almost from the time the legislation was enacted, the courts recognized that 'there is nothing in the statute itself indicating any intent other or less extensive than the unequivocal language imports' (*Hyatt v. Taylor,* 42 N.Y. 258, 261). So we by no means tread the quicksand that surrounds a case in which less than definitive statutory language requires a choice among differing interpretations, the resolution of which, in turn, compels a choice among differing canons of construction [citation omitted]. Rather, when, as here, a state is free from ambiguity and its sweep unburdened by qualification or exception, we must do no more and no less than apply the language as it is written [citations omitted].

"Thus read, the statute offers the innkeeper an option: 'provide' a safe for your guests and sharply restrict your liability; or, feel free to do absolutely nothing about a safe and continue the risk of exposure to open-ended common-law liability. But, whichever choice you make, since the statute is in derogation of the common-law rule, to obtain the benefit of the more circumscribed liability which section 200 affords, you must conform strictly with its conditions (*see Millhiser v. Beau Site Co.,* 251 N.Y. 290).

"The statute fixes no time when a safe may or must be provided. Nor does it mandate availability around the clock. A fortiori, it does not limit the operation of a safe to a 'reasonable time.' These matters are left entirely up to the hotel. The statute makes no effort to evaluate cost or convenience. Neither does it distinguish between large and small inns, between those that cater to the large convention and those that cater to the individual patron, between those that come alive at night and those that do so in the day, between those that have a wealthy clientele and those that do not. The legislative formula is uncomplicated. It says, straightforwardly, that 'whenever' a safe is provided, the liability limitations shall be applicable. Conversely, at those times when an innkeeper chooses not to provide a safe for the use of its guests, he cannot claim the statutory protection. . . .

"The defendant would have us read the statute as though the phrase 'as soon as' had been substituted for the word 'whenever' and, similarly, 'equip' for 'provide.' But neither the express language of the statute nor its avowed purpose permits us to sanction what, in effect, would amount to a substantive change, indeed, a literal rewriting of a carefully conceived and well-weathered statute. Had the Legislature meant to incorporate such qualifications, it easily could have done so. To the contrary, in the 125 years of the legislation's long life, no such restriction has ever been essayed despite periodic legislative tinkering in other respects.

"More specifically, nowhere does section 200 suggest that an innkeeper may provide a safe part of the time and yet gain the benefit of the exemption all the time. Taken to its logical conclusion, this would not only deprive guests of their common-law right to seek recovery of their full losses against the innkeeper. But, by curtailing the period during which the surrogate medium of a safe is to be available, it also would leave the guests bereft of a full-time replacement for the innkeeper's former round-the-clock incentive to maintain security. Had a statute as explicit in concept and form as is the one here been intended to give a hotel the advantages of a dramatic limitation on its liability for losses while still retaining the privilege to encroach on the temporal scope of the quid pro quo—a safe such as would afford the guests protection—surely it would have said so.

"The defendant, therefore, may not have been entitled to base an affirmative defense under section 200, and certainly was not entitled to receive summary judgment on that account. Nevertheless, on the record before us, it was correct to withhold granting summary judgment to plaintiffs. . . . [Citations omitted.] [T]he further development of relevant facts may be in order, including, *inter alia*, ones relating to the circumstances surrounding the actual disappearance of the rings, to whether the theft occurred at the time when the safe was not available to these guests and, of course, to the value of the rings.

"From all this flows our conclusion that the order of the Appellate Division should be modified, by reversing the grant of summary judgment to defendant and by reinstating the complaint, and otherwise should be affirmed. . . .

"Order modified, with costs to plaintiffs-appellants, in accordance with the opinion herein and, as so modified, affirmed."

If the guest does deposit his valuables, there are two basic patterns to the statutory protection for the innkeeper. Some statutes hold the innkeeper strictly liable for any loss, but only to a maximum amount fixed by the statute. In other jurisdictions, the innkeeper may inquire as to the value of the goods which the guest seeks to deposit. If he accepts the goods, he is liable for the full value if they are lost, but the statute allows him to refuse to accept goods of a value greater than a maximum amount fixed by the statute.

Since the purpose of these statutes is to grant relief from the harsh common-law rules of insurer's liability, most jurisdictions provide that limitation is available only if the goods are lost without fault or negligence of the innkeeper; if the guest can show negligence by the innkeeper, he may recover fully without regard to the statutory maximum. Some states, such as Florida, go even further and relieve the innkeeper of all liability for deposited valuables, except if the loss is the fault of the innkeeper.

The defendant in *Durandy v. Fairmont Roosevelt Hotel, Inc.*[37] was denied the protections of the Louisiana statute limiting innkeepers' liability because no employee was on duty at 5:30 A.M. to deposit plaintiff's jewelry in plaintiff's safe deposit box.

---

[37]523 F. Supp. 1382 (E.D. La. 1981).

In the following case, the New York Court of Appeals indicated that it would inquire into the *adequacy* of an inn's safe before it would allow the innkeeper to avail himself of the protections afforded by New York statutes, which condition a limitation of innkeepers' liability on the provision of a safe.

GONCALVES V. REGENT INTERNATIONAL HOTELS, LTD.[38]
58 N.Y.2d 206, 447 N.E.2d 693
reh'g denied, 59 N.Y.2d 761, 450 N.E.2d 254 (1983)

COOKE, C.J.: "A hotel will not be availed of limited liability provided by section 200 of the General Business Law for the loss of destruction of a guest's property delivered to it for safekeeping unless the hotel establishes that it provided a 'safe' within the meaning of that section. The hotel may be charged with its failure to provide an adequate facility.

"Plaintiffs in these two consolidated cases were guests in late November, 1979, at the Mayfair Regent, a Manhattan luxury hotel owned and operated by defendants. Each plaintiff was traveling with an extensive jewelry collection allegedly worth $1,000,000. As required by law, notices were posted in the hotel that a safe was available in the office for the secure storage of money, jewels, and other valuable items. Plaintiffs each delivered their jewelry over to the management for deposit. In doing so, they signed a 'Safe Deposit Box Receipt' which set forth certain terms and conditions.

"The security device provided by defendants consisted primarily of rows of safe-deposit boxes that required two keys—one held by the guest—to open. The safe-deposit boxes were housed in a room built of plasterboard with access controlled only by two hollow-core wood doors, one of which had an ordinary residential tumbler lock and the second of which had no lock at all. Plaintiffs claim that this room is unlocked, unattended, and open to the general public. Also, it is alleged that the card file, showing which guest was using each box and when property had been deposited and removed, was exposed to public scrutiny.

"On November 25, 1979, thieves entered the hotel and broke into a limited number of safe-deposit boxes, including those used by plaintiffs. The boxes were emptied of their valuables.

"Plaintiffs independently commenced these actions to recover for the theft of their jewelry. Plaintiff Goncalves stated four theories for relief in her third amended complaint: (1) gross negligence in providing security; (2) breach of contract by defendants' failure to fulfill an earlier promise to install a secure area for their safe-deposit boxes; (3) breach of duty as a bailee; and (4) breach of section 200 of the General Business Law by defendants' failure to provide a safe as required by that statute. Plaintiff Cecconi relied on two theories: (1) breach

---

[38]In 1986 New York amended section 200 of the General Business Law to add safety deposit boxes to the word *safe* for the purpose of limiting liability of hotels, motels, and inns regarding deposit of valuables in the office of such premises. This was done to answer the doubt raised by the *Goncalves* majority opinion as to whether the legislation intended to include safety deposit boxes within the coverage of the statute.

of duty as a bailee; and (2) negligence in providing security. Each plaintiff prayed for damages in the amount of $1,000,000.

"Defendants denied plaintiffs' allegations and raised three affirmative defenses in their answers. First, they relied on section 200 of the General Business Law as limited plaintiffs' recovery to $500. Defendants also claimed breaches of the safe-deposit agreements occasioned by plaintiffs' deposit of goods worth more than $500. Last, defendants relied on the agreement to limit their liability to $500.

"The two actions were consolidated and defendants moved to dismiss the complaints or, in the alternative, have judgment entered against them in the amount of $500. Plaintiffs cross-moved to strike defendants' affirmative defenses and for summary judgment. Special Term directed entry of judgment of $500 against defendants in favor of each plaintiff. The cross motions to strike and for summary judgment were denied. The Appellate Division unanimously affirmed. This court granted leave to appeal, 57 N.Y.2d 601, 454 N.Y.S. 2d——, 439 N.E.2d 1245. The order below is now modified, 87 A.D.2d 1010, 450 N.Y.S.2d 644.

"The centerpiece of this appeal is section 200 of the General Business Law, which places a limitation on the absolute liability for the loss or destruction of a guest's property to which a hotelkeeper was subject at common law. That statute provides:

"§ 200. Safes; limited liability

"Whenever the proprietor or manager of any hotel, motel, inn or steamboat shall provide a safe in the office of such hotel, motel or steamboat, or other convenient place for the safe keeping of any money, jewels, ornaments, bank notes, bonds, negotiable securities or precious stones, belonging to the guests of or travelers in such hotel, motel, inn or steamboat, and shall notify the guests or travelers thereof by posting a notice stating the fact that such safe is provided, in which such property may be deposited, in a public and conspicuous place and manner in the office and public rooms, and in the public parlors of such hotel, motel, or inn, or saloon of such steamboat; and if such guest or traveler shall neglect to deliver such property, to the person in charge of such office for deposit in such safe, the proprietor or manager of such hotel, motel, or steamboat shall not be liable for any loss of such property, sustained by such guest or traveler by theft or otherwise; but no hotel, motel or steamboat proprietor, manager or lessee shall be obliged to receive property on deposit for safe keeping, exceeding five hundred dollars in value; and if such guest or traveler shall deliver such property, to the person in charge of such office for deposit in such safe, said proprietor, manager or lessee shall not be liable for any loss thereof, sustained by such guest or traveler by theft or otherwise, in any sum exceeding the sum of five hundred dollars unless by special agreement in writing with such proprietor, manager or lessee.

"Several issues requiring the explication of section 200 are raised. Plaintiffs argue that the statute limits absolute liability only, but does not exonerate a hotelkeeper whose negligence is the proximate cause of the loss of the goods delivered for safekeeping. Alternatively, plaintiffs propose that a hotelkeeper who does not provide a 'safe' within the meaning of the statute may not claim the benefits of section 200. Defendants argue that section 200 limits their liability no matter what the cause of loss and that they provided a 'safe' as required. Defendants further posit that the statute does not require a safe, but that '[an] other convenient place' will satisfy the conditions for invoking the section.

"At common law, an innkeeper was an insurer of goods delivered into his or her custody by a guest, and so was absolutely liable for the loss or destruction of such goods 'unless caused by the negligence or fraud of the guest, or by the act of God or the public enemy.' (*See Hulett v. Swift*, 33 N.Y. 571, 572.) . . .

"The common-law rule placed a heavy burden on the hotelkeeper, who could be held liable for a guest's loss although not having any culpability for the property's theft or destruction (*see* Edwards, Bailments [2d ed. 1978], § 463, pp. 336–337; *see*, also, Browne, Bailments [1896], pp. 83–84; 2B Warren's Negligence [3d ed.], *Hotelkeepers*, § 5.01). The New York Legislature early acted to restrict the innkeeper's exposure by providing a statutory exception to the common-law rule. In 1855, the predecessor statute to section 200 of the General Business Law was enacted (L.1855, ch. 421 § 1). . . .

"Being in derogation of the common law, section 200 is to be strictly construed (*see Ramaley v. Leland*, 43 N.Y. 539, 541 . . .). Moreover, to obtain its protection, the hotelkeeper must strictly adhere to its provisions (*see Millhiser v. Beau Site Co.*, 251 N.Y. 290, 295–296, 167 N.E. 447 [limitation not available when innkeeper's posted notices do not include information about limitation on liability]; *see*, also, *Zaldin v. Concord Hotel*, 48 N.Y.2d 107, 113–114, 421 N.Y.S.2d 858, 297 N.E.2d 370).

"Given this statutory framework, negligence by the hotelkeeper may arise in two ways. First, the hotelkeeper may be negligent in such a way that he or she fails to satisfy the conditions of the statute. Second, the hotelkeeper may fulfill the statute's conditions, but by some other negligent act cause the loss of property. The former may be charged against the hotelkeeper and the benefits of section 200 denied, but the latter does not remove the protection of the limited liability accorded to the hotelkeeper by the statute.

"Assuming that the proprietor meets the requirements of section 200, the statutory scheme limits his or her liability for general negligence. The terms of section 200 make no exception for loss caused by the negligence of the hotelkeeper. In contrast, sections 201 and 202 of the General Business Law each limit liability unless the loss occurs through the fault or negligence of the hotelkeeper. The Legislature has maintained these distinctions for at least 100 years (*compare* L.1855, ch. 421, § 1, with L.1866, ch. 658, and with L.1883, ch. 227). They should not be disturbed now.

"A sound basis for the statutory distinctions can be divined. Section 200 is concerned with property—'money, jewels, ornaments, bank notes, bonds, negotiable securities or precious stones'—which items tend to have a value disproportionate to their size and are easily stored in facilities to protect them against theft or destruction. The statute's message to hotelkeepers is clear: If you provide a facility that will protect such property against theft or destruction, then your absolute liability will be limited (unless you expressly agree to assume greater financial responsibility). This is economically sensible as well, as it encourages a hotel to initially invest in the construction of a secure receptacle, but permits long-term savings through lower insurance premiums and lower payments if losses do occur.

"The premise underlying this discussion is that an adequate facility is available to the guest. Section 200 requires that the proprietor 'provide a safe' as one of the conditions for receiving the protection of the statute. As recently noted in *Zaldin v. Concord Hotel*, 48 N.Y.2d 107, 113, 421 N.Y.S.2d 858, 397 N.E.2d 370, *supra,* the hotel is free to determine the extent to which it 'provides' a safe, but there must be strict conformity with the terms of section 200 in order to obtain the benefit of the statute. . . .

"What, then, is a 'safe' within the meaning of section 200 of the General Business Law? The Legislature has provided no definition. And while other sources provide guidance (*see, e.g.,* Black's Law Dictionary [5th ed.], p. 1199 ['(a) metal receptacle for the preservation of valuables']; Webster's Third New International Dictionary [unabridged], p. 1998 ['a metal box or chest sometimes built into a wall or vault to protect money or other valuables against fire or burglary']), their terms lack the perspective necessary to determining whether any particular receptacle is adequate.[2] Nor is the question one that may be answered by prescribing uniform technical specifications and measurements. A large, luxury hotel has far different security needs than a small, low-priced motel catering to a different clientele. It would be inappropriate for this court, with its lack of expertise, to specify a single safe that must be used by all hotels and motels, not only because of their varying needs but also because of the flexibility that is left to the proprietor (*see Zaldin v. Concord Hotel,* 48 N.Y.2d 107, 113–114, 421 N.Y.S.2d 858, 397 N.E.2d 370, *supra; see, also, Akins v. Glens Falls City School Dist.,* 53 N.Y.2d 325, 331, 441 N.Y.S.2d 644, 424 N.E.2d 531).

"In determining an appropriate definition of a 'safe', there must be taken into account the risks that commonly threaten the type of property covered by section 200. Fire and theft, of course, come immediately to mind. Other dangers may also exist. To come within the contemplation of section 200 of the General Business Law, therefore, a 'safe' should be a receptacle that, under the circumstances, provides adequate protection against fire, theft, and other reasonably foreseeable risks. In deciding this question, all aspects of a hotel's security system may be considered.

"Section 200 is an affirmative defense [citations omitted] and so the burden of proof lies on the defendant [citation omitted]. Whether a 'safe' was provided is a question of fact [citations omitted]. . . .

"In the present case, it was improper to award summary judgment. Plaintiffs submitted an affidavit by an expert having 29 years' experience in the design, installation, and sale of safes and vaults. This witness expressed his opinion that defendants' facilities were inadequate, stating that safe-deposit boxes can be invaded in less than 30 seconds and that they should be housed in a vault, not a room of plasterboard and wooden doors. Defendants relied on the existence and operation of the safe-deposit boxes. Under the circumstances, there exists a material issue of fact as to whether defendants' safe-deposit boxes constituted a 'safe' within the meaning of section 200.

"Defendants, relying on the language in the first clause requiring 'the proprietor . . . [to] provide a safe in the office . . . or other convenient place' (General Business Law, § 200), argue that a safe per se is not required by the statute. Defendants propose that this authorizes the hotel to provide a safe or another convenient place for storing valuables. This is not persuasive. Such an interpretation would allow a box or a bag kept behind the counter or a common coat closet to be interchangeable with a state-of-the-art steel vault. Clearly, this would defeat the policy underlying the statute, as discussed above. In addition, it is contrary to the long-standing comprehension that 'other convenient place' refers only to the *location* of the safe, and not to the nature of the receptacle itself (*see* Edwards, Bailments [2d ed. 1878], § 467, p. 341). To put it another way, the words 'other convenient place' relate to 'the office', not to the 'safe'; both the 'office' and the 'convenient place' specify the area in which the 'safe' is to be located. Finally, it is noted that the statute itself is entitled 'Safes; limited liability'; it does not refer to 'safes or other convenient places'. This may be taken as some indication that the Legislature intended that a safe, and nothing else, would suffice as a security device (*see* McKinney's Cons. Laws of N.Y., Book 1, *Statutes*, § 123, subd. a, p. 246).

"As the matter must be returned for further proceedings, the court shall address the contention that defendants should not be allowed to take advantage of the agreements that were signed by the plaintiffs when they obtained the use of the safe-deposit boxes. Defendants assert that plaintiffs breached these contracts or, alternatively, that the agreements establish a maximum value of $500 for the property left in the boxes. . . .

" . . . The agreement recites: 'In consideration of the privilege herewith granted me by Mayfair House whereby I am allowed the sole use of an individual safe deposit box'. The contract is manifestly void for failure of consideration. To obtain the $500 limitation, the proprietor is required by statute to provide a safe to the guest. This statutory obligation cannot be transformed into a contractual performance, nor may the guest's statutory right be transformed into a contractual privilege. A promise to perform an existing legal obligation is not valid consideration to provide a basis for a contract (*see Ripley v. International Rys. of Cent. Amer.*, 8 N.Y.2d 430, 441, 209 N.Y.S.2d 289, 171 N.E.2d 443).

"Assuming that defendants did not provide the security required by section 200, then the agreements are unenforceable as against public policy. Allowing such agreements to be enforced would encourage hotels to provide lesser protection that is required by the statute. In addition, the present agreements result in a guest's waiver of rights without warning. Certainly, when the guest is justified in believing that the facilities are constructed to provide adequate protection against fire or theft or other reasonably foreseeable risk, the hotel should not be allowed to obtain a waiver of rights without revealing that it is actually proffering a lesser security (*cf. Gross v. Sweet,* 49 N.Y.2d 102, 108–110, 424 N.Y.S.2d 365, 400 N.E.2d 305).

"In summary, defendants may not invoke the protection of section 200 of the General Business Law without proving that [they] provided a 'safe' within the meaning of that law. There exists a material question of fact as to whether defendants supplied a receptacle that, under the circumstances, provided adequate protection against fire, theft, and other reasonably foreseeable risks. The safe-deposit box receipts, signed by each plaintiff, are unenforceable agreements and so may not be relied on by defendants in their defense.

"The parties' other contentions have been considered and are found to be without merit.

"Accordingly, the order of the Appellate Division should be modified, with costs to plaintiffs, by denying defendants' motion for summary judgment and by granting plaintiffs' cross motions to dismiss defendants' affirmative defenses to the extent of dismissing the second and third affirmative defenses, and, as so modified, affirmed.

JASEN, J. (dissenting): . . .

"Certainly, in a common-law negligence action, the question of whether a person is crippled or whether there was physical contact between two vehicles or whether a hotel provided a safe could present factual questions calling for resolution by a jury. (*See Akins v. Glens Falls City School Dist.,* 53 N.Y.2d 325, 441 N.Y.S.2d 644, 424 N.E.2d 531.) A critical distinction, which the majority fails to perceive, must be drawn, however, where the Legislature has used such terms in a statute, in which case a purely legal question is presented, requiring the court, rather than a jury, to construe their meaning. . . .

"It is abundantly clear, therefore, based on . . . long-established principles of statutory construction, that the question whether or not the facility provided by defendant for the storage of its guests' valuables is a 'safe', as that term is used in section 200 of the General Business Law, is a pure question of law to be decided by this court.

"Turning to the case before us, I would hold that the subject facility is a 'safe' within the meaning of the statute. In arriving at this conclusion, it is necessary to first consider 'the context of the statute, the purpose and spirit of it, the surrounding circumstances, and—above all—the intention of the lawmakers.' McKinney's Cons. Laws of N.Y., Book 1, *Statutes,* § 235, citing *Mangam v. City of Brooklyn,* 98 N.Y. 585; *People ex rel. Lichtenstein v. Langan,* 196 N.Y. 260, 89 N.E. 921; and *People v. City of Buffalo,* 57 Hun. 577.) . . .

"While it would go too far to say that the Legislature cared nothing for the security of property belonging to the guests of a hotel, especially since the Legislature required that a safe be provided, it is imperative that the statute be construed in light of the fact that the *primary* concern of the lawmakers in enacting section 200 was to 'protect the hotel from an undisclosed excessive liability'. (*Millhiser v. Beau Site Co.,* 251 N.Y. 290, 294, 167 N.E. 447, *supra; Zaldin v. Concord Hotel,* 48 N.Y.2d 107, 112, 421 N.Y.S.2d 858, 397 N.E.2d 370, *supra.*)

"In light of the conceded purpose of the statute, I believe that the facility provided by the defendant here clearly falls within the meaning of the term 'safe' as it is used in section 200,[4] since it was more than sufficient to safeguard $500 worth of property per guest. . . .

"There can be little doubt that the defendant's safe-deposit box facility was a 'safe' as that term is commonly defined, as it has been construed by other courts and, most especially, as the New York Legislature intended it to be construed. Nor is it insignificant that in the century and a quarter that this statute has been on the books, there is nothing in the reported cases to suggest, until now, that the availability of the statutory protection might turn on the type of 'safe' provided by the innkeeper. . . .

"For the reasons stated, I would hold that defendant's liability is limited to $500 and affirm the order of the Appellate Division awarding both plaintiffs said sum.

"2. It is worth noting, however, that the term 'safe' has long enjoyed a similar definition. Thus, the 1940 edition of Bouvier's Law Dictionary defines the word as follows: 'A place for keeping things in safety. Specifically, a strong and fireproof receptacle (as a movable chest of steel, etc., or a closet or vault of brickwork) for containing money, valuable papers, or the like.' A similar definition is employed in the 1900 edition of Webster's Dictionary of the American Language.

"4. The record reveals that defendant provided individually locked metal safety-deposit boxes for the use of its guests. The guest and the hotel each held a key to the guest's box. The safety-deposit boxes were housed in a separate room with sheetrock walls. Access to the room could be had only by passing through two-inch thick wooden doors, at least one of which was secured by an iron tumbler-type lock."

13:16 *Provision of Security Box in Guest Room*

Recently, hotel operators have voluntarily installed in-room security boxes as an added means of protecting guest valuables. Their use has raised the issue of whether such devices nullify innkeeper statutes requiring guests to deposit valuables in a hotel safe or vault or in most instances forgo the right to hold the innkeeper liable for their loss.

In 1981, Hawaii amended its hotel statute (Hawaii Revised Statutes, chapter 486K) to add a new subdivision (5) to section 486K–1:

(5) "Security box" means any metal or alloy box, used in a hotel for the safe-keeping of any valuables, which may be securely locked with a locking mechanism that meets or exceeds Underwriters Laboratories standards and which shall be secured in a manner which precludes its removal from the room.

Section 486K–4 was also amended to add a new subdivision (b):

(b) If the keeper of a hotel provides a security box in the room of any guest and prominently posts a notice stating that a security box is provided in which valuables may be deposited and explains the liability for losses therefrom, the keeper of the hotel shall not be liable in any sum for any loss sustained by the guest unless the loss is due to the negligence or fault of the keeper of the hotel.

Conference Committee Report No. 12, dated April 21, 1981, set forth the reasons for the amendments as follows:

> The purpose of this bill is to limit the liability of hotels that provide security boxes for the safekeeping of guests' valuables.
>
> Presently, hotels are not liable for any sum for any loss of valuables if: (1) a safe or vault is provided for the safekeeping of guests' valuables; (2) a notice stating that fact is posted in a conspicuous place in the room; and (3) the guest nevertheless fails to make use of the safe or vault. If a guest does deposit his valuables in the safe or vault, the hotel's liability is limited to $500.
>
> Hotels find, however, that most patrons are not willing to take the time and effort of placing their valuables in the office safe. Consequently, burglaries in hotels have become a serious and growing problem for the tourist industry. In addition to the possibility of burglary, there is the growing threat of mugging and robbery for the visitor.
>
> Your Committee finds that another means of security for hotel room guests should be made available. Though security devices have been available to hotels for several years, the question of liability has prevented their installation and use. This bill is intended to encourage hotels to provide their guests with this added measure of security.

In the absence of similar statutory changes by other states, innkeepers would be well advised to follow the Hawaii model so as to make it clear that the installation and use by the guest of such in-room security boxes is for the guest's convenience only and in no way affects the guest's continuing duty to deposit valuables in the hotel safe or vault.

13:17   *Notices Required to Be Posted*

Most statutes require that the innkeeper post notice of the availability of the safe or vault. Requirements as to the placement, form, and content of the notice vary considerably. Some states require that the statutory provisions themselves be posted. The statutory protection is available only if the innkeeper complies with the posting requirements. However, at least one state (Alabama) sets a maximum recovery even if no notice is posted, though the limit is higher than if there had been proper posting.

In order to come within the protection of the New York statute, the innkeeper must strictly comply with the mandatory posting requirements of the statute. Posting requirements for hotels are prescribed in sections 206 and 203-b of the General Business Law; a posting requirement is also included in section 201.

The notice to be posted must be a printed copy of sections 200 and 201 of the statute. The required notice must be posted in the office or public room and in the public parlors of the hotel or inn. The "office" is the registration or reception office. A copy may also be posted in the front office or credit office, if there be one, the public rooms or restrooms for men and women, the ballrooms, function rooms, the elevator lobbies on the several floors, and the checkrooms and parcel rooms. Individual guest rooms are not public rooms and, except in motels, require no posting of notices. In case of doubt as to the nature or type of a room, it is better to err on the side of posting.

To "post," as used in the New York statute, means "to nail, attach, affix or otherwise fasten up physically and to display in a conspicuous manner, and not theoretically . . . and a posting is not made by printing or recording a notice in a book or on a card and keeping it on a desk."[39]

"Conspicuous" means what it says, plainly visible and obvious to the eye, not hidden.

Where a notice in a guest's bedroom merely warned guests to take care of their property and contained a statement that the innkeeper would not be responsible for valuables, money, or personal effects missing from guest's rooms and neither mentioned the availability of a safe nor suggested that valuables be turned over to innkeeper for safekeeping, it was not sufficient notice under the statute to protect the innkeeper from liability for the loss of a guest's undeposited valuables.

The fact that a safe is provided is not sufficient. Notice to that effect must be posted in conformity with the statute and posting in a bedroom is not sufficient where there has been no posting "in a public and conspicuous place and manner in the office and public rooms, and in the public parlors of" the hotel.[40]

It has been held, though, that an actual personal notice to a guest that a safe was provided for the safekeeping of the guest's money and valuables is equivalent to the constructive notice required to be posted by the statute. Where such a personal notice is given, the innkeeper's failure to post the statutory notice will not make him liable for the loss of the guest's undeposited valuables.[41]

The posting requirements for motels and motor courts are prescribed in section 206-b.

It should be noted that in motels and motor courts, the notices must be posted "in each and every rental unit." "Rental unit" means one or more rooms offered for rent as a unit for occupancy by one or more persons.

The distinction between a hotel and a motel is discussed in Chapter 2. In case of any doubt as to the type of operation, the best practice is to post the notices conspicuously in every guest room, in addition to the office and public rooms. Posting on the inside of the bathroom door, or inside a closet, does not satisfy the requirements of the statute.

DEPAEMELAERE V. DAVIS

77 Misc. 2d. 1, 351 N.Y.S.2d 808 (Civ. Ct. N.Y. Co. 1973)

NUSBAUM, J.: "In the case at bar which was transferred from the Supreme Court pursuant to the provisions of CPLR 325(d) the plaintiff, a Belgium na-

---

[39]Epp v. Bowman-Biltmore Hotels Corp., 171 Misc. 338, 342, 12 N.Y.S.2d 384, 388 (N.Y.C. Mun. Ct. 1939).

[40]Slater v. Landes, 172 N.Y.S. 190 (Sup.Ct. 1918).

[41]Purvis v. Coleman, 21 N.Y. 111 (1860).

tional, sues to recover the sum of ten thousand dollars allegedly missing from two envelopes deposited for safe keeping in a safe containing individual safe deposit box compartments maintained by the hotel for the use and convenience of its guests.

"The defendant pleads by way of defense that its liability is limited to five hundred dollars by reason of the provisions of sections 200, 201 and 206 of the General Business Law. It further pleads as a defense, the plaintiff's contributory negligence and its own freedom from negligence.

"From the testimony adduced during the trial, it would appear that on April 14, 1971, the plaintiff, a guest at the hotel, requested the use of a safe deposit box in which he placed an envelope containing eighteen thousand dollars in cash. Again, on April 30th, he deposited another envelope in the safe deposit box containing eight thousand dollars in cash. I am satisfied from the testimony of the plaintiff, his wife, and one of the plaintiff's customers, who paid a part of the sums in question to the plaintiff, that the plaintiff did in fact deposit the sum of twenty-six thousand dollars in the hotel safe deposit box in the safe maintained by the hotel for that purpose.

"On May 12, 1971, the day before the plaintiff was scheduled to return to Belgium, he requested the safe deposit box in order to remove the money therefrom. Upon opening the box, he noticed that a rubberband placed by him around one of the envelopes was askew. He thereupon immediately sat down with his wife on a bench near the hotel desk, opened up the envelopes and counted the money. He found five thousand dollars in old bills missing from each envelope for a total of ten thousand dollars. The loss was immediately reported to the hotel employees and the police department whose investigation of the loss proved fruitless.

"It is alleged by the hotel that the sole key to the box remained in the possession of the plaintiff during the period from April 14th through May 12th except for the brief periods the key was given to the desk clerk for the removal and locking of the box in the safe on April 14th, April 30th and May 12th.

"The process of removing and locking up the safe deposit box in question was similar to that employed generally by banks. Two keys are required to do so, the customer's key and the hotel master key. Neither key by itself could effect a removal of the box from the safe. However, unlike bank procedures, the box at the time it is removed from the safe and returned to the safe is hidden from the view of the depositor by the safe door which opens in such a manner as to obstruct any view into the room housing the safe.

"These facts virtually undisputed except by implication, leave two unanswered questions, the resolution of which will be dispositive of the matter: (1) Were the notices of limitation of liability conspicuously posted as required by law so as to effect notice to the plaintiff which would limit the defendant's liability? (2) Did the defendant as bailee of the plaintiff's property come forward with a suitable explanation of the claimed loss which would free it from the implication of lack of ordinary care?

"I am of the opinion that both of these questions must be answered in the negative. The applicable sections of the General Business Law, Sections 200, 201 and 206 must be read together, and those sections when read together require not only that a notice be posted advising the guests of the hotel that a safe is available for the deposit and safe keeping of money, jewels, negotiable securities and precious stones belonging to the guests, but also that notice be given to the guests of the hotel's limitation of liability imposed by law upon the guests when such facility is used. . . .

"The facts with respect to the notices posted by the hotel in the instant case appear to be as follows:

"In the guest's room in the hotel, a notice is posted which advises him in legible clear type: 'We have safety deposit boxes that are available for you without charge. We will appreciate your cooperation.'

"At the time the guest registered at the hotel, there was printed legibly and clearly on the registration card the following legend: 'Money, jewels and other valuables, packages must be placed in the safe in the office, otherwise, the management will not be responsible for any loss.'

"It is to be noted that in both of these instances, the guest is not advised of any limitation of liability or of the fact that the hotel is not required to take for deposit money, jewels or other valuables valued in excess of $500.00. The only notices which allegedly notified the guest of this limitation of liability are contained in a notice to guests which is posted at the right hand side of the registration desk, which notice is not in his direct line of vision and which he will see only if he turns to face that wall; and a notice in one other place vaguely described as being in the lobby of the hotel near the elevators.

"These notices, which are on a 7″ by 9″ card contained in black large type approximately a quarter of an inch tall, a legend which reads as follows: 'NOTICE TO GUESTS. A SAFE IS PROVIDED IN THE OFFICE FOR THE SAFE KEEPING OF MONEY, JEWELS, ORNAMENTS, BANK NOTES, BONDS, NEGOTIABLE SECURITIES AND PRECIOUS STONES BELONGING TO GUESTS.' There then follows in clear type a space for the posting of daily rates and charges, and then in letters approximately a sixteenth of an inch high or less, the provisions of the General Business Law which to my mind are illegible and unreadable except from a distance of ten to twelve inches.

"Thus the guests of the defendant's hotel are advised of the existence of the safe, requested to place their valuables in the safe, warned of the consequences if such request is not complied with but notified of the hotel's limited liability with respect to such property deposited in the safe by notices posted only in technical compliance with the law, which in effect give no notice of the limitations.

"In my opinion it was the intention of the legislature to see to it that real and effective notice of the hotel's limitation of liability was given to its guests. This conclusion is reached and bolstered by the provisions contained in each of the sections dealing with limitations of liability which state that a printed copy of the section be posted 'in a public and conspicuous place and manner.' In the case at bar I do not regard the posting of the notice setting forth the hotel's limitation of liability as a posting in a 'public and conspicuous place and manner,' sufficient to effect a limitation of liability. In fact, it is my belief that the notice and warning on the registration card and the notice in the guest's room would lead a guest to the conclusion that he must deposit his valuables in the hotel safe in order to be safeguarded. . . . and that no limitation of liability exists if he complies with this request.

"However muddy and unclear the law may be with respect to what constitutes posting in 'a public and conspicuous place and manner,' it is clear that the failure to deposit property for safeguarding pursuant to the provisions of Section 200 of the General Business Law will free the hotel of any liability for loss even if such loss occurred through its own negligence. . . . The corollary must therefore be held to be equally true. A finding that the guest did not receive proper notice of the limitation of the hotel's liability should render it fully liable if the guest's valuables are deposited pursuant to the provisions of Section 200 of the General Business Law. . . .

"Under the common law, the liability of an innkeeper was that of an insurer of the property of a guest unless it could be shown that such loss was occasioned by the fault or negligence of the guest. As the sections in question are in derogation of the Common Law Rule relative to the liability of innkeepers, they must be strictly construed.

"These facts have been established to my satisfaction. The money was deposited as claimed by the plaintiff in this action. Upon his attempted withdrawal of the monies deposited ten thousand dollars was found to be missing and no adequate explanation has been proffered by the hotel for the mysterious disappearance of the money. I am of the opinion therefore that the hotel's liability for such loss has been established. . . .

"Not having been notified of the necessity of advising the hotel if the property deposited exceeded $500 in value or of the necessity of making a separate agreement with respect to such property if it exceeded $500 in value, the plaintiff cannot be held to have been contributorily negligent with respect to its loss.

"Judgment is accordingly awarded to the plaintiff in the sum of $10,000 with interest, as demanded in the complaint."

The Appellate Term, First Department, affirmed *DePaemelaere* without opinion. *See* 79 Misc. 2d 800, 363 N.Y.S.2d 323 (1974).

In *Insurance Co. of North America, Inc. v. Holiday Inns of America, Inc.*,[42] the innkeeper asserted the statutory defense of nonliability where guest jewelry was found missing from the guest room, claiming the total exemption from responsibility available where the guest fails to deposit his valuables in the hotel

---

[42]40 A.D.2d 885, 337 N.Y.S.2d 68 (3d Dep't 1972).

safe. The trial court granted the guest's motion to dismiss the affirmative defense on the ground that the defendant had failed to prove that the posting requirements had been fully complied with. In affirming the trial court, the appellate division reasoned:

> In support of its motion, respondent introduced the transcript of the examination before trial of appellate's general manager. This testimony clearly indicated that appellant had not posted the required notice in all of the public rooms of the motel, although such notices were posted in the guest rooms. In opposition, appellant submitted only the affidavit of its attorney, which was not based on personal knowledge and asserted no evidentiary facts. Special Term properly found that this affidavit was of no probative value. [Citation omitted.]
>
> On this appeal, appellant urges that the defense based on section 200 should not have been dismissed because there were unresolved questions of fact. This contention is without merit. No facts have been alleged which would tend to establish the existence of the statutory defense. We have examined the remainder of appellant's contentions and find them to be without merit.

In *Latini v. Loews Corp.*,[43] the federal District Court for the Southern District of New York held that absent proof that the hotel had strictly complied with conspicuous posting requirements of the New York General Business Law, section 200, it was improper to grant the hotel's motion for summary judgment dismissing the action. A substantial amount of jewelry left in a purse in the guests' hotel room was discovered missing, and the guests sued for its full value.

13:18   *Articles Required to Be Deposited in Safe*

An innkeeper who complies with the New York statute, posts the required notices, and maintains a safe is protected against liability for the loss of money, jewels, ornaments, bank notes, bonds, negotiable securities, or precious stones, unless they are deposited in the hotel safe.

Other states follow this general pattern, but are free to vary from the precise categories set forth in New York. Utah, for example, uses the phrase "other articles of unusual value and small compass" as a catchall inclusion within its definition of valuables.

In *Martin v. Holiday Inns, Inc.*,[44] the California Court of Appeals reversed a judgment for the hotel which had been based on the applicability of the California statute requiring that a plaintiff file his action within 90 days after leaving a hotel. The lost articles were a Ford Bronco and a Ford U-Haul trailer, which the hotel had directed the guest to park in a designated area. The court ruled that a van and trailer were not equivalent to "wearing apparel, trunks, valises or baggage" set forth in the statute and that the statutory limitation for filing claims did not apply to the guest's lawsuit.

---

[43]657 F. Supp. 475 (S.D.N.Y. 1987).
[44]199 Cal. App. 3d 1434, 245 Cal. Rptr. 717 (Cal. App. 1988).

13:19 *Deposit of Watch*

The question has arisen whether a watch and chain come within the description "jewels and ornaments" as used in most statutes. In New York it is held that they do not. In *Briggs v. Todd,*[45] the plaintiff, a guest, lost from his room in the inn a watch on the cover of which a state coat of arms had been engraved. The picture of the owner's mother was inside the case. The watch had been laid for a short time inside the owner's trunk. In spite of these facts the court held that the watch was not an ornament.

The reason for this interpretation of the words is forcibly put by Justice Allen in *Ramaley v. Leland:*[46]

> Certain property, particularly valuable in itself, taking but small space compared with its value for its safe keeping, easy of concealment and removal, holding out great temptation to the dishonest, and not necessary to the comfort or convenience of the guest while in his room, is made the subject of the statutory exemption. Property of a different description, including all of which is useful or necessary to the comfort and convenience of the guest, that which is usually carried and worn as a part of the ordinary apparel and outfit, or is ordinarily used, and is convenient for use, by travelers as well in as out of their rooms, is left, as before the statute, at the risk of the innkeeper. The words of the statute must be taken in their ordinary sense, in the absence of any indication that they were used, either in a technical sense or a sense other than that in which they are popularly used. A watch is neither a jewel or ornament, as these words are used and understood, either in common parlance or by lexicographers. It is not used or carried as a jewel or ornament, but as a timepiece or chronometer, an article of ordinary wear by most travelers of every class, and of daily and hourly use by all. It is as useful and necessary to the guest in his room as out of it, in the night as the daytime. It is carried for use and convenience and not for ornament. But it is enough that it is neither a jewel or ornament in any sense in which these words have ever been used. The question of negligence, and whether the plaintiff could and did bolt his door, were properly submitted to and passed upon by the jury.

A watch ornamented with diamonds is nevertheless regarded as an article of daily use and not a jewel, ornament, or precious stone, within the meaning of the New York statute. Nor would the fact that a broken clasp made it unsafe to wear the watch on the day of its loss change the nature of the article.[47]

WALLS v. COSMOPOLITAN HOTELS, INC.
13 Wash. App. 427, 534 P.2d 1373 (1975)

MUNSON, J.: "Plaintiff, Paul Walls, instituted this action against defendant Cosmopolitan Hotels, Inc., to recover the value of a wristwatch he claimed had

---

[45]28 Misc. 208, 59 N.Y.S. 23 (Sup. Ct. 1899).

[46]43 N.Y. 539, 541–42 (1881).

[47]Kennedy v. Bowman Biltmore Hotel Corp., 157 Misc. 416, 283 N.Y.S. 900 (Sup. Ct. 1935) (per curiam); Federal Insurance Co. v. Waldorf-Astoria Hotel, 60 Misc. 2d 996, 303 N.Y.S.2d 297 (City Civ. Ct. 1969).

been stolen from his room while he was a guest in the defendant's hotel. The trial court granted summary judgment to the defendant, based upon the failure of Mr. Walls to deposit his watch with the hotel as required by RCW 19.48.030. Plaintiff appeals. We affirm.

"Plaintiff was a registered guest in the defendant's hotel. Plaintiff contends that when he left his hotel room for dinner he had locked the door and left the watch on a nightstand. However, upon his return the watch was gone. He noticed that the door was damaged, and upon closer inspection, had been severely damaged on some prior occasion. Apparently the screws holding the repaired portions to the lock were loose and one could easily obtain entry by merely pushing gently upon the door, even though it was locked.

"Plaintiff contends that the maintenance of the door in this condition constituted willful and wanton misconduct and such a disregard for the protection of plaintiff's property that the defendant should be liable for the loss of his watch, which he values at $3,685. On the other hand, defendant contends that the failure of the plaintiff to deposit his watch pursuant to RCW 19.48.030 is dispositive of all issues, namely: (1) whether a wristwatch is an includable item, subject to the terms of RCW 19.48.030; and (2) whether the alleged willful and wanton misconduct of the defendant in allowing the disrepair of the door to exist entitles plaintiff to recover within the terms of RCW 19.48.030.

"We realize that RCW 19.48.030, being in derogation of the common law, must be strictly construed. *Goodwin v. Georgian Hotel Co.,* 197 Wash. 173, 179, 84 P.2d 681, 199 A.L.R. 788 (1933); [citations omitted].

"As to the first issue, we hold that a wristwatch valued at $3,685 is 'valuable property of small compass' and therefore subject to the provisions of RCW 19.48.030.

"As to the second issue, we hold that when the plaintiff failed to deposit his 'valuable property of small compass' with the hotel pursuant to RCW 19.48.030, the defendant was relieved of all liability regardless of the cause of the loss. The statute specifically states that 'if such guests, . . . shall neglect to deliver such property to the person in charge of such . . . safe . . . the proprietor, . . . shall not be liable for any loss . . . of . . . such property, . . . sustained by such guests, . . . by negligence of such proprietor, . . . or by fire, theft, burglary, or *any other cause whatsoever;* . . .' (Italics ours.) Therefore, plaintiff's contention that the cause of his loss was the willful and wanton misconduct of the defendant is not well taken in that he claimed cause of plaintiff's loss is contained within the terms 'any other cause whatsoever.' . . .

"Plaintiff contends that *Goodwin v. Georgian Hotel Co., supra,* is supportive of his theory of recovery based upon willful and wanton misconduct. We disagree. In *Goodwin* the court held that once the guest had proven the deposit of his property with the innkeeper, the burden shifted to the innkeeper to show that the loss was not the result of theft or gross negligence on the part of the innkeeper or his employees. There being no deposit in this case, *Goodwin* is not applicable.

"Judgment is affirmed."

13:20   *Deposit of Valuables of Daily Use: Jewels and Ornaments*

As regards money in the possession of the guest, the innkeeper is not responsible for loss, however small the amount and irrespective of the inconvenience of depositing it in the safe.[48] As regards jewels and ornaments it has been held in New York that a gold pen and pencil are not considered either jewelry or ornaments and need not be deposited[49] and also that a chain, a purse, and a rosary are all articles of use, and not of ornament.[50]

Although the courts are free to interpret the word "ornaments" contained in their statutes broadly or narrowly, the test of inclusion or exclusion is generally based on whether the article is one of personal utility rather than one that is purely decorative. If found to be the former, it is most often held not to fall within the applicable statute, regardless of its extrinsic value. Under South Carolina law, a guest must deposit in the innkeeper's safe jewels "not ordinarily carried upon the person" before the innkeeper will be held liable for their loss. In *Bischoff v. Days Inns of America, Inc.*,[51] the court held that, though the diamond rings at issue could have been ordinarily "worn upon the person or clothing;[52] the court would consider them "not ordinarily carried upon the person" for purposes of the law's application.

In the following case, the Supreme Judicial Court of Maine distinguished between a watch as ornament and as an object of utility in regard to the loss of a guest's diamond wristwatch from her hotel room arising out of an assault upon her person inflicted by an intruder. The court's discussion of the inn's nonliability for personal injuries is omitted.

BREWER V. ROOSEVELT MOTOR LODGE
295 A.2d 647 (Me. 1972)

DUFRESNE, C.J.: " . . . Absent statutory regulations limiting their liability, innkeepers and hotel keepers are by the common law insurers of the property of their guests committed to their care and are liable for its loss by theft or otherwise, or for injury to it, except when caused by the act of God, the public enemy, or the neglect or fault of the guest or his servants. And the liability extends to all types of personal property of the guest, including moneys and watches, which are placed within the inn or hotel, and is not limited to such as are reasonably necessary for the current use of the guest. *Wagner v. Congress Square Hotel Co.*, 115 Me. 190, at 191–192, 98 A. 660 (1916); *Levesque v. Columbia Hotel*, 141 Me. 393, 44 A.2d 728 (1945).

"The evidence disclosed that the defendant motel corporation was 'duly licensed' as an innkeeper within the City of Waterville. . . . Thus, were it not for

---

[48]Hart v. Mills Hotel Trust, 144 Misc. 121, 258 N.Y.S. 417 (N.Y.C. Mun. Ct. 1932).
[49]Gile v. Libby, 36 Barb. 70 (N.Y. Sup. Ct. 1861).
[50]Jones v. Hotel Latham Co., 62 Misc. 620, 115 N.Y.S. 1084 (Sup. Ct. 1909).
[51]568 F. Supp. 1065 (D.S.C. 1983).
[52]*Id.* at 1067.

our present statute regulating the nature and extent of liability for loss or injury to guests' property (30 M.R.S.A., § § 2901, 2902, 2903 and 2904), the defendant's responsibility in the instant case for the loss of Mrs. Brewer's watch would be unquestionable. . . .

"Our present Act displaces the common law except where, within the statutory ceiling of liability, the common law remains operative. Section 2901, as interpreted by this Court in *Wagner, supra,* limits the innkeeper's liability to $300 for the loss of any of the articles or property of the kind specified therein and this, whether the conditions of the section respecting safe, vault, locking doors, windows and transoms, the posting of the law itself, have been complied with or not. The property covered by section 2901 includes the guest's money, bank notes, *jewelry,* articles of gold and silver manufacture, precious stones, *personal ornaments,* railroad mileage books or tickets, negotiable or valuable papers and bullion.

"Section 2902 permits the innkeeper to make special arrangements to receive for deposit in the safe or vault *any* property upon such terms as they may in writing agree. But, under this section, liability for loss of the articles or property accepted for deposit under section 2901, where all the conditions of section 2901 have been met, within the limit of $300 as provided by section 2901 (exclusive of the situation where by specific terms a different arrangement is made in writing between the innkeeper and his guest), is not that of absolute liability under the common law, but the innkeeper is liable for theft or negligence on his part or that of any of his servants.

"[Reference to section 2903 omitted as inapplicable.]

"Section 2904 determines the responsibility of any innkeeper for loss of or injury to his guest's personal property other than the property described in sections 2901, 2902 and 2903 and unequivocally states that liability within the limits therein provided shall be that of a depository for hire (excepting losses by fire not intentionally produced by the innkeeper or his servants). This section permits an innkeeper to assume greater liability by agreement in writing. It also covers property of the guest kept by the innkeeper after the relationship of innkeeper and guest has ceased or property received by him prior to the inception of the relationship, where the holding of the baggage or property may be, at the option of the innkeeper, at the risk of the owner. It is to be noted that section 2904 is general in scope and covers *all* innkeepers.

"The plaintiff contends that the defendant corporation never qualified for the statutory exemption from the common law rule of absolute liability, because, although licensed as an innkeeper, it never furnished the proper bond pursuant to 30 M.R.S.A., § 2753. . . . Assuming for the purposes of this decision that the bond was statutorily insufficient . . . ,nevertheless, we conclude that the plaintiff's contention must fail. . . . Proper licensing pursuant to statute was not included as one of the required conditions under which the exemption from common-law absolute liability was granted to innkeepers in case of loss of or injury to their guest's property. The legislative language is clearly to the contrary.

"Thus, before she can recover the maximum amount of $300 under the terms of the statute for her diamond wrist watch regarding which she testified to a fair market value of approximately $400 at the time of loss on the theory of common-law absolute liability because the defendant innkeeper had not complied with the conditions of section 2901, the plaintiff must bring herself within the terms of that section. Otherwise, her recovery would be governed by the limitations of section 2904. The plaintiff's diamond wrist watch, to be covered under section 2901, must be either 'jewelry' or a 'personal ornament.' The evidence does not reveal of what metal manufacture the watch was; we cannot surmise or conjecture that it might be an article of gold or silver manufacture as described in the reference section.

"In *Ramaley v. Leland*, 43 N.Y. 539, 3 Am. Rep. 728 (1871), the New York Court said:

"A watch is neither a jewel or ornament, as these words are used and understood, either in common parlance or by lexicographers. It is not used or carried as a jewel or ornament, but as a timepiece or chronometer, an article of ordinary wear by most travelers of every class, and of daily and hourly use by all. It is as useful and necessary to the guest in his room as out of it, in the night as the day-time. It is carried for use and convenience and not for ornament. But it is enough that it is neither a jewel or ornament in any sense in which these words have ever been used.

" . . . The Nebraska Court in *Leon v. Kitchen Bros. Hotel Co.*, 1938, 134 Neb. 137, 277 N.W. 823, 115 A.L.R. 1078, after citing *Wagner v. Congress Square Hotel Co.*, supra, with approval, reached the same result as did the New York Court in the case of a lady's platinum diamond wrist watch. It concluded that if the Legislature had intended to include in that part of the statute an article of such general and common use as a watch, it would have used the word 'watch' and not relied on the terms 'jewelry' and 'personal ornaments.' We fully agree. We are aware that the Tennessee Court has ruled to the contrary. *Rains v. Maxwell House Co.*, 1904, 112 Tenn. 219, 79 S.W. 114, 64 L.R.A. 470, 2 Ann. Cas. 488.

"By this conclusion we do not suggest that a given article is, ipso facto, precluded from qualifying as 'jewelry' or 'personal ornaments' solely because it includes a 'watch.' A time-piece might be designed and arranged as a part of an item such that it, and its practical function of telling time, are truly incidental to a manifestly predominant overall purpose of the article as an adornment—in which situation it might legitimately qualify as 'jewelry' or 'personal ornament' within the meaning of the present statute. On the other hand, that which in its objective nature is revealed as primarily and essentially aimed at the practical function of telling time and, is, therefore, basically a 'watch' does not become transformed into 'jewelry' or a 'personal ornament', for purposes of the present statute, solely because it might be rendered interesting or unusual by some accompanying decoration even in the form of precious stones.

"The criterion of judgment, therefore, is the predominant function of the article as disclosed objectively by its nature, construction and assemblage.

"Our conclusion in the instant situation is that the evidence is insufficient—insofar as it has shown the article here involved to be only a 'diamond wrist watch' of market value of approximately $400.00 at the time of the loss—to sustain the ultimate burden of proof reposing upon plaintiff to establish that the article was 'jewelry' or a 'personal ornament' because its predominant function was other than that normally conveyed by the basic designation that it was a 'watch'—a mechanism to serve the utilitarian function of providing its wearer with information as to the time of day.

"Since the plaintiff's wrist watch did not come within any of the types of property enumerated in sections 2901, 2902 or 2903 of the statute, it came within the terms of section 2904 which limits the responsibility of the innkeeper to that of a depository for hire, and in the case of miscellaneous effects including personal belongings to the limit of $50. As stated in *Wagner v. Congress Square Hotel Co., supra,* at page 195 of volume 115 of the Maine reports, at page 662 of volume 98 of the Atlantic Reporter, '[a] depository for hire is liable only for failure to exercise ordinary care, or, as it is sometimes expressed, such care as men of ordinary prudence usually exercise over their own property under like circumstances.' The Justice below ruled as a matter of law that there was no obligation on the part of the defendant innkeeper to anticipate the unforeseeable intrusion of the plaintiff's assailant into her chambers through the open bathroom window and thus there was no breach of due care for which the defendant was responsible in damages . . . for the theft of her property. In this, there was no error.

"The entry will be [:]

"Appeal denied.

"All Justices concurring."

13:21 *Extent of Liability for Property Deposited in Safe*

The following case reiterates the settled doctrine that in order for a hotel to avail itself of the innkeeper's statutory limitation of liability for losses of deposited guest valuables, it must strictly comply with the statutory requirements.

ZACHARIA V. HARBOR ISLAND SPA, INC.
684 F.2d 199 (2d Cir. 1982)

WINTER, C.J.: " . . . Florida provides hotels with a statutory method of limiting their liability for the loss of valuables which they accept for safekeeping from guests. The pertinent statutory language reads:

"liability . . . shall be limited to $1,000 for such loss, if the [hotel] gave a receipt for the property (stating the value) on a form which stated, in type large enough to be clearly noticeable, that the [hotel] was not liable for any loss exceeding $1,000 and was only liable for that amount if the loss was the proximate result of fault or negligence of the operator. "Fla. Stat. § 509.111(1) (1979).

"On November 17, 1979, the plaintiff, Mrs. Sarah Zacharia, checked into defendant's Harbor Island Spa Hotel in Miami Beach. She signed a registration card which stated 'HOTEL'S LIABILITY IS LIMITED AS PROVIDED IN POSTED "IMPORTANT NOTICE TO GUESTS".' Soon thereafter, she sought the use of a Hotel safe deposit box to store her valuables. At the Hotel's request, she signed two cards. The first, Card (1), was entitled 'Harbor Island Spa, Inc.—Statement of Value.' The second, Card (2), was entitled 'Safe Deposit Box—Statement of Value.' . . . Both cards state that the Hotel's liability is limited to $1,000 for loss of valuables deposited in a safe deposit box. Each contains language certifying that the aggregate value of items on deposit will at no time exceed $1,000. The limitation provisions of Card (1), however, were crossed out and Zacharia was not asked to fill in the blanks on Card (2) for her name, the Hotel's name and the date of deposit. The parties dispute what she was told by Hotel employees, Zacharia claiming the desk clerk told her not to worry about the cards which were merely for the Hotel's record, the Hotel denying such statements were made.

"On some 36 occasions Zacharia sought access to the safe deposit box and signed the reverse side of Card (2) in order to verify her identity. Neither on the first nor on any later occasion was she given any document evidencing either a deposit of valuables or the potential limitation on the Hotel's liability.

"On December 7 or 8, 1979, many safe deposit boxes, including Zacharia's, were emptied by a thief, apparently a desk clerk who vanished at the same time as the contents of the boxes. Zacharia's claim of loss is in excess of $10,000. The Hotel, on the other hand, is prepared to present evidence that her original claim escalated sharply after a phone call to New York from the Hotel lobby.

" . . . Section 509.111(1) provides that a hotel's liability may be limited only if the hotel 'gave a receipt for the property (stating the value).' Plaintiff was given no document of any kind in connection with use of the safe deposit box. All of the documentation was retained by the Hotel in accord with its established practices. Moreover, on Card (1), 'Harbor Spa, Inc.—Statement of Value,' the critical portion relating to limitation of liability was crossed out. Finally, the blanks within the text of Card (2) 'Safe Deposit Box—Statement of Value,' relating to plaintiff's name, the name of the Hotel, and date of deposit, were not filled in.

"We can only speculate as to the result a Florida court would reach on these facts. Relevant Florida decisions, however, emphasize that the burden of compliance is on the hotel rather than on the guest, since the hotel has 'superior position and knowledge . . . with regard to the mandates of the statute,' *Garner v. Margery Lane, Inc.*, 242 So. 2d 776, 778 (Fla. 4th Dist. Ct. App. 1970), and that compliance by the hotel must be 'strict.' *Id.* at 779 (quoting *Fuchs v. Harbor Island Spa*, 420 F.2d 1100, 1103 (5th Cir. 1970)). In a case decided under an earlier but pertinent version of the statute, *Safety Harbor Spa, Inc. v. High*, 137 So. 2d 248 (Fla. 2d Dist. Ct. App. 1962), limitation of liability was denied where the hotel failed to keep track of continuing deposits and withdrawals by a guest. The Court noted that such a step was for the hotel's own protection and held it liable for an amount in excess of $1,000 because it was not in 'strict compliance.' *Id.* at 249. The most recent Florida case, *Great American Insurance Co. v. Coppedge*, 405 So. 2d 732 (Fla. 4th Dist. Ct. App. 1981) indicates *in dicta* that documentation must be given to the guest if liability is to be limited under the present statute. *Id.* at 735.

"We hold that the Hotel's casual attitude toward even the plainest requirement of the statute deprives it of the benefit of the limitation of liability. There is no ambiguity as to the statute's requiring that a document constituting a statutory receipt must be *given* to the guest depositing valuables. This receipt requirement is obviously designed to emphasize to the guest the statutory limitation since access to the valuables on each occasion is only by production of this document to Hotel officials. No document was given to Zacharia then or on any of the numerous occasions on which she entered the box. Although additional valuables might have been deposited at any time, the Hotel made no attempt to give direct notice to Zacharia of its purported limited liability except on the first deposit. While the Hotel asked plaintiff to sign two forms indicating future deposits would leave the aggregate value under $1,000, these forms were never completed, and on Card (1), the critical language was crossed out. Whether the desk clerk actually said not to worry about the cards since they were only for Hotel records is less significant than the conduct of the Hotel in keeping the cards, for that conduct expressed exactly the same idea.

"The non-compliance here was more than technical, yet defendant has not cited a single Florida case in support of its position. Florida decisions dealing with related issues directly hold that hotels seeking the shelter of the statute bear a 'burden' of 'strict compliance.' *Garner, supra,* and imply that compliance must be in connection with every use, *High, supra.* While no absolutely dispositive Florida decision has been rendered, existing case law clearly weighs in plaintiff's favor.

"We hold therefore, that the statutory limitation of liability is inapplicable. Defendant may use documents signed by Zacharia at trial to attack her assertions as to the value of the items deposited.

"Reversed and remanded."

CARLTON V. BEACON HOTEL CORP.
3 A.D.2d 28, 157 N.Y.S.2d 744 (1st Dep't 1956), *aff'd mem.,*
4 N.Y.2d 789, 149 N.E.2d 527 (1958)

BREITEL, J.: "Plaintiff, a guest of the defendant hotel, brought this action to recover for the loss of a package of jewelry and a package of foreign currency which she had deposited for safekeeping with the defendant's desk clerk. Defendant appeals from a judgment entered after a jury verdict in the amount of $10,000 in the plaintiff's favor. The judgment should be modified to limit the plaintiff's recovery to $500.

"At the time plaintiff registered as a guest at the defendant hotel, she asked the desk clerk whether he had a safe deposit box, as she 'wanted to put some things away.' The clerk replied that there were none presently available, but that he would store her valuables safely, until a safe-deposit box became vacant. He gave plaintiff an envelope specifically designed to receive guests' valuables. She placed her package of jewelry (worth $23,000, according to her verified bill of particulars) in the envelope but left blank the item 'Declared Valuation.' She then gave the clerk the sealed envelope. Plaintiff, during her six-weeks stay at the hotel, on five occasions utilized this procedure to deposit and redeposit her jewelry and on one occasion to deposit a package of English and French currency.

"The hotel had a large iron safe containing, among others, some 66 individual safe-deposit compartments and three larger compartments. One of the larger compartments, number 45, was used exclusively for envelopes containing guests' valuables. The desk clerk testified that according to the routine prescribed by the management, the envelopes were placed in compartment 45. He further testified that he could recall no deviation by him from this general practice. On the other hand, the clerk had no specific recollection of the several deposits of valuables made by plaintiff. Neither the packages of jewelry, nor the currency, nor even the envelopes in which they were deposited, were ever recovered.

"After both sides rested, defendants moved for a directed verdict in favor of plaintiff in the amount of $500. This motion was based on the provisions of Section 200 of the General Business Law. In denying the motion, the trial court stated that defendant had met two of the conditions imposed by that section, namely: (1) providing an adequate safe for the deposit of guests' valuables; and (2) posting effective notices to inform the guests that such a safe was provided. The trial court, however, went on to deny the motion, because it construed section 200 as requiring the hotel to actually deposit the valuables in the safe in order to take advantage of the limited liability provisions of that section. Accordingly, on the issue of liability, the trial court submitted to the jury the single question, namely, whether the defendant actually put the plaintiff's property in the safe.

"Even apart from the absence of any evidence in the record to indicate that in fact defendant did not deposit plaintiff's valuables in its safe, the verdict and judgment must be reduced. Section 200 of the General Business Law, in language that is quite clear, states that a hotelkeeper who provides a safe and posts requisite notices is not liable at all for the loss of guests' valuables unless the guest delivers the valuables for deposit in the safe. Where the valuables have been delivered to the person in charge of the safe 'for deposit in such safe,' the hotel's liability is limited to $500, unless it otherwise agrees in writing.

"Section 200 was enacted 'to relieve innkeepers of the heavy burden placed upon them by the common law. . . . The purpose of the section is to protect the hotel from an undisclosed excessive liability.' (*Millhiser v. Beau Site Co.*, 251 N.Y. 290, 293, 294). It is conceded in this case that the hotel complied with the posting requirements of sections 200 and 206 of the General Business Law.

There is likewise no contention that the safe here provided by the hotel did not adequately comply with the statutory requirements.

"The trial court, however, read into the statute a further requirement that the hotel prove actual deposit of the valuables in the safe. Neither the language of the section or the precedents thereunder support that view. It has been held by the Court of Appeals that section 200 limits the liability of the hotel, even in instances when the loss is occasioned by a theft committed by an employee of the hotel. (*Millhiser v. Beau Site Co., supra*). As construed by the trial court, the statute would not protect the hotel from unlimited liability when the desk clerk himself converts the valuables upon receipt from the guest. In the *Millhiser* case the court noted that the risk of loss by theft is greater as regards theft by employees than as regards theft by strangers. Similarly, the risk of theft by the employee receiving the property is greater than the risk of theft by other employees. (Of course there is no evidence in this case that plaintiff's loss was occasioned by a theft, or any implication that the loss was caused by the desk clerk.) The opinion in the *Millhiser* case indicates that the hotel's ability to claim the benefits of section 200 did not turn on whether the larcenous clerk perpetrated the theft before or after guests' valuables were placed in the safe.

"The record here demonstrates that plaintiff, with knowledge of the limited liability imposed on defendant by statute, deposited her jewelry and other property without making any declaration of value. Defendant, having complied with all the expressed conditions of section 200, is entitled to the benefit of the limited liability therein provided. . . .

"Judgment unanimously modified so as to limit plaintiff's recovery to $500 and, as so modified, affirmed, with costs to the appellant."

KALPAKIAN V. OKLAHOMA SHERATON CORP.
398 F.2d 243 (10th Cir. 1968)

PICKETT, Cir. J.: "Appellants, Edward Kalpakian and Lucy Kalpakian, instituted this action to recover damages in the amount of $286,546.00, incurred as a result of the disappearance of jewelry belonging to them from a safety deposit box provided for guests by appellee, Oklahoma-Sheraton Corporation, the operator of a hotel in Oklahoma City, Oklahoma. . . . Upon consideration of the pleadings, affidavits and depositions, the trial court concluded that a recovery by Kalpakian could not exceed $1500.00, and granted the hotel's motion for summary judgment. . . . The principal issue raised on this appeal is whether the Oklahoma statutes relating to liability of hotel operators preclude recovery by a hotel guest for loss of property from the hotel's safety deposit boxes resulting from negligence of the hotel.

"While on a selling trip, Edward Kalpakian, who with his wife Lucy is engaged in the wholesale and retail jewelry business, registered at the Sheraton in Oklahoma City on the evening of September 25, 1962. He immediately requested a deposit box in the hotel vault in which to deposit his jewelry. Apparently he informed the hotel employee at the cashier's cage that he had 'valuables' he wished to protect. The hotel maintained several sizes of deposit boxes, and at that hour no box of sufficient size to hold the case containing Kalpakian's jewelry was available. It was necessary, therefore, to use a smaller box, which entailed removing the chamois rolls containing the jewelry from the bag prior to placing them in the safety deposit box. The following morning a larger box became available, and after removing his jewelry from the smaller box, he reserved the larger box for use later that day. A different employee was on duty at that time, and upon request Kalpakian signed a printed form then used by the hotel in connection with its safety deposit service. The form was designated 'Oklahoma Biltmore Hotel Safe Deposit Box Agreement.' In addition to stating that safety deposit boxes were available for hotel guests and referring to the return of the key, the instrument contained the following statement: 'The maximum value of the property deposited shall not exceed $1500.00.' The boxes could be opened only by the joint use of the hotel's master key and the key to the particular box issued to the guest. When Kalpakian returned later in the day, this procedure was followed and the case containing the jewelry was deposited. After the box was locked, Kalpakian retained his key. Upon opening the box the next morning, the case and jewelry had been removed and have not been subsequently found. It appears from the record that during the night a person other than Kalpakian appeared at the clerk's desk with a key to Kalpakian's box and requested entrance thereto, which was granted by the clerk. . . .

"15 Okl. St. Ann. § § 501, 503, 503a and 503b fix the liability of the operator, manager or owner of a hotel in Oklahoma for loss of personal property belonging to guests. Section 503 makes it the duty of the hotel to equip the doors of all guest rooms with suitable night latches, night chains or bolts, placed on the inside of the doors to prevent opening from the outside by key or otherwise. Section 503a relates to hotels which provide a safe, vault or other depository for the safekeeping of valuables described therein. Notice that such safe, vault or other depository is available to guests shall be given by posting a notice in a public and conspicuous place and manner in the office or public rooms, or in the parlors or guest rooms of the hotel. The statute provides that if after notice, a hotel guest neglects to deposit valuables in the hotel depository, the hotel shall not be liable for any loss of property belonging to a guest, regardless of the cause. But when valuables are delivered for deposit, the statute requires that the guest shall at that time advise the person in charge of the hotel office of the actual value of the property, and the hotel is not required to accept property for deposit exceeding the value of $300. If there is a loss of deposited property, the hotel is liable only for the actual value thereof 'in no event exceeding the sum of Three Hundred Dollars ($300.00).' The hotel, however, may by special agreement in writing with a guest, receive property of greater value than $300 and assume liability as shall be provided for in the written agreement.

"The manifest purpose of Section 503a is to protect a hotel against undisclosed excessive liability when it furnishes for its guests safety deposit facilities, and to provide a method for accepting greater liability by written agreement if the hotel management desires. The decision to accept greater responsibility can be made only after the hotel guest has notified the hotel of the actual value of the deposited property. The statutory duty to give the notice of value is upon the guest. When the hotel knows the value of the property to be deposited, it may then determine whether it desires to accept the deposit and assume responsibility for its loss. Until the notice of value is given there is no liability for loss of the property beyond the $300.00 limit, regardless of the cause of the loss. As we said in *Solomon v. Downtowner of Tulsa, Inc.* with reference to a similar notice provision in Section 503b, 'Under the Oklahoma Statute, the limitation of liability for loss of merchandise samples depends . . . upon the giving of the required notice by the guest.' 357 F.2d 449, 451. The trend of the decisions considering state statutes relating to a hotel's liability for lost property deposited with it, is to strictly construe the obligation of a hotel guest to disclose the value of deposited property and to refuse to impose on hotels without notice a greater liability than the statutory amount, regardless of negligence. [Citations omitted.] The practice of pleading tort or negligence to avoid the restriction on liability was rejected in *Eichberg & Co. v. Van Orman Fort Wayne Corp.*, 7 Cir., 248 F.2d 758, *cert. denied* 356 U.S. 927, . . . and *Ricketts v. Morehead Co.*, 122 Cal. App. 2d 948, 265 P.2d 963. Kalpakian argues that the statutory provisions do not relieve the hotel from liability for loss of deposited articles if caused by negligence whatever their value. To accept this construction would permit a guest to accomplish by nondisclosure what he could not accomplish by giving notice of value.

"Kalpakian, when he requested a safety deposit box for his valuables, admittedly did not advise the person in charge of the hotel as to the actual value of the property. He signed an instrument submitted by the hotel which stated that the value of his property did not exceed $1500.00, and there is no evidence that the clerk who accepted the deposit knew that the value of the jewelry was greater than that amount. This instrument amounts to a notice upon which the hotel could rely on concluding whether it would accept liability for the deposited articles and limits recovery to $1500.00 in case of loss for any reason, including negligence.

"The purpose of the statutory requirement that notice of the availability of safety deposit boxes be posted in a conspicuous place is to limit liability of the hotel when there are losses by guests who do not deposit their valuables. Kalpakian had been a guest at the Sheraton on previous occasions. He knew that the safety deposit box facilities were available. He not only used them, but also signed an instrument acknowledging that the value of the property being deposited did not exceed $1500.00. Although the record indicates that the posted notices satisfied the statute, Kalpakian had actual notice and cannot complain of lack of the statutory constructive notice. [Citations omitted.]

"The hotel's liability being limited to $1500.00, the court did not err in dismissing the action. . . .

"Affirmed."

13:22 *Extent of Liability for Failure to Deposit Valuables*
         Where Loss Is Caused by Negligence of Innkeeper

A significant conflict among the authorities exists as to whether statutes limiting the liability of the innkeeper where the guest fails to deposit valuables in the hotel safe were intended to limit such liability only where the guest's theory of liability was that of common-law insurer's responsibility, or whether the statute was intended to limit all liability, including actions predicated on negligence. The Nebraska, Rhode Island, and West Virginia authorities adopt the reasoning that their statutes apply only to the innkeeper's liability as an insurer. The California, Louisiana, Maine, and Washington authorities have ruled that their statutes apply to all theories of liability. The conflict rests on a finding of ambiguity as to the legislative intention, which must be resolved by each state court on the basis of its own interpretation of its statutory language.

Additionally where negligence of the innkeeper is mentioned in statutes limiting liability for property losses, so as to override the limitation and restore full liability, there is a split of authority as to whether such negligence must be active in order to permit recovery without limitation. The Court of Appeals of Arizona, in the case that follows, held that negligence triggering the resumption of full liability had to occur after valuables had been deposited in the hotel safe, such as a theft from the safe by a hotel employee or third party caused by the innkeeper's negligent act or omission. Where the guest failed to deposit valuables in the safe, the negligence had to be active, an act of misfeasance, rather than an omission or failure to act, the legal term for which is nonfeasance. A failure to provide adequate security and failure to warn guests about prior thefts were deemed claims of nonfeasance, requiring dismissal of such claims.

The distinction between misfeasance and nonfeasance in regard to losses of valuables from the guest room, where the guest fails to deposit such valuables in the hotel safe, deserves fuller treatment. The Arizona case *Terry v. Linscott Hotel Corp.* is a leading opinion favoring innkeeper nonliability.

TERRY V. LINSCOTT HOTEL CORP.
126 Ariz. 548, 617 P.2d 56 (1980)

O'CONNOR, J.: "Jewelry and other items belonging to appellants were stolen from their rooms while they were guests at the Scottsdale Hilton Inn. They brought suit for the loss against appellees, owners of the Inn. Appellees moved for partial summary judgment as to that portion of the loss which was jewelry based on A.R.S. § 33–302(A), which restricts the liability of innkeepers. The trial court granted appellees' motion for partial final summary judgment. We affirm.

"The loss occurred on December 28, 1977. Some unknown thieves stole the jewelry and other items while appellants were away from their rooms. The first count of appellants' complaint simply alleges the loss, appellees' status as innkeepers, and appellants' status as guests, and seeks recovery for the loss. Count two of the complaint alleges a cause of action for negligence, as follows:

"The theft of plaintiffs' personal property from their locked room is the direct and proximate result of the defendants' negligence, carelessness and recklessness in failing to provide adequate security, failing to provide plaintiffs with the degree of care and protection to which they were entitled as paying guests, and in failing to warn plaintiffs of the series of thefts and burglaries which had occurred at the Scottsdale Hilton prior to December 28, 1977.

"Appellees served interrogatories on appellants asking them to state each act or omission which appellants alleged constituted negligence on appellees' part. Appellants answered as follows:

"Failure to provide adequate security including the use of security guards, interior hall security personnel and adequate locking and securing devices on the doors.

"Failure to increase effective security measures with full knowledge of the high incident rate of theft in the Scottsdale Hilton.

"Failure to warn the plaintiffs of the number of thefts and burglaries committed in the Scottsdale Hilton prior to December 28, 1977.

"A.R.S. § 33–302 reads in part as follows:

"A. An innkeeper who maintains a fireproof safe and gives notice by posting in a conspicuous place in the office or in the room of each guest that money, jewelry, documents and other articles of small size and unusual value may be deposited in the safe, is not liable for loss of or injury to any such article not deposited in the safe, *which is not the result of his own act.*

"B. An innkeeper may refuse to receive for deposit from a guest articles exceeding a total value of five hundred dollars, and unless otherwise agreed to in writing shall not be liable in an amount in excess of five hundred dollars for loss of or damage to property deposited by a guest in such safe *unless the loss or damage is the result of the fault or negligence of the innkeeper.*

"C. The innkeeper shall not be liable for loss of or damage to merchandise samples or merchandise for sale displayed by a guest unless the guest gives prior written notice to the innkeeper of having and displaying the merchandise or merchandise samples, and the innkeeper acknowledges receipt of such notice, but in no event shall liability for such loss or damage exceed five hundred dollars *unless it results from the fault or negligence of the innkeeper.* [Emphasis added.]

"The notice placed in appellants' rooms reads as follows in large size print:
"PLEASE

"Safety Deposit Boxes for your valuables are available at the Reception Desk. We recommend that you deposit all valuables.

"We also suggest you double bolt your door when using the patio door to the swimming pool.

"Arizona Statutes do not hold hotels liable for missing valuables, nor do we have insurance coverage.

"So . . . ,

"please deposit your valuables.

"There is no dispute that the hotel maintained a fireproof safe as required by A.R.S. § 33–302(A).

"On appeal, appellants argue that partial summary judgment for appellees was improper for two reasons. First, they argue that A.R.S. § 33–302(A) was intended to relieve an innkeeper of his common law strict liability for the guest's property, but not for the effects of his own negligence. Second, appellants contend that the trial court erred in holding as a matter of law that the notice placed in appellants' rooms complied with the statute.

Innkeeper Liability

"The common law rule imposed a strict rule of liability upon an innkeeper and was founded upon the public policy of an earlier day. . . .

"Statutes such as A.R.S. § 33–302 were enacted as . . . [t]he need to limit an innkeeper's potential liability became apparent. As it stated in an annotation at 37 A.L.R.3d 1276, 1279–80 (1971):

"The statutes defining the limits of an innkeeper's liability for loss of or injury to his guest's property represent a legislative intent to soften what has been termed an unduly harsh common-law rule.

"In former times, there were a number of sound reasons to justify the public policy of imposing a strict rule of liability on innkeepers. And so, at common law, the innkeeper was practically an insurer of property brought by a guest to his inn and he was relieved of liability for the loss of such property only where the loss occurred through an act of God, through an act of a public enemy, or through the fault of the guest himself.

"Since the passing of years has erased much of the need for such absolute liability, the modern innkeeper is often permitted by statute to lessen his responsibility to certain limits, if he provides suitable locks on his guests' rooms, provides a safe for the protection of their valuables, and provides adequate notice of the presence of that safe and, in some cases, of his limited liability.

"A.R.S. § 33–302(A) provides that an innkeeper who maintains a fireproof safe and posts the required notice is not liable for loss of jewelry or articles of unusual value 'which is not the result of his own act.' Subsection B provides that the innkeeper is not liable for more than $500.00 for the loss of jewelry or valuable items placed in the innkeeper's fireproof safe unless otherwise agreed to in writing, or unless the loss is 'the result of the fault or negligence of the innkeeper.' Subsection C has a separate provision limiting liability of the innkeeper for loss or damage to merchandise samples unless it 'results from the fault or negligence of the innkeeper.'

"Appellant argues that the phrase in subsection A, 'which is not the result of his own act,' preserves a cause of action against the innkeeper for his negligent inaction in failing to provide adequate security and in failing to warn appellant of the number of thefts within the hotel.

"There are cases from some jurisdictions holding that innkeeper's liability statutes were intended to relieve only the innkeeper's liability as an insurer, but not to preclude recovery for loss caused by the innkeeper's negligence. *See, e.g., Shiman Bros. & Co. v. Nebraska Nat. Hotel Co.,* 143 Neb. 404, 9 N.W.2d 807 (1943); *Hoffman v. Louis D. Miller & Co.* 83 R.I. 284, 115 A.2d 689 (1955); *Shifflette v. Lilly,* 130 W. Va. 297, 43 S.E.2d 289 (1947). Other jurisdictions have interpreted the provisions of particular statutes as limiting the amount of recovery for loss of a guest's property even when caused by the innkeeper's negligence. *See, e.g., Ricketts v. Morehead Co.,* 122 Cal. App. 2d 948, 265 P.2d 963 (1954); *Pfennig v. Roosevelt Hotel,* 31 So. 2d 31 (La. 1947); *Levesque v. Columbia Hotel,* 141 Me. 393, 44 A.2d 728 (1945); *Goodwin v. Georgian Hotel Co.,* 197 Wash. 173, 84 P.2d 681 (1938).

"We are guided in our analysis of the statute in question by the customary principles of statutory construction. Statutes are not to be construed as effecting any change in the common law beyond that which is clearly indicated. [Citations omitted.] Where a statute is in derogation of the common law, and is also remedial in nature, the remedial application should be construed so as to give effect to its purpose. . . . *Albuquerque Hilton Inn v. Haley,* 90 N.M. 510, 512, 565 P.2d 1027, 1029 (1977). *See also* A.R.S. § 1–211; *State v. Allred,* 102 Ariz. 102, 425 P.2d 572 (1967).

"In interpreting a statute, full effect is to be given to the legislative intent, 'and each word, phrase, clause and sentence must be given meaning so that no part will be void, inert, redundant or trivial.' *Adams v. Bolin,* 74 Ariz. 269, 276, 247 P.2d 617, 621 (1952). [Citation omitted.]

"The term 'negligence' includes both action and inaction, commission and omission. A.R.S. § 1–215(20); *Salt River Valley Water Users' Association v. Compton,* 39 Ariz. 491, 8 P.2d 249, on rehearing 40 Ariz. 282, 11 P.2d 839 (1932). The word 'act,' however, 'denotes the affirmative. Omission denotes the negative. Act is the expression of will, purpose. Omission is inaction. Act carries the idea of performance. Omission carries the idea of refraining from action.' *Randle v. Birmingham Railway, Light & Power Co.,* 169 Ala. 314, 324, 53 So. 918, 921 (1910). W. Prosser, Law of Torts § 56, at 338–39 (4th ed. 1971) states:

"In the determination of the existence of a duty, there runs through much of the law a distinction between action and inaction. In the early common law one who injured another by a positive, affirmative act, was held liable without any great regard even for his fault. But the courts were far too much occupied with the more flagrant forms of misbehavior to be greatly concerned with one who merely did nothing, even though another might suffer harm because of his omission to act. Hence there arose very early a difference, still deeply rooted in the law of negligence, between 'misfeasance' and 'non-feasance'—that is to say, between active misconduct working positive injury to others and passive inaction or a failure to take steps to protect them from harm. The reason for the distinction may be said to lie in the fact that by 'misfeasance' the defendant has created a new risk of harm to the plaintiff, while by 'non-feasance' he has at least made his situation no worse, and has merely failed to benefit him by interfering in his affairs.

"Applying these concepts to A.R.S. § 33–302, we hold that the legislature, by using the word 'act' in subsection A, intended to eliminate the common law liability of innkeepers and to encourage hotel guests to deposit their jewelry and valuable possessions in the innkeeper's fireproof safe, failing which the guest may not recover a loss from the innkeeper unless the loss results from some *active misfeasance* of the innkeeper, or unless adequate notice of the existence of the safe has not been provided to the guest. Concerning loss of items which are in fact deposited by the guest for keeping in the innkeeper's safe, the legislature, by using the words 'fault or negligence' in subsection B, intended to make the innkeeper liable to the guest for any loss occurring thereafter which is the result of the innkeeper's negligent action or inaction.

"Since appellants did not deposit their valuables in the safe, active misfeasance of the innkeeper must be shown. Appellants' only allegations of fault by appellees for the loss of their jewelry are allegations of failure of appellees to provide adequate security precautions and failure to warn appellants about the number of thefts in the hotel. These are allegations of non-feasance or acts of omission. Therefore, assuming adequate compliance by appellees with the statutory notice requirements, no cause of action exists in favor of appellants for the loss of their jewelry, which was not deposited in the safe while they were guests at appellees' hotel, based on appellees' failure to warn them of the number of thefts and to provide adequate security. . . .

"[The court's discussion of adequacy of notice to the guest of the statutory limitation is omitted.]

"For the foregoing reasons, the partial summary judgment of the trial court is affirmed."

The following Nevada cases explore innkeeper responsibility for losses of guest valuables caused by gross negligence.

LEVITT v. DESERT PALACE, INC.
601 F.2d 684 (2d Cir. 1979)

MULLIGAN, Cir. J.: "William Levitt and his wife Simone Levitt were nonpaying guests at Caesar's Palace Hotel and Casino in Las Vegas, Nevada from May 16 through May 19, 1975. They had been invited by the Hotel to attend the Alan King Tennis Tournament which features professional players and celebrities (i.e., movie stars, theatrical and business personalities). Unfortunately as it developed, Mrs. Levitt brought with her an assortment of her jewelry including a 24 carat diamond engagement ring, a diamond wedding band, a sapphire necklace, sapphire earrings and a sapphire ring, claimed in all to be worth in excess of $1,300,000. She also brought other gold and diamond jewelry of lesser value. Shortly after registering, the Levitts deposited the jewelry in the Hotel's safe deposit box where it remained until Saturday, May 18 when the Levitts were to attend a costume ball. Prior to the ball, Mr. Levitt retrieved the jewelry from the box and his wife selected the large diamond engagement ring, the diamond wedding band, the sapphire pieces and several others. Mr. Levitt then returned the case and the rejects to the safe deposit box.

"After the ball was over at 1:00 or 1:30 A.M., the Levitts dropped in at the Noshorium, an all-night restaurant off the hotel lobby. Thirty minutes later they returned to their room where Mrs. Levitt placed the jewelry on top of a dresser near the bed. Mr. Levitt then engaged the night lock, or 'dead bolt' and they retired. Upon arising late the next morning, Mrs. Levitt instructed her husband to collect the jewelry on the dresser and return it to the safe deposit box. Mr. Levitt scooped up the jewelry, placed it in a handkerchief, and returned the contents to the box. He failed to notice that the major pieces—two diamond rings, the sapphire ring, necklace and earrings—were missing. Not until later that afternoon after the jewelry case had been brought back to the room did Mrs. Levitt become aware in the course of packing that the five valuable pieces were gone. After the local police and hotel security people were summoned it was discovered that the dead bolt had been tampered with and rendered inoperable.

" . . . Plaintiffs sought a substantial punitive award and compensatory damages of $1,300,000, and the alleged value of the stolen jewelry. The trial was bifurcated—one jury found the defendant liable for the loss and a second returned a verdict of $548,599 in favor of the Levitts. The hotel then moved for judgment notwithstanding the verdict or, in the alternative, for a new trial. The Levitts moved for a new trial solely on the issue of damages. All motions were denied in a memorandum decision and order of the Hon. Lee P. GAGLIARDI, District Judge, on September 27, 1978. Judgment in favor of the Levitts in the sum of $548,599 was entered on October 3, 1978. This appeal by the Hotel ensued. The Levitts have cross-appealed for a new trial on the issues of damages only if this court orders a new trial on the issue of liability.

The Standard of Care

"The extraordinary standard of care imposed upon the innkeeper at common law originated in the feudal conditions of the Middle Ages, R. Brown, The Law of Personal Property § 102 at 482 (2d ed. 1955), and has long since been ameliorated by state legislation. *Id.* § 106 at 501. Nevada's pertinent statute provides: 'No owner or keeper of any hotel, inn, motel, motor court, or boarding house or lodginghouse in this state shall be civilly liable after July 1, 1953, for the loss of any property left in the room of any guest of any such establishment by reason of theft, burglary, fire or otherwise, in the absence of *gross neglect* upon the part of such keeper or owner.' Nev. Rev. Stat. § 651.010 (emphasis supplied).

Gross Negligence

"The state courts of Nevada have not yet construed its Innkeepers Statute, Nev. Rev. Stat. § 651.010. Judge GAGLIARDI did charge the jury, however, in the language employed by the highest court of the State in *Hart v. Kline,* 61 Nev. 96, 116 P.2d 672 (1941), which construed the phrase 'gross negligence' in the context of the Nevada automobile guest statute:

"Gross negligence is substantially and appreciably higher in magnitude and more culpable than ordinary negligence. Gross negligence is equivalent to the failure to exercise even a slight degree of care. It is materially more want of care than constitutes simple inadvertence. It is an act or omission respecting legal duty of an aggravated character as distinguished from a mere failure to exercise ordinary care. It is very great negligence, or the absence of slight diligence, or the want of even scant care. It amounts to indifference to present legal duty, and to utter forgetfulness of legal obligations so far as other persons may be affected. It is a heedless and palpable violation of legal duty respecting the rights of others. The element of culpability which characterizes all negligence is, in gross negligence, magnified to a higher degree as compared with that present in ordinary negligence. Gross negligence is manifestly a smaller amount of watchfulness and circumspection than the circumstances require of a prudent man.

" . . . [T]he issue for this court is whether on the evidence adduced at trial the jury could reasonably have found that the Hotel failed to exercise even a slight degree of care to safeguard the Levitts against the loss incurred.

" . . . After reviewing the entire record we are persuaded that the evidence presented was insufficient to warrant submission to the jury of the issue of gross neglect and that a jury could not rationally find that the hotel did not exercise even slight care in protecting the Levitts' property.

"The jury could reasonably have inferred from the evidence adduced that someone entered the Levitts' room when it was unoccupied early in the day on May 18 and removed the dead bolt by taking out the screws which held it to the door. It was replaced with a mechanism which appeared to function but which in fact was inoperative. While the Levitts were asleep the cylinder door lock was again 'picked' and the jewelry stolen, the dead bolt having provided no protection at all against entry. There was evidence by one of plaintiffs' expert witnesses, a New York City Police Department Detective, that all cylinder locks are ineffective when manipulated or picked by an experienced thief. He also testified that a dead bolt which is operative and set by the room occupant cannot be picked and can only be overcome from the outside by literally breaking down the door. The jury could reasonably find therefore that the dead bolt in the Levitts' room had been tampered with and was inoperative on the night in question.

"The record is further clear that there had been two instances of dead bolt doctoring at the hotel a year before the Levitts' visit and a third just a few weeks before they arrived. In essence this case turns on whether in the face of this risk the Hotel responded with at least a slight degree of care.

"After the first two incidents of dead bolt tampering, some five or six months before the Levitts' visit, the Hotel commenced a program to make their dead bolts 'tamper proof.' The screws which held the dead bolt were replaced with rivets which could not be unscrewed. To make extraction even more difficult a screw was inserted sideways through the dead bolt and into the door. The indentation over the screwhead was filled with putty and covered. The Hotel's program for upgrading the dead bolts for its 1200 rooms was proceeding on an almost daily basis but had not yet reached the room assigned to the Levitts.

"The evidence establishes without doubt that the Hotel had recognized the possibility of dead bolt tampering and had responded in a way which would have virtually eliminated the problem. There was no evidence at all in the case that other hotels in the area had done more or, in fact, had done anything at all to cure the problem. The Levitts' expert witness on hotel security admitted that the cylinder locks in Caesar's Palace were rekeyed every six months, far more frequently than the one and one-half to two year intervals for rekeying locks in the hotel which he managed. He further testified that at his hotel, defective dead bolts were simply replaced individually as they were discovered. In contrast, appellant was engaged in a program to replace the dead bolt locks in every room in the Hotel. Moreover, although the dead bolt in the Levitts' room had not yet been reworked, there was testimony that the house-keeping staff had been given instructions to check the dead bolts daily to ensure that the mechanisms were functioning properly.

"Furthermore, the evidence demonstrated that the Hotel had undertaken other substantial security measures. In addition to a regular force of 55 Hotel guards, 39 additional security personnel patrolled the premises during the tennis tournament week. One guard was stationed at the first floor of the elevator bank which serviced the new addition of the Hotel where the Levitts were quartered. Upstairs, plainclothes guards made unscheduled rounds of the corridors outside the guest rooms. These random patrols were supplemented by a fire watch from 10 P.M. to 6 A.M. during which uniformed guards made hourly patrols through every corridor. Although their function was to detect fires, they were also told to watch for suspicious persons. In addition to augmenting its security force by 70% for the event, the Hotel informed its patrons by a notice on their guest registration forms as well as by signs posted in every guest room of the availability of safe deposit boxes for the storage of valuables. Upon request the Hotel provided an escort service (of which the Levitts did not deny they were aware) so that guests would feel secure in making the trip from their rooms to the safe deposit boxes located off the lobby. Certainly the Hotel could reasonably expect that its guests who had precious jewelry and other valuables would avail themselves of these facilities. Indeed, the Levitts conceded that on every night during their stay at the Hotel except that on which the theft occurred they had stored the jewelry in one of the Hotel's safe deposit boxes.

"With the inevitable advantages of hindsight it can be argued that the Hotel would have been more prudent to implement speedier albeit somewhat less effective methods of hindering dead bolt tampering. But the issue before us is simply whether the Hotel exercised even slight care to insure the safety of its guests' property from that risk. The record overwhelmingly supports the conclusion that the Hotel not only satisfied that standard but responded with more than slight care. Viewing the evidence most favorably to the Levitts we are nonetheless constrained to find as a matter of law that there was insufficient evidence on this record to support the verdict of the jury and that the trial judge erred in failing to grant the motion to set aside the judgment notwithstanding the jury verdict.

''Judgment for plaintiffs is reversed and the case remanded for entry of judgment in favor of the defendant.''

In 1979, Nevada amended its statute by adding the following new paragraph:

> If an owner . . . of any hotel . . . provides a fireproof safe or vault in which guests may deposit property for safekeeping, and notice of this service is personally given to a guest or posted in the office and the guest's room, the owner . . . is not liable for the theft of any property which is not offered for deposit in the safe or vault by a guest unless the owner or keeper is grossly negligent.[53]

To the same effect, construing Nevada law, see *Kabo v. Summa Corp.*,[54] and *Levin by Levin v. Desert Palace Inc.*[55]

In *Owens v. Summa Corporation*,[56] the federal court of appeals held that Nevada's innkeeper's statute absolved a hotelkeeper of liability for theft, absent proof of gross negligence, of jewelry and cash stolen from a room occupied by sleeping guests. The guests' contention that the statute was intended to apply only to thefts from empty guest rooms was rejected, based on the *Levitt* case, *supra*, cited with approval and followed. The statute was held to apply to property left in the guest rooms whether occupied or not, in the absence of any deposit of valuables for safekeeping.

In *Kahn v. Hotel Ramada of Nevada*,[57] the Federal Court of Appeals for the Fifth Circuit interpreted the Nevada statute limiting liability for loss of guest property to place a $750 ceiling on recovery for jewelry samples lost when left with a bellman while the guest was preparing to depart, even if the guest proved that the hotel was grossly negligent. In other words, the innkeeper's liability for guest property lost within or without the hotel room owing to gross negligence is limited to $750.

In *Laubie v. Sonesta International Hotel Corp.*,[58] the Supreme Court of Louisiana interpreted its innkeepers' civil code provisions to limit liability arising out of contracts of deposit of guest property for safekeeping but not to limit liability arising out of innkeeper negligence or other torts causing loss of guest property. This decision was cited and followed in a federal lawsuit where guest jewelry was lost through theft from the guest room by violence. There was no one present at the front desk to accept the guest's jewelry for safekeeping before

---

[53]Nev. Rev. Stat., section 651.010(2) (1979).
[54]523 F. Supp. 1326 (E.D. Pa. 1981).
[55]465 A.2d 1019 (Pa. Super. 1983).
[56]625 F.2d 600 (5th Cir. 1980).
[57]799 F.2d 199 (5th Cir. 1986).
[58]398 So. 2d 1374 (La. 1981).

she retired for the night. This omission was held to constitute negligence, to which the Louisiana civil code limiting liability for undeposited valuable property was held not to apply.[59]

The Louisiana legislature thereupon amended the statute,[60] to limit liability under either theory. (*See* Appendix B, this chapter, for state limitation of liability statutes.) Most jurisdictions adopt this solution.

13:23 *Extent of Liability for Valuables Deposited in Gambling Casino Safe*

Special note must be made of the liability of hotels that operate licensed gambling casinos. As a general rule, the innkeeper's responsibility as a bailee is not affected by statutes limiting his liability for money lost where the guest avails himself of the hotel safe provided for that purpose. This is so because a hotel guest who patronizes the casino makes known to the hotel casino bank the amount of money he deposits for gambling and receives a written receipt for the amount deposited. Since the hotel casino operator wishes to encourage high-stakes gambling, the amounts receipted for far exceed the statutory limit. The recovery of a patron not a guest is in no way limited by statute. The duty to a patron is always that of a common-law bailee. A hotel guest who fails to deposit money or valuables is, however, severely restricted in recovering for such losses.

Nevada's general innkeeper's statute is unique because it exempts the innkeeper from liability for any property that the guest fails to deposit unless the *gross negligence* of the owner or hotelkeeper can be established, with the burden of proof resting upon the guest. The owner or hotelkeeper, however, is not obliged to receive property exceeding $750 in value, unless he consents to do so in a written agreement wherein the guest specifies the value of the property.

The Supreme Court of Nevada had occasion to pass on the responsibility of an innkeeper to a hotel guest who made such a deposit in the hotel's casino bank for an amount in excess of the statutory ceiling, duly acknowledged by the innkeeper. In *Kula v. Karat, Inc.*,[61] an action was brought by a hotel guest who had deposited funds with the hotel casino to recover the amount deposited. The hotel defended on the ground that the guest had orally agreed to be responsible for the gambling debts of his companion up to the amount of the deposit. In an unreported oral opinion, the district court held that title to the balance of the deposit passed to the hotel. The Nevada Supreme Court reversed:

> The trial court properly found a bailment had been created by the deposit of the money with the respondent. A bailment of money is as well recognized as the bailment of any other personal property. . . .
>
> The respondent is estopped to claim that Goldfinger had any right, title or interest in the money on deposit and it would have been error for the trial court to find any.

---

[59]Durandy v. Fairmont Roosevelt Hotel, Inc., 523 F. Supp. 1382 (E.D. La. 1981). To the same effect, *see* Kraaz v. La Quinta Motor Inns, Inc., 410 So. 2d 1048 (La. App. 1982).

[60]La. Civ. Code Ann., article 2971 (West).

[61]91 Nev. 100, 531 P.2d 1353 (Nev. 1975).

There is authority for the broad rule that as long as the relationship exists a bailee may not, in any case, dispute or deny the title of the bailor, or his ultimate right to possession, either by claiming title in himself, or as a justification for his refusal to return the property, or by asserting title in a third person.

Where a bailee, either for hire or gratuitously, is entrusted with care and custody of goods, it becomes his duty at the end of the bailment to return the goods or show that their loss occurred without negligence on his part. Failing in this, there arises a presumption that the goods have been converted by him, or lost as a result of his negligence, and he is accountable to the owner for them. [Citation omitted.]

It is difficult to discern from the record whether or not the trial court, in reaching its decision, relied upon the disputed evidence purporting to show an oral commitment by appellant to be financially responsible for the gambling losses of Goldfinger to the extent of the amount of money in safekeeping. However, if it did, such reliance was in error because NRS 111.220 renders void an agreement to answer for the debts of another which is not in writing. . . .

Although appellant is bound by the admission contained in his pleadings that $1,000 be retained by respondent [citation omitted], he is entitled to recover the $17,000 which was converted.

This matter is reversed and remanded with instructions to enter a judgment in favor of appellant not inconsistent with this opinion.[62]

13:24 *Valuables Stolen from Safe or Guest Room by Hotel Employee or Intruder*

An innkeeper is not necessarily liable in excess of the statutory limitation for valuables of a guest stolen by an employee from the hotel safe.

In *Millhiser v. Beau Site Co.,*[63] the plaintiff, Regina Millhiser, a transient guest in defendant's hotel, delivered to the clerk at the desk a package containing jewelry of the value of $369,800. She did not notify him of the value of the package. He gave her a key to a safety deposit box and placed the package in it. The box could be unlocked only by the use of a master key and the key, or a duplicate thereof, that had been given to the plaintiff. Later the plaintiff called for the package. When the box was opened, the jewelry to the value of $50,000 was missing. Thereafter the clerk who had received the package from the plaintiff was convicted of stealing the missing jewelry.

The defendant had posted in the public rooms and guest rooms a notice which read: "A safe is provided in the office of this hotel for the use of guests in which money, jewels, or other valuables may be deposited for safekeeping." No other or different notice was posted.

The Appellate Division held that section 200 of the General Business Law does not protect a hotel or limit its liability for the loss of jewelry stolen by its own employee.

---

[62]*Id.*
[63]251 N.Y. 290, 167 N.E. 447 (1929).

The Court of Appeals disagreed. "the purpose of the section," said the court, "is to protect the hotel from an undisclosed excessive liability."[64] It was to enable hotels, without notice of value, to avoid liability in excess of $500. The statute provides that if a guest desires to impose liability in excess of $500, he must give notice of value and obtain a written agreement making the hotel liable for more than $500.

However, the court continued, section 200 is not intended to limit a hotelkeeper's liability to $500 where the articles deposited are stolen by the hotelkeeper from the guest. "We read the statute to mean a theft of the articles from the hotelkeeper and not a theft by the hotelkeeper from the guest. The act of the defendant's employee in stealing the jewelry was a wrongful act, outside the scope of his employment and for his own enrichment. It was not in any guise the act of the defendant. [Citation omitted.]"[65]

Notwithstanding the exculpation of the hotel from liability because of the theft of the jewelry by its own employee, the court of appeals agreed with the result reached by the appellate division holding the hotel liable, but on another ground, namely, that it failed and neglected to post the statutory notice required by section 206 of the General Business Law.

The *Millhiser* rationale rests on the court's explicit finding that the hotel employee's criminal misconduct was not imputable to the innkeeper under the theory of *respondeat superior* (*see* section 11:6, *supra*). Unlike merely negligent conduct, the criminal conduct of an employee in general does not implicate his employer, unless the employer participated in that conduct or condoned or ratified it. However, this question is often left to the jury, with the outcome necessarily unpredictable. Independently of imputed liability, an employer who negligently hires an untrustworthy employee, or one known to have criminal propensities related to the theft of guest property, may be found liable on that ground alone.

In *Link-Simon, Inc. v. Muehlebach Hotel, Inc.*,[66] the federal district court, interpreting the Missouri innkeeper's liability statute, held that the statute completely altered the common-law liability of innkeepers as insurers of the property of guests, regardless of whether the guest sued on a negligence theory or a strict liability theory. A jewelry salesman was precluded from recovering for jewelry samples deposited in the hotel safe, the key to which had been forcibly removed from his person by robbers who thereafter used the key to secure the jewelry. The statute required written notice to the hotel that the guest had such merchandise in his possession, in order to impose any liability, and in the absence of such notice, the guest was unable to hold the innkeeper liable.

More recently, in *de Saric v. Miami Caribe Investment, Inc.*,[67] the federal Court of Appeals for the Fifth Circuit held that under Florida law a guest who

---

[64]*Id.* at 294, 167 N.E. at 448.
[65]*Id.* at 295, 167 N.E. at 448.
[66]374 F. Supp. 789 (W.D. Mo. 1974).
[67]512 F.2d 1013 (5th Cir. 1975).

failed to deposit valuables with the innkeeper was absolutely barred from recovering for his loss caused by a holdup in his guest room by masked intruders even though the innkeeper did not post the statutory notices of its limitation of liability. The Florida statute[68] provides that "in no event" will a hotel be liable for a loss of valuables not deposited with the hotel.

The guests argued that such an interpretation would violate their federal and state constitutional rights to equal protection if in fact the notices had not been posted.

The circuit court in *de Saric* remanded to the trial court the questions whether the statutory notices had been posted and, if not, whether the circuit court's prior interpretation[69] of the relevant Florida statute violated either the federal or state constitutions and was thus invalid.

The language of a particular statute governs whether the innkeeper is responsible for theft or robbery from the hotel room, and thus no general rule is available that would apply in every state. It is fair to conclude, however, that a failure to deposit valuables would severely limit the guest's right to recover (*see* section 13:22, *supra*).

In *Nova Stylings, Inc. v. Red Roof Inns, Inc.,*[70] the Supreme Court of Kansas interpreted the Kansas innkeeper's statute limiting liability for loss of deposited property to apply to a jewelry saleswoman's samples which were entrusted to a desk clerk by a guest and stored in the manager's office. The contents of the case which contained the samples were never identified, but the clerk was advised that the contents were valuable and that the case was to be released only to the guest. The high court, in an exhaustive opinion, ruled that the Kansas statute governed actions for negligence; that the provisions covering merchandise for sale or sample governed the guest's claim; that the guest was required to disclose the nature of the property left with the innkeeper; that where the guest fails to provide an itemized list of the property, the innkeeper is not responsible; and that the statute applied to the property of a nonguest, where her companion, a guest, failed to notify the innkeeper that the property belonged to the nonguest.

13:25 *Instructions to Safe Clerks*

Innkeepers who use the individual lock boxes of the double key type will find the following admonitions to safe clerks helpful:

(*a*) Never, never, never let any guest have access to the guard key.

(*b*) Keep the guard key under the care and supervision of the safe clerk at all times.

(*c*) When a guest requests access to the box, always ask his name, room number, and key number.

---

[68]Ch. 16042, Florida Acts, § 40 (1933).
[69]Ely v. Charellen Corp., 120 F.2d 984 (5th Cir. 1941) (citing Florida authorities).
[70]242 Kan. 318, 747 P.2d 107 (Kan. 1987).

(*d*) Always witness the guest's signature, compare the access signature with the guest's original signature, and always affix your initials to witness every access signature.

(*e*) It is best that you let the guest remove his box from the safe; if you do it, be sure that it is done in the presence and in full view of the guest.

(*f*) Afford the guest privacy to use his box, but be in a position at all times to observe the actions of the guest in the safe area.

(*g*) Never use the guest's key; after you partially release the locking mechanism with the guard key ask the guest to open the box with his own key.

(*h*) Ask the guest to return the box into the safe and assist only with locking the safe.

(*i*) If you are aware that the guest is checking out, be sure to obtain his signature for the surrender of the box on the safe deposit card, and obtain the key.

(*j*) Follow the standard procedure *every time with every guest*. Laxity is dangerous.

13:26 *Liability for Valuables in Guest's Possession When Guest's Departure Is Imminent*

SPILLER V. BARCLAY HOTEL
68 Misc. 2d 400, 327 N.Y.S.2d 426 (Civ. Ct. 1972)

SANDLER, J.: "Plaintiff, a guest of the Barclay Hotel, sues for the value of property, primarily wearing apparel and jewelry, lost on the steps of the hotel while she was in the process of leaving.

"Plaintiff testified that after her two bags were brought to the lobby floor, she asked a bellboy to take them to the cab area and to watch them while she checked out. When she came to the cab area, only one of her bags was there and the bellboy was not present. A search failed to disclose the missing bag or its contents. . . .

"Accordingly, I find that the property was lost through the actual negligence of the Defendant. No doubt the bellboy was under no inherent duty to watch the bags, and it may well be that his implicit undertaking to do so violated his instructions. Nonetheless, when he accepted the bags with the accompanying request to watch them, without explicitly declining the latter request, an obligation of care was assumed which quite clearly was not fulfilled.

"As to the claim for lost property other than jewelry, it is clear that the limitations of value set forth in Section 201 of the General Business Law, are not applicable because of the actual negligence of the Defendant. That section, relating to loss of clothing and other personal property, explicitly exempts from its coverage losses due to 'fault or negligence.' [Citation omitted.]

"The claim for the items of lost jewelry presents a more troublesome problem. Section 200 of the General Business Law excludes recovery by a hotel guest for loss of, among other categories enumerated, jewels, ornaments and precious stones where the hotel provides a safe for such items, gives appropriate notice of that fact, and the guest does not use that facility. It has been conceded that the hotel maintained such a safe and had posted the required notice.

"Preliminarily, I find that the items of jewelry here involved, which included a necklace, a pendant, earrings and the like, come within the definition of 'jewels' and 'ornaments,' as these terms are used in Section 200. The distinction drawn in the leading case of *Ramaley v. Leland,* 43 N.Y. 539, 542 (1871), which has been consistently followed, is between articles 'carried for use and convenience' and articles worn as an 'ornament.' [Citation omitted.]

"Moreover, although the question is less clearly settled than one would have supposed, it now appears to be the law that a guest who has failed to deposit property for safekeeping in accordance with the requirement of Section 200 may not recover for the loss even if the hotel was actually negligent. [Citation omitted.]

"What seems to me decisive here is that Section 200 was not designed to apply to a loss occurring under the circumstances of this case. Section 200 clearly contemplates a procedure for safeguarding the specified categories of property during a guest's stay at a hotel. Its provisions do not seem to me to be reasonably applied to a loss that takes place when a guest is about to leave, has gathered together her property preparatory to an imminent departure, and is arranging for the transfer of luggage to a vehicle for transportation.

"Although that situation presents some conceptual difficulties, I am satisfied that the sensible and fair approach is to consider a loss occurring at that point in time neither in terms of the provisions of Section 200, nor in terms of the traditional common law liability of innkeepers, but rather on the basis of the presence or absence of actual negligence. [Citation omitted.]

"Having found that the loss here resulted from the negligence of a hotel employee, acting within the scope of his employment, I hold that Plaintiff is entitled to recover the value of the lost jewelry. . . . ''

The above New York case is representative of the prevailing rule, since it rests on the tacit assumption that the guest cannot be expected to deposit valuables in the hotel safe when the guest is about to depart. Any such requirement would impose an unreasonable burden on the guest, contrary to the innkeeper's obligation not to interfere unjustifiably with the continuation of the guest's journey.[71]

13:27 *Liability for Guest's Property after Guest's Departure*

In *Great American Insurance Co. v. Coppedge,*[72] the plaintiff hid her jewelry in her nightstand while she was a guest at the Diplomat Hotel. After she checked out, a maid found her jewelry and turned it over to the director of hotel security, who claimed, at trial, that he had misplaced it. For purposes of examining the

[71]But *see* Kahn v. Hotel Ramada of Nevada, 799 F.2d 199 (5th Cir. 1986), noted at p. 524.
[72]405 So. 2d 732 (Fla. App. 1981). *rev. denied,* 415 So. 2d 1359 (1982).

hotel's liability, the Florida Appeals Court deemed plaintiff a "guest" at the time the jewels became missing. The court noted that to do otherwise would bring about the absurd result under Florida statutory law of limiting the hotel's liability while plaintiff was actually a guest and not limiting its liability when plaintiff had departed.

13:28   *Statutory Exemption Applies Only to Property of Guests*

Sections 200 and 201 of the New York General Business Law were intended only as a limitation of the liability of an innkeeper as an insurer of the property of his guest. These sections do not ordinarily apply to the relationship of landlord and tenant.[73]

This interpretation is universally followed since the extraordinary common-law liability of the innkeeper was asserted to protect only guests, not those accommodated in a different capacity. The statutes limiting the excessive liability of the innkeeper were intended to mitigate the harshness of the common law. Since the origin of the common-law rule was to protect the traveler, understood to mean a transient not having a permanent home in the locality in which the inn was situated, the permanent inhabitant of the inn was not in need of such protection and thus not afforded these rights. (*See* section 2:4, *supra*.)

13:29   *Waiver of Statutory Limitation*

The innkeeper may waive the statutory limitation in his favor and having once done so, he cannot afterwards ask for its protection.

Mitsuya v. Croydon Management Co.
448 F. Supp. 811 (S.D.N.Y. 1978)

Metzner, D.J.: "Plaintiff seeks to recover damages for the loss of her jewelry after it had been entrusted for safekeeping to the hotel at which she had been a guest. This court has jurisdiction by reason of the diversity of citizenship of the parties.

"Plaintiff asserted . . . that a desk clerk in the hotel approached her, commented upon her jewelry and informed her that the hotel had safe deposit boxes that she could use free of charge to keep her valuables in for safekeeping. Plaintiff further stated that until that time she had been unaware that the hotel had such facilities, or that there was a limitation of liability.

"Plaintiff contends that this oral inducement may act as an estoppel to the defendants' defense of a statutory limitation of liability under N.Y. Gen. Bus. Law § 200 (McKinney 1968) (the statute), even assuming that defendants complied with the other requirements of the statute.

---

[73]Jacobs v. Alrae Hotel Corp., 4 Misc. 2d 665, 161 N.Y.S.2d 972 (Sup. Ct. 1956), *rev'd on other grounds*, 4 A.D.2d 201, 164 N.Y.S.2d 330 (1st Dep't 1957), *aff'd mem.*, 4 N.Y.2d 769, 149 N.E.2d 337 (1958).

"The statute provides that defendants' liability is limited to $500 if jewelry is turned over to them and they have complied with the notice requirements. Of course, if jewelry is not turned over and there has been compliance with the notice requirements, any loss must be borne by the guest. The statute further provides that the limitation of liability imposed by the statute can be modified only by a writing. Defendants contend that they complied with the notice requirements of the statute and thus their liability is limited to a maximum of $500 despite any oral representations by their agents.

"Defendants are correct in that the limitation of liability imposed by the statute could not be 'modified' by an oral representation in light of the specific statutory requirement that all changes be in writing. *See Gray v. Met Contracting Corp.*, 4 A.D.2d 495, 167 N.Y.S.2d 498 (1st Dept. 1957); Williston on Contracts § 591 (3d ed. 1961). However, plaintiff's contention is not that the statement allegedly made by defendants' agent modified the contract, but rather that it bars defendants from asserting the statutory limitation by the principle of equitable estoppel.

"In *Gray v. Met Contracting Corp., supra,* it was held that the principles of equity could be applied to estop a party from asserting a statutory defense even in the absence of a required writing. In that case the court held that: '[E]stoppel would not be in conflict with [the statute] since it would not constitute an oral modification of a written contract, but the application of an ancient equitable principle whereby a person whose conduct has induced reliance thereon may not thereafter bring an action which is inconsistent with that conduct.' *Id.* at 497, 167 N.Y.S.2d at 501.

"The New York courts have not decided the issue of equitable estoppel with regard to the statute involved in this action. However, they found hotels to have waived their rights under the statute, *e.g., Friedman v. Breslin,* 51 App. Div. 268, 65 N.Y.S. 5 (1st Dept.), *aff'd,* 169 N.Y. 574, 61 N.E. 1129 (1900), and therefore it is clear that the holding in *Gray* would be applicable to the case at bar.

"Since it is possible for defendants to be barred from asserting the statutory defense by the principle of equitable estoppel, we must examine the alleged conduct in this case to see if it is sufficient to invoke the bar.

"Assuming that plaintiff's version of the facts is true, the hotel clerk's conduct did indeed induce her to deposit her jewels with the hotel. However, these statements were no more than would appear on notices of availability of safekeeping boxes posted by a hotel pursuant to the statute. There appears to be nothing in plaintiff's version of what the hotel clerk said to her that would require equity to estop the hotel from asserting the limitation of liability. It might be different if the clerk had indicated that there was no limitation of liability.

"If in fact defendants complied with all of the notice requirements mandated by the statute, and this is the disputed issue in the case that can only be decided by the jury, then they are free to assert the $500 limitation of liability clause of the statute. . . .

"So ordered."

13:30 *Statutory Limitations of Liability for Property Other Than Valuables*

In some states,[74] including New York,[75] the innkeeper is afforded protection against excessive liability with respect to property other than valuables, such as clothing left in the guest room or property stored or deposited temporarily on the premises. These limitations are intended to regulate the loss of or damage to guest property that may be extremely valuable, such as a mink or sable coat or a vicuna coat or suit, but which are not specifically enumerated as "valuables" required to be deposited in the hotel safe, or which are too bulky or otherwise unsuitable for deposit in the typical hotel safe.

The treatment of such property in New York differs from the treatment of valuables under the statute in one significant manner. Whereas a failure to deposit valuables in the safe exonerates the innkeeper from liability irrespective of the cause of the loss, if nonvaluables are lost, the limitation otherwise applicable does not apply if the guest proves that the loss "occurred through the fault or negligence of such keeper." This provision governs any loss of guest property other than valuables from the guest room, lobby, or hallways.[76]

If the property is deposited for safekeeping in a storage room, luggage room, or other place than the guest room, such as a parcel or checkroom, then two further requirements apply: (1) the guest must declare value in excess of the statutory ceiling, and the innkeeper must agree in writing, evidenced by a written receipt, to be bound by such a declaration, and (2) in order for the guest to recover in excess of the otherwise applicable ceiling, the loss must be caused by the fault or negligence of the innkeeper. In no case can the guest recover an amount greater than the value declared and accepted by the innkeeper.

Under Section 201 of the New York General Business Law, the amount of the statutory ceiling in the absence of a declared value accepted by the innkeeper is fixed by the following considerations:

1. *The nature of the property.* Merchandise samples and merchandise for sale are treated as a special case. The innkeeper is under no liability whatever for loss of or damage to such property, either in the guest's possession or delivered to the innkeeper for storage, unless the guest provides prior written notice stating value to the innkeeper, who accepts the liability in writing. The applicable limitation is in effect irrespective of value stated and acknowledged, unless the guest proves that the loss or damage was due to the fault or negligence of the innkeeper.

2. *The location of the property.* Storerooms and parcel rooms are treated as separate entities. A higher ceiling on the amount recoverable is provided for the former. There is a stated ceiling on the amount recoverable for property lost or

---

[74]*See, e.g.,* Mass. Ann. Laws. ch 140, § 10 (Mitchie/Law Co-op 1935).
[75]N.Y. General Business Law, § 201 (McKinney 1968).
[76]*Id.*

damaged in transport to and from the hotel or motel. If the guest declares excess value and the hotelkeeper issues a written receipt stating such value, then double the stated ceiling governs, unless the guest can prove that the loss or damage was caused by the negligence of the innkeeper, in which case he may recover the full declared value. In no case may the guest recover an amount greater than the stated value, and the recovery of the stated value is dependent upon proof of negligence.

3. *Whether the innkeeper charges for property stored, deposited, or checked.* In the case of a storeroom or baggage room, the innkeeper may impose a reasonable charge for storage. But in the case of a parcel room or checkroom, no charge may be made if the innkeeper wishes the protection of the statutory ceiling.

4. *The nature of the storage or checkroom facility.* Whereas no requirements exist with respect to the kind of storeroom or baggage room that must be provided, the checkroom or parcel room facility must be completely enclosed and capable of being locked. Movable racks in an open space in front of elevators or at the entrance to a dining room do not constitute a checkroom, and the innkeeper cannot claim the benefit of the statutory ceiling in cases involving such racks.

5. *The identity of the owner or operator of the facility.* New York makes its checkroom or parcel room statutory scheme available to restaurant keepers as well as innkeepers. But the courts have not extended the protection to concessionaires who operate such checking facilities as independent contractors under lease or other contract with the innkeeper or restaurateur. Moreover, the existence of such an agreement does not itself insulate the innkeeper or restaurateur from liability for the negligence or other misconduct of the concessionaire. There must be proof that the patron or guest was aware that the concessionaire was the sole operator and this is a question for the jury.

6. *The cause of the loss.* Absent acts of God, which relieve the innkeeper of any liability, even as insurer, New York does not deal with causation except with respect to fire. The innkeeper is exempt from liability for loss or damage to wearing apparel or other personal property caused by fires but only if it can affirmatively prove freedom from fault or negligence causing such loss or damage. This exemption governs fires within the lobby, hallways, or guest rooms of the inn. Another provision governs outbuildings, such as bathhouses, golf club-houses, or any other sports facility where the guest is invited to store appropriate equipment. The statute governing outbuildings adds one additional element of proof upon the innkeeper, namely, that the fire was caused by arson or other willful incendiary causes not attributable to the innkeeper.

A separate provision limits liability for loss or damage to pets caused by fire to a fixed amount ($300) unless a higher value agreed upon can be proved, regardless of whether the fire was caused by negligence or fault of the innkeeper.[77]

---

[77]*Id.* § 203.

DeBANFIELD v. HILTON HOTELS CORP.

35 Misc. 2d 967, 231 N.Y.S.2d 906 (City Ct. 1962)

[Plaintiff sues defendant hotel to recover for the loss for his belongings which were taken by some unknown person during plaintiff's absence from his room.]

LEONFORTE, J.: "It appears that while plaintiff was a guest of defendant's hotel and while he was away from his hotel room on April 22, 1959, someone unknown to the parties gained access therein and removed all of his belongings, valued by plaintiff at about $3,500.

"It is plaintiff's contention that, by reason of the fault, negligence and carelessness of the defendant, the property of plaintiff totally disappeared and was lost to plaintiff without any fault or negligence on his part and that plaintiff was thereby damaged in said sum of $3,500. . . .

" . . . Defendant . . . claims that . . . its liability under Section 201 of the General Business Law is limited to $500. . . .

"As to the amount of plaintiff's recovery in this case, he is bound by the provisions of Section 201 of the General Business Law. . . .

" . . . [T]he burden of proof is upon plaintiff to show defendant's negligence and . . . before any recovery can be made in an amount over $500 the negligence of the defendant must be established by plaintiff.

"It is plaintiff's contention that defendant's negligence has been satisfactorily shown by either or both of two factors which could have resulted in plaintiff's loss. First, plaintiff showed the possibility that a nonguest could obtain a key to a guest's room merely by going to the desk clerk and by posing as the guest. . . . Secondly, plaintiff claimed that his hotel room was easily accessible to strangers and other guests since a balcony adjacent to plaintiff's room and upon which a window of plaintiff's room and those of 12 other adjacent rooms opened gave strangers and other guests the opportunity of entering plaintiff's room. Accordingly, plaintiff contends that the maintenance of the balcony under such conditions constituted negligence on defendant's part sufficient to warrant a recovery for the entire loss sustained by plaintiff.

"It is to be noted that neither plaintiff nor defendant testified as to how the alleged loss occurred. Therefore, assuming but not conceding that a nonguest could possibly obtain a key to plaintiff's room by posing as plaintiff, no evidence was submitted at the trial to show that . . . any . . . person did in fact obtain a key to plaintiff's room with the resulting loss. Nor was there any evidence to show that plaintiff's room was entered by way of the balcony. In fact, in the absence of proof of tampering with the window, if the court was of the opinion that the plaintiff's loss was occasioned because plaintiff's window was easily accessible from the balcony adjacent thereto, under such circumstances plaintiff's entire complaint would have to be dismissed because of the plaintiff's own contributory negligence in failing to close the window with the catch lock thereon contained.

"Accordingly, the court finds that plaintiff has failed to sustain the burden required of him under section 201 of the General Business Law and that he is therefore bound by the limitation of $500 provided thereunder."

The following case applies the statutory limitations to a bailment of guest property.

ALBUQUERQUE HILTON INN V. HALEY
90 N.M. 510, 565 P.2d 1027 (1977)

EASLEY, J.: "The facts pertinent to disposition are as follows. On September 18, 1974, the plaintiff, Mrs. Haley, arrived in Albuquerque on a Texas International Airlines (TIA) flight. The airline informed her that her luggage had been inadvertently transferred to Los Angeles. Mrs. Haley told TIA that she was staying at the Hilton. The next morning, her retrieved luggage was delivered to the Hilton; a receipt was signed by the desk clerk, the luggage placed on the bell stand and a bellhop called to carry the bags to Mrs. Haley's room. By the time the bellhop arrived, the luggage had disappeared. It has never been found. Mrs. Haley made repeated inquiries at the desk as to the whereabouts of her luggage and was repeatedly informed that it had not yet been delivered. When she finally contacted TIA, she was shown the receipt indicating delivery to the hotel.

"Mrs. Haley sued the Hilton for compensatory ($5,000.00) and punitive ($25,000.00) damages, basing her complaint on Hilton's alleged wrongful refusal to return her luggage or compensate her for its loss (Count I) and also for its refusal to assist her as promised in her attempts to locate her luggage (Count II). Nowhere in the complaint do allegations of theft or negligence appear, nowhere does the claim for relief purport to be based on or limited by the hotelkeeper's liability statute, § 49–6–1, [citation omitted]. Hilton moved for partial summary judgment as to any liability beyond the $1,000.00 maximum allowed by that statute. Mrs. Haley's motion in opposition to Hilton's motion claimed that the statute did not apply (1) because it pertained only to loss of property 'brought by . . . guests into the hotel' and she had not so brought the missing luggage. . . . The trial court granted Hilton's motion, declared that the hotelkeeper's statute applied to limit liability, awarded Mrs. Haley judgment against Hilton for $1,000.00 accordingly, and granted judgment for Hilton as to any liability in excess of that amount.

"Mrs. Haley appealed the judgment. . . . The Court of Appeals reversed agreeing with appellant that the statute did not apply and that there were genuine issues of material fact requiring trial.

"We decline to adopt the reasoning of the Court of Appeals (LOPEZ, J.) that the statute only applies to property brought physically into the hotel by the guest or his agent. . . . [W]e agree with the trial court that the statute does apply and reverse the Court of Appeals accordingly.

"The statute in question provides in pertinent part that the liability of hotelkeepers for loss of guests' property is not to exceed the sum of $1,000.00. It is beyond question that the statute is in derogation of the common law rule, which provided sternly that the innkeeper was answerable as an insurer (regardless of absence of negligence) for loss of the goods, money, and baggage of his guest, except for the acts of God, the public enemy or the guest himself. . . .

"As a general rule, statutes in derogation of the common law are to be strictly construed. [Citations omitted.] However, this statute was obviously enacted to ameliorate the effect of the harsh common law rule, and as a remedial statute in derogation of the common law a different rule applies. *In re Gossett's Estate*, 46 N.M. 344, 351, 129 P.2d 56, 60 (1942) sets forth that rule: 'Where a statute is both remedial and in derogation of the common law it is usual to construe strictly the question of whether it does modify the common law, but its application should be liberally construed.' [Citations omitted.]

" 'There are three points to be considered in the construction of all remedial statutes; the old law, the mischief, and the remedy; that is, how the common law stood at the making of the act; what the mischief was, for which the common law did not provide; and what remedy the parliament hath provided to cure this mischief. And it is the business of the judges so to construe the act as to suppress the mischief and advance the remedy.' 1 Cooley's Blackstone, p. 86.

"Applying this rule, it becomes clear that the liberal construction of the statute, the construction which the Legislature obviously intended and which would 'suppress the mischief and advance the remedy,' should be applied here. This entails looking through the form of the pleadings to the substance of the action and applying the statute to limit defendant's liability.

"Under circumstances similar to those involved here the Supreme Court of Hawaii held that an analogous statute applied to limit the defendant hotel's liability for the loss of a guest's mink coat to the $50.00 statutory amount . . . [*Minneapolis Fire & Marine Ins. Co. v. Matson Nav. Co.*, 44 Haw. 59, 67, 352 P.2d 335, 340 (1960)]. . . .

"The trial court did not err in awarding summary judgment on the basis of the statute.

"The decision of the Court of Appeals is reversed, and the summary judgment of the trial court is affirmed."

Sosa, J. (dissenting): "I respectfully dissent.

"Although I agree with the majority's interpretation of § 49–6–1, N.M.S.A. 1953 (Repl. Vol. 7, 1966), I would not apply that statute under these circumstances. In my opinion a constructive bailment arose when Albuquerque Hilton Inn accepted custody of the plaintiff's luggage, transported by an independent carrier at Texas International Airlines' request. Plaintiff was a paying guest, thus the bailment was one for hire. *See Shamrock Hilton Hotel v. Caranas*, 488 S.W.2d 151 (Tex. Civ. App. 1972); *cf. Kula v. Karat, Inc.*, 531 P.2d 1353 (Nev. 1975). Thus I concur with the court of appeals and I would reverse the judgment of the trial court with direction to reinstate the case for trial.

"PAYNE, J., concurs in this dissent."

The following case illustrates the unwillingness of a federal district court to extend New York's innkeeper's liability statute governing losses of guest property from the room to luggage intentionally taken from the room by the innkeeper's employees, and intentionally transported to Saudi Arabia by mistake.

BHATTAL v. GRAND HYATT–NEW YORK
563 F. Supp. 277 (S.D.N.Y. 1983)

BRIEANT, D.J.: "Defendant, an innkeeper, seeks summary judgment in its favor in this alienage case, regulated by New York law. Plaintiffs, residents and citizens of India, registered as guests in defendant's Grand Hyatt Hotel in Midtown Manhattan on July 19, 1981 and were assigned Room 2946.

"Following the customary practice in first class hotels in this City of the sort operated by defendant, plaintiffs turned over to the bell captain various pieces of personal luggage, which are now said to have contained valuables of great significance, and this luggage was duly transferred by defendant's employees to plaintiffs' assigned hotel room.

"Plaintiffs did not request that any of their valuables be placed in the safe depository provided by the hotel, nor did they enter into any 'special agreement' with the hotel concerning their valuables, as is contemplated by § 200 of the New York General Business Law.

"Shortly after arriving at their room with the luggage, plaintiffs left the hotel for luncheon with friends, locking their door with a key provided by defendant. On returning earlier the same evening, plaintiffs discovered that their luggage and the contents thereof were missing.

"All things in the modern world which go wrong for reasons other than the application of Murphy's Law, seem to go wrong because of a particular sort of mechanical malevolence known as 'computer error.' Apparently defendant's front desk relies heavily on computer support, and as a result of computer error, employees of defendant transported plaintiffs' luggage from plaintiffs' room to JFK International Airport, along with the luggage of aircraft crew members of Saudi Arabian nationality, who had previously occupied Room 2946. In other words, the computer omitted to notice that the room had been vacated and relet to plaintiffs, and hotel employees responding to computer direction, included plaintiffs' luggage along with the other luggage of the departing prior guests. This is not to suggest that the Grand Hyatt-New York is a hotbed house, but apparently it was operating at 100% occupancy with no lost time between the departure of the Saudi Arabian aircraft crew members who had previously occupied the room, and the arrival of plaintiffs.

"Needless to say, plaintiffs' luggage departed for Saudi Arabia and has not since been seen. A missing pearl is always a pearl of the finest water, and accordingly plaintiffs demand damages in the amount of $250,000.00, together with costs and attorneys' fees.

"There seems to be no disputed issue of fact as to what happened to the luggage.

"Defendant's motion relies on § 200 [and 201] of the New York General Business Law. . . .

"Section 201 of the New York General Business Law, . . . provides in relevant part that:

"§ 201. *Liability for loss of clothing and other personal property limited*

"1. No hotel or motel keeper except as provided in the foregoing section shall be liable for damage to or loss of wearing apparel or other personal property in the lobby, hallways or in the room or rooms assigned to a guest for any sum exceeding the sum of five hundred dollars, unless it shall appear that such loss occurred through the fault or negligence of such keeper. . . .

"The motion thereby presents the question of whether these statutes limit the liability of an innkeeper, in a case where the innkeeper, by his own agents, intentionally and without justification, took custody and control of plaintiffs' luggage and contents, without plaintiffs' authorization, and intentionally, although inadvertently, caused the luggage to be transported to Saudi Arabia. The Court concludes that the statutes do not extend so far as to protect the innkeeper under these facts.

"Essentially what has taken place here is a common law conversion of property by defendant's agents. A fair reading of the amended complaint as amplified by the papers submitted on this motion indicates that plaintiffs state a claim for unintentional conversion under New York law, although not specifically so labelled. *See Meese v. Miller*, 79 A.D.2d 237, 436 N.Y.S.2d 496 (4th Dept. 1981). Intentional use of property beyond the authority which an owner confers upon a user or in violation of instructions given is a conversion. *Quintal v. Kellner*, 264 N.Y. 32, 189 N.E. 770 (1934).

"Here, defendant's employees entered plaintiffs' locked room, without plaintiffs' permission or knowledge, and removed their luggage, commingled it with the luggage of the Saudi Arabian aircraft crew members and placed it on a bus headed for Kennedy Airport. The Court infers that if the luggage was not stolen at Kennedy Airport, it arrived in Saudi Arabia and was eventually stolen by a Saudi thief who still had the use of at least one good hand. In this instance, the intentional acts of the defendant clearly constituted conversion under New York law.

"Sections 200 and 201 of the New York General Business Law were adopted in the middle of the nineteenth century to relieve an innkeeper from his liability at common law as an insurer of property of a guest lost by theft, caused without negligence or fault of the guest. *Millhiser v. Beau Site Co.*, 251 N.Y. 290, 167 N.E. 447 (1929). These statutes and the cases cited thereunder by the defendant extend to the situation where there is a mysterious disappearance of valuable property, either as a result of a theft by an employee of the hotel—or a trespass or theft by an unrelated party, for whose acts the innkeeper is not responsible. The statutes are also intended to protect the innkeeper from the danger of fraud on the part of a guest in a situation where the property said to have disappeared never existed at all, or was taken or stolen by or with the privity of the guest. [Citations omitted.]

"The reason for providing a hotel safe in compliance with § 200 and the reason for limiting a hotel's liability under § 201 is to protect against just such situations. When a hotel room is let to a guest, the innkeeper has lost a large measure of control and supervision over the hotel room and its contents. While housekeeping and security staff can enter the room at reasonable hours and on notice to any persons present therein, essentially, for most of the time at least, property of a guest which is present in a hotel room can be said to be under the exclusive dominion and control of the hotel guest, rather than the innkeeper.

"We have been cited to no case extending the limited immunity provided by statute against the common law liability of innkeepers, where the liability sought to be founded on the innkeeper was based on the exercise of unlawful dominion and control by the innkeeper himself, or his agents and employees acting in the course of their employment; as contrasted with mysterious disappearances due to causes unknown, or criminal acts of third parties or employees acting for themselves rather than for the employer. As noted above, it was only for the latter class of cases that the statutes granted immunity.

"Since §§ 200 and 201 of the New York General Business Law operate in derogation of the common law liability of an innkeeper as insurer, courts have traditionally construed their application strictly. *Millhiser v. Beau Site Co., supra; Ramaley v. Leland*, 43 N.Y. 539 (1871); *Jones v. Hotel Latham Co.*, 62 Misc. 620, 115 N.Y.S. 1084 (Sup. Ct. N.Y. Co. 1909).

"In *Millhiser v. Beau Site Co.*, the plaintiff placed a package containing jewelry worth $369,800 in a safety deposit box maintained by the defendant hotel pursuant to § 200 of the New York General Business Law, without disclosing to the defendant's desk clerk the contents of the package or the value thereof. Upon retrieving the package, the plaintiff discovered that $50,000 worth of jewelry was missing. Subsequently, an employee of the defendant was arrested and convicted for the theft of the gems but the jewelry was never recovered.

"In construing § 200, the New York Court of Appeals held that this provision limited the liability of an innkeeper for thefts of guests' property committed by its employees. However, the Court also stated that § 200 did not operate to limit the liability of an innkeeper for thefts committed by the innkeeper itself:

" . . . [S]uch a theft would be by the hotel keeper from the guest and not a theft from the hotel keeper. We read the statute to [limit the liability of the hotel keeper for] . . . a theft of . . . articles from the hotel keeper and not a theft by the hotel keeper from the guest. The act of the defendant's employee in stealing the jewelry was a wrongful act, outside the scope of his employment and for his own enrichment. It was not in any sense the act of the defendant. [Citations omitted.] 251 N.Y. at 295, 167 N.E. 447.

"Applying this rationale to the case at bar, the Court is compelled to conclude that §§ 200 and 201 do not limit the liability of an innkeeper for its conversion of guests' property. In this case, the plaintiff's luggage was not converted or stolen from the hotel by means of an employee theft or a fraud perpetrated by a third party. *See Adler v. Savoy Plaza, Inc.*, 279 App. Div. 110, 108 N.Y.S.2d 80 (1st Dep't. 1951). Rather, employees of the defendant, acting *within* the scope of their employment and relying on the accuracy of their employer's computer, intentionally converted the luggage of the plaintiffs by removing it from plaintiff's room and delivering it to an aircraft bound for Saudi Arabia. The theft (by unknown parties) occurred after the conversion. . . .

"The Court finds no genuine issue as to any material fact concerning the liability of the defendant for the conversion of the property of the plaintiffs. Accordingly, on the Court's own motion and pursuant to Rule 56(d), F.R. Civ. P., partial summary judgment is granted in favor of the nonmoving plaintiffs against defendant Hyatt Corporation. *Doe v. United States Civil Service Commission,* 483 F. Supp. 539, 571 (S.D.N.Y. 1980).

" . . . So ordered."

Appendix A. *Hawaii Revised Statutes*

Chapter 486K, Hotels

[§486K-1] Definitions. As used in this chapter, the following terms shall have the following meanings:

(1) "Guest" means a person who is registered at the hotel and to whom a bedroom is assigned. The term "guest" shall include not only the guest, but the members of the guest's family who accompany the guest.

(2) "Hotel" applies to any and all buildings or structures used by the keeper thereof for the accommodation of guests therein.

(3) "Keeper" includes any person, firm, or corporation actually operating a hotel.

(4) "Valuables" includes money, bank notes, bonds, precious stones, jewelry, ornaments, watches, securities, transportation tickets, photographic cameras, checks, drafts, and other negotiable instruments, business papers, documents, and other papers, and other articles of value.

[§486K-2] Hotelkeepers lien on baggage, etc., of guests; summary ejectment of delinquents. All hotelkeepers shall have a lien on all baggage and other property in the possession of the hotel belonging to guests at the hotel, for the amount of their proper charges against guests for the hire of rooms or board or other services or accommodation in the hotel, and shall have the right, without the process of law, to retain the same until the amount of indebtedness is discharged. All parties indebted for rooms or board in the hotel may be summarily ejected by the keeper thereof from the premises upon the keeper giving to the parties so indebted a written notice of the amount of indebtedness and his demand for the same, unless the parties shall have entered into an agreement with the keeper for a mode and manner of payment for room or board other than that announced by notice in the hotel, the right of summary ejectment to be without prejudice to the lien on the guest's baggage or other property.

[§486K-3] Sale of detained baggage; notice; disposition of proceeds. All baggage and property so held by the keeper of the hotel shall, after the expiration of three months from the date of the detention, be sold at public auction, after notice thereof published three times in a newspaper of general circulation in the county where the hotel is kept. The proceeds thereof shall be applied to the payment of the amount due and the expenses of the notice and sale. The balance, if any remaining, shall be paid over to the owner of the property or his representative. If the balance is not claimed by the owner within sixty days after sale, then the balance shall be paid over to the director of finance of the State and shall be kept by him in a special deposit for payment to the owner and shall be disposed of as provided in chapter 523.

[§486K-4] Safe for valuables; limitation of liability for deposited valuables. Whenever the keeper of any hotel provides a safe or vault in the office thereof, for the safekeeping of any money, jewels, bank notes, precious stones, transportation tickets, negotiable or valuable papers, or ornaments belonging to the guests of the hotel, and posts a notice stating the fact that a safe or vault is provided in which valuables may be deposited, in the room or rooms occupied by the guests in a conspicuous position, if any guest neglects to deliver valuables to the person in charge of the safe, the keeper of the hotel shall not be liable in any sum for any loss of valuables sustained by the guest by theft or otherwise. If the guest delivers valuables to the person in charge of the office for deposit in the safe, the keeper shall not be liable for any loss thereof sustained by the guest, by theft or otherwise, in any sum exceeding $500; provided that the keeper's liability is limited to $500 only if he gives a receipt for the valuables on a form which states, in type large enough to be clearly noticeable, that the keeper is not liable for any loss exceeding $500 except by special agreement in writing in which the keeper agrees to accept liability for losses in excess of $500. The keeper may accept liability for losses in excess of $500 by special agreement in writing between a guest and the keeper or his duly authorized representative.

[§486K-5] Hotelkeeper's liability for personal property. No keeper of any hotel shall be liable in any sum to any guest of the hotel for the loss of wearing apparel, goods, merchandise, or other personal property not mentioned in section 486K-4, unless it appears that the loss occurred through the fault or negligence of the keeper. Nor shall any keeper be liable in any event in any sum for the loss of any article or articles of wearing apparel, cane, umbrella, satchel, valise, bag, box, bundle, or other chattel belonging to any guest of, or in, any hotel, and not within a room or rooms assigned to him, unless the same is specially intrusted to the care and custody of the keeper or his duly authorized agent, and if so specially intrusted with any such article belonging to the guest, the keeper shall not be liable for the loss of the same in any sum exceeding $500 except that his liability may be in excess of $500 by special agreement in writing with the keeper or his duly authorized representative.

[§486K-6] Hotelkeeper's responsibility in case of fire, etc. The keeper of any hotel shall only be liable to any guest of the hotel, for ordinary and reasonable care in the custody of money, jewels, bank notes, precious stones, transportation tickets, negotiable or valuable papers, ornaments, baggage, wearing apparel, or other chattels or property belonging to any guest, whether specially intrusted to the keeper or his agent, or deposited in the safe of the hotel, for any loss occasioned by fire or by any other cause or force, over which the proprietor had no control.

[§486K-7] Posting copy of law; damages recoverable by guests. The keeper of every hotel shall post in a conspicuous place in the office or public room and in every bedroom of the hotel a printed copy of sections 486K-1 to 486K-8 and a statement of charge or rate of charges by the day for lodging. No charge or sum shall be collected or received by any keeper for any service not actually rendered, or for any item not actually delivered or contracted for, or for any greater or other sum than he is entitled to by the general rules and regulations of the hotel. For any intentional violation of this or any provision herein contained, the offender shall forfeit to the injured party three times the amount of the sum charged in excess of what he is entitled to.

[§486K-8] Extension of stay provision. Any guest who intentionally continues to occupy an assigned bedroom beyond the scheduled departure without the prior written approval of the keeper, shall be deemed a trespasser.

[§486K-9] Valuation of property. Whenever the value of property is to be determined under sections 486K-4 and 485K-5, the following shall apply:

(1) Value means the market value of the property.

(2) Whether or not they have been issued or delivered, certain written instruments, not including those having a readily ascertained market value, shall be evaluated as follows:

   (A) The value of an instrument constituting an evidence of debt, such as a check, traveler's check, draft, or promissory note, shall be deemed the amount due or collectible thereon or thereby, that figure ordinarily being the face amount of the indebtedness less any portion thereof which has been satisfied;

   (B) The value of any other instrument that creates, releases, discharges, or otherwise affects any valuable legal right, privilege, or obligation shall be deemed the greatest amount of economic loss which the owner of the instrument might reasonably suffer by virtue of the loss of the instrument.

(3) When property has value but that value cannot be ascertained pursuant to the standards set forth above, the value shall be deemed to be an amount not exceeding $50.

[§486K-10] Registration required. Every keeper covered by this chapter shall keep and maintain or cause to be maintained a register in which shall be inscribed the name of each and every guest renting or occupying a bedroom or apartment in such hotel. Such register shall be preserved for a period of not less than 6 months from the date of departure.

Appendix B. *Limitation of Liability Statutes*

Ala. Code § 34-15-15
Alaska Stat. §§ 08.56.50 & 08.56.60
Ariz. Rev. Stat. Ann. § 33-302
Ark. Stat. Ann. § 71-1107
Cal. Civ. Code § 1859 (West)
Colo. Rev. Stat. § 12-44-106
Conn. Gen. Stat. § 44-1
Del. Code Ann. tit. 24, § 1502
Fla. Stat. Ann. § 509.111
Ga. Code Ann. §§ 52-104 to -111
Hawaii Rev. Stat. §§ 486K-4 & -5
Idaho Code § 39-1823
Ill. Rev. Stat. ch. 71, § 1
Ind. Code § 32-8-28
Iowa Code § 105.1
Kan. Stat. Ann. §§ 36-402 & -403
Ky. Rev. Stat. §§ 306-020 & -030
La. Civ. Code Ann. § 2971 (West)
Me. Rev. Stat. tit. 30, § 2901
Md. Ann. Code art. 71, § 3
Mass. Ann. Laws ch. 140, §§ 10-11 (Michie/Law. Co-op)
Mich. Stat. Ann. §§ 18-311 & -312
Minn. Stat. §§ 327.01 to .04
Miss. Code Ann. §§ 75-73-5 & -7
Mo. Ann. Stat. §§ 419-010 to -030 (Vernon)
Mont. Rev. Codes Ann. § 70-6-501
Neb. Rev. Stat. § 41-123
Nev. Rev. Stat. § 651.010
N.H. Rev. Stat. Ann. § 353:1
N.J. Stat. Ann. §§ 2A:44 to 50 and 29:2-2 to -4
N.M. Stat. Ann. § 57-6-1
N.Y. Gen. Bus. Law §§ 200 & 201
N.C. Gen. Stat. §§ 72-1 to -7
N.D. Cent. Code §§ 60-01-28 to -33
Ohio Rev. Code Ann. § 4721.01 to .03
Okla. Stat. Ann. tit. 15, § 503 (West)
Or. Rev. Stat. §§ 699.020 to .040
Pa. Stat. Ann. tit. 37, §§ 61 to 64 (Purdon)
R.I. Gen. Laws §§ 5-14-1 & -2
S.C. Code § 45-1-40
S.D. Comp. Laws Ann. § 43-40-5
Tenn. Code Ann. § 62-704
Tex. Rev. Civ. Stat. Ann. art. 4592 & 4593 (Vernon)

Utah Code Ann. §§ 29-1-1 to -3
Vt. Stat. Ann. tit. 9, §§ 3141 & 3142
Va. Code §§ 35-10 to -13
Wash. Rev. Code Ann. §§ 19.48.030 & .070
W. Va. Code § 16-6-22
Wis. Stat. Ann. §§ 160.31 to .33
Wyo. Stat. § 33-17-101

D.C. Code Encycl. § 34-101 (West)
Guam Civ. Code § 1859
P.R. Laws Ann. tit. 10, §§ 711 to 714
V.I. Code Ann. tit. 27, §§ 402 & 403

Addendum to Hawaii Rev. Stat. §§ 486K-1, 486K-4 pp. 551, 552. amended by L. 1981, c. 83, § 1. Only significant changes are noted.

Addendum to Ind. Code § 32-8-28-2, p. 554: amended by P.L. 187, § 97, 1982

Addendum to La. Civ. Code Ann. § 2971 (West), p. 554; amended by Acts 1982, No. 382 § 1

Addendum to Minn. Stat. §§ 327.01 to .04, p. 554: repealed by Laws 1982, c. 517, § 9. See now § 327.70 *et seq.*

Addendum to Wis. Stat. Ann. §§ 160.31 to .33, p. 555: renumbered 50.80 to 50.82 by L. 1975, c. 413, § 15

14 Innkeeper's Duty to Nonguests

14:1 *Duty to Admit Nonguests Not Seeking Accommodations or Service: "Lobby Lizards"*

Someone who is not a guest or does not intend immediately to become a guest has, generally speaking, no right to enter or remain in the inn against the objection of the innkeeper.[1] Idlers who remain in the inn's "public rooms," taking up space properly set aside for paying guests, are known as "lobby lizards." To be sure, there are public rooms in every inn, and persons not guests are often in the habit of resorting to such rooms, but they are admitted to them only by the consent of the innkeeper. If that consent is withdrawn, a person who is not a guest has no more right to enter a public room in an inn than he has to enter the private room of a guest. "[B]arring the limitation imposed by holding out inducements to the public to seek accommodation at his inn, the proprietor occupies it as his dwelling-house, from which he may expel all who have not acquired rights, growing out of the relation of guest."[2]

The same idea was vigorously expressed by Judge Parsons in *Commonwealth v. Mitchell.*[3]

> If it should be held, as was contended on the argument, that because a man keeps a public house all who choose have a right to enter and occupy the hall or bar-room, or even the public parlour in a hotel, and that the proprietor has not a right to request them to leave, and if they do not, and he gently lays his hands on one to lead him out, he is guilty of an assault and battery but few persons would be found as lodgers in public houses. For where is the distinction to be drawn? If one may enter the inn and tarry there, all may. The pickpocket, the burglar, gambler and horse-thief, can come and take his seat by the side of the most virtuous man in the community in the gentleman's common parlour at the hotel, and the proprietor cannot eject him (no matter how annoying it may be to the guest) without being indicted for an assault and battery. Nor would the line of distinction be drawn here—the filthy and unclean would claim the same right. It is only necessary to state such a proposition to show its absurdity.

[1]State v. Whitby, 5 Harr. (5 Del.) 494 (Ct. Gen. Sess. 1854).
[2]Avery, J., in State v. Steele, 106 N.C. 766, 783, 11 S.E. 478, 484 (1890).
[3]2 Parsons 431, 435 (Pa. Ct. C.P. 1850).

14:2 *Nonguest Coming to Inn for Convenience of Guest*

While the general principle just stated is unquestioned, there are certain cases in which a stranger may desire to enter the inn, not merely for his own pleasure or business, but because the convenience of a guest of the inn calls him there. While no right to enter the inn can be based on his own claim, he can under certain circumstances claim to be exercising a right of the guest. It must be borne in mind, however, that in order to show a right to admittance he must base his claim on a right of the guest whom he comes to see.

If, either in his own right or the right of a guest, the party is permitted by the law to enter the inn, the innkeeper can probably not justify the use of force to exclude him.

14:3 *Nonguest Coming for Social Call on Guest*

Though there is no direct authority in favor of such a right, it seems that a nonguest coming to make a social call upon the guest at the guest's request would have a right to be admitted for that purpose. Any other rule would deprive the guest of one privilege necessary for his comfort while at the inn.

14:4 *Nonguest Coming by Appointment to Do Business with Guest*

In the ordinary case it is clear that a person who comes by appointment to do business with a guest has a right to be admitted. To be sure, if the visitor misconducts himself after his entrance, he may be excluded. As Judge Avery said in *State v. Steele:*

> If it be conceded that the prosecutor went into the hotel, at the request of a guest, for the purpose of conferring with the latter on business, still, in any view of the case, if, after entering, he engaged in "drumming" for his employer when he had been previously notified to desist, in obedience to a regulation of the house, the defendant had a right to expel him, if he did not use more force than was necessary.[4]

Judge Parsons, in *Commonwealth v. Mitchell,* appeared to recognize the general right of the guest to have a proper person visit him at the inn on business, while qualifying it by his doctrine that the innkeeper might lawfully use force to keep the visitor from making use of this right:

> When a guest had been admitted to a hotel and has taken a room, if any one calls to see him upon business, fair dealing would seem to require that the proprietor should communicate the intelligence to the guest, and if he consented to see the visitor, let him enter. But this, I apprehend, would be more by courtesy than a sheer claim of right. And if the proprietor of the house should refuse to suffer the visitor

[4]106 N.C. 766, 784, 11 S.E. 478, 485 (1890). *Cf.* Davis v. Garden Services Inc., 155 Ga. App. 34, 270 S.E.2d 228 (1980), discussed at section 9:3, *supra.*

to come in, or if he had entered should request him to depart, and on his refusal, gently lead him out, I am not prepared to say he would be guilty of an assault and battery for so doing. That the proprietor would be liable to an action, both to the guest and the visitor for an injury either might sustain in consequence thereof, I have no doubt. And probably might be liable to an indictment upon the same principle he would be for refusing to entertain a traveller when he had room. But because one should allege he had business with a guest, and the guest desire to see a visitor that was obnoxious to the keeper of the house, and therefore any one can enter the hotel on such a pretext and stay as long as he pleases without the proprietor possessing the power to remove him, is a principle which cannot be sanctioned on any clear legal ground.[5]

This 1850 opinion, however, would probably not apply today. If, either in his own right or the right of a guest, the party is permitted lawfully to enter the inn, the innkeeper cannot reasonably justify the use of force to exclude him.

14:5 *Nonguest Coming to Solicit Business from Guest*

If a person seeks admittance to an inn for the purpose of soliciting the patronage of guests, he may clearly be excluded from the inn.[6] The innkeeper is certainly under no obligation to furnish his inn as a free place of business for all tradespeople who wish to use it for that purpose. If the privilege of carrying on business in the inn is a valuable one, there is no reason why the innkeeper should not secure for himself that benefit. Accordingly, the innkeeper may either conduct himself, or make an exclusive contract with another to conduct, a barbershop, newsstand, or other business in the inn.

14:6 *Public Carriers Coming to Solicit Guest's Patronage*

There is one situation in which the innkeeper's right to use the inn for his own benefit may be limited. In any business not connected with travel he may do as he pleases, and the guest has no right to complain. But because the inn is established for the comfort and safety of travelers, and the innkeeper is under a public duty to secure that comfort and safety, he owes his guests protection in all that concerns traveling. Thus he is not permitted to do anything that might bring his own private interests into competition with those of his guest in any matter connected with the guest's journey. The guest's departure from the inn is a matter in which the innkeeper must act solely for the benefit of the guest. Any arrangement by which he permits one carrier to enter the inn and solicit the patronage of the guest, in connection with his departure, and refuses to permit other competing carriers to do the same is not permitted. Since giving the exclusive privilege of soliciting patronage to one carrier would be acting to the detriment of his guest in a matter that concerns the continuation of his journey,

[5]2 Parsons 431, 436 (Pa. Ct. C.P. 1850).
[6]State v. Steele, 106 N.C. 766, 11 S.E. 478 (1890).

the innkeeper's action would be illegal, and the competing carrier would have a right to demand admittance for the purpose of soliciting the patronage of the guests. This right, it will be noticed, is based on the right of the guest not to be subjected to a monopoly; the carrier would have no right to demand admittance if all carriers were equally excluded from the inn.

The leading case is *Markham v. Brown*,[7] in which it was held that an innkeeper who admitted to his inn the representative of one common carrier that passed through the town could not lawfully exclude the representative of another competing line.

14:7 *Right of Nonguest Forfeited by Misconduct*

It is clear that the rights of the nonguest at the inn, like the right of the guest himself, may be forfeited by the misconduct of the visitor and may even be denied because of the bad character or bad intentions of the visitor. The language of Judge Parsons to this effect has already been quoted (*see* section 14:4, *supra*). A similar opinion was given by the New Hampshire Supreme Court in *Markham v. Brown:*

> [T]he defendant might forfeit this right by his misconduct, so that the plaintiff might require him to depart, and expel him; and if, by reason of several instances of misconduct, it appeared to be necessary for the protection of his guests or of himself, the plaintiff might prohibit the defendant from entering again, until the ground of apprehension was removed. . . .
>
> So, if, after a lawful entry of the defendant, he committed an assault upon the plaintiff, or any trespass upon his property; the plaintiff might treat him as having entered for the unlawful purpose, and as a trespasser *ab initio*. [Citations omitted.][8]

When a person otherwise having a right to enter is refused admittance because it is suspected that he intends to do wrong after he enters, or because he is a person of bad character or reputation, the responsibility of the innkeeper is evidently large. So far as the authorities go, the innkeeper may undoubtedly justify exclusion on such a ground. Yet it is a difficult matter to establish a mere evil intention; and in the ordinary case it is the wiser course to admit the applicant, subject to the rules of the inn, and eject him when he violates a rule or does any act justifying exclusion.

KELLY v. UNITED STATES
348 A.2d 884 (D.C. App. 1975)

YEAGLEY, A.J.: "Appellant was convicted in a nonjury trial of unlawful entry a violation of D.C. Code 1973, § 22–3102. This appeal followed.

---

[7] 8 N.H. 523 (1837).
[8] *Id*. at 531.

"Between the months of January and March, 1974, appellant was seen by the chief of security at the Statler Hilton Hotel on approximately five occasions. He first noticed her in the hotel bar speaking with a guest with whom she later went upstairs. On one occasion when she was in the lobby all night, a police officer assigned to the vice squad told the hotel's security officer that appellant was a prostitute and showed him a copy of her criminal record and her mug shot.

"On March 18, hotel security officers again noticed appellant in the hotel. At that time she was once more observed going upstairs with a guest. After about an hour in the guest's room, she came out of the room alone. She was stopped by the hotel security officers and informed of the hotel policy of not allowing any unregistered guests above the lobby. She was also told of the conversation with the police vice squad officer and was read a 'barring notice.' Furthermore, she was told that if she returned to the hotel, she would be arrested and charged with unlawful entry.

"On August 19, security officers were called to the fifth floor of the hotel. They waited outside one of the rooms until appellant emerged with two male companions. She was then placed under arrest.

"Appellant was tried without a jury and on her motion for judgment of acquittal counsel argued that the statute was not applicable to a hotel and accordingly a hotel could not issue a valid barring notice. The court denied the motion relying on *Drew v. United States,* D.C. App., 292 A.2d 164, *cert. denied,* 409 U.S. 1062 . . . (1972), and Chief Judge GREENE's opinion in *United States v. Bean,* 99 Wash. D. L. Rep. 965 (June 2, 1971). We discern no error in that ruling.

"Appellant challenges the reliance of the trial court on *Drew* and *Bean* contending that the cases are not applicable and cannot stand scrutiny. . . . Appellant argues that the instant case is factually distinguishable from the other cases since it involved a hotel rather than a restaurant or retail store and the hotel management was no longer 'in lawful charge' of the room occupied by appellant's companion, who had leased it.

" . . . Even if we were to assume *arguendo,* however, that the person she was visiting was legally registered at the hotel, we could still not agree with appellant's contention. It is a general rule that ' . . . "an innkeeper gives a general license to all persons to enter his house. Consequently, it is not a trespass to enter an inn without a previous actual invitation," but, "Where persons enter a hotel or inn, not as guests, but intent on pleasure or profit to be derived from intercourse with its inmates, they are there, not of right, but under an implied license that the landlord may revoke at any time." The respondent did not enter the hotel as a guest nor with the intention of becoming one and it was his duty to leave peaceably when ordered by the landlord to do so, and in case of his refusal to leave on request appellant was entitled to use such force as was reasonably necessary to remove him.' [*Hopp v. Thompson,* 72 S.D. 574, 38 N.W.2d 133, 135 (1949)]. [Citations omitted]. The court in *State v. Steele,* 106 N.C. 766, 11 S.E. 478 (1890), expressed the rule this way: ' . . . The right to demand admission to the hotel is confined to persons who sustain the relation of guests, and does not extend to every individual who invades the premises. . . . The landlord is not only under no obligation to admit, but he has the power to prohibit the entrance of, any person or class of persons into his house for the purpose of plying his guests with solicitations for patronage in their business. . . . ' [11 S.E. at 482.] *See also Raider v. Dixie Inn.*, 198 Ky. 152, 248 S.W. 229 (1923). [Additional citations omitted.]

"It necessarily follows that if a hotel has the right to exclude someone, and he, or she, receives appropriate notice of his exclusion, that person's subsequent presence in the hotel is without lawful authority. Thus he or she is subject to arrest for the crime of unlawful entry."

Whatever rights a nonguest may acquire upon lawful admission to business premises open to the public, such entry is not unrestricted. Lawful entry is lost when a person refuses to obey a lawful demand to leave by the owner, operator, or other person in charge.

In *Safeway Stores Inc. v. Kelly*, the District of Columbia Court of Appeals reviewed the authorities on the question of what constitutes unlawful entry upon commercial premises. The following excerpt restates the applicable law, including mention of hotel and restaurant cases:

> . . . Absent a constitutional or statutory right to remain, a person lawfully on the premises of a commercial establishment is guilty of unlawful entry if he refuses to leave the premises after a demand by the person lawfully in charge. *Grogan v. United States*, D.C. App., 435 A.2d 1069, 1071 (1981) (individuals protesting abortions declined to leave clinic after ordered to do so); *Kelly v. United States*, D.C. App., 348 A.2d 884, 886 (1975) (unregistered guest failed to leave after returning to hotel despite warning not to); *Feldt v. Marriott Corp.*, D.C. App., 322 A.2d 913, 915 (1974) (barefoot woman refused manager's request to leave restaurant); *Drew v. United States*, D.C. App., 292 A.2d 164, 166, *cert. denied*, 409 U.S. 1062, 93 S. Ct. 569, 34 L. Ed. 2d 514 (1972) (man failed to leave restaurant after owner asked him to leave despite previous warning not to return); *United States v. Bean*, D.C. Sup. Ct. (Cr. No. 50426-70, May 12, 1971) (GREENE, C.J.) (man with prior arrest for shoplifting failed to leave store after ordered to do so). *See O'Brien v. United States*, D.C. App., 444 A.2d 946, 948 (1982).[9]

14:8 *Nonguest Entering to Make Inquiry*

In one class of cases, one who is neither a guest nor a person having business with a guest may enter an inn. One may have occasion to inquire at the office of an inn into some matter connected with the business of the inn or even to ask for a letter or message addressed to himself. Wherever more than one inn is found in a town, the traveler needs information before he can choose which inn to patronize. It must be his right, therefore, before deciding to become a guest, to enter and inquire what room he can get and what price will be charged and to

[9]448 A.2d 856, 863 (D.C. 1982).

make such other investigation as is possible. While no decided case has been found in which this subject is discussed, the right is believed to be beyond question; and in the analogous case of a common carrier it has been so held. A person going to a railroad station in order to get a timetable, but not at that time to take a train, has been held to have a right on the premises.[10]

It is the custom of inns to receive letters and telegrams addressed to strangers and to keep them a reasonable time to be called for. While, of course, an innkeeper cannot be compelled to accept such communications, still if he makes a practice of doing so (as in fact is true of most innkeepers) it seems to be clear that he must admit to the office bona fide persons coming to make inquiries for such communications. This is, of course, not a duty placed upon the innkeeper by reason of any provision of the law of innkeepers, but results necessarily from the practice of innkeepers. In the English case of *Strauss v. County Hotel and Wine Co., Ltd.,*[11] a person came to an inn intending to stay overnight and found waiting for him a telegram summoning him to another city. If the innkeeper as a matter of good business policy consents to receive such messages, he leads travelers to depend on being admitted to inquire for them and cannot therefore refuse to admit them.

14:9 *Responsibility for Property of Nonguest: Loss of Property from Tenant's Apartment*

The innkeeper may, and commonly does, provide accommodations not only for transient guests, but also for other persons who make their residence at the inn. Such persons, whether they are tenants, boarders, lodgers, or roomers, are not entitled to the exceptional responsibility of the innkeeper as insurer of the goods of his guests. (*See* section 5:22, *supra.*)

In the absence of negligence, there is no liability on the part of an innkeeper for loss of the property of such residents from the premises occupied by them.

In *Hackett v. Bell Operating Co.,*[12] the plaintiff occupied a suite of rooms in the Netherland Hotel in New York City, pursuant to a written agreement, for a term of six months and not to exceed a year, at a weekly rental of $90. During plaintiff's absence for two or three days from the hotel, certain tennis trophies were stolen from his room by some unknown thief. Plaintiff sued claiming liability on account of the duty he alleged was owing to him as defendant's guest. Defendant answered that plaintiff was not a guest, but a roomer or tenant, to whom defendant owed no duty other than that of reasonable care.

The court, in granting judgment for the defendant, said that "an innkeeper's liability, which is sought here to be enforced, exists only in the case of one who is a traveler and seeks the hospitality of the inn as a transient guest."[13]

---

[10]Bradford v. Boston & Maine R.R., 160 Mass. 392, 35 N.E. 1131 (1894).
[11][1883] 12 Q.B.D. 27.
[12]181 App. Div. 535, 169 N.Y.S. 114 (1st Dep't 1918).
[13]*Id.* at 536, 169 N.Y.S. at 115.

In *Rosenbluth v. Jamlee Hotel Corp.*,[14] the jury awarded damages to the plaintiffs because of the theft of their jewelry from the room rented to them by the defendant in its hotel. The rental was on a monthly basis. The cause of action of the plaintiffs was founded on the theory that the defendant was negligent in not having changed the lock after a prior theft and that this negligence caused the theft of the jewelry involved in the case. The court, granting defendant's motion to dismiss the complaint on its merits and directing judgment in favor of defendant, said (per Capozzoli, J.):

> It is well settled that where the original negligence of the defendant is followed by the independent act of a third person which directly results in injurious consequences to the plaintiff, the defendant's earlier negligence may be found to be the direct and proximate cause of those injurious consequences, if, according to human experience and in the natural course of events the defendant ought to have seen that the intervening act was likely to happen. But if this is not the case, if the intervening act which was the immediate cause of the injury complained of was one which it was not incumbent on the defendant to have anticipated as reasonably likely to happen, even though a high degree of caution would have shown him that it was possible, then he owed no duty to the plaintiff to anticipate such further acts. The chain of causation is broken, and the original negligence cannot be said to have been the proximate cause of the final injury. [Citations omitted.]
>
> The proximate cause of the plaintiffs' loss was not the alleged failure of the defendant to change the lock, but, rather, the independent criminal act of a third person in the stealing of the property. . . .
>
> A finding that the thief gained admittance to the room by the use of a key to the old lock is mere speculation, because there was no proof submitted as to how the thief gained admission. For all that is known, the thief might have stolen the property while defendant's servants were in and out of the room, engaged in its cleaning. As a matter of law, if an employee of the defendant, who had the right of entry into plaintiff's room, had stolen the property, the defendant would not be responsible (*Millheiser* [sic] *v. Beau Site Co.*, 251 N.Y. 290; *Castorina v. Rosen*, 290 N.Y. 445).

14:10 *Responsibility as Bailee: Loss of Tenant's Valuables Deposited in Hotel Safe*

JACOBS V. ALRAE HOTEL CORP.

4 A.D.2d 201, 164 N.Y.S.2d 330 (1st Dep't 1957), *aff'd mem.*, 4 N.Y.2d 769, 149 N.E.2d 337 (1958)

FRANK, J.: "This is an appeal from a judgment in favor of the plaintiff, in an action predicated upon negligence. There is virtually no dispute upon the proven facts as they concern the question of liability. The problem arises from the inferences to be drawn from the proof with respect to reasonable care, causation and foreseeability.

---

[14]122 N.Y.L.J. no. 103, 1439 (N.Y. County Civ. Ct. 1949).

"The defendant operated a hotel in the borough of Manhattan, occupied by permanent tenants and transient guests.

"On October 7, 1954, the plaintiff placed a quantity of her jewelry in a deposit box contained in a large safe which was located in the second room off a corridor behind the clerk's desk. The safe was not visible from the lobby. The safe-deposit box allotted to the plaintiff was one of 35, which could not be opened except by the use of two keys, one in the custody of the hotel clerk, the other in the exclusive possession of the person to whom the box was assigned. The method of access to and the appearance of the boxes were similar to those in the vaults maintained by safe-deposit companies.

"After placing her jewelry in her safe-deposit box, the plaintiff left the city and did not return for 11 days.

"On October 12, 1954, at approximately 4 o'clock in the morning, three unknown armed men entered the lobby and by a display of firearms, cowed the night clerk, a guest and his woman companion, trussed them with wire, gagged and confined them in a closet behind the desk. At the time the safe doors were open. No one actually saw the acts performed by the gunmen after they herded the persons whom they had subdued into the closet. After the robbery was completed and the perpetrators had left, it was found that a number of the individual boxes had been chiseled open and abandoned. A section of the safe which contained 15 boxes had been physically removed from the safe and the premises. The remaining section containing 20 boxes had also been removed from the safe but was abandoned on the hotel floor. All of the plaintiff's jewelry was contained in one of the 15 boxes which were carted off by the criminals. The defendant, too, sustained a loss of about $2,000 of its own funds kept in the safe.

"The hotel manager testified in effect that the safe itself showed evidence of force having been applied to remove the sections. Through the testimony of one of its officers, the defendant's uncontradicted proof was that it had not been aware that the sections containing the boxes were not bolted or welded to the safe and could be physically removed therefrom.

"The trial court predicated its determination upon the finding that the safe doors were not kept locked and the sections were removable. There was no proof that the practice of leaving the safe doors open was not the customary and accepted method used by hotels, nor that the unlocked safe doors were the competent producing cause of the loss occasioned by the robbery. It cannot be urged that negligence would be imputed to the defendant, assuming that the doors were locked and the clerk had opened them at the direction of armed criminals capable of using force to compel acquiescence to their demands. We cannot therefore predicate negligence upon the distinction of locked or unlocked safe doors under the circumstances here present. The proximate cause of the loss was not the open safe doors but the robbery from which the loss resulted. The same consequence would have followed even if the doors were closed, so long as the clerk could have been forced to open the safe. The crime and the loss were cause and result. [Citations omitted.] The plaintiff might have been in a stronger position had she offered proof that the defendant knew that the sections of boxes in the safe were removable. But no such evidence was adduced.

"The facts here are quite different from those in the cases relied upon by the trial court and by the respondent, in which there was no one in attendance at the time the burglary or theft occurred.

"It cannot be said on the proven facts in this case that the defendant could have foreseen or should have been aware, in the exercise of reasonable care, that the plaintiff's property could be removed as it was. Nor can the inference be drawn that the defendant should have provided greater security. If a hindsight test were applied, the plaintiff's position might be sound. But the record is barren of any proof to indicate that prior to the occurrence the defendant could have foreseen the event and could have taken precautionary measures to prevent it.

"Essentially the basis of liability is the ability to reasonably anticipate the risk. Not included in such a premise is every possible occurrence due to unusual or unforeseeable situations. [Citation omitted.] Under ordinary circumstances no one is chargeable with damages because he has not anticipated the commission of a crime by some third party. [Citations omitted.]

"While the defendant is not a true bailee, its status being more in the nature of a warehouseman, nevertheless, even as a bailee it is not an insurer of the plaintiff's property. [Citation omitted.] It can only be held to the same degree of care as would be required from a reasonably prudent person under the same or similar circumstances. [Citation omitted.] Where a warehouseman accounts for the failure to deliver the property left in its possession by demonstrating that the loss resulted from theft, the burden of proving negligence and freedom from contributory negligence is upon the plaintiff. [Citation omitted.] The Court of Appeals expressly rejected the theory 'that sound principles of law and considerations of expediency combine to require that the bailee be held liable.' [Citation omitted.]

"Upon the facts in this case, it must be held that the plaintiff has failed to establish the negligence of the defendant. Under the circumstances, therefore, we are constrained to reverse the judgment and dismiss the complaint.

"We do not reach the other question posed on this appeal in view of our determination with respect to liability.

"The judgment should be reversed and the complaint dismissed."

[Judgment reversed and the complaint dismissed. Settle order on notice. All concur except BOTEIN, J.P., who dissents and votes to affirm in a dissenting opinion.]

BOTEIN, J.P. (dissenting): "Defendant hotel corporation permitted a safe containing the valuables of its guests to remain open at 4:00 A.M., the time when the robbery occurred. Access to the safe would seldom be required at that hour in a residential-type hotel which evidently did not cater to transient guests. Also, the section containing 15 safe-deposit boxes—one of which held plaintiff's valuables—was not in any way attached to the sides of the safe. The detective assigned to the case and an insurance company investigator both testified that there were not marks indicating that the section had been forced or pried out of the safe. It is evident that after hacking away and opening several boxes in the lower section, which consisted of 20 boxes, the holdup men found that the smaller upper section was readily removable, and they proceeded gratefully to walk away with it.

"These combined circumstances spell out a strong *prima facie* case of negligence on the part of defendant which it made no effort whatsoever to rebut. The only witness defendant produced was its officer, who testified to a technical compliance with the posting of notice required under section 200 of the General Business Law. Another officer, whose duties were never revealed, was examined before trial by plaintiff, and expressed surprise on learning that the upper section was removable. The conclusion is irresistible that if defendant did not know that the section was removable, then in the exercise of reasonable prudence it should have known that fact.

"Plaintiff has presented actual proof of negligent acts and omissions to act that combined directly to cause the loss of her jewelry—proof of facts not based on conjecture that amply justified the trial court's findings. We should not reject such findings on the basis of speculation as to what might have happened had the safe door been closed and the missing section attached to the safe itself. To illustrate how double-edged such speculation can be, it might be argued on plaintiff's behalf that since the holdup men had tried to pry open the boxes in the lower section, they would never have reached the upper section in which the plaintiff's box was located had that section been attached securely to the safe.

"The judgment should be affirmed."[15]

The following case adopts the opposite solution.

WALLINGA v. JOHNSON
269 Minn. 436, 131 N.W.2d 216 (1964)

ROGOSHESKE, J.: "This appeal concerns an action to recover the value of two diamond rings owned by plaintiff. They were delivered and accepted for safekeeping by the Commodore Hotel, operated by defendant partnership, and were subsequently taken from the hotel safe by robbery. Plaintiff had occupied an apartment in the hotel for some years. On July 9, 1960, having been confined in a hospital with a broken leg, she directed her son to take two rings from her apartment and deposit them with the hotel clerk for safe keeping. In accordance with customary practice in performing this service, the rings were exhibited to the clerk and placed in a sealed 'safety deposit envelope' used by the hotel for depositing valuables belonging to guests. A numbered stub attached to the envelope was signed by the clerk and plaintiff's son, and a 'depositor's check' containing the same number was detached from the signed stub and given to him. This 'depositor's check' was to be presented when the envelope and contents were called for, at which time the depositor was required to sign it so that the

---

[15]A provision of the lease exempting landlord from liability for the loss of tenant's property was held unenforceable by section 234 of the Real Property Law. Nor was the landlord entitled to the benefit of the statutory limitation of liability in section 200 of the General Business Law for the reason that the statute applies only to property losses of transients.

signatures could be compared. The envelope containing the rings was placed in a large safe located in the hotel's front office 4 or 5 feet behind the registration desk and about the same distance from the hotel switchboard. The safe was used not only to keep the valuables of guests, but also cash for use in the hotel's cafe, bar, and coffee shop. Although it was equipped with a combination lock, during the 16 years that defendants operated the hotel the safe door, while customarily closed, was never locked. A clerk was on duty at the registration desk at all times.

"On July 10 at 3:45 A.M., two armed men surprised the night clerk then on duty, rifled cash drawers in the registration desk, and took the contents of the unlocked safe, including the envelope containing plaintiff's rings. The rings have not been recovered.

"The question of defendants' liability was submitted to a jury upon the sole issue of whether defendants were negligent in failing to keep the rings safely locked up and, if they were, whether such negligence was the proximate cause of the loss. The jury returned a verdict for defendants, and plaintiff appeals from an order denying her motion for a new trial.

"The primary question presented is whether the court erred in refusing to hold as a matter of law that the relationship between plaintiff and defendants was that of bailor and bailee.

"Bailment is the legal relation arising upon delivery of goods without transference of ownership under an express or implied agreement that the goods be returned. The actions of plaintiff's son and the hotel clerk—inserting the rings in the safety deposit envelope, signing the numbered stub, detaching the companion presentation stub, and placing the envelope in the safe—plainly indicate that the parties intended the rings to be kept for safekeeping until called for. This was a bailment as a matter of law.

"The error at trial lay in assuming that *Asseltyne v. Fay Hotel*, 222 Minn. 91, 23 N.W. (2d)357, applied to the facts of this case. In that case, the plaintiff was a residential guest of the defendant hotel. Her personal property, located in her rented room, was destroyed by fire. The pivotal issue was whether plaintiff's relationship to the hotel was that of a residential lodger or a transient guest. Unlike this case, the owner did not surrender exclusive possession and control of the property to the hotel. Thus, a bailment was not created and the case is inapplicable. We agree with plaintiff that *Peet v. Roth Hotel Co.*, 191 Minn. 151, 253 N.W. 546, controls. There, plaintiff, who had no relationship to the hotel, left a ring with the hotel clerk for the purpose of delivering it to a jeweler, a guest of the hotel. We held that a bailment was established as a matter of law.

"Application of the *Asseltyne* case and the court's refusal to find a bailment resulted in its erroneously instructing the jury that plaintiff bore the burden of proving defendant's negligence. Since *Rustad v. G.N. Ry. Co.*, 122 Minn. 453, 142 N.W. 727, the rule in Minnesota has been that where the plaintiff has shown a bailment relationship to exist, the defendant must assume not only the burden of going forward with evidence to show lack of negligence but also the burden of ultimate persuasion.

"The record reveals that plaintiff's proof was not wholly consistent with her theory that defendant's liability was governed by the law of bailment. In addition to proving delivery and nonreturn of the rings, she went forward with evidence tending to establish defendants' negligence. Contrary to defendants' contention, however, she did not thereby waive any right to object to the erroneous instructions. At most, she may have waived the right to have defendants assume the burden of going forward with the evidence. The error in instructing the jury as to the burden of proof is one of fundamental law and controlling principle and was properly assigned in plaintiff's motion for a new trial. Moreover, it appears from counsel's affidavit in support of plaintiff's motion for a new trial that he made oral requests to charge the jury on the theory of a bailment which were refused. Clearly, plaintiff is not precluded from asserting the error on appeal.

"While the burden of proof in a bailment case rests on the defendant, the basis of his liability remains ordinary negligence. Failure to lock the safe, at least during the night, is very strong evidence tending to show negligence. The hotel, however, established that a clerk was on duty at all times and the unlocked door was, to some extent, a convenience for guests who wished to retrieve valuables without delay. This evidence, we believe, falls short of establishing defendants' negligence as a matter of law and the question is for the jury under proper instructions.

"Since the case must be retried, defendants' contention that their actions, even if negligent, do not result in liability because the robbery was a superseding cause should be put at rest. As a general rule, a criminal act breaks the chain of causation and insulates the primary actor from liability. A criminal intervening force, however, cannot be legally effective superseding cause unless it possesses the attribute of unforeseeability. . . . The primary purpose of depositing the rings for safekeeping was to guard against theft; defendants must have, or at least should have, foreseen the possibility of their loss in the manner in which they were taken. We therefore hold that the robbery could not as a matter of law be a superseding cause.

" ' . . . Only when there might be a reasonable difference of opinion regarding the foreseeability of the intervening act should the question of intervening cause be submitted to the jury.'

"Reversed and new trial granted."

14:11 *Loss of Tenant's Property from Storage Room*

DALTON v. HAMILTON HOTEL OPERATING CO.
242 N.Y. 481, 152 N.E. 268 (1926)

HISCOCK, C.J.: "Plaintiff brought this action to recover the value of the contents of two trunks claimed to have been lost through the fault of the defendant. The facts which are claimed to sustain liability are as follows:

"The defendant operates an apartment hotel in the city of New York. In August the plaintiff desired to rent one of the apartments but the latter was then so occupied that possession could not be given to plaintiff until October 1, and a lease was subsequently made for the term of one year commencing on the latter date. Plaintiff had several trunks which she desired to store in the meantime and an oral agreement was made between her and the defendant under which the latter without compensation undertook to store said trunks until she should be entitled to possession of her apartment under the lease aforesaid. After this arrangement was made and after the execution of the lease the trunks were delivered to defendant, and the last seen or known of two of them was that they were sent to the basement of the apartment house where there was a room for the storage of such things. When the time arrived for the plaintiff to take possession of her apartment under her lease she sent word to the defendant to deliver her trunks at such apartment but two of them were not delivered and they have never been found. Defendant gave evidence to the effect that it had adopted a system covering the storage of baggage like that which prevailed in other similar buildings and under which articles were to be stored in the room above mentioned where they were under the custody and watch at all times of reliable employees. The only explanation of the loss of the trunks approaching definiteness was a statement said to have been made to plaintiff by one of defendant's officers in substance that the trunks must have been delivered at the apartment of some one other than the plaintiff.

"The lease contained a provision that the defendant should be under no obligation to accept or receive for safekeeping any property of the tenant, but in case any such property should be accepted or received it should be 'accepted, received and held entirely at the risk and hazard of the tenant and the landlord should [shall] not be liable or responsible for any damage thereto or loss or theft thereof whether arising from negligence or otherwise.' In addition to this the plaintiff received for each package delivered to defendant a check or receipt, which, in addition to describing the property, contained the following: 'Read conditions on the reverse side. . . . The property enumerated on the reverse side hereof being received and stored gratuitously it is expressly agreed by the guest that the said receipt and storage shall be entirely at the risk of the owner thereof and that the hotel shall not be liable for loss or injury thereto whether caused by negligence, fire, theft, or any other cause whatsoever. . . . Said hotel is further authorized to deliver said property to any person presenting said receipt without identification.'

"Upon these facts, which we do not understand to be disputed, the plaintiff recovered a judgment for the alleged value of the contents of her two trunks on the ground that defendant was a gratuitous bailee and was guilty of gross negligence, which judgment has been set aside by the Appellate Division both on the law and the facts with dismissal of the complaint and, thereby, several questions are presented to us for consideration.

"A majority of the court are of opinion that the complaint as a whole . . . does allege after a fashion the cause of action upon which recovery was had at the trial and this conclusion eliminates various questions discussed by counsel.

"We then come to the question whether the arrangement claimed to have been made by plaintiff with defendant for the storage of her trunks was one for gratuitous independent bailment as claimed by her, or was one incidental to and merged in the written lease so that the liability of the defendant is to be decided by the terms of that lease, especially including the exemption clause already quoted. We think that it was the former. The simple facts are that plaintiff rented an apartment but could not obtain possession thereof for several weeks; that she had several trunks which in the meantime must be stored, and that she made the arrangement with the defendant thus to store them until she could obtain possession of her apartment. Of course this arrangement for storage had a certain relation to her lease and undoubtedly never would have been made except for the fact that she made such a lease. But even so, the situation for which the arrangement provided was entirely separate and distinct from that which was covered by the lease. The lease covered occupation of the apartment from a certain future date. The arrangement for storage of the trunks covered the intervening period and the necessities for it and the rights secured were entirely different than those provided for by the lease. We are unable to see how either as a matter of technical law or as a matter of common sense it can be said that when a proposed tenant has rented a house or an apartment of which he cannot secure possession for the purpose of accommodating his property for some time to come, and says in effect that he wants to make another arrangement for storing such property until he can put it in his apartment or house, the latter agreement is covered by or merged in the former one. Therefore, we conclude that defendant accepted the lost trunks without promise of compensation and as a gratuitous bailee and, that being so, we encounter the question whether plaintiff's evidence has established any default in defendant's obligations as such bailee which entitles her to judgment.

"The obligations of defendant as gratuitous bailee are commonly described as involving the exercise of slight care and as being violated only when there has been gross negligence. The distinction between 'slight' and 'reasonable' care and between 'ordinary' negligence and 'gross' negligence is oftentimes shadowy and unsatisfactory. But the courts, however fortunate or otherwise they may have been in expressing the distinction, do recognize that it exists. . . . [I]n *Weld v. Postal Telegraph-Cable Co.* (210 N.Y. 59, 72) it was said: 'The cases cited recognize a distinction between ordinary and gross negligence, from which it may be said that gross negligence is the commission or omission of an act or duty owing by one person to a second party which discloses a failure to exercise slight diligence. In other words, the act or omission must be of an aggravated character as distinguished from the failure to exercise ordinary care.'

"When plaintiff demanded that her trunks be delivered to her at her apartment and the defendant failed to do this, a *prima facie* case was established against the latter even of gross negligence which amounted to a breach of its obligations and which called for an explanation. [Citations omitted.] And we do not think that defendant made such explanation as rebutted the presumption and destroyed the *prima facie* case. It attempted to do this by giving evidence of a system under which trunks were placed in a room under the constant watchfulness of competent and reliable employees. As a matter of fact there is no evidence that the plaintiff's trunks ever came within the operation of this system for they were traced no further than to show that they were taken to the basement of the apartment house. But if we assume that the trunks were placed in the proper depository under the watchfulness provided by the defendant, we do not think that this fact answers the presumption arising in favor of plaintiff on failure to deliver her trunks or satisfactorily explains their disappearance. Presumptively under this system the trunks should have been in defendant's possession and ready for delivery when called for and it is the failure of what was to be expected that defendant is called on to explain. So far as we can see their loss could naturally be accounted for on any one of three theories. They might have been abstracted by some external means not within the control of defendant, as larceny by an outsider. But there is no suggestion of any such occurrence as this. They might have been stolen by an employee whom the defendant had the right to regard as reliable and responsible. But again there is no suggestion of this, and the only remaining theory which occurs to us is the one that defendant voluntarily and without production of the appropriate checks delivered the trunks to some one other than the plaintiff or, as suggested by defendant's official, sent them to the wrong apartment when plaintiff called for them and wherefrom they were abstracted instead of being returned. Unless excused by special circumstances, a voluntary delivery of the trunks to a person other than plaintiff without production of checks, which at all times remained in possession of plaintiff, or the delivery of them to a different apartment than plaintiff's would not be a sufficient excuse for failure to deliver to plaintiff but would be affirmative evidence of a failure to exercise a very slight degree of care and would amount to gross negligence, if not willful misconduct.

"The exemption clauses in the lease and on the checks respectively do not become material elements in the disposition of the case. Regarding as we do the arrangement for storage of the trunks as an agreement outside of the lease, the provisions of the latter are not material. So far as concerns the exemption clause on the checks, independent of any other answer, we do not think it is to be assumed that it was the intention of the parties that it should relieve the defendant from its own gross negligence. Argument or authorities are not necessary to fortify this view, for defendant's counsel in his brief concedes its correctness. . . .

" . . . [T]he judgment of the Appellate Division should be modified so as to provide for a new trial and as so modified should be affirmed, with costs to abide event."

14:12 *Authority of Employee to Accept Property from Nonguests*

Where goods are accepted by an employee from one who is not a guest the question of the innkeeper's liability for loss of the goods often depends on the authority of the employee to bind the innkeeper. The authority may be actual, or it may be apparent or implied from the position the employee occupies. The question of authority is one of fact for the jury to determine.

In *Coykendall v. Eaton*,[16] plaintiff attended a dance at defendant's hotel. Upon leaving the hotel premises, plaintiff's carriage was involved in an accident. Plaintiff returned to the hotel, where he checked a robe and a cushion seat from the carriage with the attendant in charge of the coatroom. There was conflicting testimony as to the authority of the attendant to accept property from persons other than those in actual attendance at the dance and as to whether the deposit was made on the authority of a bartender. Judgment in favor of defendant was reversed for failure of the trial court to submit the attendant's authority to bind defendant to the jury. Said the court, "The rule is that a bailee for hire, or a gratuitous bailee, who delivers the goods he has as such bailee, to a wrong party, or who, after they are demanded of him, does not in any way account for their loss, is liable to the true owner for their value." [Citations omitted.][17]

In the early New York case of *Booth v. Litchfield*,[18] a person occupying an apartment of a hotel tenant as an accommodation upon his departure left his property with a hotel clerk to hold until his return in order to catch a train. He explained that he did not want to be burdened with his suitcase and outerwear during an intervening dinner engagement. In reversing a judgment for the plaintiff below, the Court of Appeals said: "The act of the clerk in receiving and assuming the care of the goods, after the plaintiff had ceased to be a guest at the hotel, was proven to be beyond the authority which the defendants by their words or acts had given or appeared to have given him, as between the plaintiff and the defendants he and not they must sustain his loss."

14:13 *Liability for Misdelivery*

A misdelivery of goods bailed is ordinarily held to make even a gratuitous bailee liable. The bailee is obviously liable if the misdelivery was negligent and also if he delivers goods to an apparent stranger without making an effort to verify the stranger's claim to them.[19] Thus where the goods were wrongly delivered to an expressman who brought a slip of paper with the owner's name on it, the innkeeper was held liable.[20]

The innkeeper is equally liable for a misdelivery the circumstances of which are unexplained. The burden is upon him to explain the loss.[21] And there is good authority and reason for the view that even a gratuitous bailee is liable in case of a misdelivery, however careful he may have been to secure a good delivery,

[16]55 Barb. 188 (N.Y. Sup. Ct. 1869).
[17]*Id.* at 193.
[18]201 N.Y. 466, 94 N.E. 1078 (1911).
[19]Wear v. Gleason, 52 Ark. 364, 12 S.W. 756 (1890).
[20]George v. Depierris, 17 Misc. 400, 39 N.Y.S. 1082 (Sup. Ct. 1896).
[21]Murray v. Clarke, 2 Daly 102 (N.Y. Ct.C.P. 1886).

for by delivering goods to the wrong person he is departing from the terms of his bailment.[22]

14:14 *Goods Deposited outside Inn*

Where the goods of a guest are left in charge of the innkeeper outside the precincts of the inn, though the innkeeper is not as such liable for the goods, he is nevertheless responsible for the exercise of due care. So where an innkeeper provided bath rooms, outside the inn, for his guests, and the guest's goods were lost from the bath room, while the innkeeper is not liable on a declaration charging him as innkeeper,[23] he is liable for loss by his negligence or misdelivery.[24]

[22]Jenkins v. Bacon, 111 Mass. 373 (1873).

[23]Minor v. Staples, 71 Me. 316 (1880).

[24]Tombler v. Koelling, 60 Ark. 62, 28 S.W. 795 (1894). The defendant was the keeper of the bathhouse, not an innkeeper, but the same principle is involved.

15 Responsibility of Restaurant Keeper for Patron's Property

15:1 *Difference between Restaurant and Inn*

A restaurant is a house for the entertainment of anyone, whether resident or traveler, and the entertainment furnished is food and drink, without lodging. It differs in this respect from inns and boardinghouses, which furnish lodging as well as food. An innkeeper may carry on, under the same roof, a restaurant, to which he invites all persons to come for food and drink only.

That sections 200, 201, and 206 of the New York General Business Law, limiting innkeeper liability for loss of personal property, apply only to guests was underscored in the following case. A patron of a seminar sponsor who had rented facilities from a hotel lost a cashmere coat, which the patron had placed on a rack outside the seminar room and which was missing at the conclusion of the seminar. The court found for the hotel for the reasons set forth below.

AUGUSTINE V. MARRIOTT HOTEL
132 Misc. 2d 180, 503 N.Y.S.2d 498 (N.Y. Town Ct. 1986).

BESTRY, J.: "Plaintiff attended, for a fee, a dental seminar at the Marriott Hotel. The seminar sponsor rented a banquet room, furnished with seats, from the Defendant.

"At request of the sponsor, Defendant furnished a movable coat rack, placing it outside the room, in the public lobby.

"Plaintiff placed his coat on the rack, before entering the seminar. At the noon recess, Plaintiff exited the seminar room, but found that the rack had been moved a distance down the lobby and around a corner, near an exit.

"Unfortunately, his cashmere coat was missing. He then commenced this action in the Small Claims Part of this court.

"Under the common law an innkeeper-hotel keeper was an insurer of property, *infra hospitium*, of his guests, and liable for the loss thereof or damage thereto unless the loss was caused by negligence of the guest, act of God, or the public enemy (*see Purvis v. Coleman*, 21 N.Y. 111; *Millhiser v. Beau Site Co.*, 251 N.Y. 290, 167 N.E. 447; *Lader v. Warsher*, 165 Misc. 559, 1 N.Y.S.2d 160).

"By statute, such liability has been limited (see General Business Law § 200, § 201 and § 206).

"The relationship of guest on the part of Plaintiff, and that of hotel keeper on the part of Defendant, vis-a-vis each other never arose. The occupancy by Plaintiff of a private room was never contemplated by the parties.

"Plaintiff was a patron of the seminar sponsor, who rented facilities from the Defendant. The status of Plaintiff was like that of a wedding guest of individuals who rent banquet facilities from a hotel (*see Ross v. Kirkeby Hotels,* 8 Misc. 2d 750, 160 N.Y.S.2d 978). Furthermore, Plaintiff was not a patron of Defendant; he was not a customer of any of its services.

"Therefore, General Business Law Sec. 201 is in no way applicable to the facts presented here.

"The relationship of bailor and bailee never came into existence because Plaintiff did not entrust his coat to Defendant. Not only was there never a delivery to Defendant, but Defendant never was in actual nor constructive custody of Plaintiff's coat (*Wentworth v. Riggs,* 159 A.D. 899, 143 N.Y.S. 955 *reversing* 79 Misc. 400, 139 N.Y.S. 1082, based on dissenting opinion).

"The sole question remaining is whether Defendant owed a duty to Plaintiff to provide a guard for the coat rack. Defendant placed the rack in a position near the door to the seminar room, at the request of the seminar sponsor. This created not only an opportunity but an implied invitation on the part of the sponsor, to patrons of the seminar to use the rack.

"However, there was no evidence to indicate that users of the rack were led to believe either by the sponsor or by the Defendant that there would be a guard for the rack. Under the circumstances presented, it was clear that there was merely a rack available for those who wished to use it. The Defendant did not lull Plaintiff into a sense of security, by which there was created a duty to provide a guard.

"There being no duty on the part of the Defendant, there can be found no breach of duty upon which to underpin a finding of negligence.

"Furthermore, a reasonable man would have wondered about the safety of his coat which he hung on a rack in a public lobby of a hotel, without ascertaining if there were a guard.

"The claim must be dismissed."

15:2 *Responsibility as Bailee for Patrons' Property*

By the custom of the restaurant, the guest's coat and hat may be taken by a servant at the entrance to the restaurant. In that case there is an express bailment to the restaurant keeper, and the bailment is for hire, or, as it sometimes put, for the mutual benefit of bailor and bailee. Though there is nothing specially paid to the restaurant keeper for taking charge of the goods, still it is done as a business matter: "for such a system might obviously add to the popularity of the establishment, and would probably be adopted with that very object in view."[1] The

---

[1]Ultzen v. Nicols, [1894] 1 Q.B. 92, 94 (1893) (Charles, J.).

restaurant keeper in such a case is therefore liable for any loss caused by his neglect of reasonable care.[2]

The same principle is involved where the waiter takes the guest's coat and hat and hangs them on a hook when the guest sits at the table; then, too, there is held to be a bailment for mutual benefit, so that the restaurant keeper is liable for a loss which happens by reason of his negligence.[3]

15:3 *Responsibility on an Implied Bailment*

An "implied bailment" may be established by circumstantial proof of delivery to the servant of the restaurant keeper, for example, by evidence that an overcoat was necessarily laid aside in sight of or at the direction of the restaurant keeper or his employees.[4]

If there is a bailment, the restaurant keeper is responsible for a loss caused by his negligence, even though the words "not responsible for hats and coats" are printed on the bill of fare and the waiters are forbidden to take hats and coats. The customer may be affected by a rule of this sort only if it is properly published so as to be called to his attention.[5]

WENTWORTH V. RIGGS

159 A.D. 899, 143 N.Y.S. 455 (1st Dep't 1913)

[Action by Reginald de M. Wentworth against Leon C. Riggs. From a Municipal Court judgment in favor of plaintiff, affirmed at the Appellate Term (79 Misc. 400, 139 N.Y. 1082), defendant appeals. Reversed, and complaint dismissed, with costs, on the following dissenting opinion of SEABURY, J., at the Appellate Term, 79 Misc. at 403–408, 139 N.Y.S. at 1085–1088.]

"I am unable to agree with the views expressed in the prevailing opinion.

"In view of the precautions taken by the defendant to police and care for the property of his patrons, I think it is evident that he cannot be held liable for the loss of the overcoat upon any theory of negligence unless there was a bailment. If the defendant is to be held liable at all, it can only be upon this latter theory. Confusion had been engendered by certain cases, which seem to discuss constructive bailment as if it were identical with constructive delivery. The two things are distinct. Formerly, delivery was regarded as the essence of a bailment. As this branch of the law has developed, cases of constructive bailment have been recognized covering cases where there had been no delivery either actual or constructive, as where one held the possession of a chattel under such circumstances that the law placed upon the person having the possession of the

---

[2]LaSalle Restaurant & Oyster House v. McMasters, 85 Ill. App. 677 (1899); Buttman v. Dennett, 9 Misc. 462, 30 N.Y. 247 (N.Y. Ct. C.P. 1894) (per curiam).

[3]Ultzen v. Nicols, [1894] 1 Q.B. 92 (1893); Appleton v. Welch, 20 Misc. 343, 45 N.Y. 751 (Sup. Ct. 1897).

[4]Montgomery v. Ladjing, 30 Misc. 92, 61 N.Y.S. 840 (Sup. Ct. 1899).

[5]LaSalle Restaurant & Oyster House v. McMasters, 85 Ill. App. 677 (1899).

chattel the obligation to deliver it to another. The typical instance of such a constructive bailment is where one sells a chattel to another, who pays the price thereof, and the vendor refuses to deliver it to the vendee. Here the law implies the contract of bailment, and holds the vendor answerable as bailee. In such a case it is apparent that there has been no delivery by the bailor to the bailee, and yet the bailment exists constructively. All the other examples of constructive bailment which are given in the books, as in the case of a finder, of a captor, or salvor, of an attaching officer, are cases where the person having the *possession* of the chattel is held to be a bailee, although there has never been either an actual or a constructive delivery of the chattels to the bailee by the bailor. In other words, the essential fact of legal significance in all these cases is possession. It certainly is not delivery, for, in none of these cases of constructive bailment, is there either an actual or a constructive delivery. . . .

"In an actual bailment there must be a delivery of the chattels to the bailee or his agent. The delivery may be either actual or constructive.

"(a) An actual delivery consists in giving to the bailee or his agents the real possession of the chattel. [Citation omitted.]

"(b) A constructive delivery comprehends all of those acts which, although not truly comprising real possession of the goods transferred, have been held *constructione juris* equivalent to acts of real delivery, and in this sense includes symbolical or substituted delivery. [Citations omitted.]

" . . . A constructive bailment arises where the person having the possession of a chattel holds it under such circumstances that the law imposes upon him the obligation of delivering it to another.

"From the definition of the two subdivisions of actual bailment, and from the definition of a constructive bailment, there ought to be no difficulty in determining whether there was in the case at bar a bailment of the plaintiff's overcoat. Neither the defendant nor his agents ever had the real possession of the overcoat, and, therefore there was not an *actual* delivery of the coat. The facts proved are inconsistent with the hypothesis that the plaintiff intended to transfer to the defendant or his servants such a possession of the coat as would exclude, for the time of the bailment, the possession of the owner. The overcoat hung upon a hook within two feet of where the plaintiff was sitting during the meal, and it does not seem to be capable of dispute that during that time the defendant did not have such a possession of it as to exclude the possession of the plaintiff. If the plaintiff had wished to reach his overcoat at any time during the meal, either to take something from one of the pockets of the coat or for any other purpose, he was entirely free to do so, without requiring any act on the part of the defendant or his servants. The presence of the hooks may be construed into an invitation to the patron to hang his coat upon them, but hanging the coat upon the hook cannot be reasonably held to constitute a delivery of the coat to the *exclusive* possession of the defendant. The hooks were obviously placed there for the convenience of the patron, provided he wished to retain possession of his coat. If he wished to deposit the coat in the exclusive possession of the defendant, he should have availed himself of the accommodations which the defendant provided for that purpose. If he had done this, the defendant would have been liable. *Buttman v. Dennett,* 9 Misc. Rep. 462. The frequency with which the plaintiff was accustomed to visit the defendant's restaurant leaves no room for doubt that he knew of the accommodations provided by the defendant for caring for the hats, coats, and other articles of his patrons. . . .

"The facts of this case, viewed in the light of the foregoing authorities, seem to me to establish that there was no actual bailment, because there was neither an actual or constructive delivery of the coat. That this is not a case of constructive bailment is apparent from the fact that the defendant never had the actual possession of the coat.

"It follows that there was neither an actual nor constructive bailment, and, as there is no other ground under the facts in this case upon which defendant's liability can be predicated, the judgment should be reversed and a new trial ordered, with costs to appellant to abide the event.''

In *Apfel v. Whyte's, Inc.,*[6] the reasoning of the *Wentworth* case was adopted, namely, that no bailment was created where the patron's coat had not been placed in the exclusive possession of the restaurateur. Absent proof of an express bailment by special agreement, a judgment for the plaintiff was reversed where his coat was hung by an employee within close proximity to his dining table. The fact that a restaurant employee took charge of the coat, a fact absent in *Wentworth,* was dismissed as of no legal significance, but was treated as a matter of courtesy rather than proof of entrustment sufficient to constitute a bailment.

BLACK BERT LOUNGE AND RESTAURANT v. MEISNERE
336 A.2d 532 (D.C. App. 1975)

NEBEKER, A.J.: "Appellee won a judgment in the amount of $90 in the Small Claims and Conciliation Branch for the loss of his coat at appellant-restaurant. The trial judge based his award on a determination that a bailment of the coat had occurred. We granted appellant's application for allowance of appeal to review that conclusion. We reverse.

"The record reveals that appellee hung his coat in an unattended cloakroom at the request of one of appellant's waitresses. Appellant made no charge for the use of this cloakroom and gave no claim check to appellee. A notice was posted in appellant's cloakroom disclaiming any responsibility for lost belongings. Appellee testified that he did not see any such notice.

"We hold on these facts that there was no delivery of the coat to appellant resulting in a change of possession and control. Therefore, there was no bailment. [Citations omitted.] That the appellee used the cloakroom at a waitress' request, since the coat had fallen from a chair—a fact to which the trial judge

---

[6]110 Misc. 670, 180 N.Y.S. 712 (Sup. Ct. 1920).

attached considerable importance—has been held not to impose liability on the restaurant keeper for appellee's loss. [Citation omitted.] *See generally* 43 C.J.S. *Innkeepers* § 20b and n. 49. [Citation omitted]; *Apfel v. Whyte's, Inc.*, 110 Misc. 670, 180 N.Y.S. 712 (1920).

"Accordingly, we conclude that there was no bailment. The judgment of the trial court is

"Reversed with instructions to enter judgment for appellant."

FORTE v. WESTCHESTER HILLS GOLF CLUB, INC.
103 Misc. 2d 621, 426 N.Y.S.2d 390
(Westchester County Small Claims Ct. 1980)

BLAUSTEIN, J.: "Plaintiff Diane Forte was a dinner guest of Mr. LaRue Buchanan and his son at defendant's private country club, Westchester Hills Golf Club, Inc. on January 5, 1979.

"Miss Forte was concerned about having her full-length raccoon coat hung in the club's cloak room. She personally walked into the room, and saw other fur coats hanging there. The club did not provide an attendant in the cloak room or at the entrance to screen visitors or prevent unwanted guests, although to a limited extent the function of attendant was performed by Doris Cummings, Secretary of the club, who was on duty. No notice disclaiming liability was posted.

"Miss Forte was told by Mr. Buchanan that there was no need for concern; the club would be responsible for any loss. Seeing other fur coats in the cloak room and relying upon the assurance of Mr. Buchanan, she gave him her coat to hang up. Miss Forte's coat was missing when Mr. Buchanan later returned to the cloak room after dining; apparently, the coat had been stolen.

"Mr. Buchanan had been told a number of times by club employees over the past years, usually in the presence of his wife who also had a fur coat, that there was no need to worry about having coats hung in the cloak room, as the club would bear responsibility for any loss. The club's responsibility was confirmed, or admitted, albeit after Miss Forte's coat was stolen on the evening in question, by an employee of the club, Mr. Abbott (the bartender), who had informed Miss Forte that there was no need for concern; the club would be responsible. Defendant controverts the evidence as to the club's responsibility by offering the by-laws, which are to the contrary. These by-laws, however, are not binding upon the plaintiff, Miss Forte, who is a third party guest.

"The question thus arises as to whether the club is responsible for the theft of Miss Forte's coat. Before liability may be found, a bailment relationship must exist. Ordinarily, there must be (1) an actual delivery of the coat by its owner (as bailor) to the club (as bailee), and (2) circumstances where the bailee retains possession and control of the coat and in which it may be implied that the coat will be returned in proper condition. (*Wentworth v. Riggs*, 159 App. Div. 899, 143 N.Y.S. 955 (1 Dept. 1913); *see also* this Court's decision in *Morse v. Systems for Dining, Inc.*, Small Claims No. 36-1978 (City Court of the City of

White Plains, March 21, 1978.) For the purpose of determining delivery, Mr. Buchanan cannot be considered as a representative or agent of defendant. It is more accurate to consider Mr. Buchanan to be Miss Forte's agent rather than the defendant's agent.

"The circumstances here are different from those presented in cases involving restaurants and night clubs open to the general public, where bailment is usually found only if there is delivery to an employee-agent of the restaurant or night club. However, in *Laval v. Leopold,* 47 Misc. 2d 624, 262 N.Y.S.2d 820, *aff'd,* 47 Misc. 2d 625, 263 N.Y.S.2d 46 (App. Term, 1st Dep't 1965), a patient visiting her psychiatrist's office deposited her fur coat in the closet of the reception room. There was no secretary or other employee in the reception room. The Court held that the maintenance of a closet in the defendant psychiatrist's office created an implied invitation to the patient to deposit her coat there, and that the defendant psychiatrist was thus a bailee. The private office of a physician is more analogous to the private facilities of a country club, since both are open to the clientele of the physician or club and not to the general public.

"In summary, under the facts presented here, Miss Forte's coat was hung in the cloak room of an exclusive private country club. Miss Forte had seen other fur coats hanging in the cloak room, and Mr. Buchanan had communicated to her the statements as to the club's responsibility. This was her first visit to the club, and she believed her coat would be safe or the club would be responsible. The absence of a notice disclaiming liability is not dispositive, but the country club's case would be stronger if such a notice was posted and seen by its guests. Had Miss Forte seen such a notice, this case would not be in court. As in *Laval,* there is here an implied invitation for a member or guest to deposit his or her coat in the cloak room. There is no significant evidence to the contrary. This implied invitation would apply for a man's topcoat or raincoat as well as for a woman's fur coat. It is not customary for men to wear their coats into a dining room of a country club. Liability should not depend on the sex of the owner of the coat or the coat's value.

"This Court holds that it was implicit in the relationship between the guest of a member and the defendant country club that the club became a bailee of that guest's coat. The bailment was for hire, as opposed to a gratuitous bailment, and required only ordinary reasonable care by the bailee. Monetary consideration was present in (1) the use of the club's facilities by Mr. Buchanan, a paying member of the club, and his guests, and (2) the dining expenses themselves. The lack of attendants to keep unwanted persons from the club and the lack of any safeguards to protect coats of the members and guests who use the cloak room was ordinary negligence, and defendant is thus liable.

"The equities, as well as 'substantial justice,' are surely on the side of plaintiff. [Citation omitted.] She paid $1,132.92 for her coat, and was quite concerned about the safety of that coat when she asked Mr. Buchanan to hang it up. They both relied upon statements of club employees and the prevailing appearances. The Court therefore finds for the plaintiff the amount of $1,000.00 plus costs.''

15:4 *Loss of Overcoat in Self-Service Cafeteria*

WIELAR V. SILVER STANDARD, INC.
263 A.D. 521, 33 N.Y.S.2d 617 (1st Dep't 1942)

GLENNON, J.: "The defendant was the owner of a self-service cafeteria at No. 38 Park row, borough of Manhattan, city of New York. The cafeteria consisted of two large dining rooms, one on the street floor and the other in the basement. A patron upon entering received a food check and went to a counter where food was selected and placed upon a tray. The tray was then carried to a table of the patron's own choice.

"Plaintiff entered the cafeteria on December 10, 1940, and was handed a food check. He testified, 'I selected some food, placed it on a table; took off my hat and coat, and hung my coat on a hook on a post, which was about three or four feet off my table.' In answer to a question of the court, he stated, 'I never checked it.' Further he testified, 'I got up to get a drink of some beverage. I was probably less than a minute getting the beverage, and when I turned around and went back to my seat, my coat was gone. I spoke to the manager, who is here in court. I told him of the loss of my coat. I went around with him thinking, perhaps, it might be found in some other place in the restaurant but which couldn't be found. I then asked—someone came up to me and spoke to me while I was walking around, and said that coats had been stolen before.' He brought this action on the theory of negligence to recover the value of the coat.

"The manager of the restaurant testified that in the cafeteria there were two different kinds of signs, one of which read, 'Not responsible for personal property unless checked,' and the other, 'Watch your overcoat, we are not responsible.' The following question was asked of him: 'Do you check coats of customers in that store?' to which he replied, 'Only if they are requested.'

"The case was tried in the Small Claims Part of the Municipal Court, Borough of Manhattan, by an official referee who, after hearing the evidence, directed a judgment in favor of the defendant. Upon appeal to the Appellate Term of the Supreme Court, the judgment was reversed by a majority of the court with one justice dissenting.

"Outside of the fact that the case now under consideration was tried on the theory of negligence, the situation here presented is similar to that which was before the Appellate Term of the Supreme Court, both in *Wentworth v. Riggs* (79 Misc. 400), which was reversed upon the dissenting opinion of one of the justices and reported in 159 Appellate Division 899, and *Apfel v. Whyte's Inc.* (110 Misc. 670). Both of those cases were tried on the theory of bailment. In the latter case, . . . [t]he restaurant there in question was located in the lower part of Manhattan. The food served was not inexpensive and it is fair to assert that during the winter months it was the common practice for each one of the diners to remove his hat and coat. We know from experience that in a self-service cafeteria, such as we are dealing with here, removal of overcoats by patrons while eating is by no means a common practice. Customers usually are in a hurry and the food is inexpensive. It would be well nigh impossible for the management to guard its customers' unchecked hats and overcoats during the rush hour periods without employing such a large force of special policemen or watchmen as to make the cost almost prohibitive.

"While there is evidence in the record to the effect that on a prior occasion in the month of October an overcoat had been stolen, still it seems to us that the failure of the management to detect the larceny of plaintiff's coat would not, in and of itself, under the circumstances constitute negligence. The referee properly could have found that if there were negligence on the part of the owner of the cafeteria, by the same token there was contributory negligence on the part of the customer.

"The determination of the Appellate Term should be reversed, and the judgment of the Municipal Court affirmed, with costs to the defendant in this court and in the Appellate Term."

15:5 *Loss by Reason of Insufficient Supervision of Premises*

The restaurant keeper, though not a bailee in any sense, may be held responsible for loss of the goods of his guest if the loss happened by reason of the insufficiency of the general supervision exercised by the keeper of the restaurant for the protection of his customer's goods; the burden of proving neglect of duty is on the plaintiff.[7] The kind and amount of supervision required of the restaurant keeper and the question of his neglect of due care depend, of course, upon the special circumstances of each case. And where sufficient general supervision is exercised by the restaurant keeper, he is not liable when the guest himself hangs his overcoat on a hook, without calling the waiter's attention to it, and it is stolen from the hook.[8]

MONTGOMERY v. LADJING

30 Misc. 92, 61 N.Y.S. 840 (Sup. Ct. 1899)

FREEDMAN, J.: "This action was brought by the plaintiff to recover the value of an overcoat lost in a restaurant, kept by defendant, while the plaintiff was upon the premises as a customer. At the trial the plaintiff had judgment, and the defendant appealed. The defendant was not shown to be an innkeeper, but merely a restaurant keeper. As such, he cannot be subjected to the liabilities of an innkeeper. [J. Story, Commentaries on the Law of Bailments, 4th ed. (Boston, 1846).]

"In *Carpenter v. Taylor*, 1 Hilt. 193, it was held that a person who enters a restaurant to procure a meal or refreshments is not to be deemed a guest or

---

[7]Harris v. Childs' Unique Dairy Co., 84 N.Y.S. 260 (Sup. Ct. 1903); Montgomery v. Ladjing, 30 Misc. 92, 61 N.Y.S. 840 (Sup. Ct. 1899); Simpson v. Rourke, 13 Misc. 230, 34 N.Y.S. 11 (Ct. C.P. 1895).

[8]*See* the three cases cited in note 7. In both *Harris* and *Montgomery*, the guest had notice that articles might be deposited with the cashier, but the cases seem to have turned on the absence of a bailment.

traveller entitled to the protection which the law gives against innkeepers. In *Buttman v. Dennett,* 9 Misc. Rep. 462, it was held that a restaurant keeper in whose custody wraps and other articles of wearing apparel have been temporarily placed for safekeeping is liable as a bailee. This liability has been enforced where a waiter took the hat and coat of a customer when he entered the restaurant and seated himself at a table. *Appleton v. Welch,* 20 Misc. Rep. 343.

"But in *Simpson v. Rourke,* 13 Misc. Rep. 230, it was held that a restaurant keeper is not an insurer of the effects of customers who may have accepted the invitation held out by him, but at most is required to use only the ordinary care called for by the circumstances. In that case the plaintiff had not placed his overcoat in the physical custody of the defendant or his servant, but had it removed after having selected a seat and personally placed it on a rack, and it was, therefore, held that the question merely was as to the sufficiency of the general supervision exercised over the restaurant for the protection of the customer's property placed therein, and it not appearing that the size of the restaurant or any special conditions called for greater vigilance than was actually exercised, the judgment in favor of the defendant was affirmed. . . .

" . . . [B]efore a restaurant keeper will be held liable for the loss of an overcoat of a customer while such customer takes a meal or refreshments, it must appear either that the overcoat was placed in the physical custody of the keeper of the restaurant or his servants, in which case there is an actual bailment, or that the overcoat was necessarily laid aside under circumstances showing at least notice of the fact and of such necessity to the keeper of the restaurant or his servants, in which case there is an implied bailment or constructive custody, or that the loss occurred by reason of the insufficiency of the general supervision exercised by the keeper of the restaurant for the protection of the property of customers temporarily laid aside. . . . [E]ach case must largely depend upon its particular facts and circumstances, for it is well known that there are all kinds of restaurants. In some of them good taste and etiquette require that a customer should take his hat and overcoat off while taking a meal, while in others, especially the so-called quick-lunch establishments, customers frequently remove neither hat nor overcoat.

"In the case at bar the testimony on the part of the plaintiff is to the effect that, on the day of the loss, the plaintiff entered the restaurant kept by the defendant with a party of friends and removed his overcoat, which was a light spring overcoat; that he hung it on a hook fixed to a post near the table at which he seated himself; that the attention of neither the defendant nor of any of his employees was called to the coat in any way; and that some fifteen minutes later the coat was missing. The plaintiff testified that he would not say that the waiter who waited on him ever saw the overcoat. It was not shown how the loss occurred. These facts do not establish an actual bailment. . . . There was not even an implied bailment or constructive custody on the theory that the overcoat was necessarily removed under circumstances which gave notice of such fact and of the necessity to the defendant or his servants. . . .

"Neither actual nor implied bailment or constructive custody having been established, it remains to be seen whether the plaintiff sufficiently proved negligence on the part of the defendant in the general supervision exercised over the restaurant, such as it was, for the protection of customers' property in general. The burden of proof upon this point was upon the plaintiff, for it is only in the case of a bailment that the burden is cast upon a bailee to account for the loss of the goods. But the plaintiff rested his case, upon this point, upon the bare fact of the loss.

"The defendant, on the other hand, testified, and it was not disputed, that he had kept a restaurant for the past fifteen years; that this was the first loss that had ever occurred in his establishment; that the plaintiff had visited the place for about six months prior to the date of the loss; that he, the defendant, gave his personal attention and supervision to the restaurant and allowed no suspicious characters to enter, and that there was a place immediately behind the cashier's desk reserved for the care of the property of customers that might be given to him or to his employees for safekeeping. The plaintiff admitted that in this place he 'may have seen one of the other fellows leave a sample case.' Upon the whole case it did not appear that the size of the restaurant or any special conditions therein called for greater vigilance than was actually exercised, and the plaintiff wholly failed to show failure on the part of the defendant to exercise ordinary care in the general management of his establishment. In every aspect of the case, therefore, the defendant is entitled to a reversal of the judgment against him. . . .

"Judgment reversed, new trial ordered, with costs to the appellant to abide event."

15:6 *Loss or Damage Caused by Negligence of Employees*

In *Block v. Sherry,*[9] it was recognized that the spilling of water by a waiter, causing property damage to a patron's wearing apparel, can constitute negligence and that the determination of the court as trier of the facts in a nonjury case will not be upset where the evidence was sufficient to warrant the court's finding of liability. This form of employee misconduct represents the typical restaurant hazard with respect to damage to property. The imposition of a bailment by operation of law with respect to a loss of property is noted in *Shamrock Hilton Hotel v. Caranas*, which follows. (A finder of lost property of another person, illustrated by *Caranas*, holds such property as an involuntary bailee for the true owner. The bailment is imposed by law, not, as in the normal case, by agreement of the parties.)

SHAMROCK HILTON HOTEL V. CARANAS
488 S.W.2d 151 (Tex. Civ. App., 1972)

BARRON, J.: "This is an appeal in an alleged bailment case from a judgment *non obstante veredicto* in favor of plaintiffs below.

---

[9]43 Misc. 342, 87 N.Y.S. 160 (Sup. Ct. 1904).

"Plaintiffs, husband and wife, were lodging as paying guests at the Shamrock Hilton Hotel in Houston on the evening of September 4, 1966, when they took their dinner in the hotel restaurant. After completing the meal, Mr. and Mrs. Caranas, plaintiffs, departed the dining area leaving her purse behind. The purse was found by the hotel bus boy who, pursuant to the instructions of the hotel, dutifully delivered the forgotten item to the restaurant cashier, a Mrs. Luster. The testimony indicates that some short time thereafter the cashier gave the purse to a man other than Mr. Caranas who came to claim it. There is no testimony on the question of whether identification was sought by the cashier. The purse allegedly contained $5.00 in cash, some credit cards, and ten pieces of jewelry said to be worth $13,062. The misplacement of the purse was realized the following morning, at which time plaintiffs notified the hotel authorities of the loss.

"Plaintiffs filed suit alleging negligent delivery of the purse to an unknown person and seeking a recovery for the value of the purse and its contents.

"The trial was to a jury which found that the cashier was negligent in delivering the purse to someone other than plaintiffs, and that this negligence was a proximate cause of the loss of the purse. The jury further found that plaintiffs were negligent in leaving the purse containing the jewelry in the hotel dining room, and that this negligence was a proximate cause of the loss.

" . . . [J]udgment was entered by the trial court for plaintiffs in the amount of $11,252.00 plus interest and costs. Shamrock Hilton Hotel and Hilton Hotels Corporation have perfected this appeal.

"We find after a full review of the record that there is sufficient evidence to warrant the submission of appellees' issues complained of and to support the jury findings on the special issues to the effect that the misdelivery was negligence and a proximate cause of the loss to appellees. Article 4592, Vernon's Tex. Rev. Civ. Stat. Ann. (1960), does not apply to limit the hotel's liability to $50.00 since its proviso declares that the loss must not occur through the negligence of the hotel, and such limiting statute is not applicable under the circumstances of this case.

"Contrary to appellants' contention, we find that there was indeed a constructive bailment of the purse. The delivery and acceptance were evidenced in the acts of Mrs. Caranas' unintentionally leaving her purse behind in the hotel restaurant and the bus boy, a hotel employee, picking it up and taking it to the cashier who accepted the purse as a lost or misplaced item. The delivery need not be a knowingly intended act on the part of Mrs. Caranas if it is apparent that were she, the quasi or constructive bailor, aware of the circumstances (here the chattel's being misplaced) she would have desired the person finding the article to have kept it safely for its subsequent return to her. See 8 Am. Jur. 2d Bailments Sec. 53, p. 959 (1963); and 8 C.J.S. Bailments § 15, pp. 360–362 (1962).

"As stated above, the evidence conclusively showed facts from which there was established a bailment with the Caranases as bailors and the hotel as bailee. The evidence also showed that the hotel, as bailee, had received Mrs. Caranas' purse and had not returned it on demand. Such evidence raised a presumption that the hotel had failed to exercise ordinary care in protecting the appellees' property. When the hotel failed to come forward with any evidence to the effect that it had exercised ordinary care, that the property had been stolen, or that the property had been lost, damaged or destroyed by fire or by an act of God, the appellees' proof ripened into proof by which the hotel's primary liability was established as a matter of law. [Citations omitted.] . . .

" . . . [T]his bailment was one for the mutual benefit of both parties. Appellees were paying guests in the hotel and in its dining room. Appellant hotel's practice of keeping patrons' lost personal items until they could be returned to their rightful owners, as reflected in the testimony, is certainly evidence of its being incidental to its business, as we would think it would be for almost any commercial enterprise which caters to the general public. Though no direct charge is made for this service there is indirect benefit to be had in the continued patronage of the hotel by customers who have lost chattels and who have been able to claim them from the management.

"Having found this to have been a bailment for the mutual benefit of the parties, we hold that the appellants owed the appellees the duty of reasonable care in the return of the purse and jewelry, and the hotel is therefore liable for its ordinary negligence. [Citation omitted.]

"Appellants urge that if a bailment is found it existed only as to 'the purse and the usual petty cash or credit cards found therein' and not to the jewelry of which the hotel had no actual notice. This exact question so far as we can determine has never been squarely put before the Texas Courts, but as appellants concede, the general rule in other jurisdictions is that a bailee is liable not only for lost property of which he has actual knowledge but also the property he could reasonably expect to find contained within the bailed property. *See and compare* Note, *Bailment—Articles Left in Automobiles*, 10 Baylor L. Rev. 216, 217–218 (1958). . . . [Opinions to the contrary noted but disapproved are omitted.]

"We believe appellants' contention raises the question of whether or not it was foreseeable that such jewelry might be found in a woman's purse in a restaurant of a hotel such as the Shamrock Hilton under these circumstances.

" . . . We cannot say as a matter of law that there is no evidence upon which a jury could reasonably find that it was foreseeable that such jewelry might be found in a purse under such circumstances as here presented. It is known that people who are guests in hotels such as the Shamrock Hilton, a well-known Houston hotel, not infrequently bring such expensive jewelry with them, and it does not impress us as unreasonable under the circumstances that one person might have her jewelry in her purse either awaiting a present occasion to wear it or following reclaiming it from the hotel safe in anticipation of leaving the hotel . . .

" . . . [W]e deem it to be found that one might reasonably expect to find valuable jewelry within a purse under the circumstances of this case in support of the judgment below. It follows that the findings of negligence and proximate cause of the loss of the purse apply to the jewelry as well, which is deemed to be a part of the bailment. . . .

"Appellant's final point of error complains of the trial court's granting of appellees' motion for judgment notwithstanding the verdict and disregarding the jury's findings on special issues that appellees' leaving the purse was negligence and a proximate cause of the loss of the jewelry. In support of this contention appellants cite *Southwestern Hotel Co. v. Rogers,* 183 S.W.2d 751 (Tex. Civ. App.—El Paso 1944), *aff'd* 143 Tex. 343, 184 S.W.2d 835 (1945) and *Driskill Hotel Co. v. Anderson,* 19 S.W.2d 216 (Tex. Civ. App.—Austin 1929, no writ), for the proposition that contributory negligence of a guest of a hotel is an absolute defense to a claim for jewelry or money lost in the hotel. Both cases, however, are distinguishable on the facts in that here the loss occurred *after* appellees had relinquished possession of the purse and its contents, and the hotel alone had assumed responsibility for the items. . . .

"We find *Vollmer v. Stoneleigh-Maple Terrace,* 226 S.W.2d 926 (Tex. Civ. App.—Dallas 1950, writ ref'd), cited by appellees, to be in point. There the plaintiff was a guest in the Stoneleigh Hotel and paid monthly to park his automobile in the hotel's adjacent garage. On the evening in question he drove his car to the hotel entrance and turned it over to an employee of the defendant who parked it in its usual spot. While the employee was parking another car, he heard the noise of the starting motor and arrived just in time to see plaintiff's car being driven away. The jury found that the defendant was guilty of several acts of negligence, each of which was a proximate cause of the loss of the vehicle. It also found that the plaintiff, Vollmer, was negligent in accepting the garage facilities as furnished by the defendant; in failing to keep a proper lookout for his own automobile; in failing to remove the keys from the automobile; and in failing to see that there was a sufficient number of attendants to guard his automobile. Each of these acts was found to be a proximate cause. The Court of Civil Appeals reversed the judgment of the trial court in favor of defendant and rendered judgment for plaintiff, holding that the plaintiff's contributory negligence was not a proximate cause as a matter of law. The Court stated: 'As appellant (plaintiff) aptly points out, while the car was in the possession of defendant the duty of care as between the parties rested solely upon it, plaintiff being relieved of further duties in connection with a proper lookout, safeguarding of keys, etc.' 226 S.W.2d at 928.

"The bus boy and cashier assumed possession and control of the purse per instructions of the hotel with respect to articles misplaced or lost by customers. This assumption of possession was as complete as that of defendant's employee in *Vollmer v. Stoneleigh-Maple Terrace, supra.* In each instance, once the bailee assumed possession he alone had the duty to safeguard the bailed article. We find therefore under these facts that the negligence of Mrs. Caranas was not a cause ' . . . which in a natural and continuous sequence produces an event . . . ' of this nature. . . .

" . . . The active cause which produced the loss was wholly independent of the negligence of Mrs. Caranas, and the hotel's primary duty of ordinary care to its paying guest was clear.

"The judgment of the trial court is affirmed."

15:7 *Limitation of Liability for Articles Checked*

For articles of personal property accepted for safekeeping, the restaurant keeper is responsible as bailee, bound to exercise ordinary care in keeping and safeguarding the property. The measure of liability for loss through negligence is the reasonable value of the property. The parties to a bailment may, however, contract to diminish the bailee's common-law liability provided the contract is not in violation of law or of public policy. Such a contract must be a special contract spelling out the limitation in clear language and it must appear that the bailor (the customer) has had reasonable notice of the terms and that he has assented to them.

It has been held[10] that a parcel check of the usual cardboard type ($3'' \times 2 \ 1/2''$) in size upon the face of which there appeared in legible red letters the word "Contract" together with terms and conditions limiting the parcel room owner's liability to $25, was not sufficient to charge the depositor with knowledge that he was contracting for a limitation of liability for loss. There was no proof in the case that there were conspicuous signs or large placards about the parcel room (nor any other form of notice) calling attention to the limitation of liability.

The parcel room check with the usual legend printed either on its face or on the reverse side thereof that "the restaurant (or hotel, as the case may be) will not be liable for loss of or damage to the property as a result of fire, theft, ordinary or gross negligence, or otherwise, unless it shall appear that the loss or damage was caused by willful act or misappropriation by the restaurant (hotel) or its employees" is insufficient to limit liability *unless* there is adequate notice by a conspicuous large placard at the parcel room calling attention to the contract for limited liability.

In New York, section 201 of the General Business Law does limit the restaurant keeper's liability, as it does that of an innkeeper, for articles checked in the checkroom or parcel room of any hotel *or restaurant*, the delivery of which is evidenced by a check or receipt therefor and for which no fee or charge is exacted. The posting requirements of the statute do not specifically refer to restaurants as they do to hotels.

In the following landmark case, the New York Court of Appeals, among other rulings, reaffirmed its prior holding in *Honig v. Riley*[11] limiting liability for the loss of articles checked in a restaurant checkroom to $75 absent any declaration of excess value, regardless of the fact that the loss was caused by the gross negligence of the restaurant.

WEINBERG V. D-M RESTAURANT CORP. [WEINBERG II]
53 N.Y.2d 499, 426 N.E.2d 459 (1981)

MEYER, J.: "Section 201 of the General Business Law has no bearing upon an action against a restaurant owner sued for the conversion of a coat checked by a

---

[10]Klar v. H. & M. Parcel Room, Inc., 270 A.D. 538, 61 N.Y.S.2d 285 (1st Dep't 1946), *aff'd mem.*, 296 N.Y. 1044, 73 N.E.2d 912 (1947).
[11]244 N.Y. 105, 155 N.E. 65 (1926).

patron. It does limit recovery by a patron who sues for negligence: to the value of the coat if negligence be shown, a fee or charge is exacted for checking the coat, and a value in excess of $75 is declared and a written receipt stating such value is issued when the coat is delivered to the checkroom attendant; to $100 if a value in excess of $75 is declared and the other conditions are met but negligence cannot be shown; to $75 in any event if no fee or charge is exacted or a value in excess of $75 is not declared and a written receipt obtained when the coat is delivered. . . .

I

"Plaintiff's complaint contained but one cause of action predicated upon the negligence of defendant restaurant owner. Defendant moved for summary judgment limiting plaintiff's recovery to $75. The affidavits presented by defendant established that neither defendant's president nor anyone else in his employ could explain the disappearance of the Russian sable fur coat which plaintiff checked with defendant's checkroom attendant, that no value had been declared by plaintiff nor had any writen receipt stating a value been given, acknowledged that no sign had been posted but stated that section 201 of the General Business Law did not require posting by a restaurant, and quoted a portion of plaintiff's deposition in which she acknowledged that no charge had been made for the checking of the coat. Plaintiff cross-moved for summary judgment. Her affidavit noted the admission of defendant's president that tipping was discretionary and characterized it as contrary to common knowledge. Attached to it also was the deposition of the coatroom attendant in which she conceded that on the night in question she received $20 to $30 in tips.

"Special Term denied both the motion and cross motion. On appeal the Appellate Division modified and remanded for trial as to damages, holding that plaintiff was entitled to judgment on liability but that on the issue of damages there existed questions of fact concerning whether defendant restaurant had 'exacted' a fee or charge and whether the loss was the result of theft by defendant, its agent, servants or employees (60 A.D.2d 550, 400 N.Y.S.2d 524). On remand the Trial Judge, after testimony by defendant's president that the checkroom attendant received an hourly rate of pay plus a percentage of the tips given her, the owner receiving the balance of the tips, ruled that notwithstanding that there was no sign concerning tips nor other open solicitation of them and that some people received their coats without leaving any tip, the gratuities paid the checkroom attendant constituted, as a matter of law, the exaction of a fee within the meaning of the section. He noted further that the issue of theft by defendant or its employees had become academic, that were that not so he would have directed a verdict for plaintiff on that ground also because defendant had presented no evidence on the question of theft. He submitted to the jury, therefore, only the question of the value of plaintiff's coat. The jury fixed that value at $7,500 and judgment was entered for that sum plus interest and costs.

"On appeal from the judgment entered on the jury's verdict, the Appellate Division affirmed, without opinion, but granted defendant leave to appeal to our court from the final judgment. . . . For the reasons stated below we hold that (1) the tip or gratuity customarily given a checkroom attendant is not a 'fee or charge . . . exacted' for the checking service within the meaning of section 201 of the General Business Law; (2) restaurants are not required to post the provisions of section 201 in order to be entitled to its limitation of liability; and (3) in granting summary judgment to plaintiff rather than defendant and in affirming the judgment entered February 7, 1979 the Appellate Division erred; its order of affirmance must, therefore, be modified and judgment directed to be entered for plaintiff in the amount of $75 with interest from March 3, 1975.

II

"Subdivision 1 of section 201 of the General Business Law provides in relevant part: '[A]s to property deposited by guests or patrons in the parcel or check room of any hotel, motel or restaurant, the delivery of which is evidenced by a check or receipt therefor and for which no fee or charge is exacted, the proprietor shall not be liable beyond seventy-five dollars, unless such value in excess of seventy-five dollars shall be stated upon delivery and a written receipt, stating such value, shall be issued, but he shall in no event be liable beyond one hundred dollars, unless such loss occurs through his fault or negligence.' In a case strikingly similar to the instant case, *Honig v. Riley*, 244 N.Y. 105, 155 N.E. 65, that language was construed by this court. Plaintiff Honig sought to recover the value of the fur coat she left at the checkroom of defendant's restaurant on New Year's Eve 1925. She received a check but was not questioned as to value and made no statement to the attendant concerning value. The Trial Judge charged that plaintiff was entitled to full value of the coat if they found defendant to have been negligent. On appeal by defendant from a judgment of $850 entered on the jury's verdict and affirmed by the Appellate Term and the Appellate Division, this court reversed and directed reduction of the judgment to $75. In an opinion by Judge CARDOZO, we said (244 N.Y., at pp. 108–109, 155 N.E. 65):

"The defendant maintains that where property is deposited in a parcel or check room without statement of value or delivery of the prescribed receipt, there is a limit of liability to $75 for loss from any cause. Disclosure of the value, if followed by a receipt, will extend liability for fault or negligence up to the limit of the value stated, though even then the liability, if any, as insurer will be $100 and no more. The plaintiff on her side maintains, and the courts below have held, that the exemption from liability in excess of $75 where the value is not disclosed, is not to be read as a limitation of liability for loss from any cause, but is confined to losses not due to the fault or negligence of the proprietor.

"We think the defendant's construction is the true one, however clumsy and inartificial may be the phrasing of the statute. A limitation of liability affecting merely the measure of recovery is applicable, if not otherwise restrained, to loss for any cause. . . . From the beginning of the section to the end, the exemption from liability in excess of the prescribed maximum is absolute where value is concealed. Only where value is stated and a receipt delivered is the exemption made dependent upon freedom from negligence or other fault.

"Under that reading of the statute plaintiff's recovery is limited to $75, no value having been declared or receipt obtained, unless it can be found that a 'fee or charge [was] exacted.' The ruling of the lower courts that the acceptance by the checkroom attendant of a gratuity in which the restaurant owner shares constitutes an 'exaction', made not as a finding of fact but as a matter of law was, however, erroneous. Though tips may constitute compensation to an employee for purposes of the Workers' Compensation Law [Citations omitted]; [(]*see* Ann., 75 A.L.R. 1223), of the income tax (Ann., 10 A.L.R.2d 191) and of unemployment compensation taxes (Ann., 83 A.L.R.2d 1024), it does not follow that a tip to an employee may be regarded for all purposes as compensation to the employee [citations omitted] or as a part of the employer's income (Ann., 73 A.L.R.3d 1226 [sales tax]). As to the employer the test generally is whether the payment is a 'service charge' exacted by the employer or a voluntary payment by the patron to the employee (*Beaman v. Westward Ho Hotel Co.*, 89 Ariz. I, 357 P.2d 327; *see* Ann., 73 A.L.R.3d 1226, 1231). So in *Beaman* the Arizona Supreme Court held a service charge collected by the hotel, where direct tipping of employees was not permitted, to be subject to sales tax. In so doing, it distinguished the customary employee gratuity saying (89 Ariz. at pp. 4–5, 357 P.2d 327) 'A tip is in law, if not always in fact, a voluntary payment' (*see, also, Peoria Hotel Co. v. Department of Revenue*, 87 Ill. App. 3d 176, 179, 408 N.E.2d 1182, 42 Ill. Dec. 473). The United States District Court for the Southern District of New York reached a result similar to *Beaman* in *Restaurants & Patisseries Longchamps v. Pedrick*, D.C. 52 F. Supp. 174, but noted (at pp. 174–175) that 'A patron in a restaurant is under no compulsion to leave a "tip" (*see, also, United States v. Conforte*, 9th Cir. 624 F.2d 869, 874, cert. den. 449 U.S. 1012, 101 S. Ct. 568, 66 L. Ed. 2d 470).

"The more clearly should such a distinction be made when, as here, we deal with a statute not at all concerned with the compensation of the *employee* or the taxes payable to the State, but rather with whether the *employer* in permitting gratuities to be paid to the employee has exacted a fee or charge [citation omitted]. So a restaurant owner or hotel that imposes a fixed charge for the service of checking a coat and does not leave to the patron the decision whether to give and what amount to give may properly be said to have exacted a service charge or fee (*semble Aldrich v. Waldorf Astoria Hotel*, 74 Misc. 2d 413, 414, 343 N.Y.S.2d 830 [35 cents per garment paid; held a 'fee or charge']).

"When the service cannot be obtained without the payment of a fixed sum a fee has been exacted, but when, as the papers on the summary judgment motions showed, plaintiff acknowledges that no charge was made and presents no evidence that there was a sign indicating a fixed charge, or of solicitation of any kind, or that the giving and the amount were other than discretionary with the customer, there has, as a matter or law, been no exaction of a fee or charge.

III

"Plaintiff argued on the original motions, and the dissenter in this court agrees, that section 201 is not applicable because defendant failed to comply with subdivision 2 of the section. That subdivision requires that 'A printed copy of this section shall be posted in a conspicuous place and manner in the office or public room and in the public parlors of such hotel or motel.' While that provision was not added to the section until 1960 (L. 1960, ch. 840), section 206 has since 1909 required posting of a printed copy of section 201. Section 206 is by its terms limited, however, to a 'hotel or inn' just as subdivision 2 of section 201 is limited to a 'hotel or motel.' To read subdivision 2 to require posting by a restaurant because subdivision 1 groups 'hotel, motel or restaurant' together is to fly in the face of usual rules of statutory construction that a statute (in this instance, subdivision 2's posting requirement) is to be read and given effect as it was written, and that the courts under guise of interpretation may not enlarge or change the scope of a legislative enactment [citations omitted]. Nor is the dissent's reliance upon the language of *Honig v. Riley (supra)* a proper basis for concluding otherwise. No issue of posting was presented in that case. Moreover, since section 201 contained no posting requirement when *Honig* was decided and no mention was made in the opinion of section 206, the phrases from that opinion quoted by the dissent cannot be fairly read as having been written with respect to the point for which those phrases are now cited. If posting by restaurants is to be required as a condition of the limitation of liability granted them by subdivision 1 of section 201, it is the Legislature rather than this court that must impose the requirement.

IV

"Though neither the posting nor the fee exaction provisions of section 201 limit defendant's right to the benefits of its provisions, plaintiff, pointing to the statement in *Honig v. Riley supra,* 244 N.Y. at p. 110, 155 N.E. 65, that 'The statute is aimed at loss or misadventure. It has no application to theft by the defendant or his agents,' contends she is entitled to affirmance of the judgment because defendant failed to come forward with proof that the coat had not been stolen by its employees. The difficulty with plaintiff's position is that the complaint declares for negligence only and has never been amended either by motion addressed to Special Term or by a motion to conform pleadings to proof at the end of the trial. Quite simply, plaintiff cannot recover on a conversion theory which she has never pleaded.

"Accordingly, the Appellate Division's order of February 7, 1979 should be modified, with costs to defendant in all courts, by reducing the amount awarded to plaintiff to $75 with interest from March 3, 1975."

FUCHSBERG, J. (dissenting):

"Invited, of course, to do so by its management, plaintiff, a restaurant patron, deposited her fur coat, now found to have been worth $7,500, at the defendant's cloakroom at the plush Rainbow Grill in Rockefeller Center. Without explanation, it was never to be returned. Yet, the majority would relegate her to a recovery of $75. Neither the history or public policy of the statutory scheme which governs such a case, nor the common sense or the elementary fairness that go with a living law will abide such a result. I therefore vote to uphold the Trial Term award to the plaintiff for the full amount of her loss as thereafter unanimously affirmed by the Appellate Division. Here follow my reasons, grounded, I would like to believe, on principle, practicality and, withal, sound law. . . .

" . . . [H]istory and policy lead to inexorable conclusions: The Legislature did not intend to extend the salutary benefits of section 201 of the General Business Law to the proprietors of either restaurants, hotels or motels without appropriate notice of the condition—exaction of a receipt containing a statement of value—without which the most extensive loss would bring but a pittance. When the bill was originally enacted, it would have served nothing but an impermissibly overprecious and overliteral reading to assume it intended to charge only hotels with its posting requirement, when, though its hotel sponsors had ignored restaurants, the Legislature affirmatively and expressly took the trouble to include them within the 'connected' statutory scheme [citation omitted].

"Therefore, while, no doubt, the statutory language could be clearer, it surely is remiss not to give effect to the clearcut underlying intent that, at least for checkroom posting purposes, restaurants are in the 'same class' with the other kinds of establishments to be found in the related subdivisions of the statute. . . . "

Since *Weinberg*, the New York State legislature has amended section 201 of the General Business Law to increase the liability limitations for checkrooms in hotels, motels, and restaurants. Chapter 182 of the Laws of 1983 relating to such increased limits reads (changes indicated with italics):

> . . . as to property deposited by guests or patrons in the parcel or *checkroom* of any hotel, motel or restaurant, the delivery of which is evidenced by a check or receipt therefor and for which no fee or charge is exacted, the proprietor shall not be liable beyond *two hundred* dollars, unless such value in excess of *two hundred* shall be stated upon delivery and a written receipt, stating such value, shall be issued, but he shall in no event be liable beyond *three* hundred dollars, unless such loss occurs through his fault or negligence.

Subsection 2 of section 201 was also amended, adding the following language:

> No hotel, motel or restaurant proprietor shall post a notice disclaiming or misrepresenting his liability under this section.

In a 1982 case, the court addressed a number of important issues, not the least of which was whether a discotheque may avail itself of the protection afforded under section 201(1) of the New York General Business Law. The reasoning of the court follows.

CONBOY V. STUDIO 54, INC.
113 Misc. 2d 403, 449 N.Y.S.2d 391 (City Civ. Ct. 1982)

SAXE, J.: "The issue that I must decide is whether the statutory limitation on liability in subdivision 1 of section 201 of the General Business Law provides a monetary haven for a discotheque.

"The section states in part: '[A]s to property deposited by guests or patrons in the parcel or check room of any *hotel, motel* or *restaurant*, the delivery of which is evidenced by a check or receipt therefor *and for which no fee or charge is exacted*, the proprietor shall not be liable beyond seventy-five dollars, unless such value in excess of seventy-five dollars shall be stated upon delivery and a written receipt, stating such value, shall be issued, but he shall in no event be liable beyond one hundred dollars, unless such loss occurs through his fault or negligence.' (Emphasis supplied.)

"On January 23, 1982, the claimant, his wife and a group of friends convened for a party at Studio 54 (Studio) in Manhattan. Studio, licensed by the New York City Department of Consumer Affairs as a cabaret, is a discotheque, where patrons dance to recorded music usually played continuously on high fidelity equipment. (Random House Dictionary of the English Language [unabridged ed. 1973].) Often a psychedelic light show accompanies the music and provides background and impetus for the free-spirited patrons who pay $18 per person to dance to the deafening and often overwhelming disco music played continuously on the sophisticated sound system. A cabaret is defined as 'Any room, place or space in the city in which any musical entertainment, singing, dancing or other form of amusement is permitted in connection with the restaurant business or the business of directly or indirectly selling to the public food or drink'. (Administrative Code of City of New York, § B32–296.0, subd. 3.)

"No food is sold or served here—not even a single peanut or pretzel to accompany the alcoholic and soft drinks available for purchase.

"The Conboy party checked their coats, 14 in all, with the coatroom attendant. They received seven check stubs after paying the 75 cent charge per coat. A bailment of the coats was created. (*See, generally,* 9 N.Y. Jur. 2d, *Bailments and Chattel Leases,* § 1.) Mr. Conboy did not issue a statement concerning the coat's value to the attendant.

"After their evening of revelry, they attempted to reclaim their coats. Mr. Conboy's one-month-old $1,350 leather coat was missing. It has not been found and, accordingly, he has sued Studio for $1,350.

"Under traditional bailment law, once the goods were delivered, the failure of the bailee (Studio) to return them on demand, created a prima facie case of negligence. The burden of coming forward with evidence tending to show due care shifted to Studio. (*Claflin v. Meyer,* 75 N.Y. 260, 264; *Singer Co. v. Stott & Davis Motor Express,* 79 A.D.2d 227.) Studio did not come forward with any evidence to meet this burden. Mr. Conboy is entitled to a judgment.

"Studio, relying on subdivision 1 of section 201 of the General Business Law, contends that its liability is limited to $75 since no value was declared for the coat. Its argument is incorrect for two reasons.

"First, the statute applies to a hotel, motel or restaurant and then only to property deposited by a patron in a checkroom 'the delivery of which is evidenced by a check or receipt therefor and for which no fee . . . is exacted'. The statute offers innkeepers and restaurant proprietors who comply with it a reduction of the innkeeper's common-law insurer liability as to guests' property deposited with them. (*See, generally,* Navagh, *A New Look at the Liability of Inn Keepers for Guest Property under New York Law,* 25 Fordham L. Rev., 62; *Steiner v. O'Leary,* 186 Misc. 236, *aff'd* 186 Misc. 577.) Compliance with the terms of the statute relieves the innkeeper or restaurant owner of this common-law responsibility, where applicable. (*Weinberg v. D-M Rest. Corp.,* 53 N.Y.2d 499; *Zaldin v. Concord Hotel,* 65 A.D.2d 670, mod. on other grounds 48 N.Y.2d 107.) The statute is in derogation of the common law and is therefore strictly construed. (*Briggs v. Todd,* 28 Misc. 208 [App. Term, 1st Dept.].)

"That being said, it need only be noted that the statute offers its protection to restaurants, hotels, and motels, *not* discotheques which appear to be modern-day versions of dance halls. (*Cf.* Administrative Code, § B32–296.0, subd. 1.)

"Simply put, a discotheque may qualify as a restaurant but there is no logic in giving it that classification unless one of its principal activities is the furnishing of meals. Certainly, Studio should not be classified as a restaurant, because it serves no food. A licensed cabaret, such as Studio, is permitted to engage in the restaurant business (Administrative Code, § B32–296.0, subd. 3) but is not required to.

"The term 'restaurant' was first used in America to refer to dining rooms found in the best hotels and to certain high-class *a la carte* restaurants. (*People v. Kupas,* 171 Misc. 480.) Today, a restaurant would be thought of as an establishment that sells food and drink or where meals may be purchased and eaten. (*People v. Gobeo,* 6 N.Y.S.2d 937; *see, also, Donahue v. Conant,* 102 Vt. 108.) The limitations on liability set forth in the statute are therefore not applicable here. (McKinney's Cons. Laws of N.Y., Book 1, *Statutes,* § 240.) It may be illogical to condition limitation of liability on the sale of meals, but that is what the statute says and it is for the Legislature to change, not this court.

"Even if I might have concluded that Studio could be treated as a restaurant, it still would not have benefited from the liability limitation provided by the statute because of the fact that a charge was exacted for each coat checked. (*Aldrich v. Waldorf Astoria Hotel,* 74 Misc. 2d 413.)

"Studio claims however that their liability may nevertheless be limited by the posting of a sign in the coatroom. The sign states: 'Liability for lost property in this coat/check room is limited to $100 per loss of misplaced article. This notice is posted pursuant to Section 201, General Business Law of New York State.'

"My holding to the effect that subdivision 1 of section 201 of the General Business Law is not applicable here, does not make the posting of the sign a useless act, for it may still function as a common-law disclaimer. To bind Conboy to this limitation, I must find however that he had notice of the terms of the disclaimer and agreed to it. (*Klar v. H. & M. Parcel Room,* 270 App. Div. 538, 541, *aff'd* 296 N.Y. 1044.) Studio did not establish that the sign was posted in a conspicuous manner. (*Klar v. H. & M. Parcel Room, supra,* at 542; *Aldrich v. Waldorf Astoria Hotel, supra.*)

"I hold that Conboy is not bound by the posted disclaimer of liability.

"As to damages, Conboy is entitled to the 'real value' of the coat. (*Alebrande v. New York City Housing Auth.,* 44 Misc. 2d 803, rev'd on other grounds 49 Misc. 2d 880 [App. Term, 1st Dep't].) Real value, especially with respect to used clothing or household furnishings that are lost or damaged is not necessarily its market value which presumably would reflect a deduction for depreciation. (*Supra,* at p. 808; *Teich v. Andersen & Co.,* 24 A.D.2d 749.) In fact, the real value may be measured by the price paid when new for the lost or damaged goods. (*Lobell v. Paleg,* 154 N.Y.S.2d 709, 713.)

"One commentator has offered a reason that the strict value approach is not favored: 'No judge buys his clothing second hand and none would expect any owner to replace his clothing in a second hand store. Hence no judge expects to limit the cost of replacing clothing to a market no one should be expected to use.' (Dobbs, *Remedies,* § 5.12, p. 397.)

"I therefore hold that Conboy may be compensated on a basis that will permit him to replace the very same coat purchased new—$1,350.

"Judgment for claimant in the sum of $1,350."

15:8 *Summary*

A restaurant keeper is not absolutely liable as insurer for the safety of the property of his customers. He is liable for negligence as bailee or for damage inflicted where he accepts the property for safekeeping either in a checkroom or elsewhere in the premises and fails to return it when called for or where he assumes responsibility for lost property. He is also liable for losses occasioned by failure adequately to supervise the premises. He is not liable for loss of an overcoat or hat left on a chair or hung on a hook by the customer himself. He is well advised to maintain a checking facility in the premises and to post adequate notices in conspicuous places in the establishment that he will be "Not Responsible for Personal Property Unless Checked with the Management." Disregard of such conspicuous notices may well charge the customer with contributory negligence.

PART IV

Government Regulation of
the Hospitality Industry

16   Civil and Criminal Responsibility for Anticompetitive Marketing Activities

16:1   *Introduction*

In the field of hospitality marketing, it is quite common to find close association among hospitality executives who compete for business within a given market. The term *market* in this sense includes not only a given geographic area but also specific services within that area, such as convention services. It is quite natural for sales executives in the hospitality industry to enter into informal arrangements with other sales executives in their area to coordinate rates, facilities, and ancillary services in hopes of garnering a top convention that requires services beyond the capacity of each of the various hospitality units. Such arrangements benefit not only the hospitality industry but the community as a whole. They may benefit the convention sponsor as well because a package price is often substantially lower than the sum of the prices that would be charged by each hospitality unit separately. Very often trade associations, convention bureaus, and municipal tourism boards actively solicit such convention business and support the efforts of the local hotels, restaurants, and travel bureaus. In fact, in major cities and convention sites, the competition for this form of business is fierce and vitally important to the economic viability of the community at large.

At first glance, the standard operating procedure set forth above would appear an acceptable if not a necessary practice to ensure the survival as well as serve the best interests of the entrepreneur, the industry, and the consumer. Why then have various governmental regulatory bodies raised such a furor over such activities? What specifically is acceptable activity, what is prohibited, and how does one distinguish between the two? This chapter provides a basic overview of marketing law as it affects the hospitality industry and highlights specific problem areas.

16:2   *Administrative Law: An Overview*

Government regulation of industry in general has become a pervasive fact of economic life in recent years. Emphasis has shifted from outright regulation of rates and routes previously manifest in the airline, rail, and trucking industries, to regulation of consumer and worker safety and welfare in the form of federal,

[589]

state, and local oversight over business personnel and practices. The federal Occupational Safety and Health Administration (OSHA), the federal Environmental Protection Agency, and state health and safety codes and their local counterparts are but examples of this trend.

The hospitality industry, too, is regulated in this fashion, but its regulation also takes the form of admission and service of the public, worker civil rights, licensing of public activities, and, recently, specific fire-safety measures aimed at protection of the public. Illustrative examples are federal, state, and local civil rights laws; food-service, health, and alcoholic-beverage control laws; and expanded federal discouragement of use by federal employees of hotels and motels that are not equipped with fire sprinkler systems.

The following chapters address these issues, including judicial review of regulatory activities and redress by private citizens adversely affected by regulatory violations.

16:3 *Historical Antecedents of the Antitrust Movement*

Early in the development of the American capitalist economic system the doctrine of laissez faire was embraced and encouraged by the business community. The market for products and services was to be regulated by competition, not by government intervention. Survival would then be based on the accumulation of market power, and the fittest products would gain dominance. Expansion meant the elimination of competition; no public regulation was thought necessary or desirable. The practices tolerated in the quest for survival included: buying out or driving out competition and establishing a monopoly over production or service; establishing pooling arrangements to split the market and eliminate competition; granting customer rebates to increase the market for the product or service; price discrimination in favor of designated customers; and horizontal and vertical price fixing.

Implicit in these practices was an unabashed attempt by industry to eliminate competition and replace it with a monopolistic system (within one industry) or an oligarchical system (a group of monopolies) of marketing.

16:4 *The Governmental Response*

The first major legislative effort to attack the problem of anticompetitive practices was the Sherman Act of 1890,[1] by which Congress prohibited (1) "Every contract, combination or conspiracy, in restraint of trade or commerce among the several states, or with foreign nations" and (2) "monopolies or attempts to monopolize."

In 1914 Congress passed the Clayton Act,[2] which provided more specific guidelines to the courts and permitted anticompetitive practices to be halted in

---

[1]26 Stat. 209, 15 U.S.C.A. § § 1-7 (1890).
[2]38 Stat. 730, 15 U.S.C.A. § § 12-17 (1914).

their infancy. Price discrimination, exclusive agreements (tying contracts, reciprocal agreements, and requirements contracts), and mergers (through stock acquisition) were prohibited, but only "where the effect of the practice may be to substantially lessen competition or tend to create a monopoly in any line of commerce."[3]

During the Depression the Robinson-Patman Act[4] was passed as an amendment to the Clayton Act to restrict discriminatory practices between sellers of products or services and large-scale buyers by preventing such buyers from obtaining a competitive advantage over small buyers solely because of the large-scale buyers' quantity purchasing ability.

Of particular interest to the hospitality industry are sections 2(d) and 2(e) of the Clayton Act, as amended, which prohibit providing services, facilities, and promotional allowances to a buyer unless the same are offered to all competing buyers on proportionally equal terms. Section 2(f) prohibits a person or company from seeking or receiving any increase or decrease in price not otherwise permitted under sections 2(a) and 2(b). Sections 2(a) and 2(b) allow price increases or decreases made in good faith to meet the equally low price of a competitor or as justified by changes in market conditions or where it costs the seller less to deal with a particular buyer.

In 1950 the Celler-Kefauver Act[5] amended section 7 of the Clayton Act to prohibit acquisition of assets of another entity if the effect would be to lessen competition substantially or to create a monopoly. Previously only stock purchases having this effect were prohibited.

Under the Hart-Scott-Rodino Antitrust Improvement Act of 1976,[6] the attorney general is empowered to secure antitrust information from a third party, and any state attorney general may sue on behalf of the citizens of the state against entities that violate the Sherman Act. This latter provision is known as the *parens patriae* doctrine, and it means that the state is empowered to sue to protect the interests of all of its affected citizens as a class.

16:5 *What Conduct Is Proscribed*

The Sherman Act, as interpreted by the courts, distinguishes between conduct that constitutes a *per se* violation of the Act and conduct that is governed by the "rule of reason." That rule rests on findings of lack of intent to eliminate competition and lack of any substantial adverse effect upon competition in the marketplace.[7]

---

[3]15 U.S.C.A. § § 2, 3, 7 (1936).

[4]Section 2 of the Act is 49 Stat. 1526, 15 U.S.C.A. § 13 (1936). Section 3 of the Act is 49 Stat. 1528, 15 U.S.C.A. § 13a (1936).

[5]64 Stat. 1125, 15 U.S.C.A. § 18 (1950).

[6]Pub. L. No. 94-435, 90 Stat. 1383, 15 U.S.C.A. § 16 (1976).

[7]United States v. Arnold, Schwinn & Co., 388 US 365 (1967).

16:6 Per Se *Illegality: Price Fixing*

Any form of price fixing of products or services that is not otherwise exempted from the Sherman Act by Congress is illegal *per se*.[8] Thus all joint efforts to raise, depress, fix, peg, or stabilize prices are outlawed,[9] regardless of their "purpose, aim or effect in the elimination of so called competitive ends."[10] No proof of lack of monopolistic impact or proof that the members of the price-fixing group were in no position to control the market could excuse or justify the illegal conduct. *Per se* illegality is unrelated to motive, however laudible or necessitated by market conditions.

Illegal price fixing without benefit of the rule of reason is called "horizontal price fixing," that is, fixing prices of goods or services at the same market level, whether manufacturing, wholesale, or retail. For example, one hotel-keeper would agree with his competitors to fix the rates for guest rooms, function rooms, and ancillary services for a convention package that was to be offered to a prospective host organization. The agreement could be established in writing, but an oral agreement, standing alone, would be sufficient, even though no concerted action was taken to offer the rooms and services at the rate agreed upon. Silence constitutes agreement where there is knowledge of the terms of the agreement and adoption of the rate agreed upon within a reasonable time thereafter. The courts define this silent agreement as the "knowing wink." The silent member of the group, to show that he was not involved in the agreement, must prove that he did not agree to go along, objected vociferously, and departed at the earliest opportunity.

Related to the knowing wink doctrine is the question whether identical actions among business competitors imply a scheme or conspiracy to fix prices in the absence of any direct proof of such a conspiracy to agree or actual agreement. The courts have not yet concluded that evidence of such actions without corroboration will support a finding of a conspiracy to fix prices. It may be used to show the possible existence of price fixing, which would compel the accused to prove that the charges are false and that no conspiracy exists.

How can one draw the line between illegal, conscious price fixing and legal price setting followed by competitive price adjustments to meet or undercut the competition? The answer is that in the latter case, there is no agreement, arrangement, or conspiracy by competitors prior to the announced price change. The leadership price announced at the beginning of a new season is presumably independently determined and logically arrived at; likely competitive reactions are taken into account.

The key to the legality of setting prices is the exercise of independent judgment by each business entity on its pricing policies, based on information available and lawfully acquired in the normal course of its operation. Unless that

---

[8]United States v. Socony-Vacuum Oil Co., 310 U.S. 150 (1940).
[9]*Id.*
[10]*Id.*

business qualifies as a monopoly or threatens substantially to lessen competition, such conduct should be above reproach.

What constitutes unmistakably illegal activities is a joint effort among competitors to exchange price lists and use such lists as the basis for joint pricing decisions. In practice, then, any effort, no matter how well intended, to solicit or respond to requests for prices by competitors or by trade organizations or similar groups that would identify the source of the information and publish it for the benefit of competitors must be studiously resisted. Providing general room rates and other information to professional organizations that compile the data, without identifying the source, for general trade and public consumption is proper and will not violate the Sherman Act.

The following case illustrates the treatment of a variety of antitrust problems in a typical fast-food franchise. The franchisees sought certification for class-action status. All references to that procedural issue are omitted.

KREHL V. BASKIN-ROBBINS ICE CREAM CO.
78 F.R.D. 108 (C.D. Cal. 1978)

WILLIAMS, D.J.: "Twenty store franchise owners have brought this antitrust action against Baskin-Robbins Ice Cream Co., its subsidiaries and its area franchisors alleging violations of § 1 of the Sherman Act (15 U.S.C. § 1) and § 3 of the Clayton Act (15 U.S.C. § 14). . . . The complaint was filed on June 4, 1976. A first amended complaint was filed August 3, 1976, alleging that the defendants conspired to restrain trade by: (1) tying sales of ice cream products, store leases, equipment, supplies and advertising to the sale of the Baskin-Robbins trademark; (2) by fixing the wholesale prices of ice cream products; and (3) by maintaining the resale price of ice cream products. Plaintiffs have raised an additional allegation of territorial market division and propose to amend their complaint appropriately to include this allegation. As to each of the claims, the plaintiffs pray for treble damages, injunctive relief, costs and reasonable attorneys' fees. . . .

1. The Tying Claim

"Plaintiffs have alleged that the following products have been illegally tied to the sale of the Baskin-Robbins trademark: (1) ice cream products, (2) store leases, (3) equipment package, (4) supplies, (5) advertising. The *prima facie* case is the same for each of these claims. There are five elements of a per se tying violation: (1) there must be a tying arrangement between two distinct products or services, (2) the defendant must have sufficient economic power in the tying market to impose significant restrictions in the tied product market, (3) the amount of commerce in the tied product market must not be insubstantial, (4) the seller of the tying product must have an interest in the tied product, and (5) there must be a modicum of coercion shown. *Moore v. Jas. H. Matthews & Co.*, 550 F.2d 1207, 1212 and 1216-17 (9th Cir. 1977). In addition to showing the tie, plaintiffs must demonstrate fact of damage as an element of the *prima facie* case. *Windham v. American Brands, Inc.*, 565 F.2d 59 (4th Cir. 1977). The final element of proof is the quantum of damages. The defendants contest the predominance of common questions as to each element except the third; it is conceded that a substantial amount of commerce in the tied products is involved.

a. Existence of the Tie and Coercion

"The existence of the tie and proof of coercion can be addressed together since they are functionally linked. In the typical franchise case there are two ways in which a tying arrangement can be demonstrated. The first is by express provision in the franchise agreement conditioning the sale of one product, the tying product, on the sale of the second, or tied product. When the tie is a term of the franchise agreement, the plaintiff does not need to show that he was coerced, coercion is implied. *See Siegel v. Chicken Delight, Inc.*, 448 F.2d 43, 46 (9th Cir. 1971), *cert. denied*, 405 U.S. 955, 92 S. Ct. 1172, 31 L. Ed.2d 232 (1972). The second method of showing the tie, in the absence of an express agreement, is by proving a course of conduct. *Abercrombie v. Lum's Inc.*, 345 F. Supp. 387, 391 (S.D. Fla. 1972). In this second instance the buyer must show that he was coerced into purchasing the tied item.

"As to the first claim, that the sale of Baskin-Robbins ice cream products was tied to the purchase of the franchise trademark, this term appears in the franchise agreements. The terms of the Store Franchise Agreement specify that the franchisee may sell only Baskin-Robbins ice cream products. By virtue of the Area Franchise Agreement, the area franchisor is the exclusive source of Baskin-Robbins products in his region. Reading the terms together, the store owner is compelled to buy his ice cream products from his area franchisor as a condition of his franchise. The defendants do not challenge this conclusion, but argue that the trademark and the ice cream are not separate products. Even if such a contention is plausible after *Siegel v. Chicken Delight, Inc., supra,* it is a legal question common to the class.

"The alleged tie of the store lease and the equipment package can be aggregated since, upon aquisition of a franchise, the store owner obtains both a sublease from 31 Flavors Realty Inc., and the full equipment package. Neither the lease nor the equipment package are expressly tied to the trademark in the franchise agreements. Plaintiff's support for this tie is provided by documents submitted by BRICO [Baskin-Robbins Ice Cream Co.] to the Security Exchange Commission and the Federal Trade Commission in which it is admitted that 31 Flavors Realty Inc. is the prime lessor on all stores and that each store is fully equipped and ready for operation before it is turned over to the franchisee. *See* Plaintiffs' exhibits 1 and 2. These documents are offered as proof of coercion . . .

"The standard for showing coercion in a tying case is established by *Moore v. Jas. H. Matthews & Co., supra* at 1216-1217.

"Although some cases in other circuits have required a showing of actual coercion, . . . our reading of the Supreme Court's opinions supports the view that coercion may be implied from a showing that an appreciable number of buyers have accepted burdensome terms, such as a tie-in, and there exists sufficient economic power in the tying product market. . . . Coercion occurs when the buyer must accept the tied item and forego possibly desirable substitutes . . . (citations omitted).

"BRICO possesses sufficient economic power in its trademark, as will be discussed in more detail *infra*, that, coupled with a showing of 100% franchise adherence, . . . coercion is conclusively demonstrated by the BRICO documents supplied to the SEC and FTC. . . .

b. Economic Power

"A per se showing of tying violations requires that defendants have sufficient economic power in the tying market to impose restrictions in the tied product market. The focus in determining economic power is whether the seller has sufficient power to raise prices or to impose onerous terms that could not be expected in a completely competitive market. *See Moore v. Jas. H. Matthews*, *supra*, at 1215. One cannot look at the tied product in isolation to determine if the terms are onerous; one must look at the attractiveness of the package. *See United States Steel Corp. v. Fortner Enterprises, Inc.* 429 U.S. 610, 97 S. Ct. 861, 51 L. Ed. 2d 80 (1977) (*Fortner II*). As in the *Fortner* case in which supracompetitive credit was tied to marginally competitive prefabricated housing, the package can be viewed as a legitimate form of price competition. *Id.*, 429 U.S. at 618–619, 97 S. Ct. at 867, 51 L. Ed.2d at 88–89 n. 10.

"The difficulties of proving that the tying packages in this case were burdensome in accordance with *Fortner II* standard can be avoided if the Baskin-Robbins trademark itself is sufficiently unique that economic power can be inferred. It has long been recognized that in the cases of patents and copyrights economic power is presumed. *United States v. Loew's Inc.*, 371 U.S. 38, 83 S. Ct. 97, 9 L. Ed. 2d 11 (1962); *United States v. Paramount Pictures, Inc.*, 334 U.S. 131, 68 S. Ct. 915, 92 L. Ed. 1260 (1948); *International Salt Co. v. United States*, 332 U.S. 392, 68 S. Ct. 12, 92 L. Ed. 20 (1947). The Ninth Circuit has extended the presumption that exists in the case of patents and copyrights to trademarks. *Siegel v. Chicken Delight, Inc., supra* at 50. . . .

" . . . [T]his Court finds that the Baskin-Robbins trademark is coupled with such nationwide preeminence in the retail sale of ice cream market that . . . sufficient economic power is present as a matter of law. . . .

d. Damages

" . . . Fact of damage requires proof that the alleged tying violation caused actual injury. In the case of the tie of ice cream products, plaintiffs will be required to show that alternate sources of comparable quality products would have been available, but for the tie. It is possible that such a showing will require proof of the conditions of the wholesale ice cream market in each locality in which there is a franchise. It is, however, more likely that potential competitors to the Baskin-Robbins area franchisors will themselves have to operate on a comparable scale if they are to supply the variety and volume demanded by the

Baskin-Robbins franchisee. It is reasonable to assume that such a competitor would, in many cases, compete not only as to individual stores, but as to regions. If this is the case, the Court's burden as to fact of damage will be reduced considerably. . . .

2. Price-fixing

"Plaintiffs allege that BRICO, its subsidiaries, and its area franchisors conspired among themselves and with various suppliers and distributors to fix the wholesale prices at which ice cream products, the equipment package and other supplies were sold to the franchisees. To prove such a price-fixing allegation, plaintiffs must show: (1) an agreement to set prices at a noncompetitive level, (2) fact of damage, and (3) quantum of damage. *See United States v. Socony-Vacuum Oil Co.*, 310 U.S. 150, 60 S. Ct. 811, 84 L. Ed. 1129 (1940); *Windham v. American Brands, Inc.*, *supra*, 565 F.2d at 59.

"As noted in *In re Sugar Antitrust Litigation*, 1977-1 Trade Cases ¶61,373 at 71,329 (N.D. Cal. 1977) class action petitions on wholesale price-fixing claims have generally been given favorable treatment.

"Courts have consistently held that antitrust price-fixing conspiracy litigations, by their nature, involve common legal and factual questions concerning the existence, scope and effect of the alleged conspiracy.

" . . . It appears that proof of the conspiratorial agreement to fix prices in the sale of ice cream products at its most complex, would involve only nine agreements and proof of a common objective. Proof of fact of damage as to the price-fixing claim of ice cream products would not be sufficiently complex to justify the *Windham* type exception. It may be possible to prove fact of damage as to ice cream products by relating increases in prices to increases in costs for each of the area franchisors. If this type of common proof does not work, then individualized proof of the competitive prices in each ice cream product may be necessary.

3. Resale Price Maintenance

"Plaintiffs allege that BRICO and the area franchisors conspired to fix the maximum price at which the franchisees could sell ice cream products. The crucial element of a resale price maintenance claim is an agreement between a manufacturer and the retailer to restrict the resale price to a maximum level. *Santa Clara Valley Dist. Co. v. Pabst Brewing Co.*, 556 F.2d 942 n.3 (9th Cir. 1977). That agreement may be demonstrated by contract or by a course of conduct. In the absence of a contractual term evidencing the retailer's commitment to maintain prices, there must be a showing that the retailer's participation was involuntary for the scheme to be actionable. *Gray v. Shell Oil Co.*, 469 F.2d 742, 747–48 (9th Cir. 1972). As stated in *Hanson v. Shell Oil Co.*, 541 F.2d 1352, 1357 n.4 (9th Cir. 1976), *cert. denied*, 429 U.S. 1074, 97 S. Ct. 813, 50 L. Ed. 2d 792 (1977):

"[A] supplier may suggest retail prices to its dealers and use 'persuasion' to get them to adopt the suggested prices. No violation is made out unless plaintiff can show that the supplier's conduct rose to the level of coercion to deprive the dealers of their free choice.

"Plaintiffs claim that the resale price maintenance program was conducted by the area franchisors through indirect restrictions on the store owners in the Store Franchise Agreement. The Agreement provides that store owners may post only those signs supplied by the company. Among the approved signs are price stickers designed to be affixed on the wall behind the ice cream counter. Along with the list of suggested retail prices which the store owner is supplied from time to time, the new franchisee is given the back board with the price stickers already affixed. Plaintiffs have adduced testimony that some franchises were not given any price stickers in addition to those initially affixed to the back board and that they were denied permission to raise their retail prices above the suggested prices.

"It appears that any resale price maintenance practices that might have existed were limited to the McDonald area in Michigan. Other than in Michigan, there was little price uniformity among franchisees in the same franchise area. . . .

4. Territorial Market Division Claim

"In presenting this motion, plaintiffs have introduced a claim that was not stated in the first amended complaint—that defendants violated the antitrust laws by horizontal market division. Plaintiffs stated at oral argument that they would move to amend their complaint to include this claim. . . .

"The essence of the claim is that the Baskin-Robbins franchise system which divides the country into nine different regions and appoints each area franchisor as the exclusive supplier of ice cream products in his region violates § 1 of the Sherman Act.

"Defendants contend that the territorial market division is vertical in character and that such agreements are governed by the 'Rule of Reason.' *Continental TV, Inc. v. GTE Sylvania, Inc.*, 433 U.S. 36, 97 S. Ct. 2549, 53 L. Ed.2d 568 (1977). Defendants argue that proof under a Rule of Reason test would necessarily be so individual as to each alleged restriction that class procedures would be unmanageable. The Court need not decide whether individual questions would predominate under a Rule of Reason test since the challenged territorial restriction is horizontal in nature.

"Horizontal restrictions on competition are per se illegal. This includes territorial market allocations between competitors, *Timken Roller Bearing Co. v. United States*, 341 U.S. 593, 71 S. Ct. 971, 95 L. Ed. 1199 (1951) and territorial market allocations as part of a franchising system when the allocatur is controlled by the franchisees, *United States v. Sealey, Inc.*, 388 U.S. 350, 87 S. Ct. 1847, 18 L. Ed. 2d 1238 (1967). Defendants contend that *Sealey* and the similar holding in *United States v. Topco Associates, Inc.*, 405 U.S. 596, 92 S. Ct. 1126, 31 L. Ed. 2d 515 (1972) are inapposite since the area franchisees do not own or control BRICO and it is BRICO that makes the territorial allocations. If BRICO were the franchisor and nothing more, this system would indeed be vertical. *Tomac, Inc. v. The Coca Cola Co.*, 418 F. Supp. 359 (C.D. Cal. 1976). BRICO is not, however, strictly a franchisor. It is connected to the manufacture and supply of Baskin-Robbins ice cream products through its subsidiary, Baskin-Robbins, Inc. which is the area franchisor for much of the country. An entity occupying such a dual role is forbidden per se from imposing territorial market restrictions. *American Motor Inns, Inc. v. Holiday Inns, Inc.*, 521 F.2d 1230, 1254 (5th Cir. 1975). In the latter case, Holiday Inns, Inc. was acting both as a franchisor of its trademark and as an operator of inns. The Court found that restrictions in its franchise agreements prohibiting franchisees from establishing competing Holiday Inns or competing non-Holiday Inns in cities in which Holiday Inn, Inc. operated an establishment, unless done with Holiday Inn, Inc.'s permission, constituted market allocation agreements among competitors and was per se illegal. Except for the absence of a clause waiving the territorial restrictions on the area franchisor's with BRICO's permission, the territorial allocation provision of BRICO is indistinguishable from that of Holiday Inn.

''The only possible individual issue with reference to the horizontal territorial restriction claim is fact of damage. Plaintiffs may be able to show fact of damage as to this claim by demonstrating that a neighboring area franchisor is a potential competitor. If it could be shown that a neighboring area franchisor had sufficient capacity to handle excess demand at lower prices, fact of damage would be proven. If transportation problems do not prevent such a showing, proof of fact of damages could be relatively mechanical. Even if fact of damage must be demonstrated by other means, the showing will be no more involved than that required to prove the price-fixing or tying claim as to ice cream products. . . . ''

16:7   *Who Are Competitors under the Sherman Act?*

The law does not limit the term *competitor* to a hotel or other entity that is separately owned and operated under a separate trade name or service mark. Assume that two chain units wholly owned by a national corporate entity operate in a given locality. Does that fact preclude a finding that they are competitors for purposes of determining whether their joint pricing arrangements violate the Act? No. Two competing units owned by the same chain may not agree to fix prices if the public is led to believe that the units compete against each other in the same market. In other words, the fact that the revenues derived from the two units ultimately find their way into the same corporate treasury does not mean that they are not competitors under the terms of the Sherman Act. Franchised units may also be considered competitors because each franchisee usually builds and equips the property with his own funds and merely uses the corporate name under the terms of the agreement with the corporate franchise owner. Because the units are separately owned and operated, they are competitors according to the antitrust laws. [*See* section 17:1, *infra.*]

16:8   Per Se *Illegality: Division of the Market*

It is also a *per se* violation of the law for the sellers of a product or service to get together and divide the market among themselves. Thus any attempt by competing hotelkeepers to allocate among themselves specific segments of a market, whether geographically, territorially, or by the nature of the services performed, is prohibited, regardless of good motive or economic necessity. This horizontal market division, consistently declared illegal, may be contrasted with vertical market division, by which the seller of the product or service gives dealers or franchisees the exclusive right to market the product or service in a designated area. In the latter case, the Supreme Court has recently ruled that the rule of reason must be applied to determine whether a significant or substantial portion of the competition in that market is restrained by such a distribution system.[11] If competition is significantly restricted, the system will be declared illegal and enjoined.

16:9 Per Se *Illegality: Group Boycotts*

Very often hotelkeepers wish to establish a convention bureau or association in their market to promote room sales so as to compete more effectively with other areas for convention business. Such activities are legal so long as the hotels do not agree to fix the price of services, conditions for the sale of rooms, uniform commissions to be paid to travel agents, and the like. But where an association insisted that the inns' suppliers were to be assessed one percent of their sales to finance the promotional costs of the association, and favored those suppliers who complied and curtailed purchases from those who failed or refused to do so, this scheme was declared to be a group boycott, and as such a *per se* violation of the Sherman Act.[12] Put another way, any concerted joint refusal to deal with a potential supplier or customer or any joint agreement to add or delete, discount, or otherwise alter the suppliers' services will run afoul of the law. Thus the addition of a telephone surcharge on all incoming guest calls by agreement among a large number of hotelkeepers violates the law.[13] Such a surcharge constitutes a fraud by each individual hotelkeeper upon the guest, for which legal liability will theoretically ensue. In practice, the guest may not be aware of the surcharge and in any case would not sue since the amount involved would not warrant legal recourse. But where concerted action exists, the government can step in and sue on behalf of all affected persons.

16:10 Per Se *Illegality: Tying Contracts*

Tying contracts are best exemplified by the typical franchise hotel or fast-food restaurant agreement. The franchise owner agrees to license or furnish the franchise the tying product on condition that the franchisee agrees to buy the franchisor's other products, such as bedding, locks, and food or beverage items,

---

[11]White Motor Co. v. United States, 372 U.S. 253 (1963); Continental TV, Inc. v. GTE Sylvania, Inc., 433 U.S. 36 (1977). *See also* Broadcast Music, Inc. v. Columbia Broadcasting System, Inc., 441 U.S. 1 (1979).

[12]United States v. Hilton Hotels Corp., 467 F.2d 1000 (9th Cir. 1972), *cert. denied*, 409 U.S. 1125 (1973).

[13]Colson v. Hilton Hotels Corp., 50 F.2d 86 (9th Cir. 1974); State v. Waldorf-Astoria, 67 Misc. 2d 90, 323 N.Y.S.2d 917 (Sup. Ct. 1971).

either directly from the franchisor or exclusively from designated sources. These other products are called the tied products.

Tying contracts of this sort are not illegal *per se*, that is, are not automatically violative of law. The following four conditions must exist in order to establish illegality in a tying arrangement:

(*a*) Two separate products, the tying and the tied product.

(*b*) Sufficient economic power in the tying market to coerce purchase of the tied product.

(*c*) Involvement of a not insubstantial amount of interstate commerce in the tied market.

(*d*) Anticompetitive effects in the tied market.[14]

The rationale for declaring such arrangements illegal *per se* when the above conditions are established is that they curb competition on the merits in the tied products, that is, competitors are denied free access to the market for the tied product not because the party imposing the tying requirement has better products or lower prices, but because of his power of leverage in another market.[15]

Where none of these conditions exists and the tying arrangement is otherwise proven to be reasonable on economic grounds, such a contract will be sustained.[16] The reasonableness of the arrangement is a jury question under these circumstances.

It is also important to note that where products involving trade secrets not otherwise available constitute the tied items, the tying arrangement may be sustained. However, the existence of a patent or trademark on the tying product which is the subject of a tying contract makes such a contract illegal in virtually all cases.[17]

This is not to say that a franchisor may not protect his legitimate economic interest in quality-control standards, which is a proper objective. If such standards are allowed to deteriorate, consumer satisfaction will dissipate, and the competitive standing of the product or service will be damaged. The reputation of the franchisor is what makes the franchise valuable. Thus if a guest finds product or service standards inferior with one franchisee, the guest is not likely to patronize any other franchisee carrying that name, regardless of whether his unhappy experience is duplicated at other franchised properties or indicative of quality standards found at those establishments. The guest associates the inferior product or service with the name, not necessarily the property where the name exists, and the franchisor suffers accordingly.

Every owner-operator of franchised premises is an independent entrepreneur, a legal entity not owned by the franchisor. This independence is what distinguishes the franchisee from a wholly owned subsidiary. (Franchise agreements are discussed in more detail in Chapter 17.) As an independent businessperson, the franchisee is entitled to make the most efficient use of the resources available

---

[14]Northern Pacific R. v. United States, 356 U.S. 1 (1958).
[15]*Id.*
[16]Times Picayune Publishing Co. v. United States, 345 U.S. 594 (1953).
[17]International Salt Co. v. United States, 332 U.S. 392 (1947).

to run that business. In practice, the entrepreneur would wish to buy standard, readily available products of the required quality at the lowest possible prices so as to insure the highest economic return on his investment.

The law takes into account these competitive interests by sanctioning the franchisor's right to set appropriate quality standards but permitting the franchisee to buy products in the open market, from any independent producer, grower, or manufacturer.[18] Otherwise, if the price charged by the franchisor were appreciably higher than for competing products of comparable quality sold by independents, legitimate competitors in the tied product or service would be effectively precluded from competing for the franchisee's business.

The following case illustrates the cumulative effect of various marketing devices used by a national hotel franchisor as well as the legality of the devices used independently of each other.

In *American Motor Inns, Inc. v. Holiday Inns, Inc.*,[19] the United States Court of Appeals for the Third Circuit held that Holiday Inns, Inc., committed a *per se* violation of the Sherman Act when it involved other Holiday Inn motel franchisees in the decision whether to grant a new franchise to American Motor Inns, Inc., in their respective territories. This practice constituted a ''concerted refusal to deal'' violative of the Sherman Act. Had Holiday Inns acted independently in refusing to deal with the prospective franchisee, that conduct would have been approved, regardless of whether the competing Holiday Inns affected were company-owned.

The court, however, reversed and remanded the lower court's ruling that the franchisor's ''non–Holiday Inn clause'' alone constituted an unreasonable restraint of trade. That clause prohibited franchisees from owning or operating motels other than Holiday Inns. The Court of Appeals concluded that the rule of reason applied to the clause and that the lower court had failed to explore the impact of the restraint on competition within the relevant market, a critical determinant in applying the reasonableness test. In its analysis, the court stated that the relevant market would depend on (1) whether Holiday Inns were reasonably interchangeable with other motels or hotels, insofar as the traveling public is concerned, and (2) whether Holiday Inns' franchises are reasonably interchangeable with other motels or hotels as potential franchisees for other hotel-motel chains.

Finally, the court concluded that the combined effect of the ''radius letter procedure,'' whereby competing Holiday Inn franchisees were asked to approve or veto the entry of a potential franchisee within their geographic area, the ''company-town policy,'' whereby a potential franchisee could not operate in any area in which a company-owned Holiday Inn was established, and the non–Holiday Inn clause previously noted created a horizontal allocation of territories which is *per se* unlawful.

---

[18]Siegel v. Chicken Delight, Inc. 448 F.2d 43 (9th Cir. 1971), *cert. denied*, 405 U.S. 955 (1972); Hawkins v. Holiday Inns, Inc. 1975 T.C. 60, 153 (W.D. Tenn. 1975); *cf.* Kentucky Fried Chicken v. Diversified Packaging Corp., 1 T.C. ¶61, 339 (5th Cir. 1972).

[19]521 F.2d 1230 (3d Cir. 1975).

Holiday Inns argued that these provisions protected the parent against a franchisee referring customers to non–Holiday Inns owned by the franchisee. The court rejected this claim and concluded that a "best efforts" clause contained in the franchise agreement, whereby the franchisee promised to exhaust all reasonable efforts to refer the customer to another Holiday Inn prior to accommodating him in a non-Holiday Inn property, was sufficient to protect the legitimate economic interests of the parent.

In that connection, the question arises whether the legitimate economic interests of the existing franchisee should be protected against the introduction of new competition by the franchisor in violation of a noncompetitive covenant in which the franchisor promises not to do so. Clearly such a covenant should be honored; failure to honor it deprives the franchisee of the economic value of the consideration paid by him for his franchise. In a recent case a federal district court held that no implied covenant not to compete existed where the parties did not agree to restrict the entry of a company-owned motel. In *Snyder v. Howard Johnson's Motor Lodges, Inc.*,[20] the motel franchisee alleged that the franchisor had opened a nearby company motel in violation of an implied noncompetition covenant. The court rejected this argument, and held for the franchisor, finding that although the matter had been discussed, no promise not to compete was included in the franchise agreement. The court recognized only the implied covenant of good faith and fair dealing in every contract and held that the franchisor must operate the competing company property in accordance with this implied covenant.

16:11   *The Rule of Reason: Monopolies or Attempts to Monopolize*

The Sherman Act, particularly section 2, interpreted literally, outlaws all restraints of trade, regardless of their reasonableness in terms of their effect on competition in the relevant market for the goods or services being sold, leased, or licensed.

The term *monopoly* is of particular significance to innkeepers. By definition, a monopoly results from gaining by one means or another sufficient economic power to effectively dictate prices or other terms of purchase or licensing of the product or service, presumably through other unfair methods. Because every innkeeper operates in one geographic locality, even though ownership of that inn and others operating under the same franchise may exist in a single corporation, partnership, or joint venture, every innkeeper monopolizes those services that are unique to the property within his local market. If the innkeeper is the only convention-size hotel in the market, he necessarily has a monopoly of that market's convention business. Such a monopoly does not violate the law, since there is no competition to restrict or eliminate. It is only when the innkeeper, either singly or collectively, seeks to perpetuate his lawful monopoly by compelling the owner of the franchise under which he operates not to allow competition

---

[20]412 F. Supp. 724 (N.D. Ill. 1976).

to enter his market by the use of his veto that he violates the law.[21] Similarly, attempts by an innkeeper to coerce suppliers not to deal with a potential competitor by blacklisting any supplier who does so also constitute illegal, anticompetitive conduct.[22] Any action on the part of one innkeeper which would restrict competition other than by the free play of supply and demand in the market would violate the law. The fact that the monopoly is of insignificant size compared with the national market for the product or service is immaterial. The size and significance of any monopoly affects only the likelihood of prosecution by the appropriate government authorities; it does not preclude a finding that the monopoly is illegal.

The paucity of litigation affecting service industries in general and the hospitality industry in particular must not be understood as a seal of approval of current conduct. It is more likely the result of the past fragmented nature of the industry and the fact that most innkeepers are independent entrepreneurs. Recent experience in Hawaii[23] demonstrates the fallacy of that assumption.

16:12 Horizontal Merger: The Clayton Act

A horizontal merger is the acquisition by one company of another company or group of companies selling the same product or service. If such an acquisition is thought to threaten competition, a company may have to divest itself of some existing properties. In 1956 the government instituted litigation against Hilton Hotels, Inc.[24] on the theory that Hilton's acquisition of the Statler Hotels chain gave Hilton an undue concentration of convention hotel space in the cities in which the hotels of the two chains were situated. At that time Hilton owned or operated a majority of the total convention hotel space situated in New York City, Washington, D.C., St. Louis, Los Angeles, and Beverly Hills. Although it was conceded that the ratio of Hilton and Statler hotels to the total number of hotels existing in those areas did not even approximate a monopoly or the threat

---

[21]American Motor Inns, Inc. v. Holiday Inns, Inc., 521 F.2d 1230 (3d Cir. 1975).

[22]United States v. Hilton Hotels Corp., 467 F.2d 1000 (9th Cir. 1972), *cert. denied*, 409 U.S. 1125 (1973).

[23]In November of 1976, the Department of Justice filed a criminal indictment (Case NV. 76-0182) and a civil complaint (Case 76-0418) against the Sheraton Corporation; Hilton Hotels Corporation; Western International, Inc.; Interisland Resorts Ltd.; Island Holidays Ltd., d.b.a. Island Holiday Resorts and Hawaii Hotels Association, charging them with violating the Sherman Antitrust Act during the period 1966 to 1974. The illegal conduct and conspiracy alleged consisted of fixing hotel room rates, exchanging information for that purpose, and fixing the sale of hotel rooms; fixing commissions paid to retail travel agents, tour operators, and others for such sales and fixing the terms of commissions to be given to retail travel agents, tour operators, and others for the sale of hotel rooms. Criminal penalties and a permanent injunction prohibiting such conduct was sought by way of relief. The defendants pleaded *nolo contendere*, meaning that they did not contest the charges and threw themselves on the mercy of the court. Judge Samuel King levied fines of $50,000 against both Sheraton and Hilton. Flagship and Cinerama were fined $25,000 each. The Hawaii Hotel Association was fined $10,000. The court deemed the collective fines adequate in "hitting them in the pocketbook and getting the message across." The civil case was dropped, since the alleged price fixing had ceased in 1974.

[24]1956 Trade Cases ¶68, at 253.

of a monopoly, the government argued that the ratio of convention hotels to total convention space did unduly concentrate control in that more narrowly defined market. The case did not result in a court decision because the parties entered into a consent decree whereby Hilton sold one hotel in each area. Under this form of court-approved settlement, Hilton did not admit guilt or liability, but did agree to certain government demands to avoid the time and costs of litigation and to avoid the risk of an adverse judgment and potentially more serious sanctions that might result.

16:13 Enforcement Mechanisms: The Antitrust Division of the Department of Justice

The Antitrust Division is the investigatory, regulatory, and enforcement arm of the Department of Justice and has sole responsibility for prosecuting businesses that violate the Sherman Act. It has joint responsibility with the Federal Trade Commission for oversight of price discrimination under the Clayton Act. The division deals primarily with criminal prosecutions, but has the authority to undertake civil suits where it determines that changes in company or industry policy are needed but there is insufficient evidence to support a finding that the company or industry willfully violated the law.

A fine or imprisonment resulting from criminal prosecution and conviction can clearly punish the wrongdoer for past misconduct, but cannot alter current or future conduct. Through civil litigation, however, it is possible to enjoin or prohibit current conduct and compel divestiture of monopolistic concentrations and thus drastically alter future conduct. As noted in the following sections, the impact on a particular business or industry can be severe in either case.

16:14 Criminal and Civil Sanctions

Where criminal misconduct is established, the court may impose the following penalties:

(a) A maximum jail term of three years.

(b) A maximum corporate fine of $1 million.

(c) A maximum fine per individual of $100,000.

Current policy within the Antitrust Division is to request minimum 18-month prison sentences for individuals who are found guilty of willfully violating the Sherman Act. Moreover, the courts, taking cognizance of the change in the law making Sherman Act violations felonies, are increasing fines as well. Effective 1987 and 1991, the United States Sentencing Commission's (USSC) guidelines on individual and organizational offenders authorized increased fines for the individuals and organizations of eight to sixteen times those of past practice.[25]

---

[25]See Sentencing Guidelines for Felony Cases under the Sherman Act, Antitrust Division, Department of Justice, February 24, 1977, and USSC Guidelines Manual, section 1Q1.1 et seq.

On the civil side, available remedies include dissolution, the elimination of any unlawful association between companies and groups (holding company and its subsidiaries); divorcement, the result of an order to divest; and divestiture, the sale of company assets.

16:15 *Treble Damage Remedies*

The Sherman Act authorizes both an injured competitor of the company or industry found guilty of a violation and the state attorney general, acting on behalf of injured consumers within his jurisdiction, to recover three times (treble) the appropriate damages. This sanction is intended not only to compensate the victims of the violation for their losses of profits or for compensatory damages, but also to punish the transgressor by inflicting a very severe penalty, which must be paid to those injured, rather than to society as a whole. The treble damage penalty is intended to deter future wrongdoing because the benefits of the anticompetitive behavior are lost to the guilty party.

As a matter of mitigation, the courts have sanctioned a plea of *nolo contendere*, or no contest, in both criminal and civil cases brought by the government. This in effect is a plea of guilty, since the defendant does not deny the charges, but the plea cannot itself be used as evidence of guilt in private treble damages suits. The court can and does sentence or otherwise penalize the defendant as if a full trial on the merits had been conducted, with a verdict in favor of the Antitrust Division.[26] Private treble damage action is not precluded, but the allegedly injured party must, independently of the plea of *nolo contendere*, prove that the defendant violated the law and that the violation was causally related to his injuries. The consent order or decree has the same effect. The advantage of the plea or entry of a consent decree is meant not only to forestall time-consuming and expensive litigation but also to preclude adverse publicity that might result from lengthy trial and appellate procedures.

16:16 *Enforcement Mechanisms: The Federal Trade Commission*

The FTC[27] has traditionally had wide latitude with respect to regulation of the operation of American business. It has the dual function of overseeing unfair competitive practices and protecting consumer interests. In a practical sense this means that the agency can regulate unfair trade activities and intervene on behalf of affected consumers.

Where the Federal Trade Commission Improvements Act of 1980[28] has limited or circumscribed the original authority of the FTC, appropriate mention will be made.

---

[26]*See* United States v. Sheraton Corp. *et al., supra* note 23.

[27]The Commission was established under the Federal Trade Commission Act, 38 Stat. 717, 15 U.S.C.A. § § 2, 3, 7, 8, and the Clayton Act, § 11, and was also authorized to proceed against "unfair methods of competition" in interstate or foreign commerce (FTC Act, § 5). *See* Thompson and Brady, Antitrust Fundamentals 14–15 (1974).

[28]Pub. L. No. 96–221, 94 Stat. 174 (Mar. 31, 1980).

16:17 *Penalties*

Assuming that (1) a consent order or voluntary compliance is not accepted by the company against whom a formal complaint has been issued, (2) the case is heard by an FTC administrative law judge, (3) an adverse decision is rendered against the company and affirmed by the full Commission, and (4) the appropriate U.S. Court of Appeals sustains the decision if an appeal is taken, the following penalties may be imposed by the FTC:

(*a*) The FTC may impose a $10,000 fine per violation to persons or companies that violate a *cease and desist* order given to any other firm in the industry as well as to the firm found in violation of the order. A cease and desist order is an injunction or order to stop a practice found to be in violation of law. It has the authority of law, unless within 60 days of its issue the company appeals the decision to the appropriate judicial tribunal. The court may overturn the order or affirm the order by entering judgment enforcing it. Every day of noncompliance with the order constitutes a separate violation, meaning that the $10,000 fine imposed upon the violator accumulates on a *per diem* basis until the violation ceases or is cured. Under the FTC Improvements Act of 1980, the FTC must reconsider such orders on the application of any firm subject to it and issue a decision thereon within 120 days after the filing of any such application.

(*b*) The FTC may rescind or cancel as well as reform or rewrite contracts of a company in violation to protect and remedy injuries to consumers and to companies victimized by deceptive or unfair practices or in violation of FTC rules.

(*c*) The FTC may compel companies in violation to refund money to injured consumers, to pay damages, and to notify the public of wrongdoing. However, the Commission lacks authority to award punitive damages in such cases.

16:18 *FTC Rule-making Authority*

In addition to its authority to issue cease and desist orders to halt specific violations caused or committed by named companies, the Commission may issue a *trade regulation rule,* which specifically defines acts or practices deemed unfair or deceptive. Such a rule may encompass an entire industry and thus be binding to all members, not just those named in a complaint preceding a cease and desist order. Moreover, rule making permits the Commission to attack the problem of future wrongdoing, not merely adjudicate a single case of present wrongdoing. In this sense it is a more comprehensive and thoroughgoing means of regulation than the issuance of cease and desist orders, but fraught with potentially more serious problems for the affected industry because it may adversely affect the industry's overall performance and future existence. The same penalties are levied for the violation of such rules as in the case of cease and desist orders. (*See* section 16:17, *supra*).

As a result, Congress enacted, as a part of the FTC Improvements Act of 1980, legislation to suspend the operation of any such rule for a period of 90 legislative days after final action by the FTC. If during that period both the House of Representatives and the Senate pass a concurrent resolution disapproving the rule, it is deemed vetoed and rendered ineffective. (The Improvements Act also barred the FTC from using existing authority to promulgate new rules for unfair commercial advertising until July 1983.) Finally, the Act bars the FTC from promulgating trade regulation rules establishing standards and certification criteria in any industry at any time. To illustrate, the FTC may not establish standards in the hotel industry governing overbooking practices, but may investigate and issue a cease and desist order against any hotel or group of hotels found to be in violation of law and impose appropriate sanctions.

16:19   *State Anticompetition Enactments*

Because of the vast number of businesses and industries that comprise the American economic system, it is apparent that neither the Justice Department nor the FTC has the personnel or financial resources to attack the problem of anticompetitive price fixing and related activities. Moreover, these enforcement and regulatory agencies are further hampered because their jurisdiction is limited to activities among the various states as opposed to activities within a single state. Even though the commerce clause of the federal Constitution has been given sweeping breadth by the courts to effectuate national policies affecting local activities of hospitality entrepreneurs,[29] the supplementary efforts of state authorities are needed, although the states often do not make such efforts. Officials in California, New York, Texas, and Wisconsin are more active than their counterparts in other states in this respect.

16:20   *Monopoly Updated in New York*

A problem of recurrent concern in New York is to what extent the innkeeper may refuse to deal with tradespersons selected by the guest or patron if the hotel is under an exclusive contract to have those functions performed by tradespersons of the innkeeper's choice. A recent inquiry by the assistant attorney general in charge of consumer protection prompted an informal hearing on the legality under the Donnelly Act, New York's antimonopoly statute, of a hotel's refusal to deal with florists and others whom the patron at a wedding wished to use in place of the hotel's purveyors.[30] No formal complaint or other legal action has arisen to date by reason of the hearing, but the fact that the attorney general felt obliged to investigate such a complaint establishes that the Donnelly Act does literally apply. The remaining question is whether a rule of reason will govern its interpretation or whether this practice common among innkeepers constitutes a *per se* violation of law.

[29]*See, e.g.*, Heart of Atlanta Motel v. United States, 379 U.S. 241 (1964) and Katzenbach v. McClung, 379 U.S. 294 (1964), where the Supreme Court majority applied the commerce clause to sustain the constitutionality of the Federal Civil Rights Act of 1964 as to hotels and restaurants.

[30]N.Y. Gen. Bus. Law § 340 (McKinney supp. 1975): "Every contract, agreement, arrangement or combination whereby . . . competition or the free exercise of any activity in the conduct of any business, trade or commerce or in the furnishing of any service in this state is or may be restrained . . . is hereby declared to be against public policy illegal and void."

There is no specific standard by which to judge which rule will apply in New York. Such exclusive dealings are tested against the more general prohibition of monopoly under the Donnelly Act, restraint of competition, or interference with the free exercise of business activity.

In *Eagle Springs Water Co. v. Webb & Knapp, Inc.*,[31] the defendant landlord of a commercial office building in New York City contractually barred all tenants from accepting for use in the premises drinking water and other services from any persons not authorized by the landlord. The plaintiff sued for and obtained injunctive relief against the landlord. The court applied the rule of reason and made the following observations by which it concluded that the defendant landlord had contravened the Donnelly Act: "[T]he restraint cannot be said to relate to the protection of any legitimate property interest of the landlord. The landlord itself was not in the water supply business nor was it seeking to protect the interests of any tenants so engaged. Nor was there present any unusual circumstance concerning either the locale of the buildings or some peculiar condition prevailing therein that required such a restraint. . . . "[32]

A similar distinction was noted by the Appellate Division, First Department, in *American Consumer Industries, Inc. v. City of New York*.[33] In that case the court said that the city of New York, in the guise of regulation of a market established by the city and occupied by private tenants, could not create a monopoly by granting an exclusive franchise so as to force the tenants to deal with only one supplier of ice. The court added: "Nor can the present situation be equated, as the city urges, with the right of a property owner to select his tenants or to make a covenant in a lease to a store owner that he will not rent any other store in a building or group of buildings to anyone who sells similar goods. The situation obviously is vastly different."[34]

The same point was raised and disposed of in *Big Top Stores, Inc. v. Ardsley Toy Shoppe, Ltd.*[35] in which a tie-in sale of products requiring a franchisee to purchase 90 percent of his products from his franchisor exclusively was held violative of the Donnelly Act. Once again, the court noted that the franchisor did not manufacture the products required to be purchased.

An individual refusal to deal or the right to give a lessee an exclusive on an item for sale or service offered has been invariably recognized in New York. The leading case is *Locker v. American Tobacco Co.*,[36] in which the court said:

> It is the well-settled law of this State that the refusal to maintain trade relations with any individual is an inherent right which every person may lawfully exercise, for the reason he deems sufficient or for no reasons whatever, and it is immaterial whether such refusal is based on reason or is the result of mere caprice, prejudice

---

[31]236 N.Y.S.2d 266 (Sup. Ct. 1962).

[32]*Id*. at 278.

[33]28 A.D.2d 38, 281 N.Y.S.2d 467 (1st Dep't 1967).

[34]*Id*. at 42, 281 N.Y.S.2d at 474.

[35]64 Misc. 2d 894, 315 N.Y.S.2d 897 (Sup. Ct. 1970), *aff'd*, 36 A.D.2d 582, 318 N.Y.S.2d 924 (2d Dep't 1971).

[36]121 A.D.443, 106 N.Y.S. 115 (2d Dep't 1907), *aff'd*, 195 N.Y. 565, 88 N.E. 289 (1909).

or malice. It is part of the liberty of action which the Constitutions, State and Federal, guarantee to the citizen. It is not within the power of the courts to compel an owner of property to sell or part with his title to it, without his consent and against his wishes, to any particular person.[37]

The refusal to do business except on one's own terms has been held not unlawful, even in the case of a national television network.[38] In *Revlon Products Corp. v. Bernstein*,[39] the court concluded that a manufacturer need not go into competition with himself, and if he elects to deal with a certain class of customers personally, his action in forbidding his distributors to compete with him for those customers is not in restraint of trade. In another context, it was held that the mere fact that the parties to an agreement eliminate competition between themselves does not mean that the agreement violates the Donnelly Act.[40]

Even allegedly concerted action has been sanctioned in the absence of a sufficient showing of monopolistic practices under the guise of an individual refusal to deal. In *Rothschild v. World Wide Automobiles Corp.*,[41] a would-be Volkswagen dealer alleged a conspiracy between existing Volkswagen dealers and a wholesale Volkswagen distributor to prevent him from obtaining a dealership in a particular location. The majority found only an attempt by one dealer to prevent plaintiff from obtaining a franchise to sell the products of a single manufacturer in close competition with a territory in which the dealer had an interest. In so doing, the majority applied the rule of reason and found the activity concerted but allowable conduct.

The rule of reason applied by the court of appeals in *Rothschild* to a seller's right to impose restrictions on buyers in the context of the Donnelly Act has been explored thoroughly and approved by Thomas J. Maroney in his article entitled *Antitrust in the Empire State: Regulation of Restrictive Business Practices in New York State*:[42] "It is the writer's opinion that a *per se* rule of illegality should not be applied to exclusive dealings. Tying and other restrictions on buyers may be imposed for legitimate commercial purposes, and an accommodation must be made between those purposes and protection of the competitive process. The Rule of Reason can be the vehicle for such an accommodation, as some of the New York cases have recognized. [Citations omitted.]"[43]

The innkeeping practice of making exclusive lease arrangements with selected concessionaires, thereby eliminating competition over the sale of the concessionaire's product and requiring potential patrons to accept a function package "as is," does serve a legitimate commercial purpose. It protects the

---

[37]*Id.* at 452, 106 N.Y.S. at 121.

[38]American Broadcast-Paramount Theatres, Inc. v. Hazel Bishop, Inc., 31 Misc.2d 1056, 223 N.Y.S.2d 178 (Sup. Ct. 1961).

[39]204 Misc. 80, 119 N.Y.S.2d 60 (Sup. Ct. 1953).

[40]State v. Milk Handlers & Processors Ass'n, Inc., 52 Misc.2d 658, 276 N.Y.S.2d 803, 812–13 (Sup. Ct. 1967).

[41]18 N.Y.2d 982, 224 N.E.2d 724 (1966) (per curiam).

[42]19 Syracuse L. Rev. 819 (1968).

[43]*Id.* at 861.

exclusive environment the hotel seeks to create and maintain and upon which its livelihood depends. The environment cannot be maintained if the hotel is compelled to accept the patron's choice of services or forego offering these amenities. So long as all patrons are treated alike, and the prices charged are consistent with those offered for comparable services in establishments of a similar class, the restrictive conduct is reasonable and thus allowable. Every entrepreneur can be said to have a monopoly over his goods and services. It is concerted action with others that furthers a monopolistic scheme that is condemned under the Donnelly Act. The activities an innkeeper seeks to protect are vital and necessary to the innkeeping business, not totally foreign to that business, which was the basis for the finding of a violation in the *Eagle Springs* case.

The defense or justification of pecuniary gain alone may not immunize an innkeeper's monopoly over its own function services from the sanctions of the Donnelly Act, under a literal interpretation of the statute. This is not the case, however, if the innkeeper seeks to protect its own legitimate business interests. Those interests are established by proof that the innkeeper legitimately promotes function business, provides ancillary services in connection with that business, and protects the interests of his commercial tenants engaged in that business. Such proof would meet the tests of restrictive but allowable restraints of trade, militating against any finding of illegality.

In states that have antimonopoly provisions similar to the Donnelly Act, the above analysis could also apply. Therefore it is suggested that the innkeeper obtain legal advice as to whether such refusals to deal would violate those laws.

The interplay between the Sherman and Donnelly acts is reviewed in the following case.

BUSINESS FOODS SERVICE, INC. v. FOOD CONCEPTS CORP.
533 F. Supp. 992 (E.D.N.Y. 1982)

McLAUGHLIN, D.J.: "The parties to this antitrust action compete in the employee or commissary catering business in the States of New York and New Jersey. They supply their respective customers with daily deliveries of a wide variety of food, except for items such as milk, eggs, and bread, and they do almost no on-premises cooking. In the overall cafeteria service industry, commissary catering lies somewhere between vending machines and extensive on-premises cooking.

"Plaintiff has moved for summary judgment alleging that the defendant utilizes a restrictive covenant that is both an unreasonable restraint of trade under Section 1 of the Sherman Act, 15 U.S.C. § 1, and a violation of Section 340 of the New York General Business Law. Since there are disputes as to the size of the geographic market and the scope of the relevant product market, the reasonableness of the alleged restraint cannot be presently assessed. Accordingly, summary judgment is denied.

I. The Covenant

"The restrictive covenant [footnote omitted] in question is atypical. It is a hybrid provision incorporating aspects of both a traditional employer-employee covenant not to compete and an exclusive dealing arrangement. While the covenant restricts the employment opportunities of former employees of the defendant, the covenant itself appears in contracts entered into by the defendant and its customers, rather than in contracts between the defendant and its employees. If a competitor of the defendant hires a former employee of the defendant, the controversial covenant bars the defendant's customers from using the services of the defendant's competitor for one year after the termination of the service contract between that customer and the defendant.

II. The Companies and Their Employees

" . . . The plaintiff alleges that the covenant goes beyond what is necessary to protect the defendant's business. It claims that the duration of the provision's restriction is potentially infinite. The plaintiff also notes that the employees involved were not privy to business secrets nor did they hold unique positions while employed by the defendant.

"Furthermore, plaintiff claims that it has lost at least three customers directly as a result of the restrictive covenant in question. According to the plaintiff, these customers failed to make contracts with the plaintiff because they feared that the defendant would start litigation over the restrictive covenant. Indeed, since the commencement of this action, the defendant has in fact brought two lawsuits against several of its customers and in each case has joined the plaintiff in order to enforce the provision.

"The defendant counters by asserting that the covenant is fair, reasonably warranted, and necessary for its protection. It asserts that the purpose of the restrictive covenant is to prevent the unfair use of information (e.g., business secrets) gleaned by employees while in the employ of the defendant. . . .

III. The Law

A. The Sherman Act

"Although the reasonableness of employee covenants not to compete is seldom raised in the federal courts, such restrictive covenants are 'proper subjects for scrutiny under section 1 of the Sherman Act.' *Newburger, Loeb & Co. v. Gross,* 563 F.2d 1057, 1082 (2d Cir. 1977). [Citations omitted.] So too, the reasonableness of an exclusive dealing contract may also be measured against Section 1. [Citations omitted.]

"While Section I applies both to covenants not to compete and to exclusive dealing arrangements, neither of these potentially anticompetitive contractual provisions is per se illegal. The per se rule has not been extended to restrictive covenants primarily because of the limited experience courts have had in judging the competitive impact of such covenants within the rubric of Section 1 of the

Sherman Act. *Bradford v. New York Times Co.*, 501 F.2d 51, 59–60 (2d Cir. 1974). *See also, United States v. Topco Assoc., Inc.*, 405 U.S. 596, 607–08, 92 S. Ct. 1126, 1133–34, 31 L. Ed. 2d 515 (1972). Similarly, the benefits to sellers and buyers as well as to society from exclusive dealing arrangements must be balanced against possible anticompetitive effects. [Citations omitted.]

"Thus, the legality of restrictive covenants and exclusive dealing contracts turns on the reasonableness of the provision in question. Consideration must, therefore, be directed to the nature of the business in which the restraint is used as well as the reasons for and the competitive impact of the restraint. [Citations omitted.]

"The rule of reason has recently been revitalized in Section 1 cases. *See Continental TV, Inc. v. GTE Sylvania, Inc.*, 433 U.S. 36, 97 S. Ct. 2549, 53 L. Ed. 2d 568 (1977); 2 Von Kalinowski, Antitrust Laws and Trade Regulation, § 6.02(3) (1981). In light of this resurgence, identifying the relevant market and isolating the effect of the challenged restraint on that market become essential since these are the dominant considerations in determining whether the restraint is reasonable. [Citations omitted.] Without market analysis, the competitive impact of the challenged restraint cannot be assessed. [Citations omitted.]

"Although the parties concur that they compete in the commissary catering business in the Greater New York Metropolitan Area ('GNYMA'), and that the number of people employed by a customer determines the type of cafeteria service chosen, they disagree over the geographic and product markets. . . .

"The plaintiff contends that the provision is overbroad and therefore unreasonable. It argues, for one thing, that the duration of the restriction is potentially infinite. Considering that the ban against competition lasts until one year after the termination of the contract between the defendant and its customer, the provision obviously restricts the employment opportunities of defendant's former employees long after their employment with the defendant has ended. While the plaintiff's argument has appeal, 'the duration of the restriction is not the essential inquiry here. . . . Of primary importance is the "market impact" of the alleged restraint and "the challenged restraint's impact on competitive conditions." ' *Lektro-Vend Corp. v. Vendo Corp.*, 500 F. Supp. [332] at 354–55, *quoting GTE Sylvania*, 433 U.S. at 50, 97 S. Ct. at 2557. *See National Society of Professional Engineers v. United States*, 435 U.S. at 688, 98 S. Ct. at 1363. Since there is a dispute as to the boundaries of the relevant product and geographic markets, summary judgment under Section 1 of the Sherman Act is inappropriate.

B. The Donnelly Act

"Although the Court has determined that summary judgment is inappropriate with respect to the Sherman Act claim, this does not end the inquiry. The plaintiff has also alleged a violation of New York law, specifically the Donnelly Act, and this issue may be reached under the Court's pendent jurisdiction. [Citation omitted.]

"Whether summary judgment should be granted on the Donnelly Act claim is problematic. The clear public policy of New York, as reflected in the Donnelly Act, is against restrictive covenants in the employment contract. [Citations omitted.] To constitute a violation of the Donnelly Act, however, the provision must still be found to be unreasonable. [Citation omitted.]

"Although the duration of a covenant not to compete may be a more important factor under New York law than under the Sherman Act, [citation omitted] the covenant's effect on competition and the business justification for the restraint must still be assessed. *Horne v. Radiological Health Services, P.C.,* 83 Misc. 2d 446, 371 N.Y.S.2d 948, 958, *aff'd,* 379 N.Y.S.2d 374 (1975). The harm to the general public cannot be assessed in a vacuum; it must be weighed on the scales of the relevant market. Moreover, it is significant that this case does not strictly involve a covenant not to compete. As already noted, the restrictive covenant is incorporated into contracts entered into by the defendant with its customers rather than contracts between the defendants and its employees. As stated by the plaintiff's own economist, 'by restricting the choices of some customers, the restrictive covenant is equivalent to targeted exclusive dealing.' . . .

"Even if the competitive impact of the restraint is not the crucial consideration in weighing the reasonableness of a restrictive covenant under New York law, it is clear that such an assessment is of primary importance when determining the legality of an exclusive dealing arrangement. *See, e.g., Big Top Stores, Inc. v. Ardsley Toy Shoppe,* 64 Misc. 2d 894, 315 N.Y.S.2d 897, *aff'd,* 36 A.D.2d 582, 318 N.Y.S2d 924 (1971). Considering that the restrictive covenant in this case is actually a hybrid of these two types of contractual arrangements, the dispute as to the relevant market again precludes the granting of the plaintiff's motion for summary judgment. . . .

"The reasonableness of the challenged restraint must be viewed in the light of its competitive impact on the relevant market. Because the parties disagree as to the product and geographic markets, these material issues must be resolved at trial. Plaintiff's motion for summary judgment is, therefore, denied.

"SO ORDERED."

17 Franchise Agreements: Legal Rights and Responsibilities of Franchisor and Franchisee

17:1 *Regulation of Franchising*

Section 5 of the Federal Trade Commission Act authorizes the FTC to regulate business practices found to be unfair or deceptive. As part of its ongoing responsibilities, the Commission, after lengthy investigation, issued a trade regulation effective October 2, 1979, having the force and effect of law, entitled "Disclosure Requirements and Prohibitions Concerning Franchising Business and Opportunity Ventures."[1]

Under that regulation the Commission defines a *franchise* as "an arrangement in which the owner of a trademark, tradename or copyright licenses others, under specified conditions or limitations, to use the owner's trademark, tradename, or copyright in purveying goods or services." The *franchisor* is the party granting the franchise, and the *franchisee* is the person or entity to whom the franchise is granted.

Previous mention has been made of anticompetitive activities of franchisors which are deemed violative of the antitrust laws in regard to prices, the purchase of materials and supplies, and geographic limitations that the franchisor imposes upon his franchisees.[2] What requires further examination is the disclosure of pertinent information to a prospective franchisee and regulation of the duration and termination of such agreements by the franchisor, subjects dealt with in the FTC trade regulation.

Under settled principles of contract law, the parties to any agreement may fix its terms and conditions. In theory the relationship between franchisor and franchisee is that of two independent contractors[3] dealing at arm's length; thus they

---

This chapter reproduces in part my article "The Inn-Side of the Law: The Franchisor's Liability for a Franchisee's Negligence" from the November 1979 issue of The Cornell Hotel and Restaurant Administration Quarterly, with permission from the Cornell University School of Hotel Administration. © 1979. No attempt is made to review comparable state regulations.

[1] 16 C.F.R. 436 (1978) (effective Oct. 21, 1979).

[2] *See, e.g.,* Chapter 16, *supra,* esp. 16:6–16:8, 16:10.

[3] An independent contractor is defined as a party said to pursue an independent occupation or enterprise, generally supplying his own materials and servants, being responsible to his employer only for the result of the task entrusted to him. A standard clause is contained in H. Brown, Franchising Realities and Remedies, app. A, Sample Agreement XXII, at 393–94 (2d ed. 1978). The traditional test of independent contractor status is the right to control over the party employed in respect to the manner in which his work is to be done. A. Rotwein, Law of Agency, § 8 at 4–5 (2d ed. 1949).

may specify the causes for which the franchisor may terminate the franchise, such as death, disability, insolvency, failure to make required payments, or failure to meet sales quotas. In many cases such contracts contain arbitration clauses under which a neutral party is authorized to make a final, binding determination as to whether a breach of contract has occurred sufficient to authorize its termination by the party adversely affected.

Under the FTC trade regulation, the franchisor is required to give every prospective franchisee a disclosure statement ten days before the franchisee executes a contract or makes any payment for a franchise, whichever is sooner. This statement must provide detailed information as to the franchisor's finances, experience, size of operation, and involvement in litigation; total costs to the franchisee, including whether any parts thereof are refundable; recurring expenses of the franchise; specific limitations, if any, on the franchisee's operations regarding goods and services that may be offered, customers to whom the franchisee may sell, geographic-area limitations and territorial protection granted; conditions of termination, renewal, and transfer of ownership; and detailed verification of any claims as to sales, income, and gross or net profits.

The FTC has refrained from mandating the prefiling of such statements for screening and approval for accuracy and completeness. The Commission has suggested that a private cause of action for breach of the regulation exists, but no court has ruled on this issue yet.

False statements as to sales, income, or profits are prohibited, punishable by a maximum $10,000 fine for each violation.

17:2 *The Nature of the Franchise Agreement*

A typical franchise agreement between a hotel chain and a franchisee contains language making the franchisee an independent contractor[4] and freeing the franchisor of liability to third parties for the negligence of the franchisee or his employees. Such contracts often specify that the franchisee will hold the franchisor harmless from any third-party claims and will indemnify the franchisor for any payments the latter is compelled to pay. The burden of obtaining liability insurance[5]—in which the franchisor is named as a beneficiary, both for the costs of legal defense and the payment of claims found legally sufficient—is normally placed upon the franchisee. (Some franchisors, however, including Holiday Inns, establish and manage self-insurance programs, thereby reducing the costs of coverage to all concerned.)

17:3 *Responsibility of Franchisee to Franchisor and Third Persons*

Franchisee and franchisor are bound to observe and fulfill the terms and conditions set forth in the contract existing between them and to do nothing that would interfere with its performance by the other party. The contract is pre-

[4]Rotwein, *supra* note 3 at § 8.
[5]*See, e.g.,* H. Brown, *supra* note 3, Sample Agreement XI, at 381–82.

sumed valid until declared unenforceable, in whole or in part, by a court of competent jurisdiction or an appropriate governmental regulatory agency. In the relationship between the franchisee and his patrons, guests, or other invitees, the franchisee is primarily liable for any breach of reservation or other contract, breach of implied warranty, negligence, or intentional tort, and, as an innkeeper, is subject to statutory limitations, as is any private party. The franchise agreement does not itself insulate the franchisee from responsibility, and the franchisor does not voluntarily assume such liability in the absence of proof of control evidencing apparent authority or representations of control communicated to third persons.

17:4 *Derelictions Imputable to Franchisor: Factors Creating Liability*

The sensible business practice of holding the franchisor harmless for franchisee-caused injuries to invitees is now being threatened by the tendency of some courts to theorize—despite contract provisions—that a guest or other third party is not precluded from suing the franchisor (in addition to the franchisee) for the derelictions of the franchisee's employees or agents.[6] The franchisor can be held liable only if it can be shown that the franchisor exercised a "sufficient degree of control" over the franchisee's activities giving rise to the injury or damage claim. What constitutes "sufficient control"? Among the factors taken into consideration in establishing the degree of operational control are: the construction and maintenance of the facility as specified by the franchisor; strict adherence to the rules of conduct promulgated by the franchisor (as well as granting the franchisor permission to make regular inspections of the unit to ensure compliance with the rules of operation); and, especially noteworthy, granting the franchisor permission to cancel the agreement for any substantial violation of its terms. In one case, the court concluded that these factors, taken collectively, represented sufficient evidence to hold a franchisor liable for the actions of its franchisee's employee in the wrongful revocation of a guest's credit.[7]

The Supreme Court of Virginia reached the contrary conclusion in *Murphy v. Holiday Inns,*[8] and to the same effect, see *Slates v. International House of Pancakes, Inc.*[9]

17:5 *Manifestations of Authority: Estoppel*

Independently of this finding of sufficient control over the franchisee, two courts[10] have authorized recovery on another theory: that of *apparent authority*

---

[6]Peters v. Sheraton Hotels and Inns, N.Y.L.J., July 6, 1979 (N.Y. Civ. Ct.). "The parties to an agreement may not determine the nature of their relationship by mere fiat; with respect to a third person it depends on the facts." *See also, e.g.,* Wood v. Holiday Inns, Inc., 508 F.2d 167, 175–77 (5th Cir. 1975) (interpreting Alabama Law).

[7]Wood v. Holiday Inns, Inc., 508 F.2d 167, 175–77 (5th Cir. 1975).

[8]216 Va. 490, 219 S.E.2d 874 (1975).

[9]90 Ill. App. 3d 716, 413 N.E.2d 457 (1980).

[10]Peters v. Sheraton Hotels and Inns, N.Y.L.J., July 6, 1979 (N.Y. Civ. Ct.); Wood v. Holiday Inns, Inc., 508 F.2d 167, 175–77 (5th Cir. 1975).

or *authority by estoppel*. Essentially, authority by estoppel is based on the franchisor's manifestations to guests, and guests' reasonable belief that the franchisee is authorized to bind his franchisor. These "manifestations" need not be communicated directly to the third parties, but may be communicated to the community—for example, through signs or advertising. The existence of apparent authority may be established on the basis of such factors as contract terms under which the franchisee is readily recognized by the public as a member of the national franchisor's system of inns (for example, through the required use of service marks, trademarks, and elements of interior and exterior decor). Once the requisite "manifestations" have been established, the franchisor is "estopped," that is, prevented from denying authority over the franchisee sufficient to make the franchisor liable to the invitee.

Sapp v. City of Tallahassee
354 So. 2d 985 (1977)

ERVIN, J.: " . . . Ms. Sapp's second amended complaint alleges Holiday Inns, Inc. is jointly and severally liable with the local owners of the Tallahassee Holiday Inn for her injuries. The sole ground relied upon by Holiday Inns in its motion to dismiss was that there was no operational responsibility exercised by Holiday Inns over the motel facility. No legal relationship between Holiday Inns, Inc. and the local establishment was alleged in the amended complaint. We agree with the trial court that the complaint is legally insufficient in the absence of such allegations, but find the dismissal should be without prejudice. While Ms. Sapp had filed a complaint, a first amended complaint and finally a second amended complaint, the count alleging negligence by Holiday Inns, Inc. in the second amended complaint was for the first time dismissed by the court. No prior orders had been entered dismissing her cause of action against Holiday Inns, Inc. without prejudice. We are of course committed to the rule 'that amendments to pleadings be liberally allowed in the interest of justice so that the merits of the case may be reached for adjudication whenever possible. . . . '
Conklin v. Smith, 191 So. 2d 311, 313 (Fla. 1st DCA 1966). [Citation omitted.]

"As argued in her brief, Ms. Sapp can show an agency relationship between the local motel operation and the national Holiday Inn, Inc. by properly alleging control and domination on the part of the franchisor. [Citations omitted.]

"Ms. Sapp should have an opportunity to pursue her discovery and establish what, if any, direct control Holiday Inns, Inc. exercised over the operations of the hotel, particularly in security matters. This of course should not be construed as a comment by this court on the merit of Ms. Sapp's claim.

"Holiday Inns, Inc. argues its franchise agreement with the local owners precludes as a matter of law the finding of an agency relationship. That agreement provides in part:

"(h) That Licensee, in the use of the name 'Holiday Inn,' the service marks, trade marks, color scheme and pattern, signs and the System and in Licensee's own advertising, *shall identify Licensee as being the owner and operator of Licensee's particular 'Holiday Inn' or 'Holiday Inns' under li-*

*cense from Licensor; that the parties hereto are completely separate enti-
ties, are not partners, joint adventurers, or agents of the other in any sense,
and neither has power to obligate or bind the other;* that Licensee shall not
use the words 'Holiday Inn,' or any combination of such words, in its corporate name or partnership name, if a corporation or partnership, nor allow
the use thereof by others; that Licensee will sell or provide no products or
services under the said service marks or trade marks, except inn service of
lodging, foods, and other accommodations and conveniences for the public, of the same nature, type quality and distinguishing characteristics as
are sold or provided, or may hereafter be sold or provided at the 'Holiday
Inns' in and around Memphis, Tennessee. [Emphasis supplied.]

"Notwithstanding its assertion that it and its licensees were separate entities,
other provisions of the agreement indicate varying degrees of control by Holiday
Inns, Inc.; as examples, the requirement of regular inspection of the facilities by
Holiday Inns' inspectors, the requirement that the licensee strictly observe the
operational rules of Holiday Inns, and a provision that the existing rules of operation may be amended in the wisdom of Holiday Inns. Another provision
states that Holiday Inns shall maintain supervision over licensees 'to assure
compliance with "Holiday Inn" standards as established in the System.'

"When we compare that portion of the agreement disavowing any agency relationship between the licensor and licensee with the other pertinent portions
establishing control, it is obvious that the contract's terms are inconsistent and
ambiguous. We have recently held, in construing an insurance contract, that
where clauses are hopelessly irreconcilable and inconsistent, we would follow
the rule resolving such ambiguities against the insurer, the drafter of the contract. [Citation omitted.]

"However the agreement's provisions are not necessarily dispositive of the
agency question. While agency is normally a contractual relationship created by
agreement of the parties, it may also be inferred from past dealings between the
parties. It may be proved by the facts and circumstances of each particular case,
including the words and conduct of the parties. [Citations omitted.]

"In addition, control and domination need not be actual but may be binding
upon the principal if apparent. That is, if the principal has held the agent out to
the public as being possessed of the requisite authority, and a third person is
aware of his authority and has relied on it to his detriment, then the principal is
estopped from denying the agency relationship. *Mercury Cab Owners' Association v. Jones,* 79 So. 2d 782 (Fla. 1955); *H.S.A. Inc. v. Harris-In-Hollywood,
Inc.,* 285 So. 2d 600 (Fla. 4th DCA 1973). *Compare Wood v. Holiday Inns, Inc.,*
508 F.2d 167 (5th Cir. 1975), in which it was held there was not only sufficient
control by Holiday Inns, Inc. over the licensee in its license agreement to subject
Holiday Inns to liability for injury which occurred to an invitee caused by the
licensee's employee, but that Holiday Inns might also be liable on a theory of
apparent authority. The court concluded that because the license agreement between Holiday Inns and its licensee provided that the facility should be constructed and operated so that it would readily be recognized by the public as part

of the national system of Holiday Inns, a jury could reasonably conclude that the license agreement required that the motel facility be of such an appearance that travelers would believe it was owned by Holiday Inns, Inc. It further observed that when the plaintiff contracted with the Phenix City Holiday Inn for lodging, he contracted for proper treatment by the servants of the innkeeper, but there was virtually no way he could have known that the servants in the facility were servants of the licensee, not of Holiday Inns, Inc.

"The same situation controls here. There is nothing in the record before us to indicate that Ms. Sapp, employed on a temporary fill-in basis at the restaurant of the Inn at the time the incident occurred, was aware the facility was operated by the licensees.

"The order of dismissal is therefore . . . reversed in part and remanded as to Holiday Inns, Inc. for further proceedings not inconsistent with this opinion."

In the case below, the Federal Court of Appeals for the Fourth Circuit reviewed the question of apparent agency.

CRINKLEY v. HOLIDAY INNS, INC.
844 F.2d 156 (4th Cir. 1988)

PHILLIPS, C.J.: [*See* section 11:1 at p. 367 for a brief statement of facts. All other intervening discussion is omitted.]

"Finally, Holiday Inns contends that the district court erred in submitting the claim against it to the jury on a theory of apparent agency. They argue first that because, as the district court properly held, the evidence would not support a finding of actual agency, they could not therefore be found liable on the basis of apparent authority. They then contend that in any event the evidence was insufficient to support a finding of apparent agency.

"On the first point, Holiday Inns is simply confused. It is true that apparent authority presupposes actual agency, and only operates to extend the scope of an actual agent's authority. *See generally* Restatement (Second) of Agency § 8 (1958); *see, e.g., S.F. McCotter & Son, Inc. v. O.H.A. Indus., Inc.*, 54 N.C. App. 151, 282 S.E.2d 584, 586 (1981).

"But there is the related principle of apparent agency or agency by estoppel under which agency itself may be imposed by law on legal relations. Though no actual agency exists, a party may be held to be the agent of another on the basis that he has been held out by the other to be so in a way that reasonably induces reliance on the appearances. *See, e.g., Fike v. Board of Trustees*, 53 N.C. App. 78, 279 S.E.2d 910, 912 (1981) (citation omitted) (recognizing that a party may be liable for the acts of another under the theory of agency by estoppel even where no agency relationship in fact exists); *see generally* Restatement (Second) of Agency § 267. It is clear here that the theory submitted to the jury by the district court was agency by estoppel; the issue submitted was whether TRAVCO had the power to bind Holiday Inns by virtue of its appearance as Holiday Inns' agent. Holiday Inns in fact accepts this in its brief by arguing that there was insufficient evidence to establish apparent agency, and we will review the record on that basis.

"In establishing liability based on apparent agency, a plaintiff must show that (1) the alleged principal has represented or permitted it to be represented that the party dealing directly with the plaintiff is its agent, and (2) the plaintiff, in reliance on such representations, has dealt with the supposed agent. *Fike, supra; see also* Restatement (Second) of Agency§ 267 (1958) (justifiable reliance and change of position). We believe the evidence sufficed to support submission of this theory.

"By virtue of the franchise agreement, Holiday Inns retained a significant degree of control over the operation of the Holiday Inn–Concord. This control included the use of the Holiday Inns trade name and trademarks, which appeared on numerous items in and about the motel. The motel itself was originally designed and built by Holiday Inns and sold in 1976 to a group that later conveyed it to the current owners. The company engages in national advertising that promotes its national system, without distinguishing between company owned and franchised properties. It also apparently publishes a directory listing the properties within its system, also without distinguishing between company owned and franchised properties. The only indication that the Holiday Inn–Concord was not owned by Holiday Inns was a sign in the restaurant that stated that the motel was operated by TRAVCO under a franchise agreement. Holiday Inns contends that the franchise agreement disclaims any agency relationship. However, the denial of an agency relationship in a franchise agreement is not alone determinative of liability. *See Drummond v. Hilton Hotel Corp.*, 501 F. Supp. 29, 31 (E.D. Pa.1980). As indicated, agency by estoppel specifically applies to situations where no actual agency relationship exists. We think that a jury could reasonably conclude that the Holiday Inn–Concord was operated in such a way as to create the appearance that it was owned by Holiday Inns, Inc. and that this was one of the purposes of the franchise agreement.

"As to the reliance prong of the test, Sarah Crinkley testified that she and her husband had previously stayed at Holiday Inns and that she was familiar with its national advertising. She also testified that they originally attempted to make reservations at a Holiday Inn in Charlotte because they thought it would be a good place to stay. Rather than looking for another Charlotte area hotel when they could not get a room at the Holiday Inn near their destination, they used a Holiday Inn directory to find another convenient motel. James Crinkley testified that he did not know the difference between a franchise inn and a company owned inn at the time of February 27, 1981, and noted that he would be greatly surprised to find out that Holiday Inns was not involved in the operation of the Holiday Inn–Concord beyond the franchise agreement. While the Crinkleys' evidence of actual reliance may be marginal, we think it sufficed under the applicable substantive principles to raise a jury issue.[3]

"*AFFIRMED.*

"3. The recent North Carolina decision by a divided panel in *Hayman v. Ramada Inn, Inc.*, 86 N.C. App. 274, 357 S.E.2d 394 (1987), *rev. granted in part*, 320 N.C. 631, 360 S.E.2d 87 (1987), rejecting a comparable apparent agency claim against a motel franchisor, is distinguishable. In that case, the motel guest was required by her employer to stay at the franchised motel. On this basis the court held as a matter of law that necessity rather than reliance on the franchisor's representations dictated the guest's choice. Here, by contrast, the guests were exercising free choice so that their reliance on the franchisor's representations as the controlling factor in this choice was reasonably inferable as a matter of fact. The *Hayman* majority also thought that the evidence failed as a matter of law to establish that there was any effective misrepresentation of the franchisor-franchisee relationship. Again, in the instant case, the only indication that a franchisor-franchisee relationship existed was a sign in the restaurant which the Crinkleys had had no occasion to see before they checked in."

17:6 *Contractual Disclaimers of Liability*

Is there any means by which a franchisor can conclusively avoid liability for the legal wrongs of his franchisee? One method might be to provide conspicuous public notice that the franchisee is solely responsible for injuries sustained or contract damages inflicted upon the franchisee's guests. Through a notice of this kind, the franchisor could establish the third party's awareness that the franchisor did not voluntarily assume any responsibility for the derelictions of its franchisee. But the question of authority would still require resolution, because the notice might be construed as a contractual disclaimer of responsibility for all acts or omissions of the franchisee—and such broad disclaimers are considered contrary to public policy by the law.[11]

One possible rejoinder is that there must be adequate proof of the guest's reliance on the representation of authority, because one can argue that the guest was seeking the franchisor's quality, not his liability. But this too has been held as a question of fact.[12] Furthermore, the franchisor is not allowed to claim economic ruin in the event liability is foisted on him.[13]

17:7 *A Possible Solution*

The problem of franchisor's liability must be dealt with by the legislature. The courts cannot furnish a satisfactory solution because questions of control and apparent authority are decided by a jury. As a result, there is no possibility of predicting the outcome of a case or establishing adequate precedents on which franchisors could rely. A legislative effort to relieve or curtail the third-party liability of the franchisor would allow the most expeditious and uniform resolution of this thorny issue.

[11]*See, e.g.*, W. Prosser, The Law of Torts, § 68 at 442 (4th ed. 1971). This is especially so where the party asserting the limitation is in a public calling. *See* § 13:12, infra.
[12]Peters v. Sheraton Hotels and Inns, N.Y.L.J., July 6, 1979 (N.Y. Civ. Ct.).
[13]*Id.*

18 Regulation Governing the Sale of Food, Beverages, and Intoxicants

18:1 *Introduction*

From the earliest times society has adopted legislation regulating the sale of food, drugs, and other substances ingested or applied to the human skin. Historically such legislation dealt first with false weights and measures, then adulteration, then misbranding, and ultimately false advertising. The current federal Food, Drug and Cosmetic Act is vast in size, scope, and significance. It includes a multitude of legislative enactments, administrative regulations, and judicial decisions. Yet its basic purpose is remedial, to protect the health and economy of the consuming public. In essence, what the Act does is outlaw those products that are harmful, prohibit misrepresentation, and require that certain information be disclosed when they are sold. The common-law rule of *caveat emptor*, let the buyer beware, has yielded to regulation because foodstuffs are necessities of life and because impurities or other abuses can have a disastrous effect upon the public health and welfare. In the complex economic system of the twentieth century, the ability of consumers to protect themselves from such products has been whittled down to the vanishing point but for federal regulation. The Food and Drug Administration spends much of its time determining the truthfulness and the sufficiency of representations made to the public at large concerning food and related articles of human consumption.

18:2 *Adulteration*

Section 402(a) of the Food, Drug and Cosmetic Act provides: "A food shall be deemed to be adulterated. . . (4) if it has been prepared, packed or held under unsanitary conditions whereby it may have become contaminated with filth, or whereby it may have been rendered injurious to health."

The Act goes beyond prohibiting commerce in products that are carriers of disease. It prohibits the distribution and sale of foods that may contain repulsive or offensive matter classed as filth regardless of whether such substances can be detected by laboratory procedures or are likely to be present because of the conditions under which the goods were prepared and handled. Exposure to unsanitary conditions in the preparation, packaging, and storage of foods, in addition to unclean or decomposed foods, is sufficient to support a violation.

Overall, the maintenance of sanitary conditions requires extermination and exclusion of rodents, inspection and sorting of raw materials to eliminate the insect-infested and decomposed portions, fumigation, quick handling and proper storage to prevent insect development or contamination, the use of clean equipment, control of possible sources of sewage pollution, and supervision of the conduct of food preparers and handlers.

18:3　*Economic Adulteration of Food*

Section 402 further provides: "A food shall be deemed to be adulterated. . . (b)(1) If any valuable constituent has been in whole or in part omitted or distracted therefrom; or (2) if any substance has been substituted wholly or in part therefor; or (3) if damage of inferiority has been concealed in any manner; or (4) if any substance has been added thereto or mixed or packed therewith so as to increase its bulk or weight, or reduce its quality or strength, or make it appear better or of greater value than it is."

Economic adulteration has to do with consumer deception and fraud; it refers to the substitution of less expensive ingredients or the diminution of more expensive ingredients so as to make the product, although not in itself deleterious, inferior to that which the consumer expected to receive when purchasing that product under the name by which it was sold. The test for economic adulteration is whether the consumer is deceived. The fact that merchants or vendors are not deceived is immaterial.

Falsification by means of substitution of a product or a product component may result in a real saving in cost of production. Many imitation products and, occasionally, adulterated goods, are useful, serviceable, and produced at low cost. "Without the intervention of the food law purchasers would be deceived; they would be defrauded also until competition forced down the price. At that point purchasers would not be penalized because they would be paying a competitive price based on production costs. They would be deceived, it is true, and yet, viewed solely from the national welfare, there would be economies rather than wastes."[1]

This early statement represents the argument against regulation of economic adulteration. Other critics of regulation have argued that consumers should have to fend for themselves, since no health hazard is involved; that the cost to the food dispenser, the producer, and the consumer is too high to justify the limited degree of protection afforded by regulation; and that the industry is better able than the government to educate the public.[2]

In spite of these opinions, the consistent interpretation of the law is that it is designed to protect the public from deception, regardless of whether the deception results in harm to health.

[1]Alsberg, *Economic Aspects of Adulteration and Imitation,* 46 Q.J. Econ. 1, 17, 29 (1931–32).
[2]T. Christopher, Cases and Materials on Food and Drug Law, ch. 2, subd. 5, at 102 (1966).

18:4 *Misbranding of Food*

Section 403 of the Food, Drug and Cosmetic Act reads, in part, as follows:

Section 403. A food shall be deemed to be misbranded
  (a) If its labeling is false or misleading in any particular.
  (b) If it is offered for sale under the name of another food. . . .
  (d) If its container is made, formed or filled as to be misleading. . . .
  (f) If any word, statement, or other information required by or under authority of this Act to appear on the label or labeling is not prominently placed thereon with such conspicuousness. . . and in such terms as to render it likely to be read and understood by the ordinary individual under customary conditions or purchase and use. . . .

The question whether written representations and advertising may constitute labeling violative of the Act was answered in the affirmative by the United States Supreme Court in *Kordel v. United States,*[3] in which the defendant had mailed drugs and explanatory pamphlets to his retailers in separate packages. In affirming his conviction the Court held that physical attachment is not necessary where the writing is intended to be a substitute for the labeling:

Petitioner points out that in the evolution of the Act the ban on false advertising was eliminated, the control over it being transferred to the Federal Trade Commission. 52 Stat. 114, 15 U.S.C. § 55(a). We have searched the legislative history in vain, however, to find any indicating that Congress had the purpose to eliminate from the Act advertising which performs the function of labeling. Every labeling is in a sense an advertisement. The advertising which we have here performs the same function as it would if it were on the article or on the containers or wrappers. As we have said, physical attachment or contiguity is unnecessary. . . .

It has been held that the Act was only intended to deal with misleading claims when made in immediate connection with the sale of the product. *United States v. An Undetermined Number of Cases.* . . [of] *Vinegar and Honey.* But the Act is not limited to positive misstatements; concealment of omissions are equally violative of the law. ''People have a right to assume that fraudulent advertising traps will not be laid to ensnare them. 'Laws are made to protect the trusting as well as the suspicious.' *Donaldson v. Read Magazine, Inc. 33 U.S. 178, 185–189. . . (1948).*''

Whether the product itself is beneficial or useful is immaterial. The vice is the manner in which it is represented and the claims that are made for it, tested by the understanding of people or ordinary understanding and discrimination, allowance being made for the susceptibility to the claims of the groups or types of people at whom it is peculiarly aimed.

Offer for Sale under the Name of Another Food
The Supreme Court[4] has held that section 403(b) states a separate and distinct offense so that the offer for sale of one food under the name of another food is

---

[3]397 U.S. 1 (1970).
[4]Weeks v. United States, 245 U.S. 618 (1918).

itself a violation of this section, without proof of a false or misleading label. The offer must be intentional, but proof that the offer was made by or under the authority of the producer and vendor of the food is sufficient in such cases.

Misleading Container

Section 403(d) is intended to cover food containers that are "slack filled," that is, partly filled with the product and partly filled with wrapping so that the ordinary consumer is deceived about the quantity of the product in the container. Actual deception need not be proved.[5] Proof that the packaging or container is misleading or is likely to mislead the ordinary buyer, not one who is particularly attentive or prudent, is the appropriate standard.[6] The defense that the container was designed for safety to the consumer and economy of manufacture is valid, but the defendant must prove that these qualities outweigh the deceptive qualities of the container or wrapper.

The Fair Packaging and Labeling Act of 1966 authorizes the secretary of health and welfare to augment existing regulations so as to provide "truth in packaging and labeling" standards to food products. In essence, the Food and Drug Administration is requiring more information on food labels regarding the origin of the product (for example, if canned juices are made from a concentrate), the origin of ingredients (the type of oil or fat used in the product), and the nature of the product (percentage of natural fruit juices in a fruit drink). If a product is an imitation of a known substance, that fact must be clearly disclosed.[7]

Providing information on nutritional standards is voluntary for producers and processors of food unless nutrients are added to the foods or foods are advertised for nutritional properties.[8] Food and Drug Administration nutritional regulations are designed to give the consumer adequate information about nutritional qualities of various products,[9] and they must be strictly adhered to.

18:5 Seizure of Adulterated or Misbranded Food

Section 304(a) authorizes the seizure and judicial condemnation of any adulterated or misbranded food product "where the Secretary has probable cause to believe from facts found, without hearing, by him or any officer or employee of the Department that the misbranded article is dangerous to health, or that the labeling of the misbranded article is fraudulent, or would be in a material respect misleading to the injury or damage of the purchaser or consumer." After

---

[5]United States v. Cataldo, 157 F.2d 802 (1st Cir. 1946).

[6]United States v. 116 Boxes. . . Arden Assorted Candy Drops, 80 F. Supp. 911 (D. Mass. 1948).

[7]J. Welch, Marketing Law, ch. 6, at 132–33 (1980).

[8]V. Packard, Processed Foods and the Consumer, ch. 11, at 178–80 (1976).

[9]The FDA established mandatory standards in other areas, with respect to package size, price discounts, and common names of ingredients and has prohibited slack-filling if nonfunctional, that is, if done for any reason other than protection of contents or requirements of packaging machinery. The FDA also has authority to require specification of product identity, name and place of business, and net quantity of contents. Welch, Marketing Law, *supra* note 7, at 128–29.

entry of a court decree the product may be disposed of by destruction or sale as the court may direct.

18:6 *Penalties*

Sections 303(a) and 303(b), read together, provide that any violation of section 301, that is, any adulteration, misbranding, or mislabeling, constitutes a misdemeanor, and the violator is subject to a maximum one-year term of imprisonment and a fine of no more than $1,000, or both, upon conviction. A violation with intent to defraud or mislead increases the maximum penalties to a three-year term of imprisonment and a $10,000 fine, or both. Section 303(c) immunizes any person receiving such adulterated or misbranded food who delivers it or proffers it for delivery in good faith if he has received from the shipper a guaranty that the article in question is not adulterated or misbranded.

In *United States v. Park,*[10] the United States Supreme Court reaffirmed and amplified its holding in *United States v. Dotterweich.*[11] The president of a national supermarket chain was held criminally responsible under the federal Food, Drug and Cosmetic Act for unsanitary conditions (rodent infestation) found to exist in one of the chain's food warehouses. The high court ruled that the act requires every corporate officer exercising authority and supervisory responsibility not only to seek out and remedy violations but also, indeed primarily, to implement measures that will ensure that violations do not occur. The court held that the strictest standard governs the merchandise of food distributors.

The following Texas case, another typical adulteration situation, illustrates the recurring problem of the constitutional validity of the health inspector's search of the premises.

JEAN PIERRE, INC. v. STATE
635 S.W.2d 548 (Tex. Crim. App. 1982)

DALLY, J.: ". . .The appellant, Jean Pierre, Inc., is a wholesale and retail bakery. On November 14, 1978, Charles Palmer, an inspector for the Texas Department of Health went to the premises of the company for the purpose of making a routine sanitation inspection. On arrival, Palmer was directed to the back room of the bakery where François Goodhuys, the proprietor of the bakery, was working. Palmer, who made four previous inspections of the bakery and who was acquainted with Goodhuys, stated he was there to do an FDA inspection, to which Goodhuys replied, 'Fine.' Palmer did not ask permission or present any authority to inspect. Their conversation was at all times friendly and business-like. Goodhuys did not object to the entry into the bakery or the subsequent

[10]421 U.S. 658 (1975).
[11]320 U.S. 277, *reh'g denied,* 320 U.S. 815.

gathering of samples and taking of photographs. In fact, he accompanied Mr. Palmer 'on and off' during the inspection, which lasted approximately four hours, and the two talked over some of the alleged violations at that time. There is nothing on the record to suggest any coercion.

"Prior to trial, appellant filed a Motion to Suppress, contending that the warrantless search violated appellant's rights under the Fourth and Fourteenth Amendments to the United States Constitution and under Article I, Section 9 of the Texas Constitution. However, the record amply indicates that Mr. Goodhuys gave his consent to the search. A similar inspection was upheld in *United States v. Hammond Milling Co., 413 F.3d 608 (5th Cir. 1969), cert. denied,* 396 U.S. 1002, 90 S. Ct. 552, 24 L. Ed. 2d 494 (1970). The court there additionally held that there was no requirement that the appellant be aware of the right to refuse the inspection order to give valid consent to the inspection. *Id.* at 611. Although the consent to inspect was tacit or implied, it was no less valid. The inspection was lawful. *United States v. Hammond Milling Co., supra; United States v. Del Campo Baking Mfg. Co.,* 345 F. Supp. 1371 (D. Del. 1972); *United States v. Thriftmart,* 429 F.2d 106 (9th Cir. 1970), *cert. denied,* 400 U.S. 926, 91 S. Ct. 188, 27 L. Ed. 2d 185 (1970). The samples and photographs taken as part of the inspection are thus admissible. *United States v. Acri Wholesale Grocery Co.,* 409 F. Supp. 529 (S.D. Iowa 1976). This ground of error is overruled.

"Appellant attacks the sufficiency of the evidence to sustain the conviction. Specifically he contends that the evidence is insufficient to prove the elements of 'selling an adulterated product' and the required culpable mental state. The elements of the offense as alleged are:

"(1) a person

"(2) in the course of business

"(3) intentionally or knowingly

"(4) sells an adulterated product.

"V.T.C.A. Penal Code, Section 32.42(a)(1) defines 'adulterated' as 'varying from the standard of composition or quality prescribed by law or set by established commercial usage' and the Texas Food, Drug, and Cosmetic Act, supra, deems food to be adulterated 'if it has been produced, prepared, packaged or held under unsanitary conditions whereby it may have been rendered injurious to health.'

"Inspector Palmer testified he found several violations of sanitary standards at the Jean Pierre bakery including weevil infestation of flour, rodent feces, urine, and hair in and around flour sacks and cooking utensils, dirty and unsanitized cooking utensils, and a dead rat near the oven. He further testified that he observed actual sales of bakery goods take place during his inspection. The record also indicates that Mr. Goodhuys was stipulated as the owner of the bakery. Palmer testified that Goodhuys was present during this and previous inspections, and that Goodhuys indicated to Palmer that he was aware of the rodent problem in the bakery.

"Upon these facts there was sufficient proof of each element of the offense, and the evidence supports the trial court's judgment that the appellant is guilty of committing a deceptive trade practice beyond a reasonable doubt. This ground of error is overruled.

"The judgment is affirmed."

Judicial interpretation of the scope of the guaranty under section 303(c)(2) illustrates the limited nature of this defense. One court[12] has held unequivocally that the exemption clause protects a shipper only if he passes the product on in the same form as he receives it, without repacking it or subjecting it to any new hazards of adulteration not present when the original guaranty was given by the producer or manufacturer. Thus, a commercial food service operator who altered or further processed food products would also be guilty of a violation, even though he relied on a manufacturer's or producer's guaranty in good faith.

18:7 Injunctive Relief

Section 302(a) authorizes the appropriate court to prohibit violation of section 301 by issuing an injunctive order. This legislation was intended to halt repetitious offenses. Prior to its adoption, the guilty party was free to continue to violate the law once he had served his sentence or paid his fine. The misdemeanor penalty was not a substantial deterrent to a corporate defendant and in fact was an encouragement to maintain the *status quo*. Section 302(a) was also intended to relieve the government from the necessity of bringing multiple proceedings to secure compliance.[13]

When seeking injunctive relief, the government need not prove that the violations committed were willful or performed with knowledge that the acts or omissions violated the law. The significant issues are the probability of the continuance of the illegal conduct and the seriousness of that conduct.[14]

18:8 False Advertising

The Federal Trade Commission Act, sections 12 through 15, prohibits the dissemination of false food advertisements and empowers the Federal Trade Commission to enjoin food advertisers from disseminating advertisements that fail affirmatively to reveal that such products are dangerous or that their use under certain conditions can cause bodily injury. Such an injunction may be issued by means of an FTC cease and desist order, but where the public interest would be served, the Commission may bring suit in an appropriate court to enjoin such advertisements.

The dissemination of a false advertisement for food, where the use of the product may be injurious to health or where the dissemination is with intent to

---

[12]United States v. Crown Rubber Sundries Co., 67 F. Supp. 92 (N.D. Ohio 1946).

[13]Dunn, *The Food, Drug and Cosmetic Law*, 3 Food Drug Cosmetic L. Q. 308, 571 (1948).

[14]United States v. Dotterweich, 320 U.S. 277 (1943); United States v. Parfait Powder Puff Co., 163 F.2d 1008 (7th Cir. 1947), *cert. denied*, 332 U.S. 851 (1948).

defraud or mislead, constitutes a misdemeanor. A conviction carries a maximum penalty of a $10,000 fine or imprisonment for six months, or both. Succeeding convictions carry a maximum penalty of a $10,000 fine or imprisonment for one year, or both.

The term *food* is defined under section 15(b) to mean: "(1) articles used for food or drink for man or other animals, (2) chewing gum, and (3) articles used for components of any such article."

In the following case a federal district court construed the Food, Drug and Cosmetic Act to make starchblockers subject to regulation as a drug. In so doing the court differentiated between the treatment of foods and drugs under the act.

AMERICAN HEALTH PRODUCTS CO., INC. V. HAYES
574 F. Supp. 1498 (S.D.N.Y. 1983), *aff'd*, 744 F.2d 912 (2d Cir. 1984)

SOFAER, D.J.: ". . .Finally, a court's responsibility to construe the statute in accord with its protective purposes does not confer a license to ignore congressional judgments reflected in the classification scheme. *See 62 Cases of Jam v. United States*, 340 U.S. 593 600, 71 S. Ct. 515, 520, 95 L. Ed. 566 (1951); *NNFA v. Mathews*, 557 F.2d at 336–37. Items classified as foods by no means escape regulations. Though food manufacturers need not obtain premarketing approval for their products, they are still subject to the Act's provisions on adulteration and misbranding. 21 U.S.C. §§ 342, 343. To enforce these provisions, the FDA may inspect factories, *id*. § 374; commerce seizures of adulterated foods, *id*. § 334; seek injunctions against the sale of adulterated or misbranded food, *id*. § 332; and seek criminal penalties in appropriate cases, *id*. § 333. Though these provisions do not bear directly on the threshold question whether an item is a food or a drug, they do support the inference that congress determined that a different level of regulation was adequate to protect the public in the case of an article commonly used for food, even though marketers of the product claim that it produces specific physiological effects. . . .

"Thus if an article affects bodily structure or function by way of its consumption as a food, the parenthetical [§ 321 (g) (1) (C)] precludes its regulation as a drug notwithstanding a manufacturer's representations as to physiological effect. The Act evidences throughout an objective to guarantee accurate information to consumers of foods, drugs, and cosmetics. *See, e.g.*, 21 U.S.C. § 343. The presence of the parenthetical in part (C) suggests that Congress did not want to inhibit the dissemination of useful information concerning a food's physiological properties by subjecting foods to drug regulation on the basis of representations in this regard. . . .

"The Seventh Circuit recently considered the identical question of the status of starchblockers. . . and concluded that they are drugs. *Nutrilab, Inc. v. Schweiker*, 713 F.2d 335 (7th Cir. 1983), *aff'g* 547 F. Supp. 880 (N.D. Ill. 1982). The *Nutrilab* district court had treated the issue as one of intended use, and held that ' "food" refers only to those items actually and solely. . . consumed either for taste, aroma, or nutritional value.' 547 F. Supp. at 883. The

Circuit Court found this definition 'unduly restrictive' because, it observed, 'some products such as coffee or prune juice are undoubtedly food but may be consumed on occasion for reasons other than taste, aroma, or nutritive value.' 713 F.2d at 338. It instead defined food as articles used '*primarily* for taste, aroma, or nutritive value.' *id.* (emphasis added), properly rejecting also any suggestion that the source of the product makes it a food, *id.* at 337.

"Here the manufacturers contend that starchblockers must be deemed a food because their biochemical composition varies from that of the bean flour used for making bread—a paradigmatic food—only by the percentage of each component and the addition of excipients and binders. This argument fails for the same reasons articulated in *Nutrilab.* The concentration of certain components during processing effects a significant physical change. The Supreme Court recently ruled in fact that the marketing of an established drug with different excipients and binders will necessitate submission of an application for approval as a new drug. *See United States v. Generix Drug Corp.*, [460] U.S. [453], 103 S. Ct. 1298, 75 L. Ed. 2d 198 (1983). Most fundamentally, the argument fails to address the Act's focus on usage."

In *State v. Glassman,*[15] the court interpreted New York's food-service deceptive advertising law to require proof of intention (*scienter*) to sustain a conviction of both a hotel coffee-shop operator and the owner of the hotel premises. The fact that Kosher food items purchased and advertised as Kosher were non-Kosher when offered to the public because they were not prepared in accordance with Orthodox Hebrew religious requirements did not constitute intent to defraud.

Section 15(a)(1) of the Act defines a false advertisement as one "which is misleading in a material respect." The advertiser need not intend to defraud in order to be found guilty of a violation of this section. The burden rests on the advertiser to prove that his advertisement is not misleading. It is not mandatory that the advertiser state anything. The only requirement is that if he does advertise, he shall not make statements that are materially misleading. This includes the duty to reveal facts that are material in light of representations made in the advertisement. The criterion is the capacity to deceive. Deception may be implied; it need not be explicitly stated, nor must any consumers be misled.[16]

The Supreme Court[17] has held that the Act confers upon the Commission not only the specific powers prescribed but all powers falling within the penumbra of meaning in the statute. "The courts will not interfere except where the remedy selected has no reasonable relation to the unlawful practices found to exist."[18] This means that the Commission may limit claims of benefits to the causes for

---

[15]109 Misc. 2d 1088. 441 N.Y.S.2d 346 (N.Y. Co. Ct. 1981).
[16]Christopher, *supra* note 2, at 733–34.
[17]Jacob Siegel Co. v. Federal Trade Commission, 327 U.S. 608 (1946).
[18]*Id.*

which the product or commodity is helpful. One court[19] refused to extend the Commission's authority to require affirmative disclosure of shortcomings where the product was not found harmful or injurious, but subsequent authorities[20] upheld Commission orders that included a specific finding that the failure to make the affirmative disclosure required by the order was itself deceptive.

Where a recognized trade name of otherwise good standing is sought to be enjoined, the Commission itself will apply a less drastic sanction if that remedy will adequately protect the public interest. Each case is judged on its individual merits, but an affirmative disclaimer in conjunction with the use of the name will suffice and not destroy the legitimate economic interest of the owner of the trade name. But the fact that the name is a registered trademark is not controlling.[21]

In the area of food products, the Commission[22] has enjoined a commercial baker of bread from informing the public that the bread contains fewer calories than other commercial breads or that the bread will cause a loss of weight or prevent weight gain or that such bread is useful in a weight control diet, unless the baker affirmatively disclosed in immediate conjunction with such advertising that the bread has no fewer calories than other commercial breads and that its usefulness in a weight control diet derives from the fact that it is sliced thinner. The FTC order was affirmed on appeal.[23]

In *Federal Trade Commission v. Colgate-Palmolive Co.*,[24] the Supreme Court sustained an FTC order that prohibited an advertiser from giving the viewing public the false impression that a test, experiment, or demonstration shown in a television commercial is proof of performance claims of the product if the commercial shows a mock-up rather than the actual test. In other words, where the means used to demonstrate claims are themselves materially misleading, the advertisement is equally misleading, even though the advertiser honestly believes that the means used will prove a certain product claim.

The prohibition against the false advertising is not limited to the producer or manufacturer of the product or commodity. Advertising agencies are equally liable. "The agency more so than its principal should have known whether the advertisements had the capacity to mislead or deceive the public. . . . Its responsibility. . . cannot be shifted to the principal who is liable in any event."[25]

Nor is the retailer immune from responsibility. The FTC has recently taken a retail drug store to task for disseminating false and misleading advertising material when it underwrote the cost of advertising weight-loss pills carried by the

---

[19]Alberty v. Federal Trade Commission, 182 F.2d 36 (D.C. Cir. 1950).

[20]Wybrant System Products Corp. v. Federal Trade Commission, 266 F.2d 511 (2d Cir. 1959); Erikson Hair and Scalp Specialists v. Federal Trade Commission, 276 F.2d 952 (2d Cir. 1960).

[21]Charles of the Ritz Distributors v. Federal Trade Commission, 143 F.2d 676 (2d Cir. 1944).

[22]Matter of National Bakers Services, Inc. v. Federal Trade Commission, FTC docket 7480 (1963).

[23]National Bakers Services, Inc. v. Federal Trade Commission, 329 F.2d 365 (7th Cir. 1964).

[24]380 U.S. 374 (1965). Called into doubt by Puerto Rico Tele-Con, Inc. v. Ocasio Rodriques, ——F. Supp.——, WC 145 743 (July 24, 1990).

[25]Federal Trade Commission v. Merck & Co., 69 F.T.C. 526 (1966).

retailer. What was found especially reprehensible was the message that the consumer could avoid changing his eating habits, when weight reduction by reducing calorie intake was critical to the success of the total dietary program.[26]

18:9   *Remedial Consumer Advertising*

Independently of existing FTC authority to order false advertisers to include an affirmative disclaimer of shortcomings in future advertisements, a 1978 decision[27] reaffirmed such authority and enabled the Commission to disregard any prior arbitrary limit on the amount of money the manufacturer would be compelled to expend for this purpose. The length of time such a corrective message must be disseminated before the harm to the public has dissipated is determined on a case-by-case basis. One criterion may be the length of time the advertiser utilized in making the original claims that are the subject of FTC remedial action. No question exists that the cost of the remedy to the advertiser will be substantial in any case.

18:10   *Emergence of Truth-in-Menu Acts*

In the majority of the statutes previously reported and analyzed, the thrust of the governmental effort to ensure protection of public health has been aimed at the manufacturer, producer, or grower of the food and beverage product, rather than the retail commercial dispenser of the product, either in its original form or as an ingredient in a dish or beverage, prepared and served for consumption on or off the premises. The statutes themselves are not so circumscribed, nor does the fact that the appropriate regulatory body chooses to forego prosecution or other action against a particular segment of the industry forestall or inhibit later actions against other parties in the industry.

In practice, however, regulation of retail food service establishments has been left to the states, and the typical method of ensuring compliance with appropriate standards has been the enactment and enforcement of a state or municipal health and sanitation code that prescribes what is required and authorizes civil and criminal penalties for violations. This authority is coupled with the administrative power to issue, deny, suspend, and revoke health permits for food service establishments found not in conformity with or in violation of law. The most severe sanction, outright revocation, is usually reserved for willful violations after due notice and opportunity to comply have been deliberately ignored and if the violations create a reasonably imminent apprehension of harm to the public.

All the states have a general food and drug act. Some are patterned after the original federal Pure Food and Drugs Act of 1906, some after the current Food,

---

[26]*In re* Porter and Deitsch, Inc., noted in *Legal Developments in Marketing*, 42 J. Mkting. 90 (Oct. 1978).

[27]Warner-Lambert v. Federal Trade Commission, 62 F.2d 749 (7th Cir. 1977), *cert. denied*, 435 U.S. 950 (1978).

Drug and Cosmetic Act of 1938. Half of the states have substantially adopted the Uniform State Food, Drug and Cosmetic Bill, which is consistent with the 1938 act. Enforcement varies markedly from state to state. In addition, the states have enacted special laws that involve another layer of regulation affecting the food industry. No attempt will be made to review these enactments, other than to call attention to their existence and to the need to be aware of their general requirements, which often are modeled on federal provisions previously noted. It is beyond the scope of this chapter to attempt to list the overlapping sections of state laws that supplement the federal act. It is worth noting, though, that Congress has not totally preempted the power to regulate through adoption of the federal Food, Drug and Cosmetic Act and that the states are free to legislate so long as they do not attempt to regulate interstate commerce or do not contravene the federal act.

In the case below, the California Supreme Court applied its own consumer-protection statutes, including California's Sherman Food, Drug and Cosmetic Law, to allow consumer organizations to sue food manufacturers, retailers, and advertising agencies to halt deceptive trade practices in the sale of sugared cereals as nutritive food rather than as confections. In so doing, the court interpreted the statutes broadly to protect the public interest.

COMMITTEE ON CHILDREN'S TELEVISION, INC. v. GENERAL FOODS CORP.
35 Cal. 3d 197, 197 Cal. Rptr. 783, 673 P.2d 660 (1983)

BROUSSARD, J.: "The Plaintiffs appeal from a judgment of dismissal following a trial court order sustaining demurrers without leave to amend to their fourth amended complaint. The complaint essentially charges defendants—General Foods Corporation, Safeway Stores, and two advertising agencies—with fraudulent, misleading and deceptive advertising in the marketing of sugared breakfast cereals. The trial court found its allegations insufficient because they fail to state with specificity the advertisements containing the alleged misrepresentations. We review the allegations of the complaint and conclude that the trial court erred in sustaining demurrers without leave to amend to plaintiffs' causes of action charging fraud and violation of laws against unfair competition and deceptive advertising. . . .

Causes of Action Based on Consumer Protection Statutes

"Plaintiffs' first cause of action in the fourth amended complaint seeks injunctive relief and restitution under Business and Professions Code section 17200 and subsequent sections (the unfair competition law). The operative language appears in section 17203: 'Any person performing or proposing to perform an act of unfair competition within this state may be enjoined in any court of competent jurisdiction. The court may make such orders or judgments. . . as may be necessary to prevent the use or employment by any person of any practice which constitutes unfair competition. . . or as may be necessary to restore to any person in interest any money or property, real or personal, which may have been acquired by means of such unfair competition.'

"The term 'unfair competition' receives a broad definition. A recent Court of Appeal decision summarized its breadth. 'Historically, the tort of unfair business competition required a *competitive* injury. However the language of section 17200. . . "demonstrates a clear design to protect consumers as well as competitors by its final clause, permitting inter alia, any member of the public to sue on his own behalf or on behalf of the public generally." (*Barquis v. Merchants Collection Assn.* (1972) 7 Cal. 3d 94, 110 [101 Cal. Rptr. 745, 496 P.2d 817].) Thus, section 17200 is not confined to anti-competitive business practice but is equally directed toward " 'the right of the *public* to protection from fraud and deceit.' " (*Ibid.*) Furthermore, the section 17200 proscription of "unfair competition" is not restricted to deceptive or fraudulent conduct but extends to any *unlawful* business practice (*id.*, at p. 111 [101 Cal. Rptr. 745, 496 P.2d 817]). The Legislature apparently intended to permit courts to enjoin ongoing wrongful business conduct in whatever context such activity might occur (*id.*, at p. 111 [101 Cal. Rptr. 745, 496 P.2d 817]; *People v. McKale* (1979) 25 Cal. 3d 626, 632 [159 Cal. Rptr. 811, 602 P.2d 731]; *see also* Howard, *Former Civil Code, Section 3369: A Study in Judicial Interpretation* (1979) 30 Hastings L.J. 705. Note, *Unlawful Agricultural Working Conditions as Nuisance or Unfair Competition* (1968) 19 Hastings L.J. 398, 408–409). (*Stoiber v. Honeychuck* (1980) 101 Cal. App. 3d 903, 927, 162 Cal. Rptr. 194.)

"Plaintiffs' second cause of action is based on Business and Professions Code section 17500 and subsequent sections (the false advertising law), which prohibits the dissemination in any advertising media of any 'statement' concerning real or personal property offered for sale, 'which is untrue or misleading, and which is unknown, or which by the exercise of reasonable care should be known, to be untrue or misleading.' (Bus. & Prof. Code, § 17500.) Section 17535 authorizes injunctive relief and restitution. (*See Fletcher v. Security Pacific National Bank* (1979) 23 Cal. 3d 442, 450, 153 Cal. Rptr. 28, 591 P.2d 51.) Any violation of the false advertising law, moreover, necessarily violates the unfair competition law.

"In addition to the causes of action asserted in the fourth amended complaint, plaintiffs' second amended complaint also asserted a cause of action based on the Sherman Food, Drug and Cosmetic Law (Health & Saf. Code, § 26000 *et seq.*). Section 26460 provides that '[i]t is unlawful for any person to disseminate any false advertising of any food, drug, device, or cosmetic. An advertisement is false if it is false or misleading in any particular.' Unlike the Business and Professions Code provisions cited earlier, this act does not expressly provide for private enforcement. The parties vigorously dispute whether a private right of action should be implied under this statute, but the question is immaterial since any unlawful business practice, including violations of the Sherman Law, may be redressed by a private action charging unfair competition in violation of Business and Professions Code sections 17200 and 17203.

"In sum, plaintiffs rely on three statutes—the unfair competition law, the false advertising law, and the Sherman Food, Drug and Cosmetic Law—all of which in similar language prohibit false, unfair, misleading, or deceptive advertising. In the present context we discern no difference in the scope of these enactments (apart from the fact that the Sherman law is limited to food, drugs, and cosmetics) or the meaning of their provisions. We proceed, therefore, on the basis that any advertising scheme involving false, unfair, misleading or deceptive advertising of food products equally violates all three statutes.

"To state a cause of action under these statutes for injunctive relief, it is necessary only to show that 'members of the public are likely to be deceived.' (*Chern v. Bank of America,* (1976) 15 Cal. 3d 866, 876, 127 Cal. Rptr. 110, 544 P.2d 1310; *see Payne v. United California Bank* (1972) 23 Cal. App. 3d 850, 856, 100 Cal. Rptr. 672 and cases there cited.) Allegations of actual deception, reasonable reliance, and damage are unnecessary. The court may also order restitution without individualized proof of deception, reliance, and injury if it 'determines that such a remedy is necessary "to prevent the use or employment" of the unfair practice. . . .' (*Fletcher v. Security Pacific National Bank, supra,* 23 Cal. 3d 442, 453, 158 Cal. Rptr. 591 P.2d 51.)

"Insofar as plaintiffs seek injunctive relief and restitution under the cited consumer protection statutes, defendants' principal basis for demurrer is the charge that the complaint fails to describe the alleged deceptive practices with sufficient particularity. Defendants assert that plaintiffs should not merely describe the substance of the misrepresentations, but should state the specific deceptive language employed, identify the persons making the misrepresentations and those to whom they were made, and indicate the date, time and place of the deception. . . .

"The fourth amended complaint in the present case describes the alleged deceptive scheme in considerable detail. Paragraph 35 alleges some 19 misrepresentations—some general, others relatively specific. Paragraph 42 lists material facts which are not disclosed. Finally, plaintiffs allege that each misrepresentation appears (and every listed material fact is concealed) in every advertisement for the specified product during the period in question. There is thus no doubt as to what advertisements are at issue, nor as to what deceptive practices are called into question. We believe these allegations are sufficient to notify the defendants of the claim made against them, and to frame the issues for litigation. . . ."

Because the appropriate federal authorities had neither the resources nor the inclination to pursue the retail segment of the industry, particularly with respect to consumer fraud and misrepresentation in menus and advertising promotions, coupons, flyers, and the like, the states began to adopt legislation aimed at regulating the advertising of foods. California, the first to adopt such regulations, defined the term *adulteration* as including fraudulent or misleading statements in connection with the preparation and service of foods.

The following are the pertinent provisions of the California Business and Professions Code and the Health and Safety Code:

1. *Business and Professions Code.* Section 17500, False or Misleading Statements Generally.

It is unlawful for any person, firm, corporation or association, or any employee thereof with intent directly or indirectly to dispose of real or personal property or to perform services, professional or otherwise, or anything of any nature whatsoever or to induce the public to enter into any obligation relating thereto, to make or disseminate or cause to be made or disseminated before the public in this State, in any newspaper or other publication, or any advertising device, or by public outcry or proclamation, or in any other manner or means whatever any statement, concerning such real or personal property or services, professional or otherwise, or concerning any circumstance or matter of fact connected with the proposed performance or disposition thereof, which is untrue or misleading and which is known, or which by the exercise of reasonable care should be known, to be untrue or misleading, or for any such person, firm or corporation to so make or disseminate or cause to be so made or disseminated any such statement as part of a plan or scheme with the intent not to sell such personal property or services, professional or otherwise so advertised at the price stated therein, or as so advertised. Any violation of the provisions of this section is a misdemeanor punishable by imprisonment in the county jail not exceeding six months, or by a fine not exceeding two thousand five hundred dollars ($2,500), or by both.

In addition, any violator is subject to a $2,500 maximum civil penalty. These penalties are not cumulative, but apply to each violation.

2. *Health and Safety Code.* Sections 26460, 26461, 26528, and 26534

Section 26460. It is unlawful for any person to disseminate any false advertisement of any food. . . . An advertisement is false if it is false or misleading in any particular.

Section 26461. It is unlawful for any person to manufacture, sell, deliver, hold, or offer for sale any food. . . that is falsely advertised. . . .

Section 26528. Any food is adulterated if any one of the following conditions exists:

(a) If any valuable constituent has been in whole or in part omitted or abstracted therefrom.

(b) If any substance has been substituted wholly or in part therefor.

(c) If damage or inferiority has been concealed in any manner.

(d) If any substance has been added thereto or mixed or packed therewith so as to increase its bulk or weight to reduce its quality or strength or make it appear better or of greater value than it is. . . .

Section 26534. It is unlawful for any person to manufacture, sell, deliver, hold, or offer for sale any food that is adulterated.

Violations of these sections of the Health and Safety Code are misdemeanors that subject violators to imprisonment in the county jail for not more than six months or the imposition of a fine of not more than $1,000, or both. Subsequent convictions or violations committed with intent to defraud or mislead subject violators to one year in jail or a $1,000 fine, or both.

The policy memorandum issued by the Environment Management Staff of the Los Angeles County Department of Health Services on September 27, 1976, is excerpted below. It reflects the enforcement of truth-in-menu legislation in a jurisdiction with a substantial number of restaurants.

Purpose:

One of the goals of this Department is to assure that food provided for human consumption is safe, free of adulteration, sanitary and properly labeled and advertised. The purpose of this policy statement is to specify those types of violations which constitute false advertising (menu misrepresentation) and to delineate enforcement policy for such violations.

Types of Violations:

There are many types of misrepresentations found on restaurant menus. The most common violations are:

Quality or grade of products misrepresented which includes:

Adulteration of products.

Substitution of food which is of lesser quality or which is different than advertised (i.e., grade or brand name, species of fish or meat, type or cut of meat not as advertised).

Hamburger not meeting definition specifications.

Imitation hamburger not meeting definition specifications and/or list of ingredients, if required, not posted.

Dairy products not meeting definition specifications.

Point of origin of food products not as advertised.

Size, weight or portion of food not as advertised.

Merchandising term of advertised food not accurate.

Products advertised as fresh which have been frozen, canned or preserved.

Enforcement Policy:

Strict Enforcement: Violations regarding adulteration; substitution; hamburger/imitation hamburger; dairy products; point of origin; size or weight; and products advertised as fresh *shall* be referred to the appropriate District/City Attorney for criminal or civil prosecution.

Any type of intentional or negligent violation may be strictly enforced.

General Enforcement: Violations involving misleading or unsubstantiated merchandising terms; and violations involving method of preparation shall call for issuance of orders with not more than 30 days for compliance. District/Program Directors may elect to hold hearings where partial compliance has been achieved. Prosecution shall follow if full compliance is not obtained. Under appropriate circumstances, referral to District/City Attorney may be made even if full compliance is obtained.

Menu Misrepresentation—Violation Guidelines:

This policy statement will provide guidelines for terminology, outline enforcement codes and sections and clarify policy interpretations for violations involving misrepresentations found on restaurant* menus. It is a guideline only and is not all-inclusive.

Enforcement Codes and Sections:

I. Substitution:

Restaurants offering food of a lesser quality or value than advertised in the menu or any substitution of one food item for another whether or not of lesser quality or value, *without informing the customer,* are false advertising and this constitutes a civil violation of Section 17500, Business and Professions Code (B & P Code) and of Section 3369 of the Civil Code and a criminal violation of Sections 26460 & 26461 Health & Safety Code (H & S Code–Sherman Food & Drug Law). Such violations include but are not limited to the following:

Substituting a grade product lower than that advertised.

Substituting a brand name other than that advertised.

Substituting a species of fish or meat other than that advertised.

Substituting a type/cut of meat other than that advertised.

II. *Hamburger (ground beef):*

Restaurants offering food identified as "hamburger," "burger" or any other cognate thereof on the menu or any other advertising which does not meet the specifications defining hamburger in Section 26595(a), H & S Code constitutes a civil violation of Section 17500, B & P Code and a criminal violation of Sections 26460 & 26461 H & S Code.

III. *Imitation hamburger:*

Restaurants offering food identified as "imitation hamburger" in the menu or any other advertising which does not meet the specifications defining imitation hamburger in Section 26595(b), H & S Code or where a list of ingredients is not on the menu or posted as required in Section 26595, H & S Code, this constitutes a civil violation of Section 17500, B & P Code and a criminal violation of Sections 26460 & 26461, H & S Code.

IV. *Points of origin:*

Restaurants offering food advertised in the menu or any other advertising as originating from a specific geographic place or area must be substantiated as originating from that place or area. Where it cannot be substantiated by observing the labels, bulk packages or boxes in which the product was shipped or by the invoice or other means that such advertised products originate from the advertised place or area, this constitutes a civil violation of Section 17500, B & P Code and criminal violation of Sections 26460 & 26461 H & S Code.

V. *Size or weight of portions:*

Restaurants offering food advertised in the menu or any other advertising as of a specified size or weight portion must be verified by checking the labels or invoices or in-field weighing of food portions prior to preparation.

Where it cannot be verified that such food products are of the advertised size or portion, this constitutes a civil violation of Section 17500, B & P Code and a criminal violation of Sections 26460 & 26461 H & S Code.

VI. *Merchandising terms:*

Restaurants whose menu or other advertising contain merchandising terms relating to a particular food product offered for sale must state these terms accurately. Merchandising terms relating to the quality, quantity, method of preparation or characteristics of the food product served to the consumer which cannot be verified by the owner or by observation, checking the product, label or invoice or discussion with the chefs or cooks are questionable and misleading. This includes merchandising statements as: Best Blend; Our Own Special Sauce; Finest Quality; Fresh Daily; homestyle or homemade style, etc. Where such representations cannot be verified this constitutes a civil violation of Section 17500, B & P Code and a criminal violation of Sections 26460 & 26461, H & S Code.

It should be emphasized that no food or beverage prepared in a private home shall be permitted to be used in preparation of foods or beverages, offered for sale, sold or given away in a restaurant. If products are found which are actually made in a private home, a complaint shall be issued immediately for violation of Section 28571 H & S Code. If food is prepared in the restaurant kitchen from a recipe under conditions and with ingredients similar to those used in the home, the food may be advertised as "homestyle" or "homemade style."

*"Restaurant" as used in this procedure statement means—restaurant, itinerant restaurant, vehicles, vending machines, or institutions including schools, etc. as defined in Section 26595(c) California Sherman Food, Drug and Cosmetic Law.

No judicial decision has yet dealt with the constitutionality of the California truth-in-menu statute, undoubtedly because the legislative authority to regulate false and misleading advertising claims of businesses is too well settled for citation. This inherent exercise of the power to police commercial conduct in the public interest is especially justified when the subject is public health.

New Jersey, Nebraska, and Missouri on the state level and Chicago and the District of Columbia on the municipal level have made a considerable effort to police such violations under existing or new guidelines. Both New York State and New York City have prepared, but not yet introduced, legislation that would not only prohibit misrepresentations, but would also forbid making substitutions without informing the consumer; require descriptions of beverages to state the serving size; require MSG (monosodium glutamate) to be listed on the menu; require that a menu be posted which is visible outside the premises and which includes prices per item; and forbid the use of descriptive terms unless the accuracy of such terms could be verified. Each violation would carry a penalty ranging from $25 to $250.

18:11　*Regulation of Smoking in Restaurants and Similar Public Places*

Public health regulation of smoking and the rights of smokers and nonsmokers in places of public accommodation, particularly in food-service enterprises, have become more numerous at the state and municipal levels since Minnesota adopted its Indoor Clean Air Act in 1975. One of the most comprehensive of its type, the law prohibits smoking in public places except in designated smoking sections. At least 25 percent of restaurant tables must be set aside for nonsmoking patrons. Bars and taverns are excepted, but signs to that effect must be posted. Violators are subject to civil fines of not more than $100.

New York State enacted its own far-reaching Clean Indoor Air Act (Article 13, section 1399n–x of the Public Health Law) in 1989. Section 1399o (5) requires all food-service establishments with a seating capacity of greater than fifty persons to designate 70 percent of the seating capacity as a nonsmoking area and to prominently post a notice at the entrance of each such establishment advising customers of the availability of the nonsmoking area and permitting each customer to state his or her preference. It also permits each establishment to designate a separate enclosed room or rooms for use by smokers. Bars are exempt, as are convention rooms. Local governments are permitted to enact more-stringent antismoking laws. Hotels and motels that choose to develop and implement a smoking policy for guest rooms must post at the reception area a notice as to the availability, upon request, of no-smoking rooms.

Forty-two states have adopted laws restricting smoking. Other than the Minnesota law, the New York law is the most stringent.

The question of whether freedom from tobacco smoke in public places is a civil right is the subject of the following case.

GASPER v. LOUISIANA STADIUM AND EXPOSITION DISTRICT
418 F. Supp. 716 (E.D. La. 1976), *aff'd*, 577 F.2d 897 (5th Cir. 1978)

GORDON, D.J.: "This action is brought pursuant to the provisions of 42 U.S.C., § 1983, and 28 U.S.C., § 1343, in an attempt by the named plaintiffs [Gasper is a pseudonym for the class of nonsmoker plaintiffs] to enjoin the Louisiana Stadium and Exposition District from continuing to allow tobacco-smoking in the Louisiana Superdome during events staged therein. The Louisiana Superdome is an enclosed arena located in New Orleans, Louisiana, owned and maintained by a political subdivision of the State of Louisiana known as the Louisiana Stadium and Exposition District (hereinafter referred to as "LSED"). The building is a public, multipurpose facility, and, since its completion, has been used for many events ranging from concerts to Mardi Gras parades.

"The Plaintiffs. . ., individually and as representatives of other nonsmokers who have attended, or who will attend, such functions in the Louisiana Superdome, challenge LSED's permissive attitude toward smoking as being constitutionally violative of their right to breathe smoke-free air while in a State building. In support of their complaint, the plaintiffs aver that by allowing patrons to smoke in the Louisiana Superdome, LSED is causing other nonsmokers involuntarily to consume hazardous tobacco smoke, thereby causing physical harm and discomfort to those nonsmokers, as well as interfering with their enjoyment of events for which they have paid the price of admission, all in violation of the First, Fifth, Ninth and Fourteenth Amendments to the United States Constitution.

"The defendants have filed a motion to dismiss the complaint pursuant to Rule 12(b)(6), Federal Rules of Civil Procedure, contending the plaintiffs have failed to state claims upon which relief can be granted, in that nothing in the United States Constitution grants unto plaintiffs the rights they claim to have been violated.

"Just as the First Amendment protects against the making of any law which would abridge the freedom of speech or the press, it also protects against any law or activity which would interfere with or contract the concomitant rights to receive those thoughts disseminated under the protection of the First Amendment. As the Court in *Griswold v. State of Connecticut*, 381 U.S. 479, 85 S. Ct.

1678, 14 L. Ed. 2d 510 (1965) said, 'Without those peripheral rights the specific rights would be less secure.' *See also, Stanley v. Georgia,* 394 U.S. 557, 89 S. Ct. 1243, 22 L. Ed. 2d 542 (1969).

"It is this peripheral right to receive others' thoughts and ideas that the plaintiffs herein contend is being subverted by the State's condoning tobacco-smoking in the Louisiana Superdome. The nonsmokers argue that the existence of tobacco smoke in the Superdome creates a chilling effect upon the exercise of their First Amendment rights, since they must breathe that harmful smoke as a precondition to enjoying events in the Superdome.

"To say that allowing smoking in the Louisiana Superdome creates a chilling effect upon the exercise of one's First Amendment rights has no more merit than an argument alleging that admission fees charged at such events have a chilling effect upon the exercise of such rights, or that the selling of beer violates First Amendment rights of those who refuse to attend events where alcoholic beverages are sold. This Court is of the opinion that the State's permissive attitude toward smoking in the Louisiana Superdome adequately preserves the delicate balance of individual rights without yielding to the temptation to intervene in purely private affairs. Hence, this Court finds no violation of the First Amendment to the United States Constitution.

"In further support of his [*sic*] argument that the State is violating Title 42, § 1983 of the United States Code, the plaintiffs cite the Fifth and Fourteenth Amendments to the Constitution, alleging that the State of Louisiana is unlawfully depriving those nonsmoking patrons of the Louisiana Superdome of their life, liberty and property without due process of law. The plaintiffs contend that the penumbral protection of the Fifth and Fourteenth Amendments includes the right to be free from hazardous tobacco smoke while in State buildings. . . .

"This Court is of the. . . opinion that the process of weighing one individual's right to be left alone, as opposed to other individuals' alleged rights under the Fifth and Fourteenth Amendments, is better left to the processes of the legislative branches of Government. For this reason, the rationale of *Tanner v. Armco Steel Corporation,* 340 F. Supp. 532 (S.D. Texas 1972) is more persuasive to this Court. In *Tanner,* the plaintiffs brought suit to recover for injuries allegedly sustained as a result of the exposure of their persons to air pollutants emitted by defendant's petroleum refineries and plants located along the Houston Ship Channel. As in the instant case, the plaintiffs in *Tanner* cited a potpourri of federal constitutional and statutory provisions to establish jurisdiction. The Court found both 'state action' and 'constitutional deprivation' lacking.

"After the Court acknowledged a recent boom of claims asserting the right of the general populace to enjoy a decent environment, it explained,

". . .the judicial process, though constitutional litigation, is peculiarly ill-suited to solving problems of environmental control. Because such problems frequently call for the delicate balancing of competing social interests, as well as the application of specialized expertise, it would appear that their resolution is best consigned initially to the legislative and administrative processes. Furthermore, the inevitable trade-off between economic and ecological values presents a subject matter which is inherently political, and which is far too serious to relegate to the ad hoc process of 'government by lawsuit' in the midst of a statutory vacuum. . . .

"No legally enforceable right to a healthful environment, giving rise to an action for damages, is guaranteed by the Fourteenth Amendment or any other provision of the federal Constitution. [*Tanner v. Armco Steel Corp., supra,* 340 F. Supp. at 536, 537.]

"*Accord, Hagedorn v. Union Carbide Corp.,* 363 F. Supp. 1061 (N.D. West Va., 1973), (holding that plaintiff's allegations that emissions from Union Carbide Corporation's plant in West Virginia were fouling the air did not present a controversy arising under the Fifth, Ninth or Fourteenth Amendments to the Constitution); *see also, Doak v. City of Claxton, Georgia,* 390 F. Supp. 753 (S.D. Ga. 1975.)

"This language accurately reflects the fact that the courts have never seriously considered the right to a clean environment to be constitutionally protected under the Fifth and Fourteenth Amendments. It is well established that the Constitution does not provide judicial remedies for every social and economic ill. *Lindsey v. Normet,* 405 U.S. 56. . . (1972). Accordingly, if this Court were to recognize that the Fifth and Fourteenth Amendments provide the judicial means to prohibit smoking, it would be creating a legal avenue, heretofore unavailable, through which an individual could attempt to regulate the social habits of his neighbor. This Court is not prepared to accept the preposition that life-tenured members of the federal judiciary should engage in such basic adjustments of individual behavior and liberties.

"Citing the Ninth Amendment to the United States Constitution and *Griswold v. State of Connecticut,* 381 U.S. 479, 85 S. Ct. 1678, 14. L. Ed. 2d 510 (1965), the plaintiff finally argues that the right to breathe clean air is a fundamental right, although not specifically enumerated in the Bill of Rights, and is thus protected by the Constitution. The Ninth Amendment reads, 'The enumeration in the Constitution of certain rights, shall not be construed to deny or disparage others retained by the people.' U.S.C.A. Const. Amend. 9.

"The Ninth Amendment renaissance began with *Griswold v. State of Connecticut, supra,* wherein the Court recognized that the right of privacy in a marital relationship is a fundamental right protected by the Constitution. The plaintiffs herein contend that the right to be free from hazardous smoke fumes caused by the smoking of tobacco is as fundamental as the right of privacy recognized in the *Griswold* decision. This Court does not agree. . . .

"This Court feels that, unlike the right of privacy as it relates to the institution of marriage, the 'right' to breathe smoke-free air while attending events in the Louisiana Superdome certainly does not rise to those constitutional proportions envisioned in *Griswold v. State of Connecticut.* To hold otherwise would be to invite government by the judiciary in the regulation of every conceivable ill or so-called 'right' in our litigious-minded society. The inevitable result would be that type of tyranny from which our founding fathers sought to protect the people by adopting the first ten amendments to the Constitution.

''Pretermitting the issue of state involvement, this Court is satisfied that the plaintiffs herein have failed to allege a deprivation of any right secured by the United States Constitution and, hence, have failed to state a claim upon which relief could be grated under 42 U.S.C. § 1983. It is worth repeating that the United States Constitution does not provide judicial remedies for every social and economic ill. For the Constitution to be read to protect nonsmokers from inhaling tobacco smoke would be to broaden the rights of the Constitution to limits heretofore unheard of, and to engage in that type of adjustment of individual liberties better left to the people acting through legislative processes.

''Accordingly, it is ordered that the defendants' motion to dismiss the plaintiffs' complaint be and is hereby granted.''

Until there is conclusive medical evidence that smoking poses a serious health threat to nonsmokers, a total legislative ban on smoking in places of public accommodation is not likely, except in airplanes, buses, and similar public conveyances with ''captive audiences,'' Such proscriptions would necessarily infringe upon smokers' rights, noted in the *Gasper* opinion, *supra*.

Although smoking in a dining area may be annoying to some patrons, it is a source of relaxation and pleasure to others. Current legislation reflects traditional tenets of freedom of choice; it creates separate but equal seating, with a minimum number of seats required for nonsmokers, and exempts bars and taverns from such limitations so long as tavern operators post signs to that effect. This accommodation undoubtedly reflects a legislative compromise, since the risk to health, if any, is the same to both the bar patron and food service customer. Indeed, drinking establishments may become the final refuge for the smoker who eschews sharing breathing space with the nonsmoker.

18:12 *Workplace Smoking Laws*

The New York Indoor Clean Air Act also governs smoking in the workplace. All employers must adopt and implement a written smoking policy that (1) provides nonsmoking employees with a smoke-free work area; (2) provides a contiguous nonsmoking area in employee cafeterias, lunch rooms, and lounges; (3) prohibits smoking in conference rooms and meeting rooms unless all employees in that room agree to permit smoking; and (4) in the event an employer cannot otherwise comply with an employee's request for a smoke-free work area, requires that the employee's work area be designated as a smoke-free area. Prominent posting of the smoking policy is mandated.

Forty-two states regulate workplace smoking. The federal government restricts smoking in government buildings in eating areas and other public places. The Federal Aviation Act prohibits smoking on all domestic airline flights of two hours' or less duration.

In a related context, a federal circuit court of appeals rejected the claim that the federal Constitution sanctions federal courts to impose no-smoking rules in the workplace.

KENSELL V. STATE OF OKLAHOMA
716 F.2d 1350 (10th Cir. 1983)

LOGAN, C.J.: "After examining the briefs and the appellate record, this three-judge panel has determined unanimously that oral argument would not be of material assistance in the determination of this appeal. *See* Fed. R. App. P. 34(a); Tenth Cir. R. 10(e). The cause is therefore ordered submitted without oral argument.

"Plaintiff L. Anthony Kensell appeals a judgment granting a motion to dismiss his amended complaint for failure to state a claim upon which relief can be granted. Fed. R. Civ. P. 12(b)(6). Alleging that he suffers from respiratory and cardiovascular ailments, the plaintiff brought a suit under 42 U.S.C. § 1983, claiming that the State of Oklahoma and various officers and employees of the State of Oklahoma violated his constitutional rights under the First, Fifth, Ninth, and Fourteenth Amendments by failing to prohibit smoking in the area where plaintiff worked at the Oklahoma Department of Human Services. He sought damages and injunctive relief.

"A complaint should not be dismissed for failure to state a claim unless it appears beyond doubt that the plaintiff can prove no set of facts that would entitle him to recover. *Conley v. Gibson,* 355 U.S. 41, 78 S. Ct. 99, 2 L. Ed. 2d 80 (1957). We affirm the district court's dismissal of the complaint; clearly the plaintiff could not prove that he was deprived of a federal right.

"The plaintiff asserts that the defendants' failure to provide a smoke-free workplace violated his First Amendment rights because the smoke interfered with his ability to think. In support of that argument, appellant cites only *Rogers v. Okin,* 478 F. Supp. 1342 (D. Mass. 1979), *aff'd in part, rev'd in part,* 634 F.2d 650 (1st Cir. 1980), *vacated sub nom. Mills v. Rogers,* 457 U.S. 291, 102 S. Ct. 2442, 73 L. Ed. 2d 16(1982), a class action brought by patients at a Massachusetts state mental institution. Part of the relief those patients sought was an injunction against the forcible injection of psychotrophic drugs. The district court held that the right to think was an aspect of the right of privacy, with its roots in the First Amendment, and that, absent an emergency, forcible injections of such drugs violated the patients' right to think. *Id.* at 1367.

"The plaintiff also claims that by allowing smoking in his workplace the defendants assaulted him and thereby deprived him of his constitutional rights. In support he cites cases in which police and prison personnel have been held liable under section 1983 for assaults against persons in their custody. Finally, the plaintiff alleges that he was deprived of property right in his state job because his only options were to endure cigarette smoke or quit. We note that the plaintiff still is an employee of the Department of Human Resources; thus, he has no constructive discharge claim. His contention that he must quit his job or endure the smoke is legally distinguishable from his claim that his constitutional rights are violated by his being assaulted on the job by cigarette smoke.

"The intrusions upon the plaintiff's person resulting from working with fellow servants who smoke is a far cry from forcible injections of mind altering drugs and assaults committed by police or prison officials to intimidate or punish persons in their custody. This is not a case in which governmental officers are abusing power they posses only because the government is sovereign. In essence, the plaintiff has voluntarily accepted employment in an office in which he knew or should have known other employees smoke. Upon discovering that he is allergic to smoke or that it exacerbates his health problems, instead of quitting or transferring he seeks to force his employer to install a no-smoking rule in the office or to segregate smokers from nonsmokers. The state as his employer no doubt has the power to grant his request. As sovereign, it can make exposing him to smoke a tort, *see Shimp v. New Jersey Bell Telephone Co.*, 145 N.J. Super. 516, 368 A.2d 408 (1976), or a crime. *See* Okla. Stat. Ann. tit. 21, § 1247. We are certain, however, that the United States Constitution does not empower the federal judiciary, upon the plaintiff's application, to impose no-smoking rules in the plaintiff's workplace. To do so would support the most extreme expectations of the critics who fear the federal judiciary as a superlegislature promulgating social change under the guise of securing constitutional rights. *Accord Fed. Employees for Nonsmokers' Rights (FENSR) v. United States*, 446 F. Supp. 181 (D.D.C. 1978), *aff'd mem.*, 598 F.2d 310 (D.C. Cir. 1979); *Gasper v. Louisiana Stadium and Exposition Dist.*, 418 F. Supp. 716 (E.D. La 1976), *aff'd*, 577 F.2d 897 (5th Cir. 1978). . . .

"AFFIRMED."

The District of Columbia Court of Appeals has likewise ruled that no common-law duty exists to require an employer to provide a smoke-free environment for an employee who is especially sensitive to tobacco smoke.[28]

18:13 *Public Health Provisions Regarding Emergency First Aid to Food-Service Patrons Choking on Food*

In 1980, New York adopted Public Health Law 1532–b, requiring all public food-service establishments to post first-aid instructions regarding assistance to patrons choking on food lodged in their throats. Failure to post the instructions, known as the Heimlich maneuver, does not itself impose liability upon the operator or the employees in any civil lawsuit brought by a patron injured in a choking emergency. Nor does the statute impose any legal duty on any operator, employee, or other person to remove or assist in removing food from the throat of a choking victim. Regardless of any contrary local law or ordinance, any operator, employee, or other person who voluntarily and without expectation of compensation removes, assists in removing or attempts to remove food from a choking victim in accordance with the instructions adopted by the Department of Public Health may not be held liable for personal injuries or for the wrongful death of the victim by reason of any act or failure to act in the rendering of emergency assistance unless the resulting injuries or death was caused by gross negligence of the operator, employee, or other person. Local counsel should be

---

[28]Gordon v. Raven Systems & Research, Inc., 462 A.2d 10 (D.C. App. 1983).

consulted to determine whether or not similar laws have been adopted in other states and, if so, what requirements must be met.

18:14 *Licensing and Regulation of Alcoholic Beverage Dispensers*

No subject has aroused moral outrage and regulatory zeal than intoxication. The pursuit of temperance and the coopting of the liquor trade by notorious criminal elements during the Prohibition era prompted almost all states to establish and enforce alcoholic beverage control laws. These laws involve licensing and regulation of commercial traffic in all such commodities. They also cover activities that are associated with the consumption of alcoholic beverages, such as gambling, prostitution, drug sales, and other disorderly conduct. Because the proscribed conduct of the licensee, such as sale to minors and habitual drunkards, as well as of the patron, is made criminal by the legislature, the administrative authority of the appropriate liquor board or commission to suspend or revoke the license is supplemented by the threat of criminal prosecution, with a fine or imprisonment imposed in the event of a conviction.

Because a criminal prosecution or civil action can relate only to the violation or other wrong involved and usually results in but one conviction and penalty, the risk of conviction to the licensee may not be as serious as the administrative revocation of his license. Even if he has been found guilty of a violation, he may still continue to operate under his license until renewal time and may not be required to give it up unless he has committed a felony or other crimes involving moral turpitude which the legislature has deemed appropriate grounds for non-renewal. But the liquor control authority, independently of the judiciary, may revoke that license for reasons set forth in its grant of legislative powers and is not bound by any prior judicial determination favorable to the licensee. Since the revocation of a license terminates the operation of a bar or tavern, with limited likelihood of reconsideration by the authority, it is a much more serious sanction than either criminal prosecution or personal liability for inadequate supervision or injuries sustained by reason of the inebriation of a patron. Thus the governing bodies have wide latitude in regulating the industry and have an enormous effect upon the life blood of the licensee.

It is important to distinguish between the broad discretion given the regulatory body to deny any initial application for a license and the more limited discretion to suspend or revoke an existing license for alleged misconduct. The following New York authorities illustrate the general principle that presently the courts are prone to apply the more stringent judicial review traditionally reserved for license revocation to the denial of a new license. The liquor authority must establish noncompliance with express legislative mandates, with less discretion permitted the liquor authority to expand those mandates by implication. The distinction in treatment between applicants and existing licensees is based on the premise that an applicant who meets all express requirements should not be denied the right to do business simply because of concern about potential future violations of the applicable liquor law and regulations of the authority promulgated in conformity with that law. In *Show Boat of New Lebanon, Inc. v. N.Y. State Liquor Authority,*[29] the New York Court of Appeals stated: "The discretion of the Authority in denying a new application is broader than in revoking or suspending a license, and [judicial] review is limited to a determination whether the record discloses circumstances which leave no possible scope for the reasonable exercise of that discretion. . . . However, even this broad discretion must rest on a foundation of rationality."

Thus determinations to deny licenses have been annulled in New York where the history of the disorderliness of the premises under prior owners did not warrant the conclusion that the location would inevitably lead to disorderliness; where the neighborhood was found "sensitive" but there was no showing that the applicant would be unable to maintain orderly premises; or where speculation that the operation of the premises would in the future be in violation of the rules of the authority was unjustified.[30]

In another case on this subject, the same high court has held that the authority's discretion to deny an application is not unbridled, and has clarified the limits on the exercise of that discretion. Untimely disclosure of increased expenditures of an applicant does not require denial in the absence of evidence that the funds are from improper sources. Nor may the authority use the 200-foot distance requirement from churches and schools as a minimum, allowing itself to extend this statutory standard. Nor may the authority make assumptions about possible noise, traffic, and parking problems. These problems, should they materialize, can properly be considered at renewal. Finally, adverse community responses are legitimate only insofar as they present "objections otherwise cognizable" under the statute.[31]

18:15 *Disorderly Conduct*

All states treat the problem of allowing disorderly conduct as a violation of state alcoholic beverage control laws, either because the statute explicitly prohibits such conduct or because courts have interpreted the term *disorderly conduct* to include misconduct not otherwise defined.

Whereas the term *disorderly conduct* found in section 106 of the New York Alcoholic Beverage Control Law is not defined, the courts have interpreted the statutory language to include permitting fighting or assaults by either patrons or employees on the premises, a breach of the peace or other violation of public order, or disorderliness that constitutes a nuisance.[32]

Suffering the premises to become disorderly means something more than a mere happening on one occasion. There must be a showing of a continuous course of conduct or a demonstrated attitude toward the happening which es-

---

[29]33 A.D.2d 954, 306 N.Y.S.2d 859 (3d Dep't 1970), *aff'd,* 27 N.Y.2d 676, 262 N.E.2d 211 (1970) (mem. decision).
[30]Matter of Sled Hill Cafe v. Hostetter, 22 N.Y.2d 607, 612, 241 N.E.2d 714, 719 (1968).
[31]Circus Disco Ltd. v. N.Y. State Liquor Auth., 51 N.Y.2d 24, 409 N.E.2d 963 (1980).
[32]People ex rel. Fasone v. Arnella, 139 N.Y.S.2d 186 (Mag. Ct. 1954).

tablishes acquiescence. The test is what a reasonably perceptive and alert management ought to know about the conduct of its patrons.[33] Thus mere profanity on the premises does not constitute disorderly conduct if it can be shown that such language was commonplace in the neighborhood and not objected to by other patrons.[34]

California has also treated the problem by statute,[35] and the term *disorderly conduct* has been applied to a broad range of activities that involve threats to the safety or tranquillity of the surrounding neighborhood or conduct either independently illegal or constituting overt public displays of and attempts to gratify sexual urges.[36] The courts have construed the term both in common parlance and at common law to mean keeping any licensed premises as a place where acts prohibited by statute are habitually indulged in or permitted or where acts are performed which tend to corrupt the morals of the community or promote breaches of the peace.[37]

California and New York are representative of jurisdictions which make disorderly conduct grounds for the suspension or revocation of a retail alcoholic beverage license.

Following are examples of conduct or activities that either violate the statutes or have been found by court interpretation to fall under the term *disorderly conduct.*

18:16 *Gambling*

Section 106(6) of the New York Alcoholic Beverage Control Law, a representative enactment, provides that: "no person licensed to sell alcoholic beverages shall suffer or permit any gambling on the licensed premises, or suffer or permit such premises to become disorderly. The use of the licensed premises or any part thereof, for the sale of lottery tickets, playing of bingo or games of chance, when duly authorized and lawfully conducted thereon, shall not constitute gambling within the meaning of this subdivision."

In order to sustain a gambling violation, the regulatory body must establish that the misconduct was of sufficient duration to warrant the implication that the licensee suffered or permitted gambling upon its premises.[38] An isolated incident without the reasonable knowledge of the licensee is insufficient; the question is whether the licensee should have known. Actual knowledge need not be proved.

---

[33]Chipman Assoc., Inc. v. N.Y. State Liquor Auth., 47 A.D.2d 585, 363 N.Y.S.2d 162 (4th Dep't 1975).

[34]*See also* Castelluccio v. N.Y. State Liquor Auth., 14 N.Y.2d 702, 199 N.E.2d 157 (1964) (mem. decision), which deals with vulgar and obscene words by patrons and assault in nature of horseplay.

[35]Deering's Business and Professions Code, § 25601.

[36]Boreta Enterprises, Inc. v. Department of Alcoholic Beverage Control, 2 Cal. 3d 85, 465 P.2d 1 (1970).

[37]Los Robles Motor Lodge, Inc. v. Department of Alcoholic Beverage Control, 246 Cal. App. 2d 198, 54 Cal. Rptr. 547 (1966).

[38]Martin v. N.Y. State Liquor Auth., 41 N.Y.2d 78, 359 N.E.2d 389 (1976).

The knowledge of an employee is imputable to the licensee where the employee exercises managerial authority, that is, is given responsibility for the operation of the premises and the conduct of the activities thereon on more than a casual or temporary basis.[39] The fact that the employee does not have an official managerial title does not affect his status; it is his responsibilities that determine his managerial status.[40] In the case of a corporate licensee, there must be proof that the manager or a corporate officer had knowledge of or the opportunity through reasonable diligence to acquire knowledge of the illegal conduct.[41]

18:17   Employee Assault upon Inebriated Patron

Normally the licensee is responsible for the actions of his agents and employees where the employee is instrumental in creating disorder, regardless of whether the pattern of conduct is foreseeable. However, a single isolated act, occurring on the spur of the moment, does not establish that the licensee suffered or permitted his premises to become disorderly, unless the licensee or his manager knew or should have known of the asserted disorderly condition and tolerated its existence.[42]

The question whether the licensed premises had become disorderly is factual. If the authority has introduced substantial evidence in support of its determination, the courts must affirm it.[43]

A general guide for determining whether the licensee permitted or suffered disorderly conduct is whether the incident out of which the charge grew occurred without warning and was an isolated and spontaneous event which no amount of supervision was likely to prevent.[44]

18:18   Homosexual Activity

The mere presence of homosexuals upon the premises, known as such to the licensee, does not, standing alone, constitute disorderly conduct. To be considered disorderly conduct, gay dancing must be indecent, and there must be fondling which is open and obvious.[45] Thus where a licensee employed bouncers and a security system to detect and discourage gay patrons who were either soliciting or engaged in open sexual activities, and to remove the same, a single isolated incident in which an employee observed homosexual conduct was

---

[39]Id.

[40]Matter of Falso v. State Liquor Auth., 43 N.Y.2d 721, 372 N.E.2d 325 (1977).

[41]Triple S Tavern, Inc. v. N.Y. State Liquor Auth., 40 A.D.2d 522, 334 N.Y.S.2d 289 (1st Dep't 1972), aff'd, 31 N.Y.2d 1005, 294 N.E.2d 204 (1973).

[42]I.B.R. Enterprises, Inc. v. N.Y. State Liquor Auth., 67 A.D.2d 922, 413 N.Y.S.2d 36 (1st Dep't 1979).

[43]Peanut Butter Jam, Inc. v. N.Y. State Liquor Auth., 58 A.D.2d 703, 396 N.Y.S.2d 104 (1st Dep't 1979).

[44]Id.

[45]Becker v. N.Y. State Liquor Auth., 21 N.Y.2d 289, 234 N.E.2d 443 (1967).

deemed insufficient to sustain a violation. Nor would knowledge of instances of homosexual touching that were in isolated, concealed areas of the premises unperceived by the employees of the licensee sustain a violation.[46]

ONE ELEVEN WINES & LIQUORS, INC. v. DIVISION OF ABC
50 N.J. 329, 235 A.2d 12 (1967)

JACOBS, J.: "The Division of Alcoholic Beverage Control disciplined the appellants for permitting apparent homosexuals to congregate at their licensed premises. It suspended the licenses of One Eleven Wines & Liquors, Inc. and Val's Bar, Inc. and revoked the license of Murphy's Tavern, Inc. On One Eleven's Appeal to the Appellate Division the suspension of its license was sustained [citations omitted]. We granted certification on the licensee's application. [Citation omitted.]. . .

"The disastrous experiences of national prohibition led to the adoption of the twenty-first amendment and to the return of liquor control to the states in 1933. *See Grand Union Co. v. Sills,* 43 N.J. 390, 399, 204 A.2d 853 (1964). When our Legislature during that year first created the Department of Alcoholic Beverage Control, it vested broad regulatory powers in a state commissioner who immediately set about to insure that abuses which had originally contributed so heavily in bringing about national prohibition, would not be permitted to recur. He adopted stringent regulations which he rigidly enforced and which the courts supported with great liberality. [Citations omitted.] He concerned himself not alone with matters of lawfulness but also with matters of public sensitivity for he firmly believed that the effectiveness of the new mode of control would turn on the extent of the public's acceptance of the manner in which licensed establishments were conducted. Here again the courts sustained his pertinent regulatory actions with broad sweep. [Citations omitted.]

"Among the commissioner's early regulations were Rules 4 and 5 which were adopted in 1934. Rule 4 provided that no licensee shall allow in the licensed premises 'any known criminals, gangsters, racketeers, pick-pockets, swindlers, confidence men, prostitutes, female impersonators, or other persons of ill repute.' And Rule 5 provided, that no licensee shall allow 'any disturbances, brawls, or unnecessary noises' or allow the place of business to be conducted 'in such manner as to become a nuisance.' In 1936 Rule 5 was revised to include an express prohibition of 'lewdness' and 'immoral activities,' and in 1950 it was again revised to include an express prohibition of 'foul, filthy, indecent or obscene language or conduct.' [Citations omitted.]

"During the years prior to 1954 the department instituted proceedings under Rule 4 on the basis of evidence that apparent homosexuals had been permitted to congregate at the licensed premises. Apparently the department considered that the effeminate manifestations of the patrons brought them within the pro-

---

[46]Chipman Assoc., Inc. v. N.Y. State Liquor Authority, 47 A.D.2d 585, 363 N.Y.S.2d 162 (4th Dep't 1975).

hibition of 'female impersonators' although that term relates more properly to transvestites who are, for the most part said to be non-homosexuals. *In re M. Potter, Inc.,* ABC Bulletin 474, Item 1 (August 7, 1941) the investigators had observed a group of male patrons, 'whose voices, gestures and actions were effeminate,' dancing and kissing among themselves. Although there was an express finding that 'no actual acts of immorality' were committed at the licensed premises, the license was nonetheless suspended. In the course of his formal opinion, the acting commissioner said that the mere 'presence of female impersonators in and upon licensed premises presents a definite social problem'; and in line with the then widespread intolerance and limited public understanding of the subject, he made reference to 'the deep-rooted personal contempt felt by a normal red-blooded man' and to the notion that 'the mere thought of such perverts is repugnant to the normal person.'

"Since 1954 and despite increasing public tolerance and understanding, departmental proceedings aimed at the congregation of apparent homosexuals have continued apace but have been brought under Rule 5 rather than Rule 4. They have not been based on any specific and individualized charges of lewd or immoral conduct but rather on general charges that by permitting the apparent homosexuals to congregate, the licensees had allowed their places of business to be conducted in such a manner 'as to become a nuisance' within the contemplation of Rule 5. *In re Polka Club, Inc.,* ABC Bulletin 1045, Item 6 (December 27, 1954) the then director, in suspending a license on a charge of violation of Rule 5, said that he would not permit licensed premises to become 'havens for deviates.' *In re Kaczka and Trobiano,* ABC Bulletin 1063, Item 1 (April 21, 1955) the licensee introduced expert testimony that homosexuality is not contagious and that seeing groups of homosexuals would not affect normal people but the license was nonetheless suspended. As illustrated in many of his rulings, including *In re Louise G. Mack,* ABC Bulletin 1088, Item 2 (November 2, 1955), the director entertained the view that since exposure to homosexuals might be harmful to '*some* members of the public' the congregating of homosexuals must be prohibited as a 'threat to the safety and morals of the public.' [Citation omitted.]

"In the very cases before us the Division of Alcoholic Beverage Control made it clear that it has not in anywise moderated its long standing position that permitting the congregation of apparent homosexuals, without more, is violative of Rule 5. . . .

"In the One Eleven proceeding there was no charge and no substantial evidence that lewd or immoral conduct was permitted at the licensed premises. There was a charge and sufficient evidence that the licensee had permitted apparent homosexuals to congregate there. Investigators had visited the premises on several occasions and had observed the patrons; the testimony included the following partial account of their behavior:

"They were conversing and some of them in a lisping tone of voice, and during certain parts of their conversation they used limp-wrist movements to each other. One man would stick his tongue out at another and they would laugh and they would giggle. They were very, very chummy and close. When they drank their drinks, they extended their pinkies in a very dainty manner. They took short sips from their straws; took them quite a long time to finish their drinks. . . .

"They were very, very endearing to one another, very, very delicate to each other. . . .

"They looked in each other's eyes when they conversed. They spoke in low tones like an effeminate male. When walking, getting up from the stools, they very politely excused each other, hold on to the arm and swish and sway down to the other end of the bar and come back. . . .

"Their actions and mannerisms and demeanor appeared to me to be males impersonating females, they appeared to be homosexuals commonly known as queers, fags, fruits and other names.

". . .The investigators acknowledged that for the most part the patrons were 'normally dressed' and showed 'very good behavior.' Dr. Wardell B. Pomeroy, called as an expert witness by the licensee, testified that, although it could not be said from mere observation that any given individual was a homosexual, he would be of the opinion that tavern patrons with the characteristics described by the investigators were apparent homosexuals.

"Dr. Pomeroy as associated with the Kinsey Institute for twenty years and was the co-author of several books dealing with sexual behavior and offenses. He referred to the Kinsey studies which contained startling indications that 13% of the males in the country were 'more homosexual than heterosexual' and that 37% had 'at least one homosexual experience to the point of orgasm in the course of their life.' He also referred to indications that 55% of the population was neutral on the subject of homosexuality and there is now 'a more acceptance attitude' than there was twenty years ago. *See* Mosk, *Foreword to the Consenting Adult Homosexuals and the Law,* 13 U.C.L.A. Rev. 644, 645 (1966). . . . [*S*]*ee also* Schur, Crimes Without Victims 86, 87 (1965) where Dr. Schur dealt with the so-called 'gay' bars operating in our neighboring states and elsewhere:

" 'Although such establishments are sometimes condemned as breeding grounds of homosexuality, the charge is not convincing. Most of the people who go there (apart from tourists and some 'straight' friends) already are involved in the homosexual life. Anyone who wanders in and is offended by what he sees is perfectly free to leave. . . .'

"The views expressed by Doctors Pomeroy and Schur find significant legal support in various judicial holdings, notably those of the California Supreme Court. In *Stoumen v. Reilly,* 37 Cal. 2d 713, 234 P.2d 969 (1951) the license was suspended because the licensee had permitted 'persons of known homosexual tendencies' to patronize and meet at the licensed premises. Under Section 58 of the California Alcoholic Beverage Control Act, it was unlawful to permit the licensed premises to be conducted as a disorderly house or as a place 'to which people resort for purposes which are injurious to the public morals, health, convenience or safety.' The court, in setting aside the suspension, held that mere patronage 'without proof of the commission of illegal or immoral acts on the premises, or resort thereto for such purposes' was not sufficient to show a violation of section 58. Elsewhere in its opinion it stressed that in order to establish 'good cause' for suspension of the license, something more must be shown than that many of the patrons were homosexuals and used the premises 'as a meeting place.' 234 P.2d at 971.

"After the *Stoumen* case was decided, the California Legislature enacted the provision in section 24200, subdivision (e) of the Business and Professions Code under which licensed premises were prohibited from being used as resorts for 'sexual perverts.' In *Vallerga v. Dept. of Alcoholic Beverage Control*, 53 Cal. 2d 313, 1 Cal. Rptr. 494, 347 P.2d 909 (1959) a license was revoked because the licensee had permitted his premises to become a resort for homosexuals. The revocation was set aside by the California Supreme Court which held that the legislative provision was unconstitutional under *Stoumen*. . . .

"While the New York cases contain obscurities, many of them seem to take an approach comparable to that taken by the California Supreme Court. Thus in *People on Complaint of Fasone v. Arenella*, 139 N.Y.S.2d 186 (N.Y.C. Mag. Ct. 1954) the court, in dealing with a criminal charge that a licensee had allowed his premises to become disorderly, differentiated cases deemed disorderly where the premises were frequented by homosexuals in 'open and notorious manner, for the purpose of soliciting others to commit lewd and indecent acts' from others, not deemed disorderly, where the evidence established nothing more than that homosexuals patronized the premises without engaging in prohibited acts therein. 139 N.Y.S.2d at 189. . . .

"*In re Revocation of License of Clock Bar, Inc.*, 85 Dauph 125 (Pa. 1966) the court sustained a suspension grounded on evidence of improper solicitations by homosexuals at the licensed premises. However, in the course of its opinion it pointed out there was 'no law which forbids homosexuals from being patrons of licensed premises,' that the mere, though open, congregation of homosexuals at the licensed premises would not sustain a charge that the licensee maintained 'a disorderly house,' and that homosexuals at licensed premises become objectionable only 'when they make a nuisance of themselves' by improper solicitation or other overtly offensive conduct. 85 Dauph at 131. [Citations omitted.]

"Though in our culture homosexuals are indeed unfortunates, their status does not make them criminals or outlaws. *Cf. Robinson v. State of California*, 370 U.S. 660, 82 S. Ct. 1417, 8 L. Ed. 2d 758 (1962). So long as their public behavior violates no legal proscriptions they have the undoubted right to congregate in public. And so long as their public behavior conforms with currently acceptable standards of decency and morality, they may, at least in the present context, be viewed as having the equal right to congregate within licensed establishments such as taverns, restaurants and the like. *See Stoumen v. Reilly, supra*, 234 P.2d at 971. In sustaining the suspension of One Eleven's license, the Appellate Division took the position that it was not concerned with the rights of the patrons since technically the legal issue before it was the validity of Rule 5 under which the license was suspended. But the asserted rights of the homosexuals to assemble in an patronize licensed establishments are intertwined with the asserted rights of licensed establishments to serve them. Surely in these circumstances, the licensees are properly to be viewed as having standing to seek vindication of the various rights involved in order that the Court's ultimate determination may soundly rest on the complete mosaic. [Citations omitted.]. . .

"When in the 1930's the Department of Alcoholic Beverage Control first took its severe position, it acted on the assumption that the mere congregation of apparent homosexuals had to be outlawed to achieve effective control. It of course had no experience to support the assumption but it took the prohibitory course as the safer one for the then fledgling system. At the time, the interests of the patrons in question were given little consideration and were in any event overwhelmed by the then highly felt transitional need for sweeping restraint. Now, in the 1960's, the transitional need as such is long past and it is entirely appropriate that full sweep be given to current understanding and concepts. Under them it seems clear that, so long as the division can deal effectively with the matter through lesser regulations which do not impair the rights of well behaved apparent homosexuals to patronize and meet in licensed premises, it should do so. Such narrower course would be consonant with the settled and just principle that restrictions adopted in the exercise of police powers must be reasonable and not go beyond the public need. [Citations omitted.]

"It must be borne in mind that the division has produced nothing to support any need for continuance of its flat prohibition. Nor has it produced anything to indicate that it could not readily prepare and enforce a fair and sensible regulation which, while permitting apparent homosexuals to assemble in and patronize licensed establishments, prohibits overtly indecent conduct and public displays of sexual desires manifestly offensive to currently acceptable standards of propriety. Such a regulation might well be adopted forthwith to the end that future proceedings would rightly be based on specific charges of improper conduct at the licensed premises rather than, as here, upon general charges of mere congregation which we deem to be unreasonable and legally unsupportable. In the meantime, the discipline imposed in the three cases before us must be set aside, without prejudice, however, to any new charges which the division may prefer against the licensees, or any of them, clearly describing the individual acts alleged to be violative of the provisions in Rule 5 aimed at lewd and immoral conduct within the licensed premises. [Citation omitted.]

"Reversed."

18:19 *Sexual Misconduct in General*

Solicitation of patrons for immoral purposes and prostitution fall within the term *disorderly conduct* and as such constitute violations permitting the authority to suspend or revoke the license. Again, however, the incident giving rise to the violation must be more than an isolated, unanticipated one not reasonably foreseeable, unless the licensee had actual knowledge or reasonable opportunity to perceive it, and thus had tolerated the misconduct.[47]

---

[47]Italiano v. N.Y. State Liquor Authority, 59 A.D.2d 820, 399 N.Y.S.2d 727 (1977).

The New York Court of Appeals has set limits on the traditional rule that exonerates a licensee from license revocation because of a lack of any pattern of conduct or actual knowledge of an employee's misconduct in tolerating prostitution on the premises. A critical factor noted by the court was the numerous warning letters sent to the licensee by the authority about the problem.

AWRICH RESTAURANT, INC. v. NEW YORK STATE LIQUOR AUTHORITY
60 N.Y.2d 645, 454 N.E.2d 1307 (1983)

MEMORANDUM: "The judgment of the Appellate Division should be affirmed, with costs. 92 A.D.2d 925, 460 N.Y.S.2d 347.

"Where an employee is found to have been vested with managerial authority over the operation of premises licensed to serve liquor and the conduct of the licensed activity thereon on other than a casual or temporary basis, his conduct may be imputed to the licensee in establishing a violation of subdivision 6 of section 106 of the Alcoholic Beverage Control Law despite the lack of a pattern of conduct or any actual knowledge by the licensee of the bartender's conduct (*Matter of Falso v. State Liq. Auth.*, 43 N.Y.2d 721, 401 N.Y.S.2d 484, 372 N.E.2d 325). Here the licensee testified that the bartender left in charge was responsible for, among other things, dealing with any disorder which might come up on the premises and making sure that the premises were operating in orderly fashion. Based on this testimony, there was substantial evidence to support the hearing officer's determination that the bartender had been delegated sufficient managerial authority to hold the licensee responsible for his conduct. Moreover, the licensee admitted that he had been aware of the problems with prostitutes coming on the premises, and he had been sent numerous warning letters by the authority with regard to subdivision 6 of section 106 violations. This evidence provides further support for the hearing officer's ruling that the licensee should, with due diligence and proper supervision, have known of the events that took place on the premises which give rise to the violation.

"COOKE, C.J., and JASEN, JONES, WACHTLER, MEYER and SIMONS, JJ., concur."

18:20 Sexually Explicit Entertainment

Section 106(6a) of the New York Alcoholic Beverage Control Law prohibits nudity on any retail premises licensed to sell alcoholic beverages: "No retail licensee for on premises consumption shall suffer or permit any person to appear on licensed premises in such a manner or attire as to expose any portion of the pubic area, anus, vulva or genitals, or any simulation thereof, nor shall suffer or permit any female to appear on licensed premises in such a manner or attire as to expose to view any portion of the breast below the top of the areola, or any simulation thereof."

The New York courts have recognized the distinction between lewd, indecent, or obscene entertainment or nudity or nude dancing as such, holding the latter beyond the purview of regulation on First Amendment constitutional grounds governing freedom of speech.[48]

However, in *California v. La Rue*,[49] the Supreme Court held that the Twenty-first Amendment to the Federal Constitution gave the states unfettered authority to outlaw all forms of nude entertainment, including nude dancing, even though nude dancing *per se* had been recognized previously as entitled to some limited constitutional protection.

In response to *La Rue*, New York enacted the above subdivision 6a of section 106 of the Alcoholic Beverage Control Law, patterned on the California model, which was the first enactment to outlaw all forms of nude entertainment on licenced premises. But the New York Court of Appeals has ruled that enactment inapplicable insofar as topless dancing is afforded some constitutional recognition.

BELLANCA v. NEW YORK STATE LIQUOR AUTHORITY
50 N.Y.2d 524, 407 N.E.2d 460 (1980), *rev'd*, 452 U.S. 714 (1981)[50]

WACHTLER, J.: "The question on this appeal is whether a provision of the Alcoholic Beverage Control Law (§ 106, subd 6-a) is unconstitutional insofar as it prohibits topless dancing at premises licensed by the State Liquor Authority. The Supreme Court, Erie County, held this portion of the statute unconstitutional. The State has appealed directly to this court pursuant to CPLR 5601 (subd [b], par 2).

"The plaintiffs are the owners of nightclubs, bars and restaurants which, for several years, have featured topless dancing. The plaintiffs also sell alcoholic beverages to their patrons for consumption on the premises, pursuant to licenses issued by the State Liquor Authority. That agency has adopted rules prohibiting nudity and 'lewd or indecent conduct' on premises licensed to sell alcohol. The rules also specifically prohibit the licensee from permitting 'any female' to appear with breasts 'expose[d] to view' but, as originally adopted, contained an exception for topless dancing which, although not prohibited, was subject to strict regulation.

"In 1977 the Legislature added nearly identical provisions to the Alcoholic Beverage Control Law (L 1977, ch 321, § 1). However, this statute (Alcoholic Beverage Control Law, § 106, subd 6-a) did not carry forward the exception permitting topless dancing. No criminal penalty is provided for violating this statute (*see* Alcoholic Beverage Control Law, § 130, subds 3–5). But a violation of this law may result in a loss of the liquor license (9 NYCRR 53.1 [s]).

"The plaintiffs commenced this declaratory judgment action claiming that subdivision 6-a is unconstitutional to the extent it prohibits all topless dancing at

---

[48]Beal Properties, Inc. v. N.Y. State Liquor Authority, 37 N.Y.2d 861, 340 N.E.2d 476 (1975) (mem. decision).

[49]409 U.S. 109 (1972).

[50]The Supreme Court, *per curiam*, reversed June 22, 1981, on the reasoning of the dissenting opinion of Gabrielli, J.

premises licensed by the State Liquor Authority. The plaintiffs stated that they had always complied with the Liquor Authority's rules and restrictions with respect to topless dancing. In addition it was alleged that this activity is not observable from the public streets and the fact that it is featured is clearly noted on signs posted outside the plaintiffs' premises. 'Consequently,' the complaint states, 'no person has been exposed to topless dancing performances at Plaintiffs' premises except by choice.' In their first cause of action they argued that the topless dancing featured at their establishments 'is not lewd or obscene within the meaning of the United States Constitution and is a form of protected expression under the First Amendment.' In the remaining three causes of action the plaintiffs claimed that subdivision 6-a is also overbroad, violates the equal protection clause and infringes on their freedom of expression guaranteed by section 8 of article 1 of the State Constitution. They therefore asked the court to declare subdivision 6-a unconstitutional to the extent that it prohibits topless dancing in licensed premises and also sought an injunction barring the State from enforcing this law in the future.

"In response the State contended that 'notwithstanding the Constitutional provisions which guarantee freedom of expression' it may, pursuant to the Twenty-first Amendment of the United States Constitution, 'regulate the type of entertainment in establishments licensed in this State to sell alcoholic beverages.'

"The trial court recognized the State's broad power to control and regulate the sale of liquor in order to protect the public from its effects (*California v. La Rue*, 409 U.S. 109). It found, however, that topless dancing is 'a type of expression protected by the First Amendment' and that the State had failed to 'show some serious and compelling reason to limit it. Bland reliance on the Twenty-first Amendment is insufficient.' Thus the court declared subdivision 6-a unconstitutional as applied to topless dancing in licensed premises, and to that extent, enjoined its enforcement.

"On this appeal the State contends that this judgment is inconsistent with the United States Supreme Court's holding in *California v. La Rue (supra)*.

"In *La Rue* the court held facially valid certain administrative rules regulating the type of entertainment that might be presented in bars and nightclubs licensed by the State. The rules prohibited what the court described as acts of 'gross sexuality' including display of the genitals and live or filmed performances of sexual acts. They noted that before the rules were promulgated, hearings were held and it was shown that at premises where these acts were performed, 'numerous incidents of legitimate concern to the Department had occurred' (*California v. La Rue, supra,* at p. 111). These incidents included 'bacchanalian revelries' involving public sexual acts between customers and entertainers, as well as assaults, rape and indecent exposure committed at or near such premises.

"In upholding the regulations the court observed that the Twenty-first Amendment, granting the States power over the sale and distribution of liquor within their borders, has been recognized as conferring on the States something more than the normal authority inherent in the police power. Although that amendment did not nullify the other provisions of the Constitution whenever the State seeks to regulate the sale of liquor, it did serve to 'strengthen' the State's authority in that particular area. The court conceded that some of the performances prohibited by the regulators would be entitled to constitutional protection but noted that the regulations claimed to be invalid on their face, in 'substance' prohibited performances 'that partake more of gross sexuality than of communication' (*California v. La Rue, supra*, at p. 118). The State's conclusion that these acts should not be permitted at places authorized to sell liquor was held not to be 'an irrational one' in light of 'the evidence from the hearings' (*California v. La Rue, supra*, at pp. 115, 116). 'Given the added presumption in favor of the validity of the state regulation in this area that the Twenty-first Amendment requires, we cannot hold that the regulations on their face violate the Federal Constitution' (*California v. La Rue, supra*, at pp. 118–119).

"In the case now before us the plaintiffs do not claim a right to offer performances of explicit sexual acts, live or filmed, real or simulated. Nor are we concerned with nude dancing. There is no contention that the plaintiffs should have a right to present their dancers entirely unclothed, and thus they do not challenge that portion of the statute which prohibits nudity. Nor do they contest the statute insofar as it would prohibit women other than dancers from appearing barebreasted on their premises. Similarly the plaintiffs do not contest the State's right to place some restrictions on topless dancing performances as the Liquor Authority's regulations have done in the past. Finally, of course, the plaintiffs do not claim that they are exempted from the obscenity laws or that topless dancing should always be allowed no matter how, or where performed. The only question before us is whether the statute is constitutional to the extent that it absolutely prohibits liquor licensees from presenting nonobscene topless dancing performances to willing customers under all circumstances.

"Thus unlike the court in *La Rue*, we are not confronted with a broad attack on the facial validity of a statute which in 'substance' prohibits acts of 'gross sexuality,' most of which are probably criminally obscene as well. Here the challenge narrowly focuses on a rule prohibiting a single activity, topless dancing, which is not inherently obscene. On the contrary it has been legally recognized as a form of expression (*Doran v. Salem Inn*, 422 U.S. 922) like nudity in art and sculpture. Of course involving conduct, as it does, it is undoubtedly subject to more restrictions than the more static arts. But although offensive to some, as all nudity or partial nudity is, it is nevertheless entitled to at least minimal protection under the First Amendment. Certainly the State could not prohibit topless dancing under all circumstances (*Doran v. Salem Inn, supra*). Neither, in our view, may the State arbitrarily prohibit it at all places licensed to sell alcohol.

"Here there is nothing in the record to show that the State's conclusion, that this activity should not take place at licensed premises, was rationally based on evidence demonstrating a need for the rule. Indeed it appears that the law was not prompted by hearings or any legislative awareness of deficiencies in the prior regulation permitting topless dancing subject to restrictions and the continued supervision of the State Liquor Authority.

"The State urges however that we indulge an additional presumption and assume that the Legislature did investigate and find sufficient facts to support the legislation [citations omitted]. But even if the presumption could be held to be equivalent to the actual findings made in *La Rue*—a question we need not decide—it would be inappropriate in this case to presume that topless dancing posed a problem in premises licensed by the State Liquor Authority. It is, in fact, hard to imagine that the agency, which is so vigilant in enforcing the liquor laws and its own regulations would have continued to permit topless dancing at premises authorized to sell liquor if the audiences degenerated into 'bacchanalian revelries' or became involved in 'incidents of legitimate concern' to the State. Notably, even in California where such incidents occurred in bars permitting gross sexuality, the State found no need to prohibit topless dancing. It simply imposed restrictions similar to those previously found acceptable by the State Liquor Authority in this State (*see La Rue v. California*, 326 F. Supp. 348, 359).

"The State's power to control and regulate the sale of alcoholic beverages is designed to protect the public from abuses related to alcohol consumption. It is not a license to censor whatever occurs at premises authorized to sell alcohol. Thus when the State employs this power in such a way as to infringe on activities entitled to some constitutional protection, it must at least demonstrate that there is a rational connection between the activity sought to be prohibited and the State's legitimate concern in controlling liquor consumption. On the record before us there is nothing which would rationally support a conclusion that in this State it is dangerous to mix alcohol and topless dancing.

"Accordingly the judgment of the Supreme Court, Erie County, should be affirmed. . . .

"Judges JONES, FUCHSBERG and MEYER concur with Judge WACHTLER; Judge GABRIELLI dissents and votes to reverse in a separate opinion in which Chief Judge COOKE and Judge JASEN concur.

"Judgment affirmed, with costs."

Other states are free to ban all forms of explicit entertainment or not as they see fit. Virtually all states outlaw lewd and indecent performances on licensed premises.[51] Similarly, an Alcoholic Beverage Control Commission regulation prohibiting entertainers from mingling with bar patrons does not violate the entertainers' rights of freedom of speech or assembly.[52]

The *Bellanca* case, *supra*, is now *Bellanca I*. Two later cases—*Bellanca II and Bellanca III*—follow chronologically. The trilogy of decisions is important

[51]*See* Rules 143.3–143.5 of the California Department of Beverage Control issued in 1970 and approved in California v. LaRue, 409 U.S. 109 (1972). *Cf.* Doran v. Salem Inn, 422 U.S. 922 (1975).
[52]Aristocrat Restaurant of Mass., Inc. v. Alcoholic Beverage Control Commission, (1) 374 Mass. 547, 374 N.E.2d 1181 (Mass. 1978); (2) 374 Mass. 564, 374 N.E.2d 1192 (1978); *appeal dismissed*, 439 U.S. 803 (1978).

as it represents a conflict between federal and state constitutional interpretations over the issue of regulation of entertainment within licensed premises.

NEW YORK STATE LIQUOR AUTHORITY V. BELLANCA [BELLANCA II]
452 U.S. 714, 101 S. Ct. 2599, 69 L.Ed. 2d 357 (1980)

PER CURIAM: "The question presented in this case is the power of a State to prohibit topless dancing in an establishment licensed by the State to serve liquor. In 1977, the State of New York amended its Alcoholic Beverage Control Law to prohibit nude dancing in establishments licensed by the State to sell liquor for on-premises consumption. N.Y. Alco. Bev. Cont. Law, § 106 (subd. 6a) (1977). The statute does not provide for criminal penalties, but its violation may cause an establishment to lose its liquor license.

"Respondents, owners of nightclubs, bars, and restaurants which had for a number of years offered topless dancing, brought a declaratory judgment action in state court, alleging that the statute violates the First Amendment of the U.S. Constitution insofar as it prohibits all topless dancing in all licensed premises. The New York Supreme Court declared the statute unconstitutional and the New York Court of Appeals affirmed by a divided vote. It reasoned that topless dancing was a form of protected expression under the First Amendment and that 'the State had not demonstrated a need for prohibiting licensees from presenting nonobscene topless dancing performances to willing customers.' The dissent contended that the statute was well within the State's power, conferred by the Twenty-first Amendment, to regulate the sale of liquor within its boundaries. We agree with the reasoning of the dissent and now reverse the decision of the New York Court of Appeals. This Court has long recognized that a State has absolute power under the Twenty-first Amendment to prohibit totally the sale of liquor within its boundaries. *Ziffrin, Inc. v. Reeves,* 308 U.S. 132, 138, 84 L. Ed. 128, 60 S. Ct. 163 (1939). It is equally well established that a State has broad power under the Twenty-first Amendment to regulate the times, places and circumstances under which liquor may be sold. In *California v. La Rue,* 409 U.S. 109, 34 L. Ed. 2d 342, 93 S. Ct. 390 (1972), we upheld the facial constitutionality of a statute prohibiting acts of 'gross sexuality,' including the display of the genitals and live or filmed performances of sexual acts, in establishments licensed by the State to serve liquor. Although we recognized that not all of the prohibited acts would be found obscene and were therefore entitled to some measure of First Amendment protection, we reasoned that the statute was within the State's broad power under the Twenty-first Amendment to regulate the sale of liquor.

"In *Doran v. Salem Inn, Inc.,* 422 U.S. 922, 45 L. Ed. 648, 95 S. Ct. 2561 (1975), we considered a First Amendment challenge to a local ordinance which prohibited females from appearing topless not just in bars, but 'any public place.' Though we concluded that the District Court had not abused its discretion in granting a preliminary injunction against enforcement of the ordinance, that decision does not limit our holding in *LaRue.* . . . [T]he ordinance involved either in *LaRue* or here, since it proscribed conduct at 'any public place,' a term that 'could include the theatre, town hall, opera place, as well as a marketplace, street or any place of assembly indoors or outdoors.' 422 U.S. at 933, 45 L. Ed. 2d 648, 95 S. Ct. 2561. Here, in contrast, the State has not attempted to ban topless dancing in 'any public place': As in *LaRue,* the statute's prohibition applies only to establishments which are licensed by the State to serve liquor. Indeed, we explicitly recognized in *Doran* that a more narrowly drawn statute would serve judicial scrutiny:

> "Although the customary 'barroom' type of nude dancing may involve only the barest minimum of protected expression, we recognized in *California v. LaRue,* 409 U.S. 109, [34 L. Ed. 2d 342, 93 S. Ct. 390] (1972), that this form of entertainment might be entitled to First and Fourteenth Amendment protection under some circumstances. In *LaRue,* however, we concluded that the broad powers of the States to regulate the sale of liquors conferred by the Twenty-first Amendment, outweighed any First Amendment interest in nude dancing and that a State could therefore ban such dancing as part of its liquor license control program. 422 U.S., at 932–933, 45 L. Ed. 2d 648, 95 S. Ct. 2561.

"Judged by the standards announced in *LaRue* and *Doran,* the statute at issue here is not unconstitutional. What the New York Legislature has done in this case is precisely what this Court has said a State may do in *Doran.* Pursuant to its power to regulate the sale of liquor within its boundaries, it has banned topless dancing in establishments granted a license to serve liquor. The State's power to ban the sale of alcoholic beverages entirely includes the lesser power to ban the sale of liquor on premises where topless dancing occurs.

"Respondents nonetheless insist that *LaRue* is distinguishable from this case, since the statute there prohibited acts of 'gross sexuality' and was well-supported by legislative findings demonstrating a need for the rule. They argue that the statute here is unconstitutional as applied to topless dancing because there is no legislative finding that topless dancing poses anywhere near the problem posed by acts of 'gross sexuality.' But even if explicit legislative findings were required to uphold the constitutionality of this statute as applied to topless dancing, those findings exist in this case. The purposes of the statute have been set forth in an accompanying legislative memorandum, N.Y. State Legislative Annual, 150 (1977).

> "Nudity is the kind of conduct that is a proper subject of legislative action as well as regulation by the State Liquor Authority as a phase of liquor licensing. It has long been held that sexual acts and performances may constitute disorderly behavior within the meaning of the Alcoholic Beverage Control Law. . . .

> "Common sense indicates that any form of nudity coupled with alcohol in public place begets undesirable behavior. This legislation prohibiting nudity in public will once and for all, outlaw conduct which is now quite out of hand.

"In short, the elected representatives of the State of New York have chosen to avoid the disturbances associated with mixing alcohol and nude dancing by means of a reasonable restriction upon establishments which sell liquor for on-premises consumption. Given the 'added presumption in favor of the state regulation' conferred by the Twenty-first Amendment, *California v. LaRue, supra,* at 118, 34 L. Ed. 2d 342, 93 S. Ct. 390, we cannot agree with the New York Court of Appeals that the statute violates the United States Constitution. Whatever artistic or communicative value may attach to topless dancing is overcome by the State's exercise of its broad powers arising under the Twenty-first Amendment. Although some may quarrel with the wisdom of such legislation and may consider topless dancing a harmless diversion, the Twenty-first Amendment makes that a policy judgment for the state legislature, not the courts.

"Accordingly, the petition for certiorari is granted and the judgment of the New York Court of Appeals is reversed for further proceedings not inconsistent with this opinion.

"Justice MARSHALL concurs in the judgment."

On remand, the New York Court of Appeals held that some forms of topless dancing are constitutionally protected under the New York Constitution, in spite of the validity of the state ban on such activities permitted under the Twenty-first Amendment to the United States Constitution.

BELLANCA v. NEW YORK STATE LIQUOR AUTHORITY [BELLANCA III]
54 N.Y.2d 228, 429 N.E.2d 765 (1981)
cert. denied, 456 U.S. 1006 (1982)

JONES, J.: "The guarantee of freedom of expression declared in our State Constitution mandates invalidation of the blanket proscription against all topless dancing in premises licensed by the State Liquor Authority presently stated in subdivision 6-a of section 106 of the Alcoholic Beverage Control Law. Although that statutory ban has been held to be valid under the Federal Constitution in consequence of the provisions of its Twenty-first Amendment, it is invalid under the guarantee of freedom of expression of our State Constitution, as to which the Twenty-first Amendment has no application.

"This case is now before us on remand from the Supreme Court of the United States (—— U.S. ——, 101 S. Ct. 2599, 69 L. Ed. 2d 357). On our prior consideration a majority in our court held that subdivision 6-a of section 106 of the Alcoholic Beverage Control Law was unconstitutional under the First Amendment of the United States Constitution insofar as it prohibits topless dancing at premises licensed by the State Liquor Authority (50 N.Y.2d 524, 429 N.Y.S.2d 616, 407 N.E.2d 360, rearg. and amdt. of remittitur den. 51 N.Y.2d 879). On that occasion we found it unnecessary to consider the parallel contention that the statute was unconstitutional under section 8 of article I of our State Constitution (50 N.Y.2d 524, 528, n. 5, 429 N.Y.S.2d 616, 407 N.E.2d 460, *supra*).

"The rationale of the majority then was that the Supreme Court had recognized dancing as a form of expression and had held that topless dancing, like nudity in art and sculpture, was to be accorded at least limited protection under the First Amendment (*Doran v. Salem Inn,* 422 U.S. 922, 95 S. Ct. 2561, 45 L. Ed. 2d 648). We explicitly took note of what we considered a critical circumstance in the case, namely, that the statutory provision under scrutiny barred *all* topless dancing—'The only question before us is whether the statute is constitutional to the extent that it absolutely prohibits liquor licensees from presenting nonobscene topless dancing performances to willing customers under all circumstances' (50 N.Y.2d 524, 529, 429 N.Y.S.2d 616, 407 N.E.2d 460, *supra*). We then recognized, as we do now, the right of the Legislature or the State Liquor Authority without infringement of the constitutional proscriptions to prohibit or to regulate topless dancing on either of two bases. If the dancing is itself found to be obscene there can be no question but what it falls outside the shelter of any constitutional right of expression. Or, topless dancing although not obscene may be regulated, even to the extent of its prohibition, in circumstances so functionally related to the exercise of the State's authority to regulate the sale and consumption of alcoholic beverages as to overcome the applicable constitutional guarantee of freedom of expression, as for instance, by a rule, such as that of the State Liquor Authority in effect prior to the legislative enactment of subdivision 6-a, prohibiting topless dancing performed on a stage or platform less than 18 inches above the immediate floor level or removed by less than 6 feet from the nearest patron (9 N.Y.C.R.R. 53.1[s] prior to its amendment. . . .

"The posture in which we confront this case on remand can thus be summarized as follows. When the case was previously before us the majority held subdivision 6-a unconstitutional as violative of the First Amendment of the United States Constitution; the dissenters would have held that in view of the authority granted the States by the Twenty-first Amendment to regulate the sale and use of liquor, the provision of subdivision 6-a was not irrational and accordingly should be upheld. The Supreme Court similarly upheld subdivision 6-a against challenge under the Federal Constitution on the ground that the broad provisions of the Twenty-first Amendment substantially curtailed the operative scope of the First Amendment. Nothing in its opinion intimates, however, that it would have upheld the subdivision against First Amendment challenge had there been no Twenty-first Amendment.

"We are, of course, bound by the decision of the Supreme Court as to the validity of subdivision 6-a under the provisions of the Federal Constitution. We are now called on to consider the validity of the subdivision under the provisions of our State Constitution, an issue which we did not address when the case was before us on the prior occasion and which, of course, was not within the scope of the Supreme Court's review.

"We perceive no reason to depart from our conclusion, reached before, that subdivision 6-a in its present form is violative of a constitutional guarantee of freedom of expression. In arriving at this result we had no occasion to consider whether our State constitutional guarantee is broader than the guarantee of the Federal Constitution. For present purposes it suffices to observe that, at the very least, the guarantee of freedom of expression set forth in our State Constitution is of no lesser vitality than the set forth in the Federal Constitution (considered without reference to the curtailing effect of its Twenty-first Amendment). Our State Constitution contains no provision modifying the State guarantee of freedom of expression corresponding to what the Supreme Court has held is the diminishing effect of the Twenty-first Amendment with respect to the Federal guarantee of freedom of expression. We therefore hold that subdivision 6-a is unconstitutional under the provisions of our State Constitution.

"Nor is there anything in the Twenty-first Amendment itself which inhibits or modifies the right of freedom of expression assured by our State Constitution. As read by the Supreme Court, the Twenty-first Amendment recognizes, so far as the restrictive provisions of the Federal Constitution are concerned, the absolute power of a State to prohibit totally, and consequently to regulate, the sale of alcoholic beverages. Appellants do not assert, however, that the source of the State's authority to regulate the sale and consumption of alcoholic beverages is to be found in the Twenty-first Amendment. Contrary to the position now advanced by one of the dissenters, the authority of our State in this respect stems not from any grant to be found in the Federal Constitution but derives from the inherent police power of the State as a sovereign (see 9 N.Y. Jur., Constitutional Law, § 143; U.S. Const., 10th Amdt.). The exercise of the police power by the State Legislature is necessarily subject to the strictures of our State Constitution, of which the guarantee of freedom of expression found in section 8 of article I is controlling in this instance. The Supreme Court has never espoused the proposition that the Twenty-first Amendment of the Federal Constitution confers a power on the States which is superior to or free from the constraints of their own Constitutions, and nothing cited by the dissenters is to the contrary.

"Accordingly, we hold that the present statutory ban against topless dancing in premises licensed by the State Liquor Authority is prohibited by the guarantee of freedom of expression declared in section 8 of article I, there being no legislative findings or declaration in this instance providing warrant for the judicial conclusion that the categorical ban is sufficiently functionally related to the exercise of the State's police power in the discharge of the responsibilities vested in the State Liquor Authority.

"For the reasons stated, the judgment of Supreme Court should be affirmed, with costs."

FUCHSBERG, J. (concurring).

"Because Judge JONES' analysis of the controlling constitutional and procedural issues—with all of which I agree—does not focus on the practical nature of the imposition on freedom of expression which we strike down anew today, I add this additional comment for myself:

"Licensed liquor establishments, regardless of whether they provide nonobscene topless dancing entertainment, may not dispense alcoholic beverages to minors (Alcoholic Beverage Control Law, § 65).

"As to adults, such performances are not thrust upon the patrons. Those who, understandably, do not choose to attend, should be, and are, perfectly free to stay away, and, presumably, they exercise that right. Our profound commitment to personal liberty demands not only that we respect their right to do so, but, correlatively, that we evince like respect for the right of adults who elect to attend. In a free society, one such right could not long exist without the other.

"The protection of both is implicit in section 8 of article I of our State Constitution. Its guarantee is not confined to the expression of ideas that are conventional or those shared by a majority.

"[Dissenting opinions of GABRIELLI, J., and JASEN, J., omitted.]"

The state supreme courts that have adopted the rationale of the New York Court of Appeals are Alaska: *Mickens v. City of Kodiak;* California: *Morris v. Municipal Court for San Jose–Milipitas;* and Maine: *Gabriele v. Town of Old Orchard Beach.*[53] Massachusetts had done so prior to *Bellanca III: Commonwealth v. Sees.*[54]

18:21   *Private Club Exemption under New York Alcoholic Beverage Control Law*

N.Y. STATE LIQUOR AUTHORITY V. SALEM SOCIAL CLUB
76 A.D.2d 908, 429 N.Y.S.2d 235 (2d Dep't 1980)

MEMORANDUM: "The New York State Liquor Authority (hereafter the authority) commenced this proceeding to enjoin the Salem Social Club, Inc. and its officers and directors from permitting liquor to be served on the premises of the corporation in violation of section 64-b of the Alcoholic Beverage Control Law. Appellants' position was that they were not in violation of section 64-b, inasmuch as subdivision 7 thereof exempts the club because it is a duly incorporated not-for-profit social club, as defined by section 3 (subd. 9) of the Alcoholic Beverage Control Law and section 102 of the Not-for-Profit Corporation Law.

"In their answer to the petition, appellants stated that when the liquor license of the Salem Inn, Inc. was canceled by the authority (and the cancellation ultimately sustained by the Court of Appeals in *Matter of Salem Inn v. New York State Liq. Auth.,* 43 N.Y.2d 713, 401 N.Y.S.2d 205, 372 N.E.2d 40, . . .former customers of the Inn joined together to organize a not-for-profit social club. The club's purpose is to provide a meeting place where 'consenting, forewarned adults' may view 'live erotic dance performances.' Membership is open to persons over the age of 18 years who 'comport themselves properly when on the premises.' The membership fee is $20 a year if paid in advance, $24 a year if paid in monthly installments of $2 per month. A one-time temporary membership, upon payment of $2, is permitted to allow a person to visit before committing himself to full membership.

"Following a hearing on the question of whether the Salem Social Club, Inc. is a bona fide, not-for-profit social club within the meaning of sections 64-b

---

[53]640 P.2d 818 (1982); 32 Cal.3d 553, 652 P.2d 51 (1982); 420 A.2d 252 (1980).
[54]374 Mass. 532, 373 N.E.2d 1151 (1978). *Contra:* Inturri v. Healy, 426 F. Supp. 543 (D.C. Conn. 1977) applying Connecticut law.

(subd. 7) and 3 (subd. 9) of the Alcoholic Beverage Control Law and section 102 of the Not-for-Profit Corporation Law, the trial court determined that appellants maintained no bona fide membership, and it was thus not a club within the meaning of section 64-b (subd.7). In addition the court found that the record established, by way of the testimony of one of the club's officers, that there was a distribution of income in violation of section 508 of the Not-for-Profit Corporation Law. We affirm.

"We observe at the outset that appellants are confusing the authority's purpose. The law permits the authority to regulate the sale and service of alcoholic beverages. Appellants are not being regulated as to the presentation of 'live erotic dance performances.'

"Appellants' disavowal of any pecuniary gain by the club is not supported by the record. Edward Akam, the president, testified that John Savage, the secretary-treasurer, operated the talent agency from which the dancing girls were obtained *and* that Savage derived a profit from the dancers. The statutes are clear that a 'club,' to be exempt pursuant to section 64-b (subd. 7) of the Alcoholic Beverage Control Law, must not be operated for pecuniary gain (Alcoholic Beverage Control Law, § 3, subd. 9). The realization by Savage of a profit from the activity for which the club was formed, i.e., the viewing of dancing girls, means that there is a 'pecuniary gain' derived from the club's operation in contravention of the statute. In addition, such a profit is in violation of section 508 of the Not-for-Profit Corporation Law which provides that if a lawful activity involves an incidental profit, '[a]ll such incidental profits shall be applied to the maintenance. . . of the lawful activities of the corporation, and in no case shall be divided or distributed in any manner whatsoever among the members, directors, or officers of the corporation.'

"It is also clear from the testimony that the Salem Social Club does not conform to the definition of a club in another way. A club, as defined by the relevant statute, means 'an organization of persons incorporated pursuant to the provisions of the not-for-profit corporation law. . . and which does not traffic in alcoholic beverages for profit and is operated solely for a recreational purpose but not for pecuniary gain' (Alcoholic Beverage Control Law, § 3 subd. 9). A member of a club 'shall mean a person who whether a charter member or admitted in agreement with the by-laws of the club, has become a bona fide member thereof, who maintains his membership by the payment of his annual dues in a bona fide manner in accordance with the by-laws and whose name and address is entered on the list of members' (Alcoholic Beverage Control Law, § 3, subd. 9).

"Appellants insist that the definition of a 'member' has nothing to do with whether or not the Salem Social Club is a 'club.' It would be absurd, in our view, to ignore the definition of the persons who comprise a 'club,' contained in the very same subdivision, in a determination of whether there is, in fact a club as defined by that subdivision.

"Whether or not the charge made is appropriate, it is clear that a 'club' and a 'member' as defined in the Alcoholic Beverage Control Law do not exist. There is no payment of 'annual dues in a bona fide manner in accordance with the by-laws' and there is no 'list' of such bona fide payees that comprises a list of members with names and addresses (*see* Alcoholic Beverage Control Law, § 3, subd. 9).

". . .[F]rom the manner of entry gained by Kahn and the three other investigators who testified, it is obvious that there is no bona fide membership list. A 'member' at the Salem Social Club is anyone who walks in and pays $2. It is not an organization of persons existing under prescribed rules of membership—no matter how purposefully open the membership is intended to be. The inescapable conclusion is that the club is a place open to the public at large. In that circumstance, the club is not entitled to the exemption as provided by the law inasmuch as it does not meet the statutory definition which qualifies for the exemption (*see* Alcoholic Beverage Control Law, § 64-b, subd. 7; § 3, subd. 9)."

18:22 *Trafficking in Narcotics*

Sale of narcotic drugs on the premises has been held to constitute disorderly conduct under New York Alcoholic Beverage Control Law, section 106(6). Actual knowledge on the part of the licensee is not required; proof that he should have known of such activities is sufficient. Lack of willfullness, however, may warrant the court in reducing a revocation to a suspension, where revocation was an excessive sanction disproportionate to the offense.

The Supreme Court of New Jersey[55] has held that the sale and use of narcotics in a licensed tavern does not support license revocation where the activity is due to the physical location of the tavern rather than the culpable conduct of the proprietor.

The following New York case illustrates the burden of proof required to sustain a license revocation in contrast to a license disapproval.

COLLINS V. STATE LIQUOR AUTHORITY
48 A.D.2d 848, 368 N.Y.S.2d 859 (2d Dep't 1975)

MEMORANDUM: "Proceeding pursuant to CPLR article 78 to review two determinations of respondent, both dated November 26, 1974, (1) one (a) revoking petitioner's special on-premises liquor license, effective December 3, 1974, and (b) imposing a $1,000 bond claim and (2) the other, *inter alia*, (a) disapproving petitioner's renewal application and (b) recalling the license theretofore issued to petitioner pursuant to a renewal stipulation. . . . The first above-mentioned determination is modified, on the law, by (1) annulling respondent's findings numbered '1' and '4' and (2) reducing the penalty to a forfeiture of petitioner's $1,000 bond. As so modified, determination confirmed, without costs. The second above-mentioned determination is confirmed, without costs. Petitioner is the sole owner of a tavern located in Bay Shore, New York. In September, 1973, respondent instituted a proceeding to revoke petitioner's special on-premises li-

---

[55]Ishmal v. Division of Alcoholic Beverage Control, 58 N.J. 347, 277 A.2d 532 (1971).

quor license. After a lengthy hearing the tavern owner's license was revoked and a $1,000 bond forfeited because he (a) permitted the premises to become disorderly on April 4–5, 1973, when petitioner's employee assaulted a patron (Alcoholic Beverage Control Law, § 106, subd. 6), (b) sold alcoholic beverages to two minors on December 12, 1972 (Alcoholic Beverage Control Law, § 65) and (c) suffered and permitted the premises to become disorderly on September 24, 1973, when another of petitioner's employees and petitioner's brother sold narcotics to an undercover detective. As to the assault, the record reveals that on the evening in question a fight broke out between a patron and one of petitioner's bartenders. After the combatants had been separated and restrained another bartender struck the patron on the head with an ax handle. Although petitioner was present when the altercation took place, we find no basis upon which he can be held to have 'suffered or permitted' the disorder. It is well settled that a licensee cannot be held liable for every single act of his employees (*see Matter of Playboy Club of N.Y. v. State Liq. Auth.*, 23 N.Y.2d 544). It must be shown that the licensee knew or should have known of the disorderly condition and nevertheless tolerated its existence. In the present case the bartender who assaulted the patron had been employed on a part-time basis for approximately four months. Absent in the record is any showing of a similar occurrence by this or any other employee or a showing that petitioner had participated in or sanctioned the bartender's conduct, or even that he was aware of it until it was too late. Moreover, the mere fact that the ax handle was found behind the bar, hence establishing that the licensee had constructive knowledge of its presence, is inadequate to demonstrate that he should have known that his employee would use the instrument injudiciously. Similarly, petitioner cannot be held liable for the events which transpired on September 24, 1973. On that occasion an undercover detective obtained a marijuana cigarette concealed in a package of ordinary cigarettes from a different bartender. Later that evening the same detective purchased narcotics from petitioner's brother, a mere patron, in the presence of that bartender. At the time of the transaction petitioner was not present in the premises. Significantly, the purchases took place at a time when the licensee was regularly absent. Thus it cannot be said that he can be charged with actual or constructive knowledge of the incident. Indeed, respondent predicated its finding upon the ground that the employee 'in charge' of the premises participated in and condoned the prohibited conduct, thereby imputing his knowledge to the licensee. However, 'an employee's illegal activities will not necessarily be imputed to the corporate licensee. It must be demonstrated that the manager or a corporate officer had knowledge or the opportunity through reasonable diligence to acquire knowledge of the illegal acts' (*Matter of Triple S Tavern v. New York State Liq. Auth.*, 40 A.D.2d 522, *aff'd*, 31 N.Y.2d 1006). Although petitioner admitted that the bartender was 'in charge' during his brief absence, there is no evidence in the record that the bartender is a manager, officer or one possessed with managerial authority [citation omitted]. Conversely, we find substantial evidence in the record to support the charge of selling alcoholic beverages to minors. The question now becomes whether the penalty of revocation, based upon that single charge, is excessive. The standard of review is whether the punishment was 'so disproportionate to the offense, in the light of all the circumstances, as to be shocking to one's sense of fairness' [citations omitted]. In our opinion, revocation would be entirely disproportionate and the penalty has therefore been reduced to a bond forfeiture of $1,000. Finally, petitioner argues that to annul or modify the determination revoking his license and yet uphold the nonrenewal of his license would constitute an incongruous decision. Petitioner fails to grasp the essential difference between the two administrative actions. An application for renewal of a liquor license is to be regarded in the same light as the original application for a license [citation omitted]. Here the standard for review is 'whether the record discloses circumstances which leave no possible scope for the reasonable exercise of that discretion' [citations omitted]. In addition to the charges sustained at the revocation hearing and incorporated as part of the nonrenewal proceeding, other specifications, including the fact that a letter of warning had been sent to petitioner because of an altercation in the licensed premises on May 5, 1971, a seven-day suspension for sale of alcoholic beverages to minors on February 24, 1973, and a sale of alcoholic beverages on credit in violation of subdivision 5 of section 100 of the Alcoholic Beverage Control Law, were also sustained. Prior adverse history may properly be considered in determining whether a license should be renewed [citation omitted]. Considering this adverse history in conjunction with the charge properly sustainable, it cannot be said that respondent's actions were arbitrary and capricious. . . .''

The seriousness with which violations of the New York Alcoholic Beverage Control laws concerning supervision of licensed premises are viewed is illustrated dramatically by the following case. The views expressed are representative of judicial thinking in regard to strict regulation of licensees by the states.

17 CAMERON ST. RESTAURANT CORP. v.
NEW YORK STATE LIQUOR AUTHORITY
48 N.Y.2d 509, 399 N.E.2d 907 (1979)

JASEN, J.: ''On this appeal, the sole issue presented for our consideration is whether the penalty imposed on a corporate licensee by the State Liquor Authority is excessive.

''On June 1, 1974, respondent State Liquor Authority issued petitioner 17 Cameron St. Restaurant Corp., doing business as Dillons, a restaurant liquor license for the on-premises consumption of alcoholic beverages. That license was renewed annually, the last such renewal having been made for the license period expiring February 28, 1979. However, on June 26, 1978, respondent commenced a proceeding pursuant to sections 118 and 119 of the Alcoholic Beverage Control Law to revoke petitioner's license upon the ground that one of petitioner's coprincipals, Howard Kolbenhayer, a 50% shareholder of petitioner, had been convicted of a felony, to wit: criminal sale of a controlled substance in the fifth degree. Petitioner entered a plea of no contest and offered evidence of mitigating circumstances. Thereafter, on November 1, 1978, respondent ordered that petitioner's license be revoked, that petitioner forfeit a $1,000 bond which had been given to ensure compliance with the Alcoholic Beverage Control Law and that a two-year proscription against the sale of alcoholic beverages be entered on the premises at 17 Cameron Street, Southampton, New York.

"Petitioner commenced the instant CPLR article 78 proceeding contending that the penalty ordered by respondent was excessive. Upon transfer from Supreme Court, the Appellate Division granted the petition to the extent that it modified, on the law, the determination of the State Liquor Authority by reducing the penalty to bond forfeiture alone. As so modified, the determination of respondent was affirmed. Respondent appeals from this judgment. There should be a reversal.

"It should be noted at the outset that petitioner does not deny the existence of the facts underlying the revocation proceeding, nor does it now contend that a disciplinary proceeding could not properly be based upon these facts. Rather, petitioner's sole contention is that the sanction imposed by respondent was excessive. In this situation, the role of the courts in reviewing the penalty imposed by an administrative agency is extremely limited. Indeed, it is well settled that 'where the finding of guilt is confirmed and punishment has been imposed, the test is whether such punishment is " 'so disproportionate to the offense, in light of all the circumstances, as to be shocking to one's sense of fairness'." ' *Matter of Pell v. Board of Educ.*, 34 N.Y.2d 222, 233, 356 N.Y.S.2d 833, 841, 313 N.E.2d 321, 327; *Matter of Stolz v. Board of Regents of Univ. of State of N.Y.*, 4 A.D.2d 361, 165 N.Y.S.2d 179.) We cannot say, as a matter of law, that the penalty imposed was excessive in this case.

"It is beyond dispute that the liquor industry has a significant impact upon the health, welfare and morals of the people of this State and that it must, of necessity, be strictly controlled. Further, the power of the State to regulate every facet of this industry has long been recognized by the courts. (*See e.g., Seagram & Sons v. Hostetter,* 16 N.Y.2d 47, 56, 262 N.Y.S.2d 75, 79, 209 N.E.2d 701, 704, *aff'd* 384 U.S. 35, 86 S. Ct. 1254, 16 L. Ed. 2d 336.) As a result, those who engage in the sale of intoxicants do so with the knowledge that their business conduct will be subject to constant scrutiny and that any violation of the law governing their trade is subject to a penalty commensurate with the nature of the offense. Thus, where it has been shown that a coprincipal of a corporate licensee has engaged feloniously in the sale of illegal drugs, it cannot be said that the penalty of license revocation and the entry of a two-year proscription against the premises formerly operated by the guilty coprincipal is so disproportionate as to be shocking to one's sense of fairness. Trafficking in narcotics is a serious national problem and the authority, in imposing the sanctions, took cognizance of this fact.

"Nor can it be said that the inability of the remaining coprincipal to do business under the corporate license requires us to reach a contrary conclusion. As we have noted in a case involving the operation of a nursing home, another regulated industry, the disqualification of only one of two partners authorized to operate the nursing home does not oblige the licensing agency to continue such authorization for the benefit of the remaining partner alone. (*Matter of Spiegel v. Whalen*, 44 N.Y.2d 745, 405 N.Y.S.2d 679, 376 N.E.2d 1323.) The innocence of one co-owner of petitioner does not diminish the wrongdoing of his associate, nor does it obviate the necessity of penalizing this corporate petitioner where its president, who held 50% of its stock, has been shown to have engaged feloniously in the sale of illegal drugs. In our view, this penalty against the corporate licensee does not become excessive merely because it may have a financial effect upon [a] shareholder of the guilty corporation. This is a risk any shareholder assumes when a corporation operates a licensed premises.

"For the above reasons, the judgment of the Appellate Division should be reversed, with costs, and the determination of the State Liquor Authority reinstated."

19 Responsibility Arising from the Sale of Food, Beverages, and Intoxicants

19:1 *Liability for Serving Unfit Food*

The liability of an innkeeper for serving unfit food does not arise from the innkeeper-guest relationship. An innkeeper's liability to a guest or to a nonguest arising from the sale of food is the same as that of a restaurant keeper to a patron. Such liability is based on principles of the law of torts and contracts.

The general rule of tort law is that a person is responsible for any injury or damage caused by his own negligence. By virtue of the master-servant relationship, a hotel or restaurant keeper will be held vicariously liable for the negligent acts of his employees committed within the scope of their employment.

Negligence is generally defined as a failure to exercise reasonable care. Thus if a chef were to open a can of meat which appeared green and emitted an offensive odor, which he then cooked, the innkeeper or restaurateur would be liable to a patron who became ill from eating the meal so prepared. The action of the chef in preparing food which a reasonable man would know to be unfit for consumption would constitute negligence, making his employer liable to a person harmed by such negligent action.

Negligence, however, is an element in only a small minority of unwholesome food cases. Since negligence must be shown to establish tort liability, and since employees generally will not serve food which is known, or should be known to a reasonable person, to be spoiled, in the vast majority of cases tort recovery based on negligence will be unavailable to patrons who have been served unwholesome food.[1]

19:2 *The Implied Warranty of Fitness*

In the absence of negligence, the recovery of a plaintiff who has been served unwholesome food can be based on the implied warranties of merchantability and fitness. In order for there to be a warranty claim there must be a sale. Tra-

---

[1]It is not quite true that negligence must be shown to establish tort liability. There are circumstances in which strict tort liability, that is, liability without negligence, will be imposed, notably if defendant engages in an ultrahazardous activity, such as the use of dynamite. The serving of food, however, is not an activity that gives rise to strict liability, and for our purposes it is fair to say that tort recovery must be founded upon a showing of negligence.

ditionally, the furnishing of food and drink to a guest or a restaurant patron was held not to be a sale.

> In neither case does the transaction, insofar as it involves the supply of food or drink to customers, partake of the character of a sale of goods. The essence of it is not an agreement for the transfer of the general property of the food and drink placed at the command of the customer for the satisfaction of his desires, or actually appropriated by him in the process of appeasing his appetite or thirst. The customer does not become the owner of the food set before him. . . . He is privileged to eat and that is all. The uneaten food is not his. He cannot do what he pleases with it. That which is set before him or placed at his command is provided to enable him to satisfy his immediate wants, and for no other purpose. He may satisfy those wants; but there he must stop. He may not turn over unconsumed portions to others at his pleasure, or carry away such portions. The true essence of the transaction is service in the satisfaction of human need or desire—ministry to a bodily want. . . . What he thus pays for includes all that enters into the conception of service, and with it no small factor of personal service. It does not contemplate the transfer of the general property in the food supplied as a factor in the service rendered.[2]

Today, however, the rule is that furnishing of food by a restaurant does constitute a sale. In 1924, the New York Court of Appeals in *Temple v. Keeler*[3] held that a restaurant owner sells the food which he serves to his guests. "[W]here a customer enters a restaurant, receives, eats and pays for food, delivered to him on his order, the transaction is the purchase of goods. . . . Consequently there is an implied warranty that the food is reasonably fit for consumption."[4]

The Uniform Commercial Code (UCC) has now been enacted in all fifty states, the District of Columbia, Guam, and the Virgin Islands as the law governing commercial transactions. Section 2-314 provides that:

> (1) . . . a warranty that the goods shall be merchantable is implied in a contract for their sale if the seller is a merchant with respect to goods of that kind. Under this section the serving for value of food or drink to be consumed either on the premises or elsewhere is a sale.
> (2) Goods to be merchantable must be at least such as . . .
>   (c) are fit for the ordinary purposes for which such goods are used.

The enactment of the UCC by the legislatures of the various states replaced the prior case law, which in some jurisdictions followed the *Merrill v. Hodson* approach until the enactment of the code, while others had adopted a *Temple v. Keeler* approach. Now the provision of food or drink by a restaurateur or innkeeper is held to be a sale, subject to the warranty of merchantability in all American jurisdictions.[5]

---

[2]Merrill v. Hodson, 88 Conn. 314, 317–18, 91 A. 533, 534–35 (1914).
[3]238 N.Y. 344, 144 N.E. (1924).
[4]*Id.* at 346, 144 N.E. at 635.
[5]For a discussion of the service-of-food-as-a-sale controversy before the enactment of the UCC,

19:3 *The Privity of Contract Requirement*

The privity of contract requirement concerns who may recover for the breach of an implied warranty. Liability of a seller for breach of an implied warranty of fitness arises, if at all, by contract and a sale accomplished by the making of the contract. That is to say that the breach of warranty occurs when the unfit (i.e., unmerchantable) food is served (i.e., sold) to a customer.

In the course of the development of the law of warranties, a principle of law became established whereby recovery for breach of warranty was limited to a plaintiff who had a contractual relationship with the defendant-seller. This relationship is known as privity of contract. Suppose a guest in a hotel invites a friend as her guest for dinner, and the guest of the hotel guest is injured as a result of deleterious food served to her. The food is ordered and paid for by the hotel guest. Would lack of privity of contract be a good defense in an action for breach of warranty by the injured guest of the guest? Again, we see that the law has changed. Traditionally, such an action would have been barred, but the following case illustrates the modern approach to this question.

CONKLIN v. HOTEL WALDORF ASTORIA CORP.
5 Misc. 2d 496, 161 N.Y.S.2d 205 (City Ct. 1957)

STARKE, J: "This case was tried with a jury. Plaintiff sued for breach of warranty and the defendant contended that there was a lack of privity between the plaintiff and the defendant.

"The following facts were conceded: Plaintiff was invited as a guest of a friend to lunch in the Peacock Alley Restaurant of the Hotel Waldorf. During the course of eating her lunch, plaintiff bit into a roll and sustained certain injuries due to a piece of glass concealed and imbedded in the roll. Plaintiff's friend signed the luncheon check and paid for the lunch for herself as well as for the plaintiff. Plaintiff did not reimburse her friend for the cost of the meal.

"Defendant rested at the end of plaintiff's case and moved for a dismissal of the complaint, which motion was denied. Both sides then moved for a directed verdict. The court directed a verdict for the plaintiff and asked the jury to assess damages, albeit in an advisory capacity, for by consent determination of the question of damages was left for the court. The jury recommended the sum of $1,415 in favor of the plaintiff, and the court took the recommendation under advisement. Decision was also reserved on the renewed motion by the defendant to dismiss the complaint as a matter of law, with 10 day for briefs to both sides.

"Defendant contends that plaintiff cannot be successful on the breach of warranty theory because there was no privity or contractual relationship between the plaintiff and the defendant under subdivision 2 of section 96 of the Personal Property Law. Defendant claims that plaintiff is not to be deemed the 'pur-

---

see Sofman v. Denham Food Service, Inc., 37 N.J. 304, 308–14, 181 A.2d 168, 170–73 (1972) (Schettino, J. concurring).

chaser' because her friend paid the check. Defendant further urges that plaintiff's remedy was in negligence instead of in contract and that plaintiff has made the wrong election. . . .

"The sole issue is whether plaintiff should be barred from recovery in a breach of warranty action because her friend paid the check. . . .

"In order to determine whether there was privity between the plaintiff and the defendant, let us examine these question: When was the contract formed? When were the obligations of the respective parties created?

"A contractual relationship existed between the plaintiff and the defendant long before payment of the restaurant check. The contract did not first come into being when the check was paid. An implied contract was formed when plaintiff and her friend became patrons of the restaurant, placed their orders for food and their orders were accepted. At that moment, an implied obligation on the part of both the plaintiff and her friend was individually created to pay for whatever was individually ordered. Simultaneously, the defendant impliedly agreed to serve each of them food fit for human consumption. The warranty arose then and ran to both of them. The warranty does not run only to the one who eventually pays the check. The actual payment of the check does not determine the time when the contract comes into being.

"Even if plaintiff's friend placed the order, the hotel knew it was serving an order for two persons. When one person undertakes to give the order for several people, that person is acting as the agent for the others. Which person pays the check and whether they reimburse each other or not is only a matter of private arrangement between the customers themselves. This is of no concern to therestaurateur as long as he is paid. The plaintiff and her friend relied on defendant's implied promise to serve each of them with fit and wholesome food. Consequently, it makes no difference whether the plaintiff or her friend paid the check. . . .

"Assume that plaintiff and her friend had taken violently ill in the middle of the meal as a result of harmful or contaminated food necessitating their removal to a hospital by ambulance and that the check was not paid at all. The nonpayment would not bar their action. Even if the check were not paid, it would not alter the obligation of each to pay, nor would it alter the obligation owed to each patron not to breach the warranty of fitness. In the event of a failure or refusal to pay the check, the defendant would not be without remedy. The restaurant could enforce collection against each person who ordered food, or assert a counterclaim with respect thereto in an action by the patron. . . .

"A careful analysis of the makeup of the contract and the formation thereof can produce only one sensible conclusion. A patron impliedly obligates himself to pay when the order is taken by the waiter, at which time the warranty likewise commences. No less an authority than Dean Prosser says: When a customer orders food in a restaurant, 'the understanding certainly is that the guest owns the food and must pay for it *from the moment it reaches his table*, and is free to wrap it up in a newspaper and carry it away if he likes.' (27 Minn. L. Rev. 152.) (Italics mine).

"The precise issue did arise in *Jenson v. Berris* (31 Cal. App. 2d 537) where the plaintiff, in company with other members of a card club, allegedly sustained injuries from the eating of unwholesome food in a restaurant, and was allowed a recovery as against the restaurateur for breach of warranty, *although she did not pay for the food herself.*

"The same issue also arose in *Coca-Cola Bottling Works v. Lyons* (145 Miss. 876). There the donee of a sub-vendee of food was given the right to recover for breach of warranty. The bottling company sold the bottled drink to the drugstore, where Mrs. Lyons and her friend procured two bottles. *The friend had ordered and paid for both.* . . .

"Defendant's counsel has overextended the use of the word 'privity' here. He has confused the restaurant situation with the store purchase as to when the contract is formed in each case. When a woman purchases food in a store, the contract of sale takes place when she either pays for the purchase or when the storekeeper permits a charge to her account.

"Consequently, I find that plaintiff is deemed to be a 'purchaser' even though her friend paid the check. The warranty ran to each from the time the order was placed and accepted. Aside from this finding, it is to be noted that the defendant admitted in its answer that plaintiff was a patron and did not deny this allegation in plaintiff's complaint; nor did defendant ever amend its answer.

"Viewed as a direct breach of contract, or under the theory of agency, . . . plaintiff is nonetheless entitled to recover. . . .

"With respect to the jury's recommendation of $1,415, the court finds that this sum is inadequate and will not fairly and reasonably compensate the plaintiff. Plaintiff sustained the loss of her upper right lateral tooth which broke off irregularly at the gum line when she bit into the roll. The stump of the tooth was extracted. Another tooth was slightly damaged. . . . " [The court increased plaintiff's recovery to $3,000.]

19:4 What Is "Fit to Eat"?

In determining whether there has been a breach of warranty of fitness for consumption, one must determine whether the food was legally fit to eat. An upset stomach is not necessarily a cause of action, even where it can be traced to food served by a restaurateur. The injured patron must show that his discomfort was caused by something that the law considers to be a defect.

The clearest case of a legal defect is that of the unanticipated foreign object. A centipede in tomato soup, pebbles in canned beans, a piece of glass in a roll are defects and clearly actionable. But a bone in fish or chicken which the patron ingests and chokes upon is not a defect that will give rise to an action for breach of warranty.

A common test of whether an injurious substance in food constitutes a legal defect is the test of "naturalness," that is, whether the substance is natural or foreign to the food.

WEBSTER V. BLUE SHIP TEA ROOM, INC.
347 Mass. 421, 198 N.E.2d 309 (1964)

REARDON, J.: "This is a case which by its nature evokes earnest study not only of the law but also of the culinary traditions of the Commonwealth which bear so heavily upon its outcome. It is an action to recover damages for personal injuries sustained by reason of a breach of implied warranty of food served by the defendant in its restaurant. An auditor, whose findings of fact were not to be final, found for the plaintiff. On a retrial in the Superior Court before a judge and jury, in which the plaintiff testified, the jury returned a verdict for her. The defendant is here on exceptions to the refusal of the judge (1) to strike certain portions of the auditor's report, (2) to direct a verdict for the defendant, and (3) to allow the defendant's motion for the entry of a verdict in its favor under leave reserved.

"The jury could have found the following facts: On Saturday, April 25, 1959, about 1 P.M., the plaintiff, accompanied by her sister and her aunt, entered the Blue Ship Tea Room operated by the defendant. The group was seated at a table and supplied with menus.

"This restaurant, which the plaintiff characterized as 'quaint,' was located in Boston 'on the third floor of an old building on T Wharf which overlooks the ocean.'

"The plaintiff, who had been born and brought up in New England (a fact of some consequence), ordered clam chowder and crabmeat salad. Within a few minutes she received tidings to the effect that 'there was no more clam chowder,' whereupon she ordered a cup of fish chowder. Presently, there was set before her 'a small bowl of fish chowder.' She had previously enjoyed a breakfast about 9 A.M. which had given her no difficulty. 'The fish chowder contained haddock, potatoes, milk, water and seasoning. The chowder was milky in color and not clear. The haddock and potatoes were in chunks' (also a fact of consequence). 'She agitated it a little with the spoon and observed that it was a fairly full bowl. . . . It was hot when she got it, but she did not tip it with her spoon because it was hot . . . but stirred it in an up and under motion. She denied that she did this because she was looking for something, but it was rather because she wanted an even distribution of fish and potatoes.' 'She started to eat it, alternating between the chowder and crackers which were on the table with . . . [some] rolls. She ate about 3 or 4 spoonfuls then stopped. She looked at the spoonfuls as she was eating. She saw equal parts of liquid, potato and fish as she spooned it into her mouth. She did not see anything unusual about it. After 3 or 4 spoonfuls she was aware that something had lodged in her throat because she couldn't swallow and couldn't clear her throat by gulping and she could feel it.' This misadventure led to two esophagoscopies at the Massachusetts General Hospital, in the second of which, on April 27, 1959, a fish bone was found and removed. The sequence of events produced injury to the plaintiff which was not insubstantial.

"We must decide whether a fish bone lurking in a fish chowder, about the ingredients of which there is no other complaint, constitutes a breach of implied warranty under applicable provisions of the Uniform Commercial Code, the annotations to which are not helpful on this point. As the judge put it in his charge, 'Was the fish chowder fit to be eaten and wholesome? . . . [N]obody is claiming that the fish itself wasn't wholesome. . . . But the bone of contention here—I don't mean that for a pun—but was this fish bone a foreign substance that made the fish chowder unwholesome or not fit to be eaten?'

"The plaintiff has vigorously reminded us of the high standards imposed by this court where the sale of food is involved (*see Flynn v. First Natl. Stores Inc.* 296 Mass. 521, 523) and has made reference to cases involving stones in beans (*Friend v. Childs Dining Hall Co.* 231 Mass. 65), trichinae in pork (*Holt v. Mann*, 294 Mass. 21,22), and to certain other cases, here and elsewhere, serving to bolster her contention of breach of warranty.

"The defendant asserts that here was a native New Englander eating fish chowder in a 'quaint' Boston dining place where she had been before; that '[f]ish chowder, as it is served and enjoyed by New Englanders, is a hearty dish, originally designed to satisfy the appetites of our seamen and fishermen'; that '[t]his court knows well that we are not talking of some insipid broth as is customarily served to convalescents.' We are asked to rule in such fashion that no chef is forced 'to reduce the pieces of fish in the chowder to miniscule size in an effort to ascertain if they contained any pieces of bone.' 'In so ruling,' we are told (in the defendant's brief), 'the court will not only uphold its reputation for legal knowledge and acumen, but will, as loyal sons of Massachusetts, save our world-renowned fish chowder from degenerating into an insipid broth containing the mere essence of its former stature as a culinary masterpiece.' Notwithstanding these passionate entreaties we are bound to examine with detachment the nature of fish chowder and what might happen to it under varying interpretations of the Uniform Commercial Code.

"Chowder is an ancient dish preëxisting even 'the appetites of our seamen and fishermen.' It was perhaps the common ancestor of the 'more refined cream soups, purées, and bisques.' Berolzheimer, The American Woman's Cook Book (Publisher's Guild Inc., New York, 1941) p. 176. The word 'chowder' comes from the French 'chaudière,' meaning a 'cauldron' or 'pot.' 'In the fishing villages of Brittany . . . "faire la chaudière" means to supply a cauldron in which is cooked a mess of fish and biscuit with some savoury condiments, a hodgepodge contributed by the fishermen themselves, each of whom in return receives his share of the prepared dish. The Breton fishermen probably carried the custom to Newfoundland, long famous for its chowder, whence it has spread to Nova Scotia, New Brunswick, and New England.' A New English Dictionary (MacMillan and Co., 1893) p. 386. Our literature over the years abounds in references not only to the delights of chowder but also to its manufacture. A namesake of the plaintiff, Daniel Webster, had a recipe for fish chowder which has survived into a number of modern cookbooks and in which the removal of fish bones is not mentioned at all. One old time recipe recited in the New English Dictionary study defines chowder as 'A dish made of fresh fish (esp. cod) or clams, stewed with slices of pork or bacon, onions, and biscuit. "Cider and champagne are sometimes added." ' Hawthorne, in The House of the Seven Gables (Allyn and Bacon, Boston, 1957) p. 8, speaks of '[a] codfish of sixty pounds, caught in the bay, [which] had been dissolved into the rich liquid of a chowder.' A chowder variant, cod 'Muddle,' was made in Plymouth in the 1890s by taking 'a three or four pound codfish, head added. Season with salt and pepper and boil in just enough water to keep from burning. When cooked, add milk and piece of butter.' The recitation of these ancient formulae suffices to indicate that in the construction of chowders in these parts in other years, worries about fish bones played no role whatsoever. This broad outlook on chowders has persisted in more modern cookbooks. 'The chowder of today is much the same as the old chowder. . . . '' The American Woman's Cook Book, *supra*, p. 176. The all embracing Fannie Farmer states in a portion of her recipe, fish chowder is made with a 'fish skinned, but head and tail left on. Cut off head and tail and remove fish from backbone. Cut fish in 2-inch pieces and set aside. Put head, tail, and backbone broken in pieces, in stewpan; add 2 cups cold water and bring slowly to a boiling point. . . . ' The liquor thus produced from the bones is added to the balance of the chowder. Farmer, The Boston Cooking School Cook Book (Little Brown Co., 1937) p. 166.

"Thus, we consider a dish which for many long years, if well made, has been made generally as outlined above. It is not too much to say that a person sitting down in New England to consume a good New England fish chowder embarks on a gustatory adventure which may entail the removal of some fish bones from his bowl as he proceeds. We are not inclined to tamper with age old recipes by any amendment reflecting the plaintiff's view of the effect of the Uniform Commercial Code upon them. We are aware of the heavy body of case law involving foreign substances in food, but we sense a strong distinction between them and those relative to unwholesomeness of the food itself, e.g., tainted mackerel (*Smith v. Gerrish*, 256 Mass. 183), and a fish bone in a fish chowder. Certain Massachusetts cooks might cavil at the ingredients contained in the chowder in this case in that it lacked the heartening lift of salt pork. In any event, we consider that the joys of life in New England include the ready availability of fresh fish chowder. We should be prepared to cope with the hazards of fish bones, the occasional presence of which in chowders is, it seems to us, to be anticipated, and which, in the light of a hallowed tradition, do not impair their fitness or merchantability. While we are buoyed up in this conclusion by *Shapiro v. Hotel Statler Corp.*, 132 F. Supp. 891 (S.D. Cal.), in which the bone which afflicted the plaintiff appeared in 'Hot Barquette of Seafood Mornay,' we know that the United States District Court of Southern California, situated as are we upon a coast, might be expected to share our views. We are most impressed, however, by *Allen v. Grafton*, 170 Ohio St., 249, where in Ohio, the Midwest, in a case where the plaintiff was injured by a piece of oyster shell in an order of fried oysters, Mr. Justice TAFT (now Chief Justice) in a majority opinion held that 'the possible presence of a piece of oyster shell in or attached to an oyster is so well known to anyone who eats oysters that we can say as a matter of law that one who eats oysters can reasonably anticipate and guard against eating such a piece of shell. . . . ' (P. 259.)

"Thus, while we sympathize with the plaintiff who has suffered a peculiarly New England injury, the order [denying defendant's motion for a directed verdict] must be [reversed].

"Exceptions sustained.

"Judgment for the defendant."

The foreign-natural test probably originated in *Mix v. Ingersoll Candy Co.*,[6] in which plaintiff sued for injuries sustained in eating a chicken pot pie which contained "a dangerous, harmful and injurious subject, to-wit, a sharp and pointed fragment and/or sliver of chicken bone."[7] Said the court:

> We have examined a great many cases dealing with the question of liability of restaurant keepers which arose out of the serving of food which was held to be unfit for human consumption, and we have failed to find a single case in which the facts are similar to the instant case, or in which a court has extended the liability based upon an implied warranty of a restaurant keeper to cover the presence in food of bones which are natural to the type of meat served. All of the cases are instances in which the food was found not to be reasonably fit for human consumption, either by reason of the presence of a foreign substance, or an impure or noxious condition of the food itself, such as for example [*sic*], glass, stones, wires or nails in the food served, or tainted, decayed, diseased, or infected meats or vegetables. . . . [A]s a matter of common knowledge chicken pies occasionally contain chicken bones. We have no hesitancy in so holding, and we are of the opinion that despite the fact that a chicken bone may occasionally be encountered in a chicken pie, such chicken pie, in the absence of some further defect, is reasonably fit for human consumption. Bones which are natural to the type of meat served cannot legitimately be called a foreign substance, and a consumer who eats meat dishes ought to anticipate and be on his guard against the presence of such bones. . . . Certainly no liability would attach to a restaurant keeper for the serving of a T-bone steak, or a beef stew, which contained a bone natural to the type of meat served, or if a fish dish should contain a fish bone, or if a cherry pie should contain a cherry stone—although it be admitted that an ideal cherry pie would be stoneless.[8]

In *Musso v. Picadilly Cafeterias, Inc.*[9] plaintiff encountered a cherry stone or pit in a slice of cherry pie. The court expressed the foreign-natural rule as follows:

[6]Cal. 2d 674, 59 P.2d 144 (1936).

[7]*Id.* at 676, 59 P.2d at 145.

[8]*Id.* at 681–82, 59 P.2d at 148. California has now joined other states in voiding the foreign-natural test of food fitness and adopting the "reasonable expectations" test to determine whether a foodserver has breached the warranty of fitness for human consumption. See Mexicali Rose v. Superior Court of Alameda, 4 Cal. Rptr. 2d 145, 822 P.2d 1292 (1992).

[9]178 So. 2d 421 (La. App. 1965).

The rationale of the majority rule as expressed in the cited authorities is that substances which are a natural part of the food served are not considered foreign matter or substances if inadvertently left therein. On this premise it is reasoned that the presence of substances natural to the ingredients or finished product does not constitute breach of the vendor's implied warranty that the food is wholesome and fit for human consumption. . . . In this respect it is further reasoned common experience dictates that one eating the meat of animals, fowl or fish should do so with the knowledge such foods may contain pieces of bone.[10]

However, not all jurisdictions follow this foreign-natural rule in determining whether there has been a breach of the warranty of fitness for consumption. Some states apply a reasonable expectation test to determine fitness.[11] Compare the treatment of the cherry pit in *Musso* with a Florida court's handling of a walnut shell in *Zabner v. Howard Johnson's, Inc.*[12] The court held for a plaintiff who had been injured by a piece of walnut shell concealed in a dish of maple walnut ice cream.

The reasoning applied in this [foreign-natural] test is fallacious because it assumes that all substances which are natural to the food in one stage or another of preparation are, in fact, anticipated by the average consumer in the final product served. It does not logically follow that every product which contains some chicken must as a matter of law be expected to contain occasionally or frequently chicken bones or chicken-bone slivers because chicken bones are natural to chicken meat and both have a common origin. . . . A nutshell natural to nut meat can cause as much harm as a foreign substance, such as a pebble, piece of wire or glass. All are indigestable and likely to cause the injury. Naturalness of the substance to any ingredients in the food served is important only in determining whether the consumer may reasonably expect to find such substance in the particular type of dish or style of food served. . . . The test should be what is "*reasonably expected*" by the consumer in the food as served, not what might be natural to the ingredients of that food prior to preparation.[13]

One should not assume from these cases that plaintiffs only win in states which employ a reasonable expectation test to determine fitness. In *Spencer v. Good Earth Restaurant Corp.*[14] plaintiffs who were injured by eating chow mein that contained pieces of glass recovered under the foreign-natural rule. The difference is that a reasonable expectation test holds a server of food to a higher standard of care than a foreign-natural test. Foreign matter will make food legally unfit under either standard, but a reasonable expectation standard will impose liability in certain cases even for natural material. You should become aware which test will be employed by the courts in your state.

[10]*Id.* at 426–27.
[11]For a discussion and comparison of these two tests, *see* Matthews v. Campbell Soup Co., 380 F. Supp. 1061 (S.D. Tex. 1974).
[12]201 So. 2d 824 (Fla. App. 1967).
[13]*Id.* at 826.
[14]164 Conn. 194, 319 A.2d 403 (1972).

MATTHEWS V. CAMPBELL SOUP CO.
380 F. Supp. 1061 (S.D. Tex. 1974)

SEALS, D.J.: "This action is before the Court on a Motion for Summary Judgment filed by Defendant. In this diversity suit, 28 U.S.C. § 1332(a)(1), Plaintiff seeks to recover for injuries to his teeth and gums which were allegedly suffered while he was eating the contents of a can of Defendant's Oyster Stew Soup. Plaintiff claims that the injuries were caused by a small deleterious object in the soup. Plaintiff surrendered this object to Defendant for examination and it has been identified as a small irregularly shaped oyster pearl.

"Plaintiff sets forth two theories of recovery: strict liability in tort and negligence in the manufacture and labeling of this product. Defendant contends that on the undisputed facts before the Court, Plaintiff cannot prevail on a theory of strict liability and that there is no evidence in the record to raise an issue of negligence. . . .

"Texas courts have long recognized that the manufacturers of food products warrant that they are wholesome and fit for human consumption. [Citations omitted.] The warranty was imposed by operation of law as a matter of public policy: "It seems to be the rule that where food products sold for human consumption are unfit for that purpose, there is such an utter failure of the purpose for which the food is sold, and the consequences of eating unsound food are so disastrous to human health and life, that the law imposes a warranty of purity in favor of the ultimate consumer as a matter of public policy.' [Citation omitted.]

"In *McKisson v. Sales Affiliates, Inc.*, 416 S.W.2d 787 (Tex. 1967), this strict liability concept applicable to foodstuffs was extended to include consumer products generally. [Citation omitted.] The *McKisson* court adopted the Restatement, Second, Torts § 402A which provides as follows:

"Special Liability of Seller of Product for Physical Harm to User or Consumer

"1. One who sells any product in a defective condition unreasonably dangerous to the user or consumer or his property is subject to liability for physical harm thereby caused to the ultimate user or consumer, or to his property, if

"(a) the seller is engaged in the business of selling such a product, and

"(b) it is expected to and does reach the user or consumer without substantial change in the condition in which it is sold.

"2. The rule stated in Subsection (1) applies although

"(a) the seller has exercised all possible care in the preparation and sale of his product, and

"(b) the user or consumer has not bought the product from or entered into any contractual relation with the seller.

"In order to prevail under this strict liability standard Plaintiff must establish that: (1) the product in question was defective; (2) the defect existed at the time the products left the hands of the defendant; (3) that because of the defect the product was unreasonably dangerous to the user or consumer (plaintiff); (4) that the consumer was injured or suffered damages; (5) and that the defect (if proved) was the proximate cause of the injuries suffered.

"Defendant argues that, as a matter of law, the can of Oyster Stew Soup at issue here was not unfit, unwholesome, defective, or unreasonably dangerous. . . . [I]n light of the Texas Supreme Court's adoption of Section 402A of the Restatement in *McKisson, supra*, it is apparent that a food product is defective or unreasonably dangerous if it is unwholesome or unfit for human consumption and vice versa.

"Defendant's position is bottomed on what may be labeled the 'foreign-natural' doctrine. This doctrine, which has been neither accepted nor rejected by Texas courts, apparently first emerged in *Mix v. Ingersoll Candy Co.*, 6 Cal. 2d 674, 59 P.2d 144 (1936). . . .

"Probably a majority of jurisdictions having occasion to treat the problem have adopted the *Mix* rationale. . . .

"Not all jurisdictions have followed the foreign-natural view; it has been rejected by several courts in favor of a 'reasonable expectation' test. . . . [Citations omitted.]

"Texas courts have never been in a position requiring an election between these two competing doctrines. A great number of cases involving harmful objects have been litigated but the objects were so obviously 'foreign' that the issue did not arise.

" . . . [T]his Court holds that, if faced with the problem, Texas courts would follow the reasonable expectation rule. . . . It is obvious that the 'reasonable expectation' approach is considerably more compatible and consistent with Section 402A which has been adopted as the law of Texas in product liability cases. Section 402A makes the seller liable for injuries caused by defective or unreasonably dangerous products. 'Defective condition' is defined in Comment (g) as ' . . . a condition not contemplated by the ultimate consumer, which will be unreasonably dangerous to him.' An article is 'unreasonably dangerous' according to Comment (i) if it is ' . . . dangerous to an extent beyond that which would be contemplated by the ordinary consumer who purchases it, with the ordinary knowledge common to the community as to its characteristics.' These Comments have been viewed as persuasive if not controlling in the application of Section 402A. [Citation omitted.]

"If Texas courts were to follow the 'reasonable expectation' test they logically should reach a result consistent in every case with the Restatement definitions of 'defective condition' and 'unreasonably dangerous.' This would not necessarily be true under the foreign-natural doctrine. It would be possible under that approach only if it is assumed that consumers *always* contemplate the presence of every species of object which might be categorized as natural to the food they are eating regardless of how infrequently the object might appear in common experience. That is obviously a faulty assumption which Texas courts are not at all likely to make. . . .

" . . . [T]he only way of avoiding misapplication of the foreign-natural theory is to focus on what the consumer might reasonably expect to find in the final product. This being the case it would make even more sense to discard the foreign-natural distinction and go directly to the reasonable expectation issue. The use of these labels does not advance the inquiry and unnecessarily increases the possibility of confusion on the ultimate issue.

"Having settled on the 'reasonable expectation' standard the question before this Court can be restated. Can it be said, as a matter of law, that the consumer can reasonably expect to encounter a pearl in a can of Defendant's Oyster Stew Soup. This Court thinks not. It is clearly an issue for the jury to decide. . . . Defendant's Motion For Summary Judgment on the issue of strict liability is therefore denied.

"Defendant's motion going to Plaintiff's negligence theory of recovery is also denied. Even where there are no facts in dispute, it is usually for the jury to decide whether the conduct in question meets the reasonable man standard. [Citation omitted.] On the facts reflected in this record the Court cannot say that Defendant was not negligent in the manufacture and labeling of this product as a matter of law."

The question of whether the dispenser of a food product should be held liable for a defect where the food was not prepared by the dispenser and the defect was not discoverable except by destruction of the goods was answered in the affirmative in *Cushing v. Rodman*.[15] The court's argument may be summarized as follows:

Courts holding against strict liability under a warranty theory argue that the evil should be corrected at its source through pure food and drug laws and inspection laws at the production center and that the dispenser, therefore, should not be liable. However, the dispenser of food and the consumer have a contractual relationship which must be considered. The consumer relies on the dispenser's experience and trade skill in preparing and serving food. There is no effective opportunity for the consumer to inspect or select the food as far as wholesomeness is concerned. In fact, nothing will protect the consumer effectively except wholesome food.

Social interest in individual safety is the key here. It was the opinion of the *Cushing* court that were courts to require negligence on the part of the dispenser before liability was imposed, then plaintiffs simply would not be able to get the necessary proof. The burden on the dispenser is not really so great since he can pass it on to the public as part of his price of service. Inspection at the source of the food is not enough; the public should get double protection in this area. That the dispenser bought the food from someone else is no reason not to apply the warranty. Besides the dispenser can sue his vendor. Regardless of who bears the initial burden, the cost will be spread at large in the price of the goods. It would be altogether too difficult for the consumer to sue the source of supply, and there may well be privity problems.

[15]82 F.2d 864 (D.C. Cir 1936).

In *Hochberg v. O'Donnell's Restaurant, Inc.,*[16] a jury was permitted to determine whether the restaurant owner breached an implied warranty of merchantability in selling the consumer a martini containing an unpitted olive. The consumer, thinking it had no pit, broke a tooth upon biting it. He argued that he was reasonably led to this conclusion because the olive contained a hole in one end. In rejecting the foreign-natural test on which the claim had been dismissed below and remanding the case for trial, the appellate court stated that the naturalness of a substance "to a product at one stage of preparation does not mean necessarily that it will be reasonably anticipated by the consumer in the final product served."

A jury decision denying recovery to a consumer who broke a tooth on a cherry pit in a pie purchased from a restaurant vending machine, where the trial court, sitting without a jury, applied both tests, was affirmed on appeal. The court, refusing to make a choice between the two rules, upheld the lower court on the issue of fact.[17]

The case to follow is significant in that the Supreme Court of Alabama ruled that the presence of a one-centimeter bone in a fish fillet did not render the fish unfit or unreasonably dangerous, as a matter of law. Thus the restaurant keeper was held not liable to a patron under a reasonable expectations warranty theory of liability, contrary to a jury verdict for the patron.

Ex Parte Morrison's Cafeteria of Montgomery, Inc.
431 So. 2d 975 (Ala. 1983)

Shores, J.: "This case presents a question of first impression in this state. Morrison's Cafeteria of Montgomery, Inc., petitioned this Court for a writ of certiorari to the Court of Civil Appeals following that court's affirmance of the trial court's judgment entered on a jury verdict totalling $6,000.78 against Morrison's for injuries sustained when Rodney Haddox, a minor, choked on a fishbone while dining at the restaurant.

"The facts as found by the Court of Civil Appeals and by which we are bound are as follows:

"Mrs. Haddox testified that around 2:00 or 3:00 P.M. one afternoon in May 1980, she and her three-year-old son Rodney went to Morrison's Cafeteria. Rodney wanted some fish. Mrs. Haddox took one tray and she and Rodney proceeded down the food line. Mrs. Haddox's testimony as to how she received a portion of fish almondine is conflicting. At one point in her testimony she stated that she pointed to a piece of fish and told the man behind the counter that she would take that piece of fish. At another point she stated that she asked for fried fish. At yet another point she stated that she asked for fried fish fillet. She received a portion of the fish and put it on her tray together with another food and drink. She saw no signs advertising the

[16]272 A.2d 846 (D.C. App. 1971).
[17]Hunt v. Ferguson-Paulus Enterprises, 243 Or. 546, 415 P.2d 13 (1966).

fish dish. No one told her that it was a fillet or that it was boneless. She subjectively believed it to be a fillet because of its shape and her prior experience with eating fish dishes at Morrison's. When she and Rodney were seated, Mrs. Haddox cut off a portion of the fish and put it on a plate for Rodney. She testified that she pulled it apart with her knife and fork into very small pieces. At one point Mrs. Haddox testified that she pulled Rodney's portion apart to check for bones. Later in her testimony she stated that she was merely cutting it into bite-sized pieces and not checking for bones. Rodney apparently became choked on the first bit of fish. When Rodney was taken to the hospital, it was discovered that a fishbone approximately one centimeter in length was lodged in his tonsil. The bone was removed after Rodney stayed in the hospital overnight. He suffered no permanent physical injury as a result of the incident. Mrs. Haddox stated that she did not know how Morrison's could have known there was a small bone in the fish. She testified however, that the manager and other personnel at Morrison's were extremely rude to her during the course of Rodney's difficulty. She could not persuade anyone to take her to the hospital and was told at the checkout counter that she must pay her bill before she left.

"The manager of Morrison's at the time of Rodney's injury testified that the fish which Mrs. Haddox bought was Spanish Mackerel fillet. Morrison's bought the fish from Pinellas Seafood Company, Inc. (Pinellas). Pinellas ships the fish to Morrison's in five- to ten-pound boxes. Morrison's uses this fish to prepare a dish they advertise as Fish Almondine. It is not advertised as boneless and employees are instructed not to tell customers that the dish is boneless. Morrison's does not offer the fish on a child's plate because the fish does sometimes contain bones.

"An employee of Pinellas at the time of Rodney's injury testified that Pinellas used machines to fillet the Spanish Mackerel bought by Morrison's. Such machines are commonly used by other wholesale fish processors. Machine filleting strips the sides of the fish away from the backbone. Using this method it is impossible to prevent the occasional presence of small bones in the fillets. Government regulations allow for the presence of small bones in fillets. The employee stated that Morrison's had not been told that Pinella's fillets were boneless. Approximately ninety-nine percent of the fillets which Pinellas produces are sold to Morrison's, and Pinellas is aware that Morrison's in turn sells the fillets to its customers. He further testified that in order for Pinellas or Morrison's to check for bones in the fillets they would have to cut them into tiny pieces. This would destroy the fillets.

"Another witness, an employee of a fish wholesaler and retailer, stated that a whole fillet of Spanish Mackerel could be recognized by its shape.

"Mrs. Haddox brought suit on behalf of Rodney and herself against Morrison's and Pinellas to recover medical expenses and to compensate Rodney for his pain and suffering. . . . Morrison's filed a cross claim against Pinellas. . . .

"The trial court submitted the case to the jury on the theories of implied warranty of fitness for human consumption and the Alabama Extended Manufacturer's Liability Doctrine (AEMLD) against Morrison's; the AEMLD as against Pinellas; and implied warranty as to Morrison's cross claim against Pinellas.

"The jury returned a verdict in favor of Mrs. Haddox and against Morrison's in the amount of $1,000.78. Rodney was awarded a verdict against Morrison's for $5,000.00. The jury found in favor of Pinellas on the cross claim. . . .

"Morrison's appealed to the Court of Civil Appeals. . . . Morrison's urged the Court of Civil Appeals to adopt the so-called 'foreign-natural' rule and determine as a matter of law that a bone in a piece of fish does not breach the implied warranty of fitness.

"A divided Court of Civil Appeals, in affirming the trial court's decision, rejected the 'foreign-natural' rule in favor of the 'reasonable expectation' test. Judge Holmes, dissenting in part, agreed with the majority's adoption of the reasonable expectation test, but did not agree that the test under the present facts mandated an affirmance of the trial court.

"This Court granted Morrison's petition for certiorari on October 19, 1982. We reverse.

"The issue concerns the interpretation to be given Ala. Code 1975, § 7-2-314, which provides in part:

"(1) Unless excluded or modified (section 7-2-316), a warranty that the goods shall be merchantable is implied in a contract for their sale if the seller is a merchant with respect to goods of that kind. Under this section the serving for value of food or drink to be consumed either on the premises or elsewhere is a sale.

"(2) Goods to be merchantable must be at least such as: . . .

"(c) Are fit for the ordinary purposes for which such goods are used. . . .

"The issue also concerns the Alabama Extended Manufacturer's Liability Doctrine, which requires that 'a plaintiff must prove he suffered injury or damages to himself or his property by one who sold a product in a defective condition unreasonably dangerous to the plaintiff as the ultimate user or consumer. . . . ' *Atkins v. American Motors Corp.*, 335 So. 2d 134, 141 (Ala. 1976).

"The two standards go hand-in-hand, for it is apparent that a food product is defective or unreasonably dangerous if it is unmerchantable or unfit for human consumption. *See Matthews v. Campbell Soup Co.*, 380 F. Supp. 1061 (S.D. Tex. 1974).

"The Court of Civil Appeals rejected the adoption of the so-called 'foreign-natural' rule urged by Morrison's. This rule first appeared in *Mix v. Ingersoll Candy Co.*, 6 Cal. 2d 674, 59 P.2d 144 (1936), . . .

"The undesirability of the foreign substance test lies in the artificial application at the initial stage of processing the food without consideration of the expectations of the consumer in the final product served. Surely it is within the expectation of the consumer to find a bone in a T-bone steak; but just as certainly it is reasonable for a consumer not to expect to find a bone in a package of hamburger meat. It is entirely possible that a natural substance found in processed food may be more indigestible and cause more injury than many 'foreign' substances.

"The 'reasonable expectation' test as adopted by the Florida courts in *Zabner v. Howard Johnson's, Inc.*, 201 So. 2d 824 (Fla. Dist. Ct. App. 1967), appears to us a more logical approach. Under that test, the pivotal issue is what is reasonably expected by the consumer in the food as served, not what might be natural to the ingredients of that food prior to preparation. *Id.* at 826 'Naturalness of the substance to any ingredients in the food served is important only in determining whether the consumer may reasonably expect to find such substance in the particular type of dish or style of food served.' *Id.*

"Adoption in this jurisdiction of the reasonable expectation test is compatible with the Alabama Extended Manufacturer's Liability Doctrine and the implied warranty of merchantability (§ 7-2-314). The terms 'defect,' 'unreasonably dangerous,' and 'merchantable' all focus upon the expectations of the ordinary consumer, possessed of the ordinary knowledge common to the community. *Casrell v. Altec Industries, Inc.*, 335 So. 2d 128, 133 (Ala. 1976), quoting *Welch v. Outboard Marine Corp.*, 481 F.2d 252 (5th Cir. 1973).

"The Court of Civil Appeals held that what a consumer is reasonably justified in expecting is a question for the jury. *Morrison's Cafeteria of Montgomery, Inc. v. Haddox*, 431 So.2d 969 (Ala. Civ. App. 1982), citing *Hochberg v. O'Donnell's Restaurant, Inc.*, 272 A.2d 846 (D.C. App. 1971). We agree that in most instances this would be true. . . . As the court concluded in *Hochberg, supra*, after holding the question of reasonable expectation to normally be a jury question: 'It is a different matter if one is injured by a bone while eating a chicken leg or steak or a whole baked fish. There, it may well be held as a matter of law that the consumer should reasonably expect to find a bone.' 272 A.2d at 849.

"We agree with Judge HOLMES in the instant case that, on the facts presented, the Court should find as a matter of law that a one-centimeter bone found in a fish fillet 'makes that fish neither unfit for human consumption nor unreasonably dangerous.' *Morrison's Cafeteria of Montgomery, Inc. v. Haddox*, 431 So. 2d 969 (Ala. Civ. App. 1982), HOLMES, J., dissenting.

"Courts cannot and must not ignore the common experience of life and allow rules to develop that would make sellers of food or other consumer goods insurers of the products they sell. As has been pointed out, 'consumers do have rather high expectations as to the safety of the products which are offered for sale to them . . . [and] they have a rather low threshold for the frustration of these expectations.' Rheingold, *What Are the Consumer's 'Reasonable Expectations?'*, 22 Bus. Law. 589 (1967).

"On the facts presented here, we find as a matter of law that the presence of a one-centimeter bone did not render the piece of fish unreasonably dangerous. As Judge HOLMES stated:

"I base this conclusion on several factors that are present in this case. First of all, it is common knowledge that fish have many bones. Furthermore, government regulations regarding fillets recognize this and allow for the presence of some bones in fillets. As one centimeter bone does not violate any of the government regulations regarding fillets. 50 C.F.R. § 263.101-.104 (1979). Finally, it was undisputed that, in light of the process used to mass produce fillets, it was commercially impractical to remove all bones.

"I stress that my opinion is based solely upon the facts of this case. For instance, if there had been a representation that the fish was boneless or if the bone had been larger or if there had been many bones, my conclusion might well be different. Under these facts, however, I would hold as a matter of law that the implied warranty of merchantability was not breached and that the AEMLD was not violated.

" . . . For these reasons, the judgment of the Court of Civil Appeals is due to be reversed and the cause remanded.

"REVERSED AND REMANDED."

The Supreme Court of Oregon has made the reasonable expectations test a jury question, as have courts in Oklahoma, Ohio, and New York.[18]

19:5   *Proof of Proximate Cause*

It is not enough for a consumer to prove that the food or beverage served was unfit or deleterious. The consumer must also prove that the unfitness caused his injury. If he fails to eliminate reasonable alternative causes equally or substantially likely to be the competent producing cause of his injury, he may not recover. A plaintiff who sued a professional caterer for injuries sustained when he bit into an olive pit in steak sauce furnished by the caterer was denied recovery because he was unable to establish lack of third-party responsibility for the presence of the pit in the sauce.[19] Since the injury was equally likely to have been caused by the third party, he failed to establish that the defendant's breach of warranty caused the harm suffered.

As with proof of unfitness, the mere happening of the accident does not establish causation, except where proximate cause can reasonably be inferred from the surrounding circumstances. In the case of the consumption of a bottled beverage plaintiff testified that she consumed two or three swallows "of the drink and then noticed that it had a vile smell and taste." On examination she discovered "a large mass of unidentified foreign substance" in the bottom of the

---

[18]*See* Gardyjan v. Tatone, 270 Or. 678, 528 P.2d 1332 (1974); Williams v. Braum Ice Cream Stores, Inc., 534 P.2d 700 (Okla. App. 1974); Thompson v. Lawson Milk Co., 48 Ohio App. 2d 143, 356 N.E.2d 309 (1976); Stark v. Chock Full O'Nuts, 77 Misc. 2d 553, 356 N.Y.S.2d 403 (1st Dep't 1974).

[19]Wintroub v. Abraham Catering Service, 186 Neb. 450, 183 N.W.2d 741 (1971).

bottle. She became sick immediately thereafter, although she was in good health prior to the incident. The bottle with its remaining foreign matter was introduced into evidence. The court concluded that on these facts plaintiff need not introduce medical proof to establish that the beverage "most probably" caused her illness. The injury was sufficiently related to the deleterious condition of the product so that proof of alternative causes could be disregarded.[20]

In *Jiles v. Church's Fried Chicken, Inc.*,[21] the Louisiana Court of Appeals found no liability, as a matter of law, for the salmonella poisoning of a child patron upon consuming defendant's chicken, absent proof that the presence of the salmonella bacteria was caused by defendant rather than by other sources of contamination.

19:6   *Statutory Violation*

Compliance with relevant statutory or other regulatory requirements does not relieve the food or beverage dispenser of liability in unfit products cases as a matter of law. Failure to comply with a required governmental health or other standard may be regarded as negligence *per se*, that is, as conclusive presumption of negligence or evidence of negligence. In order to avail himself of the doctrine of negligence *per se*, the consumer must prove (1) the statutory violation, (2) that he is within the class of persons the statute sought to protect, and (3) that the harm inflicted was one that the statute intended to prevent.

Thus the sale of "contaminated and unwholesome food" in violation of the criminal provisions of a state pure food and drug law, "may be made the basis of a civil action" by an injured consumer of that product because the intention of the statute was to protect consumers.[22] Because of the recent proliferation of consumer protection statutes at the federal and state level which deal with the product itself as well as with false advertising or fraud in connection with its sale, it behooves every food service operator to comply with all relevant regulations. Failure to do so may greatly increase the likelihood of legal liability.

19:7   *Defenses to Actions for Breach of Implied Warranty of Fitness*

Unlike cases based strictly on tort responsibility or express warranty, under which the courts virtually unanimously refuse to allow a consumer's own negligence or assumption of risk to bar recovery or comparatively reduce recovery, the authorities are divided where the action is predicated on breach of implied warranty. Some courts apply the Uniform Commercial Code, section 2-316(3)(b), which provides that a buyer who has had reasonable opportunity to examine the product before buying it, or who refuses to make such an examination, may not rely on any implied warranty "with regard to defects an examination ought in the circumstances to have revealed to him." Thus the consumer

---

[20]Miller v. Atlantic Bottling Corp., 259 S.C. 278, 191 S.E.2nd 518 (1972).
[21]441 So. 2d 393 (La. App. 1983).
[22]White v. East Tenn. Packing Co., 15 Negligence Cases 272 (Tenn. Sup. Ct. 1947).

may not recover where the food or beverage to be consumed is patently or obviously unfit to consume or where that unfitness or other risk is known to the consumer, or can be detected by reasonable examination prior to consumption.

California and the majority of states do not follow the UCC, but apply the same rule adopted for actions grounded in strict liability or express warranty. In *Kassouf v. Lee Bros. Inc.,*[23] plaintiff, who was reading her paper, began to eat a candy bar furnished by the defendant without examining it, although she stated that it "didn't taste just right." Proceeding to consume one-third of the candy, she looked at it and "saw that it was covered with worms and webbing." The court refused to allow the defense of contributory negligence, ruling that implied warranty of fitness was governed by principles derived from "absolute liability for ultrahazardous activities" and from fraud and deceit cases, where the "ultrahazardous activities" defense is disallowed.

The following case illustrates the application of the reasonable expectations test to the consumption of fish poisonous in its natural condition.

HOCH V. VENTURE ENTERPRISES, INC.
473 F. Supp. 541 (D.V.I. 1979)

YOUNG, D.J.:

Factual Background

"This lawsuit stems out of an alleged case of fish poisoning suffered by plaintiff after consuming native hind fish at defendant's restaurant, Venture Enterprises, Inc., d/b/a Daddy's Restaurant (hereafter 'Daddy's'). Plaintiffs, their wives and two other couples went to Daddy's for dinner on the evening of March 4, 1976. Stephen Hoch and Joseph Gubernick ordered the native hind fish, all the other members of the group ordered non-fish dinners. The dinners were served at approximately 10:00 P.M. and another member of the group, Alice Fioto, tasted a small amount of the native hind fish served to Gubernick. Around 1:00 A.M. the following morning, Gubernick and Hoch became ill, suffering stomach cramps, nausea, diarrhea malaise and a severe sensitivity to temperature changes. When the symptoms persisted, plaintiffs went to the emergency room at Knud Hansen Hospital where they were diagnosed and treated by Dr. Harold Hanno. Dr. Hanno diagnosed the plaintiffs as demonstrating symptoms of 'typical ciguatera poisoning.' Later, Alice Fioto reported that she felt slightly nauseous and suffered diarrhea the morning of March 5, 1976. Plaintiffs subsequently brought this suit against the Daddy's on the theory that Daddy's breached its express and implied warranty that the fish was wholesome and fit for human consumption. . . .

Motion for Partial Summary Judgment

"Plaintiffs move for entry of partial summary judgment in their favor on the issue of liability and assert three theories of liability in support, to wit: breach of

---

[23]209 Cal. App. 2d 568, 26 Cal. Rptr. 276 (1962).

defendant's express and implied warranty that the fish was fit for human consumption, and negligence *per se* relying on a safety regulation which prohibits the sale of contaminated food to the public. Defendant opposes said motion, arguing that material issues of fact are in dispute as to the issue of proximate causation; whether the cooked fish was unfit within the meaning of § 2-314 of the Uniform Commercial Code (hereafter U.C.C.) and whether the assumption of risk defense is applicable under the facts in the instant case.

"After carefully reviewing the memoranda of the parties and their supporting affidavits and documents, I conclude that there are material issues of fact which will be necessary for the jury to decide. First of all, on the record before me, I cannot find that plaintiffs have conclusively established the element of proximate causation. Rather, under the case authority cited by plaintiff, plaintiff has merely demonstrated that there is sufficient evidence in the matter *sub judice* to submit the issue of proximate cause to the jury. . . .

"Judge Christian's recent decision in *Battiste v. St. Thomas Diving Club,* 1979 St. Thomas Supp. 164 (D.C.V.I. 1979) provides as alternate basis for denying plaintiff's motion. *Battiste* involved a fish poisoning action for damages brought against Villa Olga Restaurant, wherein the parties filed cross motions for summary judgment. The defendant restaurant had argued that the implied warranty statute was inapplicable to fish poisoning because ciguatera fish poisoning is a latent natural condition in fish. The Court framing the issue as 'what legal standard governed the applicability of the implied warranty provisions of § 2-314 and § 2-315 to ciguatera fish poisoning' (1979 St. Thomas Supp. at 164) adopted a 'reasonable expectations test', which holds it is a question of fact whether a buyer could reasonably expect to find the substance in the food consumed. Only if the plaintiff did not reasonably expect to find such a substance, could it prevail on an implied warranty theory. Thus, under the *Battiste* rationale, there remains a factual question as to whether plaintiffs in the matter *sub judice* might have reasonably expected that their dinner would be contaminated by fish poisoning.

"There is yet a third basis on which to promise denial of plaintiff's motion. In *Bronson v. Club Comanche, Inc.,* 286 F. Supp. 21, 6 V.I.R. 683 (D.C.V.I. 1968), an action was brought against Club Comanche for alleged fish poisoning suffered after plaintiffs consumed a fish dinner in the restaurant. There, as here, plaintiffs sued on an implied warranty theory, relying on § 2-314 of the U.C.C. The Court held that the assumption of risk defense should be available to the defendant, noting:

"[t]he form of contributory negligence which consists in voluntarily and unreasonably proceeding to encounter a known danger may be a defense in a case of strict liability, such as this. If the consumer is fully aware of the danger and nevertheless proceeds voluntarily to make use of the product and is injured by it, he is barred from recovery. This has sometimes, perhaps more accurately been described as ceasing to place any reliance on the implied warranty rather than as assuming the risk. 286 F. Supp. at 23, 6 V.I.R. at 687–688.

"Thus, in the matter *sub judice*, there remains a factual issue of whether in the instant case, the assumption of risk defense should be available to defendant. This will require a full factual development of the pertinent considerations, which the record presently lacks and, accordingly, Rule 56 [summary judgment] relief is not appropriate.''

19:8 *Damages*

As a rule, upon a determination of tort liability, the wrongdoer is subject only to those direct and consequential compensatory damages proven by the victim. However, punitive damages to punish the wrongdoer and to deter others from misconduct are available in appropriate situations. In the following case, punitive damages against both the hotelkeeper and the hotel's franchisor were awarded to a food-service patron. The case arose out of food poisoning suffered from the on-premises consumption of food at the hotel.

AVERITT V. SOUTHLAND MOTOR INN OF OKLAHOMA
720 F.2d 1178 (10th Cir. 1983)

LOGAN, C.J.: "Defendants Sheraton Inns, Inc. and Southland Motor Inn Corporation of Oklahoma d/b/a Sheraton Inn-Skyline East Hotel (Southland) appeal from a judgment awarding punitive damages to plaintiff William Michael Averitt. Averitt brought this diversity suit against the defendants after he contracted shigella from eating at the Sheraton-Inn Skyline East Hotel in Tulsa, Oklahoma.

"On March 28, 1978, Averitt stayed at the Southland and dined at the hotel restaurant. Averitt became ill the next day. After he returned home to Dallas, his condition worsened. On April 5, after suffering from diarrhea for several days, he was admitted to a hospital. He was diagnosed as having ulcerative colitis, a chronic disease of the colon. On April 4, 1978, the manager of Southland was notified of an outbreak of food poisoning among guests of the hotel. That day the Tulsa City-County Health Department secured stool cultures from the hotel's employees. These cultures indicated that a hotel employee involved in food preparation had shigella. Although there was local publicity about the shigella outbreak, the hotel made no attempt to notify Averitt or other hotel guests that they had been exposed to shigella. Averitt did not learn of his exposure until a return trip to Tulsa some time later.

"Averitt brought suit against Southland on theories of negligence, strict liability, and breach of warranty, alleging that Southland sold Averitt food contaminated with shigella. Averitt also sued Sheraton Inns, Inc. on the theory that Southland was Sheraton's agent and that Sheraton was therefore responsible for Southland's torts. During trial, the plaintiff introduced into evidence health department inspection reports covering the period from January 8, 1974, to May 19, 1978. The reports indicated that Southland had committed numerous health and sanitary violations. The jury found against Sheraton and Southland and awarded the plaintiff $375,000 compensatory damages and $500,000 punitive damages. The defendants moved for a new trial challenging both the compensatory and punitive damages but then agreed with the plaintiff to pay compensatory damages and to 'forego their argument on their Motion for New Trial as to compensatory damages only, and their right to appeal as to only the amount of compensatory damages.' . . .

"Both defendants contend that the district court erred in admitting into evidence the health department inspection reports, that the evidence did not support an award of punitive damages, and that insufficient evidence of negligence existed to support any award. Sheraton asserts that the trial court erred in submitting the issue of agency or apparent agency to the jury and that Sheraton was thus wrongly held vicariously liable for the torts of Southland. . . .

"The jury verdict on the issue of compensatory damages represents a determination that the defendants breached a duty of care they owed to the plaintiff, that the breach caused the plaintiff's injury, and that Sheraton was liable for the torts of Southland because of an agency relationship. *See generally Chavez v. Sears, Roebuck & Co.*, 525 F.2d 827, 831 (10th Cir. 1975). In failing to appeal the award of compensatory damages, the defendants have left these determinations unchallenged.[1] We therefore address only whether the district court properly admitted into evidence the health department inspection reports on the issue of punitive damages and whether Southland's actions or omissions justify an award of punitive damages under Oklahoma law.

"Punitive damages are recoverable under Oklahoma law '[i]n any action for the breach of an obligation not arising from contract, where the defendant has been guilty of oppression, fraud or malice, actual or presumed.' Okla. Stat. tit. 23, § 9. Punitive damages are also recoverable when a defendant has been guilty of gross negligence that indicates a reckless disregard for the rights of others. [Citations omitted.] Whether punitive damages should be awarded is a question for the jury. 'Only where there is no evidence whatsoever that would give rise to an inference of actual malice or conduct deemed equivalent to actual malice may a trial court refuse to submit an exemplary damage instruction to the jury.' *Sopkin v. Premier Pontiac, Inc.*, 539 P.2d 1393, 1397 (Okl. App. 1975); *accord, Chavez v. Sears, Roebuck & Co.*, 525 F.2d 827, 829–30 (10th Cir. 1975); *Amoco Pipeline Co. v. Montgomery*, 487 F. Supp. 1268, 1272 (W.D. Okl. 1980).

"The defendants contend that the plaintiff introduced insufficient evidence that Southland was grossly negligent to justify submitting the question of punitive damages to the jury. We disagree. The plaintiff introduced evidence that Southland had repeatedly violated health department regulations by permitting unsanitary conditions to exist in the restaurant. The plaintiff also introduced evidence that Southland took no steps to notify guests of the hotel that they had been exposed to shigella, apparently because Southland feared that the publicity would hurt its business. We believe that this evidence justifies submitting the issue to the jury and that the jury could have found that Southland acted in reckless and conscious disregard for the rights of the plaintiff.

"AFFIRMED.

"1. Even if these issues are properly before us, we conclude that the record provides sufficient evidence to support the jury's conclusions. The law is settled in Oklahoma that a principal can be held liable for punitive damages based on the conduct of its agent. *See Taxicab Driver's Local Union No. 889 v. Pittman,* 322 P.2d 159, 168 (Okl. 1957); *Kurn v. Radencie,* 193 Okl. 126, 141 P.2d 580, 581 (1943); *Schuman v. Chatman,* 184 Okl. 224, 86 P.2d 615, 618 (1938). We are satisfied that sufficient evidence supports the jury's verdict against Sheraton under the general agency principles set out in the trial court's order denying a new trial. *See Restatement (2d) of Agency* § 267 (1958). We are also satisfied that the record sufficiently supports the jury's verdict on the issues of negligence and causation."

[The circuit court's review of the district court's admission of the health reports is omitted.]

19:9   Civil Liability for Injury Caused by Illegal Sale of Intoxicating Liquor: Dram Shop Acts or Common Law

At common law the seller of intoxicating liquors was not generally liable for injuries resulting from intoxication of one of his customers where such injuries were inflicted on a third party through the action of the customer while inebriated or were sustained by the customer himself.[24] In reaching this conclusion, the courts have held that the consumption of the liquor rather than its sale was the proximate cause of any damage resulting from the intoxication of the one who consumed it.

A notable exception is in New Jersey, the first state in which it was held that a tavernkeeper who serves alcoholic beverages when he knows or should know that the patron is intoxicated may properly be found to have created an unreasonable risk of harm, and thus to have engaged in negligent conduct on which a common-law claim for damages may be grounded.[25]

Illinois, Iowa, Minnesota, Ohio, Oregon, and Washington are in accord in imposing liability upon commercial vendors on the theory of common-law negligence. Nebraska and Wisconsin reject common-law liability. In *McClennan v. Tottenhoff,*[26] the Wyoming Supreme Court overruled its prior common-law doctrine immunizing a liquor vendor from liability to a third party arising out of the illegal sale of alcohol to a patron.

The Supreme Court of California[27] had adopted this reasoning in 1971 in abrogating its prior common-law of nonliability. According to provisions of the Business and Professions Code, section 25602, which was enacted to protect the public from injuries to person and property resulting from the excessive use of intoxicating liquor, a tavern owner owes a duty of reasonable care to members of the public. A violation of the code created a presumption of negligence.

In a far-reaching subsequent decision, *Coulter v. Superior Court,* presented below, the high court extended the rule of liability to include social or noncommercial suppliers of alcoholic beverages for serving an obviously intoxicated person whose inebriation creates a reasonably foreseeable danger or risk of injury to third persons.

[24]*Recent Developments,* 60 Colum. L. Rev. 544 (1960).
[25]Rappaport v. Nichols, 31 N.J. 188, 202–203, 156 A.2d 1, 9 (1959).
[26]666 P.2d 408 (1983).
[27]Vesely v. Sager, 5 Cal. 3d 153, 486 P.2d 151 (1971).

COULTER v. SUPERIOR COURT
21 Cal. 3d 144, 577 P.2d 669 (1978)[28]

RICHARDSON, J.: "In *Vesely* [5 Cal. 3d 153, 486 P.2d 151 (1971)], we further expressly reserved the question 'whether a noncommercial furnisher of alcoholic beverages may be subject to civil liability under section 25602. . . . ' (5 Cal. 3d at p. 157.) That question is now before us and, although defendants herein urge us to confine application of the *Vesely* rule to commercial vendors, we see no reasonable or logical basis for doing so. As will appear, section 25602 is not limited by its terms to persons who furnish liquor to others for profit. Furthermore, well established general negligence principles lead us to conclude, independently of statute, that a social host or other noncommercial provider of alcoholic beverages owes to the general public a duty to refuse to furnish such beverages to an obviously intoxicated person if, under the circumstances, such person thereby constitutes a reasonably foreseeable danger or risk of injury to third persons. We examine more closely the statutory and common law bases for our conclusion.

1. Business and Professions Code Section 25602

"Section 25602 provides, that '*Every person* who sells, furnishes, gives, or causes to be sold, furnished, or given away, any alcoholic beverage to . . . any obviously intoxicated person is guilty of a misdemeanor.' (Italics added.) Referring as it does to 'every person,' the section on its face appears to apply to both commercial and noncommercial suppliers of alcoholic beverages. Although it might be urged that the placement of section 25602 in the Business and Professions Code suggests a legislative intent to confine the section's application to the commercial sellers of liquor only, thus excluding social hosts, other sections of the same code belie any such intent. For example, unlike section 25602, the immediately preceding section, 25601, contains specified restrictions imposed upon activities of a 'licensee' as opposed to any 'person.' Section 23008 defines 'person' as including '*any individual*, firm, copartnership, [etc.] . . . ' whereas section 23009 defines 'licensee' as '*any person holding a license* issued by the department.' (Italics added.) Since all commercial vendors of alcoholic beverages in this state must be licensed (see § 23300 *et seq.*), the use of the broader term 'person' in section 25602 strongly suggests that the latter section must have been intended to apply whether or not the supplier of such beverages was engaged in commercial, and therefore licensed, activities.

"Nonetheless, defendants insist that the Legislature, by enacting section 25602, could not have intended to impose civil liability upon social hosts, given the long line of earlier cases which had denied liability even against commercial vendors. Such an argument, however, underestimates the historic force of our *Vesely* holding. As we have explained, in 1971 the Legislature was put on notice by *Vesely* that (1) section 25602 could form the basis for imposition of civil liability upon social hosts because, identifying the object of the statute, we rec-

---

[28]Superseded by statute as stated in Cartwright v. Hyatt Corp., 460 F. Supp. 80 (D.D.C. 1987).

ognized that it was 'adopted for the purpose of protecting members of the general public from injuries to person and damage to property resulting from the excessive use of intoxicating liquor' (5 Cal. 3d at p. 165); and (2) the noncommercial supplier's civil liability for a violation of section 25602 remained an open question (*id.,* at p. 157). We think it of some, but not controlling, significance that, following *Vesely,* the Legislature has failed to amend section 25602 to exclude such liability.

"We further note that the Legislature has clearly expressed its desire that the Alcoholic Beverage Control Act shall be liberally construed to accomplish its stated purposes of 'protection of the *safety, welfare,* health, peace, and morals of the people of the State, . . . and to promote temperance. . . . ' (§ 23001, italics added.) Further, 'It is hereby declared that the subject matter of this division [which includes § 25602] involves *in the highest degree* the economic, social, and moral well-being *and the safety* of the State and of all its people.' (*Ibid.,* italics added.) Our interpretation of section 25602 in authorizing imposition of civil liability is entirely consistent with these broad legislative policies, and may well further induce social hosts to take those reasonable preventive measures calculated to reduce the risk of alcohol-related accidents. [Citation omitted.]

"For all of the foregoing reasons, we conclude that section 25602 affords a sufficient statutory basis upon which civil liability may be imposed upon a noncommercial supplier who provides alcoholic beverages to an obviously intoxicated person, thereby creating a reasonably foreseeable risk of harm to third persons.

2. Common Law Principles

"Wholly apart from the provisions of section 25602, imposition of civil liability in the present case is fully compatible with general negligence principles. It is true that in *Vesely* we based the requisite *duty* to the plaintiff upon the provisions of section 25602 alone. (5 Cal. 3d at pp. 164–165.) However, as we recently explained in *Bernhard v. Harrah's Club* (1976) 16 Cal. 3d 313 [128 Cal. Rptr. 215, 546 P.2d 719], 'Although we chose to impose liability on the *Vesely* defendant on the basis of his violating the applicable statute, the clear import of our decision was that there was no bar to civil liability *under modern negligence law.*' (P. 325, italics added.)

"It has long been a fundamental principle of California law that a person is liable for the foreseeable injuries caused by his failure to exercise reasonable care. [Citations omitted.] Although we have, on occasion, described the foregoing rule as having civil rather than common law origins [citation omitted], the principle has most frequently been expressed in the negligence formulation that the defendant owes the plaintiff a 'duty' of reasonable care. The existence of a duty is primarily a question of law, and dependent upon a variety of relevant factors, of which 'foreseeability of the risk is a primary consideration. . . . ' [Citation omitted.] We think it evident that the service of alcoholic beverages to an obviously intoxicated person by one who knows that such intoxicated person intends to drive a motor vehicle creates a *reasonable foreseeable* risk of injury to those on the highway. [Citation omitted.] Simply put, one who serves alcoholic beverages under such circumstances fails to exercise reasonable care.

"We have previously identified certain factors other than foreseeability in determining the ultimate existence of a 'duty' to third persons. These factors include: ' . . . the degree of certainty that the plaintiff suffered injury, the closeness of the connection between the defendant's conduct and the injury suffered, the moral blame attached to the defendant's conduct, the policy of preventing future harm, the extent of the burden to the defendant and consequences to the community of imposing a duty to exercise care with resulting liability for breach, and the availability, cost, and prevalence of insurance for the risk involved.' [Citation omitted.]

"Application of several of the . . . elements to the circumstances herein alleged fully supports a rule establishing a duty of care and imposing civil liability. Plaintiffs' injuries are asserted to be substantial. . . . [Citation omitted.] Where such circumstances exist, as are herein alleged, it is not difficult to discern a close connection between defendant's conduct and the injury suffered by plaintiffs. Unquestionably, as we amplify below, there exists a strong public policy to prevent future injuries of this nature, and we may assume that insurance coverage (doubtless increasingly costly) will be made available to protect the social host from civil liability in this situation. While, traditionally, no moral blame attaches to the social host who entertains his guests by serving cocktails to them, it is not unfair to ascribe such blame to anyone who increases the obvious intoxication of a guest under conditions involving a reasonably foreseeable risk of harm to others. In this connection, we further note that it is small comfort to the widow whose husband has been killed in an accident involving an intoxicated driver to learn that the driver received his drinks from a hospitable social host rather than by purchase at a bar. The danger of ultimate harm is as equally foreseeable to the reasonably perceptive host as to the bartender. The danger and risk to the potential victim on the highway is equally as great, regardless of the source of the liquor.

"Finally, we do not conclude that the burden upon the noncommercial suppliers of intoxicating beverages and the consequences to the community of imposing civil liability are so serious as to justify a contrary holding. Doubtless, the spectre of civil liability may temper the spirit of conviviality at some social occasions, especially when reasonably observant hosts decline to serve further alcoholic beverages to those guests who are obviously intoxicated and perhaps becoming hostile. Nonetheless, in this context, we must surely balance any resulting moderation of hospitality with the serious hazard to the lives, limbs, and property of the public at large, and the great potential for human suffering which attends the presence on the highways of intoxicated drivers. In doing so we need not ignore the appalling, perhaps incalculable, cost of torn and broken lives incident to alcohol abuse, in the area of automobile accidents alone.

"Defendants have argued that the term 'obviously intoxicated' is too broad and subjective to serve as a satisfactory measure for imposition of civil liability. However, the phrase is contained in section 25602, a *criminal* statute, and the courts have experienced no discernible difficulty in applying it [Citations omitted.] . . . 'The use of intoxicating liquor by the average person in such quantity as to produce intoxication causes many commonly known *outward* manifestations which are "plain" and "easily seen or discovered." If such outward manifestations exist and the seller still serves the customer so affected he has violated the law, whether this was because he failed to observe what was plain and easily seen or discovered, or because, having observed, he ignored that which was apparent.' [*People v. Johnson* (1947), 81 Cal. App. 2d Supp. 973, 975, 976, 185 P.2d 105, italics in original.] We think the . . . observations made in the context of a sale of liquor have equal application when the liquor is served by a noncommercial social host.

"Let a peremptory writ of mandate issue directing respondent court to overrule defendants' demurrers to the first cause of action of plaintiffs' complaint."

The California legislature reestablished the common-law rule of nonliability except in the case of an obviously intoxicated minor in 1978 by amending the Business and Professions Code as follows:

Chapter 929
An act to amend Section 25602 of the Business and Professions Code, and to amend Section 1714 of the Civil Code, relating to proximate cause.

[Approved by Governor September 19, 1978. Filed with
Secretary of State September 20, 1978.]

LEGISLATIVE COUNSEL'S DIGEST
SB 1645, Ayala. Alcoholic beverage liability: proximate cause.

The California courts have recently interpreted existing law as imposing civil liability upon persons who sell, furnish, give or cause to be given alcoholic beverages to an intoxicated person when such person inflicts injury upon a third party.

This bill would specifically prohibit the imposition of civil liability in such instance.

This bill would also state a legislative declaration that prior judicial interpretation shall be reinstated so that such civil liability to a third party is incurred solely by the intoxicated person. The bill would also provide specifically that no social host who furnishes alcoholic beverages to any person shall be held legally accountable for damages suffered by such person, or for injury to the person or property of, or death of, any third person, resulting from the consumption of such beverages.

The people of the State of California do enact as follows:
SECTION 1. Section 25602 of the Business and Professions Code is amended to read:

25602. (a) Every person who sells, furnishes, gives, or causes to be sold, furnished, or given away, any alcoholic beverage to any habitual or common drunkard or to any obviously intoxicated person is guilty of a misdemeanor.

(b) No person who sells, furnishes, gives, or causes to be sold, furnished, or given away, any alcoholic beverage pursuant to subdivision (a) of this section shall be civilly liable to any injured person or the estate of such person for injuries inflicted on that person as a result of intoxication by the consumer of such alcoholic beverage.

(c) The Legislature hereby declares that this section shall be interpreted so that the holdings in cases such as *Vesely v. Sager* (5 Cal. 3d 153), *Bernhard v. Harrah's Club* (16 Cal. 3d 313) and *Coulter v. Superior Court* (21 Cal. 3d 144) be abrogated in favor of prior judicial interpretation finding the consumption of alcoholic beverages rather than the serving of alcoholic beverages as the proximate cause of injuries inflicted upon another by an intoxicated person.

SEC. 2. Section 1714 of the Civil Code is amended to read:

1714. (a) Every one is responsible, not only for the result of his willful acts, but also for an injury occasioned to another by his want of ordinary care or skill in the management of his property or person, except so far as the latter has, willfully or by want of ordinary care, brought the injury upon himself. The extent of liability in such cases is defined by the Title on Compensatory Relief.

(b) It is the intent of the Legislature to abrogate the holdings in cases such as *Vesely v. Sager* (5 Cal. 3d 153), *Bernard v. Harrah's Club* (16 Cal. 3d 313), and *Coulter v. Superior Court* (21 Cal. 3d 144) and to reinstate the prior judicial interpretation of this section as it relates to proximate cause for injuries incurred as a result of furnishing of alcoholic beverages to an intoxicated person, namely that the furnishing of alcoholic beverages is not the proximate cause of injuries resulting from intoxication, but rather the consumption of alcoholic beverages is the proximate cause of injuries inflicted upon another by an intoxicated person.

(c) No social host who furnishes alcoholic beverages to any person shall be held legally accountable for damages suffered by such person, or for injury to the person or property of, or death of, any third person, resulting from the consumption of such beverages.

Chapter 930

An act to add Sections 25602.1, 25602.2, and 25602.3 to the Business and Professions Code, relating to alcoholic beverages.

[Approved by Governor September 19, 1978. Filed with
Secretary of State September 20, 1978.]

LEGISLATIVE COUNSEL'S DIGEST

SB 1175, Foran. Alcoholic beverages.

Existing law prohibits furnishing alcoholic beverages to drunkards or obviously intoxicated persons.

This bill would create a cause of action against a licensee who furnishes alcoholic beverages to an obviously intoxicated minor if the minor causes personal injury or death, would authorize the Director of Alcoholic Beverage Control to enjoin certain violations of law, and would prohibit petitions for an offer in compromise for a second or subsequent violation of specified provisions within 36 months of an initial violation.

The people of the State of California do enact as follows:

SECTION 1. Section 25602.1 is added to the Business and Professions Code, to read:

25602.1 Notwithstanding subdivision (b) of Section 25602, a cause of action may be brought by or on behalf of any person who has suffered injury or death against any person licensed pursuant to Section 23300 who sells, furnishes, gives or causes to be sold, furnished or given away any alcoholic beverage to any obviously intoxicated minor where the furnishing, sale or giving of such beverage to the minor is the proximate cause of the personal injury or death sustained by such person.

SEC. 2. Section 25602.2 is added to the Business and Professions Code, to read:

25602.2 The director may bring an action to enjoin a violation or the threatened violation of subdivision (a) of Section 25602. Such action may be brought in the county in which the violation occurred or is threatened to occur. Any proceeding brought hereunder shall conform to the requirements of Chapter 3 (commencing with Section 525) of Title 7 of Part 2 of the Code of Civil Procedure, except that it shall be presumed that there is no adequate remedy at law, and that irreparable damage will occur if the continued or threatened violation is not restrained or enjoined.

SEC. 3. Section 25602.3 is added to the Business and Professions Code, to read:

25602.3 Notwithstanding any other provision of this division, no licensee may petition the department for an offer in compromise pursuant to Section 23095 for a second or any subsequent violation of subdivision (a) of Section 25602 which occurs within 36 months of the initial violation.

In the following case, a California court of appeals broadly construed the 1978 amendments to the California Civil and Business and Professions Codes to protect the alcohol server. The amendments reaffirm the traditional common-law rule that the consumption of alcohol, not its service, is the proximate cause of injuries arising therefrom.

CALENDRINO V. SHAKEY'S PIZZA PARLOR COMPANY, INC.
151 Cal. App. 3d 370, 198 Cal. Rptr. 697 (1984)

EVANS, A.J.: "Plaintiff appeals from a summary judgment entered upon defendant's motion. We affirm.

"On June 14, 1979, plaintiff, a minor, was served a number of mugs of beer over a two-hour span by defendant, a licensed purveyor. Thereafter, at approximately midnight, plaintiff went to a private party where he consumed large amounts of beer and hard liquor for six to six and one-half hours. Plaintiff remained at the party until 6:45 the following morning; at the time he was intoxicated. He accepted a ride home from Anthony Triggs, who was also intoxicated. Plaintiff was injured when Triggs' car was engaged in a single car accident.

"Triggs' intoxication was the direct cause of plaintiff's injuries. Plaintiff's theory of liability as against defendant, however, is that defendant served alcoholic beverages to plaintiff who was allegedly intoxicated. As a result of intoxication, plaintiff was alleged to be unable to care for and supervise his own conduct, and accepted a ride from an obviously intoxicated person to his physical detriment.

"Defendant's motion for summary judgment is based on the laws affecting liability for furnishing alcoholic beverages.

"The current law in California precludes plaintiff from establishing proximate cause which is the predicate to liability.

"It is now the law of this state that the consumption of alcoholic beverages rather than the furnishing of them is the proximate cause of injuries arising after the consumption of alcohol. The 1978 amendments to Civil Code section 1714 and Business and Professions Code section 25602 operate to bar a suit against providers of alcoholic beverages, social and licensed, brought by the intoxicated consumer as well as third persons injured by that consumer (*see Cory v. Shierloh* 29 Cal. 3d 430, 439 174 Cal. Rptr. 500, 629 P.2d 8). . . . .

"As the Supreme Court stated in *Cory v. Shierloh, supra,* 29 Cal. 3d in page 437, 174 Cal. Rptr. 500, 629 P.2d 8, '[t]he 1978 amendments are hardly models of draftsmanship.' However, in order to dispel any doubts harbored about the intent of the sections, the court expressly restated the result of the amendments was to preclude any actions by the consumer of alcoholic beverages or third persons from stating a cause of action for injuries against either the licensed purveyor or the social host providing the alcohol for consumption. (P. 437, 174 Cal. Rptr. 500, 629 P.2d 8.) The decision makes clear the amendments to Business and Professions Code section 25602 and Civil Code section 1714 reinstated the common law theory which precluded liability against a purveyor of alcoholic beverages prior to the *Vesely,* et al., decision.

"Defendant's motion for summary judgment successfully relied upon the provisions of Business and Professions Code section 25602 and Civil Code section 1714. Plaintiff relies on Business and Professions Code section 25602.1, which was added by the Statutes of 1978 (Stats. 1978, ch. 930, p. 2905, § 1). That section provides: 'Notwithstanding subdivision (b) of Section 25602, a cause of action may be brought by or on behalf of any person who has suffered injury or death against any person licensed pursuant to Section 23300 who sells, furnishes, gives or causes to be sold, furnished or given away any alcoholic beverage to any obviously intoxicated minor where the furnishing, sale or giving of such beverage to the minor is the proximate cause of the personal injury or death sustained by such person.'

"Plaintiff asserts that he has stated a good cause of action because he was a minor at the time his injuries were incurred and that the injuries were proximately caused by defendant serving him alcoholic beverages which impaired his judgment, causing him to ride with an intoxicated driver.

"However, we read section 25602.1 as providing a cause of action only for other persons injured by the intoxicated minor, and not for the intoxicated minor himself. The section '[e]xpresses a single exception to the . . . sweeping immunity' provided by section 25602 (*Cory v. Shierloh, supra,* 29 Cal. 3d at 436, 174 Cal. Rptr. 500, 629 P.2d 8), and, as an exception to the general rule, section 25602.1 must be narrowly construed (*see Goins v. Board of Pension Commissioners* (1979) 96 Cal. App. 3d 1005, 1009, 158 Cal. Rptr. 470, citing *Marrujo v. Hunt* (1977) 71 Cal. App. 3d 972, 977, 138 Cal. Rptr. 220). Section 25602.1

provides a cause of action for '*any person* who has suffered injury or death . . . where the furnishing, sale or giving of [an alcoholic] beverage to [an obviously intoxicated] minor is the proximate cause of the personal injury or death sustained by *such person*' (Emphasis added.) Interpreting the statute narrowly, we cannot construe the terms 'any person' and 'such person' to include the intoxicated minor himself. The purpose of the legislation amending Business and Professions Code section 25602 and Civil Code section 1714 was to abrogate the liability of the commercial purveyor of alcoholic beverages for injuries inflicted by the consumer of such beverages. If the narrow exception of Business and Professions Code section 25602.1 was intended to provide a cause of action not only for those injured by intoxicated minors, but also for the minors themselves, the Legislature would have specifically expressed such intention. . . .

"The judgement is affirmed.

"BLEASE, A.J., dissenting. . . .

"I dissent from the majority opinion because I do not see how 'person' can be read to exclude minors.

"Section 25602.1 excepts from the provisions of section 25602 '*any person* who has suffered injury or death . . . where the furnishing, sale or giving of [an alcoholic] beverage to [an obviously intoxicated] minor is the proximate cause of the . . . injury or death sustained by *such person*. (Emphasis added.) The majority opinion reads 'any person' to exclude the intoxicated minor, notwithstanding there are no words or context on which to hinge the claim. '[A]ny person who has suffered injury or death' plainly does not distinguish between a minor and other persons. Nor does 'such person,' referring to 'any person,' do the job.

"Moreover, I cannot see any reason for reading 'any person who has suffered injury' in section 25602.1 differently from 'any injured person' in section 25602 (which encompasses the consumer of alcohol; *Cory v. Shierloh, supra,* 29 Cal. 3d at p. 437, 174 Cal. Rptr. 500, 629 P.2d 8), the section to which 25602.1 is an exception.

"Nor does a rule of construction come to the aid of a statute plain on its face. There is no ambiguity in the statute. It should be applied as it reads."

Many states have abrogated the common-law rule of nonliability by statute. These several civil damage or dramshop acts create a right of action against the sellers of intoxicating liquors.

In New York, the statute (formerly section 16 of the Civil Rights Law) is now part of the General Obligations Law, and read as follows:

SECTION 11-101. *Compensation for Injury Caused by the Illegal Sale of Intoxicating Liquor*

1. Any person who shall be injured in person, property, means of support, or otherwise by any intoxicated person, or by reason of the intoxication of any person, whether resulting in his death or not, shall have a right of action against any person who shall, by unlawful selling to or unlawfully assisting in procuring liquor for such intoxicated person, have caused or contributed to such intoxication; and in any such action such person shall have a right to recover actual and exemplary damages.

2. In case of the death of either party, the action or right of action given by this section shall survive to or against his or her executor or administrator, and the amount so recovered by either wife or child shall be his or her sole and separate property.

3. Such action may be brought in any court of competent jurisdiction.

4. In any case where parents shall be entitled to such damages, either the father or mother may sue alone therefor, and recovery by one of such parties shall be a bar to suit brought by the other.

An unlawful sale, standing alone, does not impose absolute liability in New York. Thus the sale of liquor to a minor does not violate the Act: there must be a sale causing intoxication or a sale to an intoxicated minor to impose liability.[29] Needless to say, the sale may result in a criminal prosecution or the loss or suspension of the guilty owner's liquor license by the State Liquor Authority, but civil liability does not *ipso facto* result by operation of law.

Section 11-101 encompasses every liquid or solid containing alcohol from whatever source or by whatever process produced capable of being consumed by a human being. California has also recently ruled that candies containing alcohol fall within its own statutory definition of an alcoholic beverage.

Intoxication is governed by an objective test in New York. Outward appearances giving adequate notice to the dispenser of the customer's near intoxicated condition must be established. Subjective conjecture absent some visual or audible manifestations of inebriation are insufficient to satisfy this requirement. The Act neither imposes liability upon the inebriated person nor authorizes the inebriant to sue the licensee on his or her own behalf.

A common-law tort remedy for negligent or intentional conduct resulting in injury to the person or property of another exists independently of the Dram Shop Act to enable the injured party to sue the intoxicated party.[30]

The intoxication need not be the sole proximate cause of the occurrence which caused the injury. Proof that the sale or dispensing of the liquor contributed to the intoxication in the slightest is sufficient. The fact that the injured person had drinks in other establishments does not absolve the licensee of full responsibility if his violation of the statute is established. In practice, this means that each dispenser is liable, even though his establishment was merely one of many such visited by the customer prior to the incident giving rise to the lawsuit.

Recovery is limited to injury to the person, property, or means of support of the plaintiff. The phrase "or otherwise" under point (1) in section 11-101 was added to permit recovery for mental distress. Damages, however, are not limited to actual loss of wages, medical expenses, pain and suffering, and the like, but may include exemplary or punitive damages where the plaintiff can show that the unlawful sale was prompted by malice or by proof of defiance or contempt for the law.

---

[29]McNally v. Addis, 65 Misc. 2d 204, 317 N.Y.S.2d 157 (Sup. Ct. 1970).
[30]Berkeley v. Park, 47 Misc. 2d 381, 262 N.Y.S.2d 290 (Sup. Ct. 1965).

To maintain an action under section 11-101, the following minimal factors must be present:

1. An intoxicated person.

2. Injury or damage either (*a*) caused by the intoxicated person or (*b*) arising out of the intoxication.

3. Defendant seller whose illegal sale or furnishing of the liquor caused or contributed in whole or in part to the intoxication.

4. Plaintiff victim of the injury or damage.

It has been held that section 11-101 must be read in conjunction with section 65 of the Alcoholic Beverage Control Law which prohibits the sale for which section 11-101 affords the remedy.[31] Section 65 of the ABC Law provides:

SECTION 65. *Prohibited Sales*

No person shall sell, deliver or give away or cause to permit or procure to be sold, delivered or given away any alcoholic beverage to

1. Any minor, actually or apparently, under the age of eighteen years;

2. Any intoxicated person or to any person, actually or apparently, under the influence of liquor;

3. Any habitual drunkard known to be such to the person authorized to dispense any alcoholic beverages.

Neither such person so refusing to sell or deliver under this section nor his employer shall be liable in any civil or criminal action or for any fine or penalty based upon such refusal, except that such sale or delivery shall not be refused, withheld from or denied to any person on account of race, creed, color or national origin.

MITCHELL v. THE SHOALS, INC.
19 N.Y.2d 338, 227 N.E.2d 21 (1967)

FULD, C.J.: "On February 2, 1960, after having dinner together, the plaintiff, Yvonne Mitchell, her escort, Robert Taylor, and another couple drove to The Shoals, a restaurant on Staten Island, at about 9:00 P.M. for 'a few drinks' and some dancing. Between dances, they had their drinks. Miss Mitchell, after consuming several, passed out and remained asleep for the rest of the evening. Taylor, who was on a diet of 'double' bourbons 'straight,' became drunk and noisy. At one point, after he had fallen to the floor, the bartender was told not to let him have anything more to drink. Despite this admonition and Taylor's obviously intoxicated condition, the bartender—responding with 'Don't bother me; he is having a good time . . . let him enjoy himself'—served him three or four more double straight bourbons. The two couples left the restaurant at about 1 o'clock in the morning. The plaintiff, still asleep, was assisted to the car and placed in the front seat and Taylor, not to be dissuaded from driving, got behind the wheel and drove off. He apparently lost control of the car some nine miles from the restaurant; it left the roadway and crashed into a building. He was

---

[31]Moyer v. Lo Jim Cafe, Inc., 14 N.Y.2d 729, 200 N.E.2d 212 (1964); Kinney v. 1809 Forest Ave., Inc., 7 Misc. 2d 1, 165 N.Y.S.2d 149 (Sup. Ct. 1957) (mem. opinion).

killed and the plaintiff was seriously injured. She brought this action for damages, under New York's version of the 'Dram Shop Act' (Civil Rights Law, § 16, now General Obligations Law, § 11-101), against the defendant restaurant. The jury returned a verdict in her favor, and a divided Appellate Division affirmed the resulting judgment. [The verdict was for $30,000; however, since the plaintiff had settled her claims against Taylor's estate for $6,000, the judgment was reduced, by that amount, to $24,000.]

"The Alcoholic Beverage Control Law renders it a crime for any person to sell or deliver any alcoholic beverage to one who is intoxicated or under the influence of liquor (§ § 65, 130 subd. 3). . . .

"Although the statute—its forerunner goes as far back as 1873 (L. 1873, ch. 646; see Note, 8 Syracuse L. Rev. 252)—does not give the inebriated person a cause of action if he is himself injured [Citations omitted], it does entitle anyone else injured 'by reason of intoxication' of such person to recover damages from the party dispensing the liquor. There is no justification, either in the language of the legislation or in its history, for exonerating the latter simply because he had also served, and brought about the inebriety of, the third person who was hurt. As long as the latter does not himself cause or procure the intoxication of the other, there is no basis, under the statute, for denying him a recovery from the party unlawfully purveying the liquor.

"In the case before us, the plaintiff had herself become drunk while with Taylor but she had not, in any sense, caused or procured his intoxication. She had neither purchased the drinks nor encouraged him to take more than he could weather. The plaintiff had simply had a few drinks and passed out before her escort's inebriacy became really serious. This did not amount to a guilty participation in his intoxication. To deny her a remedy because her own alcoholic capacity was limited would impair, if not go a long way toward defeating, the purpose of the statute.

"In two or three states [Illinois, Michigan], the courts have held that the plaintiff's mere participation in drinking with the person whose drunkenness caused the injury may be sufficient to prevent recovery under the Dram Shop Acts of those states. [Citations omitted.] We need not, and do not, go that far. It is our view that the injured person must play a much more affirmative role than that of drinking companion to the one who injures him before he may be denied recovery against the bartender or tavern keeper who served them. The plaintiff before us comes within the coverage of the statute and the defendant was properly held accountable. . . . "

[Affirmed.]

In the more recent case of *McNally v. Addis*,[32] the father of a seventeen-year-old boy who met his death in an auto accident sued defendant tavern keeper pursuant to section 11-101 of the General Obligations Law. Part of the cause of action was predicated upon the unlawful sale of liquor to the minor.

[32]65 Misc. 2d 204, 317 N.Y.S.2d 157 (Sup. Ct. 1970).

The deceased borrowed the family car and drove with parental consent ostensibly to a church social. He picked up a friend, twenty years old, whose military leave was about to expire and who was to celebrate his imminent departure.

After leaving the social, the two visited a bar where the deceased had at least one beer, and being unsuccessful in getting served at a second bar, decedent and his friend arrived at defendant's bar at about 11:30 P.M., where deceased was observed to consume at least one beer. In getting to defendant's place, decedent appeared normal, sober, and operated the vehicle without incident. At about 12:55 A.M., deceased was involved in a motor vehicle accident when the car driven by him struck two parked vehicles. Decedent was taken to a hospital where he was pronounced dead on arrival.

The court, sitting without a jury, found as a fact that beer was sold by the defendant to the decedent and consumed by him.

Neither the consumer nor his estate has a cause of action. Under the Dram Shop Act, the burden of proof rests with the plaintiff. He must establish that there was an unlawful sale of liquor to an intoxicated person which caused him injury.

The intoxication need not be the proximate cause of the occurrence which caused the injury. A remote proximate cause between the sale and the injury is sufficient to impose liability upon the vendor. Plaintiff must establish that the accident occurred while the consumer was intoxicated and that the sale contributed to the intoxication in the slightest.

The fact that the decedent had drinks in other establishments does not absolve a defendant vendor from full liability if his violation of the statute is established.

The sale of beer is the sale of an alcoholic beverage within the meaning of section 65 of the Alcoholic Beverage Control Law. It is also a "liquor" within the meaning of section 11-101 of the General Obligations Law (Dram Shop Act).

Although an autopsy established that the decedent was intoxicated at the time of his death, he appeared to be perfectly sober when he was served beer on defendant's premises. That the beer served by defendant may have contributed to decedent's subsequent intoxication is beside the point because liability is fastened upon the seller only where he sells to an intoxicated person, or to one actually or apparently under the influence of liquor.

The legislature did not intend to impose absolute liability without some notice having first been accorded the vendor regarding the dangers attendant upon a prohibited sale. The seller must have notice of a consumer's near intoxicated condition by means of objective outward appearances for the sale to be unlawful and hence within the Dram Shop Act.

The proof in the record indicated that decedent was not intoxicated or under the influence of liquor at the time of the sale and, absent sufficient proof on this point signifying otherwise, the complaint must be dismissed.

The court considered the question whether an unlawful sale to a minor must be read into the Dram Shop Act notwithstanding the condition of the consumer at the time of the sale; liability following, if the minor subsequently becomes intoxicated.

It has been held that in the absence of a statute creating liability, the violation of a provision prohibiting sale of liquor to minors does not create a cause of action in favor of third persons. This is merely a restatement of the general principle that the violation of a statute designed to protect the public-at-large, as concededly section 65 of the Alcoholic Beverage Control Law is to be so classified, does not constitute negligence *per se*, but must be the proximate cause of the accident to impose responsibility.

The court further held that a parent's cause of action for damages for unlawful sales to his minor child does not lie under the Dram Shop Act. Nor does a person standing in the shoes of a minor, sober when served, such as a parent suing essentially for loss of services, have a cause of action under the Dram Shop Act.

The action for damages under the Dram Shop Act is separate and distinct from the usual wrongful death action.

PAUL v. HOGAN
56 A.D.2d 723, 392 N.Y.S.2d 766 (4th Dep't 1977)

MEMORANDUM: "Plaintiff, individually and as administratrix of decedent's estate, commenced this negligence action to recover damages for pain and suffering and wrongful death occurring as a result of fatal injuries suffered by decedent on May 25, 1975 when he was struck by a motorcycle owned and operated by Ronald Austin and on which Frederick Frew was a passenger. Defendants in this action are Robert B. and Elizabeth Hogan who, on the evening of the accident, had given a party which decedent, Austin and Frew had attended and at which alcoholic beverages were served. . . .

"A liberal reading of plaintiff's complaint discloses three possible theories upon which liability may be founded. The first is defendants' alleged negligence under either the Dram Shop Act or general principles of common law negligence in serving alcoholic beverages to decedent. However, insofar as plaintiff attempts to plead a cause of action under the Dram Shop Act, it must be dismissed since aside from the failure to allege any unlawful sale of alcoholic beverages it is well settled that '[n]o cause of action exists in favor of the party whose intoxication has resulted from the illegal sale' (*Moyer v. Lo Jim Cafe, Inc.*, 19 A.D.2d 523–524, 240 N.Y.S.2d 277, 279, *aff'd*, 14 N.Y.2d 792, . . . 200 N.E.2d 212). Nor is this theory of recovery permissible under the general principles of common law negligence since 'there is no special duty resting on an owner of premises to protect a party from the results of his voluntary intoxication' [citations omitted].

"The second possible theory of recovery is defendants' alleged negligence in serving alcoholic beverages to Austin and Frew. This theory is based solely upon the Dram Shop Act. As such it is not enough for plaintiff to allege the serving of alcoholic beverages; plaintiff must also allege a sale of alcoholic beverages and her failure to do so is fatal to the pleading and necessitates dismissal [citations omitted].

"The final possible theory of recovery is defendants' alleged negligence in failing to supervise adequately and control the guests at their home. While it is well settled that such a duty does exist, this duty only 'arises when the one in possession knows that he can and has the opportunity to control the third party's conduct and is reasonably aware of the necessity of such control' [citation omitted]. Furthermore, such a duty of supervision by its very nature extends only to those persons who are physically present on defendant's property. Since in the instant case it appears from the pleadings that at the time of the accident decedent, Austin and Frew were on a public highway and not on defendants' property, insofar as plaintiff's complaint is based upon this theory, it must also be dismissed.

"Since the pleadings do not state a valid cause of action under any possible interpretation, it is not necessary to discuss whether sufficient papers were presented to the court to justify the grant of a summary judgment motion."

MATALAVAGE v. SADLER

77 A.D.2d 39, 432 N.Y.S.2d 103 (2d Dep't 1980)

TITONE, J.: "The issue is whether the infant child of an intoxicated person who is killed by reason of his intoxication, may institute a cause of action under section 11-101 of the General Obligations Law.

I. Facts

"Mary Ann Paskey commenced the present action as 'natural mother and guardian' of Mark Matalavage, and 'Guardian and Administratrix of the Goods, Chattels and Credits' of the decedent (Mark Matalavage's father), against Robert Sadler, d/b/a Maybrook Inn, and John and Clara Marshall. Plaintiff alleged *inter alia* that the defendants were responsible to Mark, under section 11-101 of the General Obligations Law (commonly known as the Dram Shop Act or Civil Damages Act), for losses of companionship and comfort and for monetary support. Plaintiff also alleged that Sadler 'was an employee, agent, and/or servant of John W. Marshall and Clara Marshall, his employer,' and that John and Clara Marshall 'operate, control and maintain' the Maybrook Inn bar and grill.

"The circumstances underlying this action arose as follows: Defendants John and Clara Marshall are the owners of a two-family building in Maybrook, New York, in the first floor and cellar of which is located a bar and grill known as the Maybrook Inn. . . . Mr. Marshall operated the bar until 1974. From 1967 to 1974 he employed Robert Sadler as a part-time bartender and Maud Gleason as a barmaid. In 1974 Marshall closed the bar and grill. . . .

"In January, 1975 Sadler re-opened the bar and grill, using Maybrook Inn as its name. Sadler, in September of 1976, entered into a written lease agreement for the bar and grill with Marshall. Sadler continued as bartender and Maud Gleason remained as barmaid of the Inn. . . .

"At approximately 10 P.M. on November 12, 1976, William Matalavage entered the Maybrook Inn. During that evening and the early hours of the next morning he consumed a quantity of draft beer served by Sadler. Matalavage left the bar at about 4 A.M. and thereafter entered his automobile. After traveling a short distance he struck a telephone pole and died instantly. Surviving Matalavage were his son Mark, born on January 6, 1962, whom he was apparently supporting, and his divorced wife, Mary Ann Paskey.

"After issue was joined in the present action, defendants Marshall made a motion for summary judgment. Special Term (FERRARO, J.) denied this motion, with leave to renew after examinations before trial.

"After the examinations, the Marshalls again moved for summary judgment. The court thereupon dismissed the complaint, stating that section 11-101 of the General Obligations Law 'does not create a right of action in favor of the party whose intoxication has resulted from the illegal sale of liquor and, accordingly, his administrator is also not vested with any such cause of action by EPTL 5-4.1.' I disagree with such reasoning and determination.

"Special Term misperceived the thrust of plaintiff's complaint. Notwithstanding the partially inaccurate title of the case ('Mary Ann Paskey . . . Administratrix of the Goods, Chattels and Credits of William J. Matalavage, Deceased'), for all intents and purposes the action was brought on behalf of the decedent's infant son and not on behalf of the decedent's estate. The issue presented before Special Term, and on appeal, is whether the child of one who is killed due to self-induced intoxication has a cause of action under the Dram Shop Act.

II. Statutory History

"The origin of the current Dram Shop Act, embodied in section 11-101 of the General Obligations Law, is found in the excise law of 1857 (L. 1857, ch. 628), entitled 'An Act to Suppress Intemperance and to Regulate the Sale of Intoxicating Liquors.' Pursuant to section 28 of the excise law, any person who sold 'any strong or spirituous liquors' to any individual to whom that act declared such sale to be unlawful, was held 'liable for all damages which may be sustained in consequence of such sale.' Further, the law declared that the offending parties could be sued by any individual sustaining the injuries or by the overseers of the poor for his benefit.

"The first actual 'Dram Shop Act' was not passed until 1873 (L. 1873, ch. 646). It was denominated 'An Act to Suppress Intemperance, Pauperism and Crime.' This act provided that:

"Every husband, wife, child, parent, guardian, employer or other person who shall be injured in person, or property, or means of support, by any intoxicated person, or in consequence of the intoxication, habitual or otherwise, of any person, shall have a right of action in his or her name, against any person or persons who shall, by selling or giving away intoxicating liquors, [have] caused the intoxication, in whole or in part, of such person or persons, and any person or persons, owning or renting or permitting the occupation of any building or premises, and having knowledge that intoxicating liquors are to be sold therein, shall be liable . . . for all damages sustained and for exemplary damages.

"The constitutionality of this act was upheld in 1878 in *Bertholf v. O'Reilly*, 74 N.Y. 509.

"Between 1873 and 1921, the act underwent several minor revisions and modifications [citations omitted]. In 1921 the act was incorporated into section 16 of the Civil Rights Law (L. 1921, ch. 157). Therein it was stated, in part, that:

> "Any person who shall be injured in person, property, means of support, or otherwise by any intoxicated person, or by reason of the intoxication of any person, whether resulting in his death or not, shall have a right of action against any person who shall, by unlawful selling to or unlawfully assisting in procuring liquor for such intoxicated person, have caused or contributed to such intoxication; and in any such action such person shall have a right to recover actual and exemplary damages.

"Additionally, to determine whether there was an unlawful sale of liquor under the statute, it was held that the statute must be read and considered in conjunction with section 65 of the Alcoholic Beverage Control Law (*Moyer v. Lo Jim Cafe*, 19 A.D.2d 523, 240 N.Y.S.2d 277 *aff'd*, 14 N.Y.2d 792, . . . 200 N.E.2d 212). . . .

"Finally, effective September 27, 1964, the provisions of section 16 of the Civil Rights Law were transferred to section 11-101 of the General Obligations Law without any change in language (L. 1963, ch. 576). The 1963 statute must likewise be read in conjunction with section 65 of the Alcoholic Beverage Control Law (*Manfredonia v. American Airlines*, 68 A.D.2d 131, 135, 416 N.Y.S.2d 286).

III. Purpose

"The object of the early act was to correct the evils resulting from intemperate indulgence in intoxicating liquors, such as impoverishment of families, injuries to others, and the creation of public burdens (Joyce, The Law Relative to Intoxicating Liquor 476 [1910]). The Legislature believed that by imposing civil liability upon the seller he would be more careful in his sales and would demonstrate a greater consideration for the purchaser and his dependents. *One major purpose of this type of statute was to protect the wife and children of an intoxicated person when they were deprived of their means of support as a result of his intoxication* (*id.*, p. 476).

"Moreover, the Court of Appeals has held that the intent and purpose of the act is to suppress the sale and use of intoxicating liquor and to protect and provide a remedy for dependents and persons injured by the unlawful sale of liquor (*Mead v. Stratton*, 87 N.Y. 493). This statute, which is remedial in nature [citation omitted], thus creates an expansive cause of action completely unknown at common law (*see* [citation omitted]; *Mead v. Stratton, supra*).

IV. Conclusion

"In view of the history and purpose of the statute, I believe that the clear intent of the Legislature in enacting the Dram Shop statute was to permit the institution of actions such as the one at bar.

"It is well established that this act does not create a cause of action in favor of the individual whose intoxication resulted from the unlawful sale of liquor (*Mitchell v. The Shoals*, 19 N.Y.2d 338, 280 N.Y.S.2d 113, 227 N.E.2d 21; *Moyer v. Lo Jim Cafe, supra; Paul v. Hogan*, 56 A.D.2d 723, 392 N.Y.S.2d 766; *Scatorchia v. Caputo*, 263 App. Div. 304, 32 N.Y.S.2d 532). Hence, no cause of action is transmitted to his estate (*Mitchell v. The Shoals, supra; Scatorchia v. Caputo, supra*). However, a review of the complaint involved in the present action reveals that, notwithstanding the inaccurate title, the action was brought by Mary Ann Paskey in the name of the decedent's son, and not as the administratrix of the decedent's estate. Thus, Special Term incorrectly dismissed the plaintiff's cause of action on the ground that it was brought by the administratrix of the intoxicated individual.

"With respect to whether a cause of action accrues to the infant child of an intoxicated person under the Dram Shop Act, courts have, in dicta, held in the affirmative (*see Scatorchia v. Caputo, supra*, 263 App. Div. p. 305, 32 N.Y.S.2d 532; [citations omitted]. Moreover, appellate courts in early cases have upheld such right of action under the prior statutes [citations omitted].

"In view of such judicial precedent . . . and the statutory history of the various Dram Shop Acts enacted in this State over the years, it is clear that, despite the inaccurate title of the within action, the mother of the infant herein was entitled to institute the suit on his behalf under section 11-101 of the General Obligations Law [citation omitted]. . . .

"Order of the Supreme Court, Westchester County, entered December 27, 1979, reversed, on the law, and defendants' motions for summary judgment denied."

The case to follow interprets the New York Dram Shop Act not to apply to service of alcohol by a social host in a noncommercial setting. The court recognized a landowner's common law duty to supervise his or her premises, to include the conduct of social guests, but held that no notice of violent propensities of the guest was established, a necessary predicate to liability.

KOHLER v. WRAY

114 Misc. 2d 856, 452 N.Y.S.2d 831 (N.Y. Sup. Ct. 1982), *aff'd*, 92 A.D.2d 757, 461 N.Y.S.2d 665 (4th Dep't 1983)

BOEHM, J.: "This is a motion to dismiss the complaint of plaintiff, Donald Kohler, Jr., or, in the alternative, for summary judgment. Plaintiff's claim against defendants Jack and Vicki Wray is grounded upon common law negligence and violation of the Dram Shop Act (General Obligations Law § 11–101).

"It appears that on February 21, 1981, the defendants invited several friends to their home for a housewarming party which featured a band and several kegs of beer. After the party had been in progress for some time the plaintiff arrived and was told by Jack Wray to help himself to the beer that was downstairs in the cellar. Plaintiff claims that at this time he was also encouraged by Wray to contribute some money so that more beer could be purchased.

"Not long after his arrival at the party, plaintiff approached Kelly Piersons who, unbeknown to plaintiff, was married and in the company of her husband, and asked her to dance. There is some dispute as to the intervening details, but within a short time plaintiff and Mr. Pierson exchanged blows, with the result that plaintiff's jaw was broken.

"Thereafter, the plaintiff commenced these lawsuits against the Wrays, alleging that they negligently caused or permitted Mr. Piersons to become intoxicated and that, knowing he was intoxicated, they negligently permitted him to assault and injure the plaintiff. In his bill of particulars, plaintiff also raises a violation of the General Obligations Law (GOL), presumably referring to § 11–101, New York's 'Dram Shop Act.' . . .

"GOL § 11–101 authorizes recovery for injuries caused by an intoxicated person from 'any person' who unlawfully contributes to his intoxication. It is settled, however, that liability under the statute does not flow from the mere service of alcohol to an intoxicated person, but instead requires a 'prohibited sale' as that term is defined by Alcoholic Beverage Control Law (ABCL) § 65 (*Gabrielle v. Craft*, 75 A.D.2d 939, 428 N.Y.S.2d 84; *Huyler v. Rose*, 88 A.D.2d 755, 451 N.Y.S.2d 478; *Paul v. Hogan*, 56 A.D.2d 723, 392 N.Y.S.2d 766). No such sale has been alleged or shown to have occurred here.

"Although ABCL § 65 provides that 'no person shall sell, deliver or give away' alcohol to certain persons, the courts of this state have uniformly held that the law has no application to a social host in a non-commercial setting (*see, Huyler v. Rose, supra; Gabrielle v. Craft, supra; Paul v. Hogan, supra; Edgar v. Kajet*, 84 Misc. 2d 100, 375 N.Y.S.2d 548, aff'd, 55 A.D.2d 1026, 362 N.E.2d 626). Although the words 'give away' are included, the plain purpose of this statutory language was to include within the ambit of the sanctions 'those instances where the proprietor of a licensed establishment . . . provides the customer with the traditional "drink on the house.' The statute's title [Prohibited Sales] and its terms manifest the obvious intent to exclude from its coverage the social host who gratuitously provides his guest with an alcoholic beverage.' (*Gabrielle v. Craft, supra*, at 940, 428 N.Y.S.2d 84).

"Plaintiff's suggestion that defendant forsook the protection of the 'social host' exception to ABCL § 65 when they asked their guests to 'chip in' for the beer served is unpersuasive. In the circumstances of this case such conduct alone, unaccompanied by any exception of pecuniary gain, falls far short of the type of commercial activity that ABCL § 65 was intended to prohibit [citations omitted]. Accordingly, plaintiff's actions based upon a violation of GOL § 11–101 are dismissed.

"Nor does the common law recognize a right of action against a host based upon his serving alcohol to one who later injures another (*Paul v. Hogan, supra.*), and, insofar as plaintiff's second cause of action asserts such a claim, it, too, is dismissed.

"The common law recognizes a landowner's duty to take reasonable precautions to supervise a guest to prevent him from harming others, provided that the host 'knows that he can and has the opportunity to control the third party's conduct and is reasonably aware of the necessity of such control' (*id.*, 724, 392 N.Y.S.2d 766; *Huyler v. Rose, supra; Mangione v. Dimino*, A.D.2d 128, 332 N.Y.S.2d 683). In addition, a landowner is under a duty to act in a reasonable manner to prevent harm to those on his property, and the standard of care must be determined in view of all the circumstances of the case (*Basso v. Miller*, 40 N.Y.2d 233, 241, 386 N.Y.S.2d 564, 352 N.E.2d 868; *Scurti v. City of New York*, 40 N.Y.2d 433, 437 387 N.Y.S.2d 55, 354 N.E.2d 794; unreported decision, *Treat v. Ponderosa Systems*, Index No. 81-2682, Special Term of Supreme Court, Sixth Judicial District, Broome County, April 27, 1982). Sympathetically read, the complaint adequately states a claim against defendants based upon breach of this duty (*see Huyler v. Rose, supra*).

"However, defendants also seek summary judgment. Although they have submitted nothing to relieve defendants, Vicky Wray, of liability, they have offered proof that Jack Wray had neither reason to anticipate nor opportunity to prevent Piersons from assaulting plaintiff. . . .

"In short, plaintiff has offered nothing to rebut defendant's proof that Jack Wray had neither notice of, nor an opportunity to prevent, the assault alleged by Kohler (*see, Burgess v. Garfield*, 1 Misc. 2d 60, 149 N.Y.S.2d 55).

"Plaintiff cites several cases which in his opinion foreclose a grant of summary judgment here. They are, however, distinguishable. Two of plaintiff's cases, *Huyler v. Rose (supra)* and *Molloy v. Coletti*, 114 Misc. 177, 186 N.Y.S. 730 dealt only with the sufficiency of the complaint, an issue which in this case has already been resolved in plaintiff's favor. The others, to the extent that they dealt with a host's liability for the torts of his guests, involved circumstances in which the defendant had been given advance notice of his guest's violent propensities and had an opportunity to guard against them (*see, e.g., Betancourt v. 141 East 57th St. Corp.*, 56 A.D.2d 823, 393 N.Y.S.2d 35 [assailant permitted to re-enter premises within minutes of his involvement in a violent fight]; *Treat v. Ponderosa Systems*, Sup. Ct. Broome County, 4/27/82 [unreported] [assailant had become 'high' on alcohol which he had unlawfully introduced and consumed in defendant restaurant with approval of defendant's employees]). In fact, in *Nallan v. Helmsley-Spear Inc.*, 50 N.Y.2d 507, 429 N.Y.S.2d 606, 407 N.E.2d 451 the Court of Appeals was careful to point out:

"Of course, a possessor of land, whether he be a landowner or a leaseholder, is not an insurer of the visitor's safety. Thus, even where there is an extensive history of criminal conduct on the premises, the possessor cannot be held to a duty to take protective measures unless it is shown that he either knows or has reason to know from past experiences 'that there is a likelihood of conduct on the part of third persons . . . which is likely to endanger the safety of the visitor' (Restatement, Torts 2d, § 344, Comment *f*). Only if such conditions are met may the possessor of land be obliged to 'take precautions . . . and to provide a reasonably sufficient number of servants to afford a reasonable protection' (*id.*). (*Id.* at 519, 429 N.Y.S.2d 606, 407 N.E.2d 451.)

''Plaintiff here has shown nothing in either Pierson's conduct on the night of the party or his prior history which could have put defendants on notice that he was likely to be a danger to anyone at their party. In the absence of such proof, and considering defendant Jack Wray's showing of non-liability, plaintiff's claim against him must fall. . . . ''

An appellate court has interpreted New York's Dram Shop Act as prohibiting a tavern owner from avoiding or reducing liability, where an action is brought by a dependent of the intoxicated person (vendee), on the basis of the patron's contributory negligence. *Weinheimer v. Hoffman.*[33]

The objective test governing a commercial vendor's duty not to serve a patron alcohol, that the vendor knew or reasonably should have known that the patron was intoxicated, was reaffirmed by the Supreme Judicial Court of Massachusetts. Violation of a statute governing illegal sale of liquor was held to be some evidence of negligence. The prior requirement that the injured party prove scienter (guilty knowledge) was overruled. A parent was authorized to recover for emotional distress suffered as an on-the-scene bystander who witnessed his son's wrongful death.[34]

The Washington Supreme Court has created a common-law cause of action in favor of the estate of an obviously intoxicated minor in a case arising out of an illegal commercial sale of liquor that caused the minor's death. The court stated that the illegal sale of alcohol to such a patron constitutes negligence *per se.*[35] The Nevada Supreme Court has ruled otherwise in *Yoscovitch v. Wasson.*[36]

In the following case, the California Court of Appeals reiterated the virtually absolute bar to liability arising from commercial sales of alcoholic beverages to adult consumers which was imposed by the California legislature in 1978. The facts and reasoning are excerpted below.

HEPE v. PAKNAD

199 Cal. App. 3d 412, 244 Cal. Rptr. 823 (Cal. App. 1988)

BRAUER, Associate Judge: ''Plaintiff and appellant Paul Hepe appeals a judgment dismissing the action against defendants and respondents David Paknad, Joyce Hoist, and the 'Woodshed' (collectively 'respondents') after a demurrer was sustained without leave to amend. We affirm.

Facts

''On September 22, 1984, Paul Hepe was injured in a traffic accident. Hepe, who was riding a motorcycle, was struck by James Shimer, who was driving a

---

[33]470 N.Y.S.2d 804 (3d Dep't. 1983).

[34]Cimino v. Milford Keg, Inc., 385 Mass. 323, 431 N.E.2d 920 (1982).

[35]Young v. Caravan Corp., 99 Wash. 2d 655, 663 P.2d 834, *opinion amended,* 672 P.2d 1267 (1983). Also see Yost v. State, 640 P.2d 1044 (Utah 1981).

[36]645 P.2d 975 (1982).

car. Before the accident, Shimer had consumed alcoholic beverages in the 'Woodshed,' a bar owned by David Paknad. Joyce Hoist, a waitress at the Woodshed, had served Shimer.

"Hepe alleges that Shimer was intoxicated at the time of the accident and that the respondents are liable for serving Shimer. Ordinarily, of course, Business & Professions Code section 25602 makes the servers of alcoholic beverages immune from civil liability for injuries caused by intoxication. Hepe seeks to avoid the statutory immunity with the following allegations: respondents 'knew, or should have known, that [Shimer] was afflicted with an exceptional physical and mental condition, to wit, alcoholism, so that he should not have been furnished alcoholic beverages; that the beverages were nevertheless furnished to [Shimer] with the result that he engaged in the foreseeable conduct of an alcoholic of consuming alcohol in excess which, to turn, affected his mental and physical judgment and coordination.'

"Following the accident Shimer allegedly 'returned to [the Woodshed] where he had been drinking and the owner [Paknad] drove him away from the area with the knowledge and intent that this would make it difficult to establish [that Shimer's] operation of his vehicle [had been] under the influence [of alcohol].'

"In his complaint, Hepe named respondents Paknad, Hoist, and the Woodshed as defendants. Based upon respondents' service of alcoholic beverages, Hepe attempts to state causes of action for negligence, assault, battery, negligent hiring, and products liability. Based upon the events following the accident, Hepe attempts to state additional causes of action for fraud and interference with prospective economic advantage. Respondents demurred to Hepe's complaint, and the court sustained the demurrers without leave to amend.

Discussion

" . . .

Business and Professions Code Section 25602

"Hepe's claims for negligence, assault, battery, negligent hiring, and products liability are all premised upon respondents' service of alcoholic beverages to Shimer, the driver at fault. Each of these claims depends upon the theory that respondents' service of alcohol was a proximate cause of Hepe's injuries. The claim for negligence challenges the wisdom of serving alcohol to Shimer in light of his alleged alcoholism. The claims for assault and battery are designed to trace responsibility for the vehicular collision back to those who served alcohol. The claim for negligent hiring relates to the waitress who served the drinks. The claim for products liability is based on the absence of warning labels on the alcoholic beverages that respondents served.

"These claims might have survived a demurrer a decade ago. Today, however, section 25602 bars each claim. Section 25602, as amended by the Legislature in 1978, confers a 'sweeping immunity' upon the servers of alcoholic beverages through a legislative determination that 'the consumption of alcoholic beverages rather than the serving . . . [is] the proximate cause of injuries inflicted upon another by an intoxicated person.' (§ 25602, subd. (c); *see also* Civ. Code, § 1714, subd. (b); *see Strang v. Cabrol* (1984) 37 Cal. 3d 720, 725, 209 Cal. Rptr. 347, 691 P.2d 1013; *Cory v. Shierloh* (1981) 29 Cal. 3d 430, 436, 174 Cal. Rptr. 500, 629 P.2d 8 [holding that § 25602 is constitutional].)

"Prior to 1971, persons injured by intoxicated persons could not state a justiciable claim against those who had served the alcoholic beverages. A typical decision on point is *Cole v. Rush* (1955) 45 Cal. 2d 345, 289 P.2d 450, in which the Supreme Court held that 'as to a competent person it is the voluntary consumption, not the sale or gift, of intoxicating liquor which is the proximate cause of injury from its use.' (*Id.* at p. 356, 289 P.2d 450.) In 1971, the Supreme Court changed its position to allow injured persons to state causes of action based upon a violation of former section 25602, which made it a misdemeanor to serve alcoholic beverages to 'any habitual or common drunkard or to any obviously intoxicated person.' (§ 25602, subd. (a); *Vesely v. Sager* (1971) 5 Cal. 3d 153, 95 Cal. Rptr. 623, 486 P.2d 151.) In subsequent decisions, the Supreme Court further expanded the tort liability of persons who served alcohol by holding that the usual rules of proximate cause and foreseeability would govern. (*Bernhard v. Harrah's Club* (1976) 16 Cal. 3d 313, 128 Cal. Rptr. 215, 546 P.2d 719; *Coulter v. Superior Court* (1978) 21 Cal. 3d 144, 145 Cal. Rptr. 534, 577 P.2d 669.)

"In 1978, however, the Legislature directly intervened in the development of court-created law in this area by amending section 26502 with the addition of two new subdivisions. The first new subdivision, in the following language, precludes use of the misdemeanor prohibition as a standard of care in tort actions: '(b) No person who sells, furnishes, gives, or causes to be sold, furnished, or given away, any alcoholic beverage pursuant to subdivision (a) of this section shall be civilly liable to any injured person or the estate of such person for injuries inflicted on that person as a result of intoxication by the consumer of such alcoholic beverage.' (§ 25602, subd. (b).)

"The second new subdivision expressly abrogates the line of judicial decisions imposing liability on persons who serve alcohol: '(c) The Legislature hereby declares that this section shall be interpreted so that the holdings in cases such as [*Vesely v. Sager, supra,* 5 Cal. 3d 153, 95 Cal. Rptr. 623, 486 P.2d 151, *Bernhard v. Harrah's Club, supra,* 16 Cal. 3d 313, 128 Cal. Rptr. 215, 546 P.2d 719 and *Coulter v. Superior Court, supra,* 21 Cal. 3d 144, 145 Cal. Rptr. 534, 577 P.2d 669] be abrogated in favor of prior judicial interpretation finding the consumption of alcoholic beverages rather than the serving of alcoholic beverages as the proximate cause of injuries inflicted upon another by an intoxicated person.' (§ 25602, subd. (c).)

"The effect of these amendments was to return California law to the earlier rule typified by *Cole v. Rush, supra.* In 1981, however, one court resumed judicial activity in this area with a new, nonstatutory exception to section 25602. In *Cantor v. Anderson* (1981) 126 Cal. App. 3d 124, 178 Cal. Rptr. 540, the court held that, 'where a social host knows his guest is one who because of some exceptional physical and mental condition should not be served alcoholic beverages and is or should be aware of the risks included in providing such person with alcohol, the host is not protected by [the immunity statute].' (*Id.* at p. 132, 178 Cal. Rptr. 540.)

"The plaintiff in *Cantor,* who ran a home for developmentally disabled persons, was injured by a resident of the home. The plaintiff's neighbors had served alcohol to the resident, Edward, 'with full knowledge of his disability.' (*Id.* at p. 126, 178 Cal. Rptr. 540.) After consuming alcohol, 'Edward fell into a seizure, lost consciousness, was rendered unable to control his actions, and subsequently became violent.' (*Ibid.*) When the plaintiff attempted to aid Edward, he injured her.

"In the *Cantor* court's view, the defendants, who had served the alcohol, 'should have known the effect that liquor would have on [Edward] by reason of his disability.' (*Id.* at p. 131, 178 Cal. Rptr. 540.) Reasoning that section 25602 does not preclude liability based upon a 'concurrent proximate cause,' the *Cantor* court viewed service of alcohol to a person with an exceptional condition as a proximate cause of injury distinct from service of alcoholic beverages to ordinary persons. The Legislature provided only a single exception to the immunity statute for service of alcohol to 'obviously intoxicated minor[s].' (§ 25602.1.) But the court found authority for a new, judicial exception in the idea that, 'in returning to the rule of *Cole [supra],* we also return to the limitations of the rule.' (*Cantor v. Anderson, supra,* 126 Cal. App. 3d at p. 130, 178 Cal. Rptr. 540.) *Cole* did not involve an incompetent person, but the court had included the word 'competent' in its formulation of a rule about proximate causation. Specifically, the *Cole* court made—and *Cantor* is based upon—the following statement: 'as to a competent person it is the voluntary consumption, not the sale or gift, of intoxicating liquor which is the proximate cause of injury resulting from its use.' (*Cole v. Rush, supra,* 45 Cal. 2d at p. 356, 289 P.2d 450 (emphasis added), quoted in *Cantor v. Anderson, supra,* 126 Cal. App. 3d at p. 130, 178 Cal. Rptr. 540.)

"In this case, plaintiff Hepe relies on *Cantor* to preserve his claims. Paraphrasing that decision, Hepe alleges respondents knew that Shimer 'was afflicted with an exceptional physical and mental condition, to wit, alcoholism, so that he should not have been furnished alcoholic beverages; that the beverages were nevertheless furnished to defendant [Shimer] with the result that he engaged in the foreseeable conduct of an alcoholic of consuming alcohol to excess which, in turn, affected his mental and physical judgment and coordination; with the further foreseeable result that said [Shimer] operated a motor vehicle under the influence of alcohol.'

"We are disinclined to expand the *Cantor* decision, which does not have a sound statutory basis. As the Supreme Court categorically held in *Strang v. Cabrol, supra,* 37 Cal. 3d 720, 209 Cal. Rptr. 347, 691 P.2d 1013, 'the Legislature abolished tort liability against the furnisher of alcoholic beverages except in only one situation, namely, providing alcohol to an obviously intoxicated minor. No other exceptions to this immunity exist.' (*Id.* at p. 728, 209 Cal. Rptr. 347, 691 P.2d 1013.) The court reasoned as follows: 'The maxim *expressio unius est exclusio alterius* applies here. Under this familiar rule of construction, an express exclusion from the operation of a statute indicates the Legislature intended no other exceptions are to be implied. [Citations omitted.] The "single exception" to the "sweeping immunity" afforded by the 1978 amendments (*Cory v. Shierloh, supra,* at p. 436, 174 Cal. Rptr. 500, 629 P.2d 8) is in cases of sale by a licensee to an obviously intoxicated minor (§ 25602.1).' (*Strang v. Cabrol, supra,* at p. 725, 209 Cal. Rptr. 347, 691 P.2d 1013.) . . .

"So, after reading the Supreme Court opinion up to that point, one is startled to note a laudatory reference to *Cantor.* (*Id.* at p. 726, 209 Cal. Rptr. 347, 691 P.2d 1013.) How can the same high court opinion affirm that there is only one exception and then seemingly approve of a court of appeal decision which, by judicial fiat, engrafted a second one upon the law? What is the duty of an intermediate appellate court when confronted with irreconcilable language in the same binding precedent? . . . We therefore fashion our own answer: we follow the holding rather than the dictum, especially where the holding is so manifestly compelled by the expressed intent of the Legislature. To repeat: ' . . . the Legislature abolished tort liability against the furnisher of alcoholic beverages except in only one situation, namely, providing alcohol to an obviously intoxicated minor. No other exceptions to this immunity exist.' (*Strang v. Cabrol, supra,* at p. 728, 209 Cal. Rptr. 347, 691 P.2d 1013.) It follows that plaintiff Hepe cannot state a cause of action. . . .

Dismissal without Leave to Amend

" . . .

"Since section 25602 bars Hepe's claims for negligence, assault, battery, negligent hiring, and products liability, no amendment will permit him to state a cause of action. Hepe argues to the contrary that, if permitted to amend, he could allege that the respondents' service of alcohol was reckless. However, reckless conduct does not constitute an exception to the immunity statute. The statute's determination that the service of alcoholic beverages is not a 'proximate cause of injuries' is not limited to actions for negligence. . . .

"Hepe has not suggested that amendment would allow him to remedy the deficiencies in his pleading of fraud and interference with prospective economic advantage. Since the events underlying his complaint do not fall within the traditional scope of these torts, there is no reasonable possibility that he can state a cause of action, and the court did not abuse its discretion by denying leave to amend.

Disposition

"The judgment of dismissal is affirmed. . . . "

The necessity of proving that at the time a commercial vendor served alcoholic beverages, the person appeared to be intoxicated is noted in *Cartwright v. Hyatt Corporation.*[37] In that case, the federal district court for the District of

---

[37] 460 F. Supp. 80 (D.C. 1987).

Columbia dismissed a cause of action against a vendor for the death of a patron served at defendant's hotel bar.

The statutes of the various states are not uniform in interpretation or express language as to who may sue and the type of conduct that will give rise to liability. Therefore, caution must be exercised in dealing with the subject. For example, in at least two states, a plaintiff who merely participates in drinking with the person whose inebriation causes him injury may preclude recovery under their respective statutes. This is not the law in New York or Minnesota, but apparently governs in Michigan and Illinois.

What are the ramifications in this area of growing concern? Are illegal sales limited to the actual premises in which the liquor is dispensed, such as a hotel bar or cocktail lounge, or does the statutory scheme extend to room-service sales or deliveries of alcoholic beverages? No definitive answer to this question exists, but if the statutory policy is to be carried out, then the innkeeper who authorizes room-service sales of its own liquor inventory might logically be held responsible if the room service waiter knowingly served a minor who became drunk, or an intoxicated guest or patron, or one who became intoxicated later by reason of the sale or dispensing of liquor ordered by the guest. Having voluntarily proffered the beverages for sale, and having thereafter voluntarily relinquished any supervision over the consumption of the beverages, the innkeeper could be held responsible if inebriation ensued which later resulted in harm to a third person.

The same principle would apply if the guest hired a hotel bartender to serve beverages to guests from the hotel's liquor stock at a private party or other function held in his guest's room. It would also apply to the service of alcoholic beverages at any formal function supervised by hotel personnel in hotel function rooms.

Another more intriguing problem is that posed by the installation of self-service liquor-dispensing bars in guest rooms. The room guest, free of any supervision, dispenses his own drinks in any quantity or amount desired by activating the device and serving himself. The only control is the amount of stock loaded into such devices and the fact that each serving is recorded automatically at the front desk, for purposes of posting such charges to his bill. The disturbing aspect of this promotional scheme is that it necessarily precludes meaningful supervision and invites abuse. Having made liquor available to guests in this fashion, the innkeeper is needlessly exposing himself to a severe risk of liability totally disproportionate to the supposed benefit to be derived from their installation.

19:10 A Defense to Dram Shop or Common-Law Liability: Voluntary Intoxication of Patron

Generally the injured person's own intoxication will preclude liability under dram shop act statutes or at common law, on the theory that one should not hold another party liable for the foreseeable consequences of the actor's own voluntary intoxication.[38] Such activity constitutes either contributory negligence or an assumption of known risks, affirmative defenses which may bar recovery.

However, in the landmark case of *Ewing v. Cloverleaf Bowl*, which follows, both of these defenses were held inapplicable to reckless misconduct in serving grossly excessive quantities of alcohol to one who had only recently attained the legal drinking age. The thrust of the California high court ruling was that the patron's own intoxication does not, as a matter of law, preclude recovery where the intoxication is deliberately induced by the dispenser's own willful misconduct. Involuntary intoxication caused by the acts or omissions of the dispenser relegates such defenses to questions of fact for the jury to determine.

Contributory negligence, in this context, is synonymous with voluntary intoxication. Such intoxication is relevant on the issue of liability caused by the dispenser's failure to exercise reasonable care in serving alcohol, but is not conclusive.

Assumption of risk, which might otherwise permit dismissal of a patron's cause of action as a matter of law, must be viewed in the context of the patron's appreciation of the specific danger confronting him. The appreciation of danger is proportionate to the magnitude of the risk. A patron may be said to appreciate the risks of his own intoxication, but not the risk of acute alcohol poisoning, reasoned the high court. Here the inexperience of the patron, based on his turning twenty-one years of age on the day of the incident, when weighed against the experience of the dispenser, caused the court to reverse the judgment of dismissal and remit the case for trial.

EWING V. CLOVERLEAF BOWL
20 Cal. 3d 389, 572 P.2d 1142 (1978)[39]

TOBRINER, J.: "In this case, an experienced bartender, knowing that a patron had just turned 21 years of age that very day, served his young customer 10 straight shots of 151 proof rum, as well as a vodka collins and 2 beer chasers, during a period of less than an hour and a half; as a result, the 21-year-old patron died the next day, leaving 2 small children on whose behalf the instant wrongful death action was brought.

"Faced with these undisputed facts, the trial court granted defendant's motion for nonsuit, finding as a matter of *law*, that the patron's conduct amounted to contributory negligence and that the bartender's conduct did not constitute willful misconduct. We shall explain that this ruling represents an illogical and unwarranted limitation of this court's holding in *Vesely v. Sager* (1971), 5 Cal. 3d 153 [95 Cal. Rptr. 623, 486 P.2d 151], and improperly immunizes a bartender from all responsibility for a senseless death that the jury could have found foreseeably flowed from the bartender's reckless conduct.

---

[38]Robinson v. Bognanno, 213 N.W.2d 530 (Iowa 1973), *overrruled* by Lewis v. State, 256 N.W. 2d 181 (Iowa 1977).
[39]Superseded by statute in Hepe v. Paknad, 199 Cal. App. 3d 412, 244 Cal. Rptr. 823 (Cal. App. 1988).

1. The facts in this case.

"In this wrongful death action, Robert and Anthony Ewing, the sons of the decedent, Christopher Ewing, brought suit through their mother and guardian *ad litem,* Katherine Ewing, against Cloverleaf Bowl, a California corporation. At the close of plaintiff's presentation of evidence, the trial court granted defendant's motion for nonsuit, dismissed the jury, and entered judgment for defendant. Plaintiffs appeal.

"Dr. Allan McNie took a sample of Christopher Ewing's blood at the time of the autopsy. He found that the level of alcohol in the blood sample was .47 percent. As Dr. McNie subsequently testified, alcohol acts as a depressant on the central nervous system. If the level of alcohol in a person's blood exceeds .20 percent a casual observer will be able to detect signs that the person is drunk. If the level of alcohol is between .30 and .40 percent, the person will begin to become comatose. If the level of alcohol exceeds .42 percent, the person will die as a result of paralysis of the centers of the brain controlling heart rhythm and respiration. Dr. McNie concluded that Chris Ewing died of acute alcohol poisoning.

"Dr. McNie calculated the amount of liquor Chris must have consumed in order to achieve an alcohol level of .47 percent. Taking into account Chris' weight, the amount of food he had eaten, and other factors, Dr. McNie found that Chris must have drunk 21.6 ounces of 86 proof liquor, 18.6 ounces of 100 proof liquor, or 11.2 ounces of 151 proof liquor.

"Christopher Ewing's sons, in bringing this wrongful death action, charged the Cloverleaf Bowl with both negligence and willful misconduct. In our review of the trial court's nonsuit, we shall assess plaintiffs' allegations against the background of the facts which we have set forth above. Specifically, we shall consider three issues: whether defendant, as represented by its bartender, owed a duty of care to Christopher Ewing, its customer; whether a jury could reasonably conclude that the bartender's conduct amount to a willful misconduct in breach of that duty; and whether a jury could also reasonably conclude that Ewing's conduct, even if it did constitute contributory negligence, nonetheless amounted to neither willful misconduct nor assumption of the risk.

2. A bartender owes a duty to a patron to exercise due care and incurs liability to the patron for the foreseeable injuries caused by the bartender's failure to exercise such care.

" . . .

"Insofar as the customer is concerned, defendant asserts, it still remains true that consumption of liquor, and not the sale, is the sole cause of any injury.

"This argument fails on its face. . . . We hold that *Vesely* [*v. Sager,* 5 Cal. 3d 153, 486 P.2d 151] and *Bernhard* [*v. Harrah's Club,* 16 Cal. 3d 313, 546 P.2d 719] govern regardless of whether a third party injured by an intoxicated customer or a customer himself sues a bartender: the bartender's liability in both circumstances depends upon the application of the principle that an individual is liable for foreseeable injuries caused by his failure to exercise reasonable care.

As we noted at the outset, the applications of this principle turns on the facts of each case.

"If a jury could reasonably find only that the bartender was negligent and that Ewing was also negligent, Ewing's contributory negligence would of course bar plaintiffs' recovery and justify the trial court's nonsuit. If, however, a jury could find that Lamont's conduct amounted to willful misconduct, while Ewing's conduct was merely negligent, plaintiffs could recover [citation omitted], and the trial court's nonsuit would be erroneous. Finally, if a jury could reasonably conclude only that Lamont's conduct and Ewing's conduct constituted similarly willful misconduct, plaintiffs would again be barred. [Citation omitted.]

"We must also consider the question of assumption of risk. Specifically, we must decide whether a jury, on the basis of plaintiffs' evidence, could reasonably conclude *only* that Christopher Ewing assumed the risk of acute alcohol poisoning, the cause of his death. If assumption of risk is thus established as a matter of law, plaintiffs could not recover even if a jury could find that the bartender's conduct amounted to willful misconduct. [Citation omitted.]

> *3. In this case, the jury could reasonably conclude that the bartender engaged in willful misconduct, while the patron engaged only in negligent conduct.*

"Because our inquiry here is ultimately a search for willful misconduct, we state the appropriate standard at the outset . . . 'If conduct is sufficiently lacking in consideration for the rights of others, reckless, heedless to an extreme, and indifferent to the consequences it may impose, then, regardless of the actual state of mind of the actor and his actual concern for the rights of others, we call it willful misconduct. . . . ' [Citations omitted.]

"Lamont plainly acted intentionally in serving liquor to Chris Ewing. He also acted intentionally in serving Ewing 151 proof rum. [Chris Ewing's companion] asked only for 'the strongest drink in the house'; it was Lamont who initially selected the rum. Moreover, because Lamont had to remove the rum from its shelf below the bar before serving Chris, and reshelve it after each serving, the jury could reasonably conclude that Lamont did not serve Chris even the last shots of rum without knowledge of the specific drink he was serving.

"Lamont knew the significance of differences in proof. He knew, further, that the rum which he served Chris was anywhere from twice to half again the potency of ordinary liquors. Moreover, Lamont knew that Chris was probably an inexperienced drinker; not only his age, which Lamont knew, but the apparent novelty he saw in drinking, suggested this fact. Lamont could conclude, therefore, that Chris was not fully aware of the radical difference in potency between the rum and ordinary liquor; indeed, Lamont's own warnings to Chris evidence Lamont's knowledge of this relative disparity in experience.

"Lamont knew that Chris intended to get drunk; Chris said so. Lamont also knew that his own warning to Chris to take it easy, urged after pouring the third round, had been without effect. Knowing that Chris probably did not fully comprehend the implications of the high potency of the liquor he was drinking, and knowing as well of Chris' intent to get drunk, Lamont could have concluded, or should have concluded, that Chris might consume an amount of liquor hazardous to his health. As a bartender with 11½ years of experience, Lamont knew or should have known that, beyond a certain level, consumption of alcohol creates an immediate health hazard.

"Finally, Lamont acted in violation of two rules of practice at the Cloverleaf Bowl. He repeatedly filled the shot glasses beyond the seven-eights line, in contravention of ordinary policy. Moreover, in view of . . . [other testimony], he continued to serve Chris after Chris was manifestly intoxicated, in violation of a posted rule, and even attempted to serve Chris after his brother Doug's arrival, at a point at which Chris was barely conscious.

"This description of Lamont's acts suggests not merely a want of ordinary care, but willful misconduct. Lamont acted intentionally, aware of the health hazard created by Chris' relative inexperience and continued drinking, without regard for Cloverleaf Bowl's standard practices, which if followed would have stopped Chris' drinking short of its fatal conclusion. We emphasize that this interpretation is not the only rendition that a jury could reasonably attach to Lamont's conduct; it is, however, *one* reasonable interpretation.

"Chris intended to get drunk; he did not intend to consume a fatal overdose of alcohol. Although a prudent man would no doubt have inquired into the consequences of differences of proof, Chris' failure to so inquire hardly rises to the level of recklessness. In view of his evident inexperience, Chris had no reason to know of the possibility of alcohol poisoning. Since Chris' companions warned him he would get drunk, perhaps he could be said to have acted in reckless disregard of the usual consequences of intoxication as such. His companions, however, did not warn him that he would die. Indeed, one associate, . . . indicated that he himself had in the past consumed great quantities of 151 proof rum. Plainly, therefore, Chris did not recklessly court the risk of acute alcohol poisoning.

"In sum, a reasonable jury could conclude that Christopher Ewing was merely negligent. If plaintiffs establish defendant's willful misconduct, contributory negligence does not bar recovery. [Citation omitted.] Here, we have already seen that a reasonable jury could conclude that Lamont, defendant's employee, engaged in willful misconduct. Unless Christopher Ewing assumed the risk of acute alcohol poisoning, the trial court erred in granting defendant's motion for nonsuit.

4. In this case, the jury could reasonably conclude that the patron did not assume the risk of the bartender's willful misconduct since the specific risk to which the bartender's misconduct exposed the patron was not one which the patron appreciated.

"Defendant argues that, notwithstanding any possible willful misconduct on the part of its bartender, the trial court could nonetheless properly grant defendant's motion for nonsuit on a theory of assumption of risk. . . .

"To warrant the application of the doctrine [of assumption of risk] the evidence must show that the victim appreciated the specific danger involved. He does not assume any risk he does not know or appreciate. . . . Stated another way, before the doctrine is applicable, the victim must have not only general knowledge of a danger, but must have knowledge of the particular danger, that is, knowledge of the magnitude of the risk involved.' [Citations omitted.] 'Under ordinary circumstances the plaintiff will not be taken to assume any risk of either activities or conditions of which he is ignorant.' [Citation omitted.]

"The specific risk in this case is the risk of acute alcohol poisoning. To hold that Christopher Ewing assumed this risk we would be required to reach either of two conclusions. On the one hand, we would have to conclude (1) that plaintiffs, in presenting their case, introduced evidence which suggests that Chris Ewing knew that, by consuming 10 shots of 151 proof rum, he would subject himself to acute alcohol poisoning, and (2) that plaintiffs introduced no evidence which would rebut this suggestion. Alternatively, we would be compelled to conclude that, as a matter of law, any patron of a bar who consumes 10 shots of 151 proof alcohol must know of the risk of acute alcohol poisoning.

"As we have already seen, however, the facts of this case, as plaintiffs developed them, refute both alternatives. Plaintiff's evidence suggests that Christopher Ewing was an inexperienced drinker. As plaintiffs' evidence shows, both the bartender Lamont and the waitress . . . recognized Chris Ewing's naivete. We cannot conclude, therefore, that plaintiffs, in presenting their own case, conclusively established defendant's claim of assumption of risk. Nor can we conclude, in light of plaintiffs' evidence to the contrary, that it must necessarily be the case that *all* consumers of great quantities of 151 proof rum know of their peril. Accordingly, we hold that the trial court's nonsuit is not justified upon the theory of assumption of the risk.

5. Conclusion

"In this case, a commercial vendor of liquor, an experienced bartender, knowing that the youthful patron standing before him had become 21 years of age that day, served the young customer in the course of one and a half hours lethal quantities of the 'strongest drink in the house.' The youth died of acute alcohol poisoning. Yet the trial court cast an armour of protection around this entrepreneur based upon an inflexible rule that a patron who suffers injury from his own intoxication cannot recover from a bartender, no matter how negligent or reckless the bartender's conduct may be. Even assuming the negligence of the young patron, a jury could very well find willful misconduct on the part of the bartender; such conduct would remove the bar of contributory negligence. A jury could also very well conclude that, while contributorily negligent, the youthful patron did not assume the risk of acute alcohol poisoning, the risk of his own death.

"The trial court erred in granting defendant's motion for nonsuit. The judgment is reversed."

The *Ewing* decision is particularly noteworthy because the intoxication of minors and those who have just attained drinking age, as well as adults, is of growing social and economic concern. The California Dram Shop Act specifically exempts the intoxication of minors from the nonliability otherwise afforded commercial dispensers. Whether the California courts will interpret the Act to encompass a person newly emancipated remains an open question. A similar approach has been applied in New York to authorize recovery by a seventeen-year-old minor who was served thirteen drinks in one hour by a licensed tavern keeper against the argument that the minor's own voluntary consumption precluded recovery. The court nevertheless sustained a cause of action based on a violation of section 65 of the Alcoholic Beverage Control Law, making it *malum prohibitum* to serve alcohol to a minor. The statute was intended to encompass a minor's inexperience and lack of judgment and to protect minors against their own negligence, which presumably attach to their immaturity.[40]

Irrespective of what activities of the dispenser of alcohol would suffice to constitute involuntary intoxication in New York, which would presumably enable the inebriated customer to recover, New York has abrogated the doctrine of contributory negligence, which at common law would totally bar recovery, regardless of the degree of negligence imputable to the claimant. In its place New York has adopted a statutory comparative negligence rule, according to which the amount otherwise recoverable is diminished by the amount of negligence attributable to the claimant.[41] Although no New York authority exists on the applicability of the comparative negligence rule to Dram Shop Act claims, it is clear that it would be available to support any negligence actions brought as an independent ground of recovery, and would most likely be applied to the statutory claim. This prognosis is buttressed by the Judicial Conference recommendation, in support of the rule, that it should apply to all personal injury, death, and property claims regardless of the legal theory on which the claim is predicated.[42]

The conclusion is inescapable that illegal service of intoxicants to a minor creates civil liability, not only to injured third persons but in exceptional cases to the intoxicated minor. Almost all jurisdictions recognize this exception, whether at common law, through the vehicle of a dram shop act, or by reason of the existence of legislation criminalizing sale of intoxicants to minors. Lack of any evil motive is no defense, and the sanctions can be extremely severe, not only in terms of civil and criminal responsibility, but more destructively, in terms of the ultimate and permanent loss of one's liquor license.

Furnishing alcohol to minors in any case not only implicates the licensed vendor or dispenser, but also has been held to impose liability upon social hosts and

---

[40]Santuro v. De Marco, 65 Misc. 2d 817, 320 N.Y.S.2d 132 (D.C. Nassau Co. 1971), *reversed*, 80 Misc. 2d 276 (Sup. Ct. 1972). *See also* Marusa v. District of Columbia, 484 F.2d 828 (D.C. Cir. 1973).

[41]N.Y. Civil Practice Law § § 1411–1413.

[42]N.Y. Judicial Conference Report, 1975.

nonprofit organizations in Indiana, Montana, New Jersey, Oregon, Michigan, and Pennsylvania. California, Florida, Iowa, and New York reject such liability.

In the following landmark case, the Supreme Court of Arizona overruled its prior common-law rule of tavern owner nonliability for alcohol-related injuries either to the intoxicated drinker or to third persons caused by the intoxicated drinker.

BRANNIGAN V. RAYBUCK

136 Ariz. 513, 667 P.2d 213 (1983)[43]

FELDMAN, J.: "Plaintiffs are the surviving parents of three boys, Michael William Brannigan, Michael J. Roberts and Danny Jordan, who were killed in a motor vehicle accident which occurred on October 8, 1978. The parents of all three filed wrongful death actions against the Raybucks (defendants), who operated a business under the style of 'Good Time Inn.' The parents alleged that the defendants had breached a duty of care by furnishing liquor to the boys and that this had been the cause of the accident in which all three were killed.

"Defendants moved for summary judgment in each of the cases, claiming that under the common law of Arizona a tavern owner was not liable for negligence in furnishing intoxicants to patrons who were underage or already intoxicated. The two trial judges who considered the cases in the superior court quite properly agreed that this was the law of Arizona and granted the motions for summary judgment. The cases were consolidated on appeals and in a memorandum decision [citations omitted] the court of appeals held that prior case law required it to apply the common law rule that a tavern owner is not liable for negligence in furnishing intoxicants to an underage or intoxicated patron who, as a result, subsequently injures either himself or some third person. The court of appeals therefore affirmed the summary judgments granted the defendants.

"All three plaintiff's joined in a petition for review to this court. We accepted review of this case and the transfer of the companion case of *Ontiveros v. Borak*, 136 Ariz. 500, 667 P.2d 200 (1983) in order to reconsider the common law rule of tavern owner's nonliability and to determine whether that rule should be retained as the common law of this state. . . .

"The facts are set out in the opinion of the court of appeals; we borrow their language: Roberts and Brannigan were passengers in a pickup truck driven by Jordan when the truck was involved in a one-car accident in which all three young men died. Roberts and Brannigan were both sixteen years of age and Jordan was seventeen years of age at the time of the accident. Viewing the evidence in a light most favorable to the plaintiffs, it is established that Jordan went to the Good Time Inn with his girlfriend on the evening of October 7, 1978, where he consumed several drinks of intoxicating liquor. He took his girlfriend home around midnight and returned to the bar, where he started drinking with Bran-

---

[43]Superseded by statute as stated in Carrillo v. El Mirage Roadhouse, Inc., 164 Ariz. 364, 793 P. 2d 121 (Ariz. 1990).

nigan, Roberts and other friends. Several pitchers of beer and numerous drinks of tequila were consumed by the boys. By the time they all left the bar at 1:00 A.M. on Sunday they were all intoxicated. The Maricopa County Medical Examiner's Report indicates that Jordan, the driver of the pickup, had a blood-alcohol level of .23. Within minutes of leaving the parking lot, Jordan crashed the pickup into a wall. There is testimony that the employees of the bar did not check for age cards and that the Good Time Inn, owned by Mr. and Mrs. Raybuck, was patronized by Jordan and other teenagers because they were not checked for proof of their ages.

"The grant of summary judgment by the trial court and affirmance by the court of appeals was predicated upon the principle that it is not the act of selling, but, rather, the act of consuming liquor that is the proximate cause of the injury sustained by either the intoxicated customer or some third person, so that the tavern owner is therefore not liable for negligence in selling the liquor. This is the common law rule which has obtained in Arizona. *Ontiveros, supra.* We have today abolished that rule, holding that it is unsuitable to present society and is based on reasoning repugnant to modern tort theory. We held that causation in dram shop cases 'should ordinarily be a question of fact for the jury under usual principles of Arizona tort law.'

Duty

"In *Ontiveros, supra,* we held today that the tavern owner was under a duty, imposed both by common law principles and statute, to exercise care in serving intoxicants to a patron who later injured a third party. The facts of the case at bench present a different question, since here one of the persons served, Jordan, inflicted the harm on himself as well as third persons. The third persons involved were not completely innocent participants, as in *Ontiveros,* but had participated with Jordan at the same 'party.'

"Thus, these cases present the question of whether the tavern owner has a duty to the patron to withhold intoxicants in order to prevent the patron from injuring himself. While this question is of particular significance in the Jordan case, it also exists in the other cases since one might well argue that Brannigan and Roberts contributed to their own demise by drinking with Jordan and getting in the truck with him. There was evidence that Jordan's state of intoxication was easily recognizable by both the barkeep and the passengers. In fact, the evidence indicates that Jordan 'staggered' from the saloon to the parking lot and a witness testified on deposition that as Jordan drove away, Mrs. Raybuck mentioned that 'those boys will be lucky if they make it home alive tonight.' While we have indicated above and in *Ontiveros, supra,* that we consider the act of furnishing liquor to be part of the chain of cause and effect leading to the accident, it is certainly to be acknowledged that the voluntary consumption is also part of that cause and effect. Therefore, we examine the question of duty in the context that the act of consumption by all three boys contributed to the occurrence of the accident.

"There are cases holding that the seller of liquor is not liable for the mere sale of liquor to an intoxicated person who subsequently causes injury to himself as the result of intoxication. *Noonan v. Galick,* 19 Conn. Supp. 308, 310, 112 A.2d 892, 894 (1955); *see* 48A C.J.S. *Intoxicating Liquors* § 428 at 134 (1981). A growing number of cases, however, have recognized that one of the very hazards that makes it negligent to furnish liquor to a minor or intoxicated patron is the foreseeable prospect that the patron will become drunk and injure himself or others. *See Vesely v. Sager,* 5 Cal. 3d 153, 164, 486 P.2d 151, 159, 95 Cal. Rptr. 623, 631 (1971). Accordingly, modern authority has increasingly recognized that one who furnishes liquor to a minor or intoxicated patron breaches a common law duty owed both to innocent third parties who may be injured and to the patron himself. *See Nazareno v. Urie,* Alaska, 638 P.2d 671 (1981); *Rappaport v. Nichols,* 31 N.J. 188, 156 A.2d 1 (1959); *Jardine v. Upper Darby Lodge No. 1973, Inc.,* 413 Pa. 626, 198 A.2d 550 (1964). . . .

"We believe, therefore, that a supplier of liquor is under a common law duty of reasonable care in furnishing liquor to those who, by reason of immaturity or previous over-indulgence, may lack full capacity of self-control and may therefore injure themselves, as well as others.

"Most courts have, however, relied on statutes to find the existence of duty upon which to base a cause of action. *See Davis v. Shiappacossee,* 155 So. 2d 365 (Fla. 1963); *Elder v. Fisher,* 247 Ind. 598, 217 N.E.2d 847 (1966); *Soronen v. Old Milford Inn, Inc.,* 46 N.J. 582, 218 A.2d 630 (1966); *Smith v. Evans,* 421 Pa. 247, 219 A.2d 310 (1966); *Majors v. Brodhead Hotel,* 416 Pa. 265, 205 A.2d 873 (1965). . . .

"We believe that A.R.S. § 4-244(9), which prohibits furnishing 'spirituous liquor' to those under 19 years of age, and § 4-241(A), which requires a licensee to demand certain types of identification from those requesting service, constitute legislative recognition of the foreseeable danger to both the patron and third parties, and an effort to meet that danger by enactment of laws designed to regulate the industry, to protect third persons, and to protect those who are underage from themselves. Accordingly we find here, as in *Ontiveros, supra,* that the licensee and his employees have a duty recognized both by common law and statute to refrain from selling intoxicants to those whose subnormal capacity for self-control is or should be known or who are prohibited by statute from using alcoholic beverages. We hold, therefore, that defendants were under a duty to all three of the decedents.

Standard of Care

"Defendants argue with some persuasive force that in many cases unjust results will be reached by recognizing that the statute is, in part at least, a safety measure designed for protection of patrons and third parties. They contend that the statute will thus be considered to set the standard of care so that its violation will always result in a finding of negligence per se. It is the prevailing rule, recognized in Arizona, that a breach of a statute intended as a safety regulation is not merely evidence of negligence but is negligence per se. *Orlando v. Northcutt,* 103 Ariz. 298, 300, 441 P.2d 58, 60 (1968); W. Prosser, Handbook of the Law of Torts § 36 at 197-200 (4th ed. 1971). It is true that *if* the statutory standard of conduct were applied rigidly, one who furnished liquor to a minor might be held to have breached his duty even though the minor produced false identification to satisfy the requirements of § 4-241, and one who furnished further intoxicants to an already intoxicated patron might be held liable even though the supplier had no way of knowing the patron had reached the point of intoxication.

"As in most things, however, the common law is not so rigid as to demand injustice. The actual rule on the negligence per se doctrine is that unless the statute is construed to impose an absolute duty, its violation may be excused when, for example, the defendant was 'unable after reasonable dilligence to comply.' Restatement of Torts, *supra,* § 288 A. . . .

"[Citations omitted.]

"We think this concept is applicable to the situation presented here. The legislature has not enacted a civil damage statute eliminating all excuse for the violation of the statute; thus, we are free to recognize that rule which we consider most likely to achieve just results. Prosser, *supra,* § 36, at 198. The statutes in question do not impose strict criminal liability. *Spitz v. Municipal Court,* 127 Ariz. 405, 407–08, 621 P.2d 911, 913-14 (1980). Even if they did, this would not prevent us from recognizing excusable violations when the statute is used to define a standard of care in civil cases. *See* Restatement of Torts, *supra,* § 288 A, comment b; Prosser, *supra.* We therefore hold that where a violation of the statutes pertaining to furnishing liquor to those who are underage or already intoxicated is shown, negligence exists as a matter of law, but under proper facts the jury may be allowed to find that the violation was excusable. *O'Donnell v. Maves,* 108 Ariz. 98, 100, 492 P.2d 1205, 1207 (1972); *Platt v. Gould,* 26 Ariz. App. 315, 316-17, 548 P.2d 28, 29-30 (1976).

"In dram shop cases, then, a licensee who has violated the statute may be able to show such violation excusable if he can establish, for instance, that the minor appeared to be of age and had what appeared to be proper identification as required by A.R.S. § 4-241 or that the demeanor or conduct of the person served was such that there was no reason to believe that he or she was intoxicated. The situations cited are intended as examples, and not as an exhaustive list.

Contributory Negligence—Assumption of the Risk

"We acknowledge that the boys in question were apparently of an age to understand and to control their conduct. The present record does not indicate that they were addicted to alcohol and therefore not responsible for their conduct. *Cf. Pratt v. Daly,* 55 Ariz. 535, 104 P.2d 147 (1940). The evidence establishes that they voluntarily obtained and consumed large amounts of intoxicating liquor and knew or should have known the danger involved in driving in that condition or riding with someone who was in that condition. No doubt their voluntary consumption was a cause of the accident. However, even assuming that the defenses of contributory negligence and assumption of the risk are available, under our constitution these defenses 'shall, in all cases whatsoever, be a question of fact and shall, at all times, be left to the jury.' Ariz. Const. art. 18, § 5. In Arizona, therefore, the court cannot find as a matter of law that the legal defenses of contributory negligence or assumption of risk exist; the jury is free to find in favor of the plaintiff even though the court ordinarily would find as a matter of law that the plaintiff has been contributorily negligent, or has assumed the risk. *Layton v. Rocha*, 90 Ariz. 369, 370, 368 P.2d 444, 445 (1962). We therefore do not reach the question of contributory negligence.

Other Arguments

"Here, as in *Ontiveros*, defendants raise various examples which they claim militate in favor of nonrecognition of liability. For instance, defendants argue that there will be difficulty in administering a rule of liability in hypothetical situations where: (1) a patron has one drink in the first saloon and 19 drinks in a second saloon; (2) the patron has 19 drinks in the first saloon and one drink in the second; (3) the patron has 10 drinks in each saloon. We find these hypothetical situations no more vexatious than in other cases. . . . These and similar situations present the same problems of causation which exist in other tort actions. They are not beyond the ability of our system to handle. *Lewis v. Wolf*, 122 Ariz. 567, 572, 596 P.2d 705, 710 (App. 1979). We acknowledge that the system will not handle each case perfectly, but we think it better to adopt a rule which will permit courts to attempt to achieve justice in all cases than to continue to rely on one which guarantees injustice in many cases.

"Defendants argue that by changing the common law rule we will impose upon the liquor business a special duty of care not imposed on sellers of most other products. To an extent that is true, but alcohol is more dangerous than most products. We do no more than place upon those who furnish alcohol the burden of responding in damages for failure to use due care in furnishing a dangerous product. However, we do not place upon them any greater burden in conducting themselves than that which had already been imposed by the requirements of statute which makes it unlawful to sell liquor to minors or intoxicated patrons. We agree with the New Jersey Supreme Court:

"Liquor licensees, who operate their businesses by way of privilege rather than as of right, have long been under strict obligation not to serve minors and intoxicated persons and if, as is likely, the result we have reached in the conscientious exercise of our traditional judicial function substantially increases their diligence in honoring that obligation then the public interest will indeed be very well served.

"*Rappaport v. Nichols*, 31 N.J. at 205-06, 156 A.2d at 10.

"Defendants next argue, as did those in *Ontiveros*, that this court should await legislative action and should not abandon the common law rule in the absence of such action. As we indicated in *Ontiveros, supra*, we do not think lack of legislative intent with regard to the existence of a civil remedy is determinative. We believe there is a legislative objective to keep drunk drivers off the roads. The magnitude of the problem is documented in the statistics quoted in *Ontiveros*. The problem in Arizona seems, if anything, to be greater than in other parts of the country. According to the statistics cited in the amicus brief filed in this case by Mothers Against Drunk Drivers, between one-third and one-half of all fatal automobile accidents in Arizona involve alcohol and Arizona ranks fourth highest in the country in alcohol-related deaths and injuries. *See, also, State ex. rel. Ekstrom v. Justice Court*, 136 Ariz. 1, 4, 663 P.2d 992, 996 (1983) (concurring opinion). Adoption of a rule which will make those who furnish alcohol to those who are forbidden to use it civilly responsible to pay damages for the injuries caused by their violation of law is a step designed to meet a problem which has become acute. This is not judicial legislation, but merely the response of the common law to changed social conditions. If the legislature considers it to be unwise, it has the means of so informing us. . . .

[The court's reasoning as to retroactive application of its decision is omitted.]

"We hold, therefore, that the former rule of nonliability based on causation is abolished, and the duty of a licensee to refrain from selling alcohol to minors and intoxicated patrons who may, as a result, injure themselves or others is recognized for this case, for all other pending cases, for those not yet filed which are not barred by the statute of limitations, and for all causes of action which may arise in the future.

"The decision of the court of appeals is vacated. The judgments below are reversed. The cases are remanded for further proceedings not inconsistent with this opinion."

CONGINI BY CONGINI v. PORTERSVILLE VALVE CO.
504 Pa. 157, 470 A.2d 515 (1983)

MCDERMOTT, J.: "This appeal arises from an action in trespass for personal injuries sustained by Mark Congini in an automobile accident which occurred on December 22, 1978. His parents instituted suit on his behalf, and on their own behalf, in the Court of Common Pleas of Lawrence County against the Portersville Valve Company (Portersville). The defendant filed preliminary objections in the nature of demurrer. The trial judge, the Honorable William R. Balph, sustained the preliminary objections and the Conginis' complaint was dismissed on August 18, 1980.

"On appeal the Superior Court affirmed, relying in part on our decision in *Manning v. Andy*, 454 Pa. 237, 310 A.2d 75 (1973). Appellants petitioned this Court for allowance of appeal and we granted allocatur. . . .

"At the time of the accident in question Mark Congini was eighteen (18) years of age and an employee of Portersville. On December 22, 1978 Portersville held a Christmas party for its employees at which alcoholic beverages were served. Mark attended the party and, as a result of consuming an undisclosed amount of alcohol, became intoxicated.

"Mark's car was parked at Portersville plant, which was the scene of the party, and appellee, through one of its agents, had possession and custody of the car keys. Although Portersville's agent was aware of Mark's intoxicated condition, the keys were given to Mark upon his request so that he could drive from the plant to his home.

"While Mark was operating the car on the highway, he drove it into the rear of another vehicle which was proceeding in the same direction. As a result of this accident Mark suffered multiple fractures and brain damage which have left him totally and permanently disabled.

"In their appeal appellants have alleged several grounds of liability; first, that defendant was negligent in providing Mark with alcoholic beverages to the point that he became intoxicated; second, that defendant was negligent in surrendering the car keys to Mark, knowing that Mark was intoxicated and that he would drive; and third, that appellee, as a landowner, was negligent in breaching a duty owed to Mark as an invitee. Appellants have not alleged that appellee was a licensee of the Pennsylvania Liquor Control Board.

"The first issue before us is similar to that raised in *Klein v. Raysinger*, decided this day at ——Pa.——, 470 A.2d 507 (1983), i.e., the extent to which a social host can be held liable for injuries sustained by his guest to whom he has served intoxicating liquors. This case, however, differs in two respects: that the guest here was a minor; and that the plaintiff here is the guest to whom the intoxicants were served, rather than a third person injured by a person who was served alcoholic beverages. *See Klein, id.*

"As we note in *Klein*, our sister state jurisdictions are virtually unanimous in refusing to extend common law liability to an adult social host serving intoxicants to his adult guests. *Id.* at 510 (collected cases). However, there is no such unanimity in cases where an adult host has knowingly served intoxicants to a minor. [Citations omitted.]

"In *Klein v. Raysinger, supra,* we held that there exists no common law liability on the part of a social host for the service of intoxicants to this adult guests. In arriving at this decision we relied upon the common law rule that in the case of an ordinary able bodied man, it is the consumption of alcohol rather than the furnishing thereof, that is the proximate cause of any subsequent damage.

"However, our legislature has made a legislative judgment that persons under twenty-one years of age are incompetent to handle alcohol. Under Section 6308 of the Crimes Code, 18 Pa. C.S. § 6308, a person 'less that 21 years of age' commits a summary offense if he 'attempts to purchase, purchases, consumes, possesses or transports any alcohol, liquor or malt or brewed beverages.' Furthermore, under Section 306 of the Crimes Code, 18 Pa. C.S.A. § 306, an adult who furnishes liquor to a minor would be liable as an accomplice to the same extent as the offending minor.

"This legislative judgment compels a different result than *Klein*, for here we are not dealing with ordinary able bodied men. Rather, we are confronted with persons who are, at least in the eyes of the law, incompetent to handle the effects of alcohol. *Accord, Burke v. Superior Court, 129* Cal. App. 3d 570, 181 Cal. Rptr. 149 (1982); *Thaut v. Finely,* [50 Mich. App. 611, 213 N.W.2d 820 (1973];

Lover v. Sampson, 44 Mich. App. 173, 205 N.W.2d 69 (1972). *See Davis v. Shiappacossee*, 155 So. 2d 365 (Fla. 1963); *Chausse v. Southland Corp.*, La. App. 400 So. 2d 1199 (1981) *cert. denied*, La., 404 So. 2d 497 (1981); *Munford, Inc. v. Peterson*, Miss., 368 So. 2d 213 (1979); *Wiener v. Gamma Phi Chapter of Alpha Tau Omega Fraternity*, 258 Or. 632, 485 P. 2d 18 (1971). *See also, Cantor v. Anderson*, 126 Cal. App. 3d 124, 178 Cal. Rptr. 540 (1981).

"Section 286 of the Restatement of Torts Second provides:

"§ 286. When Standard of Conduct Defined by Legislation or Regulation Will Be Adopted

"The court may adopt as the standard of conduct of a reasonable man the requirements of a legislative enactment or an administrative regulation whose purpose is found to be exclusively or in part

"(a) to protect a class of persons which includes the one whose interest is invaded, and

"(b) to protect the particular interest which is invaded, and

"(c) to protect that interest against the kind of harm which has resulted, and

"(d) to protect that interest against the particular hazard from which the harm results.

"We have previously relied upon this Section and accepted it as an accurate statement of the law. *See Majors v. Brodhead Hotel*, 416 Pa. 265, 268, 205 A.2d 875 (1965); *Jardine v. Upper Darby Lodge, No. 1973*, 413 Pa. 626, 198 A.2d 550 (1964). *See also, Frederick L. v. Thomas*, 578 F.2d 513 (3d Cir. 1978).

"Section 6308 of the Crimes Code represents an obvious legislative decision to protect both minors and the public at large from the perceived deleterious effects of serving alcohol to persons under twenty-one years of age. Thus, we find that defendants were negligent per se in serving alcohol to the point of intoxication to a person less than twenty-one years of age, and that they can be held liable for injuries proximately resulting from the minor's intoxication.

"Our inquiry, however, cannot stop here. As noted above the plaintiff here was not an unwitting third party to the actor's negligence, but the person to whom the intoxicants were allegedly served. Nevertheless, for the purpose of deciding whether a cause of action exists, we see no valid distinction which would warrant a limitation on the action to third parties alone. [Citation omitted.]

"Under our analysis, an actor's negligence exists in furnishing intoxicants to a class of persons legislatively determined to be incompetent to handle its effects. It is the person's service which forms the basis of the cause of action, not whether or not a putative plaintiff is entitled to recover. Resolution of this latter issue requires a fuller record than the one which we have on demurrer.

"We note, however, that under the scheme set up by this Court in *Kuhns v. Brugger*, 390 Pa. 331, 135 A.2d 395 (1957) an eighteen year old person is 'presumptively capable of negligence.' We further note that an eighteen year old is liable as an adult for the offenses which he commits, and that by knowingly consuming alcohol an eighteen year old is also guilty of a summary offense. *See* 18 Pa. C.S. § 6308.

"Thus, although we recognize that an eighteen year old minor may state a cause of action against an adult social host who has knowingly served him intoxicants, the social host in turn may assert as a defense the minor's 'contributory' negligence. Thereafter, under our Comparative Negligence Act [citation omitted] it will remain for the fact finder to resolve whether the defendant's negligence was such as to allow recovery. *Accord, Munford v. Peterson, supra; Chausse v. Southland Corp., supra.*

"Appellants have also asserted two separate issues, neither of which do we find meritorious. The first involves the alleged negligent entrustment of an automobile to one who is intoxicated. However, this cause of action has been recognized only in those situations where the person sought to be held liable was 'the owner or other person responsible for its (automobile) use.' *See* Anno.: *Liability Based on Entrusting Automobile to One Who Is Intoxicated or Known to be Excessive User of Intoxicants.* 19 A.L.R.3d 1175 (1968). Appellants have cited no cases which extend this liability to persons who were not the owner or otherwise responsible for the automobile in question. *See e.g., Mills v. Continental Parking Corp.*, 86 Nev. 724, 475 P.2d 673 (1970) (holding parking lot attendant not liable for surrendering car to owner who was intoxicated.) The appellee here had no right of control over Mark Congini's car, and we see no basis upon which to extend liability to the situation posited here.

"Finally, appellants have argued that the defendants breached a duty as a landowner to Mark Congini. The Superior Court refused to discuss this issue, as they found that it was not fairly raised by the pleadings.

"Since there was nowhere pleaded that Mark Congini was required by his employer to attend the party in question, it appears at most that he was a gratuitous licensee. To such a person Section 341 of the Restatement of Torts, Second provides:

"§ 341. Activities Dangerous to Licensees

"A possessor land is subject to liability to his licensees for physical harm caused to them by his failure to carry on his activities with reasonable care for their safety, if, but only if,

"(a) he should expect that they will not discover or realize the danger, and

"(b) they do not know or have reason to know of the possessor's activities and the risk involved.

"Appellants did not plead that Mark Congini was without knowledge of the possessor's activities, or of the risks involved in consuming alcoholic beverages. Indeed, it would have been impossible to contend that Mark Congini was ignorant of the appellee's activities, since that was the reason for his presence.

"Furthermore, appellant's injuries at most would seem to have resulted from 'existent conditions upon the premises' (i.e., the availability of alcohol), as opposed to 'any affirmative or "active" negligence on [the defendant's] part.' *See Potter Title and Trust Co. v. Young*, 367 Pa. 239, 244, 80 A.2d 76, 79 (1951). In such case a possessor of land is not liable to a licensee in the absence of willful and wanton injury. *Knapp v. R.S. Noonan, Inc.*, 385 Pa. 460, 123 A.2d 429

(1956); *Potter Title and Trust Co. v. Young, supra*. Such liability was not pleaded by the appellants. We therefore, agree with the Superior Court that a cause of action under this theory was not stated.

"In light of appellee's potential liability as a social host, we reverse the order of the Superior Court and remand this case to the court of common pleas for proceeding not inconsistent with our opinion. As to appellants' other contentions, we affirm the order of the Supreme Court. . . .''

[Concurring opinion omitted.]

ZAPPALA, J. (dissenting).

"In *Klein v. Raysinger*, ———Pa.———, 470 A.2d 507 (1983), we held that no duty exists under the common law which would impose liability upon a social host who serves alcohol to an adult guest for conduct of the guest which results in injury to himself or to a third party. We recognized that it is the consumption of alcohol, rather than the furnishing of alcohol to an individual, which is the proximate cause of any subsequent occurrence.

"In the instant case, however, the majority opinion concludes that liability of a social host may arise from the act of furnishing alcohol to a minor and that such liability may extend to harm suffered by the minor. By adopting this legal premise, the majority today is effectively overruling *Klein*. The analysis employed by the majority is clearly inconsistent with that enunciated in *Klein*, and for that reason I must dissent.

"The majority attempts to reconcile the inconsistency based upon a perceived public policy to protect minors and the public from the potentially harmful effects of alcohol. This public policy is gleaned from § 6308 of the Crimes Code which imposes criminal liability on a person under 21 who attempts to purchase, purchases, consumes, possesses or transports alcohol. Although the legislature may have determined that persons under 21 are incompetent to handle alcohol, as the majority suggests, it is evident that the legislature has defined the offense so as to render the minor culpable for his own conduct which violates the statute. A minor could not defend his conduct by demonstrating that an adult had furnished him with the alcohol. Thus, the statute which the majority interprets as evincing a policy to protect minors does not shield them from their acts which contravene the statute.

"The majority attempts to distinguish underage drinkers from those over 21 years by stating that minors are deemed incompetent to handle the effects of alcohol. This distinction is irrelevant, however, to the issue of whether a social host who furnishes alcohol to a minor may be held liable for injuries sustained by the minor or a third party as a result of the minor's actions.

"It is not knowledge of a social host of the ability or inability of a guest to handle the effects of alcohol, or knowledge of a person's condition, which would give rise to a duty not to furnish alcohol to the guest. We declined to impose liability on that basis in *Klein*, when we refused to recognize a cause of action, urged by the Appellants therein, against a social host who serves alcohol to a visibly intoxicated person who the host knows, or should know, intends to drive a motor vehicle. I cannot agree, therefore, that liability should be imposed on a social host serving alcohol to a person under 21 based upon the rationale that minors are incompetent to handle alcohol. If it is consumption by an adult guest, rather than the furnishing of alcohol by a host, which is the proximate cause of subsequent occurrences, then it is not less compelling to conclude that it is the minor's voluntary consumption of alcohol which is the proximate cause of harm which results.

"I find it inconceivable that a minor or an innocent third party who suffers harm under the factual circumstances alleged in the instant case may assert a cause of action against a social host who has dispensed the alcohol, yet an innocent third party who suffers harm under the factual circumstances set forth in *Klein* would be precluded from asserting a similar cause of action. These inapposite results arise solely from the fortuitous circumstances of the age of the tortfeasor, rather than the conduct of the social host. I would hold, consistent with *Klein,* that no cause of action exists against a social host for providing alcohol to a guest under the facts alleged in this action. This matter is better left to legislative action than to judicial gymnastics."

The Connecticut Supreme Court extended the liability of venders and social hosts for the wanton and reckless sale to or service of an intoxicated person that causes that person to injure or cause death of a third party.[44]

The extent to which a social host can be made responsible for alcohol "otherwise supplied" to a minor, in violation of the Iowa Code, was held not to apply to a property owner who permitted a beer party to be held on his property when he knew or should have known that minors would be present and as a result of which a minor plaintiff was injured.[45]

In *Sager v. McClenden,*[46] the Oregon Supreme Court ruled that no cause of action exists for patrons injured off the premises by reason of their own intoxication. This decision reaffirms the traditional voluntary intoxication doctrine applicable to adults and patrons,[47] in contrast to the judicial solicitude extended to minor patrons.[48]

In *Brookins v. The Round Table, Inc.,*[49] the Tennessee Supreme Court made a jury question of the issue of whether a minor's own intoxication, arising out of an illegal sale of alcohol, actively contributed to his own injuries.

The following case poses the question whether a social host can use the defense of contributory negligence in a dram shop action.

WILLIAMS V. KLEMSRUD
197 N.W.2d 614 (Iowa 1972)

REYNOLDSON, J.: " . . . Plaintiffs, injured in a vehicle collision, brought a law action for damages against defendant, alleging he sold or gave liquor to the

---

[44]Kowal v. Hofher, 181 Conn. 355, 436 A.2d 1 (1980).
[45]DeMore by DeMore v. Dieters, 334 N.W.2d 734 (Iowa 1983).
[46]296 Or. 33, 672 P.2d 697 (1983).
[47]*See* Wright v. Mofitt, 437 A.2d 554 (Del. 1981).
[48]*See* Cogini by Congini, *supra.*
[49]624 S.W.2d 547 (Tenn. 1981).

driver of the other colliding auto, causing his intoxication, in violation of §
129.2, Code, 1966. . . . Trial court held the statute *did* provide a right of action
in this situation, and ruled the contributory negligence defense was not available. We affirm.

"On September 30, 1967 the 21 year old defendant was attending college at
Mason City, Iowa. His friend . . . , age 20, provided money and solicited defendant to purchase a pint of vodka for him at the state liquor store, which he
did. On submission below the parties stipulated defendant was neither engaged
in liquor traffic for profit nor a licensee or permittee for sale of liquor or beer. It
was further stipulated defendant made no profit from the transaction, which had
no business purpose and was purely social. The parties agreed [his friend] consumed the liquor and became intoxicated on the above date and subsequently,
while driving an auto, was involved in the collision causing plaintiffs' injuries
and damages.

[Point I omitted. Iowa currently exempts social hosts from liability by statute.
See Iowa Code § 123.92 (1975).—J.E.H.S.]

*II. Is the defense of contributory negligence available to this dram shop
defendant?*

"Presented here are plaintiffs who carry no taint of complicity or participation in the intoxication of [the friend]. Defendant does not contend the stipulated
intoxication of [the friend] was unconnected with the collision and resulting injury and damage to plaintiffs. The sole issue is whether plaintiffs' alleged contributory negligence is a defense available to defendant, sued under the dram
shop statute, § 129.2.

"It should be initially noted plaintiffs invoke a statutory right of action not
found at common law. [Citation omitted.] Such statutes are characterized in 45
Am. Jur. 2d, *Intoxicating Liquors* § 561, p. 859, as follows: 'These statutes,
commonly known as "civil damage acts" or "dramshop acts," afford remedies
unknown to the common law. The remedies created by the statutes are not in any
sense common-law negligence actions. New, separate, and distinct rights of action are conferred.'

"To the same effect, *see* 48 C.J.S. *Intoxicating Liquors* § 432, p. 718.

"Contributory negligence is ordinarily defined as ' . . . conduct on the part
of the plaintiff which falls below the standard to which he should conform for his
own protection, and which is a legally contributing cause *co-operating with the
negligence of the defendant* in bringing about the plaintiff's harm.' Restatement
(Second) of Torts § 463, p. 506 (1965). (Italics added.) However, defendant's
negligence is not an element in this case. Herein lies the reason appellant's brief,
although well prepared, cites no decision holding contributory negligence a defense to the statute-based action.

"On the other hand, numerous jurisdictions have rejected that defense in
dram shop litigation, reasoning contributory negligence is inapplicable as a defense because the statutory right is not necessarily based upon fault or negli-

gence. [Citations from 2d and 3d federal circuit courts of appeal, Conn., Ill., Mich., Minn., N.J., and Pa. omitted.]

"This rule was inferentially recognized by our decision in *Berge v. Harris,* 170 N.W.2d 621, 625 (Iowa 1969) where we said,

"The authorities cited by plaintiff in support of her contention hold contributory negligence is no defense to an action under the dramshop act as such action is based on the breach of a statutory duty and does not require a showing of negligence. (citing cases)

" 'The same line of cases recognizes the *equally well established rule* of complicity. . . .' (Italics added.)

"The Iowa Supreme Court has declined to hold a common-law tort liability arises out of a sale of intoxicating liquor [citation omitted]. Dram shop statutes impose strict liability, without negligence, upon the seller. W. Prosser, Law of Torts § 81, p. 538 (4th ed. 1971). The ordinary concepts of proximate cause are not strictly applied. [Citations omitted.] Similarly, we now hold the stereotype contributory negligence defense has no application.

"Affirmed."

Although the authorities imposing liability upon dispensers usually involve the intoxication of minors or those who have just reached the legal drinking age, a Michigan appellate court, in a case of first impression (presented below), has ruled that a common-law cause of action for gross negligence or willful, wanton, and intentional misconduct was stated against a tavern owner who sold intoxicants to an intoxicated, elderly compulsive alcoholic contrary to an agreement not to serve that person. The victim suffered injuries causing his death when he lost his balance and fell eight feet to the ground while walking on an unguarded narrow concrete projection to a bridge he was crossing after having left the tavern. No action under the Michigan dram shop act was cognizable under settled Michigan decisional law.

GRASSER v. FLEMING

74 Mich. App. 338, 253 N.W.2d 757 (1977)

KELLY, J.: "The question is, to what extent is the dramshop act the exclusive remedy against a tavern owner for wrongful service of intoxicants? In *Manuel v. Weitzman,* 386 Mich. 157, 163; 191 N.W.2d 474 (1971), the Supreme Court recognized that the remedy of the dramshop act is not exclusive since there exists a common law cause of action for breach of duty to maintain a safe place of business. The Court noted:

"The common-law duty of a liquor establishment to maintain a safe place of business for its customers is the same duty any business owes to those it invites upon its premises. The dramshop act was not intended to affect that duty. Dramshop acts were passed because under the common law it was not a tort to sell or furnish intoxicating liquor to an ordinary able-bodied man, even though as a result of his becoming intoxicated injury resulted to himself or to others. Their purpose was to fill a void in the law, not to remove the well-recognized duty of a tavern keeper to exercise due care for the welfare and safety of invited patrons. [386 Mich 157, 163.]

"We are in doubt as to whether the Supreme Court intended . . . to preclude a common law cause of action for gross negligence or wilful, wanton, and intentional misconduct in the sale of alcoholic beverages under the circumstances of this case. We conclude that it did not for the following four reasons: (1) in *Manuel,* . . . *supra,* a customer was assaulted and the question became whether the plaintiff could maintain an action under the dramshop act, as well as a common law action for negligence against the tavern owner in failing to maintain the premises in a reasonably safe condition. The holding . . . was that the plaintiff could. . . .

" . . . (2) [T]he Supreme Court in *Manuel, supra,* p. 163, stated that the 'Dramshop acts were passed because under the common law it was not a tort to sell or furnish intoxicating liquor to an ordinary able-bodied man.' In the present case, plaintiff alleges that decedent was a sick elderly man, an habitual drunkard, unable to tolerate drink; (3) an exception to the general rule was recognized at common law where the consumer was in such a helpless state as to have lost his free will; (4) it would be inequitable not to allow a consumer a remedy for the intentional, reckless or grossly negligent conduct of a tavern owner. Therefore, we hold that the dramshop act is not an exclusive remedy such that a tavern owner has no liability under the circumstances alleged. . . .

"In *Mason v. Roberts,* 33 Ohio St. 2d 29; 294 N.E.2d 884 (1973), the Ohio Supreme Court found a common law cause of action for wrongful death against a tavern operator, although the dramshop act was inapplicable. The Court held that the dramshop act was not the exclusive remedy against a tavern operator for harm caused to a third person by a patron who was served intoxicating beverages. The Court stated: ' . . . the issue of proximate cause has been properly left to the jury where the allegations, supported by the evidence, are such that, to the seller's knowledge, the purchaser's will to refrain is so impaired that it is not possible for him to refrain from drinking the liquor when it is placed before him. [Citation omitted.] This court applied this rationale in *Flandermeyer v. Cooper* (1912), 85 Ohio St. 327, 98 N.E. 102, involving the intentional sale of morphine to one known to be so weak in mind as to be unable to refuse it.'

"In the present case plaintiff's allegations which we accept as true are sufficient to come within the first exception set forth in *Mason.* Further, it is important to note that in *Mason,* as in this case, a dramshop act existed which was inapplicable and the Court found a common law cause of action. *See also Berkeley v. Park,* 47 Misc. 2d 381; 262 N.Y.S.2d 290 (Sup. Ct. 1965).

"We thus recognize a common law cause of action for serving a known drunk that other jurisdictions have also similarly found independent of the dramshop act. Not surprisingly there is a split of authority. We hold that plaintiff has stated a cause of action for gross negligence and wilful, wanton, and intentional misconduct independent of the dramshop act.

"Affirmed. . . . "

In *Carrillo v. El Mirage Roadhouse, Inc.*,[50] the Supreme Court of Arizona extended its prior decisions[51] that held that a drinker as well as a third person could recover against a bar or tavern owner by reason of illegal sales of alcohol resulting in intoxication and physical harm. The earlier decisions were extended to include drinker liability for knowingly allowing others to intoxicate the drinker who thereafter is injured by reason of such intoxication. The court noted that the Arizona legislature had eliminated drinker liability (A.R.S. Section 4-312), but that this death claim was not barred because the claim arose prior to the enactment of the statute.

In the case below, the Supreme Court of Hawaii discussed the pros and cons of imposing liability upon social hosts for injuries suffered as a result of their serving alcoholic beverages to a driver who subsequently injured a third party (the plaintiff) in an automobile accident. The high court decided against imposing such liability judicially.

JOHNSTON V. KFC NATIONAL MANAGEMENT CO.
71 Haw. 229, 788 P.2d 159 (1990)

WAKATSUKI, J.: "In *Ono v. Applegate,* 62 Haw. 131, 612 P.2d 533 (1980), this court 'allow[ed] a person injured by an inebriated tavern customer to recover from the tavern that provided liquor to the customer.' *Id.* at 136, 612 P.2d at 538. Appellant, in his case, would have this court extend liability to non-commercial suppliers of alcoholic beverages, i.e., the social host. We decline.

I.

"The employees of the Kentucky Fried Chicken (KFC), Aiea branch, had planned a Christmas party for themselves to take place on December 19, 1986. KFC management was aware of the planned party and gave approval for the party to be held on the premises of the Aiea branch after normal closing hours. Management even permitted the use of paper goods from the store and allowed the participants to eat any leftover unsold chicken. Alcoholic beverages, however, were supplied solely by the party participants.

"Sandra Joan Parks was as KFC employee at another branch. Mikilani Travis, the restaurant manager of the Aiea branch and a friend of Sandra, invited Sandra to the Aiea branch Christmas party. It is alleged that Sandra was visibly intoxicated at the time she left the Aiea branch party. She managed, however, to drive to the Cuis' residence in Wahiawa.

"Andrea Cui, who was 19 years old at the time, was an employee of the Aiea KFC. Though Andrea had met Sandra that evening for the first time, when Andrea invited several of her friends to continue the Christmas party at Andrea's home, Sandra joined them. Andrea brought out an ice chest containing beer which Sandra and others drank.

[50]164 Ariz. 364, 793 P.2d 121 (Ariz. 1990).
[51]Ontiveros v. Borak, 136 Ariz. 500, 667 P.2d 200 (1983) and Brannigan v. Raybuck, 136 Ariz. 513, 667 P.2d 213 (1983).

"While the Christmas party was continuing on the Cuis' premises but outside the home, Andrea's parents, James and Marion Cui, were asleep in their bedroom.

"Eventually, at an early hour in the morning of December 20th, Sandra drove home to Ward Avenue in Honolulu. She then took a shower, changed her clothes, and proceeded to drive her friend, Pinky Len Wai, home. While driving Pinky home, Sandra drove into oncoming traffic on Kapiolani Boulevard and crashed into a moped operated by Donna Johnston. As a result of the accident, Johnston was severely and permanently injured.

"Johnston brought suit for damages and compensation against several defendants, including KFC, Andrea Cui, and Andrea's parents. As against KFC, Johnston claims that it was negligent in permitting alcoholic beverages to be consumed on its premises, in failing to prevent Sandra from becoming intoxicated, and in failing to prevent Sandra from driving while intoxicated. Johnston claims that Andrea's negligence was in continuing to provide Sandra with alcoholic beverages when Sandra was already intoxicated. The claim against Andrea's parents is premised on either the negligent failure to supervise the party, or on the theory that parents are liable for the torts in their minor children.

"The trial court entered summary judgments in favor of KFC, Andrea Cui, and James and Marion Cui, ruling that these defendants owed no duty to Johnston for which liability could be found in this case. Johnston appeals. We affirm.

II.

"In this case, different factual considerations are associated with each of the defendant groups. KFC and the Cui parents were not 'hosts' in the sense that neither provided or served any alcohol to Sandra, although alcohol was consumed on the premises belonging to them. KFC, however, was Sandra's employer, and allegedly knew or should have known of Sandra's drinking habit. Andrea Cui was the only defendant who allegedly 'provided and served' alcoholic beverage to Sandra.

A.

"A necessary element in a negligence action is '[a] duty, or obligation, recognized by the law, requiring the actor to conform to a certain standard of conduct for the protection of others against unreasonable risks.' *Ono v. Applegate,* 62 Haw. at 137, 612 P.2d at 538.

"This court has often pointed out 'that duty is not sacrosanct in itself, but only an expression of the sum total of those considerations of policy which lead the law to say that the particular plaintiff is entitled to protection.' *Cootey v. Sun Investment,* 68 Haw. 480, 484, 718 P.2d 1086, 1090 (1986); *Waugh v. University of Hawaii,* 63 Haw. 117, 135, 621 P.2d 957, 970 (1980); *Kelley v. Kokua Sales & Supply, Ltd.,* 56 Haw. 204, 207, 532 P.2d 673, 675 (1975).

"[A]s our ideas of human relations change the law as to duties changes with them. . . . Changing social conditions lead constantly to the recognition of new duties.' Prosser and Keeton on The Law of Torts § 53 at 359 (5th ed. 1984). This court, however, is reluctant to impose a new duty upon members of our society without any logical, sound, and compelling reasons taking into consideration the social and human relationships of our society.

"As the Connecticut Supreme Court aptly stated: 'Experience can and often does demonstrate that a rule, once believed sound, needs modification to serve justice better. . . . The adaptability of the common law to the changing needs of passing time has been one of its most beneficient characteristics. . . . If, however, stare decisis is to continue to serve the cause of stability and certainty in law—a condition indispensable to any well-ordered system of jurisprudence—a court should not overrule its earlier decisions unless the most cogent reasons and inescapable logic require it.' [Citations omitted.] *Ely v. Murphy,* 207 Conn. 88, 91, 540 A.2d 54, 57 (1988) (quoting *Herald Publishing Co. v. Bill,* 142 Conn. 53, 62, 111 A.2d 4, 8 (1955); *Ozyck v. D'Atri,* 206 Conn. 473, 482–83, 538 A.2d 697, 702 (1988)."

HEALEY, J. (concurring).

B.

"Traditionally, the common law held that when a person consumes alcohol to a point of being intoxicated and injures another, he is the sole proximate cause of that injury. Thus, no liability could be attributed to the supplier of the alcoholic beverages. *See Ono v. Applegate,* 62 Haw. at 134, 612 P.2d at 537. In *Ono v. Applegate,* however, this court modified the traditional common law rule by imposing a duty upon commercial suppliers of alcohol to injured third parties. In adopting this modification, this court relied upon 'the clear trend' across the country to impose such duty, and also by reference to a statute establishing a standard of conduct for liquor licensees. However, as to the non-commercial supplier of alcoholic beverages—the social host—we find no clear judicial trend toward modifying the traditional common law, nor any statutory enactment or policy which leads this court to conclude that a change in the common law is appropriate at this time.

1.

"Many courts, faced with many different factual permutations, have dealt with the issue of social host liability. The clear trend has been a refusal to impose a duty upon a social host to protect third parties from risk of injuries that may be caused by an adult who is provided and served alcohol beverages. To date, only the courts in New Jersey and Massachusetts impose such a duty. *Kelly v. Gwinnell,* 96 N.J. 538, 476 A.2d 1219 (1984); *McGuiggan v. New England Telephone & Telegraph Co.,* 398 Mass. 152, 496 N.E.2d 141 (1986). . . .

"In Minnesota and Iowa, where the courts relied upon civil damages statutes to find a duty running from social hosts to injured third parties, the legislatures in those states amended the statutes to effect the opposite result.

2.

"Among state legislatures, the 'predominant trend has been to preclude social host liability.' Comment, *Third Party Liability for Drunken Driving: When 'One for the Road' Becomes One for the Courts*, 29 Vill. L. Rev. 119, 1149 (1983–84). . . .

"Our state legislature, over the past years, has demonstrated an active and ongoing interest in enacting heavier punishment for alcohol abusers and drunk drivers. But our legislature has not enacted any statute imposing liability upon social hosts or establishing standards of conduct for social hosts upon which this court may hold a social host civilly liable for a breach of duty to protect third persons from risks of injury from 'drunk' driving accidents.

3.

"We fail to see any judicial trend to impose a 'change in the law which has the power to so deeply affect social and business relations.' *Garren v. Cummings & McCrady*, 289 S.C. 348, 350, 345 S.E.2d 508, 510 (S.C. App. 1986) (quoting *Miller v. Moran*, 96 Ill. App. 3d 596, 600–601, 52 Ill. Dec. 183, 186, 421 N.E.2d 1046, 1049 (1981)).

"Although we are well acquainted with the arguments for and against social host liability, [t]he nature of the judicial role prevents us from capably deciding the merits of social host liability. Evaluating the overall merits of social host liability, with its wide sweeping implications, requires a balancing of the costs and benefits for society as a whole, not just the parties of any one case. *Burkhart v. Harrod*, 110 Wash. 2d 381, 385, 755 P.2d 759, 761 (1988).

"Social host liability implicates changes in social relations in a society where consumption of alcohol is a pervasive and deeply rooted part of our social life. *See* Comment, *Social Hosts and Drunken Driving: A Duty to Intervene?*, 133 U. Penn. L. Rev. 867, 872 (1985); *Gariup Construction Co., Inc. v. Foster*, 519 N.E.2d 1224, 1232–1233 (Ind. 1988) (dissenting opinion of PIVARNIK, J.); *Edgar v. Kajet*, 84 Misc. 2d 100, 375 N.Y.S.2d 548, 552 (1975).

"From an economic perspective, there needs to be consideration of the effect social host liability would have on homeowners' and renters' insurance rates, and the economic impact on those not wealthy or foresighted enough to obtain such insurance. 133 U. Penn. L. Rev. at 873; *Burkhart v. Harrod*, 110 Wash. 2d at 386, 755 P.2d at 761. Furthermore, cost considerations are not limited to an ultimate finding of liability against the social host. A host will, in all probability, be made a defendant in a civil suit for damages and compensation brought by a third person who is injured in a car accident involving a friend, invitee or guest of the host who provided and served the alcoholic beverage, thereby incurring the cost of defending against such a suit even though the host may not be liable.

III.

"We hold that, as a matter of law, Andrea Cui, James and Marion Cui, and KFC, as an alleged social host or an employer, owed no duty to Johnston under the facts of this case.

"Affirmed."

19:11   *Trends and Implications*

The marketing of alcoholic beverages is fraught with stringent regulation by the states, especially with respect to illegal sales to patrons. As an ancillary remedy to license revocation and criminal sanctions to punish violators available in almost all states, the public is afforded individual protection through the legal device of a civil damage action, whether by statute or by decisional law.

This trend toward increased civil responsibility imposes a severe burden upon all dispensers of alcoholic beverages. As deaths and severe injuries inflicted by inebriated vehicle drivers, including minors, to cite the most common type of occurrence, continue to mount, the political pressure to make the liquor dispenser pay for the resultant harm, predicated on illegal conduct proximately causing or contributing to that harm, will grow apace. This liability cannot help but increase dramatically the cost of alcoholic drinks served on premises. Damage payments are a cost of doing business, and that cost must be passed on to the vendee or consumer of the beverage. Higher prices represent the cost to society, at least to those persons presumably of legal drinking age, of having a strong affinity for alcoholic beverages and of tolerating those few who would manipulate that affinity for selfish economic motives.

PART V

Innkeeper Creditor-Debtor
Protection

20 The Innkeeper's Lien

20:1 *Nature of Innkeeper's Lien*

The innkeeper, being obliged by law to receive travelers and entertain them, is given by law not merely the right to compensation from the guest, but also the right to a lien on the goods of the guest in the inn, to the extent of his charges. This lien differs in one respect from other liens created by the common law in that technical possession on the part of the innkeeper is not necessary for the enforcement of the lien. Although the goods remain in the possession of the guest, the innkeeper may prevent their being carried from the inn, take them into his own actual possession, and hold them as security for his charges. In other respects, this lien is in its nature and incidents like other liens given by the common law to persons carrying on a public employment, such as carriers and public warehousemen.

Innkeeper's lien statutes are codifications of the common-law lien adopted by almost all states. As discussed later (*see* section 20:21), these statutes have been abrogated in California, Florida, Nebraska, and New York on the ground that the statutory procedures to enforce them violate the due process rights afforded guests under the federal and applicable state constitutions. Relatively few courts have ruled on this precise question, and those courts that have are in conflict. In those states that have not ruled such statutory procedures unconstitutional, the innkeeper's lien is presumptively valid and enforceable, at least until such time as the courts of last resort of the states or the United States Supreme Court have ruled otherwise. Even in those states whose courts have struck down such statutes as violative of due process, the state legislatures are free to amend the statue to eliminate the due process violation. However, the innkeeper may not utilize his lien rights in the interim, since any unauthorized taking of a guest's property constitutes a conversion (wrongful taking) of such property subjecting the innkeeper to liability.

20:2 *General Rule*

At common law, an innkeeper is entitled to a lien for the amount of his charges on all the goods of his guest which are found in the inn.[1] The charges

---

[1]Waters & Co. v. Gerard, 189 N.Y. 302, 82 N.E. 143 (1907), overruled in part by Blye v. Globe-Wernicke Realty Co., 33 N.Y.2d 15, 300 N.E.2d 710 (1973).

secured by the lien include not merely compensation for entertainment, but also charges connected with the guest's stay at the inn, for example, money lent to the guest by the innkeeper.[2] The lien is restricted to charges between the innkeeper and the one who is his guest in the strict sense. Thus an innkeeper at common law has no lien on the goods of a boarder,[3] except of course by special agreement.[4]

20:3 *Lien Does Not Require a Binding Contract*

This lien is, properly speaking, not created by a contract, but by law; the innkeeper, being obliged by law to receive, is given by law the lien. Consequently, an innkeeper may maintain his lien even against a guest who is incapable of making a binding contract.[5]

20:4 *Lien Does Not Cover Prior Charges*

The innkeeper's lien is not a general lien, in that it covers only charges accrued during the last period of entertainment. If the innkeeper once waives his lien by allowing the guest to depart and take away his goods without paying his bill, the charges then due can never afterwards be secured by a detainer of goods brought to the inn by the same guest on a subsequent occasion. This principle was established in the early case of *Jones v. Thurloe.*[6]

20:5 *Property to Which Lien Extends*

Generally speaking, the lien extends to all property of every kind brought to the inn by the guest, or left at the inn for the guest, each article of property being security for the whole bill. There is one debt and one lien in respect to the whole of the innkeeper's charges.

The lien secures not merely compensation for care extended to the very goods over which it is exercised, but compensation for charges incurred by the guest for his own entertainment. The innkeeper is bound to receive and entertain the guest, and if he chooses to receive with him goods he is not obliged to receive, his right in those goods, after he chooses to receive them, is the same as his right in any other goods of the guest. "[T]hey are in the same position as goods properly offered to the innkeeper according to the custom of the realm. . . . "[7]

No lien exists if it would be impossible to exercise it without violating the law. For the above reason no lien can be exercised over clothes actually on the person

---

[2]Proctor v. Nicholson, 173 Eng. Rep. 30 (K.B. 1835); Watson v. Cross, 63 Ky. (2 Duv.) 147 (1865).

[3]Singer Mfg. Co. v. Miller, 52 Minn. 516, 55 N.W. 56 (1893).

[4]Regina v. Askin, 20 U.C.Q.B. 626 (1861).

[5]Watson v. Cross, 63 Ky. (2 Duv.) 147 (1865).

[6]88 Eng. Rep. 126 (K.B. 1723).

[7]Lord Esher, M. R. in Robins v. Gray, [1895] 2 Q.B. 501, 504.

of the guest, since they could not be detained without a breach of the peace and the risk, at any rate, of indecency.[8]

20:6   *No Lien on Person of Guest*

The lien is restricted to the goods of the guest; the guest himself cannot be detained as security for the charges. This lien has never been extended at common law to any class of property other than tangible personal property, and there is not the slightest authority for extending it to the person of the debtor.

20:7   *Property Exempt from Execution*

The principle that the lien cannot apply to property otherwise protected by law, however, does not extend so far as to cover property exempt by law from execution (that is, property covered by a judicial order empowering an officer to carry out a judgment disposing of property), and the lien may be exercised over such property. The privilege of exemption granted to a debtor does not prevent him from voluntarily giving another an interest in such property or subjecting it voluntarily to a lien, as the guest does by taking it with him to an inn.[9]

20:8   *Goods of Third Person Brought by Guest to Inn*

The innkeeper's lien attaches to property brought to the inn by a guest ostensibly as his, though they were in fact the goods of a third person, unless the innkeeper knew or had notice that such property was not then the property of the guest.

In Ohio, the innkeeper's lien does not extend to stolen property in possession of a hotel guest, whether or not the innkeeper had knowledge of the ownership of the property at the time he extended credit to the guest.[10]

20:9   *Goods of Guest Who Is Not Responsible for Charges*

Where several people go together to an inn, but only one of them is responsible for paying the bill, only property which is really or ostensibly the property of the responsible party can be held on lien for the charges. Thus where a father and his daughter went to an inn, under such circumstances that the father alone was responsible for the bill, the host could not hold the daughter's goods as security for the payment of the bill.[11] And so where a husband and wife go together to an inn, the credit being extended to the husband, there is no lien on

---

[8]Sunbolf v. Alford, 150 Eng. Rep. 1135, 1138 (Ex. 1838).

[9]Swan v. Bournes, 47 Iowa 501 (1877); Thorn v. Whitbeck, 11 Misc. 171, 32 N.Y.S. 1088 (Greene County Ct. 1895), *aff'd*, 37 N.Y.S. 1150 (1896).

[10]M & M Hotel Co. v. Nichols, 21 Ohio L. Abs. 66, 32 N.E.2d 463 (Ct. App. 1935).

[11]Clayton v. Butterfield, 18 S.C. 100 (1857).

property evidently belonging to the wife,[12] though if the credit were extended to the wife, her goods could be held and not the husband's.[13] Where the wife goes alone to the inn, but the husband is liable, the wife's goods cannot be held.[14]

20:10 Lien Attaches When Charges Accrue

The lien attaches as soon as the charge is incurred, that is, as soon as the guest is received, even if the time for payment has not arrived. So in a Massachusetts case it appeared that the defendant was a boarder at the plaintiff's house, paying his board by the week at the end of the week. A week's board was to become due on Saturday night. On Saturday morning the defendant undertook, against the will of the plaintiff and without paying anything for board during the week, to remove his baggage. When the plaintiff interfered, the defendant boarder forcibly removed her from the room. The plaintiff brought an action for assault and battery, and the defendant set up in defense his right to remove his property. The Supreme Court, however, held that the lien existed, and the plaintiff could recover. Justice Morton said: "Otherwise a guest who had obtained credit upon the strength of the lien, might destroy the security . . . by a sale or by removing the goods, at any time before the bill for board became payable by the contract; a result which is inconsistent with the nature of the lien."[15]

20:11 Sale of Goods by Owner Does Not Affect Lien

A sale of the property by the guest to a third person does not terminate the lien; the innkeeper may retain the goods against the purchaser for all charges accrued (even after the sale) until notice of the sale is received by the innkeeper.[16]

20:12 Removal of Goods to Another State Does Not Affect Lien

The lien is not lost by taking the goods into another state, even if no such lien would be created by the law of the latter state. The lien once having attached to the goods remains, wherever they may be taken by the innkeeper. In a New Hampshire case, the facts were that one S., in Massachusetts, held a trunk belonging to plaintiff's son under a lien for board; at plaintiff's request, she sent the trunk to him, in New Hampshire, by the defendant express company, C.O.D. The plaintiff tendered the charges for carriage only, and demanded the trunk;

---

[12]Birney v. Wheaton, 2 How. Prac. (n.s.) 519 (N.Y. City Ct. 1885).
[13]Id.
[14]Baker v. Stratton, 52 N.J.L. 277, 19 A. 661 (1890).
[15]Smith v. Colcord, 115 Mass. 70, 71 (1874). (Although the case dealt with a statutory boardinghouse keeper's lien, the reasoning would apply equally to the common-law lien of an innkeeper).
[16]Bayley v. Merrill, 92 Mass. (10 Allen) 360 (1865).

upon the defendant refusing to give it up, he brought this action of replevin. The Supreme Court gave judgment for the defendant, Justice Stanley saying: "In this case, there is an attempt to divest S. of her lien, and there is no reason why she may not defend her title as well as if she were the absolute owner residing in Massachusetts and a suit were brought to take the property from her. The lien of S. was as perfect as the lien under a mortgage made and executed in Massachusetts in accordance with their laws would be. In such cases the title under the mortgage could be shown, and would be a defence."[17]

20:13 Care of Goods Held on Lien

An innkeeper holding goods on lien is bound to take due care of the goods, which is said to be the care which he takes of his own goods of a similar description. So where an innkeeper who was holding clothing and furs on a lien put them into a closet with similar goods of his own, and they were injured by moths and mice, it was held that the amount of negligence which would make an innkeeper liable had not been shown.[18] He may make reasonable use of the goods if such use is beneficial to the owner, for example, the care and exercise of pets, or the cleaning and repair of personal apparel, but in that case he is bound to account for the value of the use. The value of the use must be credited on the lien. "The defendant, having lawfully used the property, must account for the use upon his charges for trouble and expense of keeping the property; and the court having found that it is a full equivalent, the defendant had no lien upon the property."[19]

20:14 End of Lien by Delivery of Goods to Guest

The lien is at an end when the innkeeper voluntarily delivers the goods to the guest.[20] But a mere executory agreement to give up the goods, made without consideration, does not put an end to the lien.[21]

20:15 End of Lien through Delivery Induced by Fraud

If the innkeeper is induced to give up the goods by fraud, the lien continues in spite of the delivery, or rather the innkeeper has the right to renew it. He may recover the goods by legal process, or otherwise, and the lien will again attach to them.[22]

---

[17]Jaquith v. American Express Co., 60 N.H. 61, 62 (1880).

[18]Angus v. McLachlan, [1883] 23 Ch. D. 330.

[19]Alvord v. Davenport, 43 Vt. 9, 11 (1870).

[20]Jones v. Thurloe, 88 Eng. Rep. 126 (K.B. 1723); Danforth v. Platt, 42 Me. 50 (1856); Ginnell v. Cook, 3 Hill 485 (N.Y. Sup. Ct. 1842).

[21]Danforth v. Platt, 42 Me. 50 (1856).

[22]Manning v. Hollenbeck, 27 Wis. 202 (1870).

20:16   *Lien Does Not End upon Delivery for Temporary Use*

The innkeeper may allow the guest to take the goods temporarily without parting with his lien. In such a case the better view appears to be that the lien continues even during the temporary possession of the guest.

20:17   *End of Lien by Payment of Bill*

The lien is, of course, destroyed by payment of the debt. And so where the innkeeper owes the guest for labor more than the guest owes for food, and the guest has a right to set off the amount due him against his debt, there is no lien.[23] But a mere agreement to accept security for the bill, if it is not inconsistent with the lien, does not put an end to it.[24]

20:18   *End of Lien by Conversion of Goods*

Conversion of the goods or wrongful dealing with them by the innkeeper while he holds them on lien puts an end to the lien. Thus if the innkeeper refuses to give up the goods upon a good tender of the amount due, he is guilty of a conversion, but not where the tender is not a good one.[25]

20:19   *Extension of Time for Payment Is Not Waiver of Lien*

PEOPLE EX REL. KLAMT V. LOEFFLER
153 Misc. 781, 276 N.Y.S. 698 (Magis. Ct. 1934)

AURELIO, City Magistrate: " . . . Complainant seeks to hold the defendant for larceny for his refusal to return to her certain baggage belonging to her. The defendant is the manager of the Hotel Gladstone and claims a lien on the property under Section 181 of the Lien Law for an unpaid bill for accommodation and food furnished. . . .

"The evidence shows that before complainant was accepted as a guest she informed the defendant that she had no money, and that one Schlatter, a friend of hers, arranged with defendant to grant her at least one month's time to pay her bill while she was a guest as she was then expecting funds from some source, and said Schlatter also guaranteed the payment of the bill. Complainant remained in the hotel from April 6 to June 5, 1934, when she was locked out [for nonpayment of the bill]. . . . Thereafter, complainant was arrested, tried and acquitted in the court of Special Sessions for a violation of section 925 of the Penal Law which deals with hotel frauds. The acquittal evidently was based on the ground that credit was extended, because the section also provides that: 'this provision shall not apply where there has been a special agreement for delay in payment.'

---

[23]Hanlin v. Walters, 3 Colo. App. 519, 34 P. 686 (1893).
[24]Angus v. McLachlan, [1833] 23 Ch. D. 330.
[25]Gordon v. Cox, 173 Eng. Rep. 76 (Nisi Prius 1835).

"There is some dispute as to whether the credit was extended for one month only or for the entire period. In view of the conclusion that I have reached I think it is immaterial as to how long credit was extended.

"When Schlatter arranged with defendant to give complainant time to pay her bill nothing was said about defendant waiving his innkeeper's lien on the baggage. The court cannot assume that the lien was waived without some evidence from which that inference may be drawn. Otherwise, every time a hotelkeeper allows a guest a few more days to pay he would run the risk of waiving his lien, 'a result which is inconsistent wit the nature of the lien and which defeats the purpose of the statute.' (*Smith v. Colcord*, 115 Mass. 70). . . .

"Complainant also urges that the agreement made by Schlatter with defendant created the relation of landlord and tenant, and, therefore, the Lien Law does not apply, and cites the case of *Kuszewska v. Steiger Hotel Operating Co., Inc.* (152 Misc. 80) as authority for this proposition. . . . There is nothing before me indicating an intention to create the relation of landlord and tenant. All that defendant did was to grant complainant more time within which to pay her bill than was usual. This, in itself, did not operate to create the relation of landlord and tenant. Nor did the defendant by his act of kindness waive his legal right to the lien. True, payment was postponed, but this did not nullify the lien.

"The complaint is dismissed."

20:20 *Statutory Lien of Innkeepers*

The common-law lien of innkeepers has been codified, with some modifications and extensions, by statutes in all states.

The statutes grant a lien to the keepers of apartment hotels and boarding, rooming, and lodging houses, in addition to common-law innkeepers. The statutes do not, however, apply where the relationship is landlord and tenant.[26]

20:21 *Statutory Lien as Disposition of Property without Due Process of Law*

The cases that follow illustrate conflicting decisions on innkeepers' lien statutes in different jurisdictions.

BLYE v. GLOBE-WERNICKE REALTY CO.
33 N.Y.2d 15, 300 N.E.2d 710 (1973)

JASEN, J.: "In August, 1971, Judy Blye took up residence at the Van Rensselaer Hotel in Manhattan. In October of that year, she was locked out of her room for nonpayment of one week's hotel charges amounting to $60.60. Pur-

---

[26]Kuszewska v. Steiger Hotel Operating Co., Inc., 152 Misc. 80, 272 N.Y.S. 659 (Sup. Ct. 1934), *aff'd*, 244 A.D. 709, 279 N.Y.S. 733; Scott v. Browning Business Services, Inc., 175 Misc. 630, 24 N.Y.S.2d 227 (N.Y. Mun. Ct. 1941).

suant to the innkeeper's lien law (Lien Law, § 181), the hotel summarily seized her personal property (valued by her at about $700) without notice and without an opportunity for a hearing. She was left with only the clothes she was wearing, her purse with some personal identification, and small change.

"An action was then commenced seeking a declaratory judgment of the unconstitutionality of section 181 of the Lien Law, a permanent injunction and damages for mental distress. Special Term dismissed the action on the authority of *Waters & Co. v. Gerard* (189 N.Y. 302), and the Appellate Division unanimously affirmed. The appeal is before us as of right on constitutional grounds. [Citation omitted.]

"Plaintiff asks that we reconsider our holding in the *Gerard* case (*supra*), wherein the predecessor of section 181 of the Lien Law was upheld against a due process challenge. We are also urged to hold that section 181 is violative of the constitutional guarantees against unreasonable searches and seizures. . . .

"We conclude that section 181 of the Lien Law is irreconcilable with evolving concepts of due process and is unconstitutional. Insofar as *Gerard* holds to the contrary, it is overruled. On this view, we do not reach the search and seizure question. . . .

"Turning to the contention that this summary remedy denies due process, we note that plaintiff's property was not seized by a State official, but by private persons—i.e., hotel personnel, acting pursuant to State law. The threshold question is, therefore, whether the requisite 'State action' is present.

"It is clear that private conduct will not invoke the constitutional guarantees of due process. But it is equally without doubt that, in some circumstances, the actions of a private citizen can become the actions of the State for purposes of the due process clause. (*Adickes v. Kress & Co.*, 398 U.S. 144, 169–171; *Burton v. Wilmington Parking Auth.*, 365 U.S. 715, 722.) For instance, State action, or action under color of State law, has been readily found in racial discrimination cases. (*E.g.*, *Reitman v. Mulkey*, 387 U.S. 369; *Shelley v. Kraemer*, 334 U.S. 1; *see, generally*, Honan, *Law and Social Change; The Dynamics of the 'State Action' Doctrine*, 17 J. Pub. L. 258; Comment, *Current Developments in State Action and Equal Protection of the Law*, 4 Gonzaga L. Rev. 233.) And in recent years, another theory of State action has emerged. It holds that the actions of private persons, when performing traditionally public functions, may be attributed to the State for purposes of the Fourteenth Amendment. [Citation omitted.]

"In this State, the execution of a lien, be it a conventional security interest, a writ of attachment, or a judgment lien traditionally has been the function of the Sheriff [citations omitted]. On this view, 'State action' can be found in an innkeeper's execution on his own lien. (*Collins v. Viceroy Hotel Corp.* . . . [338 F. Supp. 390 (N.D. Ill. 1972)]; *Klim v. Jones* . . . [315 F. Supp. 109 (N.D. Cal. 1970)]; [citation omitted]. Then, too, it cannot be gainsaid that innkeepers are possessed of certain powers by virtue of section 181 of the Lien Law. By that token, their actions are clothed with the authority of State law [citation omitted] and their actions may be said to be those of the State for purposes of the due process clauses.

"Procedural due process requires notice and an opportunity for a hearing before the State may deprive a person of a possessory interest in his property. [Citation omitted.] Such protection is not limited to necessaries [citation omitted], although the relative weight of the property interest involved may be relevant to the form of notice and hearing required by due process. Nor does the availability of the right turn on the relative degree of permanence of the deprivation, nor may it be defeated by provision for recovery of the property. Only an extraordinary or truly unusual situation will justify postponing notice and opportunity for a hearing. [Citations omitted.] Thus, for example, summary seizure may be permissible where necessary to secure an important governmental or general public interest or where the need for prompt action is paramount. [Citations omitted.]

"It cannot be said that the statute before us serves such an important governmental or general public interest. As the Supreme Court noted in an analogous context in *Fuentes* [*v. Shevin*, 407 U.S. 67] (at p. 92), 'no more than private gain is directly at stake.' And as this case well illustrates, summary seizure of a guest's property may deprive him of the sum of his possessions. Consequently, it may affect his ability to hold a job, making him a burden to family or friends, or perhaps even a public charge.

"Practically speaking, it is difficult to perceive how this statue affords the innkeeper any real protection against the transient intent on absconding and defaulting on his bill. Rather, the statute falls hardest on people such as this plaintiff who work in the community and make their residence at a hotel or other like establishment. With respect to this class of persons at least, the extraordinary remedy of summary seizure is especially harsh, oppressive, and, it would seem unnecessary. Nor does this statute limit summary seizure to those extraordinary situations necessitating prompt action—e.g., to secure the creditor's interest in obtaining jurisdiction for purposes of bringing a nonpayment suit or in preventing the debtor from removing or concealing his property to prevent future execution on any judgment that might be obtained. (*See Ownbey v. Morgan*, 256 U.S. 94.) The fact is that the statutory scheme does not contemplate the bringing of a nonpayment suit, or any judicial determination, pre or post seizure, of the validity of the keeper's claim. The statute sweeps broadly and, as a matter of course, permits the unchecked summary seizure of a guest's property without regard to the validity of the particular claim and without regard to whether the particular guest is likely to remove or conceal himself and his property if given notice and opportunity for a hearing. In resolving the conflicting interests and in light of the feasible alternatives, we believe the guest's interest in possession and use of his property outweighs the innkeeper's interest in summarily seizing that property to secure the payment of charges.

"Conditioning the innkeeper's lien with procedural due process safeguards will not destroy it or leave the keeper at the mercy of the defaulting guest. The keeper's right under the Lien Law to seize a defaulting guest's property and to sell it at public auction (and the State's power to confer that right) is not questioned. All that is necessary is that the fundamentals of due process be observed.

This imports that, absent extraordinary circumstances, the guest be afforded notice and the *opportunity* to be heard before being deprived of the possession of his property.

"Accordingly, the order of the Appellate Division should be reversed, without costs, and the innkeeper's lien law declared unconstitutional."

ANASTASIA V. THE COSMOPOLITAN NATIONAL BANK OF CHICAGO
527 F.2d 150 (7th Cir. 1975), *cert. denied*, 424 U.S. 928 (1976)

MOORE, Senior Cir. J.: "Illinois Revised Statutes ch. 82, § 57 and ch. 71, § 2 give hotelkeepers a lien on the personal property brought into their establishments by guests to the extent of charges incurred for lodging, board or other services. Ch. 71, § 2 also authorizes the hotelkeeper to detain and eventually, upon continued nonpayment of charges, after notice to the guests to sell such property in order to realize on the lien. Such a sale bars any subsequent action against the hotel proprietor for the recovery of the property or the value thereof. This case represents a constitutional challenge to these provisions.

"The named plaintiffs in this class action were residents of hotels located in Chicago. In each instance they returned to their rooms one day to find that the hotelkeeper had either changed or 'plugged' the lock on the door to the room so that the plaintiffs were unable to gain admittance. Upon inquiry, each plaintiff was told by their respective hotelkeepers that they would not be readmitted and the personal property that had been located in the room would not be released until such time as arrearages in rent had been paid. When efforts by the plaintiffs and their attorneys to regain possession of their property proved unavailing, this lawsuit was filed.

"The suit . . . challenged the seizures of the personal possessions of the plaintiffs as both a deprivation of property without due process of law in violation of the Fourteenth Amendment in that no notice or hearing in which the plaintiffs could raise defenses to the alleged nonpayments of rent was provided, and an unreasonable search and seizure in contravention of the Fourth Amendment. In addition to damages, the plaintiffs sought a declaration that ch. 82, § 57 and ch. 71, § 2 were unconstitutional and an injunction restraining the defendants from acting pursuant to these sections. On January 6, 1973, the district court granted leave to intervene as defendant to several of Chicago's large hotels, and on June 5, 1973, granted plaintiffs' motion to proceed as a plaintiff and defendant class action.

"After the plaintiffs had submitted a motion for summary judgment, the district court *sua sponte* raised the issue of state action and issued a memorandum dismissing the complaint for lack of jurisdiction upon concluding that the action of the defendant hotels was not taken 'under color' of law within the meaning of 42 U.S.C. § 1983. From the judgment entered thereon, the plaintiffs appealed. We affirm.

"Ever since the *Civil Rights Cases*, 109 U.S. 3 (1883), it has been recognized that the Fourteenth Amendment serves as a limitation only on governmental action and does not affect purely private conduct. But while this proposition is easily stated, the distinction between governmental and private action is seldom very clear. With increasing frequency in recent years, the federal courts have been drawn into the sphere of creditor-debtor relations to decide whether certain statutorily authorized creditor conduct constitutes action 'under color of' state law within the meaning of section 1983, or, what is essentially the same question, whether the conduct is 'state action' under the Fourteenth Amendment. A number of cases have considered the issue in the context of the self-help repossession remedy provided to secured creditors by sections 9–503 and 9–504 of the Uniform Commercial Code. Only last year this court considered an Indiana common law and statutory mechanic's lien, finding no state action where an automobile repairman detained a car after the owner refused to pay the bill for repairs. *Phillips v. Money*, 503 F.2d 990 (7th Cir. 1974), *cert. denied*, 420 U.S. 934 (1975). And the context in which the state action question in this case arises—detention of personal property pursuant to a statutory landlords' or innkeeper's lien—is by no means unique, having been the subject of a number of court decisions. In fact, detention of property under authority of the very statutes challenged herein has in another case been declared unconstitutional by the United States District Court for the Northern District of Illinois. *Collins v. Viceroy Hotel Corp.*, 338 F. Supp. 390 (N.D. Ill. 1972).

"Before moving to an analysis of the plaintiffs' contentions, it is important to note that this case involves only the seizure of personal property by the defendant hotels. There have been no sales of the property of the named plaintiffs although ch. 71, § 2 authorizes sales under certain conditions. And the plaintiff class is defined as '[t]hose persons . . . whose personal property is now detained by a hotel. . . . ' There is no mention made of a sale. Therefore, we have in this case no occasion to consider whether a statutorily authorized sale, with the concomitant bar on any subsequent action by a guest against a hotel proprietor for the recovery of any property or the value thereof, would constitute state action. [Citations omitted.] It is appropriate, however, to note Mr. Justice CLARK's caveat made with regard to state action cases: ' "Differences in circumstances . . . beget appropriate differences in law. . . . " ' *Burton v. Wilmington Parking Authority*, 365 U.S. 715, 726 (1961), *quoting, Whitney v. Tax Commission*, 309 U.S. 530, 542 (1940).

"The plaintiffs advance two theories under which they contend that state action is present in this case. The first might properly be termed an 'entwinement' theory whereby the state has assertedly significantly involved itself in the action of the hotelkeepers, so as to make the acts of these private individuals state action for the purposes of the Fourteenth Amendment and section 1983. The second theory is the so-called 'public function' theory: that the State of Illinois has allowed hotel proprietors to perform a governmental function in enforcing their lien, and therefore that their actions must be governed by constitutional limitations.

A. Entwinement

"The proper focus for determining whether state action exists under this theory was recently stated by the Supreme Court as follows: '[T]he inquiry must be whether there is a sufficiently close nexus between the State and the challenged action of the regulated entity so that the action of the latter may be fairly treated as that of the State itself.' *Jackson v. Metropolitan Edison Co.*, 419 U.S. 345, 351 (1974). . . . The test is whether the state has significantly involved itself in the challenged conduct. *Moose Lodge No. 107 v. Irvis,* 407 U.S. 163, 173 (1972). And a conclusion as to degree of involvement can be reached only by 'sifting facts and weighing circumstances.' *Burton v. Wilmington Parking Authority, supra,* 365 U.S. at 722.

"The plaintiffs argue that by passing a statute authorizing the private seizure of the possessions of hotel residents, the State of Illinois has lent affirmative support and encouragement to hotel proprietors. They point out that ch. 71, § 2 in particular has altered the nature of the common law innkeepers' lien by expanding the class of establishments which can invoke it—a fact acknowledged by the defendants. At common law, the lien existed only in favor of innkeepers— one who took in transient guests, was bound by law to do so, and was absolutely liable for injury to the guest's person or property. Keepers of boardinghouses or lodginghouses had no corresponding obligations and liabilities, and possessed no comparable lien until granted by statute. Plaintiffs observe as well that Illinois has eliminated the principal *raison d 'être* of the common law innkeepers' lien by placing dollar ceilings on the extent of a hotelkeeper's liability and for some types of property abolishing absolute liability by requiring a showing of fault on the part of the hotelkeeper. *See* Ill. Rev. Stat. ch. 71, § § 1, 3, 3.1, 4.

"Primary reliance is placed on *Reitman v. Mulkey,* 387 U.S. 369 (1967), where the Supreme Court found state action in an amendment (art. 1, § 26 [Proposition 14]) to the California constitution providing that the state could not limit a person's right to rent or sell real estate to whomever he chooses. . . . The trial court rendered summary judgment for the defendants on the ground that the statutes had been rendered void by the adoption of art. 1, § 26. The California Supreme Court reversed the trial court, and the Supreme Court affirmed that decision. While superficially *Reitman* is similar to this case—in both instances a state enactment authorized the actions of private individuals—we consider it by no means controlling. . . .

"What is present in this case differs substantially from *Reitman.* The statutes involved here were not enacted in contravention of a constitutional goal. Ch. 82, § 57 was passed in 1874 and ch. 71, § 2 in 1909. Both provisions remain unchanged from their original form. To be sure, these provisions allowed hotel proprietors to take action that the common law did not previously permit. But we do not attach overriding significance to this limited expansion of the common law. It is but one consideration to be included in the mix. The First Circuit has recently failed to be persuaded that a statutory expansion of the common law innkeepers' lien was a basis for finding state action: 'The statute at issue is a fairly unremarkable product of the continuing legislative function to define creditors' rights. . . . If it goes beyond the common law, it does so merely by broadening the class (innkeepers) having traditional right to a possessory lien. And even this modest change occurred 115 years ago.' *Davis v. Richmond,* 512 F.2d 201, 203

(1st Cir. 1975), [citation omitted]. . . . At the turn of the century, the concept of due process had not evolved to its present-day point where summary repossession of property with participation of state officers is constitutionally impermissible in all but the most limited circumstances. And it cannot be persuasively argued, in light of the then existing remedy of self-help for innkeepers and others, that the Fourteenth Amendment upon its enactment was intended to do away with summary self-help procedures. *Adams v. Southern California First National Bank, supra,* 492 F.2d at 337.

"Nor do the hotelkeepers' remedies possess an exalted constitutional status where they are insulated from the possibility of legislative reforms. They are subject to the operation of normal political forces. This is also not a case in which the state has actively involved itself in the affairs of hotel proprietors. There is no continuing interdependence such as characterized the lessor-lessee relationship between the parking authority and the coffee shop in *Burton v. Wilmington Parking Authority.* Nor is there even an ongoing regulatory scheme such as the liquor licensing in *Moose Lodge . . . ,* which the Supreme court found were in any event an insufficient basis for finding state action. All that the State of Illinois has done is to enact statutes which permit a private hotel proprietor to detain the property of guests in an establishment owned by him. The statutes do not compel such a procedure. [Citations omitted.] . . . They merely permit it. . . . This degree of involvement falls short of the significant degree of encouragement or affirmative support necessary to the existence of state action.

B. Public Function

" . . . The Plaintiffs argue that by allowing hotel proprietors to seize the personal property located in a resident's room without any prior adjudication to the proprietor's claim for charges, the state has delegated a state function traditionally performed by officers of the law and court. The plaintiffs rely most heavily on *Hall v. Garson,* 430 F.2d 430 (5th Cir. 1970). There a private landlord had entered the dwelling of a tenant and removed a television set pursuant to a Texas statute giving landlords a lien on the personal property of their tenants. The court found state action on the ground that the landlord was performing what was ordinarily a state function: 'In this case the alleged wrongful conduct was admittedly perpetrated by a person who was not an officer or official of any state agency. But the action taken, the entry into another's home and the seizure of another's property, was an act that possessed many, if not all, of the characteristics of an act of the State. The execution of a lien, whether a traditional security interest or a quasi writ of attachment or judgment lien, has in Texas traditionally been the function of the Sheriff or constable.' *Id.* at 439.

" . . . Fundamentally, we simply disagree with the result in *Hall.* The historical accuracy of that case's assertion that the execution of liens was traditionally a state function has been questioned. [Citations omitted.] And this assessment seems correct, except insofar as *Hall* may have relied on particular characteristics of prior Texas law. Plaintiffs freely acknowledge the hoary nature of the innkeepers' lien, and a landlord's right to seize property of a tenant whose rent is in arrears has common law roots as well. Thus, while the sheriff unquestionably is often the party who executes a lien, the function can hardly be said to be traditionally and exclusively that of the state. At most it is one that has been shared by the state with private persons. We see little similarity between this case and the public function cases decided by the Supreme Court and therefore find no basis for concluding that there is state action here.

"Because we hold that there is no state action, we have no occasion to consider whether the actions of the hotel proprietors would be violative of the Fourth or Fourteenth Amendments had state action been present.

"Affirmed."

In footnote 19 of its opinion the court noted that under Illinois law the plaintiffs could sue to replevy their property and collect appropriate damages if their property was seized without just cause. Thus they were not left remediless by the court's disposition of the constitutional issues.

To the same effect, the Federal Court of Appeals for the First Circuit has ruled constitutional the Massachusetts Boardinghouse Lien Statute (Mass. G.L.C. 255 § 23) in *Davis v. Richmond.*[27]

In *Culbertson v. Leland,*[28] the Ninth Circuit Court of Appeals held that, under the Arizona Innkeeper's Lien Statute, the hotel manager's seizure by self-help of lodgers property constituted state action requiring constitutional due process, which was not afforded the affected hotel lodgers.

The Supreme Court has not yet resolved this issue, but language contained in *Flagg Brothers, Inc. v. Brooks,*[29] in which the New York Warehouseman's Lien Statute (N.Y. U.C.C. 7–210) was held not violative of constitutional due process requirements because of the lack of requisite "state action" is supportive of the innkeeper's lien for two reasons: (1) the statute permits but does not compel a sale of property seized, and (2) the lien holder has not been delegated a power reserved exclusively to the state. The rationale of the majority is expressed in footnote 10 of the Court's opinion: "It would intolerably burden beyond the scope of any of our previous cases, the notion of state action under the Fourteenth Amendment to hold that the mere existence of a body of property law in a State, whether decisional or statutory, itself amounted to 'state action' even though no state officials or state process was ever involved in enforcing that body of law."[30]

In footnote 11 the Court continues: "The conduct of private actions in relying on the rights established under these liens to resort to self-help remedies does not permit their conduct to be ascribed to the State."[31]

In the main body of the majority opinion, the Court reiterates the importance it ascribes to traditional self-help arrangements in the context of state action:

[27]512 F.2d 201 (1st Cir. 1975).
[28]528 F.2d 426 (9th Cir. 1975).
[29]436 U.S. 149 (1978).
[30]*Id.* at 160.
[31]*Id.* at 162.

"Thus, even if we were inclined to extend the sovereign function doctrine outside of its present carefully confined bounds, the field of private commercial transactions would be a particularly inappropriate area into which to expand it. We conclude that our sovereign function cases do not support a finding of state action here."[32]

However, in *Sharrock v. Dell Buick-Cadillac, Inc.*,[33] the New York Court of Appeals noted *Flagg Brothers*, but held it inapplicable, because of the inherent differences it found between state and federal due process analysis, in striking down the New York statutory garage keeper's lien for repair and storage charges. The innkeeper's lien found unconstitutional in *Blye* was held more analogous to the garage keeper's lien than to the warehouseman's lien. A strong dissenting opinion concurred in by the chief justice and one other justice took issue with the reasoning of the court, finding *Flagg Brothers* controlling and also cogently pointing out that *Blye* dealt with a seizure of property initiated by the innkeeper, whereas here the vehicle owner voluntarily transferred possession the garage keeper in the first instance.

Dell Buick stands for the general proposition that states are free to apply their own due process standards in interpreting their respective state constitutions. This means that those jurisdictions that have overturned innkeepers' lien statutes are not required to reverse themselves should the Supreme Court rule otherwise, but may do so by reason of the persuasive authority of such a ruling.

A federal district court in California was the first to invalidate that state's statutory lien in 1970.[34] The court was especially concerned about the disproportionate impact of the statute on poor persons; the fact that the statute authorized the seizure of the tools of the guest's trade with the resultant loss of the guest's means of livelihood; the possible misuse of the law to encourage dubious and fraudulent claims; and the fact that virtually no exemptions from coverage existed (except musical instruments and orthopedic appliances used by guest). Florida[35] and Nebraska[36] have followed suit, but the Illinois statute has been sustained in *Anastasia, supra,* despite a prior declaration of unconstitutionality by a federal district court.[37] Minnesota[38] has also upheld its innkeeper's lien statute. Prior to the Minnesota case, only Missouri had dealt with this issue. The Missouri Supreme Court sustained its statute, reasoning simply that its lien law, a codification of the ancient common right accorded the innkeeper, was constitutional, since it created no new rights inconsistent with it.[39]

The wisest course for the innkeeper is to consult with local counsel before utilizing the lien if the constitutionality of the statute has not been interpreted.

[32]*Id.* at 163.
[33]45 N.Y.2d 152, 379 N.E.2d 1169 (1978).
[34]Klim v. Jones, 315 F. Supp. 109 (N.D. Cal. 1970).
[35]Johnson v. Riverside Hotel, Inc., 399 F. Supp. 1138 (D. Fla. 1975).
[36]Dielen v. Levine, 344 F. Supp. 823 (D. Neb. 1972).
[37]Collins v. Viceroy Hotel Corp., 338 F. Supp. 390 (N.D. Ill. 1972).
[38]McPherson v. University Motors, Inc., 193 N.W.2d 616 (Minn. 1972).
[39]L.E. Lines Music Co. v. Holt, 332 Mo. 749, 60 S.W.2d 32 (1933).

20:22   *Statutory Requirements for Enforcement of Lien*

Where the lien is valid and enforceable, any sale or other disposition must conform with the express requirements of the statute. No sale or pledge of goods is authorized in the absence of such authority.

21 Compensation of the Innkeeper

21:1 *An Innkeeper's Charges Must Be Reasonable*

The innkeeper is not only obliged by law to receive all proper travelers for whom he has room, but is obliged to entertain them for a reasonable compensation. "[O]ne who becomes a guest at an inn renders himself liable for his entertainment at the usual and customary rate of charges made by the innkeeper. . . . ."[1] The requirement that the compensation should be reasonable is a necessary corollary of the requirement that the guest should be received, for if it were open to the innkeeper to charge what he pleased he might exclude such applicants as he did not care to entertain by the mere device of demanding from them an unreasonable payment. "They do not deal upon *contracts* as others do, they only make bills, in which they cannot set unreasonable rates; if they do, they are indictable for extortion. . . . ."[2]

The amount of the charge cannot easily be fixed by rule; nor is it usual to find the amount charged by an innkeeper disputed in court. The charge made by the innkeeper would, it seems, be upheld if it were not extravagant; "a person residing in a hotel cannot live so cheaply as at his own house."[3]

ARCHIBALD v. CINERAMA HOTELS
73 Cal. App. 3d 152, 140 Cal. Rptr. 599 (1977),
overruled by Koire v. Metro Car Wash, 40 Cal. App. 3d 24,
219 Cal. Rptr. 153 (1985)

REGAN, J.: "This is a plaintiff's appeal from a judgment of dismissal entered upon an order sustaining demurrers without leave to amend. The first amended complaint, to which the demurrers were sustained, is for breach of an innkeeper's duty. It contains three causes of action. It asserts a class action by plaintiff as a member of a class of persons who are citizens and residents of California and who have been guests of hotels and motels in Hawaii which are owned or operated by a multitude of named defendants who do business in California.

[1]Baldwin v. Webb, 121 Ga. 416, 418, 49 S.E. 265, 266 (1904).
[2]Newton v. Trigg, 89 Eng. Rep. 566 (K.B. 1691) (emphasis in original).
[3]Proctor v. Nicholson, 173 Eng. Rep. 30, 31 (K.B. 1835).

Also included is a named travel agency and several other fictitiously named travel agencies who make reservations for California visitors at such hotels.

"The first cause of action alleges that the rate charged to plaintiff for rooms in the hotels is higher than a so-called 'Kamaaina' (local resident) rate, which is offered or available to residents of Hawaii. It is alleged that this is 'unlawfully discriminatory.' The second cause of action alleges a conspiracy among defendants in furtherance of the discriminatory acts described in the first cause of action. The third cause of action alleges that defendants 'violated certain laws, statutes, rules and regulations and the policies of the State of California and engaged in unfair and deceptive acts and practices and principles contrary to the public policies of the State of California.'

"The demurrers to all the causes of action were sustained on the ground that none set forth facts sufficient to constitute a cause of action. . . .

"Plaintiff contends the first cause of action is good since it alleges a breach of the common law duties of an innkeeper not to discriminate; and also, impliedly if not directly, by alleging 'unlawful discrimination' it has alleged violations of constitutional rights under equal protection, privileges and immunities, and commerce clauses of the United States Constitution. To bolster these contentions, plaintiff has prepared a selective dissertation on the common law duties of an innkeeper, a short treatise on the economic doctrine of laissez-faire as it relates to the modern emphasis on equality of contract between providers and consumers, a discussion of certain state equal rights legislation pertaining to places of accommodation of travelers, a discussion of certain constitutional rights as they may pertain to residents versus travelers or nonresidents, and an exposition of the assertedly illusory distinction between 'discount' and 'overcharges' pertaining to hotels. Plaintiff's efforts have left us unpersuaded that the trial court erred.

"It is alleged in the first cause of action that the rates charged plaintiff and members of her class are higher than those charged to residents of the State of Hawaii. It is not alleged that the rates charged Californians are different than the rates charged any person or class of persons from anywhere else in the world, nor is it alleged that the rates charged plaintiff are unreasonable or excessive. While the complaint categorizes the rate charged her and other nonresidents as a "surcharge' which is 'discriminatory,' the 'preferential treatment' described in the complaint consists of a discount known as the 'Kamaaina rate,' and is so designated in the complaint. This is an unspecified rate presumably lower than the regular rate paid by all nonresidents and is illustrated by advertisements in the yellow pages of the telephone book placed by certain hotels such as 'Ask about our Kamaaina rates' or 'Kamaaina discounts.'

"Plaintiff has based her case in large part on the common law pertaining to innkeepers. She asserts there was, and is, a duty to charge exactly the same rates to everyone. Reliance is placed by plaintiff principally on text-book authority that innkeepers must provide lodging for *all* at a *reasonable price* and that all should be served equally and without discrimination. (*See* Beale, The Law of Innkeepers and Hotels Including Other Public Houses, Theatres, Sleeping Cars

(1906) § § 52–55, pp. 36–38; Sherry, the Law[s] of Innkeepers—For Hotels, Motels, Restaurants, and Clubs (1972) at pp. 23–24, 34.) However, looking at plaintiff's authorities, including cases cited and with her text-book references, we observe that the concern of the common law was and is limited to assuring each traveler freedom from unreasonably high rates. Since travel upon the highway at night was hazardous and there was little choice of lodging for the night, the common law approved restrictions upon innkeepers to insure a charge of 'reasonable value' for services, to prevent them from extorting exorbitant rates. (*See, e.g., Munn v. Illinois* (1877) 94 U.S. 113, 125, 134. . . .)

"We have found no authority holding that the offering of a discount to certain clients, patrons or customers based on an attempt to attract their business is unlawful under the common law, whether the discount be for salesmen, clergymen, armed services personnel, or local residents. In fact it has ben indicated in court decisions that even the common law duty to charge reasonable value for services is inapplicable where the guest is not one who might be stranded on a road in the nighttime or might otherwise be at the mercy of a single innkeeper, but rather is one who has made an advance reservation, thereby agreeing to a price before arrival. [Citations omitted.]

"Insofar as text authorities are concerned, those favored most by plaintiff recognize an innkeeper's freedom or common law right to make any reasonable charge, allowing him to frame his own schedule of rates, provided they are 'reasonable.' (Beale, *op. cit. supra*, § § 241, 243, pp. 168–169, 170; Sherry, *op. cit. supra*, at pp. 433–435.)

"All of the textual authorities and the case law cited by plaintiff, and other authorities we have examined, indicate to us that the common law was and is concerned with assuring that travelers will be received on a basis of equality in the sense that no one will be excluded by the device of demanding unreasonable rates or payment. We do not perceive that the common law is concerned with rates as such, except that they not be unreasonable; nor is it concerned with charges *lower* than reasonable charges, or discounts to induce patronage from certain groups or classes. The case before us does no present any compelling or even rational reason for us to either enlarge or depart from common law principles or concerns as to innkeepers.

"It should be added that plaintiff's reliance on *Neptune City v. Avon-By-The-Sea* (1972) 61 N.J. 296 [294 A.2d 47, 57 A.L.R.3d 983], is misplaced. The court in *Neptune* held the state could not abdicate its obligation to permit equal access to public trust (beach) lands for all state residents by permitting a beach municipality to grant preferences to residents of the municipality. At issue in *Neptune* was a beach user fee system under which residents of the municipality could purchase season badges entitling them to use the beach all season, but nonresidents were only permitted to purchase daily badges. (*See* 294 A.2d at pp. 50, 54–55.) The *Neptune* decision is clearly distinguishable. The public trust doctrine applicable to beaches owned by the sovereign does not apply to hotels located on land which is privately owned. Although hotel owners have certain common law obligations to travelers, hotels are by no means owned in public trust like public beaches. Moreover, *Neptune* did not concern itself with any question of equal access for nonstate residents.

"There is no legitimate constitutional law issue here. Plaintiff attempts to bring into play the equal protection clause, commerce clause, and the privileges and immunities clause of the United States Constitution and the so-called constitutional 'right to travel.' These constitutional provisions and rights apply only to state action, or to acts by individuals abridging rights pursuant to specific state laws so that to a significant extent the state has become involved as a governmental entity. (16 Am. Jur. 2d *Constitutional Law*, § 491, pp. 854–857 (equal protection); [citation omitted]; *Shapiro v. Thompson* (1969) 394 U.S. 618, 631 . . . (travel).) Here we have no allegation of a Hawaiian statute or any state activity under which the assertedly unlawful discrimination in hotel rates has taken place. It is not alleged that the State of Hawaii has in any way by express or implied statutory enactments caused, brought about, or taken any part in the rate discount policies or practices of the defendants.

"Plaintiff points to California Civil Code sections 51 and 52 (the Unruh Civil Rights Act) as a form of recognition and extension of the common law rules applied to innkeepers. She asserts these statutes were violated by defendants. It is true, as emphasized by plaintiff, that the California Supreme Court has construed Civil Code section 51 as prohibiting any *arbitrary* exclusion of *any* person from a business premise, even though the exclusion is based on something (such as long hair and strange garments) other than sex, race, color, religion, ancestry or national origin. (*In re Cox* (1970) 3 Cal.3d 205, 216–217 [90 Cal. Rptr. 24, 474 P.2d 992].) Plaintiff attempts to equate the Supreme Court decision in *Cox* with the case now before us. It cannot be done. Section 51 by its express language applies only within California. It cannot (with its companion penalty provisions in § 52) be extended into the Hawaiian jurisdiction. [Citation omitted.] A state cannot regulate or proscribe activities conducted in another state or supervise the internal affairs of another state in any way, even though the welfare or health of its citizens may be affected when they travel to that state. (*Bigelow v. Virginia* (1975) 421 U.S. 809, 824–825. . . .)

"Even if the legal barriers to application of Civil Code sections 51 and 52 are put aside, statutory construction indicates they are not applicable here. The language in the *Cox* case, *supra*, does not make them applicable. Plaintiff was not arbitrarily excluded from any business premise, nor was she arbitrarily discriminated against in any way. Plaintiff has alleged no tort, breach of contract or other actionable wrong. The trial court therefore did not err in sustaining the demurrers to the first cause of action."

21:2 *The Innkeeper May Fix Rates*

The innkeeper is entitled to frame a schedule of rates, provided that such rates are reasonable. Or, without having a formal rate schedule, he may make any reasonable charge on an individual basis. This may be a customary rate, or in the absence of a schedule of rates or any custom, it may be such amount as the innkeeper pleases to charge, subject to the condition that it not be more than the entertainment is reasonably worth.

21:3 *Posting of Rate Schedule*

Many states have enacted statutes requiring innkeepers to post their schedule of rates and charges. Such statutes impose this duty of posting and fix a penalty for noncompliance, but do not attempt to fix by law what the rates may be. Some statutes also create a cause of action for guests based on the innkeeper's failure to post rates. Typical is the following from the tourism-oriented state of Nevada:

651.030 Posting of rates; liability for overcharge
1. Every keeper of any hotel, inn, motel or motor court in this state shall post, in a conspicuous place in the office and in every bedroom of such establishment, a printed copy of [this section], and a statement of charge or rate of charges by the day for lodging.
2. No charge or sum shall be collected for any greater or other sum than he is entitled to by the general rules and regulations of such establishment.
3. For any violation of this section, or any provision herein contained, the offender shall forfeit to the injured party 3 times the amount of the sum charged in excess of what he is entitled to charge.[4]

Like statutory limitation of liability, this is an area in which the law varies considerably from state to state. The innkeeper should familiarize himself with the posting requirements in his own state and the penalties for noncompliance and be guided accordingly.

21:4 *Payment May Be Required in Advance*

The innkeeper has a right, if he chooses, to demand payment in advance of his charges, that is, before he receives the guest.[5] This is, of course, a more awkward rule for the innkeeper than for the carrier, yet it is quite clear that it is within the rights of the innkeeper. Whether the traveler applies for a room or for board he can undoubtedly be required, as a condition of his reception, to pay in advance for entertainment he intends to receive for a reasonable time; that he must pay for one night's lodging at the time of being received is quite clear.

Doubtless he could be compelled to pay his board for a day in advance if the inn were conducted on the "American plan," but whether the innkeeper could demand payment for a longer period in advance than a single day is doubtful. A bill for entertainment at an inn accrues "de die in diem," and the day's charge would seem to be the unit of charge and the limit of the innkeeper's demand.

This general rule applies to the typical walk-in guest seeking accommodation. In the case of a reservation confirmed in advance of arrival, the innkeeper may

[4]Nev. Rev. Stat. § 651.030 (1953).
[5]Mulliner v. Florence, 3 Q.B.D. 484 (C.A. 1878); Fell v. Knight, 151 Eng. Rep. 1039 (Exch. 1841).

insist on a minimum payment covering a longer period. New York resort hotels use this practice over holiday weekends.[6] The justification is that it ensures reimbursement for any loss suffered by the innkeeper in the event the guest fails to appear. The deposit must be reasonable and should be refunded to the guest in the event the innkeeper suffers no loss.[7]

21:5 *Compensation Due as Soon as Relation Is Established*

The right to receive compensation for his services accrues to the innkeeper at the moment of the reception of a guest, and indeed the creation of the relation of host and guest and the right to make a charge for services performed are necessarily coincident. From this it would follow that as soon as the guest signs the register and is received into the inn, he is bound to pay some compensation, even though he receives no further entertainment than the mere right of remaining in a common room; the liability to pay compensation continues until the guest ceases to bear that character. If he temporarily leaves the inn, intending to return and remaining meanwhile a guest, the innkeeper is entitled to make reasonable charge, even though neither food nor lodging is meantime furnished him.

In an English case a traveler on applying for a room at an inn was told that the inn was full, but that he might occupy a room which would not be needed until night. He went to the room and dressed there. The court intimated that the innkeeper was entitled to compensation, Bowen, L. J., saying: "I think that, as soon as he had taken the plaintiff's luggage up to the room, and had placed it in the room, the innkeeper became entitled to charge the plaintiff for the use of the room—a charge which would be expanded or contracted, according as the plaintiff's occupation of the room was prolonged or not."[8]

When the guest leaves the inn and ceases to be a guest, the innkeeper's right to charge for his services as such comes to an end, although circumstances may exist which would give the innkeeper a right to compensation for services rendered. Thus, if upon leaving, a guest desires that his room be reserved for him or for someone else whom he may send to the inn, he would be responsible for the rental value of the room. These services, however, are not innkeeper's services, and the amount of charge and the methods of enforcing the charge would be governed by the ordinary law of debtor and creditor, not by the law of innkeepers.

21:6 *Services for Which Innkeeper Is Entitled to Compensation*

The obligation of an innkeeper to his guest includes the obligation to render without extra charge the usual and reasonable personal attention to the health

[6]Freeman v. Kiamesha Concord, Inc., 351 N.Y.S.2d 541 (N.Y. Civ. Ct. 1974).
[7]*Cf.* King of Prussia Enterprises, Inc. v. Greyhound Lines, Inc., 457 F. Supp. 56 (E.D. Pa. 1978), *aff'd*, 595 F.2d 1212 (3d Cir. 1979) (without opinion). *See* section 7:6, *supra*.
[8]Medawar v. Grand Hotel Co. [1891] 2 Q.B. 11, 26 (C.A.).

and comfort of the guest. For extraordinary services, however, the innkeeper is entitled to make a special, additional charge. For instance, if the guest is nursed by the innkeeper through a severe and protracted illness, compensation for the service as nurse is due the innkeeper.

The innkeeper must perform his entire obligation before he is entitled to any compensation. For instance, if he undertakes to furnish room and board, he can make no charge for the room, although he furnishes it, if in point of fact he does not supply the guest with the reasonable board.[9] Where, however, there is a separate charge for separate articles of entertainment, the innkeeper may be entitled to charge for some of the articles furnished, though he is not entitled to charge for others. For instance, if an innkeeper unlicensed to sell liquor is unable to recover compensation for liquor furnished, he may, nevertheless, recover such amount as he is legally entitled to charge for board.

21:7 Who Is Liable for Payment?

Where a party of several persons dines together, and there is no agreement to give credit to any particular one, they are, it would seem, jointly liable for all the charges, not merely liable each for his own share.[10] If, however, the host knew that one member of the party had invited the others to dine with him, he could hold only the one who is entertaining his friends. And where the party forms a family, the head of the family is the person liable for the whole charge and not the separate members of the family; thus, where a father went to an inn with his daughter, it was held that the daughter was not liable for her father's entertainment, nor, it would seem, for her own.[11] And so where a husband and wife go to an inn together, the wife is not chargeable with any part of the bill, unless indeed it can be shown that the credit was extended to her and not to the husband.[12]

In such cases, it is well to render all bills not to the husband alone, but to "Mr. & Mrs.," so as to create a reasonable basis for the contention that credit was extended to both husband and wife and that a lien exists on the property of both.

Where two men or two women occupy a room together, they both should be required to register and all bills should be rendered to them jointly. Such procedure will help to make the lien applicable to the property of both persons.

21:8 "Necessaries" Furnished Married Persons and Minors

A married woman may, by agreement, obligate herself for accommodations furnished to her. A husband is liable for the obligations of a wife where he has

[9]Wilson v. Martin, 1 Denio 602 (N.Y. Sup. Ct. 1845).
[10]Forster v. Taylor, 3 Camp. 49 (Eng. Nisi Prius 1811).
[11]Clayton v. Butterfield, 18 S.C. 100 (1857).
[12]Birney v. Wheaton, 2 How. Prac. (n.s.) 519 (N.Y. City Ct. 1885).

expressly agreed to pay or where apparent authority is given either from prior transactions which he had ratified or where the accommodations constitute "necessaries" furnished. In order that a husband be held liable for hotel accommodations furnished as "necessaries," it must appear that such accommodations are suitable in quality and character to the wife's station in life, the means of the husband, and the manner in which she lives. It must further appear that the wife was not supplied with such necessaries by the husband.

A minor[13] cannot be held liable for accommodations furnished at his request unless they are "necessaries." The principles of law just outlined with respect to the liability of a husband for accommodations furnished to a wife are equally applicable to the liability of a parent for necessaries furnished to a minor.

Although not as well established, in appropriate cases a wife may be held liable for her husband's "necessaries," so long as she is able to do so and her spouse is unable to support himself.[14]

21:9 Employees of Corporations

Employees of corporations may incur hotel charges on their personal account, in which case they are treated as other individual guests are. They may also incur charges on the account of the employer corporation. In order to hold a corporation liable for charges incurred by an employee, it must appear that:

(a) The corporation has specifically authorized such charges.

(b) The employee has actual or apparent authority to bind the corporation. Apparent authority may be inferred from a course of prior dealings between the innkeeper and the corporation.

(c) The accommodations rendered to the guest were in fact for corporate purposes and for the benefit of the corporation.

21:10 Extension of Credit: Account Stated

It is customary for guests who have established credit with the innkeeper to charge their hotel bill. It is advisable in such instances to request the guest, at the time of checking out, to sign a statement on the bill certifying to its correctness. Such procedure has been found to eliminate many a dispute and vexatious argument, and will obviate the need for proof as to all details making up the bill, in case of a lawsuit. The statement may be printed or rubber-stamped on the guest's bill in the following form:

---

[13]The age of majority varies from state to state; usually, it is set at 18 for transactions other than those involving real property, where the age is 21. Some statutes exempt leases from the 21-or-over requirement. Local counsel should be consulted on this question.

[14]Clark, The Law of Domestic Relations 181–92 (1968) noted with approval in Davidson et al., Sex-Based Discrimination 139–48, text note (1974).

The above account showing a balance due of
$_____ , is correct.

Date_____   _____
                                                 Guest's Signature

In the presence of:

_____

In the event the bill is not available at the time of checkout, the following
statement, preferably in printed form, may be used:

Hotel_____
Having heretofore examined bills rendered by
Hotel_____ in due course, showing
accommodations rendered and payments on account,
I find there is a balance now due the hotel on my
account, in the sum of $_____ .

_____
                                                 Guest's Signature

In the presence of:

_____

21:11   *Guaranty of Guest's Account*

An innkeeper, as a condition of extending credit, or to ensure collection where
credit has already been extended, may insist on a guaranty of the guest's account
by a reliable third party. It should be remembered that a guaranty is a contract
which, like other contracts, requires a consideration in order to be enforceable.
Also, it must be in writing and signed by the guarantor.[15]

There are two kinds of guaranty; one is a guaranty of payment, the other is a
guaranty of collectibility. A guaranty of payment is an absolute promise to pay
the guest's bill when it is due, unless paid by the guest. A guaranty of collectibility is a conditional promise, the condition being that the innkeeper creditor
first exhaust his remedies against the debtor guest and if he fails, then and only
then will the guarantor pay. A statement that a check is "good and collectible"
is a mere guaranty of collectibility. On the other hand, a letter stating "Cash his
check; I'll make it good if it bounces" is a guaranty of payment. A guaranty of
collectibility is obviously undesirable since it involves the time and expense of
an unsuccessful effort to collect directly from the guest before action can be
taken against the guarantor.

[15]N.Y. Gen. Oblig. Law § 5–701 (McKinney Supp. 1978).

Examples of enforceable guaranties are: (1) a guaranty of payment of an account for food, lodging, and hotel accommodations to become due *in the future;* (2) a guaranty of payment of an account for accommodations already furnished where, in reliance upon said guaranty, the innkeeper waives his lien and permits the guest to remove his baggage from the hotel; (3) a guaranty of an account already due where, in reliance upon said guaranty, the innkeeper agrees not to institute suit for the amount due for a specific period of time. The following is suggested as a form of a guaranty of payment:

GUARANTY

Date_____

For value received and in consideration of the extension of credit for hotel accommodations by Hotel_____ to Guest_____ . I hereby waive notice of the nonpayment of said account by said Guest_____ and consent to all extension of time that said Hotel_____ may grant to said Guest_____ and I agree to pay said account upon demand.

(Signed)_____
                    Guarantor

In the presence of:

_____

In *Chemical Bank v. Bright Star Holdings,*[16] a bank sought to hold Rudy's Restaurant Group as a guarantor of payment of debts that Bright Star owed the bank. The court rejected Rudy's argument that Chemical must first proceed against Bright Star and then only against Rudy's on Bright Star's guaranty:

> With respect to Chemical's claim based on Rudy's guarantee of Bright Star's debts, defendants similarly argue that it depends on an adjudication that Chemical has a right to demand payment from Bright Star; and that only then should a claim proceed against Rudy's as a guarantor. Yet Chemical has alleged that the guarantee is one of payment, and it is well-settled New York law that proceeding against the principal debtor is not a condition precedent to an action upon such a guarantee. *General Phoenix Corporation v. Cabot* (1949) 300 N.Y. 87, 93, 89 N.E.2d 238. . . .

[16]1989 U.S. District Ct. Lexis 6633.

22 Crimes against Innkeepers

22:1 *Fraudulently Obtaining Credit or Accommodation*

In the early days of innkeeping, the protection of the traveler was the principal concern of the law. With the development of rapid means of travel, the type and number of travelers and of hotels and motels built to accommodate them increased tremendously. As criminal elements discovered the comparative ease of obtaining hotel accommodations on credit and, with airplanes, railroads, and automobiles within easy reach, of making a swift getaway, more and more innkeepers became victimized by "deadbeats," who would make free use of their hospitality and surreptitiously depart without paying their bills. Thus the protection of the innkeeper became a vital concern to the state. To protect the essential and growing hotel industry, the legislatures of most states enacted penal statutes making criminal the fraudulent obtaining of credit or lodging, food, or other accommodations and services in hotels, motels, inns, and boarding, rooming, and lodging houses. Such statutes are commonly referred to as hotel fraud acts, or "deadbeat" statutes.

The revised New York Penal Code,[1] representative of legislation universally adopted governing hotel fraud, classifies the crime of fraud on innkeepers as a type of larceny which does not, however, in law, amount to larceny, for the reason, among others, that the subject of the theft is not "property." It is an offense relating to theft and is now designated as "theft of services." It covers, in addition to hotel accommodations, restaurant services, credit cards, and a variety of other services, including transportation by railroad, subway, bus, air, or taxi; telecommunications service; services for which compensation is measured by a meter or other mechanical equipment, such as gas, electric, water, or telephone services; and commercial or industrial equipment or facilities.

A theft of services under the New York statute constitutes (1) obtaining services or attempting to induce a supplier of a rendered service to accept payment on a credit basis, using a credit card known to be stolen or (2) intentionally avoiding or attempting to avoid payment by unjustifiably failing or refusing to pay, by stealth, or by any misrepresentation of fact known to be false. Any failure or refusal to pay for services creates a presumption of intention to avoid payment. Such unlawful conduct is made a misdemeanor.

[1]N.Y. Penal Law § 165:15 (McKinney Supp. 1978), § 165:17 (McKinney 1969).

In addition, New York makes an unlawful use of a credit card, defined as use or display of a credit card known to have been revoked or canceled to obtain or attempt to obtain services, a misdemeanor also.[2]

The New York statute applies only to transient guests; it may not be invoked against permanents and certainly not against tenants. Unlike the earlier New York statute (section 925 of the Penal Law), section 165.15 applies to restaurant patrons as well as hotel guests. This practice of limiting the criminal sanction to hotel guests (transients), rather than to boarders, lodgers, or tenants is uniform, but the state legislatures are free to expand or contract its scope.

The California statute[3] encompasses an additional class of offenders: those who, after obtaining credit or accommodation, abscond and surreptitiously remove their baggage without paying their bills.

A number of hotel fraud statutes have been challenged on the grounds that they constitute imprisonment for debt in violation of the applicable constitutional guarantee against this practice. The Wisconsin Supreme Court rejected this argument, holding that "the offense under the [hotel fraud] statute is not the debtor's nonpayment but rather the fraud through which payment is evaded."[4] The Texas Court of Criminal Appeals[5] sustained the constitutionality of its state statute.

22:2 Hotel Fraud Acts Are Not Collection Aids

Innkeepers, in addition to their lien on the baggage of guests, are given further substantial protection by these penal statutes. Great care should be exercised, however, in the enforcement of these statutes, lest persons, who, without fraudulent intent, are temporarily unable to pay their bills, be unjustly arrested and prosecuted. The statute should not be used, in other words, as a weapon to force the prompt payment of hotel bills. The innkeeper must always be prepared to prove actual fraud in case the presumption arising out of nonpayment of the hotel bill on demand is rebutted. The courts are reluctant to be used as collection agencies and even more reluctant to imprison hotel guests for nonpayment of debts.

Because hotel fraud statutes by definition are penal statutes affecting the liberty of persons charged with their violation upon conviction, they are strictly construed. Thus any failure to set forth the elements of the crime required by statute will mean the dismissal of any such conviction.

AGNEW v. STATE
474 S.W.2d 218 (Tex. Crim. App. 1971)

DAVIS, Commissioner: "This is an appeal from a conviction under Article 1551(b), Vernon's Ann. P.C., which makes it unlawful for a person who has ob-

---

[2]N.Y. Penal Law § 155.00 (McKinney Supp. 1978).
[3]Cal. Penal Code § 537 (West's Ann. 1979).
[4]State v. Croy, 145 N.W.2d 118 (Wis. 1966).
[5]Rhodes v. State, 441 S.W.2d 197 (Tex. Crim. App. 1969).

tained lodging to depart the premises with the intent not to pay for such services. Punishment was assessed by the jury at a fine of $150.

"At the outset, the appellant contends that the court erred in overruling his motion to quash the information. The pertinent portion of the information recites:

"that on or about the 27th day of July, A.D. 1970, and before the making and filing of this information, in the County of Gaines and the State of Texas, one Johnny Agnew did then and there unlawfully and willfully: *did obtain lodging* from C. M. McCain, owner and operator of 51 Motel of Seminole, Gaines County, Texas with the intent not to pay for such lodging and departed from the premises of the said injured party. (Emphasis added.)

"Article 1551 (b) provides:

"It shall be unlawful for any person who has obtained lodging, meals or other lawful service at any hotel, motor hotel, inn, tourist court, or mobile home park *to depart from the premises thereof with the intent not to pay for such services.* Failure of any person who has departed from such premises without paying the amount due for such services, and without personally appearing before the room clerk or other agent of the establishment before departing and protesting the amount alleged to be due, to pay the amount due within ten (10) days after being given written notice of the amount due, shall be *prima facie* evidence of departure with intent not to pay for such services. Any person who violates any provision of this paragraph shall be punished by a fine of not more than Five Hundred Dollars ($500), or by confinement in the county jail for not more than one year, or by both such fine and confinement. (1965) (Emphasis added.)

"The information fails to comply with the requirements of the statute by alleging that: 'did obtain lodging from C. M. McCain, owner and operator of 51 Motel of Seminole, Gaines County, Texas with the intent not to pay for such lodging. . . .'

"It is apparent from the statute that 'departure from the premises thereof with the intent not to pay' is an essential element of the offense. Therefore, it must be averred in the information. *Pannell v. State*, Tex. Cr. App., 384 S.W.2d 350, 1 Branch's 2d 495, § 513.

"The information being fatally defective as pointed out, the judgment is reversed and the prosecution ordered dismissed.

"Opinion approved by the Court."

Any error in the choice of the proper criminal statute will also vitiate such a conviction. This was the holding of the Supreme Court of Washington in *State v. Walls.*[6]

The following case illustrates the unwillingness of courts to convict for mere nonpayment in a nonhotel food-service context.

[6]81 Wash. 2d 618, 503 P.2d 1068 (1972).

STATE V. WAGENIUS
99 Idaho 273, 581 P.2d 319 (1978)

BAKES, J.: " . . .

V

"In No. 12070, *State v. DeVoe,* we are also presented with substantive questions of law as well as procedural issues already discussed.

"The magistrate found DeVoe guilty of a violation of I.C. § 18-3107, which provides in pertinent part:

"18-3107. FRAUDULENT PROCUREMENT OF FOOD, . . . —It shall be unlawful for any person to obtain food . . . at any . . . restaurant . . . with intent to defraud the owner of keeper thereof by not paying for the same. . . .

"I.C. § 18-3108 establishes the following presumption for proof of fraudulent intent:

"18-3108. PROOF OF FRAUDULENT INTENT IN PROCURING FOOD . . . —Proof that . . . any person absconded without paying or offering to pay for such food . . . shall be prima facie proof of the fraudulent intent mentioned in the preceding section.

"At trial DeVoe admitted that he and a companion had left the restaurant without paying for the food and drinks they had ordered and consumed, but maintained that he had not intended to defraud the restaurant, but had merely forgotten to pay the bill, primarily because he had been intoxicated at the time. At the close of the testimony, the magistrate stated:

"I think what it really boils down to is the question as to whether there was an intent to defraud and as to whether intoxication is any excuse for that. I think the law is pretty clear on it that intoxication is no defense. It doesn't appear to me apart from what I've heard here today that either one of you were so intoxicated and so drunken that you could not have possibly formed the necessary intent to violate the law.

"I would merely point out under 18-3108 of the Idaho Code it does say that if you abscond without paying or offering to pay for the food, lodging or other accommodations, that's prima facie evidence of a fraudulent intent. And it does appear to the Court that you did, even from your own admissions, leave without paying for it. Apparently, your basis of defense was that you merely forgot and didn't have the intent or that you were so intoxicated, you didn't know what you were doing. However, I have to draw the question of intent from the the circumstantial evidence and the facts as it appears to the Court. . . .

"And, again, I don't think intoxication under the law is any defense, and certainly it doesn't appear to me that either one of you was so drunk that you couldn't possibly form the necessary intent. You both knew what you were doing. . . .

"And, therefore I do feel beyond a reasonable doubt it has been shown that you did fraudulently procure the food and lodging and that you did abscond or leave without paying for it.

"It is clear from a reading of I.C. § 18-3107 that fraudulent intent is a necessary element of the crime with which the defendant is charged. I.C. § 18-3108 further provides that a *prima facie* case of fraudulent intent is made by 'proof that . . . any person *absconded* without paying or offering to pay for such food.' (Emphasis added.) Since the state's case was based upon the *prima facie* case resulting from the defendant's alleged absconding, the question which this appeal poses is whether or not there is any evidence in the record to support the trial court's finding that the defendant 'absconded.'

"All of the dictionary definitions of 'abscond' indicate that to abscond means to depart clandestinely, secretly, or surreptitiously. *See* Black's Law Dictionary (4th ed. 1968); Webster's New International Dictionary (3d ed.). It is not sufficient that the state prove merely that the defendant left the premises without paying. There must be some evidence, either direct or circumstantial, that the departure was secretive, clandestine, or surreptitious in order for it to constitute 'absconding.' The record suggests that the magistrate may not have recognized this distinction when he stated, 'I do feel beyond a reasonable doubt that it has been shown that you did fraudulently procure the food and lodging and that you did *abscond or leave* without paying for it.' (Emphasis added). The appellant alleges that there is no evidence in the record to show that he 'absconded,' i.e., that he left secretly, clandestinely or surreptitiously.

"The entire case of the prosecution consisted of the testimony of the security guard who observed the defendant and his companion enter the restaurant in an 'intoxicated condition' at approximately 11:00 P.M. and stay until roughly 1:45 A.M.

"His testimony is not clear as to whether or not he observed them leave. On direction examination he stated,

"I observed these two gentlemen get up and walk out of the coffee shop and then proceed to walk out of the building itself.

"When asked if he followed them immediately, he said:

"No, I did not. The waitress came over and told me that they had left their ticket on the table. I went over and picked it up and followed them and caught them outside as they were proceeding to leave.

"However, in response to a later question by the prosecuting attorney in his direct examination as to whether or not he picked up the meal ticket as soon as the defendant and his companion left the table, he answered:

"No, I was doing—I was in the other part of the building at the time checking the bar and everything. And I came back in and the waitress told me that these two gentlemen had walked out on their ticket. So I went over there and got the ticket off the table and proceeded to get these gentlemen back inside.

"On cross examination, by the defendant, who appeared *pro se*, the security guard testified:

"Q. You didn't see us actually leave walking out of the building—from like over by the restaurant area?

"A. No, I did not.

"Q. So you wouldn't be able to see that we were like running out of there or something like that?

"A. No, I didn't cause—at the time the waitress said you just walked out.

"Q. And when we were outside, we didn't try to run or take off, split up or divide. . . .

"A. No, no, I didn't.

"Q. And when you first called to us, it wasn't like 'You're under arrest'. You just called and said 'Come on back' and we went back just to see what was going on or what was happening.

"A. Right.

"The foregoing testimony is the only evidence relating to the manner in which the defendant and his companion left the restaurant. The question which we must decide is whether or not, based upon that evidence, the magistrate was justified in finding that the defendant 'absconded' as we have defined that term above. We think not. There is nothing in that testimony which would justify a finding that what the defendant did was secretive, clandestine or surreptitious. Without such evidence the defendant's conduct would not constitute 'absconding' within the meaning of I.C. § 18-3108, and therefore there was no 'prima facie case of fraudulent intent.' There is nothing else in the record from which the Court would be justified in finding the necessary element of fraudulent intent required by I.C. § 18-3107. The magistrate's finding that defendant DeVoe was guilty of violating I.C. § 18-3107 is not supported by the evidence and is therefore reversed. *See State v. Erwin*, 98 Idaho, 736, 572 P.2d 170 (1977). . . ."

22:3 *Accommodations Must Be Actually Obtained*

The accommodations must be actually obtained in order to constitute an offense under these acts; it is not enough that a contract for board has been made. Thus, where one has contracted to stay at an inn for a certain time and leaves before the time, paying for all the board he has had, these acts cannot apply. In *Sundmacher v. Block*,[7] it appeared that the guest registered at night, and, on being asked how long he was to stay, said he should stay at least until after breakfast. He had notice of a rule that a guest staying until after the beginning of a meal must pay for that meal. The next morning, a few minutes after breakfast was served, he tendered to the clerk the amount due for his supper and room; the clerk, though he knew the guest had not eaten breakfast, demanded payment for breakfast under the rule, and, upon the guest's refusing to pay, caused his arrest and prosecution under the statute. The guest, having been acquitted, brought this action for malicious prosecution, and the court held that he might recover, there being no reasonable cause to suppose him guilty. Judge Pleasants said:

[7]39 Ill. App. 553 (1891).

[H]e did not obtain the breakfast. Nor can it be held that there was a contract, as to either, that he would positively remain for any definite time. They were transients, whose present purpose in that regard, though stated as represented, would not be contracts for the time mentioned, but lawfully changeable at their option for any reason thereafter arising. Nor, if they were contracts would it affect the question under consideration. This statute is not to be extended by any liberality of construction in favor of innkeepers; and we hold that in no proceeding under it is the civil liability of the guest for any accommodation not actually "obtained" at all pertinent. If he definitely contracted to remain for a week, and left without fault of the innkeeper, at the close of the first day, paying or tendering payment for all that he had actually obtained, evidence of his refusal to pay for the further time contracted for would not be admissible as tending to prove an offense, or probable cause for a prosecution, under this act.[8]

22:4   *Hotel Accommodations Must Have Been Obtained by Fraud*

There must be some element of fraud in obtaining hotel service in order to bring it within these statutes. So where the only evidence was that the defendant, after being entertained for a week, was unable to pay; that the innkeeper forbade him to go until he paid; that he asserted that money was due him in a neighboring city, and the innkeeper allowed him to go get it; and that he did not return with the money, it was held that a conviction could not be supported.[9] Judge Ross said:

If an impecunious guest who has been guilty of no fraud except inability to pay, is unable to pay the amount of a board bill already incurred, it would seem from the contention of the complainant that he must either remain and increase his liability and the landlord's loss, or if he goes away openly, and for the ostensible purpose of obtaining the money to pay the amount of the bill, that he is liable to arrest and conviction. This would amount practically to liability to conviction in every case of inability to pay a board bill. I do not think that the statute contemplates such a result. A hotel-keeper can require payment in advance from his guests; he has a common-law and statutory lien upon the baggage of his guest, and he is protected from actual fraud, and this is all. The mere fact of inability to pay a hotel bill is not made a crime.[10]

The statutes are akin to the statutes punishing one who obtains property by false pretenses, and are to be interpreted in the same way. The false pretense by means of which the board is obtained must therefore be made with reference to a past or existing fact; a promise to do something in the future is not such a false pretense as to justify a conviction under the statutes, even if the promise was not kept. Thus, where a boarder promised to pay his board as soon as he drew his

---

[8]*Id.* at 563.
[9]People v. Nicholson, 25 Misc. 266, 55 N.Y.S. 447 (Onondaga County Ct. 1898).
[10]*Id.* at 267–68.

pay as clerk of the general assembly, but when he drew his pay, he left the inn and the city without paying his board, the statute was not violated.[11]

COTTONREEDER V. STATE
389 So. 2d 1169 (Ala. Crim. App. 1980)

[The facts are omitted. In reviewing a conviction for violating Alabama's hotel fraud statute, the Court of Criminal Appeals reviewed the issue of whether a mere failure to pay constituted a fraudulent misrepresentation by a guest sufficient to sustain the state's burden of proving a *prima facie* case of fraud.]

BOOKOUT, J.: "Alabama, however, is not unique in recognizing the need for criminal legislation for the protection of the innkeeper or hotel owner against fraudulent guests. Indeed, every state in the union and the District of Columbia have enacted legislation to combat this evil. It should be noted that much of the legislation directed toward those who defraud innkeepers had been enacted or revised recently. Some of the original such statutes have been repealed and replaced with theft of services statutes which pay special attention to hotel or lodging accommodations. All such statutes require an intent to defraud, and many statutes, like our own, include *'prima facie'* provisions specifying that proof of certain enumerated acts by the accused will raise a rebuttable presumption of fraudulent intent.

"The validity of these statutes has been upheld, as against contentions that they violate the constitutional provisions of equal protection, or freedom from imprisonment for debt, or that they make the failure to pay a contractual debt a crime. 43A C.J.S. *Inns, Hotels, etc.* § 12 (1978).

"Turning our attention now to our statute in particular, which is worded in the disjunctive, it would be an easy matter to show that appellant 'represented' to Ms. Allred [the motel manager] that he would pay his bill on a weekly basis and then simply 'failed' to pay as promised. Such action on his part, without more, would not amount to an offense under § 34–15–18 [the relevant statute]. If such action were a crime, without a fraudulent intent, it would be unconstitutional in that it would punish persons by imprisonment for the mere failure to pay a debt.

"It is obvious that the 'misrepresentation' referred to in § 34–15–18 is a *fraudulent* misrepresentation. . . . [*Chauncey v. State*, 130 Ala. 71, 30 So. 403 (1901).]

"*If misrepresentations are relied upon as the inducement for the furnishing by the proprietor of the board or lodgings, they must, of necessity, have been made before the board is furnished.* If made after the board has been obtained, they could not have possibly induced the furnishing of it. *Again, the misrepresentation must have been relied upon by the proprietor and have been the controlling inducement to his furnishing the board and lodging.* In short, the proprietor must be shown to have been deceived to his injury. If he knew the representations were false, or if he believed they were

[11]State v. Tull, 42 Mo. App. 324 (1890).

false, or if he did not believe the statement or representation to be true, or if he believed the representation but if they had no influence upon his conduct, no deception was practiced. . . .

"*Deception and injury are of the very essence of the crime.* . . . (Emphasis added.) 130 Ala. at 73, 74, 30 So. 403.

" . . . It should be recognized that fraudulent intent need not be proven by direct substantive evidence, but can be inferred from the accused's conduct and the circumstances of the case. 37 Am. Jur. 2d *Fraud and Deceit* § 439 (1968); *State v. Wagenius*, 99 Idaho 273, 581 P.2d 319, 327 (1978). When a material element of a crime is the fraudulent intent of the accused, both the State and the accused are allowed broad scope in introducing evidence with even the slightest tendency to establish or negate such intent, including evidence of similar fraud. *Brooks v. Commonwealth*, 220 Va. 405, 258 S.E.2d 504 (1979). It has been said that the fertility of man's invention in devising new schemes of fraud is so great that courts have been reluctant to define it, reserving to themselves the liberty to deal with it in whatever form it may present itself. 37 Am. Jur. 2d *Fraud and Deceit* § 1 (1968). Intent to defraud is a question of fact for the jury to be determined from all the facts and circumstances of the case. *People v. Hedrick*, 265 Cal. App. 2d 392, 71 Cal. Rptr. 352 (1968). However, before a jury is permitted to find a verdict of guilty where fraudulent intent is an element of the crime, there must be in connection with the act done attending circumstances which bespeak fraud, a situation where common experience finds a reliable correlation between the act and the corresponding intent. *State v. Inscore*, 592 S.W.2d 809 (Mo. 1980). The State must prove more than the mere failure, refusal, or inability to pay in order to establish a fraudulent intent. [Citations omitted.]

"Since such statutes are penal in nature, they are subject to strict construction, and will not be applied to persons, acts, or omissions not coming within their terms. A mere failure, refusal, or inability to pay does not constitute the offense contemplated by the statutes. Such a statute requires specific intention on the part of the wrongdoer, which cannot be inferred solely from the naked fact of nonpayment. The intention must exist at the time the board of other accommodation is obtained. A conviction cannot be had in the absence of fraud on the part of accused. Where false representations are relied on as the inducement for the furnishing of board, they must have been made before, rather than after, the board is obtained. . . . 43A C.J.S. *Inns, Hotels, etc.* § 12 (1978).

"There was certainly no evidence tending to make out a *prima facie* presumption of fraud pursuant to [the applicable statute]. There is no contention on the part of the State (1) that accommodations were obtained by a false or fictitious show of baggage, (2) that appellant absconded or left the state without paying, (3) that appellant gave a 'bad check' in payment or (4) that he surreptitiously removed his baggage or attempted to do so.

"The State never proved a misrepresentation by the appellant to Ms. Allred, and neither did the State prove that she relied upon a misrepresentation between August 24 and September 21. . . .

"At the end of the State's case in chief, the defense moved to exclude the State's evidence for failure to prove a *prima facie* case. . . . The evidence only shows that appellant promised to pay on each inquiry of Ms. Allred between August 24 and September 21, and on the later date explained that a check from the Southern Christian Leadership Conference was missing. There is no showing by the State that during that period the appellant knew he had no check due him or coming to him from that organization. His explanation for the late payment was never disputed. There was no showing that the appellant knew when he repeatedly promised future payment that he had no means with which to pay. The record is void as to why he failed to pay other than his explanation to Ms. Allred concerning the Southern Christian Leadership Conference check. Therefore, in order to reach the conclusion that appellant had a fraudulent intent, a jury would have to resort to speculation and conjecture rather than rely upon the evidence. The State, therefore, failed to prove a *prima facie* case, and the appellant's motion to exclude should have been granted. . . .

"Reversed and remanded."

In the following case, a finding of statutory hotel fraud was affirmed over the guest's argument that the innkeeper had agreed to defer payment until the end of the guest's stay. Such an agreement was held other than an "express agreement for credit" found in the statute exempting the guest from criminal prosecution.

COMMONWEALTH V. WILSON
16 Mass. App. 369, 451 N.E.2d 727 (1983)

HALE, C.J.: "The defendant was charged with violating G.L. c. 140, § 12, under a complaint which alleged that the defendant 'did without an express agreement for credit, procure food, entertainment or accommodation from an innkeeper without paying therefor and with intent to cheat and defraud the owner, thereof.' A jury of six in a District Court returned a verdict of guilty, and the defendant was sentenced. He claims error in the denial of his motion for a required finding of not guilty.

"It is agreed that in May of 1981, the defendant arrived at the complainant's motel in Ipswich and said that he was in the process of moving and wanted a room at the motel for an indefinite period. The defendant was known to the owner. The defendant asked if he could pay for the charges upon leaving the motel, and the owner said that was fine with her. Thereafter the defendant stayed at the motel for a total of thirty-three days until June 24, 1981. A day or two prior to checking out, the defendant had informed the owner of his intention, and she had instructed her bookkeeper to prepare a bill. The owner was not present when the defendant checked out on June 24, but the motel manager gave the defendant a bill dated that day. The bill was not paid. When several attempts to obtain payment failed, the owner filed the complaint.

"General Laws c. 140, § 12, as amended through St. 1977, c. 284 § 1, provides in pertinent part:

"Whoever puts up in a hotel, motel . . . and, without having an express agreement for credit, procures food, entertainment or accommodation without paying therefor, and with intent to cheat or defraud the owner or keeper thereof . . . shall be punished. . . .

"If there was not an express agreement for credit, that payment for such . . . accommodation . . . was refused upon demand, shall be presumptive evidence of the intent to cheat or defraud referred to herein.

"The only express agreement between the parties was that the defendant could pay his bill when he checked out.

"The defendant contends (1) that the agreement was an express agreement for credit as contemplated by the first paragraph of G.L. c. 140, § 12, and (2) that the Commonwealth cannot take advantage of the 'presumption' in the second paragraph of § 12 as it did not introduce evidence that would 'indicate that the defendant failed to make an agreement for credit.' We treat the two contentions together.

"There is nothing in the arrangement made at the time the defendant arrived at the motel that speaks to an extension of credit beyond the defendant's time of departure from the motel. The charges became due when the defendant checked out. A bill was presented to the defendant at check out, and it was not paid. We construe the agreements for credit referred to in § 12 as contemplating an agreement to delay payment until some time after a person terminates his relation as a guest at the place of accommodation. *See Cottonreeder v. State,* 389 So. 2d 1169, 1171 (Ala. Cr. App. 1980). We regard such a credit agreement to be separate and distinct from the normal procedure of deferring payment until all requested services have been received.

"The jury were warranted in finding beyond reasonable doubt (*Commonwealth v. Latimore,* 378 Mass. 671, 677–678, 393 N.E.2d 370 [1979]), that the presentation of the bill was a demand for payment for the motel accommodations furnished to the defendant, which was refused. They could have inferred from the facts which are set out in the 'Agreed Statement' that there was no agreement for credit with respect to that bill and that the defendant had the intent to cheat the owner of the motel.

"*Judgment affirmed.*"

22:5 *Fraud Must Have Been Committed for Purpose of Obtaining Hotel Accommodations*

The pretense under such statutes must be made for the purpose of obtaining the accommodations. In a Missouri case, *State v. Kingsley,*[12] the defendant registered at the Southern Hotel On July 29 and was assigned to a room. On July 31, she sent for the manager, rented a room as a studio, stating that she was an artist, and inquired when the bills were payable. Being told that they were payable weekly, she said that it would be inconvenient to pay at the end of the week

[12]108 Mo. 135, 18 S.W. 994 (1891).

because she expected a remittance in two weeks, and asked that her bill might be payable then. The manager, without asking from whom she expected the remittance, assented. No remittance coming at the end of two weeks she was, after a few days, excluded from the hotel and indicted under the statute. The Supreme Court held that upon this evidence she should be discharged. Justice Thomas said:

> We do not think it can be fairly inferred from the evidence that defendant in this case stated to the manager of the Southern Hotel that she expected a remittance, for the purpose of obtaining board. She registered at the hotel on June [*sic*] [July] 29, and without being questioned or making any statement she was assigned a room. In this manner she obtained board in the first instance. On June [*sic*] [July] 31, she sent for the manager, and upon inquiry she was informed that bills for board were payable weekly. She replied that she could not pay till the end of two weeks, at which time she expected a remittance. It appears, therefore, that she got board for two days, and she could have continued there for one week, at least, without saying a word about payment of the bills. Persons intending to perpetrate tricks or obtain money, property or other valuable thing[s] by means of a false pretense, do not ordinarily proceed in this way. They usually defer their false statements till they are forced to the wall. Here defendant made the statements voluntarily.[13]

22:6 *Surreptitious Removal of Baggage as Element of Crime*

It is usual for such enactments to make failure to pay the bill or absconding without paying the bill and surreptitiously removing or attempting to remove baggage *prima facie* evidence of guilt. This language must be so interpreted as not to constitute practically an imprisonment for debt, since such imprisonment would be unconstitutional. It cannot therefore be so interpreted as to make the mere refusal to pay a bill sufficient reasonable cause for prosecution and imprisonment. The removal of the baggage surreptitiously must accompany the refusal to pay, in order to have such effect.[14]

A "surreptitious" removal of baggage involves some concealment; if done openly, though at a time when no one was watching, the removal would not be surreptitious, for "the fact that neither appellant nor any of his agents knew that he was going away, or taking his baggage away, does not, of itself, establish that the removal was surreptitious. He may have gone and taken his baggage in the most open and public manner, and yet neither appellant nor any of his agents saw the removal.[15] The approved definition of the word is "done by stealth, or without legitimate authority, made or produced fraudulently; characterized by concealment or underhand dealing; clandestine." Though one of the definitions mentions fraud, the fraud meant is obviously a fraud used to escape the notice of the person interested as, in an example given, the surreptitious edition of a book. The word, by derivation, means taken away secretly. It is therefore ob-

[13]*Id.* at 141.
[14]Hutchinson v. Davis, 58 Ill. App. 358 (1895).
[15]*Id.* at 363.

vious that surreptitious removal is one which is done clandestinely so as to escape the notice of the innkeeper by reason of the method of doing it.

22:7 Rebutting the Presumption of Fraudulent Intent

In *People v. Dukatt*,[16] the complainants alleged that, with intent to defraud, defendants had registered as guests at the Hotel New Yorker in the city of New York and had failed, upon demand, to pay for room rent, restaurant, laundry, telephone, and valet service. There was evidence that each defendant, carrying baggage, had registered at the hotel with his wife and family; that neither had established credit; that when one defendant had been at the hotel for three days and the other for five days, demand had been made upon them for payment of their bills; that they had failed to make such payment but had tendered a check on the Riggs National Bank of Washington, D.C., to cover both bills, which the hotel refused to accept.

Testimony that the hotel had learned by telephone that neither defendant had an account in the Riggs Bank was stricken as hearsay. The credit manager of the Waldorf-Astoria Hotel testified that the defendant Hillman had been a guest there on a number of occasions. Just prior to registering at the Hotel New Yorker, the defendant Hillman had been registered at the Waldorf-Astoria and upon failure to pay his bill upon demand had been "locked out" and his baggage withheld. The defendant Dukatt offered to go out and get the cash to pay his bill but was refused permission to do so. No attempt was made by either of the defendants to leave the hotel to avoid payment of their bills.

A memorandum decision by the court stated: "Judgments reversed and new trials ordered upon the ground that the undisputed evidence is that defendants tendered a check in payment for their lodging and other accommodations upon demand by the hotel; in the absence of competent evidence that the check was worthless, such tender overcomes the presumption created by section 925 [now section 165.15—J.E.H.S.] of the Penal Law."

This approach is generally followed in other states as well.

22:8 Abuse of Statute as Malicious Prosecution: Representative Cases

COOPER v. SCHIRRMEISTER
176 Misc. 474, 26 N.Y.S.2d 668 (N.Y. City Ct. 1941)

MADIGAN, J.: "This is a non-jury action for malicious prosecution. The plaintiff was charged with a misdemeanor under Section 925 of the Penal Law, relating to frauds on hotelkeepers and others.

"He and his family occupied, under a lease for a term of six months, a small furnished apartment in a building at 305 West Eighty-eighth Street, New York

---

[16]298 N.Y. 545, 81 N.E.2d 93 (1948).

city, called the Hotel Oxford, owned and operated by the corporate defendant. The other defendant was in charge of the premises. . . .

"In the Court of Special Sessions it was held, in effect, that Section 925 of the Penal Law could not under the circumstances be successfully invoked inasmuch as the relationship between the corporate defendant and plaintiff was not that of hotel keeper and guest as these defendants assert. That court dismissed the charge at the end of the People's case. No evidence was taken from this plaintiff. No finding of fact was made as to any contest issue. . . .

"It is held that, so far as concerns the demise to this plaintiff, the premises did not constitute a hotel within the meaning of Section 925 of the Penal Law.

"As to plaintiff the corporate defendant was either the keeper of an apartment hotel or the landlord of an apartment house.

"For defendants it is urged that Section 925 of the Penal Law applied to apartment hotels; that as employed in such statute the term 'hotel' includes an 'apartment hotel.' . . .

"Defendants, however, are confronted with the fact that the Legislature has not inserted the term 'apartment hotel' in Section 925 of the Penal Law. This must be held deliberate in the absence of any expression or action on the part of the Legislature which might be deemed a sufficient basis for ascribing a different intent to the lawmakers.

"It is well to note, moreover, that statutes antecedent to the present Section 925 of the Penal Law apparently go back some sixty years, to a time when 'hotel' could not mean 'apartment hotel' inasmuch as the apartment hotel of this day was then unknown.

"As indicating the fraud which defendants charged in support of the prosecution under Section 925 of the Penal Law, they assert that plaintiff and members of his family removed their belongings, on a night in August, 1939, after nine o'clock, through a service exit without passing the desk near the main entrance. Plaintiff denies that anything was taken out surreptitiously. However, he had hired an apartment in another building and he had stipulated there for free occupancy until October 1, 1939. He apparently did not announce at the desk in the building conducted by the corporate defendant that he was leaving and he left no forwarding address.

"It is found that plaintiff departed from the 'Hotel Oxford' with his effects and those of his family without the knowledge or consent of defendants, though it had been suspected that he was about to leave somewhat as he did. It is also found that his purpose was to avoid paying his bill for rent, electricity and telephone service. . . .

" . . . [E]lements in the evidence lead to the conclusion that defendants knew that it was venturesome to institute and prosecute the criminal charge and that nevertheless they proceeded in the hope that, by pressing plaintiff, they might bring him to pay his debt to them.

"Lack of probable cause and actual malice are found.

"Plaintiff is entitled to punitive damages.

"Plaintiff's motion to dismiss the defense set up in the answer is granted. . . .

"Defendants' motions to dismiss are denied.

"The claim as to humiliation has been considered, but it is believed that plaintiff suffered but very little humiliation.

"Judgment for $350 in favor of plaintiff and against defendants. That amount includes exemplary damages."

The following case discusses the elements of a cause of action for malicious prosecution by a user of hotel services who was criminally charged with hotel fraud under the applicable Puerto Rico law. Note that the user failed in his attempt to hold the hotel legally responsible.

VINCE V. POSADAS DE PUERTO RICO, S.A.
683 F. Supp. 312 (D. Puerto Rico 1988)

ACOSTA, District Judge: "Plaintiffs brought this action pursuant to our diversity jurisdiction, 28 U.S.C. § 1332, seeking over one billion dollars in damages for defendants' alleged malicious prosecution.

"Before the Court is a motion for dismissal and/or summary judgment filed by defendants. . . .

"Defendants argue that plaintiffs have not and cannot, as a matter of the applicable Puerto Rico law, prove a cause of action for malicious prosecution. Plaintiffs, in opposition, do little more than rest on their allegations.

"The record is now complete and the Court is fully briefed and ready to adjudicate this matter. . . .

Factual Background

"1. On or about August 26, 1983, Mr. Mohan Vyas Sanguida registered as a guest at the Condado Holiday Inn. From August 1983 to late January 1984, co-plaintiff Vito Vince ('Vince') paid all monies owed for lodging, food, and services provided to Vyas (and Vince) by the Hotel. (Vince's Aff. pp. 1–3) The credit manager of the Hotel would communicate with Vince, who then proceeded to periodically make partial payments towards the Hotel debt incurred by Vyas and/or Vince. (Vince's Aff. p. 2; Pérez's Aff. p. 2). However, a pattern of late payments occurred.

"2. By April 10, 1984 the rising hotel bill for room and services, for a three-month period, was $21,037.96. Throughout that period Vince repeatedly refused to pay the sums demanded by the Hotel and, according to Vince, he advised the credit manager in conversations held on late January and early March 1984, that he would not be responsible, after January 1984, for Vyas' account at the Hotel (Vince's Aff. pp. 2–3). Vince also states that he refused responsibility for the hotel bill because after late January 1984 he was not, despite many requests, an officially registered guest at the Hotel due solely to the lack of vacancies (Vince's Aff. pp. 2–3). However, it is undisputed that from February to April 1984, Vince and Vyas shared the same hotel room and jointly used the hotel services (Vince's Aff. pp. 2–3; Pérez's Aff. pp. 2–4).

"3. After numerous unsuccessful attempts by defendants to collect the monies owed by Vyas and Vince for room and services provided by the Hotel, defendants informed the police of a potential violation of the Innkeeper's Law. On April 10, 1984, almost four months after Vince stopped making partial payments to the hotel, the police went to the Hotel to investigate Vyas and Vince's nonpayment of their hotel bill.

"4. As a result of the above-mentioned police investigation, police agent Lucas Aponte (Badge No. 9380) pursuant to the Innkeeper's Law filed a criminal complaint ('denuncia') on April 10, 1984, against Vyas and Vince for their nonpayment of the sum of $21,037.96 owed for room and services provided by the Hotel. Immediately afterwards, Vyas and Vince were taken by the police before a district court judge who determined that the evidence gathered by the police was sufficient to establish the existence of probable cause to arrest Vyas and Vince for violation of the Innkeeper's Law. The judge ordered the arrest of Vyas and Vince and set bail. At that time, neither Vyas nor Vince were [*sic*] able to post bail and thus the judge ordered their incarceration. At no time did the Hotel itself file a criminal complaint against either Vyas or Vince.

"5. On May 10, 1984, at a preliminary hearing, another district court judge determined that the evidence gathered by the district attorney ('Fiscal') was sufficient to establish the existence of probable cause for trial against Vyas, but not against Vince, for violation of the Innkeeper's Law. The district attorney appealed to the superior court the decision of the district court judge regarding Vince. The superior court vacated the district court's decision and found probable cause for trial against Vince for violation of the Innkeeper's Law.

"6. On June 15, 1984, the charges against Vyas and Vince were dismissed by the Superior Court of Puerto Rico, San Juan Part.

"7. On September 12, 1984, plaintiffs herein filed the instant action for damages for alleged malicious prosecution.

"8. On June 14, 1985, Vyas filed suit against the Hotel, among others, for damages caused by the Hotel's alleged malicious prosecution. On May 5, 1987, this Court (Judge FUSTÉ) found that the facts of the case entitled defendants to summary judgment because ' . . . the mere *bona fide* reporting to the police of a *prima facie* violation of the law does not establish a tort cause of action. . . . ' The Court's judgment became firm and final on June 4, 1987.

Discussion

" . . .

"After viewing the record in the light most favorable to plaintiffs, *see Poller v. Columbia Broadcasting System*, 368 U.S. 464, 473, 82 S. Ct. 486, 491, 7 L. Ed. 2d 458 (1962), we find that they will be unable to discharge their burden at trial of establishing the existence of at least one, if not more, of the elements essential to sustain their cause of action for malicious prosecution. Hence, summary judgment is appropriate. Fed. R. Civ. P. 56; [Citations omitted]. And no further exploration of the facts (beyond the record) is necessary since there is no genuine dispute as to the material facts leading up to Vince's arrest. [Citation omitted.]

"To maintain an action for malicious prosecution plaintiff must prove *all* of the following elements: (1) the criminal action was initiated and instigated by defendants; (2) the criminal action terminated in favor of plaintiffs; (3) defendants acted with malice; (4) defendants acted without probable cause; *and* (5) as a consequence plaintiffs suffered damages. Art. 1802 of the Puerto Rico Civil Code, 31 L.P.R.A. 5141; *Raldiris v. Levitt & Sons of P.R., Inc.*, 103 D.P.R. 778 (1975); *Parés v. Ruiz*, 19 P.R.R. 323 (1913). *See also Ayala v. San Juan Racing Corp.*, 112 D.P.R. 804, 810 (1982).

"After more than three (3) years conducting discovery, defendants are entitled to judgment as a matter of law because plaintiffs have failed, when put to the task by defendants' motion, to make a sufficient showing on at least one essential element of their action for malicious prosecution for which they have the burden of proof. The main element they have completely failed to support in their opposition is that defendants acted without probable cause.

"Where, as here, there is sufficient evidence to establish the existence of probable cause to arrest, plaintiffs' action for malicious prosecution is effectively barred. *Palhava De Varella-Cid v. Boston Five Cents Savings Bank*, 787 F.2d 676 (1st Cir. 1986). In the instant case, the courts of Puerto Rico found probable cause to arrest and to initially process Vince. This finding of probable cause not only justifies defendants' actions in terms of reasonableness, but exonerates them of civil liability as well.

"Under Puerto Rico law, the standard of probable cause in an action for malicious prosecution is whether or not the circumstances surrounding the arrest would cause a reasonable person to believe the charge made by defendants. *See Parés, supra* at 330. Worded differently, the issue is whether or not defendants acted reasonably in calling the police regarding Vince's nonpayment of his hotel bill.

"In essence, the defendants, as the superior court later determined based on the same evidence, had probable cause to act the way they did, i.e., defendants were reasonably prudent, as was the police officer who filed the complaint against Vince, in suspecting that Vince was violating the Innkeeper's Law. The fact that the evidence was insufficient to convict Vince does not undermine the reasonableness of defendants' actions since the evidentiary standards for conviction are higher than those for arrest insofar as the Innkeeper's Law creates a *presumption* of fraudulent intent upon evidence that payment was demanded but not made whereas at trial the *actual* intent to defraud must be conclusively proven. 10 L.P.R.A. § 716(a) ('evidence that any person refused or neglected to pay for /hotel services/ on demand . . . shall be deemed to constitute presumptive evidence of fraudulent intent.') *See also Palhava*, 787 F.2d at 679; Herminio Brau, Daños y Perjuicios Extracontractuales, page 111 (2nd ed. 1987) (the subsequent acquittal of defendant does not comprise evidence of lack of probable cause). . . .

" . . . Moreover, Vince's argument that he was not an officially registered guest at the Hotel is of no consequence. The Innkeeper's Law prohibits 'any person' from fraudulently refusing or neglecting to pay for hotel services. 10 L.P.R.A. § 716(a). In addition, the law defines a 'guest' as including 'not only those individuals who are registered at the hotel and to whom bedrooms are assigned but /also/ . . . (2) any person entering the premises of a hotel with the intent of being a guest, whether or not he becomes said guest, and (3) any person found in the premises of a hotel with the purpose of enjoying the facilities provided for recreation and amusement. . . . '' Not only was Vince enjoying the facilities of the Hotel at all times, he has also admitted that he intended, at all times, to become an officially registered guest. (Vince's Aff. pp. 2–3) . . .

" . . . In the present case plaintiff admits that the Hotel repeatedly demanded payment and that he did not pay. These demands made by the Hotel over an extended period at the very least gave Vince notice that whatever continuing credit line he thought he had, in fact no longer existed. Moreover, defendants' attempts to institute a payment schedule with Vince are not inconsistent with their later attempt to achieve payment in full once the schedule had obviously failed. In any case, the Innkeeper's Law authorizes a hotel to demand and receive immediately, under penalty of criminal prosecution, payment for services rendered regardless of a guest's expectations of credit. So long as that demand is made clearly and reasonably and a debt is valid and due, then a guest such as Vince must simply pay their bill. Defendants acted reasonably in attempting to secure Vince's payment of hotel services he was enjoying and they continued to act reasonably by notifying the police when their efforts to get Vince to pay his bill failed. The information provided to the police was true, and made with reasonable basis. It is undisputed that Vince was sharing the hotel room with Vyas, and using the hotel services at all relevant times. When the police was contacted by the Hotel, Vyas and Vince owed in excess of $21,000.00 for food, services, and lodging. Once the competent authorities were informed that a reasonable basis existed to believe a felony (violation of the Innkeeper's Law) had been committed, the action taken by the police was not only beyond defendants' control, but did not entail any civil responsibility. *García Calderón v. Galinañez Hnos.*, 83 P.R.R. 307, 309 (1961), *Jiménez v. Sánchez*, 76 P.R.R. 347 (1954). In addition, there exists a social interest in having a citizen inform the authorities about the commission of potential crimes. *Raldiris, supra,* 103 D.P.R. at 781; *Jiménez v. Sánchez*, 60 P.R.R. 406 (1942). . . .

Conclusion

"In accordance with the above, the complaint is DISMISSED with prejudice. . . .

"IT IS SO ORDERED."

22:9 *Bad-Check Laws*

Statistics prove that the vast majority of checks in circulation are paid when presented to the drawee banks. With growing frequency it happens, however, that someone, who may well be an innkeeper, takes a loss upon a ''bad check.'' He then learns that, although a check is a substitute for money, it is not money.

All states have enacted statutes making the issuing and passing of bad checks a punishable crime. Since the statutes vary from state to state, it is necessary to consult the statute of each particular state in relation to bad checks passed or accepted in that state.

PART VI

Innkeeper's Rights and
Responsibilities on the
International Level

23 International Aspects of Innkeeper-Guest Liability

23:1 *Introduction*

Since the early 1930s there has been a significant multinational effort to rationalize the myriad conflicting and often contradictory international laws governing the international traveler in his relations with the hotelkeeper. This movement stemmed from the recognition that international travel represented a growing segment of foreign income vital to the development of many nations' economies. The elimination of unnecessary travel barriers to individuals and groups whose presence was sought to stabilize international economic and cultural relations was also viewed as desirable. This chapter makes brief mention of these developments, identifying areas of present concern and noting a possible vehicle for their solution.

Three major concerns, described in sections 23:2, 23:3, and 23:4, confront both innkeeper and guest where the traveler makes known to the innkeeper his wish to secure accommodations and the innkeeper agrees to accommodate the traveler on terms and conditions mutually agreed upon.

23:2 *Breach of Reservation*

A breach of the reservation contract by either party is possible for causes over which the breaching party has no control or for causes attributable to his negligence or willful conduct. Either or both parties may suffer loss as a result. For example, a prospective guest, upon arrival in a distant, foreign country, tired after a long journey and unfamiliar with the language and customs of his host, finds that there is no room at the inn. No doubt, if he can establish that the failure to honor his reservation was caused by the act or omission of the innkeeper, he may eventually recover damages, assuming that the legal system of his host authorizes such a recovery. But recovery of damages is not his immediate concern. He needs some assurance that reasonably comparable accommodations

This chapter is a synopsis of "The UNIDROIT Draft Convention on the Hotelkeeper's Contract: A Major Attempt to Unify the Law Governing Innkeeper-Guest Liability," by Rodney E. Gould, Thomas J. Ramsey, and John E. H. Sherry, from the Cornell International Law Journal, volume 13, winter 1980, with permission.

can be found for the night, at no additional cost, to carry him over until matters can be rectified the following day.

The innkeeper also bears certain risks in his relations with the traveler, particularly if the traveler is not known to him from previous dealings. The traveler may fail to appear to honor his bargain at the place, date, and time agreed upon. If the innkeeper is unable to recoup the lost income, which could be extensive in the case of a group booking for a summer season, he may undergo severe financial hardship. The traveler or travelers, whether a group of businesspersons or sojourners or a single family on holiday, may never show up. A lawsuit, theoretically possible, may be rendered futile if the breaching party cannot be located and if, in the event that the complaint can be served, the claim must be litigated in a foreign jurisdiction. Thus some mechanism is necessary to assure the innkeeper some advance compensation to secure performance and at the same time to give the traveler a means of canceling his reservation in the event of illness, breakdown in transportation, or other cause beyond his control. This same kind of remedy must also be made available to the innkeeper to relieve him of responsibility in cases of fire, flood, earthquake, or other natural calamity, as well as other defined circumstances beyond his control.

23:3 *Personal Injury*

Assuming that our hypothetical traveler has gained entrance to the inn and has been accommodated, it is necessary to provide him a reasonable measure of personal protection, including courteous and considerate treatment by the innkeeper and his employees. He should have redress for a variety of possible physical injuries caused by acts or omissions attributable to the innkeeper. Each potential cause of action can and often is treated differently by each country in which the traveler may reside. Some may recognize a specific cause of action; some may not. Further, different jurisdictions may provide different remedies in identical circumstances. The applicable standard of care for both parties may vary as well. Different rules regarding conduct or circumstances excusing or mitigating liability may apply.

To illustrate, our traveler would be entitled to rely on a breach of implied warranty theory of responsibility for food and beverages served him by the innkeeper in the United States. This means that the innkeeper guarantees that the items served are fit for human consumption by operation of law, even absent any express guarantee communicated to the guest. This doctrine is not recognized generally in civil law countries. Some fault or negligence has to be proven in order to secure compensation for such injuries—a task that may prove impossible in a foreign jurisdiction.

23:4 *Property Loss or Damage*

If our traveler has escaped the pitfalls of a breach of his reservation and potential personal injuries, he still may succumb to a loss of his personal property.

All jurisdictions provide remedies for property losses, limiting liability for particular types of property to relieve the innkeeper of excessive liability arising by reason of the traditional strict responsibility for property losses otherwise imposed.

However, as is the case with breach of reservation and personal injury claims, the right to recover may depend on the fortuitous situs of the loss, often with startlingly different results, even if the property involved and the cause of the loss are identical.

For example, a British tourist traveling in New York who brings negotiable securities with him is required by New York law to deposit the securities in the hotel safe. If he does not deposit the securities, he cannot recover for their loss so long as the innkeeper has posted the required statutory notices in the public rooms of the hotel. Furthermore, the innkeeper's liability for deposited valuables is limited to $500. If the same British tourist were to stay in a London hotel, the London hotelkeeper would be fully and absolutely liable for the loss of any property he accepts for deposit.

Common sense dictates that the guest will wish to recover for property lost or damaged in proportion to the value of that property. Business sense dictates that the innkeeper will wish to limit his liability to the bare minimum regardless of the value of the property lost or damaged. Laws in the United States reflect the industry view and fix monetary ceilings at relatively low levels that are unrelated to changes in economic conditions. Some civil law systems use a variable system of compensation tied to the current room rate times a multiplier, but do not limit liability for deposited valuables. Others employ a fixed compensation ceiling, but again make no attempt to limit liability for deposited valuables.

A reasonable compromise between the two systems is desirable and feasible. A variable system based on current room rates and a multiplier that would distinguish between valuables deposited for safekeeping and other property left in the room or checked with the innkeeper has merit for a number of reasons. First, it involves self-regulation by the industry; each innkeeper remains free to set room rates in accordance with his individual requirements in his relevant market. No governmental regulation is required. Second, the method reflects current economic realities and the overall principle that the innkeeper should provide a standard of security geared to the nature, class, and size of his property. The luxury owner charging a higher room rate would be expected to compensate for property lost or damaged at a higher rate. The innkeeper of a more modest family inn would not assume the same burden.

Third, the system is flexible; no single jurisdiction is required to alter its own regulatory scheme governing hotel rates and classifications. Thus the adoption of any system of variable monetary ceilings would not be a disadvantage to those countries that regulate rates.

The only controversial feature of any such system is how high the multiplier for each category of property should be. There is no argument that the multiplier for deposited valuables should be higher than the multiplier for other guest property. The size of the multiplier should be a matter for negotiation and resolution through compromise. It is not an insurmountable problem in view of the equity of the system as a whole to innkeeper and guest.

23:5 *A Possible Solution*

After many years of discussion and review, the International Institute for the Unification of Private Law (UNIDROIT) drafted a Convention on the Hotel-keeper's Contract dealing with these broad concerns and interrelated issues. The draft convention was circulated among the participating countries with the hope that a diplomatic conference would be convened so that the convention could be approved and opened for signature. The convention, upon ratification by the required number of countries, would then enter into force. Such ratification has not yet occurred.

23:6 *A Uniform Approach to the Legal Aspects of Tourism and Travel Abroad*

In 1987 UNIDROIT convened its Third World Congress on Uniform International Law in Practice. For the published proceedings of the Congress, the United States representative submitted a paper on the final drafting session of the Draft Convention on the Hotelkeeper's Contract.[1] Essentially, the paper examined recent international tourism and travel matters, including a proposal to revise the convention governing tourists and travel agents (CCV), the current status of the draft Hotelkeeper's Contract, the parallel work of the World Tourism Organization on security and legal protection of tourists, as well as an examination of China's wish to regularize its laws concerning international tourists and its international hotel and tourism industry. A brief reference is made to terrorism as it affects tourism and the need to establish a mechanism to combat its effects. No further action on the Draft Convention on the Hotelkeeper's Contract was taken at the Congress.

---

[1] J. E. H. Sherry, *A Uniform Approach to Legal Aspects of Travel and Tourism Abroad.* International Uniform Law in Practice, 506–508 (1988).

PART VII

Selected Hospitality-related
Legal Concerns

24 Employment Law

24:1 *Employer Rights at Common Law*

At common law, employers had virtually unlimited authority to hire, discipline, or discharge their employees for any or no reason. This right, often called the employment-at-will doctrine,[1] has been eroded by a growing number of courts that recognize a cause of action for wrongful discharge based on public policy. A sampling of cases from various jurisdictions which have grappled with this issue, not only in terms of employer liability, but also in terms of the proper damage remedy, is presented below.

In the case that follows, the Supreme Court of Illinois held that a tort action for retaliatory discharge of a managerial employee who reported to law enforcement authorities that other employees were involved in criminal wrongdoing was improperly dismissed as a matter of law. Excerpts from the majority and dissenting opinions follow.

PALMATEER V. INTERNATIONAL HARVESTER CO.
85 Ill. 2d 124,421 N.E.2d 876 (1981)

SIMON, J.: "The plaintiff, Ray Palmateer, complains of his discharge by International Harvester Company (IH). He had worked for IH for 16 years, rising from a unionized job at an hourly rate to a managerial position on a fixed salary. Following his discharge, Palmateer filed a four-count complaint against IH, alleging in count II that he had suffered a retaliatory discharge. According to the complaint, Palmateer was fired both for supplying information to local law-enforcement authorities that an IH employee might be involved in a violation of the Criminal Code of 1961 (Ill. Rev. Stat. 1979, ch. 38, par. 1–1 *et seq.*) and for agreeing to assist in the investigation and trial of the employee if requested. The circuit court of Rock Island County ruled the complaint failed to state a cause of action and dismissed it; the appellate court affirmed in a divided opinion. (85 Ill. App. 3d 50, 40 Ill. Dec. 589, 406 N.E.2d 595.) We granted Palmateer leave to appeal to determine the contours of the tort of retaliatory

---

[1]The enunciation and justification of the doctrine is contained in Payne v. Western and Atlantic R.R. Co., 81 Tenn. (13 Lea) 507, at 518–20 (1884).

discharge approved in *Kelsay v. Motorola, Inc.* (1978), 74 Ill. 2d 172, 23 Ill. Dec. 559, 384 N.E.2d 353.

"In *Kelsay* the plaintiff was discharged in retaliation for filing a worker's compensation claim. The court noted that public policy strongly favored the exercise of worker's compensation rights; if employees could be fired for filing compensation claims, that public policy would be frustrated. Despite a dissent urging that the creation of a new tort should be left to the legislature, the court said, 'We are convinced that to uphold and implement this public policy a cause of action should exist for retaliatory discharge.' (74 Ill. 2d 172, 181, 23 Ill. Dec. 559, 384 N.E.2d 353.) The court then considered the claim for damages, and decided that punitive damages would be allowed in retaliatory discharge cases, but only in the future.

"With *Kelsay*, Illinois joined the growing number of States recognizing the tort of retaliatory discharge. The tort is an exception to the general rule that an 'at-will' employment is terminable at any time for any or no cause. (*Pleasure Driveway & Park District v. Jones* (1977), 51 Ill. App. 3d 182, 190, 9 Ill. Dec. 677, 367 N.E.2d 111.) This general rule is a harsh outgrowth of the notion of reciprocal rights and obligations in employment relationships—that if the employee can end his employment at any time under any condition, then the employer should have the same right. (Summers, *Individual Protection against Unjust Dismissal: Time for a Statute*, 62 Va. L. Rev. 481, 484–85 (1976).) As one 19th century court put it:

"May I not refuse to trade with any one? May I not forbid my family to trade with any one? May I not dismiss my domestic servant for dealing, or even visiting, where I forbid? And if my domestic, why not my farm-hand, or my mechanic or teamster? . . .

" . . . All may dismiss their employees at will, be they many or few, for good cause, for no cause or even for cause morally wrong, without being thereby guilty of legal wrong. *Payne v. Western & Atlantic R.R. Co.* (1884), 81 Tenn. (13 Lea) 507, 518–20.

"Recent analysis has pointed out the shortcomings of the mutuality theory. With the rise of large corporations conducting specialized operations and employing relatively immobile workers who often have no other place to market their skills, recognition that the employer and employee do not stand on equal footing is realistic (Blades, *Employment At Will vs. Individual Freedom: On Limiting the Abusive Exercise of Employer Power*, 67 Colum. L. Rev. 1404, 1405 (1967).) In addition, unchecked employer power, like unchecked employee power, has been seen to present a distinct threat to the public policy carefully considered and adopted by society as a whole. As a result, it is now recognized that a proper balance must be maintained among the employer's interest in operating a business efficiently and profitably, the employee's interest in earning a livelihood, and society's interest in seeing its public policies carried out.

"By recognizing the tort of retaliatory discharge, *Kelsay* acknowledged the common law principle that parties to a contract may not incorporate in it rights and obligations which are clearly injurious to the public. (*See People ex rel. Peabody v. Chicago Gas Trust Co.* (1889), 130 Ill. 268, 294, 22 N.E. 798.) . . .

" . . . But the Achilles heel of the principle lies in the definition of public policy. When a discharge contravenes public policy in any way the employer has committed a legal wrong. However, the employer retains the right to fire workers at will in cases 'where no clear mandate of public policy is involved' (*Leach v. Lauhoff Grain Co.*, (1977), 51 Ill. App. 3d 1022, 1026, 9 Ill. Dec. 634, 366 N.E.2d 1145). But what constitutes clearly mandated public policy?

"There is no precise definition of the term. In general, it can be said that public policy concerns what is right and just and what affects the citizens of the State collectively. It is to be found in the State's constitution and statutes and, when they are silent, in its judicial decisions. (*Smith v. Board of Education* (1950), 405 Ill. 143, 147, 89 N.E. 893.) Although there is no precise line of demarcation dividing matters that are the subject of public policies from matters purely personal, a survey of cases in other States involving retaliatory discharges shows that a matter must strike at the heart of a citizen's social rights, duties, and responsibilities before the tort will be allowed.

"The cause of action is allowed where the public policy is clear, but is denied where it is equally clear that only private interests are at stake. Where the nature of the interest at stake is muddled, the courts have given conflicting answers as to whether the protection of the tort action is available. Compare the inconsistent results where the discharge was for opposition to sexual discrimination or harassment (*McCluney v. Jos. Schlitz Brewing Co.* (E.D. Wis. 1980), 489 F. Supp. 24, and *Monge v. Beebe Rubber Co.* (1974), 114 N.H. 130, 316 A.2d 549), for refusal to falsify official reports (*Hinrichs v. Tranquilaire Hospital* (Ala. 1977), 352 So. 2d 1130, and *Trombetta v. Detroit, Toledo & Ironton R.R. Co.* (1978), 81 Mich. App. 489, 265 N.W.2d 385), and over internal company disputes regarding product safety (*Geary v. United States Steel Corp.* (1974), 456 Pa. 171, 319 A.2d 174, and *Pierce v. Ortho Pharmaceutical Corp.* (1979), 166 N.J. Super. 335, 399 A.2d 1023).

"It is clear that Palmateer has here alleged that he was fired in violation of an established public policy. The claim is that he was discharged for supplying information to a local law-enforcement agency that an IH employee might be violating the Criminal Code, for agreeing to gather further evidence implicating the employee, and for intending to testify at the employee's trial, if it came to that. . . . There is no public policy more basic, nothing more implicit in the concept of ordered liberty (*see Palko v. Connecticut* (1937), 302 U.S. 319, 325, 58 S. Ct. 149, 152, 82 L. Ed. 288, 292), than the enforcement of a State's criminal code. (*See Hewitt v. Hewitt* (1979), 77 Ill. 2d 49, 61–62, 31 Ill. Dec. 827, 394 N.E.2d 1204; *Jarrett v. Jarrett* (1979), 78 Ill. 2d 337, 345, 36 Ill. Dec. 1, 400 N.E.2d 421.) There is no public policy more important or more fundamental than the one favoring the effective protection of the lives and property of citizens. *See* Ill. Const. 1970, Preamble; *Marbury v. Madison* (1803), 5 U.S. (1 Cranch) 137, 163, 2 L. Ed. 60, 69 . . .

"The foundation of the tort of retaliatory discharge lies in the protection of public policy, and there is a clear public policy favoring investigation and prosecution of criminal offenses. Palmateer has stated a cause of action for retaliatory discharge.

"IH contends that even if there is a public policy discouraging violations of the Criminal Code, that public policy has too wide a sweep. IH points out that the crime here might be nothing more than the theft of a $2 screwdriver. It feels that in the exercise of its sound business judgment it ought to be able to properly fire a managerial employee who recklessly and precipitously resorts to the criminal justice system to handle such a personnel problem. But this response misses the point. The magnitude of the crime is not the issue here. It was the General Assembly, the People's representatives, who decided that the theft of a $2 screwdriver was a problem that should be resolved by resort to the criminal justice system. IH's business judgment, no matter how sound, cannot override that decision. '[T]he employer is not so absolute a sovereign of the job that there are not limits to his prerogative.' (*Tameny v. Atlantic Richfield Co.* (1980), 27 Cal. 3d 167, 178, 164 Cal. Rptr. 839, 845, 610 P.2d 1330, 1336.) The law is feeble indeed if it permits IH to take matters into its own hands by retaliating against its employees who cooperate in enforcing the law . . .

"*Appellate court affirmed in part and reversed in part; circuit court affirmed in part and reversed in part; cause remanded, with directions.*"

RYAN, J. (dissenting):

"Although I authored the opinion in *Kelsay v. Motorola, Inc.* (1978), 74 Ill. 2d 172, 23 Ill. Dec. 559, 384 N.E.2d 353, I cannot agree to extend the cause of action for retaliatory discharge approved in that case into the nebulous area of judicially created public policy, as has been done by the opinion in this case. I fear that the result of this opinion will indeed fulfill the prophesy of Mr. Justice UNDERWOOD's dissent in *Kelsay*. 'Henceforth, no matter how indolent, insubordinate or obnoxious any employee may be, . . . [the] employer may thereafter discharge him only at the risk of being compelled to defend a suit for retaliatory discharge and unlimited punitive damages. . . . ' *Kelsay v. Motorola, Inc.* (1978), 74 Ill. 2d 172, 192, 23 Ill. Dec. 559, 384 N.E.2d 353.

"*Kelsay* relied on the fact that the legislature had clearly established the public policy that injured workers had a right to file claims for compensation with the Industrial Commission. We there held that discharging the employee for filing such a claim violated that public policy. Here the public policy supporting the cause of action cannot be found in any expression of the legislature, but only the vague belief that public policy requires that we all become 'citizen crime-fighters' (85 Ill. 2d at 132, 52 Ill. Dec. at 17, 421 N.E.2d at 880). . . .

"Because of the vagueness of the concept of public policy, most of the jurisdictions that have allowed a discharged employee to maintain a cause of action for retaliatory discharge have required that the public policy against such discharge be *clear* and *well-defined*, that the mandate of public policy be *clear* and *compelling*, and that there be *strong public policy* against such discharge. *Percival v. General Motors Corp.* (E.D. Mo. 1975), 400 F. Supp. 1322, *aff'd* (8th

Cir. 1976), 539 F.2d 1126; *Campbell v. Ford Industries, Inc.* (1976), 274 Or. 243, 546 P.2d 141; *Jones v. Keogh* (1979), 137 Vt. 562, 409 A.2d 581; *Harless v. First National Bank* (W. Va. 1978), 246 S.E.2d 270; *Geary v. United States Steel Corp.* (1974), 456 Pa. 171, 319 A.2d 174. . . .

"In two cases usually discussed by courts considering retaliatory discharge, recovery was permitted in actions for retaliatory discharge based on 'bad faith.' In *Monge v. Beebe Rubber Co.* (1974), 114 N.H. 130, 316 A.2d 549, a female employee was discharged after she refused to go out with her foreman. The New Hampshire Supreme Court held that the termination of employment motivated by bad faith or malice was based on retaliation, constituting a breach of the employment contract. In *Fortune v. National Cash Register Co.* (1977), 373 Mass. 96, 364 N.E.2d 1251, a salesman sued his former employer after he was discharged. The court held that the contract of employment contained an implied covenant of good faith and fair dealing and that a termination not made in good faith constitutes a breach of the contract. These cases are readily distinguishable from the strong-public-policy line of cases, in that, in the last two cases discussed, recovery was sought and allowed for breach of contract and not for a tort, and punitive damages were not sought. . . .

"By departing from the general rule that an at-will employment is terminable at the discretion of the employer, the courts are attempting to give recognition to the desire and expectation of an employee in continued employment. In doing so, however, the courts should not concentrate solely on promoting the employee's expectations. The courts must recognize that the allowance of a tort action for retaliatory discharge is a departure from, and an exception to, the general rule. The legitimate interest of the employer in guiding the policies and destiny of his operation cannot be ignored. The new tort of retaliatory discharge is in its infancy. In nurturing and shaping this remedy, courts must balance the interests of employee and employer with the hope of fashioning a remedy that will accommodate the legitimate expectations of both. In the process of emerging from the harshness of the former rule, we must guard against swinging the pendulum to the opposite extreme. In *Percival v. General Motors Corp.* (8th Cir. 1976), 539 F.2d 1126, 1130, the court stated:

"It should be kept in mind that as far as an employment relationship is concerned, an employer as well as an employee has rights; . . .

"The district court opinion in *Percival* stated:

"The courts which have recognized this nonstatutory cause of action have done so *cautiously,* recognizing that a *proper balance* must be maintained between the employee's interest in earning his livelihood and the employer's interest in operating his business efficiently and profitably. (Emphasis added.) *Percival v. General Motors Corp.* (E.D. Mo. 1975), 400 F. Supp. 1322, 1323.

" . . . In order to establish the necessary balance between employer and employee interests, I would hold that the employee may maintain an action for retaliatory discharge only when the discharge has been violative of some *strong* public policy that has been *clearly* articulated. Usually, that clear articulation would be found in legislative enactment. I do not think that an employer should be compelled to defend a tort action and possibly, be forced to pay a disgruntled discharged employee compensatory, and possibly substantial, punitive damages because of a violation of some vague concept of public policy that has never been articulated by anyone except four members of this court.

"I therefore respectfully dissent."

The Supreme Court of California, in the following case, affirmed the dismissal of an executive employee claim for wrongful termination of employment, saying that no substantial public policy was violated when the employee was dismissed for reporting matters of interest to his employer (suspected criminal conduct of fellow employee). However, an oral implied-in-fact contractual promise not to fire without good cause stated a cause of action. But no independent tort remedy for breach of such an implied covenant of good faith and fair dealing exists in such a case. The high court's reasoning for this limitation is noted.

FOLEY V. INTERACTIVE DATA CORP.
47 Cal. 3d 654, 254 Cal. Rptr. 211, 765 P.2d 373 (1988)

LUCAS, C.J.: " . . .

"We . . . conclude that the employment relationship is not sufficiently similar to that of insurer and insured to warrant judicial extension of the proposed additional tort remedies in view of the countervailing concerns about economic policy and stability, the traditional separation of tort and contract law, and finally, the numerous protections against improper terminations already afforded employees.

"Our inquiry, however, does not end here. The potential effects on an individual caused by termination of employment arguably justify additional remedies for certain improper discharges. The large body of employment law restricting an employer's right to discharge based on discriminatory reasons or on the employee's exercise of legislatively conferred employee rights, indicates that the Legislature and Congress have recognized the importance of the employment relationship *and* the necessity for vindication of certain legislatively and constitutionally established public policies in the employment context. . . . In the quest for expansion of remedies for discharged workers which we consider here, however, the policies sought to be vindicated have a different origin. The most frequently cited reason for the move to extend tort remedies in this context is the perception that traditional contract remedies are inadequate to compensate for certain breaches. (*See, e.g.,* Putz & Klippen, . . . , 21 U.S.F. L. Rev. at pp. 470–471; Trayner, *Bad Faith Breach of a Commercial Contract: A Comment on the Seaman's Case* (Cal. State Bar, Fall 1984) 8 Bus. L. News 1.) Others argue that the quest for additional remedies specifically for terminated workers also has its genesis in (1) comparisons drawn between the protections afforded nonunion employees and those covered by collective bargaining agreements, (2) changes in the economy which have led to displacement of middle-level management employees in 'unprecedented numbers,' and (3) the effect of antidiscrimination awareness and legislation that has 'raised expectations and created challenges to employer decision making.' (Gould, *Stemming the Wrongful Discharge Tide: A Case for Arbitration* (1988) 13 Emp. Rel. L. J. 404, 408–410 [hereafter *Stemming the Tide*].

"The issue is how far courts can or should go in responding to these concerns regarding the sufficiency of compensation by departing from long established principles of contract law. Significant policy judgments affecting social policies and commercial relationships are implicated in the resolution of this question in the employment termination context. Such a determination, which has the potential to alter profoundly the nature of employment, the cost of products and services, and the availability of jobs, arguably is better suited for legislative decisionmaking. (*See Wagenseller v. Scottsdale Memorial Hospital*, . . . , 710 P.2d 1025, 1040; Gould, *The Idea of the Job as Property in Contemporary America: The Legal and Collective Bargaining Framework* 1986 B.Y.U.L. Rev. 885, 898, 908 [hereafter *The Idea of the Job*]; *cf. Sabetay v. Sterling Drug, Inc.*, . . . , 506 N.E.2d at p. 923.) . . .

"As we have reiterated, the employment relationship is fundamentally contractual, and several factors combine to persuade us that in the absence of legislative direction to the contrary contractual remedies should remain the sole available relief for breaches of the implied covenant of good faith and fair dealing in the employment context. Initially, predictability of the consequences of actions related to employment contracts is important to commercial stability. In order to achieve such stability, it is also important that employers not be unduly deprived of discretion to dismiss an employee by the fear that doing so will give rise to potential tort recovery in every case. . . .

"Finally, and of primary significance, we believe that focus on available contract remedies offers the most appropriate method of expanding available relief for wrongful terminations. The expansion of tort remedies in the employment context has potentially enormous consequences for the stability of the business community.

"We are not unmindful of the legitimate concerns of employees who fear arbitrary and improper discharges that may have a devastating effect on their economic and social status. Nor are we unaware of or unsympathetic to claims that contract remedies for breaches of contract are insufficient because they do not fully compensate due to their failure to include attorney fees and their restrictions on foreseeable damages. These defects, however, exist generally in contract situations. As discussed above, the variety of possible courses to remedy the problem is well demonstrated in the literature and include increased contract damages, provision for award of attorney fees, establishment of arbitration or other speedier and less expensive dispute resolution, or the tort remedies (the scope of which is also subject to dispute) sought by plaintiff here.

"Plaintiff may proceed with his cause of action alleging a breach of an implied-in-fact contract promise to discharge him only for good cause; his claim is not barred by the statute of frauds. His cause of action for a breach of public policy [citation omitted] was properly dismissed because the facts alleged, even if proven, would not establish a discharge in violation of public policy. Finally, as to his cause of action for tortious breach of the implied covenant of good faith and fair dealing, we hold that tort remedies are not available for breach of the implied covenant in an employment contract to employees who allege they have been discharged in violation of the covenant. . . . ''

Mosk, J. (dissenting):

"I dissent. . . .

"When an employee learns that one in a supervisorial position is an embezzler, he has the choice of two immediate courses of action. He can remain silent and thus avoid the enmity of the embezzler and embarrassment to the employer. That apparently is the approach preferred by my colleagues in order to assure the employee's retention of his job. Or, as a dutiful employee concerned with the image of his company, he can report his knowledge to the employer. That is the course of action I would encourage.

"My colleagues insist that reporting the presence of an embezzler to an employer is solely to the benefit of the employer. While undoubtedly it is to the employer's benefit, it is not exclusively so. It is my opinion that such action— i.e., advising a state-created corporation of the employment in a supervisorial position of a person chargeable with a potential felony—is in the best interests of society as a while, and therefore covered by the public policy rule.

"Under Labor Code section 1102.5, subdivision (b), an employer is prohibited from retaliating against an employee for disclosing information to a law enforcement agency when there is reasonable cause to believe a violation of state or federal laws has been committed. It seems incongruous to permit retaliation and discharge when the employee chooses to go directly to his employer with the information, rather than to circumvent the employer, go behind his back and directly to a public agency. In either event, it seems clear to me that the law and public policy are implicated. . . . ''

The Supreme Court of New Jersey refused to apply its newly created cause of action for wrongful discharge to a physician who was dismissed for refusing to continue research on a controversial formulation of a drug on the ground that doing so violated her Hippocratic Oath.[2] This conclusion supports the general judicial reticence to impose liability for violations of ethical standards in employment discharge cases, unless otherwise sanctioned by legislation.

24:2 *Discrimination in the Workplace: In General*

In addition to placing limitations on the common-law employment-at-will doctrine, the federal government and state and local entities have adopted specific civil rights enactments dealing with a variety of workplace issues. The first major federal initiative was Title VII of the Civil Rights Act of 1964, which deals with employee rights by prohibiting discrimination on the basis of race, color, religion, sex, or national origin. The new 1990 Aid to Disabled Ameri-

---

[2]*See* Pierce v. Ortho Pharmaceutical Corp., 94 N.J. 58, 417 A.2d 505 (1980).

cans Act extends this coverage to disabled workers. Most states and major municipalities have enacted their own legislation patterned on Title VII. A few issues which have particular pertinence to hospitality entrepreneurs will be examined briefly below.

Before proceeding, a few words concerning the procedure and elements which plaintiff and defendant must allege and prove to support or successfully defend against a claim of discrimination lodged in court are in order.

Illegal discrimination may be established by an employee's showing that the employer has engaged in intentional discrimination—also called *disparate treatment*. Discrimination may also be shown to have a *disparate effect* or impact on the employee. Either of these kinds is sufficient if proved and not rebutted.

The first kind, disparate treatment, is illustrated by a hotel employer's refusal to permit non-Caucasions of either sex to apply for and be admitted to an advanced training program without which they could not be promoted. Lack of explicit discrimination does not necessarily shield the employer. Thus a *prima facie* violation of Title VII can be established by proving that (1) the applicant is a member of a protected class (non-Caucasion or female), (2) the applicant applied for a job for which the employer was seeking applicants, (3) the applicant was qualified for the job, (4) the applicant was not hired, and (5) the employer filled the job with a nonminority applicant or continued trying to do so.

At this point the employer may rebut by proof of a legitimate, nondiscriminatory reason for the applicant's rejection; that is, the person hired had superior qualifications. The higher the employment level being sought, the greater the degree of subjective evaluation the courts will permit, so long as those qualities are in fact necessary for job performance (for example, creativity, initiative, ability to delegate responsibilities). If the applicant can prove, after rebutted evidence, that such evidence was mere pretext for discrimination, then the applicant will prevail. Where the evidence of both legitimate and pretextual grounds for a refusal to hire or promote exists, the employer must prove that the employee would not have been hired or promoted irrespective of his or her race or gender.[3]

In·disparate impact cases, proof of statistical disparities between employable population and numbers of employees hired claiming discrimination are valid, unless the job requires special qualifications or training. Once a *prima facie* case had been established, the employer, until recently, had to rebut by showing "business necessity" (genuine need; practice actually achieves this need; and no other reasonable alternative). However, in *Ward Cove Packing Co. v. Antonio*,[4] the United States Supreme Court ruled that rebuttal is adequate that establishes merely plausible evidence of a legitimate reason justifying the policy or practice. To prevail, the applicant must show that the employer could have achieved its legitimate purpose in a manner that would not have created such a discriminatory impact. The Civil Rights Act of 1991 alters the *Price Waterhouse* and

---

[3]*See* Price Waterhouse v. Hopkins, 109 S. Ct. 1775, 104 L. Ed. 2d 268.
[4]109 S. Ct. 2115, 104 L. Ed. 2d 733.

Ward Cove, supra, decisions by restoring prior rights limited by those cases. It also permits recovery of compensatory *and* punitive damages for intentional discrimination.

In *Imperial Diner, Inc., v. State Human Rights Appeal Board,*[5] the New York Court of Appeals applied the New York Human Rights Law to obscene anti-Semitic remarks made to a waitress by her employer in the presence of customers. The employer refused repeatedly to apologize, and the employee voluntarily quit. The high court ruled that the State Board was justified in ordering her reinstatement with back pay for two years, the payment of compensatory damages, and the issuance of a written apology. Three dissenters argued that the remedy requiring a written apology was unjustified because it infringed on First Amendment (free speech) rights, though money damages were appropriate. They also deemed the back pay award excessive because the victim had secured other employment during the two-year period.

24:3 *Age Discrimination*

In 1967, the federal Age Discrimination in Employment Act (ADEA) was enacted. In many respects it is similar to Title VII in that it prohibits disparate treatment and disparate impact forms of discrimination.[6] The age threshold is 40. Statutory defenses include discharge for good cause other than age, as well as a bona fide occupational qualification like that found in Title VII. Whereas these defenses are narrowly construed in Title VII cases, courts are more liberal in treating them under the ADEA.

In the case that follows, the United States Supreme Court held that a transfer system that did not afford captains disqualified from flying because of age the same "bumping" privileges as captains disqualified for reasons other than age violated the federal Age Discrimination in Employment Act. The high court also held that the airline did not willfully violate the Act, and that recovery of double damages provided for in such cases was not warranted.

TRANS WORLD AIRLINES V. THURSTON
469 U.S. 111, 105 L. Ed. 2d 613 (1985)

POWELL, J.: " . . .

"The ADEA 'broadly prohibits arbitrary discrimination in the workplace based on age.' *Lorillard v. Pons,* 434 U.S. 575, 577 (1978). Section 4(a)(1) of the Act proscribes differential treatment of older workers 'with respect to . . . [a] privileg[e] of employment.' 29 U.S.C. §623(a). Under TWA's transfer policy, 60-year-old captains are denied a 'privilege of employment' on the basis of age. Captains who become disqualified from serving in that position for reasons

---

[5]52 N.Y.2d 72, 417 N.E.2d 525 (1980).

[6]Although beyond the scope of this overview, the ADEA applies specifically to overseas branches of U.S. employers. The Civil Rights Act of 1991 provides the same protection by overruling EEOC v. Arabian American Oil Co., 111 S. Ct. 1227 (1991), which held that Title VII does not apply to United States citizens employed abroad by United States corporations.

other than age automatically are able to displace less senior flight engineers. Captains disqualified because of age are not afforded this same 'bumping' privilege. Instead, they are forced to resort to the bidding procedures set forth in the collective-bargaining agreement. If there is no vacancy prior to a bidding captain's 60th birthday, he must retire.

"The Act does not require TWA to grant transfer privileges to disqualified captains. Nevertheless, if TWA does grant some disqualified captains the 'privilege' of 'bumping' less senior flight engineers, it may not deny this opportunity to others because of their age. In *Hishon v. King & Spalding*, 467 U.S. 69 (1984), we held that '[a] benefit that is part and parcel of the employment relationship may not be doled out in a discriminatory fashion, even if the employer would be free . . . not to provide the benefit at all.' *Id.*, at 75. This interpretation of Title VII of the Civil Rights Act of 1964, 42 U.S.C. §2000(e) *et seq.*, applies with equal force in the context of age discrimination, for the substantive provisions of the ADEA 'were derived *in haec verba* from Title VII.' *Lorillard v. Pons, supra*, at 584. . . .

"Although we find that TWA's transfer policy discriminates against disqualified captains on the basis of age, our inquiry cannot end here. Petitioners contend that the age-based transfer policy is justified by two of the ADEA's five affirmative defenses. Petitioners first argue that the discharge of respondents was lawful because age is a 'bona fide occupational qualification' (BFOQ) for the position of captain. 29 U.S.C. §623(f)(1). Furthermore, TWA claims that its retirement policy is part of a bona fide seniority system, and thus exempt from the Act's coverage. 29 U.S.C. §623(f)(2).

"Section 4(f)(1) of the ADEA provides that an employer may take 'any action otherwise prohibited' where age is a 'bona fide occupational qualification.' 29 U.S.C. §623(f)(1). In order to be permissible under §4(f)(1), however, the age-based discrimination must relate to a 'particular business.' *Ibid.* Every court to consider the issue has assumed that the 'particular business' to which the statute refers is the job from which the protected individual is excluded. In *Weeks v. Southern Bell Tel. & Tel. Co.*, 408 F.2d 228 (CA5 1969), for example, the court considered the Title VII claim of a female employee who, because of her sex, had not been allowed to transfer to the position of switchman. In deciding that the BFOQ defense was not available to the defendant, the court considered only the job of switchman.

"TWA's discriminatory transfer policy is not permissible under §4(f)(1) because age is not a BFOQ for the 'particular' position of flight engineer. It is necessary to recognize that the airline has two age-based policies: (i) captains are not allowed to serve in that capacity after reaching the age of 60; and (ii) age-disqualified captains are not given the transfer privileges afforded captains disqualified for other reasons. The first policy, which precludes individuals from serving as captains, is not challenged by respondents. The second practice does not operate to exclude protected individuals from the position of captain; rather it prevents qualified 60-year-olds from working as flight engineers. Thus, it is the 'particular' job of flight engineer from which the respondents were excluded by the discriminatory transfer policy. Because age under 60 is not a BFOQ for the position of flight engineer, the age-based discrimination at issue in this case cannot be justified by §4(f)(1). . . .

"TWA also contends that its discriminatory transfer policy is lawful under the Act because it is part of a 'bona fide seniority system.' 29 U.S.C. §623(f)(2). The Court of Appeals held that the airline's retirement policy is not mandated by the negotiated seniority plan. We need not address this finding; any seniority system that includes the challenged practice is not 'bona fide' under the statute. The Act provides that a seniority system may not 'require or permit' the involuntary retirement of a protected individual because of his age. *Ibid.* Although the FAA 'age 60 rule' may have caused respondents' retirement, TWA's seniority plan certainly 'permitted' it within the meaning of the ADEA. *Ibid.* Moreover, because captains disqualified for reasons other than age are allowed to 'bump' less senior flight engineers, the mandatory retirement was age-based. Therefore, the 'bona fide seniority system' defense is unavailable to the petitioners.

"In summary, TWA's transfer policy discriminates against protected individuals on the basis of age, and thereby violates the act. The two statutory defenses raised by petitioners do not support the argument that this discrimination is justified. The BFOQ defense is meritless because age is not a bona fide occupational qualification for the position of flight engineer, the job from which the respondents were excluded. Nor can TWA's policy be viewed as part of a bona fide seniority system. A system that includes this discriminatory transfer policy permits the forced retirement of captains on the basis of age. . . .

"Section 7(b) of the ADEA, 81 Stat. 604, 29 U.S.C. §626(b), provides that the rights created by the Act are to be 'enforced in accordance with the powers, remedies, and procedures' of the Fair Labor Standards Act. *See Lorillard v. Pons*, 434 U.S., at 579. But the remedial provisions of the two statutes are not identical. Congress declined to incorporate into the ADEA several FLSA sections. Moreover, §16(b) of the FLSA, which makes the award of liquidated damages mandatory, is significantly qualified in ADEA §7(b) by a proviso that a prevailing plaintiff is entitled to double damages 'only in cases of willful violations.' 29 U.S.C. §626(b). In this case, the Court of Appeals held that TWA's violation of the ADEA was 'willful,' and that the respondents therefore were entitled to double damages. 713 F.2d, at 957. We granted certiorari to review this holding.

"The legislative history of the ADEA indicates that Congress intended for liquidated damages to be punitive in nature. . . .

"This Court has recognized that in enacting the ADEA, 'Congress exhibited . . . a detailed knowledge of the FLSA provisions and their judicial interpretation. . . . ' *Lorillard v. Pons, supra*, at 581. The manner in which FLSA §16(a) has been interpreted therefore is relevant. In general, courts have found that an employer is subject to criminal penalties under the FLSA when he 'wholly disregards the law . . . without making any reasonable effort to determine whether the plan he is following would constitute a violation of the law.'

Nabob Oil Co. v. United States, 190 F.2d 478, 479 (CA10), *cert. denied,* 342 U.S. 876 (1951); *see also Darby v. United States,* 132 F.2d 928 (CA 5 1943). This standard is substantially in accord with the interpretation of 'willful' adopted by the Court of Appeals in interpreting the liquidated damages provision of the ADEA. The court below stated that a violation of the Act was 'willful' if 'the employer . . . knew or showed reckless disregard for the matter of whether its conduct was prohibited by the ADEA.' 713 F.2d, at 956. Given the legislative history of the liquidated damages provision, we think the 'reckless disregard' standard is reasonable. . . .

"As noted above, the Court of Appeals stated that a violation is 'willful' if 'the employer either knew or showed reckless disregard for the matter of whether its conduct was prohibited by the ADEA.' 713 F.2d, at 956. Although we hold that this is an acceptable way to articulate a definition of 'willful,' the court below misapplied this standard. TWA certainly did not 'know' that its conduct violated the Act. Nor can it fairly be said that TWA adopted its transfer policy in 'reckless disregard' of the Act's requirements. The record makes clear that TWA officials acted reasonably and in good faith in attempting to determine whether their plan would violate the ADEA. *See Nabob Oil Co. v. United States, supra.* . . .

"There simply is no evidence that TWA acted in 'reckless disregard' of the requirements of the ADEA. The airline had obligations under the collective-bargaining agreement with the Airline Pilots Association. In an attempt to bring its retirement policy into compliance with the ADEA, while at the same time observing the terms of the collective-bargaining agreement, TWA sought legal advice and consulted with the Union. Despite opposition from the Union, a plan was adopted that permitted cockpit employees to work as 'flight engineers' after reaching age 60. Apparently TWA officials and the airline's attorneys failed to focus specifically on the effect of each aspect of the new retirement policy for cockpit personnel. It is reasonable to believe that the parties involved, on focusing on the larger overall problem, simply overlooked the challenged aspect of the new plan. We conclude that TWA's violation of the Act was not willful within the meaning of §7(b), and that respondents therefore are not entitled to liquidated damages. . . .

"The ADEA requires TWA to afford 60-year-old captains the same transfer privileges that it gives to captains disqualified for reasons other than age. Therefore, we affirm the Court of Appeals on this issue. We do not agree with its holding that TWA's violation of the Act was willful. We accordingly reverse its judgment that respondents are entitled to liquidated or double damages.

"*It is so ordered.*"

In the case to follow, the federal Circuit Court of Appeals for the Fifth Circuit affirmed a violation of the ADEA by a company that compelled a store manager to resign. In doing so, the court set forth the governing principles as to proof of age discrimination and constructive discharge, as well as the defense of legitimate, nondiscriminatory business reasons for a company's actions.

GUTHRIE V. J.C. PENNEY CO., INC.
803 F.2d 202 (5th Cir. 1986)

JOHNSON, C.J.: " . . .

Sufficiency of the Evidence of Age Discrimination

"When a plaintiff in an ADEA case cannot present direct evidence of discrimination, the courts have developed a three-part test modeled on the one used by Title VII plaintiffs. *McDonnell Douglas Corp. v. Green*, 411 U.S. 792, 802, 93 S. Ct. 1817, 1824, 36 L. Ed. 2d 668 (1973). First, the plaintiff must make a *prima facie* case by proving that he was in the age group protected by the Act (forty to seventy years old), he was qualified for the position, he was discharged, and he was replaced by a younger employee. In the second stage, the burden shifts to the employer to produce evidence that dismissal was due to a business reason other than age. At the third stage, the plaintiff can prevail by showing that the articulated reason was a pretext. *Sherrod v. Sears, Roebuck & Co.*, 785 F.2d 1312, 1314–16 (5th Cir. 1986); *Elliott v. Group Medical & Surgical Service*, 714 F.2d 556, 565–66 (5th Cir. 1983), *cert. denied*, 467 U.S. 1215, 104 S. Ct. 2658, 81 L. Ed. 2d 364 (1984); *Reeves v. General Foods Corp.*, 682 F.2d 515, 520–24 (5th Cir. 1982). Penney attacks the sufficiency of the evidence supporting the jury's verdict for Guthrie at two points: constructive discharge and the pretextual nature of Penney's business reasons.

"Factual findings in employment discrimination cases are reviewed on the same standard as in other cases. *United States Postal Service Board of Governors v. Aikens*, 460 U.S. 711, 716, 103 S. Ct. 1478, 1482, 75 L. Ed. 2d 403 (1983); *Sherrod*, 785 F.2d at 1314. Consequently, the Court will not overturn the jury verdict unless it is not supported by substantial evidence. *Reeves*, 682 F.2d at 518–19; *Boeing Co. v. Shipman*, 411 F.2d 365, 374–75 (5th Cir. 1969) (en banc). An employee can prove constructive discharge by showing that his employer created conditions so intolerable that 'a reasonable person in the employee's shoes would have felt compelled to resign.' *Bourque v. Powell Electrical Manufacturing Co.*, 617 F.2d 61, 65 (5th Cir. 1980), *quoting Alicea Rosado v. Garcia Santiago*, 562 F.2d 114, 119 (1st Cir. 1977). *See also Kelleher v. Flawn*, 761 F.2d 1079, 1086 (5th Cir. 1985); *Shawgo v. Spradlin*, 701 F.2d 470, 481 (5th Cir.), *cert. denied*, 464 U.S. 965, 104 S. Ct. 404, 78 L. Ed. 2d 345 (1983); *Junior v. Texaco, Inc.*, 688 F.2d 377 (5th Cir. 1982).

"The inquiry focuses on the employee's state of mind, and the employer's intent in creating the allegedly intolerable conditions is irrelevant at this stage. *See, e.g., Kelleher*, 761 F.2d at 1086; *Shawgo*, 701 F.2d at 481 n. 12; *Junior*, 688 F.2d at 379. However, the test remains objective, because it turns, not on the plaintiff's actual reaction, but on the reaction of a 'reasonable employee' in his position. *Id.*

"In the instant case, the jury did hear substantial evidence supporting constructive discharge. All of the witnesses to District Manager Moore's two visits testified that he strongly criticized Guthrie in front of his staff. Guthrie and several of his staff members stated that morale was low and that Guthrie's authority suffered as a consequence. Moore's downgrade of Guthrie from a three to a four was a recognized first step toward dismissal, although witnesses disputed how long Guthrie had to make improvements before he would be fired. Guthrie testified that he believed it impossible to improve so long as the store was operating with a reduced staff, breaking in a new inventory control system, and undergoing remodeling. The jury had substantial evidence to find this perception reasonable, as well as Guthrie's conclusion that termination was inevitable.

"Secondly, Penney asserts that it acted as it did for business reasons, and that Guthrie did not prove these reasons to be pretextual. Specifically, Penney says that its repeated inquiries about Guthrie's retirement plans were due to the need to anticipate staff vacancies; that Moore's decision to criticize and downgrade Guthrie formed a part of a general 'get tough' attitude on his part; and that it had the right to assign little weight to the sales and profit performance of Guthrie's store. Penney is correct in pointing out that the ADEA is not a license to second-guess legitimate business judgments. *Thornburgh v. Columbus & Greenville Railroad Co.*, 760 F.2d 633, 645–46 (5th Cir. 1985). Thus, the courts would not interfere if Penney in fact decided to ignore sales and profit performance in evaluating store managers. However, the question here is what Penney's motive actually was, not what it could have been. In reaching this determination, the jury is entitled to weigh the credibility of witnesses and to disbelieve self-serving testimony. *Thornburgh*, 760 F.2d at 645–46; *Elliott*, 714 F.2d at 564; *Reeves*, 682 F.2d at 524.

"In this case, the jury could have believed that Penney's need to plan for vacancies motivated its first inquiry into Guthrie's retirement plans. However, the jury could also have believed that the later, repeated inquiries were unnecessary and constituted intentional harassment. Moreover, the jury heard considerable evidence tending to show that Moore singled out Guthrie for criticism and applied tougher standards to him than to his younger colleagues. For example, Guthrie's younger successor experienced the same problems and received a three rating. While Penney may choose to downplay sales and profit performance in evaluating a manager, its own company manual lists them as key factors. Finally, the jury may have chosen to believe Guthrie's testimony that he was told that the Company wanted him to retire at age sixty, over Penney's witnesses who testified to the contrary.

"In sum, the jury heard substantial evidence from which to conclude that Guthrie met his burden of showing that he was constructively discharged and that Penney's stated reasons for doing so were pretextual.

Prejudicial Evidence

"During the trial, Guthrie and his wife testified that his mental and physical health deteriorated under the strain of the last months before his retirement. . . .

"Damages for pain and suffering are not recoverable under the ADEA, and evidence concerning such suffering is not admissible in a case brought only under the Act. *Walker v. Petit Construction Co.*, 605 F.2d 128, 131 (4th Cir.

1979), *modified on other grounds,* 611 F.2d 950 (1979); *Haskell v. Kaman Corp.,* 743 F.2d 113, 121 (2d Cir. 1984); *Hill v. Spiegel, Inc.,* 708 F.2d 233, 236 (6th Cir. 1983). . . .

"In the instant case, the evidence on Guthrie's physical and mental suffering was relevant when offered. The district court did not clearly abuse the wide discretion that it enjoys in deciding whether the jury has been so confused that a new trial is needed. *Dawsey v. Olin Corp.,* 782 F.2d 1254, 1261 (5th Cir. 1986). . . . Penney cannot show that the trial judge's instructions, which correctly stated what evidence is relevant to an ADEA claim, were plainly erroneous merely because they did not also recite what evidence is *not* relevant.

ADEA Damages

"The trial court awarded Guthrie reinstatement, costs, attorney's fees, and $179,550 in back pay. It also granted Guthrie 'liquidated damages' equal to the back pay award, as authorized by the statute. 29 U.S.C. §626(b) (1982). The Supreme Court has held that a jury can award double back pay as liquidated damages if an employer acted willfully, either knowing that it was violating the ADEA or showing 'careless disregard' of whether it was or not. *Trans World Airlines v. Thurston,* 469 U.S. 111, 105 S. Ct. 613, 624–25, 83 L. Ed. 2d 523 (1985).

"Penney argues that the jury did not have substantial evidence to find willfulness. However, the jury heard evidence that Penney had a previous early retirement policy, evidence that some managers considered that policy still in effect, and evidence that Guthrie was subjected to several years of pressures not imposed on younger store managers. We decline to disturb the factual finding of willfulness.

"Penney also protests the district court's failure to deduct Guthrie's retirement and social security benefits from his back pay award. The ADEA empowers the district court to grant 'such legal or equitable relief as may be appropriate to effectuate the purposes of this chapter,' *i.e.,* to discourage age discrimination and to compensate its victims. 29 U.S.C. §626(b). Most courts have refused to deduct such benefits as social security and unemployment compensation from ADEA awards. *Marshall v. Goodyear Tire & Rubber Co.,* 554 F.2d 730, 736 (5th Cir. 1977); *Maxfield v. Sinclair International,* 766 F.2d 788, 793–94 (3d Cir. 1985), *cert. denied,*——U.S.——, 106 S. Ct. 796, 88 L. Ed. 2d 773 (1986); *McDowell v. Avtex Fibers, Inc.,* 740 F.2d 214, 215–17 (3d Cir. 1984), *vacated and remanded on other grounds,* 469 U.S. 1202, 105 S. Ct. 1159, 84 L. Ed. 2d 312 (1985); *Wise v. Olan Mills, Inc. of Texas,* 495 F. Supp. 257 (D. Colo. 1980). . . .

" . . . While district courts' decisions to deduct social security and similar benefits have been upheld as exercises of discretion, no appellate court has reversed a district court that refused to make a deduction. *Equal Employment Opportunity Commission v. Wyoming Retirement System,* 771 F.2d 1425 (10th Cir. 1985); *Orzel v. City of Wauwatosa Fire Department,* 697 F.2d 743, 756 (7th

Cir.), *cert. denied,* 464 U.S. 992, 104 S. Ct. 484, 78 L. Ed. 2d 680 (1983); *Naton v. Bank of California,* 649 F.2d 691, 699–700 (9th Cir. 1981). In the instant case, the trial court did not abuse its discretion in refusing to deduct social security.

"Penney's retirement plan presents a more difficult problem. While the Third Circuit has refused to set off pension plan benefits, other circuits have held that such benefits, coming from the employer, are not collateral and should be set off. *McDowell,* 740 F.2d at 217 (no set-off for pension benefits); *Hagelthorn v. Kennecott Corp.,* 710 F.2d 76 (2d Cir. 1983) (set-off for lump-sum pension payment); *Fariss v. Lynchburg Foundry,* 769 F.2d 958, 966–67 (4th Cir. 1985); [*Equal Employment Opportunity Commission v.*] *Sandia Corp.,* 639 F.2d at 626–27 [10th Cir. 1980] (set off for 'lay off allowances'). . . . [L]ooking to the practice of the majority of the other circuits, we hold that Guthrie's back pay award should be reduced by payments received from Penney's retirement fund. We remand to the district court to separate these amounts from nondeductible social security benefits. . . .

"Remanded."

24:4 *Disability and Handicap Discrimination*

Before 1990, the major federal legislation governing handicap discrimination was the Rehabilitation Act of 1973. This Act had a much narrower focus than other federal employment initiatives, in that it was limited to federal agencies, federal contractors with contracts of over $25,000, and employers receiving any form of federal assistance. Nonetheless the Rehabilitation Act was intended to serve as a model for all employers and has a broad reach, commensurate with growing federal economic activity affecting the private sector.

The Act protects employees and those seeking employment who have "a physical or mental impairment which substantially affects one or more of such person's major life activities." Especially significant is the provision of protection to those individuals "regarded as having such an impairment." The Act defines "impairments" to include virtually all diseases and disabilities that might subject a person to discrimination. The Act requires a person to be "qualified" for the job. Whereas the term *qualified* is not specifically defined, the employer is required to provide reasonable accommodation for a particular handicap, so long as the cost of doing so is not unreasonable. The 1990 Americans with Disabilities Act (ADA) significantly expands federal rights for disabled persons. Title I, governing employment, contains coverage (fifteen or more employees as size of entity) similar to Title VII. However, until 1992, the ADA applied only to employers with twenty-five or more employees.

Under Title I, no covered entity may discriminate against a "qualified individual with a disability" because of that disability. This prohibition applies to job applications, hiring, advancement, discharge, compensation, training, and other terms, conditions, and privileges of employment. The term "qualified individual with a disability" means disabled individuals who, with or without reasonable accommodation, can perform the essential functions of the job in question. The statute permits consideration to be given to the employer's judgment as to functions of a job that are essential.

Disabilities covered include those found in the Rehabilitation Act, and individuals are covered who have a *record* of a physical or mental impairment that substantially limits one or more of their major life activities. Title I also includes individuals who are *regarded* as having such an impairment. The legislative history indicates that Congress included AIDS (HIV infection), drug addiction, alcoholism, cancer, and specific learning disabilities, as well as speech and hearing impairments within the term "disabilities." The *regarded* as having such an impairment builds upon the United States Supreme Court decision in *School Board of Nassau County v. Arline,*[7] which specifically included within the definition of handicap under the Rehabilitation Act anyone discriminated against because of others' negative perception of his or her impairment. "Others" includes coworkers and customer. The Chapman Amendment, which was dropped from the bill before its final passage, permitted employers lawfully to transfer an employee in a food-handling job who has an "infectious or communicable disease of public health significance" provided the transfer would cause the employee no economic damage.

Medical examinations or inquiries by employers may not be made of job applicants as to whether the individual has a disability or the nature or severity of that disability. However, "employment entrance examinations" are authorized after an offer of employment has been tendered but before the commencement of employment duties so long as all employees are examined regardless of disability. The information obtained must be treated as a confidential medical record, and the results must be used to determine job-related performance functions and must be consistent with business necessity.

The proper treatment of an alcoholic federal employee who was terminated by the Department of Labor was reviewed in the case below. The court, in holding that reinstatement with back pay was inappropriate, carefully noted the statutes and regulations that apply in such cases, including reasonable accommodation. Because these provisions serve as a model for the 1990 Americans with Disabilities Act, which governs the private-sector workplace, they are set forth below.

WHITLOCK v. DONOVAN
598 F. Supp. 126 (U.S.D.C. D.C. 1984)

GESELL, D.J.: [Procedural aspects of case omitted.]

I. Introduction

"Plaintiff was fired by the Department of Labor in May 1983, because of repeated absences after various efforts had been made to counsel him toward treatment for his alcoholism. Whitlock was a GS-6, step 8 supervisor who had had

---

[7]480 U.S. 273 (1973).

23 years of federal service prior to his discharge. Other than alcoholic absences his work performance was not only satisfactory but often deemed superior.

"There is no dispute that plaintiff is an alcoholic. He joined the Department of Labor in 1975 but indeed had been an alcoholic since the age of 10. An alcoholic has a disease. He is the victim of a handicap which becomes progressively worse unless successfully treated. Alcoholics typically deny their handicap and conceal, excuse and even lie about their drinking and the problems it causes them at home and at work. Treatment of alcoholism focuses initially on a basic need to force the alcoholic to recognize his handicap. In employment situations, both private and public, this is usually done by presenting the employee, hopefully at an early stage, with a clear choice between either accepting intervening therapy designed to break the barriers of denial and avoidance or facing the definite loss of job and status.

"The nature of the intervening therapy provided varies considerably. There is peer support such as provided by Alcoholics Anonymous and many types of counseling which employ intensive outpatient therapy or a mixture of in-patient care for a period of time followed by careful monitoring on an out-patient basis. All programs require continuous counseling after the initial detoxification, and of course such counseling can only work if the patient is motivated to seek it and to continue it, having accepted that he has an alcoholism problem.

"Plaintiff has now been sober for more than a year following seven months of intensive in-patient treatment at St. Elizabeth's Hospital. He contends that the Department of Labor failed in several respects to meet its statutory obligation reasonably to accommodate to his handicap before termination. First, he contends that the Department should have more forcefully presented to him at an earlier stage than it did a clear choice between entering treatment or losing his job. Second, he contends the Department failed to follow up on the treatment he did enter when he stopped attending after a few successful months of therapy. In these two respects, he contends the Department's intervention was 'too little, too late.' Finally, he contends that when he was fired nearly a year after he stopped the recommended treatment, he was not presented with the reasonable option of taking a long leave without pay for intensive in-patient treatment or accepting disability retirement.

"Before reviewing plaintiff's federal employment experience, with particular reference to his alcohol problems, it is necessary to untangle the variety of laws and regulations that establish a federal employer's obligation to its alcoholic employees. That will bring into focus the basis for plaintiff's claims.

II. Applicable Statutes and Regulations

"Alcoholism is a handicapping condition for purposes of the handicap discrimination protections of the Rehabilitation Act of 1973. Both the Attorney General, 43 Op. Att'y Gen. No. 12 (1977), and the Secretary of the then Department of Health, Education and Welfare, 42 Fed. Reg. 22686 (May 4, 1977), have so concluded, and the courts are in accord. *See, e.g., Tinch v. Walters,* 573

F. Supp. 346, 348 (E.D. Tenn 1983); *Simpson v. Reynolds Metals Co.*, 629 F.2d 1226, 1228, 1231 n. 8 (7th Cir. 1980); *Davis v. Bucher*, 451 F. Supp. 791, 796 (E.D. Pa. 1978). Federal alcoholic employees who are using alcohol excessively are protected only under one section of the Act, Section 501, whereas other federally employed individuals who are handicapped by other conditions or are rehabilitated alcoholics also enjoy the protection of Section 504 of the Act.

"Under Section 501 of the Act, federal agency employers such as the Department of Labor have a duty of affirmative action toward handicapped employees and applicants. Indeed, the statute was strengthened in 1978 to make clear that any handicapped federal employee had a private right of action to enforce his right to receive affirmative action *See* section 505(a), 29 U.S.C. §794(a)(1). Members of Congress indicated in 1978 that Section 501 was intended to make the federal government a 'leader' or 'model employer' of the handicapped. In addition, regulations of the Equal Employment Opportunity Commission under the statute emphasize the general policy of the federal government to 'become a model employer of handicapped individuals.' 29 C.F.R. §1613.703. Thus this affirmative-action obligation is more than a requirement of non-discrimination or even-handed treatment. *See Shirey v. Devine*, 670 F.2d 1188, 1201 (D.C. Cir. 1982); *Southeastern Community College v. Davis*, 442 U.S. 397, 410, 99 S. Ct. 2361, 2369, 60 L. Ed. 2d 980 (1979). Federal agency employers are required to make 'reasonable accommodation' to the limitations of a handicapped employee unless the agency can show such accommodation would impose an 'undue hardship' on its operations. 29 C.F.R. §1613.704.

"Additional protection for alcoholic federal employees is found in the Comprehensive Alcohol Abuse and Alcoholism Prevention, Treatment, and Rehabilitation Act of 1970. That Act requires federal agencies to have alcoholism treatment programs for their employees. 42 U.S.C. §290dd-1(a). The Act also provides that '[n]o person may be denied or deprived of Federal civilian employment . . . solely on the ground of prior alcohol abuse or prior alcoholism.' 42 U.S.C. §290dd-1(c)(1). While the Act states that '[t]his section shall not be construed to prohibit the dismissal from employment of a Federal civilian employee who cannot properly function in his employment, '42 U.S.C. § 290dd-1(d), the legislative history indicates that dismissal was intended to apply only to employees who refused treatment altogether or who had repeatedly failed in treatment.

"These statutes viewed together in the light of their legislative history show Congress's firm intention to require federal employers to exert substantial affirmative efforts to assist alcoholic employees toward overcoming their handicap before firing them for performance deficiencies related to drinking. It is this duty, which is subsumed under the 'reasonable accommodation' requirement of Section 501(b) of the Rehabilitation Act and the regulations of 29 C.F.R. § 1613.704, that plaintiff has invoked. . . .

"The most extensive statement of reasonable accommodation duties to alcoholic employees is found in Federal Personnel Manual System Supplement 792-

2, Alcoholism and Drug Abuse Programs (1980). This provides that where a supervisor suspects alcohol is the reason for poor performance by an employee, the supervisor is directed among other things to

"Conduct an interview with the employee focusing on poor work performance and inform the employee of available counseling services if poor performance is caused by any personal or health problem.

"If the employee [subsequently] refuses help, and performance continues to be unsatisfactory; provide a firm choice between accepting agency assistance through counseling or professional diagnosis of his or her problem, and cooperation in treatment if indicated, or accepting consequences provided for unsatisfactory performance.

"*Id*. at S2-2. Supervisors are instructed not to raise directly the possibility of a drug or alcohol problem with the employee except where the employee does not seem in full control of his or her faculties or where the employee seems to be involved in criminal conduct. *Id*. Rather, it is contemplated that supervisors will make referrals to trained counselors within the agency or on contract to the agency, where the direct confrontation with the employee about his alcoholism is expected to be made. . . .

"When an agency suspects that deficiencies in an employee's performance, attendance or behavior are caused by a health problem the agency is required to take steps to confirm a connection between the deficiencies and the health problem before instituting removal. If available medical evidence is insufficient to make a final determination, the agency is required to order a fitness-for-duty examination in the form of a general physical examination, a specialized physical, or a psychiatric examination. The employee may participate in the selection of the medical examiner. A second examination may take place only if the first examiner recommends one. *See* Federal Personnel Manual Supplement 831-1 S10-10a(5) (1978).

"The agency then must make a tentative determination 'on the basis of all available evidence' whether the deficiencies 'are caused by illness or injury.' Federal Personnel Manual Supplement 831-1 S-10-10a(7) (1980). If not, the agency may institute adverse action procedures . . . if warranted.' *Id*. However, if it does find the deficiencies are caused by disease or injury, it must notify the employee in writing, giving him an opportunity to reply and other rights. After certain other steps, the agency then may apply to the Office of Personnel Management to have the employee retired on disability. *Id*. at S10-10-a(8), (9).

"Until 1980, disability retirement under these procedures was not available for alcoholic employees because the statutory definition of disability excluded anyone whose disabling disease or injury was 'due to vicious habits, intemperance, or willful misconduct.' 5 U.S.C. §8331(6). This exclusion was repealed by Pub. L. 96–499, section 403(b) (1980). The statutory definition of disability, as amended by the same act, now provides

"Any employee shall be considered to be disabled only if the employee i[s] found by the Office of Personnel Management to be unable, because of disease or injury, to render useful and efficient service in the employee's position and is not qualified for reassignment. . . .

5 U.S.C.A. §8337(a) (1984 Supp.). *See also* 5 C.F.R. §831.502(a) (conforming regulation).

"To summarize, this review of the major statutory and regulatory obligations of federal employers toward their alcoholic employees establishes that when an employee's performance deficiencies are suspected to be due to alcohol, the agency is obligated first to offer counseling to the employee. If the employee rebuffs the offer, and if the deficiency in his work is such that discipline would be warranted, the agency should offer a 'firm choice' between treatment and discipline. An agency is obligated to follow through with its firm choices. Since it is recognized that relapse is predictable in treatment of alcoholics, an agency is not justified in automatically giving up on an employee who enters treatment but who subsequently relapses. In such a case, the agency may follow through with discipline short of removal. However, the agency is obligated before removing the employee from its work force to evaluate whether keeping the employee presents an undue hardship under 29 C.F.R. §1613.704. If removal seems to be the only feasible option, the agency is obligated to conduct a formal evaluation, including a fitness-for-duty examination if necessary, to confirm whether the employee's alcoholism disease is in fact responsible for the employee's poor performance. If so, the agency must offer leave without pay if the employee will seek more extensive rehabilitative therapy that seems promising, and the agency must also counsel the employee regarding disability retirement.

"It is plain that the Department of Labor treated George Whitlock with compassion and tolerance, and more patience than many employers would have shown. However, it is also apparent that the Department fell short of the statutory mandate for accommodating handicapped employees. . . .

" . . . Based on the evidence available at that time to the agency, it is obvious that the agency should not have abandoned the fitness-for-duty process but should have made a tentative determination that his job deficiencies were caused by his alcoholism disease. That would have triggered the formal procedures for reasonably accommodating handicapped employees who can no longer perform their job duties, including an offer of an extended leave without pay for in-patient treatment, presumably at St. Elizabeth's or at the Veterans Administration, where he was also eligible. *See Doe v. Hampton*, 566 F.2d 265, 283–84 (D.C. Cir. 1977), remanding a discharge based on inadequate fitness-for-duty examination and inadequate consideration of leave without pay.

"This is not to say that in every instance where an agency confronts an alcoholic employee who has failed in treatment that it must offer leave without pay or some other specific arrangement. But if there is evidence, as there is here, that such a leave, providing opportunity to enter St. Elizabeth's of some other intensive alcoholism treatment program, might have been beneficial, the reasonable accommodation duty requires the agency to evaluate whether such a leave, or alternative arrangement, would have imposed an undue hardship on the agency. The agency made no such evaluation. Moreover, plaintiff has met his burden of showing evidence that he could have been reasonably accommodated by a leave without pay. Once an employee has shown evidence that his handicap can be accommodated, the burden of persuasion is on the agency to show that it cannot accommodate the employee. 29 C.F.R. §1613.704; *Treadwell v. Alexander,* 707 F.2d 473, 478 (11th Cir. 1983). The agency has failed to show undue hardship and thus it violated its duty to this handicapped employee. . . .

"Given the circumstances, the Court believes the most appropriate remedy is to allow the plaintiff to reapply at the Department of Labor and promptly undergo a comprehensive fitness-for-duty examination at the Department's expense. . . . If he is now found fit for re-employment in his prior position, or in another position at an equivalent or lower grade, the Department shall offer to rehire him at that grade. If not, the Department shall allow him to seek disability retirement as of the date of his application for re-employment."

24:5 *AIDS (HIV Infection) Discrimination*

As noted in section 24:4, people with AIDS and HIV (human immunodeficiency virus) infection are protected from employment discrimination under the Americans with Disabilities Act upon its effective date, 1992, (two years after enactment), because such a person's major life activities of procreation and intimate sexual relationships would be substantially limited. The fact that the individual had a record of such infection or was negatively viewed by coworkers or customers would not exempt the infected individual from the provisions of the 1990 Act. The only test for employment that the individual must meet is whether he can perform the essential functions of the job in question. The act also provides that appropriate "qualification standards" for the job may include a requirement that an individual does not pose a direct threat to the health or safety of other individuals in the workplace. However, that determination must be made on a case-by-case basis and may not be predicated upon ignorance, prejudice, irrational fears, or other similar criteria derived from coworkers or customers.

24:6 *Sexual Harassment*

As part of the comprehensive administration of Title VII of the federal Civil Rights Act, the Equal Employment Opportunity Commission (EEOC) has issued regulations governing sexual harassment of employees in the workplace by coworkers or supervisors. This form of harassment takes two forms: (1) *quid pro quo* and (2) *hostile environment* harassment.

Quid pro quo harassment involves unwelcome requests for sexual favors which are a term or condition of employment or reasonably perceived by the employee as such a term or condition. For example, continued employment, a promotion, favorable review, or other tangible job benefit is explicitly or implicitly conditioned upon the employee's positive response to a requested sexual favor by a supervisor.

Hostile environment harassment involves requests for sexual favors that do not involve tangible job benefits, but create an intimidating, hostile, or offensive working environment. Usually more than one such incident must occur in order to establish this form of discrimination.

The leading case interpreting the scope of workplace sexual harassment under Title VII of the federal Civil Rights Act of 1964 is *Meritor Savings Bank v. Vinson,* excerpted below, in which the Untied States Supreme Court first recognized that the Act governed *hostile environment* as well as *quid pro quo* harassment. However, the Supreme Court declined to rule on the issue of employer liability and rejected the view that employers are automatically liable for sexual harassment or, conversely, the view that absence of notice automatically insulated employers from liability. Agency principles would govern in such cases. The court's analysis of these and other issues follows.

MERITOR SAVINGS BANK v. VINSON
477 U.S. 57, 91 L. Ed. 2d 49 (1986)

REHNQUIST, J.: " . . .

" . . . Title VII of the Civil Rights Act of 1964 makes it 'an unlawful employment practice for an employer . . . to discriminate against any individual with respect to his compensation, terms, conditions, or privileges of employment, because of such individual's race, color, religion, sex, or national origin.' 42 U.S.C. §2000e–2(a)(1). . . .

"Respondent argues, and the Court of Appeals held, that unwelcome sexual advances that create an offensive or hostile working environment violate Title VII. Without question, when a supervisor sexually harasses a subordinate because of the subordinate's sex, that supervisor 'discriminate[s]' on the basis of sex. Petitioner apparently does not challenge this proposition. It contends instead that in prohibiting discrimination with respect to 'compensation, terms, conditions, or privileges' of employment, Congress was concerned with what petitioner describes as 'tangible loss' of 'an economic character,' not 'purely psychological aspects of the workplace environment,' Brief for Petitioner 30––31, 34. In support of this claim petitioner observes that in both the legislative history of Title VII and this Court's Title VII decisions, the focus has been on tangible, economic barriers erected by discrimination.

"We reject petitioner's view. First, the language of Title VII is not limited to 'economic' or 'tangible' discrimination. The phrase 'terms, conditions, or privileges of employment' evinces a congressional intent ' "to strike at the entire spectrum of disparate treatment of men and women" ' in employment. *Los An-*

geles Dept. of Water and Power v. Manhart, 435 U.S. 702, 707, n. 13, 98 S. Ct. 1370, 1375, n. 13, 55 L. Ed. 2d 657 (1978), quoting *Sprogis v. United Air Lines, Inc.,* 444 F.2d 1194, 1198 (CA7 1971). Petitioner has pointed to nothing in the Act to suggest that Congress contemplated the limitation urged here.

"Second, in 1980 the EOC issued Guidelines specifying that 'sexual harassment' as there defined, is a form of sex discrimination prohibited by Title VII. As an 'administrative interpretation of the Act by the enforcing agency,' *Griggs v. Duke Power Co.,* 401 U.S. 424, 433–434, 91 S. Ct. 849, 855, 28 L. Ed. 2d 158 (1971), these Guidelines, ' "while not controlling upon the courts by reason of their authority, do constitute a body of experience and informed judgment to which courts and litigants may properly resort for guidance," ' *General Electric Co. v. Gilbert,* 429 U.S. 125, 141–142, 97 S. Ct. 401, 410–11, 50 L. Ed. 2d 343 (1976), quoting *Skidmore v. Swift & Co.,* 323 U.S. 134, 140, 65 S. Ct. 161, 164, 89 L. Ed. 124 (1944). The EEOC Guidelines fully support the view that harassment leading to noneconomic injury can violate Title VII. . . .

"In concluding that so-called 'hostile environment' (*i.e.,* non *quid pro quo*) harassment violates Title VII, the EEOC drew upon a substantial body of judicial decisions and EEOC precedent holding that Title VII affords employees the right to work in an environment free from discriminatory intimidation, ridicule, and insult. *See* generally 45 Fed. Reg. 74676 (1980). *Rogers v. EEOC,* 454 F.2d 234 (CA5 1971), *cert. denied,* 406 U.S. 957, 92 S. Ct. 2058, 32 L. Ed. 2d 343 (1972), was apparently the first case to recognize a cause of action based upon a discriminatory work environment. In *Rogers,* the Court of Appeals for the Fifth Circuit held that a Hispanic complainant could establish a Title VII violation by demonstrating that her employer created an offensive work environment for employees by giving discriminatory service to its Hispanic clientele. . . .

"Since the Guidelines were issued, courts have uniformly held, and we agree, that a plaintiff may establish a violation of Title VII by proving that discrimination based on sex has created a hostile or abusive work environment. . . .

"Of course, as the courts in both *Rogers* and *Henson* [*v. City of Dundee,* 682 F.2d 897] recognized, not all workplace conduct that may be described as 'harassment' affects a 'term, condition, or privilege' of employment within the meaning of Title VII. . . .

"For sexual harassment to be actionable, it must be sufficiently severe or pervasive ' to alter the conditions of [the victim's] employment and create an abusive working environment.' [*Henson,* 689 F.2d at 904.] Respondent's allegations in this case—which include not only pervasive harassment but also criminal conduct of the most serious nature—are plainly sufficient to state a claim for 'hostile environment' sexual harassment.

"The question remains, however, whether the District Court's ultimate finding that respondent 'was not the victim of sexual harassment,' 22 EPD ¶30,708, at 14,692–14,693, 23 FEP Cases, at 43, effectively disposed of respondent's claim. The Court of Appeals recognized, we think correctly, that this ultimate finding was likely based on one or both of two erroneous views of the law. First, the District Court apparently believed that a claim for sexual harassment will not lie absent an *economic* effect on the complainant's employment. . . . Since it appears that the District Court made its findings without ever considering the 'hostile environment' theory of sexual harassment, the Court of Appeals' decision to remand was correct.

"Second, the District Court's conclusion that no actionable harassment occurred might have rested on its earlier 'finding' that '[i]f [respondent] and Taylor did engage in an intimate or sexual relationship . . . , that relationship was a voluntary one.' *Id.*, at 14, 692, 23 FEP Cases, at 42. But the fact that sex-related conduct was 'voluntary,' in the sense that the complainant was not forced to participate against her will, is not a defense to a sexual harassment suit brought under Title VII. The gravamen of any sexual harassment claim is that the alleged sexual advances were 'unwelcome.' 29 CFR § 1604.11(a) (1985). While the question whether particular conduct was indeed unwelcome presents difficult problems of proof and turns largely on credibility determinations committed to the trier of fact, the District Court in this case erroneously focused on the 'voluntariness' of respondent's participation in the claimed sexual episodes. The correct inquiry is whether respondent by her conduct indicated that the alleged sexual advances were unwelcome, not whether her actual participation in sexual intercourse was voluntary.

"Petitioner contends that even if this case must be remanded to the District Court, the Court of Appeals erred in one of the terms of its remand. Specifically, the Court of Appeals stated that testimony about respondent's 'dress and personal fantasies,' 243 U.S. App. D.C., at 328, n. 36, 753 F.2d, at 146, n. 36, which the District Court apparently admitted into evidence, 'had no place in this litigation.' *Ibid.* The apparent ground for this conclusion was that respondent's voluntariness *vel non* in submitting to Taylor's advances was immaterial to her sexual harassment claim. While 'voluntariness' in the sense of consent is not a defense to such a claim, it does not follow that a complainant's sexually provocative speech or dress is irrelevant as a matter of law in determining whether he or she found particular sexual advances unwelcome. To the contrary, such evidence is obviously relevant. The EEOC Guidelines emphasize that the trier of fact must determine the existence of sexual harassment in light of 'the record as a whole' and 'the totality of circumstances, such as the nature of the sexual advances and the context in which the alleged incidents occurred.' 29 CFR §1604.11(b) (1985). Respondent's claim that any marginal relevance of the evidence in question was outweighed by the potential for unfair prejudice is the sort of argument properly addressed to the District Court. In this case the District Court concluded that the evidence should be admitted, and the Court of Appeal's contrary conclusion was based upon the erroneous, categorical view that testimony about provocative dress and publicly expressed sexual fantasies 'had no place in this litigation.' 243 U.S. App. D.C., at 328, n. 36, 753 F.2d, at 146, n. 36. While the District Court must carefully weigh the applicable considerations in deciding whether to admit evidence of this kind, there is no *per se* rule against its admissibility.

"Although the District Court concluded that respondent had not proved a violation of Title VII, it nevertheless went on to consider the question of the bank's liability. Finding that 'the bank was without notice' of Taylor's alleged conduct, and that notice to Taylor was not the equivalent of notice to the bank, the court concluded that the bank therefore could not be held liable for Taylor's alleged actions. The Court of Appeals took the opposite view, holding that an employer is strictly liable for a hostile environment created by a supervisor's sexual advances, even though the employer neither knew nor reasonably could have known of the alleged misconduct. The court held that a supervisor, whether or not he possesses the authority to hire, fire, or promote, is necessarily an 'agent' of his employer for all Title VII purposes, since 'even the appearance' of such authority may enable him to impose himself on his subordinates. . . .

"Petitioner argues that respondent's failure to use its established grievance procedure, or to otherwise put it on notice of the alleged misconduct, insulates petitioner from liability for Taylor's wrongdoing. A contrary rule would be unfair, petitioner argues, since in a hostile environment harassment case the employer often will have no reason to know about, or opportunity to cure, the alleged wrongdoing.

"The EEOC, in its brief as *amicus curiae,* contends that courts formulating employer liability rules should draw from traditional agency principles. Examination of those principles has led the EEOC to the view that where a supervisor exercises the authority actually delegated to him by his employer, by making or threatening to make decisions affecting the employment status of his subordinates, such actions are properly imputed to the employer whose delegation of authority empowered the supervisor to undertake them. Brief for United States and EEOC as *Amici Curiae* 22. Thus, the courts have consistently held employers liable for the discriminatory discharges of employees by supervisory personnel, whether or not the employer knew, should have known, or approved of the supervisor's actions. *E.g., Anderson v. Methodist Evangelical Hospital, Inc.,* 464 F.2d 723, 725 (CA6 1972). . . .

"This debate over the appropriate standard for employer liability has a rather abstract quality about it given the state of the record in this case. We do not know at this stage whether Taylor made any sexual advances toward respondent at all, let alone whether those advances were unwelcome, whether they were sufficiently pervasive to constitute a condition of employment, or whether they were 'so pervasive and so long continuing . . . that the employer must have become conscious of [them],' *Taylor v. Jones,* 653 F.2d 1193, 1197–1199 (CA8 1981) (holding employer liable for racially hostile working environment based on constructive knowledge).

"We therefore decline the parties' invitation to issue a definitive rule on employer liability, but we do agree with the EEOC that Congress wanted courts to look to agency principles for guidance in this area. While such common-law principles may not be transferable in all their particulars to Title VII, Congress' decision to define ' employer' to include any 'agent' of an employer, 42 U.S.C. §2000e(b), surely evinces an intent to place some limits on the acts of employees for which employers under Title VII are to be held responsible. For this reason, we hold that the Court of Appeals erred in concluding that employers are always automatically liable for sexual harassment by their supervisors. See generally Restatement (Second) of Agency §§219–237 (1958). For the same reason, absence of notice to an employer does not necessarily insulate that employer from liability. *Ibid.*

"Finally, we reject petitioner's view that the mere existence of a grievance procedure and a policy against discrimination, coupled with respondent's failure to invoke that procedure, must insulate petitioner from liability. While those facts are plainly relevant, the situation before us demonstrates why they are not necessarily dispositive. Petitioner's general nondiscrimination policy did not address sexual harassment in particular, and thus did not alert employees to their employer's interest in correcting that form of discrimination. App. 25. Moreover, the bank's grievance procedure apparently required an employee to complain first to her supervisor, in this case Taylor. Since Taylor was the alleged perpetrator, it is not altogether surprising that respondent failed to invoke the procedure and report her grievance to him. Petitioner's contention that respondent's failure should insulate it from liability might be substantially stronger if its procedures were better calculated to encourage victims of harassment to come forward.

"In sum, we hold that a claim of ' hostile environment' sex discrimination is actionable under Title VII, that the District Court's findings were insufficient to dispose of respondent's hostile environment claim, and that the District Court did not err in admitting testimony about respondent's sexually provocative speech and dress. As to employer liability, we conclude that the Court of Appeals was wrong to entirely disregard agency principles and impose absolute liability on employers for the acts of their supervisors, regardless of the circumstances of a particular case.

"Accordingly, the judgment of the Court of Appeals reversing the judgment of the District Court is affirmed, and the case is remanded for further proceedings consistent with this opinion.

"*It is so ordered.*"

In *Rabidue v. Osceola Refining Co.,* below, the federal Circuit Court of Appeals for the Sixth Circuit affirmed the dismissal of a claim of sexual hostile environment harassment. In doing so, the court adopted the test that the victim must prove that (1) the workplace was hostile to a reasonable person, (2) the prevailing social attitude condoning vulgar language and sexually oriented posters in the workplace did not meet the hostile environment standard, and (3) the employer had knowledge of the hostile environment (*respondeat superior*). The dissent took exception to this three-part test and would require proof that the workplace was hostile to a reasonable victim, not simply a reasonable person. The dissent also disagreed that plaintiff bears the burden of proving employer knowledge. Both opinions are noted.

RABIDUE V. OSCEOLA REFINING CO.
805 F.2d 611 (6th Cir. 1986)

KRUPANSKY, C.J.: " . . .

"Thus, to prove a claim of abusive work environment premised upon sexual harassment a plaintiff must demonstrate that she would not have been the object of harassment but for her sex. *Henson* [*v. Dundee*], 682 F.2d at 904 (citations omitted). It is of significance to note that instances of complained of sexual conduct that prove equally offensive to male and female workers would not support a Title VII sexual harassment charge because both men and women were accorded like treatment. *Id.* (citing, *inter alia, Barnes v. Costle*, 561 F.2d 983, 990 n. 55 (D.C. Cir. 1977); *Bradford v. Sloan Paper Co.*, 383 F. Supp. 1157, 1161 (N.D. Ala. 1974); *Note, Sexual Harassment and Title VII*, 76 U. Mich. L. Rev. 1007, 1020–21 & n. 99, 1033 & n. 178 (1978); *Comment, Sexual Harassment and Title VII*, 51 N.Y.U. L. Rev. 148, 151–52 (1976).

"Unlike *quid pro quo* sexual harassment which may evolve from a single incident, sexually hostile or intimidating environments are characterized by multiple and varied combinations and frequencies of offensive exposures, which characteristics would dictate an order of proof that placed the burden upon the plaintiff to demonstrate that injury resulted not from a single or isolated offensive incident, comment, or conduct, but from incidents, comments, or conduct that occurred with some frequency. To accord appropriate protection to both plaintiffs and defendants in a hostile and/or abusive work environment sexual harassment case, the trier of fact, when judging the totality of the circumstances impacting upon the asserted abusive and hostile environment placed in issue by the plaintiff's charges, must adopt the perspective of a reasonable person's reaction to a similar environment under essentially like or similar circumstances. Thus, in the absence of conduct which would interfere with that hypothetical reasonable individual's work performance and affect seriously the psychological well-being of that reasonable person under like circumstances, a plaintiff may not prevail on asserted charges of sexual harassment anchored in an alleged hostile and/or abusive work environment regardless of whether the plaintiff was actually offended by the defendant's conduct. Assuming that the plaintiff has successfully satisfied the burden of proving that the defendant's conduct would have interfered with a reasonable individual's work performance and would have affected seriously the psychological well-being of a reasonable employee, the particular plaintiff would nevertheless also be required to demonstrate that she was actually offended by the defendant's conduct and that she suffered some degree of injury as a result of the abusive and hostile work environment.

"Accordingly, a proper assessment or evaluation of an employment environment that gives rise to a sexual harassment claim would invite consideration of such objective and subjective factors as the nature of the alleged harassment, the background and experience of the plaintiff, her coworkers, and supervisors, the totality of the physical environment of the plaintiff's work area, the lexicon of obscenity that pervaded the environment of the workplace both before and after the plaintiff's introduction into its environs, coupled with the reasonable expectation of the plaintiff upon voluntarily entering that environment. Thus, the presence of actionable sexual harassment would be different depending upon the personality of the plaintiff and the prevailing work environment and must be considered and evaluated upon an *ad hoc* basis. As Judge NEWBLATT aptly stated in his opinion in the district court:

> "Indeed, it cannot seriously be disputed that in some work environments, humor and language are rough hewn and vulgar. Sexual jokes, sexual conversations and girlie magazines may abound. Title VII was not meant to— or can—change this. It must never be forgotten that Title VII is the federal court mainstay in the struggle for equal employment opportunity for the female workers of America. But it is quite different to claim that Title VII was designed to bring about a magical transformation in the social mores of American workers. Clearly, the Court's qualification is necessary to enable 29 C.F.R. § 1604.11(a)(3) to function as a workable judicial standard.

"*Rabidue*, 584 F. Supp. at 430.

"To prevail in an action that asserts a charge of offensive work environment sexual harassment, the ultimate burden of proof is upon the plaintiff to additionally demonstrate *respondeat superior* liability by proving that the employer, through its agents or supervisory personnel, know or should have known of the charged sexual harassment and failed to implement prompt and appropriate corrective action. *See Barrett v. Omaha National Bank*, 726 F.2d 424, 427–28 (8th Cir. 1984); *Katz v. Dole*, 709 F.2d 251, 255–56 (4th Cir. 1983); *Henson*, 682 F.2d 905, 910 n. 20. *Cf. Erebia v. Chrysler Plastic Products Corp.*, 772 F.2d 1250, 1254 (6th Cir. 1985) (racial hostile working environment). *See generally* 1 Larson, Employment Discrimination §41.65 (1985). The promptness and adequacy of the employer's response to correct instances of alleged sexual harassment is of significance in assessing a sexually hostile environment claim and the employer's reactions must be evaluated upon a case by case basis. *See, e.g., Barrett*, 726 F.2d at 427. . . .

"A review of the Title VII sexual harassment issue in the matter *sub judice* prompts this court to conclude that the plaintiff neither asserted nor proved a claim of 'sexual advances,' 'sexual favors,' or ' physical conduct,' or sexual harassment implicating subparts (a)(1) or (a)(2) of the EEOC definition, more specifically, those elements typically at issue in a case of *quid pro quo* sexual harassment. Thus, the plaintiff to have prevailed in her cause of action against the defendant on this record must have proved that she had been subjected to unwelcomed verbal conduct and poster displays of a sexual nature which had unreasonably interfered with her work performance and created an intimidating, hostile, or offensive working environment that affected seriously her psychological well-being.

"In the case at bar, the record effectively disclosed that Henry's [supervisor] obscenities, although annoying, were not so startling as to have affected seriously the psyches of the plaintiff or other female employees. The evidence did not demonstrate that this single employee's vulgarity substantially affected the totality of the workplace. The sexually oriented poster displays had a *de minimis* effect on the plaintiff's work environment when considered in the context of a society that condones and publicly features and commercially exploits open displays of written and pictorial erotica at the newsstands, on prime-time television, at the cinema, and in other public places. In sum, Henry's vulgar language, coupled with the sexually oriented posters, did not result in a working environment that could be considered intimidating, hostile, or offensive under 29 C.F.R. §1604.11(a)(3) as elaborated upon by this court. The district court's factual findings supporting its conclusion to this effect were not clearly erroneous. It necessarily follows that the plaintiff failed to sustain her burden of proof that she was the victim of a Title VII sexual harassment violation. Accordingly, the trial court's disposition of this issue is AFFIRMED. . . . ''

KEITH, C.J. (concurring in part, dissenting in part): '' . . .

'' . . . I dissent because I am unable to accept key elements of the standard for sexual harassment set forth in the majority opinion. Specifically, I would not impose on the plaintiff alleging hostile environment harassment an additional burden of proving *respondeat superior* liability where a supervisor is responsible for the harm. In *Meritor Savings Bank v. Vinson*, 477 U.S. 57, 106 S. Ct. 2399, 91 L. Ed. 2d 49 (1986), the Supreme Court instructed courts to determine employer liability according to agency principles. *Id.*——U.S.——, 106 S. Ct. at 2407. Agency principles establish that an employer is normally liable for the acts of its supervisors and agents. *Id.* Because a supervisor is 'clothed with the employer's authority' and is responsible for the 'day-to-day supervision of the work environment and with ensuring a safe, productive workplace,'his abusive behavior in violation of that duty should be imputed to the employer just as with any other supervisory action which violates Title VII. *Id.*——U.S. at——, 106 S. Ct. at 2410–11 (J. MARSHALL concurring, joined by JJ. BRENNAN, BLACK-MUN and STEVENS). The creation of a discriminatory work environment by a supervisor can only be achieved through the power accorded him by the employer. I see insufficient reason to add an element of proof not imposed on any other discrimination victim, particularly where agency principles and the 'goals of Title VII law' preclude the imposition of automatic liability in all circumstances. *Id.* . . .

"In cases of hostile work environment harassment by coworkers, I would follow guidelines set forth by the Equal Employment Opportunity Commission:

"With respect to conduct between fellow employees, an employer is responsible for acts of sexual harassment in the workplace where the employer (or its agents or supervisory employees) knows or should have known of the conduct unless it can show that it took immediate and appropriate action.

"29 C.F.R. §§ 1604.11(d)(1985).

"Nor do I agree with the majority holding that a court considering hostile environment claims should adopt the perspective of the reasonable person's reaction to a similar environment. At 619. In my view, the reasonable person perspective fails to account for the wide divergence between most women's views of appropriate sexual conduct and those of men. *See Comment, Sexual Harassment Claims of Abusive Work Environment under Title VII*, 97 Harv. L. Rev. 1449, 1451 (1984). As suggested by the *Comment*, I would have courts adopt the perspective of the reasonable victim which simultaneously allows courts to consider salient sociological differences as well as shield employers from the neurotic complainant. *Id.* at 1459. Moreover, unless the outlook of the reasonable woman is adopted, the defendants as well as the courts are permitted to sustain ingrained notions of reasonable behavior fashioned by the offenders, in this case, men. *Id.*

"Which brings me to the majority's mandate to consider the 'prevailing work environment,' 'the lexicon of obscenity that pervaded the environment both before and after plaintiff's introduction into its environs,' and plaintiff's reasonable expectations upon 'voluntarily' entering that environment. At 620. The majority suggests through these factors that a woman assumes the risk of working in an abusive, anti-female environment. Moreover, the majority contends that such work environments somehow have an innate right to perpetuation and are not to be addressed under Title VII. . . .

"In my view, Title VII's precise purpose is to prevent such behavior and attitudes from poisoning the work environment of classes protected under the Act. To condone the majority's notion of the 'prevailing workplace' I would also have to agree that if an employer maintains an anti-semitic workforce and tolerates a workplace in which 'kike' jokes, displays of nazi literature and anti-Jewish conversation 'may abound,' a Jewish employee assumes the risk of working there, and a court must consider such a work environment as 'prevailing.' I cannot. As I see it, job relatedness is the only additional factor which legitimately bears on the inquiry of plaintiff's reasonableness in finding her work environment offensive. In other words, the only additional question I would find relevant is whether the behavior complained of is required to perform the work. . . .

"As I believe no woman should be subjected to an environment where her sexual dignity and reasonable sensibilities are visually, verbally or physically assaulted as a matter of prevailing male prerogative, I dissent. . . .

"In conclusion, I dissent because the record shows that defendant's treatment of plaintiff evinces anti-female animus and that plaintiff's gender played a role in her dismissal. I also believe the hostile environment standard set fourth in the majority opinion shields and condones behavior Title VII would have the courts redress. Finally, in my view, the standard fails to encourage employers to set up internal complaint procedures or otherwise seriously address the problem of sexual harassment in the workplace."

In the following case, the federal District Court for the District of Columbia found for a female government staff attorney who alleged sexual hostile environment harassment in her workplace, the United States Securities and Exchange Commission (SEC) at the Washington Regional Field Office (WRO). The court made the following conclusions of law.

BRODERICK V. RUDER
685 F. Supp. 269 (D.D.C. 1988)

PRATT, J.: [Facts and procedural aspects omitted.]

Plaintiff's Sexual Harassment Claim

"2. The parties stipulated that the definition of sexual harassment contained in the Equal Employment Opportunity Commission's Guidelines on Discrimination Because of Sex. 29 C.F.R. §1604.11 (1986), is the definition that should be applied in this case. Section 1604.11(a) defines sexual harassment as follows: 'Unwelcome sexual advances, requests for sexual favors, and other verbal or physical conduct of a sexual nature constitute sexual harassment when (1) submission to such conduct is made either explicitly or implicitly a term or condition of an individual's employment, (2) submission to or rejection of such conduct by an individual is used as the basis for employment decisions affecting such individual, or (3) *such conduct has the purpose or the effect of unreasonably interfering with an individual's work performance or creating an intimidating, hostile or offensive working environment.*' (emphasis supplied.) Additionally, section 1604.11(g) provides that '[w]here employment opportunities or benefits are granted because of an individual's submission to the employer's sexual advances or requests for sexual favors, the employer may be held liable for unlawful sex discrimination against other persons who were qualified for but denied that employment opportunity or benefit.

"3. The United States Supreme Court recently held that a violation of Title VII may be predicted on either of two types of sexual harassment: (a) harassment that involves the conditioning of concrete employment benefits in return for sexual favors, and (b) harassment that, while not directly affecting economic benefits, creates a hostile or offensive working environment. *Meritor Savings Bank, F.S.B. v. Vinson,* 477 U.S. 57, 62–67, 40 FEP Cases 1822 (1986); [citations omitted].

"4. A 'hostile work environment' claim is actionable under Title VII if unwelcome sexual advances, requests for sexual favors, and other verbal or physical conduct of a sexual nature are so pervasive that it can reasonably be said that they create a hostile or offensive work environment. *Meritor,* 477 U.S. at 65–67. Whether the sexual conduct is sufficiently pervasive to amount to harassment and create a hostile or offensive work environment must be determined from the totality of the circumstances. . . . Additionally, Title VII is also violated when an employer affords preferential treatment to female employees who submit to sexual advances or other conduct of a sexual nature and such conduct is a matter of common knowledge. *King v. Palmer,* 778 F.2d 878, 880, 39 FEP Cases 877 (D.C. Cir. 1985); *Priest v. Rotary,* 634 F. Supp. 571, 581, 40 FEP Cases 208 (N.D. Cal 1986); *Toscano v. Nimmo,* 570 F. Supp. 1197, 1199, 32 FEP Cases 1401 (D. Del. 1983); *see also* 29 C.F.R. § 1604.11(g).

"5. Evidence of the general work atmosphere, involving employees other than the plaintiff, is relevant tot he issue of whether there existed an atmosphere of hostile work environment which violated Title VII. *Vinson v. Taylor,* 753 F.2d 141, 146, 36 FEP Cases 1423 (D.C. Cir. 1985), *aff'd in relevant part and rev'd in part,* 477 U.S. 57, 40 FEP Cases 1822 (1986); *Delgado v. Lehman,* 665 F. Supp. 460, 43 FEP Cases 593 (E.D. Va. 1987). *See also Rogers V. EEOC,* 454 F.2d 234, 4 FEP Cases 92 (5th Cir. 1971), *cert. denied,* 406 U.S. 957, 4 FEP Cases 771 (1972). This is so because '[e]ven a woman who was never herself the object of harassment might have a Title VII claim if she were forced to work in an atmosphere in which such harassment was pervasive.' *Vinson v. Taylor,* 753 F.2d at 146.

"6. Ms. Broderick established a *prima facie* case of sexual harassment because of having to work in a hostile work environment. The evidence at trial established that such conduct of a sexual nature was so pervasive at the WRO that it can reasonably be said that such conduct created a hostile or offensive work environment which affected the motivation and work performance of those who found such conduct repugnant and offensive. Ms. Broderick was herself sexually harassed by Leonard, Hunter, Kennedy and possibly others. But we need not emphasize these isolated incidents. More importantly, plaintiff, without any doubt, was forced to work in an environment in which the WRO managers by their conduct harassed her and other WRO female employees, by bestowing preferential treatment upon those who submitted to their sexual advances. Further, this preferential treatment undermined plaintiff's motivation and work performance and deprived plaintiff, and other WRO female employees, of promotions and job opportunities. The record is clear that plaintiff and other women working at the WRO found the sexual conduct and its accompanying manifestations which WRO managers engaged in over a protracted period of time to be offensive. The record also establishes that plaintiff and other women were for obvious reasons reluctant to voice their displeasure and, when they did, they were treated with a hostile response by WRO's management team.

Plaintiff's Opposition and Retaliation Claims

"7. Title VII makes it an unlawful employment practice for an employer to discriminate against an employee 'because [s]he has opposed any practice made an unlawful practice by this title. . . . ' 42 U.S.C. §2000e-3(a). As this court has recognized. ' "[t]he opposition clause" protects opposition expressed in a wide variety of forms and is not limited to the filing of charges.' *Jones [v. Lyng],* 669 F. Supp. at 1121–22. *See also Armstrong v. Index Journal Co.,* 647 F.2d 441, 448, 25 FEP Cases 1081 (4th Cir. 1981); *Novotny v. Great American Federal Savings and Loan Assoc.,* 584 F.2d 1235, 1260–61, 17 FEP Cases 1252 (3rd Cir. 1978). *vacated on other grounds,* 442 U.S. 366, 19 FEP Cases 1482 (1979); *Gresham v. Waffle House, Inc.,* 586 F. Supp. 1442, 1446, 35 FEP Cases 763 (N.D. Ga. 1984). Title VII also prohibits an employer from retaliating against an employee who 'has made a charge, testified, assisted or participated in any manner in an investigation, proceeding, or hearing . . . ' 42 U.S.C. §2000e-3(a).

"8. To establish a *prima facie* case of unlawful retaliation, a plaintiff must show (1) that she engaged in protected activity; (2) that she was subject to an adverse action by her employer after engaging in the protected activity, and (3) that there was a causal connection between the two. *Burrus v. United Telephone Co. of Kansas, Inc.*, 683 F.2d 339, 343, 29 FEP Cases 663 (10th Cir.), *cert. denied*. 459 U.S. 1071, 30 FEP Cases 592 (1982). [Citations omitted.]

"9. Plaintiff met the first element of her *prima facie* case by showing that she repeatedly protested the hostile work environment at the WRO and that she ultimately filed an EEO claim because of the office environment. Plaintiff complained to Hilton Foster about Hunter's insistence on giving her a ride and touring her apartment, the ridicule to which he subsequently subjected her and her transfer from his branch. She also told Foster about Hunter's attempt to proposition Karen Nelson and his efforts to get her fired after she rebuffed his overtures. She also informed him about the sexual remarks and gestures management made towards her and other female employees at the WRO. Furthermore, plaintiff made known her opposition to the Hunter-Bour affair, the Brooks-McDonald affair, the Kennedy-Sarles affair and the employment benefits awarded to these women because of their relationships with members of WRO's management team. Finally, when all else had failed, plaintiff, after more than two years of frustration, filed an EEO charge on February 16, 1984. These activities of plaintiff are clearly protected by Title VII against retaliation. *Jones*, 669 F. Supp. at 1121; *Spence v. Local 1250, United Auto Workers*, 595 F. Supp. 6, 10, 35 FEP Cases 1666 (N.D. Ohio 1984); *Garcia v. Rush-Presbyterian-St. Luke's Medical Center*, 80 F.R.D. 254, 262, 23 FEP Cases 165 (N.D. Ill. 1978); *Eichman v. Indiana State Univ. Bd. of Trustees*, 597 F.2d 1104, 1107, 19 FEP Cases 979 (7th Cir. 1979).

"10. Plaintiff met the second element of her *prima facie* case by demonstrating that she was subjected to adverse employment action after she made known her opposition to the WRO managers' conduct: to wit, promotion from GS-12 to GS-13 was delayed without explanation. *Hickman v. Flood & Peterson Ins., Inc.*, 29 Fair Empl. Prac. Cas. (BNA) 1467, 1469 (D. Colo. 1982). In addition, she was given adverse performance appraisals after she complained about the improper conduct of WRO managers, and she was reprimanded and threatened with termination when her complaints persisted. [Citations omitted.]

"11. Plaintiff also established the third element of the *prima facie* case by proving that the Commission was aware of the protected activities, and that the adverse actions followed *after* she made known her opposition and *after* she filed her EEO charge. For instance, the complaint of Foster in February 1984 concerning plaintiff's lack of punctuality, his threat of discharge and the adverse performance evaluation of 1984 are examples of defendant's retaliation. The proximity of the adverse actions taken against her and her protected activity establishes the necessary nexus to meet the third element of the required *prima facie* case. [Citations omitted.]

The Defendant's Failure to Rebut the *Prima Facie* Case

"12. In the ordinary gender bias case, once the plaintiff has established a *prima facie* case of discrimination or retaliation, the burden shifts to the defendant 'to articulate some legitimate non-discriminatory reason' for the actions taken. *Texas Dept. of Community Affairs v. Burdine*, 450 U.S. 248, 252, 25 FEP Cases 113 (1981); *McDonell Douglas Corp. v. Green*, 411 U.S. 797, 802-05, 5 FEP Cases 965 (1973); *Williams v. Boorstin*, 663 F.2d 109, 23 FEP Cases 1669 (D.C. Cir. 1980), *cert. denied*, 451 U.S. 985, 25 FEP Cases 1192 (1981). In a sexual harassment case involving the claim of hostile work environment, the burden on the defendant employer is markedly heavier. Once a plaintiff has established a *prima facie* case of sexual harassment or retaliation for opposing sexual harassment, the burden shifts to the employer to rebut the plaintiff's harassment claims and to show *by clear and convincing evidence* that the plaintiff would not have been treated differently if she had not opposed the harassment. [Citations omitted.] This is a higher standard than that required of an employer in a simple gender discrimination case. [Citation omitted.] The reason for this different rule in sexual harassment cases is that ' once a plaintiff establishes that she was harassed . . . it is hard to see how an employer can justify [the] harassment.' *Moffett v. Gene B. Glick Co., Inc.*, 621 F. Supp. 244, 266, 41 FEP Cases 671 (N.D. Ind. 1985).

"13. In this case, the Commission failed to rebut Ms. Broderick's hostile atmosphere, sexual harassment and retaliation claims by clear and convincing evidence, or even by a preponderance of the evidence. The Commission attempted to meet Ms. Broderick's harassment claims by arguing that Ms. Broderick 'was paranoid.' Admittedly, plaintiff had problems of personal adjustment before being employed by the Commission in 1979. Whether diagnosed either as 'paranoia' or as a 'post traumatic stress disorder', we are satisfied that plaintiff's mental condition was caused and exacerbated by the hostile atmosphere in which she worked. Even assuming that the assertion that plaintiff was a paranoid personality has support in Dr. Stein's testimony, it does not rebut similar testimony from other witnesses presented by the plaintiff as to the conditions of sexual harassment and retaliation at the WRO.

"14. With respect to plaintiff's opposition and retaliation claims, the Commission's argument that Ms. Broderick's tardiness and her diminished work performance accounted for her performance evaluations and were legitimate reasons for reprimands and threats to terminate her are not persuasive in the overall context of this case. The Commission's allegations of excessive tardiness when tardiness by others was overlooked is sheer 'make weight' and pretext. Ms. Broderick amply demonstrated, through both lay and expert witnesses, that any alleged deficiencies in her work performance, which rested largely on her failure to interact with her supervisors, were directly attributable to the atmosphere in which she worked.[10]

"15. Defendant in effect argues that this is a '*quid pro quo*' sex harassment case and, except for isolated instances, plaintiff was not sexually harassed. This contention is in error and misses the mark. The Commission's attempt to justify the sexual misconduct on the part of supervisory personnel as 'social/sexual interactions between and among employees' which Title VII never intended to regulate is unacceptable on the facts of this case. However relaxed one's views of sexual morality may be in a different context, such views do not cover the pattern of conduct disclosed by the record in this case. We hold, and plaintiff has proved, that consensual sexual relations, in exchange for tangible employment benefits, while possibly not creating a cause of action for the recipient of such sexual advances who does not find them unwelcome, do, and in this case did, create and contribute to a sexually hostile working environment.

"16. The SEC was the employer of, and had authority over, the personnel who persisted in this activity of which it had actual, as well as constructive, knowledge. It took no action. It is therefore liable under agency principles for the acts of these high-ranking subordinates.

The Court's Order

" . . .

"ORDERED that judgment be and the same hereby is entered in favor of plaintiff for defendant's violation of Title VII of the Civil Rights Act of 1964.

"10. Plaintiff's diminished performance cannot be asserted as a legitimate basis for her removal when that diminution is the direct result of the employer's discriminatory behavior. *Delgado v. Lehman*, 665 F. Supp. at 467; *Moffett*, 621 F. Supp. at 281; *Weiss v. United States*, 595 F. Supp. 1050, 1057, 36 FEP Cases 1 (E.D. Va. 1984); *Lamb v. Drilco Div. v. Smith Int'l*, 32 Fair Empl. Prac. Cas. (BNA) 105, 107 (S.D. Tex. 1983). *See also Henson v. City of Dundee*, 682 F.2d 897, 910, 29 FEP Cases 787 (11th Cir. 1982)."

The federal Circuit Court of Appeals for the Third Circuit dealt with the *quid pro quo* type of sexual harassment in *Craig v. Y and Y Snacks, Inc.*, excerpted below. On the issue of actual or constructive notice to impose employer liability for supervisory harassment, the court ruled as follows.

CRAIG V. Y AND Y SNACKS, INC.
721 F.2d 77 (3rd Cir. 1983)

SLOVITER, Cir. J.:

Facts and Procedural History

"Valerie A. Craig worked for Y & Y Snacks, Inc. in the packaging department, where popcorn and other snack foods were packed and bagged in a small assembly-line operation. Her supervisor at all relevant times was Harris Hughes, who, by his own testimony and that of the company president, exercised 'complete discretion' over hiring, firing, scheduling and disciplining employees in the department.

"On July 15, 1978, Hughes joined Craig and several other employees for drinks after work, and then gave Craig a lift. In the car Hughes proposed that they go to Craig's house for the purpose of sexual relations. Craig refused. Hughes persisted, Craig persisted in refusing, and before he dropped her off Hughes said he would 'get even' with her. Craig's account of the events of July 15 stand uncontradicted.

"The following week Hughes was noticeably cool to Craig and several times refused to excuse her to use the restroom, a departure from his previous practice. On July 25 Craig did not report to work, having left a message before the shift started that she was ill and had gone to her doctor's office. She returned the next day with a doctor's note to find that Hughes had dismissed her.

"Craig testified, and the district court found, that she immediately told David Yaffe, Y & Y's President, of her discharge and of her suspicion that it was motivated by the events of July 15. Yaffe told her he would look into the matter, but when she called him several days later he said that her record justified her dismissal and that he would not reinstate her. Yaffe testified he knew nothing of the incident until months later, when he received a complaint that Craig had filed with the Equal Employment Opportunity Commission. The district court credited Craig's account regarding notice, and determined liability in her favor. The court subsequently issued an order directing Craig's reinstatement, enjoining Y & Y from making future reprisals against Craig, and granting Craig back pay, reduced by the amount of interim earnings and unemployment compensation that she received after her dismissal.

Liability

" . . . Y & Y claims that the court failed to apply the requirement of *Tomkins v. Public Service Electric & Gas Co.*, 568 F.2d 1044 (3d Cir. 1977), that the employer have actual or constructive knowledge of the harassment before it may be held liable. . . .

"Y & Y complains . . . that the district court failed to follow this court's ruling in *Tomkins v. Public Service Electric & Gas, supra.* In *Tomkins*, the district court, characterizing sexual harassment as an 'abuse of authority . . . for personal purposes' outside the scope of Title VII, had dismissed the employee's complaint. In reversing the dismissal and directing reinstatement of the complaint, Judge ALDISERT, in a seminal opinion on the issue of sexual harassment, distinguished between 'complaints alleging sexual advances of an individual or personal nature' and 'those alleging direct employment consequences flowing from the advances', which do constitute Title VII violations. He stated two elements are necessary to find a violation of Title VII: ' first, that a term or condition of employment has been imposed and second, that it has been imposed by the employer, either directly or vicariously, in a sexually discriminatory fashion.' 568 F.2d at 1048.

"Y & Y suggests that *Tomkins* imposed a requirement that an employer have actual or constructive knowledge of the sexual harassment at the time the advance was made. Y & Y Brief at 13. Nothing in *Tomkins* imposes such an unreasonable burden on an employee. In the relevant, and oft-quoted, language, the court stated:

"Applying these requirements to the present complaint, we conclude that Title VII is violated when a supervisor, with the actual or constructive knowledge of the employer, makes sexual advances or demands toward a subordinate employee and conditions that employee's job status . . . on a favorable response to those advances or demands, and the employer does not take prompt and appropriate remedial action. . . .

"568 F.2d at 1048–49 (emphasis added). As the *Tomkins* opinion noted, the complaint filed in that case alleged that the plaintiff's employer 'either knowingly or constructively, made acquiescence in her supervisor's sexual demands a necessary prerequisite of, or advancement in, her job.' *Id.* at 1046. The holding on appeal was that these allegations, if proven, would establish a Title VII violation.

"The district court in this case found that Yaffe, Y & Y's President, had actual notice of the harassment immediately after the discharge, and failed to take adequate remedial steps. Actual knowledge at the time of the employment decision at issue satisfied the *Tomkins* ruling.

"Furthermore, when a supervisor who has plenary authority over hiring, discipline and dismissal makes an employment decision, that decision may be imputed to the employer. Title VII itself defines 'employer' to include 'any agent of such a person.' 42 U.S.C. §2000e(b). . . .

"It is also the prevailing view in other circuits that employer liability follows when the supervising employee has broad authority over employment decisions. *See* Waks and Starr, *Sexual Harassment in the Work Place: The Scope of Employer Liability,* 7 Employee Relations L.J. 369, 377–78 (1981). *See, e.g., Henson v. City of Dundee,* 682 F.2d 897, 910 (11th Cir. 1982) (employer strictly liable for sexual harassment by supervisors that results in 'tangible job detriment'); *Miller v. Bank of America,* 600 F.2d 211, 213 (9th Cir. 1979) (*respondeat superior* applies to harassment by supervisor authorized to hire, fire, discipline or promote, even if harassment violates company policy); *Barnes v. Costle,* 561 F.2d 983, 993 (D.C. Dir. 1977) (employer generally liable for Title VII violations 'occasioned by discriminatory practices of supervisory personnel'); *see also Ferguson v. E.I. duPont de Nemours and Co.,* 560 F. Supp. 1172, 1198–99 n. 62 (D. Del. 1983).

"We conclude that the imputation of knowledge to an employer in situations, such as this one, in which an offending supervisor has unbridled authority to retaliate against an employee is in accord with *Tomkins.* To hold otherwise would vitiate the reference to 'constructive notice' in *Tomkins* and would lead to incongruous results. It would compel an employee who is subjected to a supervisor's sexual advances to notify the chief executive officer of each incident in order to preserve the employee's rights in the event of future retaliation. It would also, as the district court commented, permit an employer to insulate itself from Title VII liability 'by sealing off its ultimate executive officials from those with the fullest form of day to day operational authority to govern at the plant level.' We do not believe that this course is mandated by *Tomkins,* or was envisioned by Congress when it enacted the Equal Employment Opportunity Act.

"Affirmed as to finding of sex discrimination. Reversed as to deduction of unemployment benefits from award."

24:7 *Alcohol and Drug Testing*

The Americans with Disabilities Act (ADA) excludes from protection those individuals who are involved in the illegal use of drugs when the employer acts to remove, discharge, or discipline on that basis. The ADA itself does not affect the ability of covered employers to mandate a drug- or alcohol-free workplace environment as a condition of employment by all employees. Employers can require all employees not to be under the influence of alcohol or engaged in illegal drug use at work and may further require employees to comply with the Drug-Free Workplace Act of 1988. The ADA does not require the employer to treat an employee who is a drug user or alcoholic to any lesser employment performance standard than that to which it holds other employees.

However, those individuals who have successfully completed a supervised drug or alcohol rehabilitation program and are no longer engaged in illegal drug use or are alcohol-free are protected under the ADA. Reasonable employer policies and procedures, including drug testing, are permitted to ensure that rehabilitated employees are drug- and alcohol-free.

As to drug testing, the ADA provides that a test to determine illegal drug use shall not be considered a "medical examination" under the law. The ADA is neutral on this problem, and the statute states that its provisions should not be construed to encourage, prohibit, or authorize drug testing for job applicants or employees or for making employment decisions on the basis of such test results.

In legal questions of the propriety of drug or alcohol testing in private workplaces, there is no constitutional prohibition that can be asserted against private employer testing on the ground of the Fourth Amendment's prohibition against unreasonable searches and seizures. That amendment is limited to state or federal government testing as a form of public employment action.[8]

In the private sector, the Supreme Court of Alaska recently dismissed a complaint of wrongful discharge based upon an oil drill rigger's refusal to submit to a urinalysis drug test mandated by his private employer. First, the high court determined that no federal constitutional right to be free of unreasonable searches and seizures was raised in this case. Second, the high court determined that Alaska's constitutional privacy provision was not involved, but that a common law right of privacy protected by public policy exists in Alaska. Finally, the court concluded that in this case weighing the balance between employee privacy and employer responsibility to support public health and safety, the employer must prevail. The court's rationale is extracted below.

LUEDKE V. NABORS ALASKA DRILLING COMPANY
768 P.2d 1123 (1989)

COMPTON, J.: [Facts and procedural aspects are omitted.]

" . . . [T]here is a sphere of activity in every person's life that is closed to scrutiny by others. . . . The boundaries of that sphere are determined by bal-

---

[8]*See* National Treasury Employees Union v. Von Raab, 816 F.2d 170 (5th Cir. 1987).

ancing a person's right to privacy against other public policies, such as 'the health, safety, rights and privileges of others. . . . ' Luedtke claim[s] that whether or not [he] use[s] marijuana is information within that protected sphere into which his employer, Nabors, may not intrude. We disagree. As we have previously observed, marijuana can impair a person's ability to function normally:

> "The short-term physiological effects are relatively undisputed. An immediate slight increase in the pulse, decrease in salivation, and a slight reddening of the eyes are usually noted. There is also impairment of psychomotor control. . . .
>
> " . . .

"Where the public policy supporting [Luedtke's] privacy in off-duty activities conflicts with the public policy supporting the protection of the health and safety of other workers, and even [Luedtke himself], the health and safety concerns are paramount. As a result, Nabors is justified in determining whether [Luedtke is] possibly impaired on the job by drug usage off the job.

"We observe, however, that the employer's prerogative does have limitations. First, the drug test must be conducted at a time reasonably contemporaneous with the employee's work time. The employer's interest is in monitoring drug use that may directly affect employee performance. The employer's interest is not in the broader police function of discovering and controlling the use of illicit drugs in general society. In the context of this case, Nabors could have tested [Luedtke] immediately prior to [his] departure for the North Slope, or immediately upon [his] return from the North Slope when the test could be reasonably certain of detecting drugs consumed there. Further, given Nabors' need to control the oil rig community, Nabors could have tested [him] at any time [he was] on the North Slope.

"Second, an employee must receive notice of the adoption of a drug testing program. By requiring a test, an employer introduces an additional term of employment. An employee should have notice of the additional term so that he may contest it, refuse to accept it and quit, seek to negotiate its conditions, or prepare for the test so that he will not fail it and thereby suffer sanctions."

24:8 OSHA: Employee Safety and Health

Because such traditional workplace remedies as workers' compensation laws are aimed at compensating for workplace accidents and disease after the fact and are necessarily reactive, as is most private litigation involving personal injuries, Congress sought to establish a means of preventing industrial injuries. Thus in 1970 Congress enacted the Occupational Safety and Health Act. The Act created the Occupational Safety and Health Administration (OSHA), which is authorized to administer health and safety standards in virtually every workplace in the United States. Although OSHA initially dealt with a myriad of seemingly obvious safety standards, its current focus is on prevention of occupational diseases. To illustrate: OSHA issued a stringent standard for the inhalation of benzene, a carcinogenic petroleum derivative, without specifying the magnitude of the harm created by the risk. The United States Supreme Court nullified that standard, telling OSHA that it could not involve itself with other than significant risks and that it must attempt to measure the size of a risk before initiating standards.[9]

Because it would be impossible for OSHA to establish rules against all workplace hazards, Congress provided a "general duty clause" in the Act. That clause requires all employers to provide a place of employment free from recognized hazards that can cause death or serious bodily harm, regardless of whether a federal standard governs the situation.

The Act's enforcement provisions permit OSHA to halt or enjoin serious risks and to fine violators up to $1000 per violation. The following cases highlight salient interpretations of the Act.

In *American Textile Manufacturers Institute, Inc. v. Donovan*,[10] the United States Supreme Court had to decide whether OSHA in promulgating a standard that reduces health and safety risks in the workplace was required to apply a cost-benefit analysis and whether its failure to do so rendered a cotton-dust standard legally inoperative. The court ruled that such an analysis need not be present and that a technological and economic feasibility analysis is sufficient. Justice Brennan reviewed the legislative history and concluded:

> When Congress passed the Occupational Safety and Health Act in 1970, it chose to place pre-eminent value on assuring employees a safe and healthful working environment, limited only by the feasibility of achieving such an environment. We must measure the validity of the Secretary's actions against the requirements of that Act. For "[t]he judicial function does not extend to substantive revision of regulatory policy. That function lies elsewhere—in Congressional and Executive oversight or amendatory legislation." *Industrial Union Dept. v. American Petroleum Institute*, 448 U.S., at 663 (BURGER, C.J., concurring); see *TVA v. Hill*, 437 U.S. 153, 185, 187–188, 194–195 (1978).

In *Whirlpool Corp. v. Marshall*,[11] the United States Supreme Court held that a regulation promulgated by the Secretary of Labor under the Occupational Safety and Health Act (OSHA) which granted an employee the right not to perform an assigned task because of reasonable apprehension of death or serious injury coupled with belief that no less drastic action is available is within the purview of the Act. This being so, the antiretaliation provisions of the Act prohibit firing or disciplining the employee.

In the case below, the federal Circuit Court of Appeals for the Sixth Circuit ruled that the specific duty provision of the Occupational Health and Safety Act is not limited to an employer's own employees, but protects the employees of an independent contractor working at the other employer's worksite. That issue is noted below.

---

[9]Industrial Union Dept. v. American Petroleum Institute, 448 U.S. 607, 65 L. Ed. 2d 1010 (1980).
[10]452 U.S. 490, 101 L. Ed. 2d 2478 (1981).
[11]445 U.S. 1, 160 L. Ed. 2d 883 (1979).

TEAL V. E.I. DUPONT DE NEMOURS AND CO.
728 F.2d 799 (6th Cir. 1984)

CELEBREEZE, C.J.: " . . .

"The second issue on appeal concerns the trial court's refusal to instruct the jury on the issue of negligence *per se*. Pursuant to Tennessee case law, a breach of a duty imposed by statute or regulation is negligence *per se* if the party injured is a member of the class of persons the statute or regulation was intended to protect. *E.g., Alex v. Armstrong*, 215 Tenn. 276, 385 S.W.2d 110 (1964); *Taylor v. Coburn*, 597 S.W.2d 319, 322 (Tenn. App. 1980); *Berry v. Whitworth*, 576 S.W.2d 351, 353 (Tenn. App. 1978). In this case, the parties agree that Richard Teal was, at the time of the accident, an employee of Daniel Construction, an independent contractor, and that Teal fell from a permanently affixed ladder in DuPont's plant. Further, the parties agree that the OSHA regulation established a duty owed by DuPont and that DuPont breached its duty to conform with the specifications of the regulation. Accordingly, the primary dispute is whether an employee of an independent contractor is a member of the class of persons that the OSHA regulation was intended to protect.

"DuPont argues that the stated purposes for the Occupational Safety and Health Act of 1970 reveal that Congress did not intend to impose a duty upon employers to protect the safety of an independent contractor's employees who work in the employer's plant. In support of this proposition, DuPont relies upon the plain language of the Act which provides that 'each employer shall furnish to each of *his* employees employment and a place of employment which are free from recognized hazards that are causing or are likely to cause death or serious physical harm to *his* employees.' 29 U.S.C. Sec. 654 (a)(1) (emphasis added). Although DuPont's legal position is not without support, *see Melerine v. Avondale Shipyards, Inc.*, 659 F.2d 706 (5th Cir. 1981), we believe that an employer's duty to comply with OSHA regulations is broader than DuPont suggests.

"Congress' primary purpose for enacting the Occupational Safety and Health Act is ' to assure so far as possible every working man and woman in the Nation safe and healthful working conditions.' 29 U.S.C. Sec. 651(b). To further this primary goal, Congress imposed statutory duties on employers and employees. Under the Act, an employer's duty is two-fold:

"Each employer—

"(1) Shall furnish to each of his employees employment and a place of employment which are free from recognized hazards that are causing or are likely to cause death or serious physical harm to his employees;

"(2) Shall comply with Occupational Safety and Health standards promulgated under this chapter.

"29 U.S.C. Sec. 654(a). The first duty is a 'general duty' imposed on an employer to protect its employees from hazards that are likely to cause death or serious bodily injury. The second duty is a 'specific duty' imposed on employers to comply with the OSHA regulations. . . .

"In this case, DuPont is accused of breaching the specific duty imposed on employers by Sec. 654(a)(2). Accordingly, DuPont's reliance on the plain language of the general duty clause is misplaced. The very narrow question on appeal does not concern the scope of an employer's general duty to protect employees from exposure to recognized hazards, but rather, the scope of an employer's duty to comply with the specific OSHA regulations. If the special duty provision is logically construed as imposing an obligation on the part of employers to protect *all* of the employees who work at a particular job site, then the employees of an independent contractor who work on the premises of another employer must be considered members of the class that Sec. 654(a)(2) was intended to protect. In other words, one cannot define the scope of an employer's obligation under Sec. 654(a)(2) as including the protection of another's employees and at the same time, claim that those 'other' employees are unintended beneficiaries.

"We believe that Congress enacted Sec. 654(a)(2) for the special benefit of *all* employees, including the employees of an independent contractor, who perform work at another employer's workplace. The specific duty clause represents the *primary* means for furthering Congress' purpose of assuring 'so far as possible every working man and woman in the Nation safe and healthful working conditions.' 29 U.S.C. Sec. 651(b). (Emphasis added). The broad remedial nature of the Occupational Health and Safety Act of 1970 is the Act's primary characteristic. E.g., *Southern Ohio Building Systems, Inc. v. OSHRC*, 649 F.2d 456, 458 (6th Cir. 1981); *Marshall v. Whirlpool Corporation*, 593 F.2d 715, 722 (6th Cir. 1979). Consistent with the broad remedial nature of the Act, we interpret the scope of intended beneficiaries of the special duty provision in a broad fashion. In our view, once an employer is deemed responsible for complying with OSHA regulations, it is obligated to protect every employee who works at its workplace. *See, e.g., Marshall v. Knutson Construction Co.*, 566 F.2d 596, 599 (8th Cir. 1977) (duty of general contractor extends to protection of all employees). Thus, Richard Teal, an employee of an independent contractor, must be considered a member of the class of persons that the special duty provision was intended to protect. . . . "

The importance of pleading and proving and affirmative defense in an employment safety context was reiterated in the following case. Under OSHA, an abatement order for a safety violation may be vacated under the greater hazard doctrine; that is, abatement would cause a greater hazard to employees than the safety hazard itself. In reinstating the original abatement order of the Administrative Law Judge, the federal Circuit Court of Appeals for the Eighth Circuit made the following observations.

DOLE v. WILLIAMS ENTERPRISES, INC.
876 F.2d 186 (D.C. Cir. 1989)

WALD, C.J.: [The facts of the case establish that the defendant violated a serious safety standard in exposing Dole to a construction site fall hazard of 20–30 feet, which could lead to serious physical harm. This fact clearly influenced the court's ultimate conclusion.]

II. Analysis

" . . .

" 'Greater hazard' refers to a well-established Commission doctrine that, in brief, allows employers to escape sanctions for violations of otherwise applicable safety regulations if they can establish that the act of abating a violation would itself pose an even greater threat to the safety and health of their employees. 'Greater hazard' is an affirmative defense that is subject to certain specific pleading requirements under the Commission's procedures. *See* 29 C.F.R. § 2200.36(b). Moreover, commission precedent clearly requires that to prevail on the 'greater hazard' defense, an employer must establish the three substantive elements of the defense: '(1) the hazards of compliance with a standard are greater than the hazards of noncompliance, (2) alternative means of protection are unavailable, and (3) a variance was unavailable or inappropriate.' *Lauhoff Grain Co.*, 1986–1987 O.S.H. Dec. (CCH) ¶27,814, at 26,397–98 (Rev. Comm'n 1987) (citations omitted). *See also M.J. Lee Constr. Co.*, 1979 O.S.H. Dec. (CCH) ¶23,330, at 28,227 (Rev. Comm'n 1979). This three-part test, each prong of which employers must satisfy, has been recognized and approved by several federal courts of appeals. *See, e.g., Brock v. L.R. Willson & Sons, Inc.*, 773 F.2d 1377, 1389 n. 13 (D.C. Cir. 1985) (denying the availability of the affirmative defense of 'greater hazard' because '[t]here [was] no indication in the record that Willson attempted to obtain a variance'); *Modern Drop Forge Co. v. Secretary of Labor*, 683 F.2d 1105, 1116 (7th Cir. 1982); *General Electric Co. v. Secretary of Labor*, 576 F.2d 558, 560–62 (3d Cir. 1978). . . .

"Just as it is clear to us that the substance of the 'greater hazard' defense was invoked by the Commission, so too it is clear that the requirements of the defense were not met. First, as a procedural matter, Williams never pleaded 'greater hazard,' and thus it was never properly brought into the case. 'Greater hazard' is an *affirmative defense,* which, according to Commission regulations, '[t]he employer shall state in its answer in [a] separate numbered paragraph[].' 29 C.F.R. § 2200.36(b)(1). Furthermore, our understanding of affirmative defenses, buttressed by years of experience under Rule 8(c) of the Federal Rules of Civil Procedure, is that these defenses place the burden on the party raising them to affirmatively plead the claim in order to bring them into the action. *See, e.g., Camalier & Buckley-Madison, Inc. v. The Madison Hotel, Inc.*, 513 F.2d 407, 419 n. 92 (D.C. Cir. 1975). A party's failure to plead an affirmative defense does not merely put him at a strategic disadvantage vis-à-vis the claim; rather, it generally 'results in the waiver of that defense and its *exclusion from the case.*' 5 C. Wright & A. Miller, Federal Practice and Procedure § 1278 (1969 & Supp. 1986) (emphasis added). This rule suffices to demonstrate the error of the ALJ's decision. . . .

" . . . The Secretary undertakes to show that the ALJ's finding as to the existence of a more serious threat to safety from abatement—the first element of the 'greater hazard' defense—is not supported by substantial evidence. We do not address that issue, because for purposes of our holding it suffices that the record reveals *no* evidence to support any findings pertaining to the second and third elements—namely, the unavailability of alternative means of protection, and the unavailability (or inappropriateness) of a variance. Without a showing on these elements of the claim, it was patently improper for the Commission to vacate the Secretary's citation on the ground that abatement posed a more serious hazard to Williams' employees.

III. Conclusion

" . . . The record clearly reflects that Williams violated § 1926.750(b)(1)(iii). Moreover, although the Commission did not make a finding as to the 'serious-[ness]' of the violation, a serious violation exists 'if there is a substantial probability that death or serious physical harm could result.' 29 U.S.C. § 666(k). We find that the Secretary has established a serious violation of § 1926.750(b)(1)(iii), because she has shown that workers were exposed to a fall hazard of 20–30 feet, which could lead to serious physical harm. [Citation omitted.] We see no other supportable conclusion from the record before us. The citation vacated . . . is therefore remanded with directions that it be reinstated, and the petition for review is

"*Granted*."

24:9 *Workers' Compensation: Emerging Stress-related Psychological Claims*

Historically the common law, based on a fault concept of liability, was found inadequate to deal with industrial injuries caused by accidents or occupational diseases. Employer defenses of contributory negligence, assumption of risk, and the fellow-servant doctrine (barring recovery for workplace injuries caused by a coworker) precluded recovery even where employer fault could be established. To remedy the harshness of the result in such cases, which grew proportionately to the rise of the Industrial Revolution, the states and the federal government enacted workers' compensation laws. These laws uniformly provide compensation irrespective of fault. Compensation is paid by a predetermined schedule depending on the nature and scope of the injury. These benefits include medical costs, income replacement, death benefits, and rehabilitation expenses. Although the scheduled payments are lower than the common law would provide, the elimination of fault and the defenses previously mentioned in most cases are felt to justify the lower awards.

The one requirement that a worker must meet is to prove that the injury arose "out of and in the course of employment." The nature of the job determines the scope of that requirement, and the courts tend to support a compensation award where the employer requires off-worksite duties as part of the job.

Another more serious problem arises where a claim is based on mental or emotional injuries for which a worker seeks compensation. Normally most state courts permit recovery where a job-related physical injury causes or contributes to mental illness. Some courts also permit recovery where a job-related mental illness causes physical disability. The major problem where the courts divide is job-related mental illness causing mental illness. The issues in this situation are whether the perceived mental condition is genuine, or actual, and whether a perceived illness is compensable. The following case reviews these issues and reaffirms the Minnesota rule barring recovery for emotional depression. In this case the Supreme Court of Minnesota reaffirmed its prior holding in *Lockwood v. Independent School District No. 877*,[12] which precluded recovery of workers' compensation benefits for mental depression. However, the Court noted that recovery could be had for stress-induced ulcer, in a case of first impression. The claimant was a police officer who argued that his ulcer and depression were causally related to his police activities. The court reasoned as follows.

EGELAND V. CITY OF MINNEAPOLIS
344 N.W.2d 597 (Minn. 1984)

AMDAHL, C.J.: " . . .

"The employee, Raymond Egeland, formerly a policeman with the Minneapolis Police Department, claims that he suffers from peptic ulcer disease and chronic anxiety and depression which were caused by job-associated stress. Workers' Compensation Judge PARKER found that Mr. Egeland suffered personal injury in the nature of depression and a duodenal ulcer arising out of and in the course of employment. The stresses of his job as a policeman were found to be a substantial contributing factor toward such injury. The judge concluded that our determination in *Lockwood v. Independent School Dist. No. 877*, 312 N.W.2d 924 (Minn. 1981), precluded compensation for disability resulting from the depression. . . .

"On appeal, the judgment was upheld. . . . The majority on the Appellate Court was divided as to the rationale for the noncompensability of the depression. Two of the judges determined that Mr. Egeland suffered from 'perceived' rather than 'actual' stress and that 'perceived' stress was not compensable. A third judge refused to accept the distinction between 'perceived' and 'actual' stress but found that our *Lockwood* decision precluded compensation for solely mental injury.

"The dissenting judges believed that the employee had not carried his burden of showing objective significant manifestations of stress as a causal factor in both the ulcer disease and the depression. One judge refused to accept the tenet that work as a police officer was inherently stressful or that the evidence established that Mr. Egeland's work caused either his ulcer or his depression.

"We do not accept the majority's adoption of a distinction between 'perceived' and 'actual' stress. Nor do we need to decide whether Egeland's depression arose out of and in the course of his employment. That determination has no relevance to the decision here because, even if it did, under *Lockwood* such mental injury is not compensable under the Workers' Compensation Act, Minn. Stat. § 176.-021, subd. 1 (1980). We affirm the award . . . for the physical injury in the form of a duodenal ulcer and we note that this is the first time in

[12]312 N.W.2d 924 (Minn. 1981).

Minnesota that a stress-induced ulcer has been found to be compensable under the Workers' Compensation Act.

"The City . . . contends that Mr. Egeland has not established a causal relationship between the nature of his work and his illnesses because he cannot point to any specific episodes of ulcer activity that were linked with specific incidents at work. But, as the City itself points out, 'the exact causative factors of peptic ulcer disease are not understood and no single factor can be said to be responsible.' The statute only requires that Egeland's work as a police officer be a significant contributing factor in the development of the disease, not the sole factor. *See Aker v. State of Minn. Dept. of Natural Resources,* 282 N.W.2d 533, 535–36 (Minn. 1979). Nor does the statute require a finding of a single precipitating incident which caused the disease. *Cf. Forseen v. Tire Retread Company,* 271 Minn. 399, 403, 136 N.W.2d 75, 77 (1965) (disablement compensable if work aggravates preexisting infirmity even if work did not do so because of violent strain or exertion). . . .

"The WCCA, in holding that Egeland's depression was caused by 'perceived' and not 'actual' stress and hence was not compensable, was applying a test it has itself just recently developed but which has never been articulated or accepted by this court. In *Applequist v. Insurance Co. of North America,* 33 W.C.D. 245 (1980), the employee's contention that her hysterical psychosis was caused by an environment that was stressful because of an overload of work and continuous noise distractions was refuted by a fellow employee who testified that the workload was not overwhelming and the noisy environment was not even close to the employee's work station. Judge RIEKE of the WCCA, in his concurrence, rejected the Michigan court's acceptance of an 'honest perception' subjective test of stress formulated in *Deziel v. Difco Laboratories, Inc.,* 403 Mich. 1, 268 N.W.2d 1 (1978). . . . He concluded that the use of the Michigan test would diminish the causal connection to employment test required of the statute to a 'meaningless ruse.' *Id.* at 254. Hence, Judge RIEKE attempted to adopt a test based on objective facts and standards, refusing compensation because the emotional disability was precipitated by incidents or experiences which were honestly perceived but in reality nonexistent. . . .

"As previously discussed, the facts as established in the record of Mr. Egeland's case do not coincide with the fact of the WCCA decisions. At trial, there was a great deal of evidence of outward manifestations of stress and of specifics in the work situation such as continual changes in shifts that were actually stress-producing. This distinction between actual and perceived stress seems to be purely semantical and does not square with lay or professional experience. To say that one person suffers from perceived stress and another from real stress makes as little sense as saying that one person has perceived back pain while another has real back pain. Professor Larson, in his article *Mental and Nervous Injury in Workmen's Compensation,* 23 Vanderbilt L. Rev. 1243, 1243 (1970), speaks of the 'poignant judicial cry of the past'; 'how could it be real when . . . it was purely mental?' The *Deziel* court stated in response: 'This "poignant judicial cry'' can only be explained if it is understood that *all* people manufacture their own concepts of reality.' 403 Mich. at 30, 268 N.W.2d at 12. (Emphasis in original). Moreover, all stress experienced by a person is necessarily 'perceived' before it can cause any reaction within the person at all. The theoretical position advanced by the Workers' Compensation Court of Appeals in so far as it applies a 'perceived' versus an 'actual' reality test is therefore unacceptable.

"What seems to be the crux of the WCCA's earlier three decisions is the idea that is it important to establish factually the existence of stress in the workplace other than by means of the disabled employee's own testimony . . .

"To prove legal causation, the employee must produce evidence that the stress was extreme . . . or at least 'beyond the ordinary day-to-day stress to which all employees are exposed.' *Lockwood v. Independent School District No. 877.* 312 N.W.2d 924, 926 (Minn. 1981).

"The test of *extreme* stress logically applies to cases . . . where a single precipitating cause is at issue. But the test of 'beyond day-to-day' stress applies to employees such as Mr. Egeland who have experienced stress that has accumulated over a long period of time.

"Mr. Egeland presented sufficient evidence to meet the above-stated test. Two of the judges constituting a majority of the WCCA seem to imply that police work is inherently stressful as compared to other occupations. The fact that under the occupational disease section, Minn. Stat. § 176.011, subd. 15 (1982), police officers are granted a presumption of a causal link between their employment and some specific diseases (myocarditis and coronary sclerosis) which can be stress-induced is an indication that the legislature views police work as *sui generis.* Indeed, this court so stated very forcefully in our recent decision in *Linnell v. City of St. Louis Park,* 305 N.W.2d 599, 601 (1981):

"We construe section 176.011(15) however, to embody the legislature's presumably informed acceptance of the thesis that the occupations of fireman, policeman . . . *are likely to involve greater stress,* whether physical or emotional, or both, than other occupations. . . .

" . . .

"It is certainly the case that these types of pressures do not incapacitate the majority of police officers and Mr. Egeland was probably constitutionally predisposed to such injuries. But this fact does not influence compensability under the workers' compensation laws. *See Walker v. Minnesota Steel Co.,* 167 Minn. 475, 209 N.W. 635 (1926):

"The compensation act was designed for the protection of all laborers coming within its purview. That is, it does not apply to those only who are strong in body. Neither is it limited to those only who are normal. Those who are below normal, have a weakness, or carry perchance a disease, are also within its protection. Compensation is not dependent upon any implied assumption of perfect health. It does not exclude the weak or physically unfortunate.

"167 Minn. at 476, 209 N.W. at 635.

''Compensation Judge PARKER and WCCA Judge ADEL are correct in holding that compensation for stress-induced depression is precluded by our recent decision in *Lockwood*.

''Workers' compensation cases which involve mental conditions such as emotional, nervous, psychoneurotic or psychotic disorders have been classified into there groups by Professor Larson: (1) mental trauma which results in physical injury; (2) physical trauma which results in mental injury, and (3) mental trauma which results in mental injury. In Minnesota, coverage has been extended to the first two categories . . . but not to the third, although we recognized in *Lockwood* that the majority of courts in the country have held such injury to be compensable. In *Lockwood*, this court refused to permit compensation for work-related stress-induced mental disability in the absence of a clear legislative intent to extend coverage to such disability.

''The policy determination as to whether workers' compensation coverage should be extended to employees who are mentally disabled by employment-related stress is best left to the legislature. We affirm the award of permanent partial disability to Mr. Egeland for his stress-induced ulcer and deny compensation for the claimed depression. . . .

''Affirmed.''

25 Environmental Law and Land Use

25:1 *Common-Law Liability in General*

At common law, the courts developed the doctrine of nuisance to prevent or provide compensation for conduct that unreasonably interferes with the use and enjoyment of land by another. The fact that the conduct is lawful and conducted lawfully does not preclude judicial injunctive or other relief. It is how the conduct affects others that determines whether it is a nuisance. Nuisances apply to public as well as private activity.

The courts attempt to balance the economic and social utility of the activity of the defendant with the economic and social utility of protecting the alleged injured party seeking relief. The harm must be more than inconvenient or annoying. Mere evidence of harm, standing alone, is insufficient to make out a claim. Note that this doctrine differs from statutory environmental protection in that the latter is more concerned with harm to the environment and less concerned with the utility of the alleged wrongdoer's conduct. Moreover, violation of a statutory environmental duty may be deemed negligence *per se,* itself wrongful, whereas the nuisance doctrine requires balancing conflicting interests.

The following case raises the question of whether environmental protection laws preclude claims based on a federal common-law nuisance theory. One of the issues posed was whether a substantial Nevada hotel casino development could be halted on the ground that it constituted a federal common-law nuisance. Only that portion of the decision of the federal Circuit Court of Appeals for the Ninth Circuit follows.

CALIFORNIA TAHOE REGIONAL PLANNING AGENCY v. JENNINGS
594 F.2d 181 (9th Cir. 1979), *cert. denied* 444 U.S. 864, 62 L. Ed. 2d 86

SNEED, Cir. J.: "Appellants appeal from the district court's grant of appellees' motion to dismiss and denial of appellants' motions for a temporary injunction and for summary judgment in this suit to prevent the construction of four hotel-casinos at the south shore of Lake Tahoe. The appellants are California Tahoe Regional Planning Agency (CTRPA) and the State of California, the League to Save Lake Tahoe (League), and the Sierra Club. The appellees are Douglas County, Nevada, Ted Jennings, Oliver Kahle, Harvey's Wagon Wheel, Inc.

[853]

(Harvey's), and Park Cattle Co. (Park), five in all. In their complaints, all appellants assert that certain administrative action of Douglas County violated the relevant portion of the California-Nevada interstate compact to regulate the Lake Tahoe Basin. The CTRPA and the State of California allege a second cause of action in which they assert a nuisance under federal common law against all appellees except Park. After a hearing, the district court refused all relief to appellants and granted appellees' motion to dismiss. We affirm. . . .

Federal Common Law Nuisance Claim

"Finally, we turn to the request by the State of California and the CTRPA that Jennings', Kahle's and Harvey's projects be enjoined on the ground that their development will result in an interstate nuisance. They premise this claim not on any statute, but upon federal common law. The district court dismissed the claim. As we hold that the appellants did not state a claim for common law nuisance under these circumstances, we affirm.

"Appellants do not seek to stop an existing activity on the part of appellees that constitutes a nuisance extending across state boundaries. Instead they seek to enjoin a threatened or apprehended nuisance. Before determining whether appellants' action will be such under these circumstances, we must decide whether this common law remedy has been precluded by Congressional action.

"Appellees contend that even if an action for federal common law nuisance exists, such action is precluded either by the Compact [California-Nevada Interstate Compact] itself, the Clean Air Act, or the Federal Water Pollution Control Act (FWPCA). When Congress approved the Compact, it appended Article VIII, § 5 to the Compact specifically providing:

"[N]othing contained in this Act or in the compact consented to shall in any way affect . . . the applicability of any law or regulation of the United States in, over, or to the region or waters which are the subject of this compact. . . .

"We believe this provision clearly indicates that the Compact itself does not preclude the application of federal common law nuisance doctrines. However, although the Compact does not affect the applicability of federal common law nuisance principles, the operation of the Compact may influence the factors that should be weighed in applying these principles and doctrines. It is clear, however, that given an appropriate situation, such an action may be maintained.

"The federal pollution control laws do not preclude this action. The Clean Air Act and the FWPCA each have 'citizen suits' provisions professing not to 'restrict any right which any person—may have under any statute or common law—.' 42 U.S.C. § 7604(e), 33 U.S.C. § 1365(e). This exclusion is even broader than that present in the Compact. Moreover the Supreme Court held in 1972 that the FWPCA had not yet occupied the field. *Illinois v. City of Milwaukee*, 406 U.S. 91, 92 S. Ct. 1385, 31 L. Ed. 2d 712 (1972), and courts have continued so to hold even after the enactment of the 1972 amendments—[citations omitted]. We decline the invitation to draw a different conclusion.

"The Supreme Court has recognized the validity of federal common law nuisance actions instituted by one state to enjoin damaging activities carried on in another. *Illinois v. City of Milwaukee*, [*supra*]; *Georgia v. Tennessee Copper Co.*, 206 U.S. 230, 27 S. Ct. 618, 51 L. Ed. 1038 (1907); *Missouri v. Illinois*, 180 U.S. 208, 21 S. Ct. 331, 45 L. Ed. 497 (1901). And the equitable powers of the federal courts are not limited to stopping nuisances already in operation. Long ago the Supreme Court noted that courts of equity 'can, not only prevent nuisances that are threatened, and before irreparable mischief ensues, but arrest or abate those in progress. . . . ' *Mugler v. Kansas*, 123 U.S. 623, 673, 8 S. Ct. 273, 303, 31 L. Ed. 205 (1887). The exercise of these equitable powers, however, requires great certainty, and the standards for enjoining a threatened nuisance are stricter than those for stopping an existing nuisance."

"[I]t is settled that an injunction to restrain a nuisance will issue only in cases where the fact of nuisance is made out upon determinate and satisfactory evidence; that if the evidence be conflicting and the injury be doubtful, that conflict and doubt will be a ground for withholding an injunction; and that, *where interposition by injunction is sought, to restrain that which it is apprehended will create a nuisance . . .* the proofs must show such a state of facts as will manifest the danger to be *real and immediate.*

"*Missouri v. Illinois*, 180 U.S. at 248, 21 S. Ct. at 346 (emphasis added).

"Appellants assert that appellees' projects indirectly will create a nuisance—that they will attract more people and cars to the Basin, and that inevitably a nuisance will result. We cannot agree. Appellants' allegation is insufficient to establish that the danger of a nuisance in this case is real and immediate. Without more, appellants at this preliminary stage have not met the requirements set forth in *Missouri v. Illinois, supra.* In so holding we must remember that these projects have passed through the gauntlet of approval established by the Compact and the Ordinance. The record before the district court manifests the conflicting evidence as to the degree of potential injury. This court cannot set its face against these facts merely because we as citizens might prefer that all development be barred from the Tahoe Basin. Much of modern life is distasteful, but the federal common law of nuisance bestows upon us no power to root out that which happens to offend both us and a vigorous plaintiff. . . .

"This case is unique. California entered a Compact, later approved by Congress, to help coordinate and control growth and development in the Tahoe Basin. As equal parties in the interstate agency developed under the Compact, California participated in the adoption of a regional plan and ordinances to regulate new construction in the Basin. Pursuant to established procedures the appellants' projects, which do not violate the ordinances' substantive provisions, have been approved. Now California seeks to prevent construction of these projects by invoking the equitable powers of the federal courts to enjoin interstate nuisances. Fundamentally, it contends the projects will harm the environment of the region. This may be so, but not every injury to the environment is a nuisance under the federal common law. A fortiori, not every threatened injury can be enjoined as a potential nuisance. The line is not a bright one, but we cannot consider high rise hotels and their occupants as indistinguishable from untreated sewage, noxious gases, and poisonous pesticides.

''We therefore affirm the judgment of the district court and lift our injunction preventing Harvey's from commencing construction.
''AFFIRMED.''

25:2 *Government Regulation of Toxic and Hazardous Substances: Penalties*

In 1970, amid growing concern for the welfare of the environment, in particular the effects of human intrusions upon the ecosphere (the earth's living things and the water, air, and soil that support them), Congress established the Environmental Protection Agency (EPA) to consolidate federal environmental activities into one agency.[1] A whole range of pollutants, including toxic chemicals, was to be reviewed and managed, with a twofold objective: creation of national standards and enforcement, together with the states, of those standards.

Two examples of federal pollution statutes and their penalties are the 1977 Clean Water Act and the 1976 Toxic Substances Control Act. The Clean Water Act (CWA) was to control effluent or waste discharges and to provide water clean enough for swimming and other recreational uses by 1983. Quality standards based on water use were established for human consumption and for recreational and industrial use. Dischargers of effluent were to install the best practicable control devices and the best technology economically achievable by 1983. The CWA defined pollutants as conventional (sanitary waste), toxic (sixty-five designated chemicals), and nonconventional (all others). The EPA was required to publish regulations and to set limits on discharge of conventional pollutants. More stringent limitation requirements were set for toxic chemicals. In both cases the requirements were to meet the best available technology (BAT) economically achievable.

The enforcement sections establish both criminal and civil penalties, which are substantial. The Act permits states to use their own environmental laws in the absence of federal preemption in the field.

The 1976 Toxic Substances Control Act (TSCA) permits the government to control and halt the production or use of chemical substances that may present an unreasonable risk of injury to health or the environment. Once again a range of civil and criminal enforcement provisions exist to compel compliance.

These two statutes are only two of a host of laws passed governing air, water, hazardous wastes, noise, pesticides, and endangered species, to name the major ones. State counterpart legislation also exists, which also applies to municipal and private activities subject to control. A major concern for management is the degree of worker disclosure of hazardous wastes or materials required for workers who are exposed to these substances. Also, when a private party engages in activities which impact upon this overall regulatory scheme, the party may be required to comply, even though his activity is negligible or local in scope.

In the following case, the New Jersey federal District Court issued a preliminary injunction to halt a hazardous condition imposed by dry asbestos found in

---

[1]Reorg. Plan #3, of 1970, 35 Fed. Reg. 15, 623, 84 Stat. 2086 (1970).

an old hotel being renovated by its owners. The court discussed various defenses raised, which are excerpted below.

U.S. v. Tzavah Urban Renewal Corp.
696 F. Supp. 1013 (D.N.J. 1988)

LECHNER, J.: [Facts and other issues omitted.]

"Section 113 of the Act gives the Administrator of EPA [Environmental Protection Agency] authority to seek injunctive relief and/or the assessment of civil penalties whenever he finds that an owner or operator of a facility violates or fails or refuses to comply with any NESHAP [National Emission Standard for Hazardous Air Pollutants] regulation or any order issued pursuant to 42 U.S.C. § 7413(a). Defendants' violations of the asbestos NESHAP requirements and failure to comply with EPA orders have been well documented. It is very likely that the Government will succeed in imposing penalties upon defendants.

"Defendants counter this claim with two arguments. First, because defendants' violations were not 'knowing or intentional' the Government is not entitled to relief under the statute. . . . In the alternative, defendants claim that the Government has not substantiated its allegations regarding their alleged violations.

No *Mens Rea* is Required under the Clean Air Act and NESHAP Regulations

"Defendants' first contention is not supported by the Clean Air Act's underlying objectives. The District Court for the Eastern District of California has held that the Act and asbestos NESHAP 'provide strict liability for civil violations of their provisions.' *U.S. v. Ben's Truck and Equipment, Inc.*, 25 E.R.C. 1295, 1298 (E.D. Cal. 1986) [available on WESTLAW, 1986 WL 15402]. I agree with the California court's finding that strict liability is 'essential to meet the purpose of the Act and to protect and improve the quality of the nation's air.' *Id.* Furthermore, the statute and regulations themselves do not indicate that scienter is required for establishing violations of the Act. . . .

"Imposing a strict liability standard for violations of the asbestos NESHAP is also supported by well accepted principles of tort law. Under the rule of *Rylands v. Fletcher*, L.R. 1 Ex. 265 (1866), *aff'd*, L.R. 3 H.L. 330 (1868), a landowner is strictly liable for any damages caused by ultrahazardous activities conducted on his land. This principal has recently been acknowledged by the New Jersey Supreme Court in *State Dept. of Environ. Protec. v. Ventron Corp.*, 94 N.J. 473, 488, 468 A.2d 150 (1983) (a landowner is strictly liable to others for harm caused by toxic wastes that are stored in his property and flow onto the property of others). . . .

"The NESHAP regulations clearly bring the emission of asbestos within this concept of 'ultrahazardous activity.' Asbestos is regarded as extremely dangerous to human health, threatening individuals who reside in the vicinity of an asbestos source like the Old Military Park Hotel. . . . While the NESHAP regulations do not hold defendants liable to individuals harmed by the [asbestos level] found in the hotel, they are concerned with preventing the possibility of this harm. The imposition of strict liability for the defendants' conduct is both appropriate and well supported.

Defendants' Violations are Well Documented

" . . .

"The Government's evidence of asbestos NESHAP violations at the facility has been well substantiated. Defendants even admit that the amount of friable asbestos materials at 16 Park Place exceeded the 260 linear feet or 160 square feet minimum set by the regulations. . . . They also acknowledge their failure to provide EPA with written notification of their intention to renovate as required by 40 C.F.R. § 61.146 and their failure to wet the friable asbestos materials stripped from the facility. . . . Thus, the Government has established a reasonable probability of success on the merits.

B. The Likelihood of Irreparable Injury and the Public Interest

"As injury to the environment is especially difficult to remedy, injunctive relief is appropriate when a defendant's conduct poses a continued threat to environmental well being. 'Environmental injury, by its nature, can seldom be adequately remedied by money damages and is often permanent or at least of long duration, *i.e.*, irreparable.' *Amoco Production Company v. Village of Gambell*, 480 U.S. 531, 107 S. Ct. 1396, 1404, 94 L. Ed. 2d 542 (1987); *see also PIRG of New Jersey v. Top Notch Metal Finishing Co.*, 26 E.R.C. 2012, 2015 (D.N.J. 1987) [available on WESTLAW, 1987 WL 44393] (violations of pretreatment requirements of Clean Water Act by metal finishing company poses irreparable injury to environment). The presence of ACM within the hotel and the continued emission of asbestos dust into the surrounding community pose a significant health risk to the squatters who intermittently inhabit the hotel as well as the residents and workers who are present in the area. . . .

"As defendants point out, injunctive relief should not be issued as a matter of course. Rather, an injunction should only issue 'when the intervention of a court of equity "is essential in order effectively to protect property rights against injuries otherwise irremediable." ' *Weinberg v. Romero-Barcelo*, 456 U.S. 305, 312, 102 S. Ct. 1798, 1803, 72 L. Ed. 2d 91 (1982) (citing *Cavanaugh v. Looney*, 248 U.S. 453, 39 S. Ct. 142, 63 L. Ed. 354 (1919)). However, in this case the Government has met its burden of establishing a threat to public health which may very well prove irremediable. *Getty Oil Co. v. Ruckelshaus*, 467 F.2d 349, 357 (3d Cir. 1972), *cert. denied*, 409 U.S. 1125, 93 S. Ct. 937, 35 L. Ed. 2d 256 (1973) (In an enforcement proceeding under the Clean Air Act, 'the burden of establishing a violation of the applicable regulation would be carried by the government'). . . .

C. Balancing of Hardships

"This prong of the test for injunctive relief is easily met: the danger of asbestos has been established, while no potential for hardship to the defendants has been suggested. In fact, defendants contend that they have made good faith efforts at compliance and have continually asserted that they intend to comply with the asbestos NESHAP. . . . If this is the case, the relief requested will not harm them at all, it will only comport with their professed intentions. A preliminary injunction mandating defendants' compliance, then, poses no cognizable risk of hardship to defendants. . . .

Conclusion

"Defendants are 'owners and/or operators' within the meaning of the Clean Air Act. From the time they purchased the Old Military Park Hotel in 1986, they have committed numerous violations of the Act and the asbestos NESHAP regulations. Defendants have also failed to comply with the compliance orders issued to them by EPA. The Government has established a reasonable probability of success on the merits, the likelihood of irreparable injury if the asbestos in the hotel is not properly disposed of, and that a balancing of hardships favors granting an injunction. Because it is so clearly in the public interest to grant a preliminary injunction enjoining defendants to secure the facility, properly dispose of the [asbestos], and comply with EPA's orders, the Government's motion is granted."

25:3 *Private Enforcement of Environmental Regulations*

Absent specific legislative authority granting private citizens or organizations the right to sue to enforce various environmental laws such as the Clean Air Act (authorizing private lawsuits against any person, including the federal government) and the Clean Water Act (likewise), federal courts have the power to determine whether a citizen has standing to sue. Two requirements must be satisfied. First, injury in fact: that is, some governmental approval causing esthetic or other environmental damage. Second, zone of interest: that is, the injury was within the protective shield that the law was intended to govern. In the absence of such proof, courts are reluctant to authorize private attorneys in general to sue.

The United States Supreme Court, in an early decision, held that, absent express environmental statutory authority, the Administrative Procedure Act (APA) did not authorize the Sierra Club to obtain judicial review of federal agency action approving and extending skiing development in Mineral King Valley in the Sequoia National Forest. Specifically, the Court found that the Club lacked judicial standing to sue because the Club was not one of those parties itself injured by the challenged action of the U.S. Forest Service.[2]

In the following case, the federal Circuit Court of Appeals for the Second Circuit reviewed a challenge by a citizens' group to the 42nd Street Development Project in New York City. In affirming the dismissal of their complaint, the Circuit Court held that the citizens' suit was not specific enough to state a cause of action.

---

[2]Sierra Club v. Morton, 405 U.S. 727, 31 L. Ed. 2d 636 (1972).

WILDER v. THOMAS
854 F.2d 605 (2nd Cir. 1988),
cert. denied 489 U.S. 1053, 103 L. Ed. 2d 583

PRATT, C.J.: "This appeal arises from the most recent in a long series of actions that have been brought in state and federal courts by these plaintiffs and others similarly situated, who seek to forestall construction of the proposed 42nd Street Development Project ('the project') in New York City. . . . The goal of the project is to eliminate 'physical, social and economic blight' in the Times Square area, *Rosenthal & Rosenthal, Inc. v. N.Y. State Urban Dev. Corp.*, 771 F.2d 44, 45 (2d Cir. 1985) . . . , *cert. denied*, 475 U.S. 1018, 106 S. Ct. 1204, 89 L. Ed. 2d 317 (1986). After extensive study and review pursuant to state statute, the City of New York, the New York State Urban Development Corporation ('UDC'), its subsidiary, the Times Square Redevelopment Corporation, and various private developers have decided that this goal will be achieved by the construction of four office towers, a hotel, eight renovated theatres, a wholesale mart, restaurants, retail spaces, and a renovated subway station. [Citation omitted.] The project area has been divided into twelve sites between 40th and 43rd streets.

"Opposition to the project by area business owners and residents, historical preservationists, and environmentalists has so far produced more than two dozen actions against the project. Residents fear that they will be driven out by skyrocketing property values; environmentalists claim that the project will exacerbate traffic congestion, thereby increasing levels of air pollution; others seek to preserve landmark theatres from demolition. . . .

"Plaintiffs appeal from a judgment of the United States District Court for the Southern District of New York, Thomas P. GREISA, Judge, that dismissed their action brought under the citizen suits provision of the Clean Air Act ('CAA'), 42 U.S.C. § 7401 *et seq.*, on the ground that the proposed amended complaint failed to state a claim. Plaintiffs alleged that defendants violated requirements of the CAA relating to transportation control measures set out in New York State's implementation plan, which was adopted pursuant to CAA § 7410. In essence, plaintiffs claim that construction of the project will lead to further violations of the CAA, and they seek an injunction against construction of the project.

"Plaintiffs rely in particular on § 7604(a) which provides, in pertinent part, that 'any person may commence a civil action on his own behalf . . . against any person . . . (or) governmental instrumentality or agency . . . who is alleged to be in violation of . . . an emission standard or limitation under this chapter'. 42 U.S.C. § 7604(a)(1)(A). 'Emission standard or limitation' is defined as including 'any condition or requirement under an applicable implementation plan relating to transportation control measures', § 7604(f)(3). A citizen may also commence a civil action against the administrator of the Environmental Protection Agency ('EPA') where the administrator fails to perform any nondiscretionary duty under the CAA. § 7604(a)(2). . . .

"The provisions of the SIP [State Implementation Plan] are crucial to this appeal because plaintiffs bringing a citizen suit 'must allege a violation of a specific strategy or commitment in the SIP and describe, with some particularity, the respects in which compliance with the provision is deficient.' *Council of Commuter Orgs. v. Metro. Transp. Authority,* 683 F.2d 663, 670 (2d Cir. 1982). *See Action for Rational Transit v. Westside Highway [Project],* 699 F.2d 614, 616 (2d Cir. 1983).

"The 1984 SIP was submitted pursuant to that portion of § 7410 that allows states to include provisions for review of 'indirect sources'. An 'indirect source' includes structures that 'may attract mobile sources of pollution', 42 U.S.C. § 7410(a)(5)(C), presumably cars, buses, etc. Under an 'indirect source review program', the state may provide for a review of indirect sources of air pollution and for the development of measures that will 'assure, or assist in assuring,' that a new or modified indirect source will not lead to nonattainment of the NAAQS or prevent the maintenance of the NAAQS. 42 U.S.C. § 7410(a)(5)(D).

"In exercising its discretion under the CAA to include an indirect source review program in its SIP, the state chose to use the SEQRA EIS process as the means by which the environmental impact of an indirect source would be evaluated. The 1984 SIP, which was approved by the EPA in 1985, see 40 C.F.R. § 52.1673(a), provides that '(t)he primary mechanism for comprehensive evaluation of major projects which may have a significant impact on air quality is the environmental impact statement (EIS). EIS's are required by either the National Environmental Policy Act (NEPA), the State Environmental Quality Review Act (SEQRA), or the New York City Environmental Quality Review (CEQR).' 1984 SIP at § 3.6 (Changing Traffic Patterns). SEQRA, in turn, requires that, in preparing an EIS, agencies 'choose alternatives which, consistent with social, economic and other essential considerations, to the maximum extent practicable, minimize or avoid adverse environmental effects, including effects revealed in the environmental impact statement process.' N.Y. Envtl. Conserv. Law § 8–0109.1 (McKinney 1984). Thus, project approval was subject to the indirect source review program that New York voluntarily included in the 1984 SIP, which it adopted pursuant to CAA requirements. The SEQRA EIS process was the mechanism that the UDC used to evaluate the potential impact of the project on air quality. . . .

"In the discussion to follow we will, first, examine the scope of the citizen suits provision to determine whether the plaintiffs' first claim falls within that scope. . . .

Scope of the Citizen Suits Provision/The First Claim for Relief

"Citizen suits are an important aspect of the CAA enforcement scheme. *See Friends of the Earth v. Carey,* 535 F.2d 165, 172 (2d Cir. 1976); *Natural Resources Defense Council, Inc. v. Train,* 510 F.2d 692, 699–700 (D.C. Cir. 1974). In enacting this provision, congress expanded federal court jurisdiction by circumventing the diversity of citizenship, jurisdictional amount, and traditional standing requirements, *see* 535 F.2d at 172–73; 510 F.2d at 700; S. Rep. No. 91–1196, 91st Cong., 2d Sess., reprinted at Appendix B, 510 F.2d at 725, in order to allow citizens to bring suit against the administrator of EPA for failure to perform nondiscretionary duties, or against polluters, including government agencies and the United States, for violation of specific requirements of an SIP. *See* 510 F.2d at 700; S. Rep. No. 91–1196, reprinted at 510 F.2d at 725.

''Congress intended citizen suits to 'motivate governmental agencies charged with the responsibility to bring enforcement and abatement proceedings' against violators. S. Rep. No. 91–1196, reprinted at 510 F.2d at 723. *See* 510 F.2d at 700. In order to avoid either overburdening the courts or unduly interfering with implementation of the act, however, congress carefully circumscribed the scope of the provision by authorizing citizens to bring suit only for violations of specific provisions of the act or specific provisions of an applicable implementation plan. *See* S. Rep. No. 91–1196, reprinted at 510 F.2d at 723, *see also Friends of the Earth v. Consolidated Rail Corp.*, 768 F.2d 57, 63 (2d Cir. 1985) (discussing congressional purpose in limiting citizen suits). By the specificity requirements Congresssought to establish an objective evidentiary standard (that) would have to be met by the citizen who brings an action under (§ 7604)', and thereby eliminate the need for 'reanalysis of technological or other considerations at the enforcement stage.' *See Citizens Ass'n of Georgetown the Committee of 100 on the Fed. City v. Washington*, 535 F.2d 1318, 1322 (D.C. Cir. 1976) (citation omitted).

''(1) Thus, plaintiffs are limited under § 7604 to seeking relief from specific violations of existing SIPs; they may not, through a citizen suit, obtain modification of an SIP to conform with their own 'notion of proper environmental policy.' *Action for Rational Transit v. West Side Highway Project*, 699 F.2d 614, 616 (2d Cir. 1983). Such a claim must be addressed directly to the court of appeals, which has exclusive jurisdiction to review EPA approval of SIPs. *See id.*, 42 U.S.C. § 7607(b)(1).

''Section 7604(a)(1)(A) allows any person to bring a suit against an individual or government agency who violates an 'emission standard or limitation' under the CAA. The statutory definition of 'emission standard or limitation' includes 'any condition or requirement under an applicable implementation plan relating to transportation control measures'. 42 U.S.C. § 7604(f)(3). . . .

'' . . . Plaintiffs' first claim, which alleges, in essence, that the city has failed, or will fail, to attain the NAAQS in the project area thus falls short of this requirement of specificity.

''Plaintiffs' construction of the CAA would eliminate the distinction between the NAAQS and measures that are designed to assure attainment of the NAAQS. The CAA and the regulations promulgated thereunder, however, emphasize the distinction between the attainment of the NAAQS, which is a goal of the CAA, and the specific provisions of an SIP which are the only permissible subjects of a citizen suit. . . . The statutory and regulatory language indicates that a 'transportation control measure' is designed to help achieve the goal of reducing pollution, and to assure attainment of the NAAQS.

''The NAAQS for carbon monoxide, by contrast, is the standard established by the EPA pursuant to congressional directive, *see* 42 U.S.C. § 7409(a); 40 C.F.R. § 50.8 (1987), that the EPA determined the states must attain in order to effectuate Congress's goal: 'to protect and enhance the quality of the Nation's air resources so as to promote the public health and welfare and the productive capacity of its population'. § 7401(b)(1). [Citation omitted.] Section 7604 does not provide for citizen suits based on violation of, or failure to attain, the NAAQS itself. . . .

"Contrary to plaintiffs' contention, our interpretation does not trivialize or emasculate the citizen suits provision; rather, it adheres to the statutory language while effectuating both the congressional purpose of fostering enforcement and the equally important purpose of providing specific, objective standards for citizen suits. . . .

"The order of the district court is affirmed."

25:4 Scope of Judicial Review

The United States Supreme Court ruled that once the Department of Housing and Urban Development (HUD) had considered alternative sites for a low-income housing project before redesignating a site in a middle-income area for the project, the National Environmental Policy Act (NEPA) was satisfied. The court held that it was error to require HUD to give highest priority to environmental concerns. Consideration of the consequences is all that NEPA requires, and under NEPA the proper scope of review of an agency's action is to see that such concerns are addressed.

STRYCKER'S BAY NEIGHBORHOOD COUNCIL V. KARLEN
444 U.S. 223, 100 L. Ed. 2d 497 (1980)

PER CURIAM: [Facts and other issues omitted.]
"In *Vermont Yankee Nuclear Power Corp. v. NRDC*, 435 U.S. 519, 558 (1987), we stated that NEPA, while establishing 'significant substantive goals for the Nation,' imposes upon agencies duties that are 'essentially procedural.' As we stressed in that case, NEPA was designed 'to insure a fully informed and well-considered decision,' but not necessarily 'a decision the judges of the Court of Appeals or of this Court would have reached had they been members of the decision making unit of the agency.' *Ibid.*, *Vermont Yankee* cuts sharply against the Court of Appeals' conclusion that an agency in selecting a course of action must elevate environmental concerns over other appropriate considerations. On the contrary once an agency has made a decision subject to NEPA's procedural requirements the only role for a court is to insure that the agency has considered the environmental consequences; it cannot 'interject itself within the area of discretion of the executive as to the choice of the action to be taken.' *Kleppe v. Sierra Club*, 427 U.S. 390, 410, n. 21 (1976). *See also FPC v. Transcontinental Gas Pipe Line Corp.*, 423 U.S. 326 (1976).

"In the present litigation there is no doubt that HUD considered the environmental consequences of its decision to redesignate the proposed site for low-income housing. NEPA requires no more. The petitions for certiorari are granted and the judgment of the Court of Appeals is therefore reversed.''

25:5   Liability of Private Parties for Violations of Environmental Regulations: Environmental Impact Statements

Private developers or others wishing to establish or expand a business such as a hotel or resort within a community or environmentally protected area must see to it that a proper Environmental Impact Statement (EIS) is submitted to a municipal or other agency having authority to issue the necessary permit or approval before new construction or renovation can commence. Failure to file a complete EIS may cause a reviewing court to cancel the improperly issued permit with substantial economic loss to the developer or sponsor.

''In the case below, the New York Court of Appeals held that New York City's City Environmental Quality Review (CEQR) regulations required application for a special permit to construct a high-rise luxury apartment building in Chinatown to meet stringent State Environmental Quality Review Act (SEQRA) provisions. Any EIS pursuant to that law must include population concentration, distribution, or growth and existing community or neighborhood character. Moreover, the failure of the city to include these factors in its EIS rendered the special permit null and void. The high court's reasoning follows.

CHINESE STAFF AND WORKERS ASSOCIATION v. CITY OF NEW YORK
68 N.Y. 2d 359, 535 N.E.2d 566 (1986)

ALEXANDER, J.: [Facts and other issues omitted.]

''This controversy arises out of the proposed construction of Henry Street Tower, a high-rise luxury condominium, on a vacant lot in the Chinatown section of New York City. This building is to be the first construction in the Special Manhattan Bridge District (SMBD), a special zoning district created by the City of New York designed to preserve the residential character of the Chinatown community, encourage new residential development on sites requiring minimal relocation, promote the rehabilitation of existing housing stock, and protect the scale of the community (*see* New York City Zoning Resolution § 116–00 *et seq.*; *Asian Am. Equality v. Koch*, 129 Misc. 2d 67, 71–74). An application for a special permit for Henry Street Tower was submitted by the developer, Henry Street Partners, to the Department of City Planning and the Department of Environmental Protection, the colead agencies responsible for implementing SEQRA in the City of New York (*see*, CEQR 1 [k]). Following a thorough environmental review of the effects of the project on the physical environment, the agencies issued a conditional negative declaration asserting that the project will not have any significant effect on the environment if certain modifications were adopted by the developer (*see* CEQR 1 [d]; 7 [b] [2]). The modifications were accepted by the developer and the application for a special permit was thereafter approved by the City Planning Commission and the Board of Estimate.

"A combined plenary action and article 78 proceeding was commenced by various members of the Chinatown community challenging the Board of Estimate approval of the special permit. . . .

"As limited by their brief to this court, petitioners argue that the city's environmental review was arbitrary and capricious because of the failure of the lead agencies to consider whether the introduction of luxury housing into the Chinatown community would accelerate the displacement of local low-income residents and business or alter the character of the community. Respondents contend that absent a determination that the proposed action will have significant adverse impact on the area's physical environment, SEQRA and CEQR do not require consideration of any social or economic impacts such as those asserted by petitioners.

"The initial determination to be made under SEQRA and CEQRA is whether an EIS is required, which in turn depends on whether an action may or will not have a significant effect on the environment (ECL 8–0109 [2]; CEQR 7 [a]). In making this initial environmental analysis, the lead agencies must study the same areas of environmental impacts as would be contained in an EIS, including both the short-term and long-term effects (ECL 8–0109 [2] [b]) as well as the primary and secondary effects (CEQR 1 [g]) of an action on the environment. The threshold at which the requirement that an EIS be prepared is triggered is relatively low: it need only be demonstrated that the action may have a significant effect on the environment (*see, Oak Beach Inn Corp. v. Harris*, 108 A.D.2d 796, 797; *J.O.M.E.S. v. New York State Urban Dev. Corp.*, 69 A.D.2d 222, 232, . . .).

"The dispute here concerns the reach of the term 'environment', which is defined as 'the physical conditions which will be affected by a proposed action, including land, air, water, minerals, flora, fauna, noise, objects of historic or aesthetic significance, existing patterns of population concentration, distribution, or growth, and existing community or neighborhood character' (ECL 8–0105 [6]; CEQR 1 [f]). Petitioners argue that the displacement of neighborhood residents and businesses caused by a proposed project is an environmental impact within the purview of SEQRA and CEQRA, and the failure of respondents to consider these potential effects renders their environmental analysis invalid. Respondents contend that any impacts that are not either directly related to a primary physical impact or will not impinge upon the physical environment in a significant manner are outside the scope of the definition of 'environment', and that the lead agencies were therefore not required to investigate the potential effects alleged by petitioners.

"Respondents' limited view of the parameters of the term 'environment' is contrary to the plain meaning of SEQRA and the city's regulations and must be rejected. It is clear from the express terms of the statute and the regulations that environment is broadly defined and expressly includes as physical conditions such considerations as 'existing patterns of population concentration, distribution, or growth, and existing community or neighborhood character'. By their express terms, therefore, both SEQRA and CEQRA require a lead agency to consider more than impacts upon the physical environment in determining whether to require the preparation of an EIS. In sum, population patterns and neighborhood character are physical conditions of the environment under SEQRA and CEQRA regardless of whether there is any impact on the physical environment (*see* Ulasewicz, *Department of Environmental Conservation and SEQRA: Upholding Its Mandates and Charting Parameters for the Elusive Socio-Economic Assessment*, 46 Alb. L. Rev. 1255, 1266, 1282).

"Having concluded that the environmental analysis of respondents was arbitrary and capricious, it is necessary to consider the appropriate remedy for their violation of the statutory mandate imposed by SEQRA. Although this issue was neither briefed nor argued in this court, we conclude, contrary to the conclusion tendered by our recent decision in *Matter of Tri-County Taxpayers Assn. v. Town Bd.* (55 N.Y.2d 41, *modfg.* 79 A.D.2d 337). . . .

" . . . Respondents have failed to comply with the requirements of SEQRA and CEQR and the appropriate remedy is to grant petitioners' motion for summary judgment declaring the special permit null and void. The suggestion in the dissenting opinion that the omission here can be cured by 'an amended negative declaration' (dissenting opn. at p. 371) finds no support in the carefully drafted procedures of the statute and would effectively allow the municipality to comply with SEQRA and CEQR only as an afterthought following a successful challenge to their prior action. Such result is directly contrary to our holding in *Matter of Tri-County Taxpayers Assn. v. Town Bd.*, *supra*, and moreover, would contravene the important purposes underlying SEQRA. Indeed, 'it would allow a project to initially be approved without the benefit of a valid environmental review.' In order to further thestrong policies serve by SEQRA and to not frustrate its important objectives, we hold that the appropriate remedy here is the annulment of the special permit.

"Accordingly the order of the Appellate Division affirming the Supreme Court's grant of summary judgment to respondents is reversed and petitioners' cross motion for summary judgment granted."

25:6 *Regulation of Land Use: Hotel and Resort Development*

Regulation of land use by state and local governments has normally taken the form of zoning regulation. Zoning authorizes various government authorities to exercise their power to protect the public health, morals, and safety. This exercise of the police power does not require the government to compensate the affected landowner unless the regulation amounts to a taking of property, which must be compensated. Regulation may include land classifications for industrial, commercial, and residential uses, what types of business or other occupations may be conducted, or what types of occupants may use the property. A taking occurs when the owner is denied any use of his or her property or is compelled to transfer the property to another. A mere regulation of an existing or future use does not amount to a taking. A taking for a public purpose constitutes the exercise of government power under eminent domain, usually by condemnation. Such an exercise in the public interest is also a taking.

The following cases represent a variety of hotel and resort development fact patterns involving federal and state environmental issues. They are not intended as definitive but merely illustrate typical problems and judicial solutions.

The California Court of Appeal ruled that the California Coastal Commission had properly refused to approve the city's local coastal development program for part of South San Diego Bay, which included a 700-room hotel. The Court of Appeal held that the standard of review of this sort of administrative action was the existence of substantial evidence to support the Commission's ruling, and there was substantial evidence in the record to support the Commission's refusal to approve the plan.

CITY OF CHULA VISTA V. SUPERIOR COURT OF SAN DIEGO COUNTY
133 Cal. App. 3d 472, 183 Cal. Rptr. 909 (Cal. App. 1982)

COLOGNE, J.: [Facts and other issues omitted.]

Summary

"The City does not deny the possibility of any of the predicted adverse effects of its development which the Commission foresees. Rather, it contends first, it will take all economically feasible mitigating measures and, second, the remaining risks are justified by the gain in public access to and enjoyment of the bayfront area as a result of the planned development. It says the various alternatives for development suggested by the commission such as, for instance, moving the 700-unit hotel from. . . [Gunpowder] Point to the adjacent less environmentally significant Vener farms area, are not economically feasible. . . .

"We conclude the record is replete with substantial evidence of risk to the marsh environment if the proposed development is allowed. As stated at the outset of this discussion, the Coastal Act presents competing values: local planning options and needs versus statewide concerns in the preservation of the unique California coastal zone. The Commission as representative of the state and protector of the statewide interests in conservation and coastal management must have an effective role when it comes to balancing these values, else the agency has no real purpose. Local government is not expected to concern itself with statewide interests to the same extent that a statewide agency would and here, the statewide interests to be protected clearly appear. The Commission must be permitted to decide the necessary level of protection. If it is compelled to accept risks it regards as unjustified in the name of economic necessity, it cannot carry out its statutory mandate to provide permanent protection for the state's distinctive and valuable coastal zone for the benefit of the people of California. . . .

"PETITION DENIED."

The federal Circuit Court of Appeals for the District of Columbia affirmed administrative decisions below to permit private interests to expand and develop the government-owned ski area on the San Francisco Peaks in the Coconino National Forest. In doing so, the court reviewed alleged violations of the federal Endangered Species Act, the Wilderness Act, the National Historic Preservation Act, and Land Use Permits.

WILSON v. BLOCK
708 F.2d 735 (D.C. Cir. 1983)

LUMBARD, Senior Cir. J.: [All other issues omitted.]

"The San Francisco Peaks are within the Coconino National Forest and are managed by the Forest Service. A 777 acre portion of the Peaks, known as the 'Snow Bowl,' has been used for downhill skiing since 1937 when the Forest Service build [*sic*] a road and ski lodge. The lodge was destroyed by fire in 1952 and was replaced in 1956. Ski lifts were built at the Snow Bowl in 1958 and 1962. Since 1962 the facilities have changed very little.

"In April 1977 the Forest Service transferred the permit to operate the Snow Bowl skiing facilities from Summit Properties, Inc. to the Northland Recreation Company. In July 1977 Northland submitted to the Forest Service a 'master plan' for the future development of the Snow Bowl, which contemplated the construction of additional parking and ski slopes, new lodge facilities, and ski lifts. The Forest Service, pursuant to the National Environmental Policy Act, conducted public workshops and solicited alternatives to Northland's plan. The Forest Service evaluated the proposed alternatives and identified six which were feasible and represented the spectrum of public opinion. These alternatives ranged from complete elimination of artificial structures in the Snow Bowl to full development as proposed by Northland. On June 23, 1978 the Forest Service filed a draft Environmental Impact Statement evaluating the six alternatives. Between June 23 and September 30, 1978 the Forest Service solicited public opinion on the draft Environmental Impact Statement. Special efforts were made to solicit the views of the Hopis and Navajos.

"On February 27, 1979 the Forest Supervisor of the Coconino National Forest issued his decision to permit moderate development of the Snow Bowl under a 'Preferred Alternative,' which in fact was not one of the six alternatives previously identified. The Preferred Alternative envisions the clearing of 50 acres of forest for new ski runs, instead of the 120 acres requested by Northland. The Preferred Alternative also authorizes construction of a new day lodge, improvement of restroom facilities, reconstruction of existing chair lifts, construction of three new lifts, and the paving and widening of the Snow Bowl road.

"At the request of various persons, including certain of the plaintiffs, the Regional Forester on February 7, 1980 overruled the Forest Supervisor and ordered maintenance of the status quo. The Chief Forester on December 31, 1980 reversed the Regional Forester and reinstated the Forest Supervisor's approval of the Preferred Alternative. . . .

"The plaintiffs alleged that expansion of the Snow Bowl facilities would violate the Indians' First Amendment right to the free exercise of religion, the American Indian Religious Freedom Act, the fiduciary duties owed the Indians by the government, the Endangered Species Act, two statutes regulating private use of national forest land (16 U.S.C. §§ 497, 551), the National Historic Preservation Act, the Multiple-Use Sustained Yield Act, the Wilderness Act, the National Environmental Policy Act, and the Administrative Procedure Act. . . .

" . . . After a hearing, Judge RICHEY on June 15, 1981 granted summary judgment to the defendants on all issues except the plaintiffs' claim under the National Historic Preservation Act. Finding that the Forest Service had failed to comply with certain requirements of that Act, Judge RICHEY remanded the cause to the Forest Service for further proceedings and stayed development until compliance. After the defendants reported back, Judge RICHEY on May 14, 1982 ruled that the Forest Service had achieved compliance and he entered final judgment for the defendants on all issues and vacated his stay. These appeals followed promptly and the defendants have agreed to delay development pending their disposition.

"From our review of the record we are convinced that Judge RICHEY's conclusions of law are in accordance with precedent and not in error. Accordingly, we affirm the judgments. . . .

Endangered Species Act

"The plaintiffs claim that the Forest Service violated section 7(a)(2) of the Endangered Species Act, 16 U.S.C. § 1536(a)(2) (Supp. IV. 1980), by failing to insure that the Preferred Alternative will not be likely to jeopardize the continued existence on the Peaks of a small yellow-flowered plant called *senecio franciscanus*, or the 'San Francisco Peaks groundsel.' *Senecio franciscanus* exists only in an elongated area of approximately 2.6 square kilometers at the top of the Peaks. This elongated area extends into the Snow Bowl permit area. As an alpine plant, *senecio franciscanus* is particularly susceptible to damage from human activity. The plant's population, once reduced by human activity, would not recover for decades or even centuries. The approved development will extend into a small portion of the plant's habitat and will destroy a small number of plants. The greatest threat to the plant's continued existence, however, is posed not by construction, or by skiers, but by summer hikers who walk off-trail and trample the fragile plants. Expansion of the ski lifts will significantly increase the threat to the plant by allowing a greater number of hikers to reach its habitat.

"On June 16, 1976 the Secretary of the Interior proposed *senecio franciscanus* for formal listing as an endangered species under section 4 of the Endangered Species Act of 1973, 16 U.S.C. § 1533. Section 4 requires the Secretary to publish in the Federal Register a list of those species determined by him or by the Secretary of Commerce to be endangered or threatened within the meaning of the Act. The Endangered Species Act amendments of 1978 required the withdrawal of all listing proposals over two years old. A one year grace period was extended to proposals already over two years old. On December 10, 1979 the Secretary withdrew the proposal to list *senecio franciscanus* because no action had been taken on the proposal since its submission. At the time the plaintiffs commenced this suit *senecio franciscanus* was neither listed nor proposed for listing.

"Section 7(a)(2) of the Endangered Species Act requires each federal agency, with the assistance of the Secretary, to insure that its actions are not likely to jeopardize the continued existence of any endangered or threatened species. Section 7(a)(2) provides:

> "Each Federal agency shall, in consultation with and with the assistance of the Secretary, insure that any action authorized, funded, or carried out by such agency . . . is not likely to jeopardize the continued existence of any endangered species or threatened species or result in the destruction or adverse modification of habitat of such species which is determined by the Secretary, after consultation as appropriate with affected States, to be critical. . . . In fulfilling the requirements of this paragraph each agency shall use the best scientific and commercial data available.

"Section 7(a)(2) requires an agency, prior to project implementation, formally to consult the Secretary about any agency action that might affect a protected species. Section 7(b), 16 U.S.C. § 1536(b), requires the Secretary to provide to an agency that consults him under section 7(a)(2) a written opinion indicating how the agency's proposed action would affect the protected species and identifying means of protecting the species. The Forest Service has not formally consulted the Secretary about *senecio franciscanus,* and it has not obtained the written opinion required by section 7(b). The plaintiffs' claim would therefore have merit if section 7(a)(2) in fact protected *senecio franciscanus.* We, however, agree with Judge RICHEY, who held that § 7(a)(2) applies only to species listed pursuant to section 4, and hence had no application to the unlisted *senecio franciscanus.* . . .

Wilderness Act

"On May 2, 1979 President Carter, on the advice of the Secretary of Agriculture, recommended to Congress that it designate as wilderness under the National Wilderness Preservation System Act of 1964, 16 U.S.C. §§ 1131–36 (1976), some 14,650 acres of the San Francisco Peaks. Congress has not yet acted upon that recommendation. The area recommended for wilderness designation abuts the Snow Bowl permit area on the north, south, and east, but includes no part of the permit area. A substantial part of the permit area is still undeveloped; in particular, a strip of land approximately 500 feet wide along the area's northern border, adjacent to the recommended wilderness area, remains heavily forested. Under the Preferred Alternative that strip of land will be partially developed for skiing. The plaintiffs contend that the Secretary of Agriculture, in approving development of pristine land adjacent to a recommended wilderness area, infringed Congress' exclusive authority to determine wilderness area boundaries. The plaintiffs base their claim upon § 3(b) of the Wilderness Act, 16 U.S.C. § 1132(b) (1976), and argue that the Secretary may not, by authorizing expansion of the ski area, impair Congress' discretion to include undeveloped portions of the Snow Bowl in the San Francisco Peaks wilderness area. As Judge RICHEY found, the plaintiffs' claim is without merit.

"Section 1132(b) authorizes the President to recommend for inclusion in designated wilderness areas lands contiguous to areas formerly designated as 'primitive' by the Secretary of Agriculture. It provides:

"The Secretary of Agriculture shall, within ten years after September 3, 1964, review, as to its suitability or nonsuitability for preservation as wilderness, each area in the national forests classified on September 3, 1964 by the Secretary of Agriculture or the Chief of the Forest Service as 'primitive' and report his findings to the President. The President shall advise the United States Senate and House of Representatives of his recommendations with respect to the designation as 'wilderness' or other reclassification of each area on which review has been completed. . . . Each recommendation of the President for designation as 'wilderness' shall become effective only if so provided by an Act of Congress. . . . *Nothing herein contained shall limit the President in proposing, as part of his recommendations to Congress, the alteration of existing boundaries of primitive areas or recommending the addition of any contiguous area of national forest lands predominantly of wilderness value.* (Emphasis supplied.)

"In *Parker v. United States*, 448 F.2d 793, 797 (10th Cir. 1971), *cert. denied*, 405 U.S. 989, 92 S. Ct. 1252, 31 L. Ed. 2d 455 (1972), the Tenth Circuit held that the italicized language reflects 'the clear intent of Congress . . . that both the President and the Congress shall have a meaningful opportunity to add contiguous areas predominantly of wilderness value to existing primitive areas for final wilderness designation.' A 'meaningful opportunity' can be preserved only if lands within the ambit of § 1132(b) remain undeveloped until such time as the President and Congress act. Thus in *Parker,* the Tenth Circuit affirmed a district court order enjoining the Secretary from authorizing lumbering of certain virgin land contiguous to a primitive area, where the President and Congress had not yet considered whether to designate the land in question as wilderness.

"*Parker* indicates that § 1132(b) can restrict the Secretary's discretion to approve development of wilderness land contiguous to a designated primitive area. The defendants, however, contend that § 1132(b) does not apply to national forest land which is neither contained in nor contiguous to a primitive area, and that the plaintiffs' claim must therefore fail, as neither the Snow Bowl permit area nor any other part of the San Francisco Peaks has ever been designated primitive. We agree. . . .

National Historic Preservation Act

"In his June 15, 1981 opinion, Judge RICHEY found that the Forest Service had committed three violations of the National Historic Preservation Act (NHPA), 16 U.S.C. § 470 *et seq.* (1976), and implementing regulations . . . Judge RICHEY remanded the case to the Forest Service for compliance with NHPA, and stayed development pending compliance. Upon remand, the Forest Service conducted archaeological surveys of the permit area and consulted the SHPO [State Historic Preservation Officer]. On September 22, 1981, the Chief Forester determined that the project area contained no properties either listed or eligible for listing on the National Register; that expansion of the ski area would not affect the historic qualities of the Merriam Base Camp or the Fern Mountain Ranch; and that the San Francisco Peaks themselves were not eligible for listing.

The SHPO had concurred in these findings by letter dated September 11, 1981. After the plaintiffs failed to obtain administrative reversal of the Chief Forester's determination, the defendants returned to court to show compliance to Judge RICHEY. On May 14, 1982 Judge RICHEY ruled that the Forest Service had complied with NHPA in all respects. He granted the defendants final judgment on all counts and lifted the stay against development. . . .

"The plaintiffs argue that the Forest Service breached its NHPA duty to identify *all* eligible properties by failing to survey 100% of the impact area. They contend that the Forest Service's partial surveys may have left some eligible properties undetected. We think that the partial surveys were sufficient. The regulations do not expressly require agencies in all cases completely to survey impact areas, and in fact recognize that the need for surveys will vary from case to case. *See* C.F.R. §§ 800.4(a)(1),(2). We believe that a complete survey is not required where both the partial survey, and all other evidence, indicate that a complete survey would be fruitless. . . .

Land Use Permits

"In 1977 the Forest Service issued two permits to Northland for use of the Snow Bowl permit area, which on May 18, 1982 were amended to reflect the development approved under the Preferred Alternative. One of the amended permits, covering 24 acres, is a term permit valid until May 1, 1997. The Forest Service granted this permit under the Act of March 4, 1915, as amended, 16 U.S.C. § 497 (1976), which provides:

"The Secretary of Agriculture is authorized, under such regulations as he may make and upon such terms and conditions as he may deem proper, (a) to permit the use and occupancy of suitable areas of land within the national forests, not exceeding eighty acres and for periods not exceeding thirty years, for the purpose of constructing or maintaining hotels, resorts, and any other structures or facilities necessary or desirable for recreation, public convenience, or safety; . . .

"Northland will build the ski lodge and all other permanent facilities upon the land covered by the term permit. The other permit, an annual or revocable permit covering the remaining 753 acres of the permit area, was issued by the Forest Service under the authority of the Act of June 4, 1897, as amended, 16 U.S.C. § 551 (1976), which authorizes the Secretary of Agriculture to 'make such rules and regulations . . . as will insure the objects of such reservations, namely, to regulate their occupancy and use and to preserve the forests thereon from destruction.' The land covered by the revocable permit will be used only for ski slopes.

"The plaintiffs challenge the validity of the 'dual permit' system employed by the Forest Service. They contend that 16 U.S.C. § 497, which authorizes permit areas no larger than 80 acres, constitutes the sole authority under which the Secretary may grant permits for the private recreational development of national forest lands. They accordingly claim that the Forest Service exceeded its authority in issuing a revocable permit under 16 U.S.C. § 551 and in granting permits covering 777 acres to a single developer. We agree with Judge RICHEY that § 497 does not limit the Secretary's authority under § 551 and that Congress has sanctioned the use of dual permits. . . .

"In *Sierra Club v. Hickel,* 433 F.2d 24, 35 (9th Cir. 1970), *affd. on other grounds sub nom. Sierra Club v. Morton,* 405 U.S. 727, 92 S. Ct. 1361, 31 L. Ed. 2d 636 (1972), the Ninth Circuit approved the practice of issuing dual permits to ski resort operators and, in language highly instructive here, stated:

> "The fact that the record discloses that there are now a total of at least eighty-four recreational developments on national forest lands in which there is such a combination of the term permit and the revocable permit is convincing proof of their legality. Many of these developments are ski developments making use of the maximum acres of the term permit plus revocable permits for additional acreage in amounts in some cases in excess of 6,000 acres. . . . It seems apparent, as was obvious to both [the 1956] Senate and House Committees, that the eighty-acre long-term permit was a necessity to obtain proper financing for substantial permanent improvements, while developments of less magnitude and permanency, such as trails, slopes, corrals, could be placed upon lands held under revocable permits.

"The Forest Service has continued, following the decision in *Sierra Club,* to grant dual permits to ski resort operators. There are presently about 200 ski developments in the national forests and most of them employ dual permits. . . .

"We conclude, then, that the Secretary has consistently interpreted the Act of 1915 as *not* limiting his authority to issue revocable permits under the Act of 1897 [discussion omitted]; that Congress has for decades had knowledge of the Secretary's interpretation, but has never objected; and that on the one occasion when Congress did comment on the Secretary's interpretation and practice, in 1956, it expressed approval. Under these circumstances the Secretary's authority to issue revocable permits under § 551, whether or not exercised in connection with dual permits, cannot be doubted. As this court stated in *Kay v. FCC,* 443 F.2d 638, 646–47 (1970), 'a consistent administrative interpretation of a statute, shown clearly to have been brought to the attention of Congress and not changed by it, is almost conclusive evidence that the interpretation has congressional approval.'

"Accordingly, we affirm the judgment of the district court."

The importance of exhausting all administrative agency remedies as a prerequisite to seeking judicial review of environmental approval by a city of a university's new hotel project and sports stadium improvement was set forth in the following case.

The California Court of Appeal's conclusions are presented here.

COALITION FOR STUDENT ACTION V. CITY OF FULLERTON
153 Cal. App. 3d 1194, 200 Cal. Rptr. 855 (Cal. App. 1984)

CROSBY, A.J.: "Two individuals and an unincorporated association appeal a judgment denying a petition for writ of mandate to compel respondent public entities to set aside approval of plans to construct a twelve-story, two-hundred room hotel and conference center on the campus of California State University, Fullerton, and to improve and expand the existing football/soccer stadium and baseball field. Petitioners' challenge was based on respondents' alleged violations of the California Environmental Quality Act (CEQA). Petitioners claimed no CEQA violation at the administrative level, however, and may not do so for the first time in a petition of writ of mandate. Thus, we affirm the judgment without reaching the merits of the appeal.

"In compliance with the California Administrative Code, title 14, section 15080, the City of Fullerton prepared 'Initial Studies' in October and November 1982 'to determine if the project[s] may have a significant effect on the environment.' The Initial Study for the hotel project determined there were no significant environmental effects and a Negative Declaration would be appropriate (Pub. Resources Code, § 21080, subd. (c)(1). . . .

"The Fullerton Planning Commission held a noticed public hearing concerning the proposed hotel on December 8, 1982; no member of the public objected to the project or the environmental data. The Fullerton City Council and Redevelopment Agency noticed joint public hearings on the projects on January 4 and 18, 1983. Again, no one criticized the recommendation to prepare Negative Declarations or claimed EIR's [Environmental Impact Reports] were required. The Negative Declarations were approved at the conclusion of the second hearing.

"The petition for writ of mandate was timely filed several weeks later. (§ 21167.) There petitioners alleged for the first time the failure to prepare EIR's violated CEQA. Respondents answered, and the court determined respondents complied with CEQA requirements and substantial evidence supported their actions. The petition was denied.

"The essence of the exhaustion doctrine is the public agency's opportunity to receive and respond to articulated factual issues and legal theories *before* its actions are subjected to judicial review. The doctrine was not satisfied here by a relatively few bland and general references to environmental matters. The city was entitled to consider any objection to proceeding by Negative Declaration in the first instance, if there was one. Mere objections to the *project,* as opposed to the procedure, are not sufficient to alert an agency to an objection based on CEQA. Petitioners, having failed to raise their CEQA claims at the administrative level, cannot air them for the first time in the courts.

"Judgment affirmed. Respondents to recover costs on appeal."

In *Nollan v. California Coastal Commission,*[3] property owners brought an action against the commission to overturn a requirement that they provide lateral access to the public to pass and repass across their property in order to obtain approval of a rebuilding permit. The United States Supreme Court ruled that such a creation of a beachfront public easement was a taking which must be

[3]107 S. Ct. 3141 (1987).

compensated under the federal Constitution. Were it not for the rebuilding permit, California could have lawfully required the owners to create such an easement in order to increase public access to the beach without compensation.

In *Citizens of Croleta Valley v. Board of Supervisors,*[4] the California Court of Appeal reversed the denial of a motion to set aside the board's certification and approval of a proposed hotel resort project on seventy-three acres of beachfront land in Santa Barbara County. In setting aside the board's actions, the court ruled that the failure to prepare an adequate environmental impact report (EIR) was an abuse of discretion as a matter of law. In this case, such an EIR required consideration of an alternative smaller project. The local county zoning ordinance required that the smaller alternative, if economically viable, be approved if it would have fewer significant environmental impacts and there was no showing that the alternative was economically infeasible.

In the next case, an environmental group sought to overturn the implementation of a 1981 plan restricting but not prohibiting off-road vehicles on the Cape Cod National Seashore, arguing that the plan would cause significant damage to the coastal ecosystem and conflict with other recreational activities. In affirming the granting of summary judgment to the Secretary by the district court, the federal Circuit Court of Appeals for the First Circuit ruled that the plan was appropriate and sufficient under both the Cape Code National Seashore Act and Executive Order 11644. The latter order is noted below.

CONSERVATION LAW FOUNDATION OF NEW ENGLAND, INC. V.
SECRETARY OF THE INTERIOR
864 F.2d 954 (1st Cir. 1989)

CAFFREY, Senior District Judge: [All other issues omitted.]

IV. Executive Order 11644

"Executive Order No. 11644, 37 Fed. Reg. 2877 (1972) ('Use of Off-Road Vehicles on Public Lands'), *as amended by* Executive Order No. 11989, 42 Fed. Reg. 26959 (1977), *both reprinted in note following* 42 U.S.C. § 4321 (1981), provides that ORV use on federal lands must be consistent with 'the protection of the resources of the public lands, promotion of the safety of all users of those lands, and minimization of conflicts among the various uses of those lands.' E.O. 11644, § 3(a). Section 3(a) of the Order requires that ORV trails be located in areas of the National Park System only 'if the respective agency head determines that off-road vehicle use in such locations will not adversely affect their natural, aesthetic, or scenic values.' *Id.* § 3(a)(4). Executive Order 11989, the 1977 amendment to Executive Order 11644, further provides that the agency head must,

"whenever he determines that the use of off-road vehicles will cause or is causing considerable adverse effects on the soil, vegetation, wildlife habitat

[4]197 Cal. App. 3d 1167, 243 Cal. Rptr. 339 (Cal. App. 1988).

or cultural or historic resources of particular areas or trails of the public lands, immediately close such areas or trails to the type of off-road vehicle causing such effects until such time as he determines that such adverse effects have been eliminated and that measures have been implemented to prevent future recurrence.

"E.O. 11644 § 9(a). These provisions, then, restrict the Secretary's discretion regarding ORV use on the Seashore, along with Section 7 of the Seashore Act.

"CLF [Conservation Law Foundation] maintains that Executive Order 11644 requires the defendants to close the Seashore to ORV use because of alleged ecological damage and aesthetic degradation at the Seashore. CLF challenges the Secretary's finding that current regulations on ORV use effectively protect the ecology of the Seashore and that limited ORV use does not adversely affect natural or scenic values at the Seashore. The plaintiff argues in particular that numerous violations of the National Park Service regulations cause considerable damage to the Seashore ecology and aesthetics, and require that a ban be imposed on ORV travel, unless the violations can be prevented.

"The Secretary determined that limited ORV use under the 1985 Plan does not adversely affect natural, aesthetic or scenic values at the Seashore. Amended Record of Decision at 30. We agree with the district court that there is adequate support for this determination. The defendants considered the protection of natural values in arriving at the current regulations restricting ORV use on the Seashore. The extent and location of ORV trails were set under the 1985 Plan consistent with these values. Though unregulated ORV travel on the Seashore might well threaten the natural or scenic values of the Seashore, the restrictions imposed under the 1985 Plan are substantial and were designed specifically to protect those values that would otherwise be at risk.

"The Secretary also determined that ORV use has caused no significant ecological damage at the Seashore since the adoption of the 1981 Plan. The district court correctly explained in its June 27, 1984 decision that an agency's technical conclusions are to be upheld by a reviewing court where they are 'founded on supportable data and methodology, and meet minimum standards of rationality.' *CLR I, 590* F. Supp. at 1483 (quoting *South Terminal Corp. v. Environmental Protection Agency,* 504 F.2d 646, 655 & 665 (1st Cir. 1974)). We agree with the district court that the defendants' conclusion regarding effective protection of the Seashore ecology under the Management Plan is based on supportable data and methodology, and meets minimum standards of rationality. Accordingly, the defendants' finding as to adequate ecological protection should not be disturbed. . . .

"AFFIRMED."

25:7 *The Emerging Role of the Environmental Impact Statement*

However we view global and national economic developments as we approach the twenty-first century, one issue exists as a given: our natural open land areas are shrinking, and the remaining areas will be more greatly impacted by environmental concerns than in the past. Increased population, increased demand for scarcer land resources for habitation, recreation, and resort development by growing numbers of leisure-time users, and tourism development worldwide, will require closer and more stringent land use to maintain current environmental standards and to ration available land already sorely afflicted by myriad ecological problems. In essence, our industry must develop creative methods of land use so as to maintain a rational, economically feasible supply of properties in the face of environmental demands to preserve and enhance the *status quo*.

The Environmental Impact Statement is one device that communities will use to justify control over land-use development by the hospitality industry, among other land developers. The day of uncontrolled commercial sprawl is over, a relic of the past, when our country was young, untamed, and in need of rapid economic stimulation by public and private sources. Now we confront a mature economy, far less open space, and the aftermath of rapid economic growth: damage to the existing ecosystem that sustains us. That acknowledged fact does not spell no hospitality growth, but merely more regulation, where we must justify development to the overall community. We must compete more effectively for land-use resources so as to enhance our preeminent position as a worldwide industry that promotes human well-being.

In sum, environmental demands expressed by the EIS requirement need not dismay us. Rather they challenge us to develop qualitative standards that are both cost beneficial in the economic sense to our investors and environmentally beneficial in the regulatory sense to consumers. The achievement of that balance between creative enterprise and legal constraints is well within our means and will help to define our economic posture into the next century.

26 Catastrophic Risk Liability

26.1 *Introduction*

During the 1980s a series of disasters beset the hotel industry. The MGM-Grand fire in Las Vegas, a similar occurrence at the DuPont Plaza in San Juan, the collapse of a lobby walkway at the Hyatt in Kansas City, and the 1989 earthquake that struck the San Francisco Bay Area illustrate but do not exhaust the number of such occurrences. The resultant deaths; serious injuries to guests, patrons, and staff; as well as extensive damage to hotel buildings and furnishings and economic losses due to business interruption are all causes for concern. Normally, the potential for harm is associated with high-rise convention and resort properties. However, the 1980 Stouffer Inn fire in Harrison, New York, demonstrates that such risks are shared alike by all properties, irrespective of size. That fire occurred in the third-floor public rooms of a medium-sized property, not in upper-story guest rooms.

What makes these risks extraordinary is the attendant publicity and public outcry for increased safety measures. These demands often result in new legislation and greater government regulation. Whereas this activity was once considered a state or local responsibility, the federal Hotel and Motel Safety Act of 1990 indirectly compels installation of fire-suppression sprinklers and smoke-detection alarm systems in all properties of over three floors by prohibiting government employees from staying at covered properties that lack such devices after 1996. This is the most dramatic example of government intervention establishing minimum nationwide standards involving one serious potential disaster, a fire on the premises.

These occurrences, though infrequent, are severe in terms of likelihood and size of legal claims. In addition to the burst of tort litigation involving death or physical and emotional harm to guests and patrons, the loss of ability to perform preexisting convention and function contracts and group tour packages, raises the possibility of breach of contract litigation. These subjects and proposed containment measures will be reviewed in the sections to follow.

26:2 *General Rule of Nonliability: Contract Theory*

As a general rule, there are circumstances beyond the control of the parties to a contract which will cause a court to discharge or relieve the parties of any liability to each other assumed under their agreement. These circumstances are external or extrinsic to the contract. The mere financial inability of the party obligated to perform is not such a case. Riots and shortages of material or labor also fall outside the rule of nonliability and do not excuse performance. This is so because the shortage can be made up from other sources, even though at greater cost to the obligated party. To illustrate, a hotel having booked a convention on a certain date cannot excuse performance on the ground that present occupants are overstaying their departure, unless that fact was a condition which excused performance by the hotel. Absent such a contractual condition, the hotel would be obligated to provide alternate space at its own expense or to pay damages. Likewise an overbooking of space by the hotel under contract to provide the same does not bar recovery by a convention group with whom the hotel obligated itself.

What may cause a discharge of performance is the destruction of the subject matter upon the existence of which performance was based, but only where the specific subject matter was expressed and no substitution was authorized. Thus, where a convention host by contract expressly specified the only resort existing on the Falkland Islands as its convention site, and no other, and the resort was destroyed by fire absent fault by either party, the contract would be discharged. Note that it is not the nature of the catastrophe that triggers discharge, but the impossibility of substituting other comparable performance. By contrast, if a convention host contracts for any available space of a certain class and quality, and the tour operator or destination convention representative promises to deliver that type of accommodation, there is no discharge due to catastrophic damage because the source of supply was not limited to a single property. Only if the catastrophe were so serious as to destroy all properties of that class in that specific destination would discharge be appropriate.

26:3   *General Rule of Nonliability: Tort Theory*

In the case of tort or personal injury liability arising by operation of law, catastrophic occurrence such as an unexpected earthquake, flood, or tornado, may excuse liability on the ground that the risk of unreasonable harm was unforeseeable. There is no contract guaranteeing safety and security of guests to discharge, since innkeepers are normally not insurers but only need to exercise ordinary or reasonable care to safeguard their guests and patrons. Past similar occurrences of the catastrophic hazard may give rise to proof of actual notice of such risks sufficient to create foreseeability and the duty to warn or take other appropriate measures. Likewise, statutes adopted to prevent or minimize risks (earthquake, fire, and safety building codes; swimming pool safety codes; and the like) create actual notice whether understood or not and must be obeyed. Their violation in some cases creates proof of negligence *per se,* or conclusively against the hotel.

Thus under both contract and tort theories of liability, catastrophic occurrences may or may not relieve the obligated party or party at fault from responsibility. Thus the best managerial rule is to prepare for these contingencies on the basis of experience. Contracts for reservations or functions should condition performance or otherwise apportion risks among the parties. In the case of possible tort responsibility the innkeeper or other owner or operator should consider the use of disclaimers of liability or hold-harmless clauses. These are most useful when dealing with human risks of a severe kind, such as resort-sponsored white-water rafting, the use of health club facilities, scuba diving, hang gliding, and other such activities. A sample form is included below:

Sample Waiver (Indemnity) Clause

User agrees to indemnify and hold _____ (name of hotel owner/operator) free and harmless from all injuries to persons, including death, damages to property, loss of time and/or any and all other loss or damages, whether caused or occasioned by the negligence of _____ (name of hotel owner/operator), its employees or servants, or any other persons whatsoever, arising or flowing from the use, operation, or rental of the said (item) by User.

In addition, signs should also be conspicuously posted warning users with health problems to use exercise or other equipment at their own risk. Not all states recognize the validity of such clauses, and those that do require them to be specific and unequivocal.[1]

26:4 *Acts of God and the Public Enemy*

A special rule, more limited in scope than the foregoing analysis, applies to protect innkeepers from the unlimited common-law liability they assume over the property of their guests brought within the four walls of the premises (*infra hospitium*) or under the exclusive supervision and control of the management.

In these more restrictive circumstances, the innkeeper is exonerated from property losses or damage suffered by guests due to acts of God or the "public enemy." This means that unforeseen natural catastrophes (acts of God) that are solely to blame for property losses or damage excuse the innkeeper from liability. Likewise acts of war or declaration of martial law (acts of the public enemy) also exonerate the innkeeper in cases where they cause loss or destruction of guest property. Criminal activity by individuals or groups does not constitute public enemy acts irrespective of how they may be characterized by the media.

26:5 *Terrorism*

Terrorist activities have horrific if not catastrophic consequences. The explosion of Pan Am Flight 103 over Lockerbie, Scotland, is vivid testimony to their destructive effect. The fact that to date terrorists have vented their fanaticism

---

[1]*See* Gimpel v. Host Enterprises, Inc. 640 F. Supp. 972 (D. Pa 1986) (bicycle); *Contra:* Calarco v. YMCA, 501 N.E.2d 268 (Ill. 1986) (weightroom equipment).

against air and marine carriers is no reason for hotels to ignore preventive measures. Because of their size and location, major convention hotels and resorts present an inviting target for assassination, kidnapping, bombing, and inciting panic in the large numbers of persons assembled there. The near death in 1984 of former Prime Minister Margaret Thatcher in a terrorist bombing of her Brighton, England, hotel suite is a sobering example. The hotel was severely damaged, and Mrs. Thatcher would certainly have been killed had she been present when the bomb exploded. The blast killed three politicians and wounded thirty-four others.

To respond by ignoring such doomsday forecasts as pure speculation until such a tragedy occurs is one way of dealing with the issue, on grounds of tortious, lack of foreseeability (personal injuries), or contract discharge (destruction of premises). However, events in the British Isles, where hotels have been targeted and damaged, should give pause to that traditional conclusion. It is true that United States innkeepers have not experienced any serious physical damage or loss of life in a hotel as yet, but the motive exists as does the means of accomplishment. Only the proper opportunity need manifest itself.

How the courts would deal with ultimate responsibility is as yet unknown. However, some general observations, noted hereafter, are in order.

26:6 *Failure to Rescue or Inadequate Rescue of Guests and Patrons*

Regardless of lack of foreseeability of the terrorist-inspired event, hotels are under a duty to secure the safety and security of their occupants in a reasonable fashion. This translates into the duty to provide reasonable rescue, first aid, and other assistance so as to diminish, to the extent possible, the consequences of a terrorist event. Performance of that duty is viewed in light of what was possible under the circumstances, not the hindsight test of what could have been done under normal conditions.

In this perspective, terrorism must be viewed as any other catastrophic occurrence or event. It differs only in that most natural calamities are caused by forces beyond our control; they are true acts of God. Terrorism, like criminal activities of individuals on the premises, are intended to harm or at least panic those at whom directed as well as the general population. Yet in either case, the innkeeper's legal duty is to mitigate that harm, so long as to do so does not threaten the lives of management or other employees. What constitutes a reasonable response will depend on the nature of the emergency, and emergency situations do not always dictate a normal response. Thus, it may not be possible to follow the standard operating procedure in every case. However, what is necessary is that a catastrophic rescue plan is developed with proper training and practice and reviewed and changed to meet new situations or to improve established techniques. Any operator who fails to have such a plan in place will more likely be dealt with more harshly by the courts than an operator who does his best to make his plan work under trying circumstances.

26:7 *The Emerging Role of Crisis Management*

It is an economic fact of life that as we develop plans to house larger numbers of persons in our existing or new hospitality facilities, and as we offer a greater number of recreational facilities and amenities, the increased hotel and resort population we generate will increase the risk of the occupancy and facilities' use. That risk must be scrutinized with the same level of competence and concern that drives our marketing activities. For the large convention and resort operator, the possibility of crisis events is magnified by the size and scope of the operation. But even the small operator must take crisis management into account not only because of state and municipal laws governing severe risks irrespective of number of victims but because that operator, too, is required by the common law to exercise a reasonable degree of care for his guest's safety and security, not exhausted by compliance with statutory regulations.

Therefore, as the industry grows, the risk grows commensurately. This fact is part and parcel of our goal of providing every guest and patron with increased expectations of service and amenities. We need not fear that responsibility, but need only devote the same time, funds, and support to that task as we provide our other responsibilities. Crisis management is emerging from the back of the house to the general manager's and corporate executive's offices. How well we perform this task will be the barometer of our ability to enhance public confidence and thus lessen further government regulatory activities.

Law Review Articles

Responsibilities of Innkeeper to Guests and Patrons

1. *Civil Rights—Civil Rights Act of 1964—A Bar Containing Various Mechanical Means of Amusement Held to Be a "Place of Entertainment" and therefore a Place of Public Accommodation within the Meaning of the Act,* 7 Ind. L. Rev. 752 (1974).
2. *Club Visitors as Innkeepers' "Guests,"* 43 L.J. 748 (1908).
3. *The Common Lodging House,* 110 Just. Peace 551 (1946).
4. Molot, *The Duty of Business to Serve the Public: Analogy to the Innkeeper's Obligation,* 46 Can. B. Rev. 612 (1968).
5. *Guests and Lodgers at Inns,* 17 Modern L. Rev. 272 (1954).
6. *Holiday Bookings,* 106 Solicitors' J. 499 (1962).
7. *Holiday Problems,* 115 L.J. 379, 397 (1965).
8. *Hotel Law in Virginia,* 38 Va. L. Rev. 815 (1952).
9. *Innkeeper and Guest,* 188 L. Times 91 (1939).
10. *Innkeeper: Status or Contract?* 114 Just. Peace 233 (1950).
11. *Innkeepers—Definition for Purpose of Statutory Provision,* 37 Yale L.J. 265 (1927).
12. *Innkeepers—Duties to Guests—§ 200 and § 206 of New York General Business Law,* 7 N.Y.U.L.Q. 536 (1929).
13. *Innkeepers' Liability,* 14 Modern L. Rev. 352 (1951).
14. *Innkeeper's Liability,* 74 Solicitors' J. 697 (1930).
15. *Innkeepers' Liability,* 101 Solicitors' J. 137 (1957).
16. Misner, *Innkeeper Liability,* 22 Trial 70 (1986).
17. *Innkeepers Liability and the Hospitium of the Inn,* 4 Chitty's L.J. 231 (1954).
18. Hemphling, *Innkeeper's Liability at Common Law and under the Statutes,* 4 Notre Dame Law. 421 (1929).
19. *Innkeepers—Liability to Guests,* 93 Cent. L.J. 156 (1921).
20. *An Innkeeper's "Right" to Discriminate,* 15 U. Fla. L. Rev. 109 (1962).
21. *Innkeeper's Right to Exclude or Eject Guests,* 7 Fordham L. Rev. 417 (1938).
22. Wyman, *The Law of the Public Callings as a Solution of the Trust Problem,* 17 Harv. L. Rev. 156 (1903).
23. *The Liability of Innkeepers,* 79 L.J. 146, 166, 185, 201 (1935).
24. *Modern Liability of Innkeepers—Under Virginia Statute,* 1 Wm. & Mary L. Rev. 121 (1957).
25. *A Proposed Analysis for Gender-based Practices and State Public Accommodation Laws,* 16 U. Mich. J.L. Reform 135 (1982).
26. *Public Accommodations in New Mexico: The Right to Refuse Service for Reasons Other than Race or Religion,* 10 Natural Resources J. 635 (1970).
27. Hartmann, *Racial and Religious Discrimination by Innkeepers in U.S.A.,* 12 Modern L. Rev. 449 (1949).
28. *Recent Developments,* 45 Fordham L. Rev. 682 (1976).

29. *Registration of Visitors at Hotels*, 72 Solicitors' J. 358 (1928).
30. *Sex Discrimination in Private Clubs*, 29 Hastings L.J. 417 (1977).
31. *Tort—Innkeeper—Refusal to Receive Guest—Action on Case—No Need to Prove Special Damage*, 9 Cambridge L.J. 123 (1945).
32. *Torts—Innkeeper Liability—Duty to an Infant Guest*, 18 Mercer L. Rev. 480 (1967).
33. *Torts—Liability of Hotel Keeper for Refusing Dining Service to Person Not Lodging in Hotel [Virginia]*, 4 Wash. & Lee L. Rev. 107 (1946).
34. Dickerson, *Travel Law*, 24 Prac. Law 13 (1978).
35. Clark, *Wyatt Earp and the Winelist: Is a Restaurant an "Open Saloon"?* 47 J. Kan. B.A. 63 (1978).

Liability for Guest's Safety

1. Maroney, *Antitrust in the Empire State: Regulation of Restrictive Business Practices in New York State*, 19 Syracuse L. Rev. 819 (1968).
2. Manby, *Assumption of Risk after Sunday vs. Stratton Corporation: The Vermont Sports Injury Liability Statute and Injured Skiers*, 3 Vt. L. Rev. 129 (1978).
3. *Banks v. Hyatt Corporation (722 F.2d. 214): Degree, Nature and Extent of Innkeeper's and Business Proprietor's Duties to Protect Invitees from Criminal Assault*, 30 Loy. L. Rev. 1040 (1984).
4. Steinfeld, *The Hotel—Always the Insurer?* [in the event of fire], 1947 Ins. L.J. 316.
5. *Innkeepers—Assault by One Guest on Another—Liability of Landlord*, 3 Wash. L. Rev. 194 (1928)
6. Taylor, *Innkeeper, Guest and Outlaw: A Very Old Triangle*, 21 S. Tex. L.J. 355 (1981).
7. *Innkeepers—Injury to Person of Guest*, 11 U. Cin. L. Rev. 536 (1937).
8. *Innkeepers—Liability for Acts of Servant without the Scope of Employment*, 24 Alb. L. Rev. 433 (1960).
9. *Innkeeper Liability for Criminal Acts of Third Parties: Should Negligence of the Franchisee Extend to the Franchisor?* 14 Mem. St. L. Rev. 189 (1984).
10. *Innkeepers—Liability for Injuries to Guest Caused by Defective Premises*, 22 Miss. L.J. 246 (1951).
11. *Innkeepers—Liability for Negligence of Porter in Transporting Guest's Baggage*, 1 Brooklyn L. Rev. 120 (1932).
12. *Knodle v. Waikiki Gateway Hotel, Inc. (742 P. 2d 377 (Haw.)): Imposing a Duty to Protect against Third Party Criminal Conduct on the Premises*, 11 Haw. L. Rev. 231 (1989).
13. *Landlord and Tenant—Innkeeper—Liability of Proprietor for Injury to Occupant*, 21 St. Louis L. Rev. 91 (1935).
14. *Liability of Hotel to Pedestrian for Misconduct of Guests*, 44 Minn. L. Rev. 584 (1960).
15. *Liability of Innkeeper for Offensive Acts of Employees*, 69 Alb. L.J. 313 (1907).
16. *Liability of Innkeepers, Judicial Amendment of Statutes, and Theory-of-the-Case Pleading: Kraaz v. La Quinta Motor Inns, Inc.*, 43 La. L. Rev. 1573 (1983).
17. *Liability of Innkeeper to Guest Insulted by Employee*, 13 Bench & Bar 90 (1908).
18. *The Modern Innkeeper's Liability for Injuries to the Person of His Guest*, 19 St. Louis L. Rev. 232 (1934).
19. *Offenses and Quasi-Offenses—Innkeepers—Liability for Objects Thrown into Streets Causing Injury*, 26 Tul. L. Rev. 394 (1952).
20. *Reducing the Slipperiness of Slip and Fall Litigation: Establishing Strict Liability for Hotels*, 25 Santa Clara L. Rev. 591 (1985).

21. *Personal Safety of Innkeepers' Guests*, 102 L.J. 689 (1952).
22. Farrow, *Ski Operators and Skiers—Responsibility and Liability*, 14 New Eng. L. Rev. 262 (1978).
23. *Torts—Innkeeper's Liability for Personal Injuries of Guest*, 25 Geo. L.J. 200 (1936).
24. *Torts—Liability of an Innkeeper for Personal Injuries to Guests*, 28 Fordham L. Rev. 559 (1959).
25. *Torts—Negligence—Liability of Innkeeper for Acts of Transient Guests*, 3 Mercer L. Rev. 351 (1952).

Government Regulation

1. *A Sobering New Approach to Liquor Vendor Liability in Florida*, 13 Fla. St. L. Rev. 827 (1985).
2. *Applying Concepts of Indemnification between Active and Passive Tortfeasors to Actions Brought under the Illinois Dram Shop Act*, 3 Loy. Chi. L.J. 345 (1972).
3. *Bar Owners, Inebriates, and Last Clear Chance*, 37 La. L. Rev. 617 (1977).
4. Quint, *Basis for Liability of a Restaurateur for Serving Unwholesome Food*, 8 N.Y.U. Intra L. Rev. 77 (1953).
5. *Beyond the Dram Shop Act: Imposition of Common-Law Liability on Purveyors of Liquor*, 63 Iowa L. Rev. 1282 (1978).
6. Silver, *Bulk Sales and the Sale of Restaurants under U.C.C. Section 6–102*, 80 Com. L.J. 520 (1975).
7. *California's 1978 Liquor Legislation and the Ewing Case: The Status of the Patron Plaintiff*, 11 Sw. U.L. Rev. 1451 (1979).
8. *Campbell v. Carpenter: Tavern Owner Liability for Serving Visibly Intoxicated Patrons*, 14 Williamette L.J. 327 (1978).
9. *The Case for Tavern Keeper Liability in Georgia*, 9 Ga. L. Rev. 239 (1974).
10. Hanbury, *The Changing Face of the British Pub*, 134 Solicitors' J. 466 (1990).
11. *The Casino Act: Gambling's Past and the Casino Act's Future*, 10 Rut.-Cam. L.J. 279 (1979).
12. *Civil Liability for Furnishing Alcohol in California*, 5 Pacific L.J. 186 (1974).
13. *Common Law Liability of Tavern Owners*, 1971 Wash. U.L.Q. 645.
14. Hagglund and Arthur, *Common Law Liquor Liability*, 7 Forum 73 (1972).
15. *Constitutional Law—First and Twenty-first Amendments—State Can Proscribe Sexual Entertainment at On-Sale Liquor Establishments—California v. LaRue*, 6 Geo. L.J. 1577 (1973).
16. *Constitutional Law—Freedom of Speech—Liquor Licensing Regulations Governing Nightclub Entertainment Are a Rational Exercise of the State's Authority under the Twenty-first Amendment. Even Though Expression Protected by the First Amendment is Proscribed*, 19 Vill. L. Rev. 177 (1973).
17. *Construction of the Illinois Dram Shop Act Imposing Liability upon Tavernkeeper and His Lessor for Injuries Caused by Intoxicated Persons*, 14 Notre Dame Law. 295 (1939).
18. *Copyright: Twentieth Century Music Corp. v. Aiken, Infringement Liability of a Restaurant Owner for Reception of Radio Broadcast for the Enjoyment of His Customers*, 30 Okla. L. Rev. 201 (1977).
19. Alsberg, *Economic Aspects of Adulteration and Imitation*, 46 Q.J. Econ. 1 (1931–32).
20. Dunn, *The Food, Drug and Cosmetic Law*, 3 Food, Drug, Cosmetic L.Q. 308 (1948).
21. Lightman, *Hotels and VAT*, 1982 Brit. Tax Rev. 233.

22. *The Illinois Dram Shop Act and the Common Law: A Continuing Drama*, 5 J. Mar. J. 342 (1972).
23. *Implied Warranty and the Sale of Restaurant Food*, 63 W. Va. L. Rev. 326 (1961).
24. *Intoxicating Liquors—Dram Shop Act—Tavern Owner Held Liable for Injuries of an Intoxicated Patron*, 54 N.D. L. Rev. 301 (1977).
25. *Intoxicating Liquors—Increasing the Liability of New Jersey Taverns: Where to Draw the Line?* 3 Seton Hall L. Rev. 233 (1971).
26. *Intoxicating Liquors—Proximate Cause of Injury—Liability of Tavern Owner for Torts Committed by Intoxicated Patron*, 48 N.D. L. Rev. 505 (1972).
27. *Intoxication—Liability and Recovery: A Practical Look at New York's Dram Shop Act*, 39 Alb. L. Rev. 15 (1974).
28. *Intoxication No Longer a Bar to a Patron's Action against Tavern Owner*, 22 Loy. L. Rev. 867 (1976).
29. Schubert, *The Iowa Dram Shop Act—Causes of Action and Defenses*, 23 Drake L. Rev. 16 (1973).
30. *Judicial Prohibition? Erosion of the Common Law Rule of Non-Liability for Those Who Dispense Alcohol*, 34 Drake L. Rev. 937 (1985).
31. *Legal Developments in Marketing*, 42 J. Marketing 90 (1978).
32. *Legal Effects of Serving Impure Food by a Restaurant Keeper to His Guests*, 24 Yale L.J. 73 (1914).
33. Rose, *Legalization and Control of Casino Gambling*, 8 Fordham Urb. L.J. 245 (1979).
34. *The Liability of Purveyors of Alcoholic Beverages for Torts of Intoxicated Consumers*, 47 Mont. L. Rev. 495 (1986).
35. *Liability of Liquor Vendors to Third Party Victims*, 56 Neb. L. Rev. 951 (1977).
36. *Liability of Restaurant Owner for Fitness of Food Served*, 10 S. Cal. L. Rev. 188 (1937).
37. *Liability of Tavern Owners under the New York State Dram Shop Act*, 30 Alb. L. Rev. 271 (1966).
38. *Liquor Law Liability—Comparative Negligence—Drunk Bar Patron Denied Recovery for His Injuries in a Suit against the Bar*, 17 Santa Clara L. Rev. 469 (1977).
39. Keenan, *Liquor Law Liability in California*, 14 Santa Clara L. Rev. 46 (1973).
40. *Liquor Vendor Liability for Injuries Caused by Intoxicated Patrons—A Question of Policy*, 35 Ohio St. L.J. 630 (1974).
41. *Louisiana Supreme Court Revises Its Position on Bar Owners Liability*, 26 Loy. L. Rev. 431 (1980).
42. *More Than a Mouthful: Libel and the Restaurant Review*, 7 Car. Arts and Ent. L.J. 409 (1989).
43. *Negligence Actions against Liquor Purveyors: Filling the Gap in South Dakota*, 23 S.D. L. Rev. 227 (1978).
44. *Negligence—Intoxicating Liquors—Vendor's Liability for Damages by Intoxicated Patrons*, 74 W. Va. L. Rev. 408 (1972).
45. Fastiff and Durant, *New Rules for Determining Bargaining Units in the Hotel Industry*, 11 Labor L.J. 971 (1960).
46. *One More for the Road: Civil Liability of Licensees and Social Hosts for Furnishing Alcoholic Beverages to Minors*, 59 B.U. L. Rev. 725 (1979).
47. *Products Liability—Restaurant Patron—Implied Warranty—Foreign-Natural Test*, 40 Tul. L. Rev. 928 (1966).
48. *Recent Developments*, 60 Colum. L. Rev. 544 (1960).
49. *The Status of Hotels under the Federal Housing and Rent Act*, 16 U. Chi. L. Rev. 554 (1949).

50. Ellentock, *Tax Aspects of Organizing and Operating Hotels and Motels*, 29 N.Y.U. Inst. Fed. Tax. 887 (1971).
51. *Tort—Bar Owner's Liability to Patron for Injuries arising from Sale of Intoxicating Liquor*, 51 Tul. L. Rev. 394 (1977).
52. *Tort Liability for Serving Alcohol: An Expanding Doctrine*, 46 Mont. L. Rev. 381 (1985).
53. *Tort Liability for Suppliers of Alcohol*, 44 Mo. L. Rev. 757 (1979).
54. *Tort Liability: Liability of Liquor Vendors for Injuries to Intoxicated Persons*, 14 Akron L. Rev. 350 (1980).
55. *Torts—A Bartender Owes a Duty of Due Care in Serving Alcohol to a Patron and Incurs Liability for Foreseeable Injuries Suffered by a Patron Which Result from the Failure to Exercise Such Care*, 28 Drake L. Rev. 728 (1979).
56. *Torts—Common Law Dramshop Liability—Liquor Vendor Who Illegally Sells Intoxicants in California to a Visibly Intoxicated Person Is Liable for the Injurious Results of Such Sales to Third Persons*, 5 L. J L.A.L. Rev. 441 (1972).
57. *Torts—The Common Law Negligence Liability of Commercial Purveyors of Alcohol: Campbell v. Carpenter*, 57 Ore. L. Rev. 357 (1978).
58. *Torts—Liability of Suppliers of Alcohol*, 58 Ore. L. Rev. 387 (1979).
59. Richmond, *Vicarious Liability of Purveyors of Liquor for the Torts of Their Drunken Minor Patrons*, 13 Stet. L. Rev. 267 (1984).

Innkeeper's Liability for Property of Guests

1. *Bailment—An Innkeeper Is Liable for the Unknown Contents of Bailed Property Which He Could Reasonably Expect to Find Contained within the Bailed Property*, 5 Tex. Tech. U.L. Rev. 141 (1973).
2. *Bailment—Liability of Innkeepers*, 31 Tenn. L. Rev. 499 (1964).
3. *Bailments—Innkeeper—Liability for Damage to Automobile of Guest*, 80 U. Pa. L. Rev. 122 (1931).
4. *Bailments—Innkeepers—Liability for Loss of Baggage*, 30 Mich. L. Rev. 1107 (1932).
5. *Bailments—Statutory Limitation of Liability of Innkeeper Where Value of Goods, Deposited for Safe-Keeping, Has Not Been Revealed*, 3 Temp. L.Q. 316 (1929).
6. *Damaged Goods at the Inn*, 19 Modern L. Rev. 408 (1956).
7. *Hoteliers' Liability for Stolen Goods*, 134 Solicitors' J. 466 (1990).
8. *Hotelkeepers Liability for Negligent Loss of Property of a Guest*, 57 Dick. L. Rev. 348 (1953).
9. *Hotel Keeper's Liability—Property in Transport*, 6 Fordham L. Rev. 489 (1937).
10. *Hotels: Liability of Innkeepers for Property of Guests and Tenants*, 1 U. Fla. L. Rev. 283 (1948).
11. *The Illinois Innkeeper and the Goods of His Guests*, 7 De Paul L. Rev. 102 (1957).
12. *An Innkeeper and His Guest's Car*, 75 Solicitors' J. 68 (1931).
13. *Innkeeper-Guest Relationship—Statutory Limitation of Liability*, 23 Fordham L. Rev. 209 (1954).
14. *Innkeeper—Liability of Innkeepers for Employee's Theft of Guest's Automobile*, 29 Rocky Mtn. L. Rev. 136 (1956).
15. *Innkeeper Negligence—Inapplicability of the Limitation of Liability of Article 2971*, 57 Tul. L. Rev. 412 (1982).
16. *Innkeeper—Statute Limiting Liability for the Property of Guests*, 52 Harv. L. Rev. 334 (1938).
17. *Innkeepers—Failure of Guest to Disclose Character of Contents of Baggage as Negligence*, 44 Mich. L. Rev. 1148 (1946).

18. *Innkeepers—Hotel Providing Lodging Only—Liability for Valuables Deposited,* 21 Colum. L. Rev. 95 (1921).
19. *Innkeepers—Injury to Property of Guest—Care Required of Innkeeper,* 12 Notre Dame Law. 463 (1937).
20. *Innkeepers—Liability as Modified by Statute,* 28 Mich L. Rev. 345 (1930).
21. *Innkeepers—Liability for Damage to Automobile of Guest,* 14 Tenn. L. Rev. 289 (1936).
22. *Innkeepers—Liability for Guest's Personal Property—Automobiles,* 15 Alb. L. Rev. 236 (1951).
23. *Innkeepers—Liability for Guest's Property,* 24 S. Cal. L. Rev. 319 (1951).
24. *Innkeepers—Liability for Loss of Guest's Property—Effect of Statutory Limitation,* 26 Texas L. Rev. 541 (1948).
25. *Innkeepers—Liability for Loss of Property of Guest—Ohio Statutes Limiting Liability,* 19 U. Cin. L. Rev. 531 (1950).
26. *Innkeepers—Liability for Property of Guest,* 9 N.Y.U.L.Q. Rev. 237 (1931).
27. *Innkeeper's Liability for Theft of a Guest's Automobile,* 31 Mo. L. Rev. 459 (1966).
28. *Innkeeper's Liability to a Permanent Guest for Loss of Goods by Fire,* 32 Iowa L. Rev. 95 (1946).
29. *Innkeepers—Limitation of Liability for Loss of Guests' Property—Article 2971, Louisiana Civil Code of 1870,* 22 Tul. L. Rev. 333 (1947).
30. *Innkeepers—New York General Business Law, Section 201, Applicability of Statute Where Guest Has Merely a Right to Possession,* 31 Colum. L. Rev. 166 (1931).
31. *Innkeepers—Personal Property—Innkeepers' Relationship with Clientele,* 11 Baylor L. Rev. 329 (1959).
32. *Innkeepers—Statutory Limitation of Liability—Effect of Maximum Liability Clause When Guest's Property is Stolen by Servant,* 13 Minn. L. Rev. 615 (1929).
33. *Innkeepers—Statutory Limitation of Liability—Necessity of Strict Compliance as a Condition Precedent to Exemption,* 33 Mich. L. Rev. 127 (1934).
34. *Innkeepers—Statutory Limitations of Liability—Application Where Valuables Deposited by Guest Are Stolen by Employee of Innkeeper,* 14 Minn. L. Rev. 419 (1930).
35. *Liability of Innkeeper for Damage to Goods of Guest,* 171 Law Times 115 (1931).
36. Hirsch, *Limited Liability of Innkeepers under Statutory Regulations,* 76 U. Pa. L. Rev. 272 (1928).
37. *Negligence—Innkeepers—Liability for Loss of or Injury to Goods of Guest,* 6 Texas L. Rev. 545 (1928).
38. Navagh, *A New Look at the Liability of Inn Keepers for Guest Property under New York Law,* 25 Fordham L. Rev. 62 (1956).
39. *Personal Property—Bailee—Innkeeper—Damage to Guest's Car—Injury by Frost—Liability of Innkeeper,* 4 Cambridge L.J. 376 (1932).
40. *Personal Property—Innkeeper—Liability for Loss of Guest's Property by Theft—Question of Guest's Negligence,* 7 Cambridge L.J. 271 (1940).
41. *Personal Property—Innkeeper—Liability for Loss of Guest's Property—Question Whether Loss Caused by Guest's Negligence,* 9 Cambridge L.J. 246 (1946).
42. Montague, *Personal Property—Innkeeper's Liability for Loss of—Burden of Proof under Modifying Statute,* 13 S. Cal. L. Rev. 164 (1939).
43. *Personal Property—Statutory Liability of an Innkeeper for Personal Property of a Guest,* 1 Ark. L. Rev. 86 (1946).
44. *Statutory Limitation of Innkeepers' Liability,* 14 Wash. L. Rev. 217 (1939).
45. Arnold, *A Summary of Rights and Liabilities of Innkeepers regarding Property of Guests,* 1 S. Tex. L.J. 63 (1954).
46. *Theft by Hotel Servant,* 72 Solicitors' J. 127 (1928).
47. *Theft by Motor-Car—Hotel Parking Ground—Liability of Hotel Company,* 5 Can. B. Rev. 440 (1927).

Creditor-Debtor Relations

1. *Color of State Law and State Authorized Self-Help under Innkeeper's Lien Statutes: Culbertson v. Leland*, 9 Sw. U.L. Rev. 235 (1977).
2. *Constitutional Law—Due Process of Law—Innkeeper's Lien—Appellate Jurisdiction*, 22 Geo. L.J. 101 (1933).
3. *Evolving Concepts of the Innkeepers Lien*, 61 Cornell L. Rev. 587 (1976).
4. *Fraud on the Innkeeper: The Need for Legislative Reform*, 16 U. Fla. L. Rev. 622 (1964).
5. Berry, *Hoteliers' Liability for and Lien on the Property of Their Guests*, 131 New Law J. 795 (1981).
6. *The Innkeeper and His Lien*, 91 Solicitors' J. 488 (1947).
7. *Innkeepers Lien and Due Process*, 5 U. Richmond L. Rev. 447 (1971).
8. Hogan, *The Innkeeper's Lien at Common Law*, 8 Hastings L.J. 33 (1956).
9. *Innkeeper's Lien in Missouri*, 36 Mo. L. Rev. 431 (1971).
10. *The Innkeeper's Lien in the Twentieth Century*, 13 Wm. & Mary L. Rev. 175 (1971).
11. *An Innkeeper's Lien on Letters Addressed to His Guest*, 55 Solicitors' J. 199 (1911).
12. *Innkeepers—Lien on Stolen Property Brought to Hotel by Guest*, 21 B.U. L. Rev. 559 (1941).
13. *Innkeeper's Liens and the Requirements of Due Process*, 28 Wash. & Lee L. Rev. 481 (1971).
14. *Innkeeper's Remedy against Unruly Guest*, 94 Just. Peace 649 (1930).
15. *Inns and Innkeepers—Innkeeper's Lien—An Innkeeper May Not Enforce a Statutory Innkeeper's Lien Unless the Lodger Is Given Notice and Has an Opportunity to Test the Validity of the Seizure at a Hearing*, 39 U. Cin. L. Rev. 815 (1970).
16. *Liens—Innkeepers—Lien of Innkeeper on Stolen Goods Brought into His Hotel by Guest*, 10 U. Cin. L. Rev. 495 (1936).
17. *Personal Property—Innkeeper's Lien—Lien over Stolen Property—Held: Innkeeper Entitled to Exercise Right of Lien over Such Property*, 9 Cambridge L.J. 122 (1945).
18. *Proposal for a Constitutional Innkeeper's Lien Statute*, 24 Buffalo L. Rev. 369 (1975).

Innkeeper's Rights and Responsibilities on the International Level

1. *Boardinghouses: Liability for Loss of Guest's Property*, 19 N.Z.L.J. 89 (1943).
2. *Hotel Proprietors Act, 1956*, 20 Modern L. Rev. 153 (1957).
3. *Innkeeper and the Edict*, 75 Scot. L. Rev. 4 (1959).
4. *Innkeeper—Liability for Loss of Goods Left in Car of Guest—Whether Goods Left by Guest in Car Parked in Hotel Parking Lot Are Infra Hospitium—Innkeeper Liability Acts*, 34 Can. B. Rev. 1203 (1956).
5. *Innkeeper—Liability for Loss of Guest's Car—Traveller—Infra Hospitium—Contracting Out of Liability—Innkeepers Liability Act*, 29 Can. B. Rev. 768 (1951).
6. *Innkeeper—Liability—Injury to Guest's Goods—Insurer—Negligence*, 9 Can. B. Rev. 750 (1931).
7. *Innkeepers' Guests: Their Personal Safety*, 29 N.Z.L.J. 43 (1953).
8. *The Innkeeper's Legal Obligations*, 85 Ir. L. Times 285 (1951).
9. *Innkeeper's Liability at Common Law—What Amounts to Carelessness by a Guest*, 13 Austl. L.J. 358 (1939).
10. Stirling, *Innkeepers' Liability for Guests' Lost Goods*, 4 Austl. L.J. 319 (1931).
11. *An Innkeeper's Liability for the Safety of His Guests—Some New Considerations*, 74 Ir. L. Times 123 (1940).
12. *Innkeeper's Liability—Negligence of Guest*, 4 Austl. L.J. 293 (1931).
13. *Innkeeper's Liability: The Need for Reform*, 23 Ir. Jur. 5 (1957).

14. Silberberg, *Intoxicated Patron: A Re-Appraisal of the Duty of Care*, 20 McGill L.J. 491 (1974).
15. *Isaac v. Hotel de Paris Ltd.*, 1 Tasmanian U.L. Rev. 512 (1960).
16. *Legislation—Innkeepers—Limitation of Liability for Loss of Guest's Vehicle*, 32 Can. B. Rev. 1149 (1954).
17. *The Liabilities of Innkeepers*, 5 Austl. L.J. 21 (1931).
18. Winder, *Liability of an Innkeeper in Recent Cases*, 1952 Scots. L. Times 58.
19. *The Liability of an Innkeeper to Supply Reasonable Refreshment*, 82 Ir. L. Times 59 (1948).
20. *The Licensing Amendment Bill*, 36 N.Z.L.J. 390 (1960).
21. *Negligence—Innkeeper and Lodger—Lodger Giving False Name for Immoral Purpose—Whether Invitee or Trespasser*, 19 Austl. L.J. 372 (1946).
22. *Refusal of Reasonable Refreshment by Innkeeper*, 81 Ir. L. Times 193 (1947).
23. Angus, *Some Reflections on the Edict*, 1959 Scots L. Times 63.
24. *Tort—Negligence—Breach of Statutory Duty—Common Law Duty of Care—Affirmative Duties—Contributory Negligence—Volenti Non Fit Injuria—Ex Turpi Causa Non Oritur Actio—Drink Now—Sue Later*, 53 Can. B. Rev. 344 (1975).
25. *Tort—Negligence—Innkeeper's Liability for Customer's Goods Stolen Whilst in Custody—Customer Not a Guest at Common Law—No Liability*, 6 Res. Judicatae 537 (1954).
26. Gould, Ramsey and Sherry, *UNIDROIT Draft Convention on the Hotelkeeper's Contract: A Major Attempt to Unify the Law Governing Innkeeper-Guest Liability*, 13 Cornell Int'l L.J. 33 (1980).
27. Sherry, *A Uniform Approach to Legal Aspects of Tourism and Travel Abroad*, in INTERNATIONAL UNIFORM LAW IN PRACTICE, 506–508 (1988).

Table of Cases

Index

Library of Congress Cataloging-in-Publication Data

Sherry, John E. H.
   The laws of innkeepers : for hotels, motels, restaurants, and clubs / John E. H. Sherry.—3rd ed.
      p. cm.
   Rev. ed. of: The laws of innkeepers / John H. Sherry. Rev. ed. 1981.
   Includes bibliographical references and index.
   ISBN 0-8014-2508-5
   1. Hotels, taverns, etc.—Law and legislation—United States—Cases.   I. Sherry, John Harold.
Laws of innkeepers.   II. Title.
KF951.A7S48   1993
343.73'07864794—dc20
[347.3037864794]   92-30561

Milton Keynes UK
Ingram Content Group UK Ltd.
UKHW010653280723
425913UK00003B/143